Australia

a Lonely Planet travel survival kit

Hugh Finlay
Mark Armstrong
Michelle Coxall
Jon Murray
Jeff Williams

Australia

7th edition

Published by
Lonely Planet Publications
Head Office: PO Box 617, Hawthorn, Vic 3122, Australia
Branches: 155 Filbert St, Suite 251, Oakland, CA 94607, USA
10 Barley Mow Passage, Chiswick, London W4 4PH, UK
71 bis rue du Cardinal Lemoine, 75005 Paris, France

Printed by
McPherson's Printing Group Ltd, Australia

Photographs by

Greg Alford (GA)	Mark Armstrong (MA)	Ross Barnett (RB)
Glenn Beanland (GB)	John Chapman (JC)	Michelle Coxall (MC)
David Curl (DC)	Hugh Finlay (HF)	Mark Fraser (MF)
Healesville Sanctuary	Richard I'Anson (RI)	Matt King (MK)
Chris Klep (CK)	James Lyon (JL)	Jon Murray (JM)
Richard Nebesky (RN)	NT Tourist Commission (NTTC)	Tom Smallman (TS)
Ray Stamp (RS)	Paul Steel (PS)	Valerie Tellini (VT)
Tony Wheeler (TW)	Jeff Williams (JW)	

Front cover: *Old Man – Young Man – Very Big Story* by Djambu Barra Barra, born about 1946;
language group Wagilak related to Ritangu; domicile Ngukurr, NT;
synthetic polymer paint on lanaquarelle paper; 63 x 67cm; 1992;
represented by Alcaston House Gallery, Melbourne.
Back cover: Landscape, Keep River National Park, Northern Territory (RI)

First Published
February 1977

This Edition
October 1994

Although the authors and publisher have tried to make the information as accurate as possible, they accept no responsibility for any loss, injury or inconvenience sustained by any person using this book.

National Library of Australia Cataloguing in Publication Data

Australia – a travel survival kit.

7th ed.
Includes index.
ISBN 0 86442 233 4.
1. Australia – Guidebooks.
I. Finlay, Hugh.
(Series: Lonely Planet travel survival kit)

919.40463

text & maps © Lonely Planet 1994
photos © photographers as indicated 1994
climate charts compiled from information supplied by Patrick J Tyson, © Patrick J Tyson, 1994

Hugh Finlay

After deciding there must be more to life than a career in civil engineering, Hugh first took off around Australia in the mid-1970s, working at everything from spray painting to diamond prospecting, before hitting the overland trail. Since joining Lonely Planet in 1985, Hugh has written *Jordan & Syria*, co-authored *Morocco, Algeria & Tunisia* and *Kenya*, and has contributed to other Lonely Planet guides including *Africa* and *India*. Hugh co-ordinated this edition of *Australia* and updated the chapters on Tasmania and the Northern Territory, and the section on the far north in the South Australia chapter. Hugh lives in central Victoria, Australia, with Linda and daughters Ella and Vera.

Mark Armstrong

Mark was born in Melbourne and completed his tertiary studies at Melbourne University. Amongst other things, he has worked in computer sales and marketing, as a restorer of old houses, as a fencing contractor and in the hospitality industry. He lived in Barcelona for a while and has travelled in South-East Asia, Europe and North America. In 1992 he researched, wrote and published *Where to Wine, Dine and Recline in Central Victoria*, before beginning work for Lonely Planet on the *Victoria* and *Melbourne* guides. Mark updated the chapters on Victoria and Queensland for this edition of *Australia*.

Michelle Coxall

Michelle Coxall was born in the mighty metropolis of Buninyong in country Victoria. She worked for five years as a travel consultant before deciding the people on the other side of the desk were having more fun than her. After various trips overseas and the completion of a degree in humanities, she washed up at Lonely Planet where she trained as an editor. She is currently working in the Tibetan community in Dharamsala, northern India. Michelle updated the South Australia chapter.

Jon Murray

After trying everything from syrup-mixing in a soft-drink factory to buying Christmas-tree lights for the Australian army, Jon achieved a balance of long-distance cycling, travel in Asia and working for various publishing houses in Melbourne. He has contributed to several Lonely Planet guides, co-authored *South Africa, Lesotho & Swaziland*, written the *New South Wales* travel survival kit and updated the *Sydney* city guide. For this edition of *Australia*, he updated the chapters on New South Wales and the Australian Capital Territory.

Jeff Williams

Since Jeff started working for Lonely Planet, he has divided his time between writing, chasing one-year-old Callum (who single-handedly chases cars and trams in Melbourne's streets) and wishing for a rest. He has languished in New Zealand and Western Australia, researching and updating this book and contributing to *New Zealand*, *Tramping in New Zealand* and *Outback Australia*. When not working for Lonely Planet, Jeff amuses himself mountaineering, skiing and bird-watching on whichever continent will have him. Jeff updated the chapter on Western Australia.

From the Authors

Hugh Finlay Hugh would like to thank the many people who gave generously of their time and knowledge, which greatly simplified the task of updating. In particular, thanks to Peter Yates of the NT Tourism Commission, Alan Withers of the NT Conservation Commission in Borroloola (Did you ever get that croc?), Andrew Morley & Rowan of Milikapiti on Melville Island (NT) for arranging a visit there, Nick & Kerry Bryce for their hospitality in both Auburn (SA) and the Granites (NT), Ian Fox in Darwin (known far and wide for his bottomless fridge) and to Linda, who accompanied him for much of the time and gave many valuable insights.

Mark Armstrong Mark would like to thank Julian and Yvonne Cavanagh, Mandy and Paul Cranage, Ashley and Nicole (Brisbane), Harry and Barb Kemp for the loan of the apartment, Andrew McKenzie of the Wet Tropics Management Authority, and Rob Kemp (Bendigo). Special thanks to Paul and Hope Hayes (Cairns) for their warm and enduring hospitality. Also, thanks to the mechanic, panel beater and publican at the outback town of Winton, and apologies to the kangaroo. And thanks to all the staff at LP.

Michelle Coxall Michelle would like to thank Kate Oka and Lisa Berardo, Tourism SA; Charlene Coulthard, at the Rangers Office, Wilpena Pound; Stephen Gregov for the Mexican dinner; the friendly fellows at the Elbow Inn, Eyre Peninsula who let her jump fully clothed into their swimming pool to escape the 43° heat; to LP editors Janet Austin and Lyn McGaurr; and to Pam Coxall, who saw her safely over the border. To the police officer who picked her up after 5000 km and only 30 km from home – thanks a lot!

Jeff Williams Jeff would like to thank his wife, Alison, and son, Callum; the WATC in Perth; Alan Morley and Rita Stinson; Jim and Collette Truscott and their kids in Karratha; Helen and Albert Innes in Perth for their hospitality; Neil McLeod of Ningaloo Safari Tours in Exmouth; George Swann in Broome for pointing out the waders as they arrived from Siberia; Russell Wilson in Melbourne; Stef and Angela Frodsham of East Fremantle; and Pete Flavelle for keeping an eye on the tides near Cottesloe Beach.

This Book

Australia was first written by Tony Wheeler in 1977 and has been through successive transformations. Among the major contributors to past editions were Simon Hayman and Alan Samalgalski (3rd edition), Mark Lightbody and Lindy Cameron (4th edition), Susan Forsyth, John Noble, Richard Nebesky and Peter Turner (5th edition), and Alan Tiller and Charlotte Hindle (6th edition).

From the Publisher

This edition was edited by Janet Austin, Lyn McGaurr and Katie Cody. Thanks to Bruce Cameron, Vicky Wayland, Dave Colquhoun and Rob van Driesum for their assistance. Lyn McGaurr, Sharan Kaur and Tom Smallman helped with the proofing. Chris Love co-ordinated the mapping with help from Louise Keppie and Chris Lee-Ack. Glenn Beanland did the layout and designed the section on Australian fauna, and Jane Hart designed the cover. Matt King co-ordinated the Aboriginal art section and Vicki Beale handled the design. Sharon Wertheim produced the index.

Thanks to all the readers whose letters helped us with this update. Their names are listed at the back of the book.

Warning & Request

Things change – prices go up, schedules change, good places go bad and bad places go bankrupt – nothing stays the same. So if you find things better or worse, recently opened or long since closed, please write and tell us and help make the next edition better! Your letters will be used to help update future editions and, where possible, important changes will also be included as a Stop Press section in reprints.

All information is greatly appreciated and the best letters will receive a free copy of the next edition, or any other Lonely Planet book of your choice.

Contents

INTRODUCTION 11

FACTS ABOUT THE COUNTRY 12

History 12
Geography 23
Climate 24
Flora 24
Fauna 29
National Parks & Reserves 45
Government 46

Economy 47
Population &
People 48
Arts & Culture 48
Religion 51
Language 51
Aboriginal Art **57**

Central Australian Art 60
Arnhem Land Art 67
Tiwi Island Art 72
Kimberley Art 74
North Queensland
Art 75
Urban Art 75

FACTS FOR THE VISITOR 77

Visas & Embassies 77
Customs 78
Money 79
When to Go 81
Tourist Offices 81
Useful Organisations 82
Business Hours & Holidays 87
Cultural Events 87
Post & Telecommunications 89

Time 91
Electricity 91
Weights & Measures 91
Books & Maps 91
Media 94
Film & Photography 94
Health 95
Women Travellers 96
Emergency 96

Dangers & Annoyances 96
Work 98
Activities 99
Highlights 100
Accommodation 100
Food 106
Drinks 107
Entertainment 109
Things to Buy 111

GETTING THERE & AWAY 113

Discount Tickets 113
Round-the-World
Tickets 114
Circle Pacific Tickets 114

To/From the UK 114
To/From North America 115
To/From New Zealand 115
To/From Asia 116

To/From Africa & South
America 116
Arriving & Departing 116

GETTING AROUND 118

Air 118
Bus 121
Train 123

Car 125
Bicycle 133
Hitching 135

Boat 136
Tours 136
Student Travel 136

AUSTRALIAN CAPITAL TERRITORY 137

Canberra .... **137**   **Around Canberra** .... **154**   Queanbeyan 155

NEW SOUTH WALES 156

Geography 158
Information 158
National Parks 158
Activities 158
Getting There &
Away 160
Getting Around 160
Sydney **160**
Around Sydney **204**
Botany Bay 204
Royal National
Park 204
Parramatta 206
Penrith 207
Camden Area 207

Ku-ring-gai Chase National
Park 207
Hawkesbury River 208
Windsor Area 209
Blue Mountains **210**
Glenbrook to Katoomba 212
Katoomba 214
Blackheath Area 216
Mt Victoria & Beyond 217
Jenolan Caves 217
North Coast **218**
Sydney to Newcastle 218
Newcastle 219
Hunter Valley 223
Newcastle to Port Macquarie ... 225

Port Macquarie 227
Port Macquarie to Coffs
Harbour 231
Coffs Harbour 234
Coffs Harbour to Byron Bay . 238
Byron Bay 241
Byron Bay to Tweed Heads ... 247
Tweed Heads 248
Far North Coast
Hinterland **249**
Lismore 249
Nimbin 251
Around Nimbin 252
Mullumbimby 253
Mt Warning National Park 254

Border Ranges National
Park 254
New England 255
Tamworth 256
Tamworth to Armidale 256
Armidale 257
North of Armidale 258
South Coast 259
Wollongong 259
Around Wollongong 262
Wollongong to Nowra 262
Shoalhaven 263
Batemans Bay to Bega 264
South to the Victorian
Border 265
Snowy Mountains 266
Cooma 268
Jindabyne 269
Kosciusko National Park 269

Skiing & Ski Resorts 270
The Alpine Way 272
Tumut Area 272
South-West &
the Murray 273
Along the Hume
Highway 273
Albury 275
Wagga Wagga 276
Narrandera 276
Griffith 277
Around Griffith 278
Hay 278
Deniliquin 279
Along the Murray 279
Central West 280
Lithgow 280
Bathurst 280
Around Bathurst 281

Mudgee & Around 281
Orange 282
Dubbo 282
Cowra 284
Forbes 284
North-West 285
Along the Newell 285
Along the Castlereagh 285
Along the Mitchell 286
Outback 286
Bourke 286
Back of Bourke – Corner
Country 287
Barrier Highway 288
Broken Hill 289
Around Broken Hill 293
Mungo National Park 294
Lord Howe Island 294

NORTHERN TERRITORY 296

Northern Territory Aborigines 296
Climate 299
Information 300
National Parks 300
Activities 300
Getting There & Away 301
Getting Around 301
Darwin 302
The Top End 318
Around Darwin 319
Kakadu National Park 323
Bathurst & Melville Islands ... 330

Cobourg Peninsula 331
Arnhem Land & Gove 331
Down the Track 333
Darwin to Katherine 333
Katherine 334
Around Katherine 337
Katherine to
Western Australia 338
Mataranka 339
Mataranka to Threeways 339
Threeways 340
Tennant Creek 340

Tennant Creek to
Alice Springs 341
Alice Springs 342
The MacDonnell Ranges 355
Eastern MacDonnell Ranges 355
Western MacDonnell Ranges 358
South to Uluru (Ayers
Rock) 361
Uluru National Park 364
Uluru (Ayers Rock) 364
Kata Tjuta (the Olgas) 366
Yulara 367

QUEENSLAND 373

Aborigines & Kanakas 376
Geography 376
Climate 377
Information 377
National Parks 377
State Forests 378
Activities 378
Getting Around 379
Brisbane 380
Moreton Bay 401
The Bayside 401
North Stradbroke Island 402
Moreton Island 404
St Helena Island 406
Other Islands 406
Gold Coast 406
Gold Coast Hinterland 416
Sunshine Coast 418
Caboolture 419
Glass House Mountains 420
Caloundra 420
Maroochydore 420
Noosa 421
Cooloola Coast 425

Nambour 426
Sunshine Coast Hinterland 426
Darling Downs 426
Ipswich 427
Ipswich to Warwick 427
Warwick Area 428
Goondiwindi & further West . 428
Toowoomba 428
Roma 429
Hervey Bay Area 429
Gympie 429
Rainbow Beach 429
Maryborough 430
Hervey Bay 430
Fraser Island 433
Childers 437
Bundaberg 437
Capricorn Coast 438
Southern Reef Islands 439
Gladstone 441
Rockhampton 441
Around Rockhampton 444
Yeppoon 444
Yeppoon to Emu Park 445

Great Keppel Island 445
Other Keppel Bay Islands 450
Capricorn Hinterland 450
Whitsunday Coast 452
Mackay 453
Around Mackay 456
Airlie Beach & Shute Harbour 458
Whitsunday Islands 463
Bowen 467
North Coast 468
Ayr 468
Townsville 468
Magnetic Island 476
Townsville to Mission Beach 480
Mission Beach 482
Dunk Island & the Family
Islands 484
Mission Beach to Cairns 485
North Coast Hinterland 486
Far North Queensland 488
Cairns 489
Islands off Cairns 501
Atherton Tableland 501
Cairns to Port Douglas 508

Port Douglas 508
Mossman.................................. 511
Daintree 511
Cape Tribulation Area 512
Cape Tribulation to
Cooktown 515
Cairns to Cooktown –
The Inland Road 516

Cooktown................................ 516
Lizard Island 519
**Cape York &
the Gulf 520**
Cape York Peninsula.............. 520
Gulf of Carpentaria................ 525
Outback 527
Cloncurry 527

Cloncurry to Mt Isa................ 528
Mt Isa 528
Mt Isa to Threeways 531
Mt Isa to Longreach............... 532
Longreach 533
Longreach to Charleville 534
The Channel Country............. 534

SOUTH AUSTRALIA 537

South Australian Aborigines .. 537
Geography 539
Information............................. 539
National Parks 539
Activities................................ 539
Getting There & Away 540
Getting Around 540
Adelaide............................. 541
Adelaide Hills 556
National Parks & Scenic
Drives 557
Birdwood 558
Hahndorf................................. 558
Strathalbyn.............................. 559
Clarendon 559
Fleurieu Peninsula........... 559
Gulf St Vincent Beaches 560
Southern Vales 561
Port Elliot............................... 562
Victor Harbor 562
Goolwa 563
Kangaroo Island............... 564
Kingscote 567
American River 567
Penneshaw 568
North Coast............................. 568
Flinders Chase National Park. 568
South Coast............................. 569
Barossa Valley 569
Lyndoch 571
Tanunda 572
Nuriootpa................................ 572
Angaston................................. 573
Other Barossa Valley Towns .. 573
Mid-North.......................... 573

Kapunda...................................573
Auburn 573
Clare...574
Burra...574
Port Pirie 576
Other Mid-North Towns 576
South-East........................577
The Coorong 577
Kingston SE 578
Robe..578
Beachport.................................578
Millicent...................................579
Mt Gambier..............................579
Port Macdonnell 579
Along the Dukes Highway 580
Naracoorte 580
Coonawarra & Penola 580
Murray River......................581
Renmark...................................582
Berri 582
Loxton 582
Barmera....................................583
Waikerie 583
Morgan.....................................583
Swan Reach 584
Mannum....................................584
Murray Bridge 584
Tailem Bend 585
Yorke Peninsula................585
West Coast 586
East Coast 587
Innes National Park 587
Eyre Peninsula..................588
Port Augusta 588
Whyalla.....................................589

Whyalla to Port Lincoln 590
Port Lincoln 590
Around Port Lincoln 591
Port Lincoln to Streaky Bay ...591
Streaky Bay..............................592
Smoky Bay................................592
Ceduna 592
Flinders Ranges 593
Mt Remarkable
National Park 596
Melrose 596
South of the Flinders
Ranges......................................596
Quorn 596
Kanyaka 597
Hawker 597
Wilpena Pound.........................598
Blinman 599
Around Blinman 599
Leigh Creek..............................600
Arkaroola 600
Outback.............................601
Routes North 601
Woomera 602
Andamooka...............................602
Glendambo................................603
Coober Pedy.............................603
Around Coober Pedy 606
Marla...606
Marree 606
Oodnadatta...............................607
Birdsville Track 607
Strzelecki Track 607
Innamincka...............................608
The Ghan..................................608

TASMANIA...609

Tasmanian Aborigines 611
Geography 611
Information............................. 612
National Parks 612
Activities................................ 613
Getting There & Away 614
Getting Around 616
Hobart............................... 617
Around Hobart 627
Taroona 627
Kingston 627

Bridgewater 627
Pontville...................................627
New Norfolk 628
Mt Field National Park 628
Richmond.................................629
South-East Coast.............630
Kettering 630
Bruny Island 630
Cygnet......................................631
Grove 631
Huonville 631

Geeveston.................................632
Hartz Mountains National
Park 632
Dover..632
Hastings....................................632
Lune River 633
Tasman Peninsula 633
Port Arthur 633
Around the Peninsula...............635
East Coast & North-East. 636
Buckland 637

Orford 637
Triabunna............................... 637
Maria Island National Park 637
Swansea 638
Coles Bay & Freycinet
National Park......................... 639
Bicheno.................................. 640
St Marys................................. 641
St Helens................................ 641
Weldborough 642
Gladstone 642
Derby 643
Scottsdale............................... 643
Ben Lomond National Park.... 643
Midlands 644
Oatlands................................. 644
Ross 644
Campbell Town 645
Launceston..................... 645
Around Launceston........ 651
Hadspen 651
Liffey Valley 652
Evandale................................. 652

Longford 652
Tamar Valley 653
Notley Gorge State
Reserve 653
Deviot.....................................653
Beaconsfield 653
Low Head................................653
George Town...........................654
Hillwood 654
Lilydale...................................654
North-Central 654
Westbury.................................654
Deloraine................................655
Mole Creek 655
Sheffield.................................656
Devonport...............................656
Around Devonport..................660
North-West 660
Ulverstone..............................660
Penguin..................................661
Burnie 661
Wynyard..................................663
Around Wynyard 664

Stanley....................................664
Around Stanley 665
Marrawah 665
Arthur River............................666
Hellyer Gorge.........................666
Savage River 666
Corinna...................................666
Rosebery 667
West Coast....................... 667
Zeehan....................................668
Queenstown 668
Strahan...................................670
Franklin-Gordon Wild Rivers
National Park 672
South-West National Park.......673
Lake Pedder 673
Strathgordon...........................673
Cradle Mountain-Lake St
Clair 673
Lake Country 677
Bass Strait Islands 678
King Island..............................678
Flinders Island........................679

VICTORIA 681

Geography 683
Climate 683
Information............................. 683
National & State Parks 684
Activities................................. 684
Getting There & Away 685
Getting Around....................... 685
Melbourne...................... 685
Around Melbourne.......... 721
South-West to Geelong........... 721
Geelong.................................. 722
Bellarine Peninsula 724
North-West to Bendigo........... 726
Healesville & Around............. 726
The Dandenongs.................... 727
Mornington Peninsula 728
Phillip Island.......................... 730
Great Ocean Road 734
Torquay................................... 735
Anglesea 736
Anglesea to Lorne 736
Lorne...................................... 736
Lorne to Apollo Bay 739
Apollo Bay 739
Otway Ranges......................... 739
Port Campbell National
Park 740
South-West...................... 741
Warrnambool 741
Tower Hill State Game
Reserve 742
Port Fairy 742
Portland.................................. 743

Portland to the South
Australian Border 743
The Western District.............. 743
The Wimmera 745
Ararat 745
Stawell 745
Grampians (Gariwerd)
National Park 746
Horsham..................................749
Mt Arapiles 749
Dimboola 750
Little Desert National
Park...750
The Mallee 750
Murray River.................... 751
Mildura 753
Around Mildura 754
Swan Hill 755
Kerang.....................................755
Gunbower State Forest 756
Echuca....................................756
Barmah State Forest 757
Yarrawonga.............................757
Gold Country.................... 758
Ballarat....................................759
Clunes.....................................765
Maryborough...........................765
Moliagul, Tarnagulla &
Dunolly...................................765
Daylesford...............................766
Hepburn Springs 767
Castlemaine 767
Around Castlemaine 769

Maldon 769
Bendigo 770
Around Bendigo......................775
Along the Calder
Highway 776
Rushworth...............................776
North-East.......................... 776
Lake Eildon.............................776
Mansfield 777
Goulburn Valley 777
Glenrowan...............................778
Wangaratta 778
Chiltern...................................779
Rutherglen...............................779
Wodonga 780
Corryong 780
Yackandandah..........................780
Beechworth 781
Bright......................................782
The Alps 783
Alpine National Park 783
Mt Buffalo National
Park 785
Harrietville 785
Omeo 785
Ski Resorts 786
Gippsland 789
West Gippsland & the
Latrobe Valley 789
South Gippsland 792
Wilsons Promontory 793
The Gippsland Lakes 795
East Gippsland 796

WESTERN AUSTRALIA..800

Geography 802
Information 802
Wildflowers 802
Activities................................. 802
Getting There & Away 803
Getting Around 804
Perth.................................... 805
Around Perth.................. 819
Fremantle 819
Rottnest Island 823
North Coast............................ 825
South Coast............................ 828
Avon Valley 829
The Darling Range 831
Wheatlands...................... 831
Cunderdin & Kellerberrin 832
Merredin 832
Southern Cross 832
Hyden & Wave Rock.............. 832
Other Towns 832
Gold Country.................. 833
Coolgardie 834
Kalgoorlie-Boulder................ 835
North of Kalgoorlie 839
Kambalda................................ 841
Norseman................................ 841
The Nullarbor 841
The Eyre Highway 843
The South-West 845
Australind 845
Inland...................................... 846
Bunbury 846

Busselton................................. 847
Dunsborough 847
Yallingup................................ 848
Margaret River....................... 848
Augusta................................... 849
Nannup.................................... 850
Bridgetown 850
Manjimup................................ 850
Pemberton 851
Northcliffe............................... 852
Walpole-Nornalup National
Park 852
Denmark 853
Mt Barker............................... 854
Porongurup & Stirling Range
National Parks........................ 854
Albany..................................... 855
Around Albany 858
Esperance............................... 860
Around Esperance 862
Up the Coast 863
Geraldton 864
Houtman Abrolhos Islands 867
Northampton.......................... 867
Kalbarri 867
Shark Bay 869
Carnarvon 871
Gascoyne Area........................ 874
North-West Cape 874
Exmouth.................................. 874
Ningaloo Reef........................ 877
Cape Range National Park 878

Coral Bay 878
The Pilbara 879
Onslow 879
Dampier...................................879
Karratha...................................881
Roebourne Area 881
Millstream-Chichester
National Park 883
Wittenoom...............................883
Karijini (Hamersley Range)
National Park 884
Tom Price & Paraburdoo 885
Port Hedland 886
The Great Northern
Highway..................................888
Port Hedland to Broome.........889
Broome............................. 890
Around Broome 895
The Kimberley................. 896
Derby......................................898
Gibb River Road.....................900
Devonian Reef National
Parks.......................................901
Fitzroy Crossing......................902
Halls Creek 903
Wolfe Creek Crater National
Park 903
Bungle Bungle (Purnululu)
National Park 904
Wyndham................................904
Kununurra...............................905
Lake Argyle.............................908

INDEX 909

Maps 909   Text 910

Map Legend

BOUNDARIES

············· International Boundary
·············· State Boundary
·············· Marine Park Boundary

ROUTES

··············· Freeway
··············· Highway
··············· Major Road
··············· Unsealed Road or Track
··············· City Road
··············· City Street
·+·+·+·+·+·+· Railway
··············· Underground Railway
··············· Tram
··············· Walking Track
··············· Ferry Route
·+·+·+·+·+·+· Cable Car or Chairlift

AREA FEATURES

··············· Park, Gardens
··············· National Park
··············· Forest
··············· Pedestrian Mall
··············· Market
·+·+·+·+·+· Cemetery
··············· Reef
··············· Beach or Desert
··············· Aboriginal Land

HYDROGRAPHIC FEATURES

··············· Coastline
··············· River, Creek
··············· Intermittent River or Creek
··············· Lake, Intermittent Lake
··············· Canal
··············· Swamp

SYMBOLS

Symbol	Label	Symbol	Label
✪ CAPITAL	National Capital	✈ ✠	Airport, Airfield
◉ Capital	State Capital	⌨ ✿	Swimming Pool, Gardens
⬤ CITY	Major City	◆ 🐖	Shopping Centre, Zoo
● City	City	⚘ ⚑	Winery/Vineyard, Golf Course
● Town	Town	← 33	One Way Street, Route Number
● Village	Village	⁙	Archaeological Site or Ruins
■	Place to Stay	⛫ ⚱	Stately Home, Monument
▼	Place to Eat	P ⚲	Petrol Station, Bicycle Track
♟	Pub, Bar	⌒ ⌂	Cave, Hut or Chalet
✉ ☎	Post Office, Telephone	▲ ✳	Mountain or Hill, Lookout
❶ ⑤	Tourist Information, Bank	🗼 ⚓	Lighthouse, Shipwreck
⊖ P	Transport, Parking	)(⚲	Pass, Spring
🏛 🏠	Museum, Youth Hostel	Ⓤ	Underground Railway Station
⚕ ⛺	Caravan Park, Camping Ground		Ancient or City Wall
✝ 🚻 ✝	Church, Cathedral		Rapids, Waterfalls
☪ ✡	Mosque, Synagogue		Cliff or Escarpment, Tunnel
⊕ ★	Hospital, Police Station		Railway Station

Note: not all symbols displayed above appear in this book

Introduction

It may be cliched to say Australia is a big country, but there are few places on earth with as much variety as Australia has to offer. And not just variety in things to see – in things to do, places to eat, entertainment, activities and just general good times.

What to see and do while tripping around our island continent is an open-ended question. There are cities big and small, some of them amazingly beautiful. If you fly in over its magnificent harbour, for example, Sydney is a city which can simply take your breath away. To really get to grips with the country, however, you must get away from the cities. Australian society may be a basically urban one but, myth or not, it's in the outback where you really find Australia – the endless skies and red dirt, and the laconic Aussie characters. And when you've seen the outback, that still leaves you mountains and coast, bushwalks and big surf, the Great Barrier Reef and the Northern Territory's 'top end'.

Best of all, Australia can be far from the rough and ready country its image might indicate. In the big cities you'll find some of the prettiest Victorian architecture going; Australian restaurants serve up an astounding variety of national cuisines with the

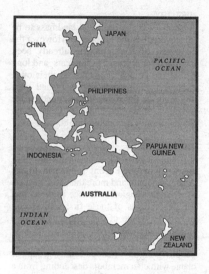

freshest ingredients you could ask for (it's all grown here) and it's no problem at all to fall in love with Australian wines. Australia is not just exciting and invigorating, it's also very civilised. There's some fantastic travelling waiting for you around Australia: go for it.

Facts about the Country

HISTORY

Australia was the last great landmass to be 'discovered' by the Europeans. However the continent of Australia had already been inhabited for at least 50,000 years, and long before the British claimed it as their own, European explorers and traders had been dreaming of the riches to be found in the unknown, some said mythical, Great South Land – if only they could find it.

The Aborigines

It is believed that the ancestors of the Aborigines journeyed from Indonesia to the Australian mainland more than 50,000 years ago. Archaeological evidence suggests that the descendants of these first settlers colonised the whole of the continent within a few thousand years.

Traditionally, the Aborigines were tribal people living in extended family groups or clans, with clan members descending from a common ancestral being. Tradition, rituals and laws linked the people of each clan to the land they occupied and each clan had various sites of spiritual significance on their land, places to which their spirits would return when they died. Clan members came together to perform rituals to honour their ancestral spirits and the creators of the Dreaming. These traditional religious beliefs were the basis of the Aborigines' ties to the land they lived and thrived in for thousands of years before the coming of the Europeans.

It was the responsibility of the clan, or particular members of it, to correctly maintain and protect the sites so that the ancestral beings were not offended and would continue to protect the clan. Traditional punishments for those who neglected these responsibilities was often severe, as their actions could easily affect the well-being of the whole clan – food and water shortages, natural disasters or mysterious illnesses could all be attributed to disgruntled or offended ancestral beings.

Many Aboriginal communities were almost nomadic, others sedentary, one of the deciding factors being the availability of food. Where food and water were readily available, the people tended to remain in a limited area. When they did wander, however, it was to visit sacred places to carry out rituals, or to take advantage of seasonal foods available elsewhere. They did not, as is still often believed, roam aimlessly and desperately in the search for food and water.

The traditional role of the men was that of hunter, tool-maker and custodian of male law; the women reared the children, and gathered and prepared food. There was also female law and ritual for which the women would be responsible.

Wisdom and skills obtained over millennia enabled Aborigines to use their environment to the maximum. An intimate knowledge of the behaviour of animals and the correct time to harvest the many plants they utilised ensured that food shortages were rare. They never hunted an animal species or harvested a plant species to the point where it was threatened with extinction. Like other hunter-gatherer peoples of the world, the Aborigines were true ecologists.

Although Aborigines in northern Australia had been in regular contact with the farming peoples of Indonesia for at least 1000 years, the farming of crops and the

domestication of livestock held no appeal. The only major modification of the landscape practised by the Aborigines was the selective burning of undergrowth in forests and dead grass on the plains. This encouraged new growth, which in turn attracted game animals to the area. It also prevented the build-up of combustible material in the forests, making hunting easier and reducing the possibility of major bush fires. Dingoes were domesticated to assist in the hunt and to guard the camp from intruders.

Similar technology – for example the boomerang and spear – was used throughout the continent, but techniques were adapted to the environment and the species being hunted. In the wetlands of northern Australia, fish traps hundreds of metres long made of bamboo and cord were built to catch fish at the end of the wet season. In the area now known as Victoria, permanent stone weirs many km long were used to trap migrating eels, while in the tablelands of Queensland finely woven nets were used to snare herds of wallabies and kangaroos.

Contrary to the common image, some tribes did build permanent dwellings, varying widely depending on climate, the materials available and likely length of use. In western Victoria the local Aborigines built permanent stone dwellings; in the deserts semicircular shelters were made with arched branches covered with native grasses or leaves; and in Tasmania large conical thatch shelters which could house up to 30 people were constructed. Such dwellings were used mainly for sleeping.

The early Australian Aborigines were also traders. Trade routes crisscrossed the country, dispersing goods and a variety of produced items along their way. Many of the items traded, such as certain types of stone or shell, were rare and had great ritual significance. Boomerangs and ochre were other important trade items. Along the trading networks which developed, large numbers of people would often meet for 'exchange ceremonies', where not only goods but also songs and dances were passed on.

When Sydney Cove was first settled by Whites, around 200 years ago, there were about 300,000 Aborigines in Australia and around 250 different languages were spoken, many as distinct from each other as English is from Chinese. Tasmania alone had eight languages, and tribes living on opposite sides of present-day Sydney Harbour spoke mutually unintelligible languages.

In such a society, based on family groups with an egalitarian political structure, a co-ordinated response to the European colonisers was not possible. Despite the presence of the Aborigines, the newly arrived Europeans considered the new continent to be *terra nullius* – a land without people. Conveniently, they saw no recognisable system of government, no commerce or permanent settlements and no evidence of land ownership. Thus, when Governor Phillip raised the British flag at Sydney Cove in 1788, the laws of England became the law governing all Aborigines in the Australian continent. All land in Australia was from that moment the property of the English Crown.

If the Aborigines had had a readily recognisable political system and had resisted colonisation by organised force of arms, then the English might have been forced to recognise a prior title to the land and therefore legitimise their colonisation by entering into a treaty with the Aboriginal land owners.

Without any legal right to the lands they once lived on, Aborigines throughout the country became dispossessed; some were driven from their country by force, and some succumbed to exotic diseases. Others voluntarily left their lands to travel to the fringes of settled areas to obtain new commodities such as steel and cloth, and experience hitherto unknown drugs such as tea, tobacco, alcohol and narcotics.

At a local level, individuals resisted the encroachment of settlers. Warriors including Pemulwy, Yagan, Dundalli, Pigeon and Nemarluk were, for a time, feared by the colonists in their areas. But although some settlements had to be abandoned, the effect of such resistance only temporarily postponed the inevitable.

By the early 1900s legislation designed to segregate and 'protect' Aboriginal people was passed in all states. The legislation imposed restrictions on the Aborigines' right to own property and seek employment, and the Aboriginals Ordinance of 1918 even allowed the state to remove children from Aboriginal mothers if it was suspected that the father was non-Aboriginal. In these cases the parents were considered to have no rights over the children, who were placed in foster homes or childcare institutions. Many Aborigines are still bitter about having been separated from their families and forced to grow up apart from their people. An up-side of the Ordinance was that it gave a degree of protection for 'full-blood' Aborigines living on reserves, as non-Aborigines could enter only with a permit, and mineral exploration was forbidden.

The process of social change was accelerated by WW II, and 'assimilation' became the stated aim of postwar governments. To this end, the rights of Aborigines were subjugated even further – the government had control over everything, from where Aborigines could live to whom they could marry. Many people were forcibly moved to townships, the idea being that they would adapt to the European culture, which would in turn aid their economic development. It was a dismal failure.

In the 1960s the assimilation policy came under a great deal of scrutiny, and White Australians became increasingly aware of the inequity of their treatment of Aborigines. In 1967 non-Aboriginal Australians voted to give Aborigines and Torres Strait Islanders the status of citizens, and gave the Commonwealth government power to legislate for them in all states. The states had to provide them with the same services as were available to other citizens, and the Federal government set up the Department of Aboriginal Affairs to identify the special needs of Aborigines and legislate for them.

The assimilation policy was finally dumped in 1972, to be replaced by the government's policy of self-determination, which for the first time enabled Aborigines to participate in decision-making processes. In 1976 the Aboriginal Land Rights (Northern Territory) Act gave Aborigines in that region undisputable title to all Aboriginal reserves (about 20% of the Territory) and a means for claiming other Crown land. It also provided for mineral royalties to be paid to Aboriginal communities. This legislation was supposed to be enacted federally but the political upheavals of 1975 (see later) put paid to that prospect.

Only in the last couple of years did the non-Aboriginal community, including the Federal government, come to grips with the fact that a meaningful conciliation between Australia's White and indigenous populations was vital to the psychological well-being of all Australians. In 1992 the High Court handed down what became known as its Mabo ruling. It was the result of a claim by a Torres Strait Islander, Eddy Mabo, challenging the established concept of *terra nullius* – that Australia was basically uninhabited when Europeans arrived here more than 200 years ago. The court ruled that, where there was continuous association with Crown land, Aborigines did have a right to claim it. The ruling resulted in some fairly hysterical responses, with non-Aborigines fearing their precious backyard was suddenly going to be subject to an Aboriginal land claim.

In December 1993 the Federal government introduced its Native Title legislation, which basically formalised the High Court's Mabo ruling. The content of the bill had, somewhat surprisingly, been agreed upon by all the major players involved – the miners, the farmers, the government and, of course, the Aborigines. While the Native Title legislation can do nothing to solve the injustices of the past, it does go a long way towards creating for the first time in the country's history the conditions for just land dealings between Aboriginal and non-Aboriginal groups.

Although there is much to be optimistic about, many Aborigines live in appalling conditions, and alcohol and drug problems remain widespread, particularly among the

Australian Capital Territory
Top Left: Black Mountain tower, Canberra (JL)
Top Right: Waterfall near Canberra (JL)
Bottom Left: National Gallery of Australia, Canberra (TW)
Bottom Right: Vietnam War Memorial detail, Canberra (RI)

AUSTRALIA

0   250   500 km

Australian Capital Territory
Top: New Parliament House, Canberra (PS)
Middle: High Court building, Canberra (TW)
Bottom: Old Parliament House, Canberra (RI)

young and middle-aged men. Aboriginal communities have taken up the challenge to try and eradicate these problems – many communities are now 'dry', and there are a number of rehabilitation programs for alcoholics, petrol sniffers and others with drug problems.

All in all it's been a bloody awful 200 years for Australia's Aborigines – one can only be thankful for their resilience, which enabled them to withstand the pressures placed on their culture, traditions and dignity, and that after so many years of domination they've been able to keep so much of that culture intact.

European Discovery & Exploration
Captain James Cook is popularly credited with Australia's discovery, but it was probably a Portuguese who first sighted the country, while credit for its earliest coastal exploration must go to a Dutchman.

Portuguese navigators had probably come within sight of the coast in the first half of the 16th century; and in 1606 the Spaniard Torres sailed through the strait between Cape York and New Guinea that still bears his name, though there's no record of his actually sighting the southern continent.

In the early 1600s Dutch sailors, in search of gold and spices, reached the west coast of Cape York and several other places on the west coast. What they found was a dry, harsh, unpleasant country, and they rapidly scuttled back to the kinder climes of Batavia in the Dutch East Indies (now Jakarta in Indonesia).

In 1642 the Dutch East India Company, in pursuit of fertile lands and riches of any sort, mounted an expedition to explore the land to the south. Abel Tasman made two voyages from Batavia in the 1640s during which he discovered the region he called Van Diemen's Land (which was renamed Tasmania some 200 years later), though he was unaware that it was an island, and the west coast of New Zealand. Although Tasman charted the coast of New Holland from Cape York to the Great Australian Bight, as well as the southern reaches of Van Diemen's Land, he did not sight the continent's east coast.

The prize for being Australia's original Pom goes to the enterprising pirate William Dampier, who made the first investigations ashore about 40 years after Tasman and nearly 100 years before Cook. He returned with sensational, but accurate, reports of the wildlife and the general conclusion that New Holland was a lousy place inhabited by the 'miserablest people in the world'. Of these people and their land he wrote:

They have no houses, but lie in the open air, without any covering, the earth being their bed and the heaven their canopy...the earth affords them no food at all...nor (is there) any sort of bird or beast that they can catch, having no instruments wherewithal to do so. I did not perceive that they did worship anything...

Dampier's records of New Holland, from visits made to Shark Bay on the west coast in 1688 and 1698, influenced the European idea of a primitive and godless land and that perspective remained unchanged until Cook's more informed and better documented voyages of discoveries spawned romantic and exotic notions of the South Seas and the idealised view of the 'noble savage'.

This dismal continent was forgotten until 1768, when the British Admiralty instructed Captain James Cook to lead a scientific expedition to Tahiti, to observe the transit of the planet Venus, and then begin a search for the Great South Land. On board his ship *Endeavour* were also several scientists including an astronomer and a group of naturalists and artists led by Joseph Banks.

After circumnavigating both islands of New Zealand, Cook set sail in search of the Great South Land, planning to head west until he found the unexplored east coast of the land known as New Holland.

On 19 April 1770 the extreme southeastern tip of the continent was sighted and named Point Hicks, and when the *Endeavour* was a navigable distance from shore Cook turned north to follow the coast and search for a suitable landfall. It was nine days before an opening in the cliffs was sighted and the ship and crew found sheltered anchorage in a harbour they named Botany Bay.

During their forays ashore the scientists recorded descriptions of plants, animals and birds, the likes of which had never been seen, and attempted to communicate with the few native inhabitants, who all but ignored these, the first White people to set foot on the east coast. Cook wrote of the Blacks: 'All they seemed to want was for us to be gone.'

After leaving Botany Bay Cook continued north, charting the coastline and noting that the fertile east coast was a different story from the inhospitable land the earlier explorers had seen to the south and west. When the *Endeavour* was badly damaged on a reef off north Queensland, Cook was forced to make a temporary settlement. It took six weeks to repair the ship, during which time Cook and the scientists investigated their surroundings further, this time making contact with the local Aborigines.

Unlike the unimpressed Dampier, Cook was quite taken with the indigenous people and wrote:

They may appear to some to be the most wretched people upon the earth: but in reality they are far more happier than we Europeans...They live in a tranquillity which is not disturbed by the inequality of condition...they seem to set no value upon anything we gave them, nor would they ever part with anything of their own...

After repairing the *Endeavour*, navigating the Great Barrier Reef and rounding Cape York, Cook again put ashore to raise the Union Jack, rename the continent New South Wales and claim it for the British in the name of King George III.

James Cook was resourceful, intelligent, and popularly regarded as one of the greatest and most humane explorers of all time. His incisive reports of his voyages make fascinating reading, even today. By the time he was killed, in the Sandwich Islands (now Hawaii) in 1779, he had led two further expeditions to the South Pacific.

Convicts & Settlement

Following the American Revolution, Britain was no longer able to transport convicts to North America. With jails and prison hulks already overcrowded, it was essential that an alternative be found quickly. In 1779 Joseph Banks suggested New South Wales as a fine site for a colony of thieves and in 1786 Lord Sydney announced that the king had decided upon Botany Bay as a place for convicts under sentence of transportation. The fact that the continent was already inhabited was not considered significant.

Less than two years later, in January 1788, the First Fleet sailed into Botany Bay under the command of Captain Arthur Phillip, who was to be the colony's first governor. Phillip was immediately disappointed with the landscape and sent a small boat north to find a more suitable landfall. The crew soon returned with the news that in Port Jackson they had found the finest harbour in the world and a good sheltered cove.

The fleet, comprised of 11 ships carrying about 750 male and female convicts, 400 sailors, four companies of marines and enough livestock and supplies for two years, weighed anchor again and headed for Sydney Cove to begin settlement.

For the new arrivals New South Wales was a harsh and horrible place. The reasons for transportation were often minor and the sentences, of no less than seven years with hard

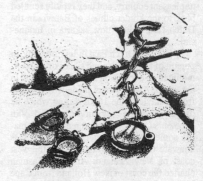

Convict cuffs and leg fetters

labour, were tantamount to life sentences as there was little hope of returning home.

Although the colony of soldiers, sailors, pickpockets, prostitutes, sheep stealers and petty thieves managed to survive the first difficult years, the cruel power of the military guards made the settlement a prison hell.

At first, until farming could be developed, the settlers were dependent upon supplies from Europe and a late or, even worse, a wrecked supply ship would have been disastrous. The threat of starvation hung over the colony for at least 16 years.

The Second Fleet arrived in 1790 with more convicts and some supplies, and a year later, following the landing of the Third Fleet, the population increased to around 4000.

As crops began to yield, New South Wales became less dependent on Britain for food. There were still, however, huge social gulfs in the fledgling colony: officers and their families were in control and clinging desperately to a modicum of civilised British living; soldiers, free settlers and even emancipated convicts were beginning to eke out a living; yet the majority of the population were still in chains, regarded as the dregs of humanity and living in squalid conditions.

Little of the country was explored during those first years; few people ventured further than Sydney Cove, and though Governor Phillip had instructed that every attempt should be made to befriend the Blacks, this was not to be.

Phillip believed New South Wales would not progress if the colony continued to rely solely on the labour of convicts, who were already busy constructing government roads and buildings. He believed prosperity depended on attracting free settlers, to whom convicts could be assigned as labourers, and in the granting of land to officers, soldiers and worthy emancipists (convicts who had served their time).

This began to happen when Phillip returned to England and his second in command, Grose, took over. In a classic case of 'jobs for the boys', Grose tipped the balance of power further in favour of the military by granting land to officers of the New South Wales Corps.

With money, land and cheap labour suddenly at their disposal the officers became exploitative, making huge profits at the expense of the small farmers. To encourage convicts to work, the officers were given permission to pay them in rum. The officers quickly prospered and were soon able to buy whole shiploads of goods and resell them for many times their original value. New South Wales was becoming an important port on trade routes, and whaling and sealing were increasing.

The officers, meeting little resistance, continued to do virtually as they pleased, all the while getting richer and more arrogant. They – and in particular one John Macarthur – managed to upset, defy, out-manoeuvre and outlast three governors, including William Bligh of the *Bounty* mutiny fame.

Bligh actually faced a second mutiny when the officers rebelled and ordered his arrest. This rebellion was the final straw for the British government, which dispatched Lieutenant-Colonel Lachlan Macquarie with his own regiment and orders for the return to London of the New South Wales Corps.

John Macarthur, incidentally, was to have far-reaching effects on the colony's first staple industry. It was his understanding of the country's grazing potential that fostered his own profitable sheep breeding concerns and prompted his introduction of the merino in the belief that careful breeding could produce wool of exceptional quality. Though it was his vision, it was his wife, Elizabeth, who did most of the work – Macarthur remained in England for nearly a decade for his part in what became known as the Rum Rebellion.

Governor Macquarie, having broken the stranglehold of the New South Wales Corps officers, set about laying the groundwork for social reforms. He felt that the convicts who had served their time should be allowed rights as citizens, and began appointing emancipists to public positions.

While this meant the long-term future for convicts didn't appear quite so grim, by the end of Macquarie's term in 1821 New South Wales was still basically a convict society and there were often clashes between those who had never been imprisoned and those who had been freed.

During the 1830s and 1840s the number of free settlers to the colonies of New South Wales, Western Australia, Van Diemen's Land (present-day Tasmania) and Port Phillip (Victoria) was increasing, although it was the discovery of gold in the 1850s that was truly to change the face of the young country.

By the time transportation was abolished (to the eastern colonies in 1852 and to the west in 1868) more than 168,000 convicts had been shipped to Australia.

Colonial Expansion

Australia never enjoyed the systematic push westward that characterised the European settlement of America. Exploration and expansion basically took place for one of three reasons: to find suitable places of secondary punishment, like the barbaric penal settlements at Port Arthur in Van Diemen's Land; to create another colony in order to occupy land before anyone else arrived; or in later years because of the quest for gold.

By 1800 there were only two small settlements in Australia – at Sydney Cove and Norfolk Island. While unknown areas on world maps were becoming few and far between, most of Australia was still one big blank. It was even suspected that it might be two large, separate islands and it was hoped that there might be a vast sea in the centre.

In the ensuing 40 years a great period of discovery started as the vast inland was explored and settlements were established at Hobart, Brisbane, Perth, Adelaide and Melbourne. Some of the early explorers, particularly those who braved the hostile centre, suffered great hardship.

George Bass had charted the coast south of Sydney almost down to the present location of Melbourne during 1797-98, and in 1798, with Matthew Flinders, he sailed around Van Diemen's Land, establishing that it was an island. Flinders went on in 1802 to sail right round Australia.

The first settlement in Van Diemen's Land, in 1803, was close to the present site of Hobart; by the 1820s Hobart Town rivalled Sydney in importance. The island was not named Tasmania, after its original European discoverer, until 1856 when, after the end of transportation, the inhabitants requested the name be changed to remove the stigma of what had been vicious penal colonies.

On the mainland, the Blue Mountains at first proved an impenetrable barrier, fencing in Sydney to the sea, but in 1813 a track was finally forced through and the western plains were reached by the explorers Blaxland, Wentworth and Lawson.

Port Phillip Bay in Victoria was originally considered as a site for the second settlement in Australia but was rejected in favour of Hobart, so it was not looked at again until 1835 when settlers from Tasmania, in search of more land, selected the present site of Melbourne. Perth was first settled in 1829, but as it was isolated from the rest of the country, growth there was very slow.

The first settlement in the Brisbane area was made by a party of convicts sent north from Sydney because the (by then) good citizens of that fair city were getting fed up with having all those crims about the place. By the time the Brisbane penal colony was abandoned in 1839, free settlers had arrived in force.

Adelaide, established in 1837, was initially an experiment in free-enterprise colonisation. It failed due to bad management and the British government had to take over from the bankrupt organisers and bail the settlement out of trouble.

In 1824 the explorers Hume and Hovell, starting from near present-day Canberra, made the first overland journey southwards, reaching the western shores of Port Phillip Bay. On the way they discovered a large river and named it after Hume, although it was later renamed the Murray by another great explorer, Charles Sturt. In 1829 it was Sturt who established how the Murrumbidgee and Darling River systems tied in with the Murray, and where the Murray met the sea.

Up until that time there had been much speculation that many of the inland rivers might in fact drain the anticipated inland sea.

Twelve years later the colony's surveyor-general, Major Mitchell, wrote glowing reports of the beautiful and fertile country he had crossed in his expedition across the Murray River and as far south as Portland Bay. He dubbed the region (now called Victoria) Australia Felix, or 'Australia Fair'.

In 1840 Edward Eyre left Adelaide to try to reach the centre of Australia. He gave up at Mt Hopeless and then decided to attempt a crossing to Albany in Western Australia. The formidable task nearly proved too much as both food and water were virtually unobtainable and his companion, Baxter, was killed by two of their Aboriginal guides. Eyre struggled on, encountering a French whaling ship in Rossiter Bay, and reprovisioned managed to reach Albany. The road across the Nullarbor Plain from South Australia to Western Australia is named the Eyre Highway.

From 1844 to 1845 a German scientist by the name of Ludwig Leichhardt travelled through northern Queensland, skirting the Gulf of Carpentaria, to Port Essington, near modern-day Darwin. He turned back during an attempt in 1846 and 1847 to cross Australia from east to west, only to disappear on his second attempt; he was never seen again.

In 1848 Edmund Kennedy set out to travel by land up Cape York Peninsula while a ship, HMS *Rattlesnake*, explored the coast and islands. Starting from Rockingham Bay, south of Cairns, the expedition almost immediately struck trouble when their heavy supply carts could not be dragged through the swampy ground around Tully. The rugged land, harsh climate, lack of supplies, hostile Aborigines and missed supply drops, all took their toll and nine of the party of 13 died. Kennedy himself was speared to death in an attack by Aborigines when he was only 30 km from the end of the fearsome trek. His Aboriginal servant, Jacky Jacky, was the only expedition member to finally reach the supply ship.

Leaving Melbourne in 1860, the Burke

and Wills expedition's attempt to cross the continent from south to north was destined to be one of the most tragic. Unlike earlier explorers, they tried to manage without Aboriginal guides. After reaching a depot at Cooper Creek in Queensland they intended to make a dash north to the Gulf of Carpentaria with a party of four. Their camels proved far slower than anticipated in the swampy land close to the gulf and on their way back one of the party died of exhaustion.

Burke, Wills and the third survivor, King, eventually struggled back to Cooper Creek, virtually at the end of their strength and nearly two months behind schedule, only to find the depot group had given up hope and left for Melbourne just hours earlier. They remained at Cooper Creek, but missed a returning search party and never found the supplies that had been left for them. Burke and Wills finally starved to death, literally in the midst of plenty; their companion, King, was able to survive on food provided by local Aborigines until a rescue party arrived.

Departing from Adelaide in 1860, chasing a £2000 reward for the first south-north crossing, John Stuart reached the geographical centre of Australia, Central Mt Stuart, but shortly after was forced to turn back. A second attempt in 1861 got much closer to the Top End before he again had to return. Finally in 1862 he managed to reach the north coast near Darwin. The overland telegraph line, completed in 1872, and the modern Stuart Highway follow a similar route.

Gold, Stability & Growth

The discovery of gold in the 1850s brought about the most significant changes in the social and economic structure of Australia, particularly in Victoria, where most of the gold was found.

Earlier gold discoveries had been all but ignored, partly because they were only small finds and mining skills were still undeveloped, but mostly because the law stated that all gold discovered belonged to the government.

The discovery of large quantities near Bathurst in 1851, however, caused a rush of hopeful miners from Sydney and forced the government to abandon the law of ownership. Instead, it introduced a compulsory diggers' licence fee of 30 shillings a month, whether the miners found gold or not, to ensure the country earned some revenue from the incredible wealth that was being unearthed. Victorian businesspeople at the time, fearing their towns would soon be devoid of able-bodied men, offered a reward for the discovery of gold in their colony.

In 1851 one of the largest gold discoveries in history was made at Ballarat, followed by others at Bendigo and Mt Alexander (near Castlemaine), starting a rush of unprecedented magnitude.

While the first diggers at the gold fields that soon sprang up all over Victoria came from the other Australian colonies, it wasn't long before they were joined by thousands of migrants. The Irish and English, as well as Europeans and Americans, began arriving in droves, and within 12 months there were about 1800 hopeful diggers disembarking at Melbourne every week.

Similar discoveries in other colonies, in particular the Western Australian gold rush of the 1890s, further boosted populations and levels of economic activity.

The 19th-century history of Australia, however, had its shameful side. The Aborigines, who were looked upon as little more than animals, were ruthlessly pushed off their tribal lands as the White diggers and settlers continued to take up the land for mining and farming. In some places, Tasmania in particular, they were hunted and killed like vermin, while those that survived on the fringes of the new White society became a dispossessed and oppressed people.

The gold rushes also brought floods of diligent Chinese miners and market gardeners onto the Australian diggings, where violent White opposition led to a series of race riots and a morbid fear of Asian immigration which persisted well into this century. Although few people actually made their fortunes on the gold fields, many stayed to settle the country, as farmers, workers and shopkeepers. At the same time the Industrial

Revolution in England started to produce a strong demand for raw materials. With the agricultural and mineral resources of such a vast country, Australia's economic base became secure.

Besides the population and economic growth that followed the discovery of gold, the rush also contributed greatly to the development of a distinctive Australian folklore. The music brought by the English and Irish, for instance, was tuned in to life on the diggings, while poets, singers and writers began telling stories of the people, the roaring gold towns and the boisterous hotels, the squatters and their sheep and cattle stations, the swagmen, and the derring-do of the notorious bushrangers, many of whom became folk heroes.

The 20th Century

During the 1890s calls for the separate colonies to federate became increasingly strident. Supporters argued that it would improve the economy and the position of the workers by enabling the abolition of intercolonial tariffs and the protection of workers against competition from foreign labour.

Each colony was determined, however, that its interests should not be overshadowed by those of the other colonies. For this reason, the constitution that was finally adopted gave only very specific powers to the Commonwealth, leaving all residual powers with the states. It also gave each state equal representation in the upper house of parliament (the Senate) regardless of size or population. Today Tasmania, with a population of less than half a million, has as many senators in Federal parliament as New South Wales, with a population of around 6 million. As the upper house is able to reject legislation passed by the lower house, this legacy of Australia's colonial past has had a profound effect on its politics ever since, entrenching state divisions and ensuring that the smaller states have remained powerful forces in the government of the nation.

With federation, which came on 1 January 1901, Australia became a nation, but its loyalty and many of its legal and cultural ties to Britain remained. The mother country still expected to be able to rely on military support from its Commonwealth allies in any conflict, and Australia fought beside Britain in battles as far from Australia's shores as the Boer War in South Africa. This willingness to follow Western powers to war would be demonstrated time and again during the 20th century. Seemingly unquestioning loyalty to Britain and later the USA was only part of the reason. Xenophobia – born of isolation, an Asian location and a vulnerable economy – was also to blame.

The extent to which Australia regarded itself as a European outpost became evident with the passage of the Immigration Restriction Bill of 1901. The bill, known as the White Australia policy, was designed to prevent the immigration of Asians and Pacific Islanders. Prospective immigrants were required to pass a dictation test in a European language. The language in which the test was given could be as obscure a tongue as the authorities wished. The dictation test was not abolished until 1958.

The desire to protect the jobs and conditions of White Australian workers that had helped bring about the White Australia policy did, however, have some positive results. The labour movement had been a strong political force for many years, and by 1908 the principle of a basic wage sufficient to enable a male worker to support himself, a wife and three children had been established. By that time also, old age and invalid pensions were being paid.

When war broke out in Europe, Australian troops were again sent to fight thousands of km from home. The most infamous of the WW I battles in which Diggers took part, from Australia's perspective, was that intended to force a passage through the Dardanelles to Constantinople. Australian and New Zealand troops landed at Gallipoli only to be slaughtered by well-equipped and strategically positioned Turkish soldiers. Ever since, the sacrifices made by Australian soldiers have been commemorated on Anzac Day, 25 April, the anniversary of the Gallipoli landing.

Interestingly, while Australians rallied to the aid of Britain during WW I, the majority of voters were only prepared to condone voluntary military service. Efforts to introduce conscription during the war led to bitter argument, both in Parliament and in the streets, and in referenda compulsory national service was rejected by a small margin.

Australia was hard hit by the Depression. In 1931 almost a third of breadwinners were unemployed and poverty was widespread. Swagmen became a familiar sight once more, as thousands of men took to the 'wallaby track' in search of work in the country. By 1932, however, Australia's economy was starting to recover, a result of rises in wool prices and a rapid revival of manufacturing.

In the years before WW II Australia became increasingly fearful of Japan. When war did break out, Australian troops fought beside the British in Europe, but after the Japanese bombed Pearl Harbor Australia's own national security finally began to take priority.

Singapore fell, the northern Australian towns of Darwin and Broome and the New Guinean town of Port Moresby were bombed, the Japanese advanced southward, and still Britain called for more Australian troops. This time the Australian Prime Minister, John Curtin, refused. Australian soldiers were needed to fight the Japanese advancing over the mountainous Kokoda Trail towards Port Moresby. In appalling conditions Australian soldiers confronted and defeated the Japanese at Milne Bay, east of Port Moresby, and began the long struggle to push them from the conquered Pacific territories.

Ultimately it was the USA, not Britain, that helped protect Australia from the Japanese, defeating them in the Battle of the Coral Sea. This event was to mark the beginning of a profound shift in Australia's allegiance away from Britain and towards the USA. Although Australia continued to support Britain in the war in Europe, its appreciation of its own vulnerability had been sharpened immeasurably by the Japanese advance.

One result of this was the postwar immigration program, which offered assisted passage not only to the British but also to refugees from eastern Europe in the hope that the increase in population would strengthen Australia's economy and contribute to its ability to defend itself. 'Populate or Perish' became the catchphrase. Between 1947 and 1968 more than 800,000 non-British European migrants came to live in Australia. They have since made an enormous contribution to the country, enlivening its culture and broadening its vision.

As living conditions improved after the war Australia came to accept the American view that it was not so much Asia but *communism* in Asia that threatened the increasingly Americanised Australian way of life. Accordingly Australia followed the USA into the Korean War and joined it as a signatory to the treaties of ANZUS and the anti-communist Southeast Asia Treaty Organization (SEATO). Australia also provided aid to south-east Asian nations under the Colombo Plan, a scheme initiated by Australia but subscribed to by many other countries, including the USA, Britain, Canada and Japan.

In the light of Australia's willingness to join SEATO, it is not surprising that its conservative government applauded the USA's entry into the Vietnam War and, in 1965, committed troops to the struggle. Support for involvement was far from absolute, however. The leader of the Australian Labor Party, for example, believed the Vietnam conflict to be a civil war in which Australia had no part. Still more troubling for many young Australian men was the fact that conscription had been introduced during the previous year and those undertaking national service could now be sent overseas. By 1967 as many as 40% of Australians serving in Vietnam were conscripts.

The civil unrest aroused by conscription was one factor that contributed to the rise to power, in 1972, of the Australian Labor Party for the first time in more than 20 years. The Whitlam government withdrew Australian troops from Vietnam, abolished national service and higher-education fees, instituted a system of free and universally available health care, and supported land rights for Aborigines..

Labor, however, was hampered by a hostile Senate and talk of mismanagement. On 11 November 1975, the Governor-General (the British monarch's representative in Australia) dismissed Parliament and installed a caretaker government led by the leader of the Opposition, Malcolm Fraser. Labor supporters were appalled. Such action was unprecedented in the history of the Commonwealth of Australia and the powers that the Governor-General had been able to invoke had long been regarded by many as an anachronistic vestige of Australia's now remote British past, the office itself as that of an impotent figurehead.

Nevertheless, it was a conservative coalition of the Liberal and National Country parties that won the ensuing election. A Labor government was not returned until 1983, when a former trade union leader, Bob Hawke, led the party to victory. The current Labor government, pragmatic by comparison to the Whitlam government, has maintained close links with the union movement. In 1990 Hawke won a record third consecutive term in office, thanks in no small part to the lack of better alternatives offered by the Liberals. He was replaced as Prime Minister and Labor leader by Paul Keating, his long-time Treasurer, in late 1991.

In 1991 Australia found itself in recession again, mainly as a result of domestic economic policy but also because Australia is particularly hard hit when demand (and prices) for primary produce and minerals falls on the world markets. Unemployment was the highest it had been since the early 1930s, hundreds of farmers were forced off the land because they couldn't keep afloat financially, there was a four-million-bale wool stockpile that no-one seemed to know how to shift, the building and manufacturing areas faced a huge slump and there was a general air of doom and gloom. The federal election in 1993 was won by Paul Keating, against all expectations. Unemployment remains unacceptably high, but Australia is now gradually clawing its way out of its worst recession in 60 years.

Despite the problems, most non-Aboriginal Australians have a standard of living which is extremely high; it's a disgrace that the same can't be said for most of their Aboriginal counterparts. Many Aborigines still live in deplorable conditions, with outbreaks of preventable diseases and infant mortality running at an unacceptably high rate – higher even than in many Third World countries. While definite progress has been made with the Federal government's recent Native Title legislation (see earlier), there's still a long way to go before Aborigines can enjoy the lifestyle of their choice.

Socially and economically, Australia is still coming to terms with its strategic location in Asia. While it has accepted large numbers of Vietnamese and other Asian refugees during the past two decades, it has never really considered itself a part of Asia, nor has it exploited the area's economic potential. With the boom in the economies of the region, regionalism is set to become the focus for the Australian economy in the future.

Another issue which is set to dominate Australian thinking in the 1990s is that of republicanism, as increasing numbers of people feel the continued constitutional ties with Britain are no longer relevant. This is especially true now that Sydney has been awarded the Olympic Games in the year 2000. Many feel it would be fitting that the games be opened by the constitutional head of the new Republic of Australia. The issue is far from decided and there's still a deal of soul-searching to be done before the Governor-General is done away with, but change seems inevitable.

GEOGRAPHY
Australia is an island continent whose landscape – much of it uncompromisingly bleak and inhospitable – is the result of gradual changes wrought over millions of years. Although there is still seismic activity in the eastern and western highland areas, Australia is one of the most stable land masses, and for about 100 million years has been free of the mountain-building forces that have given rise to huge mountain ranges elsewhere.

From the east coast a narrow, fertile strip merges into the greatly eroded, almost continent-long Great Dividing Range. The mountains are mere reminders of the mighty range that once stood here. Only in the section straddling the New South Wales border with Victoria and in Tasmania are they high enough to have winter snow.

West of the range the country becomes increasingly flat, dry and inhospitable. The endless flatness is broken only by salt lakes, occasional mysterious protuberances like Uluru (Ayers Rock) and Kata Tjuta (the Olgas), and some starkly beautiful mountains like the MacDonnell Ranges near Alice Springs. In places, the scant vegetation is sufficient to allow some grazing, so long as each animal has a seemingly enormous area of land. However, much of the Australian outback is a barren land of harsh, stone deserts and dry lakes with evocative names like Lake Disappointment.

The extreme north of Australia, the Top End, is a tropical area within the monsoon belt. Although the annual rainfall there looks adequate on paper, it comes in more or less one short, sharp burst. This has prevented the Top End from becoming seriously productive agriculturally.

The west of Australia consists mainly of a broad plateau. In the far west there is a mountain range and fertile coastal strip which heralds the Indian Ocean, but this is only to the south. In the north-central part of Western Australia, the dry country runs right to the sea. The rugged Kimberley region in the state's far north is spectacular.

Australia is the world's sixth largest country. Its area is 7,682,300 sq km, about the same size as the 48 mainland states of the USA and half as large again as Europe, excluding the former USSR. It is approximately 5% of the world's land surface. Lying between the Indian and Pacific oceans, Australia is about 4000 km from east to west and 3200 km from north to south, with a coastline 36,735 km long.

CLIMATE

Australian seasons are the antithesis of those in Europe and North America. It's hot in December and many Australians spend Christmas at the beach, while in July and August it's midwinter. Summer starts in December, autumn in March, winter in June and spring in September.

The climatic extremes aren't too severe in most parts of Australia. Even in Melbourne, the southernmost capital city on the mainland, it's a rare occasion when the mercury hits freezing point, although it's a different story in Canberra, the national capital. The poor Tasmanians, further to the south, have a good idea of what cold is.

As you head north the seasonal variations become fewer until, in the far north around Darwin, you are in the monsoon belt where there are just two seasons – hot and wet, and hot and dry. In the Snowy Mountains of southern New South Wales and the Alps of north-east Victoria there's a snow season with good skiing. The centre of the continent is arid – hot and dry during the day, but often bitterly cold at night.

A synopsis of average maximum and minimum temperatures and rainfall follows. Note that these are *average* maximums – even Melbourne gets a fair number of summer days hotter than 40°C.

Adelaide Maximum temperatures are from 26°C to 30°C from November to March; minimums can be below 10°C between June and September. Rainfall is heaviest, 50 to 80 mm per month, from May to September.

Alice Springs There are maximums of 30°C and above from October to March; minimums are 10°C and below from May to September. Rainfall is low all year round; from December to February there's an average of 40 mm of rain per month.

Brisbane Maximums average 20°C or more year round, peaking around 30°C from December to February; minimums are around 10°C from June to September. Rainfall is fairly heavy all year round, with more than 130 mm per month from December to March.

Canberra Maximums are in the mid to high 20s in the summer and minimums often close to freezing

between May and October; rainfall is usually 40 to 60 mm a month, year round.

Cairns Maximums are about 25°C to 33°C year round, with minimums rarely below 20°C; rainfall is below 100 mm a month from May to October (lowest in July and August), but peaks from January to March at 400 to 450 mm.

Darwin Temperatures are even year round, with maximums from 30°C to 34°C and minimums from 19°C to 26°C; rainfall is minimal from May to September, but from December to March there's 250 to 380 mm a month.

Hobart Maximums top 20°C only from December to March, and from April to November minimums are usually below 10°C; rainfall is about 40 to 60 mm a month, year round.

Melbourne Maximums are 20°C and above from October to April, minimums 10°C and below from May to October; rainfall is even year round, at 50 to 60 mm almost every month.

Perth Maximums are around 30°C from December to March, but minimums are rarely below 10°C; rainfall is lightest from November to March (20 mm and below) and heaviest from May to August (130 to 180 mm).

Sydney Usually only in the middle of winter are minimums below 10°C; summer maximums are around 25°C from December to March; rainfall is in the 75 to 130 mm range year round.

FLORA

Despite vast tracts of dry and barren land, much of Australia is well vegetated. Forests cover 5%, or 410,000 sq km. Plants can be found even in the arid centre, though many of them grow and flower erratically. Human activities seriously threaten Australian flora but to date most species have survived.

Origins

Australia's distinctive vegetation began to take shape about 55 million years ago when Australia broke from the supercontinent of Gondwanaland, drifting away from Antarctica to warmer climes. At this time, Australia was completely covered by cool-climate rainforest, but due to its geographic isolation and the gradual drying of the continent,

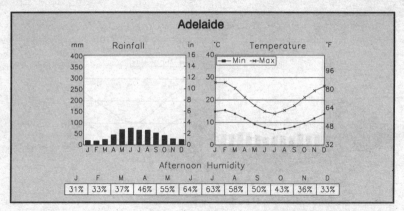

Adelaide

Afternoon Humidity

J	F	M	A	M	J	J	A	S	O	N	D
31%	33%	37%	46%	55%	64%	63%	58%	50%	43%	36%	33%

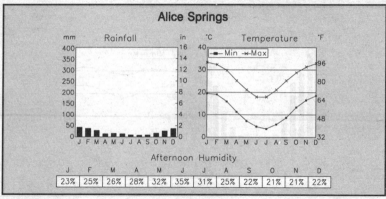

Alice Springs

Afternoon Humidity

J	F	M	A	M	J	J	A	S	O	N	D
23%	25%	26%	28%	32%	35%	31%	25%	22%	21%	21%	22%

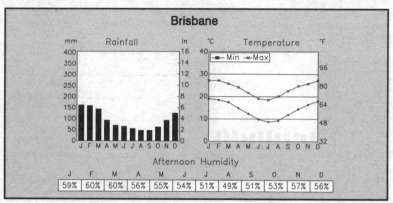

Brisbane

Afternoon Humidity

J	F	M	A	M	J	J	A	S	O	N	D
59%	60%	60%	56%	55%	54%	51%	49%	51%	53%	57%	56%

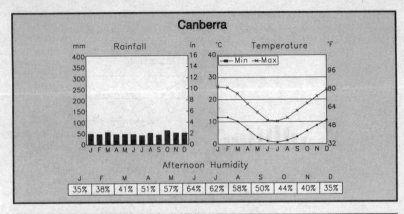

Canberra

Rainfall

Temperature

Afternoon Humidity

J	F	M	A	M	J	J	A	S	O	N	D
35%	38%	41%	51%	57%	64%	62%	58%	50%	44%	40%	35%

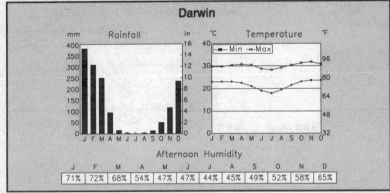

Darwin

Rainfall

Temperature

Afternoon Humidity

J	F	M	A	M	J	J	A	S	O	N	D
71%	72%	68%	54%	47%	47%	44%	45%	49%	52%	58%	65%

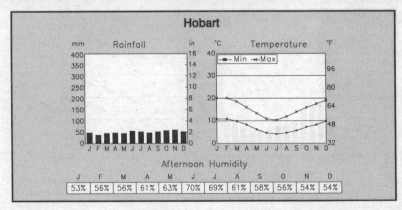

Hobart

Rainfall

Temperature

Afternoon Humidity

J	F	M	A	M	J	J	A	S	O	N	D
53%	56%	56%	61%	63%	70%	69%	61%	58%	56%	54%	54%

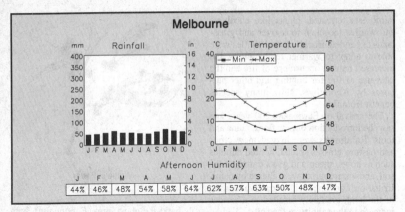

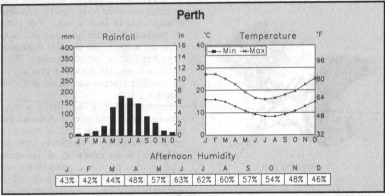

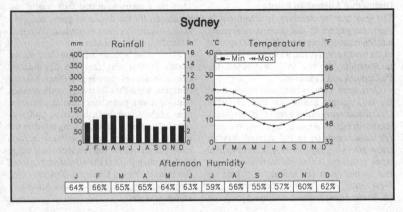

rainforests retreated, plants like eucalypts and wattles (acacias) took over and grasslands expanded. Eucalypts and wattles were able to adapt to warmer temperatures, the increased natural occurrence of fire and the later use of fire for hunting and other purposes by Aborigines. Now many species benefit from fire.

The arrival of Europeans 200 years ago saw the introduction of new flora, fauna and tools. Rainforests were logged, new crops and pasture grasses spread, hoofed animals such as cows, sheep and goats damaged the soil, and watercourses were altered by dams. Irrigation, combined with excessive clearing of the land, gradually resulted in a serious increase in the salinity of the soil.

Wattle in flower

Flowering gum

Distinctive Australian Plants

The gum tree, or eucalypt, is ubiquitous in Australia except in the deepest rainforests and the most arid regions. Of the 700 species of the genus eucalyptus, 95% occur naturally in Australia, the rest in New Guinea, the Philippines and Indonesia.

Gum trees vary in form and height from the tall, straight hardwoods such as jarrah (*Eucalyptus marginata*), karri (*E. diversifolia*), mountain ash (*E. regnans*) and river red gum (*E. camaldulensis*) to the stunted, twisted snow gum (*E. pauciflora*) with its colourful trunk striations. Other distinctive gums are the spotted gum (*E. maculata*), found on New South Wales's coast; the scribbly gum (*E. haemastoma*), which has insect tracks on

its bark; the ghost gum (*E. papuana*), with its distinctive white trunk; and the beautiful salmon-coloured Darwin woollybutt gums (*E. miniata*) of Katherine Gorge and elsewhere in the north. The gum tree features in Australian folklore, art and literature. Many varieties flower, the wood is prized and its oil is used for pharmaceuticals and perfumed products.

Fast-growing but short-lived wattles (acacias) occur in many warm countries, but around 600 species are found in Australia, growing in a variety of conditions, from the arid inland to the rainforests of Tasmania. Many wattles have deep green leaves and bright yellow to orange flowers. Most species flower during late winter and spring. Then the country is ablaze with wattle and the reason for the choice of green and gold as our national colours is obvious. Wattle is Australia's floral emblem.

Many other species of Australian native plants flower but few are deciduous. Common natives include grevilleas, hakeas, banksias, waratahs (*Telopeas*), bottlebrushes (callistemons), paperbarks (melaleucas), tea trees (*Leptospermums*), boronias, and she-oaks (casuarinas). An interesting book on the topic is *Field Guide to Native Plants of Australia* (Bay Books). You can see a wide range of Australian flora at the all-native National Botanic Gardens in Canberra. Brisbane's Mt Coot-tha Botanic Gardens features Australia's arid-zone plants.

Native Australian Fauna

Australia is blessed with a fascinating mix of native fauna, which ranges from the primitive to the highly evolved – some creatures are unique survivors from a previous age, while others have adapted so acutely to the natural environment that they can survive in areas which other animals would find uninhabitable.

Australian fauna is very distinct, partly because the Australian land mass is one of the most ancient on earth, and also because the sea has kept it isolated from other land masses for more than 50 million years. In this time the continent has suffered no major climatic upheavals, giving its various indigenous creatures an unusually long and uninterrupted period in which to evolve.

Since the European colonisation of Australia, 17 species of mammal have become extinct and at least 30 more are currently endangered. Many introduced non-native animals have been allowed to run wild, causing a great deal of damage to native species and to Australian vegetation. Introduced animals and birds include the fox, cat, pig, goat, camel, donkey, water buffalo, horse, starling, blackbird, cane toad and, best known of all, the notorious rabbit. Foxes and cats kill small native mammals and birds, rabbits denude vast areas of land, pigs carry disease and introduced birds take over the habitat of the local species.

MONOTREMES

The monotremes are regarded as virtually living fossils, and it's an exclusive little club with just two members – the platypus and the echidna. They are both egg-laying mammals which suckle their young on milk. They have survived in Australia partly thanks to the isolation already mentioned, but also because they became so specialised in their own sphere that no 'modern' creatures were able to supplant them.

Platypus

Zoological name: *Ornithorhynchus anatinus*
The platypus is certainly well equipped for its semi-aquatic life-style. It has a duck-like bill, which is actually quite soft, short legs,

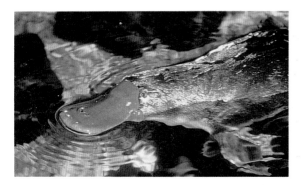

Platypus:
Ornithorhynchus
anatinus (photograph
courtesy of Healesville
Sanctuary)

webbed feet and a short but thick, beaver-like tail. Adult males are about 50 cm long, not including the 10 to 13-cm tail, and weigh around two kg; the females are slightly smaller. The males have a small hollow spur on the hind ankles which secretes a poison during the breeding season.

A platypus spends most of its time in the extensive burrows which it digs along the river banks; it spends the rest of its time in the water foraging for food with its bill or sunning itself in the open. Its diet is mainly small crustaceans, worms and tadpoles, and a mature adult will eat up to its own body weight in a day.

Separate burrows are dug for shelter and breeding. The entrance is usually just above water level and after some years the burrow can be 30 metres long. Copulation takes place in the water, and two (sometimes three) eggs are laid in the grass-lined nest. The newly hatched young measure just 17 mm.

The platypus is confined to eastern Australia and Tasmania, but within that area its environment ranges from near-freezing alpine streams to the subtropical rivers of Queensland.

Echidna (or spiny anteater)
Zoological name: *Tachyglossus aculeatus*

The echidna is a small, four-legged monotreme which is covered on the back with long, sharp spines and on the underside with fur. When fully grown they weigh around 4.5 kg and measure around 45 cm long. They have no neck, and the ears are just hairy holes on either side of the head. The elongated, beak-like snout is around 7.5 cm long and it has a long, sticky tongue which it can whip out some 15 cm beyond the snout – perfect for catching ants and termites, which comprise the major portion of its diet. It has very strong forelegs for scratching through the forest litter or

*Echidna
(or spiny anteater):
Tachyglossus
aculeatus (GB)*

digging in hard earth in search of food. At the first sign of danger, the echidna rapidly buries its body in the dirt, leaving only its formidable spines exposed.

The breeding season is from July until late September. The female echidna carries her eggs in a pouch, and, on hatching, the young remain there and suckle, only being evicted when their spines become too sharp for mum! At this time the mother hides them in thick undergrowth and tends them until they can fend for themselves.

Echidnas are found in a great range of habitats, from hot, dry deserts to altitudes of 1800 metres in the alps. A separate species exists in Tasmania, and a number of species are also found in New Guinea.

MARSUPIALS

The next major grouping of Australian mammals are the marsupials, mammals which raise their tiny young inside a pouch, or *marsupium*. Marsupials are largely confined to Australia, and included in this group of around 120 species are some of the country's most distinct and well-known animals – kangaroos, wallabies, koalas, wombats and possums – as well as others less well known, such as the numerous bandicoots and bush mice, the predatory quoll and the now-extinct thylacine (or Tasmanian tiger).

Marsupials can be considered as an intermediate step between the egg-laying monotremes and the more advanced placental mammals which give birth to developed foetuses able to survive

Brushtailed rock-wallaby:
Petrogale penicillata
(GB)

Grey kangaroo: *Macropodidae family (GB)*

(with help) in the outside world. Marsupial foetuses are usually tiny at birth and need to spend a good deal of time in the pouch before being sufficiently advanced to live outside the pouch.

Kangaroo
Zoological family: *Macropodidae*

Kangaroos are probably the most instantly recognisable Australian mammal and hardly need a description, although the name is applied to dozens of species, ranging from the tiny rufous hare-wallaby, which weighs barely half a kg, through to cat-sized wallabies and tree kangaroos right up to the 'big reds', which can be up to two metres high and weigh 90-odd kg.

There are now more kangaroos in Australia than there were when Europeans arrived, a result of the better availability of water and the creation of grasslands for sheep and cattle. Certain species, however, are threatened, as their particular environments are being destroyed or predators such as feral cats and foxes take their toll. About three million kangaroos are culled legally each year but many more are killed for sport or by those farmers who believe the cull is insufficient to protect their paddocks from overgrazing by the animals. Kangaroo meat has been exported for some time but it is only in recent years that it has started to appear on Australian menus – and in some states has only just been legalised.

The extraordinary breeding cycle of the kangaroo is well adapted to Australia's harsh and often unpredictable environment. The young kangaroo, or joey, just mm long at birth, claws its way unaided to the mother's pouch where it attaches itself to a nipple that expands inside its mouth. At this point, the mother produces two types of milk – one formula if she has a joey at heel, the other for the baby in her pouch. A day or two later the mother mates again, but the new embryo does not begin to develop until the first joey has permanently left the pouch. The embryo can also be held in a temporary state of suspended development if food or water becomes scarce.

Although kangaroos generally are not aggressive, males of the larger species, such as reds, can be dangerous when cornered. In the wild, boomers, as they are called, will grasp other males with their forearms, rear up on their muscular tails and pound their opponents with their hind feet, sometimes slashing them with their claws. Such behaviour can also be directed against dogs and, very rarely, people. It has also been said that kangaroos being pursued by dogs will sometimes hop into deep water and drown the dogs with their strong forearms.

Large kangaroos can be a hazard to people driving through the outback – hitting a two-metre kangaroo at 110 km/h is no joke.

Possum
Suborder: *Phalangerida*

There is an enormous range of possums (or phalangers) in Australia – they seem to have adapted to all sorts of conditions, including those of the city, where you'll often find them in parks. Look for them at dusk; sometimes they are so tame they'll eat from

Common brushtail
possum: Trichosurus
vulpecula (RI)

your hand. Some large species are found living in suburban roofs and will eat garden plants and food scraps. Possums are also common visitors at camp sites in heavily treed country, and will often help themselves to any food left out.

Possums are tree dwellers, clinging to branches with their hand-like feet and a tail which grips like a monkey's. They range in size from the tiny, mouse-like honey possum (*Tarsipes spenserae*), which measures barely four cm, up to the larger possums, such as the common ringtail possum (*Pseudocheirus peregrinus*) which can be as big as a domestic cat. Insects and leaves form the greater part of the possum's diet, although some have diversified and specialised; the honey possum, which lives on nectar sucked from wildflowers, has a long tubular snout like a drinking straw.

The sugar glider (*Petaurus breviceps*) has membranes between its front and rear legs, which when spread out are used for gliding from the tip of one tree to the base of the next, covering up to 100 metres in one swoop – quite a remarkable sight. The greater glider (*Petauroides volans*) has a yellow belly, and eyes which seem to glow when hit by torchlight. The eastern pygmy possum (*Cercartetus nanus*), no larger than a mouse, has a long tail by which it hangs to reach flowers to lick their nectar and pollen; when finished it climbs back up its own tail to the branch! It also has startling black eyes. Probably the most familiar of all possums is the common brushtail (or grey) possum (*Trichosurus vulpecula*), which occurs widely throughout the mainland and Tasmania. If you see a possum splattered on the highway (and unfortunately this is not an uncommon sight), chances are it's a poor old brushtail. In the past the brushtail was hunted widely for its fur.

Wombat: *Vombatidae family*

Wombat
Zoological family: *Vombatidae*

Wombats are slow, solid, powerfully built marsupials with broad heads and short, stumpy legs. These fairly placid and easily tamed creatures are legally killed by farmers, who object to the damage done to paddocks by wombats digging large burrows and tunnelling under fences.

Adult wombats are about 1.2 metres long and weigh up to 32 kg. Their strong front legs are excellent burrowing tools, and the rear legs are used for pushing the earth away. Their long burrows terminate in a nesting chamber, and it's here that the wombats live. They are nocturnal, solitary creatures and are rarely sighted. Their diet consists mainly of grasses, roots and certain tree barks. The female seeks out a mate during the breeding season, and she'll carry her single baby in the pouch for five to six months.

There are three species of wombat, the most common being the common wombat (*Vombatus ursinus*), which is distributed throughout the forested areas of south-eastern Australia. This species has a hairless snout, in contrast to the northern hairy-nosed wombat (*Lasiorhinus krefftii*), which is restricted to one small national park in tropical Queensland, and the southern hairy-nosed wombat (*Lasiorhinus latifrons*), which is also vulnerable and lives inland of the Great Australian Bight.

Koala
Zoological name: *Phascolarctos cinereus*

Australia's other instantly recognisable mammal is the much-loved koala. The name is an Aboriginal word meaning 'no water', which refers to the koala's alleged ability to meet all its moisture requirements from gum leaves, although it does drink water from pools.

The koala's cuddly appearance and slow speed have probably been its biggest liabilities. It was driven close to extinction earlier this century as its skin was highly prized, vast tracts of timbered country were cleared for agriculture and introduced viral diseases killed large numbers. Although they are protected today and their survival assured, large numbers of females are infertile due to chlamydia, a sexually transmitted disease. Their cuddly appear-

Koala: *Phascolarctos cinereus. Top: (GB) Bottom: (RI)*

ance also belies an irritable nature, and they will scratch and bite if sufficiently provoked.

Koalas are distantly related to the wombat and have a similarly solid build. When fully grown a koala measures about 70 cm and weighs around 10 kg. Their most distinctive features are their tufted ears, hard, black nose and, in common with the possums, opposable big toes which enable them to use their hind paws for gripping and climbing.

The mating season is from October to February. After birth, the young koala makes its way unaided into the pouch, where it stays for around six months until large enough to ride on its mother's back. The opening of the pouch actually faces backwards, and therefore often downwards, which would seem potentially dangerous for the young, but strong muscles around the pouch opening prevent the young marsupials from falling out.

Koalas feed only on the leaves of certain types of eucalypt and are particularly sensitive to changes to their habitat. They are found along the east coast from about Townsville down to Melbourne, and have been reintroduced in South Australia, where they had previously been driven to extinction.

Quoll
Zoological family: *Dasyuridae*

Australia's spotted quolls, or native cats, are about the size of domestic cats and are probably even more efficient killers, but are totally unrelated. Being nocturnal creatures which spend most of their time in trees, they are not often seen.

The native cats include the eastern quoll (*Dasyurus viverrinus*),

Northern quoll:
Dasyurus hallucatus
(DC)

western quoll (*Dasyurus geoffroii*) and the northern quoll (*Dasyurus hallucatus*). The eastern is now largely extinct on the mainland but is still found in numbers in Tasmania; it is brown or grey with white spots and an unspotted tail. The western is lighter in colour with a bushy, unspotted tail, and is now found only in Western Australia. The northern is the smallest of the native cats and has a combined head and body length of around 30 cm; it weighs in at birth at around a quarter of a gram!

The spotted-tailed quoll (*Dasyurus maculatus*), also known as the tiger cat, is one of the most ferocious hunters in the Australian bush. It is easily distinguishable from other species of quoll as it is quite a bit bigger, at 35 to 55 cm combined head and body length, and its spots continue onto its tail. These days it is found in Tasmania and along the east coast of the mainland.

Tasmanian Devil
Zoological name: *Sarcophilus harrisii*
The carnivorous Tasmanian devil is the largest of the dasyurids, and is as fierce as it looks. It's an ugly little creature with a nasty set of teeth and a fierce whining growl. They are hunters and scavengers, and are largely solitary and nocturnal. The body is black with a white stripe across the chest, and measures around 60 cm, while the tail is around 25 cm. They have immensely strong teeth and jaws, giving them the ability to chew through bone as easily as if it were cork, and it's this that is at the heart of its fearsome reputation. Their main diet consists of small birds and mammals, insects and carrion.

Tassie devils are found only in Tasmania, where the locals will gleefully torment visitors with morbid tales of its hideous habits.

Thylacine
Zoological name: *Thylacinus cynocephalus*
The now-extinct, striped thylacine, or Tasmanian tiger, was a dog-like, carnivorous marsupial, reared like the Tasmanian devil in the female's backward-opening pouch. At one time both the tiger and the devil were threatened with extinction. Efforts to avert this disaster ensured the survival of the latter, but the larger tiger was unable to recover its numbers. The last known specimen died in Hobart Zoo in 1936, although there is still much speculation as to whether tigers still exist. Regular 'sightings' are reported, and these are often the cause for much excitement in the press, but as yet none of these sightings has been confirmed.

Bandicoot
Zoological family: *Peramelidae*
The small, rat-like bandicoots have been among the principal victims of the introduced domestic and feral cats – a number of species have either been totally wiped out or are heading that way.

Bandicoots are largely nocturnal, but can occasionally be seen scampering through the bush. They are largely insect eaters but do also eat some plant material. The second and third toes of the hind feet are fused together, a feature they share with the kangaroo and the wombat. The large claws are put to good use scratching for insects, including centipedes and scorpions, but also make them excellent fighters.

One of the most common varieties is the southern brown bandicoot (*Isoodon obesulus*), which is found in eastern and western Australia. Others, such as the eastern barred bandicoot (*Perameles gunnii*), are these days found in very limited areas. The rare bilby (*Macrotis lagotis*) is found mainly in the Northern Territory and major efforts have been made to ensure its survival. Its rabbit-like ears have recently caused it to be promoted as Australia's own Easter animal: the Easter bilby versus the Easter bunny!

Numbat
Zoological name: *Myrmecobius fasciatus*
The attractive numbat, or banded anteater, is a pouchless marsupial and is unusual in that it is most active during the day rather than at night. It has striking rust-red fur with six or seven white stripes across the rump. Adult numbats are about the size of a rat and weigh around half a kg.

They live in hollow, fallen wandoo trees (*Eucalyptus redunca*) found in the forests of south-western Australia; their numbers are dwindling.

Dingo
Zoological name: *Canis familiaris dingo*
Australia's native dog is the dingo, domesticated by the Aborigines and thought to have arrived around 6000 years ago. It differs from the domestic dog in that it howls rather than barks and breeds only once a year (rather than twice), although the two can successfully interbreed.

Dingo: *Canis familiaris dingo (JC)*

Dingoes prey mainly on rabbits, rats and mice, although when other food is scarce they sometimes attack livestock (usually unattended sheep or calves), and for this reason are considered vermin by many farmers. Efforts to control the number of dingoes have been largely unsuccessful. For many years the government paid a bounty on each scalp brought in, and even poison is still widely used.

They are found only on the mainland, north and west of the Dogproof Fence, which is the world's longest artificial barrier. It runs for 5490 km from near the Gold Coast in Queensland to the coast near Ceduna in South Australia.

BIRDS

Australia's bird life is as beautiful as it is varied, with over 750 species recorded.

The Royal Australasian Ornithologists Union runs bird observatories in New South Wales, Victoria and Western Australia, which provide accommodation and guides. Contact the RAOU (☎ (03) 370 1422) at 21 Gladstone St, Moonee Ponds, Victoria 3039.

Emu: *Dromaius novaehollandiae (RI)*

Emu

Zoological name: *Dromaius novaehollandiae*
The only bird larger than the emu is the African ostrich, also flightless. The emu is a shaggy feathered, often curious bird found right across the country, but only in uninhabited areas. After the female lays her six to 12 large, dark green eggs the male hatches them and raises the young.

Parrots & Cockatoos

There is an amazing variety of these birds throughout Australia. The noisy pink and grey galah (*Cacatua roseicapilla*) is amongst the most common, although the sulphur-crested cockatoo (*Cacatua galerita*) has to be the noisiest. There are a number of species of rosella (*Platycercus*), most of them brilliantly coloured and not at all backward about taking a free feed from humans. The eastern rosella (*Platycercus eximius*) is the most widespread and is found throughout rural south-eastern Australia.

Rainbow lorikeets (*Trichoglossus haematodus*) are more extravagantly colourful than you can imagine until you've seen one. Budgerigars (*Melopsittacus undulatus*), native to Australia, are widespread over inland Australia but are mainly found towards the Centre; they often fly in flocks of thousands.

Other distinctive birds are the various black cockatoos. There are five varieties, the most widespread being the large red-tailed black cockatoo (*Calyptorhynchus magnificus*) which occurs right across northern and eastern Australia. The yellow-tailed black cockatoo (*C. funereus*) is similar but is confined to south-eastern Australia.

Rainbow lorikeet: *Trichoglossus haematodus (Rl)*

*Kookaburra: Dacelo
novaeguinae (JC)*

Kookaburra
Zoological name: *Dacelo novaeguinae*
A member of the kingfisher family, the kookaburra is heard as much
as it is seen – you can't miss its loud, cackling cry. Kookaburras
can become quite tame and pay regular visits to friendly house-
holds, but only if the food is excellent. It's hard to impress a
kookaburra with anything less than top-class steak.

It is common throughout coastal Australia, but particularly in the
east and south-west of the country.

Bower Bird
The stocky, stout-billed bowerbird, of which there are at least half
a dozen varieties, is best known for its unique mating practice. The
male builds a bower which he decorates with various coloured
objects to attract females. In the wild, flowers, berries or stones
are used, but if artificial objects (clothes pegs, plastic pens, bottle
tops – anything brightly coloured, but usually white, blue or green)
are available, he'll certainly use them. The female is impressed by
the male's neatly built bower and attractively displayed treasures,
but once they've mated all the hard work is left to her. He goes
back to refurbishing the bower and attracting more females while
she hops off to build a nest.

The three most common varieties are the great bowerbird
(*Chlamydera nuchalis*), which occurs right across the top of northern Australia; the spotted bowerbird (*C. maculata*), found in inland
New South Wales and southern Queensland; and the satin bowerbird (*Ptilonorhynchus violaceus*), which lives in the coastal
regions of eastern Victoria, New South Wales and southern
Queensland.

REPTILES
Snakes
Australian snakes are generally shy and try to avoid confrontations with humans. A few, however, are deadly. The most dangerous are the taipans and tiger snakes, although death adders, copperheads, brown snakes and red-bellied black snakes should also be avoided. Tiger snakes will actually attack. It's a good idea to stay right away from all snakes – and don't try stepping over them when they're asleep!

Crocodiles
There are two types of crocodile in Australia: the extremely dangerous saltwater crocodile (*Crocodylus porosus*), or 'saltie' as it's known, and the less aggressive freshwater crocodile (*C. johnstoni*), or 'freshie'.

Salties are not confined to salt water. They inhabit estuaries, and following floods may be found many km from the coast. They may even be found in permanent fresh water more than 100 km inland. It is important to be able to tell the difference between the saltie and its less dangerous relative, as both are prolific in northern Australia.

Freshies are smaller than salties – anything over four metres should be regarded as a saltie. Freshies are also more finely constructed and have much narrower snouts and smaller teeth. Salties, which can grow to seven metres, will attack and kill humans. Freshies, though unlikely to seek human prey, have been known to bite, and children in particular should be kept away from them.

Saltwater crocodile:
Crocodylus porosus
(PS)

SPIDERS

Most Australian spiders bite. In particular, two spiders to keep away from are the redback (*Latrodectus hasselti*), a relative of the American black widow, and the funnel-web (*Dipluridae* family). The latter is found only in New South Wales, particularly around Sydney, while the former is more widespread and has a legendary liking for toilet seats. Both are extremely poisonous and have been lethal.

You should also beware of the white-tailed spider, commonly found in fields and gardens. It is about the size of a dollar coin, with a distinct white spot on its grey-black back. Some people have extreme reactions to its bite and gangrene can result.

Another nasty to look out for is the wolf spider (*Lycosidae* family), which builds a trap-doored hole in the ground. The bite of the wolf spider can cause necrosis.

Funnel-web spider: *Dipluridae family*

NATIONAL PARKS & RESERVES

Australia has more than 500 national parks – nonurban protected wilderness areas of environmental or natural importance. Each state defines and runs its own national parks, but the principle is the same throughout Australia. National parks include rainforests, vast tracts of empty outback, strips of coastal dune land and long, rugged mountain ranges.

Public access is encouraged if safety and conservation regulations are observed. In all parks you're asked to do nothing to damage or alter the natural environment. Approach roads, camping grounds (often with toilets and showers), walking tracks and information centres are often provided for visitors.

Some national parks are so isolated, rugged or uninviting that you wouldn't want to do much except look unless you were an experienced, well-prepared bushwalker or climber. Other parks, however, are among Australia's major attractions and some of the most beautiful have been included on the World Heritage List (a United Nations list of natural or cultural places of world significance that would be an irreplaceable loss to the planet if they were altered).

Internationally, the World Heritage List includes the Taj Mahal, the Pyramids, the Grand Canyon and, currently, nine Australian areas: the Great Barrier Reef; Kakadu and Uluru national parks in the Northern Territory; the Willandra Lakes region of far western New South Wales; the Lord Howe Island group off New South Wales; the Tasmanian wilderness heritage area (Franklin-Gordon Wild Rivers and Cradle Mountain-Lake St Clair national parks); the east coast temperate and subtropical rainforest parks (15 national parks and reserves, covering 1000 sq km in the eastern highlands of New South Wales); the wet tropics area of far north Queensland, which is in the Daintree-Cape Tribulation area; Shark Bay on the Western Australian coast; and Fraser Island off the Queensland coast.

The Australian Conservation Foundation is one of a number of bodies lobbying to have further places listed. Currently these are Lake Eyre in outback South Australia, the

Kangaroo

Blue Mountains National Park near Sydney, the Nullarbor Plain, the mountain regions of south-west Tasmania not already listed, the Australian Alps, and Cape York Peninsula.

Before a site or area is accepted for the World Heritage List it has first to be proposed by its country and then must pass a series of tests at the UN, culminating, if it is successful, in acceptance by the UN World Heritage Committee which meets at the end of each year. Any country proposing one of its sites or areas for the list must agree to protect the selected area, keeping it for the enjoyment of future generations even if to do so requires help from other countries.

While state governments have authority over their own national parks, the Federal government is responsible for ensuring that Australia meets its international treaty obligations, and in any dispute arising from a related conflict between a state and the Federal government, the latter can override the former.

In this way the Federal government can force a state to protect an area with World

Heritage listing, as it did in the early 1980s when the Tasmanian government wanted to dam the Gordon River in the south-west of the state and thereby flood much of the wild Franklin River.

For National Park authority addresses see the Useful Organisations section of the Facts for the Visitor chapter.

State Forests

Another form of nature reserve you may discover is the state forest. These are owned by state governments and have fewer regulations than national parks. In theory, the state forests can be logged, but often they are primarily recreational areas with camping grounds, walking trails and signposted forest drives. Some permit horses and dogs.

GOVERNMENT

Australia is a federation of six states and two territories. Under the written Constitution, which came into force on 1 January 1901 when the colonies joined to form the Commonwealth of Australia, the Federal government is mainly responsible for the national economy and Reserve Bank, customs and excise, immigration, defence, foreign policy and the post office. The state governments are chiefly responsible for health, education, housing, transport and justice. There are both federal and state police forces.

Australia has a parliamentary system of government based on that of the UK, and the state and federal structures are broadly similar. In Federal parliament, the lower house is the House of Representatives, the upper house the Senate. The House of Representatives has 147 members, divided among the states on a population basis (NSW 50, Victoria 38, Queensland 25, South Australia 12, Western Australia 14, Tasmania five, ACT two and Northern Territory one). Elections for the House of Representatives are held at least every three years. The Senate has 12 Senators from each state, and two each from the ACT and the Northern Territory. State Senators serve six-year terms, with elections for half of them every three years; territory Senators serve only three years, their terms coinciding with the elections for the House of Representatives. Queensland's upper house was abolished in

Parliament House, Sydney

1922. The Commonwealth government is run by a prime minister, while the state governments are led by a premier and the Northern Territory by a chief minister. The party holding the greatest number of lower house seats forms the government.

Australia is a monarchy, but although Britain's king or queen is also Australia's, Australia is fully autonomous. The British sovereign is represented by the Governor-General and state governors, whose nominations for their posts by the respective governments are ratified by the monarch of the day.

Federal parliament is based in Canberra, the capital of the nation. Like Washington DC in the USA, Canberra is in its own separate area of land, the Australian Capital Territory (ACT), and is not under the rule of one of the states. Geographically, however, the ACT is completely surrounded by New South Wales. The state parliaments are in each state capital.

The Federal government is elected for a maximum of three years but elections can be (and often are) called earlier. Voting in Australian elections is by secret ballot and is compulsory for persons 18 years of age and over. Voting can be somewhat complicated as a preferential system is used whereby each candidate has to be listed in order of preference. This can result, for example, in Senate elections with 50 or more candidates to be ranked!

The Constitution can only be changed by referendum, and only if a majority of voters in at least four states favour it. Since federation in 1901, of the 42 proposals that have been put to referendum, only eight have been approved.

In Federal parliament, the two main political groups are the Australian Labor Party (ALP) and the coalition between the Liberal Party and the National Party. These parties also dominate state politics but sometimes the Liberal and National parties are not in coalition. The latter was once known as the National Country Party since it mainly represents country seats.

The only other political party of any real substance is the Australian Democrats, which has largely carried the flag for the ever-growing 'green' movement. Independent politicians with no affiliation to a particular party have also made it into the traditional political structure in recent times – in the 1993 federal elections two independent 'green' senators and an independent senator were elected to the Senate, and they hold the balance of power with the Democrats.

The Cabinet, presided over by the Prime Minister, is the government's major policy-making body, and it comprises about half of the full ministry. It's a somewhat secretive body which meets in private (usually in Canberra) and its decisions are ratified by the Executive Council, a formal body presided over by the Governor-General.

ECONOMY

Today, Australia is a relatively affluent, industrialised nation but much of its wealth still comes from agriculture and mining. It has a small domestic market and its manufacturing sector is comparatively weak. Nevertheless, a substantial proportion of the population is employed in manufacturing, and for much of Australia's history it has been argued that these industries need tariff protection from imports to ensure their survival.

Today, however, efforts are being made to increase Australia's international competitiveness. This has become more important as prices of traditional primary exports have become more volatile. The government has sought to restrain real wages with the assistance of the Australian Council of Trade Unions (ACTU), to make Australian products more competitive overseas and to promote employment within Australia.

This policy saw the creation of many new jobs, but the recession threw many thousands back onto the unemployment queues, with unemployment currently around 11%. However, analysts are cautiously optimistic.

One of Australia's greatest economic hopes is tourism, with the numbers of visitors rising each year and projections for even greater numbers in the future. The other bright spot is the booming economies of South-East Asia. Australia is perfectly positioned to enter these markets, providing goods and services.

POPULATION & PEOPLE

Australia's population is about 17 million. The most populous states are New South Wales and Victoria, each with a capital city (Sydney and Melbourne) with a population of around three million. The population is concentrated along the east coast strip from Adelaide to Cairns and in the similar but smaller coastal region in Western Australia. The centre of the country is very sparsely populated.

There are about 230,000 Aborigines and Torres Strait Islanders, most heavily concentrated in central Australia and the far north.

Until WW II Australians were predominantly of British and Irish descent but that has changed dramatically since the war. First there was heavy migration from Europe creating major Greek and Italian populations but also adding Yugoslavs, Lebanese, Turks and other groups.

More recently Australia has had large influxes of Asians, particularly Vietnamese after the Vietnam War. In comparison to the country's population Australia probably took more Vietnamese refugees than any other Western nation. On the whole these 'new Australians' have been remarkably well accepted and 'multiculturalism' is a popular concept in Australia.

If you come to Australia in search of a real Australian you will find one quite easily – they are not known to be a shy breed. He or she may be a Lebanese cafe owner, an English used-car salesperson, an Aboriginal artist, a Malaysian architect or a Greek greengrocer. And you will find them in pubs, on beaches, at barbecues, in mustering yards and at art galleries. And yes, you may meet a Mick (Crocodile) Dundee or two but he is strictly a rural model – the real Paul Hogan was a Sydney Harbour Bridge painter, a job where after you finish at one end you just start again at the other.

ARTS & CULTURE
Aboriginal Culture

Early European settlers and explorers usually dismissed the entire Aboriginal population as 'savages' and 'barbarians', and it was some time before the Aborigines' deep, spiritual bond with the land, and their relationship to it, was understood by White Australians.

The perceived simplicity of the Aborigines' technology contrasts with the sophistication of their cultural life. Religion, history, law and art are integrated in complex ceremonies which depict the activities of their ancestral beings, and prescribe codes of behaviour and responsibilities for looking after the land and all living things. The link between the Aborigines and the ancestral beings are totems, each person having their own totem, or Dreaming. These totems take many forms, such as caterpillars, snakes, fish and magpies. Songs explain how the landscape contains these powerful creator ancestors, who can exert either a benign or a malevolent

Bark painting of a long-necked turtle from western Arnhem Land

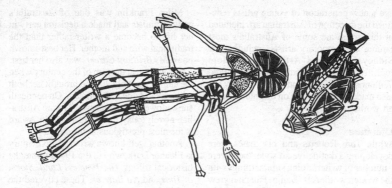

Blue Paintings at Little Nourlangie, Kakadu

influence. They tell of the best places and the best times to hunt, and where to find water in drought years. They can also specify kinship relations and correct marriage partners.

Ceremonies are still performed in many parts of Australia; many of the sacred sites are believed to be dangerous and entry is prohibited under traditional Aboriginal law. These restrictions may seem merely the result of superstition, but in many cases they have a pragmatic origin. One site in northern Australia was believed to cause sores to break out all over the body of anyone visiting the area. Subsequently, the area was found to have a dangerously high level of radiation from naturally occurring radon gas. In another instance, fishing from a certain reef was traditionally prohibited. This restriction was scoffed at by local Europeans until it was discovered that fish from this area had a high incidence of ciguatera, which renders fish poisonous if eaten by humans.

While many Aborigines still live in rural areas today, those living an urban life in towns remain distinctively Aboriginal – they still speak their indigenous language (or a creolised mix) on a daily basis, and mix largely with other Aborigines. Much of their knowledge of the environment, bush medicine and food ('bush tucker') has been retained, and many traditional rites and ceremonies are being revived.

The art of the Aborigines is detailed in a colour section at the end of this chapter.

European Art

In the 1880s a group of young artists developed the first distinctively Australian style of watercolour painting. Working from a permanent bush camp in Melbourne's (then) outer suburb of Box Hill, the painters captured the unique qualities of Australian life and the bush. The work of this group is generally referred to as the Heidelberg School, although the majority of the work was done at Box Hill. In Sydney a contemporary movement worked at Sirius Cove on Sydney Harbour. Both groups were influenced by the French plein-air painters, whose practice of working outdoors to capture the effects of natural light led directly to Impressionism. The main artists were Tom Roberts, Arthur Streeton, Frederick McCubbin, Louis Abrahams, Charles Conder, Julian Ashton and, later, Walter Withers. Their works can be found in most of the major galleries and are well worth seeking out.

In the 1940s another revolution took place at Heide, the home of John and Sunday Reed in suburban Melbourne. Under their patronage a new generation of young artists redefined the direction of Australian art. Included in this group are some of Australia's most famous contemporary artists, including Sir Sidney Nolan and Arthur Boyd. More recently the work of painters such as Fred Williams, John Olsen and Brett Whiteley has also made an impression on the international art world.

Literature

While Tom Roberts and his mates were developing a distinctive art style, there were a number of writers doing similar things with the written word. A B (Banjo) Paterson grew up in the bush in the second half of last century and went on to become one of Australia's most important bush poets. For some years he contributed ballads to the Sydney *Bulletin*, and wrote under the name of 'the Banjo', the name of a horse on his family's station. His horse ballads were regarded as some of his best, but he was familiar with all aspects of station life and wrote with great optimism. *Clancy of the Overflow* and *The Man From Snowy River* are both well known, but the Banjo is probably most remembered as the author of Australia's alternative national anthem, 'Waltzing Matilda'.

Henry Lawson was a contemporary of Paterson, but was much more of a social commentator and political thinker. Although he wrote a good many poems about the bush – pieces such as 'Andy's Gone with Cattle' and 'The Roaring Days' are among his best – his greatest legacy is his short stories of life in the bush, which seem remarkably simple yet manage to capture the atmosphere perfectly – *The Drover's Wife* and *A Day on a Selection* are good examples. Lawson published a number of short-story collections, including *While the Billy Boils* (1896) and *Joe Wilson and his Mates* (1901).

C J Dennis was another writer of the time, and his verse story, *The Songs of a Sentimental Bloke*, published in 1915, established him as a national writer with broad appeal. The tone of his writing was much lighter than that of either Lawson or Paterson.

Miles Franklin was one of Australia's early feminists and made a decision early in her life to become a writer rather than the traditional wife and mother. Her best-known book, *My Brilliant Career*, was also her first. It was written at the turn of the century when the author was only 20, and brought her both widespread fame and criticism. On her death she endowed an annual award for an Australian novel; today the Miles Franklin Award is the most prestigious in the country.

Another well-known writer of this century is Eleanor Dark, who in the 1940s wrote the historical trilogy *The Timeless Land*, *Storm of Time* and *No Barrier*. These covered the period from 1788 to 1914, and were highly unusual at the time for the sympathetic treatment they gave to the Aboriginal culture.

The works of Patrick White are arguably some of the best to come out of Australia in the last 30 years. He was a prolific writer who won the Miles Franklin Award twice, for *Voss* (1957) and *The Riders in the Chariot* (1961), and the Nobel Prize for *The Eye of the Storm* (1973).

Other contemporary writers of note include Peter Carey, who has won both the Miles Franklin Award (for *Bliss* in 1981) and the Booker Prize (for *Oscar and Lucinda* in 1988); Thomas Keneally, who has won two Miles Franklin Awards and one Booker Prize, well-known for his novels, such as *The Chant of Jimmy Blacksmith*, which deal with the suffering of oppressed peoples, in this case Aborigines; Tim Winton, a young writer from Western Australia; Elizabeth Jolley, a short-story writer and novelist with a keen eye for the eccentric; and Thea Astley.

Cinema

The Australian film industry began as early as 1896, a year after the Lumière brothers opened the world's first cinema in Paris. Maurice Sestier, one of the Lumières' photographers, came to Australia and made the first films in the streets of Sydney and at Flemington Race Course during the Melbourne Cup.

Cinema historians regard an Australian film, *Soldiers of the Cross*, as the world's first 'real' movie. It was originally screened at the Melbourne Town Hall in 1901, cost £600 to make and was shown throughout America in 1902.

The next significant Australian film, *The Story of the Kelly Gang*, was screened in 1907, and by 1911 the industry was flourishing. Low-budget films were being made in such quantities that they could be hired out or sold cheaply. Over 250 silent feature films were made before the 1930s when the *talkies* and Hollywood took over.

In the 1930s, film companies like Cinesound sprang up. Cinesound made 17 feature films between 1931 and 1940, many based on Australian history or literature. *Forty Thousand Horsemen*, directed by Cinesound's great film maker Charles Chauvel, was a highlight of this era of locally made and financed films which ended in 1959, the year of Chauvel's death.

Before the introduction of government subsidies during 1969 and 1970, the Australian film industry found it difficult to compete with US and British interests. The New Wave era of the 1970s, a renaissance of Australian cinema, produced films like *Picnic at Hanging Rock, Sunday Too Far Away, Caddie* and *The Devil's Playground*, which appealed to large local and international audiences. Since the '70s, Australian actors and directors like Mel Gibson, Judy Davis, Greta Scacchi, Paul Hogan, Bruce Beresford, Peter Weir, Gillian Armstrong and Fred Schepisi have gained international recognition. Films like *Gallipoli, The Year of Living Dangerously, Mad Max, Malcolm, Crocodile Dundee I* and *II, Proof, Holidays on the River Yarra, The Year My Voice Broke* and most recently *Strictly Ballroom* have entertained and impressed audiences worldwide.

Music

Australia's participation in the flurry of popular music which has occurred since Elvis did his thing back in 1954 has been a frustrating mix of good, indifferent, lousy, parochial and excellent. However, even the offerings of our most popular acts have done

nothing to remove the cultural cringe: the highest praise remains 'it's good enough to have come from the UK/USA'. And it's true that little of the popular music created here has been noticeably different from that coming from overseas.

Which is why the recent success of Aboriginal music, and its merging with rock, is so refreshing. This music really is different. The most obvious name that springs to mind is Yothu Yindi. Their song about the agreement dishonoured by the Whites, 'Treaty', perhaps did more than anything else to popularise the Aborigines' land rights claims.

Having written off White popular music, the live-music circuits of Australia really are something to crow about. The bands playing around the traps can be just as exciting as those found in London or LA, pardon the comparisons!

RELIGION

A shrinking majority of people in Australia are at least nominally Christian. Most Protestant churches have merged to become the Uniting Church, although the Church of England has remained separate. The Catholic Church is popular (about a third of Christians are Catholics), with the original Irish adherents now joined by the large numbers of Mediterranean immigrants.

Non-Christian minorities abound, the main ones being Buddhist, Jewish or Muslim.

Traditional Aboriginal cultures either have very little religious component or are nothing but religion, depending on how you look at it. Is a belief system which views every event, no matter how trifling, in a nonmaterial context a religion? The early Christian missionaries certainly didn't think so. For them a belief in a deity was an essential part of a religion, and anything else was mere superstition.

LANGUAGE
Australian English

Any visitor from abroad who thinks Australian (that's 'strine') is simply a weird variant of English/American will soon have a few surprises. For a start many Australians don't even speak Australian – they speak Italian, Lebanese, Vietnamese, Turkish or Greek.

Those who do speak the native tongue are liable to lose you in a strange collection of Australian words. Some have completely different meanings in Australia than they have in English-speaking countries north of the equator; some commonly used words have been shortened almost beyond recognition. Others are derived from Aboriginal languages, or from the slang used by early convict settlers.

There is a slight regional variation in the Australian accent, while the difference between city and country speech is mainly a matter of speed. Some of the most famed Aussie words are hardly heard at all – 'mates' are more common than 'cobbers'. If you want to pass for a native try speaking slightly nasally, shortening any word of more than two syllables and then adding a vowel to the end of it, making anything you can into a diminutive (even the Hell's Angels can become mere 'bikies') and peppering your speech with as many expletives as possible. Lonely Planet publishes *Australia – a language survival kit*, an introduction to both Australian English and Aboriginal languages, and the list that follows may also help:

amber fluid – beer
arvo – afternoon
avagoyermug – traditional rallying call, especially at cricket matches
award wage – minimum pay rate

back o' Bourke – back of beyond, middle of nowhere
bail out – leave
bail up – hold up, rob, earbash
banana bender – resident of Queensland
barbie – barbecue (bbq)
barrack – cheer on team at sporting event, support (as in 'who do you barrack for?')
bathers – swimming costume (Victoria)
battler – hard trier, struggler

beaut, beauty, bewdie – great, fantastic
big mobs – a large amount, heaps
bikies – motorcyclists
billabong – water hole in dried up riverbed, more correctly an ox-bow bend cut off in the dry season by receding waters
billy – tin container used to boil tea in the bush
bitumen – surfaced road
black stump – where the 'back o' Bourke' begins
bloke – man
blowies – blow flies
bludger – lazy person, one who won't work
blue (ie *have a blue*) – to have an argument or fight
bluey – swag, or nickname for a red-haired person
bonzer – great, ripper
boomer – very big, a particularly large male kangaroo
boomerang – a curved flat wooden instrument used by Aborigines for hunting
booze bus – police van used for random breath testing for alcohol
bottle shop – liquor shop
Buckley's – no chance at all
bug (*Moreton Bay bug*) – a small crab
Bullamakanka – imaginary place even beyond the back o' Bourke, way beyond the black stump
bull dust – fine and sometimes deep dust on outback roads, also bullshit
bunyip – mythical bush spirit
burl – have a try (as in 'give it a burl')
bush – country, anywhere away from the city
bush (ie *go bush*) – go back to the land
bushbash – to force your way through pathless bush
bushranger – Australia's equivalent of the outlaws of the American Wild West (some goodies, some baddies)
bush tucker – native foods, usually in the outback
BYO – Bring Your Own (booze to a restaurant, meat to a barbecue, etc)

caaarn! – come on, traditional rallying call, especially at football games, as in 'Caaarn the Blues!'

camp oven – large, cast-iron pot with lid, used for cooking on an open fire

cask – wine box (a great Australian invention)

Chiko roll – vile Australian junk food

chook – chicken

chuck a U-ey – do a U-turn

chunder – vomit, technicolour yawn, pavement pizza, curbside quiche, liquid laugh, drive the porcelain bus

clobber – clothes

cobber – mate (archaic)

cocky – small-scale farmer

come good – turn out all right

compo – compensation such as workers' compensation

counter meal, countery – pub meal

cow cocky – small-scale cattle farmer

cozzie – swimming costume (New South Wales)

crook – ill, badly made, substandard

crow eater – resident of South Australia

cut lunch – sandwiches

dag, daggy – dirty lump of wool at back end of a sheep, also an affectionate or mildly abusive term for a socially inept person

daks – trousers

damper – bush loaf made from flour and water and cooked in a camp oven

dead horse – tomato sauce

deli – delicatessen, milk bar in South Australia

dijeridu – cylindrical wooden musical instrument played by Aboriginal men

dill – idiot

dinkum, fair dinkum – honest, genuine

dinky-di – the real thing

divvy van – police divisional van

dob in – to tell on someone

donk – car or boat engine

don't come the raw prawn – don't try and fool me

down south – the rest of Australia, according to anyone north of Brisbane

drongo – worthless person

duco – car paint

dunny – outdoor lavatory

dunny budgies – blowies

earbash – talk nonstop

eastern states – the rest of Australia viewed from Western Australia

esky – large insulated box for keeping beer etc cold

fair crack of the whip! – fair go!

fair go! – give us a break

FJ – most revered Holden car

flake – shark meat, used in fish & chips

floater – meat pie floating in pea soup – yuk

fossick – hunt for gems or semiprecious stones

galah – noisy parrot, thus noisy idiot

game – brave (as in 'game as Ned Kelly')

gander – look (as in 'have a gander')

garbo – person who collects your garbage

g'day – good day, traditional Australian greeting

gibber – Aboriginal word for stony desert

give it away – give up

good on ya – well done

grazier – large-scale sheep or cattle farmer

grog – general term for alcohol

grouse – very good, unreal

hoon – idiot, hooligan, yahoo

how are ya? – standard greeting, expected answer 'good, thanks, how are *you*?'

HQ – second most revered Australian car

icy-pole – frozen lolly water or ice cream on a stick

jackaroo – young male trainee on a station (farm)

jillaroo – young female trainee on a station

jocks – men's underpants

journo – journalist

kiwi – New Zealander

knock – criticise, deride

knocker – one who knocks

Koori – Aborigine (mostly south of the Murray River)

lair – layabout, ruffian
lairising – acting like a lair
lamington – square of sponge cake covered in chocolate icing and coconut
larrikin – a bit like a lair
lay-by – put a deposit on an article so the shop will hold it for you
lollies – sweets, candy
lurk – a scheme

manchester – household linen
mate – general term of familiarity, whether you know the person or not
middy – 285 ml beer glass (New South Wales)
milk bar – general store
milko – milkman
mozzies – mosquitoes

never-never – remote country in the outback
no hoper – hopeless case
no worries – she'll be right, that's OK
north island – mainland Australia, viewed from Tasmania
northern summer – summer in the northern hemisphere
nulla-nulla – wooden club used by Aborigines

ocker – an uncultivated or boorish Australian
off-sider – assistant or partner
O-S – overseas, as in 'he's gone O-S'
outback – remote part of the bush, back o' Bourke
OYO – own your own (flat or apartment)

pastoralist – large-scale grazier
pavlova – traditional Australian meringue and cream dessert, named after the Russian ballerina Anna Pavlova
perve – to gaze with lust
pineapple (*rough end of*) – stick (sharp end of)
piss – beer
piss turn – boozy party
pissed – drunk
pissed off – annoyed

pokies – poker machines, found in clubs, mainly in New South Wales
pom – English person
possie – advantageous position
postie – mailman
pot – 285 ml glass of beer (Victoria, Queensland)
push – group or gang of people, such as shearers

ratbag – friendly term of abuse
ratshit (*R-S*) – lousy
rapt – delighted, enraptured
reckon! – you bet!, absolutely!
rego – registration, as in 'car rego'
ridgy-didge – original, genuine
ripper – good (also 'little ripper')
road train – semitrailer-trailer-trailer
root – have sexual intercourse
rooted – tired
ropable – very bad-tempered or angry
rubbish (ie *to rubbish*) – deride, tease

salvo – member of the Salvation Army
sandgroper – resident of Western Australia
scallops – fried potato cakes (Queensland), shellfish (elsewhere)
schooner – large beer glass (New South Wales, South Australia)
sea wasp – deadly box jellyfish
sealed road – surfaced road
see you in the soup – see you around
semitrailer – articulated truck
session – lengthy period of heavy drinking
sheila – woman
shellacking – comprehensive defeat
she'll be right – no worries
shonky – unreliable
shoot through – leave in a hurry
shout – buy round of drinks (as in 'it's your shout')
sickie – day off work ill (or malingering)
smoke-oh – tea break
snag – sausage
spunky – good looking, attractive (as in 'what a spunk')
squatter – pioneer farmer who occupied land as a tenant of the government
squattocracy – Australian 'old money' folk,

who made it by being first on the scene and grabbing the land

station – large farm

stickybeak – nosy person

stinger – box jellyfish

strides – daks

strine – Australian slang

stubby – small bottle of beer

sunbake – sunbathe (well, the sun's hot in Australia)

surfies – surfing fanatics

swag – canvas-covered bed roll used in the outback, also a large amount

tall poppies – achievers (knockers like to cut them down)

Taswegian – resident of Tasmania

tea – evening meal

thingo – thing, whatchamacallit, hooza meebob, doo velacki, thingamajig

tinny – can of beer; also a small, aluminium fishing dinghy (Northern Territory)

togs – swimming costume (Queensland, Victoria)

too right! – absolutely!

Top End – northern part of the Northern Territory

trucky – truck driver

true blue – dinkum

tucker – food

two-pot screamer – person unable to hold their drink

two-up – traditional heads/tails gambling game

uni – university

up north – New South Wales and Queensland when viewed from Victoria

ute – utility, pick-up truck

wag (ie *to wag*) – to skip school or work

walkabout – lengthy walk away from it all

wallaby track (*on the*) – to wander from place to place seeking work (archaic)

weatherboard – wooden house

Wet (ie *the Wet*) – rainy season in the north

wharfie – dockworker

whinge – complain, moan

wobbly – disturbing, unpredictable behaviour (as in 'throw a wobbly')

woomera – stick used by Aborigines for throwing spears

wowser – spoilsport, puritan

yabbie – small freshwater crayfish

yahoo – noisy and unruly person

yakka – work (from an Aboriginal language)

yobbo – uncouth, aggressive person

yonks – ages; a long time

youse – plural of you

Aboriginal Language

At the time of contact there were around 250 separate Australian languages spoken by the 600 to 700 Aboriginal 'tribes', and these languages were as distinct from each other as English and French. Often three or four adjacent tribes would speak what amounted to dialects of the same language, but another adjacent tribe might speak a completely different language.

It is believed that all the languages evolved from a single language family as the Aborigines gradually moved out over the entire continent and split into new groups. There are a number of words that occur right across the continent, such as *jina* (foot) and *mala* (hand), and similarities also exist in the often complex grammatical structures.

Following European contact the number of Aboriginal languages was drastically reduced. At least eight separate languages were spoken in Tasmania alone, but none of these was recorded before the native speakers either died or were killed. Of the original 250 or so languages, only around 30 are today spoken on a regular basis and are taught to children.

Aboriginal Kriol is a new language which has developed since European arrival in Australia. It is spoken across northern Australia and has become the 'native' language of many young Aborigines. It contains many English words, but the pronunciation and grammatical usage are along Aboriginal lines, the meaning is often different, and the spelling is phonetic. For example, the English sentence 'He was amazed' becomes 'I bin luk kwesjinmak' in Kriol.

There are a number of generic terms

which Aborigines use to describe themselves, and these vary according to the region. The most common of these is Koori, used for the people of south-east Australia.

Nunga is used to refer to the people of coastal South Australia, Murri for those from the north-east, and Nyoongah is used in the country's south-west.

Aboriginal Art

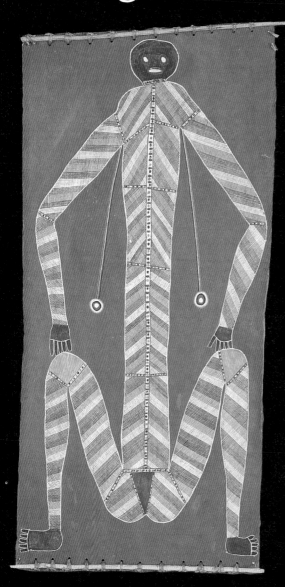

Namarrkon, Lightning Spirit by Curly Bardagubu, c. 1931-1987, Born clan; Kunwinjku language, Namokardabu, western Arnhem Land; earth pigments on bark; 156 x 75cm; 1987; purchased through the Art Foundation of Victoria with assistance from Alcoa of Australia Limited, Governor 1990; National Gallery of Victoria.

ABORIGINAL ART

Aboriginal art has undergone a major revival in the last decade or so, with artists throughout the country finding both a means to express and preserve ancient Dreaming values, and a way to share this rich cultural heritage with the wider community.

While the so-called dot paintings of the central deserts are the most readily identifiable and probably most popular form of contemporary Aboriginal art, there's a huge range of material being produced – bark paintings from Arnhem Land, wood carving and silk-screen printing from the Tiwi Islands north of Darwin, batik printing and wood carving from central Australia, and more.

The initial forms of artistic expression were rock carvings, body painting and ground designs, and the earliest engraved designs known to exist date back at least 30,000 years. Art has always been an integral part of Aboriginal life, a connection between past and present, between the supernatural and the earthly, between people and the land.

All early art was a reflection of the various peoples' ancestral Dreaming – the 'Creation', when the earth's physical features were formed by the struggles between powerful supernatural ancestors such as the Rainbow Serpent, the Lightning Men and the Wandjina. Not only was the physical layout mapped but codes of behaviour were also laid down, and although these laws have been diluted and adapted in the last 200 years, they still provide the basis for today's Aborigines. Ceremonies, rituals and sacred paintings are all based on the Dreaming.

A Dreaming may take a number of different forms – it can be a

Pampardu Jukurrpa
by Clarise Poulson;
acrylic on linen;
150 x 90cm; 1993;
Warlukurlangu Artists
Association, Yuen-
dumu, NT; courtesy of
DESART.

Left: Lightning Brothers rock art site at Katherine River; courtesy of the NT Tourist Commission.

Below: Ewaninga rock engravings, south of Alice Springs; courtesy of the NT Tourist Commission.

person, an animal or a physical feature, while others are more general, relating to a region, a group of people, or natural forces such as floods and wind. Thus Australia is covered by a wide network of Dreamings, and any one person may have connections with several.

CENTRAL AUSTRALIAN ART
Western Desert Paintings

The current renaissance in Aboriginal painting began in the early 1970s at Papunya (honey ant place), at the time a small, depressed community 240 km north-west of Alice Springs, which had grown out of the government's 'assimilation' policy. Here the local children were given the task of painting a traditional-style mural on the school wall. The local elders took interest in the project, and although the public display of traditional images gave rise to much debate amongst the elders, they eventually participated and in fact completed the *Honey Ant Dreaming* mural. This was the first time that images which were originally confined to rock and body art came to be reproduced in a different environment.

Other murals followed this first one, and before long the desire to paint spread through the community. In the early stages paintings were produced on small boards on the ground or balanced on the artist's knee, but this soon gave way to painting on canvas with acrylic paints. Canvas was an ideal medium as it could be easily rolled and transported, yet large paintings were possible. With the growing importance of art, both as an economic and a cultural activity, an association was formed to help the artists sell their work. The Papunya Tula company in Alice Springs is still one

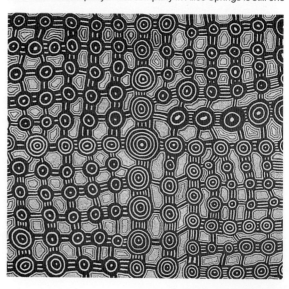

Untitled by Dini Campbell Tjampitjinpa; acrylic on linen; 182 x 152cm; 1993; Papunya Tula Artists Pty Ltd, Alice Springs, NT; courtesy of DESART.

of the few galleries in central Australia to be owned and run by Aborigines.

Painting in central Australia has flourished to such a degree that these days it is an important educational source for young kids, as they can learn aspects of religious and ceremonial knowledge. This is especially true now that women are so much a part of the painting movement.

The trademark dot-painting style is partly an evolution from 'ground paintings', which formed the centrepiece of traditional dances and songs. These were made from pulped plant material, and the designs were made on the ground using dots of this mush. Dots were also used to outline objects in rock paintings, and to highlight geographical features or vegetation. Over time the use of dots has developed, sometimes covering the entire canvas.

While the paintings may look random and abstract, they have great significance to the artist and usually depict a Dreaming journey, and so can be seen almost as aerial landscape maps. One feature which appears regularly is the tracks of birds, animals and humans, often identifying the ancestor. Various subjects, including people, are often depicted by the imprint they leave in the sand – a simple arc depicts a person (as that is the print left by someone sitting), a coolamon (wooden carrying dish) is shown as an oval shape, a digging stick by a single line, a camp fire by a circle. Males or females are identified by the objects associated with them – digging sticks and coolamons are always used by women, spears and boomerangs by men. Concentric circles are usually used to depict Dreaming sites, or places where ancestors paused in their journeys.

Liru Tjara by Mary Ungkaipai Forbes; watercolour on paper; 102 x 82cm; Kaltjiti Crafts, Fregon, SA; courtesy of DESART.

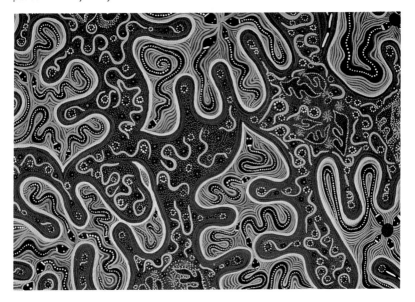

Kadaitja Man by
Ronnie Tjampitjinpa;
acrylic on linen;
122 x 61cm; 1993;
Papunya Tula Artists
Pty Ltd, Alice Springs,
NT; courtesy of
DESART.

While these symbols are widely used and are readily identifiable, their context within each individual painting is known only by the artist and the people closely associated with him or her – either by group or by the Dreaming – and different groups apply different interpretations to each painting. In this way sacred stories can be publicly portrayed, as the deeper meaning is not evident to any but those with a close association with the image.

The colours used in dot paintings from central Australia may seem overly vivid, and inappropriate to the land or story depicted. However, they are not meant to be true representations of the landscape, but variations in that landscape. The reds, blues and purples which often dominate the outback scenery, and which were so much a part of Albert Namatjira's painting (see below), feature prominently.

Albert Namatjira (1902-59) Australia's most well-known Aboriginal artist was probably Albert Namatjira. He lived at the Hermannsburg Lutheran Mission, about 130 km west of Alice Springs, and was introduced to European-style watercolour painting by a non-Aboriginal artist, Rex Batterbee, in the 1930s.

Namatjira successfully captured the essence of the Centre using a heavily European-influenced style. At the time his paintings were seen purely as picturesque landscapes. These days, however, it is thought he chose his subjects carefully, as they were Dreaming landscapes to which he had a great bond.

Namatjira supported many of his people on the income from his work, as was his obligation under tribal law. Because of his fame he was allowed to buy alcohol at a time when this was otherwise

Ngapa Manu Warna Jukurrpa (Water & Snake Dreaming) by Rosie Nangala Flemming; acrylic on linen; 180 x 120cm; 1993; Warlukurlangu Artists Association, Yuendumu, NT; courtesy of DESART.

illegal for Aborigines. In 1957 he was the first Aborigine to be granted Australian citizenship, but in 1958 he was jailed for six months for supplying alcohol to Aborigines. He died the following year aged only 57.

Although Namatjira died very disenchanted with White society, he did much to change the extremely negative views of Aborigines which prevailed at the time. At the same time he paved the way for the Papunya painting movement which emerged just over a decade after his death.

The Utopia Batik Artists

The women of Utopia, 225 km north-east of Alice Springs, have become famous in recent years for their production of batik material. In the mid 1970s the Anmatyerre and Alyawarre people started to reoccupy their traditional lands around Utopia cattle station, and this was given a formal basis in 1979 when they were granted title to the station. A number of scattered outstations, rather than a central settlement, were set up, and around this time the women were introduced to batik as part of a self-help program. The art form flourished and Utopia Women's Batik Group was formed in 1978.

Silk soon became the preferred medium for printing, and the batiks were based on the traditional women's designs which were painted on their bodies.

In the late 1980s techniques using acrylic paints on canvas were introduced to the artists at Utopia, and they have also become popular.

Other Central Australian Art

The making of wooden sculptures for sale dates back to at least early this century. In 1903 a group of Diyari people living on the Killalpaninna Lutheran Mission near Lake Eyre in South Australia

Handcrafted decorative central Australian carvings made from river red gum root; Maruku Arts & Crafts, Uluru (Ayers Rock), NT; courtesy of DESART.

were encouraged by the pastor to produce sculptures in order to raise funds for the mission.

The momentum for producing crafts for sale was accelerated by the opening up and settlement of the country by Europeans. Demand was slow to increase but the steady growth of the tourist trade since WW II, and the tourist boom of the 1980s, has seen demand and production increase dramatically.

The most widespread crafts seen for sale these days are the wooden carvings which have designs scorched into them with hot fencing wire. These range from small figures, such as possums, up to quite large snakes and lizards, although none of them have any Dreaming significance. One of the main outlets for these is the Maruku Arts & Crafts centre at the Uluru National Park rangers' station, where it's possible to see the crafts being made. Although much of the artwork is usually done by women, men are also involved at the Maruku centre. The Mt Ebenezer Roadhouse, on the Lasseter Highway (the main route to Uluru), is another Aboriginal-owned enterprise – and one of the cheapest places for buying sculpted figures.

Terracotta pots by the Hermannsburg Potters; 1992; represented by Alcaston House Gallery, Melbourne.

The Ernabella Presbyterian Mission in northern South Australia was another place where craftwork was encouraged. A 1950 mission report stated that: 'A mission station must have an industry to provide work for and help finance the cost of caring for the natives'. As the mission had been founded on a sheep station, wool crafts were the obvious way to go, and to that end the techniques of wool spinning, dyeing and weaving were introduced. The Pitjantjatjara (pigeon-jara) women made woollen articles such as rugs, belts, traditional dilly bags (carry bags) and scarves, using designs incorporating aspects of women's law (*yawilyu*). With the introduction of batik fabric dyeing in the 1970s, weaving at Ernabella virtually ceased.

The Arrernte people from Hermannsburg have recently begun to work with pottery, a craft which is not traditionally Aboriginal. They have incorporated moulded figures and surface treatments adapted from Dreaming stories.

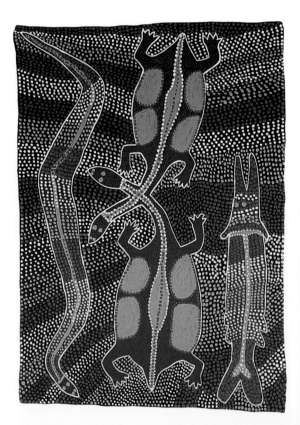

Old Man – Young Man – Very Big Story by Djambu Barra Barra, born about 1946; language group Wagilak related to Ritangu; domicile Ngukurr, NT; synthetic polymer paint on lanaquarelle paper; 63 x 67cm; 1992; represented by Alcaston House Gallery, Melbourne.

ARNHEM LAND ART

Arnhem Land, in Australia's tropical 'Top End', is possibly the area with the richest artistic heritage. It is thought that rock paintings were being made as much as 40,000 years ago, and some of the rock art galleries in the huge sandstone Arnhem Land plateau are at least 18,000 years old.

Although Arnhem Land is famous for its rock art, the tradition of bark painting is equally strong in the region. In fact in recent years, this portable art form has become very popular, probably because the boom in tourism has led to a high demand for souvenirs. As is the case in many communities throughout the country, producing art works for sale is an important form of employment in a place where there are generally few opportunities.

The art of Arnhem Land is vastly different from that of the central deserts. Here, Dreaming stories are depicted far more literally, with easily recognisable (though often stylised) images of ancestors, animals, and even Macassans – early Indonesian mariners who regularly visited the north coast long before the Europeans arrived on the scene.

Rock Art

The paintings contained in the Arnhem Land rock art sites range from hand prints to paintings of animals, people, mythological beings and European ships, constituting one of the world's most important and fascinating rock art collections. They provide a record of changing environments and Aboriginal lifestyles over the millennia.

In some places they are concentrated in large galleries, with paintings from more recent eras sometimes superimposed over older paintings. Some sites are kept secret – not only to protect them from damage, but also because they are private or sacred

Rock paintings, Nourlangie Rock, Kakadu National Park; courtesy of the NT Tourist Commission.

to the Aborigines. Some are even believed to be inhabited by dangerous beings, who must not be approached by the ignorant. However, two of the finest sites have been opened up to visitors, with access roads, walkways and explanatory signs. These are Ubirr and Nourlangie Rock. Park rangers conduct free art-site tours once or twice a day from May to October. (For more information see the Ubirr and Nourlangie Rock sections in the Northern Territory chapter.)

The rock paintings show how the main styles succeeded each other over time. The earliest hand or grass prints were followed by a 'naturalistic' style, with large outlines of people or animals filled in with colour. Some of the animals depicted, such as the thylacine (or Tasmanian tiger), have long been extinct in mainland Australia. Other paintings are thought to show large beasts which roamed the world and which were wiped out millennia ago.

After the naturalistic style came the 'dynamic', in which motion was often cleverly depicted (a dotted line, for example, to show a spear's path through the air). In this era the first mythological beings appeared – with human bodies and animal heads.

The next style mainly showed simple human silhouettes, and was followed by the curious 'yam figures', in which people and animals were drawn in the shape of yams (or yams in the shape of people/animals!). Yams must have been an important food source at this time, about 8000 years ago, when the climate was growing increasingly damp. As the waters rose, much of what is now Kakadu National Park became covered with salt marshes. Many fish were depicted in the art of this period, and the so-called 'x-ray' style, which showed the creatures' bones and internal organs, made its appearance.

By about 1000 years ago many of the salt marshes had turned into freshwater swamps and billabongs. The birds and plants which provided new food sources in this landscape appeared in the art of this time.

From around 400 years ago, Aboriginal artists also depicted the human newcomers to the region – Macassan fisherpeople and, more recently, the Europeans – and the things they brought, or their transport such as ships or horses.

Bark Paintings

While the bark painting tradition is a more recent art form than rock art, it is still an important part of the cultural heritage of Arnhem Land Aborigines. It's difficult to establish when bark was first used, partly because it is perishable and old pieces simply don't exist. European visitors in the early 19th century noted the practice of painting the inside walls of bark shelters. The bark used is from the stringybark tree (*Eucalyptus tetradonta*), and it is taken off in the wet season when it is moist and supple. The rough outer layers are removed and the bark is then dried by placing it over a fire and then under weights on the ground to keep it flat. Drying is complete within about a fortnight, and the bark is then ready for use. Most bark paintings made today have a pair of sticks across the top and bottom of the sheet to keep it flat.

The pigments used in bark paintings are mainly red and yellow (ochres), white (kaolin) and black (charcoal). Because these were

Kumoken (Freshwater Crocodile) with Mimi Spirits by Djawida, b.c. 1935, Yulkman clan; Kunwinjku language, Kurrudjmuh, western Arnhem Land; earth pigments on bark; 151 x 71cm; 1990; purchased 1990; National Gallery of Victoria.

the only colours available their source was an important place. The colour could only be gathered by the traditional owners, and it was then traded. Even today it is these natural pigments which are used, giving the paintings their superb soft and earthy finish. Binding agents such as birds' egg yolks, wax and plant resins were added to the pigments. Recently these have been replaced by synthetic agents such as wood glue. Similarly, the brushes used in the past were obtained from the bush materials at hand – twigs, leaf fibres, feathers, human hair and the like – but these too have largely been done away with in favour of modern brushes.

One of the main features of Arnhem Land bark paintings is the use of cross-hatching designs. These designs identify the particular clans, and are based on body paintings of the past. The paintings can also be broadly categorised by their regional styles. In the west the tendency is towards naturalistic images and plain backgrounds, while to the east the use of geometric designs is more common.

The art reflects Dreaming themes, and once again these vary by region. In eastern Arnhem Land the prominent ancestor beings are the Djangkawu, who travelled the land with elaborate dilly bags and digging sticks (which they used to create waterholes each time

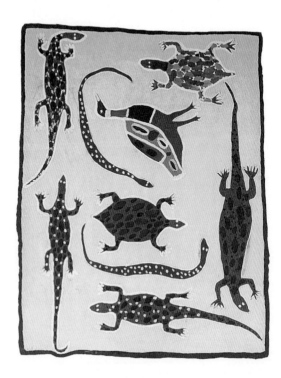

Some Animals Have Secret Songs by Amy Johnson Jirwulurr, born about 1953; language group Wagilak; domicile Ngukurr, NT; synthetic polymer paint on cotton duck; 90 x 106cm; 1988; represented by Alcaston House Gallery, Melbourne.

Gabal Ritual by Willie Gudabi, born about 1916;
language group Alawa; domicile Ngukurr, NT;
synthetic polymer paint on lanaquarelle paper;
75 x 55cm; 1993;
represented by Alcaston House Gallery, Melbourne.

they stopped), and the Wagilag Sisters, who are associated with snakes and water holes. In western Arnhem Land the Rainbow Serpent, Yingarna, is the significant being (according to some clans), but one of her offspring, Ngalyod, and Nawura are also important. The *mimi* spirits are another feature of western Arnhem Land art, both on bark and rock. These mischievous spirits are attributed with having taught the Aborigines of the region many things, including hunting, food gathering and painting skills.

Fibre Art
Articles made from fibres are a major art form among the women. While the string and pandanus-fibre dilly bags, skirts, mats and nets all have utilitarian purposes, many also have ritual uses.

Hollow-Log Coffins
Hollowed-out logs were often used for reburial ceremonies in Arnhem Land, and were also a major form of artistic expression. They were highly decorated, often with many of the Dreaming themes, and were known as *dupun* in eastern Arnhem Land and *lorrkon* in western Arnhem Land.

In 1988 a group of Arnhem Land artists made a memorial as their contribution to the movement highlighting injustices against Aborigines – this was, of course, the year when non-Aboriginal Australians were celebrating 200 years of European settlement. The artists painted 200 log coffins – one for each year of settlement – with traditional clan and Dreaming designs, and these now form a permanent display in the National Gallery in Canberra.

Ngukurr Contemporary Painting
Since the late 1980s the artists of Ngukurr (nook-or), near Roper Bar in south-eastern Arnhem Land, have been producing works using acrylic paints on canvas. Although ancestral beings still feature prominently, the works are generally much more 'modern' in nature, with free-flowing forms and often little in common with traditional formal structure.

TIWI ISLAND ART
Due to their isolation, the Aborigines of the Tiwi Islands (Bathurst and Melville islands off the coast of Darwin) have developed art forms – mainly sculpture – not found anywhere else, although there are some similarities with the art of Arnhem Land.

The *pukumani* burial rites are one of the main rituals of Tiwi religious life, and it is for these ceremonies that many of the art

Tiwi art is derived from ceremonial body painting and the ornate decoration applied to funerary poles, *yimawilini* bark baskets and associated ritual objects made for the *pukamani* ceremony, which is held at the grave site approximately six months after burial. The ceremony marks the conclusion of formal mourning and the lifting of complex taboos associated with death.

Traditionally, the participants decorate themselves with a variety of ochre designs so as to conceal their true identity from the malevolent *mapurtiti*, the spirits of the dead. Tiwi art generally avoids specific reference to totems, dreamings or stories connected with the *palaneri* (Creation period).

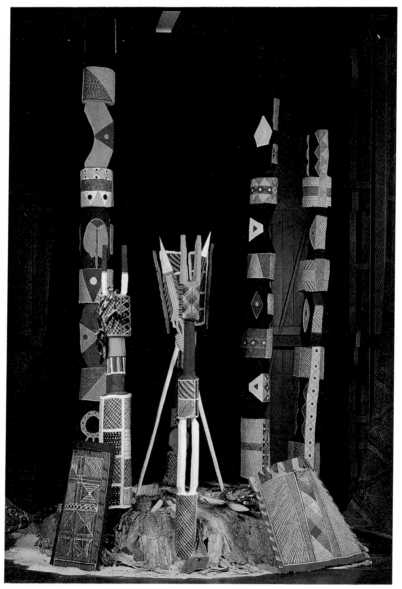

Pukamani funerary poles and bark baskets installation; Milikapiti, Melville Island, NT; represented by Alcaston House Gallery, Melbourne.

works are created – *jimwalini* (bark baskets), spears and *tutini* (burial poles). These carved and painted ironwood poles, up to 2.5 metres long, are placed around the grave, and represent features of that person's life.

In the last 50 or so years the Tiwi islanders have been producing sculptured animals and birds, many of these being Creation ancestors. (The Darwin Museum of Arts & Sciences has an excellent display.) More recently, bark painting and silk-screen printing have become popular, and there are workshops on both islands where these items are produced. (For more information see the section on the Bathurst and Melville islands in the Northern Territory chapter.)

KIMBERLEY ART

The art of the Kimberley is most famous for its Wandjina images – a group of ancestor beings who came from the sky – but other styles also exist.

The Wandjina generally appear in human form, with large black eyes, a nose but no mouth, a halo around the head (representative of both hair and clouds), and a black oval shape on the chest. These beings were responsible for the formation of the country's natural features, and were also thought to control the elements. The images of the Wandjina are found on rock as well as on more

Walker River, NT by Djitjima Ngalandarra Wilfred, born about 1927; language group Ritangu; domicile Walker River, NT; synthetic polymer paint on lanaquarelle paper; 63 x 67cm; 1992; represented by Alcaston House Gallery, Melbourne.

recent portable art media, with some of the rock images being more than six metres long.

Another art form from the western Kimberley is the engraved pearl-shell pendants which come from the Broome area. It is believed that the Aborigines of the area were using pearl shell for decoration before the arrival of Europeans, but with the establishment of the pearling industry in Broome late last century the use of pearl shell increased markedly. Traditionally the shells were highly prized, and so were engraved and then used for a number of purposes – ceremonial, personal decoration and trade – examples of this art have been found as far away as Queensland and South Australia.

The designs engraved into the shells were usually fairly simple geometric patterns which had little symbolic importance. The practice of pearl-shell engraving has largely died out, although the decorated shells are still highly valued.

Art in the eastern Kimberley also features elements of the works of the desert peoples of central Australia, a legacy of the forced movement of people during the 1970s. The community of Warmun at Turkey Creek on the Great Northern Highway has been particularly active in ensuring that Aboriginal culture through painting and dance remains strong.

NORTH QUEENSLAND ART

In North Queensland it is once again the rock art which predominates. The superb 'Quinkan' galleries at Laura on the Cape York Peninsula, north of Cairns, are among the best known in the country. Among the many creatures depicted on the walls, the main ones are the Quinkan spirits, which are shown in two forms – the long and stick-like Timara, and the crocodile-like Imjim with their knobbed, club-like tails.

A number of ceremonial items were also traditionally produced in this area, with perhaps the best known being the men's decorated shields. These were mainly used for ritual purposes, but they were also put to practical use when fighting between clans occurred. Other items included clubs, boomerangs and woven baskets, many of which also carried painted designs.

URBAN ART

While the works of rural artists based on traditional themes is the high-profile side of Aboriginal art, another important aspect is the works produced by city-based Aborigines. As much of this work has strong European influences, it was often not regarded as an authentic form of Aboriginal art – this view has since changed.

A major impetus in the development of urban art was the Aboriginal land rights movement, which started to gain momentum in the 1970s. Images depicting the dispossession of the Aborigines and the racist treatment they had received became powerful symbols in their struggle for equality.

Although much of the work being produced still carries strong political and social comment, these days the range has become broader.

David Mpetyane paints and writes within the context of his joint ancestral background and his awareness of present and past. He lives and works in Alice Springs, and is influenced by the contemporary life of the community around him, while also using first-contact stories and his strong identification with the land. His imagination is fired by the anger and beauty of the natural environment, as he relives the Creation period journeys of his ancestors and weaves their stories into his present life. David's painting *Perfect Place for Philosophy and Waste* was inspired by the following poem.

Fertility

Alice lost her virginity
Witness by
The old man gum tree
While the dog sat confused
Patiently licking its wounds
She gave birth
To one stone room
Next a shed then a house

She then stepped one step south
Before the caterpillars knew
Alice grew
With the scenery so strong
The old man gum tree
Witness Alice lose her virginity
Long before me

David Mpetyane, 1992

Perfect Place for Philosophy and Waste by David Mpetyane, born 1963; language group Central/Western Aranda; domicile Alice Springs, NT; synthetic polymer paint on linen; 110 x 183cm; 1992; represented by Alcaston House Gallery, Melbourne.

Facts for the Visitor

VISAS & EMBASSIES

Once upon a time, Australia was fairly free and easy about who was allowed to visit the country, particularly if you were from the UK or Canada. These days, only New Zealanders get any sort of preferential treatment and even they need at least a passport. Everybody else has to have a visa.

Visa application forms are available from either Australian diplomatic missions overseas or travel agents, and you can apply by mail or in person. There are several different types of visas, depending on the reason for your visit.

Australian Embassies

Australian consular offices overseas include:

Canada
  Suite 710, 50 O'Connor St, Ottawa K1P 6L2 (☎ (613) 236 0841)
  also in Toronto and Vancouver
China
  15 Dongzhimenwai Dajie, San Li Tun, Beijing (☎ (1) 532 2331)
Denmark
  Kristianagade 21, 2100 Copenhagen (☎ 3 126 22 44)
France
  4 Rue Jean Rey, Paris, 15ème (☎ (1) 40 59 33 00)
Germany
  Godesberger Allee 107, 5300 Bonn 1 (☎ (0228) 8 10 30)
  also in Frankfurt and Berlin
Greece
  37 Dimitriou Soutsou, Ambelokipi, Athens 11512 (☎ (01) 644 7303)
Hong Kong
  Harbour Centre, 24th floor, 25 Harbour Rd, Wanchai, Hong Kong Island (☎ (5) 73 1881)
India
  Australian Compound, No 1/50-G Shantipath, Chanakyapuri, New Delhi 110021 (☎ 60 1336)
  also in Bombay
Indonesia
  Jalan Thamrin 15, Gambir, Jakarta (☎ (21) 323109)
  also in Denpasar
Ireland
  Fitzwilton House, Wilton Terrace, Dublin 2 (☎ (01) 76 1517)

Italy
  Via Alessandria 215, Rome 00198 (☎ (06) 832 721)
  also in Milan
Japan
  2-1-14 Mita, Minato-ku, Tokyo (☎ (3) 5232 4111)
  also in Osaka
Malaysia
  6 Jalan Yap Kwan Seng, Kuala Lumpur 50450 (☎ (03) 242 3122)
Netherlands
  Carnegielaan 12, 2517 KH The Hague (☎ (070) 310 82 00)
New Zealand
  72-78 Hobson St, Thorndon, Wellington (☎ (4) 73 6411)
  also in Auckland
Papua New Guinea
  Independence Drive, Waigani, Port Moresby (☎ 25 9333)
Philippines
  Bank of Philippine Islands Building, Paseo de Roxas, Makati, Manila (☎ 817 7911)
Singapore
  25 Napier Rd, Singapore 10 (☎ 737 9311)
South Africa
  4th floor, Mutual & Federal Centre, 220 Vermuelen St, Pretoria 0002 (☎ (012) 325 4315)
Sweden
  Sergels Torg 12, Stockholm C (☎ (08) 613 29 00)
Switzerland
  29 Alpenstrasse, Berne (☎ (031) 43 01 43)
  also in Geneva
Thailand
  37 South Sathorn Rd, Bangkok 10120 (☎ (2) 287 2680)
UK
  Australia House, The Strand, London WC2B 4LA (☎ (071) 379 4334)
  also in Edinburgh and Manchester
USA
  1601 Massachusetts Ave NW, Washington DC 20036 (☎ (202) 797 3000)
  also in Los Angeles, Chicago, Honolulu, Houston, New York and San Francisco

Tourist Visas

Tourist visas are issued by Australian consular offices abroad; they are the most common and are generally valid for a stay of up to six months within a 12-month period. If you intend staying less than three months, the visa is free; otherwise there is a $30 processing fee.

When you apply for a visa, you need to present your passport and a passport photo, as well as signing an undertaking that you have an onward or return ticket and 'sufficient funds' – the latter is obviously open to interpretation. Like those of any country, Australian visas seem to cause their hassles, although the authorities do seem to be more uniform in their approach these days.

Working Visas

Young visitors from Britain, Ireland, Canada, Holland and Japan may be eligible for a 'working holiday' visa. 'Young' is fairly loosely interpreted as around 18 to 26, and working holiday means up to 12 months, but the emphasis is supposed to be on casual employment rather than a full-time job, so you are only supposed to work for three months. Officially this visa can only be applied for in your home country, but some travellers report that the rule can be bent.

See the section on Working later in this chapter for details of what sort of work is available and where.

Visa Extensions

The maximum stay allowed to visitors in Australia is one year, including extensions.

Visa extensions are made through Department of Immigration & Ethnic Affairs offices in Australia and, as the process takes some time, it's best to apply about a month before your visa expires. There is an application fee of $200 – and even if they turn down your application they can still keep your money! To qualify for an extension you are required to take out private medical insurance to cover the period of the extension, and have a ticket out of the country. Some offices are more strict in enforcing these conditions than others.

If you're trying to stay for longer in Australia the books *Tourist to Permanent Resident in Australia* and *Practical Guide to Obtaining Permanent Residence in Australia*, both published by Legal Books, might be useful.

Foreign Embassies & Consulates

The principal diplomatic representations to Australia are in Canberra and you'll find a list of the addresses of relevant offices in the Canberra section. There are also representatives in various other major cities, particularly from countries with major connections with Australia like the USA, UK or New Zealand; or in cities with important connections, like Darwin which has an Indonesian consulate. Big cities like Sydney and Melbourne have nearly as many consular offices as Canberra, although visa applications are generally handled in Canberra. Look up addresses in the Yellow Pages phone book under 'Consulates & Legations'.

CUSTOMS

When entering Australia you can bring most articles in free of duty provided that Customs is satisfied they are for personal use and that you'll be taking them with you when you leave. There's also the usual duty-free per person quota of one litre of alcohol, 250 cigarettes and dutiable goods up to the value of A$400.

With regard to prohibited goods, there are two areas you need to pay particular attention to. Number one is, of course, dope – Australian Customs have a positive mania about the stuff and can be extremely efficient when it comes to finding it. Unless you want to make first-hand investigations of conditions in Australian jails (not very good), don't bring any with you. This particularly applies if you are arriving from South-East Asia or the Indian Subcontinent.

Problem two is animal and plant quarantine. You will be asked to declare all goods of animal or vegetable origin – wooden spoons, straw hats, the lot – and show them to an official. The authorities are naturally keen to prevent weeds, pests or diseases getting into the country – Australia has so far managed to escape many of the agricultural pests and diseases prevalent in other parts of the world. Fresh food is also unpopular, particularly meat, sausages, fruit, vegetables and flowers. There are also restrictions on taking fruit and vegetables between states.

Weapons and firearms are either prohibited or require a permit and safety testing. Other restricted goods include products (such as ivory) made from protected wildlife species, non-approved telecommunications devices and live animals.

When it is time to leave there are duty-free stores at the international airports and their associated cities. Treat them with healthy suspicion. 'Duty-free' is one of the world's most overworked catch phrases, and it is often just an excuse to sell things at prices you can easily beat by a little shopping around.

MONEY
Currency
Australia's currency is the Australian dollar, which comprises 100 cents. The dollar was introduced in 1966 to replace the old system of pounds, shillings and pence. There are coins for 5c, 10c, 20c, 50c, $1 and $2, and paper notes for $5, $10, $20, $50 and $100. There are also nasty little indestructible plastic versions of the $5 and $10 notes, and these are far more common than the good old paper ones these days.

There are no notable restrictions on importing or exporting currency or travellers' cheques except that you may not take out more than A$5000 in cash without prior approval.

Exchange Rates
In recent years the Australian dollar has fluctuated quite markedly against the US dollar, but it now seems to hover around the 65c to 70c mark – a disaster for Australians travelling overseas but a real bonus for inbound visitors.

C$1	=	A$1.00
DM 1	=	A$0.85
HK$10	=	A$1.80
NZ$1	=	A$0.80
UK£1	=	A$2.10
US$1	=	A$1.40
Y100	=	A$1.35

Changing Money
Changing foreign currency or travellers' cheques is no problem at almost any bank. It's done quickly and efficiently and never involves the sort of headaches and grand production that changing foreign currency in the USA always entails.

Travellers' Cheques
There is a variety of ways to carry your money around Australia with you. If your stay is limited then travellers' cheques are the most straightforward and they generally enjoy a better exchange rate than foreign cash in Australia.

American Express, Thomas Cook and other well-known international brands of travellers' cheques are all widely used in Australia. A passport will usually be adequate for identification; it would be sensible to carry a driver's licence, credit cards or a plane ticket in case of problems.

Commissions and fees for changing foreign currency travellers' cheques seem to vary from bank to bank and year to year. It's worth making a few phone calls to see which bank currently has the lowest charges. Some charge a flat fee for each transaction, which varies from $2.50 (Commonwealth Bank) to $6.50 (ANZ Bank), while others take a percentage of the amount changed – Westpac charges 1% with a minimum charge of $10.

Buying Australian dollar travellers' cheques is an option worth looking at. These can be exchanged immediately at the bank cashier's window without being converted from a foreign currency and incurring commissions, fees and exchange rate fluctuations.

Credit Cards
Credit cards are widely accepted in Australia and are an alternative to carrying large numbers of travellers' cheques. The most common credit card, however, is the purely Australian Bankcard system. Visa, MasterCard, Diners Club and American Express are also widely accepted.

Cash advances from credit cards are available over the counter and from many automatic teller machines (ATMs), depending on the card.

If you're planning to rent cars while travelling around Australia, a credit card makes life much simpler; they're looked upon with much greater favour by rent-a-car agencies than nasty old cash, and many agencies simply won't rent you a vehicle if you don't have a card.

Local Bank Accounts

If you're planning to stay longer than just a month or so, it's worth considering other ways of handling money that give you more flexibility and are more economical. This applies equally to Australians setting off to travel around the country.

Most travellers these days opt for an account which includes a cash card, which you can use to access your cash from ATMs found all over Australia. You put your card in the machine, key in your personal identification number (PIN) number, and then withdraw funds from your account. Westpac, ANZ, National and Commonwealth bank branches are found nationwide, and in all but the most remote town there'll be at least one place where you can withdraw money from a hole in the wall.

ATM machines can be used day or night, and it is possible to use the machines of some other banks: Westpac ATMs accept Commonwealth Bank cards and vice versa; National Bank ATMs accept ANZ cards and vice versa. There is a limit on how much you can withdraw from your account. This varies from bank to bank but is usually $400 to $500 per day.

Many businesses, such as service stations, supermarkets and convenience stores, are linked into the EFTPOS system (Electronic Funds Transfer at Point Of Sale), and at places with this facility you can use your bank cash card to pay for services or purchases direct, and sometimes withdraw cash as well. Bank cash cards and credit cards can also be used to make local, STD and international phone calls in special public telephones, found in most towns throughout the country.

Opening an account at an Australian bank is not all that easy these days, especially for overseas visitors. A points system operates and you need to score a minimum of 100 points before you can have the privilege of letting the bank take your money. Passports, driver's licences, birth certificates and other 'major' IDs earn you 40 points; minor ones such as credit cards get you 20 points. Just like a game show really! However, if visitors apply to open an account during the first six weeks of their visit, then just showing their passport will suffice.

If you don't have an Australian Tax File Number, interest earned from your funds will be taxed at the rate of 48% and this money goes straight to my old mate, the Deputy Commissioner of Taxation.

Costs

Compared to the USA, Canada and European countries, Australia is cheaper in some ways and more expensive in others. Manufactured goods tend to be more expensive: if they are imported they have all the additional costs of transport and duties, and if they're locally manufactured they suffer from the extra costs entailed in making things in comparatively small quantities. Thus you pay more for clothes, cars and other manufactured items. On the other hand, food is both high in quality and low in cost.

Accommodation is also very reasonably priced. In virtually every town where backpackers are likely to stay there'll be a backpackers' hostel with dorm beds for $10 or less, or a caravan park with on-site vans for around $20 for two people.

The biggest cost in any trip to Australia is going to be transport, simply because it's such a vast country. If there's a group of you, buying a second-hand car is probably the most economical way to go.

Tipping

In Australia tipping isn't entrenched in the way it is in the USA or Europe. It's only customary to tip in more expensive restaurants and only then if you want to. If the service has been especially good and you decide to leave a tip, 10% of the bill is the usual amount. Taxi drivers don't expect tips (of course, they don't hurl it back at you if you decide to leave the change). In contrast, just try getting out of a New York cab, or even a London one, without leaving your 10 to 15%.

WHEN TO GO

Any time is a good time to be in Australia, but as you'd expect in a country this large, different parts of the country are at their best at different times.

The southern states are most popular during the summer months, as it's warm enough for swimming and it's great to be outdoors. In the centre of the country it's just too damn hot to do anything much, while in the far north the summer is the Wet season and the heat and humidity can make life pretty uncomfortable. To make matters worse, swimming in the sea in the north is not possible due to the 'stingers' (box jellyfish) which frequent the waters at this time. On the other hand, if you want to see the Top End green and free of dust, be treated to some spectacular electrical storms and have the best of the barramundi fishing while all the other tourists are down south, this is the time to do it.

In winter the focus swings to the north, when the humidity has faded and the temperature is perfect. This is the time for visits to far north Queensland and the Top End. Central and outback Australia are also popular at this time, as the extreme heat of summer has been replaced by warm sunny days and surprisingly cool – even cold – nights. The cooler weather also deters the bushflies, which in the warmer months can be an absolute nightmare. The southern states, however, are not without their own attractions in winter. Snow skiers can head for the Victorian Alps or the Snowy Mountains in New South Wales for good cross-country or downhill skiing – although snow cover ranges from excellent one year to virtually nonexistent the next.

Spring and autumn give the greatest flexibility for a short visit as you can combine highlights of the whole country while avoiding the extremes of the weather. Spring is the time for wildflowers in the outback (particularly Western and central Australia) and these can be absolutely stunning after rains and are worth going a long way to see.

The other major consideration when travelling in Australia is school holidays. Australian families take to the road (and air) en masse at these times and many places are booked out, prices rise and things generally get a bit crazy. Holidays vary somewhat from state to state, but the main holiday period is from mid-December to late January; the other two-week periods are roughly early to mid-April, late June to mid-July, and late September to early October.

TOURIST OFFICES

There are a number of information sources for visitors to Australia and, in common with a number of other tourist-conscious Western countries, you can easily drown yourself in brochures and booklets, maps and leaflets.

Local Tourist Offices

Within Australia, tourist information is handled by the various state and local offices. Each state and the ACT and Northern Territory have a tourist office of some form and you will find information about these centres in the various state sections. Apart from a main office in the capital cities, they often have regional offices in main tourist centres and also in other states. Tourist information in Victoria is handled by the Royal Automobile Club of Victoria (RACV) organisation in Melbourne.

As well as supplying brochures, price lists, maps and other information, the state offices will often book transport, tours and accommodation for you. Unfortunately, very few of the state tourist offices maintain information desks at the airports and, furthermore, the opening hours of the city offices are very much of the 9-to-5 weekdays and Saturday-morning-only variety. Addresses of the main state tourist offices are:

Australian Capital Territory
   Canberra Tourist Bureau, Jolimont Centre,
   Northbourne Ave, Canberra City, ACT 2601
   (☎ toll-free 1800 026 166)
New South Wales
   NSW Government Travel Centre, 19 Castlereagh
   St, Sydney, NSW 2000 (☎ (02) 231 4444)
Northern Territory
   Darwin Region Tourism Association, 33 Smith
   St, Darwin, NT 0800 (☎ (089) 81 4300)
Queensland
   Queen St Mall Information Centre, corner Queen
   and Albert Sts, Brisbane, Qld 4000 (☎ (07) 229
   5918)
South Australia
   Tourism South Australia Travel Centre, 1 King
   William St, Adelaide, SA 5000 (☎ toll-free 1800
   882 092)
Tasmania
   Tasmanian Travel & Information Centre, corner
   Davey and Elizabeth Sts, Hobart, Tas 7000
   (☎ (002) 30 8233)
Victoria
   RACV Travel Centre, 230 Collins St, Mel-
   bourne, Vic 3000 (☎ (03) 650 1522)
Western Australia
   Western Australian Tourist Centre, Forrest Place,
   Perth, WA 6000 (☎ (09) 483 1111)

A step down from the state tourist offices are the local or regional tourist offices. Almost every major town in Australia seems to maintain a tourist office or centre of some type or other and in many cases these are really excellent, with much local information not readily available from the larger, state offices. This particularly applies where there is a strong local tourist trade.

Overseas Reps

The Australian Tourist Commission (ATC) is the government body intended to inform potential visitors about the country. There's a very definite split between promotion outside Australia and inside it. The ATC is strictly an external operator; it does minimal promotion within the country and has little contact with visitors to Australia. Within the country, tourist promotion is handled by state or local tourist offices.

ATC offices overseas have a useful free magazine-style booklet called *Travellers' Guide to Australia* which is a good introduc-

tion to the country, its geography, flora, fauna, states, transport, accommodation, food and so on. They also have a handy free map of the country. This literature is intended for distribution overseas only; if you want copies, get them before you come to Australia. Addresses of the ATC offices for literature requests are:

Australia
   80 William St, Woolloomooloo, Sydney, NSW
   2011 (☎ (02) 360 1111)
Germany
   Neue Mainzerstrasse 22, D6000 Frankfurt/Main
   1 (☎ (069) 274 00 60)
Hong Kong
   Suite 6, 10th floor, Central Plaza, 18 Harbour Rd,
   Wanchai (☎ 802 7700)
Japan
   8th floor, Sankaido Building, 9-13, Akasaka 1-
   chome, Minato-ku, Tokyo 107 (☎ (03) 3582
   2191)
   4th floor, Yuki Building, 3-3-9 Hiranomachi,
   Chuo-Ku, Osaka 541 (☎ (06) 229 3601)
New Zealand
   Level 13, 44-48 Emily Place, Auckland 1 (☎ (09)
   379 9594)
Singapore
   Suite 1703, United Square, 101 Thomson Rd,
   Singapore 1130 (☎ 255 4555)
   80 William St, Woolloomooloo, Sydney, NSW
   2011 (☎ (02) 360 1111)
South Africa
   c/-Mrs Dee Mets, 6th floor, Petrob House, 343
   Surrey Ave, Randburg 2125, Johannesburg
   (☎ (011) 787 6300)
UK
   Gemini House, 10-18 Putney Hill, London SW15
   (☎ (071) 780 2227)
USA
   Suite 1200, 2121 Ave of the Stars, Los Angeles,
   CA 90067 (☎ (213) 552 1988)
   31st floor, 489 Fifth Ave, New York, NY 10017
   (☎ (212) 687 6300)

Canadian travellers should contact the offices in New York or Los Angeles; those from France, Ireland or the Netherlands should contact the London office.

USEFUL ORGANISATIONS
Automobile Associations

Australia has a national automobile association, the Australian Automobile Association, but this exists mainly as an umbrella organisation for the various state associations and to maintain international links. The day-to-day operations are all handled by the state organisations who provide an emergency breakdown service, literature, excellent maps and detailed guides to accommodation and camp sites.

The state organisations have reciprocal arrangements amongst the various states in Australia and with similar organisations overseas. So, if you're a member of the National Roads & Motorists Association (NRMA) in New South Wales, you can use RACV facilities in Victoria. Similarly, if you're a member of the AAA in the USA or the RAC or AA in the UK, you can use any of the state organisations' facilities. But bring proof of membership with you. More details about the state automobile organisations can be found in the relevant state sections. Some of the material they produce is of a very high standard. In particular there is a superb set of regional maps to Queensland produced by the Royal Automobile Club of Queensland (RACQ). The most useful state offices are:

New South Wales
  NRMA, 151 Clarence St, Sydney, NSW 2000 (☎ (02) 260 9222)
Northern Territory
  Automobile Association of the Northern Territory, 79-81 Smith St, Darwin, NT 0800 (☎ (089) 81 3837)
Queensland
  RACQ, 300 St Pauls Terrace, Fortitude Valley, Qld 4006 (☎ (07) 361 2444)
South Australia
  Royal Automobile Association of South Australia (RAA), 41 Hindmarsh Square, Adelaide, SA 5000 (☎ (08) 202 4500)
Tasmania
  Royal Automobile Club of Tasmania (RACT), corner Patrick and Murray Sts, Hobart, Tas 7000 (☎ (002) 38 2200)
Victoria
  RACV, 422 Little Collins St, Melbourne, Vic 3000 (☎ (03) 607 2137)
Western Australia
  Royal Automobile Club of Western Australia (RAC), 228 Adelaide Terrace, Perth, WA 6000 (☎ (09) 421 4444)

National Parks Organisations

Australia has an extensive collection of national parks. In fact, the Royal National Park just outside Sydney is the second oldest national park in the world; only Yellowstone Park in the USA predates it.

The Australian Nature Conservation Agency (ANCA), formerly the Australian National Parks & Wildlife Service, is a commonwealth body which is responsible for Kakadu and Uluru national parks in the Northern Territory, other offshore areas such as the Cocos (Keeling) Islands and Norfolk Island, and also international conservation issues such as whaling and migratory bird conventions. To some extent it also co-ordinates projects, such as Bob Hawke's One Million Trees initiative, which involve more than one state body.

The individual National Parks agencies are operated by the states, rather than being nationally run. The offices tend to be a little hidden away in their capital city locations, although if you search them out they often have excellent literature and maps on the parks. They are much more upfront in the actual parks where, in many cases, they have very good guides and leaflets to bushwalking, nature trails and other activities. The state offices are:

Australian Capital Territory
  Australian Nature Conservation Agency, GPO Box 636, Canberra, ACT 2601 (☎ (06) 250 0200)
New South Wales
  National Parks & Wildlife Service, 43 Bridge St, Hurstville, NSW 2220 (PO Box 1967, Hurstville, NSW 2220) (☎ (02) 585 6444)
Northern Territory
  Conservation Commission of the Northern Territory, PO Box 496, Palmerston, NT 0831 (☎ (089) 89 5511)
  Australian Nature Conservation Agency, Smith St, Darwin, NT 0800 (GPO Box 1260, Darwin, NT 0801) (☎ (089) 81 5299)
Queensland
  National Parks & Wildlife Service, 160 Ann St, Brisbane, Qld 4000 (PO Box 155, North Quay, Qld 4002) (☎ (07) 227 8185)
South Australia
  Department of Environment & Natural Resources, 77 Grenfell St, Adelaide, SA 5001 (GPO Box 667, Adelaide, SA 5001) (☎ (08) 204 1910)

Tasmania
    Department of Parks, Wildlife & Heritage, 134
    Macquarie St, Hobart, Tas 7000 (PO Box 44A,
    Hobart, Tas 7001) (☎ (002) 33 8011)
Victoria
    Department of Conservation & Natural
    Resources, 240 Victoria Parade, East Melbourne,
    Vic 3002 (PO Box 41, East Melbourne, Vic 3002)
    (☎ (03) 412 4011)
Western Australia
    Department of Conservation & Land Manage-
    ment, 50 Hayman Rd, Como, Perth, WA 6152 (☎
    (09) 367 0333)

Australian Conservation Foundation

The Australian Conservation Foundation
(ACF) is the largest nongovernment
organisation involved in conservation. Only
nine to 10% of its income is from the government; the rest comes from memberships
and subscriptions, and from donations
(72%), which are mainly from individuals.

The ACF covers a wide range of issues,
including the greenhouse effect and deple-
tion of the ozone layer, the negative effects
of logging, preservation of rainforests, the
problems of land degradation, and protection
of the Antarctic. It frequently works in conjunction with the Wilderness Society and
other conservation groups.

With the growing focus on conservation
issues and the increasing concern of the Australian public in regard to their environment,
the conservation vote has now become
increasingly important to all political parties.

Wilderness Society

The Tasmanian Wilderness Society was
formed by conservationists who had been
unsuccessful in preventing the damming of
Lake Pedder in south-west Tasmania but
who were determined to prevent the destruction of the Franklin River. The Franklin
River campaign was one of Australia's first
major conservation confrontations and it
caught the attention of the international
media. In 1983, after the High Court decided
against the damming of the Franklin, the
group changed its name to the Wilderness
Society because of their Australia-wide
focus on wilderness issues.

The Wilderness Society is involved in
issues concerning protection of the Australian wilderness, such as forest management
and logging. Like the ACF, government
funding is only a small percentage of its
income, the rest coming from memberships,
donations, the shops and merchandising.
There are Wilderness Society shops in all
states (not in the Northern Territory) where you
can buy books, T-shirts, posters, badges, etc.

Wilderness Society
    130 Davey St, Hobart, Tas 7000 (☎ (002) 34 9366)

Australian Trust for Conservation Volunteers

This nonpolitical, nonprofit group organises
practical conservation projects (such as tree
planting, track construction and flora and
fauna surveys) for volunteers to take part in.
Travellers are welcome and it's an excellent
way to get involved with the conservation
movement and, at the same time, visit some
of the more interesting areas of the country.
Past volunteers have found themselves
working in places such as Tasmania, Kakadu
and Fraser Island.

Most projects are either for a weekend or
a week and all food, transport and accommodation is supplied in return for a small
contribution to help cover costs. Most travellers who take part in ATCV join a Banksia
Package, which lasts six weeks and includes
six different projects. The cost is $650, and
further weeks can be added for $105.

Contact the head office (☎ (053) 33 1483)
at PO Box 423, Ballarat, Vic 3350, or the
state offices listed.

New South Wales
    23-33 Bridge St, Sydney, NSW 2000 (☎ (02)
    228 6461)
Northern Territory
    52 Temira St, Darwin, NT 0800 (☎ (089) 81 3206)
Queensland
    Qld Government House, QUT Grounds, George
    St, Brisbane, Qld 4000 (☎ (07) 210 0330)
South Australia
    TAFE College, Brookway Drive, Campbelltown,
    Adelaide, SA 5000 (☎ (08) 365 1612)
Victoria
    13 Duke St, South Caulfield, Vic 3162 (☎ (03)
    532 8446)

WWOOF

WWOOF (Willing Workers on Organic Farms) is a relatively new organisation in Australia, although it is well established in other countries. The idea is that you do a few hours work each day on a farm in return for bed and board. Some places have a minimum stay of a couple of days but many will take you for just a night. Some will let you stay for months if they like the look of you, and you can get involved with some interesting large-scale projects.

Becoming a WWOOFer is a great way to meet interesting people and to travel cheaply. There are about 200 WWOOF associates in Australia, mostly in Victoria, New South Wales and Queensland.

As the name says, the farms are supposed to be organic but that isn't always so. Some places aren't even farms – you might help out at a pottery or do the books at a seed wholesaler. There are even a few commercial farms which exploit WWOOFers as cheap harvest labour, although these are quite rare. Whether they have a farm or just a vegie patch, most participants in the scheme are concerned to some extent with alternative lifestyles.

To join WWOOF send $15 (A$20 from overseas) to WWOOF, W Tree, Buchan, Vic 3885 (☎ (051) 55 0218), and they'll send you a membership number and a booklet which lists WWOOF places all over Australia.

National Trust

The National Trust is dedicated to preserving historic buildings in all parts of Australia. The Trust actually owns a number of buildings throughout the country which are open to the public. Many other buildings are 'classified' by the National Trust to ensure their preservation.

The National Trust also produces some excellent literature, including a fine series of walking-tour guides to many cities around the country, large and small. These guides are often available from local tourist offices or from National Trust offices and are usually free whether you're a member of the National Trust or not. Membership of the trust is well worth considering, however, because it entitles you to free entry to any National Trust property for your year of membership. If you're a dedicated visitor of old buildings this could soon pay for itself. Annual membership costs $41 for individuals ($29 concession) and $58 for families ($41 concession), and includes the monthly or quarterly magazine put out by the state organisation that you join. Addresses of the various National Trust state offices are:

Australian Capital Territory
  6 Geills Court, Deakin, ACT 2600 (☎ (06) 281 0711)
New South Wales
  Observatory Hill, Sydney, NSW 2000 (☎ (02) 258 0123)
Northern Territory
  52 Temira Crescent, Myilly Point, Darwin, NT 0820 (☎ (089) 81 2848)
Queensland
  Old Government House, 2 George St, Brisbane, Qld 4000 (☎ (07) 229 1788)
South Australia
  Ayers House, 288 North Terrace, Adelaide, SA 5000 (☎ (08) 223 1655)
Tasmania
  39 Paterson St, Launceston, Tas 7250 (☎ (003) 31 9077)
Victoria
  Tasma Terrace, 6 Parliament Place, Melbourne, Vic 3002 (☎ (03) 654 4711)
Western Australia
  Old Observatory, 4 Havelock St, West Perth, WA 6005 (☎ (09) 321 6088)

Disabled Travellers Organisations

A number of organisations can supply advice to disabled travellers, but many of them only operate within a single state. The office of the National Industries for Disability Services, operating through the Australian Council for the Rehabilitation of the Disabled (ACROD) (PO Box 60, Curtin, ACT 2605, ☎ (06) 282 4333), produces information sheets for disabled travellers, including lists of state-level organisations, specialist travel agents, wheelchair and equipment hire and access guides. It can also sometimes help with specific queries. It would be grateful if

Wheelchair Access

Australia's level of disability awareness is encouraging, although the information about accessible accommodation and tourist attractions is fragmented and available on a regional basis only. The practical level of accessibility is generally quite high and all new facilities must satisfy the standards set down by law.

The Australian Tourist Commission (☎ (02) 360 1111, fax (02) 333 6469) has published a comprehensive information fact sheet, *Travel in Australia for People with Disabilities*. This contains the addresses of organisations in each state or territory which provide assistance to the disabled, for example the Paraplegic and Quadriplegic Association, the Multiple Sclerosis Society, the Yooralla Society, societies for the intellectually disabled, specialist tour operators and care providers. NICAN (National Information Communications Awareness Network), PO Box 407, Curtin, ACT 2605 (☎ (06) 285 3713, fax (06) 285 3714), is an Australia-wide directory providing information on accessible accommodation and sporting and recreational activities. ACROD (Australian Council for the Rehabilitation of the Disabled), PO Box 60, Curtin, ACT 2605 (☎ (06) 282 4333, fax (06) 281 3488), can provide information on state-based help organisations, accommodation and tour operators, etc.

Qantas and Ansett airlines welcome disabled travellers. Qantas planes carry the sky chair and some have accessible toilets. Before booking, disabled travellers should contact the airlines to determine any policy requirements, for example medical certification for fitness to fly. Australia's major airports all have facilities for the disabled traveller.

The new ferry which operates between Melbourne and Devonport has four accessible cabins and access to the public areas on the ship.

Interstate travel on buses and trains is not yet a viable option for the wheelchair user. Melbourne's metropolitan train system is accessible; the Met has published a useful leaflet, *Disability Services for Customers with Specific Needs*, available from Disability Services, Public Transport Corporation, Spencer St Station (☎ (03) 619 2355). Also in Melbourne, the Travellers Aid Society at Spencer St Station (☎ (03) 670 2873) and at Level 2, 169 Swanston Walk (☎ (03) 654 2600), provides advice, assistance and toilets for the disabled traveller. The Travellers Aid Support Centre (☎ (03) 654 7690) is also at 169 Swanston Walk.

Avis and Hertz offer hire cars with hand controls at no extra charge. The vehicles can be picked up at major airports; the agencies require 24 hours notice. Most of the taxi companies in the major cities and towns have modified vehicles which take wheelchairs.

The international wheelchair symbol for parking in allocated bays is generally recognised throughout Australia. These symbols are available from local councils upon production of a medical certificate. Parking in built-up areas can usually be arranged in advance by contacting the city council. City mobility maps, showing accessible routes, toilets, etc, are also available from the city council.

Accommodation in Australia is generally good, but always ask at information centres for lists of accessible accommodation and tourist attractions. Australia is well represented by international hotel chains such as Hyatt, Hilton, Sheraton and the Accor group, and by motel chains such as Flag and Best Western. The *A-Z Australian Accommodation Guide* is available from the state-based automobile association offices; the guide indicates accessible accommodation, although it is best to confirm that the facilities suit your needs before booking. A number of YHA hostels have accessible accommodation; contact the YHA Membership Centre, 205 King St, Melbourne 3000 (☎ (03) 670 7991). One of the best examples of accommodation which caters for disabled travellers is the Wheel Resort; see the Byron Bay places to stay section.

Bruce M Cameron

enquirers could send at least the cost of postage.

ANZSES

The Australian & New Zealand Scientific Exploration Society is a nonprofit organisation which undertakes scientific expeditions into wilderness areas of Australia. Each year over 100 volunteers are sent into the field, always under the guidance of an experienced leader.

The organisation offers volunteers the opportunity to participate in the collection of scientific data and the experience of living and working in remote areas of Australia generally not accessible to the average traveller.

Recent studies have included flora and fauna gathering west of Coober Pedy and in Witjira National Park (outback South Australia), Eungella National Park, Cedar Bay National Park, Fraser Island, Sturt National Park (NSW), south-west Tasmania and far-east Gippsland (Vic).

The ANZSES postal address and phone number is PO Box 174, Albert Park, Vic 3206 (☎ (03) 690 5455).

BUSINESS HOURS & HOLIDAYS
Business Hours

Most shops close at 5 or 5.30 pm weekdays, and either noon or 5 pm on Saturdays. In some places Sunday trading is starting to catch on, but it's currently limited to the major cities. In most towns there are usually one or two late shopping nights each week, when the doors stay open until 9 or 9.30 pm. Usually it's Thursday and/or Friday night.

Banks are open from 9.30 am to 4 pm Monday to Thursday, and until 5 pm on Friday. Some large city branches are open 8 am to 6 pm Monday to Friday. Some are also open to 9 pm on Fridays. Of course there are some exceptions to Australia's unremarkable opening hours and all sorts of places stay open late and all weekend – particularly milk bars, convenience stores, supermarkets, delis and city bookshops.

Holidays

The Christmas holiday season is part of the long summer school vacation and the time you are most likely to find accommodation booked out and long queues. There are three other shorter school holiday periods during the year but they vary by a week or two from state to state, falling from early to mid-April, late June to mid-July, and late September to early October.

Like school holidays, public holidays vary quite a bit from state to state. The following

is a list of the main national and state public holidays:

New Year's Day
    1 January
Australia Day
    26 January
Labour Day (Vic)
    first or second Monday in March
Labour Day (WA)
    second Monday in March
Easter
    Good Friday and Easter Saturday, Sunday and Monday (and Tuesday in Victoria)
Anzac Day
    25 April
Labour Day (Qld)
    first Monday in May
May Day (NT)
    1 May
Adelaide Cup (SA)
    third Monday in May
Foundation Day (WA)
    first Monday in June
Queen's Birthday (Qld, NT, Vic)
    second Monday in June
Bank Holiday (NSW)
    first Monday in August
Picnic Day (NT)
    first Monday in August
Queen's Birthday (WA)
    first Monday in October
Labour Day (NSW, ACT & SA)
    first Monday in October
Melbourne Cup (Vic)
    first Tuesday in November
Christmas Day
    25 December
Boxing Day
    26 December

CULTURAL EVENTS

Some of the most enjoyable Australian festivals are, naturally, the ones which are most typically Australian – like the surf-lifesaving competitions on beaches all around the country during summer; or the outback race meetings, which draw together isolated townsfolk, the tiny communities from the huge stations and more than a few eccentric bush characters.

There are happenings and holidays in Australia all year round – the following is just a brief overview. Check the relevant state tourist authorities for dates and more details.

January

Sydney to Hobart Yacht Race – Tas. The arrival (29 December to 2 January) in Hobart of the yachts competing in this annual New Year race is celebrated with a mardi gras. The competitors in the *Melbourne to Hobart Yacht Race* arrive soon after.

Australia Day – this national holiday, commemorating the arrival of the First Fleet, in 1788, is observed on 26 January.

Montsalvat Jazz Festival – Vic. Australia's biggest jazz festival is held at the beautiful Montsalvat artists' colony at Eltham.

February

Royal Hobart Regatta – Tas. This is the largest aquatic carnival in the southern hemisphere, with boat races and other activities.

Sydney Gay & Lesbian Mardi Gras – NSW. It's fun – there's a huge procession with extravagant costumes, and an incredible party along Oxford St.

Festival of Perth – WA. This huge festival features local and international artists.

March

Adelaide Arts Festival – SA. Held on even-dated years, this is three weeks of music, theatre, opera, ballet, art exhibitions, light relief and plenty of parties.

Hunter Valley Vintage Festival – NSW. Wine enthusiasts flock to the Hunter Valley (north of Sydney) for wine tasting, and grape picking and treading contests.

Moomba – Melbourne. This week-long festival culminates in a huge street procession, usually on the Victorian Labour Day holiday.

Port Fairy Folk Festival – Vic. Every Labour Day weekend the small coastal town of Port Fairy comes to life with music, dancing, workshops, storytelling, spontaneous entertainment and stalls. Australia's biggest folk music festival attracts all sorts of people and for three days the population swells from 2500 to over 10,000.

March to April

Sydney Royal Agricultural Show – NSW. Livestock contests and exhibits, ring events, sideshows and rodeos are features of this Easter show.

April

Anzac Day – This is a national public holiday, on 25 April, commemorating the landing of Anzac troops at Gallipoli in 1915. Memorial marches by the returned soldiers of both world wars and the veterans of Korea and Vietnam are held all over the country.

Melbourne Comedy Festival – Vic. The comedy capital of Australia puts on a terrific three-week festival with local, out-of-town and international comedians, plays and other funny things.

World Motorcycle Grand Prix This round of the 500 cc world championships is held in New South Wales.

June

Melbourne Film Festival – Vic. This is Australia's longest-running international film event, presenting the best in contemporary world cinema.

July

NT Royal Shows Agricultural shows in Darwin, Katherine, Tennant Creek and Alice Springs.

August

Darwin Rodeo – NT. This includes international team events between Australia, the USA, Canada and New Zealand.

Darwin Beer Can Regatta – NT. Boat races for boats constructed entirely out of beer cans, of which there are plenty in the world's beer-drinking capital.

Sydney City to Surf – NSW. Australia's biggest foot race takes place with up to 25,000 competitors running the 14 km from Hyde Park to Bondi Beach.

Shinju Matsuri (Festival of the Pearl) – WA. Held in the old pearling port of Broome, this week-long festival is a great event and includes Asiatic celebrations.

September

AFL Grand Final – Vic. Sporting attention turns to Melbourne with the Grand Final of Aussie rules football, when the MCG's 100,000 seats aren't enough to hold the spectators. It's the biggest sporting event in Australia.

Royal Melbourne Show – Vic. This attracts agricultural folk for the judging of livestock and produce, and lots of families for the sideshows.

Royal Perth Show – WA.

Western Australian Folk Festival – WA. Enjoy a weekend of music and dancing in Toodyay.

Tooheys Bathurst 1000 – NSW. Motor racing enthusiasts flock to Bathurst for the annual 1000 km, touring-car race on the superb Mt Panorama circuit.

Royal Adelaide Show – SA. One of the oldest royal shows in the country, with major agricultural and horticultural exhibits and entertainment.

October

Oktoberfests Traditional beerfests with food, plenty of beer and live entertainment for all ages are held all over the country including Darwin, Alice Springs and Melbourne.

Melbourne International Festival of the Arts – Vic. An annual festival offering the best of opera, theatre, dance and the visual arts from around Australia and the world.

Melbourne International Fringe Festival – Vic. Three weeks of theatre, dance, comedy, cabaret, writers' readings, exhibitions and other events help Melbourne celebrate the 'alternative' arts.

Henley-on-Todd Regatta – NT. A series of races

for leg-powered bottomless boats on the (usually) dry Todd River.

Royal Shows – Tas. The royal agricultural and horticultural shows of Hobart and Launceston are held this month.

November

Melbourne Cup – Vic. On the first Tuesday in November Australia's premier horse race is run at Flemington Race Course. It's a public holiday in Melbourne but the whole country shuts down for the three minutes or so when the race is on.

Australian Formula One Grand Prix – SA. This premier motor race takes place on a circuit around the streets and parklands of Adelaide. There are also festive events, concerts and street parties. The race will be moving to Melbourne in 1996.

December to January

These are the busiest summer months with Christmas, school holidays, lots of beach activities, rock and jazz festivals, international sporting events including tennis and cricket, a whole host of outdoor activities and lots of parties.

Sydney to Hobart Yacht Race – NSW. Sydney Harbour is a sight to behold on Boxing Day, 26 December, when boats of all shapes and sizes crowd its waters to farewell the yachts competing in this gruelling race. It's a fantastic sight as the yachts stream out of the harbour and head south. In Hobart there's a mardi gras to celebrate the finish of the race.

POST & TELECOMMUNICATIONS
Postal Rates

Australia's postal services are relatively efficient but not too cheap. It costs 45c to send a standard letter or postcard within Australia, while aerograms cost 70c.

Air-mail letters/postcards cost 75/70c to New Zealand, Singapore and Malaysia, 95/90c to Hong Kong and India, $1.05/95c to the USA and Canada, and $1.20/1 to Europe and the UK.

Post offices are open from 9 am to 5 pm Monday to Friday, but you can often get stamps from local post offices operated from newsagencies or from Australia Post shops, found in large cities, on Saturday mornings.

Receiving Mail

All post offices will hold mail for visitors and some city GPOs have very busy postes restantes. Cairns GPO poste restante, for example, can get quite hectic. You can also have mail sent to you at the American Express offices in big cities if you have an Amex card or carry Amex travellers' cheques.

Telephone

From the year dot the Australian phone system was wholly owned and run by the government, but these days the market has been deregulated with a second player, Optus, now offering an alternative. The system (still run by the government-owned Telecom) is really remarkably efficient and, equally important, easy to use. Local calls from public phones cost 40c for an unlimited amount of time. You can make local calls from gold or blue phones – often found in

Phone Changes
Australia is running out of phone and fax numbers! AUSTEL (the Australian Telecommunications Authority) is implementing a progressive response to the crisis, beginning in July 1994 and taking up to five years, with Sydney's Mona Vale numbers being the first to be changed. Every phone and fax number in Australia will gain an extra one or two digits, so that all numbers will have a total of eight digits. In metropolitan areas an extra digit will be added to the front of the existing seven-digit number. In regional areas, the last two digits of the current area code will be added to the front of the local number to form a new eight-digit number; for example, if the area code is (052), just ignore the 0 and add 52 to the existing number. To accommodate the changes, a very small percentage of numbers in regional areas will have to undergo two changes.

When completed, the present 54 area codes will have been merged into just four: (02) will cover New South Wales and the ACT, (03) will cover Victoria and Tasmania, (07) will cover Queensland and (08) will cover Western Australia, the Northern Territory and South Australia.

There will be a six-month period when both the old and new numbers will be accessible, followed by a further three-month period when a recorded message will refer the caller to the White Pages' information section.

The change will not affect the cost of calls: a long-distance call will still be charged at long-distance rates. If in doubt, you can call AUSTEL's information hotline on ☎ 1800 888 888, and more specific details are given at the beginning of each chapter. ∎

shops, hotels, bars, etc – and from payphone booths.

It's also possible to make long-distance (STD – Subscriber Trunk Dialling) calls from virtually any public phone. Many public phones accept the Telecom Phonecards, which are very convenient. The cards come in $2, $5 and $10 denominations, and are available from retail outlets such as newsagents and pharmacies which display the Phonecard logo. You keep using the card until the value has been used in calls. Otherwise, have plenty of 20c, 50c and $1 coins, and be prepared to feed them through at a fair old rate. STD calls are cheaper in off-peak hours – see the front of a local telephone book for the different rates.

Some public phones are set up to take only bank cash cards or credit cards, and these too are convenient, although you need to keep an eye on how much the call is costing as it can quickly mount up. The minimum charge for a call on one of these phones is $1.20.

Many businesses and some government departments operate a toll-free service, so no matter where you are ringing from around the country, it's a free call. These numbers have the prefix 1800 (or the old toll-free prefix 008) and we've listed them wherever possible throughout the book. Phone numbers with the prefixes 018, 015 or 041 are mobile or car phones. Many companies, such as the airlines, have six-digit numbers beginning with 13, and these are charged at the rate of a local call. Often they'll be Australia-wide numbers, but sometimes are applicable only to a specific STD district. Unfortunately there's no way of telling without actually ringing the number.

Other odd numbers you may come across are nine-digit numbers starting with 0055. These calls, usually recorded information services and the like, are provided by private companies, and your call is charged in multiples of 25c (40c from public phones) at a rate selected by the provider (Premium 70c per minute, Value 55c per minute, Budget 35c per minute).

STD calls are cheaper at night. In ascending order of cost:

Economy – from 6 pm Saturday to 8 am Monday; 10 pm to 8 am every night
Night – from 6 to 10 pm Monday to Friday
Day – from 8 am to 6 pm Monday to Saturday

From most STD phones you can also make ISD (International Subscriber Dialling) calls. Dialling ISD you can get through to overseas numbers almost as quickly as you can access local numbers and if your call is brief it needn't cost very much.

All you do is dial 0011 for overseas, the country code (44 for Britain, 1 for the USA or Canada, 64 for New Zealand), the city code (71 or 81 for London, 212 for New York, etc), and then the telephone number. And have a Phonecard, credit card or plenty of coins to hand.

To use Optus rather than Telecom (which may or may not be cheaper – the two are constantly trying to undercut one another), dial 1 or 1456 before the ISD country code or STD area code. The prefix differs according to preferential dialling: you dial 1456 to access Optus from a Telecom phone; those who have not yet subscribed through a ballot dial 1; and Optus subscribers dial normally (0011 etc). Optus is only available from private phones in certain areas.

A standard Telecom call to the USA or Britain costs $2.50 a minute ($2 off peak); New Zealand is $2.10 a minute ($1.40 off peak). Off-peak times, if available, vary depending on the destination – see the front of any telephone book for more details. Sunday is often the cheapest day to ring.

With the competition offered by Optus, Telecom often has discount specials to various destinations, although many of these are only available from private phones.

Country Direct is a service which gives travellers in Australia direct access to operators in 42 countries, to make collect or credit card calls. For a full list of the countries hooked into this system, check any local telephone book. They include: Canada (☎ 1800 881 150), Germany (☎ 1800 881 490), Japan (☎ 1800 881 810), New Zealand (☎ 1800 881 640), the UK (☎ 1800 881 440) and the USA (☎ 1800 881 011).

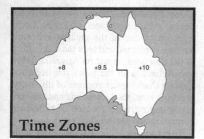

Time Zones

TIME

Australia is divided into three time zones: Western Standard Time is plus eight hours from GMT/UTC (Western Australia), Central Standard Time is plus 9½ hours (Northern Territory, South Australia) and Eastern Standard Time is plus 10 (Tasmania, Victoria, New South Wales, Queensland). When it's noon in Western Australia it's 1.30 pm in the Northern Territory and South Australia and 2 pm in the rest of the country. During the summer things get slightly screwed up as daylight saving time (when clocks are put forward an hour) does not operate in Western Australia or Queensland, and in Tasmania it lasts for one month longer than in the other states. To make matters even more confusing, Victoria and South Australia may join Tasmania in having an extra month of daylight saving in 1995, while New South Wales has decided not to join!

ELECTRICITY

Voltage is 220-240 V and the plugs are three-pin, but not the same as British three-pin plugs. Users of electric shavers or hairdryers should note that, apart from in fancy hotels, it's difficult to find converters to take either US flat two-pin plugs or the European round two-pin plugs. Adaptors for British plugs can be found in good hardware shops, chemists and travel agents. You can easily bend the US plugs to a slight angle to make them fit.

WEIGHTS & MEASURES

Australia went metric in the early '70s. Petrol and milk are sold by the litre, apples and potatoes by the kg, distance is measured by the metre or km, and speed limits are in km per hour (km/h).

For those who need help with metric there's a conversion table at the back of this book.

BOOKS & MAPS

In almost any bookshop in the country you'll find a section devoted to Australiana with books on every Australian subject you care to mention. If you want a souvenir of Australia, such as a photographic record, try one of the numerous coffee-table books like *A Day in the Life of Australia*. There are many other Australian books which make good gifts: children's books with very Australian illustrations like Julie Vivar and Mem Fox's *Possum Magic*, Norman Lindsay's *The Magic Pudding* and *Snugglepot & Cuddlepie* by May Gibbs (one of the first bestselling Australian children's books), or cartoon books by excellent Australian cartoonists such as Michael Leunig or Kaz Cooke. We've got a lot of bookshops and some of the better-known ones are mentioned in the various city sections.

At the Wilderness Society shops in each capital city and the Government Printing Offices in Sydney and Melbourne you'll find a good range of wildlife posters, calendars and books.

Aborigines

The Australian Aborigines by Kenneth Maddock is a good cultural summary. The awardwinning *Triumph of the Nomads*, by Geoffrey Blainey, chronicles the life of Australia's original inhabitants, and convincingly demolishes the myth that the Aborigines were 'primitive' people trapped on a hostile continent. They were in fact extremely successful in adapting to and overcoming the difficulties presented by the climate and resources (or seeming lack of them) – the book's an excellent read.

For a sympathetic historical account of what's happened to the original Australians since Whites arrived read *Aboriginal Australians* by Richard Broome. *A Change of*

Ownership, by Mildred Kirk, covers similar ground to Broome's book, but does so more concisely, focusing on the land rights movement and its historical background.

The Other Side of the Frontier, by Henry Reynolds, uses historical records to give a vivid account of an Aboriginal view of the arrival and takeover of Australia by Europeans. His *With the White People* identifies the essential Aboriginal contributions to the survival of the early White settlers. *My Place*, Sally Morgan's prizewinning autobiography, traces her discovery of her Aboriginal heritage. *The Fringe Dwellers* by Nene Gare describes just what it's like to be an Aborigine growing up in a White-dominated society.

Don't Take Your Love to Town by Ruby Langford and *My People* by Oodgeroo Noonuccal (Kath Walker) are also recommended reading for people interested in Aborigines' experience.

History

For a good introduction to Australian history, read *A Short History of Australia*, a most accessible and informative general history by the late Manning Clark, the much-loved Aussie historian, or *The Fatal Shore*, Robert Hughes's bestselling account of the convict era.

Finding Australia, by Russel Ward, traces the story of the early days from the first Aboriginal arrivals up to 1821. It's strong on Aborigines, women and the full story of foreign exploration, not just Captain Cook's role. There's lots of fascinating detail, including information about the appalling crooks who ran the early colony for long periods, and it's intended to be the first of a series.

The Exploration of Australia, by Michael Cannon, is coffee-table book in size, presentation and price, but it's a fascinating reference book about the gradual European uncovering of the continent.

Cooper's Creek, by Alan Moorehead, is a classic account of the ill-fated Burke and Wills expedition which dramatises the horrors and hardships faced by the early explorers.

The Fatal Impact, also by Moorehead, begins with the voyages of James Cook, regarded as one of the greatest and most humane explorers, and tells the tragic story of the European impact on Australia, Tahiti and Antarctica in the years that followed Captain Cook's great voyages of discovery. It details how good intentions and the economic imperatives of the time led to disaster, corruption and annihilation.

To get an idea of life on a Kimberley cattle station last century, *Kings in Grass Castles* and *Sore in the Saddle*, both by Dame Mary Durack, are well worth getting hold of. Other books which give an insight into the pioneering days in the outback include *Packhorse & Waterhole* by Gordon Buchanan, son of legendary drover Nat Buchanan who was responsible for opening up large areas of the Northern Territory; *The Big Run*, a history of the huge Victoria River Downs cattle station in the Northern Territory; and *The Cattle King* by Ion Idriess, which details the life of the remarkable Sir Sidney Kidman, the man who set up a chain of stations in the outback early this century.

Fiction

You don't need to worry about bringing a few good novels from home for your trip to Australia; there's plenty of excellent recent Australian literature including the novels and short stories of Helen Garner, Kate Grenville, Elizabeth Jolley, Thomas Keneally, Peter Carey, Thea Astley, Tim Winton and Beverley Farmer.

There's many Australian classics (these have also been made into films), including *The Getting of Wisdom* by Henry Handel Richardson, *Picnic at Hanging Rock* by Joan Lindsay and *My Brilliant Career* by Miles Franklin. *For the Term of his Natural Life*, written in 1870 by Marcus Clarke, was one of the first books to be made into a film, in 1926.

The works of Banjo Paterson (*The Man from Snowy River*, for example), Henry Lawson, Frank Hardy, Alan Marshall (*I Can Jump Puddles*) and Albert Facey (*A Fortunate Life*) make interesting reading.

The novels of the Nobel prizewinner Patrick White are difficult but rewarding – try *Voss*, the story of a 19th-century explorer and his lover left behind in the stifling social climate of middle-class Sydney.

Peter Carey is one of Australia's most successful contemporary writers and all of his books are worth looking out for. His rambling novel *Illywhacker* is set mostly in Melbourne, and other works include *Oscar and Lucinda* and two collections of short stories, *The Fat Man in History* and *War Crimes*.

Travel Accounts

Accounts of travels in Australia include the marvellous *Tracks*, by Robyn Davidson. It's the amazing story of a young woman who set out alone to walk from Alice Springs to the Western Australia coast with her camels – proof that you can do anything if you try hard enough. It almost single-handedly inspired the current Australian interest in camel safaris!

Quite another sort of travel is Tony Horwitz's *One for the Road*, an often hilarious account of a high-speed hitchhiking trip around Australia (Oz through a windscreen). In contrast, *The Ribbon and the Ragged Square*, by Linda Christmas, is an intelligent, sober account of a nine-month investigatory trip round Oz by a *Guardian* journalist from England. There's lots of background and history as well as first-hand reporting and interviews.

Howard Jacobson's *In the Land of Oz* recounts his circuit of the country. It's amusing at times, but through most of the book you're left wondering when the long-suffering Ros is finally going to thump the twerp!

The late Bruce Chatwin's book *The Songlines* tells of his experiences among central Australian Aborigines and makes more sense of the Dreamtime, sacred sites, sacred songs and the traditional Aboriginal way of life than 10 learned tomes put together. Along the way it also delves into the origins of humankind and throws in some pithy anecdotes about modern Australia.

The journals of the early European explorers can be fairly hard going but make fascinating reading. The hardships that many of these men (and they were virtually all men) endured is nothing short of amazing. These accounts are usually available in the main libraries. Men such as Sturt, Eyre, Leichhardt, Davidson, King (on the Burke and Wills expedition), Stuart and many others all kept detailed journals.

Travel Guides

Burnum Burnum's Aboriginal Australia is subtitled 'a traveller's guide'. If you want to explore Australia from the Aboriginal point of view, this large and lavish hardback is the book for you.

For trips into the outback in your own vehicle Brian Sheedy's *Outback on a Budget* includes lots of practical advice. There are a number of other books about vehicle preparation and driving in the outback, including *Explore Australia by Four-Wheel Drive* by Peter & Kim Wherrett (Viking O'Neil).

Surfing Australia's East Coast by Aussie surf star Nat Young is a slim, cheap, comprehensive guide to the best breaks from Victoria to Fraser Island. He's also written the *Surfing & Sailboard Guide to Australia* which covers the whole country. Surfing enthusiasts can also look for the expensive coffee-table book *Atlas of Australian Surfing*, by Mark Warren.

If you want to really understand the Barrier Reef's natural history, look for *Australia's Great Barrier Reef*. It's colourful, expensive and nearly as big as the Barrier Reef itself. There's also a cheaper abbreviated paperback version. Lonely Planet's *Islands of Australia's Great Barrier Reef* book gives you all the practical info you'll need for making the most of the reef. *Australia's Wonderful Wildlife* (Australian Women's Weekly) is the shoestringer's equivalent of a coffee-table book – a cheap paperback with lots of great photos of the animals you didn't see, or those that didn't stay still when you pointed your camera at them.

Lonely Planet's *Bushwalking in Australia*

describes 23 walks of different lengths and difficulty in various parts of the country, ranging from an easy two-day stroll along the coastline of the Royal National Park near Sydney, to a strenuous 10-day bushwalk on the exposed peaks of the Western Arthur Range in Tasmania. Lonely Planet also has guidebooks to the states of *Victoria* and *New South Wales*, city guides for Melbourne and Sydney, and a guide to the outback.

There are state-by-state Reader's Digest guides to coasts and national parks, such as the *Coast of New South Wales*, and Gregory's guides to national parks, such as *National Parks of New South Wales* (a handy reference listing access, facilities, activities and so on for all parks).

Maps

There's no shortage of maps available, although many of them are of pretty average quality. For road maps the best are probably those published by the various oil companies – Shell, BP, Mobil, etc, and these are available from service stations. The state motoring organisations are another good source of maps, and they are often a lot cheaper than the oil company maps. See earlier in this chapter for addresses. Commercially available city street guides, such as *Melways* and those produced by UBD, are also useful.

For bushwalking, ski-touring and other activities which require large-scale maps, the topographic sheets put out by the Australian Surveying & Land Information Group (AUSLIG) are the ones to get. Many of the more popular sheets are available over the counter at shops which sell specialist bushwalking gear and outdoor equipment. AUSLIG also has special interest maps showing various types of land use such as population densities or Aboriginal land. For more information, or a catalogue, contact AUSLIG, Department of Administrative Services, PO Box 2, Belconnen, ACT 2616 (☎ (06) 201 4300).

MEDIA

Australia has a wide range of media although a few big companies (Rupert Murdoch's News Corporation and Kerry Packer's Consolidated Press being the best known) own an awful lot of what there is to read and watch.

Newspapers & Magazines

Each major city tends to have at least one important daily, often backed up by a tabloid paper and also by evening papers. The *Sydney Morning Herald* and the Melbourne *Age* are two of the most important dailies. There's also the *Australian*, a Murdoch-owned paper and the country's only national daily.

Weekly newspapers and magazines include an Australian edition of *Time* and a combined edition of the Australian news magazine the *Bulletin* and *Newsweek*. The *Guardian Weekly* is widely available and good for international news.

Radio & TV

The national advertising-free TV and radio network is the ABC. In most places there are a couple of ABC radio stations and a host of commercial stations, both AM and FM, featuring the whole gamut of radio possibilities, from rock to talkback to 'beautiful music'.

In Sydney and Melbourne there are the ABC, three commercial TV stations and SBS, a government-sponsored multicultural TV station which is beamed to the capital cities and some regional centres. Around the country the number of TV stations varies from place to place; there are regional TV stations but in some remote areas the ABC may be all you can receive.

Imparja is an Aboriginal-run TV station which operates out of Alice Springs and has a 'footprint' which covers one-third of the country. It broadcasts a variety of programs, ranging from soaps to pieces made by and for Aborigines.

FILM & PHOTOGRAPHY

If you come to Australia via Hong Kong or Singapore it's worth buying film there but otherwise Australian film prices are not too far out of line with those of the rest of the

Western world. Including developing, 36-exposure Kodachrome 64 or Fujichrome 100 slide film costs around $25, but with a little shopping around you can find it for around $20 – even less if you buy it in quantity.

There are plenty of camera shops in all the big cities and standards of camera service are high. Developing standards are also high, with many places offering one-hour developing of print film. Melbourne is the main centre for developing Kodachrome slide film in the South-East Asian region.

Photography is no problem, but in the outback you have to allow for the exceptional intensity of the light. Best results in the outback regions are obtained early in the morning and late in the afternoon. As the sun gets higher, colours appear washed out. You must also allow for the intensity of reflected light when taking shots on the Barrier Reef or at other coastal locations. In the outback, especially in the summer, allow for temperature extremes and do your best to keep film as cool as possible, particularly after exposure. Other film and camera hazards are dust in the outback and humidity in the tropical regions of the far north.

As in any country, politeness goes a long way when taking photographs; ask before taking pictures of people. Note that many Aborigines do not like to have their photographs taken, even from a distance.

HEALTH

So long as you have not visited an infected country in the past 14 days (aircraft refuelling stops do not count) no vaccinations are required for entry. Naturally, if you're going to be travelling around in outlandish places apart from Australia, a good collection of immunisations is highly advisable.

Medical care in Australia is first-class and only moderately expensive. A typical visit to the doctor costs around $35. Health insurance cover is available in Australia, but there is usually a waiting period after you sign up before any claims can be made. If you have an immediate health problem, phone or visit the casualty section at the nearest public hospital.

Travel Insurance

Even if you normally carry health or hospitalisation insurance, or live in a country where health care is provided by the government, it's still a good idea to buy some travellers' insurance that covers both health and loss of baggage.

Make sure the policy includes health care and medication in the countries you plan to visit and includes a flight home for you and anyone you're travelling with, should your condition warrant it.

Medical Kit

It's always a good idea to travel with a basic medical kit even when your destination is a country like Australia where most first-aid supplies are readily available. Some of the items that should be included are: Band-aids, a sterilised gauze bandage, elastoplast, cotton wool, a thermometer, tweezers, scissors, antibiotic cream and ointment, contraceptives (if required), an antiseptic agent, burn cream, insect repellent and multivitamins. Calamine lotion, antihistamine cream and old-fashioned Tiger Balm are all useful for insect bites.

Don't forget any medication you're already taking, and paracetamol or aspirin (for pain and fever).

Health Precautions

Travellers from the northern hemisphere need to be aware of the intensity of the sun in Australia. Those ultraviolet rays can have you burnt to a crisp even on an overcast day, so if in doubt wear protective cream, a wide-brimmed hat and a long-sleeved shirt with a collar. Australia has a high incidence of skin cancer, a fact directly connected to exposure to the sun. Be careful.

The contraceptive pill is available on prescription only, so a visit to a doctor is necessary. Doctors are listed in the Yellow Pages phone book or you can visit the outpatients section of a public hospital. Condoms are available from chemists, many convenience stores such as 7-Eleven, and vending machines in the public toilets of many hotels and universities.

WOMEN TRAVELLERS

Australia is generally a safe place for women travellers, although it's probably best to avoid walking alone late at night in any of the major cities. Sexual harassment is unfortunately still second nature to some Aussie males, and it's generally true to say that the further you get from 'civilisation' (ie, the big cities), the less enlightened your average Aussie male is going to be about women's issues; you're far more likely to meet an ocker than a Snag!

Female hitchers should exercise care at all times (see the section on hitching in the Getting Around chapter.)

EMERGENCY

In the case of a life-threatening situation dial 000. This call is free from any phone and the operator will connect you with either the police, ambulance or fire brigade. To dial any of these services direct, check the inside front cover of any local telephone book.

For other telephone crisis and personal counselling services (such as sexual assault, poisons information or alcohol and drug problems), check the Community pages of the local telephone book.

DANGERS & ANNOYANCES
Animal Hazards

There are a few unique and sometimes dangerous creatures, although it's unlikely that you'll come across any of them, particularly if you stick to the cities. Here's a rundown just in case.

The best-known danger in the Australian outback, and the one that captures visitors' imaginations, is snakes. Although there are many venomous snakes there are few that are aggressive, and unless you have the bad fortune to stand on one it's unlikely that you'll be bitten. Taipans and tiger snakes, however, will attack if alarmed. Sea snakes can also be dangerous.

To minimise your chances of being bitten always wear boots, socks and long trousers when walking through undergrowth where snakes may be present. Don't put your hands into holes and crevices, and be careful when collecting firewood.

Snake bites do not cause instantaneous death and antivenenes are usually available. Keep the victim calm and still, wrap the bitten limb tightly, as you would for a sprained ankle, and then attach a splint to immobilise it. Then seek medical help, if possible with the dead snake for identification. Don't attempt to catch the snake if there is even a remote possibility of being bitten again. Tourniquets and sucking out the poison are now comprehensively discredited.

We've got a couple of nasty spiders too, including the funnel-web, the redback and the white-tail, so it's best not to play with any spider. Funnel-web spiders are found in New South Wales and their bite is treated in the same way as snake bite. For redback bites apply ice and seek medical attention.

Among the splendid variety of biting insects the mosquito and march fly are the most common. The common bush tick (found in the forest and scrub country along the east coast of Australia) can be dangerous if left lodged in the skin, as the toxin the tick excretes can cause paralysis and sometimes death – check your body for lumps every night if you're walking in tick-infested areas. The tick should be removed by dousing it with methylated spirits or kerosene and levering it out intact.

Leeches are common, and while they will suck your blood they are not dangerous and are easily removed by the application of salt or heat.

Up north saltwater crocodiles can be a real danger and have killed a number of people (travellers and locals). They are found in river estuaries and large rivers, sometimes a long way inland, so before diving into that inviting, cool water find out from the locals whether it's croc-free.

In the sea, the box jellyfish, also known as the sea wasp or 'stinger', occurs north of Great Keppel Island (see the Queensland chapter) during summer and can be fatal. The stinging tentacles spread several metres away from the sea wasp's body; by the time

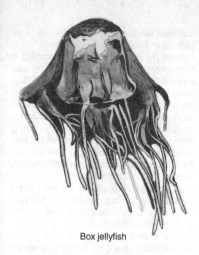

Box jellyfish

you see it you're likely to have been stung. If someone is stung, they are likely to run out of the sea screaming and collapse on the beach, with weals on their body as though they've been whipped. They may stop breathing. Douse the stings with vinegar (available on many beaches or from nearby houses), do not try to remove the tentacles from the skin, and treat as for snake bite. If there's a first-aider present, they may have to apply artificial respiration until the ambulance gets there. Above all, stay out of the sea when the sea wasps are around – the locals are ignoring that lovely water for an excellent reason.

The blue-ringed octopus and Barrier Reef cone shells can also be fatal so don't pick them up. If someone is stung, apply a pressure bandage, monitor breathing carefully and conduct mouth-to-mouth resuscitation if breathing stops.

When reef walking you must always wear shoes to protect your feet against coral. In tropical waters there are stonefish – venomous fish that look like a flat piece of rock on the sea bed. Also watch out for the scorpion fish, which has venomous spines.

Flies & Mosquitoes

For four to six months of the year you'll have to cope with those two banes of the Australian outdoors – the fly and the mosquito.

In the cities the flies are not too bad; it's in the country that it starts getting out of hand, and the further 'out' you get the worse the flies seem to be. In central Australia the flies start to come out with the warmer spring weather (late August) and last through until winter. They are such a nuisance that virtually every shop sells the Genuine Aussie Fly Net (made in Korea), which is rather like a string onion bag but is very effective. It's either that or the 'Great Australian Wave' to keep them away. Repellents such as Aerogard and Rid go some way to deterring the little bastards.

Mossies too can be a problem, especially in the warmer tropical and subtropical areas. Fortunately none of them are malaria carriers.

On the Road

Cows and kangaroos can be a real hazard to the driver. A collision with one will badly damage your car and probably kill the animal. Unfortunately, other drivers are even more dangerous, particularly those who drink. Australia has its share of fatal road accidents, particularly in the countryside, so don't drink and drive and please take care. The dangers posed by stray animals and drunks are particularly enhanced at night, so it's best to avoid travelling after dark. See the Getting Around chapter for more on driving hazards.

Bushfires & Blizzards

Bushfires happen every year in Australia. Don't be the mug who starts one. In hot, dry, windy weather, be extremely careful with any naked flame – no cigarette butts out of car windows, please. On a Total Fire Ban Day (listen to the radio or watch the billboards on country roads), it is forbidden even to use a camping stove in the open. The locals will not be amused if they catch you breaking this particular law; they'll happily dob you in, and the penalties are severe.

If you're unfortunate enough to find yourself driving through a bushfire, stay inside your car and try to park off the road in an open space, away from trees, until the danger's past. Lie on the floor under the dashboard, covering yourself with a wool blanket if possible. The front of the fire should pass quickly, and you will be much safer than if you were out in the open. It is very important to cover up with a wool blanket or wear protective clothing, as it has been proved that heat radiation is the big killer in bushfire situations.

Bushwalkers should take local advice before setting out. On a day of total fire ban, don't go – delay your trip until the weather has changed. Chances are that it will be so unpleasantly hot and windy, you'll be better off anyway in an air-conditioned pub sipping a cool beer.

If you're out in the bush and you see smoke, even at a great distance, take it seriously. Go to the nearest open space, downhill if possible. A forested ridge is the most dangerous place to be. Bushfires move very quickly and change direction with the wind.

Having said all that, more bushwalkers die of cold than in bushfires! Even in summer, temperatures can drop below freezing at night in the mountains. The Tasmanian mountains can have blizzards at almost any time of year.

WORK

If you come to Australia on a 12-month 'working holiday' visa you can officially only work for three out of those 12 months, but working on a regular tourist visa is strictly *verboten*. Many travellers on tourist visas do find casual work, but with a national unemployment rate of 11%, and youth unemployment as high as 40% in some areas, it is becoming more difficult to find a job – legal or otherwise.

To receive wages in Australia you must be in possession of a Tax File Number, issued by the Taxation Department. Forms are available from post offices and you'll need to show your passport and visa.

The best prospects for casual work include factories, bar work, waiting on tables or washing dishes, other domestic chores at outback roadhouses, nanny work, fruit picking and collecting for charities.

With the current economic downturn in Australia, casual work has become increasingly difficult to find. Gone are the days when you could rock in to practically any town or city and find some sort of paid casual work. Many travellers who have budgeted on finding work return home early, simply because the work they hoped to find just isn't available. If you are coming to Australia with the intention of working, make sure you have enough funds to cover you for your stay, or have a contingency plan if the work is not forthcoming. Having said that, it *is* still possible to find short-term work, it's just that the opportunities are far fewer than in the past.

The Commonwealth Employment Service (CES) has over 300 offices around the country, and the staff usually have a good idea of what's available where. Try the classified section of the daily papers under Situations Vacant, especially on Saturdays and Wednesdays.

The various backpackers' magazines, newspapers and hostels are good information sources – some local employers even advertise on their notice boards.

Fruit & Vegetable Picking Seasons The table here lists the main harvest times of the crops where casual employment is a possibility. Enquire at the local CES office.

New South Wales

Crop	Time	Region/s
Grapes	Feb-Mar	Griffith, Hunter Valley
Peaches	Feb-Mar	Griffith
Apples	Feb-Apr	Orange
Cherries	Nov-Jan	Orange
Oranges	Dec-Mar	Griffith
Bananas	year round	North Coast

Queensland

Crop	Time	Region/s
Bananas	year round	Innisfail
Grapes	Jan-Feb	Warwick
Pears	Feb-Mar	Warwick
Apples	Feb-Mar	Warwick
Various fruit & veg	May-Nov	Bowen

Asparagus	Aug-Dec	Warwick
Tomatoes	May-Nov	Bundaberg
Stone fruits	Dec	Warwick

South Australia

Crop	Time	Region/s
Dried fruits/ peaches	Feb-Mar	Riverland
Wine grapes	Feb-Apr	Riverland, Barossa, Clare
Apples/pears	Feb-Apr	Adelaide Hills
Strawberries	Oct-Feb	Adelaide Hills
Apricots	Dec-Feb	Riverland

Tasmania

Crop	Time	Region/s
Apples/pears	Feb-May	Huon Valley, Tasman Pen.
Soft fruit	Dec-Jan	Huon Valley, Kingston, Derwent Valley

Victoria

Crop	Time	Region/s
Peaches	Jan-Mar	Shepparton
Grapes	Jan-Apr	Mildura
Tomatoes	Feb-Apr	Shepparton, Echuca
Strawberries	Oct-Apr	Echuca, Dandenongs
Cherries	Nov-Feb	Dandenongs

Western Australia

Crop	Time	Region/s
Grapes	Feb-Apr	Albany, Midland
Apples/pears	Mar-May	Manjimup
Melons, vegies	May-Oct	Kununurra

ACTIVITIES

There are plenty of activities that you can take part in while travelling round the country.

Australia has a flourishing skiing industry – a fact that takes a number of travellers by surprise – with snowfields that straddle New South Wales's border with Victoria. There's information on the Victorian snowfields in the Victorian Alps section of the Victoria chapter, and likewise for the Snowy Mountains in the New South Wales chapter. Tasmania's snowfields aren't as developed as those of Victoria and New South Wales, but if you do want to ski while in Tassie you

can read all about it in the Activities section of the Tasmania chapter.

If skiing isn't your scene how about bushwalking? Not only is it cheap but you can do it anywhere. There are many fantastic walks in the various national parks around the country and information on how to get there is in Lonely Planet's *Bushwalking in Australia*, as well as in the Activities sections of each state.

If you're interested in surfing you'll find great beaches and surf in most states. There's great scuba diving at a number of places around the coast but particularly along the Queensland Great Barrier Reef where there are also many dive schools. Many travellers come to Australia with the goal of getting a scuba certificate during their stay.

In Victoria you can go horse riding in the High Country and follow the route of the Snowy Mountains cattle people, whose lives were the subject of the film *The Man from Snowy River*, which in turn was based on the poem by Banjo Paterson. In northern Queensland you can ride horses through rainforests and along sand dunes and swim with them in the sea. You can find horses to hire at any number of places around the country.

You can cycle all around Australia; for the athletic there are long, challenging routes and for the not so masochistic there are plenty of great day trips. In most states there are excellent roads and helpful bicycle societies, which have lots of maps and useful tips and advice. See the Getting Around chapter and individual state chapters for more details.

For the more adventurous, camel riding has taken off around the country but especially in the Northern Territory. If you've done it in India or Egypt or you just fancy yourself as the explorer/outdoors type, then here's your chance.

Windsurfing, paragliding, rafting, hot-air ballooning, bungee jumping and hang-gliding are among the many other outdoor activities enjoyed by Australians and available to travellers. For information on any of these or other activities see the relevant chapters or contact any of the state tourist bureaus.

HIGHLIGHTS
In a country as broad and geographically diverse as Australia the list of highlights is virtually endless, although one person's highlight can easily be another's disappointment. There are, however, a number of features in each state which shouldn't be missed.

In Queensland there's the Great Barrier Reef and its many water-based activities. The state's varied terrain offers visitors the choice of secluded beach and island resorts, the rainforested Daintree, inland desert and 'one-horse towns', cattle country and remote Cape York Peninsula.

Sydney, the capital of New South Wales and host for the year 2000 Olympic Games, has simply one of the most stunning locations you're likely to come across.

No visit to Victoria would be complete without a visit to the enchanting Grampians (Gariwerd) mountain range, famous for its natural beauty and great bushwalks. Other highlights include the fairy penguins at Phillip Island, the period gold-mining township of Sovereign Hill at Ballarat, and the Great Ocean Road, one of the world's most spectacular coastal routes. Melbourne, too, is often overlooked, yet it has a charm not found in other Australian cities.

Heading south to Tasmania there's the rich heritage of the convict era at places such as Port Arthur, as well as some of the most beautiful wilderness areas in the country. The beautiful World Heritage area of Cradle Mountain-Lake St Clair is popular with bushwalkers from many countries, as is the rugged south-west corner of the state.

South Australia's big drawcards are the Barossa Valley, with its excellent wineries, and the Flinders Ranges, which offer superb bushwalking and stunning scenery. In the northern areas of South Australia you can get a real taste of the outback along famous tracks such as the Strzelecki, Oodnadatta and Birdsville, while the opal-mining town of Coober Pedy, where many people not only

work underground but also live in subterranean houses, is totally unique.

The Northern Territory has the obvious attraction of Uluru (Ayers Rock), probably Australia's most readily identifiable symbol after Sydney's Opera House. There's also the World-Heritage-listed Kakadu National Park with its abundant flora and fauna and superb wetlands. The Territory is also where Australia's Aboriginal cultural heritage is at its most accessible – the rock-art sites of Kakadu, and Aboriginal-owned and run tours of Arnhem Land, Manyallaluk (near Katherine) and King's Canyon are just a few of the possibilities.

Lastly there's Western Australia with its vast distances and wide open spaces. In the south of the state there's Fremantle, an eclectic little port city not far from the state capital, Perth. The eucalypt forests of the south coast are simply spectacular, while the Kimberley region in the far north of the state is as ruggedly picturesque as any you'll find – the Bungle Bungle (Purnululu) National Park here is unforgettable.

ACCOMMODATION
Australia is very well equipped with youth hostels, backpackers' hostels and caravan parks with camp sites – the cheapest shelter you can find. Furthermore, there are plenty of motels around the country, and in holiday regions like the Queensland coast intense competition tends to keep the prices down.

A typical town of a few thousand people will have a basic motel at around $40/45 for singles/doubles, an old town centre hotel with rooms (shared bathrooms) at say $25/30, and a caravan park – probably with camp sites for around $8 and on-site vans or cabins for $25 to $30 for two. If the town is on anything like a main road or is bigger, it'll probably have several of each. You'll rarely have much trouble finding *somewhere* to lay your head in Oz, even when there are no hostels, although some surprisingly small and seemingly insignificant towns have backpackers' hostels these days. If there's a group of you, the rates for three or four people in a room are always worth checking.

Often there are larger 'family' rooms or units with two bedrooms.

There are a couple of free backpackers' newspapers and booklets available at hostels around the country, and these have fairly up-to-date listings of hostels, although they give neither prices nor details of each hostel.

For more comprehensive accommodation listings, the state automobile clubs produce directories listing caravan parks, hotels, motels, holiday flats and a number of backpackers' hostels in almost every city and town in the country. They're updated every year so the prices are generally fairly current. They're available from the clubs for a nominal charge if you're a member or a member of an affiliated club enjoying reciprocal rights. Alternatively, some state tourist offices (notably Tasmania and Western Australia) also put out frequently updated guides to local accommodation.

Camping & Caravanning

The camping story in Australia is partly excellent and partly rather annoying! The excellent side is that there is a great number of caravan parks and you'll almost always find space available. If you want to get around Australia on the cheap then camping is the cheapest way of all, with nightly costs for two of around $8 to $15.

One of the drawbacks is that camp sites are often intended more for caravanners (house trailers for any North Americans out there) than for campers and the tent campers get little thought in these places. The New Zealanders could certainly show Australian camp site operators how it's done. Over there camp sites often have a kitchen and dining area where you can eat. If it's raining you're not stuck with huddling in your car or tent. The fact that in Australia most of the sites are called 'caravan parks' indicates who gets most attention.

In many Australian caravan parks gravel is laid down to make the ground more suitable for cars and caravans, so pitching a tent becomes very hard work.

Equally bad is that in most big cities sites are well away from the centre. This is not inconvenient in small towns, but in general if you're planning to camp around Australia you really need your own transport. Brisbane is the worst city in Australia in this respect because council regulations actually forbid tents within a 22-km radius of the centre. Although there are some sites in Brisbane within that radius, they're strictly for caravans – no campers allowed.

Still, it's not all gloom; in general, Australian caravan parks are well kept, conveniently located and excellent value. Many sites also have on-site vans which you can rent for the night. These give you the comfort of a caravan without the inconvenience of actually towing one of the damned things. On-site cabins are also widely available, and these are more like a small self-contained unit. They usually have one bedroom, or at least an area which can be screened off from the rest of the unit – just the thing if you have small kids. Cabins also have the advantage of having their own bathroom and toilet, although this is sometimes an optional extra. They are also much less cramped than a caravan, and the price difference is not always that great – say $25 to $30 for an on-site van, $30 to $40 for a cabin. In winter, if you're going to be using this sort of accommodation on a regular basis, it's worth investing in a small heater of some sort as many vans and cabins are unheated.

Camping in the bush, either in national parks and reserves or in the open, is for many people one of the highlights of a visit to Oz. In the outback you won't even need a tent – swags are the way to go, and nights spent around a campfire under the stars are unforgettable.

Youth Hostels

Australia has a very active Youth Hostel Association (YHA) and you'll find hostels all over the country, with more official hostels and backpackers' hostels popping up all the time.

YHA hostels provide basic accommodation, usually in small dormitories or bunk rooms although more and more of them are providing twin rooms for couples. The nightly charges are rock bottom – usually between $8 and $15 a night.

With the increased competition from the proliferation of backpackers' hostels, many YHA hostels have done away with the old fetishes for curfews and doing chores, but still retain segregated dorms. Many even take non-YHA members, although there may be a small 'temporary membership' charge. To become a full YHA member in Australia costs $24 a year (there's also a $16 joining fee, although if you're an overseas resident joining in Australia you don't have to pay this). You can join at a state office or at any youth hostel.

The YHA has recently introduced the Aussie Starter Pack, whereby Australian residents joining the YHA will receive two vouchers worth $8 each to use at a hostel in their state. International visitors joining the YHA at a hostel will receive their first night at that hostel for free. The scheme has standardised the additional nightly fee charged to non-YHA members at $2 per night. Non-members will receive an Aussie Starter Card, to be stamped each night by the YHA. Full membership is given when the card has 12 stamps.

Youth hostels are part of an international organisation, the International Youth Hostel Federation (IYHF, also known as HI, Hostelling International), so if you're already a member of the YHA in your own country, your membership entitles you to use the Australian hostels. Hostels are great places for meeting people and great travellers' centres, and in many busier hostels the foreign visitors will outnumber the Australians. The annual *YHA Accommodation Guide* booklet, which is available from any YHA office in Australia and from some YHA offices overseas, lists all the YHA hostels around Australia with useful little maps showing how to find them. YHA members are eligible for discounts at various places and these facilities are also listed in the handbook.

You must have a regulation sheet sleeping bag or bed linen – for hygiene reasons a regular sleeping bag will not do. If you haven't got sheets they can be rented at many hostels (usually for $3), but it's cheaper, after a few nights' stay, to have your own. YHA offices and some larger hostels sell the official YHA sheet bag.

All hostels have cooking facilities and 24-hour access, and there's usually some communal area where you can sit and talk. There are usually laundry facilities and often excellent notice boards. Many hostels have a maximum-stay period – because some hostels are permanently full it would hardly be fair for people to stay too long when others are being turned away.

The YHA defines its hostels as 'simple', 'standard' or 'superior'. They range from tiny places to big modern buildings, from historic convict buildings to a disused railway station. Most hostels have a manager who checks you in when you arrive and keeps the peace. Because you have so much more contact with a hostel manager than the person in charge of other styles of accommodation he or she can really make or break the place. Good managers are often great characters and well worth getting to know.

Accommodation can usually be booked directly with the manager or through a Membership & Travel Centre. The YHA handbook tells all.

The Australian head office is in Sydney, at the Australian Youth Hostels Association, 10 Mallett St, Camperdown, NSW 2050 (☎ (02) 565 1699). If you can't get a YHA hostel booklet in your own country write to them but otherwise deal with the Membership & Travel centres:

New South Wales
   422 Kent St, Sydney, NSW 2001 (☎ (02) 261 1111)
Northern Territory
   Darwin Hostel Complex, 69A Mitchell St, Darwin, NT 0821 (☎ (089) 81 3995)
Queensland
   154 Roma St, Brisbane, Qld 4000 (☎ (07) 236 1680)
South Australia
   38 Sturt St, Adelaide, SA 5000 (☎ (03) 231 5583)
Tasmania
   1st floor, 28 Criterion St, Hobart, Tas 7000 (☎ (002) 34 9617)
Victoria
   205 King St, Melbourne, Vic 3000 (☎ (03) 670 7991)
Western Australia
   65 Francis St, Northbridge, Perth, WA 6003 (☎ (09) 227 5122)

Not all of the 140-plus hostels listed in the handbook are actually owned by the YHA. Some are 'associate hostels', which generally abide by hostel regulations but are owned by other organisations or individuals. You don't need to be a YHA member to stay at an associated hostel. Others are 'alternative accommodation' and do not totally fit the hostel blueprint. They might be motels which keep some hostel-style accommodation available for YHA members, caravan parks with an on-site van or two kept aside, or even places just like hostels but where the operators don't want to abide by all the hostel regulations.

Backpackers' Hostels

In recent years the number of backpackers' hostels has increased dramatically. The standard of these hostels varies enormously. Some are rundown inner-city hotels where the owners have tried to fill empty rooms; unless renovations have been done, these places are generally pretty gloomy and depressing. Others are former motels, so each unit, typically with four to six beds, will have fridge, TV and bathroom. When the climate allows, there's usually a pool too. The drawback with these places is that the communal areas and cooking facilities are often lacking, as motels were never originally designed for communal use. You may

also find yourself sharing a room with someone who wants to watch TV all night – it happens!

Still other hostels are purpose-built as backpackers' hostels; these are usually the best places in terms of facilities, although sometimes they are simply too big and therefore lack any personalised service. As often as not the managers have backpackers running the places, and usually it's not too long before standards start to slip. Some of these places, particularly along the Queensland coast, actively promote themselves as 'party' hostels, so if you want a quiet time, they're often not the place to be. The best places are often the smaller, more intimate hostels where the owner is also the manager. These are usually the older hostels which were around long before the 'backpacker boom'.

With the proliferation of hostels has also come intense competition. Hop off a bus in any town on the Queensland coast and chances are there'll be at least three or four touts from the various hostels, all trying to lure you in. To this end many have introduced inducements, such as the first night free, and virtually all have courtesy buses. Even the YHA hostels have had to resort to this to stay in the race in some places.

Prices at backpackers' hostels are generally in line with YHA hostels – typically $10 to $12, although the $7 bed is still alive and well in some places.

There's at least one organisation (VIP) which you can join where, for a modest fee (typically $15), you'll receive a discount card (valid for 12 months) and a list of participating hostels. This is hardly a great inducement to join but you do also receive useful discounts on other services, such as bus passes, so they may be worth considering.

As with YHA hostels, the success of a hostel largely depends on the friendliness and willingness of the managers. One practice that many people find objectionable – in independent hostels only, since it never happens in YHAs – is the 'vetting' of Australians and sometimes New Zealanders, who may be asked to provide a passport or double ID which they may not carry. Virtually all city hostels ask everyone for some ID – usually a passport – but this can also be used as a way of keeping unwanted customers out.

Some places will actually only admit overseas backpackers. This happens mostly in cities and when it does it's because the hostel in question has had problems with some locals treating the place more as a doss house than a hostel – drinking too much, making too much noise, getting into fights and the like. Hostels which discourage or ban Aussies say it's only a rowdy minority that makes trouble, but they can't take the risk on who'll turn out bad. If you're an Aussie and encounter this kind of reception, the best you can do is persuade the desk people that you're genuinely travelling the country, and aren't just looking for a cheap place to crash for a while.

The Ys

In a number of places in Australia accommodation is provided by the YMCA or YWCA. There are variations from place to place – some are mainly intended for permanent accommodation, some are run like normal commercial guesthouses. They're generally excellent value and usually conveniently located. You don't have to be a YMCA or YWCA member to stay at them, although sometimes you get a discount if you are. Accommodation in the Ys is generally in fairly straightforward rooms, usually with shared bathroom facilities. Some Ys also have dormitory-style accommodation. Note, however, that not all YMCA or YWCA organisations around the country offer accommodation; it's mainly in the big cities.

Another organisation that sometimes offers accommodation is the CWA (Country Women's Association), which operates mainly in the country and is usually for women only.

Guesthouses & B&Bs

These are the fastest growing segment of the accommodation market. New places are opening all the time, and the network of accommodation alternatives throughout the country includes everything from restored miners' cottages, converted barns and stables, renovated and rambling old guesthouses, up-market country homes and romantic escapes to a simple bedroom in a family home. Many of these places are listed throughout the book. Tariffs cover a wide range, but are typically in the $40 to $100 (per double) bracket.

Hotels & Pubs

For the budget traveller, hotels in Australia are generally older places – new accommodation is usually motels. To understand why Australia's hotels are the way they are requires delving into the history books a little. When the powers that be decided Australia's drinking should only be at the most inconvenient hours, they also decided that drinking places should also be hotels. So every place which in Britain would be a 'pub' in Australia was a 'hotel', but often in name only.

The original idea of forcing pubs to provide accommodation for weary travellers has long faded into history and this ludicrous law has been rolled back. Every place called a hotel does not necessarily have rooms to rent, although many still do. A 'private hotel', as opposed to a 'licensed hotel', really is a hotel and does not serve alcohol. A 'guesthouse' is much the same as a 'private hotel'.

New hotels being built today are mainly of the Hilton variety; smaller establishments will usually be motels. So, if you're staying in a hotel, it will normally mean an older place, often with rooms without private facilities. Unfortunately many older places are on the drab, grey and dreary side. You get a strong feeling that because they've got the rooms they try to turn a dollar on them, but without much enthusiasm. Others, fortunately, are colourful places with some real character. Although the word 'hotel' doesn't always mean they'll have rooms, the places that do have rooms usually make it pretty plain that they are available. If a hotel is listed in an accommodation directory you can be pretty sure it really will offer you a bed. If there's nothing that looks like a reception desk or counter, just ask in the bar.

You'll find hotels all around the town centres in smaller towns while in larger towns the hotels that offer accommodation are often to be found close to the railway stations. In some older towns, or in historic centres like the gold-mining towns, the old hotels can be really magnificent. The rooms themselves may be pretty old-fashioned and unexciting, but the hotel facade and entrance area will often be quite extravagant. In the outback the old hotels are often places of real character. They are often the real 'town centre' and you'll meet all the local eccentrics there.

A bright word about hotels (guesthouses and private hotels, too) is that the breakfasts are usually excellent – big and 100% filling. A substantial breakfast is what this country was built on and if your hotel is still into serving a real breakfast you'll probably feel it could last you until breakfast comes around next morning. Generally, hotels will have rooms for around $20 to $30. When comparing prices, remember to check if it includes breakfast.

In airports and bus and railway stations, there are often information boards with direct-dial phones to book accommodation. These are generally for the more expensive hotels, but sometimes they offer discounts if you use the direct phone to book. The staff at bus stations are helpful when it comes to finding cheap and convenient places to stay.

Motels, Serviced Apartments & Holiday Flats

If you've got transport and want a more modern place with your own bathroom and other facilities, then you're moving into the motel bracket. Motels cover the earth in Australia, just like in the USA, but they're usually located away from the city centres. Prices vary and with the motels, unlike hotels, singles are often not much cheaper than doubles. The reason is quite simple – in the old hotels many of the rooms really are singles, relics of the days when single men

travelled the country looking for work. In motels, the rooms are almost always doubles. You'll sometimes find motel rooms for less than $30, and in most places will have no trouble finding something for $45 or less.

Holiday flats and serviced apartments are much the same thing and bear some relationship to motels. Basically holiday flats are found in holiday areas, serviced apartments in cities. A holiday flat is much like a motel room but usually has a kitchen or cooking facilities so you can fix your own food. Usually holiday flats are not serviced like motels – you don't get your bed made up every morning and the cups washed out. In some holiday flats you actually have to provide your own sheets and bedding but others are operated just like motel rooms with a kitchen. Most motels in Australia provide at least tea- and coffee-making facilities and a small fridge, but a holiday flat will also have cooking utensils, cutlery, crockery and so on.

Holiday flats are often rented on a weekly basis but even in these cases it's worth asking if daily rates are available. Paying for a week, even if you stay only for a few days, can still be cheaper than having those days at a higher daily rate. If there are more than just two of you, another advantage of holiday flats is that you can often find them with two or more bedrooms. A two-bedroom holiday flat is typically priced at about 1½ times the cost of a comparable single-bedroom unit.

In holiday areas like the Queensland coast, motels and holiday flats will often be virtually interchangeable terms – there's nothing really to distinguish one from the other. In big cities, on the other hand, the serviced apartments are often a little more obscure, although they may be advertised in the newspaper's classified ads.

Colleges

Although it is students who get first chance at these, nonstudents can also stay at many university colleges during the uni vacations. These places can be relatively cheap and comfortable and provide an opportunity for you to meet people. Costs are typically from about $15 for B&B for students, twice that if you're not a student.

This type of accommodation is usually available only during the summer vacations (from November to February). Additionally, it must almost always be booked ahead; you can't just turn up. Many of Australia's new universities are way out in the suburbs and are inconvenient to get to unless you have transport.

Other Possibilities

That covers the usual accommodation possibilities, but there are lots of less conventional ones. You don't have to camp in caravan parks, for example. There are plenty of parks where you can camp for free, or (in Queensland at least) roadside rest areas where short-term camping is permitted. Australia has lots of bush where nobody is going to complain about you putting up a tent – or even notice you.

In the cities, if you want to stay longer, the first place to look for a shared flat or a room is the classified ad section of the daily newspaper. Wednesdays and Saturdays are the best days for these ads. Notice boards in universities, hostels, certain popular bookshops and cafes, and other contact centres are good places to look for flats/houses to share or rooms to rent.

Australia is a land of farms (known as 'stations' in the outback) and one of the best ways to come to grips with Australian life is to spend a few days on one. Many farms offer accommodation where you can just sit back and watch how it's done, while others like to get you more actively involved in the day-to-day activities. With commodity prices falling daily, mountainous wool stockpiles and a general rural crisis, tourism offers the hope of at least some income for farmers, at a time when many are being forced off the land. The state tourist offices can advise you on what's available; prices are pretty reasonable.

Finally, how about life on a houseboat? – see the Murray River sections in Victoria and South Australia.

FOOD

The culinary delights can be one of the real highlights of Australia. Time was – like 25 years ago – when Australia's food (mighty steaks apart) had a reputation for being like England's, only worse. Well, perhaps not quite that bad, but getting on that way. Miracles happen and Australia's miracle was immigration. The Greeks, Yugoslavs, Italians, Lebanese and many others who flooded into Australia in the '50s and '60s brought, thank God, their food with them. More recent arrivals include the Vietnamese, whose communities are thriving in several cities.

So in Australia today you can have excellent Greek moussaka (and a bottle of retsina to wash it down), delicious Italian saltimbocca and pastas, or good, heavy German dumplings; you can perfume the air with garlic after stumbling out of a French bistro, or try all sorts of Middle Eastern and Arab treats. The Chinese have been sweet & souring since the gold-rush days, while more recently Indian, Thai and Malaysian restaurants have been all the rage. And for cheap eats, you can't beat some of the Vietnamese places.

Australian Food

Although there is no real Australian cuisine there is certainly some excellent Australian food to try. For a start there's the great Australian meat pie – every bit as sacred an institution as the hot dog is to a New Yorker. There are a few places that do a really good job on this classic dish, but the standard pie is an awful concoction of anonymous meat and dark gravy in a soggy pastry case. You'll have to try one though; the number consumed in Australia each year is phenomenal, and they're a real part of Australian culture.

Even more central to Australian eating habits is Vegemite. This strange, dark yeast-extract substance looks and spreads like thick tar and smells like, well, Vegemite – it is something only an Australian could love. Australians spread Vegemite on bread and become so addicted to it that anywhere in the world you find an Aussie, a jar of Vegemite is bound to be close at hand. Not surprisingly, Australian embassies the world over have the location of the nearest Vegemite retailer as one of their most-asked-for pieces of information.

The good news about Australian food is the fine ingredients. Nearly everything is grown right here in Australia so you're not eating food that has been shipped halfway around the world. Everybody knows about good Australian steaks ('This is cattle country, so eat beef you bastards', announce the farmers' bumper stickers), but there are lots of other things to try.

Australia has a superb range of seafood: fish like John Dory and the esteemed barramundi, or superb lobsters and other crustaceans like the engagingly named Moreton Bay bugs! Yabbies are freshwater crayfish and very good. Even vegetarians get a fair go in Australia; there are some excellent vegetarian restaurants and, once again, the vegetables are as fresh as you could ask for.

Where to Eat

If you want something familiar and utterly predictable there are McDonald's, Kentucky Frieds, Pizza Huts and all the other well-known names looking no different than they do anywhere from New York to Amsterdam. There are also Chinese restaurants where the script is all in Chinese, little Lebanese places where you'd imagine the local PLO cell getting together for a meal, and every other national restaurant type you could imagine.

For real value for money there are a couple of dinky-di Australian eating places you should certainly try, though. For a start, Australian delis are terrific and they'll put together a superb sandwich. Hunt out the authentic-looking ones in any big city and you'll get a sandwich any New York deli would have trouble matching, and it's a safe bet it'll be half the price.

In the evening the best value is to be found in the pubs. Look for 'counter meals', so called because they used to be eaten at the bar counter. Some places still are just like that, while others are fancier, almost restau-

rant-like. Good counter meals are hard to beat for value for money, and although the food is usually of the simple steak-salad-chips variety, the quality is often excellent and prices are commendably low. The best counter meal places usually have serve-yourself salad tables where you can add as much salad, French bread and so on as you wish.

Counter meals are usually served as counter lunches or counter teas, the latter a hangover from the old northern English terminology where 'tea' meant the evening meal. One catch with pub meals is that they usually operate fairly strict hours. The evening meal time may be just 6 to 7.30 or 8 pm. Pubs doing counter meals often have a blackboard menu outside but some of the best places are quite anonymous – you simply have to know that this is the pub that does great food and furthermore that it's in the bar hidden away at the back. Counter meals vary enormously in price but in general the better class places with good serve-yourself salad tables will be in the $6 to $14 range for all the traditional dishes: steak, veal, chicken, and so on.

For rock-bottom prices, you can check out university and college cafeterias and the big department store cafeterias (Woolworth's and Coles, for example), or even try sneaking into public service office cafeterias.

Australians love their fish & chips just as much as the British and, just like in Britain, their quality can vary enormously – all the way from stodgy and horrible to superb. Fish & chip shops usually serve the other Aussie favourite – hamburgers. We've also got the full range of international takeaway foods, from Italian to Mexican, Chinese to Lebanese.

DRINKS

In the nonalcoholic department Australians knock back Coke and flavoured milk like there's no tomorrow and also have some excellent mineral water brands. Coffee enthusiasts will be relieved to find good Italian cafes serving cappuccino and other coffees, often into the wee small hours and beyond. Beer and wine need their own explanations.

Beer

Australian beer will be fairly familiar to North Americans; it's similar to what's known as lager in the UK. It may taste like lemonade to the European real ale addict, but it packs quite a punch. It is invariably chilled before drinking.

Fosters is, of course, the best-known international brand with a worldwide reputation. Each Australian state has its own beer brand and there'll be someone to sing the praises of each one: XXXX, pronounced four-ex, and Powers (Queensland); Swan (Western Australia); Tooheys (New South Wales); and VB – Victoria Bitter (Victoria).

Although most big-name beers are associated in particular with one state, they are available across the country. The smaller breweries generally seem to produce better beer – Cascade (Tasmania) and Coopers (South Australia) being two examples. Coopers also produce a stout which is popular among connoisseurs. Some Australians drink a mixture of stout and lemonade called portagaff.

Small 'boutique' brewers have also been making a comeback so you'll find one-off brands scattered around the country. Beers such as Redback, Dogbolter and Eumundi,

while being more expensive than the big commercial brands, are definitely worth a try. For the homesick European, there are a few pubs in the major cities that brew their own bitter. Guinness is occasionally found on draught, usually in Irish pubs.

A word of warning to visitors: Australian beer has a higher alcohol content than British or American beers. Standard beer generally contains around 4.9% alcohol, although most breweries now produce 'light' beers, with an alcohol content of between 2% and 3.5%. Toohey's Blue is a particularly popular light beer. And another warning: people who drive under the influence of alcohol and get caught lose their licences (unfortunately, drink-driving is a real problem in Australia). The maximum permissible blood-alcohol concentration level for drivers in most parts of Australia is 0.05%.

All around Australia, beer, the containers it comes in, and the receptacles you drink it from are called by different names. Beer comes in stubbies, long necks, bottles, tinnies and twisties, depending on where you are in Australia.

Ordering at the bar can be an intimidating business for the newly arrived traveller. A 200-ml beer is a glass (Victoria), a beer (Tasmania) or a seven (Queensland); a 285-ml beer is a pot (Victoria and Queensland),

---

The Six O'Clock Swill

Way back in WW I the government of the day decided that all pubs should shut at 6 pm as a wartime austerity measure. Unfortunately, when the war ended this wartime emergency move didn't. On one side the wowsers didn't want anybody to drink, and if Australia couldn't have prohibition like the USA, stopping drinking at 6 pm was at least a step in the right direction in their view. The other supporters of this terrible arrangement were, believe it or not, the breweries and pub owners. They discovered that shutting the pubs at 6 pm didn't really cut sales at all and it certainly cut costs. You didn't have to pay staff until late in the evening and you didn't have to worry about making your pub a pleasant place for a drink. People left work, rushed around to the pub and swallowed as much beer as they could before 6 pm. They definitely didn't have time to admire the decor.

This unhappy story didn't even end after WW II. In fact it carried right on into the '50s, before common sense finally came into play and the 'six o'clock swill' was consigned to history. Since that time the idea of the Australian pub as a bare and cheerless beer barn has gradually faded and there are now many pleasant pubs. More recently, drinking hours have been further relaxed and pubs can now open later in the evening and on Sundays. ■

a middy (New South Wales and Western Australia) or a tenner (Queensland); while in New South Wales and Western Australia they also have the 450-ml schooner. In New South Wales, they're likely to ask if you want new or old, new being ordinary beer and old being stout. A low-alcohol-content beer is called a light, while regular strength beer can be called a heavy. If in doubt, take local advice, which will readily be offered!

While Australians are generally considered to be heavy beer drinkers, per capita beer consumption has been falling faster than in any other developed country. In the past decade per capita consumption has decreased by 20%.

Wine

If you don't fancy Australian beer, then turn to wines. Australia has a great climate for wine producing and some superb wine areas. Best known are the Hunter Valley of New South Wales and the Barossa Valley of South Australia, but there are a great number of other wine-producing areas, each with its own enthusiastic promoters.

European wine experts now realise just how good Australian wines can be – exporting wines is now a multimillion dollar business in Australia and one of the few really bright lights in a generally gloomy economic climate. Furthermore, Australia's wines are cheap and readily available. We pay less for our wine than the Californians do for theirs.

It takes a little while to become familiar with Australian wineries and their styles but it's an effort worth making. All over Australia, but particularly in Melbourne, you'll find restaurants advertising that they're BYO. The initials stand for 'Bring Your Own' and it means that they're not licensed to serve alcohol but you are permitted to bring your own with you. This is a real boon to wine-loving but budget-minded travellers because you can bring your own bottle of wine from the local bottle shop or from that winery you visited last week and not pay any mark-up. In fact, most restaurants make only a small 'corkage' charge (typically 60c to $1 per person) if you bring your own, even though it's conceivable that without it they could have sold you a soft drink or similar.

An even more economical way of drinking Australian wine is to do it on the cheap (or free) at the wineries. In the wine-growing areas, most wineries have tastings: you just zip straight in and say what you'd like to try. However, free wine tastings do not mean open slather drinking – the glasses are generally thimble-sized and it's expected that you will buy something if, for example, you taste every chardonnay that that vineyard has ever produced. Many wineries, particularly in the main areas, have decided that enough is enough and now have a small 'tasting fee' of a couple of dollars, refundable if you buy any wine.

ENTERTAINMENT

Cinema

Although the cinema took a huge knock from the meteoric rise of the home-video market, it has bounced back as people rediscover the joys of the big screen.

In the big cities there are commercial cinema chains, such as Village, Hoyts and Greater Union, and their cinemas are usually found in centres which will have anything from two to 10 screens in the one complex. Smaller towns have just the one cinema, and many of these are almost museum pieces in themselves. Seeing a new-release mainstream film costs around $12 ($7.50 for children under 15) in the big cities, less in country areas and less on certain nights at the bigger cinema chains.

Also in the cities you'll find art-house and independent cinemas, and these places generally screen either films that aren't made for mass consumption or specialise purely in re-runs of classics and cult movies. Cinemas such as the Longford and Astor in Melbourne, the Valhalla and Encore in Sydney, the Chelsea in Adelaide and the Astor in Perth all fall into this category.

Discos & Nightclubs

Yep, no shortage of these either, but they are confined to the larger cities and towns. Clubs range from the exclusive 'members only' variety to barn-sized discos where anyone who wants to spend the money is welcomed with open arms. Admission charges range from around $6 to $12.

Some places have certain dress standards, but it is generally left to the discretion of the people at the door – if they don't like the look of you, bad luck. The more 'up-market' nightclubs attract an older, more sophisticated and affluent crowd, and generally have stricter dress codes, smarter decor – and higher prices.

Many suburban pubs have discos and/or live music, and these are often great places for catching live bands, either nationally well-known names or up-and-coming performers trying to make a name for themselves – most of Australia's popular bands started out on the pub circuit in one city or another.

The best way to find out about the local scene is to get to know some locals, or travellers who have spent some time in the place. Otherwise there are often comprehensive listings in newspapers, particularly on Fridays.

Spectator Sports

If you're an armchair – or wooden bench – sports fan Australia has plenty to offer. Australians play at least four types of football, each type being called 'football' by its aficionados. The season runs from about March to September.

Aussie rules is unique – only Gaelic football is anything like it. It's played by teams of 18 on an oval field with an oval ball that can be kicked, caught, hit with the hand or carried and bounced. You get six points for kicking the ball between two central posts (a goal) and one point for kicking it through side posts (a behind). A game lasts for four quarters of 20 minutes each. To take a 'mark' a player must catch a ball on the volley from a kick – in which case the player gets a free kick. A typical final score for one team is between 70 and 110.

Players cannot be sent off in the course of a game; disciplinary tribunals are held the following week. Consequently there are some spectacular brawls on field – while the crowds, in contrast, are noisy but remarkably peaceful (a pleasant surprise for visiting soccer fans).

Melbourne is the national (and world) centre for Australian Rules, and the Australian Football League (AFL) is the national competition. Ten of its 15 teams are from Melbourne; the others are from Geelong, Perth, Sydney, Adelaide and Brisbane. Adelaide is also a stronghold of Aussie Rules but it's nowhere near as big-time there as it is in Melbourne, where crowds regularly exceed 30,000 at top regular games and 70,000 at finals.

Australian rules is a great game to get to know. Fast, tactical, skilful, rough and athletic, it can produce gripping finishes when even after 80 minutes of play the outcome hangs on the very last kick. It also inspires fierce spectator loyalties and has made otherwise obscure Melbourne suburbs (Hawthorn, Essendon, Collingwood, etc) national names.

Soccer is a bit of a poor cousin: it's widely played on an amateur basis but the national league is only semiprofessional and attracts a pathetically small following. It's slowly gaining popularity thanks in part to the success of the national team. At the local level, there are ethnically based teams representing a wide range of national origins.

Rugby is the main game in New South Wales and Queensland, and it's rugby league, the 13-a-side working-class version, that attracts the crowds. The Winfield Cup competition produces the world's best rugby league – fast, fit and clever. Most of its teams are in Sydney but there are others in Canberra, Wollongong, Newcastle, Brisbane and on the Gold Coast. Rugby union, the 15-a-side game for amateurs, was less popular until Australia won the World Cup in 1991.

During the other (non-football) half of the year there's cricket. The Melbourne Cricket Ground (MCG) is the world's biggest, and international Test and one-day matches are played virtually every summer there and in Sydney, Adelaide, Perth, Brisbane and

Hobart. There is also an interstate competition (the Sheffield Shield) and numerous local grades.

Basketball too is growing in popularity as a spectator sport and there is a national league. Surfing competitions such as that held each year at Bells Beach, Victoria, are world class.

Australia loves a gamble, and hardly any town of even minor import is without a horse-racing track or a Totalisator Agency Board (TAB) betting office. Melbourne and Adelaide must be amongst the only cities in the world to give a public holiday for horse races. The prestigious Melbourne Cup is held on the first Tuesday in November.

There's also yacht racing, some good tennis and golf. The Australian Formula One Grand Prix is held in Adelaide each November (moving to Melbourne in 1996), the Australian round of the World 500 cc Motorcycle Grand Prix is held annually in April, and the Australian Tennis Open is played in Melbourne in January.

THINGS TO BUY

There are lots of things definitely not to buy – like plastic boomerangs, fake Aboriginal ashtrays and T-shirts, and all the other terrible souvenirs which fill the tacky souvenir shops in the big cities. Most of them come from Taiwan or Korea anyway. Before buying an Australian souvenir, turn it over to check that it was actually made here!

Aboriginal Art

Top of the list for any real Australian purchase, however, would have to be Aboriginal art. It's an amazingly direct and down-to-earth art which has now gained international appreciation. If you're willing to put in a little effort you can see superb examples of the Aborigines' art in its original form, carved or painted on rocks and caves in many remote parts of Australia. Now (and really just in time) skilled Aboriginal artists are also working on their art in a more portable form. Nobody captures the essence of outback Australia better than the Aborigines, so if you want a real souvenir of Australia this is

what to buy. Have a look at the spectacular Aboriginal artworks hanging in the big state art galleries before you make your choice.

Prices of the best works are way out of reach for the average traveller, but among the cheaper artworks on sale are prints, baskets, small carvings and some very beautiful screen-printed T-shirts produced by Aboriginal craft co-operatives – and a larger number of commercial rip-offs. It's worth shopping around and paying a few dollars more for the real thing.

Australiana

The term 'Australiana' is a euphemism for souvenirs. These are the things you buy as gifts for all the friends, aunts and uncles, nieces and nephews, and other sundry bods back home. They are supposedly representative of Australia and its culture, although many are extremely dubious. Some of the more popular items are:

Stuffed toy animals, especially koalas and kangaroos; wool products such as hand-knitted jumpers; sheepskin products; bush hats, with Akubra being the most famous and also the most expensive; T-shirts and other clothing, usually with Australian symbols or tacky slogans such as 'No flies on me, mate!'; Australia-shaped egg-flippers and fly swats; koala key rings; jewellery made from opal and pewter, often in the shape of native fauna or flora; rubber reptiles; boomerangs, usually made overseas, horrendously gaudy and guaranteed not to fly, but there are exceptions; painted dijeridus (tubular wooden Aboriginal musical instruments), usually one to two metres long; local glassware, pottery and ceramics, often with Aboriginal designs; and high-kitsch items such as ceramic flying pigs or koalas.

The seeds of many of Australia's native plants are on sale all over the place. Try growing kangaroo paws back home, if your own country will allow them in.

For those last-minute gifts, drop into a deli. Australian wines are well known overseas, but why not try honey (leatherwood honey is one of a number of powerful local varieties), macadamia nuts (native to Queensland) or Bundaberg Rum with its unusual sweet flavour. We have heard rumours of tinned witchetty grubs, honey ants and other bush tucker.

Aussie Clothing

While you're here, fit yourself out in some local clobber – made in Australia for Australian conditions. Start off with some Bonds undies and a singlet, a pair of Holeproof Explorer socks and Blundstone elastic-sided boots. Slip on a pair of Stubbie shorts and you've got the complete Aussie labourer's working uniform.

Then there's anything from the gear made by R M Williams – boots, moleskin trousers, shirts – to a shearer's bush shirt, a greasy-wool jumper, a Bluey (a coarse woollen worker's coat), a Driza-bone (an oilskin riding coat) or an Akubra hat.

Opals

The opal is Australia's national gemstone and opals and jewellery made with it are popular souvenirs. It's a beautiful stone, but buy wisely and shop around – quality and prices can vary widely from place to place.

Getting There & Away

Basically getting to Australia means flying, although it is sometimes possible to hitch a ride on a yacht to or from Australia.

The main problem with getting to Australia is that it's a long way from anywhere. Coming from Asia, Europe or North America there are lots of competing airlines and a wide variety of air fares, but there's no way you can avoid those great distances. Australia's current international popularity adds another problem – flights are often heavily booked. If you want to fly to Australia at a particularly popular time of year (the middle of summer, ie Christmas time, is notoriously difficult) or on a particularly popular route (like Hong Kong-Sydney or Singapore-Sydney) then you need to plan well ahead.

Australia has a large number of international gateways. Sydney and Melbourne are the two busiest international airports with flights from everywhere. Perth also gets many flights from Asia and Europe and has direct flights to New Zealand and Africa. Other international airports include Hobart in Tasmania (New Zealand only), Adelaide, Port Hedland (Bali only), Darwin, Cairns and Brisbane. One place you can't arrive at directly from overseas is Canberra, the national capital.

Although Sydney is the busiest gateway it makes a lot of sense to avoid arriving or departing there. Sydney's airport is stretched way beyond its capacity and flights are frequently delayed on arrival and departure. Furthermore the Customs and Immigration facilities are cramped, crowded and too small for the current visitor flow so even after you've finally landed you may face further long delays. If you can organise your flights to avoid Sydney it's a wise idea but unfortunately many flights to or from other cities (Melbourne in particular) still go via Sydney. If you're planning to explore Australia seriously then starting at a quieter entry port like Cairns in far north Queensland or Darwin in the Northern Territory can make a lot of sense.

DISCOUNT TICKETS

Buying airline tickets these days is like shopping for a car, a stereo or a camera – five different travel agents will quote you five different prices. Rule number one if you're looking for a cheap ticket is to go to an agent, not directly to the airline. The airline can usually only quote you the absolutely by-the-rule-book regular fare. An agent, on the other hand, can offer all sorts of special deals particularly on competitive routes.

Ideally an airline would like to fly all its flights with every seat in use and every passenger paying the highest fare possible. Fortunately life usually isn't like that and airlines would rather have a half-price passenger than an empty seat. When faced with the problem of too many seats, they will either let agents sell them at cut prices, or occasionally make one-off special offers on particular routes – watch the travel ads in the press.

Of course what's available and what it costs depends on what time of year it is, what route you're flying and who you're flying with. If you're flying on a popular route (like from Hong Kong) or one where the choice of flights is very limited (like from South America or from Africa) then the fare is likely to be higher or there may be nothing available but the official fare.

Similarly the dirt cheap fares are likely to be less conveniently scheduled, go by a less convenient route or be with a less popular airline. Flying London-Sydney, for example, is most convenient with airlines like Qantas, British Airways, Thai International or Singapore Airlines. They have flights every day, they operate the same flight straight through to Australia and they're good, reliable, comfortable, safe airlines. At the other extreme you could fly from London to an Eastern European or Middle Eastern city on one flight, switch to another flight from there to Asia, and change to another airline from there to Australia. It takes longer, there are delays and changes of aircraft along the way, the airlines may not be so good and furthermore the connection only works once a week and that means leaving London at 1.30 on a Wednesday morning. The flip side is it's cheaper.

ROUND-THE-WORLD TICKETS

Round-the-World tickets have become very popular in the last few years and many of these will take you through Australia. The airline RTW tickets are often real bargains and since Australia is pretty much at the other side of the world from Europe or North America it can work out no more expensive, or even cheaper, to keep going in the same direction right round the world rather than U-turn to return.

The official airline RTW tickets are usually put together by a combination of two airlines, and permit you to fly anywhere you want on their route systems so long as you do not backtrack. Other restrictions are that you (usually) must book the first sector in advance and cancellation penalties then apply. There may be restrictions on how many stops you are permitted and usually the tickets are valid from 90 days up to a year. A typical price for a South Pacific RTW ticket is around £816 or US$1900.

An alternative type of RTW ticket is one put together by a travel agent using a combination of discounted tickets from a number of airlines. A UK agent like Trailfinders can put together interesting London-to-London RTW combinations including Australia for between £750 and £930.

CIRCLE PACIFIC TICKETS

Circle Pacific fares are a similar idea to RTW tickets which use a combination of airlines to circle the Pacific – combining Australia, New Zealand, North America and Asia. Examples would be Qantas-Northwest Orient, Canadian Airlines International-Cathay Pacific and so on. As with RTW tickets there are advance purchase restric-

tions and limits to how many stopovers you can take. Typically fares range between US$1750 and US$2180. Possible Circle Pacific routes are Los Angeles-Bangkok-Sydney-Auckland-Honolulu-Los Angeles or Los Angeles-Tokyo-Kuala Lumpur-Sydney-Auckland-Honolulu-Los Angeles.

TO/FROM THE UK

The cheapest tickets in London are from the numerous 'bucket shops' (discount ticket agencies) which advertise in magazines and papers like *Time Out*, *City Limits*, *Southern Cross* and *TNT*. Pick up one or two of these publications and ring round a few bucket shops to find the best deal. The magazine *Business Traveller* also has a great deal of good advice on air-fare bargains. Most bucket shops are trustworthy and reliable but the occasional sharp operator appears – *Time Out* and *Business Traveller* give some useful advice on precautions to take.

Trailfinders (☎ (071) 938 3366) at 46 Earls Court Rd, London W8, and STA Travel (☎ (071) 581 4132) at 74 Old Brompton Rd, London SW7, and 117 Euston Rd, London NW1 (☎ (071) 465 0484), are good, reliable agents for cheap tickets.

The cheapest London to Sydney or Melbourne bucket-shop (not direct) tickets are about £310 one way or £572 return. Cheap fares to Perth are around £330 one way and £583 return. Such prices are usually only available if you leave London in the low season – March to June. In September and mid-December fares go up by about 30%, while the rest of the year they're somewhere in between. Average direct high-season fares to Sydney or Melbourne are £527 one way, £957 return; to Perth £478 one way and £865 return.

Many cheap tickets allow stopovers on the way to or from Australia. Rules regarding how many stopovers you can take, how long you can stay away, how far in advance you have to decide your return date and so on, vary from time to time and ticket to ticket, but recently most return tickets have allowed you to stay away for any period between 14 days and one year, with stopovers permitted anywhere along your route. As usual with heavily discounted tickets the less you pay the less you get. Nice direct flights, leaving at convenient times and flying with popular airlines, are going to be more expensive than flying from London to Singapore or Bangkok with some Eastern European or Middle Eastern airline and then changing to another airline for the last leg.

From Australia you can expect to pay around A$1200 one way, and A$1800 return to London and other European capitals, with stops in Asia on the way. Again, all fares increase by up to 30% in the European summer and at Christmas.

TO/FROM NORTH AMERICA

There is a variety of connections across the Pacific from Los Angeles, San Francisco and Vancouver to Australia, including direct flights, flights via New Zealand, island-hopping routes and more circuitous Pacific rim routes via nations in Asia. Qantas, Air New Zealand and United all fly USA-Australia; Qantas, Air New Zealand and Canadian Airlines International fly Canada-Australia. An interesting option from the east coast is Northwest's flight via Japan.

One advantage of flying Qantas or Air New Zealand is that on the US airlines, if your flight goes via Hawaii, the west coast to Hawaii sector is treated as a domestic flight. This means that you have to pay for drinks and headsets – goodies that are free on international sectors.

To find good fares to Australia check the travel ads in the Sunday travel sections of papers like the *Los Angeles Times*, *San Francisco Chronicle-Examiner*, *New York Times* or *Toronto Globe & Mail*. The straightforward return excursion fare from the USA west coast is around US$1090, and from the east coast the return fare ranges from US$1185 to US$2100. The costs vary seasonally, but plenty of deals are available. You can typically get a one-way ticket from the west coast for US$800, or US$1050 from the east coast. At peak seasons – particularly the Australia summer/Christmas time – seats will be harder to get and the price will prob-

ably be higher. In the USA good agents for discounted tickets are the two student travel operators, Council Travel and STA Travel, both of which have lots of offices around the country. Canadian west-coast fares out of Vancouver will be similar to those from the US west coast. From Toronto fares go from around C$1650 return.

The French airline Air France has an interesting island-hopping route between the US west coast and Australia which includes the French colonies of New Caledonia and French Polynesia (Tahiti, etc). The Air France flight is often discounted and is very popular with travellers because of its multiple Pacific stopover possibilities. Los Angeles to Sydney on Air France costs around US$830 one way and US$1000 return. Polynesian Airlines has a similar route (Los Angeles-Sydney via Hawaii and Apia in Western Samoa) which costs between US$800 and US$1000 return.

If Pacific island-hopping is your aim, check out the airlines of Pacific Island nations, some of which have good deals on indirect routings. Qantas can give you Fiji or Tahiti along the way, while Air New Zealand can offer both and the Cook Islands as well. See the Circle Pacific section for more details.

One-way/return fares available from Australia include: San Francisco A$1000/1650, New York A$1150/2000 and Vancouver $1150/1800.

TO/FROM NEW ZEALAND

Air New Zealand and Qantas operate a network of trans-Tasman flights linking Auckland, Wellington and Christchurch in New Zealand with most major Australian gateway cities. You can fly directly between a lot of places in New Zealand and a lot of places in Australia.

Fares vary depending on which cities you fly between and when you do it but from New Zealand to Sydney you're looking at around NZ$520 one way and NZ$650 return, and to Melbourne NZ$600 one way and NZ$720 return. There is a lot of competition on this route – with United and British Airways both flying it as well as Qantas and

Air New Zealand, so there is bound to be some good discounting going on.

Cheap fares to New Zealand from Europe will usually be for flights via the USA. A straightforward London-Auckland return bucket-shop ticket costs around £950. Coming via Australia you can continue right around on a Round-the-World (RTW) ticket which will cost from around £1050 for a ticket with a comprehensive choice of stopovers.

TO/FROM ASIA

Ticket discounting is widespread in Asia, particularly in Singapore, Hong Kong, Bangkok and Penang. There are a lot of fly-by-nights in the Asian ticketing scene so a little care is required. Also the Asian routes have been particularly caught up in the capacity shortages on flights to Australia. Flights between Hong Kong and Australia are notoriously heavily booked while flights to or from Bangkok and Singapore are often part of the longer Europe-Australia route so they are also sometimes very full. Plan ahead. For much more information on South-East Asian travel and on to Australia see Lonely Planet's *South-East Asia on a shoestring*.

Typical one-way fares to Australia from Asia include from Hong Kong for around HK$4400 or from Singapore for around S$540. These fares are to the east-coast capitals; fares to Brisbane, Perth or Darwin are sometimes a bit cheaper.

You can also pick up some interesting tickets in Asia to include Australia on the way across the Pacific. Air France were first in this market but Qantas and Air New Zealand are also offering discounted trans-Pacific tickets. On the Air France ticket you can stop over in Jakarta, Sydney, Noumea, Auckland and Tahiti.

From Australia return fares from the east coast to Singapore, Kuala Lumpur and Bangkok range from $700 to $900, and to Hong Kong from $900 to $1300.

The cheapest way out of Australia is to take one of the flights operating between Darwin and Kupang (Timor, Indonesia). Current one-way/return fares are $198/330.

See the Darwin Getting There & Away section for full details.

TO/FROM AFRICA & SOUTH AMERICA

The flight possibilities from these continents are not so varied and you're much more likely to have to pay the full fare. There is only a handful of direct flights each week between Africa and Australia and then only between Perth and Harare (Zimbabwe) or Johannesburg (South Africa). A much cheaper alternative from East Africa is to fly from Nairobi to India or Pakistan and on to South-East Asia, then connect from there to Australia.

Two routes now operate between South America and Australia. The long-running Chile connection involves a Lan Chile Santiago-Easter Island-Tahiti flight, from where you fly Qantas or another airline to Australia. Alternatively there is a route which skirts the Antarctic circle, flying from Buenos Aires to Auckland and Sydney, operated by Aerolineas Argentinas.

ARRIVING & DEPARTING
Arriving in Australia

Australia's dramatic increase in visitor arrivals has caused some severe bottlenecks at the entry points, particularly at Sydney where the airport is often operating at more than full capacity and delays on arrival or departure are frequent. Even when you're on the ground it can take ages to get through Immigration and Customs. One answer to this problem is to try not to arrive in Australia at Sydney. Sure, you'll probably have to go there sometime – but you can save yourself a lot of time and trouble by making Brisbane, Cairns, Melbourne or another gateway city your arrival point.

For information about how to get to the city from the airport when you first arrive in Australia, check the To/From the Airport section under the relevant city. There is generally an airport bus service at the international airports and there are always taxis available.

Leaving Australia

When you finally go, remember to keep $25 aside for the departure tax. The amount of the tax and the method of payment is currently under review; by the time you read this it may have been increased to $27, and the fee may have been added to the price of the air ticket rather than existing as a separate tax.

Warning

This chapter is particularly vulnerable to change – prices for international travel are volatile, routes are introduced and cancelled, schedules change, rules are amended, special deals come and go, borders open and close.

Airlines and governments seem to take a perverse pleasure in making price structures and regulations as complicated as possible and you should check directly with the airline or travel agent to make sure you understand how a fare (and ticket you may buy) works.

In addition, the travel industry is highly competitive and there are many lurks and perks. The upshot of this is that you should get quotes and advice from as many airlines and travel agents as possible before you part with your hard-earned cash. The details given in this chapter should be regarded only as pointers and cannot be any substitute for your own careful, up-to-date research.

Getting Around

AIR

Australia is so vast (and at times so empty) that unless your time is unlimited you will probably have to take to the air sometime. It has been calculated that something like 80% of long-distance trips by public transport are made by air.

There are only two main domestic carriers within Australia – Qantas (which merged with Australian Airlines) and Ansett – despite the fact that the airline industry is deregulated. For 40-odd years Australia had a 'two-airline policy'; Australian and Ansett had a duopoly on domestic flights. With this cosy cohabitation the airlines could charge virtually what they liked, and operate virtually identical schedules. All this meant that for the traveller, domestic airline travel within Australia was expensive and the choices of flights limited, particularly on the low-volume routes.

QANTAS
THE AUSTRALIAN AIRLINE

Ansett Australia.
One of the world's great airlines.

With deregulation came another player, Compass, and a fierce price war. The net result was that Compass folded (twice!) and for all intents we're back to a two-airline industry. For travellers, however, the picture is quite bright, because although the sometimes crazy fares which were offered during the Compass price war have gone, widespread fare discounting has become a feature of air travel in Australia.

Note that all domestic flights in Australia are nonsmoking. Because Qantas flies both international and domestic routes, flights leave from both the international and domestic terminals at Australian airports. Flights with flight numbers from QF001 to QF399 operate from international terminals; flight numbers QF400 and above from domestic terminals.

Cheap Fares

Random Discounting A major feature of the deregulated air travel industry seems to be random discounting. As the airlines try harder to fill planes, they are offering often substantial discounts on selected routes. Although this seems to apply mainly to the heavy volume routes, that's not always the case.

To make the most of the discounted fares, you need to keep in touch with what's currently on offer, mainly because there are usually conditions attached to cheap fares – such as booking 14 or so days in advance, only flying on weekends or between certain dates and so on. Also the number of seats available is usually fairly limited. The further ahead you can plan the better.

The places to which this sort of discounting generally applies are the main centres – Melbourne, Sydney, Brisbane, Cairns, Adelaide and Perth – but deals come and go all the time.

It is fair to say that on virtually any route in the country covered by Qantas or Ansett the full economy fare will not be the cheapest way to go. Because the situation is so fluid, the special fares will more than likely have changed by the time you read this. For that reason we list the full one-way economy fares throughout the book, although you can safely assume that there will be a cheaper fare available.

Discounts are generally greater for return rather than one-way travel.

Some Possibilities If you're planning a return trip and you have 14 days up your sleeve then you can save 45% to 50% by

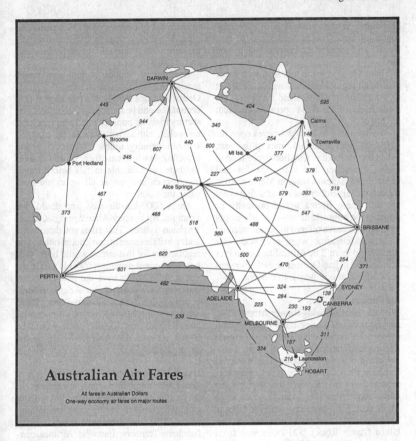

Australian Air Fares

All fares in Australian Dollars
One-way economy air fares on major routes

travelling Apex. You have to book and pay for your tickets 14 days in advance and you must stay away at least one Saturday night. Flight details can be changed at any time, but the tickets are nonrefundable. If you book seven days in advance the saving is 35% to 40% off the full fare.

For one-way travel, if you can book three days in advance a saving of 25% to 30% is offered; for immediate travel on off-peak flights the discount is 15% to 20%.

University or other higher education students under the age of 26 can get a 25% discount off the regular economy fare. An

airline tertiary concession card (available from the airlines) is required for Australian students. Overseas students can use their International Student Identity Card.

All nonresident international travellers can get a 30% to 40% discount on internal Qantas flights simply by presenting their international ticket when booking. It seems there is no limit to the number of domestic flights you can take, it doesn't matter which airline you fly into Australia with, and it doesn't have to be on a return ticket. Note that the discount applies only to the full economy fare, and so in many cases it will be cheaper to take advantage of other discounts offered. The best advice is to ring around and explore the options before you buy.

There are also some worthwhile cheaper deals with regional airlines such as Eastwest or a number of Queensland operators. On some lesser routes these operators undercut the big two.

Another thing to keep your eyes open for is special deals at certain times of the year. When the Melbourne Cup horse race is on in early November and when the football Grand Final happens (also in Melbourne) at the end of September lots of extra flights are put on. These flights would normally be going in the opposite direction nearly empty so special fares are offered to people wanting to leave Melbourne when everybody else wants to go there. The Australian Grand Prix in Adelaide in late October or early November is a similar one-way-traffic event.

Air Passes

With discounting being the norm these days, air passes do not represent the value they did in pre-deregulation days. However, there are a few worth checking out.

Qantas offers two passes. The Australia Explorer Pass can only be purchased overseas and has two formats: one is for most cities and towns (for example, Hobart to Melbourne $160 one way), and the other is for long-haul travel to destinations such as Uluru (Ayers Rock) ($210 one way from Sydney) or Perth ($210 one way from Melbourne). There is also the Qantas Backpackers Pass, which can only be bought in Australia on production of identification such as a YHA membership or a VIP Backpackers Card. A sample fare using this pass is Sydney to Uluru (Ayers Rock) $279 one way.

Ansett still has its Kangaroo Airpass, which gives you two options – 6000 km with two or three stopovers for $949 ($729 for children) and 10,000 km with three to seven stopovers for $1499 ($1149 for children). A number of restrictions apply to these tickets, although they can be a good deal if you want

to see a lot of country in a short period of time. You do not need to start and finish at the same place; you could start in Sydney and end in Darwin, for example.

Restrictions include a minimum travel time (10 nights) and a maximum (45 nights). One of the stops must be at a non-capital-city destination and be for at least four nights. All sectors must be booked when you purchase the ticket, although these can be changed without penalty unless the ticket needs rewriting, in which case there's a $50 charge. Refunds are available in full before travel commences and not at all once you start using the ticket.

On a 6000-km air pass you could, for example, fly Sydney-Alice Springs-Cairns-Brisbane-Sydney. That gives you three stops and two of them are in non-capital cities. The regular fare for that circuit would be $1498, but with current discounts it's only $1076, so you save $127 but have the restrictions. A one-way route might be Adelaide-Melbourne-Sydney-Alice Springs-Perth. There are three stops, of which one is a non-capital city. Regular cost for that route would be $1465, but with discounts it's $1016, so the saving is only $67.

Other Airline Options

There are a number of secondary airlines. In Western Australia there's Ansett WA with an extensive network of flights to the mining towns of the north-west and to Darwin in the Northern Territory. Eastwest Airlines connects the Queensland coast with the rest of eastern Australia, and Kendell Airlines services country areas of Victoria, South Australia and Tasmania, as well as Broken Hill (NSW) and Uluru (Ayers Rock) (NT).

There are numerous other smaller operators. Sunstate operate services in Queensland including some out to a number of islands. They also have a couple of routes in the south to Mildura and Broken Hill. Skywest have a number of services to remote parts of Western Australia. Eastern Australia Airlines operate up and down the New South Wales coast and also inland from Sydney as far as Bourke and Cobar.

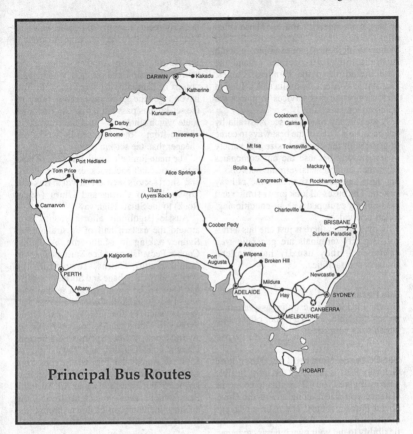

Principal Bus Routes

Airport Transport

There are private or public bus services at almost every major town in Australia. In one or two places you may have to depend on taxis but in general you can get between airport and city reasonably economically and conveniently by bus. Quite often a taxi shared between three or more people can be cheaper than the bus.

BUS

Bus travel is generally the cheapest way from A to B, other than hitching of course, but the main problem is to find the best deal.

There is only one truly *national* bus network – Greyhound Pioneer Australia, which consists of the former Greyhound/Pioneer and Bus Australia companies. All were once separate companies, and in fact the buses are still done out in their original paint-jobs.

McCafferty's, operating out of Brisbane, is probably the next biggest, with services all along the east coast as well the loop through the Centre to Adelaide, Alice Springs and Darwin to Townsville.

There are also many smaller bus companies operating locally or specialising in one or two main intercity routes. These often offer the best deals – Firefly costs $40 for Sydney to Melbourne, for example. In South Australia, Stateliner operates around the state including to the Flinders Ranges. Westrail in Western Australia and V/Line in Victoria operate bus services to places the trains no longer go to.

A great many travellers see Australia by bus because it's one of the best ways to come to grips with the country's size and variety of terrain, and because the bus companies have such comprehensive route networks – far more comprehensive than the railway system. The buses all look pretty similar and are similarly equipped with air-conditioning, toilets and videos.

In most places there is just one bus terminal. Big city terminals are generally well equipped – they usually have toilets, showers and facilities.

Bus Passes
Greyhound Pioneer Australia has a variety of passes available, so it's a matter of deciding which suits your needs.

Set-Distance Version The Greyhound Getaway Pass is probably the most flexible pass as it gives you 12 months to cover the distance you select along any of the Greyhound Pioneer routes. The main advantage of these passes is that they give you the flexibility to put your own itinerary together, which is convenient if your intended route is one not covered by the passes – Melbourne to Alice Springs or Perth, for instance.

Getaway Passes are valid for 12 months and can be used on any Greyhound Pioneer Australia service. The passes are issued in multiples of 1000 km (minimum 2000 km, no maximum) and the cost ranges from $180 for 2000 km, $360 for 4000 km, $480 for 6000 km and $750 for 10,000 km.

The trap with these passes is that the more km you buy, the more time you'll need to spend on a bus. Many travellers find that to make proper use of the passes they have to travel faster than they would wish. This par-

ticularly seems to apply to people who buy their passes before they arrive in Australia.

Set-Route Version Another option is the set-route Aussie Explorer Pass, which gives you six or 12 months to cover a set route. You haven't got the go-anywhere flexibility of the set-km bus pass but if you can find a set route which suits you – and there are 20 to choose from – then it generally works out cheaper than the set-km pass.

The main limitation with this kind of pass is that you can't backtrack, except on 'dead-end' short sectors such as Darwin to Kakadu, Townsville to Cairns and Uluru (Ayers Rock) to the Stuart Highway.

Aussie Highlights allows you to loop around the eastern half of Australia from Sydney taking in Melbourne, Adelaide, Coober Pedy, Uluru, Alice Springs, Darwin (and Kakadu), Cairns, Townsville, the Whitsundays, Brisbane and Surfers Paradise for A$690. The same trip on a set-km pass would cost you $840. Or there are one-way passes, such as the Go West pass from Sydney to Cairns via Melbourne, Adelaide, Ayers Rock, Alice Springs, Katherine, Darwin (and Kakadu), and Townsville for $590; or Across the Top, which goes from Cairns to Perth via the Top End and Kimberley, for $490. There's even an All Australia Pass which takes you right around the country, including up or down through the Centre, for $1235.

Set-Duration Version The other option is the set-duration pass – the Aussie Pass. This allows travel on a set number of days during a specified period. There are no restrictions on where you can travel. It's hard to see what advantages these passes have over the others already mentioned.

The passes range from $343 for seven days of travel in one month up to 90 days of travel in six months (what a nightmare!) for $2100.

There's also a Tassie Pass which gives you seven, 14 or 21 consecutive days of unlimited travel around the island state for $129, $152 and $174 respectively.

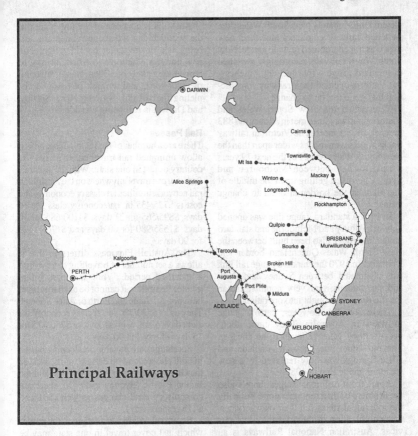

Principal Railways

(Map labels: DARWIN, Cairns, Townsville, Mt Isa, Mackay, Winton, Alice Springs, Longreach, Rockhampton, Quilpie, Cunnamulla, BRISBANE, Murwillumbah, Bourke, Tarcoola, Kalgoorlie, Broken Hill, PERTH, Port Augusta, Port Pirie, Mildura, SYDNEY, ADELAIDE, CANBERRA, MELBOURNE, HOBART)

TRAIN

Australia's railway system has never really recovered from the colonial bungling which accompanied its early days over a century ago. Before Australia became an independent country it was governed as six separate colonies, all administered from London. When the colony of Victoria, for example, wanted to build a railway line it checked not with the adjoining colony of New South Wales but with the colonial office in London. When the colonies were federated in 1901 and Australia came into existence, by a sheer masterpiece of misplanning not one state had railway lines of the same gauge as a neighbouring state!

The immense misfortune of this inept planning has dogged the railway system ever since. The situation between Victoria and New South Wales is a typical example. When New South Wales started to lay a line from Sydney to Parramatta in 1850 their railway engineer convinced the authorities it should be built to wide gauge – five feet three inches. Victoria also started to build to this gauge in order to tie in with the New South Wales system if, at some time in the future, a Melbourne-Sydney rail link was completed. Unfortunately New South Wales then switched railway engineers and their new man was not enamoured of wide gauge. New South Wales railways accordingly switched to standard gauge – four feet eight inches – but Victoria decided their railway construction had gone too far to change.

Thus when the New South Wales and Victorian railway lines met in Albury in 1883 they, er, didn't meet. The Victorian railway tracks were seven inches wider apart than the New South Wales ones. For the next 79 years a rail journey between Melbourne and Sydney involved getting up in the middle of the night at the border in order to change trains!

In 1962 a standard gauge line was opened between Albury and Melbourne and standard gauge lines have also been built between the New South Wales-Queensland border and Brisbane. In 1970 the standard gauge rail link was completed between Sydney and Perth and the famous, and very popular, Indian Pacific run was brought into operation.

There are also, however, narrow gauge railways in Australia. They came about because they were believed to be cheaper. The old Ghan line between Adelaide and Alice Springs was only replaced by a new standard gauge line in 1980.

Apart from different gauges there's also the problem of different operators. Basically the individual states run their own services, or a combination of them for interstate services. Australian National Railways is an association of the government-owned systems in Queensland, New South Wales, Victoria and Western Australia, and this body goes some way to co-ordinating the major services.

Rail travel in Australia today is basically something you do because you really want to – not because it's cheaper, especially now with the reduced air fares, and certainly not because it's fast. Rail travel is generally the slowest way to get from anywhere to anywhere in Australia. On the other hand the trains are comfortable and you certainly see Australia at ground level in a way no other means of travel permits.

Australia is also one of the few places in the world today where new lines are still being laid or are under consideration. The new line from Tarcoola to Alice Springs, to replace the rickety old Ghan, was an amazing piece of work, and the task of finally completing the rail link between Alice Springs and Darwin is still being considered.

Rail Passes

There are a number of passes available which allow unlimited rail travel either across the country or just in one state. With the Austrail Pass you can travel anywhere on the Australian rail network, in either 1st class or economy. The cost is $725/435 in 1st/economy class for 14 days, $895/565 for 21 days, $1100/685 for 30 days, $1535/980 for 60 days and $1765/1125 for 90 days.

The Austrail Flexipass differs in that it allows a set number of travelling days within a specified period. While this pass offers greater flexibility, it cannot be used for travel between Adelaide and Perth or Alice Springs. The cost is $530/320 in 1st class/economy for eight days of travel in 60 days, or $750/475 for 15 days of travel in 90 days.

Surcharges are payable on sleeping berths in both classes, and on certain trains, such as the Ghan (Adelaide to Alice Springs) and the Indian Pacific (Sydney to Perth), there are compulsory meal charges as well ($31 and $113 respectively).

For travel within a limited area, the passes which just cover travel in one state may be more suitable. These are available for Victoria, Queensland and Western Australia; see the relevant Getting Around sections for details.

The passes can be purchased at major railway stations and from travel agents. For details of passes and conditions contact Rail Australia on ☎ (08) 217 4479.

As the railway booking system is computerised, any station (other than those on metropolitan lines) can make a booking for any journey throughout the country. For reservations telephone ☎ 13 2232 during office hours; this will connect you to the nearest mainline station.

CAR

Australia is a big, sprawling country with large cities where public transport is not always very comprehensive or convenient – the car is the accepted means of getting from A to B. More and more travellers are also finding it the best way to see the country – with three or four of you the costs are reasonable and the benefits many, provided of course you don't have a major mechanical problem. As so many travellers are buying cars these days, you may find it difficult to find people who need a lift and will share costs if you buy one on your own.

Road Rules

Driving in Australia holds few real surprises. Australians drive on the left-hand side of the road just like in the UK, Japan and most countries in south and east Asia and the Pacific. There are a few local variations from the rules of the road as applied elsewhere in the West. The main one is the 'give way to the right' rule. This means that if you're driving along a main road and somebody appears on a minor road on your right, you must give way to them – unless they're facing a give-way or stop sign. This rule caused so much confusion over the years – with cars zooming out of tiny tracks onto main highways and expecting everything to screech to a stop for them – that most intersections are now signposted to indicate which is the priority road. It's wise to be careful because while almost every intersection is signposted in southern capitals, when you get up to towns in the north of Queensland, stop signs are few and far between and the old give-way rules will apply.

There's a special hazard in Melbourne – trams. You can only overtake trams from the left lane and must stop behind them when they stop to pick up or drop off passengers. Be aware of trams – they weigh about as much as the *Queen Mary* and cannot swerve to avoid foolish drivers. In central Melbourne there are also a number of intersections where a special technique, mastered only by native Melburnians, must be employed when making right-hand turns. You must wait until the light of the road you're turning into turns green, and then turn from the left-hand side of the road. Got that?

The general speed limit in built-up areas in Australia is 60 km/h and out on the open highway it's usually 100 or 110 km/h depending on where you are, although in the Northern Territory there is no speed limit outside of built-up areas. The police have radar speed traps and speed cameras and are very fond of using them in carefully hidden locations in order to raise easy revenue – don't exceed the speed limit in inviting areas where the boys and girls in blue may be waiting for you. On the other hand, when you get far from the cities and traffic is light, you'll see a lot of vehicles moving a lot faster than 100 km/h. Oncoming drivers who flash their lights at you may be giving you a friendly indication of a speed trap ahead.

Australia was one of the first countries in the world to make the wearing of seat belts compulsory. All new cars in Australia are required to have seat belts back and front and if your seat has a belt then you're required to wear it. You're liable to be fined if you don't. Small children must be belted into an approved safety seat.

Although overseas licences are acceptable in Australia for genuine overseas visitors, an International Driving Permit is preferred.

On the Road

Australia is not crisscrossed by multilane highways. There simply is not enough traffic and the distances are too great to justify them. You'll certainly find stretches of divided road, particularly on busy roads like the Sydney to Melbourne Hume Highway or close to the state capital cities – the last stretch into Adelaide from Melbourne, the Pacific Highway from Sydney to Newcastle, the Surfers Paradise-Brisbane road, for example. Elsewhere Australian roads are only well-surfaced and two lanes (though a long way from the billiard-table surfaces the Poms are used to driving on) on all the main routes.

You don't have to get very far off the beaten track, however, to find yourself on dirt roads, and anybody who sets out to see the country in reasonable detail will have to expect to do some dirt-road travelling. If you seriously want to explore, then you'd better plan on having four-wheel drive (4WD) and a winch. A few useful spare parts are worth carrying if you're travelling on highways in the Northern Territory or the north of Western Australia. A broken fan belt can be a damn nuisance if the next service station is 200 km away.

Driving standards in Australia aren't exactly the highest in the world and drink-driving is a real problem, especially in country areas. Serious attempts have been made in recent years to reduce the road toll – random breath tests are not uncommon in built-up areas. If you're caught with a blood-alcohol level of more than 0.05 (0.08 in the Northern Territory) then be prepared for a hefty fine, a court appearance and the loss of your licence.

Petrol is available from stations sporting the well-known international brand names. Prices vary from place to place and from price war to price war but generally it's in the 65 to 75c a litre range (say around $2.70 to $3.20 an imperial gallon). In the outback the price can soar and some outback service stations are not above exploiting their monopoly position. Distances between fill-ups can be long in the outback and in some remote areas deliveries can be haphazard – it's not unknown to finally arrive at that 'nearest station x hundred km' only to find there's no fuel until next week's delivery!

Between cities signposting on the main roads is generally quite OK, but around cities it's usually abysmal. You can spend a lot of time trying to find street-name signs, and as for indicating which way to go to leave the city – until recently you were halfway to Sydney from Melbourne before you saw the first sign telling you that you were travelling in the right direction.

Cows and kangaroos are two common hazards on country roads, and a collision is likely to kill the animal and seriously damage your vehicle. Kangaroos are most active around dawn and dusk, and they travel in groups. If you see one hopping across the road in front of you, slow right down – its friends are probably just behind it. Many Australians try to avoid travelling altogether between 5 pm and 8 am, because of the hazards posed by animals. Finally, if one hops out right in front of you, hit the brakes and only swerve to avoid the animal if it is safe to do so. The number of people who have been killed in accidents caused by

Distances by Road (km)							
	Adelaide	Brisbane	Canberra	Darwin	Melbourne	Perth	Sydney
Adelaide		2130	1210	3215	745	2750	1430
Alice Springs	1690	3060	2755	1525	2435	3770	2930
Brisbane	2130		1295	3495	1735	4390	1030
Broome	4035	4320	5100	1965	4780	2415	4885
Cairns	2865	1840	3140	2795	3235	6015	2870
Canberra	1210	1295		4230	655	3815	305
Darwin	3215	3495	4230		3960	4345	4060
Melbourne	755	1735	655	3960		3495	895
Perth	2750	4390	3815	4345	3495		3990
Sydney	1430	1030	305	4060	895	3990	

These are the shortest distances by road; other routes may be considerably longer. For distances by coach, check the companies' leaflets.

swerving to miss an animal is high – better to damage your car and probably kill the animal than kill yourself and others with you.

Outback Travel

Although you can now drive all the way round Australia on Highway 1 or through the middle all the way from Adelaide in the south to Darwin in the north without ever leaving sealed road, that hasn't always been so. The Eyre Highway across the Nullarbor Plain in the south was only surfaced in the 1970s, the final stretch of Highway 1 in the Kimberley region of Western Australia was done in the mid-1980s and the final section of the Stuart Highway from Port Augusta up to Alice Springs was finished in 1987.

If you really want to see outback Australia there are still lots of roads where the official recommendation is that you report to the police before you leave one end, and again when you arrive at the other. That way if you fail to turn up at the other end they can send the search parties. Nevertheless many of these tracks are now much better kept than in years past and you don't need 4WD or fancy expedition equipment to tackle them. You do need to be carefully prepared and to carry important spare parts, however. Backtracking 500 km to pick up some minor malfunctioning component or, much worse, to arrange a tow, is unlikely to be easy or cheap. When travelling to really remote areas it is advisable to travel with a high frequency outpost radio transmitter which is equipped to pick up the Royal Flying Doctor Service bases in the area.

You will of course need to carry a fair amount of water in case of disaster – around 20 litres a person is sensible – stored in more than one container. Food is less important – the space might be better allocated to an extra spare tyre.

The state automobile associations can advise on preparation and supply maps and track notes. Most tracks have an ideal time of year – in the Centre it's not wise to attempt the tough tracks during the heat of summer (November-March) when the dust can be severe, chances of mechanical trouble are much greater and water will be scarce and hence a breakdown more dangerous. Similarly in the north travelling in the wet season may be impossible due to flooding and mud.

If you do run into trouble in the back of beyond, stay with your car. It's easier to spot a car than a human being from the air, and you wouldn't be able to carry your 20 litres of water very far anyway.

Some of the favourite tracks are:

Birdsville Track Running 499 km from Marree in South Australia to Birdsville just across the border in Queensland, this is one of the best-known routes in Australia and these days is quite feasible in any well-prepared conventional vehicle.

Strzelecki Track This track covers much the same territory, starting south of Marree at Lyndhurst and going to Innamincka, 473 km north-east and close to the Queensland border. From there you can loop down to Tibooburra in New South Wales. The route has been much improved due to work on the Moomba gas fields. It was at Innamincka that the hapless early explorers Burke and Wills died.

Oodnadatta Track Parallel to the old Ghan railway line to Alice Springs, the Oodnadatta Track is now comprehensively bypassed with the new sealed Stuart Highway in operation. It's 465 km from Marree to Oodnadatta and another 202 km from there to the Stuart Highway at Marla. Any well-prepared vehicle should be able to manage this route.

Simpson Desert Crossing the Simpson Desert from Birdsville to the Stuart Highway is becoming increasingly popular but this route is still a real test. Four-wheel drive is definitely required and you should be in a party of at least three or four vehicles equipped with long-range two-way radios.

Warburton Road/Gunbarrel Highway This route runs west from Uluru (Ayers Rock) by the Aboriginal settlements of Docker River and Warburton to Laverton in Western Australia. From there you can drive down to Kalgoorlie and on to Perth. The route passes through Aboriginal reserves and permission to enter them must be obtained in advance if you want to leave the road. A well-prepared conventional vehicle can complete this route although ground clearance can be a problem and it is very remote. From the Yulara resort at Uluru to Warburton is 567 km, and it's another 568 km from there to Laverton. It's then 361 km on sealed road to Kalgoorlie. For 300 km near the Giles Meteorological

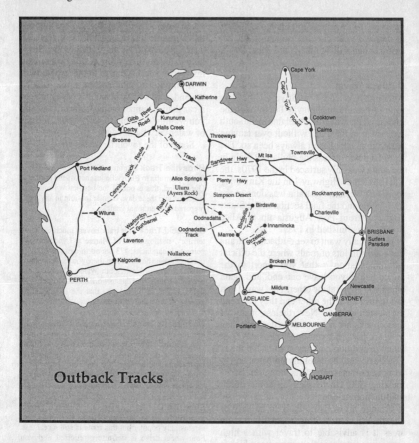

Outback Tracks

Station the Warburton Road and the Gunbarrel Highway run on the same route. Taking the old Gunbarrel (to the north of the Warburton) all the way to Wiluna in Western Australia is a much rougher trip requiring 4WD. The Warburton Road is now commonly referred to as the Gunbarrel – just to make life simple.

Tanami Track Turning off the Stuart Highway just north of Alice Springs the Tanami Track goes north-west across the Tanami Desert to Halls Creek in Western Australia. It's a popular short-cut for people travelling between the Centre and the Kimberley. The road has been extensively improved in recent years and conventional vehicles are quite OK although there are occasional sandy stretches on the WA

section. Be warned that the Rabbit Flat roadhouse in the middle of the desert is only open from Friday to Monday.

Canning Stock Route This old stock trail runs south-west from Halls Creek to Wiluna in Western Australia. It crosses the Great Sandy Desert and Gibson Desert, and since the track has not been maintained for over 30 years it's a route to be taken seriously. Like the Simpson Desert crossing you should only travel in a well-equipped party and careful navigation is required.

Plenty Highway & Sandover Highways These two routes run east from the Stuart Highway, to the north of Alice Springs, to Mt Isa in Queensland. They're suitable for conventional vehicles.

Cape York The Peninsula Developmental Road up to the top of Cape York, the furthest northerly point in Australia, is a popular route with a number of rivers to cross. It can only be attempted in the dry season when the water levels are lower. The original Cape York Rd along the old telegraph line definitely requires 4WD. Conventional vehicles can take the new 'Heathlands' road to the east beyond the Wenlock River, which bypasses the most difficult sections, but the Wenlock River itself can be a formidable obstacle.

Gibb River Road This is the 'short cut' between Derby and Kununurra, and runs through the heart of the spectacular Kimberley in northern Western Australia. Although fairly badly corrugated in places, it can be easily negotiated by conventional vehicles in the dry season and is 720 km, compared with about 920 km via the bitumen Northern Highway.

Car Rental

If you've got the cash there are plenty of car-rental companies ready and willing to put you behind the wheel. Competition in the Australian car-rental business is pretty fierce so rates tend to be variable and lots of special deals pop up and disappear again. Whatever your mode of travel on the long stretches, it can be very useful to have a car for some local travel. Between a group it can even be reasonably economical. There are some places – like around Alice Springs – where if you haven't got your own wheels you really have to choose between a tour and a rented vehicle since there is no public transport and the distances are too great for walking or even bicycles.

The three major companies are Budget, Hertz and Avis, with offices in almost every town that has more than one pub and a general store. The second-string companies which are also represented almost everywhere in the country are Thrifty and National. Then there is a vast number of local firms or firms with outlets in a limited number of locations. You can take it as read that the big operators will generally have higher rates than the local firms but it ain't necessarily so, so don't jump to conclusions.

The big firms have a number of big advantages, however. First of all they're the ones at the airports – Avis, Budget, Hertz and, quite often, Thrifty, are represented at most airports. If you want to pick up a car or leave a car at the airport then they're the best ones to deal with. In some but not all airports other companies will also arrange to pick up or leave their cars there. It tends to depend on how convenient the airport is.

The second advantage of the big companies is if you want to do a one-way rental – pick up a car in Adelaide and leave it in Sydney, for example. There are, however, a variety of restrictions on these. Usually it's a minimum-hire period rather than repositioning charges. Only certain cars may be eligible for one-ways. Check the small print on one-way charges before deciding on one company rather than another. One-way rentals are generally not available into or out of the Northern Territory or Western Australia. Special rules may also apply to one-ways into or out of other 'remote areas'.

The major companies all offer unlimited km rates in the city, but in country and 'remote' areas it's a flat charge plus so many cents per km. On straightforward off-the-card city rentals they're all pretty much the same price. It's on special deals, odd rentals or longer periods that you find the differences. Weekend specials – usually three days for the price of two – are usually good value. If you just need a car for three days around Sydney make it the weekend rather than midweek. Budget offer 'stand-by' rates and you may see other special deals available. When picking up a car in Townsville once I saw a sign offering cars free, so long as you got them to Cairns within 24 hours!

Daily rates are typically about $70 a day for a small car (Ford Laser, Toyota Corolla, Nissan Pulsar), about $90 a day for a medium car (Holden Camira, Toyota Camry, Nissan Pintara) or about $100 to $110 a day for a big car (Holden Commodore, Ford Falcon), all including insurance.

There is a whole collection of other factors to bear in mind about this rent-a-car business. For a start, if you're going to want it for a week, a month or longer then they all have lower rates. If you're in Tasmania, where competition is very fierce, there are often lower rates, especially in the low season. If you're in the really remote outback (places like Darwin and Alice Springs are only vaguely remote) then the choice of cars is likely to be limited to the larger, more expensive ones. You usually must be at least 21 to hire from most firms.

OK, that's the big hire companies, what about all the rest of them? Well some of them are still pretty big in terms of numbers of shiny new cars. In Tasmania, for example, the car-hire business is really big since many people don't bring their cars with them. There's a plethora of hire companies and lots of competition. In many cases local companies are markedly cheaper than the big boys, but in others what looks like a cheaper rate can end up quite the opposite if you're not careful.

And don't forget the 'rent-a-wreck' companies. They specialise in renting older cars – at first they really were old, and a flat rate like '$10 a day and forget the insurance' was the usual story. Now many of them have a variety of rates, typically around $35 a day. If you just want to travel around the city, or not too far out, they can be worth considering.

Moke Rental In lots of popular holiday areas – like on the Gold Coast, around Cairns and on Magnetic Island – right at the bottom of the rent-a-car rates will be the ubiquitous Moke. To those not in the know, a Moke is a totally open vehicle looking rather like a miniature Jeep. They're based on the Mini so they're FWD (front-wheel drive) not 4WD (four-wheel drive) and they are not suitable for getting way off the beaten track. For general good fun in places with a sunny climate, however, they simply can't be beaten. No vehicle has more air-conditioning than a Moke, and as the stickers say 'Moking is not a wealth hazard' – they cover lots of km on a litre of petrol.

If you do hire a Moke there are a few points to watch. Don't have an accident in one; they offer little more protection than a motorcycle. There is absolutely no place to

lock things up so don't leave your valuables inside, and the fuel tanks are equally accessible so if you're leaving it somewhere at night beware of petrol thieves – not that there are a great number in Australia, but it does happen.

4WD Rental Having 4WD enables you to get right off the beaten track and out to some of the great wilderness and outback places, to see some of the Australian natural wonders that most travellers don't see.

Renting a 4WD vehicle is within the budget range if a few people get together. Something small like a Suzuki or similar costs around $100 per day; for a Toyota Landcruiser you're looking at around $150, which should include insurance and some free km (typically 100 km). Check the insurance conditions, especially the excess, as they can be onerous.

Hertz has 4WD rentals, with one-way rentals possible between the eastern states and the Northern Territory. Budget also rents 4WD vehicles from Darwin and Alice Springs. Brits: Australia (☎ (1800) 331 454) is a company which hires fully equipped 4WD vehicles fitted out as campervans. These have proved extremely popular in recent years, although they are not cheap at $155 per day for unlimited km, plus Collision Damage Waiver ($12 per day). They have offices in all the mainland capitals, as well as in Cairns and Alice Springs, so one-way rentals are also possible.

Renting Other Vehicles

There are lots of other vehicles you can rent apart from cars. In many places you can rent campervans – they're particularly popular in Tasmania. Motorscooters are also available in a number of locations – they are popular on Magnetic Island and in Cairns for example – and you only need a car licence to ride one. Best of all, in many places you can rent bicycles.

Buying a Car

If you want to explore Australia by car and haven't got one or can't borrow one, then you've either got to buy one or rent one. Australian cars are not cheap – another product of the small population. Locally manufactured cars are made in small, uneconomic numbers and imported cars are heavily taxed so they won't undercut the local products. If you're buying a second-hand vehicle reliability is all important. Mechanical breakdowns way out in the outback can be very inconvenient (not to mention dangerous) – the nearest mechanic can be a hell of a long way down the road.

Shopping around for a used car involves much the same rules as anywhere in the Western world but with a few local variations. First of all, used-car dealers in Australia are just like used-car dealers from Los Angeles to London – they'd sell their mother into slavery if it turned a dollar. You'll probably get any car cheaper by buying privately through newspaper small ads rather than through a car dealer. Buying through a dealer does give the advantage of some sort of guarantee, but a guarantee is not much use if you're buying a car in Sydney and intend setting off for Perth next week. Used-car guarantee requirements vary from state to state – check with the local automobile organisation.

There's a great deal of discussion amongst travellers about where is the best place to buy used cars. Popular theories exist that you can buy a car in Sydney or Melbourne, drive it to Darwin and sell it there for a profit. Or was it vice versa? It's quite possible that prices do vary but don't count on turning it to your advantage. See the section on buying cars in Sydney for the situation at that popular starting/finishing point.

What is rather more certain is that the further you get from civilisation, the better it is to be in a Holden or a Ford. New cars can be a whole different ball game of course, but if you're in an older vehicle, something that's likely to have the odd hiccup from time to time, then life is much simpler if it's a car for which you can get spare parts anywhere from Bourke to Bulamakanka. When your fancy Japanese car goes kaput somewhere back of Bourke it's likely to be a two-week wait while the new bit arrives fresh from Fukuoka. On the other hand, when your rusty old Holden goes bang there's probably another old Holden sitting in a ditch with a perfectly good widget waiting to be removed. Every scrap yard in Australia is full of good ole Holdens.

Note that in Australia third-party personal injury insurance is always included in the vehicle registration cost. This ensures that every vehicle (as long as it's currently registered) carries at least minimum insurance. You're wise to extend that minimum to at least third-party property insurance as well – minor collisions with Rolls-Royces can be amazingly expensive.

When you come to buy or sell a car there are usually some local regulations to be complied with. In Victoria, for example, a car has to have a compulsory safety check (Road Worthiness Certificate – RWC) before it can be registered in the new owner's name – usually the seller will indicate if the car already has an RWC. In New South Wales and the Northern Territory, on the other hand, safety checks are compulsory every year when you come to renew the registration. Stamp duty has to be paid when you buy a car and, as this is based on the purchase price, it's not unknown for buyer and seller to agree privately to understate the price! It's much easier to sell a car in the same state that it's registered in, otherwise it has to be re-registered in the new state. It may be possible to sell a car without re-registering it, but you're likely to get a lower price.

One way of getting around the hassles of buying and selling a vehicle privately is to enter into a buy-back arrangement with a car or motorcycle dealer. However, dealers will often find ways of knocking down the price when you return the vehicle, even if a price has been agreed in writing – often by pointing out expensive repairs that allegedly will be required to gain the dreaded RWC needed to transfer the registration. The cars on offer have often been driven around Australia a number of times, often with haphazard or minimal servicing, and are generally pretty tired. The main advantage of these schemes is that you don't have to worry about being able to sell the vehicle quickly at the end of your trip, and can usually arrange insurance, which short-term visitors may find hard to get. (See the Sydney Getting There & Away section in the New South Wales chapter for more details.)

A company that specialises in buy-back arrangements on cars and motorcycles, with fixed rates and no hidden extras, is Car Connection Australia. Also known as Bike Tours Australia, it has been organising adventure holidays and expeditions covering the entire continent for over 10 years, and has recently branched into this sideline. Its program is basically a glorified long-term rental arrangement where you put down a deposit to the value of the vehicle and in the end you get your money back, minus the fixed 'usage' fee.

The bottom line is that a second-hand Ford station wagon or Yamaha XT600 trail bike will set you back a fixed sum of $1950 for any period up to six months; a Toyota Landcruiser, suitable for serious outback exploration, is $3500, also for up to six months. Prices include pick-up at Melbourne Airport and a night's accommodation in Castlemaine to help you acclimatise, and you'll be sent on your way with touring maps and advice. You can also rent camping equipment (but not sleeping bags). Car Connection Australia (☎ (054) 73 4469, fax (054) 73 4520) is at RSD Lot 8, Vaughan Springs Rd, Glenluce (near Castlemaine), Vic 3451. Information and bookings are handled by its European agent: Travel Action GmbH (☎ (0276) 4 78 24, fax 79 38), Einsiedeleiweg 16, 57399 Kirchhundem, Germany.

Finally, make use of the automobile organisations – see the Facts for the Visitor chapter for more details about them. They can advise you on any local regulations you should be aware of, give general guidelines about buying a car and, most importantly, for a fee (around $70) will check over a used car and report on its condition before you agree to purchase it. They also offer car insurance to their members.

MOTORBIKE

Motorbikes are a very popular way of getting around. The climate is just about ideal for biking much of the year, and the many small trails from the road into the bush often lead to perfect spots to spend the night in the world's largest camping ground.

The long, open roads are really made for large-capacity machines above 750 cc, which Australians prefer once they outgrow their 250 cc learner restrictions. But that doesn't stop enterprising individuals – many of them Japanese – from tackling the length and breadth of the continent on 250 cc trail bikes. Doing it on a small bike is not impossible, just tedious at times.

If you want to bring your own motorcycle into Australia you'll need a *carnet de passages*, and when you try to sell it you'll get less than the market price because of restrictive registration requirements (not so severe in Western Australia, South Australia and the Northern Territory). Shipping from just about anywhere is expensive.

However, with a little bit of time up your sleeve, getting mobile on two wheels in Australia is quite feasible, thanks largely to the chronically depressed motorcycle market. The beginning of the southern winter is a good time to strike. Australian newspapers and the lively local bike press have extensive classified advertisement sections where $2500 gets you something that will easily take you around the country if you know a bit about bikes. The main drawback is that you'll have to try and sell it again afterwards.

An easier option is a buy-back arrangement with a large motorcycle dealer in a major city (Elizabeth St in Melbourne is a good hunting ground). They're keen to do business, and basic negotiating skills allied with a wad of cash (say, $4000) should secure an excellent second-hand bike with a written guarantee that they'll buy it back in good condition minus $1500 or $2000 after your four-month, round-Australia trip. Popular brands for this sort of thing are BMWs, large-capacity, shaft-driven Japanese bikes and possibly Harley-Davidsons (very popular in Australia). The percentage drop on a trail bike will be much greater (though the actual amount you lose should be similar), but very few dealers are interested in buy-back schemes on trail bikes.

You'll need a rider's licence and a helmet. Some motorcyclists in New South Wales have special permission to ride without a helmet, ostensibly for medical reasons. A fuel range of 350 km will cover fuel stops up the Centre and on Highway 1 around the continent. Beware of dehydration in the dry, hot air – force yourself to drink plenty of water, even if you don't feel thirsty. If riding in Tasmania (a top bicycling and motorcycling destination) you should be prepared for rotten weather in winter, and rain any time of year.

The 'roo bars' (outsize bumpers) on interstate trucks and many outback cars tell you never to ride at night, or in the early morning and evening. Marsupials are nocturnal, sleeping in the shade during the day and feeding at night, and road ditches often provide lush grass for them to eat. Cows and sheep also stray onto the roads at night. It's wise to stop riding by around 5 pm.

Many roadhouses offer showers free of charge or for a nominal fee. They're meant for truck drivers, but other people often use them too.

It's worth carrying some spares and tools even if you don't know how to use them, because someone else often does. If you do know, you'll probably have a fair idea of what to take. The basics include: a spare tyre tube (front wheel size, which will fit on the rear but usually not vice versa); puncture repair kit with levers and a pump (or tubeless tyre repair kit with at least three carbon dioxide cartridges); a spare tyre valve, and a valve cap that can unscrew same; the bike's standard tool kit for what it's worth (aftermarket items are better); spare throttle, clutch and brake cables; tie wire, cloth tape ('gaffer' tape) and nylon 'zip-ties'; a handful of bolts and nuts in the usual emergency sizes (M6 and M8), along with a few self-tapping screws; one or two fuses in your bike's ratings; a bar of soap for fixing tank leaks (knead to a putty with water and squeeze into

the leak); and, most important of all, a workshop manual for your bike (even if you can't make sense of it, the local motorcycle mechanic can). You'll never have enough elastic straps (octopus or 'ocky' straps) to tie down your gear.

Make sure you carry water – at least two litres on major roads in central Australia, more off the beaten track. And finally, if something does go hopelessly wrong in the back of beyond, park your bike where it's clearly visible and observe the cardinal rule: **don't leave your vehicle**.

BICYCLE

Whether you're hiring a bike to ride around a city or wearing out your Bio-Ace chainwheels on a Melbourne-Darwin marathon, you'll find that Australia is a great place for cycling. There are bike tracks in most cities, and in the country you'll find thousands of km of good roads which carry so little traffic that the biggest hassle is waving back to the drivers. Especially appealing is that in many areas you'll ride a very long way without encountering a hill.

Bicycle helmets are compulsory wear in all states and territories.

It's possible to plan rides of any duration and through almost any terrain. A day or two cycling around South Australia's wineries is popular, or you could meander along beside the Murrumbidgee for weeks. Tasmania is very popular for touring, and mountain bikes would love Australia's deserts – or its mountains, for that matter.

Cycling has always been popular here, and not only as a sport: some shearers would ride for huge distances between jobs, rather than use less reliable horses. It's rare to find a reasonably sized town that doesn't have a shop stocking at least basic bike parts.

If you're coming specifically to cycle, it makes sense to bring your own bike. Check your airline for costs and the degree of dismantling/packing required. Within Australia you can load your bike onto a bus or train to skip the boring bits. Note that bus companies require you to dismantle your bike, and some don't guarantee that it will travel on the same bus as you. Trains are easier, but supervise the loading and if possible tie your bike upright, otherwise you may find that the guard has stacked crates of Holden spares on your fragile alloy wheels.

You can buy a good steel-framed touring bike in Australia for about $400 (plus panniers). It may be possible to rent touring bikes and equipment from a few of the commercial touring organisations.

Much of eastern Australia seems to have been settled on the principle of not having more than a day's horse ride between pubs, so it's possible to plan even ultralong routes and still get a shower at the end of the day. Most people do carry camping equipment, but, on the east coast at least, it's feasible to travel from town to town staying in hotels or on-site vans.

You can get by with standard road maps, but as you'll probably want to avoid both the highways and the low-grade unsealed roads, the Government series is best. The 1:250,000 scale is the most suitable but you'll need a lot of maps if you're covering much territory. The next scale up, 1:1,000,000, is adequate. They are available in capital cities and elsewhere.

Until you get fit you should be careful to eat enough to keep you going – remember that exercise is an appetite suppressant. It's surprisingly easy to be so depleted of energy that you end up camping under a gum tree just 10 km short of a shower and a steak.

No matter how fit you are, water is still vital. Dehydration is no joke and can be life-threatening. One Lonely Planet author rode his first 200-km-in-a-day on a bowl of cornflakes and a round of sandwiches, but the Queensland sun forced him to drink nearly five litres. Having been involved in a drinking contest with stockmen the night before may have had something to do with it, though.

It can get very hot in summer, and you should take things slowly until you're used to the heat. Cycling in 35°C-plus temperatures isn't too bad if you wear a hat and plenty of sunscreen, and drink *lots* of water. In the eastern states, be aware of the blister-ing 'hot northerlies', the prevailing winds that make a north-bound cyclist's life uncomfortable in summer. In April, when the south-east's clear autumn weather begins, the Southerly Trades prevail, and you can have (theoretically at least) tailwinds all the way to Darwin.

Of course, you don't have to follow the larger roads and visit towns. It's possible to fill your mountain bike's panniers with muesli, head out into the mulga, and not see anyone for weeks. Or ever again – outback travel is very risky if not properly planned. Water is the main problem in the 'dead heart', and you can't rely on it where there aren't settlements. That tank marked on your map may be dry or the water from it unfit for humans, and those station buildings probably blew away years ago. That little creek marked with a dotted blue line? Forget it – the only time it has water is when the country's flooded for hundreds of km.

Always check with locals if you're heading into remote areas, and notify the police if you're about to do something particularly adventurous. That said, you can't rely too much on local knowledge of road conditions – most people have no idea of what a heavily loaded touring bike needs. What they think of as a great road may be pedal-deep in sand or bull dust, and cyclists have happily ridden along roads that were officially flooded out.

Information

In each state there are touring organisations which can help with information and put you in touch with touring clubs:

Australian Capital Territory
　Pedal Power ACT, PO Box 581, Canberra, ACT 2601 (☎ (06) 248 7995)
New South Wales
　Bicycle Institute of New South Wales, 82 Campbell St, Surry Hills, NSW 2010 (☎ (02) 212 5628)
Queensland
　Bicycle Institute of Queensland, The Web, 142 Agnew St, Norman Park, Qld 4101 (☎ (07) 899 2988)
South Australia
　Bicycle Institute of South Australia, 11 Church Rd, Mitcham, SA 5062 (☎ (08) 271 5824)

Tasmania
  Pedal Power Tasmania, c/o Environment Centre, 102 Bathurst St, Hobart, Tas 7000 (☎ (002) 34 5566)
Victoria
  Bicycle Victoria, 19 O'Connell St, North Melbourne, Vic 3051 (☎ (03) 328 3000)
Western Australia
  Cycle Touring Association, PO Box 174, Wembley, WA 6014 (☎ (09) 349 2310)

There are many organised tours available of varying lengths, and if you get tired of talking to sheep as you ride along, it might be a good idea to include one or more tours in your itinerary. Most provide a support vehicle and take care of accommodation and cooking, so they can be a nice break from solo chores.

HITCHING

Hitching is never entirely safe in any country in the world, and we don't recommend it. Travellers who decide to hitch should understand that they are taking a small but potentially serious risk. Australia is not exempt from danger (Queensland in particular is notorious for attacks on women travellers), and even people hitching in pairs are not entirely safe. Before deciding to hitch, talk to local people about the dangers, and it is a good idea to let someone know where you are planning to hitch to before you set off. If you do choose to hitch, the advice that follows should help to make your journey as fast and safe as possible.

Factor one for safety and speed is numbers. More than two people hitching together will make things very difficult, and solo hitching is unwise for men as well as women. Two women hitching together may be vulnerable, and two men hitching together can expect long waits. The best option is for a woman and a man to hitch together.

Factor two is position – look for a place where vehicles will be going slowly and where they can stop easily. A junction or freeway slip road is a good place if there is stopping room. Position goes beyond just where you stand. The ideal location is on the outskirts of a town – hitching from way out in the country is as hopeless as from the centre of a city. Take a bus out to the edge of town.

Factor three is appearance. The ideal appearance for hitching is a sort of genteel poverty – threadbare but clean. Looking too good can be as much of a bummer as looking too bad! Don't carry too much gear – if it looks like it's going to take half an hour to pack your bags aboard you'll be left on the roadside.

Factor four is knowing when to say no. Saying no to a car-load of drunks is pretty obvious, but you should also be prepared to abandon a ride if you begin to feel uneasy for any reason. Don't sit there hoping for the best: make an excuse and get out at the first opportunity.

It can be time-saving to say no to a short ride that might take you from a good hitching point to a lousy one. Wait for the right, long ride to come along. On a long haul, it's pointless to start walking as it's not likely to increase the likelihood of your getting a lift and it's often an awfully long way to the next town.

Trucks are often the best lifts but they will only stop if they are going slowly and can get started easily again. Thus the ideal place is at the top of a hill where they have a downhill run. Truckies often say they are going to the next town and if they don't like you, will drop you anywhere. As they often pick up hitchers for company, the quickest way to create a bad impression is to jump in and fall asleep. It's also worth remembering that while you're in someone else's vehicle, you are their guest and should act accordingly – many drivers no longer pick up people because they have suffered from thoughtless hikers in the past. It's the hitcher's duty to provide entertainment!

Of course people do get stuck in outlandish places but that is the name of the game. If you're visiting from abroad a nice prominent flag on your pack will help, and a sign announcing your destination can also be useful. Uni and hostel notice boards are good places to look for hitching partners. The main law against hitching is 'thou shalt not stand in the road' – so when you see the law coming, step back.

Just as hitchers should be wary when accepting lifts, drivers who pick up fellow travellers to share the costs should also be aware of the possible risks involved.

BOAT

Not really. Once upon a time there was quite a busy coastal shipping service but now it only applies to freight, and apart from specialised bulk carriers, even that is declining rapidly. The only regular shipping service is between Victoria and Tasmania and unless you are taking a vehicle with you the very cheapest ticket on that often-choppy route is not all that much cheaper than the air fare. You can occasionally travel between Australian ports on a liner bound for somewhere but very few people do that.

On the other hand it *is* quite possible to make your way round the coast or even to other countries like New Zealand, Papua New Guinea or Indonesia by hitching rides or crewing on yachts. Ask around at harbours, marinas or yacht or sailing clubs. Good places on the east coast include Coffs Harbour, Great Keppel Island, Airlie Beach/Whitsundays, Cairns – anywhere where boats call. Usually you have to chip in something for food.

A lot of boats move north to escape the winter, so April is a good time to look for a berth in the Sydney area.

TOURS

There are all sorts of tours around Australia including some interesting camping tours. Adventure tours include 4WD safaris in the Northern Territory and up into far north Queensland. Some of these go to places you simply couldn't get to on your own without large amounts of expensive equipment. You can also walk, ski, boat, raft, canoe, ride a horse or camel or even fly.

YHA tours are good value – find out about them at YHA Travel offices in capital cities. In major centres like Sydney, Darwin and

Cairns there are many tours aimed specially at backpackers – good prices, good destinations, good fun.

There are several operators offering organised motorcycling tours in Australia but many of them are fly-by-night outfits. However, one that has been around for over 10 years is Bike Tours Australia, which offers a wide range of long-distance tours on Yamaha XT600 trail bikes. These include a three-week east coast tour from Melbourne to the Barrier Reef for $2870, and a variety of outback tours for which you have to be a reasonably good rider, for instance a five-week outback adventure diagonally across the continent from Perth to Cape York for $5400. Most of Bike Tours' clients are continental Europeans but other nationalities are welcome. Bike Tours Australia also operates a car and motorcycle buy-back scheme under the name Car Connection Australia; see the Buying a Car section for contact details.

STUDENT TRAVEL

STA Travel is the main agent for student travellers in Australia. They have a network of travel offices around the country and apart from selling normal tickets also have special student discounts and tours. STA Travel don't only cater to students, they also act as normal travel agents to the public in general. The STA Travel head office is in Faraday St, Melbourne, but there are a number of other offices around the various cities and at the universities. The main offices are:

Australian Capital Territory
    Arts Centre, Australian National University, Canberra, ACT 2600 (☎ (06) 251 4688)
New South Wales
    1A Lee St, Railway Square, Sydney, NSW 2000 (☎ (02) 519 9866)
Queensland
    Northern Security Building, 40 Creek St, Brisbane, Qld 4000 (☎ (07) 221 9388)
South Australia
    235 Rundle St, Adelaide, 5000 (☎ (08) 223 2426)
Victoria
    220 Faraday St, Carlton 3053 (☎ (03) 347 4711)
Western Australia
    426 Hay St, Subiaco 6008 (☎ (09) 382 3977)

Australian Capital Territory

Area   2366 sq km
Population   296,000

> ☎ From February 1998, the ACT's existing phone numbers will be prefixed by the additional digit 6 (for example, ☎ 123 4567 becomes ☎ 6123 4567). The ACT's area code will be 02. ■

When the separate colonies of Australia were federated in 1901 and became states, the decision to build a national capital was part of the Constitution. The site was selected in 1908, diplomatically situated between arch rivals Sydney and Melbourne, and an international competition to design the capital was won by the American architect Walter Burley Griffin. In 1911 the Commonwealth government bought land for the Australian Capital Territory (ACT) and in 1913 decided to call the capital Canberra, believed to be an Aboriginal term for 'meeting place'.

Development of the site was slow and it was not until 1927 that parliament was first convened in the capital. From 1901 until then, Melbourne was the seat of the national government. The Depression virtually halted development and things really only got under way after WW II. In 1960 the population topped 50,000, reaching 100,000 by 1967. Today the ACT has almost 300,000 people.

Canberra

Population 285,000

Canberra is well worth visiting. Some of the best architecture and exhibitions in Australia are here and the whole city is fascinating because it is totally planned and orderly. It also has a beautiful setting, surrounded by hills, and is close to good bushwalking and skiing country. It is a place of government with few local industries and it has that unique, stimulating atmosphere that's only to be found in national capitals.

Canberra has finally acquired the furnishings of a true centre of national life – like the exciting National Gallery, the splendid new Parliament House and the excellent National Botanic Gardens. What's more, Canberra has quite a young population, including a lot of students, and is livelier than we're usually led to expect. Finally, this is the only city in Australia that's really *Australian* – as opposed to South Australian, Victorian, Western Australian or whatever.

Orientation

Civic, the city centre, is on the northern side of Lake Burley Griffin (an artificial waterway). Civic's centre is Vernon Circle and the nearby post office, banks and bus terminals. The pedestrian malls east of the circle are Canberra's main shopping areas. The mirror-image Sydney and Melbourne Buildings flank the beginning of Northbourne Ave, the main artery north of the lake.

From Vernon Circle, Commonwealth Ave runs south over the Commonwealth Ave Bridge to Capital Circle, which surrounds the new Parliament House on Capital Hill. Capital Circle is the apex of Walter Burley Griffin's parliamentary triangle, formed by Commonwealth Ave, Kings Ave (crossing the lake on the north-eastern side) and the

ACT

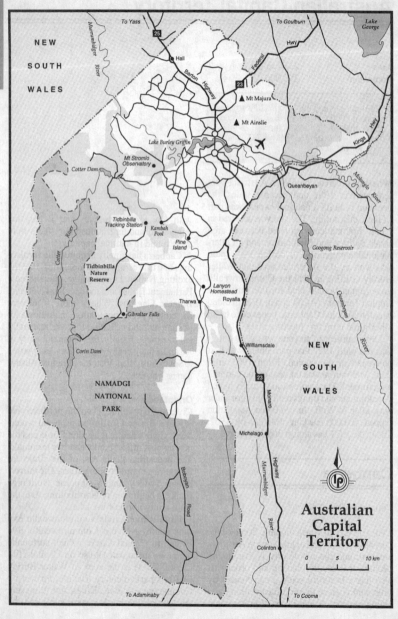

lake. Many important buildings are concentrated within this triangle, including the National Library, the High Court, the National Gallery and the old parliament house. South-east of Capital Hill is Manuka Circle, another large shopping centre.

As well as the many neighbourhoods (Canberra's basic unit of urban structure) north and south of the lake, the city includes the large 'towns' of Belconnen, Woden and Tuggeranong.

Information

Tourist Office The information centre (☎ toll-free 1800 026 166) is on Northbourne Ave, Dickson, about two km north of Vernon Circle. It's open from 9 am to 5 pm daily (from 8.30 am on weekends). There are free phones to call various places to book accommodation.

Tune to 98.9 FM for tourist information.

Post & Telecommunications Have mail addressed to poste restante at the Canberra City Post Office on Alinga St, Civic. There are plenty of payphones here and there's a credit-card phone in the nearby Jolimont Centre. Canberra's STD area code is 06.

Foreign Embassies There are about 60 embassies and high commissions in Canberra. A few are worth looking at, although many operate from rather nondescript suburban houses. Most are in Yarralumla, west and north of Parliament House. On the Sunday of long weekends in January (Australia Day), June (Queen's Birthday) and October (Labour Day) there's an embassies open day, when you can visit a few of them for about $5.

The US Embassy is a facsimile of a mansion in the style of those in Williamsburg, Virginia. The Thai Embassy, with its pointed, orange-tiled roof, is in a style similar to that of temples in Bangkok. The Indonesian Embassy is no architectural jewel but there's an exhibit on Indonesia's colourful culture, open weekdays from about 9 am to 5 pm with a break for lunch. Papua New Guinea's high commission looks like a 'haus tambaran' spirit-house from PNG's

Sepik region. There's a display room with photos and artefacts, open weekdays from about 10 am to 4.30 pm (with lunch break).

Embassy and high commission addresses include:

Austria
    12 Talbot St, Forrest (☎ 295 1533)
Canada
    Commonwealth Ave, Yarralumla (☎ 273 3844)
Germany
    119 Empire Court, Yarralumla (☎ 270 1911)
India
    3 Moonah Place, Yarralumla (☎ 273 3999)
Indonesia
    8 Darwin Ave, Yarralumla (☎ 273 3222)
Ireland
    20 Arkana St, Yarralumla (☎ 273 3022)
Japan
    112 Empire Circuit, Yarralumla (☎ 273 3244)
Malaysia
    7 Perth Ave, Yarralumla (☎ 273 1543)
Netherlands
    120 Empire Circuit, Yarralumla (☎ 273 3111)
New Zealand
    Commonwealth Ave, Yarralumla (☎ 270 4211)
Norway
    17 Hunter St, Yarralumla (☎ 273 3444)
Papua New Guinea
    Forster Crescent, Yarralumla (☎ 273 3322)
Singapore
    Forster Crescent, Yarralumla (☎ 273 3944)
Sweden
    Turrana St, Yarralumla (☎ 273 3033)
Switzerland
    7 Melbourne Ave, Forrest (☎ 273 3977)
Thailand
    111 Empire Circuit, Yarralumla (☎ 273 1149)
UK
    Commonwealth Ave, Yarralumla (☎ 270 6666)
USA
    21 Moonah Place, Yarralumla (☎ 270 5000)

Bookshops There are many good bookshops. Dalton's, in the Capital Centre near Civic's Barry Drive, and Paperchain, on Furneaux St in Manuka, are two of the best. The Commonwealth Government Bookshop, on the northern side of the Melbourne Building, has handy publications plus some glossy books which are useful as souvenirs. There's an excellent second-hand bookshop in Lyneham shopping centre. Canberra is well stocked with overseas information

ACT

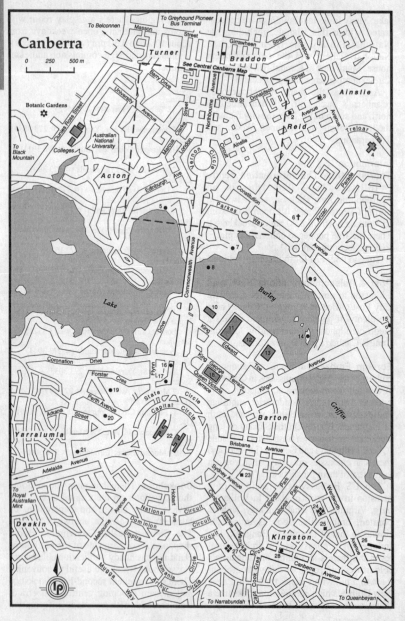

Canberra

0   250   500 m

To Belconnen
To Greyhound Pioneer Bus Terminal
Masson Street
Girrawheen
Linslse

Turner
Braddon
See Central Canberra Map
Berry Drive
Cooyong St
Donaldson
Ainslie

Botanic Gardens
University Avenue
Northbourne Avenue
Marcus Clarke Street
London
Reid

Ourles Ross Street
Ainslie
Constitution
Treloar Cres

To Black Mountain
Australian National University
Colleges
Vernon Circle
Acton
Edinburgh Ave

Parkes Way
Anzac

5
6
7

8
9
Burley

Lake
Commonwealth Avenue
Drive
10
King
11
12
13
14
15

Coronation Drive
Flynn
16
King George Terrace
Edward
Tce

Forster Cres
17
Queen Victoria Terrace
18
Kings

Perth Avenue
19
State Circle
Capital Circle

Arkana Street
20
Barton
Brisbane Avenue
Griffin

Yarralumia
21

Adelaide Avenue
22
Sydney Avenue
23

To Royal Australian Mint
Hobart Ave
Melbourne Avenue
Dominion Circuit
National Circuit
Empire Circuit
Circuit
24
Teloysa Park
Wentworth

Deakin
25
Kingston
26

27
28
Canberra Avenue

Mugga Way
Tasmania Circle
Arthur Circle
Capt Cook Cres
Circle
Telopea Park

To Narrabundah
To Queanbeyan

PLACES TO STAY

1 Kythera Motel
2 Acacia Motor Lodge
3 Olim's Canberra Hotel
23 Macquarie Private Hotel
25 Victor Lodge
28 Kingston Hotel

OTHER

4 War Memorial
5 Ferry Terminal, Bike & Boat Hire
6 Church of St John the Baptist
7 National Capital Exhibition
8 Captain Cook Memorial
    Water Jet
9 Blundell's Farmhouse
10 National Library
11 Australian Science & Technology
    Centre
12 High Court
13 National Gallery
14 Carillon
15 Australian-American Memorial
16 UK High Commission
17 PNG High Commission
18 Old Parliament House
19 Indonesian Embassy
20 US Embassy
21 Thai Embassy
22 Parliament House (on Capital Hill)
24 Kingston Shopping Centre
26 Railway Station
27 Manuka Shopping Centre

centres and libraries – good places to keep up with foreign news.

Maps The NRMA (☎ 243 8800) at 92 Northbourne Ave has excellent maps of Canberra. For topographic maps of the ACT try the information centre or the ACT Shopfront near the Civic bus interchange.

Medical Services There's a Travellers Medical & Vaccination Centre (☎ 257 7156) upstairs in the City Walk Arcade, near the Civic bus interchange. It's open only on Mondays and Fridays and on Wednesday mornings. There are several other doctors' clinics nearby.

Emergency Emergency phone numbers are ☎ 000 for ambulance, fire and police; ☎ 257

1111 for Lifeline; and ☎ 247 2525 for the Rape Crisis Centre.

Lookouts

There are fine views of Canberra from the surrounding hills. West of Civic, **Black Mountain** rises to 825 metres and is topped by the 195-metre Telecom Telecommunications Tower, complete with a revolving restaurant. There's also a display on telecommunications history. The tower is open daily from 9 am to 10 pm ($3). There are also splendid vistas from the approach road. Bus No 904 runs to the tower or you can walk there along a two-km trail through bush, starting on Frith Rd. Other bushwalks, accessible from Belconnen Way and Caswell Drive, wander round the back of the mountain. The information centre has a brochure with a map.

Other lookouts, all with roads to them, are **Mt Ainslie** (840 metres), **Red Hill** (722 metres) and, in New South Wales, **Mt Pleasant** (665 metres). Mt Ainslie is close to the city on the north-eastern side and has particularly fine views, day or night. There are foot trails up Mt Ainslie from behind the War Memorial, and out behind Mt Ainslie to **Mt Majura** (888 metres) four km away. You may see a kangaroo or two on the hike up.

Lake Burley Griffin

The lake was named after Canberra's designer but was not created until the Molonglo River was dammed in 1963. It is not recommended to swim in the lake but you can go boating (beware of sudden strong winds) or cycle around it. You can hire boats and bikes at the Acton Park Ferry Terminal, on the northern side of the lake.

There are a number of places of interest around the 35-km shore. The most visible is the **Captain Cook Memorial Water Jet** which flings a six-tonne column of water 140 metres into the air, and will give you a free shower if the wind is blowing from the right direction (despite an automatic switch-off which is supposed to operate if the wind speed gets too high). The jet, built in 1970 to commemorate the bicentenary of Captain

Cook's visit to Australia, operates from 10 am to noon and 2 to 4 pm daily, and from 7 to 9 pm during daylight saving time. At **Regatta Point**, nearby on the north shore, is a skeleton globe with Cook's three great voyages traced on it.

The **National Capital Exhibition**, also at Regatta Point, is open daily from 9 am to 6 pm and has displays on the growth of the capital. It's free and interesting. Further round the lake, to the east, is **Blundell's Farmhouse** (1858). The simple stone and slab cottage is a reminder of the area's early farming history and is open daily ($1).

A little further around the lake, at the far end of Commonwealth Park which stretches east from the Commonwealth Ave Bridge, is the **Carillon**, on Aspen Island. The 53-bell tower was a gift from Britain in 1963, Canberra's 50th anniversary. The bells weigh from seven kg to six tonnes. There are recitals on Wednesday from 12.45 to 1.30 pm and on weekends and public holidays from 2.45 to 3.30 pm.

The southern shore of the lake, along which the impressive National Gallery and High Court are situated, forms the base of the parliamentary triangle.

Parliament House

South of the lake, the four-legged flag mast on top of Capital Hill marks Parliament House. This, the most recent aspect of Walter Burley Griffin's vision to become a reality, sits at the apex of the parliamentary triangle, at the end of Commonwealth Ave. Opened in 1988, it cost $1.1 billion, took eight years to build and replaces the 'temporary' parliament house lower down the hill on King George Terrace, which served for 11 years longer than its intended 50-year life. The new Parliament was designed by the US-based Italian Romaldo Giurgola, who won a competition entered by more than 300 architects.

It's built into the top of the hill and the roof has been grassed over to preserve the shape of the original hilltop. The interior design and decoration is splendid. Seventy new Australian art and craft works were commissioned and a further 3000 were bought. A different combination of Australian timbers is used in each of its principal sections.

The building's main axis runs north-east to south-west, in a direct line from the old parliament, the War Memorial across the lake, and Mt Ainslie. On either side of this axis two high, granite-faced walls curve out from the centre to the corners of the site. The House of Representatives is to the east of these walls, the Senate to the west. They're linked to the centre by covered walkways.

Extensive areas of Parliament House are open to the public from 9 am to 5 pm daily. You enter through the white marble Great Verandah at the north-eastern end of the main axis, where Nelson Tjakamarra's *Meeting Place* mosaic, within the pool, represents a gathering of Aboriginal tribes. Inside, the grey-green marble columns of the foyer symbolise a forest, while marquetry panels on the walls depict Australian flora. From the 1st floor you look down on the Reception Hall, with its 20-metre-long Arthur Boyd tapestry. A public gallery above the Reception Hall has a 16-metre-long embroidery, created by 1000 people.

Beyond the Reception Hall you reach the gallery above the Members' Hall, the central 'crossroads' of the building, with the flag mast above it and passages to the debating chambers on each side. One of only four known originals of the Magna Carta is on display here. South of the Members' Hall are the committee rooms and ministers' offices. The public can view the committee rooms and attend some of their proceedings.

Other visitor facilities include a cafeteria, a terrace with views over the city, and a small theatre telling the story of Australian democracy. You can also wander over the grassy top of the building. If you want to make sure of a place in the House of Representatives gallery, book by phone (☎ 277 4890) or write to the Principal Attendant, House of Representatives, Parliament House, Canberra. Some seats are left unbooked but on sitting days you'd have to queue early to get one. Seats in the Senate gallery are almost always available.

On nonsitting days there are free guided tours every half-hour; on sitting days there's a talk on the building in the Great Hall Gallery every half-hour. For $3 ($5 for two people) you can hire a cassette (seven languages available) and player for a self-guided tour.

Bus Nos 901, 234 and 352 run from the city to Parliament House.

Old Parliament House

Situated on King George Terrace, halfway between the new Parliament House and the lake, this building was the seat of government from 1927 to 1988. Its parliamentary days ended in style: as the corridors of power echoed to the Defence Minister's favourite Rolling Stones records, the Prime Minister and Leader of the Opposition sang together arm in arm, and bodies were seen dragging themselves away well after dawn the next morning – and that's just what got into print! There are tours of the building and regular exhibitions in the old parliamentary library.

Old Parliament House is now home to the **National Portrait Gallery** (☎ 273 5130). The gallery is open daily from 9am to 4pm, and it includes displays of the National Museum and the Australia Archives. The admission charge (adults $2, children $1 and families $5) covers all the exhibits.

National Gallery of Australia

At the bottom of the parliamentary triangle, on Parkes Place, beside the High Court and Lake Burley Griffin, is the excellent art gallery, which opened in 1982. The Australian collection ranges from traditional Aboriginal art through to 20th-century works by Arthur Boyd, Sidney Nolan and Albert Tucker. Aboriginal works include bark paintings from Arnhem Land, *pukumani* burial poles from the Tiwi people of Melville and Bathurst islands off Darwin, printed fabrics by the women of Utopia and Ernabella in central Australia, and paintings from Yuendumu, also in central Australia. There are often temporary exhibitions from the Kimberley and other areas where Aboriginal art is flourishing.

In addition to works from the early decades of European settlement and the 19th-century romantics, there are examples of the early nationalistic statements of Charles Conder, Arthur Streeton and Tom Roberts. The collection is not confined to paintings: sculptures, prints, drawings, photographs, furniture, ceramics, fashion, textiles and silverware are all on display. The Sculpture Garden has a variety of striking sculptures.

The gallery is open from 10 am to 5 pm daily and there are tours at 11 am and 2 pm. Admission is $3, or free if you have a student card. There are two restaurants at the gallery. Free lectures are given on Tuesday, Wednesday and Thursday at 12.45 pm. On the last Thursday night of each month there's a free session beginning with a guided tour, followed by informal discussion groups, a film and then a guest lecture. Phone the gallery for details (☎ 271 2502).

High Court

The High Court building, by the lake next to the National Gallery, is open daily from 10 am to 4 pm. Opened in 1980, its grandiose magnificence caused it to be dubbed 'Gar's Mahal', a reference to Sir Garfield Barwick, Chief Justice during the building's construction. To tell the truth, there is a touch of Indian Moghul palace about the ornamental watercourse burbling alongside the entrance path to this grand building.

Questacon – National Science & Technology Centre

This is a 'hands on' science museum in the snappy white building between the High Court and the National Library. It's open daily from 10 am to 5 pm and entry is $6 ($3 students). There are 200 'devices' in the centre's five galleries and outdoor areas where you can use 'props' to get a feeling for a scientific concept, and then see its application to an everyday situation. It might be educational but it's also great fun.

National Library

Also on Parkes Place, beside the lake, is the

National Library, one of the most elegant buildings in Canberra. It has more than 4½ million books, and displays include rare books, paintings, early manuscripts and maps, a cannon from Cook's ship the *Endeavour*, a fine model of the ship itself and special exhibitions. The library is open from 9 am to 9 pm Monday to Thursday, 9 am to 4.45 pm Friday and Saturday, and 1.30 to 4.45 pm on Sunday. There are guided tours (☎ 269 1699) and free films at lunch time on Tuesday and on Thursday night – phone for programs (☎ 262 1475). There's also a restaurant and a cafe.

Royal Australian Mint

The Mint, on Denison St, Deakin, south of the lake, produces all Australia's coins. Through plate-glass windows (to keep you at arm's length from the cash) you can see the whole process, from raw materials to finished coins. There's a collection of rare coins in the foyer. The Mint is open from 9 am to 4 pm on weekdays and 10 am to 3 pm on weekends (free). Bus Nos 230 and 231 run past on weekdays; on weekends take No 267.

Australian War Memorial

The massive war memorial, north of the lake and at the foot of Mt Ainslie, looks directly along Anzac Parade to the old parliament house across the lake. It was conceived in 1925 and finally opened in 1941. It houses an amazing collection of pictures, dioramas, relics and exhibitions. For the less military-minded, the memorial has an excellent art collection. The Hall of Memory is the focus of the memorial and in 1993 the body of the Unknown Australian Soldier was brought from a WW I battlefield and entombed here.

The memorial is open from 10 am to 5 pm daily and admission is free. Several free tours are held each day, some focusing on the artworks. Phone ☎ 243 4211 for times. Bus Nos 901 and 302 run from the city; No 303 runs nearby.

Several conflicts and campaigns also have memorials along Anzac Parade.

Australian National University

The ANU's attractive grounds take up most of the area between Civic and Black Mountain and are very pleasant to wander through. There's an information centre (☎ 249 0794) on Balmain Crescent open on weekdays. The University Union on University Ave offers a variety of cheap eats and entertainment. On the corner of Kingsley St and Barry Drive is the Drill Hall Gallery, an offshoot of the National Gallery with changing exhibitions of contemporary art. It's open from noon to 5 pm Wednesday to Sunday. Admission is free.

National Film & Sound Archive

The archive is on McCoy Circuit, at the eastern edge of the university area, and is open from 9.30 am to 4 pm daily. Admission is free. Interesting exhibitions from the archive's collections are shown. Over the road is the Australian Academy of Science (not open to the public), known locally as the Martian Embassy – it looks like a misplaced flying saucer.

National Botanic Gardens

On the lower slopes of Black Mountain, behind the ANU, the beautiful 50-hectare botanic gardens are devoted to Australian flora. There are educational walks, including one amongst plants used by Aborigines. The eucalypt lawn has 600 species of this ubiquitous Australian tree. Another highlight is the rainforest area, achieved in this dry climate by a 'misting' system.

The gardens are reached from Clunies Ross St (take bus No 904) and are open from 9 am to 5 pm daily. Guided tours are held at 11 am on Wednesday, Friday and Sunday, with a 2 pm tour on Saturday and Sunday. The information centre has an introductory video about the gardens and there's a cafe.

National Museum of Australia

A site for the long-awaited museum might have finally been found on Acton peninsula, west of the Commonwealth Ave Bridge. Meanwhile, the visitor centre (☎ 256 1126) on Lady Denman Drive in Yarralumla is open from 10 am to 4 pm weekdays and from 1 to 4 pm weekends and displays items from the museum's collection.

Australian Institute of Sport
Founded in 1981 as part of an effort to improve Australia's performance at events like the Olympics, the AIS is on Leverrier Crescent, in the northern suburb of Bruce. It provides training facilities for the country's top sportspeople, who lead hour-long tours of the institute ($2) daily at 2 pm. The public can use the tennis courts and swimming pools; phone ☎ 252 1257 for times. Bus No 431 runs to the AIS from the city centre.

National Aquarium
On Lady Denman Drive near Scrivener Dam, the western end of the lake, the impressive aquarium (☎ 287 1211) also includes a wildlife sanctuary. It's open daily from 9 am to 5.30 pm and admission is $10 ($5 students).

Other Attractions
You can do no more than drive by and peek in the gates of the Prime Minister's official Canberra residence, **The Lodge**, on Adelaide Ave, Deakin – Australia's 10 Downing St. The same is true of **Government House**, the residence of the Governor-General, which is on the south-western corner of Lake Burley Griffin, but there's a lookout beside Scrivener Dam at the end of the lake, giving a good view of the building. The Governor-General is the representative of the Australian monarch – who lives in London and also happens to be the British monarch.

At the eastern end of Kings Ave the **Australian-American Memorial**, a 79-metre-high pillar topped by an eagle, is a memorial to US support of Australia during WW II.

The **Church of St John the Baptist**, in Reid, just east of Civic, was built between 1841 and 1845. The stained-glass windows show pioneering families of the region. There is an adjoining schoolhouse with some early relics, open on Wednesday morning and on weekend afternoons. The **Serbian**

Orthodox Church in Forrest is decorated with biblical murals.

The **Royal Military College, Duntroon**, was once a homestead, with parts dating from the 1830s. Tours of the grounds start at the sign in Starkey Park, Jubilee Ave, at 2.30 pm on weekdays (except public holidays), February to November.

The enterprising **Tradesmen's Union Club** in Badham St, Dickson, off Antill St, has a large collection of 'old and unusual bicycles'. The club also runs the Downer Club nearby on Hawdon St, home to 'the world's largest beer collection'. If that doesn't grab you, there's also an Antarctic igloo on display. Still not interested? Well, what about an observatory with an astronomer on duty nightly from nightfall (or 7 pm, whichever is later) until midnight. Admission to all this is free.

Bushwalking
Tidbinbilla Fauna Reserve has marked trails. For other places see the Around Canberra section. Contact the Canberra Bushwalking Club through the Environment Centre (☎ 247 3064) on Kingsley St in the city. Here you can buy *Above the Cotter*, which details walks and drives in the area. Graeme Barrow's *Twenty-five Family Bushwalks In & Around Canberra* is also useful. There are also some good rock-climbing areas.

Water Sports
Dobel Boat Hire (☎ 249 6861) at the Acton Park Ferry Terminal on the northern shore of Lake Burley Griffin rents canoes at $10 an hour and catamarans at $20, plus paddle boats and surf skis. Canoeing in the Murrumbidgee River is also popular.

It's 150 km to the nearest surf beaches at Batemans Bay in New South Wales – Murrays buses run down daily. Swimming pools around the city include the Olympic Pool on Allara St, Civic. Swimming in Lake Burley Griffin is not recommended.

River Runners (☎ 288 5610) has rafting on the Shoalhaven River, 1½ hours from Canberra, for about $110, less if you have your own transport.

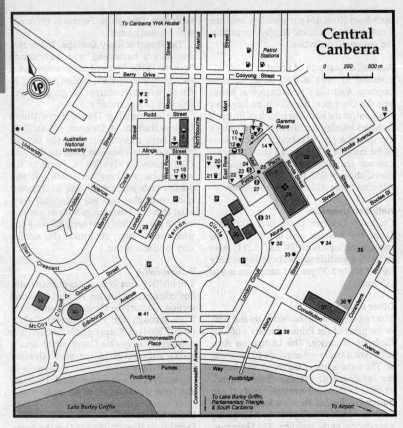

Central Canberra

0   250   500 m

Cycling
Canberra has a great series of bicycle tracks – probably the best in Australia. See Getting Around for more information.

Other Activities
Several places hire rollerblades, including Mr Spokes near the Acton Park Ferry Terminal and Canberra Blades Centre on Allara St in the city, opposite the Parkroyal Hotel. The latter doesn't rent helmets.

The New South Wales snowfields are within four hours drive of Canberra and the information centre has the latest news on conditions. There are plenty of equipment hire places. Deanes Buslines (☎ 299 3722) offers day-trip ski packages for around $60 for beginners, $70 for experienced skiers.

Organised Tours
The information centre has details of the many tours of the city and the ACT. Half-day city tours start at around $25. Canberra Cruises (☎ 295 3544) has cruises on Lake Burley Griffin from $10. Taking a flight might be a good way of seeing the grand scale of the city's plan. Several outfits offer flights, such as Aerial Adventure (☎ (006)

PLACES TO STAY		OTHER	
1	Downtown Speros Motel	3	Dalton's Bookshop
41	Lakeside Hotel	4	University Students Union
		5	Post Office
PLACES TO EAT		6	Jolimont Centre(Countrylink,
2	Fringe Benefits		Airlines & Bus Station)
7	Gus's	12	Travellers' Medical & Vaccination
8	Sammy's Kitchen & Asian Noodle		Centre
	House	13	Bus Interchange & Bus
9	Noshes, Wilderness Society		Information
	& Heaven	16	Commonwealth Government
10	Dorettes Bistro		Bookshop
11	Mama's Trattoria	18	Commonwealth Bank
14	Club Asmara & Red Sea	21	Moosehead's Bar
	Restaurant	24	ANZ Bank
15	Clarry's Restaurant & Gorman	25	Merry-go-round
	House Arts Centre	26	Supermarket
17	Zorba's Char-Grill & Charcoal	27	Westpac Bank
	Restaurant	28	Canberra Centre
19	Waffles Piano Bar & Private Bin		(Shopping Centre)
20	Thai Lotus & Canberra Vietnamese	29	Police Station
	Restaurant	30	Canberra Theatre Centre
22	Tosolini's, Australian Pizza Kitchen	31	Westpac Bank
	& Bailey's Corner	33	Electric Shadows Cinemas
23	Antigo Cafe	35	Glebe Park
32	Anarkali Restaurant	37	Casino
34	Capital Parkroyal	38	Swimming Pool
36	Glebe Park Food Hall	39	National Film & Sound Archives
		40	Academy of Science

247 4777) which charges from $35 (minimum two people).

Festivals
The Canberra Festival takes place over 10 days in March and celebrates the city's birthday with fun events, many held in Commonwealth Park. In September there's the Floriade, concentrating on Canberra's spectacular spring flowers but with many related events.

Places to Stay
Camping Canberra Motor Village (☎ 247 5466), three km north-west of the centre on Kunzea St, O'Connor, has a bush setting and charges $18 for sites, $39 a double for on-site vans and from $60 a double in cabins. There's a restaurant, kitchen, tennis court and swimming pool.

The Canberra Carotel (☎ 241 1377) off the Federal Highway in Watson, six km north of the centre, has sites from $10, on-site vans

from $40 for four people, and more expensive motel-style cabins. The Southside Motor Park (☎ 280 6176) is eight km south of the city in Fyshwick, on the main road to Queanbeyan, and for two people charges $12 for a site, from $35 for an on-site van and from $45 for cabins.

Hostels 'The best YHA I've ever seen' is how one traveller described the Canberra YHA Hostel (☎ 248 9155). It's purpose-built and well designed and equipped. There is a travel desk (☎ 248 0177) at the hostel which handles domestic and international travel. Nightly charges are $15, plus $3 if you need a sleeping sheet, and there are twin rooms with attached bathrooms for $20 a person, or $18 with shared bathroom. (Add $5 if you aren't a YHA member.) The office is open from 7 am to 10.30 pm but you can check in up until midnight if you give advance warning. The hostel is on Dryandra St, O'Connor, about six km north-west of Civic.

Bus No 380 runs from the city twice an hour on weekdays and hourly on weekends to the Scrivener St stop on Miller St, O'Connor. From there, follow the signs. From the Greyhound Pioneer terminal on Northbourne Ave take bus No 381 to the corner of Scrivener and Brigalow Sts, head north-east up Scrivener St to Dryandra St and turn right. Driving, turn west off Northbourne Ave onto Macarthur Ave and after about two km turn right onto Dryandra. You can hire bicycles at the hostel.

On the other side of town in Manuka, a couple of km from Parliament House, the *Kingston Hotel* (☎ 295 0123) on the corner of Canberra Ave and Giles St offers shared accommodation for $12 per person with non-compulsory linen hire at $4. There are cooking facilities and counter meals are available. Bus No 352 from the city runs past. The Kingston is a large and popular pub.

Guesthouses & Private Hotels *Victor Lodge* (☎ 295 7777) is a clean and friendly place at 29 Dawes St, Kingston, half a km from the railway station and a couple of km south-east of Parliament House. Rooms with shared bathrooms are $35/40 a single/double or you can share a twin room for $19 or a four-bunk room for $15, including a light breakfast. Several travellers have reported enjoying their stay here. To get here from the city take bus No 352 to the nearby Kingston shops, or phone and see if they can pick you up. They also rent bikes here.

Also south of the lake, the *Macquarie Private Hotel* (☎ 273 2325) on National Circuit at the corner of Bourke St has 500 rooms. Singles/doubles are $35/60 or $112/167 per week, including a cooked breakfast. All rooms share bathrooms. Bus No 350 from the city stops at the front door.

Entering Canberra from the north, there's a cluster of guesthouses on the east side of Northbourne Ave in Downer, just south of the junction of the Barton Highway from Yass and the Federal Highway from Goulburn. All are clean and straightforward. It's four km or so into town, but buses run

past, and Dickson shopping centre is not far away. At No 524 *Blue & White Lodge* (☎ 248 0498), which also runs *Blue Sky* at No 528, has shared rooms from $24 a person and singles between $36 and $40. Prices include cooked breakfast and all rooms have TV and a fridge but most bathrooms are shared. Rooms with attached bathrooms go for $60 a single or double. They can probably pick you up from the bus station. *Chelsea Lodge* (☎ 248 0655) at No 526 also does pick-ups and charges $38/48 a single/double including cooked breakfast, or $48/58 with private bathroom. *Northbourne Lodge* (☎ 257 2599) at No 522 is similar.

Motels Most motels are expensive and few resemble those seen elsewhere in Australia; many are ex-government guesthouses. The *Acacia Motor Lodge* (☎ 249 6955) at 65 Ainslie Ave charges from $65/70 including light breakfast, and is only half a km from the centre of Civic. *Downtown Speros* (☎ 249 1388), at 82 Northbourne Ave, and *Kythera* (☎ 248 7611), nearby at No 98, charge about the same. Other places are scattered through the suburbs, with a concentration of mid-range motels about eight km south of the city in Narrabundah, most on Jerrabomberra Ave.

Top-end places to stay include *Olim's Canberra Hotel* (☎ 248 5511) at the corner of Ainslie and Limestone Aves in Braddon. Rooms cost from $95 a single or double and it's a pleasant old place.

Colleges The ANU, just west of Civic, has a selection of colleges which may have empty rooms during the Easter (one week), June/July, September (two weeks) and late-November to late-February vacations. The uni campus is a very pleasant place to stay. Try *Toad Hall* (☎ 267 4999), $15 per night, $90 per week; *Ursula College* (☎ 279 4300), students/nonstudents $35/45 per night, $210/270 per week, including breakfast and with other meals available; or *Burgmann College* (☎ 267 5222), students/nonstudents $30/40 with breakfast or $38/48 full board.

Places to Eat

Canberra's eating scene has improved out of sight over the past few years. Most places are around Civic, with an up-market selection in Manuka and other possibilities scattered around the suburbs.

City Centre There's a small food hall in the lower section of the Canberra Centre. Main courses are in the $6.50 range. There's another food hall in Glebe Park, behind the Casino/Convention Centre.

One of the best places to eat is the *Thai Lotus* in the Sydney Building on East Row. It's open nightly for dinner, and for lunch from Tuesday to Friday. Prices are reasonable, mostly around $10 to $13. Also excellent is *Fringe Benefits*, a brasserie at 54 Marcus Clark St, with main courses around $18.

On East Row near Thai Lotus, the *Canberra Vietnamese Restaurant* has main courses for less than $10.

Bailey's Corner, at the south end of East Row on the corner of London Circuit, has a couple of places with outdoor tables. *Tosolini's* is an Italian-based bistro, good for a drink or a meal, with lunch-time specials around $10 and an evening menu with main courses under $14. It also opens for breakfast. Downstairs the *Australian Pizza Kitchen* is cheaper and has wood-fired ovens. Around the corner in Petrie Plaza, *Antigo* is a cafe and bar open daily until late. The menu is interesting and main courses are around $10.

Waffles Piano Bar, on the Northbourne Ave side of the Sydney Building, offers food of the steak, pasta, burger, pizza variety at around $10 for a main meal. Around the corner on Alinga St is *Waffles Patisserie & Bakery*, and a few doors east is the *Pancake Parlour*, open late every day and 24 hours from Thursday to Sunday. It has pancakes from $5 at lunch time on weekdays.

On the southern end of the Melbourne Building, *Zorba's Char-Grill* and *Charcoal Restaurant* are side-by-side competitors offering steaks and seafood. Zorba's is slightly cheaper, with steaks around $18. In

the Wales Centre, on the corner of London Circuit and Akuna St, the *Anarkali* Pakistani restaurant has lunch specials (around $12) on weekdays and is open for dinner as well.

The *Capital Parkroyal* on Binara St has several restaurants and an all-you-can-eat buffet for $22 at breakfast, lunch and dinner.

Garema Place is full of restaurants and cafes. *Happy's* is a reasonably priced Chinese restaurant with lunch-time specials. Upstairs is the long-running *Dorettes Bistro* with main courses around $15 and good jazz or folk most nights. Nearby *Mama's Trattoria* does home-made pasta for about $9 and other meals for about $12.

Around the corner on Bunda St *Gus's* has outdoor tables and serves cafe food, with soup about $4 and pasta and goulash around $7.50. It is open until midnight and later on weekends. Not far away, *Sammy's Kitchen* is a Chinese and Malaysian place with a good reputation and many dishes between $7 and $9; the nearby *Asian Noodle House* has many dishes under $7. *Ali Baba*, on the corner of Bunda St and Garema Place's southern arm, does Lebanese takeaways, with shwarmas and felafels for around $4 and meals around $9.

The *Red Sea Restaurant* at Club Asmara on Bunda St has some African dishes, from $12 to $16. The fruit shop just south of Club Asmara has takeaway fruit salads, fresh juices and healthy sandwiches.

Manuka South of the lake, not far from Capital Hill, is the Manuka shopping centre which services the diplomatic corps and well-heeled bureaucrats from surrounding neighbourhoods. There's a cinema centre here and several bars and cafes which stay open late, such as *Metropole* on the corner of Furneaux and Franklin Sts, and the stylish *La Grange* bar and brasserie further south on Franklin St, which has main courses between $10 and $16.

Across Franklin St is *My Cafe* with a bagel-based menu and main courses between $6 and $9. Upstairs in nearby Style Arcade, *Alanya* is a good Turkish restaurant with main courses between $10 and $15. Also up here is *Chez Daniel*, one of Canberra's better restaurants, with main courses around $20. *Timmy's Kitchen* on Furneaux St is a very popular Malaysian/Chinese place with main courses under $10 and many under $8. There are plenty of other cafes and restaurants.

Elsewhere *Clarry's*, at the back of the Gorman House Arts Centre on Ainslie Ave, a few minutes walk from Civic, is a good cafe open Monday to Saturday for lunch and Thursday to Saturday for dinner, with main courses from $8.

In Lyneham at 96 Wattle St is well-known *Tilley's*, a cafe, bar and art gallery. The food is healthy (if you don't count the great cakes) and the clientele diverse. There is often entertainment here. The *Parakeet Cafe* at Wakefield Gardens (the Ainslie shopping centre) has good vegetarian food and a good atmosphere. The menu changes regularly but main courses are always $12, salads start at $7 and desserts are $4. They also have great pizzas. It's open for dinner from Tuesday to Sunday and for lunch on weekdays; closed Monday. The Malaysian *Rasa Sayang*, at 43 Woolley St in Dickson, is quite good and reasonably priced. There are also other inexpensive Asian places in Dickson.

Cheap food can be found at the student union *Refectory* at the ANU.

Entertainment

Canberra is more lively than its reputation suggests. For one thing, liberal licensing laws allow hotels unlimited opening hours and there are some 24-hour bars. The *Good Times* section in the Thursday *Canberra Times* has full entertainment listings and the free, monthly *BMA* magazine lists bands and other events.

The new *casino* on Constitution Ave is open from 10 am on Friday all the way through to 4 am on Monday, and from 10 am to 4 am for the rest of the week. It regards itself as 'stylishly elegant yet friendly' – ie, punters wearing casual clothes such as denim, T-shirts or sports shoes don't make it through the door. Men have to wear a jacket and tie after 7 pm.

If you're tired of Oz club culture, phone one of the clubs catering to Australians of foreign descent to see if visitors are welcome – see the Yellow Pages under 'Clubs, Social'.

The *Canberra Theatre Centre*, on Civic Square, has several theatres with a varied range of events. Also check with the foreign cultural organisations like Maison de France and the Goethe Institute German Cultural Centre to find out what's on. *Gorman House Arts Centre* on Ainslie Ave, Braddon, sometimes has theatre or dance performances or exhibitions. An interesting market is held here on weekends. The *Brickworks Market*, held on weekends between 11 am and 5 pm on Denman St in Yarralumla, has antiques, junk and everything in between.

Dancing & Drinking There's live music two or three nights a week during term at the *ANU union bar*, a good place for a drink even when there's no entertainment. Big touring acts often play the *Refectory* here.

In Civic, *Moosehead's Bar* on the south side of the Sydney Building is popular. Around the corner on Northbourne Ave, the *Private Bin* is a big place popular with younger dancers. Not far away, *Pandora's*, on the corner of Alinga and Mort Sts, has a bar downstairs and a dance club upstairs. *Asylum*, upstairs at 23 East Row (near London Circuit), has live music most nights and mainly features young bands. Entry costs between $3 and $8, depending on who's playing. The *Terrace Bar*, near the Electric Shadows cinemas on Akuna St, has bands several nights a week.

Heaven, on Garema Place, is a venue popular with gays. Nearby, upstairs from Happy's restaurant, *Dorettes Bistro* is a relaxed and pleasant wine bar with live acoustic music; you can have a meal or just a drink. There's music every night, with a cover charge from Thursday to Saturday. *Club Asmara*, at 128 Bunda St near Garema Place, is home to the fairly pricey Red Sea restaurant, but if you turn up after about 9 pm you can listen to the music, sometimes live, without ordering a meal. There's a $4 cover charge on Friday and Saturday.

Olim's Canberra Hotel, on the corner of Ainslie and Limestone Aves in Braddon, has a piano/jazz bar and a popular beer garden. *Tilley's* in Lyneham often has live music, usually a cut above pub bands, on Friday, Saturday and Sunday nights. The *Southern Cross Club* in Woden sometimes has good jazz. *Bobby McGee's*, at the Lakeside Hotel south-west of Vernon Circle, is a popular dining/drinking/dancing complex.

Other places that sometimes have bands include the *Canberra Workers' Club*, on Childers St, and the *Canberra Labor Club*, on Chandler St, Belconnen. The *Southern Cross Club* in Phillip has local bands on Friday night.

Cinemas There are several cinemas in the Civic Square and London Circuit area. The *Boulevard Twin Cinemas*, on Akuna St, are collectively known as Electric Shadows and show repertory type films.

The *National Library* shows free films at lunch time on Tuesday and on Thursday evenings – phone for details (☎ 262 1475). The *National Gallery* has concerts and films on Saturday and Sunday afternoons at around 2.30 pm.

Getting There & Away
Air Canberra is not an international airport (yet). Sydney is normally just half an hour away; the standard fare with the two major airlines is $138; Melbourne is about an hour away and costs $193. Direct flights to Adelaide cost $309 and to Brisbane it's $281. There are always advance purchase tickets and other special offers available which are considerably cheaper. Ansett offers a night flight to Sydney for $59. You can't fly *from* Sydney with this deal (except back to Canberra on a return ticket for $118). Qantas (☎ toll-free 13 1313) and Ansett (☎ toll-free 13 1300) are both in the Jolimont Centre on Northbourne Ave.

Fares on Eastern Australia and Ansett Express are the same as those on the main carriers, although they fly more frequently. Other smaller airlines fly to New South Wales country destinations.

Bus Most bus lines have booking offices and their main stop at the Jolimont Centre. The Greyhound Pioneer (☎ toll-free 13 2030) terminal is on the corner of Northbourne Ave and Ipima Ave, a few blocks north of the centre, and there's a booking office in the Jolimont Centre. They have the most frequent Sydney service ($28) including one direct from Sydney Airport ($32). It takes four to five hours. They also run to Adelaide (about $99), Melbourne ($52), Cooma ($14) and the New South Wales snowfields ($32, including park entry fees). Services are frequent in winter, less so at other times. Deanes Buslines (☎ 299 3722) has day-trip ski packages.

Murrays (☎ 295 3611) has daily express (under four hours) buses to Sydney for $28 or around $20 if you pay in advance. The service also runs to Batemans Bay ($21.75) and connects with buses running up to Nowra ($39).

Transborder Express (☎ 226 1378) runs to Yass ($8). Capital Coachlines (book through Greyhound Pioneer) runs to Bathurst ($36), Orange ($36) and Dubbo ($50) as does Rendell's (☎ toll-free 1800 023 328). Sid Fogg's (☎ toll-free 1800 045 952) runs to Newcastle ($43) four times a week, or daily in school holidays.

The Countrylink Travel Centre (☎ 13 2232) is in the Jolimont Centre. Countrylink buses run to Sydney three times a day and cost $35. There's a daily service to Adelaide via Albury which involves two buses and a train and costs about $90; it's quicker and no more expensive to go by bus via Melbourne.

Train The railway station (☎ 239 0133) is south of the lake on Wentworth Ave in Kingston. To Sydney there are two trains daily, taking about 4½ hours and costing $35/48 in economy/1st class.

There is no direct train to Melbourne. The daily V/Line Canberra Link service involves a train between Melbourne and Wodonga and a connecting bus to Canberra. This costs $45 in economy and takes about 10 hours. A longer but much more interesting train/bus service to Melbourne is the V/Line Capital

Link which runs via Cooma and the forests of Victoria's East Gippsland then down the Princes Highway to Sale where you catch a train. This takes over 11 hours and costs $45.

Car Rental Avis (☎ 249 6088), Hertz (☎ 257 4877), Budget (☎ toll-free 13 2727) and Thrifty (☎ 247 7422) have offices at the airport and in town. Cheaper outfits include Rumbles (☎ 280 7444), at the corner of Kembla and Wollongong Sts in Fyshwick, and Rent a Dent (☎ 257 5947) – a few minutes walk from the Greyhound Pioneer depot, or phone to be picked up from the Jolimont Centre. Expect to pay $35 to $40 a day with 100 free km, and better deals are available on longer rentals.

Getting Around
To/From the Airport The airport is seven km from the city centre. Note all the government cars lined up outside waiting to pick up 'pollies' and public servants. Hertz, Budget, Avis and Thrifty have airport car rental desks.

The airport bus service is run by ACT Mini Buses (☎ 295 6999) which charges $4.50 and picks up from the Jolimont Centre, various hotels and the youth hostel. You have to book. The taxi fare from Civic is around $9.

Bus Action (Australian Capital Territory Internal Omnibus Network!) buses run fairly frequently. Phone (☎ 207 7611) for information from 7 am to 11 pm Monday to Saturday and from 8.30 am to 6 pm Sunday. The main interchange is on the corner of Alinga St and East Row in Civic, not far from the Jolimont Centre. The information kiosk here is open daily until about 11 pm. If you plan to use a lot of buses it's worth spending $2 on *The Bus Book*.

The flat 'one route' fare is $2 and you need the exact change. Some express buses (700 series) cost twice the normal fare. You can save money with advance purchase tickets, available from newsagents and elsewhere. Fare Go tickets cost $10.60 for 10 and a weekly ticket is $18. Daily tickets are great value as they offer unlimited travel for $4.80.

Special Services The free Downtowner service is a bus disguised as a tram which runs around the Civic shopping centre, stopping at specially designated stops.

Sightseeing Bus No 901 runs to the War Memorial, Regatta Point, Questacon, the National Gallery, Parliament House and several embassies in Yarralumla; No 904 goes to the Botanic Gardens, the aquarium and Black Mountain. Both services depart hourly from the city interchange, No 901 between 9 am and 3 pm and No 904 between 10.25 am and 3.25 pm. You'll need a day ticket ($4.80) to ride these services.

Murrays' Canberra Explorer (☎ 295 3611) runs a 25-km route around 19 points of interest and you can get on and off wherever you like. It departs hourly from the Jolimont Centre between 10.15 am and 4.15 pm daily, and tickets ($15, $8 children) are sold on the bus. If you just want to make one circuit without getting off (a good way to orient yourself) buy a one-hour tour ticket ($7, children $5).

Taxi Call Aerial Taxis (☎ 285 9222).

Bicycle Canberra is a cyclist's paradise, with bike paths making it possible to ride around the city hardly touching a road. One popular track is a circuit of the lake; there are also peaceful stretches of bushland along some suburban routes. Get a copy of the *Canberra Cycleways* map from bookshops or the information centre ($2.50).

Mr Spokes Bike Hire (☎ 257 1188), near the Acton Park Ferry Terminal, charges $6 an hour or $20 a day, plus $1 for a helmet. The rates are similar at Glebe Park, on Coranderrk St, a few blocks west of Vernon Circle. Another company is Dial a Bicycle (☎ 286 5463) which hires 10-speed mountain bikes for $20 a day, or $60 for a week, including helmet; the firm also delivers the bikes.

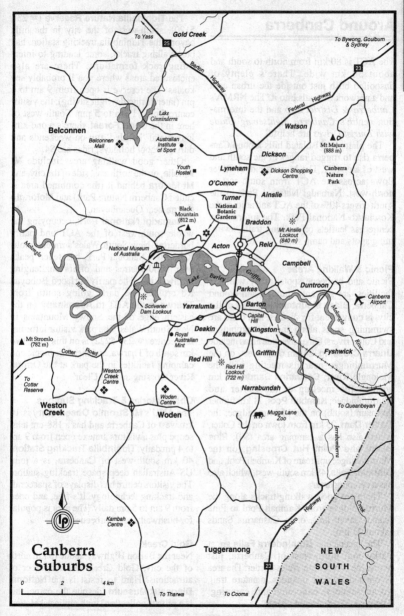

To Yass

Gold Creek

To Bywong, Goulburn
& Sydney

25

Barton Highway

23

Federal Highway

Lake Ginninderra

Belconnen

Belconnen Mall

Australian Institute of Sport

Watson

Mt Majura (888 m)

Dickson

Youth Hostel

Lyneham

Dickson Shopping Centre

Canberra Nature Park

O'Connor

Turner

Ainslie

Black Mountain (812 m)

National Botanic Gardens

Braddon

Mt Ainslie Lookout (840 m)

National Museum of Australia

Molonglo River

Acton

Reid

Campbell

Lake Burley Griffin

Parkes

Duntroon

Canberra Airport

Scrivener Dam Lookout

Yarralumia

Barton

Capital Hill

Molonglo River

Mt Stromlo (782 m)

Cotter Road

Deakin

Manuka

Kingston

Fyshwick

Royal Australian Mint

Red Hill

Griffith

To Cotter Reserve

Weston Creek Centre

Red Hill Lookout (722 m)

Narrabundah

Woden Centre

Weston Creek

Woden

Mugga Lane Zoo

To Queanbeyan

Jerrabomberra

Kambah Centre

Monaro Highway

Canberra Suburbs

0   2   4 km

Tuggeranong

NEW SOUTH WALES

23

To Tharwa

To Cooma

Around Canberra

The ACT is 80 km from north to south and about 30 km wide. There's plenty of unspoiled bush just outside the urban area and a network of roads into it. The NRMA's *Canberra & District* map and the information centre's *Canberra Sightseeing Guide with Tourist Drives* are helpful.

The plains and isolated hills around Canberra rise to rugged ranges in the south and west of the ACT. The Murrumbidgee River flows across the ACT from south-east to north-west. Namadgi National Park in the south covers 40% of the ACT and adjoins the Kosciusko National Park. The information centre has leaflets on walking trails, swimming spots and camp sites.

Picnic & Walking Areas

Picnic and barbecue spots, many with gas facilities, are scattered through and around Canberra. **Black Mountain**, just west of the city, is convenient for picnics, and there are swimming spots along the Murrumbidgee and Cotter rivers. Other riverside areas include **Uriarra Crossing**, 24 km north-west, on the Murrumbidgee near its meeting with the Molonglo River; **Casuarina Sands**, 19 km west at the meeting of the Cotter and Murrumbidgee; **Kambah Pool**, 21 km further upstream (south) on the Murrumbidgee; the **Cotter Dam**, 23 km from town on the Cotter, which also has a camping area ($9); **Pine Island** and **Point Hut Crossing**, on the Murrumbidgee upstream of Kambah Pool; and **Gibraltar Falls**, 48 km south-west, which also has a camping area.

There are good walking tracks along the Murrumbidgee from Kambah Pool to Pine Island (seven km), or to Casuarina Sands (about 21 km).

The spectacular **Ginninderra Falls** are at Parkwood, north-west of Canberra, just across the New South Wales border. The area is open daily and includes a nature trail, gorge scenery, canoeing and camping. There's a $3 admission charge.

The **Tidbinbilla Nature Reserve** (☎ 237 5120), south-west of the city in the hills beyond the Tidbinbilla tracking station, has bushwalking tracks, some leading to interesting rock formations. There are also enclosured areas where you'll probably see koalas. The reserve is open from 9 am to 6 pm (later during daylight saving); the visitor centre from 11 am to 5 pm. South-west of here in the **Corin Forest**, there's a one-km-long metal 'bobsled' run on weekends and during school holidays; rides are $4.

Other good walking areas include **Mt Ainslie**, on the north-east side of the city, and **Mt Majura** behind it (the combined area is called Canberra Nature Park) and **Molonglo Gorge** near Queanbeyan.

Namadgi National Park, occupying the whole south-west of the ACT and partly bordering New South Wales's mountainous Kosciusko National Park, has seven peaks over 1600 metres and offers challenging bushwalking. The partly surfaced Boboyan Rd crosses the park, going south from **Tharwa** in the ACT to **Adaminaby** on the eastern edge of the Snowy Mountains in New South Wales. The park visitor information centre (☎ 237 5222) is on this road, two km south of Tharwa, and there are picnic and camping facilities in the park at the Orroral River crossing and Mt Clear.

Observatories & Tracking Stations

The ANU's **Mt Stromlo Observatory** is 16 km west of Canberra and has a 188-cm telescope plus a visitors annexe open from 9 am to 4 pm daily. **Tidbinbilla Tracking Station**, 40 km south-west of Canberra, is a joint US-Australian deep-space tracking station. The visitors centre has displays of spacecraft and tracking technology. It's free, and open from 9 am to 5 pm daily. The area is popular for bushwalks and barbecues.

Gold Creek

Near the Barton Highway about 15 km north of the city, Gold Creek has a number of attractions. Hard to resist is the **National Dinosaur Museum** (despite the name, this is a private collection) with replica skeletons of 10 dinosaurs and many other bones and fossils. Admission is $7.50 ($5 children) and it's open daily from 10 am to 5 pm. **Ginninderra Village** has a collection of craft workshops and galleries. Next door is **Cockington Green**, a miniature replica of an English village, open daily; admission is $6.

Other Attractions
Mugga Lane Zoo, in Red Hill about seven km south of the city centre, has about 80 species of native and exotic animals and is open daily ($6.50). Bus No 352 runs nearby. **Rehwinkel's Animal Park** has native animals and is on Macks Reef Rd, off the Federal Highway, 24 km north of Canberra in New South Wales. It's open daily and admission is $6.

Bywong Mining Town, about 30 km north of Canberra, is a re-creation of a mining settlement. It's open daily between 10 am and 4 pm and there are tours at 11 am, and 1 and 3 pm. Entry is $7.

The beautifully restored **Lanyon Homestead** is about 20 km south of the city centre, on the Murrumbidgee River near Tharwa. The early stone cottage on the site was built by convicts and the grand homestead was completed in 1859. This National Trust homestead, which now documents the life of the region before Canberra existed, is open

from 10 am to 4 pm from Tuesday to Sunday. A major attraction is a gallery of Sidney Nolan paintings.

Cuppacumbalong, also near Tharwa, is another old homestead, now a craft studio and gallery, open from 11 am to 5 pm Wednesday to Sunday.

Day Trips
A popular drive is east into New South Wales, past Bungendore, to **Braidwood** (an hour or so) with its many antique shops, craft stores and restaurants. **Bungendore** has craft galleries such as the Bungendore Wood Works and some old buildings.

Another good route takes in **Tharwa**, situated in hilly grazing lands. From here the route goes north-west to **Gibraltar Falls** (good walking) and **Tidbinbilla Nature Reserve**. The Tidbinbilla Tracking Station is on the way back into town along a slow, winding, scenic road.

QUEANBEYAN (population 27,000)
Just across the New South Wales border east of Canberra is Queanbeyan, now virtually a suburb of the capital it predates. Until 1838 it was known as 'Queen Bean'. There's a history museum in the town and good lookouts on Jerrabomberra Hill five km west and Bungendore Hill four km east.

New South Wales

NEW SOUTH WALES

Area	802,000 sq km
Population	6,000,000

☎ From July 1995, Sydney's existing phone numbers which begin with 90 to 98 will be prefixed by an additional 9 (for example, ☎ 901 2345 becomes ☎ 9901 2345). From July 1996, all numbers in the metropolitan area will be prefixed by the additional digit 9. From 1998, in regional areas, the last two digits of the current area code will be added to the existing number (for example, ☎ (012) 123 456 becomes ☎ 1212 3456). The area code for the state will be (02). ■

New South Wales is the site of Captain Cook's original landing in Australia, the place where the first permanent settlement was established; and today it is the most populous state and has the country's largest city – Sydney. Of course the state is much more than Sydney with its Opera House and equally well-known harbour bridge – but Sydney is certainly a good place to start.

It was down at Sydney Cove, where the ferries run from today, that the first settlement was made in 1788, so it is not surprising that Sydney has an air of history which is missing from most Australian cities. That doesn't stop Sydney from being a far brasher and more lively-looking city than its younger rival, Melbourne. With a setting like Port Jackson (the harbour) to build around, it would be hard for Sydney to be unattractive.

Sydney has more than the central city going for it; Paddington is one of the most attractive inner-city residential areas in the world, and the Pacific shoreline is dotted with famous beaches like Bondi and Manly. Furthermore there are two good national parks marking the southern and northern boundaries of the city – Royal National Park and Ku-ring-gai Chase. Inland, it is a short drive to the Blue Mountains with some of the most spectacular scenery in Australia.

The Pacific Highway runs north and south from the capital, with great beaches, surf and scenery all along the coast. To the north,

Newcastle is the state's second city and a major industrial centre (but with fine beaches), and the nearby Hunter Valley is a premier wine-producing area. There are coastal resorts like Port Macquarie and Coffs Harbour, and close to the Queensland border is Byron Bay, one of the best travellers' stops on the whole east coast, with strong links to the counterculture that has taken root in the nearby hinterland. All the way up there are also long, empty, unspoiled stretches of coast, some protected as national parks, and spectacular ranges reaching up to the high plateau of the New England region.

South of Sydney and inland are the southern highlands with beautiful scenery and good bushwalks. There is plenty of unspoilt coastline on the way down to Victoria, plus Wollongong, the state's third city and another major industrial centre. In the south the Great Dividing Range climbs up into the heights of the Snowy Mountains, Australia's highest, with excellent summer bushwalking and winter skiing.

Further inland, the Great Dividing Range rolls down to the vast inland plains with their sweeping expanses of agricultural and grazing land, broken only by occasional ranges like the Warrumbungles, and finally dwindles into the harsh outback. There's some fascinating history in the old towns and settlements including, in the far west, the union-run mining town of Broken Hill.

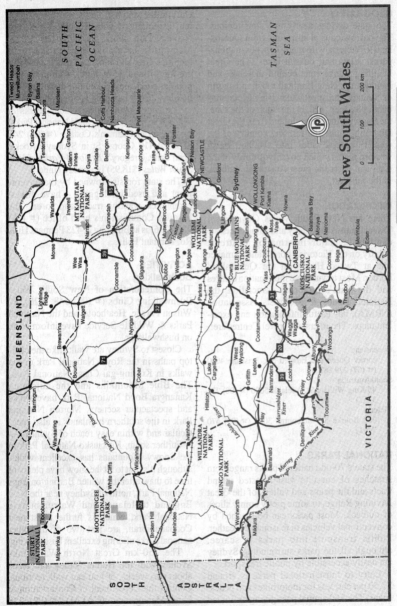

NEW SOUTH WALES

New South Wales

GEOGRAPHY

The state divides neatly into four regions. The narrow coastal strip runs from Queensland to Victoria with many beaches, national parks, inlets and coastal lakes. The Great Dividing Range runs behind the coast and includes the New England tablelands north of Sydney, the spectacular Blue Mountains behind Sydney, and, in the south of the state, the Snowy Mountains. Inland from the Great Dividing Range the farming country of the western slopes fades into the hot, harsh western plains which cover two-thirds of the state and enter the great Australian outback in the far west.

INFORMATION

There are New South Wales Government Travel Centres in Sydney and some interstate capitals, a major information centre at Albury on the Victorian border and a smaller one at Tweed Heads on the Queensland border. Most towns have information centres and the state's motoring association, the National Roads & Motorists Association (NRMA), has useful information and excellent maps. The interstate Travel Centres are:

Queensland
   corner Queen and Edward Sts, Brisbane 4000
   (☎ (07) 229 8833)
South Australia
   45 King William St, Adelaide 5000 (☎ (08) 231
   3167)
Victoria
   388 Bourke St, Melbourne 3000 (☎ (03) 670
   7461)

NATIONAL PARKS

The state's 70-odd national parks range from stretches of coast to vast forested inland tracts and the peaks and valleys of the Great Dividing Range, to some pretty empty slices of outback. Most parks can be reached by conventional vehicles in reasonable weather. Public transport into parks is scarce, although all the parks surrounding Sydney are easily accessible by public transport.

Entry to most national parks is around $7.50 per car, less for motorbikes and pedestrians. The $60 annual pass giving unlimited entry to the state's parks is worth considering, especially if you visit Mt Kosciusko National Park, where the daily fee is $12. Many parks have drive-in camp sites with facilities like showers and toilets, usually costing around $5 a night. Camp sites at popular parks are booked out during school holidays. Bush camping is often allowed.

The New South Wales National Parks & Wildlife Service (usually called National Parks) has a shop in Cadman's Cottage (☎ (02) 247 8861) at 110 George St in Sydney's Rocks, open daily. Gregory's *National Parks of New South Wales* ($18.95) is a handy guide.

The state forests – owned by the government and used for logging – have drives, camp sites, walking tracks and so on. The Forestry Commission's head office (☎ (02) 980 4296) is at Building 2, 423 Pennant Hills Rd, Pennant Hills.

ACTIVITIES
Bushwalking

The Confederation of New South Wales Bushwalking Clubs (☎ (02) 548 1228), 82 Wilson Parade, Heathcote, and the National Parks & Wildlife Service have information on bushwalking.

Closest to Sydney are walks like the clifftop paths in the Royal National Park or the walks in Ku-ring-gai Chase National Park. The Blue Mountains and the adjoining Kanangra Boyd National Park have walks and spectacular scenery. Morton National Park in the southern highlands is also spectacular and within easy reach of Sydney.

Further south, Kosciusko National Park in the Snowy Mountains has excellent walks, although it's best to let the snow have plenty of time to thaw after the winter. Barrington Tops National Park, north of Sydney near the New England tableland, and Warrumbungle National Park, which is further west near Coonabarabran, are just two of the other national parks offering excellent bushwalking.

The 250-km Great North Walk links Sydney with the Hunter Valley and takes about two weeks, or you can walk sections. Contact the Department of Conservation & Land Management (C&LM) (☎ (02) 228

The Fires of '94

In early 1994 more than 100 huge fires broke out in the Great Dividing Range and raged for nearly a fortnight. High temperatures, low humidity and strong winds produced cataclysmic conditions and when fires began to explode along Sydney's green corridors, to within a few km of the city centre, an unprecedented disaster seemed imminent.

Thanks to the heroic efforts of 20,000 volunteer firefighters from brigades from around the country, the toll of property and human life was remarkably low. Lessons had been learned in the Ash Wednesday fires in Victoria and South Australia a decade earlier, which had killed 80 people and destroyed thousands of homes.

However, with more than 800,000 hectares of national parks and state forests burnt out, the ecological effects are more serious and far-reaching. Although Australian flora and fauna are accustomed to the regularity of bushland fires, it is feared that some species may not recover because most bushland is now surrounded by towns or farmland which can't provide new stocks of plants and animals.

Fires on this scale might not recur for many years, but almost every summer there are big fires somewhere in the state's forests. ■

6111), 23-33 Bridge St, Sydney. The Hume & Hovell Track runs through high country between Yass and Albury, tracing part of the route taken by the two explorers who walked to Port Phillip in 1824-5. C&LM publishes a guide to the track ($19.95).

Lonely Planet's *Bushwalking in Australia* details some walks in New South Wales. Other useful books are *100 Walks in New South Wales* by Tyrone T Thomas ($16) and *Bushwalks in the Sydney Region* ($16.95) published by the National Parks Association.

Water Sports

Diving & Snorkelling A number of places offer excellent diving and snorkelling. North of Sydney try Terrigal (96 km), Port Stephens (235 km), Seal Rocks (325 km) or Byron Bay (850 km). Head south to Jervis Bay (190 km) or Eden (488 km). You can take diving courses in many centres including Sydney and Byron Bay.

White-Water Rafting & Canoeing Rafting takes place on the upper Murray and Snowy rivers in the south and on the Nymboida and Gwydir rivers in the north. Albury and Jindabyne are jumping-off points for the southern rivers; Coffs Harbour and Nambucca Heads for the northern. A day trip costs just under $100.

With rivers, lakes, bays and dams there are plenty of opportunities for canoeing. The Canoe Association of New South Wales (☎ (02) 660 4597) has information.

Swimming & Surfing This is the state's true-blue activity and its 1900-km coastline is crowded with great beaches, some practically deserted. The warmer north coast is more popular during the winter months at places like Seal Rocks (325 km), Crescent Head (497 km), Angourie (744 km) and Lennox Heads (823 km). Byron Bay has been a surfing Mecca for almost as long as Australia has had surfers.

South of Sydney there is Wollongong (82 km), Huskisson (187 km), Mollymook (222 km), and others. Nat Young's *Surfing Australia's East Coast* (Castle Books) details the 'wheres and whens'. You can take surfing lessons in Coffs Harbour and elsewhere.

Surf carnivals – competing lifesavers, surf rescue boats, all that stuff – start in December. Phone the Surf Life Saving Association (☎ (02) 597 5588) for dates and venues, or contact the New South Wales Travel Centre.

Sailing Sydney Harbour and the Pittwater are both excellent sailing grounds, as is Lake Macquarie just south of Newcastle. Check with the Australian Yachting Federation (☎ (02) 922 4333) about clubs and sailing instruction.

Cycling

The Bicycle Institute of New South Wales (☎ (02) 212 5628), 82 Campbell St (GPO Box 272), Surry Hills, can provide information, including cycling routes throughout the state.

Skiing

See the Snowy Mountains section for information about skiing.

GETTING THERE & AWAY

Transport into the state is discussed mainly in the Sydney section.

GETTING AROUND
Air

Smaller airlines like Ansett Express and Eastern Australia Airlines operate comprehensive networks, mostly within the state, and other airlines serve particular regions. The chart shows some routes and standard fares – much cheaper discount fares are usually available.

Bus

Within the state it is often expensive to make short bus trips, so look for cheap stopover deals if you want to make a few stops on the way. Buses are often a little quicker and cheaper than trains, but not always.

Once you've reached your destination there are usually local bus lines, though services may not be frequent. Sometimes school buses are the only option and although they will usually take you along, they aren't obliged to.

Train

Countrylink has the most comprehensive state rail service in Australia and will, in conjunction with connecting buses, take you quite quickly to most sizable towns. However, the frequency and value for money is variable: always compare with private-enterprise bus services. Most Countrylink services have to be booked (☎ (02) 217 8812 or ☎ 13 2232 outside Sydney), between 6.30 am and 10 pm daily).

There are high-speed XPT trains (some with sleepers) and the new Explorer trains.

New South Wales Air Fares

All fares in Australian Dollars
One-way economy air fares

Intrastate services and economy fares from Sydney include Albury, 643 km, $62; Armidale, 530 km, $58; Bathurst, 240 km, $25; Bourke, 841 km, $70; Broken Hill, 1125 km, $86; Byron Bay, 883 km, from $70; Coffs Harbour, 608 km, $62; Cooma, 446 km, $47; Dubbo, 431 km, $47; Griffith, 631 km, $62; Orange, 323 km, $30; Tamworth, 455 km, $51 (direct rail), $45 (coach). Frequent commuter-type trains run between Sydney and Wollongong ($8.60), Katoomba ($8.60), Lithgow ($18), Newcastle ($13.60) and, less frequently, Goulburn ($17).

At the time of writing there were no rail pass deals but Countrylink should by now have released its packages aimed at budget travellers.

Sydney

Population 3,700,000

As Australia's oldest and largest city, Sydney (Sinney to the locals) has plenty to offer. The harbour, around which the city is built, was named Port Jackson by Captain Cook in

1770 but he actually anchored in Botany Bay, a few km to the south, and only passed by the narrow entrance to the harbour. In 1788 when the convict First Fleet arrived in Sydney it too went to Botany Bay, but after a few days moved north to Port Jackson. These first White settlers established themselves at Sydney Cove, still the centre of harbour shipping, and behind the waterfront in the area known as the Rocks are some of the earliest buildings in Australia.

Because Sydney grew in a piecemeal fashion, unlike later Australian cities which were planned from the start, it has a tighter, more congested centre without wide boulevards. It's also a dazzlingly modern city, with the most energy and style in Australia. In Sydney the buildings soar higher, the colours are brighter, the nightlife's more exciting, the taxi drivers more aggressive and the consumption more conspicuous!

It all comes back to that stupendous harbour though. It's more than just the centrepiece for the city; everything in Sydney revolves around it. Would the Opera House, for example, be anything like the place it is, if it wasn't perched right beside the harbour?

Orientation

The harbour divides Sydney into north and south, the Harbour Bridge, and now also the tunnel, joining the two. The city centre and most other places of interest are south of the harbour. The central area is long and narrow, although only George and Pitt Sts (the main commercial and shopping streets) run the whole three km from the waterfront Rocks area south to Central railway station.

The Rocks and Circular Quay mark the northern boundary of the centre, Central Station is on the southern edge, the inlet of Darling Harbour is the western boundary and a string of pleasant parks border Elizabeth and Macquarie Sts on the east.

East of these parks are some of the oldest inner suburbs – Woolloomooloo, Darlinghurst, Kings Cross and Paddington. Further east again are some of the more exclusive suburbs south of the harbour and then beachfront suburbs like Bondi. The airport is south of this area, beside Botany Bay, which is Sydney's second waterway.

West of the centre is Glebe and on the next headland is Balmain. The suburbs of the inner west, such as Chippendale, Newtown and Leichhardt, are next in line for the process of gentrification which has transformed Woolloomooloo and Paddington.

Suburbs stretch a good 20 km north and south from the centre, their extent having been limited by national parks, but 50 km to the west Penrith has become part of the urban sprawl.

Information

Tourist Offices The New South Wales Government Travel Centre (☎ 231 4444) is at 19 Castlereagh St and is open weekdays from 9 am to 5 pm. The Sydney Information Booth (☎ 235 2424) is nearby in Martin Place (sharing a booth with Halftix) and is open the same hours. You might be served more quickly here.

The Tourist Information Service (☎ 669 5111) answers phone enquiries from 8 am to 6 pm daily. In the Eddy Ave bus station (outside Central Station), the Travellers' Information Service (☎ 281 9366) makes bus and accommodation bookings (not hostels).

The 2000 Olympics
Sydney will host the Olympic Games in the year 2000, the second time the games will have come to Australia (Melbourne hosted the 1956 games).

The main Olympic stadiums are under construction in the neglected suburb of Homebush, on the Parramatta River 16 km west of the city centre. Other venues will be at Darling Harbour's Exhibition Centre, the nearby Entertainment Centre, Moore Park, Parramatta and Penrith. Yachting events will of course be held on the harbour. ■

NEW SOUTH WALES

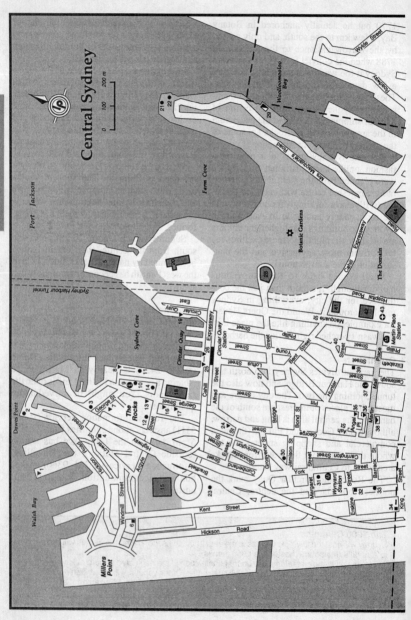

Central Sydney

0   100   200 m

Port Jackson

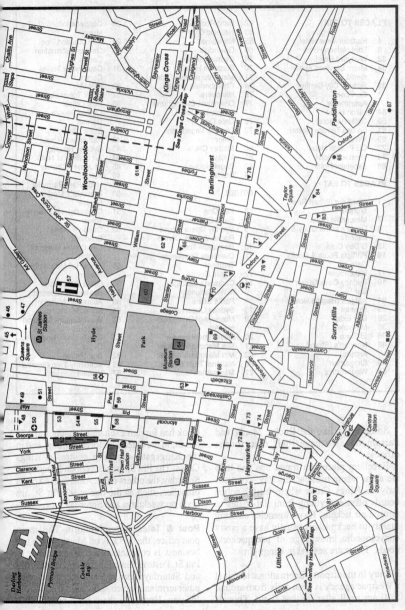

PLACES TO STAY

4	Harbour View Hotel
6	Lord Nelson Hotel
32	Wynyard Hotel
34	Metro Serviced Apartments
39	Sydney City Centre Serviced Apartments
54	Hilton Hotel
59	Criterion Hotel
61	Forbes Terrace Hostel
69	YWCA
72	CB Private Hotel
73	Westend Hotel
86	Excelsior Hotel

PLACES TO EAT

1	Pier Four (Wharf Restaurant)
7	Mercantile Hotel
8	Doyle's at the Quay & Bilson's
13	G'Day Cafe
16	Phillip's Foote & Rocks Cafe
17	Bakehouse
19	Sydney Cove Oyster Bar
24	Kable's (Regent Hotel)
25	Rossini
26	City Extra
35	Merivales
36	El Sano
48	Noonan's (Strand Arcade)
49	Skygarden
58	Woolworth's
62	Hard Rock Cafe
63	Hellenic Club
65	No Names
66	Govinda's
68	Cyprus Hellene
70	Burdekin Hotel
71	Metro Vegetarian Cafe
74	Chamberlain Hotel
76	Hanovers
77	Downtown Darlinghurst & Spanish Deli
78	Cafe Dov
79	Laurie's Vegetarian Diner
80	Mother Chu's
81	Malaya
83	Bagel House
84	Balkan

OTHER

2	Pier One
3	Earth Exchange
5	Sydney Opera House
9	Rocks Visitors' Centre
10	Rockcycle Tours
11	Overseas Passenger Terminal
12	Argyle Centre
14	Cadman's Cottage, NSW National Parks Office
15	Sydney Observatory
18	Museum of Contemporary Art
20	Government House
21	Mrs Macquarie's Point
22	Mrs Macquarie's Chair
23	National Trust Centre
27	Macquarie Place
28	Conservatorium of Music
29	Boy Charlton Pool
30	Qantas Vaccination Centre
31	Countrylink Travel Centre
33	NRMA
37	NSW Travel Centre
38	Post Office
40	Chifley Square - Qantas
41	State Library
42	Parliament House
43	Sydney Hospital
44	Art Gallery of NSW
45	St James Church
46	Mint
47	Hyde Park Barracks
50	Traveller's Medical Centre
51	Centrepoint & Sydney Tower
52	Queen Victoria Building
53	City Centre Monorail Station
55	Town Hall Monorail Station
56	Great Synagogue
57	St Mary's Cathedral
60	Australian Museum
64	Anzac Memorial
67	World Square Monorail Station
75	Greyhound Pioneer Depot
82	Bus Station
85	Academy Twin Cinema
87	Victoria Barracks

Some areas like the Rocks, Manly and Parramatta also have their own tourist offices.

Excellent places for travel tips and help are areas where backpackers stay – particularly in Kings Cross where hostel notice boards offer everything from flat-shares to unused air tickets. Travel agencies catering mainly to backpackers usually have a pretty encyclopedic knowledge of backpackers' needs. There are several in Kings Cross.

Money In the airport's international terminal a Westpac agency is open daily from around 5.30 am until after the last flight. Thomas Cook has foreign exchange branches at 175 Pitt St, in the Queen Victoria Building and in the Kingsgate shopping centre in Kings Cross. The Pitt St branch is open Monday to Saturday, the others daily. American Express branches, such as the one at 92 Pitt St, are open on weekdays and Saturday morning.

Post & Telecommunications The main post office, the GPO, is on Martin Place but business is conducted around the corner in Pitt St. Poste restante is here (open weekdays and Saturday morning) and there are computer terminals which show if mail is waiting for you. Hopefully these have helped with the delays and other frustrations travellers have experienced in the past. If not, have your mail redirected to a suburban post office ($5 a month).

Travellers Contact Point (☎ 221 8744), Suite 16, 8th floor, 428 George St (Dymocks Building), offers services such as bus bookings and mail holding and forwarding. Travel Active at 3 Orwell St in Kings Cross (☎ 357 4477) is a travel agency which offers similar services.

The Telecom Phone Centre at 100 King St, near the corner of George St, has 100 phones (some of which accept major credit cards) and is open 24 hours a day.

The STD area code for Sydney is 02.

Other Offices The YHA Membership & Travel Centre (☎ 261 1111) is at 422 Kent St in the city, between Market and Druitt Sts. Here the staff can make both national and international hostel bookings.

The NRMA's head office is at 151 Clarence St (☎ 260 9222) and there's a branch at 324 Pitt St (☎ 260 8122).

If your backpack needs repairing, try Custom Luggage (☎ 261 1099) at 317 Sussex St in the city. Camera repair places include Whilton Camera Service (☎ 267 8429) at 251 Elizabeth St opposite Hyde Park.

Bookshops The Travel Bookshop at 20 Bridge St is open daily and has guides to everywhere. Dymocks and Angus & Robertson are two chains with a reasonable range of stock. Dymocks branches include 424 George St and Darling Harbour; you'll find an Angus & Robertson in Imperial Arcade off Pitt St.

Abbey's Bookshop at 131 York St has a good range including foreign-language titles. Other shops worth checking out include Gleebooks at 191 Glebe Point Rd and New Edition at 328 Oxford St, Paddington. Ariel at 42 Oxford St is also good and stays open until midnight.

Publications *For Backpackers, By Backpackers* is a free bimonthly magazine with brief listings of budget places to stay and eat, what to see, etc. It's available from hostels and elsewhere. *Index* is a free monthly pamphlet useful for gallery and entertainment listings, with cafes, bookshops and other places also mentioned. The travel centre has copies, or you can try galleries and bookshops.

There are plenty of guidebooks to Sydney, few to the state. Lonely Planet's *Sydney City Guide* and *New South Wales – a travel survival kit* are general guides and there are plenty of specialised books such as the *Sydney Good Walks Guide* by Joan Lawrence (Kingsclear Books, paperback, about $15), *Sydney Bushwalks* by Neil Paton (Kangaroo Press, paperback, about $13) and the various Heritage Field Guides such as *Sydney by Ferry & Foot* (paperback, $13).

A great book to read while visiting is *Sydney* by Jan Morris (Penguin, about $15). For the seamy side of the city, read Peter Corris's Cliff Hardy thrillers – *White Meat* is a good example.

Maps Just about every brochure you pick up includes a map of the city centre. A more detailed map of the city centre and inner suburbs is the UBD *Sydney Tourist Map* ($4.15). For topographic maps go to the Lands Department (☎ 228 6111) at 23-33 Bridge St.

Medical Services Qantas has a medical and vaccination centre (☎ 255 6688) in the city at the World Trade Centre on Jamison St, open weekdays. You don't have to have a Qantas ticket to attend the centre. The Traveller's Medical & Vaccination Centre (☎ 221 7133) is at Level 7, 428 George St, between King and Market Sts, and the Kings Cross Travellers' Clinic (☎ 358 3066) is at Suite 1, 13 Springfield Ave. Both are open weekdays and Saturday morning. It's best to book.

Emergency Phone ☎ 000 for police, fire or ambulance. The Wayside Chapel (☎ 358 6577), 29 Hughes St, Kings Cross, is a personal crisis centre and good for all sorts of problem solving. Other emergency support services include Lifeline (☎ 951 5555) and the Rape Crisis Centre (☎ 819 6565, 24 hours).

Left Luggage There are cloakrooms at Central, Town Hall and Wynyard stations ($1.50 per item per day). At the Eddy Ave bus station there are luggage lockers ($4 a day).

Dangers & Annoyances Sydney isn't an especially dangerous city but you should remain alert. The usual big-city rules apply: never leave luggage unattended, never flaunt money and never get drunk in the company of strangers. Harassment of gays, lesbians and non-Anglo-Saxons is not rife but it does happen. Use extra caution in Kings Cross, which attracts drifters from all over Australia.

City Views

Sydney is becoming a mini-Manhattan and from up top you can look down on the convoluted streets that are a relic of the unplanned convict past.

Highest is the **Sydney Tower** (☎ 229 7444) on top of the Centrepoint complex on Market St between Pitt and Castlereagh Sts. This gigantic column has a viewing gallery and revolving restaurants on the summit, 305 metres above street level. You can see as far as the Blue Mountains to the west and Wollongong to the south. You can ride to the top for $6 daily from 9.30 am to 9.30 pm (11.30 pm on Saturday).

The **Harbour Bridge** is a good vantage point and you can climb the 200 stairs inside the south-eastern pylon for panoramic views of the harbour and city. The pylon also houses the small **Harbour Bridge Museum**. Admission to the pylon is $1.50 and it's open from 10 am to 5 pm daily. Enter from the bridge's pedestrian walkway, accessible from Cumberland St in the Rocks and from near Milsons Point Station.

For a view of the Opera House, harbour and bridge from sea level, take a trip on the harbour or go to **Mrs Macquarie's Point**,

one headland east of the Opera House. It has been a lookout since at least 1810 when Elizabeth Macquarie, wife of the governor, had a stone chair hewn into the rock, from where she would watch for ships entering the harbour or keep an eye on hubby's construction projects just across Farm Cove. The seat is still there today.

There are also excellent panoramas of the city centre from the north shore.

The Rocks

Sydney's first White settlement was on the rocky spur of land on the western side of Sydney Cove, from which the Harbour Bridge now leaps to the north shore. A pretty squalid place it was too, with overcrowding, open sewers and notoriously raucous residents. In the 1820s and '30s the nouveaux riches built their three-storey houses where Lower Fort St is today; their outlook was onto the slums below.

In the 1870s and '80s the Rocks was notorious for 'pushes', gangs of larrikins (a great Australian word) who used to haunt the area, robbing pedestrians, feuding and generally creating havoc. It became an area of warehouses and then fell into decline as more modern shipping and storage facilities were opened elsewhere. An outbreak of bubonic plague at the turn of the century led to whole streets being razed and the construction of the Harbour Bridge also resulted in much demolition.

Since the 1970s, redevelopment has made the Rocks one of Sydney's most interesting and atmospheric areas. Imaginative restorations have converted the old warehouses into places like the busy Argyle Centre and the Rocks is still a wonderful area to wander around, full of narrow cobbled streets and fine colonial buildings.

Pick up a walking tour map of the area from the Rocks Visitors Centre (☎ 247 4972, ☎ 11 606 for recorded information), 104 George St, open daily. A full walk round the area will take you to Millers Point, Walsh Bay and Dawes Point, just west of the Harbour Bridge. The centre sells the Rocks Ticket ($31.50) which includes a meal, a walking tour, a harbour cruise and entry to a couple of attractions.

The **Argyle Centre**, on the corner of Argyle and Playfair Sts, was built as bond stores between 1826 and 1881. Today it houses a collection of shops, boutiques, studios and eating places. (It has temporarily closed for a major refit, with most of the shops moving to the **Rocks Centre**, another restored building a few doors away on Argyle St.)

Just beyond the Argyle Centre is the **Argyle Cut**, an old tunnel through the hill to the other side of the peninsula. At the far end of the cut is **Millers Point**, a delightful district of early colonial homes. Close at hand are the Lord Nelson Hotel in Argyle St and the Hero of Waterloo Hotel on the corner of Windmill and Lower Fort Sts which vie for the title of Sydney's oldest pub. Also on Lower Fort St is the **Colonial House Museum** at No 53 (open daily; entry $1).

On George St near the visitor centre is **Cadman's Cottage** (1816), the oldest house in Sydney. When the cottage was built this was where the waterfront was, and the arches to the south of it once housed longboats; this was the home of the last Government Coxswain, John Cadman. The cottage now houses a National Parks & Wildlife Service information centre (☎ 247 8861), open daily.

The **Earth Exchange** at 36-64 George St is a geological and mining museum with the emphasis on interaction and participation – such as experiencing an earthquake. It's open daily from 10 am to 5 pm and admission is $7. The always interesting **Museum of Contemporary Art** (the MCA) is housed in the old Maritime Services building on George St at Circular Quay. Admission is $6 and it's open daily except Tuesday from 11 am to 6 pm. The bookshop sells good postcards.

In the park on Observatory Hill, the **Sydney Observatory** is an old building with an interesting little museum (free). It's open from 2 to 5 pm (from 10 am on weekends and school holidays). Nightly except Wednesday there's a tour with videos and telescope viewing. Night visits cost $5 and must be booked (☎ 217 0485).

Sydney Harbour Bridge from the Rocks

Close by in the old military hospital building, the **National Trust Centre** houses a museum, art gallery, bookshop and tearooms, open daily except Monday from 11 am to 5 pm (from noon on weekends). Admission is around $4.

At Dawes Point on Walsh Bay, just beneath the bridge on the western side, **Pier One** is an under-used shopping and leisure complex. Nearby, **Pier Four** is home to the prestigious Sydney Theatre and Sydney Dance companies.

Sydney Harbour Bridge

From the end of the Rocks the 'old coat hanger' rises up on its route to the north shore. It was the city's symbol until the Opera House came along. The bridge was completed in 1932 at a cost of $20 million, quite a bargain in modern terms, but it took until 1988 to pay off!

Driving south (only) there's a $2 toll. There's a cycleway across the bridge (west side) and a pedestrian walkway (east side), with stairs up to them from Cumberland St in the Rocks. The bridge's massive stone pylons are purely decorative and don't help to hold the bridge up in any way – you can climb up inside one of them (see City Views). The bridge can no longer handle the volume of traffic so a tunnel has been built under the harbour, beginning about half a km south of the Opera House and meeting the bridge road on the northern side. There's a southbound (only) toll of $2.

On the north shore is another Sydney symbol – the grinning mouth of **Luna Park** funfair. It was closed for years but will soon reopen; some of the city's best fringe artists worked on the park's restoration. Ferries from Circular Quay will probably run to the park or you can take a train (or walk) across the bridge to Milsons Point Station.

At the end of Kirribilli Point east of the bridge stand **Admiralty House** and **Kirribilli House**, the Sydney pieds-à-terre of the Governor-General and the Prime Minister respectively (Admiralty House is the one nearer the bridge).

Sydney Opera House

Whether you're at a free Sunday concert or sitting in the open-air restaurant with a carafe of wine watching the harbour life, the Opera House is a truly memorable place. It looks fine from any angle, but the view from a ferry coming into Circular Quay is one of the best.

Before the Opera House was built the site was used as a tram depot. Danish architect Jorn Utzon won a contest with his design but amidst hassles, cost overruns and construction difficulties, he quit and the building was completed (in 1973) by a consortium of Australian architects. How were the enormous additional costs covered? – not by the taxpayer but in true-blue Aussie fashion by a series of lotteries.

The Opera House has four auditoriums and puts on dance, theatre, concerts and films as well as opera. Popular performances sell out quickly but there are often 'restricted view' tickets available. For operas these tickets cost about $30.

You can often catch a free lunch-time film or organ recital in the concert hall. On Sunday there is free entertainment outside on the 'prow' of the Opera House, with jazz near the Forecourt restaurant and crafts markets near the front entrance.

There are tours of the building and although the inside is less spectacular than the outside, they are worth taking. Tours run daily between 9 am and 4 pm ($8.50, students $5.50). Not all tours can visit all theatres because of rehearsals etc. You're more likely to see everything if you take an early tour, or phone ☎ 250 7250 to see what's available. There are irregular backstage tours on Sunday ($13).

Circular Quay

Circular Quay is a busy hub for both tourists and harbour ferry commuters. It was the landing point of the First Fleet and settlement grew around the Tank Stream which ran into the harbour here. The quay was made semicircular during the 1830s. Later it was the city's shipping centre and early photographs show a forest of masts crowding the skyline. On the western side, by the Rocks, is the overseas passenger terminal where visiting liners moor.

Macquarie Place

Narrow lanes lead back from Circular Quay towards the centre of the city. At the corner of Loftus and Bridge Sts, under the shady Moreton Bay figs in little Macquarie Place, are a cannon and anchor from the First Fleet flagship, HMS *Sirius*. There are several other pieces of colonial memorabilia in this square, including an obelisk indicating distances to various points in the colony and a National-Trust-classified gentlemen's convenience. Backing Macquarie Place is the **Lands Department building** on Bridge St, a grand 19th-century edifice.

East of here at 8 Phillip St, the **Justice & Police Museum** is housed in the old Water Police station and is set up as a turn-of-the-century police station and court, with various displays on crime. It's open on Sunday from 10 am to 5 pm and admission is $4.

City Centre

Central Sydney stretches from Central Station

in the south up to Circular Quay in the north. The business hub is towards the northern end, and if anywhere is Sydney's centre it's **Martin Place**, a pedestrian mall extending from Macquarie St to George St beside the massive GPO. This is a popular lunch-time entertainment spot. In December a Christmas tree is erected here in the summer heat.

The city has some attractive shopping complexes including the old **Strand Arcade** between Pitt and George Sts just south of King St. The big **Queen Victoria Building**, on the corner of George and Market Sts, has been restored to house about 200 shops, cafes and restaurants. Other centres off George and Pitt Sts include the MLC Centre, Centrepoint and the Royal Arcade.

In the basement of the Hilton Hotel, under the Royal Arcade between George and Pitt Sts south of Market St, is the **Marble Bar**, a Victorian extravaganza built by George Adams, the fellow with the prescience to foresee Australia's gambling lust, who founded Tattersalls lotteries. When the old Adams Hotel was torn down to build the Hilton, the bar was carefully dismantled and reassembled like some archaeological wonder.

Half a block further south along George St is the 1874 **Town Hall** on the corner of Druitt St. Inside there's the impressive Grand Organ. Across the open space to the south, **St Andrew's Cathedral** was built about the same time. Today it houses an unusual two-part organ with computerised sections. Recitals are held weekly.

From here to Central Station the centre begins to fade and appears to be ripe for development. The complicated intersection of Broadway and George, Pitt and Quay Sts outside Central Station is known as **Railway Square**. Just west of George St, before the station, is the colourful **Chinatown** around Dixon St and the **Haymarket** area.

Darling Harbour

This inlet, half a km west of the city centre, has been turned into a huge waterfront leisure and tourist park.

The **monorail** circles Darling Harbour

and links it to the city centre, travelling at 1st-floor level. For sightseeing it is well worth the $2.50 fare. The full circuit takes 12 minutes and there's a train every three or four minutes. For $6 you can ride as often as you like between 9 am and 7 pm.

The main pedestrian approaches to Darling Harbour are across footbridges from Market St and Liverpool St. The one from Market St leads to **Pyrmont Bridge**, now a pedestrian-and-monorail-only route. It was famous in its day as the first electrically operated swing-span bridge in the world. It has great views of the whole complex.

Other than by monorail or on foot, you can get to Darling Harbour on the Sydney Explorer bus, the 'Tramway' shuttle bus or by ferry from Circular Quay (you a great view of Darling Harbour if you travel there by ferry).

The complex is so big that you might want to take a ride on the 'people-mover' which takes 20 minutes to get around all the sights and costs $2.50.

The centre of Darling Harbour is the **Harbourside Festival Marketplace**, a large and graceful structure by Pyrmont Bridge crammed with shops, cafes and other food outlets. The South Pavilion is a bright and noisy place which is very popular with young Sydneysiders; the North Pavilion has more-expensive restaurants and shops, catering mainly to tourists. The North Pavilion also houses the Craig Brewery, a large pub with entertainment, and the Virgin Video Cafe.

The Darling Harbour Superticket ($35.50), sold at monorail stations, the aquarium and elsewhere, gives you a harbour cruise, a trip on the monorail, entrance to the aquarium and the Chinese Garden, a 10% discount shopping voucher for some Harbourside stores plus a barbecue in the Craig Brewery. It's valid for three months.

Sydney Aquarium The aquarium is by the east end of Pyrmont Bridge. Its all-Australian inhabitants include river fish, Barrier Reef fish and coral gardens, and crocodiles. Two 'oceanarium' tanks, with sharks, rays

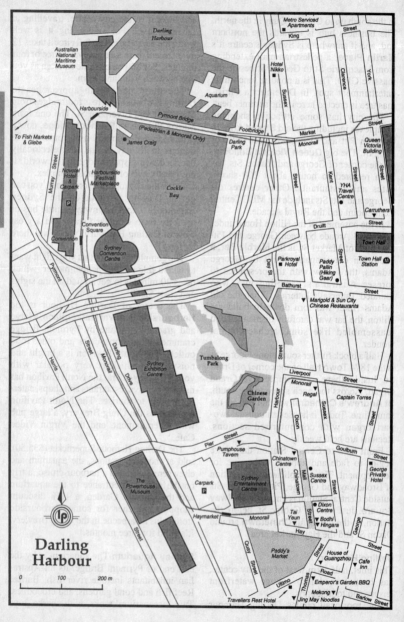

Darling Harbour

Darling Harbour

Australian National Maritime Museum

Aquarium

Harbourside

Pyrmont Bridge
(Pedestrian & Monorail Only)

To Fish Markets & Glebe

James Craig

Novotel Hotel
Carpark
P

Harbourside Festival Marketplace

Cockle Bay

Murray Street

Convention Square

Convention

Sydney Convention Centre

Pyrmont Street

Harris Street

Monorail

Sydney Exhibition Centre

Darling Drive

Tumbalong Park

Chinese Garden

Pier Street

Pumphouse Tavern

The Powerhouse Museum

Carpark
P

Sydney Entertainment Centre

Haymarket

Harris Street

Monorail

Paddy's Market

Haymarket

Ultimo

Quay Street

Thomas Street

Travellers Rest Hotel

Metro Serviced Apartments

King Street

Clarence Street

York Street

Hotel Nikko

Sussex Street

Footbridge

Market Street

Monorail

Darling Park

Kent Street

Sussex Street

Street

Queen Victoria Building

YHA Travel Centre

Carruthers Street

Druitt Street

Town Hall

Day St

Parkroyal Hotel

Paddy Pallin (Hiking Gear)

Town Hall Station

Bathurst Street

Street

Marigold & Sun City Chinese Restaurants

Liverpool Street

Monorail

Regal

Sussex Street

Captain Torres

Dixon Street

Harbour Street

Goulburn Street

George Private Hotel

Street

Pier Street

Chinatown Centre

Sussex Centre

Chinatown Mall

Dixon Centre

Bodhi
Hingara

George Street

Tai Yuen

Hay Street

House of Guangzhou

Cafe Inn

Road

Emperor's Garden BBQ

Mekong
Jing May Noodles

Barlow Street

0   100   200 m

LP

and other big fish in one, and Sydney Harbour marine life in the other, are moored in the harbour. You walk below water level to view the tanks through transparent walkways. The aquarium is open daily from 9.30 am to 9 pm ($13.50).

Australian National Maritime Museum

Across Pyrmont Bridge from the aquarium the roof of the Maritime Museum billows like sails, echoing the nautical shapes of the Opera House. The museum tells the story of Australia's relationship with the sea, from Aboriginal canoes to the America's Cup. Vessels of many different types stand inside or are moored at the wharves, including HMAS *Vampire*, a retired warship. It's open daily from 10 am to 5 pm ($7).

Just under the bridge from the museum two more ships are moored at what's called Sydney Seaport – the 1874 sailing ship *James Craig*, which is slowly being restored, and the *Kanangra*, a harbour ferry built in 1912.

Powerhouse Museum & Nearby Behind the exhibition centre is Sydney's most spectacular museum, housed in a vast building encompassing the old power station for Sydney's now defunct trams. It covers the decorative arts, science and technology and social history. The collections are superbly displayed and there are lots of opportunities for interaction. It's open from 10 am to 5 pm daily and admission is $5 (free on the first Saturday of the month).

In front of the exhibition centre, **Tumbalong Park** includes an amphitheatre with free entertainment most lunch times. In another corner is the **Chinese Garden**, the biggest outside China, which was planned by landscape architects from New South Wales's sister province, Guangdong. Admission is $2. Just south of here, the old pump house which supplied hydraulic power for many Sydney lifts has become the **Pump House Tavern**, with its own brewery.

Nearby and on the edge of Chinatown is the **Sydney Entertainment Centre**, the venue for big-name touring rock acts.

Early Central Buildings

After the founding governor, Phillip, left in 1792, the colony was run mainly by officials and soldiers intent on making a quick fortune through the rum monopoly. It was not until Lachlan Macquarie became governor in 1810 that order was restored. The narrow streets of parts of central Sydney are a reminder of the chaotic pre-Macquarie period.

Macquarie St Macquarie commissioned Francis Greenway, a convict transported for forgery, to design a series of public buildings, some of which remain among the finest in Sydney. There are good views of all Greenway's buildings from the 14th-floor cafeteria in the Law Courts building on the corner of Macquarie St and Queens Square.

St James Church (1819-24) and the **Hyde Park Barracks** (1819), two Greenway masterpieces, are on Queens Square at the northern end of Hyde Park. The Barracks, originally convict quarters, now house an interesting museum of Sydney's social history, open daily from 10 am to 5 pm, admission $6.

Next to the Barracks is the **Mint building**, built as a hospital in 1814 and known as the Rum Hospital because the builders constructed it in return for the lucrative monopoly on the rum trade. It became the Mint in 1853 and the northern end is now the state **Parliament House**. There are free weekday tours on nonsitting days; sitting-day tours include question time but are usually booked out. Phone ☎ 230 2111 for bookings. The Mint, with its collection of decorative arts, stamps and coins, is open from 10 am to 5 pm daily (from noon on Wednesday); admission is $4.

Further up Macquarie St on the Botanic Gardens side, the **Sydney Conservatorium of Music** was originally built, by Greenway again, as the stables and servants' quarters of a new government house for Macquarie. Macquarie was replaced as governor before the rest of the house could be finished, partly because of the perceived extravagance of this project. Greenway's life ended in poverty because he could never recoup the money he had put into the work. The conservatorium holds free lunch-time concerts on Wednesday and Friday during term.

Art Gallery of New South Wales

In the Domain, the art gallery has an excellent permanent display of Australian, European, Asian and tribal art, and has some inspired temporary exhibits. It's open from 10 am to 5 pm daily and there are free guided tours. Admission is free but fees may apply for special exhibitions. Sydney is packed with other galleries, particularly in Paddington and Woollahra.

Australian Museum

The Australian Museum, across from Hyde Park on the corner of College and William Sts, is a natural history museum with an excellent Australian wildlife collection and a gallery tracing Aboriginal history from the Dreamtime to the present; see this before you head off to central Australia. The bookshop has good publications on Aboriginal and Pacific arts and crafts. The museum is open from 10 am to 5 pm daily. Admission is $4, free after 4 pm.

Other Museums

On Macquarie St, just north of Parliament House, the **State Library** has a huge collection of early records and works on Australia, including Captain Cook's and Joseph Banks's journals and Captain Bligh's log from the *Bounty* (the irascible Bligh recovered from that ordeal to become an early New South Wales governor where he suffered a second mutiny!). Many items are displayed in the library galleries, which are open from 10 am to 5 pm Monday to Saturday, and from 2 to 6 pm on Sunday.

Other museums include the **Nicholson** and **Macleay** museums at Sydney University, with antiquities at the former and a curious collection ranging from stuffed birds and animals to early computers at the latter. Both are free and open on weekdays.

Sportspace (☎ 0055 21058 for bookings) is a behind-the-scenes guided tour of the Sydney Cricket Ground in Moore Park and the nearby Sydney Football Stadium. Tours are held daily and cost $15 for two hours, or $8 for one hour. Amidst construction for the Olympics, the State Sports Centre in Homebush has the **Hall of Champions**, featuring state sporting heroes since 1876. It's free and open daily. To get here take a train to Strathfield then a shuttle bus to the sports centre.

See the Rocks section for information on the Observatory and the Earth Exchange and the Darling Harbour section for the Powerhouse Museum.

Parks

Sydney has many parks which, together with the harbour, make it a surprisingly spacious city. A string of parks borders the eastern side of the city centre. Stretching back from the harbour, beside the Opera House, are the **Royal Botanic Gardens** which feature plant life from the South Pacific region. The Gardens were established in 1816 and in one corner is a wall marking the site of the colony's first vegetable patch. The tropical display ($5) in the Arc and Pyramid glasshouses is worth seeing. There's a visitor centre where guided walks start at 10 am on Wednesday and Friday and at 1 pm on Sunday. The gardens are open daily from 8 am to sunset.

The Cahill Expressway separates the Botanic Gardens from **the Domain**, another open space to the south – you can cross the expressway on the Art Gallery Rd bridge. On Sunday afternoons impassioned soapbox speakers entertain their listeners, and free events are held here during the Festival of Sydney in January, as well as Carols by Candlelight in December. This is also a rallying place for public protests.

Hyde Park, between Elizabeth and College Sts, has delightful fountains and the **Anzac Memorial**, where there's a changing of the guard ceremony on Thursday at 12.30 pm. **St Mary's Cathedral** overlooks the park from the east and the **Great Synagogue** is opposite on the western side: both are open for inspection.

Sydney's biggest park, with running, cycling and horse tracks, duck ponds, barbecue sites and lots more, is **Centennial Park**, five km from the centre and just east of Paddington. Black swans and many other birds nest here. You can hire bikes from several places on Clovelly Rd near the southern edge of the park (see Getting Around), or horses from Centennial Park Horse Hire at the Showgrounds on Lang Rd, just west of Centennial Park.

Balls Head Reserve, on the north shore of the harbour two headlands west of the Harbour Bridge, is a pocket of bushland with great views of the harbour and old Aboriginal rock paintings and carvings. Take a North Shore train to Waverton and follow the signs from the station.

As well as parks there are wilder areas. Some of these, along the harbour shores, are described in the Harbour section. Another, **Davidson Park**, is an eight-km corridor of bushland in northern Sydney stretching from Bantry Bay on Middle Harbour up to Kuring-gai Chase National Park. The **Lane Cove River** recreation area runs between the suburbs of Ryde and Chatswood, again north of the harbour. Both areas have extensive walking tracks and Lane Cove River has lots of picnic areas. You may see lyrebirds in Davidson Park; the males make their spectacular mating displays from May to August. Cadman's Cottage in the Rocks has information.

Oxford St

Branching off Liverpool St near Hyde Park, Oxford St is a famous thoroughfare through the lively inner suburbs of Surry Hills, Darlinghurst and, further east, Paddington. This whole area is full of interesting shops and fashionable but often inexpensive places to eat. Oxford St is Sydney's official gay and lesbian precinct and **Taylor Square**, the junction of Oxford, Flinders and Bourke Sts, is its heart.

Paddington

Hilly Paddington, four km east of the city centre, is a very attractive inner-city residen-

Terraced houses, Paddington

tial area. It is a tightly packed mass of late-Victorian terrace houses, built for aspiring artisans. During the lemming-like rush to the outer suburbs after WW II the area became a slum but a renewed interest in Victorian architecture (of which Australia has some gems) and the pleasures of inner-city life led to the restoration of 'Paddo' during the '60s.

Today it's a fascinating jumble of often beautifully restored terraces tumbling up and down the steep streets and a fine example of totally unplanned urban restoration. The best time to visit is Saturday when the '**Paddo Bazaar**' is held at the corner of Newcombe and Oxford Sts.

The heart of Paddo is along Oxford St east of the Victoria Barracks and in the streets north from there. A couple of blocks past the barracks, take Underwood St then Heeley St to **Five Ways**, a mass meeting of streets around which cluster interesting shops and places to eat, plus the lovely old Royal pub. Paddington St, further east, has some of the finest-looking houses, while many antique shops are on Queen St.

On Thursday morning from 10 am you can visit the old Victoria Barracks (☎ 339 3000) to hear a military band and see the Army

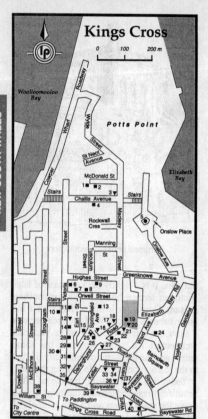

Kings Cross

0   100   200 m

Woolloomooloo Bay

Potts Point

Elizabeth Bay

Onslow Place

Barncleuth Square

To Paddington

To City Centre

PLACES TO STAY

1	Backpackers Village
2	Rucksack Rest
4	Challis Lodge
6	Kendall Private Hotel
7	Eva's Backpackers
8	Jolly Swagman Backpackers (Orwell St)
9	Downunder Hostel
10	Kanga House
11	Jolly Swagman Backpackers (Victoria St)
13	Jolly Swagman Backpackers (Springfield Mall)
14	Travellers Rest
15	Bernly Private Hotel & Springfield Lodge
22	Fountain International Hostel
23	Backpackers Connection
24	Barncleuth House
26	Fountain Plaza Hostel
28	Original Backpackers
29	Highfield House
31	Plane Tree Lodge
37	Metro Motor Inn
38	O'Malley's Hotel
39	Barclay Hotel
41	Backpackers Headquarters

PLACES TO EAT

3	Merivale Brasserie
12	Four Fingers
16	Yakidori
17	Astoria
18	Nick's Seafood
20	Fountain Cafe
21	Bourbon & Beefsteak
25	Pad Thai
27	Geoffrey's Cafe
32	Joe's
33	Dean's
34	Cafe Iguana
36	Bayswater Brasserie
40	Gado Gado

OTHER

5	Elizabeth Bay House
19	El Alamein Fountain/ Fitzroy Gardens
30	Let's Travel
35	Kings Cross Station

Museum. The museum is also open on the first Sunday of the month. Vic Barracks is still an army base so opening times can change.

Many buses run along Oxford St, such as No 378 from Central Station and No 380 from Circular Quay along Elizabeth St.

Kings Cross

'The Cross' has seedy strip joints, junkie teenage hookers, leafy old streets, lots of eateries; and it's the main travellers' centre in Sydney, with Australia's greatest concentration of hostels. Darlinghurst Rd is its main

street and many of the hostels are on or near Victoria St, which diverges from Darlinghurst Rd just north of William St. The thistle-like **El Alamein Fountain**, down in Fitzroy Gardens at the end of Darlinghurst

Rd, is the main landmark (and is known locally as the 'elephant douche').

Many travellers begin and end their Australian adventures in the Cross. It's a good place to swap information and notice boards line the hostel and shop walls and there's a car park where travellers buy and sell vehicles.

From the city you can walk straight up William St to the Cross, or grab one of the multitude of buses which run there or take the quick train. There's a quieter pedestrian route from the city: duck through Sydney Hospital from Macquarie St, cross the Domain and descend the hill on the right of the Art Gallery, then go down Palmer St from its junction with Sir John Young Crescent, turn left along Harmer St and then follow the paths and backstreets till you reach a flight of steps leading up to Victoria St, just south of its junction with Orwell St.

Between the city and the Cross is **Woolloomooloo** (the 'loo), one of Sydney's older areas. This area, extremely run down in the early '70s, has gone through a complete restoration and is now very pleasant. But I bet you can't spell it without looking at it again. Does anywhere else in the world have four double-O's in its name? Near Cowper Wharf is Harry's Cafe de Wheels, a pie cart which opened in 1945 and is still going strong.

Beyond the Cross

The harbourfront about half a km north-east of the Cross is called Elizabeth Bay. Here at 7 Onslow St is **Elizabeth Bay House**, one of Sydney's finest old homes, built in 1832 and featuring an unusual elliptical dome. It's open daily except Monday from 10 am to 4.30 pm, and admission is $5. Bus No 311 from Hunter St runs past.

The next bay east – about half a km from the Cross – is **Rushcutters Bay** which has a harbourside park and lots of boats at anchor. Then there's **Darling Point** and even trendier **Double Bay** – swish shops and lots of badly parked Porsches and Mercedes Benzes.

Next east is Rose Bay, then Nielsen Park

and Vaucluse where **Vaucluse House** (open from 10 am to 4.30 pm daily except Monday, admission $5) on Wentworth Rd is an imposing example of 19th-century Australiana in fine grounds. It was built in 1828 for the explorer and patriot William Wentworth. Take bus No 325 from Circular Quay and alight a couple of stops past Nielsen Park.

At the end of the harbour is **Watsons Bay** with fashionable Doyle's restaurant, a couple of Sydney's most 'be seen there' harbour beaches and the magnificent view across the Heads. All along this side of the harbour there are superb views back towards the city.

Other Suburbs

West of the city centre and on its own headland is **Balmain**, the arty centre of Sydney and rivalling Paddington in Victorian-era trendiness. **Glebe**, again west but closer to the centre, is also rising up the social scale but has managed to retain its bohemian atmosphere. Neighbouring suburbs such as **Chippendale**, **Newtown** and **Leichhardt** are even more studenty. **Redfern**, south of the centre and bordering Surry Hills, is also interesting but parts are Australia's closest approach to a real inner-urban slum.

The eastern suburbs (the harbour-to-ocean area east of the Cross) and the north shore (across the harbour) are the wealthy areas. **Hunters Hill** on the north shore, west of the bridge, is full of elegant Victorian houses.

Westward of the inner suburbs stretch the red-tile-roofed suburbs, the dull Bankstowns of Sydney. It's in suburbs like these that most Australians live, not around a harbour or in the outback. **Sylvania Waters**, infamous because of a pommie TV documentary series 'exposing' Aussie materialism, is on the Georges River near the southern shore of Botany Bay.

The Harbour

Sydney's harbour is best viewed from a ferry. It's extravagantly colourful and always interesting. People have often wondered which great city has the most magnificent harbour – Hong Kong, Rio, San Francisco or Sydney?

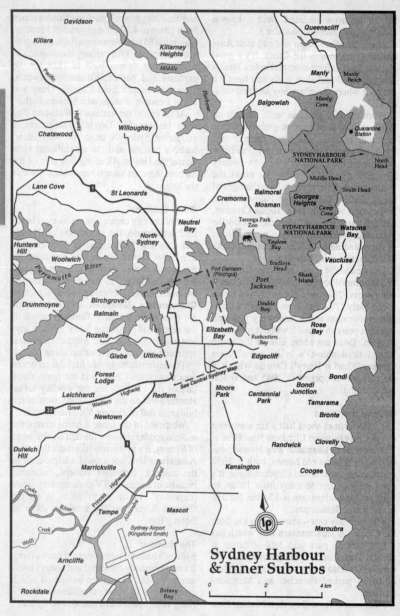

Sydney Harbour & Inner Suburbs

NEW SOUTH WALES

0   4 km

I've still to get to Rio, but of the others I'd have to give Sydney first place. Officially called Port Jackson, the harbour stretches about 20 km inland from the ocean to the mouth of the Parramatta River. The city centre is about eight km inland. The harbour shores are a maze of headlands and inlets and there are several islands. The biggest inlet, which heads off north-west a couple of km from the ocean, is called **Middle Harbour**.

Fort Denison, or Pinchgut as it was previously aptly named, is a small island which was the site of a gallows for convicts who misbehaved, and was then fortified in the mid-19th century when a Russian invasion was feared. Hegarty's Ferries (book on ☎ 206 1167 on weekends) has tours daily except Monday at 10 am, 12.15 and 2 pm. The tours leave from Jetty 6 at Circular Quay and cost $8.50. Tearooms are to be built on the island. **Goat Island**, another tiny speck in the harbour, is currently closed to tours.

On weekends the harbour is alive with yachts weaving around the ferries and freighters. Many of them compete in races and the most spectacular are the speedy 18-footers. These honed-down skiffs carry a huge sail area for their size and their agile crews leap about on outriggers to control them, chasing big prize money. A spectator ferry follows the races and you can make a bet on board. The ferry leaves from the western side of Circular Quay at 2.15 pm and costs $9. The 18-footer racing season runs from mid-September to late March.

Harbour Walks Some of the harbour shore is still quite wild and several undeveloped stretches towards the ocean have been declared the **Sydney Harbour National Park**. Most of them have walking tracks, beaches and good views. On the south shore is Nielsen Park (which covers Vaucluse Point and has a shark net), Shark Bay (very popular for swimming in summer, and also with a shark net) and the Hermitage Walk round Hermit Bay. The park headquarters (☎ 337 5355) is at Greycliffe House in Nielsen Park.

Further out there's a fine short walk round South Head from Camp Cove Beach, passing Lady Bay, Inner South Head, the Gap near Watsons Bay (a popular place for catching the sunrise and sunset), and on to Outer South Head. Bus No 325 from Circular Quay runs past Nielsen Park and the South Head area. On weekends ferries run to Watsons Bay.

On the north shore, the four-km Ashton Park track, round Bradleys Head below Taronga Zoo and up alongside Taylors Bay, is also part of the national park. Take the Taronga Zoo ferry from Circular Quay to get to Ashton Park. From Taronga you can also walk to Cremorne Point by a combination of parks, stairways, streets and bits of bush. Either way you get good views of the south shore. Georges and Middle Heads and Obelisk Bay, a little further east from Taylors Bay, are also parts of the national park. See also the Manly section.

Taronga Zoo & Koala Park

A short ferry ride from Circular Quay's Jetty 5 takes you across to Taronga Zoo, which has a superb harbourside setting. There are over 4000 critters including lots of Aussie ones. The zoo is at the top of a small hill and if you can't be bothered to walk, take a bus or cable car (the Aerial Safari, $2.50) to the top entrance. It's open daily from 9 am to 5 pm and admission is $14 ($7 children). A Zoo Pass, sold at Circular Quay and elsewhere, costs $17 ($8.50 children) and includes return ferry rides, the bus to the entrance, zoo admission and the Aerial Safari.

If koalas are your special interest, Koala Park (☎ 484 3141) on Castle Hill Rd in West Pennant Hills in north-west Sydney is open daily from 9 am to 5 pm and costs $8 ($4 children) to enter. Take a train to Pennant Hills Station and from there bus Nos 661 to 665. Other wildlife parks are covered in Around Sydney.

Manly

Manly is more like a small resort than a city suburb and all types of people head out here at weekends. The ferry ride to and from Manly is one of the most scenic harbour trips.

NEW SOUTH WALES

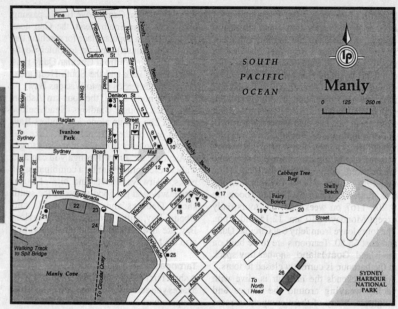

Manly

SOUTH
PACIFIC
OCEAN

0   125   250 m

SYDNEY
HARBOUR
NATIONAL
PARK

To
North
Head

To Circular Quay

Manly Cove

Walking Track
to Spit Bridge

To
Sydney

Cabbage Tree
Bay

Shelly
Beach

Fairy
Bower

PLACES TO STAY	PLACES TO EAT	OTHER
1 Manly Beach	5 Pacific Parkroyal Hotel	3 Aloha Surf
Resort Backpackers	6 Cafe Tunis	4 Manly Cycle Centre
2 Manly Astra	8 Luis	7 Post Office
Backpackers	11 Malacca Straits Satay	10 Information Office
9 Steyne Hotel	Restaurant	17 Surf Lifesaving Club
14 Eversham Private	12 Cadillac Cafe	20 Rock Pool
Hotel	13 Pan Tip Thai	21 Oceanworld
18 Manly Lodge	15 Cafe Steyne	22 Netted Swimming Area
25 Periwinkle	16 Radisson Kestrel Hotel	23 Bus Interchange
Guesthouse	19 Bower Restaurant	24 Manly Wharf/Ferries
		26 St Patrick's College

Named in 1788, after the physique of the local Aborigines, Manly is on a narrow neck of land running down to North Head at the harbour entrance. A short walk across this isthmus from the ferry terminal on Manly Cove (the inner beach) takes you to the famous ocean beach. The main street across the isthmus, the Corso, is a pedestrian mall with numerous cafes. North and South Steyne are the names of the road running along the ocean beach. The information

centre (☎ 977 1088) is on the ocean beach near the Corso and has lockers where you can leave your valuables while swimming.

Manly Museum & Art Gallery on West Esplanade (to the left when you leave the wharf) has Australian paintings and exhibitions on appropriate subjects like the history of surfing or swimming costumes. **Oceanworld** is a very good oceanarium also on West Esplanade, at the end of the beach ($11).

Beyond Oceanworld is a 10-km walking track, the **Manly Scenic Walkway**, which follows the shoreline all the way back to the Spit Bridge over Middle Harbour. Collect a leaflet detailing the walk from the information centre. Buses run from the Spit Bridge to Sydney city centre.

Spectacular **North Head** at the Sydney Harbour entrance is about three km south of Manly. Most of the headland is in Sydney Harbour National Park – including the **quarantine station** which housed suspected disease carriers from 1832 until 1984. To visit the station you have to book a guided tour (☎ 977 6522), available most afternoons ($6). Take the 1.10 pm Manly Hospital bus from Manly Wharf.

North of Manly

A string of oceanfront suburbs stretches north up the coast from Manly, ending in beautiful, wealthy **Palm Beach** and the spectacular **Barrenjoey Heads** at the mouth of **Broken Bay**, 30 km from Manly. There are lots of beaches along the way and buses run the route. From Palm Beach you can take cruises on the **Hawkesbury River** or on the **Pittwater**, a lovely inlet off Broken Bay, or take ferries to Ku-ring-gai Chase or across Broken Bay to **Patonga**. (From Patonga buses run to Gosford, from where you can catch a bus or train heading north.)

Beaches

Sydney's beaches are one of its greatest assets – they're easily accessible and usually very good. A high point of Sydney's beach life is the surf-lifesaving competitions held at various beaches throughout the summer.

There are harbour beaches and ocean beaches. Harbour beaches are sheltered and calm and generally smaller; ocean beaches often have good surf. Swimming is generally safe – at the ocean beaches you have to swim within the 'flagged' areas patrolled by the famed lifeguards. Efforts are made to keep surfers separate from swimmers.

Shark patrols operate through the summer and ocean beaches are generally netted – Sydney has had only one fatal shark attack since 1937. Sharkproof nets do not usually enclose the beaches, they run at right angles to the coast to dissuade sharks from patrolling along the beaches.

Many beaches are 'topless' but many aren't – do as the locals do to avoid hassles. There are also a couple of nudist beaches.

Harbour Beaches On the southern side, out near the heads (the harbour entrance), is trendy Camp Cove, a small but pleasant sliver of sand popular with families, and topless. This is where Governor Phillip first landed in Sydney. Just north of Camp Cove and immediately inside the heads, tiny Lady Bay Beach achieved some notoriety in the process of becoming a nude beach. It's mainly a gay scene. There's another nude beach, Reef Beach, on the north shore and accessible from the Manly Scenic Walkway.

South of Camp Cove is Watsons Bay. Two other popular harbour beaches are Balmoral, near the entrance to Middle Harbour, and Nielsen Park at Vaucluse.

Southern Ocean Beaches South of the heads a string of ocean beaches runs all the way to Botany Bay. Bondi is probably Australia's best-known beach and it's a popular gathering place, with a selection of cheap accommodation. Some of Australia's most accessible Aboriginal carvings – outlines of fish on a flat rock – are a short walk north of the beach on the golf course.

Tamarama, a little south of Bondi, has a tiny beach with strong surf. Then there's Bronte, popular with families (bus No 378 from Bondi Junction), and Coogee, a wide beach where you'll find the popular Coogee Bay Hotel with its beer garden overlooking the beach (bus No 373 from Circular Quay). Other beaches towards Botany Bay, which is more for sailing than swimming due to industry and sharks, include Maroubra.

Northern Ocean Beaches The 30-km coast up to Barrenjoey Heads is dotted with beaches, beginning at Manly. Freshwater, first up from Manly, attracts a lot of teenagers, then there's Curl Curl (families and surfers), Dee Why and Collaroy (family beaches), the long sweep of Narrabeen (surfers) backed by the Narrabeen Lakes which are home to many water birds, and further up Newport (families again). Towards Barrenjoey Heads three of the best are Avalon, Whale Beach and Palm Beach, the northern end of which is a nude beach.

Bus Nos 136 and 139 run from Manly to Freshwater and Curl Curl. Bus No 190 from Wynyard in the city centre runs to Newport and north. From Manly take a bus to Narrabeen (eg, No 155) and pick up No 190 there.

Surf Beaches Surfing is popular and with so many good beaches it's easy to see why. Apart from Bondi and Tamarama, there's Maroubra south of the heads. Beyond Botany Bay, Cronulla is another serious surf beach. North of Manly there's another dozen or so beaches, the best being Narrabeen, North Avalon and Palm Beach.

Swimming

See the earlier Beaches section for information on harbour and ocean swimming. Pools include the saltwater Boy Charlton pool near the Domain, the North Sydney pool next to Luna Park in Milsons Point and the pool in Prince Alfred Park, near Central Station.

Surfing

At the various surf beaches there are board-hire places, such as Bondi Surf Company on Campbell Parade at Bondi Beach, Surfworld at 250 Coogee Bay Rd in Coogee and Aloha Surf on Pittwater Rd in Manly.

Sailing & Boating

There are many sailing schools, such as Northside Sailing School (☎ 969 3972) at the southern end of the Spit Bridge in Mosman, which has lessons for beginners in yachts, dinghies or sailboards. The school also hires sailboards and dinghies for $15 per hour. Barrenjoey Sails & Cats (☎ 018 862 000) also teaches and rents.

The Pittwater and adjacent Broken Bay offer excellent sailing. Scotland Island Schooners (☎ 9999 3954) at Church Point cruise the area in an old 65-foot schooner, *Bon Ton*. It can drop off and pick up at the YHA's Pittwater Hostel in Ku-ring-gai Chase National Park. A day on the water costs around $30. This outfit is also a sailing school specialising in ocean-going boats.

Diving

There's good diving from ocean beaches and shipwrecks to explore from boat dives. Plenty of outfits will take you diving and many run dive courses, including Pro Dive (☎ 665 6333) in Coogee, Manly Dive Centre (☎ 977 2095) and Moby Dive (☎ 976 3297) in Manly.

Qualified divers can dive with the sharks at Manly's Oceanworld; the cost is $55 plus equipment.

Canoeing & Kayaking

The Canoe Association of New South Wales (☎ 660 4597) will point you towards clubs and hire places. Canoe Specialists (☎ 969 4590) at the south end of the Spit Bridge on Spit Rd in Mosman rent single/double sea kayaks for $10/20 an hour, less for longer.

Natural Wanders (☎ 555 9788) has kayak tours of the harbour, on which you can go paddling under the bridge and stop in secluded bays to take short walks. No kayaking experience is necessary. A tour of about five hours costs $65. You might be able to book this at YHA hostels.

Other Activities

The Blue Mountains offer activities such as bushwalking, abseiling, canyoning and climbing. See the Around Sydney section for some Katoomba-based adventure outfits.

The *Sydney Morning Herald*'s Friday *Metro* guide lists activities in its Out & About section; notice boards at hostels are usually crammed with suggestions. Wildwise (☎ 360 2099) runs adventure-style activities for women.

Organised Tours

There's a vast array of city and area tours. Ask at the New South Wales Government Travel Centre in Castlereagh St for details, and check out the free magazines from hotels and so on. Companies include AAT King's, Australian Pacific, Clipper/Gray Line and Murrays. You can join a half-day city or koala-cuddling tour from $30; a full-day 'the works' tour will cost over $80. Many companies also run tours to destinations such as the Blue Mountains (from $50), Canberra ($60) and the Hunter Valley ($75).

An interesting way to see Sydney is by helicopter – not the cheapest way to go but if you're ever going to take a helicopter flight it might as well be over this beautiful harbour. Companies include Heli-Scenic (☎ 317 3402) with a variety flights from $95 per person.

The Wonderbus runs backpacker-friendly day tours of the Blue Mountains ($30) and overnight trips ($74) which include the Blue Mountains, Jenolan Caves and a visit to the Australian Wildlife Park where you can cuddle a koala. It's possible to arrange a stopover at Katoomba. Book at the YHA Travel Centre (☎ 261 1111) or a YHA hostel in Glebe.

Oz-Trek (☎ 360 3444), 1/318 Crown St, Darlinghurst, runs popular day trips and camping tours aimed at backpackers. There's a daily tour of the Blue Mountains (about $34) and the operators will pick you up from most hostel areas in Sydney.

Festivals

The Festival of Sydney is mainly devoted to arts and lasts all January. Features include open-air opera and music in the parks. Sydney's Chinese celebrate their new year in Chinatown in January or February.

The highlight of the month-long Gay & Lesbian Mardi Gras (☎ 332 4088) is the highly colourful parade along Oxford St which ends in an incredible party at the showgrounds. The mardi gras is held in late February or early March.

The showgrounds are also the venue for the Royal Easter Show, with its livestock displays, sideshows and rodeos.

The Sydney Film Festival is held in June. The Sydney Biennale is a modern art festival held in June in even-numbered years.

On Boxing Day the harbour is a fantastic sight, as boats of all shapes and sizes crowd its waters to farewell the competitors in the Sydney to Hobart Yacht Race.

Places to Stay

There's a wide variety of accommodation including a large selection of travellers' hostels. In summer, the busy season, rates rise (or special deals vanish) just about everywhere, from caravan parks to five-star hotels. In winter it's worth hunting around for bargains. The New South Wales Government Travel Centre (☎ 231 4444) often knows of special deals.

Bed & Breakfast Sydneyside (☎ 449 4430), PO Box 555, Turramurra, arranges accommodation in private homes for about $40 to $65 a night for a single, $55 to $95 a double.

For longer-term stays there are cheap places in the 'flats to let' and 'share accommodation' ads in the *Sydney Morning Herald*, especially on Wednesday and Saturday. Many travellers find flat-shares through other travellers they meet in hostels. Hostel notice boards are good sources of information.

Camping Sydney's caravan parks are a long way out of town. Listed here are some within 25 km of the centre.

Meriton North Ryde (☎ 88 72177), corner Lane Cove and Fontenoy Rds, North Ryde; sites $18 double, cabins from $50.

East's Van Park Lane Cove River (☎ 805 0500), Plassey Rd, North Ryde; sites from $15 double, on-site vans from $44, cabins from $50.

Sheralee Tourist Caravan Park (☎ 798 7059), 88 Bryant St, Rockdale; sites from $12.

Lakeside Caravan Park (☎ 913 7845), Lake Park Rd, Narrabeen; camping from $14, cabins from $55.

The Grand Pines Caravan Park (☎ 529 7329), 289 The Grand Parade, Ramsgate; no camping, on-site vans from $40 double.

Hostels The $10-a-night barrier has been broken and average hostels now charge about $12 and some higher-quality places

---

Accommodation

When Maureen and I first set up Lonely Planet we lived in the basement of a Paddington terrace in Sydney, and since then we've made lots of trips and visits to the harbour city and tried out all sorts of areas around the city, either staying with friends or in a variety of places, more than a few of which feature here. The Cross is the backpacker centre and is great fun if you like a little raucous squalor. Bondi is Sydney's best-known beach and like the Cross it has lots of activity and plenty of places to eat. If you'd like something quieter the distance to Manly is no big deal because you ride back and forth on the best transport Sydney has to offer – a harbour ferry.

Tony Wheeler

charge $15 or more. In winter the $10 bed sometimes reappears. Most hostels are acutely aware of what the competition is charging and the prices given here could easily fluctuate by a few dollars.

The largest concentration of hostels is still in Kings Cross but hostels are appearing in some new areas such as Newtown. Some hostels have set hours for checking in and out, although all have 24-hour access once you have handed over your cash.

If you are Australian, getting into a hostel might be a problem, especially in Kings Cross. Of course, the YHA hostels (in Glebe) take members of any nationality and they are cleaner and better run than many backpackers' hostels.

City Centre The excellent *YWCA* hostel (☎ 264 2451) is on Wentworth Ave at the corner of Liverpool St. Both men and women can stay. Dorm accommodation costs $18 a night with a maximum stay of three nights. Rooms go for $42/60/75 for singles/twins/triples, $60/85/100 with bathroom. There are cheaper monthly rates.

The big *CB Private Hotel* (☎ 211 5115) at 417 Pitt St (between Goulburn and Campbell Sts) has some dorm beds at $10 per person, and occasionally other city pubs also have dorm beds.

Kings Cross & Nearby Heading north along Victoria St from Kings Cross Station, the first hostel you come to is *Plane Tree Lodge* (☎ 356 4551) at No 172. This is an average Kings Cross hostel, with a variety of rooms. Rates start at $12 ($75 weekly) in a four-bed dorm, $11 ($70 weekly) in a six-bed. There are some singles at $20 (no weekly rate), twins at $25 ($170 weekly) and doubles at $30 ($190 weekly). You'll pay more in summer.

Next down the street at No 166 is *High-field House Private Hotel* (☎ 358 1552), catering to overseas travellers and run by friendly Swedes. It's secure and clean enough and the rates stay much the same all year, with singles/doubles for $25/40

($150/240 weekly). You can share a twin for $15 per person or share a triple for $12 per person.

The *Original Backpackers* (☎ 356 3232) at No 162 *is* the original hostel in this part of the world and it's still going strong. The atmosphere is good, it's reasonably clean and there are good-sized common areas. Dorms cost between $10 and $13 (from $70 weekly), and singles/doubles are $20/28 ($120/160 weekly). There's a good notice board.

The *Travellers Rest* (☎ 358 4606) is very clean and well run, with well-equipped rooms, some with balconies overlooking Victoria St. The rates tend to stay the same year round: dorms (three-bed) $13 ($72 weekly); singles $22, twins $28, twins/doubles with bathroom $30. Across the road at No 141, *Kanga House* (☎ 357 7897) is a basic place charging from $10 ($60 weekly) for dorms and $15/24 ($90/144 weekly) for singles/doubles.

Back on the eastern side of Victoria St, at No 144 you'll find one of the three busy *Jolly Swagman* hostels, also called *Sydney Central Backpackers*. They all charge $11 ($66 weekly) for dorms, $24/26 ($144/156 weekly) for singles/doubles. These rates might drop a little in winter and rise a little in summer. The rooms have fridges and cooking facilities. As well as the Victoria St hostel (☎ 357 4733) there are Jolly Swagmen at 16 Orwell St (☎ 358 6600) and 14 Spring-field Mall (☎ 358 6400).

On Orwell St at No 6, the family-run *Eva's Backpackers* (☎ 358 2185) is clean and friendly. High-season rates are $14 in dorms, $32 for twins or doubles and $48 for a three-person room with bathroom. If you stay two nights they'll refund your airport bus fare. Prices drop in winter, when there are also weekly rates.

The big *Downunder Hostel* (☎ 358 1433) at 25 Hughes St has been renovated and is much more spruce than it once was. Dorms cost $11 or $12 ($70 weekly) and doubles are $30 ($160 weekly). There are free excursions, such as outings to Palm Beach, at least weekly, but more often in summer.

Completely renovated and refurbished, the big, squeaky-clean *Backpackers Headquarters* (☎ 331 6180) at 79 Bayswater Rd charges from $13 in dorms and from $17 per person in doubles.

Fountain International Hostel (☎ 358 6799) at 22 Darlinghurst Rd, next to the Bourbon & Beefsteak restaurant, has fairly large dorms scattered through a warren of corridors. Dorms cost from $10 ($60 weekly) and twins from $20.

One of the most popular hostels is *Barncleuth House* (☎ 358 1689), often known as the Pink House. It's east of Darlinghurst Rd at 6 Barncleuth Square. It has a courtyard garden and log fires when it's cold. Dorm beds are $11 ($70 weekly) and doubles are $12 per person (around $80 weekly). Some dorms have double-bed bunks which go for $10 per person. Winter rates are a little lower.

At 9 McDonald St, off Macleay St north of the El Alamein Fountain, *Rucksack Rest* (☎ 358 2348) is a long-established hostel, quiet, clean and in fair condition. Sam, the owner, lives-in. Dorm beds go for $12 or $13, twins/doubles are about $28 and singles are $20; it is cheaper by the week. A couple of doors away at 3 McDonald St, *Backpackers Village* (☎ 358 2808) is quite a large hostel in a block of flats.

Forbes Terrace (☎ 358 4327) is a good new hostel at 153 Forbes St in Woolloomooloo, just north of William St. It's clean and quiet and has a courtyard area. Each room has a TV, fridge and tea- and coffee-making facilities. Dorm beds go for $15, singles are $25 to $35, and twins cost from $40. Forbes Restaurant next door is owned by the same people and there are backpacker specials.

Fountain Plaza (☎ 358 6799) at the corner of Darlinghurst Rd and Llankelly Place is a private hotel now aiming at backpackers. Shared rooms cost $10 per person ($60 weekly) and singles/doubles are just $16/25 ($100/140 weekly). Similar is the nearby *Astoria* (☎ 356 3666) where all rooms have bathroom, TV, air-con and fridge – but don't expect everything to work. Per-person rates

are $13 ($75 weekly) in four-person rooms, $15 ($85) in twins and $25 ($150) for a single room. The *Lido* (☎ 358 4844), also known as *Backpackers Connection*, is just off Darlinghurst Rd at 2 Roslyn St. It's a big motel which concentrates on the backpacker trade. The rooms are large and each has TV, bathroom, ceiling fan and air-con. Dorm beds go for $12 ($73.50 weekly) and motel rooms cost $45 for a single or a double. There's a basic kitchen on the roof.

South of the Centre *Kangaroo Bakpak* (☎ 319 5915) is at 635 South Dowling St in Surry Hills, just north of the corner of Cleveland St. This is a very friendly place which gets consistently good feedback. Dorm beds go for $12 ($70 weekly). Bus Nos 372, 393 and 395 run here from Central Station.

The *Excelsior Hotel* (☎ 211 4945) is also in Surry Hills at 64 Foveaux St, on the corner of Bellevue St and only a few blocks from Central Station. It's a small pub with reasonable accommodation (with shared bathrooms) and a few large dorms. Dorm beds are $13 ($80 weekly) and doubles are $35 ($30 if you stay more than a couple of days and $180 weekly). There are cooking facilities.

Across the road from Prince Alfred Park at 207 Cleveland St in Redfern, the *Alfred Park Private Hotel* (☎ 319 4031) has been a high-quality, low-cost place for a few years, and is now concentrating on backpackers. Dorm beds cost from $15, singles from $25 to $35 and twins from $40 (around $50 with bathroom).

At 83 Regent St near Redfern Station the *Regent St Hotel* (☎ 698 2793) is a pub but also a reasonable hostel with variable rates that tend to be a little lower than those in the Cross.

Billabong Gardens (☎ 550 3236) at 5 Egan St in Newtown is a good new hostel. Dorm beds cost from $12, twins and doubles from $35 or $50 with bathroom. There are also triples ($60) and a family room ($65) with bathrooms. Weekly rates are available. They do airport pick-ups between 9 am and 9 pm. To get here from Railway Square take bus No 422, 423, 426 or 428, all of which run up Newtown's King St; get off at Missenden Rd. By train, alight at Newtown Station and turn right into King St; Egan St is about four blocks along, on the left.

Glebe Glebe is a good place to stay, with a choice of hostels, places to eat and nightlife. Bus No 431 from the city goes along Glebe Point Rd. The shortest walking route from the city is across Pyrmont Bridge at Darling Harbour then along Pyrmont Bridge Rd.

Wattle House (☎ 692 0879) at 44 Hereford St is a good little hostel, very clean and with some nice touches such as doonas (duvets). Dorm beds are $14 ($85 weekly) and twin rooms are $34 ($210 weekly). *Alishan International Guesthouse* (☎ 566 4048) at 100 Glebe Point Rd also has good shared accommodation, with dorm beds at $18 a night ($105 weekly).

The YHA has two large, clean and friendly hostels, *Hereford YHA Lodge* (☎ 660 5577) at 51 Hereford St, and *Glebe Point YHA Hostel* (☎ 692 8418) at 262 Glebe Point Rd. Hereford Lodge has a small rooftop pool and an inexpensive cafe. There are six-bed dorms at $15 ($95 weekly), four-bed at $17 ($110 weekly) and twin rooms at $44. Glebe Point has six-bed dorms for $15, four-bed for $16 ($95 weekly) and twin rooms for $40. Both hostels offer a large range of activities, and they both store luggage and deduct the airport bus fare from your bill. The YHA also operates a summer hostel at St Andrews College at Sydney University, charging $15 in dorms and $17 per person in twins.

At the northern end of Glebe Point Rd, near the YHA hostel, *Glebe Village Backpackers* (☎ 660 8133) is a large place in two big houses. There's something of a rabbit warren about it and it's well-worn but many people like the lively atmosphere. Dorms cost $14 or $15 and singles/doubles are $20/40.

Bondi Beach The most famous of Sydney's beaches, Bondi has a range of accommodation and lots of long-term working travellers. To get here from the city you could take a

bus all the way but it's quicker to take a train to Bondi Junction and bus No 380, 382 or 389 from there. Buying a combined ticket is a little cheaper than buying two fares.

Lamrock Hostel (☎ 365 0221) is at 7 Lamrock Ave, a block back from Campbell Parade on the corner of Lamrock and Jacques Aves. It's a well-worn but bright house with dorms at $15 ($80 weekly) and twins for about $40. These rates stay the same all year. They also have long-term beds in the building next door at about $60 weekly. This place has been running for years and it's friendly and popular.

Other places in Bondi have shared rooms; see the following Hotels & Guesthouses section.

Coogee It's worth ringing before setting off to Coogee as some hostels have limited office hours. Bus Nos 373 and 374 run from Circular Quay to Coogee, Nos 371 and 372 run from Railway Square (near Central Station) and Nos 314 and 315 run from Bondi Junction.

Surfside Backpackers Coogee (☎ 315 7888) at 186 Arden St (the entrance is around the corner in Alfreda St) is above McDonald's and across the road from the bus stop – and the beach. There are lots of stairs! Off-season dorm rates are around $13 ($75 weekly), rising to about $15 (no weekly rates) in summer. Doubles go for $34 all year.

A block inland at 116 Brook St, on the corner of Alfreda St, *Aaronbrook Lodge* (☎ 665 7798 or 315 8222) is in a rambling old house. Off-season dorm rates are $12 ($70 weekly) and $28 for a double or twin ($160 weekly).

Further from the beach and a short but stiff walk uphill is the popular *Coogee Beach Backpackers* (☎ 665 7735) at 94 Beach St, which runs beside the Coogee Palace centre at the northern end of the beach. The hostel is in a Federation-era house with a more modern block next door. Dorms are $15, doubles $32, and rates are a little lower in winter. There's an initial compulsory sheet-hire charge of $1. *Indy's* (☎ 315 7644) is at 302 Arden St on the corner of Dudley St. It's on the hill south of the beach and is a smaller place in a pleasant old house.

About a km up Coogee Bay Rd at No 40, the *Aegean* (☎ 398 4999), also known as *Coogee Bay Rd Backpackers*, has shared accommodation in self-contained flats for around $12 (from $65 weekly), with twins from about $26. There's a range of rates and good deals in winter.

Manly Manly has great beaches and few city hassles, and it's just 30 minutes by ferry (15 minutes by JetCat) from Circular Quay.

Manly Beach Resort Backpackers (☎ 977 4188) is part of a motel on the corner of Pittwater Rd and Carlton St, but backpackers have their own section in a newly renovated house. The four dorms ($14) are spacious and clean; by now there should be twin rooms (from $30). The long-running *Manly Astra Backpackers* (☎ 977 2092) is nearby at 68-70 Pittwater Rd. Bunks in dorms or twin rooms go for $13 per person or $78 a week.

Cremorne Point The *Harbourside Hotel* (☎ 953 7977), at 41 Cremorne Rd on Cremorne Point, isn't a hotel, but a large, loose hostel catering mainly to backpackers and young locals working in Sydney. It won't suit everyone but it's worth checking out. Dorms cost between $10 and $12, with singles/doubles from $20/25. Take a ferry to Cremorne Wharf and walk up the hill a couple of hundred metres.

Avalon For a break from inner-city life, try the relaxed northern beachside suburb of Avalon, where the purpose-built *Avalon Beach Hostel* (☎ 918 9709) at 59 Avalon Parade is a good place to stay. There are boards and bikes for hire and the hostel arranges activities such as abseiling, sailing and hiking. Dorms cost from $12 a night ($80 weekly) and singles/doubles are $28/32. Take bus No 190 from Wynyard Park on York St in the city and ask for Avalon Parade. The trip takes about 1¼ hours and costs $4.20.

Hotels & Guesthouses – bottom end
Although you might have to search for a while to find them, there are some reasonably cheap hotels and guesthouses in Sydney.

City Centre & the Rocks At 417 Pitt St near the corner of Goulburn St, the *CB Private Hotel* (☎ 211 5115) opened in 1908 and was once the largest hotel in the country with over 200 rooms, mostly singles. It's plain and fairly well maintained, although it gets a lot of wear. Singles/doubles/triples with shared bathroom are $25/40/50. Shared rooms are $10 per person. The weekly rate in single rooms (only) is $99.

A block west at 700A George St, the *George Private Hotel* (☎ 211 1800) is also plain and clean. The rooms are more spartan than the foyer suggests but they are OK. Cooking and laundry facilities are available. Singles/doubles with shared bathroom are $30/45 and a double with bathroom is $60. There are weekly rates and the daily rates might drop a little in winter.

Close to Central Station but out of the central city is the *Central Private Hotel* (☎ 212 1068) at 356 Elizabeth St, at the corner of Randle St. It's clean and comfortable enough. Singles/doubles with shared bathroom cost from $25/35 (from $120/180 a week); a double with bathroom is $45.

The *Criterion Hotel* (☎ 264 3093) on the corner of Pitt and Park Sts is a large pub with rooms from $40/50 or $60/70 with bathroom.

On the corner of Lower Fort St and Cumberland St, the small *Harbour View Hotel* (☎ 252 3769) is a hundred metres from the Rocks. There's some noise from trains on the bridge and more from the bands in the bar, but with clean rooms at $35/40 it's great value for the location.

Kings Cross & Nearby One of the accommodation bargains in the Cross is *Challis Lodge* (☎ 358 5422) at 21 Challis Ave. It's a pair of big old terraces with simple but clean and well-maintained rooms for $28/34 ($120/154 weekly) or $36/42 ($154/168) with bathroom. Larger rooms at the front have balconies and go for $54 ($266 weekly). The owners are due to open a new place at 71 Macleay St.

Springfield Lodge (☎ 358 3222) on Springfield Ave has simple guesthouse-style accommodation, clean and well maintained. All rooms have fridges, TVs and tea- and coffee-making facilities. Rooms start at $30/38 ($140/168 weekly) or from $42/44 (from $182/196 weekly) with bathroom. Close by at 15 Springfield Ave, the *Bernly Private Hotel* (☎ 358 3122) has more modern rooms. All rooms share toilets but some of them have private showers. Singles/doubles/triples cost $40/50/60 or $45/55/65 with shower. Prices haven't risen for years and the friendly manager empha-sises that the rates are negotiable.

Also in the area are *Maksim Lodge* (☎ 356 3399) at 37 Darlinghurst Rd ($55/65), *Orwell Lodge* (☎ 358 1745) at 18-20 Orwell St ($30/40), *Montpelier Private Hotel* (☎ 358 6960) at 39A Elizabeth Bay Rd (from $25/30) and *Holiday Lodge* (☎ 356 3955) at 55 Macleay St (from $48/55).

Bondi Beach The *Hotel Bondi* (☎ 30 3271) on the corner of Campbell Parade and Curlewis St is a grand old seaside hotel with low rates that stay the same year round – which means that vacancies are scarce in summer. Singles/doubles cost from $25/27.50 or $27.50/35 with bathroom. In the off season there are weekly rates.

Rates at bottom-end places in Bondi vary depending on demand. The *Thelellen Beach Inn* (☎ 30 5333), at the southern end of the beach strip at 2 Campbell Parade, dates from the 1930s and is in fair condition. Singles/doubles cost from $30/35 and shared rooms are $15 per person. From May to December there are cheaper weekly rates. These people also have *Thelellen Lodge* (☎ 30 1521), a boarding house at 11A Consett Ave. It's smallish and quite well kept. The rates are the same as at the The-lellen Beach Inn (although there are no shared rooms) with lots of off-season spe-cials. Next door at No 11 is the *Bondi Beach*

Guesthouse (☎ 389 8309) with similar rooms and rates.

On the corner of Consett and Lamrock Aves, *Merrimeads Flatettes* (☎ 30 5063) sometimes has specials such as shared 'flatettes' from $12 per person or $65 weekly.

South of the main beach area (and in the suburb of Tamarama) *Bondi Boutique Hotel* (☎ 365 2088) at 63 Fletcher St, on the corner of Dellview St, is apparently worth checking out. Their advertised rates are from $30 per person, including a big breakfast and dinner; dorm beds are from $10.

Coogee The *Grand Pacific Private Hotel* (☎ 665 6301) is right on the southern end of the beach, at the end of Carr St. It has seen much better days but it is cheap and there are kitchen and laundry facilities. Singles range from about $15 to $20 and doubles from $24 to $60. Shared rooms go for $12 per person.

North of the Bridge *St Leonards Mansions* (☎ 439 6999) at 7 Park Rd, St Leonards, occupies three well-kept old houses and has well-equipped, clean rooms for $45 a single, plus $10 for each extra person (up to six people), or $35 plus $10 with shared bath-rooms. Most rooms have a TV, phone, fridge and cooking facilities. A light breakfast is free and there are laundry facilities, parking and a garden. It's a nice place and good value. From St Leonards Station turn left (west) along the Pacific Highway and Park Rd is second on the left.

Kirribilli, just across the bridge from the city, has a number of guesthouses. You can take a ferry to Kirribilli Wharf or a train to Milsons Point Station and walk down. *Tremayne Private Hotel* (☎ 955 4155) at 89 Carabella St (near the corner of Fitzroy St) is a large, clean guesthouse with weekly rates (only) from $115/180 a single/double, including meals. Bathrooms are shared. There are some units with bathrooms for about $200 per week for a double. *Kirribilli Court Private Hotel* (☎ 955 4344) at 45 Cara-bella St has dorm beds for $10 and singles/doubles for $20/30. Further south on

Carabella St at No 12A, *Glenferrie Private Hotel* (☎ 955 1685) is a very large old house. Some rooms are pretty ordinary, others have been renovated. Rates, which include breakfast and dinner, vary a lot. Singles/doubles in the old rooms range from $90/120 a week and in the new rooms from about $110/160. Daily rates from about $20/40 are possible and you can negotiate lower rates if you don't want meals.

In Neutral Bay on the corner of Karraba Rd and Hayes St and not far from the ferry wharf, the *Neutral Bay Motor Lodge* (☎ 953 4199) is more like a guesthouse than a motel. Several travellers report that it's a reasonable place to stay and rates start at $50/55.

Manly Manly is particularly susceptible to summertime price rises.

The *Eversham Private Hotel* (☎ 977 2423) on Victoria Parade near the corner of South Steyne is a large, basic place where the rates haven't risen for years. Singles go for $123 to $133 a week (only) and doubles are $150. There are also deals which include meals. A major renovation is about to take place but they say that prices won't rise. Ask at Manly Lodge (☎ 977 8655), across Victoria Parade, about *Lansdown Court* and *Manly Cove* where dorm beds go for around $20 ($110 weekly) and singles/doubles are $40/50 ($145/180 weekly).

Hotels, Motels, Guesthouses & Serviced Apartments – middle It's always worth asking about special rates such as weekend deals.

City Centre & Nearby Right in the Rocks the *Lord Nelson Brewery Hotel* (☎ 251 4044) is on the corner of Kent and Argyle Sts, with doubles from $60 to $100.

Well worth checking out is *Sydney City Centre Serviced Apartments* (☎ 233 6677 or 223 3529) at 7 Elizabeth St, between Martin Place and Hunter St. Each apartment is fully equipped, down to a washing machine and drier. The apartments are bedsits but they are a good size. Rates start at $60 a double, plus $10 for each extra person.

The *Wynyard Hotel* (☎ 299 1330), on the corner of Clarence and Erskine Sts, is a pleasant pub with rooms for $45/55/65 a single/double/twin, with cheaper weekly rates. The rooms are plain but clean and comfortable; bathrooms are shared. Weekly guests can use the hotel's kitchen. At the recently renovated *Grand Hotel* (☎ 232 3755), at 30 Hunter St, just west of Pitt St, rooms go for $50/70. The hotel's dining room serves lunch Monday to Friday and dinner on Thursday and Friday nights.

The *Westend Hotel* (☎ 211 4822) at 412 Pitt St is a big, reasonably priced place with fully equipped motel-style rooms for $60/70. There's a bar and an inexpensive restaurant on the premises.

Close to Chinatown and Darling Harbour, the *Travellers Rest Hotel* (☎ toll-free 1800 023 071) at 37 Ultimo Rd in Haymarket has singles/doubles from $58/68 or $68/78 with bathroom. They have a four-bed room which they will let at $27 per person, which is expensive for a dorm.

The *Metro* chain has a couple of serviced apartments in the city: on the corner of Sussex and King Sts (☎ 290 9200) at $120 a double, and at 2 Francis St (☎ 360 5988) just east of Hyde Park at $100 a double. They also have a motel (☎ 319 4133) at 1 Meagher St in Chippendale, at $85 a double.

Kings Cross & Nearby On Bayswater Rd just east of Darlinghurst Rd, the *Barclay Hotel* (☎ 358 6133) has a wide range of rooms, some starting at under $50. At 40 Bayswater Rd there's a *Metro Motor Inn* (☎ 356 3511), charging $85 a double. At 30 Darlinghurst Rd, the Flag *Kingsview Motel* (☎ 358 5599) has been recently renovated and costs about $85.

On the corner of William and Brougham Sts, a block west of the Darlinghurst Rd and Victoria St junction, *O'Malley's Hotel* (☎ 357 2211) has good rooms for $50/60. A few rooms share bathrooms. At 145 Darlinghurst Rd, just south of William St, *L'Otel* (☎ 360 6868) is a stylish boutique hotel charging from $80 a double.

The *Kendall* (☎ 357 3200) at 122 Victoria

St is a comfortable private hotel in a pair of restored terrace houses. Single/double rooms go for $100/115 including continental breakfast, with occasional specials.

East of the Cross is *Bersens Cosmopolitan Hotel* (☎ 327 3207) at 2B Mona Rd, near the intersection with New South Head Rd (the continuation of William St/Kings Cross Rd). Edgewater Station is nearby. Each room has a mini-kitchen with a fridge and microwave and some have good views. Singles/doubles start at $75/85. The *Lodge* (☎ 327 8511) at 38-44 New South Head Rd in Rushcutters Bay has studio apartments for about $60 a double ($320 weekly). Check in at the Bayside Motel diagonally opposite.

In up-market Double Bay the *Savoy Double Bay Hotel* (☎ 326 1411) at 41-45 Knox St is a small place with good rooms from about $70 a double, rising when things are busy. This is good value.

Glebe *Alishan International Guesthouse* (☎ 566 4048) at 100 Glebe Point Rd is something like an up-market hostel, with good common areas including kitchen and laundry facilities, and a small garden with a barbecue. Singles/doubles with bathroom go for $65/75, dropping to around $50/65 when things are slow.

As well as hostel accommodation, the YHA's *Hereford Lodge* (☎ 660 5577) at 51 Wattle St has good motel-style rooms (lacking phones) and you don't have to be a member to stay in one. A single costs $60 plus $5 for each extra person, up to four. YHA members get a discount.

The *Rooftop Motel* (☎ 660 7777) at 146-148 Glebe Point Rd is a fairly simple motel charging $70 per room, with variations in busy or slack times. Further north at 196 Glebe Point Rd the *Haven Inn* (☎ 660 6655) is quite good, with large rooms at $140, sometimes dropping to around $90. There's a heated swimming pool, secure parking and a restaurant.

Bondi Beach The *Hotel Bondi* (☎ 30 3271), an impressive old pile on the corner of Campbell Parade and Curlewis St, has newly renovated suites from $60 to $80 and other rooms with beach views from $50. These prices stay the same year round, so it's great value in summer, when you'll have to book ahead. There are also cheaper rooms; see the Bottom End section.

The *Bondi Beach Motel* (☎ 365 5233) at 68 Gould St, a block back from Campbell Parade off Curlewis St, is reasonable and charges from $60/70, more in the summer. At 152 Campbell Parade, on the corner of Roscoe St, the *Bondi Beachside Inn* (☎ 30 5311) has older-style motel rooms which are being upgraded. They're small but each has a kitchen and a balcony and it's fair value at $69 for an older single or double, and up to $88 for a renovated room with a beach view. Across the road is the more modern *Breakers Motel* (☎ 365 3300) at 164-176 Campbell Parade with rooms from $90 to $110, rising by about 10% in summer.

Ravesi's (☎ 365 4422, 365 4483 after hours) is an interesting three-star place in a recycled building on the corner of Campbell Parade and Hall St. There are only 16 rooms and suites, some with their own terraces. Rates start at $88 but you'll have to pay at least $110 for a beach view.

Manly *Manly Lodge* (☎ 977 8655) at 22 Victoria Parade is a guesthouse but not in the usual musty sense – there's a holiday atmosphere here. Most rooms are small but well furnished. Rooms with bathroom cost from around $70 a double, more in summer. In winter or slack times there are some excellent deals.

The *Steyne Hotel* (☎ 977 4977) on the corner of the Corso and North Steyne has rooms, most with shared bathroom, from $40/60. The *Manly Beach Resort* (☎ 977 4188) at 6 Carlton St, at the corner of Pittwater Rd, is a reasonable motel with rooms for $70/75, plus $10 surcharge in December and January. There are a few other motels in this price range, such as *Manly Paradise* (☎ 977 5799) at 54 North Steyne.

Periwinkle Guesthouse (☎ 977 4668), a restored Victorian house facing the harbour beach at 19 East Esplanade, has guesthouse accommodation for $70/80. Kitchen and laundry facilities are available.

Hotels, Motels & Serviced Apartments – top end

Many expensive hotels cater to business people so their rates might be lower on weekends. Serviced apartments sometimes sleep more than two people and with lower weekly rates they can work out inexpensive among a group.

Some of the many, many hotels and serviced apartments charging between $100 and $200 a double are: *Wynyard Travelodge* (☎ 299 3000), 7 York St (from $130); the *Stafford* (☎ 251 6711), 75 Harrington St, the Rocks (serviced apartments, from $170); the *Ramada* (☎ 365 5666), Campbell Parade, Bondi Beach (from $170); the *Century Radisson* (☎ 368 4000), 203 Victoria St, Kings Cross (from $130); and *17 Elizabeth Bay Rd* (☎ 358 8999, toll-free 1800 251 917), Elizabeth Bay (serviced apartments, from $110/140).

Colleges

Many colleges at Sydney University and the University of New South Wales are eager for casual guests during vacations, mainly the long break from mid-December to late January. Most places quote B&B rates but it is often possible to negotiate a lower bed-only rate. Ask about weekly or fortnightly rates which might be much cheaper.

Sydney University This is south-west of Chippendale and not far from Glebe.

Darlington House (☎ 692 3322), terrace houses sleeping four to eight, $350 to $400 a week.
International House (☎ 950 9800), rooms for $30. During term time three serviced rooms are available for students and visitors connected with the university, from $55 B&B.
St Johns College (☎ 394 5200), doesn't always stay open for all of the long vacation. When it does, rooms with bathroom and all meals go for $250 a week; rooms with shared bathrooms are $210.
Wesley College (☎ 565 3333), rooms available during any vacation except Easter, $40 B&B (students $32.50), $51.50 full board (students $45.50).

Women's College (☎ 516 1642), students and YHA members pay $32 B&B, $37 DB&B and $42 full board. Everyone else pays $40/46/52. There are also some twin rooms which go for $53/64/72 for students and YHA members and $60/72/80 for others.
St Pauls College (☎ 550 7444).
Sancta Sophia College (☎ 519 7123).

University of New South Wales This is further from the centre but closer to the beaches and not too far from Oxford St.

International House (☎ 663 0418), full board $35 students, $45 others. For a few weeks around Christmas there are also B&B rates: $25 students, $35 others.
New College (☎ 697 8962), sometimes has accommodation at other vacations as well as the long break. B&B $25.
Kensington College (☎ 663 8111).
Shalom College (☎ 663 1366).

Places to Eat

Sydney has an enormous range of eateries offering an equally impressive range of cuisines, a reflection of the country's ethnic diversity. If you're going to explore the options a useful book is *Cheap Eats in Sydney* ($7.95).

For a splurge, consider *Kable's* at the Regent Hotel on George St. It's one of Australia's best restaurants and the prices reflect this, but there's a lunch-time deal where you can choose from the full menu and pay $37.50 for three courses or $32.50 for two. An enjoyable way to spend a lot of money is to take Doyle's lunch-time water taxi from the steps on the western side of Circular Quay ($7 return, services start at 11.30 am, weekdays only) to *Doyle's on the Beach* (☎ 337 2007) at Watsons Bay, where main courses average around $25.

City Centre There's no shortage of places for a snack or meal in the city, especially on weekdays. They are clustered around railway stations, in shopping arcades and at the bases of office towers.

If you want a quiet cuppa away from the city bustle, take the lift to *Noonan's* at Level 2 of the Strand Arcade. A wide range of teas

NEW SOUTH WALES

costs $2 for a one-person pot, there are cakes and salads and Noonan's does a good breakfast, such as bacon & eggs for $7.50, including tea or coffee. Not far away is the collection of stylish eateries and bars in the top levels of the *Skygarden*, a complex in a recycled building on Pitt St Mall.

For a lunch-time vegetarian snack, drop into *Carruthers*, a takeaway place on Druitt St near Clarence St. More substantial vegetarian meals are sold at *El Sano*, downstairs on the north-western corner of Pitt St and Martin Place.

A little way north on Pitt St in the old Angel Hotel is *Merivales*, a stylish bar, restaurant and coffee shop. There's another Merivales on Pitt St just north of the mall, at No 194.

The *Centrepoint Tavern*, downstairs on the Pitt St Mall near the corner of Market St, is a plush cafeteria with main courses between $8 and $12. Towering above Centrepoint is the Sydney Tower with a coffee shop and two pricey restaurants.

On the corner of George and Park Sts, the 2nd-floor cafeteria in *Woolworth's* has meals from $6; a roast will set you back about $7. Better value is the small food hall in the basement (enter from an arcade in Pitt St) where there's a number of shops, mainly Asian, with dishes from $4.50 or less.

There is a small collection of Spanish places along Liverpool St between George and Sussex Sts, such as *Captain Torres* which has tapas in the bar from $3.50 and main courses between $9 and $18.

At 152 Elizabeth St, just south of Liverpool St, the *Cyprus Hellene Club* is open Monday to Saturday. Most main courses are $7.50, with steaks for $8.50. A little dearer is the *Hellenic Club*, upstairs at 251 Elizabeth St, across from Hyde Park.

The streets around Central Station have Asian places spilling over from Chinatown, old-style cafes and a few pubs with counter meals, such as the *Chamberlain Hotel* on the corner of Pitt and Campbell Sts which has $5 meals. Along George St are several cafes with breakfast for less than $6, such as the *Cafe Inn* at No 768, across from Ultimo Rd.

One of Sydney's cheapest places to eat is *Mekong*, an Asian place at 711 George St, where you can choose two dishes and rice and still have change from $5. A little further south on George St at No 735 is *Mother Chu's*, more expensive but a rare Chinese restaurant which serves vegan food. It's open for lunch and dinner daily and has main courses for around $8 to $10, plus cheaper snacks. Nearby on the corner of Valentine St, the *Malaya* was once a very cheap Chinese/Indonesian/Malaysian eatery patronised by students. It has moved up market but still has plenty of main courses between $8.50 and $14, with cheaper vegetarian dishes.

Carriages in Central Station serves cafeteria-style meals which are OK if a little on the stodgy side. Roast beef and vegies goes for $7.50 and there are other dishes for much less.

Chinatown Officially, Chinatown consists only of the pedestrian mall on Dixon St but there are many good Chinese restaurants in the streets nearby. You can spend a small fortune at some outstanding Chinese restaurants with internationally famous chefs, or eat well for next to nothing in a food hall. Weekend yum cha brunch is popular in Sydney and you may have to queue to get into some of the many places offering it, such as the *Regal* on Sussex St.

For a quick sample, the best place to start is the food hall downstairs in the *Chinatown Centre*, the pagoda-style building on the corner of Dixon and Goulburn Sts. There is a wide range of eateries, including Korean and Thai, and there are many dishes for $4.50 with few above $6. The food hall is open daily from 10 am to 10 pm. There are also food halls in the *Sussex Centre*, on Dixon St diagonally across from the Chinatown Centre, and in the *Dixon Centre*, on the corner of Dixon and Little Hay Sts.

The *Hingara* at 82 Dixon St has more interesting dishes than the normal Chinese menu usually allows – fried fish with corn sauce for instance – but the favourites are there too. Nearby is *Bodhi*, a vegetarian restaurant with low prices. Others worth checking out are the large *Tai Yuen*, at 110 Hay St, which has been around a long time and has a good reputation, and the *New Tai Yuen* at 31 Dixon St – both have main courses around the $11 to $15 mark.

House of Guangzhou on the corner of Thomas St and Ultimo Rd is a long-established place with a reputation for seafood. Main courses cost around $10 to $19 (seafood can be more). Downstairs, there's an inexpensive *Japanese takeaway*, with a few tables.

Across the road, still on Thomas St, the *Emperor's Garden BBQ* is a cafe-style Chinese eatery, popular with the Chinese community, as is *Jing May Noodles* further along Thomas St, upstairs in the Princes Centre, with little over $15. Both are open daily.

Darling Harbour There are many, many food outlets in the Harbourside Festival Marketplace. The *Craig Brewery* has main courses for well under $10. Upstairs is the *Virgin Video Cafe*. Down near the Entertainment Centre, the *Pumphouse Brewery Tavern* has above-average pub meals starting under $10. In the Parkroyal Hotel on the corner of Day and Bathurst Sts, *Arizona* is one of a small chain of 'western' bar/restaurants, popular for drinking and snacking.

The Rocks & Circular Quay At 101 George St, *Phillip's Foote* has cafe meals from $6 to $10 at lunch, more at dinner, and an outdoor barbecue area where you cook your own steak or fish for $15; the price includes a glass of wine but salads are extra. Next door at No 99, *Rock's Cafe* is a bit cheaper and has snacks and light meals from 8 am to 7 pm during the week and till late on Friday and Saturday nights.

G'Day Cafe at No 83, just north of Argyle St, is similar but cheaper still – surprisingly so, with breakfast from $3.50, focaccia from $2 and other light meals. It's open from 5.30 am to midnight. Further south on George St the *Bakehouse* has good coffee and cakes as well as takeaways.

At the top of George St, just before it goes

under the bridge, the *Mercantile Hotel* is a restored pub with counter meals. Keep going up George St, turn left after you've gone under the bridge, and you'll come to the unrestored *Harbour View Hotel* where meals are basic but good value.

In Metcalfe Arcade, near the Hickson St entrance, *Pancakes at the Rocks* is open long hours and has a large menu.

Walk under the bridge to Pier One, with several eating places including the *Harbour Watch* seafood restaurant with main courses around $25. There are several other eating places here, including *Harbourside Brasserie*. Not far away on Pier Four, the *Wharf Restaurant* is pricey but interesting.

Right on Circular Quay, *City Extra* is reasonable for coffee, snacks and meals, as is nearby *Rossini*, although you pay for the position. Behind the quay, on the Alfred St median strip at the corner of Pitt St, *Nulbom Oriental Food* is a kiosk with a few outdoor tables selling reasonable Asian food starting under $5.

The *Museum of Contemporary Art* has a suitably stylish cafe with interesting food. Entrées and specials cost around $10 and main courses $13.

Two excellent seafood restaurants occupy upstairs-downstairs positions in the Overseas Passenger Terminal. Upstairs is *Bilson's*, a formal place with main courses from $20 at lunch and from $30 at dinner. *Doyle's at the Quay* is on street level, with dockside tables and a relaxed style. The minimum food order is $14.50 per person. The Doyle family has been serving seafood to Sydneysiders for generations; the family also runs *Doyle's on the Beach* at Watsons Bay and *Doyle's at the Markets*, a bistro and takeaway at the Pyrmont Fishmarkets.

Further around Circular Quay West, between the Overseas Passenger Terminal and the Park Hyatt Hotel, are several restaurants with outdoor areas in the $20-and-up region. On the other side of Circular Quay, the *Sydney Cove Oyster Bar* is a small place right on the waterfront which offers purely Australian produce, including a good wine list. Oysters cost from $16/9 a dozen/half-dozen, with other dishes from $12. It's open from mid-morning until about 8 pm during winter, and until 11 pm or later during summer.

Further around at the Opera House are three restaurants with good views, the *Forecourt* (you might have to stand up to see the water), the *Harbour* on the 'prow' of the Opera House and the expensive *Bennelong*. The *Harbour Take-Out Bar* next to the Harbour restaurant is open daily; fish & chips costs from $5.50.

Kings Cross & Nearby Victoria St is gaining some fashionable eateries. *Joe's* has breakfast from $7, focaccia from $5 and other snacks and light meals. Further down and more of a restaurant than a cafe, *Four Fingers* has a $22.50 two-course deal. For something completely different, the *Turquoise Cafe* in front of Highfield House is a small place with plain food at low prices. Cooked breakfasts start at $5, salads at $3 and pasta around $5.50.

Along William St around the corner from the Darlinghurst Rd and Victoria St junction is a string of inexpensive cafes. You can usually find breakfast for under $5 and *O'Malley's Hotel* has lunches from $5. On the southern side of wide William St, on the corner of Darlinghurst Rd, *Michaelangelos* is a 24-hour cafe.

On Llankelly Place near the corner of Darlinghurst Rd *Pad Thai* is a tiny takeaway with meals from $5 and nearby is the equally inexpensive *Yakidori*. Not far away on Darlinghurst Rd the *Astoria* has old-fashioned tucker such as roasts for just $5. A few doors away, where Darlinghurst Rd bends around to become Macleay St, *Nick's Seafood* has fish dinner (grilled fish, salad and chips) for $4.50.

On Darlinghurst Rd near the El Alamein Fountain are several popular eateries, such as the *Bourbon & Beefsteak*, open 24 hours. Breakfast is about $9, steaks about $16. Next door, the *Fountain Cafe* is similar but a little cheaper. Another place with outdoor tables is *Geoffrey's Cafe* on Roslyn St near the corner of Darlinghurst Rd. The large menu

has nothing over $10, with steaks from $7. Breakfast is $4.90.

Gado Gado is a long-established Indonesian restaurant at 57 Bayswater Rd, where most main courses are under $10 (more for some seafood). It's open nightly for dinner and for lunch on Friday. At No 32, the *Bayswater Brasserie* is a very good restaurant where you don't have to spend a fortune if you choose carefully, especially at lunch.

On Kellet St several places cater to late-night eating and drinking for those with deeper pockets, such as *Dean's* and *Cafe Iguana*. There's also a string of more up-market cafes along Macleay St north of the Cross. Perhaps the smartest is the new *Merivale Brasserie* on the corner of Macleay St and Challis Ave. Next door the *Espresso Bar* is part of the same establishment and equally fashionable.

Darlinghurst & East Sydney On the corner of Victoria and Burton Sts, *Laurie's Vegetarian Diner* is open for lunch and dinner daily. Great smoothies are $3.50, soups are $4 and there's a varied menu of vegetarian delights from about $5.50; prices are higher for dinner.

There's more vegetarian food at *Govinda's*, the Hare Krishna restaurant at 112 Darlinghurst St, just south of William St and Kings Cross. Currently they offer a $12.50 all-you-can-eat smorgasbord nightly between 6 and 10.30 pm, which includes admission to the cinema upstairs.

The northern end of Victoria St, as it nears William St and Kings Cross, has plenty of cafes and restaurants. *Una's*, just south of Surrey St, is neither new nor trendy. It's open from breakfast until about 11 pm with good, solid food at $7.50 or less.

On the corner of Forbes and Burton Sts, *Dov* is a popular BYO cafe with interesting Israeli-inspired food. There are only a couple of main courses each day (about $11) but there's a long list of very tasty cold dishes ($6.50) or you can sample a mixed plate ($8.50). Above the Arch Coffee Lounge at 81 Stanley St, *No Names* is a simple, inexpensive and popular Italian restaurant. This

New South Wales

A Sydney city from Kirribilli (RI)
B Sydney Opera House (PS)
C Gay & Lesbian Mardi Gras, Sydney (RB)

D Strand Arcade, Sydney (JM)
E Sydney city across
Rozelle Bay (RB)

New South Wales

A Darling Harbour, Sydney (MF)
B Circular Quay, Sydney (JM)
C Royal Hotel, Paddington, Sydney (GA)
D Colo River, near Windsor (JM)
E Blue Mountains (JM)

Steyne *Luis* is an Italian place with a wood-fired oven producing excellent pizzas.

At 27 Belgrave St *Cafe Tunis* has good coffee and interesting food, open most days and nights. Pasta costs from \$8.50 and main courses are between \$8 and \$14. There are a couple of seafood buffets: at the *Manly Pacific Parkroyal* on North Steyne, where a buffet lunch from Wednesday to Sunday costs \$29.50; and the *Radisson Kestrel* on South Steyne, where the Monday to Saturday buffet lunch is \$17.50.

Armstrong's on Manly Wharf has a great view and an even better reputation. Seafood is emphasised and main courses approach \$20.

Entertainment

The *Sydney Morning Herald*'s *Metro* section is published on Friday and lists most events in town for the week.

Halftix sells half-price (or thereabouts) last-minute seats to various performances and events from a booth on Martin Place near Elizabeth St. You have to buy a ticket to a show that night and Halftix doesn't post lists of which shows are available until noon. The booth is also a Ticketek agency (☎ 266 4800) so if you miss out on cheap seats you can always buy full-price ones. Halftix is open from noon to 5.30 pm on weekdays and from noon to 5 pm on Saturday. The Ticketek side of the business is open from 9 am to 5 pm on weekdays and from noon to 4 pm on Saturday.

Try to see something at the Opera House – you can choose from films, ballet, theatre, classical music, opera and even rock concerts.

A lot of evening entertainment takes place in Leagues Clubs, where the profits from the assembled ranks of poker machines – 'pokies' – enable the clubs to put on big-name acts at low prices. They may be 'members only' for locals but as an interstate or, even better, international visitor you're generally welcome. Simply ring ahead and ask, then wave your interstate driving licence or passport at the door. Acts vary from Max Bygraves to good Australian rock, but what-

ever the show you'll see a good cross-section of Sydneysiders. The most lavish is the *St George Leagues Club* on the Princes Highway, Kogarah. More centrally there's the *City of Sydney RSL Club* on George St or the *South Sydney Leagues Club* at 263 Chalmers St, Redfern.

Cinemas Mainstream shows are cheaper on Tuesday at the major city venues (eg at the southern end of George St), but not in school holidays.

For more unusual fare try independent cinemas such as the *Dendy* at 624 George St; the *Mandolin* at 150 Elizabeth St; the *Academy Twin* at 3A Oxford St, Paddington; the *Valhalla Cinema* at 166 Glebe Point Rd, Glebe; and the *Encore Cinema* at 64 Devonshire St, Surry Hills. The Australian Film Institute screens interesting new work and classics at the *AFI Cinema* on the corner of Oxford St and Oatley Rd in Paddington.

In Darlinghurst, the *Movie Room* upstairs at 112 Darlinghurst Rd shows a wide range of movies. Admission is \$12.50, which includes an all-you-can-eat smorgasbord at Govinda's, the Hare Krishna restaurant downstairs. There are two screenings a night, the first at about 7 pm. Govinda's is open from 6 pm. Phone ☎ 380 5162 for programs.

A sight in itself is the *State Movie Theatre* on Market St between Pitt and George Sts – they don't make them like this any more! It's now used for live shows, except during the Sydney Film Festival in June. There are no regular tours.

Performance The top mainstream company is the *Sydney Theatre Company*, which has its own theatre at Pier Four on Hickson Rd, across from the Rocks. The similarly prestigious *Sydney Dance Company* is also here. At *NIDA* (National Institute of Dramatic Art), 215 Anzac Parade, Kensington, student shows are staged regularly.

The *Seymour Centre* at the corner of Cleveland St and City Rd, Chippendale (near Sydney University), has varied and interesting productions. The *Footbridge Theatre* at Sydney Uni is also worth keeping an eye on.

The *Bay Street Theatre* at 75 Bay St in Glebe, the *Belvoir Street Theatre* at 25 Belvoir St, Surry Hills, and the *Rep Theatre* at 1 Brown Lane in Newtown are three of many experimental/off-beat places.

The *Tilbury Hotel* in Woolloomooloo at the corner of Forbes and Nicholson Sts often has cabaret. The *Comedy Store* on the corner of Crystal St and Parramatta Rd in Leichhardt is open from Tuesday to Saturday. Tuesday, when new comics try out, is the cheapest night.

Music Sydney doesn't have the same pub music scene as Melbourne, but there are plenty of clubs and you can count on something most nights of the week. For detailed listings of venues and acts pick up free copies of music/lifestyle papers such as *Drum Media* and *3D World*. Five-star hotels often have big-name cabaret artists and sometimes more adventurous acts at prices that aren't outrageous if you watch what you drink. A few of the many, many venues are:

The Basement, 29 Reiby Place, Circular Quay – good jazz, sometimes big international names.

Bat & Ball, corner of Cleveland and South Dowling Rds, Surry Hills – pub with young bands.

Cat & Fiddle Hotel, corner Darling and Elliott Sts, Balmain – pub rock usually Friday to Sunday nights.

Cock 'n' Bull Tavern, corner Bronte and Ebley Sts, Bondi Junction – bands (often free) or disco most nights.

Golden Sheaf Hotel, 429 New South Head Rd, Double Bay, two km east of Kings Cross – pub with free bands several nights. Good food, popular with travellers.

Harbourside Brasserie, Pier One – a variety of fairly big acts, often jazz or comedy.

Joe's Garage, Macleay St, Kings Cross – party atmosphere nightly, popular with backpackers for its happy hours, inexpensive food (at lunch) and entertainment such as horizontal bungee jumping.

Kings Cross Hotel, at the junction of Victoria St, Darlinghurst Rd and William St – open 24 hours, plenty of pokies. Several travellers have reported that this is, surprisingly, a reasonable place for a night out.

Kinselas, 383 Bourke St, Darlinghurst – a renovated funeral parlour, now a large venue with various levels and interesting acts. Sometimes free (ground floor) up to $20 (top floor), depending on who's playing. Always worth checking out.

Lansdowne Hotel, corner of Broadway and City Rd, Chippendale – lively young bands nightly except on Tuesday.

On Sight, 171 Victoria St, Kings Cross – dance club, various theme nights, from $5.

Powercuts, 150 Elizabeth St (south of Liverpool St), city – reggae and Afro club on Friday and Saturday from 10 pm.

Rose, Shamrock & Thistle Hotel (aka 'the three weeds'), 139 Evans St, Rozelle – the more gentle end of the rock spectrum (sometimes big names) plus jazz, folk etc.

Royal Hotel, Bondi Rd at Bondi Beach – bands, free.

Sandringham Hotel, King St, Newtown – young bands.

Selina's (in the Coogee Bay Hotel), Coogee Bay Rd, Coogee Bay – rock, often top Australian bands for which you can pay $20 or more. Main nights Friday and Saturday, but sometimes cheaper bands other nights.

Strawberry Hills Hotel, 451 Elizabeth St (corner Devonshire St), Surry Hills – something interesting most nights, often jazz.

Studebakers, 33 Bayswater Rd, Kings Cross – club with '50s and '60s theme.

Tom Tom Cafe, 22 Bayswater Rd, Kings Cross – bands and/or DJs Tuesday to Sunday until 7 am, busy and lively. Big-name bands sometimes play here semi-incognito. From $6 to $8, backpackers might get in for half-price midweek.

Pubs Many pubs have a totally different atmosphere during the week than they do on weekends when the hordes are out on the town.

For a drink near Kings Cross try the friendly *Darlo Bar*, taking up its own tiny block at the corner of Darlinghurst and Liverpool Sts.

The *Craig* at Darling Harbour has $1 schooners on Thursday until 10.30 pm – very popular with backpackers.

One of the nicest places for a Guinness is *Molly Bloom's Bar* at the Mercantile Hotel on George St in the Rocks. There is often Irish music here. Also in the Rocks are the *Lord Dudley* on Jersey Rd, the *Lord Nelson* in Argyle St (with its own brewery) and the *Hero of Waterloo* on Lower Fort St.

Over in Glebe, the *Friend in Hand* at 58

Cowper St has events such as crab racing, music on weekends and often generous backpackers' discounts. Glebe's other popular pub, the *Harold Park Hotel* at 115 Wigram Rd, also has a packed entertainment program. Writers at the Park presents well-known writers reading their work; on other nights there are comedy acts or bands.

Spectator Sports Sydneysiders don't place the same emphasis on spectator sports as do Melburnians – there's just too much else to do here.

Sydney is arguably the world capital of rugby league (as opposed to the more gentlemanly but more widely played rugby union) – although Brisbane might disagree. The main competition is the Winfield Cup, with the finals played at the Football Stadium in Moore Park in September.

The Sydney Cricket Ground (SCG) in Moore Park is the venue for sparsely attended Sheffield Shield matches, well-attended five-day Test matches and sell-out World Series Cup (one-day) matches.

On weekends the harbour is carpeted with yachts weaving and racing around the ferries and ships on Sydney Harbour. The sporting year ends with the Boxing Day (26 December) start of the Sydney to Hobart Yacht Race. A huge fleet of yachts compete frantically to be first out of the harbour, before turning south for the three- to five-day voyage to Hobart in Tasmania.

Things to Buy

Shopping complexes in the city include the Royal, Strand and Imperial arcades, Centrepoint and the impressive Queen Victoria Building. David Jones and Grace Brothers are city-centre department stores. The Rocks and the Harbourside Festival Marketplace at Darling Harbour teem with shops which are open daily. Oxford St has galleries and bookshops in Paddington, and more-bizarre shops and boutiques in Surry Hills. There are also many large suburban shopping complexes.

Aboriginal Art There are several Aboriginal Art Centres, including 117 George St in the Rocks and a large showroom at 7 Walker Lane, opposite 7A Liverpool St, in Paddington. They have many bark paintings which, as usual, are attractive but costly. The Aboriginal Artists Gallery in Civic House, 477 Kent St (behind the Town Hall), has a large range of traditional and contemporary Aboriginal and Islander work. Quality is high, prices competitive.

New Guinea Primitive Arts, on the 6th floor at 428 George St, and also on Level 2 of the Queen Victoria Building, has a big range of artefacts from PNG and some Aboriginal work.

Bennelong Boomerangs, at 29-31 Playfair St in the Rocks, is owned by a guy who's been the Australian Boomerang Throwing Champion a few times, so he can tell you truthfully it isn't as easy as it looks. Another champion is at 14 Blue Point Rd in McMahons Point.

Australiana Arts and crafts, T-shirts, souvenirs, designer clothing, bushgear and the like are sold practically everywhere. Much of this stuff is high quality, with prices to match, though you can pick up the odd bargain. Check out the huge range sold in the Rocks and Darling Harbour to see what's available then compare prices in other areas.

Metcalfe Arcade, at 80-84 George St, houses the Society of Arts & Crafts with a gallery and sales, and there's Australian Craftworks at 127 George St in the old police station.

For bushgear, try Morrisons at 105 George St in the Rocks, Goodwood Saddlery at 237-9 The Broadway or Thomas Cook at 790 George St.

The Wilderness Shop at 92 Liverpool St has high quality posters and books on wilderness issues, as well as great T-shirts and other good souvenirs. It's open all week. At the Gardens Shop in the Royal Botanic Gardens Visitors Centre there are souvenirs, posters and books with an Australian plant theme.

In the Strand Arcade off Pitt St Mall several leading fashion designers and craftspeople have shops. The Strand Hatters will make sure your Akubra fits properly before they sell it to you.

The Australian Wine Centre, in Goldfields House behind Circular Quay at 1 Alfred St, is open daily and stocks wines from every Australian wine-growing region. There are sometimes tastings, especially on Friday or Saturday.

Markets Sydney has lots of weekend 'flea' markets. The most interesting, Paddo Village Bazaar, is held in the grounds of the church on the corner of Oxford and Newcombe Sts on Saturday. It's quite a scene. Balmain's Saturday market is also good; it's in the church on Darling St, opposite Gladstone Park. Glebe's weekend markets are held in the school at the corner of Glebe Point Rd and Derby Place. On weekends the top end of George St in the Rocks is closed for a market and there's a Sunday craft market outside the Opera House.

Paddy's Market, an institution which was banished to the suburbs for a few years, has returned to Haymarket, at the corner of Hay and Thomas Sts, and is open on weekends. The Paddy's on Parramatta Rd in Flemington still operates (along with the Flemington fruit and vegetable market) on Friday and Sunday.

Getting There & Away

Air Sydney's Kingsford Smith Airport is Australia's busiest. It's fairly central which makes access easy, but it also means that jet flights have to stop at 11 pm due to noise regulations.

You can fly into Sydney from all the usual international points and from all over Australia. Both Qantas (☎ 13 1313) and Ansett (☎ 13 1300) have frequent flights to other capital cities and major airports. Smaller airlines, such as Ansett Express, Eastern Australia, Hazelton and Kendell, fly within the state.

Cheap international flights are advertised in the Saturday *Sydney Morning Herald*. The cheapest tickets of all are sold by travellers – check hostel notice boards – but there's a risk: most tickets are nontransferable, so the person whose name is on the ticket has to check in for the flight, and you then have to trust to luck that no-one checks your passport against the ticket. If the ticket involves a change of planes, a stopover, or otherwise checking in more than once, there's a pretty high chance you'll be caught out.

Bus It pays to shop around. When you're asking about prices mention that you're a backpacker as some companies give good discounts. As well as checking out the private operators it's worth finding out what the government Countrylink network of trains and buses has on offer; see the following Train section.

If you're doing a lot of travel check out the excellent bus pass deals – make sure you get enough time and stopovers.

On straight point-to-point tickets there are varying stopover deals. Some companies give one free stopover on interstate routes, others charge a fee of around $5 for each stopover. This might be waived if you book through certain agents, notably some of the hostels. Check hostel notice boards or contact one of the travel agencies which specialises in backpackers' needs. There are several in Kings Cross.

The biggest company is Greyhound Pioneer (☎ 13 2030) with Kirklands (☎ 281 2233) and McCafferty's (☎ 361 5125) following close behind, although the last two don't run Australia-wide. There are quite a few other companies running less-extensive routes.

The Sydney Coach Terminal (☎ 281 9366) is on Eddy Ave near Pitt St, outside Central Station. A few companies maintain their own depots, notably Greyhound Pioneer which is at the corner of Oxford and Riley Sts. McCafferty's has a depot near Kings Cross at 179 Darlinghurst Rd, but it also picks up on Eddy Ave. Many lines stop in suburbs on the way in or out of the city and some have feeder services from the suburbs.

To/From Brisbane By the coastal Pacific Highway it takes about 16 hours and can cost

$55 or less; the 'standard' cheap fare is around $60. You often need to book ahead, and not all buses stop in all the main towns en route. Some typical fares are Port Macquarie $36 (seven hours), Coffs Harbour $44 (9½ hours), Byron Bay $60 (13 hours) and Surfers Paradise $60 (14½) hours. Companies running the Pacific Highway route to Brisbane include Greyhound Pioneer, Kirklands, McCafferty's and Lindsay's (☎ toll-free 1800 027 944).

Greyhound Pioneer, McCafferty's and Border Coaches (book at the Eddy Ave terminal) also use the inland New England Highway which takes an hour or two longer but can cost about the same.

Ando's Opal Outback Experience (☎ 559 2901) travels between Sydney and Byron Bay via a week-long outback detour. Ando (John Anderson) is quite a character and his tour gets good feedback. At around $390 it's a bargain.

The Pioneering Spirit (☎ 018 751 466) is a double-decker bus (with sleeping quarters on the upper deck) which runs from Sydney to Brisbane via the coast, taking six days and costing $32 a day, plus $6 food kitty – there's a chef on board. It describes itself as a mobile hostel. As it takes six days to do a trip that regular buses do in 16 hours, there's plenty of time to explore.

To/From Canberra Murrays (☎ 252 3599) has three daily express (under four hours) buses to Canberra for $28 or around $20 if you pay in advance. Greyhound Pioneer has the most frequent Canberra service ($28) including one direct from Sydney Airport ($32).

To/From Melbourne It's a 12- to 13-hour run (more if you go via Canberra) by the most direct route, the Hume Highway. Firefly Express (☎ 211 1644) currently charges just $35, while other companies charge around $50. As well as the Hume route, Greyhound Pioneer runs up the prettier, but much longer (up to 18 hours), coastal Princes Highway route ($58).

A great way to travel to or from Melbourne is with Straycat (☎ (03) 481 2993, toll-free 1800 800 840) which runs via Canberra and the high country, taking a leisurely three days and stopping for lots of activities. The standard fare is $125, plus accommodation (two nights, about $12 per night).

To/From Adelaide Sydney to Adelaide takes 18 to 25 hours and costs from about $90. Services run via Mildura ($70) or Broken Hill ($90). Travelling Sydney-Melbourne-Adelaide with Firefly might be a little cheaper than travelling Sydney-Adelaide with other companies. Countrylink's daily Speedlink service is a train to Albury then a bus to Adelaide, and costs about $90.

To/From Elsewhere To the Snowy Mountains, Greyhound Pioneers run to Cooma ($36), Jindabyne ($45), and the resorts (about $49). The fare is about $245 for the 52- to 56-hour trip to Perth. To Alice Springs it's about 42 hours (plus some waiting in Adelaide) and costs $211.

Train The government's Countrylink rail network is complemented with coaches and it provides a good service. On point-to-point tickets prices can be comparable to the private bus lines, and there are some special deals.

All interstate and principal regional services operate to and from Central Station. Call the Central Reservation Centre (☎ 217 8812, 13 2232 outside Sydney).

Interstate trains can be faster than buses and there are often special fares which make the prices competitive, too. On interstate journeys you can arrange free stopovers if you finish the trip within two months (six months on a return ticket).

Two trains run daily to Canberra taking about 4½ hours and costing $35/48 in economy/1st class.

An XPT runs nightly between Sydney and Melbourne, taking just 10 hours and costing $49/79 for an economy/1st-class seat. Sleeping berths are available for $135.

To Brisbane there's a nightly XPT which takes about 12½ hours and costs $95 in economy ($67 Caper advance-purchase fare), $137 in 1st class ($96 Caper fare) and $217 with a sleeper. In conjunction with this train there's a connecting bus from Casino to the New South Wales far north coast and Queensland's Gold Coast. You can also take the train between Sydney and Murwillumbah, just south of the Queensland border, from where there's a connecting bus to the Gold Coast.

You can travel between Sydney and Adelaide via Broken Hill on the twice-weekly Indian Pacific for $104 in economy, $199 in an 'Econoberth' sleeper ($139 Caper fare) and $317 in a standard sleeper ($222 Caper fare). The trip takes nearly 26 hours. There's also Speedlink, a daily bus/train connection which is cheaper ($99/105 in economy/1st class) and five or six hours faster.

Sydney to Perth is on the Indian-Pacific – see the Perth section for more details.

There's an extensive rail network within the state – see the New South Wales introductory Getting Around section for details.

Car Rental Avis, Budget, Hertz and Thrifty are on William St up from the city towards Kings Cross, together with a number of local operators. The larger companies' daily metropolitan rates are typically about $80 a day for a small car (Ford Laser, Mitsubishi Lancer, Toyota Corolla, Nissan Pulsar), about $85 a day for a medium car (Holden Apollo, Toyota Camry, Nissan Pintara, Mitsubishi Magna), or about $95 a day for a big car (Holden Commodore, Ford Falcon). If you shop around you might also get insurance and unlimited km at these prices. Some places require you to be over 23 years old.

Downunder Rent-a-Car rents cars from $55 a day including insurance and 4000 free km. There's an office in Manly (☎ 976 2822) at 4/27 Belgrave St. Many other companies are in the same price range.

There's no shortage of outfits renting older cars which range from reasonable transport to frustrating old bombs. Prices start at about $30 a day, plus a few dollars for insurance. Check for things like bald tyres and bad brakes before you sign anything. Also check the fine print regarding insurance

excess (the amount you pay before the insurance takes over); it can be pretty high. You'll find lots of places listed in the Yellow Pages, and hostel notice boards often have ads.

Buying a Car or Motorbike If you want to buy a car to travel round Australia, Sydney's a good place to do it. Parramatta Rd is lined with used car lots and there are other set ups geared specially to travellers. It's illegal to sell cars on the street in Kings Cross but there's a car market at the Kings Cross Parking Station on the corner of Ward Ave and Elizabeth Bay Rd, which charges sellers $35 a week (daily rates available). This place can help with paperwork and insurance and is becoming something of a travellers' rendezvous. The Flemington Car Market (☎ 0055 21122), near Flemington Station on Sunday, charges sellers $50 and has a shuttle bus that picks up in Kings Cross.

Several dealers will sell you a car with an undertaking to buy it back at an agreed price. Always read the small print. We've heard of deals where the seller agreed to buy the vehicle back at 60% of sale price, minus 1% for every 1000 km travelled, minus the cost of repairing any damage, and the buyer ended up with next to nothing. A buy-back deal with a private seller (such as a hostel manager) is risky as they might not have enough ready cash when you want to sell.

Before you buy it's worth having the car checked by a mechanic. If you, or a friend, are a member of the NRMA you can get a vehicle checked over for $98. It costs $72 to join the NRMA (☎ 13 2132) but members of interstate and some overseas motoring organisations pay only $36. Some garages do inspections for much less.

For full details of the paperwork required to buy a car, pick up a copy of the Roads & Traffic Authority (RTA) pamphlet 'Six Steps to Buying a Secondhand Motor Vehicle', available at RTA and NRMA offices. Motor Registry offices also have information and there are many of them: for example at 88 Ebley St in Bondi Junction, 239 Pittwater Rd in Manly and at the NRMA's Clarence St office.

To be registered every vehicle needs third-party insurance – a Green Slip. This covers you against injuries you might cause but not damage to other people's property, so it's a good idea to also have third-party property insurance. The major insurance companies don't sell third-party property insurance to travellers but the Kings Cross car market (and some dealers) can arrange it, even if you didn't buy the car there.

Holiday Wheels Motorcycles (☎ 718 6668), at the rear of 589 Canterbury Rd in Belmore, sometimes have buy-back deals on bikes and they can help arrange insurance. One of the partners speaks German.

Getting Around

The State Transit Authority (STA) controls almost all public transport in Sydney. For information on STA buses, ferries and trains, phone ☎ 13 1500 between 6 am and 10 pm, daily. You'll find detailed public transport information in the front of the A-K White Pages phone book.

To/From the Airport The international and domestic terminals at Sydney airport are across the runway from each other, and about a five-km bus trip apart.

The Airport Express is a special STA service to and from the airport via Central Station, with No 300 going on to Circular Quay and No 350 going to Kings Cross. Airport Express buses have their own stops and are painted green and yellow. The one-way fare is $5 and a return ticket, valid for two months, is $8. Travel between the terminals costs $2.50. From the airport to Central Station the trip takes about 15 minutes; to Circular Quay or Kings Cross, 30 minutes.

Kingsford Smith Transport (KST) (☎ 667 0663) runs a door-to-door service between the airport and places to stay (including hostels) in the city, Kings Cross and Darling Harbour. The fare is $5. When heading out to the airport you have to book at least three hours before you want to be collected. Clipper/Gray Line (☎ 319 6600, 5.30 am to 10 pm) offers a similar service for $6 ($10 return).

A taxi from the airport to Circular Quay should cost between $15 and $20, depending on traffic.

Bus The bus information kiosk on Alfred St (running behind Circular Quay), at the corner of Loftus St, is open daily. There are other offices on Carrington St by Wynyard Park and in the Queen Victoria Building on York St.

Buses run almost everywhere but they are slow compared to trains. Some places – including Bondi Beach, Coogee and the north shore east of the Harbour Bridge – are not serviced by trains so you do need buses (or ferries) to get there. On the Eastern Suburbs line you can get a combination bus/rail ticket from some stations such as Kings Cross (but not Central) so you can change to a bus for a destination such as Bondi Beach. This works out cheaper than buying the tickets separately.

Circular Quay, Wynyard Park on York St and Railway Square are the main bus stops in the city centre.

Special Bus Services The red Sydney Explorer is an STA tourist bus which runs a circuit of many inner-city attractions. There's a bus every 20 minutes between 9.30 am and 9 pm daily. It has an on-board commentary, you can get on and off as often as you like and your ticket entitles you to discounted entry to many of the attractions. As well as seeing a lot of sights, this is a good way to orient yourself to the city. Tickets cost $20 and are sold on board the bus and at STA offices. It would be much cheaper to get around these places by ordinary buses (in fact it's possible to walk around the circuit), but the Explorer's easy as you don't have to work out routes. Its 22 stops are marked by green and red signs. You can use the Explorer ticket on ordinary buses between Central Station and Circular Quay or the Rocks until midnight. The ticket also entitles you to big discounts on some tours – conditions apply.

The Bondi & Bay Explorer operates on similar lines to the Sydney Explorer, running a much larger circle from Circular Quay to

Kings Cross, Double Bay, Vaucluse, Watsons Bay, the Gap, Bondi Beach and returning up Oxford St. Just riding around the circle takes two hours and if you want to get off at many of the 20 places of interest along the way you'll need to start early. The bus runs half-hourly (hourly after 1.30 pm on weekdays) between 9 am and 6 pm, daily. The ticket entitles you to use ordinary buses south of the harbour until midnight. Ticket prices are the same as for the Sydney Explorer or you can buy a two-day pass for $35 which gives you the use of both the Sydney Explorer and the Bondi & Bay Explorer.

Operating on similar lines to the Explorer services is a new privately run operation which runs a continuous loop between Manly and Palm Beach, stopping at 15 places of interest along the way. The whole route takes about three hours, plus whatever stops you make, and the trip includes a commentary. The Boomerang Bus Tours bus (☎ 913 8402) leaves from near Manly wharf on Thursday, Friday and Saturday, with the first bus departing at 9.15 am and the last at 5.15 pm during daylight saving time and at 2.15 pm during the rest of the year. Three buses run the route and there are nine circuits in summer, six at other times. The fare is $20 ($15 children) and there are discounts for YHA and VIP members.

The Tramway, a bus disguised as a tram, shuttles between Circular Quay and Darling Harbour every 15 minutes between 9.30 am and 6 pm daily. A one-way ticket costs $2 or you can buy an all-day pass for $3 – a good way of getting around inner Sydney at a rock-bottom price. Tramway stops are marked with yellow and black signs like railway signals.

Nightrider buses provide a skeleton service after the regular buses and trains stop running.

Train Quite a lot of Sydney is covered by the suburban rail service, which has frequent trains and is generally much quicker than the bus network. Getting around the city centre by train is feasible (if disorienting).

After 9 am on weekdays and at any time on weekends you can buy an off-peak return ticket for not much more than a standard one-way fare. A City Hopper costs $2.20 and gives you a day of unlimited rides in the central area after 9 am on weekdays and at any time on weekends. You can go as far north as North Sydney, as far south as Central and as far east as Kings Cross. If you buy a City Hopper at a suburban station it costs more but includes the return fare. If you have to change trains, buy a ticket to your ultimate destination – it's cheaper.

Automatic ticket machines are being installed at stations, for which you'll need coins (any except five-cent coins) or $5 notes.

The rail system has a central City Circle and a number of lines radiating out to the suburbs. A single trip anywhere on the City Circle or to a nearby suburb such as Kings Cross is $1.20. Suburban trains all stop at Central Station and usually one or more of the other City Circle stations as well.

Trains generally run from around 4 am to about midnight, give or take an hour. After the trains stop, Nightrider buses provide a skeleton service.

Ferry Sydney's ferries are one of the nicest ways of getting around in Australia. As well as the ferries there are JetCats to Manly ($4.60) and RiverCats running up the Parramatta River to Meadowbank ($2.60).

All the harbour ferries (and the Cats) depart from Circular Quay. The STA, which runs most of the ferries, has a ferry information office on the concourse behind Jetty 4, open daily. Many ferries have connecting bus services.

Getting to Manly you have the choice of a roomy ferry, which takes about 30 minutes and costs $3.40, or a JetCat, which does the trip in half the time and costs $4.60. The ferry trip is much more pleasant. After 7.40 pm the JetCat is the only craft running to Manly but you can take it for the normal ferry fare. If you're staying in Manly or will otherwise be using the ferry a lot, consider buying a Ferry 10 ticket or a Travel Pass.

Hegarty's Ferries (☎ 247 6606) run from Jetty 6 at Circular Quay to wharves directly across the harbour: Lavender Bay, McMahons Point and two stops in Kirribilli. These services cater to peak-hour commuters and stop early in the evening.

Fare Deals The Sydney Pass offers great value compared to buying its components separately. If you just want transport you're better off buying a Travel Pass (see below). The Sydney Pass covers bus and ferry transport, travel on Tramway and Sydney Explorer buses, harbour cruises and a return trip on the Airport Express. A three-day Sydney Pass costs $50 ($40 children), five days costs $65 ($55 children) and seven days is $75 ($65 children). Family tickets are available. The trip back to the airport is valid for a month but it must be your last trip, as you surrender the ticket.

Designed for commuters but very useful for visitors, a Travel Pass offers cheap weekly or quarterly travel. There are various colour-coded grades offering combinations of distances and services. The Green Travel Pass is valid for extensive train and bus travel and all ferries except the RiverCat and the Manly JetCat. At $24 for a week it's a bargain. If you buy a Travel Pass after 3 pm, your week doesn't begin until the next day. They're sold at railway stations and STA offices.

A Travel 10 ticket gives a sizable discount on 10 trips.

Several transport-plus-entry tickets are available, such as the Zoo Pass for $17 ($8.50 children) – these work out cheaper than paying for everything separately.

Taxi The four big taxi companies offer a reliable telephone service: Taxis Combined (☎ 332 8888), RSL Taxis (☎ 581 1111), Legion (☎ 289 9000) and Premier Radio Cabs (☎ 897 4000).

Water taxis are pricey but fun ways of getting around the harbour. Companies include Taxis Afloat (☎ 955 3222) and Harbour Taxis (☎ 555 1155).

Bicycle The Bicycle Institute of New South Wales (☎ 212 5628), at the corner of Campbell and Foster Sts in Surry Hills, publishes a handy book, *Cycling Around Sydney* ($10.50), which details routes and cycle paths. Another guide to cycling in Sydney is *Seeing Sydney by Bicycle* by Julia Thorne (Kangaroo Press, $13). The RTA map ($3.50) of recommended bike routes around greater Sydney is mainly for commuters.

Bicycle Hire Most of these places require a hefty deposit but they'll accept credit cards.

Rockcycle Tours (☎ 247 7777) on Circular Quay West, across from the Overseas Passenger Terminal and behind the Rocks visitor centre, is a friendly new outfit renting good mountain bikes for $9 an hour, $25 for half a day and $39 a day, with big discounts for students and backpackers. They have planned interesting and bike-friendly routes around the Rocks and the inner city and you get a map when you hire a bike. They can also help with information on rides further afield.

In Kings Cross on Orwell St near Eva's Hostel, Roo Bikes rents well-worn mountain bikes at $12 for a half-day, $15 for the day after 10.30 am and $20 for the whole day. Inner City Cycles (☎ 660 6605) at 31 Glebe Point Rd in Glebe rents quality mountain bikes for $30 a day, $45 for the weekend (Friday afternoon to Monday morning) and $100 a week.

The Australian Cycle Company (☎ 399 3475) at 28 Clovelly Rd in Randwick (near the three-way intersection of Darley Rd, Clovelly Rd and Wentworth St) rents bikes and there are several other places nearby, handy for rides in Centennial Park.

Over in Manly, you can hire good bikes from the Manly Cycle Centre (☎ 977 1189) at 36 Pittwater Rd for $5 an hour, $25 a day, $40 a weekend or $60 a week.

Cruises A wide range of cruises offer relatively inexpensive excursions on the harbour. You can book most at the Quayside Booking Centre (☎ 247 5151) at Jetty 2. Captain Cook Cruises (☎ 206 1111) has its own booking office at Jetty 6. STA ferries offer some good-value cruises, such as a 2½-hour trip for $16. Buy tickets from the ferry information office behind Jetty 4 at Circular Quay.

The Sydney Harbour Explorer, run by Captain Cook Cruises, is a hop-on, hop-off service around the harbour with stops at Circular Quay (Jetty 6), the Opera House, Watsons Bay, Taronga (for the zoo) and Darling Harbour. Boats run two-hourly from 9.30 am until evening and the fare is $16 ($12 students).

For $45 you can cruise on the *Bounty* (☎ 247 1789), a replica of the ship lost by Captain Bligh, made for the film *Mutiny on the Bounty* starring Mel Gibson.

Around Sydney

There are superb national parks just to the north and south of Sydney and other interesting places within easy reach. In the early days of European settlement small towns were established around the major centre, and although some have been engulfed by Sydney's urban sprawl, they're still of interest.

BOTANY BAY

It's a common misconception amongst first-time visitors that Sydney is built around Botany Bay. Actually Sydney Harbour is Port Jackson and Botany Bay is 10 to 15 km south, although the city now encompasses Botany Bay too. Botany Bay was Captain Cook's first landing point in Australia and was named by Joseph Banks, the expedition's naturalist, for the many botanical specimens he found here.

In the **Botany Bay National Park** at Kurnell, on the southern side of the bay, Captain Cook's landing place is marked with various monuments. The Discovery Centre describes Cook's life and explorations, as well as the surrounding wetlands. It's open from 10.30 am to 4.30 or 5 pm daily; the rest of the site, with bushland walking tracks and

picnic areas, is open from 7.30 am to 7 or 8 pm. From Cronulla Station (10 km away) take bus No 987. Entry costs $7.50 per car.

On the northern side of the bay entrance, beyond the oil tankers heading for the Kurnell refinery, is La Perouse where the French explorer of that name arrived in 1788, just six days after the arrival of the First Fleet. He gave the Poms a good scare as they weren't expecting the French to turn up quite so soon. **La Perouse** and his men camped at Botany Bay for a few weeks then sailed off into the Pacific and totally disappeared. Many years later the wrecks of their ships were discovered on a reef near Vanuatu. At La Perouse there's a French-built monument and a museum with relics from the expedition and a collection of antique maps. The museum is open daily ($2) and guided tours in English or French can be booked (☎ (02) 311 3379). Offshore from the museum is **Bare Island** with a decaying concrete fort built in 1885 to discourage a feared Russian (yes, Russian) invasion. Bus Nos 394 and 398 run here from Circular Quay.

ROYAL NATIONAL PARK

Thirty-six km south of the city, this is the second oldest national park in the world – only Yellowstone in the USA predates it. It stretches about 20 km south from Port Hacking and has a large network of walking tracks through varied country including a two-day, 26-km trail along the coast, with spectacular cliff-top stretches.

The scenery varies from dramatic cliffs and rocky scrubland to lush pockets of dense bush in the valleys. The park is carpeted with flowers in late winter and early spring. There are good surfing and swimming beaches (although surfing at Marley is dangerous), and some are patrolled on summer weekends. There are swimming spots along the Hacking River, which runs right through the park, and Lady Carrington Drive (a walking and cycling trail) follows the river south from Audley.

The visitor centre (☎ (02) 542 0648) is at Audley, about two km from the park's northeastern entrance, off the Princes Highway.

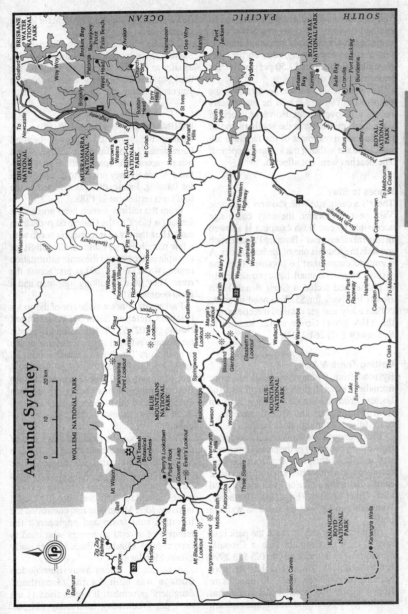

Around Sydney

NEW SOUTH WALES

You can drive through the park from end to end and down to the coast in a few places; some beach-access roads are closed at nightfall. You can hire rowing boats on the river at Audley. Entry costs $7.50 per car, free for pedestrians and cyclists.

Royal National Park was devastated in the bushfires of '94 and it will be many years before it recovers fully. However, much of the superb rainforest in the southern end of the park survives, most of the facilities are intact and the walking tracks have reopened. The beaches were not affected.

Places to Stay

There's a camp site with showers at Bonnie Vale near Bundeena, the only camp site accessible by car. Bush camping is allowed in several other areas – Burning Palms Beach towards the south is one of the best places. A permit to camp must be obtained from the visitor centre. The small, basic (no electricity or phone) and secluded *Garie Beach Youth Hostel* has beds for $5. You need to book, collect a key and get detailed directions: see the YHA Travel Centre at 422 Kent St in Sydney (☎ (02) 261 1111).

Getting There & Away

By road from Sydney you reach the park from the Princes Highway – turn off south of Loftus. From the south, the coast road up from Wollongong and Otford provides a beautiful drive through thick bush.

The Sydney to Wollongong railway forms the western boundary of the park. The closest station is at Loftus, four km from the park entrance and another two km from the visitor centre. Bringing a bike on the train is a good idea. Other stations (Engadine, Heathcote, Waterfall and Otford) are close to walking trails.

An interesting way to reach the park is to take a train to Cronulla then a Cronulla Ferries boat to **Bundeena** (☎ (02) 523 2990 for timetables). Bundeena has its own beaches, or you can walk 30 minutes to Jibbon nearer the ocean coast which has another good beach and Aboriginal rock art.

Bundeena is also the starting-point for longer coastal walks.

Cronulla Ferries cruise up the river on Sunday, Monday and Wednesday for $8, usually as far as Audley (it depends on the tide) but there's no longer a wharf there so you can't disembark.

PARRAMATTA (population 130,000)

Sydney has sprawled out well beyond Parramatta, 24 km from the centre, which was the second European settlement in Australia. When Sydney proved to be a poor area for farming, Parramatta was selected as the first farm settlement in 1788.

From the railway station head north-west for half a block to the Church St pedestrian mall. Here there's an information booth with a few pamphlets; go north on Church St for a couple of blocks and the main information centre (☎ (02) 630 3703) is just across the river. They have a walking tour map and a good booklet ($1).

Parramatta Park was the site of the area's first farm. Here you'll find **Old Government House** (☎ (02) 635 8149). A country retreat for the early rulers, it is now a museum which is open from Tuesday to Thursday from 10 am to 4 pm and on Sunday from 11 am to 4 pm; admission is $4. The **Governor's Bath House**, nearby, looks like an overgrown dovecot. Just south of the park on O'Connell St, **St Johns Cemetery** is the oldest in Australia.

There are more historic buildings east of the city centre. **Elizabeth Farm** at 70 Alice St is the oldest surviving home in the country, built in 1793 by John and Elizabeth Macarthur. Their sheep-breeding experiments formed the basis for Australia's wool industry. John Macarthur also controlled the lucrative rum trade and engineered the removal of several governors who tried to control him! Elizabeth Farm is open daily except Monday ($5).

A couple of blocks away **Hambledon Cottage** was built for the Macarthurs' daughters' governess. It's open from 11 am to 4 pm Wednesday to Sunday ($2.50).

Experiment Farm Cottage at 9 Ruse St was built for James Ruse in the early 1800s; it's another fine early homestead, furnished in 1840s style, and is open from Tuesday to Thursday from 10 am to 4 pm and on Sunday from 11 am to 4 pm ($3.50).

Featherdale Wildlife Park (☎ (02) 671 4984 for recorded information) on Kildare Rd, Doonside, about halfway from Parramatta to Penrith, is a 'koala cuddlery' which also has plenty of other native fauna. Featherdale is open daily and costs $8 ($4 children). Take a train to Blacktown and then bus No 725.

PENRITH (population 60,000)

Penrith is almost an outer suburb of Sydney, its extent bounded on the west by the serene Nepean River and the forested foothills of the Blue Mountains. The New South Wales Fire Service's **Museum of Fire** is open daily except Sunday ($3) – here in the Hall of Flame you can experience simulated fire conditions. If that's too hot, you can take a cruise on the river in the *Nepean Belle*.

Midway between Penrith and Parramatta, just south of the Western Freeway, is **Australia's Wonderland**, a large amusement park complex with a wildlife park. Admission is $27 ($20 children) and it's open daily (until 11 pm on Saturday). Admission to the wildlife park alone is $8.50 ($6.50 children). Shuttle buses meet trains at Rooty Hill.

CAMDEN AREA

South of Sydney and west of the Hume Highway, Camden is one of Australia's oldest towns. The surrounding countryside is fast filling with weekend attractions for Sydneysiders.

Camden was originally called Cowpasture because a herd of escapee cattle from Sydney Cove thrived here, but it was John and Elizabeth Macarthur's sheep, which arrived in 1805, that made the area famous. This area's main information centre (☎ (02) 821 2311) is in the outer suburb of Liverpool, at the corner of the Hume Highway and

Congressional Drive. In Camden, **John Oxley Cottage** on the northern outskirts houses an information centre (☎ (046) 58 1370), open from 10 am to 3 pm on weekends and holidays.

Gledswood at nearby Narellan is an 1810 homestead now housing a winery and a restaurant. There is also sheepshearing, boomerang-throwing and other activities. Not far away, **Australiana Park** (also called El Caballo Blanco) has an assortment of things to see and do but the star attractions are the Andalusian Dancing Stallions.

Midway between Camden and Campbelltown, the huge **Mount Annan Botanic Garden** is an offshoot of Sydney's botanic gardens which displays native flora on its 400 hectares. It's open daily from 10 am and admission is $5 per car, $2 for pedestrians. You can get here on bus No 896 which runs approximately hourly from Campbelltown railway station to Camden.

South of Camden and more rural is pretty **Picton**, an old village originally called Stonequarry. Today coal is mined in the area. In nearby Thirlmere the **Rail Transport Museum** has a huge collection of steam trains, some in working order. It's open between 10 am and 3 pm on weekdays and 9 am and 5 pm on weekends; admission is $5. The **Merigal Dingo Education Centre** (☎ (046) 84 1156), south of Picton near Bargo, is open on the first Sunday of the month between 10.30 am and 3 pm (and sometimes on other Sundays) and offers a chance to meet dingoes.

KU-RING-GAI CHASE NATIONAL PARK

Ku-ring-gai Chase (☎ (02) 457 9322 on weekdays, ☎ 457 9310 on weekends) lies to the north, between Sydney and the Hawkesbury River, 24 km from the city centre. Its eastern side borders the Pittwater. With over 100 km of shoreline, lots of forest and wildlife, walking tracks and Aboriginal rock art, this is a fine national park to find on a city's doorstep. High points in the park offer superb views across deep inlets like Cowan Water and the wide Pittwater, and from West Head at the park's north-eastern tip there's another fantastic view across the Pittwater to Barrenjoey Point at the end of Palm Beach. You might see lyrebirds at West Head during their May to July mating period.

The Kalkari visitor centre (☎ (02) 457 9853, open daily) is on Ku-ring-gai Chase Rd about four km into the park from Mt Colah, near Bobbin Head. There's an adjoining nature trail, and the road descends from the visitor centre to Bobbin Head on Cowan Water, where you can hire rowing boats, and then goes round to the Turramurra entrance.

At Akuna Bay on Coal & Candle Creek, off Cowan Water, there's a marina with a variety of craft for hire.

The popular **Waratah Park** on Namba Rd, Terrey Hills, on the edge of the park, is another place where you can meet koalas. The TV series *Skippy* was filmed here. It's open daily and admission is $10.80, or $5.80 for kids. You can get here on Forest Coachlines bus No 284, which meets trains at Chatswood, but there are only three a day and fewer on weekends. A recorded message (☎ (02) 450 1236) gives bus times.

Large areas of Ku-ring-gai Chase, especially around West Head, were burned in the fires of '94. Neither the camping area at the Basin nor the YHA hostel were directly affected.

Places to Stay

Camping ($10 for two people, $15 in school holidays) is allowed only at the Basin, on the western side of the Pittwater and a walk of about two km from the West Head road or a ferry ride from Palm Beach. Book camp sites in advance (☎ (02) 451 8124). The idyllic *Pittwater Youth Hostel* (☎ (02) 9999 2196) is a couple of km south of the Basin and is noted for friendly wildlife. Beds cost $13 or $16 per person in a twin room. If you stay only for Saturday night it's a little more. You must book.

Getting There & Away

There are four road entrances to the park – from Mt Colah (on the Pacific Highway) and Turramurra in the south-west, and Terrey Hills and Church Point in the south-east. Hornsby Buses (☎ (02) 457 8888) run fairly frequently from Turramurra Station to the nearby park entrance ($1.80), with a few services continuing on to Bobbin Head ($2.50). Roads reach Akuna Bay and West Head from the Terrey Hills or Church Point entrances, which are served by Forest Coachlines (☎ (02) 450 2277) and STA buses respectively. It's quite a walk in from these entrances.

From Palm Beach, ferries (☎ (02) 918 2747) run to the Basin hourly from 9 am to 4 pm (5 pm on weekends), costing $6 return. A ferry departs Palm Beach for Bobbin Head (running via Patonga on the northern side of the Hawkesbury River) every day at 11 am, returning at 3.30 pm. The one-way fare is $10 plus a dollar or two for bikes or big backpacks.

For the youth hostel, take a ferry from Church Point to Halls Wharf, from where it's a short walk. (YHA members get ferry discounts.) Several bus routes run from the city centre to Church Point; some involve changing buses at Mona Vale. You can get a direct bus from Manly. Scotland Island Schooners (☎ (02) 9999 3954) at Church Point will drop you off at the Basin or the hostel by arrangement.

HAWKESBURY RIVER

The Hawkesbury River enters the sea 30 km north of Sydney at Broken Bay. Dotted with coves, beaches, picnic spots and some fine riverside restaurants, it's one of Australia's most attractive rivers. The Hawkesbury's final 20-odd km before entering the ocean expand into bays and inlets like Berowra Creek, Cowan Water and the Pittwater on the southern side, and Brisbane Water on the northern. The river flows between a succession of national parks – Marramarra and Ku-ring-gai Chase to the south; Dharug, Brisbane Water and Bouddi to the north. About 100 km upstream are the towns of Windsor and Richmond (see below).

An excellent way to get a feel for the river is to go along with the river mail-boat, the *Riverboat Postman*, which runs up the river every weekday from Brooklyn at 9.30 am and returns at 1.15 pm. There's also an afternoon run on Wednesday and Friday, departing at 1.30 pm and returning at 4.15 pm. It costs $20 and the 8.16 am train from Sydney's Central Station will get you to Brooklyn in time to join the morning run. The same people run other Hawkesbury services, including Brooklyn to Windsor cruises and a cruise between Brooklyn and Patonga on the northern shore daily except Friday ($10 return). Bookings (☎ (02) 985 7566) are necessary.

There's also a daily ferry between Palm Beach, Patonga and Bobbin Head in Kuring-gai Chase National Park. From Patonga, Peninsula Bus Lines (☎ (043) 41 4133) has infrequent buses to Gosford where you can catch a bus or train going north.

Another interesting way to see the river is to hire a houseboat from an outfit such as Hawkesbury Holidays-a-Float (☎ (02) 985 7368) in Brooklyn. Renting midweek out of the peak season can be fairly cheap among a few people.

The tiny settlement of **Wisemans Ferry** (where a ferry is still the only means of crossing the river) is a popular spot up the river. Historic *Wisemans Ferry Inn* (☎ (045) 66 4301) has rooms for $50 a double. There are several caravan parks in the area; the cheapest sites ($8 a double) are at *Rosevale Farm Resort* (☎ (045) 66 4207) a couple of km north of the village centre.

Across the river, **Dharug National Park** is noted for its Aboriginal rock carvings which date back nearly 10,000 years.

A scenic road continues north from Wisemans Ferry to **St Albans** and is an example of early convict road building – it has scarcely changed since its original construction. The friendly *Settlers Arms Inn* (☎ (045) 68 2111) dates from 1836 and the public bar is worth a beer. They have a few pleasant rooms from $80 a double and there's a basic camp site opposite the pub.

WINDSOR AREA

Along with Richmond, Wilberforce, Castlereagh and Pitt Town, Windsor is one of the five 'Macquarie Towns' established by governor Lachlan Macquarie in the early 19th century on rich agricultural land on the upper Hawkesbury River. You can see them on the way to or from the Blue Mountains by the northern route along the Bells Line of Road – a more interesting and peaceful route to Katoomba than the Great Western Highway, but considerably longer.

The main information centre (☎ (045) 88 5895) for the upper Hawkesbury area is on the road between Richmond and Windsor, across from the Richmond RAAF base. It's open daily from 9 am to 5 pm. Windsor has its own information centre in the 1843 Daniel O'Connell Inn on Thompson Square. This also houses the **Hawkesbury Museum of Local History** which is open daily; admission is $2.50. You can book river cruises here.

Windsor's other old buildings include the convict-built **St Matthew's Church** completed in 1822 and designed, like the **courthouse**, by the convict architect Francis Greenway. George St has more historic buildings and the **Macquarie Arms Hotel** is reckoned to be the oldest pub in Australia (there are a few 'oldest pubs'!). On the edge of town is the **Tebbutt Observatory**, featured on the $100 note. You can look through the telescopes on Friday and Saturday night tours ($10) but you must book a fortnight in advance (☎ 018 611 232).

The **Australiana Pioneer Village** at Wilberforce is six km north of Windsor. It includes Rose Cottage (1811), probably the oldest surviving timber building in the country, and as well as other original buildings there are also native animals. The village is open daily except Monday and Friday, and admission is $7.

Richmond, eight km west of Windsor, dates from 1810 and has some more early buildings. There's a village-green-like park in the middle of town.

You can drive north to Wisemans Ferry and from there drive 70-odd km along the Hawkesbury to the Pacific Highway near Gosford, or stay on small picturesque roads all the way north to Wollombi near Cessnock in the Hunter Valley. Another scenic route from Windsor to the Hunter Valley is the road to Singleton, 160 km north. On this road about 20 km north of Windsor there's a long descent to the lovely **Colo River**. The nearby hamlet has a shop and a caravan park (☎ (045) 75 5253).

Blue Mountains

The Blue Mountains, part of the Great Dividing Range, were an impenetrable barrier to White expansion from Sydney. Despite many attempts to find a route through the mountains and a bizarre belief amongst many convicts that China, and freedom, was just on the other side, it was not until 1813 that a crossing was finally made and the western plains were opened up.

The first Whites into the mountains found evidence of Aboriginal occupation but few Aborigines. It seems likely that European diseases had travelled up from Sydney long before the explorers and wiped out most of the indigenous people.

The Blue Mountains National Park has some truly fantastic scenery, excellent bushwalks and all the gorges, gum trees and cliffs you could ask for. The hills rise up just 65 km inland from Sydney and even a century ago this was a popular getaway for affluent Sydneysiders who came to escape the summer heat. The mountains rise as high as 1100 metres and despite the intensive tourist development much of the area is so precipitous that it's still only open to bushwalkers. The blue haze which gave the mountains their name is a result of the fine mist of oil given off by eucalyptus trees.

Be prepared for the climatic difference between the Blue Mountains and the coast – you can swelter in Sydney but shiver in Katoomba. However, even in winter the days are often clear and down in the valleys it can be warm. Winter can be the best time for bushwalks but beware of sudden changes of weather and come prepared for freezing conditions.

During the '94 fires large areas on the eastern and south-eastern sides of the Grose Valley were burned but the Blue Gum Forest escaped almost intact. A low-intensity fire in the undergrowth raced through without causing too much damage to the larger trees.

The YHA hostel at North Springwood was destroyed in the fires but there are plans to replace it. The new hostel might be in a different location but it will be similarly simple and designed for people who want to experience the bush.

Orientation

The Great Western Highway from Sydney follows a ridge from east to west through the Blue Mountains. Along this less-than-beautiful road the Blue Mountains towns often merge into each other – Glenbrook, Springwood, Woodford, Lawson, Wentworth Falls, Leura, Katoomba (the main accommodation centre), Medlow Bath, Blackheath, Mt Victoria and Hartley. On the western fringe of the mountains is Lithgow – see the later Central West section.

To the south and north of the highway's ridge the country drops away into precipitous valleys, including the Grose Valley to the north, and the Jamison Valley south of Katoomba.

The old Bells Line of Road, much more scenic (and less congested) than the Great Western Highway, is a more northerly approach from Sydney; from Richmond it goes across north of the Grose Valley to bring you out on the main highway at Mt Victoria, or you can follow it all the way to Lithgow.

Information

There is an information centre on the highway at Glenbrook (☎ (047) 39 6266) and another at Echo Point in Katoomba (☎ (047) 82 0756). An excellent National Parks visitor centre – the Blue Mountains Heritage Centre (☎ (047) 87 8877) – is on Govetts Leap Rd at Blackheath, about three km off the Great Western Highway. On weekends a second National Parks visitor centre is open in Glenbrook (☎ (047) 39 2950) on Bruce Rd.

Books on the Blue Mountains include *Exploring the Blue Mountains* by M E Hungerford & J K Donald (Kangaroo Press) and, for walkers, *Walks in the Blue Mountains* by Neil Paton (Kangaroo Press) and *How to See the Blue Mountains* by Jim Smith (Megalong Books). Lonely Planet's *Bushwalking in Australia* by John & Monica Chapman includes walks in the Blue Mountains. Books and maps are sold at the visitor centres.

It usually snows sometime between June and August and the region has a Yule Festival, when many of the restaurants and guesthouses have good deals on 'Christmas' dinners.

National Parks

Large areas to the north and south of the Great Western Highway make up the **Blue Mountains National Park**. **Wollemi National Park**, north of the Bells Line of Road, is the state's largest forested wilderness area, stretching almost up to Denman in the Hunter Valley and offering good rugged bushwalking. It has lots of wildlife and similar landscape to the Blue Mountains. At the north-eastern end of Wollemi is the new **Yengo National Park**, a wilderness area with no facilities and limited road access.

Kanangra Boyd National Park, west of the southern part of the Blue Mountains National Park, has bushwalking possibilities and grand scenery, and includes the spectacular Kanangra Walls Plateau which is entirely surrounded by sheer cliffs and can be reached by unsealed roads from Oberon or Jenolan Caves.

Bushwalking

There are walks lasting from a few minutes to several days. The two most popular areas, spectacular from the top of the cliffs or the bottom of the valleys, are the Jamison Valley immediately south of Katoomba and the Grose Valley area north-east of Katoomba and Blackheath. The area south of Glenbrook is another good place. There's a fairly easy three-day walk from Katoomba to Jenolan Caves along the Six Foot Track.

Visit a National Parks visitor centre for information or, for shorter walks, ask at one of the tourist information centres. It's very rugged country and walkers sometimes get lost so it's highly advisable to get reliable information, not to go alone, and to tell someone where you're going. Most Blue Mountains watercourses are polluted so you have to sterilise water or take your own. And be prepared for rapid weather changes.

Mountain Biking

Cycling is permitted on many trails through the park, but this could change. See the Katoomba section for bike rentals.

Adventure Activities

The cliffs and gorges of the Blue Mountains offer excellent abseiling, climbing and canyoning. Most of the adventure outfits are based in Katoomba. If you drop into the Imperial Hotel in Mt Victoria on a weekend you're likely to meet climbers.

Places to Stay

There's a lot of accommodation in the Blue Mountains, from hostels to super-expensive guesthouses. Katoomba is the main centre. Most places charge more at weekends and guesthouses tend to be full on long weekends. In the national park you might need a permit to camp and in some parts camping is banned so check first.

Getting There & Away

Katoomba is almost an outer suburb of Sydney, 109 km from the centre, and trains run frequently on the two-hour trip, which costs $8.80. On weekdays you can buy a rail/bus sightseeing ticket at Sydney's Central Station for about $40.

The popular Wonderbus runs day tours of the Blue Mountains ($30) and overnight trips ($74) which include the Jenolan Caves and a visit to the Australian Wildlife Park. Book in Sydney at the YHA Travel Centre or at the YHA hostels. Another operator which gets good feedback is Oz-Trek (☎ (02) 360 3444).

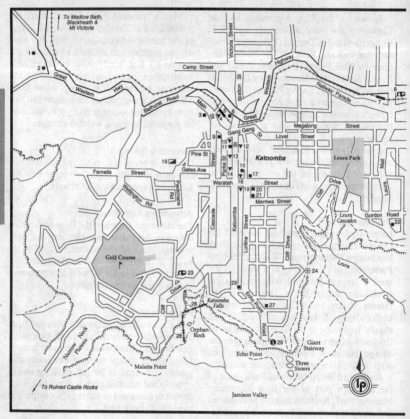

Getting Around

The Katoomba-Leura Bus Co (☎ (047) 82 3333) runs between Leura, Katoomba, Medlow Bath, Blackheath and Mt Victoria, with some services running down Hat Hill Rd and Govetts Leap Rd which lead respectively to Perrys Lookdown and Govetts Leap. They'll take you to within about one km of Govetts Leap but for Perrys Lookdown you have to walk about six km from the last stop. Services are sparse with few on Saturday and none on Sunday. In Katoomba the bus leaves from the top of Katoomba St.

The Katoomba-Woodford Bus Company

(☎ (047) 82 4213) runs between Leura and Katoomba and east as far as Woodford. They run from the Skyway and Katoomba Station daily except for Sunday and public holidays.

Ask Fantastic Aussie Tours outside Katoomba Station for details of other local bus services.

GLENBROOK TO KATOOMBA

From Marge's and Elizabeth's lookouts just north of Glenbrook there are good views back to Sydney. The section of the Blue Mountains National Park south of Glenbrook contains **Red Hand Cave**, an old

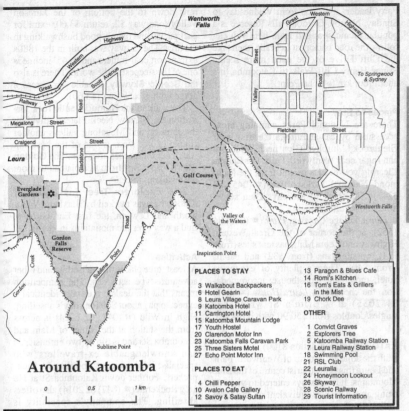

Around Katoomba

| 0 | 0.5 | 1 km |

PLACES TO STAY

3 Walkabout Backpackers
6 Hotel Gearin
8 Leura Village Caravan Park
9 Katoomba Hotel
11 Carrington Hotel
15 Katoomba Mountain Lodge
17 Youth Hostel
20 Clarendon Motor Inn
23 Katoomba Falls Caravan Park
25 Three Sisters Motel
27 Echo Point Motor Inn

PLACES TO EAT

4 Chilli Pepper
10 Avalon Cafe Gallery
12 Savoy & Satay Sultan

13 Paragon & Blues Cafe
14 Romi's Kitchen
16 Tom's Eats & Grillers
       in the Mist
19 Chork Dee

OTHER

1 Convict Graves
2 Explorers Tree
5 Katoomba Railway Station
7 Leura Railway Station
18 Swimming Pool
21 RSL Club
22 Leuralla
24 Honeymoon Lookout
26 Skyway
28 Scenic Railway
29 Tourist Information

Aboriginal shelter with hand stencils on the walls. It's an easy walk of about seven km (return) south-west of the National Parks information centre.

The famous (and infamous) artist and author Norman Lindsay lived in **Springwood** from 1912 until he died in 1969. His home at 128 Chapman Parade is now a gallery and museum (☎ (047) 51 1067) with exhibits of his paintings, cartoons, illustrations and, in the garden, sculptures. It's open from 11 am to 5 pm Friday to Sunday and public holidays; admission is $5.

Just south of the town of **Wentworth Falls**

there are great views of the Jamison Valley, and of the 300-metre Wentworth Falls themselves, from Gordon Falls Reserve which is the starting point for a network of walking tracks. In Wentworth Falls, Yester Grange is a restored 19th-century premier's home, open from Wednesday to Sunday; admission is $4.

Sublime Point, south of Leura, is another great lookout point. In **Leura**, Leuralla is an Art-Deco mansion with a fine collection of 19th-century Australian art and a model railway museum. The house is a memorial to H V 'Doc' Evatt, a former Australian Labor

Party leader; it's open from Wednesday to Sunday. Nearby, Gordon Falls Reserve is a popular picnic spot and from here you can follow the road back past Leuralla, then take the Cliff Drive or the even more scenic Prince Henry Cliff Walk to Katoomba (it's about four km to Echo Point).

Places to Stay

There are National Parks camping areas accessible by car at Euroka Clearing near Glenbrook, Murphys Glen near Woodford and Ingar near Wentworth Falls. For Euroka Clearing you need a permit from the Richmond National Parks office (☎ (045) 88 5247). The track to Murphys Glen sometimes closes after rain.

Leura Village Caravan Park (☎ (047) 84 1552), at the corner of the Great Western Highway and Leura Mall, has tent sites (from $14), on-site vans (from $32) and cabins (from $40). There's plenty of expensive hotel, motel and guesthouse accommodation; the cheapest is *Leura House* (☎ (047) 84 2035) at 7 Britain St which has singles/doubles from $50/90 with breakfast.

KATOOMBA (population 8100)

With the adjacent centres of Wentworth Falls and Leura this is the tourist centre of the Blue Mountains. It has always catered to visitors, being an Australian equivalent of an Indian 'hill station', where plains-dwellers escape the summer heat. Despite the numbers of tourists, Katoomba retains the atmosphere of a town from another time and place, with its Art-Deco and Art-Nouveau guesthouses and cafes, and its thick mists and occasional snow.

The Cliff Drive from Leura passes Honeymoon Lookout and then reaches **Echo Point** about two km south of central Katoomba. Echo Point has some of the best views of the Jamison Valley including the magnificent **Three Sisters** rock formation. The Three Sisters floodlit at night are an awesome sight. The tourist information centre (☎ (047) 82 0756) is here.

West of Echo Point, the **scenic railway** runs down to the bottom of the Jamison Valley (one way $2, return $3.60, extra for backpacks) and there's good bushwalking in the area. The railway was built in the 1880s to transport coal-miners and its 45° incline is one of the steepest in the world. There is also the **Scenic Skyway**, a cable car across a gorge with great views ($3.60).

The walk to the **Ruined Castle** rock formation on Narrow Neck Plateau, dividing the Jamison and Megalong valleys another couple of km west, is one of the best, but watch out for leeches after rain. The **Golden Stairs** lead down from this plateau to more bushwalking tracks.

The **Explorers Tree**, just west of Katoomba, was marked by Blaxland, Wentworth and Lawson, the first Europeans to find a way over the mountains in 1813.

Activities

At least three places offer abseiling and other adventure-type activities. The competition means that the deals are usually identical – expect to pay about $60 for a day's abseiling. High 'n Wild (☎ (047) 82 6224) is across from the station at the corner of Main and Katoomba Sts and is run by two enthusiastic and knowledgeable ex-travellers who specialise in introductory abseiling for backpackers. Further down Katoomba St at No 182, Rockcraft (☎ (047) 82 2014) also offers abseiling. The company's speciality is climbing and it runs the Australian School of Mountaineering. Not far away, upstairs in the Mountain Designs shop, the Blue Mountains Adventure Company (☎ (047) 82 1271) has abseiling and a variety of tours. It also has some interesting mountain-bike rides.

Extreme Mountain Bike Tours (☎ (047) 87 7281, ask for Philip) is a small outfit offering experienced mountain bikers some great riding. Blue Mountains Adventure Company (☎ (047) 82 1271) have more-gentle guided rides from $50 a day.

Places to Stay

Camping *Katoomba Falls Caravan Park*

(☎ (047) 82 1835) on Katoomba Falls Rd has tent sites from $7 and on-site vans from $35.

Hostels Katoomba's youth hostel (☎ (047) 82 1416) is in a nice old guesthouse on the corner of Lurline and Waratah Sts, near the centre of town. For members, dorm beds cost from $11 and twins/doubles are around $17 per person. Many of the rooms have attached bathrooms. Nearby *Katoomba Mountain Lodge* (☎ (047) 82 3933) at 31 Lurline St is a guesthouse and hostel charging from $22 per person for singles/doubles with shared bathrooms, and from $11 for dorm beds.

Walkabout Backpackers (☎ (047) 82 4226) at 190 Bathurst Rd (the westward continuation of Main St) is close to the railway station and has large dorms for $12 (three nights for $30) and good twins for $30. They staff will drive you to any of the trailheads in the area.

Hotels & Motels On the Great Western Highway north of the station, the *Hotel Gearin* (☎ (047) 82 4395), always known as Gearin's Hotel, is good for a local pub and has rooms for $25/45. Some of the rooms are much better than average pub rooms. The *Katoomba Hotel* (☎ (047) 82 1106), at the corner of Parke and Main Sts, has rooms for $20/40 midweek and $25/50 on Friday and Saturday nights. Both pubs sometimes have share rooms which they let to backpackers for about $20 per person.

The *Clarendon Motor Inn* (☎ (047) 82 1322) at the corner of Lurline and Waratah Sts has guesthouse-style singles/doubles from $40/60 midweek and other more expensive rooms. There's a theatre restaurant/cabaret here with shows on Friday and Saturday nights – some of the acts are big names.

Most of the more expensive places have widely varying rates depending on the time of the week and the time of the year. The *Three Sisters Motel* (☎ (047) 82 2911) at the bottom end of Katoomba St is an average cheaper motel, charging from around $50 to $85 a single or double.

At the top of the hotel scale is a superb relic of an earlier era, the *Hydro Majestic Hotel* (☎ (047) 88 1002), located a few km west of Katoomba at Medlow Bath. Doubles with breakfast cost around $130, more on weekends. The equally grand *Carrington Hotel* in the centre of Katoomba is due to reopen after a major refit.

Places to Eat
Katoomba St has plenty of good places to eat. The *Savoy* is a cafe with an interesting menu of focaccia, pasta and Asian-inspired dishes. Salads cost from $4.50 and entrée-size pastas from $6; the servings are large. It's open until 9 pm, later on weekends. Across the street is the *Blues Cafe*, a coffee shop/cafe with snacks for about $5 and main courses for about $12.

Blues Cafe has Art-Deco decor but nearby is Katoomba's undisputed Art-Deco palace, the *Paragon*. Check out the even gaudier cocktail lounge at the back. Both Blues Cafe and the Paragon are open only during the day, except perhaps on weekends and at peak times.

Not far away is *Satay Sultan*, a combination coffee shop and Malaysian restaurant. Small serves cost $6 and main courses, with rice, salad and side-dishes, are $13.50. Vegetarian meals are about $9. Open during the day, *Romi's Kitchen* is a small coffee shop also selling curries for about $6.

Towards the corner of Waratah St at 200 Katoomba St *Tom's Place* has meals for well under $10. It's open from 11 am to 11 pm during the week and till 1 am on weekends. Nearby *Grillers in the Mist* (groan) sells fresh and frozen seafood and puts together some interesting takeaways, such as grilled sardine rolls for $3.50. Across Waratah St, the Thai *Chork Dee* has vegetarian dishes for around $7 and other main courses for under $10. At 43 Waratah St the *Curry Shop* is open for dinner nightly and for weekend lunch.

On Main St next to the railway station, *Chilli Pepper* serves Asian food, with plenty of vegetarian dishes, for around $8 to $11 for a main course. It's open for dinner from Wednesday to Monday, and daily at peak times. Upstairs and along some corridors from 82 Main St, near the station, the *Avalon Cafe Gallery* is a relaxed and pleasantly eccentric place open for lunch and dinner Wednesday to Saturday and for dinner on Sunday. Main courses are around $9 for pasta and $14 for other dishes.

Both *Gearin's Hotel* and the *Katoomba Hotel* have counter meals. For late-night eating and drinking try the *Last Resort* restaurant and bar at 8 Gang Gang St, open from 6 pm to 3 am daily. Most meals are $10 or less.

At 13 Cliff Drive, near the highway towards Blackheath, the *Arjuna Cafe* has Indian and Asian food, vegetarian meals and home-made cakes. It's a pleasant place with mountain views, open for dinner from Wednesday to Monday. In Leura, the *Little Cafe* in Leura Mall has Sunday evening Indian vegetarian meals for $7.

Entertainment

The *Carrington Hotel*'s revamped bar on Main St has some dress regulations but that doesn't stop the hotel from holding events such as horizontal bungee jumping. The bar at the *Last Resort* on Gang Gang St stays open until 3 am nightly. For local bands try *Gearin's Hotel* or the *Katoomba Hotel* on weekends, and there's a blues jam at Gearin's on Monday nights.

Getting Around

You can hire mountain bikes at the YHA hostel for $20 a day ($15 for guests) and $12 for a half-day ($10 for guests). Better bikes are available from the Blue Mountains Adventure Company (☎ (047) 82 1271) on Katoomba St for $30 a day (24 hours); the rate is reduced if the bike is hired for a number of days.

A bus service (☎ (047) 82 4213) runs from opposite the Carrington Hotel to the scenic railway, approximately hourly until about 4.30 pm on weekdays and a few times on Saturday and Sunday ($1.60). On weekends and holidays the Blue Mountains Explorer Bus around Katoomba and Leura is a hop-on, hop-off service for which you buy an all-day ticket ($15, $7.50 children). Contact Fantastic Aussie Tours (also called Golden West Travel (☎ (047) 82 1866) outside Katoomba railway station; the same people run Blue Mountains and Jenolan Caves tours from Katoomba.

BLACKHEATH AREA (population 4000)

The little town of Blackheath is on the rail line from Sydney and the Great Western Highway, and is a good base for visiting – or looking at – the Grose Valley. There are superb lookouts a few km east of Blackheath, among them **Govetts Leap** with the adjacent **Bridal Veil Falls** (the Blue Mountains' highest), **Evans Lookout** to the south and **Pulpit Rock**, **Perrys Lookdown** and **Anvil Rock** to the north. The last three are all reached from Hat Hill Rd.

A long cliff-edge track leads from Evans Lookout to Pulpit Rock and there are walks down into the Grose Valley itself and on the valley bottom – all involve at least a 300-metre descent and ascent. Get details on walks from the Heritage Centre, about three km out of Blackheath on Govetts Leap Rd, shortly before Govetts Leap itself. Perrys Lookdown is the beginning of the shortest route to beautiful **Blue Gum Forest** in the valley bottom – about four hours return, but you'll want to spend longer.

The **Megalong Valley**, south of Blackheath, is largely cleared farmland but it's still a beautiful place. The road down from Blackheath passes through some lovely rainforest and there is at least one place where you can stop and walk. There are several horse-riding outfits, such as Werriberri Trail Rides (☎ (047) 87 9171) and Packsaddlers (☎ (047) 87 9150) at the end of the valley in Green Gully. Megalong Valley Farm (☎ (047) 87 9265) has displays of sheep and cattle as well as Clydesdale horses and native animals.

Places to Stay

The nearest National Parks camp site is Acacia Flat in the Grose Valley, near Blue Gum Forest and a steep walk down from

Govetts Leap or Perrys Lookdown, but you can camp in the car park at Perrys Lookdown.

The Blackheath Caravan Park (☎ (047) 87 8101) has tent sites from $7 a single and vans from $35 a double. It's on Prince Edward St, off Govetts Leap Rd, about 600 metres from the highway. *Gardners Inn* (☎ (047) 87 8347), on the highway in Blackheath just north of Govetts Leap Rd, is the oldest hotel in the Blue Mountains (1831) and charges about $35 per person, including breakfast. The *Lakeview Holiday Park* (☎ (047) 87 8534) on Prince Edward St has cabins from $40 to $60 a double.

MT VICTORIA & BEYOND

A couple of km west of Blackheath, at the top of the mountain, is the pretty National-Trust-classified town of Mt Victoria. The **museum** at the railway station is open on weekend afternoons. Interesting buildings include the Victoria & Albert guesthouse, the 1849 Tollkeeper's Cottage and the 1870s church.

Mt Vic Flicks is an old-style cinema with usherettes and door prizes. On Thursday night it costs just $5, while on Saturday night $10 gets you a double feature plus supper at interval!

Off the highway at **Mt York** there's a memorial to the explorers who first found a way across the Blue Mountains. There's a short stretch of the original road across the mountains here.

About 11 km past Mt Victoria is the tiny village of **Hartley** which flourished in the 1830s and '40s but dwindled when it was bypassed by the railway in 1887. Seventeen buildings of historic significance can be viewed and tours are available on weekdays.

Between Bell and Richmond, **Mt Tomah Botanic Gardens** is the cool-climate annexe of Sydney's Royal Botanic Gardens. They're open daily and admission is $5 per car and $2 for individuals. North of the Bells Line of Road, **Mt Wilson** is a village with many formal gardens. There's also a lovely remnant of rainforest, the **Cathedral of Ferns**. Off the Bells Line of Road between

Lithgow and Bell is the Zig Zag Railway – see the Central West section.

Places to Stay

The *Imperial Hotel* (☎ (047) 87 1233), a very fine old hotel, has backpackers' beds for about $20 – expensive but apparently worth it. The hotel also has singles/doubles from about $30/50 to $70/100 and various packages. Nearby is the *Victoria & Albert* (☎ (047) 87 1588), a very grand guesthouse with B&B for about $45/90, or $15 more for attached bathroom. There's a cafe and in the evening a good restaurant offering two-course dinners for $24.50 and three courses for $30.

JENOLAN CAVES

South-west of Katoomba and on the western edge of Kanangra Boyd National Park are the best-known limestone caves in Australia. One cave has been open to the public since

Jenolan Caves

1867 although parts of the system are still unexplored. Three caves are open for independent viewing, and you can visit a further nine by guided tours which go about 10 times a day from 10 am to 4 pm, with an evening tour at 8 pm. Tours last 1½ to two hours and prices vary from $10 to $12. At holiday time arrive early as the best caves can be 'sold out' by 10 am.

Places to Stay & Eat

You can camp near Jenolan Caves House. *Binda Bush Cabins* (☎ (063) 59 3311) are on the road from Hartley about eight km north of the caves and accommodate six people in bunks for $75 per night. *Jenolan Caves House* (☎ (063) 59 3304) has packages from $90/150 including two meals, with a minimum of two nights on weekends. It does a four-course buffet lunch for $19.50. *Forest Lodge* (☎ (063) 35 6267) is much less expensive but it's about eight km south-west of the caves.

Getting There & Away

The Six Foot Track from Katoomba to the Jenolan Caves is a fairly easy three-day walk. The Department of Conservation & Land Management has a detailed brochure.

See Getting There & Away at the start of the Blue Mountains section for information on the popular Wonderbus tour. Fantastic Aussie Tours (☎ (047) 82 1866; (02) 281 7100) has day tours to the caves from Katoomba for about $46 (plus cave entry). Walkers can be dropped off or collected from the Six Foot Track at Jenolan for $30 but you have to book. It also has day and overnight tours from Sydney.

North Coast

The New South Wales north coast is extremely popular – and with good reason. As well as the excellent beaches, the numerous national parks in the ranges offer wildlife, challenging bushwalks and superb scenery.

The Pacific Highway runs north along the coast into Queensland, and along it you'll find some great places to stop, including Byron Bay – a surfing Mecca and long-time travellers' favourite.

Most of the way north a narrow coastal strip runs between the sea and the Great Dividing Range. In places the highway runs well inland from the coast and rougher roads will take you along quite deserted stretches of beach. Some superbly scenic roads lead into the ranges and onto the New England tableland.

SYDNEY TO NEWCASTLE

The fastest route is the Sydney to Newcastle Freeway, but just as scenic are the curves of the Pacific Highway which, once across the Hawkesbury River, runs nearer to the coast.

On the Pacific Highway nine km south of Gosford, **Old Sydney Town** is a major reconstruction of early Sydney with nonstop street theatre retelling events from the colony's early history. It's open from 10 am to 4 pm Wednesday to Sunday and daily during school holidays. Admission is $14.50 (children $8). Several tours run here from Sydney.

The largest town on the densely populated central coast is **Gosford**, on Brisbane Water and connected to Sydney by suburban trains. The information centre (☎ (043) 22 4475) is on Mann St near the railway station. **Terrigal** is about 12 km east of Gosford on the ocean. There's a new hostel, *Terrigal Beach Backpackers* (☎ (043) 85 3330), with dorm beds for $14 and a double or triple room for $35. It's close to the beach at 10 Campbell Crescent. **Patonga**, a village on the northern bank of the Hawkesbury River/Broken Bay, is accessible by ferry from Sydney's Palm Beach.

Bouddi National Park is an attractive coastal park extending north from the Hawkesbury River mouth, with excellent bushwalking and swimming. The beautiful **Brisbane Water National Park** offers similar attractions south-west of Gosford, just in from the mouth of the Hawkesbury. It has many old Aboriginal rock engravings.

Further north, **Lake Macquarie** is Australia's biggest saltwater lake, popular for sailing, water-skiing and fishing. The region's information centre (☎ (049) 72 1172) is on the highway just north of Swansea.

NEWCASTLE (population 265,000)

The state's second largest city, Newcastle is also one of Australia's largest ports. At the mouth of the Hunter River, 167 km north of Sydney, it's a major industrial and commercial centre, with the massive BHP steelworks and other heavy industries. It's also the export port for the Hunter Valley coalfields.

Newcastle is a relaxed and friendly place and, despite the heavy industry, the city centre has wide, leafy streets, with clean surf beaches only a few hundred metres away.

Originally named Coal River, the city was founded in 1804 as a place for the most intractable of Sydney's convicts and was known as the 'hell of New South Wales'. The breakwater out to Nobbys Head, with its lighthouse, was built by convicts. The Bogey Hole, a swimming pool cut into the rock on the ocean's edge below the pleasant King Edward Park, was built for Major Morriset, a strict disciplinarian. It's still a great place for a dip.

In late 1989, Newcastle suffered Australia's most destructive earthquake, with 12 people killed and a lot of property damaged. Around town you can still see signs of it – props holding up facades and buildings being restored or demolished.

Orientation & Information

The city centre is a peninsula bordered by the ocean on one side and the Hunter River on the other. It tapers down to the long sandspit leading to Nobbys Head. Hunter St is the three-km-long main street, forming a pedestrian mall between Newcomen and Perkins Sts.

The tourist office (☎ (049) 29 9299) is in the waterfront Queens Wharf complex; from the Hunter St Mall take the elevated walkway. It's open from 9 am to 5 pm on weekdays and from 10 am to 3.30 pm on weekends. It sells excellent heritage walk maps.

The railway station, the long-distance bus stop, the post office, banks and some fine old buildings are at the north-eastern end of the city centre. Cooks Hill rises steeply behind the centre and offers good views.

Things to See & Do

Newcastle is well endowed with clean beaches, many with world-class surf. The main beach, **Newcastle Beach**, is adjacent to the centre of town; it has an ocean pool and good surf. Just north of here is **Nobbys Beach**, more sheltered from the southerlies and often open when other beaches are closed. South of the centre, **Bar Beach** is floodlit at night. Nearby **Merewether Beach** has two huge pools.

Just across the river/harbour from Queens Wharf is **Stockton**, a modest suburb with beaches and good views back to Newcastle city. It's minutes from the city by ferry but by road you have to wind through the docks and some dramatic industrial landscapes, a trip of about 20 km.

The **Newcastle Regional Museum** at 787 Hunter St in Newcastle West is open daily except Monday (daily in school holidays) and admission is $3. It includes the Supernova hands-on science display. There is a free maritime museum (open 10 am to 5 pm from Tuesday to Friday and during the afternoon from Saturday to Monday) and a military museum (open weekend afternoons) in **Fort Scratchley** out towards Nobbys Head, which dates from the 1880s. For $1 you can explore parts of the tunnels under the fort, which are said to run all the way to King Edwards Park.

The **Newcastle Regional Art Gallery** is on Laman St next to Civic Park. It's free and open weekdays and weekend afternoons. There are several private galleries on nearby Cooks Hill.

A couple of outfits offer infrequent cruises on the harbour. *Lady Joy* departs from Queens Wharf on Thursday at 2 pm ($12), more often in school holidays, and *William*

NEW SOUTH WALES

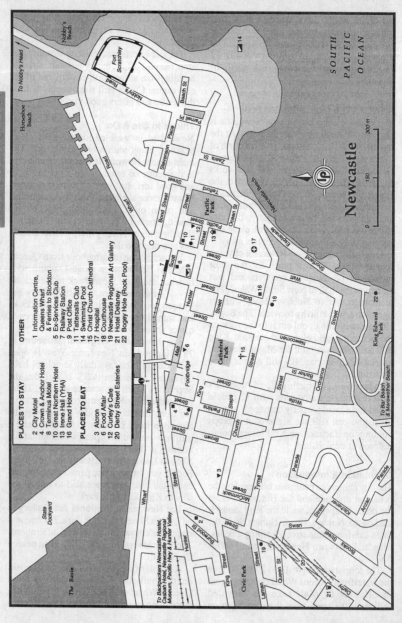

Newcastle

SOUTH PACIFIC OCEAN

Nobby's Beach

Horseshoe Beach

To Nobby's Head

Fort Scratchley

The Basin

State Dockyard

King Edward Park

Newcastle Beach

Shortland

Esplanade

To Bar Beach & Merewether Beach

Civic Park

To Backpackers Newcastle Hostel,
Casbah Hotel, Newcastle Regional
Museum, Pacific Hwy & Hunter Valley

PLACES TO STAY

2 City Motel
4 Crown & Anchor Hotel
8 Terminus Motel
10 Great Northern Hotel
13 Irene Hall (YHA)
16 Grand Hotel

PLACES TO EAT

3 Akron
6 Food Affair
12 Curley's Cafe
20 Derby Street Eateries

OTHER

1 Information Centre,
   Queens Wharf
   & Ferries to Stockton
5 Ex-Services Club
9 Railway Station
11 Tattersalls Club
14 Swimming Pool
15 Christ Church Cathedral
17 Hospital
18 Courthouse
19 Newcastle Regional Art Gallery
21 Hotel Delaney
22 Bogey Hole (Rock Pool)

the Fourth, a replica of an old steamship, leaves Merewether St near Queens Wharf at 11 am and 2 pm on the third Sunday of the month ($10).

At New Lambton Heights, approximately 10 km south-west of the centre, **Blackbutt Reserve** (☎ (049) 52 1449) is a 182-hectare bushland reserve with bushwalks and aviaries, wildlife enclosures and fern houses. Bus No 363 runs past the upper entrance, Nos 216 and 217 past the lower.

About 10 km west of the centre near Sandgate railway station, the **Shortlands Wetlands Centre** (☎ (049) 51 6466) on the edge of Hexham Swamp has lots of bird life as well as walks and canoe trails. It's open daily and admission is by a $2 donation.

Places to Stay

Camping Stockton is handy for Newcastle by ferry but it's 20 km by road. *Stockton Beach Caravan Park* (☎ (049) 28 1393) is on the beach in Pitt St. Sites are $9 a double and on-site vans cost from $30 to $50. There are several caravan parks south of Newcastle, around Belmont and on the ocean at Redhead Beach.

Hostels The YHA operates part of *Irene Hall* (☎ (049) 29 3324) at 27 Pacific St as a hostel; the rest of the building is mainly student accommodation. It's in the centre of the city and a short walk from the beach. Dorm beds are $12 (YHA members only), while singles/doubles are about $20/30.

Further from the centre (but with free pick-ups and bikes) is *Backpackers Newcastle* (☎ (049) 69 3436) at 42 Denison St. This is a clean, friendly place and is recommended. Dorm beds are $12 and doubles are $28. There are free surfboards and one of the owners is a keen surfer who can help you learn. They also have trips to beaches up the coast and possible excursions to the Lower Hunter wineries.

Hotels Once a grand hotel but now terminally past its prime, the *Great Northern Hotel* (☎ (049) 29 4961) on the corner of Scott and Watt Sts is worth a look even if you

don't stay there. Check out the foyer's murals and the 1st-floor bar. Singles/doubles are $26/41, or $33/48 with bathroom. Weekly rates are much cheaper.

The *Crown & Anchor* (☎ (049) 29 1027) on the corner of Hunter and Perkins Sts has singles/doubles for $25/35. The *Grand Hotel* (☎ (049) 29 3489) is on the corner of Bolton and Church Sts in the city centre, across from the courthouse. This fine old pub has been well renovated and the large, pleasant rooms go for $40/42, or $50/52 with bathroom.

Motels The *Terminus Motel* (☎ (049) 26 3244) at 107 Scott St, also known as the Harbourside Motel, is central with rooms at $45/50. The *City Motel* (☎ (049) 29 5855), on the corner of Darby and Burwood Sts, is reasonably central but costs $60/65. In Belmont, about 15 km south, there's a string of less expensive motels along the Pacific Highway.

Places to Eat

From Monday to Wednesday during term, you can put together a main course and dessert for around $5 at *Hunter TAFE College* on King St.

There are several good places for snacks and meals at the eastern end of Hunter St. *Vera's Cafe* on the corner of Pacific and Hunter Sts has footpath tables, and serves breakfast for around $6. *Curley's* (the illuminated sign says Vienna Cafe), just around the corner on Pacific St, is a nice place with focaccia for $4.50, pasta from about $6 and other main courses for $8. Also on Pacific St, *Irene Hall Cafeteria* has inexpensive meals.

Up the escalator on Hunter Mall is *Food Affair*, a small food hall. The Chinese place sells three dishes plus rice for $5.40.

Darby St south of Queen St is Newcastle's eat street, with a wide variety of cuisines and price ranges, including: *Voquet*, a stylish but not too expensive French cafe and restaurant; the *Taj*, an Indian grocery with a fine takeaway section; *Splash*, which claims to have 'the finest fish & chips in the known universe' for $4.20; and *Al-Oi*, a Thai place with main courses around $8.50.

Not far away, on the Church St hill, is *Alcron*, perhaps the oldest restaurant in Australia. Main courses are around $20.

Beaumont St, in Hamilton just south of the Pacific Highway as you enter the town, has a cluster of Italian restaurants, including *Little Swallow* and *Milano's*. The restaurant upstairs from the Italian Club has been recommended.

Entertainment

There's something on most nights – get the Wednesday *Newcastle Herald* for an entertainment lift-out or pick up a copy of the weekly *Wire* pocket guide. The *Cambridge Hotel* at the corner of Hunter and Dennison Sts has bands, as does *Tattersalls Club* (Tatts) on Watt St, which is popular with students. The *Kent Hotel* on Beaumont St has jazz. The *Hotel Delaney* is a relaxed little pub on the corner of Darby and Council Sts, with music most nights. The popular *Brewery*, at the Queens Wharf complex, brews its own.

In Merewether the *Beach Hotel* has bands mainly on weekends. The *Bar on the Hill* out at the university usually has bands on Thursday nights.

Getting There & Away

Air Aeropelican flies several times a day between Sydney ($68) and Belmont, just south of Newcastle. Oxley flies between Newcastle and Brisbane ($233), Lismore ($206), Port Macquarie ($126) and Taree ($106). Eastern Australia also flies out of Newcastle. Oxley and Eastern Australia fly from Williamtown, north of Newcastle.

Bus Between Sydney and Newcastle you're better off taking the train, but heading up the coast from Newcastle buses offer a much better service. Nearly all long-distance buses stop on Watt St near the railway station, although there is talk of building a bus station somewhere else. Cheapish fares from Newcastle include: Sydney $14.50, Port Macquarie $30, Byron Bay $48, Brisbane $50. Jayes Travel (☎ (049) 26 2000) at 285

Hunter St near Darby St handles most major bus lines. Sid Fogg's (☎ toll-free 1800 045 952) runs to Canberra ($43) (four times a week, daily in school holidays) and up the valley to Dubbo ($43) (three times a week). Book at Tower Travel (☎ (049) 26 3199), 245 Hunter St on the corner of Crown St, or phone the depot.

Rover Motors (☎ (049) 90 1699) runs to Maitland and Cessnock ($7).

Train Ordinary Sydney suburban trains run from Central Station to Newcastle about 25 times a day, taking nearly three hours. The one-way fare is $13.60; off-peak return is about $18. Other trains heading north from Sydney bypass central Newcastle, stopping at suburban Broadmeadow. Frequent buses run from here to the city centre. An XPT from Central Station to Broadmeadow takes about 2¼ hours and costs $17.90.

Car Rental As well as the regular places, you can hire used cars from places such as Cheep Heep (☎ (049) 61 3144) at 107 Tudor St, Hamilton, from about $20 a day, including insurance.

Getting Around

STA buses cover Newcastle and the eastern side of Lake Macquarie. There are fare deals similar to those on offer in Sydney. The bus information booth at the west end of the mall, on the corner of Perkins St, has timetables; if it's closed see the tourist office or phone the Travel Information Centre (☎ (049) 61 8933) between 8.30 am and 4.30 pm. For sightseeing try route No 348, 350 or 358 to Swansea or No 306, 307 or 327 to Speers Point.

Trains run along the western side of Lake Macquarie with connecting buses to the south-western shores.

Bus No 118 runs to Stockton but much quicker is the ferry from Queens Wharf. It costs $1.30 and departs approximately half-hourly until 11 pm from Monday to Saturday, until midnight on Friday and Saturday and until 8.30 pm on Sunday. The ferry office on Queens Wharf near the tourist office has timetables.

Bicycle Bike-hire places come and go – the tourist office will know if one is operating currently.

HUNTER VALLEY

The Hunter Valley has two curiously diverse products – coal and wine. The centre of the Hunter Valley vineyards is the Pokolbin area near Cessnock and some wineries date back to the 1860s. You'll find many of Australia's best-known wine names here.

On the southern side of the valley rise the sandstone ranges of the Wollemi and Goulburn River national parks; the northern side is bordered by the high, rugged ranges leading up to Barrington Tops National Park.

The main road through the Hunter Valley is the New England Highway running north-west from Newcastle and climbing up to the New England tablelands near Murrurundi. The 300-km-long Hunter River comes from further west and doesn't meet the highway until Singleton. The valley is wide in the Lower Hunter area, where you'll find most of the wineries; upstream from Singleton it narrows.

More than 40 vineyards in the Lower Hunter, and others in the Upper Hunter, are open for sampling and buying wines. Generally they're open for tastings daily, with slightly reduced hours on Sunday. Many have picnic and barbecue facilities.

Organised Tours

Hunter Vineyard Tours (☎ (049) 91 1659) has daily departures from Newcastle and other Hunter centres and charges $45 ($29 without lunch). Several Sydney companies have day tours of the Lower Hunter wineries. For tours of the Upper Hunter contact the Scone or Denman information centres.

Getting There & Around

Trains run up the valley en route to Armidale and Moree.

Batterhams Express (☎ (049) 90 5000, toll-free 1800 043 339) runs at least once daily between Sydney and Cessnock ($18), continuing up the valley as far as Scone. Rover Motors (☎ (049) 90 1699) runs between Newcastle and Cessnock ($7) frequently on weekdays, less often on Saturday and not at all on Sunday. Sid Fogg's (☎ toll-free 1800 045 952) has a daily bus from Newcastle to Denman ($21).

Driving from Sydney to the Lower Hunter there's an interesting back route (some unsealed roads) from Wisemans Ferry, passing through the pretty hamlet of Wollombi. A great drive from Sydney to the Upper Hunter is on the Windsor to Singleton road, known as the Putty Road.

You can hire bicycles from Grapemobile (☎ (049) 98 7639), at the corner of McDonalds and Gillards Rds near Pokolbin. They charge $25 for a day and $15 for a half-day.

Lower Hunter Wineries

The region's information centre (☎ (049) 90 4477) is in **Cessnock** on the corner of Wollombi and Mount View Rds and is open daily. If you're coming from the Newcastle direction head through town and the information centre is on your right a few blocks past the traffic lights. Drop in here for maps and brochures before you set out on a winery tour. For tourist information tune to 107.9 FM.

Several wineries run tours. On weekdays McWilliams and Rothbury have tours at 11 am and 2 pm and Tyrrells has one at 1.30 pm. Rothbury also has tours at weekends (11 am and 2 pm) as does Hunter Estate (9.30 am). Hungerford Hill bills itself as a 'wine village'. It has a restaurant and handicrafts shop as well as the usual tasting and wine sales facilities. The Hunter Valley Wine Society also has a pleasant bistro here.

The Hunter Vintage Walkabout in February and March attracts hordes of wine enthusiasts for wine tasting, and grape-picking and treading contests. In September there's the Wine & Food Affair.

Places to Stay Almost all places offering accommodation charge more at weekends and you might have to take a package (meals included). Cessnock's information centre (☎ (049) 90 4477) can book accommodation.

Cessnock is the main town and accommodation centre for the vineyards. *Valley View Carapark* (☎ (049) 90 2573) on Mount View Rd has tent sites for $8, on-site vans from $17 and cabins from $30. *Cessnock Cabins & Country Carapark* (☎ (049) 90 5819) off Allandale Rd north of Cessnock has sites for $10, on-site vans from $25 and cabins from $30.

The friendly *Black Opal Hotel* (☎ (049) 90 1070) is at the top end of Vincent St, the main shopping street, and is a popular place to stay – you're advised to book. It's also an associate-YHA hostel. Bunk beds are $13 a night for YHA members and singles/doubles in the hotel rooms are $15/30 midweek and $20/40 on weekends.

The *Wentworth Hotel* (☎ (049) 90 1364) at 36 Vincent St charges about $30/50 with breakfast. Other Cessnock hotels include the *Royal Oak* (☎ (049) 90 2366) on the corner of Vincent and Snape Sts and the *Cessnock Hotel* (☎ (049) 90 1002) on Wollombi Rd opposite the post office. There is also pub accommodation in nearby towns such as Neath and Bellbird.

Midweek prices at some Cessnock motels include $42/52 at the *Cessnock Motel* (☎ (049) 90 2699) and $40/48 at the *Hunter Valley Motel* (☎ (049) 90 1722), both on Allandale Rd. Prices at these and other motels rise steeply at weekends.

There is a lot of accommodation out among the vineyards. Most is well over $100 a night on weekends, but midweek there are a few places charging around $60 a double, such as *Hunter Country Lodge* (☎ (049) 38 1744) about 12 km north of Cessnock on Branxton Rd and *Belford Country Cabins* (☎ (049) 91 2777) on Hermitage Rd north of the Hunter Estate.

Upper Hunter Wineries

The Upper Hunter has fewer wineries than the Lower, only a half-dozen or so, but it's worth visiting because the pace is slower and the scenery more beautiful. The first weekend in August is the Upper Hunter's Wine Weekend.

The nearest town to the Upper Hunter wineries is **Denman**, a sleepy little place 25 km south-west of Muswellbrook. The area's information centre (☎ (065) 47 2731) is on Denman's main street at *Benjamin's Lock, Stock & Barrel*, a cafe/restaurant in an old railway carriage. As well as the plentiful accommodation in nearby Muswellbrook and Singleton there is camping, pub, motel and B&B accommodation in and around Denman.

Up the Valley

The New England Highway runs up the Hunter Valley through some old towns and attractive scenery. The **Goulburn River National Park** at the upper end of the valley follows the river as it cuts through sandstone gorges. This was the route used by Aborigines travelling from the plains to the sea and the area is rich in cave art and other sites. You can camp but there are no facilities. Access is from Sandy Hollow (near Denman) or Merriwa (on the Denman to Gulgong road). The Muswellbrook National Parks office (☎ (065) 43 3533) has information.

Maitland An old coal-mining centre, Maitland is now a sprawling town with a population of 46,000. It was established as a convict settlement in 1818 and at one time Sydney, Parramatta and Maitland were the main settlements in Australia.

The information centre (☎ (049) 33 2611) is in East Maitland, on the corner of the New England Highway and Banks St. Trains run to Maitland from Newcastle.

High St follows the winding route of the original track through town and part of it is now the **Heritage Mall**. **Brough House** on Church St houses the art gallery, and its neighbour, **Grossman House**, is the local history museum (open weekends).

The *Hunter River Hotel* (☎ (049) 33 7244) at 10 Melbourne St in East Maitland has singles/doubles for $20/40 and a backpackers' rate of $15 if there is a spare room. There is plenty of other accommodation and a caravan park (☎ (049) 33 2950).

Singleton This is a coal-mining town and one of the oldest towns in the state. In Burdekin Park there's a historical museum in the 1841 courthouse. The **Australian Infantry Corps Museum** is at the military camp south of Singleton. The old *Caledonian Hotel* (☎ (065) 72 1356) on the highway near the town centre has accommodation.

Muswellbrook Like other Hunter Valley towns, Muswellbrook (population 10,000) was founded early in Australia's history and has some interesting old buildings, surrounded by spreading residential areas. Historic *Eatons Hotel* (☎ (065) 43 2403) on the main street at the northern end of town charges $18/30 a single/double.

Scone With over 40 horse studs in the area, Scone dubs itself 'the horse capital of Australia'. Horse Week is held annually in May. You can arrange to visit studs ($3.50 per person) at the information centre (☎ (065) 45 2907), on the northern side of town, near the Mare & Foal statue.

The friendly *Belmore Hotel* (☎ (065) 45 2078) on Kelly St, not far from the railway station and the information centre, has good rooms for $20/30. The *Golden Fleece Hotel* (☎ (065) 45 1357) on the corner of Kelly and Liverpool Sts charges $15/24. The rural *Scone YHA Hostel* (☎ (065) 45 2072) is actually 10 km east of town at Segenhoe. Dorm beds in this historic building are $12.

At **Burning Mountain**, off the highway 20 km north of Scone, a coal seam has been burning for over 5000 years.

NEWCASTLE TO PORT MACQUARIE
Port Stephens
Port Stephens is a large and beautiful bay, home to many dolphins. The main town, near the south head, is **Nelson Bay** (population 7000), which has an information centre (☎ (049) 81 1579) near the marina. Nearby, **Shoal Bay** is on a long, sheltered beach and is a short walk from surf at Zenith Beach. Back down the Tomagee Peninsula from Nelson Bay is **Anna Bay**, with access to both the bay and ocean beaches.

Places to Stay There's a YHA hostel in the *Shoal Bay Motel* (☎ (049) 84 2315) on the beachfront road. Dorm beds are $13 and there are some motel rooms for $18 per person (minimum two people); these rates can rise during school holidays.

In Anna Bay *Samurai Beach Bungalows* (☎ (049) 82 1921) is a new backpackers' hostel with a bush setting and dorm beds in bungalows from $10. It's at the corner of Frost Rd and Robert Connell Close. Buses from Newcastle run past.

Getting There & Away Port Stephens Buses (☎ toll-free 1800 045 949) has a daily service to Sydney ($20) and there are plenty of buses to Newcastle ($6.80).

To head north up the coast it's easiest to backtrack to Newcastle and catch a long-distance bus there. If you can persuade one of the cruise boats to take you over to Tea Gardens on the northern shore (for around $8 for the short trip) you can catch an infrequent Great Lakes Coaches (☎ (049) 97 4287) service to Forster-Tuncurry.

Barrington Tops National Park
Barrington Tops is a World Heritage area of wild forest with two 1600-metre plateaus that fall away steeply to just 400 metres. There are several walking trails but be prepared for snow in winter and cold snaps at any time. Drinking water must be boiled. There are camp sites in the Gloucester River area to the east of the park or you can bush camp. Forty-three km from Dungog, *Barrington Guesthouse* (☎ (049) 95 3212) is the nearest accommodation to the park, charging about $75 per person with meals.

Easiest access to the park is via Dungog or Gloucester.

Myall Lakes National Park
This park combines some beautiful lakes with ocean beaches and is one of the few remaining coastal lagoon systems in the state.

Bombah Point, 11 km from Bulahdelah, is the main settlement within the park. At the northern end of the park, **Seal Rocks** is a small hamlet on a great beach. Just outside the southern end of the park, **Tea Gardens** and **Hawks Nest** are two sizable towns near the north head of Port Stephens. Some cruises from Port Stephens run into the Myall Lakes. The Mungo Track can be walked in one or two days or in half-day sections.

Places to Stay There are National Parks camp sites, and at Bombah Point *Myall Shores* (☎ (049) 97 4495) has tent sites from $13 for two people, shared cabins from $12.50 per person and private cabins from $40. Prices rise at peak times. There's a shop and a restaurant. If you're staying at Myall Shores the owners can organise a lift from Bulahdelah – free at 9 am and 3.30 pm during school terms, $5 at other times; you need to book.

At Seal Rocks there's a basic caravan park, located by an excellent beach, with sites for $8.50.

Getting There & Away Access is either via Bulahdelah (on the Pacific Highway) or via Tea Gardens. Tea Gardens is very close to Nelson Bay by water but very distant by road. There is no ferry but pedestrians might be able to get a lift with a cruise boat for about $8. You can drive between Tea Gardens and Bulahdelah, travelling through the national park and crossing the lake on the Bombah Point punt. It runs half-hourly from 8 am to 6 pm and the fare is $2.50 for cars and 50c for pedestrians.

Seal Rocks is accessible from the Great Lakes Way, a scenic road between Bulahdelah and Forster-Tuncurry.

Forster-Tuncurry (population 16,000)
Forster-Tuncurry are twin towns on either side of the sea entrance of Wallis Lake. Forster is the larger town and here you'll find the information centre (☎ (065) 54 8779) on Little St, the lakefront road. As well as the lake there are some excellent sea beaches right in town and many others in the area.

Aboriginal Ranger Heritage Tours (☎ (065) 55 5274) explain the traditional meaning and significance of the area. Tours cost from $20 per person, with a minimum of three people, and they are apparently good.

Places to Stay In the middle of Forster and a short walk from the lake and ocean, *Forster Beach Caravan Park* (☎ (065) 54 6269) has sites from $9 to $15 and on-site vans from $20 ($30 with en-suite) to $34 ($55).

The YHA-affiliated *Dolphin Lodge* (☎ (065) 55 8155) is at 43 Head St in Forster. Coming from the town centre it's on the left just before the road makes a right-angle turn to the right. It's clean and spacious and has a surf beach more-or-less at the back door. Dorm beds are $12 and doubles are $25. Boards and bikes are free.

In the off season there are some good deals on motels, with doubles for $35 or less, but around Christmas/January most are expensive – and booked out. Holiday apartments can also be good value outside peak times. Letting agents include Hilton Mason (☎ (065) 54 6333).

Getting There & Away Forster-Tuncurry is on the Great Lakes Way, which leaves the Pacific Highway near Bulahdelah and rejoins it south of Taree. Great Lakes Coaches (☎ toll-free 1800 043 263) run to Sydney daily for $34 and have several services to Newcastle. Some companies sometimes include Forster-Tuncurry on their Sydney to Brisbane run.

Manning Valley
From Forster-Tuncurry the highway swings inland to **Taree**, a large town serving the farms of the fertile Manning Valley. Further up the valley is **Wingham**, a timber town where you can visit Wingham Brush, a lovely seven-hectare vestige of the dense rainforest which once covered the valley. Small roads run north from Wingham to Wauchope, near Port Macquarie, passing through some interesting villages and great scenery. WWOOFers (see Facts for the Visitor chapter) have several options in the area.

On the coast near Taree there are several small resorts, such as **Old Bar**. **Crowdy Bay National Park** runs up the coast, with a long and beautiful beach. **Diamond Head** at the northern end of the national park has a basic but pretty camp site. You might need to bring your own water.

North of the national park and accessible from the Pacific Highway at Kew, **Camden Haven** is a collection of villages clustering around the wide sea entrance of Queens Lake. Just north of here the coast road runs past **Lake Cathie** (pronounced cat-eye), both a town and a shallow lake, and then enters the outer-suburbs of Port Macquarie.

PORT MACQUARIE (population 30,000)

One of the larger resorts on the New South Wales north coast, Port Macquarie makes a good stopping point on the journey from Sydney (430 km south). It was founded in 1821, making it one of the oldest towns in the state, and was a convict settlement until 1840.

'Port' has both a river frontage (the Hastings River enters the sea here) and a series of ocean beaches starting right in the town.

Orientation & Information

The city centre is at the mouth of the Hastings River, and Horton St, the main street, runs down to the water. West of the city centre at the base of the Settlement Point Peninsula is the big Settlement City shopping centre.

The information centre (☎ toll-free 1800 025 935) is at the corner of Hay and Clarence Sts and is open daily.

Things to See

The **Koala Hospital** is off Lord St about a km south of the town centre. Convalescent koalas are in outdoor enclosures and you can visit them daily. The hospital is in the grounds of **Roto**, a historic homestead which houses the National Parks office (☎ (065) 83 5518). Roto is open on weekdays from 9 am to 4 pm.

You can meet undamaged koalas and other animals at **Kingfisher Park** (☎ (065) 81 0783), off the Oxley Highway; admission is $6. **Billabong Koala Park** (☎ (065) 85 1060) is further out, just past the Pacific Highway interchange.

Other than Roto, most surviving old buildings are near the city centre: St Thomas' Church (1828) on William St near Hay St (admission $1); the Garrison (1830) on the corner of Hay and Clarence; the courthouse (1869) across the road; and the **museum** (1830) nearby at 22 Clarence St, open Monday to Saturday from 9.30 am to 4.30 pm and from 1 pm on Sunday (admission $3). An old Pilot Cottage below Town Beach houses the small **Maritime Museum**, open daily from 10 am to 4 pm (admission $2). Nearby, a small **observatory** is at the beach end of Lord St. It opens at 7.30 pm in winter and 8.30 pm in summer; admission is $2.

Five km south of the town centre, **Sea Acres Rainforest Centre** is a 30-hectare flora and fauna reserve protecting a pocket of coastal rainforest. There's an ecology centre with displays and a 1.3-km boardwalk. Entry is $8.50.

A vehicle ferry ($1) crosses the river at Settlement Point, leading to two interesting roads north. A very rough dirt road (4WD might be required) runs along the coast, past **Limeburners Creek Nature Reserve** to **Point Plomer** (good surf) and **Crescent Head**, from where you can rejoin the highway at Kempsey. The second road – better and gravelled – takes a more inland route to meet the Crescent Head to Kempsey road. The ferry runs only a few times each day. The information centre has timetables.

Activities

Port Explorer (☎ (065) 82 1235) has half-day tours of the town on Friday ($10) and several day tours of the area ($18).

You can hire watercraft at several places on Settlement Point, such as Hastings River Boat Hire (☎ (065) 83 8811) at Port Marina (powered craft and canoes) and Jordans Boating Centre (☎ (065) 83 1005) on Settlement Point Rd (cats, canoes and sailboards).

NEW SOUTH WALES

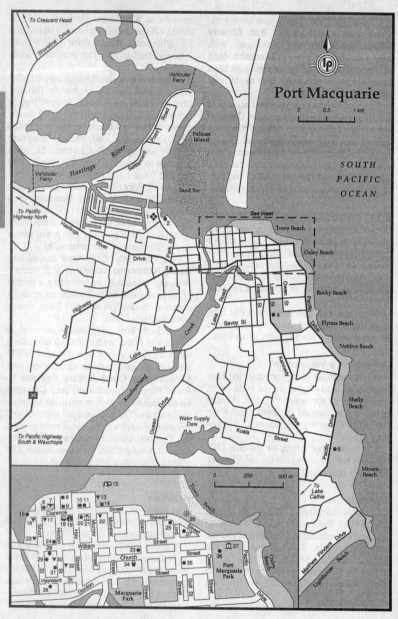

Port Macquarie

0   0.5   1 km

To Crescent Head

Shoreline Drive

Vehicular Ferry

Hastings   River

Settlement Point Road

Pelican Island

Sand Bar

SOUTH
PACIFIC
OCEAN

Vehicular Ferry

To Pacific Highway North

Hastings   River

Drive

Park St

2

See Inset

Town Beach

Oxley Beach

3

Lake   Road

Creek

Savoy St

Lake   Road

Grant St

Lord St

Owen St

Pacific   Drive

4

Rocky Beach

Flynns Beach

Nobbys Beach

Oxley   Highway

Kooloonbung

Ocean   Drive

Kennedy   Drive

Shelly Beach

34

To Pacific Highway
South & Wauchope

Water Supply
Dam

Koala   Street

Pacific   Drive

5

Miners
Beach

To Lake
Cathie

0   250   500 m

Town   Beach

Oxley Beach

Matthew Flinders Drive

Lighthouse Beach

Inset

12

6   7
8
9

10 11

13
14

15

Clarence

16

Short   Street

Horton   Street

Hay   Street

18 19

20 21   22

Murray   Street

Munster   Street

Street

Stewart   Street

Grant   Street

Street

25

Lord   Street

26

17

23

24

28

William   Street

Church   Street

33

34

35

Street

27

36

37

Port
Macquarie
Park

29

30

31

32

38

Hayward   St

Gordon   Street

Street

Street

Golf   Street

Owen   Street

Pacific   Drive

Macquarie
Park

PLACES TO STAY		OTHER	
3	Lindel Travellers Hostel	1	Settlement City Shopping
6	Flag Motel		Centre & RSL
8	Royal Hotel	2	Marina
9	Port Macquarie Hotel	4	Koala Hospital & Roto Homestead
11	El Paso Motel	5	Sea Acres Rainforest Centre
12	Sundowner Breakwall Caravan Park	7	Post Office
14	River Motel	10	Old Courthouse
25	Historic Well Motel	15	Cruises & Fishermen's Co-op
31	Backpackers Headquarters	18	Lindsay's Buses
34	Beachside Backpackers (YHA)	19	Information Office
35	Port Macquarie Cabins	20	Garrison & Cafes
		21	Museum
PLACES TO EAT		24	Jetset Travel
		26	Lookout
13	Toro's Cantina	27	Observatory
16	Intersection	28	TC's Nightclub
17	Macquarie Seafoods	29	Down Under Nightclub
22	Tickled Trout	33	Tower
23	Yum Yums	36	Bowling Club
30	Yuen Hing	37	Maritime Museum
32	Shades	38	Port Pushbikes

Diving is available with the Port Diving Centre (☎ (065) 83 8483).

There are plenty of river cruises. Everglades Tours (book at the information centre) has shallow-draught boats exploring the backwaters and wetlands from $18.

Coastal Camel Safaris (☎ toll-free 1800 025 935) has beach rides from $9 and overnight treks.

Places to Stay

Camping The most central caravan park is *Sundowner Breakwall* (☎ (065) 83 2755) at 1 Munster St, near the river mouth and Town Beach, with sites from $15 and on-site vans from $35. There are cheaper places near Flynns Beach and inland along the river or on the Oxley Highway.

Hostels *Beachside Backpackers* (☎ (065) 83 5512) is a YHA associate at 40 Church St, near the corner of Grant St. Dorm beds are $12. It's clean, friendly and popular and is about a five-minute walk from the town centre and the beach; they'll collect you from the bus stop. Water-skiing trips (about $20) are a popular activity here.

Lindel Travellers Hostel (☎ (065) 83 1791) is slightly further from the centre on

the Oxley Highway, but they meet the buses and there are free bikes to ride once you get there. They also do a daily run to the beaches and there's a small pool. Lindel has a reputation for being friendly and well run. Dorm beds are $12 and twin rooms cost $24. There's a once-only fee of $1 for linen hire.

Backpackers Headquarters at 135 Horton St (☎ (065) 83 1913) charges $10 for a dorm bed, $15 for a single, $25 for a double and $30 for a twin. The atmosphere is depressing and reportedly sleazy.

Hotels At the northern end of Horton St, the *Port Macquarie Hotel* and the *Royal Hotel* have very reasonable rates. The reception desk at the Port Macquarie (☎ (065) 83 1011) handles accommodation for both hotels. The Port Macquarie has motel-style units from $45/55 and there are pub rooms for $20/30 or $25/35 with bathroom. At the Royal there are motel-style units overlooking the water for just $32/40 and pub rooms with bathroom for $25/30. Singles aren't available at peak times and prices rise.

Motels There are more than 30 motels. The cheapest are furthest from the beaches, not surprisingly. In town, the *River Motel* at 5

Clarence St near the corner of School St has off-season doubles for around $40 and several nearby holiday apartments have similar deals. Other moderate places are along Hastings River Drive.

Cabins & Apartments *Port Macquarie Cabins* (☎ (065) 83 1115) are old fibro-cement cabins, very worn but clean enough and the prices are low: $24 for two people and just $1 for each extra person, or $120 a week. Prices rise at Christmas and other peak times. Each cabin has a double bed and three singles (all in the same room), a bathroom and cooking facilities. The cabins are at 24 Lord St, not far from the corner of Church St. The sign is small – go down a driveway next to a fish & chip shop.

There are scores of holiday apartments. Contact an estate agent such as L J Hooker (☎ (065) 83 2988) at 49 Horton St.

Places to Eat

The Fishermen's Co-op at the western end of Clarence St sells seafood straight off the boats.

For breakfast try *Yum Yums*, a small place on Short St near the corner of William St, where prices start at $4.

In the historic Garrison building on the corner of Hay and Clarence Sts, *Margo's Cafe* has tables outside and is a pleasant place for coffee and a snack. Fish & chips are $5, pastas $6.50. Diagonally opposite is the *Pancake Place* which has a large menu.

At the corner of Short and Clarence Sts, the *Intersection* has outdoor tables and a large menu of snacks and light meals. Focaccia is $6. Across Short St is *Macquarie Seafoods* with fish & chips for $3.80. On Murray St there are a couple of Mexican places: *Toro's Cantina* with main courses around $11 and nearby *Bruno's Pizza & Mexican*. *Wah Hing* and *Yuen Hing* are Chinese places on Horton St, both with special deals and sometimes smorgasbord lunches for well under $10.

The *Tickled Trout* at 2 Clarence St is open nightly and has main courses for around $12. Half-a-dozen oysters will set you back $6. It

also has takeaways in the evenings, with fish & chips for $4.

Entertainment

There are three nightspots: *Lachlans*, between the Port Macquarie and Royal hotels, *TC's* on William St and *Down Under* around the corner on Short St. When the RSL's big new complex at Settlement City opens there should be entertainment there as well.

Getting There & Away

The Oxley Highway runs west from Port Macquarie through Wauchope and eventually reaches the New England tablelands near Walcha. It's a spectacular drive.

Air There are at least three flights a day to Sydney on Oxley ($156) and Eastern Australia ($162). There are also flights to Brisbane ($196).

Bus Port Macquarie Bus Service (☎ (065) 83 2161) runs to Wauchope several times a day for $5.40. This service stops outside the Lindsay's office at the corner of Clarence and Horton Sts, as do Lindsay's buses. Other long-distance services stop outside the old RSL building on Short St but a new bus terminal might be built near the information centre.

Lindsay's (☎ toll-free 1800 027 944) runs to Newcastle ($33), Sydney ($36), Brisbane ($45), Armidale ($35) and Tamworth ($50). Prices to destinations closer to Port Macquarie are high – $30 to Coffs Harbour, $26 to Dorrigo.

Train The nearest station is at Wauchope, 19 km inland and on the line between Sydney ($51) and Brisbane ($64).

Getting Around

Port Macquarie Bus Service (☎ (065) 83 2161) runs buses around the town. There are no super-cheap car-rental outfits, only the majors. Budget (☎ (065) 83 5144) is at the corner of William and Short Sts. Port Pushbikes on Hayward St rents ungeared bikes for $8 a half-day, $15 for a day and just $25 for a week. Graham Seers Cyclery at Port Marina near Settlement City also rents bikes.

PORT MACQUARIE TO COFFS HARBOUR

Wauchope (population 4200)

Nineteen km inland from Port Macquarie and on the Hastings River, Wauchope (pronounced 'war hope') is an old timber town – its story is told at **Timbertown**, an interesting working replica of an 1880s town. It's open from 9 am to 5 pm daily ($12.50). Lilybank Canoe Hire (☎ (065) 85 1600), on the river one km east of the town, has two-person canoes for hire by the hour ($10), day or week, and can advise on camping spots. The **Big Bull**, 'the world's biggest fibreglass bull', is three km east of Wauchope and houses an animal nursery and other displays; entry is $5.

Wauchope has a range of accommodation including *Rainbow Ridge Hostel* (☎ (065) 85 6134), a quiet YHA associate, 11 km west on the Oxley Highway towards Tamworth. Dorm beds are $10 or you can camp for $5.

The Oxley Highway runs west from Wauchope up into the ranges and onto the New England tablelands, passing through some spectacular scenery.

Kempsey Area

North along the Pacific Highway from Wauchope is **Kempsey** (population 9000), a large town serving the farms of the Macleay Valley and also the home of the Akubra hat. The information centre (☎ (065) 63 1555) is off the highway at the southern end of town. Next door is the **Macleay River Historical Museum & Cultural Centre** ($2). There is plenty of accommodation here but it's worth diverting to the coast. Mercury Roadlines (☎ (065) 62 4201) runs one or two buses a day to the Trial Bay area.

Crescent Head, a small village 20 km from Kempsey, has a quiet front beach and a surf-washed back beach. *Crescent Head Caravan Park* (☎ (065) 66 0261) has sites

from $9 and cabins from $40, rising to $70 in holidays. There are plenty of holiday apartments and some can be cheaper than cabins at the caravan park – contact an estate agent (☎ (065) 66 0500). South of town, **Limeburners Creek Nature Reserve** (☎ (065) 83 5866) has walking trails and camp sites.

Hat Head is a hamlet with a caravan park and holiday flats at the foot of Hat Hill Headland. There are good beaches and walks. Part of the nearby coast is **Hat Head National Park**.

South West Rocks is another coastal resort village, near the mouth of the Macleay River, with good beaches. The *Costa Rica Motel* (☎ (065) 66 6500) sometimes has share accommodation for about $15. **Trial Bay Gaol** is on the headland three km east of South West Rocks. This imposing edifice was a prison in the late 19th century and housed German POWs in WW I. It's now a museum with wonderful views, open daily ($2.50). Trial Bay is named after the *Trial*, a brig which was stolen from Sydney by convicts in 1816 and wrecked here. **Smoky Cape Lighthouse**, a few km down the coast from the jail, can be inspected on Thursday (and Tuesday in school holidays) from 10 to 11.45 am and 1 to 2.45 pm.

By the bay behind the old jail is a caravan park (☎ (065) 66 6168), with sites from $8 and on-site vans from $18 during the week and $30 on weekends. Prices rise considerably during school holidays. In summer you can hire boats here.

Nambucca Heads (population 6000)

At the mouth of the Nambucca (pronounced 'Nambucka') River, this little resort town is one of the better stops on the north coast.

Orientation & Information The town is a km or so off the highway, and the road in, Riverside Drive, runs beside the wide estuary of the Nambucca River then climbs a steep hill to Bowra St, the main shopping street.

The helpful information centre (☎ (065)

68 6954) is on Ridge St next to the post office and is open daily. You can leave luggage here while you explore.

Main Beach, the patrolled surf beach, is about 1.5 km east of the centre. Follow Ridge St and take Liston St when it splits. The **Headland Museum** ($1) is near the Main Beach car park. If you take Parkes St at this junction you'll eventually reach North Head, with stunning views from **Pilot Lookout**. To get to the estuary and the river mouth (where there is good surf for the experienced), turn off Bowra St at the Mobil service station onto Wellington Drive, which winds scenically down past **Gordon Park**.

Places to Stay There are several caravan parks. As usual, prices rise in holidays and you might have to stay by the week at peak times. *Foreshore Caravan Park* (☎ (065) 68 6014), on Riverside Drive not far from the highway, overlooks the estuary and there is a beach nearby. Sites are from $8, on-site vans from $20 and cabins from $32.

Nambucca Backpackers Hostel (☎ (065) 68 6360) at 3 Newman St is a very good hostel and a great place to relax for a few days. Dorm beds are $13 for the first night and $12 for subsequent nights; doubles are $28 for the first night and $26 for subsequent nights; and singles, when available, are $20. There are sometimes specials in less busy times. The friendly managers offer trips in the area and can arrange white-water rafting. They lend snorkel gear and boogie boards. It's a one-km walk through bush to the beach and you might meet wallabies in the evening.

The *Ranch* (☎ (065) 68 6386) at 4 Wellington Drive is a new guesthouse (the outside is yet to be renovated) with large rooms for $35 including breakfast. Bathrooms are currently shared but that's about to change. There are also a couple of bunk rooms for backpackers (maybe not in summer), who pay $10 a night. The view from here is wonderful and sharing it from the other side of Gordon Park are the *Max Motel* (☎ (065) 68 6138) and the *Blue Dolphin Motel* (☎ (065) 68 6700) next door. Max Motel is an old-style place with few luxury touches, but it's clean and the view is worth a lot more than the $36/50 charged (less in the off season). The Blue Dolphin is newer and costs a few dollars more. Both these places are entered from Fraser St, the southern half of the main street.

Places to Eat The *Bowling Club* on Nelson St and the *RSL* on Fraser St both have restaurants with good-value meals. The *Golden Sands* has pub meals, and *Midnight Express* behind the pub is worth trying. On Wellington Drive near Gordon Park *Matilda's* has char-grill and seafood for around $15. Nearby on the waterfront is the similarly priced *Bar & Brasserie*.

Getting There & Away Most long-distance buses stop on the highway at the Shell service station (southbound) or the Aukaka Motel (northbound). With Kirklands the fare to Sydney is about $42, and to Byron Bay it's about $38.

Pells (☎ (065) 68 6106), a local company, runs to Coffs Harbour on Tuesday and Thursday, departing at 9.30 am from the police station on Bowra St. The return fare is $6. Jessup's (☎ (066) 53 4552) has a service between Bellingen and Coffs Harbour running via Nambucca Heads, Mylestom and Urunga, on school days only. Joyce's (☎ (066) 55 6330) has about four runs a day (fewer in school holidays), weekdays only, between Bellingen, Urunga and Nambucca ($6.80).

Nambucca is on the main railway line north from Sydney ($58). The station is about three km out of town – follow Bowra St north.

Bowraville
Inland from Nambucca and in the Bowra Valley, the small town of Bowraville has a folk museum and many craft shops as well as a Saturday morning market.

Bellingen (population 2300)
Bellingen is a small town on the banks of the Bellinger River, reached by turning off the

Pacific Highway near Urunga, about halfway from Nambucca Heads to Coffs Harbour. It's a pleasant and interesting place, a centre for the area's artistic/alternative population.

The Yellow Shed craft shop (☎ (066) 55 1189) on the main street has tourist information. The small **museum** is behind the old wooden library on the main street and is open from 2 to 4 pm daily and also from 10 am to noon on Wednesday and Friday; admission is 50c. There are plenty of craft shops including the **Old Butter Factory** on the outskirts which houses several workshops and galleries and a cafe.

From December to March a huge colony of flying foxes lives on Bellingen Island near the caravan park. Platypuses live in the river nearby.

The market, held in the park on the third Saturday of the month, is a major event with more than 250 stalls. People from all over the valley show up and there's live music.

You can hire canoes ($10 for the first hour, $32 for the day) at the Oasis Cafe at the Old Butter Factory. Bushwhacker Expeditions (☎ (066) 55 8607) has canoeing and other tours, including walks in the area's rainforests.

Places to Stay The caravan park (☎ (066) 55 1138) is across the river – turn onto Wharf St from the main street (the post office is on the corner), cross the bridge and follow the road around to the left, then turn left down Dowle St. You can walk from town.

Bellingen Backpackers (☎ (066) 55 1116) (also called Belfry Lodge) is on Short St behind the Federal Hotel and overlooking the river. Beds are around $15. Staff will pick you up from Urunga.

Places to Eat On the main street, towards the top end, the *Carriageway* coffee shop is open daily and in the evening from Wednesday to Saturday. It serves breakfast (muesli $3.50, omelettes from $5) and light meals. On Church St there are several other places. The *Flying Fox Cafe* is an excellent restaurant with a relaxed atmosphere and innovative food. Main courses are around $10 at lunch and $14 at dinner, with cheaper vegetarian options. To get there, head for the caravan park but keep going to the roundabout and turn left.

Getting There & Away The bus stop is at the corner of Church St and the main street, diagonally opposite the courthouse. Lindsay's (☎ toll-free 1800 027 944) comes through on its run up to Armidale but it isn't allowed to carry passengers on short sectors such as Coffs Harbour to Bellingen. It can do Coffs to Dorrigo ($9.70) or Bellingen to Armidale ($17.20). Joyce's (☎ (066) 55 6330) has about four runs a day (fewer in school holidays), weekdays only, between Bellingen, Urunga ($3.20 from Bellingen) and Nambucca Heads ($6.80). Jessup's (☎ (066) 53 4552) runs to Coffs Harbour via Nambucca Heads, Mylestom and Urunga on school days only, departing Bellingen at 8 am. On any Tuesday it has a service from Bellingen to Coffs via Urunga and Mylestom only, departing Bellingen at 9.35 am.

It might be possible to get to Dorrigo by school bus but you would have to change at least once on the way and hope for a connection.

The nearest railway station is at Urunga.

Dorrigo (population 1100)
From Bellingen the road climbs steeply up to Dorrigo, a spectacular drive. This quiet mountain town was one of the last places to be settled in the eastwards push across the New England tablelands. As the largest town on the Dorrigo Plateau it is a base for visiting the area's outstanding national parks.

The information centre (☎ (066) 57 2486) is in the Dorrigo Hotel/Motel and is usually open on weekdays. The proposed Railway Museum isn't open yet but there is a long line of steam engines queued up at the old railway station. A few km north of town on the road to Leigh are the picturesque **Dangar Falls**.

The dense rainforest of **Dorrigo National Park** is known for its orchids. There are several good walking tracks and it's well worth making the drive through thick forest to the Never Never picnic area, from where you can walk to waterfalls. Camping isn't allowed in the park. The Dorrigo Rainforest Centre has an elevated walkway and good displays as well as a National Parks office (☎ (066) 57 2309). The turn-off to the park is just south of Dorrigo.

See the New England section for information on other national parks in this area.

Places to Stay *Dorrigo Mountain Resort* (☎ (066) 57 2564), a caravan park with some substantial wooden cabins, is just out of town on the road to Bellingen. Sites cost from $8.50 and there are on-site vans and self-contained cabins. The *Dorrigo Hotel/Motel* (☎ (066) 57 2017) has motel units for about $40 and cheaper pub rooms.

Getting There & Away Lindsay's buses come through on their run from the coast to Armidale.

Urunga & Mylestom

Urunga, about 20 km north of Nambucca, is a little place on the estuary of the Bellinger/Kalang River, with surf beaches not far away. The *Ocean View Hotel* (☎ (066) 55 6221) overlooks the estuary and has rooms for $25/35 with breakfast. The double rooms are fairly large and some have views; the smaller singles and twins are at the back. On the highway is a strip of motels that can be as low as $25 a double at slow times.

North of Urunga is the turn-off to Mylestom, also called **North Beach**. This quiet hamlet is in a great location on the banks of the wide Bellinger River and also has ocean beaches. It has a caravan park (☎ (066) 55 4250) and new backpackers' hostel, *Caipera Riverside Lodge* (☎ (066) 55 4245), on the main street across from the river, the third house on the left as you enter town. It has beds in two-bed 'dorms' for $13 and can help organise activities such as white-water rafting and horse riding. It also provides bikes to explore the area. With a

day's notice someone from the hostel can probably give you a lift from Coffs.

COFFS HARBOUR (population 55,000)

Coffs Harbour (originally Korff's Harbour) is a major resort town and the centre of rampant housing development. The town centre is busy and nothing to write home about, but there's a harbour and some interesting headlands, and a string of good beaches stretch north.

Orientation & Information

The Pacific Highway is called Grafton St on its run through town, where it crosses the main shopping centre. The corner of Grafton and High Sts is just about the city centre. High St is a pedestrian mall here, but on the other side of the mall it's the main road to the waterfront Jetty area, a couple of km east.

The tourist office (☎ (066) 52 8824) is in Urana Park on Grafton St, near where Moonee St branches off.

Beaches

Diggers Beach, about three km north of the centre and reached by turning off the highway near the Big Banana, is worth travelling to. North of Diggers there's another good beach at **Korora** and then a string of them up to Woolgoolga. **Jetty Beach** is more sheltered than the others and can be good for a swim when the surf is rough.

Other Attractions

Coff's tourist symbol is the **Big Banana**, on the northern outskirts. Behind the banana is Horticulture World; entry is free but you won't see much unless you take a tour.

The **North Coast Botanic Gardens**, on Hardacre St off High St, focus on the flora of the subtropical coast and are open daily. Down at the end of High St the old jetty still stands in the harbour. There are good views from **Beacon Hill Lookout** above the harbour at the top of Edinburgh St and from **Corambirra Point** on the southern side of the harbour. You can walk out along the northern harbour wall to **Muttonbird Island**,

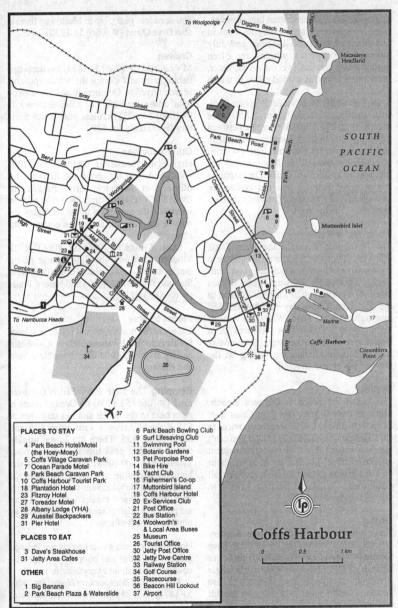

Coffs Harbour

0   0.5   1 km

PLACES TO STAY

4   Park Beach Hotel/Motel
    (the Hoey-Moey)
5   Coffs Village Caravan Park
7   Ocean Parade Motel
8   Park Beach Caravan Park
10 Coffs Harbour Tourist Park
18 Plantation Hotel
23 Fitzroy Hotel
27 Toreador Motel
28 Albany Lodge (YHA)
29 Aussitel Backpackers
31 Pier Hotel

PLACES TO EAT

3   Dave's Steakhouse
31 Jetty Area Cafes

OTHER

1   Big Banana
2   Park Beach Plaza & Waterslide

6   Park Beach Bowling Club
9   Surf Lifesaving Club
11 Swimming Pool
12 Botanic Gardens
13 Pet Porpoise Pool
14 Bike Hire
15 Yacht Club
16 Fishermen's Co-op
17 Muttonbird Island
19 Coffs Harbour Hotel
20 Ex-Services Club
21 Post Office
22 Bus Station
24 Woolworth's
    & Local Area Buses
25 Museum
26 Tourist Office
30 Jetty Post Office
32 Jetty Dive Centre
33 Railway Station
34 Golf Course
35 Racecourse
36 Beacon Hill Lookout
37 Airport

a nature reserve where mutton birds (wedge-tailed shearwaters) breed. They lay eggs in underground burrows. In June and July migrating humpback whales are often spotted and if you can't get out on the water, Muttonbird Island is a good place to watch from.

On Orlando St there's a Pet Porpoise Pool, with shows twice daily for $9.50. The **museum** at 191 High St is open between 1.30 and 4.30 pm from Tuesday to Thursday and Sunday. **Coffs Harbour Zoo** (☎ (066) 56 1330) is actually in Moonee, off the highway 12 km north of Coffs. The emphasis is on native animals and the koalas are 'presented' at 11 am and 3 pm daily. Admission is $9 ($5 children).

White-Water Rafting

The Nymboida River inland from Coffs offers excellent white-water thrills and there are a couple of outfits which get good feedback. Whitewater Rafting Professionals (☎ (066) 51 4066) at 20 Moonee St (next to the bus station) have day trips for $95 and overnight trips for $245. Wildwater Adventures (☎ (066) 53 4469) at 4 Butlers Rd in Bonville offers much the same, plus four-day trips and more challenging rafting on the Gwydir River near Inverell.

Surfing

The best local beach is **Diggers Beach**, north of Park Beach. The East Coast Surf School (☎ (066) 52 4727) teaches novices to surf. Helene Enevddson says that if you can't stand on a board after six lessons, subsequent lessons are free! The fee, about $14 an hour or a six-lesson course for $72, includes all equipment. Weekend surfing camps in school holidays cost $80.

Diving

There's interesting diving at the Solitary Islands, a few km up the coast. Jetty Dive Centre (☎ (066) 51 1611) at 396 High St has courses ($350) and dives ($25 for a single dive, plus equipment hire). The centre also rents snorkelling gear ($15 a day for the full set, including weights and wetsuit – less if you need less gear). Up in Mulloway there's also Dive Quest (☎ (066) 54 1930).

Cruises

MV *Laura E* (☎ (066) 51 1434) has deep-sea fishing trips and during the whale-spotting season (April to October) they have a two-hour cruise for $25. The *Commissioner II* (☎ (066) 51 3271) cruises past South Solitary Island daily for $20.

Other Activities

High Flyer Parasailing (☎ (066) 51 5200) will whisk you up above the harbour. Its office is at the Jetty. Direct Parasailing (☎ 018 657 034, toll-free 1800 670 417) is nearby on the harbour wall but its flights are outside the harbour, above the ocean. Both charge $40.

Outer Limits (☎ (066) 51 4066) at 22 Moonee St offers abseiling. Horse-riding outfits in the area include Bonville Forest Stables (☎ (066) 53 4537) and Valery Trails (☎ (066) 53 6217).

Places to Stay

Except in the hostels, expect prices in school holidays to rise by about 50% in midwinter and by about 100% at Christmas/New Year and Easter.

Camping The huge *Park Beach Caravan Park* (☎ (066) 52 3204) on Ocean Parade is right next to the beach and has tent sites at $12 a double, on-site vans from $26 and cabins from $35. There are lower weekly rates but not at peak times. *Coffs Harbour Tourist Park* (☎ (066) 52 1694), on the highway a couple of blocks on from the Ex-Services Club, has sites from $10, on-site vans from $20 and cabins from $30. There are plenty of other places along the highway north and south of town.

Hostels The town's two hostels are in good modern buildings and both can arrange discounts on just about everything in town.

The *Aussitel Backpackers Hostel* (☎ (066) 51 1871) at 312 High St, about 1.5 km from the town centre and 500 metres from the harbour, is a lively place with dorm beds at $13 and doubles at $15. It has all the usual hostel facilities plus a pool. The enthusiastic management will help fix up white-water rafting, diving, surfing and other activities, and will pick you up on arrival and give rides to the beach during the day or to the pub at night. There's a stretch of creek over the road and canoes are free.

The *Albany Lodge* (☎ (066) 52 6462), the YHA hostel at 110 Albany St, a block off High St and one km from the town centre, is a friendly place. Dorm beds cost $12 and there are a few double rooms for $12.50 per person. Bikes and surfboards are free and there's a spa. The hostel is open all day and someone can usually pick you up – at night phone in advance to ask. The hostel arranges trips, activities and excursions, such as day trips to the Dorrigo area.

Hotels Officially on Moonee St (although it appears to be on Grafton St) the *Fitzroy Hotel* (☎ (066) 52 3007), an old-style neighbourhood pub, has singles/doubles for $15/30. Further down Grafton St, opposite the Ex-Services Club, the *Plantation Hotel* (☎ (066) 52 3855) has rooms from $20/25 for singles/doubles. Down near the harbour on High St, the *Pier Hotel* (☎ (066) 52 2110) has a few large, clean, old-style rooms for $18 per person. The owners live-in, so they are a little choosy about their guests.

Motels There's a string of motels on Grafton St across from the tourist office, such as *Toreador* (☎ (066) 52 3887) and *Golden Glow* (☎ (066) 52 2644). In the off season prices fall as low as $40 a double.

There's another bunch of motels in the Park Beach area with similar rates. You'll pay around $40 a double at the *Ocean Parade Motel* (☎ (066) 52 6733); in the high season the rates are around $60 a double, and there are no singles. The *Park Beach Hotel/Motel* (☎ (066) 52 3833) – the Hoey-Moey – has old-style motel units for $25/30/35 a single/double/triple, less when trade is slack.

Apartments There is a huge range of holiday apartments and houses. In the off season the cheapest two-bedroom apartments cost around $45 a night (less by the week) and $90 a night in the high season, although many places are only available by the week at this time. The tourist office has a booking service (☎ toll-free 1800 025 650).

Places to Eat

Some of the best cheap eats can be found in the clubs, such as the *Ex-Services Club* on the corner of Grafton and Vernon Sts and the *Catholic Club* on High St, about one km inland from Grafton St.

There are snack places on the mall and the pubs in this area have counter meals. At the *Plantation Hotel* on Grafton St, lunch specials can include a meal and a drink for $5. The *Unicorn* Chinese restaurant, upstairs in the 176 Arcade off the mall, has deals such as $3 main courses. *Pancakes All Round*, on High St near the corner of Gordon St, has pancakes and crepes from $6 and pasta from $8.

For choice you can't beat the cluster of restaurants at the Jetty end of High St, although none are especially cheap. You can eat seafood, Italian, Indian, Chinese, French and, in the nearby shopping centre, Thai. There are bistro meals and $5 breakfasts at the *Pier Hotel*.

Le Joint, on Ocean Parade opposite the Park Beach bowling club, is basically a milk bar but it has a fine verandah where you can eat breakfast and other meals. The nearby *Hoey-Moey* has a bistro with specials such as $5 meals. At 99 Park Beach Rd, over York St, *Dave's Steakhouse* has steaks from $14 and seafood from $15.

Entertainment

Nightclubs currently popular are *High St 66* and the *Shovel*, both on the mall. *Crystal's Night Club* in the Ex-Services Club has bands and/or a disco. When top names come to Coffs they play here or at the *Hoey-Moey*, which has bands at weekends. On Grafton St, the *Plantation Hotel* has free local bands from Wednesday to Saturday.

Down at the Jetty, near the strip of eating places, *Beach Street* has party nights, usually with a beach theme. Velcro 'bar flying', a mechanical surfboard and other devices help the fun along – as do the various deals on cheap drinks.

Getting There & Away

Near the long-distance bus stop on Moonee St, Lindsay's handles bus bookings (not just Lindsay's) and a few doors away Coffs Harbour Coaches & Travel (☎ (066) 52 2686) will fix you up with bus, air and Countrylink tickets.

Air Coffs has a busy airport with direct flights to Sydney ($190) and Brisbane ($165).

Bus All the long-distance lines on the Sydney to Brisbane route stop at Coffs, and Lindsay's has services up to Armidale. The main stop is in Moonee St just west of Grafton St. Fares from Coffs include: Byron Bay $32, Brisbane $41, Nambucca Heads $10, Port Macquarie $30, Sydney $44, Dorrigo $9.70 and Armidale $18.30. As usual, it pays to ask for special deals.

Most local-area buses stop at the car park next to Woolworth's on Park Ave. Ryan's (☎ (066) 52 3201) runs several times daily except Sunday to Woolgoolga ($5) via beachside towns off the highway. Bradley's (☎ (066) 54 1516) has a weekday service between Coffs and Grafton, running via Woolgoolga and beachside towns north of there. See the Bellingen and Nambucca Heads sections for other local services.

Train The railway station (☎ (066) 52 2312) is near the harbour at the end of High St. The fare to Sydney is $62.

Car Rental As well as the majors there are some local outfits offering cheaper rates, although you should compare the deals carefully. JR's Car & Truck Rental (☎ (066) 52 8480) at 30 Orlando St rents older vehicles.

Boat Coffs is a good place to pick up a ride along the coast on a yacht or cruiser. Ask around or put a notice in the yacht club at the harbour. Sometimes the hostels know of boat owners who are looking for crew.

Getting Around

A bus service connects the centre, the Jetty and Park Beach but services are infrequent, with none on Sunday.

Taxi companies include Coffs Radio Cabs (☎ (066) 51 3944). There's a taxi rank on the corner of High and Gordon Sts.

Bob Wallis Bicycle Centre (☎ (066) 52 5102) on the corner of Collingwood and Orlando Sts rents bikes.

COFFS HARBOUR TO BYRON BAY
Woolgoolga (population 4000)

Twenty-six km north of Coffs, Woolgoolga is a fishing port and small resort with a fine surf beach. It has a sizable Indian Sikh population whose *gurdwara* (place of worship), the **Guru Nanak Temple**, is just off the highway at the southern end of town. The 'Indianesque' structure at the northern end is the Raj Mahal tourist trap.

The *Woolgoolga Beach Caravan Park* (☎ (066) 54 1373) has sites from $8, on-site vans from $22 and cabins from $33. For Indian food there's the *Koh-I-Nor* at the Raj Mahal and the *Ramblak Restaurant* near the temple.

North of Woolgoolga is **Arrawarra**, a quiet seaside village with yet another great beach and a pleasant caravan park close to the water. Sleepy **Red Rock** is on a beautiful little inlet.

Yuraygir National Park

Yuraygir covers 60 km of coast in three sections, the northern one reaching nearly to Yamba at the mouth of the Clarence River. There are several camp sites in the park, plus a range of accommodation in villages such as **Wooli** and **Minnie Water** (accessible from the highway south of Grafton) and **Brooms Head** (accessible from the highway near Maclean). The northern section of the park is also accessible from Yamba.

The Solitary Islands

This island group, strung out along the coast offshore from Yuraygir National Park, is a marine park because it is at the meeting place of the warmer tropical currents and the more temperate southern currents, with some interesting varieties of fish attracted by the unusual conditions.

Grafton (population 17,000)

Grafton is a large country town basking on the subtropical banks of the wide Clarence River. The fertile Clarence Valley is a patchwork of sugar-cane plantations. Grafton is noted for its trees and there's a Jacaranda Festival in late October. **Prentice House** (1880) on Fitzroy St is now an art gallery, and nearby **Schaeffer House** is a historical museum.

The Pacific Highway runs past Grafton and the Clarence River Tourist Centre (☎ (066) 42 4677) is on the highway south of the town. Before you cross the bridge into town a road leads off to **South Grafton**, a sleepy old riverside suburb.

Places to Stay The *Rathgar Guesthouse* on the Pacific Highway south of town had backpackers' accommodation but it seems to have at least temporarily closed.

There's no shortage of motels and many pubs have accommodation. The *Crown Hotel/Motel* (☎ (066) 42 4000) is a pleasant place on Prince St, overlooking the river. Pub rooms are $20/28 a single/double or $28/30 with bathroom. Motel units are $40/50. Another nice old pub in the same area is *Roches* (☎ (066) 44 2866) at 85 Victoria St.

Getting There & Away Long-distance buses stop on the highway in South Grafton, not far from the information centre. Fares include Sydney $52 and Byron Bay $25. Countrylink runs up the Gwydir Highway to Glen Innes four times a week for about $17.

Most local-area buses leave from the Market Square shopping centre in the town centre not far from the corner of King and Fitzroy Sts. The bus to Maclean and Yamba (☎ (066) 42 2779) leaves from the Saraton Theatre on Prince St.

The railway station is on the highway side of the river.

Grafton to Ballina

From Grafton the highway follows the Clarence River north-east, bypassing the pleasant little river port of **Maclean**. Maclean celebrates its Scottish early settlers with a Highland Gathering each Easter.

East of Maclean, off the highway and at the river mouth, **Yamba** is a fishing town and a growing resort with good beaches. The *Pacific Hotel* (☎ (066) 46 2466), on Pilot St and overlooking the main beach, has backpackers' rooms for $12.50 per person. Infrequent buses (☎ (066) 46 2019) run to Yamba from Maclean and Grafton. A ferry runs four times daily to the village of **Iluka**, on the northern bank of the Clarence, for $3.

Just south of Yamba, **Angourie** is one of the coast's top spots for experienced surfers but beware of the rips. Nat Young, legendary Aussie surfie and ex-World Champion, has *Nat's Mexican Restaurant* here.

North of Iluka, **Bundjalung National Park** lies between the highway and the coast. There are good beaches, canoeing, surfing and fishing, plus lots of wildlife and some old Aboriginal camp sites. The main access points are Iluka and Evans Head at the northern end. Near Iluka at beautiful **Woody Point** there's a large camping area with a shop but no electricity. Sites cost $10 a double, plus $2 for each extra person, and cabins go for $40/50/60 for two/four/eight people. At peak times you might need to book (☎ (066) 46 6134).

South of Woodburn (where you turn off the highway for the fishing port of Evans Head) is the **New Italy Museum** which describes the settlement formed from the tattered remnants of the Marquis de Ray's plan to colonise the New Guinea island of New Ireland. There's also an Italian Pavilion and a restaurant. Behind all this is the good Gurrigai Aboriginal Arts & Crafts shop, selling some local work along with pieces from the outback.

NEW SOUTH WALES

Ballina (population 15,000)
This busy town, on both the Pacific Highway and an island at the mouth of the Richmond River, is popular for sailing and fishing and also has some ocean beaches.

Orientation & Information The Pacific Highway runs into town, becoming River St, its long main road. The information centre (☎ (066) 86 3484) is off River St, towards the eastern end, just past the fanciful old courthouse. It's open daily. Ask here about river cruises, priced from $9. In the information centre is one of the three balsawood rafts from the La Balsa expedition that drifted across the Pacific from Ecuador to Ballina in 1973, taking 177 days.

Beaches Closest to town is the patrolled **Lighthouse Beach**, and next north is the popular **Shelly Beach**. To get to Lighthouse Beach take River St, cross the river and take the first right after the Shaws Hotel turn-off; this road will also take you to Shelly Beach or you could just continue on the main road. The small beach curving around **Shaws Bay Lagoon** is a quiet place to swim.

Places to Stay *Shaws Bay Caravan Park* (☎ (066) 86 2326) is across the bridge from the town centre, not far from Lighthouse Beach. Sites cost from $10 and cabins from $20.

Ballina Travellers Lodge (☎ (066) 86 6737/6342) is a good, modern YHA hostel at 36-38 Tamar St. Dorm beds are $12 and twins are $13.50 per person. Bikes and boogie boards are hired for $1 an hour, and there's a pool. The Travellers Lodge is worth considering if you have deeper pockets as it's also a motel and one of the few in town which doesn't have highway noise. In the low season singles/doubles go as low as $41/43, rising to around $70 a double (only).

At the Ballina Quays Marina (☎ (066) 86 4289), off the highway south of the Big Prawn, you can rent houseboats. Prices start at $90 for a weeknight in the low season ($140 in the high season) for up to four people. Longer hires are cheaper. With over 100 km of navigable river there's plenty of room to move.

Places to Eat *Shelley's on the Beach*, above Shelly Beach, has outdoor tables, good food and wonderful views. It's open from 7.30 am. In the Boulevard shopping centre off River St near the corner of Martin St, *Palm Garden Thai* has main courses for around $9. On River St east of here *Local Motion* is an above-average pasta joint, with main-course servings around $10. Nearby is *Popeye's*, a hamburger place where you can also get a sit-down curry for $5.50 and they do breakfast as well. Across the road is *Beanz*, with healthy lunches to eat in or take away.

The *RSL* on Grant St near River St has meals most days. They're not especially cheap, but how does Morton Bay bug and prawn lasagne sound?

Getting There & Away All the major bus lines service Ballina, most stopping on the highway on the western side of town, at the Life Australia Centre (the Big Prawn). The Kirklands depot (☎ (066) 86 5254) is on Cherry St at the corner of Crane St. Countrylink stops on River St near the corner of Cherry St, outside the Jetset travel agency.

Blanch's departs from the Countrylink stop on River St, travelling to Lennox Head ($2.80), Byron Bay ($4.60) and other nearby towns. The shop next to Jetset has timetables in the window.

Sunray Car Rentals (☎ (066) 86 7315) at 268 River St has cars from around $40 a day plus insurance.

Lennox Head (population 2200)
From Ballina the Pacific Highway runs a little inland but you'll hardly add one km to the journey if you follow the coast road from Ballina to Byron Bay. Long-distance buses take this route and Blanch's stops here.

Lennox Head is the name of both the small, pleasant town (with its fine beach) and the dramatic headland (a prime hang-gliding site) that overlooks it, 11 km out of Ballina

A	
B	C	D
E	

New South Wales

A Lighthouse, Byron Bay (RI)
B Sunset, Darling River (JM)
C Protesters' Falls near Nimbin (JM)

D Border Ranges National Park (JM)
E Abandoned farmhouse, Cooma (JM)

New South Wales
Top: Mootwingee National Park (JM)
Middle: Ghost town in the Riverina (JM)
Bottom: Mungo National Park (JM)

and 18 km from Byron Bay. It has some of the best surf on the coast, particularly in winter. Lake Ainsworth just back from the beach is a freshwater lake, good for swimming and windsurfing. Its dark colour is due to the tea-tree oil, good for the skin and hair, which seeps in from the surrounding vegetation.

The Lennox Point Hotel often has bands on weekends.

Places to Stay *Lake Ainsworth Caravan Park* (☎ (066) 87 7249) has tent sites (from $10) and cabins ($25; $45 in the high season).

People come back to *Lennox Beach House Hostel* (☎ (066) 87 7636), especially those who have been travelling for a while and want to put their feet up. It's purpose-built, very clean and very friendly. Both Lake Ainsworth and the beach are nearby and you can have use of a cat and a windsurfer ($5 for as long as you stay). Boards, bikes and other sporting equipment are free. Dorm beds are $14 and there's a double for $30.

BYRON BAY (population 5000)
Byron Bay is one of the most attractive stops on the whole east coast: a relaxed little seaside town with superb beaches and a great climate – warm in winter, hot in summer. Tourism is low key (although a planned Club Med might change that) and Byron is a meeting place of alternative cultures: it's a surfing Mecca thanks to the superb surf below Cape Byron, and is also close to the 'back to the land' lifestyles pursued in the beautiful far north coast hinterland. There are good music venues, wholefood and vegetarian eateries, off-beat people, distinctive craft and clothes shops, a thriving fashion and surf industry, and numerous opportunities to learn yogic dance, take a massage or naturopathic therapy, have your stars read and so on. Byron Bay market, in Butler St on the first Sunday of each month, is one of a series around the area at which the counter-culture (almost establishment up here!) gets a chance to meet and sell its wares.

Orientation & Information
Byron Bay is situated six km east of the Pacific Highway. Jonson St, which becomes Bangalow Rd, is the main shopping street. The information centre (☎ (066) 85 8050) is on Jonson St near the railway station. Across the road, you can leave packs at the muralled community centre during the day for $1. Pick up a copy of the quirky weekly paper *Echo* to get an idea of the way of life around here.

There's a lot to do in and around Byron Bay. Hostels often have the best deals but for a range of options and activities it pays to check around a few hostels.

Cape Byron
Cape Byron was named by Captain Cook after the poet Byron's grandfather, who had sailed round the world in the 1760s. One spur of the cape is the most easterly point of the Australian mainland. You can drive right up to the picturesque 1901 lighthouse, one of the most powerful in the southern hemisphere. There's a 3.5-km walking track right round the cape from the Captain Cook Lookout on Lighthouse Rd. It's circular, so you can leave bikes at the start. There's a good chance of seeing wallabies in the final rainforest stretch.

From the top you can often see schools of dolphins surfing through the waves below and during the season (best in June and July) whales sometimes pass close by.

Beaches
The Byron area has a glorious collection of beaches, ranging from 10-km stretches of empty sand to secluded little coves. **Main Beach** immediately in front of the town is a good swimming beach and sometimes has decent surf. The sand stretches 50 km or more, all the way up to the Gold Coast, interrupted only by river or creek entrances and a few small headlands.

The eastern end of Main Beach, curving away towards Cape Byron, is known as **Clarks Beach** and can be good for surfing. The headland at the end of Clarks is called the Pass and the best surf is off here and at the next beach, **Watego's Beach**. **Little**

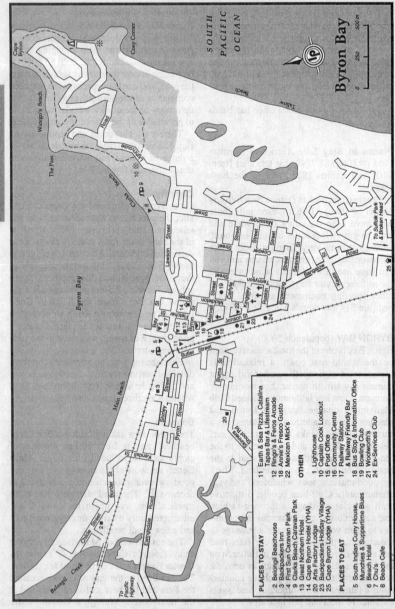

Byron Bay

SOUTH PACIFIC OCEAN

0   250   500 m

Cape Byron

Cosy Corner

Watego's Beach

The Pass

Lighthouse Road

Clarks Beach

Byron Bay

Main Beach

Belongil Creek

To Pacific Highway

Tallow Beach

To Suffolk Park & Broken Head

Lawson Street

Massinger Street

Cowper Street

Tennyson Street

Browning Street

Seaview St

Keats St

Bangalow Road

Carlyle Street

Kingsley Street

Ruskin St

Jonson St

Marvell St

Fletcher Street

Middleton Street

Bay St

Burns St

Butler Street

Shirley Street

Byron Street

Kendall St

Border St

Childe Street

Ewingsdale Road

Shirley Rd

Tennyson St

PLACES TO STAY

2 Belongil Beachouse
3 Backpackers Inn
4 First Sun Caravan Park
13 Clarks Beach Caravan Park
14 Great Northern Hotel
14 Cape Byron Hostel (YHA)
20 Arts Factory Lodge
23 Backpackers Holiday Village
25 Cape Byron Lodge (YHA)

PLACES TO EAT

5 South Indian Curry House,
   Munchies & Supertime Blues
6 Beach Hotel
7 Chu's
8 Beach Cafe
11 Earth & Sea Pizza, Catalina
   Tapas Bar & Lifestream
12 Ringo's & Feros Arcade
18 Annie's Fresco Gusto
22 Mexican Mick's

OTHER

1 Lighthouse
10 Captain Cook Lookout
15 Post Office
16 Community Centre
17 Railway Station
   & Railway Friendly Bar
18 Bus Stop & Information Office
19 Bowling Club
21 Woolworth's
24 Ex-Services Club

Watego's Beach is further round, almost at the tip of the cape. Dolphins are quite common, particularly in the surf off Watego's and Little Watego's.

South of Cape Byron, **Tallow Beach** stretches seven km down to a rockier stretch of shore around Broken Head, where a succession of small beaches (clothes optional) dot the coast before opening on to **Seven Mile Beach** which goes all the way to Lennox Head, a further 10 km south. You can reach Tallow from various points along the Byron Bay to Lennox Head road.

The turn-off to the 'suburb' of **Suffolk Park** (with more good surf, particularly in winter) is five km from Byron Bay. A further km down the Byron to Lennox road is the turn-off to the Broken Head caravan park. About 200 metres before the caravan park, the unsurfaced Seven Mile Beach Rd turns off south and runs behind the rainforest of the **Broken Head Nature Reserve**. Seven Mile Beach Rd ends after five km (at the north end of Seven Mile Beach), but several tracks lead down from it through the forest to the Broken Head beaches – **Kings Beach** (for which there's a car park 750 metres down Seven Mile Beach Rd) and **Whites Beach** (a foot track after about 3.25 km) are just two good ones.

Diving

Diving is popular at Julian Rocks, three km offshore, a meeting point of cold southerly currents and warm northerly ones, which attracts a profusion of marine species from both. There's cut-throat competition between the growing number of dive operators – ask around to see who has the best deals. Byron Bay Sport & Dive (also called Byron Bay Dive Centre) (☎ (066) 85 7149) at 9 Lawson St is the oldest established. Sundive (☎ (066) 85 7755) has moved to the new Cape Byron Hostel complex on Middleton St. Bayside Scuba (☎ (066) 85 8333), a newcomer, has taken over Sundive's old shop at 15 Fletcher St, near the corner of Lawson. Two more newcomers are North Coast Dive (☎ (066) 85 7651), which operates out of a house at 41 Cowper St, and

Byron Dive Downunder, which plans to set up at 84 Jonson St near the information centre.

Surfing

Most hostels have free boards for guests. Byron Surf Hire on Lawson St near Fletcher St hires surfboards and wetsuits for $25 a day and boogie boards for $15 a day. The weekly rates are much cheaper. Let's Go Surfing (☎ (066) 87 1358 or 85 8768) will teach you to surf from about $20 a lesson.

Rafting

Rapid Action (☎ (075) 30 8088) has whitewater rafting trips on the Nymboida River for about $95. The season is usually between November and June.

Flying

Cape Byron is a great place for hang-gliding and Flight Zone (☎ (066) 85 3178) has tandem flights and tuition. Tandem flights are $75 ($65 from Lennox Head). Ring at 10 am to find out if and when there will be flights that day.

Trike flights (ultra-light aircraft) are run by Skylimit (☎ (066) 84 3616) and cost about $70 for half an hour. Skylimit also offers tandem hang-gliding.

Kite-flying is popular here and most days around 4 pm you'll see plenty on Main Beach or Tallow Beach, depending on the wind. Byron Kites (☎ (066) 85 5299) in the Cape Byron Hostel complex will sell you a kite or you can rent one for $20, which includes tuition and five hours flying.

Alternative Therapies

There are at least two floatation-tank places: Samadhi (☎ (066) 85 6905) on Jonson St opposite Woolworth's and Relax Haven (☎ (066) 85 8304) at the Belongil Beachouse. These places also do massage – at Relax Haven you can get an hour in the tank and an hour-long massage for $35.

Several other places offer massage, acupuncture and other alternative therapies; other outfits drift into the fuzzier edges of alternative thought. If you need your chakra rebalanced see Quintessence Healing Sanctuary (☎ (066) 85 5533) at 8/11 Fletcher St. It offers a wide range of services, everything from clairvoyance to sports medicine!

Organised Tours

Byron Bay to Bush Tours (☎ (066) 85 5767) has a popular day tour which gives a taste of life on the north coast hinterland. It leaves the information centre at 9.30 am on Monday, Wednesday and Friday and costs $25. On Tuesday there's a good-value trip to Mt Warning for $15. There are plenty of other tours around, such as Damien Wilkinson's Big Scrub Tours (☎ (066) 84 5323, or see Jetset Travel on Marvell St) which has day and overnight trips to the rainforest.

Places to Stay

Prices are higher at holiday times, particularly in summer. Some cafes – especially Suppertime Blues – have notice boards where longer-term places are advertised.

Camping & Cabins Around Christmas/January and Easter you'll be lucky to find a site and it's unlikely that you can rent a cabin for less than a week at the peak times. Byron Bay Disposals in the Plaza shopping centre on Jonson St sells camping equipment.

The council has four caravan parks, all by beaches. *First Sun Caravan Park* (☎ (066) 85 6544) is on Main Beach close to the town centre. Sites start at $8 for one person, plus $4 for each extra person, rising by increments to $14 plus $6 at the peak time. There's a range of cabins, the cheapest going for $31 in the low season and $50 ($350 for a week) at the peak. *Clarks Beach Caravan Park* (☎ (066) 85 6496) is off Lighthouse Rd about a km east of the town centre and has plenty of trees. Sites are marginally more expensive here but the cabins start cheaper, from $27 rising to $42 ($295 a week).

Down at Suffolk Park on Tallow Beach *Suffolk Park Caravan Park* (☎ (066) 85 3353) is a friendly place with shady sites and cabins for marginally less than those at First

Sun. They can probably squeeze in your tent when everywhere else is full. South of here at Broken Head there's a small, superbly situated council-run caravan park (☎ (066) 85 3245). Sites cost from $8/9 for one/two people, rising by increments to $14/15 at peak times. There are on-site vans from $30 to $50. You'll need to bring all your supplies.

Other places include: *Belongil by the Sea* (☎ (066) 85 8111), an all-cabin place next to the Belongil Beachouse hostel; *Crosby's Caravan Court* (☎ (066) 85 6751) by Tallow Beach in Suffolk Park; and the good *Tallow Beach Resort* (☎ (066) 85 3303, toll-free 1800 656 817), a spacious place on Tallow Beach with self-contained cabins.

Hostels All six hostels have their good points and if you're planning a lengthy stay check them all to see which suits you best. Prices fluctuate depending on demand, peaking around Christmas/January, when you should book. At other times ask about deals and weekly rates.

The popular *Backpackers Holiday Village Hostel* (☎ (066) 85 7660) at 116 Jonson St, close to the bus stop, is a clean, friendly, well-equipped place with a small pool and spa. Dorms cost from $12, doubles for $29, and there's one double with bathroom and TV for $35. Well-maintained bicycles, surfboards and boogie boards are free and there are plenty of them.

The closest hostel to the beach is *Backpackers Inn* (☎ (066) 85 8231) at 29 Shirley St, about half a km from the town centre. It's a modern hostel with a pool and all the usual features, including free bikes and boogie boards. To get to the beach you just walk across the lawn, cross the railway line (carefully!) and climb a sand dune. The rates are $12 in eight-bed dorms, $14 in four-share ($15 for any dorm bed around Christmas/January) and there are doubles for $30 ($60 for four people in the high season).

Byron Bay has two YHA-affiliated hostels. *Cape Byron Lodge* (☎ (066) 85 6445) is clean, comfortable and well equipped. It's some way from the town centre at 78 Bangalow Rd (the southern end of Jonson St) but only about 10 minutes walk to Tallow Beach. There's a small pool and bikes are free. This is usually the cheapest hostel in town, with dorm beds at $11 or $12 in a four-bed dorm, and doubles for $15 per person.

The new YHA affiliate is the very impressive *Cape Byron Hostel* (☎ (066) 85 8788), close to the town centre and Main Beach at the corner of Byron and Middleton Sts. It's a big new building with its own mini shopping centre and a heated pool. Prices (which might rise in summer) are $13 in a 10-person dorm, $14 in a four-person dorm, $35 in a double or twin ($28 for one person when available) and $40 for a double with bathroom.

The *Belongil Beachouse* (☎ (066) 85 7868) is a great place to stay, well run, relaxed and friendly. It's off Childe St, a quiet road adjacent to the beach; bikes, surfboards and boogie boards are free. The cafe here is a big plus, with excellent healthy food served between 8 am and 10 pm. There's a nightly half-price special for guests and at about $4.50 it's great value. You can store gear here for $5 a week. Dorm beds start at $12, rising to $14 during school holidays and $15 around Christmas. Singles/doubles with shared bathroom are $25/30, rising to $34 during school holidays and $38 around Christmas. There are a few doubles/triples with bathrooms starting at $40/50.

The *Arts Factory Lodge* (☎ (066) 85 7709) is some way from the beach on Skinners Shoot Rd, but it has a nice setting and it gets quite a few travellers who have tried other places in town and want something a little looser. Prices here vary a lot, but are often a little lower than most other places in town. Camping on the small island in the hostel grounds costs $6 per person. The staff meet most buses or you can have your taxi fare (about $4) deducted from your bill.

Hotels & Motels The *Great Northern Hotel* (☎ (066) 85 6454) on Jonson St has single or double rooms for $45 year round. Motels such as the *Wollongbar* (☎ (066) 85 8200) at 19 Shirley St, the *Bay Beach* (☎ (066) 85

7708), and *Byron Sunseeker* (☎ (066) 85 7369) at 100 Bangalow Rd have singles/doubles from around $50/60 in the off season. Prices skyrocket around Christmas/January and Easter and to a lesser extent during other school holidays.

The *Wheel Resort* (☎ (066) 85 6139), 39-51 Broken Head Rd, was designed and is operated by wheelchair users for disabled travellers. They provide personal assistance and rates are between $75 and $135 per night for a single cabin (from $440 weekly), and between $100 and $180 for family cabins which sleep up to seven (weekly rate from $520). Dogs can come along too for $10 per night, by prior arrangement.

Self-Catering Holiday houses and apartments start from around $300 a week in the off season, $500 during school holidays and $800 over Christmas. Letting agents include Elders (☎ (066) 85 6222) on Jonson St near the station.

Places to Eat
There is a wide choice of restaurants, cafes and takeaways serving good food, and vegetarians are particularly well catered for.

Breakfast is served all over town. Overlooking Clarks Beach, the *Beach Cafe* isn't cheap but the views are superb. The *Jetty Cafe* on Bay St next to the Beach Hotel specialises in breakfast/brunch. Variations on bacon & eggs cost around $7. *Cafe DOC* at the Cape Byron Hostel complex has breakfast for about $5.50. At the other end of the day, the *Night Owl* is a van selling late-night takeaways behind the Great Northern Hotel.

The *Beach Hotel* has a wide range of snacks such as burgers from $4.50 and more substantial meals such as satays ($9.50) and steaks (from $11). Heading down Jonson St from here, the *South Indian Curry House* is a long-time favourite and has main courses from $8 to $13, most around $10. It's open nightly for dinner. *Munchies* is a small place with healthy snacks and meals, open during the day. Further along, *Suppertime Blues* has similarly healthy food such as vegie-burgers at $4.50 and smoothies from $2.50. Both places stay open until early evening, later in summer.

Still on Jonson St but east of the round-about, the old wooden guesthouse on the corner of Lawson St is due to be transformed into a bar and restaurant complex. Nearby, *Ringo's* is one of Byron's older cafes and has a large menu of snacks and drinks and meals from around $10. It's open from breakfast ($6 for bacon & eggs) until about 8.30 pm. If a 'meal deal' is on offer, grab it – around $7.50 for two courses of excellent food. Across the road, *Earth & Sea Pizza* has main-course pasta for about $10 and pizzas from $9.50. *Catalina* is a stylish tapas bar where you'll pay between $3 and $7 per serving. *Lifestream* is a large health-food cafe with a huge range of goodies. You can put together a decent meal for $3 to $5.

At the Railway Friendly Bar, *Annie's Fresco Gusto* opens for lunch and dinner. The food is innovative and not expensive. Further along Jonson St is the licensed *Mexican Mick's*, open for dinner from Tuesday to Saturday. It's an old favourite and is still reasonably priced, with main courses under $14 and lots of snacks on the big menu. There are sometimes special deals for back-packers.

The Chinese restaurant at the bowling club in Marvell St has various specials and none of the main courses are over $8. *Chu's* on Lawson St has no MSG in its Chinese food, with main courses under $10. *Oh! Delhi*, a popular Indian restaurant, is across the road in the Bay Centre. Nearby, the *Athena Greek Taverna* has main courses around $12.

Feros Arcade dog-legs between Lawson and Jonson Sts and has several options. The *Indian Curry Restaurant* is a small place open from Wednesday to Monday for dinner, with vegetarian main courses from $8 and others up to $13. *Annabella's Spaghetti Bar* is open weekdays for lunch and dinner (and occasionally on summer weekends), with main courses from $7 to $10. Next door, the *Raving Prawn* has an interesting modern menu with main courses ranging between $14 and $20.

Entertainment

No-one should miss the *Railway Friendly Bar* at the station. It's open daily and has music most evenings, with larger bands from Friday to Sunday. The music stops by 9.30 pm but there are other venues nearby. *Catalina* on Jonson St has music and dancing from 10 pm. There's a cover charge of about $4. On Thursdays backpackers get half-price entry (pick up a card from your hostel), a free sangria and an inexpensive meal. The *Beach Hotel* has music most nights.

The *Ex-Services Club* ('the Servo') has music on Friday and Saturday (from big touring bands to Kenny Ball) and free films on Sunday and Thursday nights.

It's always worth seeing what's on at the *Epicentre*, on Kendall St just over the railway line. Whatever it is (and its programs encompass a wide range of the weird) it's sure to be at least interesting. The *Piggery*, near the Arts Factory Lodge, might be reopening as a venue for mainly local bands.

Getting There & Away

Bus Numerous buses run through Byron Bay. There are also more-or-less direct buses to Melbourne ($117) and Adelaide ($147). Other approximate fares are Brisbane $22, Sydney $60, Coffs Harbour $32 and Surfers Paradise $18. Kirklands' Lismore to Brisbane route passes through Byron Bay and stops in other useful places such as Murwillumbah, Ballina and Tweed Heads. Blanch's serves the local area with destinations such as Mullumbimby ($4) and Ballina ($4.60).

Train Byron Bay is on the Sydney to Murwillumbah line, with a daily train in each direction, plus several rail/bus services. From Sydney ($75) the quickest service is the 7.05 am XPT, reaching Byron Bay at 7.30 pm. This train continues to Murwillumbah ($5.70) and connects with a bus to Brisbane ($24.60 from Byron Bay).

Car & Motorbike Rental Earth Car Rentals (book through a hostel or the information centre) has older cars from $35 a day (including 200 free km), more recent vehicles from $45 and eight-seater vans from $45. Jetset Travel rents small current-model cars for $35 a day plus 15c per km. You can't go more than 300 km from Byron Bay but that's enough to get around the hinterland.

Ride on Motorcyles (☎ (066) 85 6304), on Jonson St opposite Woolworth's, hires motorbikes from $45 a day. You need a motorbike licence, Australian or foreign.

Getting Around
Bicycle The hostels lend bikes of varying quality to guests. Byron Bay Cycles in the Plaza shopping centre on Jonson St has good single-speed bikes for $10 a day, including helmet, and geared bikes for $15 a day. Let's Go Bikes, nearby on Jonson St, also has single-speed bikes at $10 a day.

BYRON BAY TO TWEED HEADS
The Pacific Highway continues north from the Byron Bay turn-off to the state border at Tweed Heads. Just after the Mullumbimby turn-off is **Brunswick Heads**, a river-mouth town with a small fishing fleet and several caravan parks and motels.

A few km north is the turn-off to the coastal hamlet of **Wooyung**. The Wooyung Camel Farm has short rides for $4 and sunset rides to the beach for $20. A sealed road runs up the coast from Wooyung to Tweed Heads and makes an alternative to the Pacific Highway. This coast is known as the Tweed Coast and is much less developed than the Gold Coast to the north.

Bogangar-Cabarita and **Kingscliff** are two small resorts. Cabarita Beach has good surf and there's a good hostel, *Emu Park Backpackers Resort* (☎ (066) 76 1190). It's one of the cleanest hostels around and the rooms are large. Dorm beds are $13 and there's a 'stay two nights, get the third night free' deal, except in the peak summer season. Doubles cost $28 and there's an en-suite double with TV for $38. Bikes and boards are free and the beach is a minute away. The staff will drop you off at Mt Warning and

pick you up after your climb for about $45 – not bad among several people. Guests can be picked up from Coolangatta or Murwillumbah.

Surfside Bus Lines runs from Tweed Heads down as far as Pottsville about four times a day during the week and once on Saturday. More frequent services run as far as Kingscliff.

Murwillumbah (population 8000)
Murwillumbah is in a banana- and sugar-growing area in the broad Tweed Valley. It's also the main town in this part of the north coast hinterland and there are several communes and 'back to the land' centres in the area. You're also within reach of Mt Warning and the spectacular border ranges. You can cross into Queensland by the Numinbah road through the ranges between the Springbrook and Lamington areas (see the Queensland chapter for more details).

The tourist information centre (☎ (066) 72 1340), the main one for the whole Tweed region, is on the Pacific Highway near the railway station. The excellent **Tweed River Regional Art Gallery** is just up the road from the hostel. The **museum** is on Queensland Rd and is open from Wednesday to Friday from 11 am to 3 pm and admission is $1.

You can hire bikes from Jim's Cycle Centre for about $10 a day.

Places to Stay & Eat The associate-YHA *Mt Warning Backpackers of Murwillumbah* (☎ (066) 72 3763) is at 1 Tumbulgum Rd beside the Tweed River – you'll see it on the right as you cross the bridge into town. It has a good reputation as a relaxed and friendly place with lots of activities. Dorm beds are $13.50, singles $18, twins $26 and the double room is $29.

Several pubs have accommodation, including the solid *Imperial Hotel* (☎ (066) 72 1036) on the main street across from the post office, with rooms from $20/34.

Getting There & Away Murwillumbah is served by most buses on the Sydney (about $60) to Brisbane ($17) coastal run. Except for Kirklands, which goes into town, the long-distance buses stop at the railway station. Fulton's Bus Service (☎ (066) 21 6231) runs to Uki ($4.50), Nimbin ($12) and Lismore ($14). Surfside runs to Tweed Heads ($3.80).

A daily train from Sydney ($75) connects with a bus to the Gold Coast and Brisbane.

TWEED HEADS (population 44,750)

Sharing a street with the more-developed Queensland resort of Coolangatta, Tweed Heads marks the southern end of the Gold Coast strip. The northern side of Boundary St, which runs along a short peninsula to Point Danger above the mouth of the Tweed River, is in Queensland. This end of the Gold Coast is quieter than the resorts closer to Surfers Paradise.

The information centre (☎ (075) 36 4244) is at the northern end of Wharf St (the Pacific Highway), opposite the post office. It's open on weekdays and until 1 pm on Saturday but not at all on Sunday. There's also an information kiosk in the Beach House complex at the corner of Marine Parade and McLean St in Coolangatta, but it doesn't always open on Sunday either. The Greyhound Pioneer office, situated around the corner on McLean St, *is* open on Sunday and might be able to help.

Things to See

At Point Danger the towering **Captain Cook Memorial** straddles the state border. The 18-metre-high monument was completed in 1970 (the bicentenary of Cook's visit) and is topped by a laser-beam lighthouse visible 35 km out to sea. The replica of the *Endeavour*'s capstan is made from ballast dumped by Cook after the *Endeavour* ran aground on the Great Barrier Reef and recovered along with the ship's cannons in 1968. Point Danger was named by Cook after he nearly ran aground there too. Three km from Tweed Heads there are views over the Tweed Valley and the Gold Coast from the **Razorback Lookout**.

On Kirkwood Rd in South Tweed Heads, the **Minjungbal Aboriginal Cultural Centre**

(☎ (075) 24 2109) has exhibits on pre-contact history and culture. It's open daily and admission is $4.

Places to Stay

Accommodation in Tweed Heads spills over into Coolangatta and up the Gold Coast, where the choice is more varied. The cheaper motels along Wharf St are feeling the pinch now that the highway bypasses Tweed Heads and in the off season you might find doubles for less than $30.

See the Coolangatta section of the Queensland chapter for places to stay across the border.

Places to Eat

The *Tweed Heads Bowls Club* on Wharf St has specials such as weekday roast lunches for under $3; the other clubs are also sources of cheap eats. The smaller *Rowing & Aquatic Club* on Coral St has meals for less than $8. Next door, the *Fishermans Cove Restaurant* is known for its seafood and has main courses averaging around $16. At Rainbow Bay, on the northern side of Point Danger, *Doyle's on the Beach* has excellent seafood takeaways and a restaurant.

Getting There & Away

All long-distance buses stop in Coolangatta – Greyhound Pioneer at Beach House on McLean St near the corner of the beachfront Marine Parade, and the others at Golden Gateway Travel (☎ (075) 36 1700), a few blocks back towards Tweed Heads. Greyhound Pioneer has a $15 same-day return ticket to Brisbane; $10 one way.

Surfside (☎ (075) 36 7666) has daily services to Murwillumbah ($3.80) and to Kingscliff (some go on to Cabarita Beach but not on Sunday), and they have deals on day-return tickets up the Gold Coast. There's a stop outside the information centre.

There are several car-hire places which will get you moving for $25 a day or less, such as Tweed Auto Rentals (☎ (075) 36 8000) at the information centre.

Far North Coast Hinterland

The area stretching 60 km or so inland from the Pacific Highway in far northern New South Wales is full of interest for the beauty of its spectacular forested mountains, and its high population of 'alternative lifestylers', 'back to the landers', 'freaks', 'hippies' – whatever label you care to apply. These settlers, the first of whom were attracted to the area by the Aquarius Festival at Nimbin in 1973, have become an accepted part of the community – although there are still occasional run-ins with the Drug Squad.

The country between Lismore and the coast was once known as the Big Scrub, an incredibly inadequate description of a place that must have been close to paradise at the time of European incursion. Much of the 'scrub' was cleared for farming, after the loggers had been through and taken out all the cedar. More recent arrivals have dubbed it Rainbow Country.

A web of narrow roads covers the area and you can nearly always approach a place by one route and leave by another. Nimbin, for instance, can be reached from Lismore, Mullumbimby or Murwillumbah. If you're planning to explore the area get the Forestry Commission's Casino area map ($5) – the information centres in Byron Bay and Nimbin are two places which stock it.

Geography

The northern part of the hinterland was formed by volcanic activity (see the Mt Warning section) and is essentially a huge bowl almost completely rimmed by mountain ranges, with the spectacular peak of Mt Warning in the centre. The escarpments of the McPherson and Tweed ranges form the north-western rim, with the Razorback Range to the west and the Nightcap Range to the south-west. National parks, some World Heritage areas, protect unique and beautiful subtropical rainforests.

South of this area the country is a maze of steep hills and beautiful valleys, some still harbouring magnificent stands of rainforest, others cleared for cattle-grazing and plantations.

Markets & Music

The colourful alternative community can be seen in force at the weekend markets listed below. The biggest market is at The Channon, between Lismore and Nimbin.

Brunswick Heads
    1st Saturday of the month, behind the Ampol service station
Byron Bay
    1st Sunday, Butler St Reserve
Lismore
    1st and 3rd Sunday, Lismore Shopping Square
Murwillumbah
    1st Sunday, Sunnyside Shopping Centre
The Channon
    2nd Sunday, Coronation Park
Mullumbimby
    3rd Saturday, Museum
Uki
    3rd Sunday, Old Buttery
Bangalow
    4th Sunday, Showground
Nimbin
    4th Sunday, Showground

Many accomplished musicians live in the area and they sometimes play at the markets or in the village pub after the market (notably at Uki). Between them, the *Brunswick Byron Echo* and the *Lismore Echo* newspapers give notice of most musical and cultural events in the area.

LISMORE (population 40,000)

Thirty-five km inland from Ballina on the Bruxner Highway to New England, or 48 km in from Byron Bay, Lismore is the 'capital' of the state's far north – the centre of a productive rural district, with a student population from the Southern Cross University, and influenced by the alternative community in the country to the north.

The good Information & Heritage Centre (☎ (066) 22 0122), near Wilsons River at the corner of Molesworth and Ballina Sts, includes a rainforest display ($1). The Big

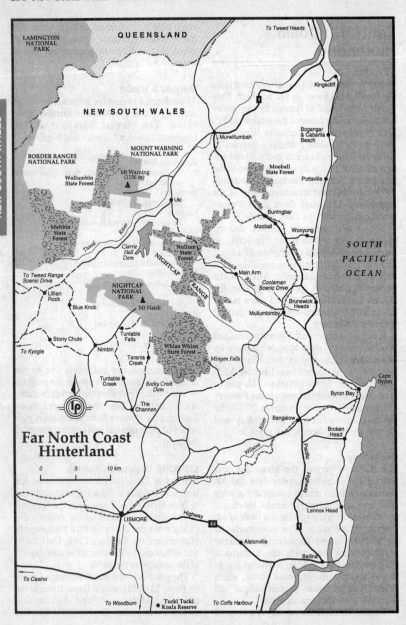

Far North Coast Hinterland

0   5   10 km

Scrub Environment Centre (☎ (066) 21 3278) on Keen St sells topographic maps of the area. The Outdoor & Disposals shop (☎ (066) 21 3371) on Keen St rents camping gear: a dome tent, a stove and a couple of sleeping bags would cost about $80 for a week.

The interesting **Richmond River Historical Society Museum** is at 165 Molesworth St and is open weekdays ($2). The **regional art gallery** next door is open from Tuesday to Saturday (free). **Tucki Tucki Nature Reserve**, 16 km south of Lismore on the Woodburn road, is a koala reserve. There's an Aboriginal **bora ring** nearby, where initiation ceremonies were held.

The MV *Bennelong* (☎ (066) 21 7729) has several cruises, from two hours ($10) to a day cruise down to the coast at Ballina ($45).

Places to Stay

Currendina Travellers Lodge (☎ (066) 21 6118) at 14 Ewing St has dorms from $12 and single/double rooms from $15/24 to $20/32. Smoking and drinking aren't permitted. This is a pleasant old wooden house and the friendly managers can organise trips to places of interest in the area.

Places to Eat

Dr Juice on Keen St is open during the day for excellent juices and smoothies, and it has vegetarian and vegan snacks for around $2. On Thursday, Friday and Saturday nights cheap Indian meals are available and there are plans to open as a music cafe on the other nights. Next door is *Fundamental Health Foods*, a big health-food shop. *Boccacio Ristorante Italiano* at 55 Keen St sometimes has all-you-can-eat pasta deals for $7.50. Not far away on Keen St, *Peppers* has cheap meals, such as pasta for under $3.

Getting There & Away

There are daily flights to Brisbane (Oxley) and Sydney (Hazelton). Kirklands (☎ (066) 22 1499) is based here and runs buses around the immediate area as well as further afield. Destinations include Byron Bay ($7.90), Murwillumbah ($12.70) and Brisbane

($25.90). There's a handy service to Tenterfield in New England ($21.60). The XPT train from Sydney ($70) stops here.

NIMBIN (population 1300)

Although Australia's 'back to the land' movement is past its heyday, Nimbin, 30 km north of Lismore, is still a very active alternative centre. This was where the move to northern New South Wales started, with the 1973 Aquarius Festival, and there are many communes ('multiple-occupancy properties') in the area. You're still likely to be asked if you want to buy some 'green' as you walk along the street.

In 1993 Nimbin celebrated the 20th anniversary of the Aquarius Festival and many murals were added to the streetscape. The same year the more conservative elements in town launched a campaign to 'reclaim the streets', in reaction to a growing transient population. Locals are quick to tell you that what goes on in town bears little relationship to the way of life of the many people living in the area.

Despite the size of its reputation, Nimbin is just a tiny village. Cullen St is the main street. The information centre (☎ (066) 89 1222) is next to the Ampol service station at the southern end of the shopping centre. Pick up a copy of the booklet *Nimbin & Environs* ($3). The Environment Centre and the Community Centre, both on Cullen St, are also good sources of information.

The weird and wonderful **Nimbin Museum** is on Cullen St near the Rainbow Cafe. Admission is $2, and it's worth it for the conversations you'll have before you get through the door. There's a good market on the fourth Sunday of the month and you may catch a local band playing afterwards.

Places to Stay

The council's basic caravan park (☎ (066) 89 1402) is near the bowling club – go down the road running past the pub. Sites cost $9 and on-site vans around $28.

Granny's Farm (☎ (066) 89 1333), an associate-YHA hostel, is a pleasantly relaxed place surrounded by farmland, with platypuses in the nearby creek. Dorm beds go for $12.50 and doubles for $15 per person. The friendly managers will sometimes give rides to places of interest. To get here go north along Cullen St and turn left just before the bridge over the creek.

Just north of town Crofton Rd branches off Blue Knob Rd, and four km along is the quiet *Nimbin Motel* (☎ (066) 89 1420) with singles/doubles for $20/35. As a motel it's pretty basic, but as a bed for the night in a quiet valley with bushland at the back door it's good value.

There are several B&B places in town and nearby. Next to the church at the southern end of Cullen St, the *Old Rectory* (☎ (066) 89 1097) is in the early stages of renovation and charges $30/40/50 for a single/double/twin. One of the owners has lived in the area intermittently since before the Aquarius Festival so she has good information on people and places.

The *Quinns* (☎ (066) 89 1113) offer B&B in their comfortable home for $20 per person, with full board for $35. There's a large garden and a spring-fed dam for swimming. To get there head south on Cullen St to the edge of town and turn left onto High St, which becomes Falls Rd, and the Quinn's place is about a km along, on the right. *Nimbin Tourist Accommodation* (☎ (066) 89 1493) is six km out of town and charges $40/60 for B&B.

Places to Eat

At the northern end of Cullen St, *Nimbin Pizza & Trattoria* has pasta from $7.50 and is open from Tuesday to Sunday for dinner. The *Rainbow Cafe* has been the most popular hang-out in town for a long time and is the best place to meet locals. Wholesome meals cost around $6 and delicious cakes are around $2. It does breakfasts, as does the nearby *Nimbin Rocks Cafe*, the closest thing you'll find to a standard country-town cafe. Across the street, *Choices* has healthy (and not so healthy) takeaways and light meals. *Freemasons Hotel* has counter meals for under $7.

A popular new place is *Jem's*, near the Ampol service station, with an interesting lunch and dinner menu. Snacks cost from $3.50 and most main courses are under $10. It's open from Wednesday to Saturday for lunch and dinner, and on Tuesday for lunch only.

Three km along Lillian Rock Rd (the turnoff is eight km from Nimbin on Blue Knob Rd), *Calurla Tea Garden* (☎ (066) 89 7297) is open between 10 am and 6 pm daily for teas and lunches.

Entertainment

If there's a dance at the town hall don't miss it – you'll meet the friendly people from the country around Nimbin, and how long is it since you heard a 20-minute guitar solo? Some time in late Autumn you might get a chance to trip the light fantastic at the *Marijuana Harvest Ball*.

The *Freemasons Hotel* often has music, or the *Bush Theatre* at the old butter factory near the bridge at the northern end of town has performances, and films on Friday and Saturday.

Getting There & Away

Several buses run between Nimbin and Lismore ($8) daily except Sunday. A Fulton's school bus runs to and from Murwillumbah on weekdays (leaving Murwillumbah at 7 am, returning in the afternoon). It takes two hours and costs $12. Students, the unemployed and travellers *might* get concessions on local buses.

AROUND NIMBIN

The country around Nimbin is superb. The 800-metre-plus Nightcap Range, originally a flank of the huge Mt Warning volcano, rises north-east of the town and a sealed road leads to one of its highest points, **Mt Nardi**. The range is part of **Nightcap National Park**. The Mt Nardi road gives access to a variety of other vehicle and walking tracks along and across the range, including the historic Nightcap Track, a packhorse trail which was once the main route between Lismore and Murwillumbah. The views from **Pholis Gap** on the Googarna road, towards the western end of the range, are particularly spectacular.

The Tuntable Falls commune, one of the biggest with its own shop and school – and some fine houses – is about nine km east of Nimbin and you can reach it by the public Tuntable Falls Rd. You can walk to the 123-metre **Tuntable Falls** themselves, 13 km from Nimbin. To get to **Nimbin Rocks**, with an Aboriginal sacred site, head south through the town and turn right at Stony Chute (Kyogle) Rd. After two km there's a turn-off to the left and three km along there's a signposted walking trail on the left. **Hanging Rock Creek** has falls and a good swimming hole; take the road through Stony Chute for 14 km, turn right at the Barker's Vale sign, then left onto Williams Rd; the falls are nearby on the right.

A tiny village off the Nimbin to Lismore road, **The Channon** hosts the biggest of the region's markets on the second Sunday of the month. A dance is sometimes held the night before the market and there's often music after the market. *The Channon Teahouse & Craftshop* is a pleasant place for a snack or a light meal and there's interesting craft to browse through. It's open daily from 10 am to 5 pm, with dinner on Friday and Saturday nights. The information centre (☎ (066) 88 6276) is here as well. *The Channon Village Campsite* is basic but pretty and costs $4 per person. Out of town on the Terania Creek road, *Mimosa Park* (☎ (066) 88 6230) has cabins for $35 a double.

About 15 km north up the Terania Creek road is the rainforest of Nightcap National Park. A stunningly beautiful 700-metre walk leads to **Protesters' Falls**, named after the environmentalists whose 1979 campaign to stop logging was a major factor in the creation of the national park. There's a beautiful camping area at Terania Creek. It's free but you're supposed to stay only one night. No fires are allowed.

MULLUMBIMBY (population 2700)

This pleasant little town, known locally as Mullum, is in subtropical countryside five km off the Pacific Highway between Bangalow and Brunswick Heads. Perhaps best known for its marijuana – 'Mullumbimby Madness' – it's a centre for the long-established farming community and for the alternative folk from nearby areas, although there's nothing like the cultural frontier mentality of Nimbin here.

West of Mullum in the Whian Whian State Forest, **Minyon Falls** drop 100 metres into a rainforest gorge. There are good walking tracks around the falls and you can get within a couple of minutes walk by conventional vehicle from Repentance Creek on one of the back roads between Mullum and Lismore. The eastern end of the historic Nightcap Track (see Around Nimbin) emerges at the north of Whian Whian State Forest.

Places to Stay & Eat

There are a couple of motels and, 12 km north, *Maca's Camping Ground* (☎ (066) 84 5211) is an idyllic place, under the lee of hills lush with rainforest. It's nothing like a commercial caravan park but the facilities are quite good, with a kitchen, hot showers and a laundry. It costs $4 per person and you can hire tents from $5 a day. To get here, take Main Arm Rd and follow the 'camping' signposts.

The *Popular Cafe* on Burringbar St is a popular place to hang out and *Buon Appetito* on Stuart St has inexpensive pasta (from $3.50) and pizzas to eat in or take away. *Mullum House* at 103 Stuart St has Chinese main courses under $10. The *Lane* is a licensed Thai restaurant down the lane next to the National Bank on Burringbar St. Most main courses are under $12.

Getting There & Away

Most Kirklands buses go through Mullum on their Lismore ($8.40) to Brisbane ($20.30) run. The newsagent at the corner of Burringbar and Stuart Sts is the Kirklands agent.

Mullum is on the Sydney ($70) to Murwillumbah railway line.

There are two road routes to Mullum from

the Pacific Highway: one turns off just south of Brunswick Heads, and the other is the longer but prettier Coolaman Scenic Drive, which leaves the highway north of Brunswick Heads near the Ocean Shores turn-off.

For a scenic drive to Uki and Mt Warning, head out to Upper Main Arm, pass Maca's Camping Ground and follow the unsealed road through the Nullum State Forest. Keep to the main road and watch for signposts at the few ambiguous intersections. Watch out for trucks and don't try it after rain or you stand a good chance of literally sliding off the mountain.

MT WARNING NATIONAL PARK

The dramatic peak of this 1156-metre-high mountain dominates the whole area. Mt Warning is solidified lava – the remains of the central vent of a volcano 20 million years old. Erosion has since carved out the deep Tweed and Oxley valleys around Mt Warning, but on the far sides of those valleys the outer flanks of the volcano remain as the Nightcap Range in the south and parts of the Border Ranges to the north. Mt Warning was named by Captain Cook as a landmark for avoiding Point Danger off Tweed Heads.

The road into the national park runs off the road between Murwillumbah and Uki. The car park at the start of the climb to the summit is about six km along this road. The walk to the summit from the car park is less than five km long, partly through rainforest, but the last section is steep (to put it mildly) so allow five hours for the round trip. Take water. If you're on the summit at dawn you'll be the first person on the Australian mainland to see the sun's rays that day! The trail is well marked but take a torch (flashlight), partly so you don't get lost and partly so you don't step on a snake.

Even if you don't want to climb Mt Warning it's worth visiting for the superb rainforest in this World Heritage area. There's a short walking track near the car park.

Places to Stay

You can't camp at Mt Warning but the *Wollumbin Wildlife Refuge & Caravan Park*

(☎ (066) 79 5120), on the Mt Warning approach road, has tent sites ($10), on-site vans (from $24) and cabins ($35). The vans and cabins cost less if you stay more than one night. There are kitchen facilities and a well-stocked kiosk – and lots of wildlife in the 120 hectare refuge.

There are several other places to stay around the bottom of Mt Warning, such as the *Village Guesthouse* (☎ (066) 79 5345) in Uki (B&B $55 for one or two people during the week, on weekends $55/75 s single/double) and *Mt Warning Forest Hideaway* (☎ (066) 79 7139), 12 km south-west of Uki on Byrrill Creek Rd (motel units with cooking facilities from $40/45 to $60/70).

Getting There & Away

A Fulton's (☎ (066) 21 6231) school bus runs from Murwillumbah to Uki, Nimbin and Lismore on weekdays. It passes the foot of the six-km Mt Warning approach road, with some services going in as far as the Wollumbin Wildlife Refuge. The hostels at Murwillumbah and Cabarita Beach organise trips to the mountain, and the Uki Village Guesthouse may have guided climbs for about $15.

BORDER RANGES NATIONAL PARK

The Border Ranges National Park covers the New South Wales side of the McPherson Range along the New South Wales-Queensland border and some of the range's outlying spurs. The Tweed Range Scenic Drive – gravel but usable in all weathers – loops through the park about 100 km from Lillian Rock (midway between Uki and Kyogle) to Wiangaree (north of Kyogle on the Woodenbong road). It's well worth the effort of finding this drive which goes through mountain forest most of the way, with some steep hills and really breathtaking lookouts over the Tweed Valley to Mt Warning and the coast. The adrenalin-charging walk out to the crag called **the Pinnacle** – about an hour from the road and back – is not for vertigo sufferers! The rainforest along **Brindle Creek** is also breathtaking, and there are several walks from the picnic area here.

There are a couple of camp sites, basic but free, on the Tweed Range Scenic Drive: Forest Tops, high on the range, and Sheepstation Creek, about six km further west and 15 km from the Wiangaree turn-off. There might be tank water but it's best to bring your own.

New England

New England is the area along the Great Dividing Range stretching north from around Newcastle to the Queensland border. It's a vast tableland of sheep and cattle country with many good bushwalking areas, photogenic scenery and, unlike much of Australia, four distinct seasons. If you're travelling up and down the eastern seaboard it's worth taking a longer route through an inland area like New England now and then, to get a glimpse of noncoastal Australia – which has a different way of life, is at least as scenic as the coast, and suffers from a great deal less tourist hype.

The New England Highway, running north from Newcastle to Warwick in Queensland, is an alternative to the Pacific Highway. Scenically the several roads climbing up the escarpment from the coast to New England are more spectacular than the tableland itself, where most of the forests have been cut down.

National Parks
The eastern side of the tableland tumbles over an escarpment to the coastal plains below, and along this edge is a string of fine national parks, some World Heritage areas. Gorges and waterfalls are a common feature.

Werrikimbe This is a large, rugged and spectacular park with remote-area gorge walking as well as gentler walks around the visitor areas. Access is on the Kangaroo Flat road, about 50 km east of Walcha off the road to Wauchope. The Armidale National Parks office (☎ (067) 73 7211) has information.

Oxley Wild Rivers A park in several sec-

tions, east of Armidale and Walcha, this park contains some of the best waterfalls and gorges. The **Wollomombi Falls**, 40 km east of Armidale, are the highest in Australia with a 457-metre drop; **Apsley Falls** are east of Walcha at the southern end of the park. Down on the bottom of the gorges is a wilderness area, accessible from Raspberry Rd which runs off the Wollomombi to Kempsey road. The Armidale National Parks office (☎ (067) 73 7211) has information.

New England & Cathedral Rock New England is a spectacular park with a wide range of ecosystems. There are 20 km of walking tracks and, at the bottom of the escarpment, a wilderness area. Access is from near Ebor and there are cabins and camp sites near the entrance. Book these through the Dorrigo National Parks office (☎ (066) 57 2309). Cathedral Rock is also near Ebor, off the Guy Fawkes to Guyra road. It's a small park with photogenic granite formations.

Dorrigo See the North Coast section.

Guy Fawkes River This is gorge country with canoeing and walking. **Ebor Falls**, near the village of Ebor on the road from Armidale to Dorrigo, are spectacular. Access to the park is from Hernani, 15 km north-east of Ebor. From here it's 30 km to the Chaelundi Rest Area, with camp sites and water. The Dorrigo National Parks office (☎ (066) 57 2309) has information.

Gibraltar Range & Washpool Dramatic, forested and wild, these parks lie south and north of the Gwydir Highway between Glen Innes and Grafton. Countrylink buses stop at the visitor centre (the start of a 10-km track to the Mulligans Hut camping area in Gibraltar Range) and at the entrance to Washpool (from where it's about three km to camping areas). The Glen Innes National Parks office (☎ (067) 32 5133) has information.

Bald Rock & Boonoo Boonoo Bald Rock is about 30 km north of Tenterfield on an unsealed (but deceptively smooth – take it easy) road which continues into Queensland. Not on the escarpment but in granite country, Bald Rock is a huge monolith which has been compared to Uluru. You can walk to the top and camp near the base. Nearby is Boonoo Boonoo, with a 200-metre-drop waterfall and basic camping.

Getting There & Away
Hazelton, Oxley and Eastern Australia are among the airlines serving New England.

Several bus lines run through New England from Melbourne or Sydney to Brisbane. Border Coaches (☎ toll-free 1800 028 937) is a local company doing the Sydney to Brisbane run. Lindsay's runs between Tamworth and Coffs Harbour ($33.30) via Armidale; Kirklands has a Lismore to Tenterfield service ($21.60). Batterhams Express (☎ toll-free 1800 043 339) runs between Sydney and Tamworth via the Hunter Valley. Trains run from Sydney to Armidale, from where Countrylink buses run up to Tenterfield.

TAMWORTH (population 35,000)
Spend much time driving the country roads of Australia and listening to a radio and you'll realise that country music has a big following. Tamworth is the country music centre of the nation, an antipodean Nashville. Each January there's a week-long country music festival culminating in the Australia Day weekend when the Australasian country music awards are handed out.

The information centre (☎ (067) 68 4462) is in CWA Park, near the corner of Kable Ave and Brisbane St. Pick up a map of the Heritage Walk or the longer Kamilaroi Walking Track which begins at the Oxley Scenic Lookout at the northern end of White St.

Country music memorabilia around town includes a collection of photos at the Good Companions Hotel, the **Hands of Fame** near the information centre and, at Tattersalls Hotel on Peel St, **Noses of Fame**!

The **Country Collection**, on the New England Highway in South Tamworth, is hard to miss – out the front is the 12-metre-high **Golden Guitar**. Inside is a wax museum ($4). Also here is the Longyard Hotel, a major venue during the festival. Recording studios, such as Big Wheel (☎ (067) 67 9499) and Hadley Records & Yeldah Music (☎ (067) 65 7813), can often be inspected by arrangement.

Places to Stay
During the country music festival most accommodation is full.

The *Paradise Caravan Park* (☎ (067) 66 3120) is by the river a few blocks east of the town centre at the corner of East and Peel Sts. Sites cost $10 and on-site vans from $25 a double.

The *Central Hotel* (☎ (067) 66 2160), on the corner of Peel and Brisbane Sts in the city centre, has singles/doubles for $20/32 or $30/38 with bathroom. Other city centre pubs include the *Good Companions* (☎ (067) 66 2850) on Brisbane St, the *Imperial* (☎ (067) 66 2613) on the corner of Brisbane and Marius Sts and the *Tamworth* (☎ (067) 66 2923) on Marius St.

Many motels are enormous but few are cheap. At slow times you might find some charging $40 or $45 but don't count on it.

Some way from Tamworth there's backpacker-style accommodation at *Echo Hills Station* (☎ toll-free 1800 810 243), a working farm. It costs $35 including meals plus an optional $25 for activities. There are also self-contained cottages.

TAMWORTH TO ARMIDALE
The timber town of **Walcha** (population 1800) is off the New England Highway on the eastern slope of the Great Dividing Range, on the winding and spectacular Oxley Highway route to the coast at Port Macquarie. East of the town is the Apsley Gorge with magnificent waterfalls; see the earlier National Parks section.

Back on the highway, the pretty town of **Uralla** (population 2300) is where bushranger Captain Thunderbolt was buried in 1870. Thunderbolt's Rock, by the highway seven km south of town, was one of his hide-outs. There are several craft shops and the big McCrossin's Mill Museum ($2). There's a fossicking area about five km north-west of Uralla on the Kingstown road. The hamlet of **Gostwyck**, a little piece of England, is 10 km south-east of Uralla.

ARMIDALE (population 22,000)

The main centre in the region and site of the University of New England, Armidale is a popular halting point. The 1000-metre altitude means it's pleasantly cool in summer and frosty (but often sunny) in winter. The town centre is attractive, with the Beardy St pedestrian mall and some well-kept old buildings.

The information centre (☎ (067) 73 8527) is just north of the city centre on the corner of Marsh and Dumaresq Sts, at the bus station. It has walking and driving tour brochures.

The **Armidale Folk Museum** is in the city centre on the corner of Faulkner and Rusden Sts and is open daily from 1 pm to 4 pm (admission by donation). The excellent **New England Regional Art Museum** ($5) is south of the centre on Kentucky St.

Saumarez Homestead, on the New England Highway between Armidale and Uralla, is a beautiful old house which still contains the effects of the rich pastoralists who built it.

The Armidale area is noted for its magnificent gorges, many of which contain impressive waterfalls when it rains enough. The **Wollomombi Falls** are 39 km east of Armidale and close to the Armidale to Kempsey road.

Places to Stay

The *Pembroke Caravan Park* (☎ (067) 72 6470) on Grafton Rd has sites from $11, on-site vans from $20/25 a single/double and cabins between $28/32 and $42/45. Grafton Rd is the eastwards continuation of Barney St and the caravan park is about 2.5 km from the bus station. The *Highlander Van Village* (☎ (067) 72 4768) on the New England Highway north of town charges similar prices.

Pembroke Caravan Park is also an associate-YHA hostel, with lots of bunk beds in one huge dorm (with partitions), costing $12.50. Families might be offered an en-suite cabin at YHA rates.

The *Wicklow Hotel* (☎ (067) 72 2421) ('the Pink Pub') is on the corner of Marsh and Dumaresq Sts, across from the bus station. Beds in shared rooms are $12, while singles/doubles start at $15/24. The rooms are unheated and small but they are clean. *Tattersalls Hotel* (☎ (067) 72 2247) is on the mall so it has little traffic noise. Rooms start at $22/34, more with attached bathroom.

There are more than 20 motels but about the only places with doubles for under $50 are *Rose Villa Motel* (☎ (067) 72 3872) which charges from $37/41, and *Armidale Motel* (☎ (067) 72 8122) which charges from $45/48. Both are on the New England Highway north of town.

Places to Eat

The central streets have a wide variety of eating places. *QC's* in Hanna's Arcade off the East Mall is a pleasant place with bacon & eggs from $7 and light meals through the day and some evenings. *Cafe Midalé* further along Beardy St has breakfast and light meals from $6. The nearby *IXL Cafeteria* has pasta from $4.

Tall Paul's on the corner of Marsh and Beardy Sts has roasts ($7.50), steaks ($10) and less expensive eats such as burgers (from $2.70) and pasta (from $4). Nearby on East Mall is *Jean-Pierre's BYO Cafe*, an odd combination of a country-town cafe and a French restaurant, with snacks and meals.

Chinese restaurants include *Mekong* on East Mall, which has weekday smorgasbord lunches for $6.50 and a smorgasbord dinner on Thursday for $8.50.

The *Beardy St Brasserie*, upstairs near Cafe Midalé, is open from 6 pm until late for dinner and supper, and sometimes for weekday lunches too. Focaccia costs from $7, pasta from $9 and main courses (including kangaroo steaks) are around $15.

Getting There & Away

Eastern Australia flies to Sydney ($179), Oxley flies to Brisbane ($180) and Hazelton flies to Melbourne ($360).

Countrylink, McCafferty's, Greyhound Pioneer and Border Coaches service Armidale, and Lindsay's runs down to Coffs Harbour and Port Macquarie, via Dorrigo. Fares from Armidale include Sydney $49, Brisbane $44, Tamworth $12.60, Glen Innes $9.90, Byron Bay $45, Dorrigo $11.90 and Coffs Harbour $18.30.

Trains run from Sydney.

Realistic Car Rentals (☎ (067) 72 8078) at Armidale Exhaust Centre on the corner of Rusden and Dangar Sts has cars from $45 a day, including insurance and 100 free km – you must be over 23 and you can't go more than 100 km from Armidale, which rules out trips to the coast.

Getting Around

The university sports union (☎ (067) 73 2783) hires 18-speed mountain bikes for $17 a day, $25 for two days or $35 for a week. They also organise cycling tours in the nearby national parks. Armidale Cycle Centre (☎ (067) 72 3718) at 248 Beardy St (near Allingham St) also hires bikes. A cycleway runs past the information centre out to the uni, about five km away.

NORTH OF ARMIDALE
Guyra

Guyra is at an altitude of 1300 metres, making it one of the highest towns in the state. There's a museum here, open only on Sunday afternoons, and a lagoon named **Mother of Ducks**, home to many birds. There are fine views from **Chandlers Peak** and, 12 km before Glen Innes, unusual 'balancing rocks' at **Stonehenge**.

Glen Innes (population 6200)

You're still at over 1000 metres at Glen Innes, which was a good place to meet bushrangers a century ago. The information centre (☎ (067) 32 2397) is on Church St and long-distance buses stop nearby.

The old hospital on the corner of Ferguson St and West Ave houses **Land of the Beardies**, a big folk museum open between 2 and 5 pm daily and also between 10 and 11 am on weekdays. Grey St, the main street, is worth strolling down for its old buildings. This area was settled by Scots and Glen Innes regards itself as the Celtic capital of New England – there are bilingual street signs and the impressive **Standing Stones** on a hill above town.

Glen Innes is still a centre for sapphire mining and you can fossick at Dunvegan Sapphire Reserve.

The **Australian Bush Music Festival** is held over the October long weekend and attracts about 100 artists; some are big names and an increasing number of them are Aboriginal. It's a fun weekend of singing, dancing and workshops. Some years a special train runs to Glen Innes from Sydney and you can travel in antique carriages with many of the performers. For more information contact the organisers (☎ (065) 32 1359).

Inverell (population 10,000)

Inverell is large country town with some impressive public buildings. The information centre (☎ (067) 22 1693) is in a converted water tower on Campbell St, a block back from the main shopping street. The **mining museum** is here too – Inverell is in a sapphire and silver mining area. **Inverell Pioneer Village** is open from 2 to 4 pm on Sunday and Monday, and from 10 am to 5 pm the rest of the week. Admission is $3.

You can tour the old Conrad and King Conrad silver mines at 9 am, noon and 3 pm, daily except Friday, for $5. Head south on the Bundarra road for 21 km, take the Lake Copeton turn-off and travel nine km to Wattle Grove (☎ (067) 23 3326), the reception area. There's a fossicking area nearby. The Smith Museum of Mining & Natural History is in nearby **Tingha**.

Tenterfield (population 3300)

At the junction of the New England and

Bruxner highways, Tenterfield is the last town of any size before the Queensland border. The information centre (☎ (067) 36 1082) is on Rouse St, the main street, at the corner of Miles St. The **Sir Henry Parkes Memorial School of Arts** is where Parkes launched the national federation movement in 1889.

Thunderbolt's Hideout, where bushranger Captain Thunderbolt did just that, is 11 km out of town. The main attractions in the area are the Bald Rock and Boonoo Boonoo national parks – see the earlier National Parks section. Across the border are several wineries in Queensland's granite belt.

Places to Stay *Tenterfield Lodge* (☎ (067) 36 1477) is a YHA-affiliated hostel/guesthouse at the western end of Manners St, near the old railway station. Shared rooms are $13 per person, while doubles are $30. You can camp for $10 and there are on-site vans from $22. The managers can help arrange farm stays in the area.

Several pubs have accommodation, such as the *Exchange Hotel* (☎ (067) 36 1054) on Rouse St with singles/doubles for $15/25.

South Coast

Though much less visited than the coast north of Sydney, the coast from Sydney to the Victorian border has many beautiful spots and excellent beaches, good surf and diving, some interesting little fishing towns and forests both lovely and spectacularly wild. The Snowy Mountains are 150 km inland from the southern part of the coast.

The Princes Highway runs along the coast from Sydney through Wollongong to the Victorian border. Although this is a longer and slower route to Melbourne than the Hume Highway, it's much more interesting.

South of Nowra the sandstone of the Sydney area gives way to granite and good soils, and the forests start to soar.

Getting There & Away
Hazelton flies to Merimbula from Sydney; Kendell flies to the area from Melbourne.

Greyhound Pioneer travels the Princes Highway route. Typical fares from Sydney include Bega $44 (eight hours), Narooma $38 (seven hours) and Batemans Bay $30 (six hours). Sapphire Coast Express (☎ (044) 73 5517) runs between Batemans Bay and Melbourne ($57) twice a week.

Pioneer Motor Service (a local company) runs buses between Eden and Sydney and for short hops between coastal towns is much cheaper than the big lines. There's also a service between Bega and Canberra. Countrylink also serves Bega, on the daily run between Eden and Canberra.

Murrays has daily buses from Canberra to Batemans Bay and south along the coast to Narooma. Their buses connect with northbound Pioneer Motor Service buses at Batemans Bay.

The railway from Sydney goes as far south as Bomaderry (Nowra).

WOLLONGONG (population 214,000)
Only 80 km south of Sydney is the state's third largest city, an industrial centre which includes the biggest steelworks in Australia at Port Kembla. Wollongong also has some superb surf beaches, and the hills soar up behind, giving a fine backdrop, great views over the city and coast, and good walks.

The name Illawarra is often applied to Wollongong and its surrounds – it refers specifically to the hills behind the city (the Illawarra Escarpment) and the coastal Lake Illawarra to the south.

Orientation & Information
The Crown St pedestrian mall is in the centre of town. Through traffic bypasses the city on the Southern Freeway.

Just east of the mall, the information centre (☎ (042) 28 0300) on the corner of Crown and Kembla Sts is open daily.

The post office is at 296-98 Crown St near the railway station, but you might find the Wollongong East post office, near the tourist

NEW SOUTH WALES

PLACES TO STAY
4 Novotel Hotel
16 Keiraleagh House
32 Piccadilly Motor Inn
33 Tattersalls Hotel

PLACES TO EAT
1 Lagoon & Kiosk
5 North Beach Gourmet
6 Jodie's
7 Beach House Restaurant
8 Ocean View Chinese
Restaurant
17 Market Street Bistro

18 Cafe on the Mall
& Terrace Cafe
19 Pot of Gold & Frenchies
20 Il Faro
22 Tannous
23 Thai Carnation
25 Lorenzo's
30 Plant Room
36 Angelo's Trattoria
37 Som Chay

OTHER
2 Stuart Park
3 Wollongong North
Railway Station
9 Swimming Pool

10 Old Lighthouse
11 Belmore Basin
12 Fishing Co-op
13 New Lighthouse
14 Bus Station
15 Church of England
Cathedral
21 Harp Hotel
24 Museum
26 Information Office
27 City Gallery
28 Oxford Tavern
29 City Bus Terminal
31 Post Office
34 Wollongong Railway
Station & Countrylink
35 Bushcraft

Wollongong

0   250   500 m

*TASMAN
SEA*

To Corrimal, Bulli
& Sydney

Fairy   Creek

Gipps

Throsby

To Kiama
& Nowra

Harbour

McCabe
Park

To Port Kembla
(8 km)

information centre, more convenient. Bushcraft on Stewart St has hiking and camping gear.

Things to See

Wollongong has an interesting harbour, with the fishing fleet based in the southern part called **Belmore Basin**, which was cut from solid rock in 1868. There's a fish market, a couple of fish restaurants and an 1872 lighthouse on the point. The **old lighthouse** is open weekends from midday to 4 pm (1 pm to 5 pm during daylight saving).

North Beach, north of the harbour, generally has better surf than the south beach. The harbour itself has beaches which are good for children. Other beaches run north up the coast.

The interesting **City Gallery** on the corner of Kembla and Burelli Sts is open from Tuesday to Friday and weekend afternoons. The Illawarra Historical Society's **museum** on Market St is open Wednesday from 10 am to 1 pm and weekend afternoons ($2). The museum includes a reconstruction of the 1902 Mt Kembla village mining disaster. Port Kembla's industrial area has been renamed **Australia's Industry World** – it sounds like a theme park!

Places to Stay

You have to go a little way out before you can camp. There are council-run camping areas on the beach at Corrimal (☎ (042) 85 5688), near the beach on Farrell Rd in Bulli (☎ (042) 85 5677) and on Fern St in Windang (☎ (042) 97 3166), with beach and lake frontage. Bulli is 11 km north, Corrimal about halfway there and Windang is 15 km south, between Lake Illawarra and the sea. All charge about $12 for camp sites (two people) and from $40 for vans or cabins, with prices rising sharply during school and Christmas holidays.

Keiraleagh House (☎ (042) 28 6765) is at 60 Kembla St, north of Market St. It's a large place catering mainly to long-term students but they will let you have a bed for $15 a night if there's room. *Piccadilly Motor Inn* (☎ (042) 26 4555) next to the railway station

has a few units available to backpackers at $20 per person sharing. Several hotels have fairly cheap accommodation such as *Tattersalls Hotel* (☎ (042) 29 1952) at 333 Crown St, just along from the station, charging $25/40/50 for singles/doubles/triples.

About the only inexpensive motel in the area is the *Cabbage Tree Motel* (☎ (042) 84 4000) at 1 Anama St (behind the Cabbage Tree Hotel) in Fairy Meadow, off the Princes Highway 3.5 km north of the city centre. Singles/doubles cost from $30/35 to $40/45. Most buses heading north from the railway station go to Fairy Meadow.

Places to Eat

For good coffee, snacks and meals it's hard to go past *Tannous*, a Lebanese cafe on Crown St at the corner of Corrimal St. Various shish kebabs, felafel and other takeaways are $3, or $5 if you eat in. Eat-in meals come with large serves of hummus, tabouli and bread. There's also a good selection of cakes and sweets.

There are plenty of other places in the area. The *Cafe on the Mall* and the *Terrace* at the corner of Church St are open long hours for snacks and meals. *Lorenzo's* on the mall near Kembla St is a highly rated restaurant with an interesting Italian-inspired menu; main courses are around $15. Nearby in Kembla St there's the Mexican *Pot of Gold* and across the street there's *Il Faro*, which serves pizzas.

Angelo's Trattoria at the International Centre, 28 Stewart St, between Kembla and Corrimal Sts, serves moderately priced Italian food plus steaks and seafood. It's popular with the local Italian community and is open for lunch and dinner daily.

The *Plant Room* on Crown St opposite the corner of Gladstone Ave, just up the hill from the railway station, opens during the day for coffee and snacks and at night for meals; main courses are around $12. It has a relaxed atmosphere and a cosmopolitan menu.

On Bourke St at North Beach, both *Jodie's* and *North Beach Gourmet* have breakfast and light meals. Further north, the *Lagoon* (☎ (042) 26 1766), in Stuart Park behind

North Beach, has a great location and is open daily for lunch and dinner, and for breakfast on Sunday. The adjacent *kiosk* is less expensive.

Entertainment
Young bands play at the *Harp* on Corrimal St and the *Oxford Tavern* nearby on Crown St. There are many clubs and pubs with live entertainment scattered throughout the area.

Getting There & Away
Bus The bus station (☎ (042) 26 1022) is on the corner of Keira and Campbell Sts. Several daily services run to Sydney ($15, sometimes much less) and one to Canberra ($28) via the southern highlands. Greyhound Pioneer's Sydney to Melbourne ($58) coastal route runs through Wollongong and direct buses to Brisbane cost $75. Pioneer Motor Service (a Nowra company) runs down to Eden ($47).

Train Many electric trains run to and from Sydney (about 80 minutes, $8.60, off-peak day-return $10.60) and a fair number continue south to Kiama, Gerringong and Bomaderry (Nowra). On weekends a tourist train runs to Moss Vale ($5), inland near the Hume Highway and Morton National Park.

Getting Around
The city bus terminal is in Crown St where it meets Marine Drive. By rail you can reach a lot of Wollongong, including some beaches, and the trains are fairly frequent. A cycle path runs from the city centre north to Bulli and south to Port Kembla and you can hire bikes in Stuart Park behind North Beach.

AROUND WOLLONGONG
The hills rise suddenly and dramatically behind Wollongong and there are walking tracks and lookouts on Mt Kembla and Mt Keira less than 10 km from the city centre, but no buses go up there. You get spectacular views over the town and coast from the **Bulli Pass** ('bull-eye') on the Princes Highway, just north of Wollongong.

The country is equally spectacular to the south if you head inland through the **Macquarie Pass National Park** to Moss Vale or through the Kangaroo Valley. The Fitzroy Falls and other attractions of mountainous **Morton National Park** can be reached by either route.

Up the coast there are several excellent beaches. Those with good surf include **Sandon Point**, **Austinmer**, **Headlands** (only for experienced surfers) and **Sharkies**.

On the road to Otford and Royal National Park, the **Lawrence Hargrave Lookout** at Bald Hill above Stanwell Park is superb for cliff-top viewing. Hargrave, a pioneer aviator, made his first attempts at flying in the area early this century. Hang-gliders fly there today and Aerial Technics (☎ (042) 94 2545) has courses. Just south of Wollongong, **Lake Illawarra** is popular for water sports.

WOLLONGONG TO NOWRA
South of Lake Illawarra, **Shellharbour** is a popular holiday resort. It's one of the oldest towns along the coast and back in 1830 was a thriving port, but it declined after the coming of the railway. There are good beaches on the Windang Peninsula north of the town.

Kiama is a pretty little seaside town famous for its blowhole: it can spout up to 60 metres high and is illuminated at night. It also has a maritime museum, good beaches and surf, and the scenic Cathedral Rock at Jones Beach.

Just south of Kiama, **Gerringong** has fine beaches and surf. Pioneer aviator Charles Kingsford Smith took off from Seven Mile Beach, immediately south of Gerringong and now a national park, to fly to New Zealand in 1933. *Chittick Lodge* is an associate-YHA hostel (☎ (042) 34 1249) on Bridges Rd, five minutes walk back up the hill from Werri Beach. Beds are $11 for members.

The village of **Berry** was an early settlement, and today it has a number of National-Trust-classified buildings, a museum and many antique and craft shops. The *Hotel Berry* (☎ (044) 64 1011) is a very pleasant pub charging $30/40/50 a single/double/triple. You'll probably have to book on weekends. Next door in an impressive building is the excellent *Bunyip Inn Guesthouse* (☎ (044) 64 2064), which charges from $90 a double. Some rooms share bathrooms. There are very scenic roads from Berry to pretty **Kangaroo Valley**, where there are more galleries and craft shops, and canoeing.

Coolangatta (no, not the Queensland Coolangatta) has a group of buildings (now a motel and theatre-restaurant) which were constructed by convicts in 1822. The town is also the home of Bigfoot (☎ (044) 48 7131), a strange vehicle which will carry you to the top of Mt Coolangatta for $10 ($5 children).

SHOALHAVEN

The coastal strip south of Gerringong down to Durras Lake, just north of Batemans Bay, is a popular holiday destination known as Shoalhaven, which also stretches up to 50 km inland to include the Morton and Budawang national parks. Inland on Shoalhaven River, the twin towns of **Nowra** and **Bomaderry** form the main population centre. The region is popular for water sports, and white-water rafting is available – phone the information centre (☎ (044) 21 0778, toll-free 1800 024 261), situated on the highway in Bomaderry. There's a National Parks office (☎ (044) 23 9800) at 24 Berry St in Nowra.

Nowra Animal Park (☎ (044) 21 3949), on the northern bank of the Shoalhaven River upstream from Nowra, is a pleasant place to meet some Australian animals and you can camp in bushland here for $9, rising to $14 at peak times. The *Barracks* (☎ (044) 23 0495) is an associate-YHA hostel in Bomaderry, near the railway station. It's a friendly, well-run place in a solid building that once housed railway workers. Dorm beds cost $12 and twin rooms are $16 per person. The managers can pick you up from the Nowra bus stop. They also run the Bushmobile, a big purpose-built 6WD vehicle that goes just about anywhere.

Inland, beyond Kangaroo Valley, Fitzroy Falls is the visitor centre for **Morton**

National Park (☎ (048) 87 7270) with many walks. South of Morton the line of mountain national parks (Budawang, Deua and Wadbilliga) stretches south to the Victorian border. They protect some outstanding wilderness areas which are good for rugged bushwalking.

South of Nowra, **Jervis Bay** is becoming suburban but **Huskisson**, one of the oldest towns on the bay, is still a nice place. The Museum of Jervis Bay, Science & the Sea is by the bay just on the Nowra side of Huskisson, and also here is Timbey's Aboriginal Arts & Crafts which sells works by the local Aboriginal community. The museum is open Tuesday to Friday afternoon and on weekends, and admission is $2; the rest of the complex is open daily. The *Lodge* (☎ (044) 41 5019) on the main street has dorm beds for $15, and there are also private rooms.

Jervis Bay National Park takes up the south-eastern spit of land on Jervis Bay. It's an interesting park with good swimming, surfing and diving on bay and ocean beaches. There are camp sites at Caves Beach ($8 to $10), where there's surf, and elsewhere – you have to book (☎ (044) 43 0977). Entry to the park costs $5 per car for a week.

Ulladulla is in an area of beautiful lakes, lagoons and beaches. There's good swimming and surfing in the area (try Mollymook beach, just north of town) or you can make the bushwalk to the top of Pigeon House Mountain (719 metres) in the impressive Budawang Range. The mountain is in the south-east of Morton National Park.

South Coast Backpackers (☎ (044) 54 0500) is in Ulladulla at 67 Princes Highway, towards the top of the hill to the north of the shopping centre. It's a small, clean place with spacious five-bed dorms and all the usual facilities. Beds cost $12.50 a night. They'll take guests to Murramarang National Park or the Pigeonhouse for $10.

Fares from Ulladulla with Pioneer Motor Service include Sydney, $12; Nowra, $11.40; Merry Beach (at the northern end of Murramarang National Park), $5.50; the North Durras turn-off at East Lynne (for Pebbly Beach in Murramarang National

Park), $6.50; Batemans Bay, $8.80; and Eden, $29.20.

Murramarang National Park is a beautiful coastal park running from about 20 km south of Ulladulla all the way south to Batemans Bay. The National Parks camp site (☎ (044) 78 6006) is at lovely Pebbly Beach and costs $10 a double (plus the $7.50 per car entry fee). A kiosk operates during school holidays – when tent sites are scarce. You should book in summer. Pebbly Beach is about 10 km off the highway and there's no public transport.

There is accommodation at settlements within the park. At **Depot Beach** the basic *Moore's Caravan Park* (☎ (044) 78 6010) has tent sites for $4 plus $3 per person and a range of on-site vans, cabins and flats from about $400 per week in summer or from $45 a night in the off season. As well as the superb beach, **North Durras** is on the inlet to Durras Lake. *Durras Lake North Caravan Park* (☎ (044) 78 6072) often has an on-site van set aside for backpackers ($8 per person) – ask at the shop.

BATEMANS BAY TO BEGA

The fishing port of **Batemans Bay** has become one of the south coast's largest holiday centres. The visitor centre (☎ toll-free 1800 802 528) is on the highway near the town centre. The *Bay View Hotel* (☎ (044) 72 4522) on Orient St in the town centre has pub rooms for $20/30. Buses run west to Canberra ($22), north to Sydney ($30) and south to Melbourne ($57).

About 80 km inland from Batemans Bay on the very scenic road to Canberra is **Braidwood**, with its many old buildings and thriving arts and crafts. From here there's road access to the superb rugged bushwalking country of the Budawang Range.

Moruya is a dairy centre but oyster farming is carried on too. There's some fairly unspoiled coast down the side roads south of Moruya, with a good camp site ($8 per vehicle, more in summer) at **Congo**, where there are beaches on both sides of a headland. Bring your own supplies and you'll need to boil drinking water.

Narooma is another oyster town, popular for seaside holidays and serious sport fishing. There are many inlets and lakes nearby. The information centre (☎ (044) 76 2881) is on the beachfront and the National Parks office (☎ (044) 76 2888) is nearby. About 10 km offshore is **Montague Island**, a nature reserve with a historic lighthouse and many seals and fairy penguins. Several times each week there's a tour of the island conducted by National Parks rangers ($40). The clear waters around the island are popular with divers.

Central Tilba, off the highway 15 km south of Narooma, is a little wooden town which has undergone little change this century. There are several craft workshops and a cheese factory which gives tastings. The village perches on the side of **Mt Dromedary** (800 metres) and you can walk to the top from the nearby village of **Tilba Tilba**. The return walk of 11 km takes about five hours, or alternatively you could ride up with Mt Dromedary Trail Rides (☎ (044) 76 3376).

South of the coastal **Wallaga Lake National Park** and off the Princes Highway, **Bermagui** is a fishing centre made famous 50 years ago by American cowboy-novelist Zane Grey. It's a handy base for visits to both Wallaga Lake and Mimosa Rocks national parks, and for Wadbilliga National Park, inland in the ranges. The information centre (☎ (064) 93 4174) is on Coluga St, the continuation of the main road north of the bridge. *Blue Pacific Flats* (☎ (064) 93 4921) at 77 Murrah St has backpacker accommodation for $12 a bed as well as regular holiday flats. It's uphill from the road running along the beach north of the town centre. The turn-off is signposted, just north of the fishing-boat wharf. Bega Valley Coaches (☎ (064) 92 2418) has a weekday service between Bermagui and Bega ($9.90) and a feeder service connects with Pioneer Motor Service's bus north to Nowra.

The largely unsealed road between Bermagui and Tathra is more interesting than the highway, running through the excellent **Mimosa Rocks National Park**. You can camp at Gillards Beach and Araunnu Beach ($5) but bring your own water.

Inland and on the Princes Highway is **Cobargo**, another unspoilt old town. The main 2WD access to **Wadbilliga National Park** is near here. It's a rugged park and the many species of animals live in surroundings which haven't changed much in thousands of years.

Bega is a sizable town near the junction of the Princes and Snowy Mountains highways. The information centre (☎ (064) 92 2045) is in Gipps St near the corner of Carp St, in a craft shop. The *Bega YHA Hostel* (☎ (064) 92 3103) is a modern mud-brick building on Kirkland Crescent (off Kirkland Ave, which is off the highway about a km west of the town centre). It's a friendly place which charges $12 a night. Countrylink's Eden to Canberra service passes through Bega daily. Pioneer Motor Service runs from Bega to Sydney. Greyhound Pioneer passes through on the coastal run between Sydney and Melbourne, as does Sapphire Coast Express on the run between Batemans Bay and Melbourne.

SOUTH TO THE VICTORIAN BORDER

The coast here is quite undeveloped, and there are many good beaches and some awe-inspiring forests full of wildlife – and loggers.

Merimbula

Merimbula is a big resort with a good 'lake' (a large inlet) and ocean beaches. Despite large-scale development the setting remains beautiful and nearby **Pambula** remains a quiet town.

The Merimbula information centre (☎ (064) 95 1129) is on the waterfront at the bottom of Market St. Around at the wharf on the eastern point there's a small **aquarium** ($5).

The *South Haven Caravan Park* (☎ (064) 95 1304) is across the bridge from the main part of town, near the surf beach. The *Merimbula Divers Lodge* (☎ (064) 95 3611) at 15 Park St, a short walk from the information centre, often has backpackers' beds in a self-contained unit for $20 per person. A new YHA hostel, *Wandarrah Lodge*, is being built at 18 Marine Parade.

Eden

At Eden the road bends away from the coast into Victoria, running through more mighty forests. The town is an old whaling port on Twofold Bay, much less touristy than towns further up the coast. The information centre (☎ (064) 96 1953) is open weekdays and weekend mornings.

There's a very intriguing **Killer Whale Museum** where you can learn about the whaler who, in 1891, was swallowed by a whale and regurgitated, unharmed, 15 hours later. Well, almost unharmed. His hair turned white and fell out due to the whale's digestive juices. There's also the skeleton of a killer whale, Old Tom, which lead a pack of other killer whales in herding baleen whales into Twofold Bay where they were killed by the whalers. The museum is open from 10.15 am to 3.45 pm on weekdays and 11.15 am to 3.45 pm on weekends. Admission is $3.

Whales still swim along the coast in October and November. Cat Balou Cruises has whale-spotting cruises from $15. Book at the information centre.

The *Australasia Hotel* (☎ (064) 96 1600) on Imlay St has backpackers' beds for $11 and singles/doubles from $15/25.

Boydtown

Boydtown, south of Eden, was founded by Benjamin Boyd – a flamboyant early settler whose land-holdings were once second only in size to the Crown's. His grandiose plans included making Boydtown the capital of Australia but his fortune foundered and so did the town – later he did too, disappearing without trace somewhere in the Pacific. Some of his buildings still stand, and the Sea Horse Inn, built by convict labour, is still in use today. You can camp nearby for $10.

Ben Boyd National Park

To the north and south of Eden is the Ben Boyd National Park – good for walking, camping, swimming and surfing, especially at Long Beach in the north.

Nadgee Nature Reserve continues down the coast from Ben Boyd National Park but it's much less accessible. **Wonboyn**, a small settlement on Wonboyn Lake at the northern end of the reserve, has a store and *Wonboyn Cabins & Caravan Park* (☎ (064) 96 9131).

Across the lake from Wonboyn but accessed from the road into Ben Boyd National Park is *Wonboyn Lake Resort* (☎ (064) 96 9162), with self-contained cabins from around $55 for four people.

Snowy Mountains

The first people to ski in Australia were the fur hunters of Tasmania in the 1830s, using three-foot boards. Norwegian miners introduced skiing in Kiandra in the 1860s, where the world's first ski races were held. The skis in those days were crude objects and the method of braking was a pole held between the two skis. Early this century the development of the sport began with lodges like the one at Charlotte Pass and the importing of European skis.

The snowfields straddle the New South Wales-Victoria border. Mt Kosciusko (pronounced 'kozzyosko' and named after a Polish hero of the American War of Independence) is in New South Wales and, at 2228 metres, its summit is Australia's highest. Much of the state's Snowies are within the Kosciusko National Park, an area of year-round interest: skiing in winter, bushwalking and vivid wildflowers in summer. The main ski resorts and the highest country are in the south-centre of the park, west of Jindabyne. Thredbo and the Perisher Valley and Smiggin Holes area are the main downhill skiing areas. Charlotte Pass, Guthega and Mt Blue Cow are smaller downhill areas, as is Mt Selwyn, towards the northern end of the park.

The upper waters of the Murray River form both the state and national park boundaries in the south-west. The Snowy, another of Australia's best-known rivers, made famous by Banjo Paterson's poem 'The Man from Snowy River' and the film based on it, rises just below the summit of Mt Kosciusko. The Murrumbidgee also rises in the national park.

You can take white-water rafting trips on the Murray and Snowy rivers in summer when the water is high enough. In summer, horse trail riding is also popular and there are stables near Cooma, Adaminaby, Jindabyne, Tumut and Tumbarumba.

Snowy Mountains Hydroelectric Scheme

This huge project, taking over 25 years, was largely built in mountainous terrain which had barely been explored, much less settled. One obstacle the scheme didn't face was environmental concerns – it was begun in the '50s, a time when the creation of 16 major dams was seen as an advance of civilisation rather the drowning of a wilderness.

Two power stations are open to visitors: Murray 1 near Khancoban (tours at 10 am,

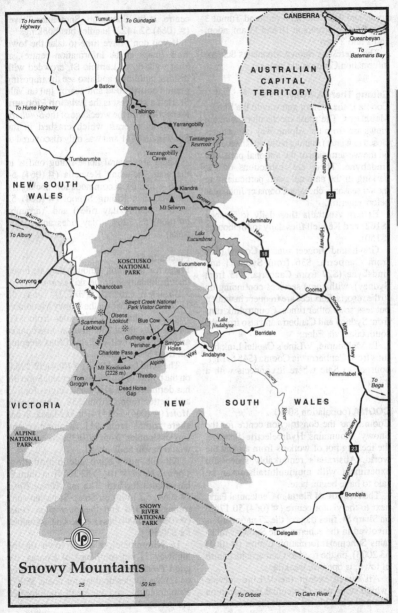

Snowy Mountains

0   25   50 km

noon, and 1.30 and 2.30 pm) and Tumut 3 near Talbingo (tours at 10 and 11 am, noon, and 1 and 2 pm).

The interesting Snowy Mountains Scheme Information Centre is in Cooma.

Getting There & Away

Cooma is the eastern gateway to the Snowy Mountains. The most spectacular mountain views are from the Alpine Way (sometimes closed in winter) running between Khancoban, on the western side of the national park, and Jindabyne. There are restrictions on car parking in the national park, particularly in the ski season – check at Cooma or Jindabyne before entering.

Eastern Australia flies daily to Sydney ($162) and Kendell flies daily to Melbourne ($150).

Greyhound Pioneer runs to Cooma ($14 from Canberra, $36 from Sydney) and Jindabyne ($27 from Canberra, $45 from Sydney), with some services continuing on to the resorts. Services are frequent in winter, but less so at other times. Countrylink runs from Sydney and Canberra and also from the south coast via Eden.

To Melbourne, V/Line's Capital Link bus runs from Canberra via Cooma ($45 to Melbourne) to Sale where it connects with a train.

COOMA (population 8000)

Cooma was the construction centre for the Snowy Mountains Hydroelectric Scheme, the melting pot of workers from around the world. Australia's remarkably successful experiment with multiculturalism can be said to have begun here.

The **Avenue of Flags** in Centennial Park, next to the visitor centre (☎ (064) 50 1742) on Sharp St, flies flags of the 27 nationalities involved in the scheme. The Snowy Mountains Scheme Information Centre (☎ (064) 53 2003), on the road to Canberra just north of town, is open on weekdays.

All buses except the V/Line service (which stops near Centennial Park) stop on Sharp St a few blocks east of the information centre, at the Snowstop. Snowliner Travel (☎ (064) 52 1422) handles bus bookings.

If you don't have time to take the town walk (maps at the information centre), at least walk down **Lambie St**, crowded with historic buildings, and also see the imposing granite **courthouse** and nearby **jail** on Vale St. Half a km west is the **Aviation Pioneers Memorial** with the wreckage of the *Southern Cloud*, an aircraft which crashed in the Snowies in 1931 and was only discovered in 1958.

There are several horse-riding outfits in the area, including Reynella (☎ (064) 54 2386 – mainly accommodation packages), the Magellan Riding School (☎ (064) 52 1110 – mainly day rides) and Yarramba (☎ (064) 53 7204 – day rides and longer treks).

Places to Stay

Prices rise in winter, although they are lower than in Jindabyne or the ski resorts.

Snowtels Caravan Park (☎ (064) 52 1828) is a big place on the Snowy Mountains Highway (Sharp St) with sites from $11, on-site vans about $30 (you can hire doonas and linen) and self-contained flats sleeping six from $50 a double.

The *Bunkhouse Motel* (☎ (064) 52 2983) on the corner of Commissioner and Soho Sts has dorm beds for $15, small singles for $25 and better rooms from $38. The *Family Motel* (☎ (064) 52 1414) at 32 Massie St has share rooms from $11 in summer and singles/doubles from $20/30. In winter it would pay to book ahead.

All the pubs have accommodation. *Coffey's Hotel* (☎ (064) 52 2064) on Short St has singles for $15. The big *Alpine Hotel* (☎ (064) 52 1466) on Sharp St has en-suite rooms for $50 and the *Australian Hotel* (☎ (064) 52 1844) has en-suite singles/doubles for $30/50.

In Nimmitabel, a small town on the highway 37 km south-east of Cooma, the good *Royal Arms* guesthouse (☎ (064) 54 6422) has singles/doubles for about $50/75 a single/double and one small room for $20 per person.

NEW SOUTH WALES

JINDABYNE (population 1800)

Fifty-six km west of Cooma and a step nearer the mountains, Jindabyne is a new town on the shore of the artificial Lake Jindabyne which covers the old town. In summer you can swim or rent boats. The information centre (☎ (064) 56 2444) is helpful. Paddy Pallin (☎ (064) 56 2922) is one of several companies running adventure activities in the Snowies.

Wombat

Places to Stay

Winter sees a huge influx of visitors; prices soar and overnight accommodation all but disappears.

The *Lake Jindabyne Caravan Park* (☎ (064) 56 2249) is in town by the lake. Sites cost $12 and on-site vans cost from $35 (two-berth) to $75 (eight-berth) in winter, from $30 to $50 at other times. In winter only there are basic rooms for $30 a double plus $5 for each extra person (up to six). The *Snowline Caravan Park* (☎ (064) 52 2099) is better equipped and has tent sites from $12 plus $3 per person, and cabins from $35 a double. Prices rise in the winter. Snowline is at the intersection of the Alpine Way and the Kosciusko road.

There's a fair range of motel-style places, some converting to longer-term accommodation in winter. *Aspen Chalet* (☎ (064) 56 2372), next to the information centre at 1 Kosciusko Rd, has doubles from $50 in summer and $130 in the peak season, which is pretty cheap for this town. *Lakeview Plaza Lodge* (☎ (064) 56 2134) on Snowy River Ave charges $50 a double in summer and up to $160 in winter.

Apartments & Lodges Many places offer ski-season accommodation but they fill up – book months in advance if possible. Letting agents include Jindabyne Reservation Centre (☎ toll-free 1800 026 356) and Jindabyne Real Estate (☎ toll-free 1800 020 657). Very approximately, apartments sleeping six cost from around $300 a week in the off season and $900 a week in the high winter season.

KOSCIUSKO NATIONAL PARK

The 6900 sq km of the state's largest national park includes caves, glacial lakes, forest and all of the state's ski resorts as well as the highest mountain in Australia. Most famous for its snow, it's also popular in summer when there are excellent bushwalks and marvellous alpine wildflowers. Outside the snow season you can drive to within eight km of the top of Mt Kosciusko, up the Kosciusko road from Jindabyne to Charlotte Pass. There are other walking trails from Charlotte Pass, including the 20-km lakes walk which includes Blue, Albina and Club lakes.

Mt Kosciusko and the main ski resorts are in the south-centre of the park. From Jindabyne the Kosciusko road leads to the National Parks visitor centre (☎ (064) 56 2102), about 15 km north-west at **Sawpit Creek**, then on to Smiggin Holes, Perisher Valley (33 km) and Charlotte Pass, with a turn-off before Perisher Valley to Guthega. The Alpine Way also runs from Jindabyne, to Thredbo (35 km from Jindabyne) and around to Khancoban on the south-western side of the mountains.

Entry to the national park (and that includes all the ski resorts) costs $12 per car, *per day*. This makes the $60 annual pass (unlimited entry to all parks in the state) seem like a very good idea. Motorbikes pay $3.50 and bus passengers $4 (usually included in the bus fare).

The CMA's useful *Snowy Kosciusko* map ($4.95) includes maps of the resorts.

Places to Stay

Bush camping is permitted in most of the park but not in ecologically fragile areas. *Kosciusko Mountain Retreat* (☎ (064) 56 2224) is just up the road from the Sawpit Creek visitor centre. It's a pleasant place in bushland with tent sites (about $7 plus $5 per person) and cabins (from $40 plus $5 per person, no overnights in the ski season or around Christmas).

There is plenty of accommodation at the ski resorts, some very cheap in summer, and there is a YHA hostel at Thredbo – see the following sections.

Getting There & Away

Greyhound Pioneer is the main carrier in this area. In winter there are plenty of services from Sydney and Canberra to Cooma and Jindabyne, from where shuttles run to the resorts. It costs $11 ($18 return) from Jindabyne to Smiggins, Perisher (45 minutes) or Thredbo (an hour). In summer buses run to Thredbo ($32 from Canberra), but not always daily.

In winter you can normally drive as far as Perisher Valley but snow chains must be carried and fitted when directed. The simplest and safest way to get to Perisher and Smiggins in winter is to take the Skitube, a tunnel railway up to Perisher Valley and Blue Cow from below the snowline at Bullocks Flat on the Alpine Way. A return trip from Bullocks Flat to either Blue Cow or Perisher costs $16 and there are deals on combined Skitube and lift tickets. You can hire skis and equipment at Bullocks Flat, and luggage lockers and overnight parking are also available. The Skitube runs a reduced timetable in summer.

SKIING & SKI RESORTS

Snow skiing in Australia can be a marginal activity. The season is short (July, August and early September is really all there is) and good snow is by no means a safe bet. Nor are the mountains ideal for downhill skiing – their gently rounded shapes mean that most long runs are relatively easy and the harder runs tend to be short and sharp. Worse, the short seasons mean the operators have to get their returns quickly and costs can be high.

Having told you the bad, here's the good: when the snow's there and the sun's shining, the skiing can be just fine. You will find all the fun (not to mention heart-in-the-mouth fear) you could ask for. Further, the open slopes of the Australian alps are a ski-tourer's paradise – nordic (cross-country or langlauf) skiing is becoming increasingly popular and most resorts now offer lessons and hire equipment.

The national park includes some of the most famous trails – Kiandra to Kosciusko, the Grey Mare Range, Thredbo or Charlotte Pass to Kosciusko's summit and the Jagungal wilderness. The possibilities for nordic touring are endless, and often old cattle-herders' huts are the only form of accommodation apart from your own tent.

In addition to touring, there is ample scope for cross-country racing (classic or skating) in the Perisher Valley. On the steep slopes of the Main Range near Twynam and Carruthers the cross-country downhill (XCD) fanatics get their adrenalin rushes. In winter, the cliffs near Blue Lake become a practice ground for alpine climbers.

The cheapest (and by far the most fun) way to get out on the slopes is to gather a bunch of friends and rent a lodge or an apartment. Costs vary enormously but can be within the bounds of reason. Bring as much food and drink as you can, as supplies in the resorts are expensive. Many agents (including most travel agents) book accommodation and packages on the snowfields. Specialists include the Jindabyne Reservation Centre (☎ toll-free 1800 026 331), the Perisher Reservation Centre (☎ toll-free 1800 020 700) and the Thredbo Resort Centre (☎ (064) 57 6360). The New South Wales Government Travel Centres in Sydney (☎ (02) 231 4444) and other capital cities also make bookings.

Accommodation is cheaper in towns like Jindabyne, and particularly in Cooma, which is some distance below the snow line. Buses shuttle from Jindabyne and Cooma to the resorts in the morning and back again in the afternoon.

Lift charges vary – see the following information on the various resorts. Class lessons cost from $25 or can be included in a package with lift tickets from about $50 a day, but much less for five days. Boots, skis and stocks can be hired for around $30 a day, but less for longer and less off the mountain. It's a trade-off whether to hire in the city and risk adjustment problems or at the resort and possibly pay more. There are hire places in towns close to the resorts and many garages hire ski equipment as well as chains. Snow chains must be carried in the mountains during winter even if there is no snow – there are heavy penalties if you haven't got them.

Australian ski resorts are short of the frenetic nightlife of many European resorts, but compensate with lots of partying among the lodges. Nor is there a great variety of alternative activities apart from toboggan runs. Weekends are crowded because the resorts are so convenient, particularly to Canberra.

For snow and road reports ring the various visitor centres. In Sydney there's a recorded service (☎ 11 539). Thredbo has its own number (☎ 0055 34320).

Thredbo (1370 metres)

Thredbo has the longest runs (the longest is over three km through 670 metres of vertical drop) and the best and most expensive skiing in Australia. A day ticket costs $52, a five-day pass $240 and a five-day lift and lesson package costs $295.

In summer Thredbo is still a good place to visit, unlike the other resorts which become ghost towns. It's a popular bushwalking centre with all sorts of excellent and scenic tracks. The chair lift to the top of Mt Crackenback runs right through the summer ($11 one way, $13 return). From the top of the chair lift it's a two-km walk or cross-country ski to a good lookout point over Mt Kosciusko, or seven km to the top of the mountain itself. Remember to carry adequate clothing and be prepared for all conditions, even in summer.

Places to Stay The *Thredbo YHA Lodge* (☎ (064) 57 6376) costs just $13 a night ($16

per person twin share) outside the ski season and $30 a night ($39 Saturday night) and $175 a week in the ski season. A ballot is held for winter places and you have to enter by April. Most people get the nights they want and even if you aren't in the ballot it's worth checking to see if there are cancellations. In June and the end of September, when snow might be scanty, there is less pressure on places at the lodge. There's plenty of room in the off season. The YHA Travel Centre in Sydney (☎ (02) 261 1111) is the best place to start making enquiries about Thredbo Lodge.

Several lodges such as the *Snow Goose* (☎ (064) 57 6222) and the *House of Ullr* (☎ (064) 57 6210) have very good deals outside the ski season, from around $14 sharing in a twin room and $25 a double.

Near Bullocks Flat there's a pretty but basic free camp site between Jindabyne and Thredbo, near the Skitube, called *Thredbo Diggings*.

Perisher Valley & Smiggin Holes (1680 metres)

Perisher Valley has a good selection of intermediate runs. Smiggin Holes is just down the road from Perisher and run by the same management so a combined ski-tow ticket is available. A shuttle bus runs between the two resorts and they are also joined by a lift system so it is possible to ski from one resort to the other. Together they have over 100 km of runs and 30 lifts. A day ticket costs $52, a five-day pass costs $218, and a five-day lesson-and-lift package costs $276 ($218 for beginners).

Mt Blue Cow (1640 metres)

Mt Blue Cow (☎ (064) 56 2890), with beginner to intermediate skiing, is between Perisher Valley and Guthega in the Perisher Range. This is a day resort (no accommodation) accessible by the Skitube, but there are accommodation packages which include shuttles and Skitube tickets (☎ toll-free 1800 251 354). Combined lift and Skitube tickets cost $50; Skitube, lifts and lessons cost $69

($55 for beginners). There are various deals available if you take more days.

Guthega (1630 metres)

This is mainly a day resort, best suited to intermediate and, to a lesser extent, beginner skiers. *Guthega Lodge* (☎ (064) 57 5383) is the only commercial accommodation. Guthega is smaller and less crowded than other places. From here cross-country skiers head out for the Main Range or Rolling Ground.

Charlotte Pass (1780 metres)

At the base of Mt Kosciusko this is the highest and one of the oldest and most isolated resorts in Australia. In winter you have to snowcat the last eight km from Perisher Valley. Five lifts service rather short but uncrowded runs, and this is good ski touring country.

Mt Selwyn (1492 metres)

This is the only ski resort in the northern end of the national park, halfway between Tumut and Cooma. It has 13 lifts and is ideal for beginners. One-day lift tickets are $38, five days costs $175 and five days plus lessons is $220. It's another day resort – most accommodation is at Adaminaby. The booking centre (☎ toll-free 1800 020 777) books accommodation, some of which is relatively cheap – self-catering units are from $40 a double, plus $12 for each extra adult, and there are caravan park units sleeping four from $50. Adaminaby Bus Service (☎ (064) 54 2318) runs between Cooma and Mt Selwyn.

THE ALPINE WAY

From Jindabyne, the Alpine Way runs past Thredbo then loops around the southern end of Kosciusko National Park to the western side of the ranges. Two of the best mountain views are from Olsens Lookout, 10 km off the Alpine Way on the Geehi Dam road, and Scammels Lookout, just off the Alpine Way.

The tiny town of **Khancoban** at the other end of the Alpine Way has backpackers' accommodation at the basic *Khancoban Backpackers & Fisherman's Lodge*, where dorm beds are $11 and singles/doubles are $15/22. Each extra person (up to six) costs $5. You need to bring your own bedding and cooking utensils. Book and check in at the nearby Khancoban Alpine Inn (☎ (060) 76 9471).

TUMUT AREA

Tumut is on the Snowy Mountains Highway on the northern side of the national park. Australia's largest commercial trout farm is at nearby Blowering Dam. The information centre (☎ (069) 47 1849) can tell you about visits to the various centres of the Snowy Mountains Hydroelectric Scheme. For a wide variety of activities, see the friendly people at Adventure Sports (☎ toll-free 1800 020 631) in the Old Butter Factory.

Talbingo Dam and the **Yarrangobilly Caves** (60 km east, about midway between Tumut and Kiandra) are other points to visit. You can visit a cave by yourself ($4) or take a tour ($8). There's also a thermal pool at a constant 27°C, some beautiful country in the reserve around the caves, and a National Parks information centre (☎ (064) 54 9597).

Batlow is south of Tumut in a fruit-growing area. Near Batlow is **Hume & Hovell's Lookout** where the two explorers did indeed pause for the view in 1824. **Paddy's River Dam** was built by Chinese gold-miners back in the 1850s. Continuing south from Batlow you reach **Tumbarumba**, site of the early exploits of bushranger Mad Dog Morgan.

South-West & the Murray

This is wide, rolling, sometimes hypnotic country with some of the state's best farming areas and some interesting history. The Murray River forms the boundary between New South Wales and Victoria – most of the larger towns are on the Victorian side. Part of this area is also known as the Riverina because of the meandering Murray and Murrumbidgee rivers and their tributaries.

Getting There & Away

The region is served by a number of airlines, such as Ansett Express, Hazelton, Kendell, Air Link and Country Connection.

Several roads run through the south-west – the Hume Highway being the obvious one. But there are quieter alternative routes like the Olympic Way running through Cowra, Wagga Wagga and Albury. There are routes to Adelaide like the Sturt Highway through Hay and Wentworth and you'll also come through the south-west if travelling direct between Brisbane and Melbourne on the Newell Highway. The Melbourne to Sydney bus services run on the Hume and trains run close to it. There are regional bus services such as Fearnes Coaches (☎ toll-free 1800 029 918) which runs between Sydney and Wagga Wagga, Gundagai and Yass (all $35 from Sydney) and Goulburn and Mittagong (both $20).

Countrylink reaches most other towns in the area. The region is also crisscrossed by major bus routes – from Sydney and Brisbane to Melbourne and Adelaide.

ALONG THE HUME HIGHWAY

The Hume Highway is the main road between Australia's two largest cities. It's the fastest and shortest road and although it's not the most interesting there are attractive places along the way, as well as some worthwhile diversions.

One of the simplest diversions is right at the beginning – take the coastal Princes Highway past Royal National Park to Wollongong. Just after Wollongong take the Illawarra Highway along the picturesque Macquarie Pass to meet the Hume near Moss Vale. Further south you can leave the Hume to visit Canberra or continue beyond Canberra through the Snowy Mountains on the Alpine Way, rejoining the Hume near Albury.

From Sydney to beyond Goulburn the Hume is a freeway but it will be a long time before the whole road is upgraded. There are long stretches of narrow, two-lane road carrying a lot of traffic.

Sydney to Goulburn

The large towns of **Mittagong** and **Bowral** adjoin each other along the Hume Highway. Four km south of Mittagong, a winding 65-km road leads west to the **Wombeyan Caves**. The drive up is through superb mountain scenery and there's a pretty camping ground at the caves. Bowral was where cricketer Sir Donald Bradman, probably Australia's greatest sporting hero, spent his boyhood. In 1926, aged 17, he scored 300 runs for Bowral in a final against Moss Vale, averaging over 100 runs per innings for the season. There's a cricket ground and museum dedicated to 'the Don'. A little further south along the Hume, **Berrima** is a tiny town which was founded in 1829 and has changed remarkably little since then.

South of Berrima are the village of **Bundanoon** and the large Morton National Park, with its deep gorges and high sandstone plateaus in the Budawang Range. There are several entry points to the park: two of the easiest are Fitzroy Falls (on the road between Moss Vale and Nowra) and Bundanoon. The pleasant *Bundanoon YHA Hostel* (☎ (048) 83 6010) on Railway Ave has dorm beds for $12. Bundanoon is on the railway line between Sydney and Canberra (and Melbourne). Countrylink buses run daily to Wollongong.

Goulburn (population 24,000)

Goulburn was proclaimed a town in 1833. It's surrounded by sheep country and as a monument to the source of its wealth there's a three-storey-high **Big Merino** in town. It looks truly diabolic with its green eyes glowing at night: by day you can climb inside to see displays on wool and sheep.

The visitor centre (☎ (048) 21 5343) is on Montague St across from Belmore Park and it has a walking tour map. The **Old Goulburn Brewery** (1836) is a large complex down on the river flats and as well as a working brewery

NEW SOUTH WALES

there's accommodation in renovated mews for $35 per person. There's plenty of other accommodation in town, in pubs, motels and caravan parks.

The *Yurt Farm*, 20 km north of Goulburn on the Grabben Gullen road (take Clinton St from central Goulburn) is an activities camp for kids with the emphasis on conservation and living simply, but travellers are welcome to stay in the yurt village for $10 a night if there's room; if not you can stay in the farmhouse for $10 and do a few hours work in exchange for meals. You'll need a sleeping bag. Phone first (☎ (048) 29 2114) to see if there's room. If you ring a few days in advance it might be possible to arrange a lift from Goulburn.

Yass (population 4500)

Yass is closely connected with the early explorer Hume, for whom the highway is named. On Comur St, next to the tourist information centre (☎ (06) 226 2557), the **Hamilton Hume Museum** has exhibits relating to him. Near Yass at **Wee Jasper** are Careys Caves, open on Sunday afternoons from 1 pm.

Just east of Yass the Barton Highway branches off the Hume for Canberra. Transborder Express (☎ (06) 226 1378) has several daily buses ($8).

Gundagai (population 2500)

Gundagai, 386 km from Sydney, is one of the more interesting small towns along the Hume. The long wooden **Prince Alfred Bridge** (now closed to traffic, but you can walk across it) crosses the flood plain of the Murrumbidgee River, a reminder that in 1852 Gundagai suffered Australia's worst flood disaster when 89 people were drowned. Gold rushes and bushrangers were also part of its colourful early history and the notorious Captain Moonlight was tried in Gundagai's 1859 **courthouse**.

Other places of interest include the **museum** on Homer St and, on Sheridan St, the **Gabriel Gallery** of historic photos and the information centre, which features the

---

Dog on the Tuckerbox

Gundagai features in a number of famous songs, including 'Along the Road to Gundagai', 'My Mabel Waits for Me' and 'When a Boy from Alabama Meets a Girl from Gundagai'. Its most famous monument is eight km east of town just off the highway. There, still sitting on his tuckerbox, is the Dog on the Tuckerbox memorial, a sculpture of the dog who in a 19th-century bush ballad (and a more recent, perhaps even better known, poem by Jack Moses) 'sat on the tuckerbox, five miles from Gundagai', and refused to help while its owner's bullock team was bogged in the creek. A popular tale has it that the dog was even less helpful, because in the original version it apparently shat on the tuckerbox. ■

Marble Marvel, a 20,000-piece cathedral model. Is it art? Is it lunacy? Is it worth the $1 entry fee? Probably. You at least get to hear a snatch of 'Along the Road to Gundagai'.

Places to Stay The *Gundagai River Caravan Park* (☎ (069) 44 1702) is by the river near the southern end of the Prince Alfred Bridge, with sites from $8 a double. In town, *Gundagai Caravan Village* (☎ (069) 44 1057) has sites from $14 and on-site vans from $28. There are several motels. On Sheridan St both the *Criterion Hotel* (☎ (069) 44 1048) and the *Royal Hotel* (☎ (069) 44 1024) have accommodation.

Holbrook (population 1400)

Holbrook is the halfway point between Sydney and Melbourne, and was known as Germanton until WW I, during which it was renamed after a British war hero. In Holbrook Park there's a replica of the submarine in which he won a Victoria Cross. The local information centre is located in the large **Woolpack Inn Museum** (admission $3).

ALBURY (population 42,500)

Albury is on the Murray River just below the Hume Weir and across the river from the large Victorian town of Wodonga. It is a good base for trips and activities in a variety of terrain: the snowfields and high country of both Victoria and New South Wales, the vineyards around Rutherglen (Victoria), and the tempestuous Upper Murray, which becomes languid below Albury as it starts its journey to the sea in South Australia. It's also a good place to break the journey between Sydney and Melbourne.

Information

The Albury information centre (☎ (060) 21 2655) is on the Hume Highway as you enter Albury from Wodonga and the larger Gateway Information Centre (☎ (060) 41 3875), with information on both New South Wales and Victoria, is on the highway in Wodonga. Tourist information is broadcast on 88 FM.

Some seasonal fruit-picking work is available in the area; see the CES (☎ (060) 21 3400) at 488 Swift St. The hostel might also know of work.

Things to See & Do

In summer there's river swimming from **Noreuil Park** behind the Albury information centre and you can take river cruises on the paddle-steamer *Cumberoona* or the newer *Discovery*. Also in the park is a tree marked by explorer William Hovell when he crossed the Murray on his 1824 expedition with Hamilton Hume from Sydney to Port Phillip (Melbourne wasn't there then). Murray River Lodge, the backpackers' hostel, has canoe trips ($15/20 a full/half-day) and you don't have to stay there to join in. The hostel can arrange longer trips – and just about anything else.

The **Ettamogah Wildlife Sanctuary**, 11 km north on the highway and open daily ($5, children $2), has a collection of Aussie fauna, most of which arrived sick or injured, so this is a genuine sanctuary. A few km north the grotesque **Ettamogah Pub** looms up near the highway – a real-life re-creation of a famous Aussie cartoon pub and proof that life (of a sort) follows art not vice versa.

The good **Jindera Pioneer Museum** is 16 km north-west of Albury in the village of Jindera and is open daily ($3). Jindera is in an area known as **Morgan Country** because of its association with the unpleasant bushranger Mad Dog Morgan. Other nice little towns in this area include **Culcairn**, west of Holbrook, where the wonderful *Culcairn Hotel* (☎ (060) 29 8501) has accommodation at $25/35.

Places to Stay

The *Albury Central Caravan Park* (☎ (060) 21 8420) is a couple of km north of the centre on North St and has tent sites from $10 and cabins from $30.

The *Murray River Lodge* (☎ (060) 41 1822) has dorm beds at $13 and a double room for $32. It's on Hume St (the highway) not far from the bus stop and Noreuil Park. You can hire bikes for $3 a day. This is a friendly place which takes care of its guests. The staff will help you get involved in adventure activities or find a farm where you can work for your board.

Places to Eat

Matilda's Family Steakhouse at the corner of David and Hume Sts has lunch specials from $8. The *Family Eating House* at 639 Dean St has all-you-can-eat smorgasbords daily, with roasts at weekends. There's a weekday lunch buffet for $9.50 at the *Carlton Motel* on the corner of Dean and Elizabeth Sts. On Dean St next to the Carlton, *Cafe Picasso* is a Spanish restaurant with main courses around $13.

Getting There & Away

The nightly Sydney to Melbourne XPT stops here. If you're travelling between the two capital cities it's much cheaper to stop over in Albury on a through ticket than to buy two separate tickets. The same applies to bus tickets. Buses stop at Vienna World (a service station/diner) on the highway on the corner of Hovell St, across from Noreuil Park. Pyles Coaches (☎ (057) 57 2024) runs to the Victorian high country. V/Line runs to Mildura along the Murray.

WAGGA WAGGA (population 54,000)

Wagga Wagga on the Murrumbidgee River is the state's largest inland city but, despite its size, the city retains a relaxed country-town feel. The name is pronounced 'wogga' and is usually abbreviated to one word (although there's a literary group called Wagga Wagga Writers Writers).

The long main street is Baylis St which runs north from the railway station, becoming Fitzmaurice St at the northern end. Pick up a driving tour map from the information centre (☎ (069) 23 5402) on Tarcutta St. The excellent **Botanic Gardens** are about 1.5 km south of the railway station. In the gardens there's a small zoo with a free-flight aviary of native birds.

The **Murray Cod Hatcheries** are on the Sturt Highway east of Wagga, just past the hamlet of Gumly Gumly. Here you can see Big Murray (a 50 kg, 100-year-old cod) and a wide range of native animals. It's open daily and admission is about $5.

On the Olympic Way, about 40 km north of Wagga, the small town of **Junee** has some historic buildings including the lovely Monte Cristo Homestead and some splendid pubs. Glass Buslines runs a local service from Wagga to Junee on weekdays and picks up along Baylis St.

Places to Stay

The *Tourist Caravan Park* (☎ (069) 21 2540) is on the river right next to the swimming beach and a couple of blocks from the town centre. Tent sites are $7 for two people, on-site vans cost from $22 and cabins are up to $40.

Several pubs have accommodation, including *Romano's Hotel* (☎ (069) 21 2013) on Fitzmaurice St, with good rooms for $30/38, some with attached bathrooms. The *Manor* (☎ (069) 21 5962) is a small, well-restored guesthouse across from the Memorial Gardens on Morrow St, near Baylis St. Singles and doubles range from $25 to $45 per person, including breakfast. There are plenty of motels, but none of them are cheap.

Places to Eat

Fitzmaurice/Baylis St has a surprisingly diverse range of places to eat. At the top of Fitzmaurice St the *Kebab Place* is an authentic Lebanese takeaway and restaurant. On Baylis St south of Tompson St is *Pancakes at Wagga Wagga* with a large menu of pancake permutations plus pasta (around $8, 15% student discount); upstairs nearby is *Bloomsbury's*, a cafe-style place with a balcony overlooking the street.

In the Baylis Centre is the plush *Wagga Thai Restaurant* with a $5 lunch-time buffet. At the *Family Eating House* you can eat as much as you like for $7.80 at lunch and $8.80 at dinner; further down is the small *Saigon Restaurant* with lunch specials for about $4.

Getting There & Away

Ansett Express (☎ 13 1300), Kendell (☎ (069) 22 0100), Western (☎ (069) 22 7777) and Air Link (☎ (069) 22 7900) connect Wagga with Sydney, Melbourne, Brisbane and many places in New South Wales.

Countrylink buses leave from the railway station but other long-distance services leave from the terminal on Gurwood St, off Fitzmaurice St. You can make bookings here. Wagga is on the railway line between Sydney ($55) and Melbourne ($49).

NARRANDERA (population 5100)

Near the junction of the Newell and Sturt Highways, Narrandera is in the Murrumbidgee Irrigation Area (MIA). The information centre (☎ (069) 59 1766) in Narrandera Park has a walking tour map.

Lake Talbot is an excellent water-sports reserve, partly a long artificial lake and partly a big swimming complex. Bush (including a koala regeneration area) surrounds the lake and walking trails wander by.

The **John Lake Centre** at the Inland Fisheries Research Station has guided tours (during which you can see a huge Murray Cod) on weekdays at 10.30 am ($5); the centre is also open for casual inspection from

9 am to 4 pm. Turn off the Sturt Highway four km south-east of Narrandera.

South of Narrandera on the Newell Highway is **Jerilderie**, immortalised by the bushranger Ned Kelly who held up the whole town for two days in 1879. Kelly relics can be seen in the **Telegraph Office Museum** on Powell St.

Places to Stay & Eat

The *Lake Talbot Caravan Park* (☎ (069) 59 1302), some way from the town centre at the eastern end of Larmer St, overlooks the Lake Talbot complex. Tent sites are $10, on-site vans cost from $25 a double and self-contained units are from $35 a double.

The *Star Lodge* (☎ (069) 59 1768), across from the railway station on Ferrier St (the Newell Highway), is an associate-YHA hostel in a fine old building. It's clean and friendly. Only YHA members can use the dorms ($12) but the good single/double rooms are available to anyone for $15/28; one room has an attached bathroom and costs $20/35.

Getting There & Away

Greyhound Pioneer buses plying the Newell Highway between Brisbane ($96) and Melbourne ($57) stop at the old railway station.

GRIFFITH (population 13,000)

Griffith was planned by Walter Burley Griffin, the American architect who designed Canberra. The information centre (☎ (069) 62 4145) is on the corner of Banna (the long main street) and Jondaryan Aves; out the front a Fairy Firefly plane perches on a pole. Ask about taking a school bus for a weekday tour of the district.

High on a hill to the north-east of the town centre, **Pioneer Park** is a re-creation of an early Riverina village and is worth seeing. It's open daily ($5).

Descendants of the Italian farmers who helped develop this area make up a large proportion of the population. Although the Hunter Valley is the best-known wine-producing area in New South Wales, the Griffith area produces 80% of the state's wine. You can visit 11 **wineries** – the information centre has a map.

Fruit Picking

Many people come to Griffith to work on the grape harvest, usually beginning around mid-February and lasting six to eight weeks. The citrus harvest begins in November and runs through to March and other crops are harvested during the year. Few vineyards and almost none of the other farms have accommodation or even space to camp so you'll need your own transport. The CES (☎ (069) 69 1100) on Yambil St can help you find work.

Places to Stay

The small *Tourist Caravan Park* (☎ (069) 62 4537) on Willandra Ave, not far from the bus stop, has tent sites from $10, on-site vans from $20 and units from $33. There's a basic camping area at the showgrounds, south of the circular western end of the city centre, which has sites for $5 ($30 per week).

Pioneer Park (☎ (069) 62 4196) has shared accommodation in the old shearers' quarters. The rooms are small and basic but there's a good kitchen and lounge. The problem with staying here is that it's a long, steep walk from the city centre and there's no public transport. During the harvest this place can fill up. The *Area Hotel* (☎ (069) 62 1322) on Banna Ave has rooms for $25/35.

Places to Eat

Italian food is the region's dominant cuisine. For good coffee and cake or pasta (from $5), try *Pasticceria Banna* at the western end of Banna Ave. It's also open daily for breakfast. A few doors away and down some steps, the Vico family's *La Scala* is open for dinner from Tuesday to Saturday.

Not far away and on the other side of Banna Ave, the *Belvedere Restaurant* has more of a cafe atmosphere and it's also a busy takeaway pizzeria. For pizzas cooked in a wood-fired oven, head out to *La Villa Bianca* at 40 Mackay Ave.

Getting There & Away

Hazelton (☎ (063) 61 5888) flies between Griffith and Sydney daily for $191.

Buses stop at the Griffith Travel & Transit Centre (☎ (069) 62 7199), in Donald's Country Restaurant on Jondaryan St. Greyhound Pioneer and Countrylink run to Sydney daily ($60), and also to Canberra ($40). MIA Intercity Coaches (☎ (069) 62 3419) runs to Melbourne three times a week. Greyhound Pioneer also runs to Melbourne ($55) and to Adelaide (about $100).

AROUND GRIFFITH

West of Griffith the last hills of the Great Dividing Range give way to endless plains.

Cocoparra National Park

Cocoparra, just east of Griffith, is not a large park but its hills and gullies provide some contrasts and there is a fair amount of wildlife. The camping area is on Woolshed Flat in the north of the park, not far from Woolshed Falls. BYO water. Bush camping is permitted away from the roads. Park entry is $7.50 and camping costs $5.

Leeton (population 7000)

Leeton is the MIA's oldest town (1913). Like Griffith, Leeton was designed by Walter Burley Griffin and it remains close to the architect's original vision because of restrictions on development.

The visitor centre (☎ (069) 53 2832) is next to the shire offices on Chelmsford Place. Ask here about tours of the rice mill and other food processing plants. Lillypilly Estate and Toorak Wines are two **wineries** near Leeton, open daily except Sunday for tastings and for tours on weekdays – 11.30 am at Toorak and 4 pm at Lillypilly.

Willandra National Park

Willandra, on the plains 160 km north-west of Griffith as the crow flies, has been carved from a huge sheep station on a system of lakes, usually dry. The World-Heritage-listed park's 20,000 hectares is less than 10% of the area which comprised Big Willandra

station in its 1870s heyday. The partially restored homestead (1918) was the third to be built on the increasingly busy station.

There are several short walking tracks in the park and the Merton Motor Trail does a loop around the eastern half of the park. The western half has no vehicular access but you can walk here if you are very sure of what you're doing.

There's a camp site near the homestead ($4) and with permission you can bush camp. Shared accommodation in the 'men's quarters' costs $8.

The main access is off the Hillston to Mossgiel road, 40-odd km west of Hillston. It takes less than 10 mm of rain to close roads around here so phone ☎ (069) 67 8159 to check conditions before setting out.

HAY (population 3000)

In flat, treeless country, Hay is at the junction of the Sturt and Cobb highways and is a substantial town for this part of the world. The information centre (☎ (069) 93 1003) is on the main street. There are some fine beaches along the Murrumbidgee and interesting old buildings like the **Hay Gaol Museum** and **Bishops Lodge**, a corrugated-iron mansion.

Most of the pubs have accommodation. The *Hay Motel* (☎ (069) 93 1804) and the *New Crown Hotel/Motel* (☎ (069) 93 1600) are the least expensive motels at about $35/45. There are several caravan parks and off the Sturt Highway 11 km east of Hay, the *Bidgee Beach Primitive Camping Area* (☎ (069) 93 1180) is a simple camping area on the banks of the Murrumbidgee. Tent sites are $10.

DENILIQUIN (population 8000)

Deniliquin is an attractive, bustling country town on a wide bend in the Edward River. Before the Whites arrived, this area was the most densely populated part of Australia.

The information centre (☎ (058) 81 2878) is on Cressy St. Nearby on the **Island Sanctuary** animals such as an over-friendly emu live in river-gum forest.

Merino sheep breeds developed in this area have long been the mainstay of Australia's wool industry and the **Peppin Heritage Centre** on George St tells the story. It's open from 10 am to 4 pm (until 2 pm on weekends) and admission is $3. The visitor centre at the **Sun Rice Mill**, the largest rice mill in the southern hemisphere, is open on weekdays from 10 am to noon and 2 to 4 pm.

You can hire canoes and other boats at Masons' Paringa Caravan & Tourist Park (☎ (058) 81 1131). For $60 the staff will drive you and your canoe up the river and you have the whole day to float back down; for a half-day trip it's $30.

Places to Stay

There are several caravan parks, such as *McLeans Beach Caravan Park* (☎ (058) 81 2448) which is on a swimming beach; head north-east on Charlotte St. The basic but clean *Deniliquin Youth Hostel* (☎ (058) 81 5025) is on the corner of Wood and Macauley Sts about a km south-west of the town centre. YHA members (only) can stay here for $7 a night.

All the hotels have accommodation. The *Globe* (☎ (058) 81 2030) is good value, with rooms at $18 per person, including a cooked breakfast. The *Federal Hotel* (☎ (058) 81 1260) on the corner of Cressy and Napier Sts has newly painted rooms for $20/35 a single/double and $40 for a twin.

There are plenty of motels. Semis growl through town all night so choose one off the highway, such as the *Wendburn Riverside* (☎ (058) 81 2311) at the north-eastern end of Charlotte St. Rooms cost from around $50.

Getting There & Away

Western Airlines (☎ toll-free 1800 804 775) has a daily service to Sydney's Bankstown airport via Wagga Wagga.

Long-distances buses stop at the Bus Stop Cafe on Whitelock St. Countrylink runs to Wagga Wagga, from where trains run to Sydney and Melbourne. McCafferty's stops here on the run between Melbourne ($33) and Brisbane ($103). Victoria's V/Line also runs to Melbourne.

ALONG THE MURRAY

Most of the important river towns are on the Victorian side – see the Victoria chapter for more on the river. It's no problem to hop back and forth across the river as in many places roads run along both sides.

Albury (see earlier) is the largest New South Wales town on the Murray and also the first big town on the river down from its source. The Murray was once an important means of communication, with paddle-steamers splashing upstream and downstream – an antipodean Mississippi.

Downstream from Albury, **Corowa** is a wine-producing centre – the Lindeman winery has been here since 1860. **Tocumwal** on the Newell Highway is a quiet riverside town with sandy river beaches and a giant fibreglass Murray Cod in the town square. The nearby airport is a gliding centre.

Wentworth is an old river port at the confluence of the Murray and Darling rivers. The riverboat *Loyalty* (☎ (050) 27 3330) has two-hour cruises to the confluence on Tuesday and Thursday, leaving the Wentworth Ex-Services Club at 1.45 pm. The fare is $12.

You can see local history in the **Old Gaol** ($3.50) and across the road in the **Pioneer Museum** ($2.50). The **Perry Dunes** are large orange sand dunes six km out of town, off the road to Broken Hill.

Central West

The central west starts inland from the Blue Mountains and continues for about 400 km, gradually fading from rolling agricultural land into the harsh far west. This region has some of the earliest inland towns in Australia. From Sydney, Bathurst is the gateway to the region, and from here you can turn north-west through Orange and Dubbo or south-west through Cowra and West Wyalong.

The Olympic Way, running from Bathurst through Cowra and Wagga Wagga to Albury, is an alternative Sydney to Melbourne route.

The Newell Highway, the most direct route between Melbourne and Brisbane, also passes through the central west. On long weekends accommodation all along the Newell is booked out.

Getting There & Away

Air The central west is well served by airlines. From Dubbo ($155 from Sydney with Eastern Australia or Hazelton) there are flights to other locations in the centre and far west of the state.

Bus Major lines have services through the region on routes between Sydney and Broken Hill or Adelaide, and from Brisbane to Melbourne or Adelaide. Local companies include Rendell's Coaches (☎ toll-free 1800 023 328). Sid Fogg's (☎ toll-free 1800 045 952) runs from Newcastle as far as Dubbo.

Train Direct trains run from Sydney to Lithgow ($18), Bathurst ($25), Orange ($35), Dubbo ($51) and Parkes ($54). From those centres connecting buses run to most other towns including Cowra ($37 from Sydney), Forbes ($45), Grenfell ($42) and Mudgee ($33).

LITHGOW (population 14,700)

On the western fringe of the Blue Mountains, Lithgow is an industrial town, a little bemused by its increasing number of visitors. The information centre (☎ (063) 51 2307) is at 285 Main St. **Eskbank House** on Bennet St is a gracious 1841 home housing a museum, open daily between 10 am and 4 pm, except Tuesday and Wednesday ($2). There are fine views from **Hassan Walls Lookout**, five km south of town.

The **Zig Zag Railway** by which, until 1910, trains descended from the Blue Mountains, was built in 1868 and was quite an engineering wonder in its day. A section has been restored and steam trains run on weekends and in school holidays. The railway is about 10 km east of Lithgow on the road to Bell; some trains to and from Sydney stop here. Phone for timetable information (☎ (02) 858 1480).

Many pubs in Lithgow have accommodation from about $15/25 for singles/doubles. There are frequent trains to Sydney.

See the earlier Blue Mountains section for information on the village of Hartley. **Newnes**, about 50 km north of Lithgow on the edge of the wild Wollemi National Park, is a ghost town where the pub still functions. There's a five-km walk to a disused railway tunnel, now full of glow-worms.

BATHURST (population 26,000)

Bathurst is Australia's oldest inland city and it was laid out to a grand scale. The Victorian-era streetscape is relatively intact and there are some impressive buildings, such as the 1880 **courthouse** on Russell St. Here you'll find the information centre (☎ (063) 33 6288) and a **museum** ($1). Eight km out of town is **Abercrombie House**, a huge Gothic mansion of the 1870s. Ask about open days at the information centre.

South-west of the city centre is the 6.2-km **Mt Panorama motor racing circuit**. It's the venue for one of Australia's best-known races, the Bathurst 1000 km for production cars, held in October. You can drive around the circuit (it's a public road) and there's a small **motor racing museum** ($3) near Pit Straight. Also on Mt Panorama are the **Sir Joseph Banks Nature Park** ($5), with koalas and other animals, and the **Bathurst Gold Diggings**, a reconstruction of a gold-mining town which is open daily except Saturday.

Places to Stay & Eat

Cheaper places to stay include the *Park Hotel* (☎ (063) 31 3399) on the corner of George and Keppel Sts and the *Capri Motel* (☎ (063) 31 2966) at 357 Stewart St, but they aren't for shoestringers. For pizza from a wood-fired oven or large servings of pasta ($7.50), try *Uncle Joe's Pizza*, opposite the post office on Howick St. *Zeigler's Cafe* on Keppel St has an interesting modern menu of not-too-expensive dishes.

AROUND BATHURST

The **Abercrombie Caves** are 72 km south of Bathurst. There are several guided tours each day.

North of Bathurst the village of **Sofala** has some interesting buildings; west of here on a narrow mountain road is **Hill End**, now almost a ghost town. It was the scene for a gold rush in the 1870s and is classified as a historic site. The information centre (☎ (063) 37 8206) is in the old hospital which also houses the **museum**. The *Royal Hotel* (☎ (065) 37 8261) has singles/doubles for $38/45 and you can camp at one of three sites for about $10. A local bus runs to and from Bathurst once a week. On school days you can get here on a series of school buses from Mudgee for a total of about $6. Contact Case's (☎ (063) 72 6622) in Mudgee.

Rockley, 34 km south of Bathurst, is another classified historic village. North-east of Bathurst is **Rylstone**, where there are sandstone buildings and Aboriginal rock paintings just outside the town (ask at the shire council).

MUDGEE & AROUND

Mudgee (population 7500), about 120 km north of both Lithgow and Bathurst, is a fine example of an old country town and is a pleasant place to stay. The information centre (☎ (063) 72 5875) is on Market St, near the old police station.

There are many young and enthusiastic **wineries** in the area and people who find the Hunter Valley too commercial will enjoy visiting them. As well as the youngsters there's Craigmore which has produced a vintage every year since 1858, making it the second oldest continually operating winery in Australia. Around 18 wineries are open six or seven days a week. In September there's a wine festival. Despite all the vineyards there isn't much harvest work as most is done by locals.

Accommodation tends to fill up on weekends, and several hotels have above-average pub accommodation. The *Paragon Hotel* (☎ (063) 72 1313), on the corner of Gladstone and Perry Sts, charges from $15 per person, as does the *Woolpack Hotel* (☎ (063) 72 1908), on Market St. The *Federal Hotel* (☎ (063) 72 2150), on Inglis St near the railway station, charges $15/24 for a single/double, and $18/34 on weekends. North of town and near the wineries, *Hithergreen Lodge* (☎ (063) 72 1022) has motel units for $48/55. On weekdays it might have backpackers' specials but phone to check first. A taxi out here costs around $4, otherwise it's a pleasant walk of about five km.

The best place for a coffee or snack is the *Last Cafe Tearooms*, through an archway on Market St near the corner of Church St. Nearby in the Woolpack Hotel, *Jumbucks* (☎ (063) 72 3159) serves good, standard food (around $10) and local wines.

Gulgong, 30 km north-west, is an old gold town once described as 'the hub of the world'. It was the boyhood home of author Henry Lawson and the **Henry Lawson Centre** on Mayne St houses a big collection of 'Lawsonia', open daily from 10 am to noon ($1). The information centre (☎ (063) 74 2078) is in the Olde Books shop at the other end of Mayne St. The huge **Gulgong Pioneer Museum** on Herbert St is one of the best country-town museums in the state ($3).

The *Centennial Hotel* (☎ (063) 74 1241) on Mayne St has singles/doubles with bathroom for $25/35. The *Heritage Centre* on Red Hill has a dorm for groups. Phone ☎ (063) 74 1202 to see whether there's space for individuals.

At **Nagundie** 11 km north there's a rock five metres above the ground which is said to hold water year round – it's an old Aboriginal water hole and you can camp there. Further east, en route to the Goulburn River National Park and the Hunter Valley, **Merriwa** has a number of historic buildings, as has nearby **Cassilis**.

Getting There & Away

Hazelton flies between Mudgee and Sydney ($140). Countrylink runs from Sydney ($40) via Lithgow; between Mudgee and Gulgong the fare is $2. There's also a daily bus to Bathurst.

NEW SOUTH WALES

ORANGE (population 30,000)

This important fruit-growing centre does not grow oranges! Rather, it was named after William of Orange. Pioneer poet Banjo Paterson (who wrote the words of 'Waltzing Matilda') was born here, and the foundations of his birthplace are in Banjo Paterson Park. Orange was considered as a site for the federal capital before Canberra was eventually selected.

The visitor centre (☎ (063) 61 5226) is on Byng St. The **museum** on McNamara St includes a 300-year-old tree carved with Aboriginal designs. The autumn apple-picking season lasts for about six weeks; contact the CES (☎ (063) 61 4144) on Anson St.

Mt Canobolas (1395 metres) is a steep, extinct volcano 20 km south-west of Orange. You can drive to the top or there are a couple of walking tracks.

Australia's first real gold rush took place at **Ophir**, 27 km north of Orange. The area is now a nature reserve and it's still popular with fossickers – you can buy a licence and hire a gold pan from the Orange visitor centre.

Places to Stay & Eat

The council's *Orange Showground Caravan Park* (☎ (063) 62 7254), on Margaret St about two km north-east of the city centre, has tent sites for $7.50, on-site vans for $25 a double and self-contained units for $35/40 a single/double.

Hotel Canobolas (☎ (063) 62 2444), on Summer St at the corner of Lords Place, was once the largest hotel outside Sydney. Most rooms have bathrooms, steam heat, TV and a fridge, and cost $35/55 or $25/40 for rooms with shared bathrooms.

Lord's Cafe on Lords Place near the corner of Summer St is a good place for breakfast, with eggs for $3. *Matilda's Family Steakhouse* at the corner of Bathurst Rd and McLachlan St, a few blocks east of the railway line, has $8 all-you-can-eat lunch specials.

Getting There & Away

Rendell's Coaches (☎ toll-free 1800 023 328) runs to Dubbo ($30) and Sydney ($25) daily. There's also a service to Canberra ($30). Selwood's Coaches (☎ (063) 62 7963) also run to Sydney daily.

DUBBO (population 32,000)

North of Parkes and Orange and 420 km from Sydney, Dubbo is a large agricultural and sheep- and cattle-raising town with some old buildings. The information centre (☎ (068) 84 1422) is at the top end of Macquarie St, the main shopping street, at the corner of Erskine St. You can hire geared bikes for $10 a day at Wheelers on the corner of Darling and Bultje Sts.

Old Dubbo Gaol ($3) on Macquarie St has 'animatronic' characters telling the story of prison life. Also on Macquarie St is the **museum** ($3).

Five km south-west of town, the **Western Plains Zoo** is the largest open-range zoo in Australia. The Bengal tigers and Asiatic lions alone are worth the price of admission. You're better off walking around the six-km circuit or hiring a bike ($8 for half a day) than joining the crawling line of cars. The zoo is open daily and admission is $12.50.

Places to Stay

The closest caravan parks to the town centre are the small *Poplars* (☎ (068) 82 4067), near the river at the western end of Bultje St, and *Dubbo City* (☎ (068) 82 4820), also on the river but on the western bank and a fair distance by road from the centre.

Kurrajong House (☎ (068) 82 0922) is a pleasant YHA hostel at 87 Brisbane St, north of the railway line. From the bus station head west on Erskine St. Dorm beds are $12 and there are a few twin rooms. Guests get 20% off zoo tickets and the hostel can often arrange a lift out there, or you can hire a bike and ride ($6 a day).

A couple of doors away is the *Hub of the West* (☎ (068) 82 5004), a spartan guesthouse where rooms with common bathroom cost from $15/30. Several pubs have accommodation, such as the good *Castlereagh Hotel* (☎ (068) 82 4877) on the corner of

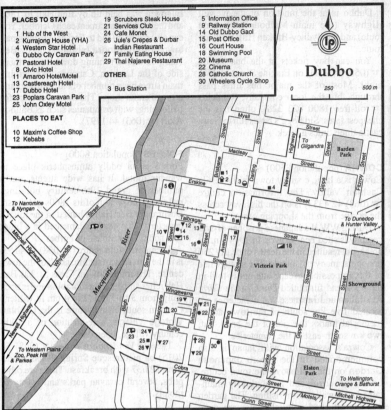

PLACES TO STAY
1 Hub of the West
2 Kurrajong House (YHA)
4 Western Star Hotel
6 Dubbo City Caravan Park
7 Pastoral Hotel
8 Civic Hotel
11 Amaroo Hotel/Motel
13 Castlereagh Hotel
17 Dubbo Hotel
23 Poplars Caravan Park
25 John Oxley Motel

PLACES TO EAT
10 Maxim's Coffee Shop
12 Kebabs

19 Scrubbers Steak House
21 Services Club
24 Cafe Monet
26 Jule's Crepes & Durbar
Indian Restaurant
27 Family Eating House
29 Thai Najaree Restaurant

OTHER
3 Bus Station

5 Information Office
9 Railway Station
14 Old Dubbo Gaol
15 Post Office
16 Court House
18 Swimming Pool
20 Museum
22 Cinema
28 Catholic Church
30 Wheelers Cycle Shop

Dubbo

0   250   500 m

Talbragar and Brisbane Sts, which has singles/doubles from $25/50, including a big cooked breakfast. Some rooms have bathrooms. Also good is the *Western Star* (☎ (068) 82 4644) on Erskine St.

The *John Oxley Motel* (☎ (068) 82 4622), towards the southern end of Macquarie St, is central and cheap for Dubbo ($41/45) but the rooms are pretty small. There are more than 20 other motels, mostly along Cobra St.

Places to Eat

The best value is the bistro at the opulent *Ex-Services Club* on Brisbane St. There's a

Family Eating House on Macquarie St, with an all-you-can-eat smorgasbord lunch for $7.50 and dinner for $12.50. *Cafe Monet* in the Kemwah Building at the corner of Macquarie and Bultje Sts has good coffee, snacks (around $7) and meals (about $15).

On Brisbane St, next to the church with the ski-jump spire, the *Thai Najaree Restaurant* is open for lunch and dinner daily except Monday. The cafe at the bus station is open 24 hours.

Getting There & Away

The air fare from Sydney is $155.

Dubbo is at the junction of the Newell Highway (the main Melbourne-Brisbane route) and the Sydney-Broken Hill/Adelaide route.

You can buy tickets at the bus station (☎ (068) 84 2411) on Erskine St until late at night. Most of the major bus lines pass through, but the local company, Rendell's (☎ toll-free 1800 023 328), often has the cheapest fares. Sid Fogg's buses run to Newcastle three times a week.

COWRA (population 8500)

Cowra is a large country town in the fertile Lachlan Valley. The information centre (☎ (063) 42 4333) is on the highway across the bridge from the shopping centre.

During WW II a Japanese prisoner-of-war camp was sited near Cowra. In 1944 a mass break-out resulted in the deaths of nearly 250 prisoners, many by suicide. The strange tale of this impossible escape attempt is told in the book and film titled *Die Like the Carp*. Australian and Japanese war cemeteries are located five km south of the town and a memorial marks the site of the break-out, two km south-east of the cemeteries.

Cowra's association with Japan is also commemorated in the superb **Japanese Garden** on the hill above the town centre. Large, beautiful and meticulously maintained, it's well worth visiting. The garden and the attached cultural centre are open daily ($4.50).

Several hotels have accommodation, including the big *Imperial Hotel* (☎ (063) 42 1588) at the western end of Kendal St (the main street) with basic rooms for $25/30/35 a single/double/triple. *Ilfracombe*, also on Kendal St, is a good restaurant and cafe.

To the west of Cowra the Lachlan River flows through fertile and pretty farming country. The road to Forbes (turn off the Western Highway about five km south of Cowra) runs along the southern bank of the Lachlan and is a pleasant drive.

At Paynters Bridge, about 45 km on from the turn-off, cross the Lachlan to **Eugowra**, a village in the shadow of bush-clad hills.

Eugowra was held up by Ben Hall in 1863 and there's a re-enactment each October. You can also get here (and to Forbes) via the small town of **Canowindra** (also held up by Ben Hall), on a road running down the northern side of the Lachlan. Canowindra's curving main street has a number of old buildings and arts and crafts shops. The town is a centre for ballooning, with companies such as Balloon Aloft (☎ (063) 44 1797).

FORBES (population 8000)

Forbes is an oddly atmospheric place to wander round. It has wide streets and a number of grand 19th-century buildings reflecting the wealth of its 1860s gold rush. Bushranger Ben Hall is buried in the town's cemetery – his death is lamented in a bitter folk song, 'The Streets of Forbes'.

The information centre (☎ (068) 52 4155) is in the old railway station, north of the town centre. The **museum**, on Cross St, has Ben Hall relics and other memorabilia and is open daily from 3 to 5 pm (2 to 4 pm in winter). One km south of the centre is the **Lachlan Vintage Village**, a re-creation of a 19th-century village, open daily.

The old *Vandenberg Hotel* (☎ (068) 52 2015) on picturesque Spring St has rooms from $23/37 with breakfast. There are other pubs, several caravan parks and plenty of motels.

North-West

From Dubbo, roads radiate out to various parts of the state. The Newell Highway runs north-east and is the quickest route between Melbourne and Brisbane. The Castlereagh Highway, forking off the Newell 66 km from Dubbo at Gilgandra, runs north into the rugged opal country towards the Queensland border, its surfaced section ending soon after Lightning Ridge.

The Mitchell Highway heads north-west to Bourke and Queensland via Nyngan. At

Nyngan the Barrier Highway forks off west to Broken Hill.

Getting There & Away
Eastern Australia and Ansett Express fly to several of the main towns. Towns on the Newell Highway are served by buses travelling to and from Brisbane, en route to Melbourne or Adelaide. Countrylink trains and/or buses connect most other towns in the area with Sydney. Fares from Sydney include Gunnedah $51, Coonabarabran $55 and Lightning Ridge $70.

ALONG THE NEWELL
Gilgandra has a small **observatory** with an audiovisual of the moon landing and other space flights, plus a historical display. Gilgandra is a junction town where the Newell and Castlereagh highways divide, and a road also cuts across to the Mitchell.

Coonabarabran (population 3000) is an access point for the spectacular domes and spires of the rugged **Warrumbungle National Park**, which offers great walking and rock climbing (permit required). The park headquarters (☎ (068) 25 4364) are at Canyon Camp, about 35 km west of Coonabarabran. Park entry costs $7.50 per car and $3 for pedestrians. Camping costs $10 for two people on-site or $1 for bush camping (permit required). There's a National Parks office in Coonabarabran (☎ (068) 42 1311).

The largest optical telescope in the southern hemisphere is at **Siding Spring**, on the edge of the national park. There's a visitor centre, open daily.

Coonabarabran has several motels and caravan parks but during school holidays they can fill up. The *Imperial Hotel* (☎ (068) 42 1023) has singles/doubles/twins for $26/40/46, including breakfast. Rooms with bathroom go for $32/45/50. There's an associate-YHA hostel ($13 a night) at the *Warrumbungles Mountain Motel* (☎ (068) 42 1832), nine km out of town on the road to the national park. The *Jolly Cauli* health-food shop on John St serves salads and snacks.

In the country around the national park are a number of places to stay. *Tibuc* (☎ (068) 42 1740, evenings best), an organic farm, sounds the most interesting.

Narrabri (population 7300) is a cotton-growing centre, with the enormous Australia Telescope (actually five linked radio telescope dishes) 25 km west on the Yarrie Lake road. The interesting visitor centre is open daily. **Mt Kaputar National Park**, good for walking, camping and climbing, is 53 km east of Narrabri by a steep, unsealed road. **Moree** is a large town on the Gwydir River with some reputedly therapeutic hot baths ($2.50).

ALONG THE CASTLEREAGH
Coonamble, 98 km north of Gilgandra, is at the edge of the Western Plains. West of here are the extensive **Macquarie Marshes** with their prolific bird life. The road continues north to **Walgett** in dry country near the Grawin and Glengarry opal fields.

A few km off the highway near the Queensland border, **Lightning Ridge** is a huge opal field which is the world's only reliable source of black opals. Despite the emphasis on tourism, with underground opal showrooms etc, Lightning Ridge remains a mining community where any battler could strike it rich. The **Moozeum** is worth a visit. There are motels (none cheap) and a few caravan parks with on-site vans. The *Tram-o-Tel* (☎ (068) 29 0448) has self-contained accommodation in old trams and caravans for $20/30.

ALONG THE MITCHELL
From Dubbo the Mitchell Highway passes through the citrus-growing centre of **Narromine**. **Warren**, further north and off the Mitchell on the Macquarie Highway, is an access point for the Macquarie Marshes, as is **Nyngan** where the Mitchell and Barrier highways divide. The huge marshes are breeding grounds for ducks, water hens, swans, pelicans, ibis and herons. Nyngan was the scene of fierce resistance by Aborigines to early White encroachment. From Nyngan the highway runs arrow-straight for 206 km to Bourke.

Outback

You don't have to travel to central Australia to experience red-soil country, limitless horizons and vast blue skies. The far west of New South Wales is rough, rugged and sparsely populated, but it also produces a fair proportion of the state's wealth – particularly from the mines of Broken Hill.

Always seek local advice before travelling on secondary roads west of the Mitchell Highway. You must carry plenty of water, and if you break down *stay with your vehicle*.

BOURKE (population 3500)

Nearly 800 km north-west of Sydney, Bourke is on the edge of the outback – 'back of Bourke' is synonymous with the outback, the back of beyond. A glance at the map will show just how outback the area beyond Bourke is – there's no town of any size for far around, and the country is flat and featureless as far as the eye can see. Bourke is a surprisingly pretty town and the surrounding country can be beautiful – the sheer space is exhilarating.

Bourke is on the Darling River as well as the Mitchell Highway and it was once a major port. Scores of paddle-steamers plied the river and in the 1880s it was possible for wool to be in London just six weeks after leaving Bourke – somewhat quicker than a sea-mail parcel today! The courthouse has a crown on its spire, signifying that its jurisdiction includes maritime cases.

The information centre (☎ (068) 72 2280) is at the railway station on Anson St. Pick up a 'Mud Maps' leaflet detailing drives to places like **Mt Gunderbooka**, which has Aboriginal cave art and vivid wildflowers in spring, and **Mt Oxley**.

Brewarrina (usually known as Bree) is 95 km east of Bourke. You can see **the Fisheries**, stone fish traps which the Ngemba Aboriginal people used to catch the fish to feed the inter-tribal gatherings they hosted. 'Brewarrina' means 'good fishing'. Nearby is the **Aboriginal Cultural Museum**.

Places to Stay

The *Paddlewheel Caravan Park* (☎ (068) 72 2277) has tent sites ($8), vans (from $18 a double), cabins (from $30 a double) and old-style self-contained units (from $30 a double).

Back o' Bourke Backpackers (☎ (068) 72 3009) is a good hostel on the corner of Oxley and Sturt Sts, close to the town centre and beside an impressive old bank building. Beds in two-bed dorms are $12 per person.

The best of Bourke's hotels is the *Old Royal* (☎ (068) 72 2544) on Mitchell St between Sturt and Richard Sts. It's renovated and the rooms are good value at $24/30/36 for singles/twins/doubles, or $52 for a self-contained suite.

Outback Accommodation Several stations in the Bourke area (a very large area) offer accommodation. The information centre has details and can make bookings. One of the best is historic *Urisino Station* (☎ (068) 74 7639), a friendly place which welcomes backpackers (and everyone else) and has camel treks. You can stay in the homestead ($35 per person or $60 with meals and activities) or in backpacker accommodation in old mud-brick cottages ($15 per person). Urisino is 230 km west of Bourke, beyond Wanaaring. It might be possible to arrange transport from Bourke.

Places to Eat

There are several cafes, such as the *Gum Blossom Tea Room* on Mitchell St. In the Post Office Hotel on Oxley St is the *Paddy Fitzgerald Coffee Lounge*, with good snacks and meals and some interesting old photos.

There are Chinese restaurants at the Bowling Club and at the Ex-Services Club. The best place for dinner is the *Old Royal Hotel Dining Room* on Mitchell St, with a touch of elegance and some interesting dishes. Main courses are around $15.

Getting There & Away

Lachlan Travel (☎ (068) 72 2092) on Oxley St is the Countrylink and Air Link agent. Countrylink buses run to Dubbo four times a week and connect with trains to Sydney ($70). It *might* be possible to go along on the biweekly mail runs to Wanaaring and Brewarrina. The post office (☎ (068) 72 2017) can put you in touch with the contractors.

BACK OF BOURKE – CORNER COUNTRY

There's no sealed road west of Bourke in New South Wales. If you cared to drive the 713 km from Bourke to Broken Hill via Wanaaring and Tibooburra it would be mostly on lonely unsealed roads. The far western corner of the state is a semidesert of red plains, heat, dust and flies, but with interesting physical features and prolific wildlife. Running along the border with Queensland is the Dogproof Fence, patrolled every day by boundary riders who each look after a 40-km section.

Tibooburra

Tiny Tibooburra, the hottest place in the state, is right in the north-western corner and has a number of stone buildings from the 1880s and '90s. There's a National Parks office (☎ (080) 91 3309), open daily. Tibooburra used to be called the Granites, after the granite outcrops nearby – these are good to visit on a sunset walk.

Although the town is so isolated, international flights bound for Sydney pass overhead. You can normally reach Tibooburra from Bourke or Broken Hill in a conventional vehicle, except after rain (which is pretty rare!).

Places to Stay & Eat There's a camp site just north of town at *Dead Horse Gully* ($5). In town, the *Granites Caravan Park* (☎ (080) 91 3305) has sites for $10, on-site vans for $24, cabins for $34 and motel units from $36/46.

The two fine old pubs, the *Family Hotel* (☎ (080) 91 3314) and the *Tibooburra Hotel* (☎ (080) 91 3310) (known as 'the two-storey'), have accommodation and both charge from $20/30. Both bars are worth a beer: the Family's has a mural by Clifton Pugh; the two-storey's has more than 60 impressively well-worn hats on the wall, left behind when their owners bought new headgear at the pub.

The hotels do good counter meals and even have tables outside where you can sit and watch the occasional 4WD pass by.

Sturt National Park

Tibooburra is an entry point for Sturt National Park in the very corner of the state. The park has 300 km of drivable tracks, camping areas and walks, particularly on the Jump Up Loop drive and towards the top of Mt Wood. It is recommended that you inform the ranger at Tibooburra before venturing into the park. The entry fee is $7.50 per car and camping costs $5 for two people.

At Camerons Corner there's a post to mark the place where Queensland, South Australia and New South Wales meet. It's a favourite goal for visitors and a 4WD is not always necessary to get there. In the Queensland corner, the *Corner Store* (!) does good sandwiches, home-made pies and even ice cream. Everybody coming by the Corner stops here and the staff give good advice on road conditions. At the time of writing you could buy fuel here but that hasn't always been the case – check in Tibooburra.

Milparinka

Milparinka, once a gold town, now consists of little more than a solitary hotel and some old sandstone buildings. In 1845 members of Charles Sturt's expedition from Adelaide, searching for an inland sea, were forced to camp near here for six months. The temperatures were high, the conditions terrible and their supplies inadequate. You can see the grave of James Poole, Sturt's second-in-command, about 14 km north-west of the settlement. Poole died of scurvy.

Country Race Meetings

Some country race meetings are real occasions – the one at Louth, on the Darling about 100 km south-west of Bourke, is particularly revered. The town's population is only about 50 and one year they recorded 29 planes 'flying in for the day'!

BARRIER HIGHWAY

The Barrier Highway is the main route in the state's west – and just about the only sealed road. It heads west from Nyngan, from where it's 594 km to Broken Hill. This provides an alternative route to Adelaide and it's the most direct route between Sydney and Western Australia.

Cobar (population 5500)

Cobar has a modern and highly productive copper mine but it also has an earlier history as evidenced by its old buildings, like the Great Western Hotel with its endless stretch of iron lacework ornamenting the verandah. Pick up a town tour map at the information centre (☎ (068) 36 2448), which is in the excellent **museum** ($3) at the eastern end of the main street. Ask here about mine tours.

Weather balloons are released at 9 am and 3 pm from the meteorological station on the edge of town, off the Louth road.

Mt Grenfell, with important Aboriginal cave paintings, is 40 km west of Cobar then 32 km north off the highway. You can't camp here.

The *Cobar Caravan Park* (☎ (068) 36 2425) has sites at $7.50, on-site vans at $20 and cabins at $28. Several pubs have accommodation, including the *New Occidental* (☎ (068) 36 2111) with singles/doubles for $15/25. The *Great Western* (☎ (068) 36 2053) has motel-style units at $28/44/55 a single/double/triple. Several motels are in the $40/50 range, such as the *Hi-Way* (☎ (068) 36 2000).

Wilcannia

Wilcannia is on the Darling River and in the days of paddle-steamers was an important port. It's a much quieter place today but you can still see buildings from that era, such as the police station. There are a couple of motels costing around $60 a double. The pubs may provide meals but are best avoided unless you are an experienced bar room brawler.

White Cliffs (population 150)

About 100 km north-west of Wilcannia is White Cliffs, an opal-mining settlement. For a taste of life in a small outback community it's worth the drive on a dirt road. You can fossick for opals around the old diggings (watch out for unfenced shafts) and there are opal showrooms and underground homes (called dugouts) open for inspection. Jock's Place is worth seeing – he has relics collected in the area and can tell you about opal mining. A tourist pamphlet is available from the general store or the showrooms.

As you enter White Cliffs you pass the high-tech dishes of the solar energy research station, where emus often graze out the front. There's a tour of the station at 2 pm daily.

Places to Stay & Eat The *White Cliffs Hotel* (☎ (080) 91 6606) has basic rooms, but they are air-con and good value at $14 per person. The management is friendly, meals are available (although they're pricey) and there is a 4WD for guests' use – around town only. Near the post office, *Opal View* (☎ (080) 91 6756) is a self-contained flat sleeping four or five and costing $50 a night. Across the road at the swimming pool there's a small camping area (☎ (080) 91 6627) where sites cost just $2 per person and showers are $1.

Up on Smiths Hill, *Rosavilla* (☎ (080) 91 6632) is a large dugout home with B&B at $26 per person. Nearby is the astounding *White Cliffs Underground Motel* (☎ toll-free 1800 021 154). It's surprisingly roomy and down here it's a constant 22°C, whether there's a heatwave or a frost up on the surface. Singles/doubles/triples cost $34/68/84; meals are expensive but the portions are reasonable.

The *Golf Club*, near the solar station, often has filling Sunday roast lunches for $5.

Mootwingee National Park

This park in the Bynguano Range, 131 km north of Broken Hill, teems with wildlife and it is a place of exceptional beauty. It is well worth the 1½- to two-hour drive from Broken Hill on an isolated dirt road. You can also get here from White Cliffs but neither route should be attempted after rain. Entry to the park is $7.50 per car.

In the park is an Aboriginal tribal ground

with important rock carvings and cave paintings – which have been badly damaged by vandals. The major site is now controlled by the Aboriginal community and is off limits except on ranger-escorted tours on Wednesday and Saturday morning ($4). The National Parks office in Broken Hill (☎ (080) 88 5933) has details.

There are walks through the crumbling sandstone hills to rock pools, which often have enough water for swimming, and rock paintings can be seen in the areas that are not off limits. There is a camp site ($10) with water for washing, but drinking water might not be always available. You should book sites, especially during school holidays.

BROKEN HILL (population 27,000)
Out in the far west, Broken Hill is an oasis in the wilderness. It's a fascinating town not only for its comfortable existence in an extremely unwelcoming environment, but also for the fact that it was once a one-company town which spawned one equally strong union.

History
The Broken Hill Proprietary Company (BHP) was formed in 1885 after Charles Rasp, a boundary rider, discovered a silver lode. Miners working on other finds in the area had failed to notice the real wealth. Other mining claims were staked, but BHP was always the 'big mine' and dominated the town. Charles Rasp amassed a personal fortune and BHP, which later diversified into steel production, became Australia's largest company.

Early conditions in the mine were appalling. Hundreds of miners died and many more suffered from lead poisoning and lung disease. This gave rise to the other great force in Broken Hill, the unions. Many miners were immigrants but all were united in their efforts to improve conditions.

The town's first 35 years saw a militancy rarely matched in Australian industrial relations. Many campaigns were fought, police were called in to break strikes and, though there was a gradual improvement in conditions, the miners lost many confrontations. The turning point was the Big Strike of 1919 and 1920, which lasted for over 18 months. The miners won a great victory, achieving a 35-hour week and the end of dry drilling, responsible for the dust that afflicted so many miners.

The concept of 'one big union', which had helped to win the strike, was formalised in 1923 with the formation of the Barrier Industrial Council, which still largely runs the town.

Today the world's richest deposit of silver, lead and zinc is still being worked, but lead and zinc have assumed a greater importance in the Silver City, as Broken Hill is known. There is enough ore left to ensure at least another 20 years of mining, but new technology has greatly reduced the number of jobs in the mines.

Orientation & Information
The city is laid out in a grid and the central area is easy to get around on foot.

The big Tourist & Travellers Centre (☎ (080) 87 6077) on the corner of Blende and Bromide Sts is open daily. This is where the buses arrive and there's a bus booking agency on the premises, as well as a cafeteria and a car-rental desk. Also here is the Broken Hill Interpretive Centre with displays on all aspects of the city. Pick up a heritage tour map ($2).

In many ways Broken Hill is closer to South Australia than New South Wales (it is 1170 km from Sydney but only 509 km from Adelaide) and clocks are set on Adelaide (central) rather than Sydney (eastern) time – half an hour behind.

The National Parks office (☎ (080) 88 5933) is at 5 Oxide St. The Royal Automobile Association of South Australia (☎ (080) 88 4999) is at 261 Argent St and provides reciprocal service to other autoclub members. You can buy your South Australian Desert Parks Pass here – see the Outback section of the South Australia chapter.

The swimming pool is in Sturt Park on Wolfram St. There's a laundromat on Argent St just east of the West Darling Hotel.

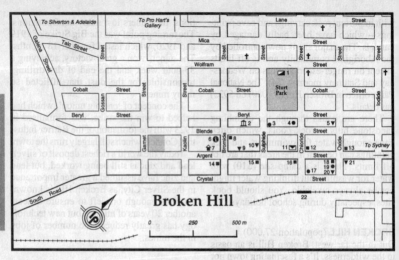

Broken Hill

0   250   500 m

PLACES TO STAY

7 Tourist Lodge (YHA)
8 Black Lion Inn
12 Royal Exchange Hotel
13 West Darling Hotel
14 Silver Spade Motel
15 Mario's Palace Hotel
16 Grand Private Hotel
18 Astra House Backpackers

PLACES TO EAT

5 International Deli
9 Barrier Social
   Democratic Club
10 Champion Pizza &
   Chinese Takeaway
20 Silver City Chinese
   Restaurant
21 Papa Joe's Pizza

OTHER

1 Swimming Pool
2 Railway Museum
3 Trades Hall
4 Broken Hill City Art Gallery
   & Entertainment Centre
6 Tourist & Travellers Centre
11 Post Office
17 RSL Club
19 National Parks Office
22 Railway Station

Mines

There are four working mines, controlled by two companies. The deepest is the North Mine, 1600 metres down. At that depth it can reach 60°C and massive refrigeration plants are needed to control the temperature. You can't visit the working mines but there are tours of old mines.

Delprat's Mine (☎ (080) 88 1064) has an excellent underground tour daily except Sunday, where you don miners' gear and descend 130 metres for a tour lasting nearly two hours. It costs $18 (students $15). Nobody under eight years of age is allowed. To get there go up Iodide St, cross the railway tracks and follow the signs – it's about a five-minute drive.

Day Dream Mine, begun in 1881, is 33 km from Broken Hill, off the Silverton Rd. A one-hour tour costs $10, or $5 for children (all ages allowed), and sturdy footwear is essential. Contact the tourist centre for bookings.

At **White's Mineral Art Gallery & Mining Museum**, 1 Allendale St, you can walk into a mining stope and see mining memorabilia and minerals. Follow Galena St out to the north-west for two km or so. Admission is $4.

Artists

Broken Hill seems to inspire artists and there is a plethora of galleries, including the Pro Hart Gallery at 108 Wyman St and Jack Absalom's Gallery at 638 Chapple St. Pro Hart, a former miner, is Broken Hill's best-known artist and a local personality. Apart from his own work, his gallery displays minor works of major artists (eg, Picasso and Dali) and his collection of Australian art is superb. He charges admission ($2) but many others don't.

The Ant Hill Gallery on Bromide St opposite the tourist centre features local and major Australian artists. In the Broken Hill City Art Gallery (in the Entertainment Centre) is the 'Silver Tree', an intricate silver sculpture commissioned by Charles Rasp. One gallery is devoted to the artists of Broken Hill.

Have a look at the murals inside Mario's Palace Hotel on Argent St.

Royal Flying Doctor Service Base

You can visit the RFDS base at the airport. The tour ($2) includes a film, and you can inspect the headquarters, aircraft and the radio room that handles calls from remote towns and stations. Tour times are Monday to Friday, 10.30 am and 3.30 pm, and weekends at 10.30 am. Bookings are made at the tourist centre.

School of the Air

You can sit in on School of the Air broadcasts to kids in isolated homesteads, on weekdays at 8.30 am. The one-hour session costs $2. You can visit during vacations, when a tape-recording is played. Book at the tourist centre.

Other Attractions

The **Sulphide St Station Railway & Historical Museum** is in the Silverton Tramway Company's old station on Sulphide St. The tramway was a private railway running between Cockburn (South Australia) and Broken Hill via Silverton until 1970. It's open from 10 am to 3 pm daily and admission is $2.

The **Afghani Mosque** is a simple corrugated-iron building dating from 1891.

Afghani cameleers helped to open up the outback and the mosque was built on the site of a camel camp. It's on the corner of William and Buck Sts in North Broken Hill and is open on Sunday between 2.30 and 4.30 pm. It no longer functions as a mosque.

The **Sculpture Symposium** was a project by 12 sculptors from several countries who carved sandstone blocks on a hilltop outside town. Drive north-west on Kaolin St and keep going on the unsealed road for a couple of km, until you get to the signposted turn-off on the right. From here it's another couple of km on a rough road, then a steep walk to the top of the hill. Apart from the sculptures there are excellent views over the plains.

This is a good place to watch one of Broken Hill's famous sunsets, as is the **Sundown Nature Trail** 10 km north-east of town off the Silver City Highway.

Organised Tours

Plenty of companies offer tours of the town and nearby attractions, some going further out to White Cliffs, Mootwingee and other outback destinations. The tourist centre has information and takes bookings.

Goanna Safari (☎ (080) 91 2518) has 4WD outback tours which get good feedback from travellers. Catherine Mould's family has worked the huge Westward Downs station, 180 km north of Broken Hill, for a century and she knows the country well. At $295 per person for three days and two nights, with a minimum of two people, it's a good introduction to the outback. Shorter and longer tours can be arranged.

An interesting way to see some of the country beyond Broken Hill is to go along on an outback mail run. Contact Crittenden Air (☎ (080) 88 5702), as far in advance as possible. The mail run departs at 6.30 am on Saturday and calls at about 14 outback stations, stopping in White Cliffs for a tour and lunch. The cost is $210. It also does various air tours.

Places to Stay

Camping The *Broken Hill Caravan Park* (☎ (080) 87 3841) on Rakow St (the Barrier

Highway) north-west of the centre has sites ($9), cabins (from $30) and on-site vans (about $25). The *Lake View Caravan Park* (☎ (080) 88 2250) on Argent St (the Barrier Highway) to the east has sites ($8) and cabins (from $30), and the small *Silverland Road-house Park* (☎ (080) 87 7389) north of here on Jabez St also has sites ($8) and cabins (about $28).

Hostels *Astra House* (☎ (080) 87 7788), in the centre of town on the corner of Argent and Oxide Sts, is a good backpackers' hostel in an ex-pub. There's still a lot of renovating to be done but it is a friendly place with huge verandahs, high ceilings and clean rooms. James, the manager, will drive you to local sights. There are bikes for hire ($5 a day) and twice a week there's a free meal for backpackers, which might be anything from kangaroo steaks to lentils. Dorm beds are $10, singles (when available) are $12 and doubles are $24.

The *Tourist Lodge* (☎ (080) 2086) at 100 Argent St, not far from the tourist centre, is an associate-YHA hostel with dorms at $14 ($12 YHA members). Singles/twins cost from $20/32, with much cheaper weekly rates.

Hotels & Motels High ceilings, wide corridors and huge verandahs come as standard equipment on pubs in this hot city. All the places mentioned here also have air-con. The nice old *Royal Exchange Hotel* (☎ (080) 87 2308) on the corner of Argent and Chloride Sts has rooms for $24/40 or $34/50 with bathroom, fridge and TV. The price drops by about 10% if you stay more than a couple of days. Diagonally opposite, the *Grand Private Hotel* (☎ (080) 87 5305) has rooms with shared bathrooms for $40/48 a single/double.

Further west on Sulphide and Argent Sts, *Mario's Palace Hotel* (☎ (080) 88 1699) is an impressive old (1888) pub covered in murals. All rooms have fridges, TVs and tea-and coffee-making facilities. Some have phones. Singles/doubles are $25/36 or $36/46 with attached bathroom. Some rooms

have thin walls. The *Black Lion Inn* (☎ (080) 87 4801), across from the tourist centre, isn't on the same scale but it has reasonable rooms for $18/28 (there's no air-con in the single rooms).

The *Sturt Motel* (☎ (080) 87 3558), on Rakow St (Barrier Highway) a few km north-west of the centre, charges from about $35/40. The *Silver Spade* (☎ (080) 87 7021), at 77 Argent St, charges around $45/55; most of the other motels charge at least $55/65.

Cottages *Beryl Cottage* (☎ (080) 88 3288) at 350 Beryl St is a small house available by the night for $65 for four people, plus $5 for each extra person (up to six). Other six-person cottages are available for $60 a night or $320 a week – contact the owner (☎ (080) 87 8488) at 143 Knox St.

Places to Eat
The cafeteria in the tourist centre is OK, with bacon & eggs for about $6 and other snacks and meals.

Broken Hill is a club town if ever there was one. The clubs welcome visitors and in most cases you just sign the book at the front door and walk in. Most have reasonably priced, reasonably good, very filling meals. The *Barrier Social & Democratic Club* ('the Demo'), 218 Argent St, has meals including a breakfast (from 6 am, or 7 am weekends) which will keep you going all day. The *Musician's Club* at 267 Crystal St is slightly cheaper, while the *RSL*, on Chloride St, is a bit more up-market.

There are lots of pubs too – this is a mining town – like the *Black Lion Inn* across from the tourist centre which has a $5 counter lunch and main courses in the evening for around $10. Many other pubs also have counter meals. At the Royal Exchange Hotel on the corner of Argent and Chloride Sts, the *Pepinella Room* restaurant has a two-course lunch special for $8 (weekdays only) and main courses from around $15 at dinner.

Papa Joe's on Argent St has pasta and pizzas, plus steaks from around $9. Further east on Argent St are the *Oceania Chinese Restaurant*, with $6 lunch specials and main courses from around $7.50; *Old Capri*, a small Italian place boasting home-made pasta; and the *Pussycat*, with pasta for $6 and steaks from about $10. Up on Sulphide St, *Champion Pizza & Chinese Takeaway* stays open late. Also good for late-night supplies is the *International Deli* on Oxide St near Beryl St, open until midnight all week. If you're after a late-night pie, head for the *Camp Oven Pie Cart*, usually parked on Oxide St outside Papa Joe's.

Entertainment

Maybe it's because this is a mining town, maybe it's because there are so many nights when it's too hot to sleep, but Broken Hill stays up late. There isn't a lot of formal entertainment but pubs stay open almost until dawn on Thursday, Friday and Saturday.

The *Theatre Royale Hotel* on Argent St has a disco, and the *Barrier Social & Democratic Club* often has music and sometimes features good bands. The *Black Lion*, across from the tourist centre, has been recommended as a good pub for a drink. It has a three-page cocktail list and two-for-one deals on some nights.

Two-up (gambling on the fall of two pennies) is played at *Burke Ward Hall* on Wills St near the corner of Gypsum St, west of the centre, on Friday and Saturday nights. Broken Hill claims to have retained all the atmosphere of a real two-up 'school' (until recently illegal), unlike the sanitised versions played in casinos.

Getting There & Around

Air Standard one-way fares from Broken Hill include $160 to Adelaide with Kendell and Sunstate, $337 to Sydney with Hazelton ($250 advance purchase), $98 to Mildura and $197 to Melbourne with Sunstate.

Bus Greyhound Pioneer runs daily to Adelaide for $50, to Mildura for about $35 and to Sydney for $90 (sometimes less). Most buses depart from the tourist centre, where you can book seats.

A Victorian V/Line bus runs to Mildura

($35) and Melbourne ($85) on Monday, Wednesday, Friday and Sunday. Book at the railway station.

Train Broken Hill is on the Sydney to Perth railway line so the Indian Pacific passes through. On Sunday and Wednesday it leaves Broken Hill at 3.05 pm and arrives in Sydney at 9.15 am the next day. The economy fare is $86. To Adelaide ($44) and Perth (from $214), it departs Broken Hill on Tuesday and Friday at 9 am.

There's a slightly faster and marginally cheaper daily service to Sydney called Laser, a Countrylink bus departing Broken Hill daily at 4 am (groan) and connecting with a train at Dubbo, arriving in Sydney at 9 pm.

The Countrylink booking office at the railway station (☎ (080) 87 1400) is open on weekdays.

Car Rental The major companies have offices here but their 'remote region' rates can work out to be very expensive.

Taxi Phone numbers which will get you a taxi include (☎ (080) 88 1144) and (☎ (080) 88 2222).

AROUND BROKEN HILL
Silverton

Silverton, 25 km west of Broken Hill, is an old silver-mining town which peaked in 1885 when it had a population of 3000 and public buildings designed to last for centuries. In 1889 the mines closed and the population (and many of the houses) moved to Broken Hill.

Today it's an interesting little ghost town, which was used as a setting in films such as *Mad Max II* and *A Town Like Alice*. A number of buildings still stand, including the old jail (now the museum) and the Silverton Hotel. The hotel is still operating and it displays photographs taken on the film sets. There are also a couple of art galleries. The information centre, in the old school, has a walking tour map.

The road beyond Silverton becomes bleak and lonely almost immediately but the

Umberumberka Reservoir, 13 km from Silverton, is a popular picnic spot.

Bill Canard (☎ (080) 88 5316) runs a variety of camel tours from Silverton. His camels are often hitched up near the hotel or the information centre. You can take a 15-minute tour of the town for $5, a one-hour ride for $20 or a two-hour sunset ride for $40. There are also overnight treks ($150) and a five-day journey through the Barrier Ranges.

There's basic camping at Penrose Park (☎ (080) 88 5307), located by a creek on the Broken Hill side of town. Bring or boil drinking water.

Menindee Lakes

This water storage development on the Darling River, 112 km south-east of Broken Hill, offers a variety of water sport facilities. **Menindee** is the town for the area. Bourke and Wills stayed at Maidens Hotel on their ill-fated trip north in 1860. The hotel was built in 1854 and has been with the same family for nearly 100 years. It still has accommodation (☎ (080) 91 4880).

Kinchega National Park is close to the town and the lakes, overflowing from the Darling River, are a haven for bird life. The visitor centre is at the site of the old Kinchega Homestead, about 16 km from the park entrance, and the shearing shed has been preserved. There are plenty of camp sites along the river.

MUNGO NATIONAL PARK

North-east of Mildura and south of Menindee is Lake Mungo, a dry lake which is the site of the oldest archaeological finds in Australia – human skeletons and artefacts dating back 45,000 years. A 25-km semicircle ('lunette') of huge sand dunes has been created by the never-ending west wind, which continually exposes fabulously ancient remains. Remember, it is illegal in Australia to remove archaeological objects or to disturb human remains.

There's a visitor centre by the old Mungo woolshed. A road leads across the dry lake bed to the Great Wall of China, a formation in the dunes, and you can drive a complete 60-km loop of the dunes – but not after rain. Park entry costs $7.50 per car.

Accommodation fills up during school holidays. There are two camp sites – Main Camp near the visitor centre and Belah Camp on the eastern side of the dunes. Camping costs $5 a night. There is also shared accommodation in the old shearers' quarters for $15 per person or $25 for a room to yourself. Book through the National Parks office in Buronga (☎ (050) 23 1278), near Mildura. On the Mildura road about four km from the visitor centre is *Mungo Lodge* (☎ (050) 29 7297). Singles/doubles go for $55/65 and there are self-contained cottages sleeping five or six for $75. There's also a restaurant.

Mungo is 110 km from Mildura and 150 km from Balranald on unsealed roads. These towns are the closest places where you can buy fuel. Mallee Outback Exploration (☎ (050) 21 1621) and Junction Tours (☎ (050) 21 4424) are two Mildura-based companies offering tours.

Lord Howe Island

Only 11 km long and 2.5-km wide, beautiful Lord Howe Island is a long way out in the Pacific, east of Port Macquarie and 600 km north-east of Sydney. Lord Howe is really off the budget track, and apart from the expense of getting there you won't find much in the way of cheap accommodation. Most visitors are on package tours.

It's heavily forested and has beautiful walks, a wide lagoon sheltered by a coral reef, and some fine beaches. It's small enough to get around on foot or by bicycle. The southern end is dominated by towering Mt Lidgbird (808 metres) and Mt Gower (875 metres). You can climb Mt Gower in around six hours (round trip). The lagoon has good snorkelling, and you can also inspect the sea life from glass-bottomed boats. On the other side of the island there's surf at Blinky Beach.

Information

For more information contact travel agents such as the Pacific Island Travel Centre (☎ (02) 262 6555), 7th floor, 39-41 York St, Sydney.

Places to Stay

You can't camp on the island but there are lodges and self-contained apartments. Even in the mid-winter low season lodges cost over $200 a day for a double room, with the cheapest apartments over $100. Food is more expensive than on the Australian mainland.

Getting There & Away

You used to get to Lord Howe by romantic old flying boats from Sydney. Today they've been retired and a small airport has been built on the island. The return fare with Eastern Australia from Sydney (daily) or Sunstate from Brisbane (weekends) is $694.

Getting Around

You can hire bicycles; there are motorbikes and a few rental cars on the island but a bike is all you need. There is an overall 25 kph speed limit.

NEW SOUTH WALES

Northern Territory

Area	1,346,000 sq km
Population	168,000

> ☎ From April 1995, Darwin numbers beginning with 89 will be changed to 99. From April 1996, the Northern Territory's existing phone numbers will be prefixed by the last two digits of the current area code (for example, ☎ (089) 12 3456 becomes ☎ 8912 3456). The area code for the Territory will be (08). ■

The fascinating Northern Territory is the least populated (with only 1% of the Australian population!) and most barren area of Australia. The populated parts of Australia are predominantly urban and coastal, but it is in the centre – the Red Heart – that the picture-book, untamed and sometimes surreal Australia exists.

The Centre is not just Uluru (Ayers Rock), bang in the middle of nowhere. There are meteorite craters, eerie canyons, lost valleys of palms, and noisy Alice Springs festivals. Where else is there an annual boat regatta on a dry river bed? The colour red is evident as soon as you arrive – in the soil, the rocks and in Uluru itself. At the other end of the Track – the 1500 km of bitumen that connects Alice Springs to the north coast – is Darwin, probably Australia's most cosmopolitan city.

Even that long, empty road between Alice Springs and Darwin isn't dull – there are plenty of interesting places along the way. As you travel up or down that single link you'll notice another of the Territory's real surprises – the contrast between the Centre's amazing aridity and the humid, tropical wetness of the Top End in the monsoon season. The wetlands and escarpments of Kakadu National Park are a treasure house of wildlife and Aboriginal rock painting.

With a small population and a more fragile economy than other parts of Australia, the Northern Territory isn't classified as a state. It was formerly administered by New South Wales and then by South Australia, but it has been controlled by the Federal government since 1911. Since 1978 the Territory has been self-governing, although Canberra still has more say over its internal affairs than over those of the states.

NORTHERN TERRITORY ABORIGINES

Around 22% of the Territory's population is Aboriginal – a higher proportion than in most southern states.

The process of White settlement in the Northern Territory was just as troubled and violent as elsewhere in Australia, with Aboriginal groups vainly trying to resist the takeover of lands on which their way of life depended. By the early 20th century, most Aborigines were confined to government-allotted reserves or Christian missions. Others lived on cattle stations where they were employed as skilful but poorly paid stockmen or domestic servants, or were living a half-life on the edges of towns, attracted there by food and tobacco, sometimes finding low-paid work, too often acquiring an alcohol habit. Only a few – some of those on reserves and cattle stations, and those in the remote outback – maintained much of their traditional way of life.

During the 1960s, Northern Territory Aborigines began to demand more rights. In 1963 the people of Yirrkala on the Gove Peninsula, part of the Arnhem Land reserve, protested against plans for bauxite mining. In 1966 the Gurindji people on Wave Hill

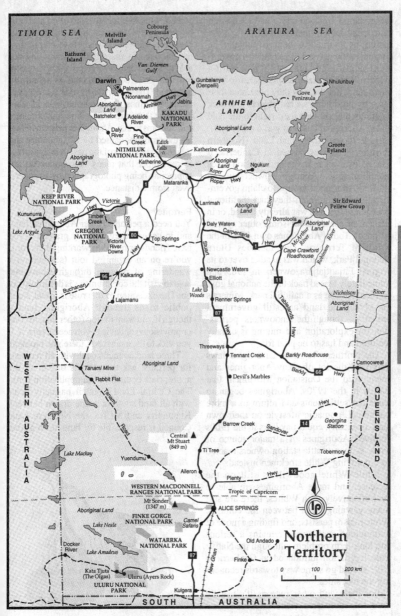

NORTHERN TERRITORY

Northern Territory

0   100   200 km

cattle station went on strike and asked that their tribal land, which formed part of the station, be returned to them. Eventually the Gurindji were given 3238 sq km in a government-negotiated deal with the station owners. The Yirrkala people failed to stop the mining, but the way they presented their case (by producing sacred objects and bark paintings that showed their right to the land under Aboriginal custom) was a milestone.

In 1976 the Aboriginal Land (Northern Territory) Act was passed in Canberra. It handed over all reserves and mission lands in the Territory to Aboriginal ownership, and allowed Aboriginal groups to claim government land with which they had traditional ties (unless the land was already leased, or in a town, or set aside for some other special purpose). Today Aborigines own 45% of the Northern Territory. This includes Uluru National Park, which was handed over to its original Pitjantjatjara owners in 1985 and immediately leased back to the national government for use as a national park. Minerals on Aboriginal land are still government property – though the landowners' permission for exploration and mining is usually required and has to be paid for.

The Northern Territory land rights laws improved the lot of many Aborigines and encouraged the Outstation Movement that started in the 1970s. Aborigines began to leave the settlements and return to a more traditional, nomadic lifestyle on their own land. Ironically, equal-pay laws in the 1960s deprived Aborigines of a major source of work, as many cattle station owners reacted by employing White stockmen instead.

While White goodwill is still on the increase, and more Aborigines are able to deal effectively with Whites, there are still many yawning gulfs between the cultures. White racism persists, and finding a mode of harmonious coexistence remains a serious and long-term problem, although the Native Title legislation introduced in Canberra in 1993 should go some way towards reconciling the two sides.

For these and other reasons it's usually hard for short-term visitors to make real contact with Aborigines, who often prefer to be left to themselves. This is gradually changing, however, as more communities feel inclined to share their culture, and are able to do it on their own terms. For this reason tourism on Aboriginal land is generally restricted. The benefits to the communities are twofold: the most obvious is the financial gain, the other that introducing Aboriginal culture and customs to non-Aborigines helps to alleviate the problems caused by the ignorance and misunderstandings of the past. It is important to remember that many Aborigines do not appreciate being photographed by strangers, even from a distance.

Permits

You need a permit to enter Aboriginal land, and in general they are only granted if you have friends or relatives working there, or if you're on an organised tour (see below) – wandering at random through Aboriginal land to visit the communities is definitely not on. The exception to this rule is travel along public roads through Aboriginal land – though if you want to stop (other than for fuel or provisions) or deviate, you need a permit. If you stick to the main roads, there's no problem.

Three land councils deal with all requests for permits: ask the permits officer of the appropriate council for an application form. The Central Land Council basically deals with all land south of a line drawn between Kununurra and Mt Isa, the Northern Land Council is responsible for land north of that

line, and the Tiwi Land Council deals with Bathurst and Melville islands.

Permits take around four to six weeks to be processed.

Northern Land Council
    9 Rowling St, (PO Box 42921), Casuarina, Darwin, NT 0820 (☎ (089) 20 5100)
Tiwi Land Council
    Unit 9, Wingate Centre, Winnellie, Darwin, NT 0800 (☎ (089) 47 1838)
Central Land Council
    33 Stuart Highway, (PO Box 3321), Alice Springs, NT 0871 (☎ (089) 52 3800)

Tours on Aboriginal Land

There are a number of tourist operations, some of them Aboriginal owned, running trips to visit Aboriginal land and communities in the Northern Territory. This is the best way to have any meaningful contact with Aborigines, even though you may feel that by being on a tour what you're getting is not the 'real thing'. The fact is that this is the way the Aboriginal owners of the land want tourism to work, so that they have some control over who visits what and when.

Arnhem Land offers the most options, mainly because of its proximity to Kakadu. The tours here generally only visit the very western edge of Arnhem Land, and take you to Gunbalanya (Oenpelli) and other places which are normally off limits. Some operators include Magela Tours, Umorrduk Safaris, AAT-Kings and Davidson's Arnhem Land Safaris (see the Kakadu and Arnhem Land sections for more details).

Other places in the Top End with similar operations include Tiwi Islands, Katherine and Borroloola, while in the Centre they are at Kings Canyon and Uluru. See those sections for details.

Aboriginal Events & Festivals

There are a number of regular festivals which are well worth attending. Although they are usually held on restricted Aboriginal land, permit requirements are generally waived for the festivals. Be aware also that alcohol is banned or restricted in many communities.

Barunga Festival
    For the four days over the Queen's Birthday long weekend in June, Barunga, 80 km south-east of Katherine, becomes a gathering place for Aborigines from all over the Territory. There's a traditional arts and crafts, as well as dancing and athletics competitions. No accommodation is provided so you'll need your own camping equipment, or visit for the day from Katherine. No permit required.
Merrepen Arts Festival
    On the fourth Sunday in July, Nauiyu Nambiyu on the banks of the Daly River is the venue for the Merrepen Arts Festival. Several Aboriginal communities from around the district, such as Wadeye, Nauiyu and Peppimenarti, display their arts and crafts. No permit required.
Yuendumu Festival
    The Yuendumu community is 270 km north-west of Alice Springs, and Aborigines from the central and western desert region meet here over the long weekend in early August. There's a mix of traditional and modern sporting and cultural events. BYO camping gear. No permit required.
Gunbalanya (Oenpelli) Open Day
    Gunbalanya is in Arnhem Land, not far from Jabiru. On the first Saturday in August an open day is held where there's a chance to purchase local artefacts and watch the sports and dancing events. No permit required.
National Aboriginal Art Award
    Every Saturday an exhibition of works entered for this award is held at the Darwin Museum of Arts & Sciences. It attracts entries from all over the country

CLIMATE

The climate of the Top End is best described in terms of the Dry and the Wet, rather than winter and summer. Roughly, the Dry is April to September, and the Wet is October to March, with the heaviest rain falling from January onwards. April, when the rains taper off, and October to December, with their uncomfortably high humidity and that 'waiting for the rains' feeling (known as the 'build-up'), are transition periods. The Top End is the most thundery part of Australia: Darwin has over 90 'thunderdays' a year, all between September and March.

In the Centre the temperatures are much more variable – plummeting below freezing on winter nights (July to August), and soaring into the high 40s on summer days (December to January). Come prepared for both extremes, and for intense sun and the occasional rainstorm at any time of the year. When it rains, dirt roads quickly become quagmires.

Ask any Territorian when the best time to visit the Territory is and invariably they'll say the wet season. The reasons they'll cite will include that everything is green, there's no dust, the barramundi fishing is at its best, prices drop at many places, there are spectacular electrical storms – and all the tourists have gone home! While it's hard to argue with this sort of logic, the Wet does present problems for the visitor – the humidity is often unbearable unless you're acclimatised, dirt roads are often impassable, swimming in the ocean is impossible because of box jellyfish (stingers), and many national parks and reserves are either totally or partially closed.

INFORMATION

Surprisingly, the Northern Territory Tourism Commission doesn't have any tourist offices either within the Territory or elsewhere in Australia, although there are regional tourist offices in Darwin, Katherine and Alice Springs.

If you want any predeparture information, contact the Northern Territory Tourism Commission (☎ (089) 89 3900) in Darwin.

NATIONAL PARKS

For detailed information on Uluru and Kakadu national parks contact the Australian Nature Conservation Agency (ANCA; formerly the Australian National Parks & Wildlife Service) (☎ (089) 81 5299) in Smith St, Darwin, which administers the two parks. There are excellent information offices in the parks themselves.

Other parks and natural and historic reserves are run by the Conservation Commission of the Northern Territory, which has offices at Alice Springs, Katherine and Darwin, plus an information desk in the tourist office in Alice Springs. The Conservation Commission puts out fact sheets on individual parks, and these are available at CCNT offices or from the parks themselves.

ACTIVITIES
Bushwalking

There are interesting bushwalking trails in the Northern Territory, but take care if you venture off the beaten track. You can climb the ranges surrounding Alice Springs – remember to wear stout shoes, as the spinifex grass and burrs are very sharp. In summer, wear a hat and carry water even on short walks. Walking is best in the Dry, although shorter walks are possible in the Wet when the patches of monsoon rainforest are at their best.

The Larapinta Trail, in the Western MacDonnell Ranges near Alice Springs, is a well laid out trail with camp sites and other basic facilities provided along the way. Trephina Gorge Nature Park, in the Eastern MacDonnells, has a few marked trails, although they are all day trips or shorter.

Gregory National Park, just off the Victoria Highway, also lends itself well to extended bushwalks, although there are no marked trails. The same applies to Kakadu.

When undertaking any bushwalks in the Territory parks and reserves it is usually necessary to contact the local ranger for permission.

The Darwin Bushwalking Club (☎ (089) 85 1484) makes weekend expeditions all year round and welcomes visitors.

Willis's Walkabouts (☎ (089) 85 2134) is a commercial tour operator in Darwin which offers bushwalks in the Top End, Kimberley and the Centre, ranging from three days to three weeks.

Swimming

Stay out of the sea during the Wet because stings from box jellyfish (stingers) can be fatal. Darwin beaches are popular, however, during the safe months. Beware too, of saltwater crocodiles in both salt and fresh waters in the Top End – though there are quite a few safe, natural swimming holes. Take local advice – and if in doubt, don't take a risk.

It is a good idea to have vinegar with you at the beach when swimming in coastal waters in the Territory, as this is the most effective way to treat stinger weals. Don't try to remove the stings.

Fishing

This is good, particularly for barramundi, a perch that often grows to over a metre long and is great to eat. Barramundi is found both offshore and inland and there are fishing tours out of a number of places for the express purpose of catching it.

Some of the best fishing is found in and around Borroloola in the Gulf country, but Kakadu and Darwin are also OK.

Some of the companies which run fishing tours include Big Barra (☎ (089) 32 1473) and Top End Sportsfishing (☎ (089) 83 1495) in and around Kakadu and Arnhem Land, and Croc Spot (☎ (089) 75 8721) in Borroloola.

There are size and bag limits on barramundi and mud crabs, so be aware of these. For information contact the Fisheries Management Section (☎ (089) 89 4395) of the Department of Primary Industry & Fisheries.

Fossicking

There are many places in the Northern Territory for the fossicker – check in advance with the Northern Territory Department of Mines & Energy for information on the best places and to check whether permission is required. Look around the Harts Range (72 km north-east of Alice Springs) for beryl, garnet and quartz; the Eastern MacDonnell Ranges (east of Alice Springs) for beryl and garnet; Tennant Creek for gold and jasper; Anthony Lagoon (215 km east of the Stuart Highway, north of Tennant Creek) for ribbonstone; Pine Creek for gold; and Brock's Creek (37 km south-west of Adelaide River, south of Darwin) for topaz, tourmaline, garnet and zircon.

The NT Department of Mines & Energy publishes *A Guide to Fossicking in the Northern Territory*, available for $9 from the department offices in Alice Springs (☎ (089) 50 3658), Tennant Creek (☎ (089) 62 2491) and Darwin (☎ (089) 81 4806).

Gliding & Parachuting

The thermals created by the dry heat of the Centre are fantastic for gliding. There is a gliding club at Bond Springs, 25 km north of

Alice Springs, and a parachuting club at Batchelor, 88 km south of Darwin.

GETTING THERE & AWAY

Transport into the Northern Territory by bus, train, car and air is discussed mainly in the Alice Springs, Darwin and Uluru sections.

GETTING AROUND
Air

Ansett's flight network is more comprehensive than the Qantas service. There are also two Ansett-affiliated feeder airlines: Air North linking Darwin, Katherine, Bathurst

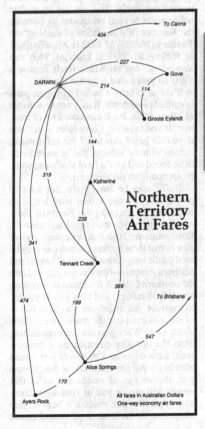

Northern Territory Air Fares

All fares in Australian Dollars
One-way economy air fares

Island, Jabiru, Gunbalanya (Oenpelli), Groote Eylandt and Gove; and Skyport, which operates between Alice Springs, Tennant Creek, Katherine and Darwin. The chart details regular fares.

Bus

Within the Territory, there's fairly good coverage given by Greyhound Pioneer. See the Getting There & Away sections for the various towns.

Car

Off the beaten track, 'with care' is the thought to bear in mind, and all the usual precautions apply. You can get up-to-date information on road conditions by phoning the Automobile Association of the Northern Territory (☎ (089) 53 1322 in Alice Springs, or ☎ (089) 81 3837 in Darwin). They can also advise you on which roads require a 4WD all year round or just in the Wet.

It's wise to carry a basic kit of spare parts in case of breakdown. It may not be a matter of life or death, but it can save a lot of time, trouble and expense. Carry spare water, and if you do break down off the main roads, remain with the vehicle; you're more likely to be found and you'll have shade and some protection from the elements.

Traffic may be fairly light, but a lot of people still manage to run into things, so watch out for the two great Northern Territory road hazards – road trains and animals. Road trains are huge trucks (a prime mover plus two or three trailers), which can only be used on the long outback roads of central and northern Australia – they're not allowed into the southern cities. A road train is very long (around 50 metres) and very big. If you try to overtake one make sure you have plenty of room to complete the manoeuvre – allow about a km. When you see one approaching from the opposite direction on a bitumen road, slow down and pull over – if a road train has to put its wheels off the road to pass you, the shower of stones and rocks that results will not do you or your windscreen any good. On dirt roads it's best to stop altogether, as the dust cloud behind a road train usually blanks your vision completely, if only for a few seconds.

Between sunset and sunrise the Territory's wildlife comes out to play. Hitting a kangaroo is all too easy and the damage to your vehicle, not to mention the kangaroo, can be severe. There are also buffaloes, cattle, wild horses and a number of other driving hazards which you are wise to avoid. There's really only one sensible way to deal with these night-time road hazards – don't drive at night. If you must drive at night, keep your speed right down, and remember that most animals travel in groups!

An added hazard in the Territory is the fact that there is no speed limit on the open roads, leading to the temptation to travel faster than the road conditions allow.

Hitching

Hitching is generally good, but once away from the main towns lifts can be few and far between. Threeways, where the road to Mt Isa branches off the Darwin to Alice Springs road, is notorious for long waits for lifts.

Darwin

Population 67,900

The 'capital' of northern Australia comes as a surprise to many people. Instead of the hard-bitten, rough-and-ready town you might expect, Darwin is a lively, modern place with a young population, an easy-going lifestyle and a cosmopolitan atmosphere.

In part this is thanks to Cyclone Tracy, which did a comprehensive job of flattening Darwin on Christmas Day in 1974. People who were there during the reconstruction say a new spirit grew up with the new buildings, as Darwinites, showing true Top End resilience, took the chance to make their city one of which to be proud. Darwin became a brighter, smarter, sturdier place, and development has continued into the 'post-post-cyclone' phase.

Darwin is still a frontier town, with a fairly

transient population and a hard-drinking one at that – it's not easy to resist a beer or two after a day in the heat – but these days it has the full trappings of civilisation too. Darwin is extremely ethnically diverse with anywhere between 45 and 60 ethnic groups represented, depending on who you listen to. Asian and European accents are almost as thick in the air as the Aussie drawl.

A lot of people only live here for a year or two – it's surprising how many people you meet elsewhere who used to live in Darwin. It's reckoned you can consider yourself a 'Territorian' if you've stuck the climate and remoteness for five years. There is a constant flow of travellers coming and going from Asia, or making their way around Australia. Backpacks seem part of the everyday scene and people always appear to be heading somewhere else.

Darwin is an obvious base for trips to Kakadu and other Top End natural attractions, such as Litchfield Park. It's a bit of an oasis too – whether you're travelling south to Alice Springs, west to Western Australia or east to Queensland, there are a lot of km to be covered before you get anywhere, and having reached Darwin many people rest a bit before leaving.

History

It took a long time to decide on Darwin as the site for the region's main centre and even after the city was established growth was slow and troubled. Early attempts to settle the Top End were mainly due to British fears that the French or Dutch might get a foothold in Australia. Between 1824 and 1829 Fort Dundas on Melville Island and Fort Wellington on the Cobourg Peninsula, 200 km north-east of Darwin, were settled and then abandoned. Victoria, settled in 1838 on Cobourg's Port Essington harbour, survived a cyclone and malaria, but was abandoned in 1849.

In 1845 the explorer Leichhardt reached Port Essington overland from Brisbane, arousing prolonged interest in the Top End. The region came under the control of South Australia in 1863, and more ambitious development plans were made. A settlement was established in 1864 at Escape Cliffs on the mouth of the Adelaide River, not too far from Darwin's present location, but it was abandoned in 1866. Finally Darwin was founded at its present site in 1869. The harbour had been discovered back in 1839 by John Lort Stokes aboard the *Beagle*, who named it Port Darwin after a former shipmate – the evolutionist Charles Darwin. At first the settlement was called Palmerston, but soon became unofficially known as Port Darwin, and in 1911 the name was officially changed.

Darwin's growth was accelerated by the discovery of gold at Pine Creek, about 200 km south, in 1871. But once the gold fever had run its course Darwin's development slowed down, due to the harsh, unpredictable climate (including occasional cyclones), and its poor communications with other Australian cities.

WW II put Darwin permanently on the map when the town became an important base for Allied action against the Japanese in the Pacific. The road south to the railhead at Alice Springs was surfaced, finally putting the city in direct contact with the rest of the country. Darwin was attacked 64 times during the war and 243 people lost their lives; it was the only place in Australia to suffer prolonged attacks.

Modern Darwin has an important role as the front door to Australia's northern region and as a centre for administration and mining. The port facilities have been expanded – but hopes of a railway line to Alice Springs have receded for the time being, although it's still much talked about. Darwin's population, after rising rapidly, has steadied in the past few years, but the place still has a go-ahead feel.

Orientation

Darwin's centre is a fairly compact area at the end of a peninsula. The Stuart Highway does a big loop entering the city and finally heads south to end under the name Daly St. The city-centre peninsula stretches southeast from here, and the main city-centre

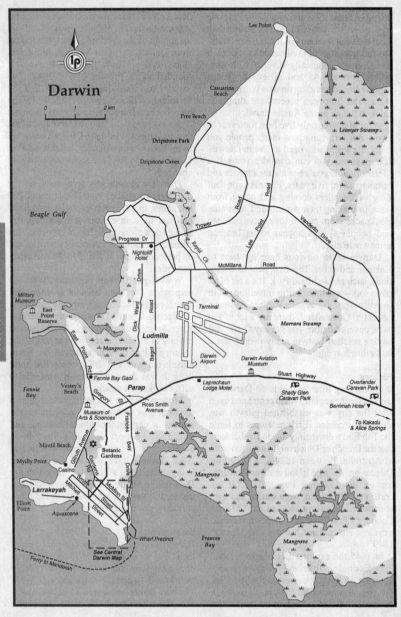

shopping area, Smith St and its mall, is about half a km from Daly St.

Long-distance buses arrive at the transit centre at 69 Mitchell St, and there is accommodation a few minutes walk away. Most of what you'll want in central Darwin is within two or three blocks of the transit centre or Smith St Mall. The suburbs spread a good 12 to 15 km away to the north and east, but the airport is conveniently central.

Information

Tourist Offices The Darwin Region Tourism Association Information Centre (☎ 81 4300) is at 33 Smith St, in the mall. It's open from 8 am to 6 pm from Monday to Friday, from 9 am to 2 pm on Saturday and 10 am to 5 pm on Sunday. It has free maps of the city and several decent booklets, and can book just about any tour or accommodation in the Territory. There's also a tourist information desk at the airport.

The NT Government Publications Centre (☎ 89 7152) at 13 Smith St, open from Monday to Friday from 9 am to 4 pm, is more for locals, but if you're interested in delving into a particular aspect of the Northern Territory it may be able to help.

There are good notice boards in the mall (a couple of doors from the tourist office) and in the backpacker hostels – these are useful for buying and selling things (like vehicles) or looking for rides. Right outside the transit centre on Mitchell St is the unofficial place for selling cars – you'll see half a dozen parked here at any one time, especially towards the end of the dry season when many visitors head for Asia or home.

Post & Telecommunications The GPO is on the corner of Cavenagh and Edmunds Sts. The poste restante is computerised and efficient; a computer-generated list of all mail held is available at the counter. You'll need some form of identification to collect any mail.

Darwin's STD telephone code is 089. (In fact the STD code for the whole Territory is 089, but calls to other towns in the Territory are still charged at the usual STD rates.)

Other Offices The Australian Nature Conservation Agency (☎ 81 5299) is in the Commercial Union building on Smith St between Lindsay and Whitfield Sts.

The National Trust (☎ 81 2848) is at 52 Temira Crescent in Myilly Point – pick up a copy of its Darwin walking-tour leaflet (also available from the tourist office). The Automobile Association of the Northern Territory (☎ 81 3837) is at 79-81 Smith St.

The Conservation Commission (☎ 89 5511) has its office way out in Palmerston, some 20 km from the city centre, which is a real nuisance. Bus No 8 gets you there.

The Department of Mines & Energy (☎ 81 4806) is in the Centrepoint Tower, Smith St Mall. For fishing info, the Department of Primary Industry & Fisheries (☎ 89 4821) has its office in the Harbour View Plaza, Bennett St.

Foreign Embassies The Indonesian Consulate (☎ 41 0048) is at 18 Harry Chan Ave (PO Box 1953, Darwin 0801) and is open weekdays from 9 am to 1 pm and 2 to 5 pm.

Bookshops Bookworld on Smith St Mall is a good bookshop, as is Angus & Robertson in the Galleria shopping centre, also in the Smith St Mall; you'll find all the Lonely Planet guides for travel to Asia here.

For maps, the NT General Store on Cavenagh St has a good range. Other places to try include the NT Government Publications Centre or the Ministry of Housing & Lands on Cavenagh St.

Medical & Emergency Services The Department of Health runs an International Vaccination Clinic (☎ 81 4792) at 43 Cavenagh St. It is open on Tuesday and Friday.

For emergency medical treatment phone the Royal Darwin Hospital on ☎ 22 8125.

The Lifeline Crisis Line is ☎ 81 9227. The Salvo Youth Line is ☎ toll-free 1800 251 008.

Dangers & Annoyances Don't swim in Darwin waters from October to May. Stingers are prevalent, and there are crocodiles

NORTHERN TERRITORY

Cyclone Tracy

The statistics are frightening. Cyclone Tracy built up over Christmas Eve 1974 and by midnight the winds began to reach their full fury. At 3.05 am the airport's anemometer cried 'enough', failing just after it recorded a speed of 217 km/h. It's thought the peak wind speeds were as high as 280 km/h. Sixty-six lives were lost. Of Darwin's 11,200 houses 50% to 60% were either totally destroyed or so badly damaged that repair was impossible, and only 400 survived relatively intact.

Much criticism was levelled at the design and construction of Darwin's houses, but plenty of places a century or more old, and built as solidly as you could ask for, also toppled before the awesome winds. The new and rebuilt houses have been cyclone-proofed with strong steel reinforcements and roofs which are firmly pinned down.

Most people say that next time a cyclone is forecast, they'll jump straight into their cars and head down the Track – and come back afterwards to find out if their houses really were cyclone-proof! Those who stay will probably take advantage of the official cyclone shelters. ■

along the coast and rivers – any crocodiles found in the harbour are removed, and other beaches near the city are patrolled to minimise the risk. There's a Marine Stinger Emergency Line on ☎ toll-free 1800 079 909.

Town Centre

Despite its shaky beginnings and the destruction caused by WW II and Cyclone Tracy, Darwin still has a number of historic buildings. The National Trust produces an interesting booklet titled *A Walk through Historical Darwin*.

Old buildings include the **Victoria Hotel** on Smith St Mall, originally built in 1894 and badly damaged by Tracy. On the corner of the mall and Bennett St, the stone **Commercial Bank** dates from 1884. The old **town hall**, a little further down Smith St, was built in 1883 but was virtually destroyed by Tracy, despite its solid Victorian construction. Today only its walls remain.

Across the road, **Brown's Mart**, a former mining exchange dating from 1885, was badly damaged but now houses a theatre. There's a **Chinese temple**, glossy and new, on the corner of Woods and Bennett Sts.

Christ Church Cathedral, nearer the harbour, was destroyed by the cyclone. It was originally built in 1902, but all that remained after Tracy was the porch, which had been added in 1944. A new cathedral has been built and the old porch retained.

The 1884 **police station** and **old court-house** at the corner of Smith St and the Esplanade were badly damaged, but have been restored and are now used as government offices. A little further south along the Esplanade, **Government House**, built in stages from 1870, was known as the Residency until 1911, and has been damaged by just about every cyclone to hit Darwin. It is once again in fine condition.

Continuing round the Esplanade you reach a **memorial** marking the point where the telegraph cable once ran from Darwin into the sea on its crossing to Banyuwangi in Java. This cable put Australia into instant communication with Britain for the first time.

Other buildings of interest along the Esplanade include the agreeably tropical **Darwin Hotel**, and **Admiralty House** at the corner of Knuckey St.

Further along at 74 The Esplanade, in Lyons Cottage, is the **British-Australian Telegraph Residence Museum**. It's free and open daily from 10 am to noon and 12.30 to 5 pm. There are displays on pre-1911 north Australian history. A short distance further on is the **Shades of Ochre** gallery which has some fine Aboriginal art for sale. Further along again is modern Darwin's architectural talking point: the pink and blue **Beaufort Darwin Centre**, housing a luxury hotel, a couple of up-market cafes, and the Performing Arts Centre.

The Esplanade is fronted by an expanse of grass and trees, and a pleasant seafront pathway runs along from the Hotel Darwin to Daly St.

Aquascene

This is one tourist attraction actually worth the cost of admission. At Doctor's Gully, near the corner of Daly St and the Esplanade, fish come in for a feed every day at high tide. Half the stale bread in Darwin gets dispensed to a horde of milkfish, mullet, catfish and batfish. Some are quite big – the milkfish grow to over a metre and will demolish a whole slice of bread in one go. It's a great sight and children love it – the fish will take bread right out of your hand. Feeding times depend on the tides (☎ 81 7837 for tide times). Admission is $3.50 ($2.50 children); the bread is free.

Botanic Gardens

The gardens' site was used to grow vegetables during the earliest days of Darwin. Tracy severely damaged the gardens, uprooting three-quarters of the plants. Fortunately, vegetation grows fast in Darwin's climate and the Botanic Gardens, with their noteworthy collection of tropical flora, have been restored. There's a coastal section over the road, between Gilruth Ave and Fannie Bay. It's an easy bicycle ride out to the gardens from the centre.

Indo-Pacific Marine & Australian Pearling Exhibition

This excellent aquarium is a successful attempt to display living coral and its associated life. Each small tank is a complete ecosystem, with only the occasional extra fish introduced as food for some of the carnivores such as stonefish or angler fish. They sometimes have box jellyfish, as well as more attractive creatures like sea horses, clown fish and butterfly fish. The living coral reef display is especially impressive.

Housed in the same building is the Pearling Exhibition, which deals with the history of the pearling industry in this area. While pearling around Darwin doesn't have the importance it has in places like Broome,

quite a bit still goes on. The exhibition has excellent displays and informative videos.

Both displays are housed in the former Port Authority garage at the Wharf Precinct, which has been completely renovated and air-conditioned. The Indo-Pacific Marine is open daily from 9 am to 5 pm (last entry 4 pm) and costs $8 ($3 for children), and the Pearling Exhibition hours are from 10 am to 6 pm (last entry 5 pm) and it costs $5 ($3); there's a joint ticket to the two attractions for $12.

Wharf Precinct

The Indo-Pacific Marine and Pearling Exhibition are actually part of the Darwin Wharf Precinct. Although still in the early stages, the precinct aims to turn what was basically the city's ugly port facilities into something attractive which will draw the tourists.

Right at the outer end of the jetty is an old warehouse, now known as the Arcade, which houses a good food centre. There's also bungee jumping on weekends. The Wharf Precinct also features the old **storage tunnels** which were dug into the cliff face below the city centre during WW II.

A shuttle bus operates between the Wharf Precinct sites and the northern end of Smith St Mall, or it's a pleasant stroll if you have a morning to spare.

Museum of Arts & Sciences

This excellent museum and art gallery is on Conacher St at Fannie Bay, about four km from the city centre. It's bright, well presented and not too big, but full of interesting displays. A highlight is the Northern Territory Aboriginal art collection, with just the right mix of exhibits and information to introduce visitors to the purpose of this art, and its history and regional differences. It's particularly strong on carvings and bark paintings from Bathurst and Melville islands and Arnhem Land.

There's also a good collection on the art of the Pacific and Asian nations closest to Australia, including Indonesian *ikat* (woven cloth) and gamelan instruments, and a sea gypsies' *prahu* (floating home) from Sabah, Malaysia.

NORTHERN TERRITORY

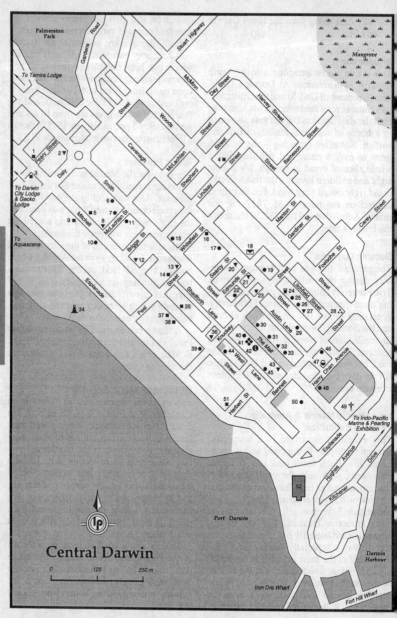

Central Darwin

0   125   250 m

Port Darwin

Iron Ore Wharf

Fort Hill Wharf

Darwin
Harbour

To Indo-Pacific
Marine & Pearling
Exhibition

Palmerston
Park

To Temira Lodge

To Darwin
City Lodge
& Gecko
Lodge

To
Aquascene

Mangrove

PLACES TO STAY	21	Inshore Water Gardens Restaurant	25	Green Turtle Environment CentreShop
1	Elke's Inner City Backpackers	23	Maharajah Indian Restaurant	26	Royal Brunei Airlines
3	YWCA	24	Roma Bar	28	Chinese Temple
4	Frogshollow Backpackers	27	Night Tokyo Japanese Restaurant	29	Garuda
5	Fawlty Towers	32	Hog's Breath Cafe	30	Paspalis Centrepoint & Singapore Airlines
9	Ivan's Backpackers Hostel	36	Golden Oldies Cafe	31	Ansett Airlines
14	Sherwood Lodge	43	Victoria Hotel	33	World of Books
16	Tiwi Lodge			34	Leichhardt Memorial
35	Larrakeyah Lodge	**OTHER**		39	Indigenous Creations
37	Darwin Transit Inn & Transit Centre			40	Darwin Plaza
38	Darwin City Youth Hostel	6	Thrifty Rent-a-Car	41	Galleria Shopping Centre
51	Darwin Hotel	7	Rent-a-Rocket	42	Darwin Region Tourism Association Office
		10	Performing Arts Centre		
PLACES TO EAT	11	Rent-a-Dent	44	Malaysian Airlines
		15	ANCA (Australian Nature Conservation Agency)	45	Natrabu Indonesian Travel Agency
2	Thai Garden Restaurant	17	International Vaccination Clinic	46	Qantas Airlines
8	Peppi's Restaurant			47	City Bus Depot
12	Sizzler Restaurant	18	General Post Office	48	Brown's Mart
13	Toots Eatery	19	NT General Store	49	Christ Church Cathedral
20	Guiseppe's	22	Squire's Tavern & Rockitz Niteclub	50	Old Town Hall
				52	Government House

Pride of place among the stuffed Northern Territory birds and animals undoubtedly goes to 'Sweetheart', a five-metre, 780-kg saltwater crocodile, who became quite a Top End personality after numerous encounters with fishing dinghies on the Finnis River south of Darwin. Apparently he had a taste for outboard motors. He died when captured in 1979. You can also see a box jellyfish – safely dead – in a jar.

The non-Aboriginal Australian art collection includes works by top names like Nolan, Lindsay and Boyd. The museum has a good little bookshop and outside, but under cover, there is an excellent maritime display with a number of vessels, including an old pearling lugger and a Vietnamese refugee boat.

Admission is free and it's open from Monday to Friday from 9 am to 5 pm, Saturday and Sunday from 10 am to 6 pm. Bus Nos 4 and 6 go close by, or you can get there on the Tour Tub (see Getting Around).

Fannie Bay Gaol Museum
Another interesting museum is a little further out of town at the corner of East Point Rd and Ross Smith Ave. This was Darwin's main jail from 1883 to 1979, when a new maximum security lock-up opened at Berrimah. You can look round the old cells and see the gallows used in the Territory's last hanging in 1952. There are also good displays on Cyclone Tracy, transport, technology and industrial archaeology. The museum is open daily from 10 am to 5 pm; admission is free. Bus Nos 4 and 6 from the city centre go very close to the museum, and it's also on the Tour Tub route.

East Point
This spit of undeveloped land north of Fannie Bay is good to visit in the late afternoon when wallabies come out to feed, cool breezes spring up and you can watch the sunset across the bay. There are some walking and riding trails as well as a road to the tip of the point.

On the northern side of the point is a series of wartime gun emplacements and the **Military Museum**, devoted to Darwin's WW II activities, open daily from 9.30 am to 5 pm ($4). Bus Nos 4 and 6 will take you five km from the city centre to the corner of East Point Rd and Ross Smith Ave; from there it's three km to the tip of the point, or you can take the Tour Tub.

Aviation Museum

Darwin's aviation museum would be unspectacular were it not for the American B52 bomber. This truly mammoth aircraft, one of only two displayed outside the USA, dominates the other displays, which include the wreck of a Japanese Zero fighter shot down in 1942 and other items of historical interest. The museum is on the Stuart Highway in Winnellie, about five km from the centre. It is open daily from 10 to 4 pm; entry is $5. Bus Nos 5 and 8 run along the Stuart Highway.

Beaches

Darwin has plenty of beaches, but you'd be wise to keep out of the water during the October to May wet season because of the deadly box jellyfish. Popular beaches include **Mindil** and **Vestey's** on Fannie Bay, and **Mandorah**, across the bay from the town (see Around Darwin).

In north Darwin, there's a stinger net protecting part of **Nightcliff** beach off Casuarina Drive, and a stretch of the seven-km **Casuarina** beach further east is an official nude beach. This is a good beach but at low tide it's a long walk to the water's edge.

Like so many places in tropical Australia, Darwin has a water slide – it's at **Parap Pool** on Ross Smith Ave and is open daily.

Organised Tours

There are innumerable tours in and around Darwin offered by a host of companies. The Information Office in the mall is the best place for information on what's available. Many tours go less frequently (if at all) in the wet season. Some of the longer or more adventurous ones have only a few departures a year: enquire in advance if you're interested.

Local Among the Darwin city tours, Darwin Day Tours' (☎ 81 8696) four-hour trip is pretty comprehensive ($29). The same company also does a five-hour Sunset Tour for the same price. Frontier Billy J's (☎ 41 0744) 1½-hour sunset harbour cruise costs $26, or for $42 you can do a two-hour Corroboree and Dinner tour. Darwin Harbour Ferries (☎ 78 5094) also offers a two-hour harbour trip for $18.

The Tour Tub (☎ 41 1656) is an open-sided minibus which tours around the various Darwin sights (see Getting Around below), and it also does a 2½-hour Sunset Tour for $12.50 which goes to the wharf and out to East Point.

One-hour Harley-Davidson tours of the town are offered by Just Looking Tours (☎ 81 5827), and these include the City Sights for $45, or a Sunset Tour for $55.

A number of operators do trips to the jumping crocodiles at Adelaide River, and to the Territory Wildlife Park on the Cox Peninsula road. For the former try Frontier Jumping Crocodile Cruises (☎ 41 0740), which cost $25 (plus transfers) and take two hours. Darwin Day Tours' (☎ 81 8696) six-hour trips to the Territory Wildlife Park cost $29.

For a view of Darwin from the air 15-minute helicopter rides are available for $50 from Heli North (☎ 45 0105).

Further Afield You can take tours from Darwin to just about anywhere of interest in the Northern Territory. With money to burn you could combine several major destinations or even make it to the Kimberley in Western Australia.

For bushwalkers, Willis's Walkabouts (☎ 85 2134) have been recommended. Organised by an ex-president of the Darwin Bushwalking Club, these are guided hikes in small groups (usually four to eight people). You can join a prearranged walk of 11 to 21 days, or a group can set its own itinerary of two or more days. Some of Willis's Walkabouts are mentioned under Kakadu National Park, but others include Keep River and the Bungle Bungles (16 days), and the Mitchell

Plateau in the Kimberley. Prices for 'choose-your-own' bushwalks start at $60 a day per person depending on the season and length of walk.

Other interesting – but not cheap – tour destinations from Darwin include Bathurst and Melville islands, the Cobourg Peninsula, Arnhem Land and Gove. See the sections on those places for further details.

Festivals

Aside from the Beer Can Regatta in late June or early July, with its sports and contests, there is the Bougainvillea Festival leading up to it, earlier in June. It's a week of concerts, dances, a picnic in the Botanic Gardens and a parade on the final day.

Darwin also goes into festive mood for May Day (International Labour Day), regarded as the start of the 'no-box-jellyfish season' and the occasion of big beach parties, rock concerts the night before, etc. Unfortunately the jellyfish don't always leave on time.

Darwinites are as fond of horse races as other Australians, and two big days at the Fannie Bay track are St Patrick's Day (17 March) and the Darwin Cup (October). The Royal Darwin Show takes place in July, and the Rodeo and Mud Crab Tying Competition are in August.

Places to Stay

Darwin has hostels, guesthouses, motels, holiday flats, and a clutch of up-market hotels. The city's many caravan parks/camp sites are unfortunately all several km out.

Camping Sadly, Darwin takes no advantage of what could be fine camp sites on its many open spaces. East Point, for instance, would be superb. To camp or get an on-site van you must go to one of the privately run caravan parks in the outer city. A second drawback is that a number of the more conveniently situated caravan parks don't take tent campers. The closest place to the city is the *Leprechaun Lodge Motel* which has a limited number of camp/caravan sites at the rear – enquire at reception.

Shady Glen Caravan Park (☎ 84 3330), 10 km east, at the corner of Stuart Highway and Farrell Crescent, Winnellie; camp sites at $12 for two ($15 with power), on-site vans $35 for two.

Overlander Caravan Park (☎ 84 3025), 13 km east at 1064 McMillans Rd, Berrimah; camp sites at $10 for two ($12 powered), on-site vans $29 to $31.

Palms Caravan Park (☎ 32 2891), 17 km south-east of town on the Stuart Highway at Berrimah; camp sites at $12 for two ($14.50 powered).

Also consider camping at Howard Springs, 26 km out, where there are two caravan parks which take campers (see Around Darwin).

Hostels There's a host of choices in this bracket, with several of the cheapest places on or near Mitchell St, conveniently close to the transit centre. Most places have guest kitchens, and the showers and toilets are almost always communal.

Very popular among travellers is the purpose-built *Frogshollow Backpackers* (☎ 41 2600) at 27 Lindsay St, about 10 minutes walk from the transit centre but still close to the centre of town. It's a new, spacious and clean place, and has three spas which guests can use. The charge is $12.50 a night in a fan-cooled, eight-bed dorm ($80 per week), and there are double rooms for $30, or $35 with attached bath. It has a well-appointed kitchen, common area with TV and travel information and, as with other hostels, it does pick-ups from the transit centre (and airport on demand). It also organises free trips for guests out to East Point at sunset, which are popular.

Ivan's Backpackers Hostel (☎ 81 5385) at 97 Mitchell St has a pool, two kitchens, frequent barbecues and good info on Timor. A dormitory bunk is $12.50 in a four- to seven-bed air-con self-contained room complete with fridge and TV. Breakfast is included in the price, there's a bar and cheap meals in the evening, and free bicycles for guests to use. Double rooms are available for $40 with attached bath.

Right across the road from Ivan's, at 88 Mitchell St, is *Fawlty Towers* (☎ 81 8363), a friendly and informal place with dorm beds for $10.50 including breakfast. There are also doubles for $29.

The *Darwin Transit Inn* (☎ 81 9733) at 69 Mitchell St has its reception actually in the transit centre. This place has definitely seen better days, but it still gets a steady stream of travellers. There's a small pool, and it costs $12 per person in twin rooms with fridge, and some with bathroom. The rate drops by $1 per night for stays of up to three nights, and it drops to $9 per night for four nights or longer. Double rooms cost $30 with air-con, or $25 with fan cooling.

The 180-bed *Darwin City Youth Hostel* (☎ toll-free 1800 814 702) is at 69A Mitchell St next to the transit centre. Its rooms are all fan-cooled twins and cost $12 per person, plus $1 for a sleeping sheet. In the dry season it's YHA members only here, and there's a three-day limit; in the Wet, nonmembers can pay a $6 'introductory membership' fee. The building has reasonably new kitchens, bathrooms and an open-air sitting area, and there's a pool.

Right across the road from the transit centre is the *Larrakeyah Lodge Backpackers* (☎ 81 7550), which has beds in dorms for $11 ($12 air-con) including breakfast, or there are double rooms (see listing below).

The smaller *Sherwood Lodge* (☎ 41 1994) is at 15 Peel St, with a kitchen and sitting area upstairs. The cost is $10 per person, which gets you a bed in a cramped six-bed dorm, or you can pay $18/24 for a single/double room.

Still on Mitchell St, but just north of Daly St, is *Elke's Inner City Backpackers* (☎ 81 8399) at No 112. It's actually in a couple of newly renovated adjacent houses, and it has a bit more of a garden feel than those right in the heart of the city. It has dorm beds for $12 ($13 air-con) in four- to six-bed dorms, or twin rooms for $30 ($34). Breakfast is free.

Further north along at 151 Mitchell St, about a 10-minute walk from the centre, is the family-run *Darwin City Lodge* (☎ 41 1295). Formerly a family home, this place is one of the Cyclone Tracy survivors and is certainly a bit rough around the edges. However, it's clean, there's a pool and the

owners are friendly. The cost is $12 in a dorm ($11 for VIP members), or $27/30 for singles/doubles. This place offers substantial discounts during the wet season.

In the same area is the *Gecko Lodge* (☎ 81 5569) at 146 Mitchell St which has dorm beds for $12, or double rooms for $30. This place receives good raves from travellers.

The big *YWCA* (☎ 81 8644) is at 119 Mitchell St. It takes women and men and has no curfew. Rooms have fans and fridges, and are clean and well kept; there are two TV lounges and a kitchen. It charges $13 per person in a twin share room, $21/35 for singles/doubles, or $26/41 with attached bath.

Guesthouses Darwin has several small guesthouses – good for longer stays as well as short ones. Among those which aren't too far from the centre is the friendly *Park Lodge* (☎ 81 5692) at 42 Coronation Drive, Stuart Park. All rooms have fan, air-con and fridge; bathrooms, kitchen, sitting/TV room and laundry are communal. Air-con doubles cost $45, and weekly rates are cheaper. Numerous city buses, including Nos 5 and 8, run to this part of Darwin along the highway; ask the driver where to get off.

Motels, Hotels & Holiday Flats There are plenty of modern places in Darwin, but prices in this range often vary between the Dry and the cheaper Wet. Many of them give discounts if you stay a week or more – usually of the seventh-night-free variety. Typically these places have air-con and swimming pools.

Three older and cheaper places in central Darwin lack pools, however. The *Larrakeyah Lodge* (☎ 81 2933) at 50 Mitchell St, right opposite the transit centre, offers comfortable air-con rooms with fridge and shared facilities for $35/49 for singles/doubles. It has a TV lounge, laundry and coffee shop.

The pleasantly tropical and centrally located *Hotel Darwin* (☎ 81 9211), on the Esplanade, offers very good value for money, with air-con twin rooms from $30, and a communal kitchen.

In the centre at 35 Cavenagh St, the *Air Raid City Lodge* (☎ 81 9214) has air-con rooms – all with shower and toilet, fridge and tea- and coffee-making facilities – for $46/56. At 53 Cavenagh St, on the corner of Whitefield St, the *Tiwi Lodge* (☎ 81 6471) is a motel with air-con rooms at $60, with the usual facilities.

The *Tops Boulevard Motel* (☎ 81 1544) at 38 Gardens Rd, the continuation of Cavenagh St beyond Daly St, is a comfortable modern motel. Double rooms cost $70, or studio rooms with cooking facilities are $80 (these sleep three people). All rooms have private bathroom, fridge and TV. There's also a pool, tennis court and restaurant.

If you have a vehicle there are places worth considering in the suburbs. The *Parap Village Apartments* (☎ 43 0500), at 39 Parap Rd in Fannie Bay, has fully equipped and furnished three-bedroom flats for $175 and two-bedroom flats for $145. The *Seabreeze Motel* (☎ 81 8433), also in Fannie Bay at 60 East Point Rd, has singles/twins for $65/75. Directly across from the airport on the Stuart Highway, the *Leprechaun Lodge Motel* (☎ 84 3400) costs $50/60 for singles/twins. It's convenient for early morning departures, but not much else.

Other than these places you're generally into the $80-plus bracket. The most expensive are the big modern hotels on Mitchell St and the Esplanade. You'll pay $140-plus for a single room at the *Atrium*, *Melia*, *Beaufort* or *Travelodge*.

Places to Eat

Darwin's proximity to Asia is obvious in its large number of fine Asian eateries, but on the whole eating out is expensive. Takeaway places, a growing number of lunch spots in and around the Smith St Mall and the excellent Asian-style markets – held two or three times a week at various sites around the city – are the cheapest.

A number of eateries around town, particularly the pubs, offer discount meals for backpackers. Keep an eye out for vouchers at the hostels.

City Centre – cafes, pubs & takeaways

Next to the transit centre on Mitchell St there's a small food centre with a couple of reasonably priced stalls and open-air tables. *Graham's*, at the far end, is popular with travellers and serves roast dinners in the evening for $5, or full-on cholesterol-packed breakfasts for $4. A couple of other places here offer a range of Asian dishes, and charge $5 for a piled-high plateful – good value.

A host of snack bars and cafes in Smith St Mall offer lots of choice during the day – but, except for Thursday, the late shopping night, they're virtually all closed from about 5 pm and on Saturday afternoon and all day Sunday.

There's a good collection of fast-food counters in Darwin Plaza towards the Knuckey St end of the mall – *Omar Khayyam* for Middle Eastern and Indian, *La Veg* for health food, lasagne and light meals, *Ozzy Burgers* for, well, burgers, and *Roseland* for yoghurt, fruit salads and ice cream.

Further up the mall the fancy new Galleria shopping centre has a few good places: *Satay King* specialises in Malaysian food and serves that excellent Nonya dish, curry laksa; *Mamma Bella* serves predictable Italian food; *Al Fresco* has gourmet sandwiches and ice cream; and the *Galleria* is a straightforward burger place. There's a good seating area in the centre, although at lunch times it can be difficult to find a spare table.

Further up the mall is Anthony Plaza where the *French Bakehouse* is one of the few places you can get a coffee and snack every day.

Opposite Anthony Plaza is the Victoria Arcade where the *Victoria Hotel* has lunch or dinner for around $6 in its upstairs Settlers Bar. The barramundi burgers ($7 including chips and salad) are excellent, as are the steaks. In the arcade the *Sate House* has good cheap Indonesian fare.

Simply Foods at 37 Knuckey St is a busy health-food place. It's a good spot with appealing decor, music and friendly service. On the corner of Mitchell and Knuckey Sts the small *Golden Oldies Cafe* is a popular breakfast spot.

In the *Green Room* at the Darwin Hotel you can have a barbecue lunch by the pool for $10; it also has menu dishes.

El Toro's is a popular Mexican restaurant in the Saloon Hotel at 21 Cavenagh St.

City Centre – restaurants The *Maharajah Indian Restaurant* at 37 Knuckey St has a good reasonably priced takeaway selection. The menu is extensive with dishes from $9 to $13. The *Pancake Palace* on Cavenagh St near Knuckey St is open daily for lunch and in the evening until 1 am. Conveniently close to many of Darwin's night spots, it has sweet and savoury pancakes from $6.

Also on Cavenagh St is *Guiseppe's*, one of the few pasta places in Darwin. Main dishes are in the $9 to $12 range, or there's pizza from $11.

Other restaurants include steakhouses, seafood specialists, and French, Greek and Italian cuisine. The numerous Chinese places are generally rather up-market. The *Jade Garden* on the Smith St Mall (upstairs, roughly opposite the Victoria Arcade) offers a nine-course meal for $12 a head.

The *Sizzler* restaurant on Mitchell St is one of the chain found Australia-wide. It's amazingly popular, with queues out onto the footpath every night. The reason is that it's very good value: for around $12 you can fill your plate from a wide range of dishes, and have a dessert too.

Probably the best restaurant in the city centre area is *Peppi's* at 84 Mitchell St. It's fully licensed and a two-course meal for two will set you back around $80 with drinks.

Out of the Centre On Smith St, just beyond Daly St, the *Thai Garden Restaurant* serves not only delicious and reasonably priced Thai food but pizzas too! It has a few outdoor tables. There's a takeaway 'Aussie-Chinese' place across the road, and a 24-hour Chinese fast-food joint next door.

Further out, the *Parap Hotel* on Parap Rd, between Gregory and Hingston Sts, does counter meals. It also has *Jessie's Bistro* where buffalo and beef steaks are around $12. It's open for lunch and dinner from Monday to Saturday, and from 2 pm on Sunday. Locals recommend the food here. There are two other Jessie's Bistro locations – one in the *Casuarina Tavern* and the other in the *Berrimah Hotel* on the Stuart Highway in Berrimah.

In the Botanic Gardens, the *Holtze Cottage* restaurant is a carnivore's delight. It's fully licensed and specialises in buffalo, kangaroo, crocodile and camel meats. It is open daily for lunch and dinner.

At the end of the jetty, the Arcade is a small, Asian-style food centre with a number of different shops selling Chinese food, pizza or excellent fish & chips. *Christo's on the Wharf* is a more up-market place, open for lunch and dinner from Tuesday to Friday.

Markets Easily the best all-round eating experience in Darwin is the bustling Asian-style market at Mindil Beach on Thursday nights during the dry season. People begin arriving from 5.30 pm, bringing tables, chairs, rugs, grog and kids to settle under the coconut palms for sunset and decide which of the tantalising food-stall aromas has the greatest allure. It's difficult to know whether to choose Thai, Sri Lankan, Indian, Chinese,

---

The Darwin Thirst

Darwin's legendary beer thirst is celebrated at the annual Beer Can Regatta in June. A series of boat races is held for boats constructed entirely of beer cans. Apart from the racing boats some unusual special entries generally turn up – like a beer-can Viking longboat or a beer-can submarine. Constructed by an Australian navy contingent the submarine actually submerged! The races also have their controversial elements – on one occasion a boat turned up made entirely of brand-new cans, delivered straight from the brewery, sealed but empty. Unfair, cried other competitors, the beer must be drunk! ∎

Two-up

The Alice and Darwin casinos offer plenty of opportunities to watch the Australian gambling mania in full flight. You can also observe a part of Australia's true cultural heritage, the all-Australian game of two-up.

The essential idea of two-up is to toss two coins and obtain two heads. The players stand around a circular playing area and bet on the coins showing either two heads or two tails when they fall. The 'spinner' uses a 'kip' to toss the coins and the house pays out and takes in as the coins fall – except that nothing happens on 'odd' tosses (one head, one tail) unless they're thrown five times in a row. In this case you lose unless you have also bet on this possibility. The spinner continues tossing until he or she either throws tails, throws five odds or throws three heads. If the spinner manages three heads then he or she also wins at 7½ to one on any bet placed on that possibility, then starts tossing all over again. When the spinner finally loses, the next player in the circle takes over as spinner. ∎

Malaysian, Greek or Portuguese. You'll even find Indonesian black rice pudding. All prices are reasonable – around $2 to $5 for a meal. There are cake stalls, fruit-salad bars, arts and crafts stalls – and sometimes entertainment in the form of a band or street theatre.

Similar food stalls can be found at the Parap market on Saturday morning, the one at Rapid Creek on Sunday morning, and in the Smith St Mall in the evening (except Thursday), but Mindil Beach is the best for atmosphere and proximity. It's about two km from the city centre, off Gilruth Ave. During the Wet, it transfers to Rapid Creek. Bus Nos 4 and 6 go past Mindil Beach: No 4 goes on to Rapid Creek, No 6 to Parap.

Entertainment

Darwin is a lively city with bands at several venues and a number of clubs and discos. More sophisticated tastes are also catered for, with theatre, film, concerts and a casino.

Live bands play upstairs at the *Victoria Hotel* from 9 pm Wednesday to Saturday. The *Billabong Bar* in the Atrium Hotel, on the corner of the Esplanade and Peel St, has live bands on Friday and Saturday nights until 1 am. Take a look at the hotel's spectacular seven-storey glass-roofed atrium while you're there.

The Darwin Hotel is pleasant in the evening for a quiet drink. There's a patio section by the pool. It's livelier on Friday night when there's a band in the *Green Room*,

or on Wednesday to Saturday nights in the *Pickled Parrot Piano Bar*.

The *Brewery Bar* in the Frontier Hotel on the corner of Mitchell and Daly Sts is another popular venue. The *Beachcomber* bar at the rear is a popular disco and nightclub.

Other popular clubs and discos, often with live bands, include *Rockitz*, *Dix*, *Sweethearts* and *Circles*. They're open nightly, with cover charges only on Saturday. Some stay open all night, and midweek they offer cheap drinks to early arrivals. There's lots of entertainment on Sunday afternoon. The Beachfront Hotel at Rapid Creek is very popular, and you can alternate between two bands – one in the outdoor bar known as the *Cage*, the other in the air-con *Colonial Bar*.

The *Nightcliff Hotel* on the corner of Bagot and Trower Rds, about 10 km north of the city centre, has live music every night except Monday and Tuesday. It's a wild place with one of the longest bars in the Northern Territory, and on Wednesday night it's 'fun night', with some bizarre entertainment. More laid back is the *Top End Folk Club* which meets every second Sunday of the month at the Gun Turret at East Point Reserve. Visitors are welcome, and you're welcome to perform also, in which case the $5 admission is waived.

The *Performing Arts Centre* (☎ 81 1222) on Mitchell St, opposite McLachlan St, hosts a variety of events, from fashion award nights to plays, rock operas, pantomimes and concerts. There are sometimes bands and other shows in the amphitheatre in the Botanic Gardens.

There are several cinemas in town and the *Darwin Film Society* (☎ 81 2215) has regular showings of offbeat/artistic films at the Museum Theatrette in the Museum of Arts & Sciences, Conacher St, Bullocky Point.

Finally, there's the *Diamond Beach Casino* on Mindil Beach off Gilruth Ave – as long as you're 'properly dressed'. That means no thongs, and long socks for men wearing shorts! It's quite good entertainment just watching people throwing away large sums of money.

Things to Buy

Aboriginal art is generally cheaper in Alice Springs, but Darwin has greater variety. The Raintree Gallery at 29 Knuckey St is one of a number of places offering a range of art work – bark paintings from Arnhem Land, and interesting carvings by the Tiwi people of Bathurst and Melville islands and by the peoples of central Australia. Shades of Ochre at 78 The Esplanade is another place with quality items.

T-shirts printed with Aboriginal designs are popular but quality and prices vary. Riji Dij at 11 Knuckey St has a large range of T-shirts for $25. They are printed by Tiwi Designs and Territoriana, both local companies using Aboriginal designs and, to a large extent, Aboriginal labour. It stocks Tiwi printed fabric and clothing made from fabric printed by central Australian Aborigines. Another place worth trying is Indigenous Creations at 55 Mitchell St.

You can find Balinese and Indian clothing at Darwin's markets – Mindil Beach (Thursday evening, dry season only), Parap (Saturday morning) and Rapid Creek (Sunday morning, and Thursday evening in the wet season). Local arts and crafts (the market at Parap is said to be the best), jewellery and bric-a-brac are on sale too.

Getting There & Away

Air Darwin is becoming increasingly busy as an international and domestic gateway.

International A popular international route is to and from Indonesia with the Indonesian airlines Merpati or Garuda. You can book on Merpati at Natrabu (☎ 81 3695), an Indonesian government travel agency at 16 Westlane Arcade (behind the Victoria Hotel on Smith St Mall). Merpati flies twice a week to and from Kupang in Timor ($198 one way, $330 return), and from there it has further flights to numerous other places in Indonesia. Kupang is a 'designated entry port' in Indonesia which means you get the normal two-month visitor permit on arrival. Garuda (☎ 81 1103), on Cavenagh St, has direct flights to Denpasar in Bali ($367 one way, $671 return). Ansett (☎ 13 1300) at 14 Smith St Mall and Qantas (☎ 13 1313) at 16 Bennett St also fly this route for the same fare.

Royal Brunei Airlines (☎ 41 0966), also on Cavenagh St, flies twice weekly between Darwin and Bandar Seri Begawan, and on to Manila and Hong Kong.

Singapore Airlines (☎ 41 1799), in the Paspalis Centrepoint building at the corner of Smith St Mall and Knuckey St, also flies to Darwin.

Malaysian Airlines (☎ 41 2323), on the 2nd floor at 38 Mitchell St, has weekly flights to Kuala Lumpur for $467 one way and $700 return.

Domestic Within Australia you can fly to Darwin from other states with Qantas and Ansett.

There are often stops or transfers at Alice Springs, Brisbane or Adelaide on longer flights. Some flights from Queensland stop at Gove or Groote Eylandt. One-way fares include Adelaide $518, Alice Springs $440, Perth $607, Broome $344, Cairns $404, Mt Isa $340, Brisbane $595 and Sydney $600. In Darwin, Qantas (☎ 13 1313) is at 16 Bennett St, Ansett (☎ 13 1300) is at 14 Smith St Mall.

For air travel within the Northern Territory see the air-fares chart in the introductory Getting Around section to this chapter. Air North's office (☎ 45 2866) is at Darwin Airport.

Bus You can reach Darwin by bus on three routes – the Western Australian route from Broome, Derby and Kununurra; the Queensland route through Mt Isa to Threeways and up the Track; or straight up the Track from Alice Springs.

Greyhound Pioneer usually runs up and down the Track daily to and from Alice Springs. Some buses connect in Alice Springs for Adelaide. It also has daily services to and from Townsville via Mt Isa, frequently with connections for Brisbane or Cairns. On Queensland services you often have to change buses at Threeways or Tennant Creek and Mt Isa. For Western Australia, Greyhound Pioneer goes to and from Perth daily through Kununurra, Broome and Port Hedland. You also have the option once or twice a week of taking the Western Australian inland route south of Port Hedland, along the Great Northern Highway through Newman. All buses stop at Katherine. McCafferty's also runs on the routes to Queensland and Adelaide.

Fares can vary quite a bit between the companies, although they are currently in the grip of a price war so anything could happen.

Although fares vary, travel times are very similar, but beware of services that schedule long waits for connections in Tennant Creek or Mt Isa. For example, you pay around $120 one way to Darwin from Tennant Creek (13 hours), $158 from Mt Isa (21 hours), $258 from Brisbane (51 hours), $135 from Alice Springs (19 hours), $169 from Broome (22 hours) and $330 from Perth (57 hours). In Darwin both Greyhound Pioneer (☎ 13 2030) and McCafferty's (☎ 41 0911) operate from the transit centre at 69 Mitchell St.

Car Rental Darwin has two budget car-rental operators, as well as several of the national companies.

Rent-a-Rocket (☎ 81 6977) and Rent-a-Dent (☎ 81 1411), both on McLachlan St, offer similar deals on their mostly 1970s and early 1980s cars. Costs depend on whether you're staying near Darwin, or going further afield to Kakadu, Katherine, Litchfield Park and so on. For local trips with Rent-a-Dent

you pay $35 a day, depending on the vehicle, and must stay within 70 km of Darwin. This includes 150 free km, with a charge of 20c per km beyond that distance. With these deals you can't go beyond Humpty Doo or Acacia Store (about 70 km down the Track). The prices drop for longer rentals.

The bigger companies usually class Darwin as 'remote', which means that cars cost about $10 a day more than they do elsewhere. Territory Rent-a-Car (☎ 81 8400) at 64 Stuart Highway, Parap, is probably the best value. Discount deals to look for include cheaper rates for four or more days hire, weekend specials (three days for roughly the price of two), and one-way hires (to Jabiru, Katherine or Alice Springs).

There are also 4WD vehicles available in Darwin, but you usually have to book ahead, and fees and deposits can be hefty. The best place to start looking is probably Territory, which has several different models – the cheapest, a Suzuki four-seater, costs around $75 a day including insurance, plus 35c a km over 100 km.

Rental companies, including the cut-price ones, generally operate a free towing or replacement service if the vehicle breaks down. But (especially with the cheaper operators) check the paperwork to see exactly what you're covered for in terms of damage to vehicles and injuries to passengers. The usual age and insurance requirements apply in Darwin and there may be restrictions on off-bitumen driving, or on the distance you're allowed to go from the city. Even with the big firms the insurance does not cover you when driving off the bitumen.

Most rental companies are open every day and have agents in the city centre to save you trekking out to the Stuart Highway. Budget (☎ 81 9800), Hertz (☎ 41 0944) and Thrifty (☎ 81 8555) also have offices at the airport.

Getting Around

To/From the Airport Darwin's busy airport, only about six km from the centre of town, handles international flights as well as domestic ones. Hertz, Budget, Thrifty and Territory Rent-a-Car have desks at the airport. The taxi fare into the centre is about $12.

There is an airport shuttle bus (☎ 41 1656) for $6, which will pick up or drop off almost anywhere in the centre. When leaving Darwin book a day before departure.

Bus Darwin has a fairly good city bus service – Monday to Friday. On Saturday, services cease around lunch time and on Sunday and holidays they shut down completely. The city services start from the small terminal (☎ 89 6540) on Harry Chan Ave, near the corner of Smith St. Buses enter the city along Mitchell St and leave along Cavenagh St.

Fares are on a zone system – shorter trips are 90c or $1.20, and the longest cost $1.70. Bus No 4 (to Fannie Bay, Nightcliff, Rapid Creek and Casuarina) and No 6 (Fannie Bay, Parap and Stuart Park) are useful for getting to Aquascene, the Botanic Gardens, Mindil Beach, the Museum of Arts & Sciences, Fannie Bay Gaol Museum and East Point. Bus Nos 5 and 8 go up the Stuart Highway past the airport to Berrimah, from where No 5 goes north to Casuarina and No 8 continues along the highway to Palmerston.

On weekdays three buses a day go to Humpty Doo from Palmerston.

The Tour Tub (☎ 85 4779) is a private bus which does a circuit of the city, calling at the major places of interest, and you can hop on or off anywhere. In the city centre it leaves from Knuckey St, at the end of the Smith St Mall. The set fare is $12.50, and the buses operate hourly from 9 am to 4 pm. Sites visited include Aquascene (only at fish-feeding times), Indo-Pacific Marine and Wharf Precinct, Diamond Beach Casino, the museum and art gallery, Military Museum, Fannie Bay Gaol, Parap markets (Saturday only) and the Botanic Gardens.

Bicycle Darwin has a fairly extensive network of bike tracks. It's a pleasant ride out from the city to the Botanic Gardens, Fannie Bay, East Point or even, if you're feeling fit, all the way to Nightcliff and Casuarina.

Darwin Bike Rentals in Top End Travel at

57 Mitchell St has bikes from $8 a day (from 8 am to 5 pm), or $10 for 24 hours – plus tandems and mountain bikes, and hourly, weekly and monthly rates. Many of the backpackers' hostels have bicycles, and these are often free for guests to use.

The Top End

There are numerous places of interest close to Darwin, and several of the more remote and spectacular Top End areas are becoming increasingly accessible. The chief glory among the latter is Kakadu National Park. Litchfield Park, a national park to the south of Darwin, and Melville and Bathurst islands to the north are other places that are worth the effort if you have the time and dollars.

A group of people can hire a vehicle in Darwin and get to most of the mainland places quite economically. There are also tours from Darwin to many of these places (see the Darwin Getting Around section). Some additional places that can be reached from Darwin are covered in the Down the Track section.

Crocodiles

There are two types of crocodile in Australia – the freshwater or 'freshie' (*Crocodylus johnstoni*) and the saltwater or 'saltie' (*C. porosus*) – and both are present in the Territory. After a century of being hunted, crocodiles are now protected in the Northern Territory – freshies were protected in 1964 and salties in 1971. They are currently thought to number around 100,000.

The smaller freshwater crocodile is endemic to Australia and is found in freshwater rivers and billabongs, while the larger saltwater crocodile can be found in or near almost any body of water, fresh or salt. Freshwater crocodiles, which have narrower snouts and rarely exceed three metres in length, are harmless to people unless provoked, but saltwater crocodiles can definitely be dangerous.

Ask locally before swimming or even pad-

Saltwater crocodile or 'saltie'

Freshwater crocodile or 'freshie'

NORTHERN TERRITORY

dling in any rivers or billabongs in the Top End – attacks on humans by salties happen more often than you might think. Warning signs are posted alongside many dangerous stretches of water. The beasts are apparently partial to dogs and can be attracted by barking some distance away.

Crocodiles have become a major tourist attraction (eating the odd tourist certainly helps in this respect) and the Northern Territory is very big on crocodile humour. Darwin's shops have a plentiful supply of crocodile T-shirts including the Darwin Crocodile Wrestling Club shirt, complete with gory blood stains and a large hole 'bitten' out of one side.

AROUND DARWIN
All the places listed here are within a couple of hours travel from the city.

Mandorah
It's only 10 km across the harbour by boat to this popular beach resort on the tip of Cox Peninsula – you can reach it by road, but that's nearly 140 km, about half of it on unsealed roads. The return ferry trip is $14,

with the first departure from Darwin at 10 am and the last one from Mandorah at 5 pm; the crossing takes about 30 minutes. The ferries leave the main Stokes Hill Wharf in Darwin three or four times a day from Monday to Friday and on weekends in the tourist season.

Howard Springs
The springs, with crocodile-free swimming, are 27 km from the city. Turn off 23 km down the Stuart Highway, beyond Palmerston. The forest-surrounded swimming hole can get uncomfortably crowded because it's so convenient to the city. Nevertheless on a quiet day it's a pleasant spot for an excursion and there are short walking tracks and lots of bird life.

Places to Stay There are two nearby caravan parks. The *Howard Springs Caravan Park* (☎ (089) 83 1169) at Whitewood Rd has tent ($10) and caravan ($14) sites only. The *Nook Van-o-Tel* (☎ (089) 83 1048) at 17 Morgan Rd has tent sites ($8) and cabins ($50).

Arnhem Highway
The Arnhem Highway branches off towards

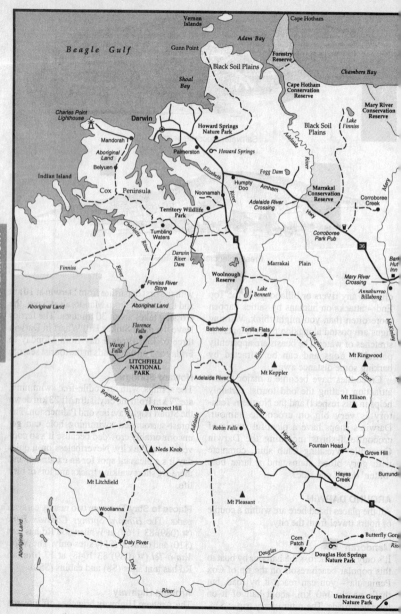

NORTHERN TERRITORY

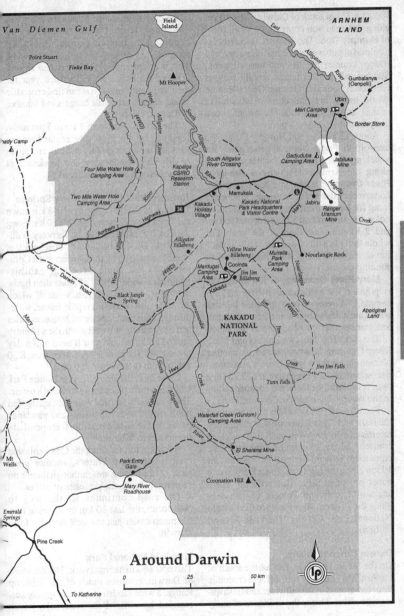

Around Darwin

0   25   50 km

Kakadu, 33 km south of Darwin. Only 10 km along this road you come to the small town of **Humpty Doo**. The *Humpty Doo Hotel* is a colourful pub with some real character, and it does counter lunches and teas all week. Sunday, when local bands usually play, is particularly popular. Graeme Gow's Reptile World has a big collection of Australian snakes and a knowledgable owner (open daily from 8.30 am to 6 pm).

About 15 km beyond Humpty Doo is the turn-off to **Fogg Dam**, a great place for watching water birds. A further eight km along the Arnhem Highway is **Adelaide River Crossing** where you can take a 2½-hour river cruise and see saltwater crocodiles jump for bits of meat held out on the end of poles. These trips cost $25 and depart at 9 am and 2.30 pm most days of the year. The whole thing is a bit of a circus really, but it's fun to see crocs doing something other than sunning themselves on a river bank.

Mary River Crossing, 47 km further on, is popular for barramundi fishing and for camping. A reserve here includes lagoons which are a dry-season home for water birds, and granite outcrops which shelter wallabies.

The *Bark Hut Inn*, two km beyond Mary River Crossing at **Annaburroo**, is another pleasant place for a halt. There's accommodation here but it's expensive at $55/75 for a twin room/unit, or there are cheaper cabins in the nearby *Annaburroo Caravan Park*.

The turn-off to Cooinda is 19 km beyond the Bark Hut. This is an unsealed road, often impassable in the Wet, and it's easier to continue along the sealed highway. The entrance to Kakadu National Park is a further 19 km along the highway. Some Darwin city buses go out as far as Humpty Doo. There are also Greyhound Pioneer bus services along the Arnhem Highway (see the Kakadu National Park Getting There & Around section).

Darwin Crocodile Farm
On the Stuart Highway, just a little south of the Arnhem Highway turn-off, the crocodile farm has around 7000 saltwater and freshwater crocodiles. This is the residence of many of the crocodiles which have been taken out of Northern Territory waters because they've become a hazard to people. But don't imagine they're here out of human charity. This is a farm, not a rest home, and around 2000 of the beasts are killed each year for their skins and meat – you can find crocodile steaks or even crocodile burgers in a number of Darwin eateries.

The farm is open from 9 am to 5 pm daily. Feedings are the most spectacular times to visit and these occur daily at 2 pm, and again on Monday, Wednesday and weekends at noon. Entry is $8.50 (children $3).

Territory Wildlife Park & Berry Springs
The turn-off to Berry Springs is 48 km down the Track from Darwin, then it's 10 km along the Cox Peninsula road to the Territory Wildlife Park. On 400 hectares of bushland this wildlife park (run by the Conservation Commission) has some excellent exhibits featuring a wide variety of Australian birds, mammals, reptiles and fish, some of which are quite rare. There's a reptile house, walk-through aquarium, nocturnal house, aviaries and nature trails. It's well worth the $10 entry fee ($5 children) and you'll need half a day to see it all. The park is open daily from 8.30 am to 4 pm (gates close at 6 pm).

Close by is the Berry Springs Nature Park which is a great place for a swim and a picnic. There's a warm thermal waterfall, spring-fed pools ringed with paperbarks and pandanus palms, and abundant bird life. It is open daily from 8 am to 6.30 pm.

A few km further along the Cox Peninsula road is **Tumbling Waters**, another good picnic and camping area, although there's no swimming due to the presence of salties.

The road continues all the way to **Mandorah**, the last 30 km or so being dirt. It's much easier just to catch the ferry from Darwin.

Litchfield National Park
This 650-sq-km national park, 140 km south of Darwin, encloses much of the Tabletop Range, a wide sandstone plateau mostly surrounded by cliffs. Four waterfalls, which

drop off the edge of this plateau, and their surrounding rainforest patches are the park's main attractions. It's well worth a visit, although it's best to avoid weekends as Litchfield is a very popular day-trip destination for locals.

There are two routes to Litchfield Park, both about a two-hour drive from Darwin. One, from the north, involves turning south off the Berry Springs to Cox Peninsula road onto a well-maintained dirt road, which is suitable for conventional vehicles except in the wet season. A second approach is along a bitumen and dirt road from Batchelor into the east of the park. The two access roads join up so it's possible to do a loop from the Stuart Highway.

If you enter the park from Batchelor it is 18 km from the park boundary to the **Florence Falls** turn-off. The waterfalls lie five km off the road along a good track. This is an excellent swimming hole in the dry season, as is Buley Rockhole, a few km away, where you can also camp.

Eighteen km beyond the turn-off to Florence Falls is the turn-off to **Tolmer Falls**, which are a 400-metre walk off the road. There's also a 1.5-km walking track here which gives you some excellent views of the area.

It's a further seven km along the main road to the turn-off to the most popular attraction in Litchfield – **Wangi Falls** (pronounced 'wong-gye'), two km along a side road. The falls here flow year round and fill a beautiful swimming hole. There are also extensive picnic and camping areas. From Wangi it's about 16 km to the rangers' station near the park's northern access point.

Bush camping is also allowed at the pretty **Tjaynera (Sandy Creek) Falls**, located in a rainforest valley in the south of the park (4WD access only). There are several other 4WD tracks in the park, and plenty of bushwalking possibilities.

As usual in the Top End, it's easier to reach and get around the park from May to October.

Organised Tours Plenty of companies offer day trips to Litchfield from Darwin. Woolly

Butt (☎ (089) 41 2600), operating out of Frogshollow Backpackers in Darwin, is popular. The price is $65, including morning tea and lunch.

KAKADU NATIONAL PARK

Kakadu National Park is one of the natural marvels not just of the Northern Territory, but of Australia. The longer you stay, the more rewarding it is.

Kakadu stretches more than 200 km south from the coast and 100 km from east to west, with the main entrance 153 km by bitumen road east of Darwin. It encompasses a variety of superb landscapes, swarms with wildlife and has some of Australia's best Aboriginal rock art.

Kakadu was proclaimed a national park in three stages. Stage One, the eastern and central part of the park including Ubirr, Nourlangie Rock, Jim Jim Falls, Twin Falls and Yellow Water Billabong, was declared in 1979 and is on the World Heritage List for both its natural and cultural importance – a rare distinction. Stage Two, in the north, was declared in 1984 and won World Heritage listing for its natural importance. Stage Three, in the south, was finally listed in 1991, bringing virtually the whole of the South Alligator River system within the park.

The name Kakadu comes from Gagadju, one of the local Aboriginal languages, and part of Kakadu is Aboriginal land, leased to the government for use as a national park. There are several Aboriginal settlements in the park and about half the park rangers are Aborigines. Enclosed by the park, but not part of it, are a few tracts of land designated for other purposes – principally three uranium-mining leases in the east.

Geography & Vegetation

A straight line on the map separates Kakadu from the Arnhem Land Aboriginal Land to its east, which you can't enter without a permit. The circuitous Arnhem Land escarpment, a dramatic 100- to 200-metre-high sandstone cliff line that provides the natural boundary of the rugged Arnhem Land plateau, winds some 500 km through east and south-east Kakadu.

Creeks cut across the rocky plateau and tumble off the escarpment as thundering waterfalls in the wet season. They then flow across the lowlands to swamp the vast flood plains of Kakadu's four north-flowing rivers, turning the north of the park into a kind of huge, vegetated lake. From west to east the rivers are the Wildman, the West Alligator, the South Alligator and the East Alligator. Such is the difference between dry and wet seasons that areas on river flood plains which are perfectly dry underfoot in September will be under three metres of water a few months later. As the waters recede in the Dry, some loops of wet-season watercourses become cut off, but don't dry up. These are billabongs – and they're often carpeted with water lilies and are a magnet for water birds.

The coastline has long stretches of mangrove swamp, important for halting erosion and as a breeding ground for marine and bird life. The southern part of the park is dry lowlands with open grassland and eucalypts. Pockets of monsoon rainforest crop up here as well as in most of the park's other landscapes.

In all, Kakadu has over 1000 plant species, and a number of them are still used by the local Aborigines for food, bush medicine and other practical purposes.

Climate

The great change between the Dry and the November-to-March Wet makes a big difference to visitors to Kakadu. Not only is the landscape transformed as the wetlands and waterfalls grow, but Kakadu's lesser roads become impassable in the Wet, cutting off some highlights, such as Jim Jim Falls. The local Aborigines recognise six seasons in the annual cycle.

The 'build-up' to the Wet (known as *Gunumeleng*) starts in October. Humidity and the temperatures rise (to 35°C or more) – and the number of mosquitoes, always high near water, rises to near plague proportions. By November the thunderstorms have started, billabongs start to be replenished and the water birds disperse.

The Wet proper (*Gudjuek*) continues through January, February and March, with violent thunderstorms and an abundance of plant and animal life thriving in the hot, moist conditions. Around 1300 mm of rain falls in Kakadu, most of it during this period.

April is *Banggereng*, the season when storms (known as 'knock 'em down' storms) flatten the spear grass, which during the course of the Wet has shot up to two metres in height.

Yekke, from May to mid-June, is the season of mists, when the air starts to dry out. It is quite a good time to visit – there aren't too many other visitors, the wetlands and waterfalls still have a lot of water and most of the tracks are open.

The most comfortable time is the late Dry, July and August – *Wurrgeng* and *Gurrung*. This is when wildlife, especially birds, congregates in big numbers around the shrinking billabongs and watercourses, but it's also when most tourists come to the park.

Wildlife

Kakadu has about 25 species of frog, 50 types of mammals, 77 fish species, 75 types of reptile, 280 bird species (one-third of all those native to Australia) and 4500 kinds of insect. There are frequent additions to the list, and a few of the rarer species are unique to the park. Kakadu's wetlands are on the UN list of Wetlands of International Importance, principally because of their crucial significance to so many types of water bird.

You'll only see a tiny fraction of these creatures in a visit to the park since many of them are shy, nocturnal or few in numbers. Take advantage of talks and walks led by park rangers – mainly in the Dry – to get to know and see more of the wildlife (details from the park information centre). Cruises are run at South Alligator River and Yellow Water Billabong to enable you to see the water life.

Reptiles The park has both types of Australian crocodile: both Twin and Jim Jim Falls, for instance, have resident freshwater crocodiles, which are considered harmless, while there are about 3500 of the dangerous salt-water variety in the park. You're sure to see a few if you take a South Alligator or Yellow Water cruise.

Kakadu's other reptiles include several types of lizard, such as the frilled lizard, and five freshwater turtle species, of which the most common is the northern snake-necked turtle. There are many snakes, including three highly poisonous types, but you're unlikely to see any. Oenpelli pythons, probably unique to the Kakadu escarpment, were only discovered in 1977.

Birds Kakadu's abundant water birds, and their beautiful wetland setting, make a memorable sight. The park is one of the chief refuges in Australia for several species, among them the magpie goose, green pygmy goose and Burdekin duck.

Other fine water birds include pelicans, darters and the Jabiru stork, with its distinctive red legs and long straight beak.

Herons, egrets, ibis and cormorants are common. You're quite likely to see rainbow bee-eaters and kingfishers (of which there are six types in inland Kakadu). Majestic white-breasted sea eagles are often seen near inland waterways too, and wedge-tailed eagles, whistling kites and black kites are common. At night you might hear barking owls calling – they sound just like dogs. The red-tailed black cockatoos are spectacular, and there are also brolgas and bustards.

Mammals Several types of kangaroo and wallaby inhabit the park, and the shy black wallaroo is more or less unique to Kakadu. You might be lucky enough to see a sugar glider in wooded areas in the daytime. Kakadu is home to 25 bat species and is a key refuge for four endangered varieties.

Water buffalo, which ran wild after being introduced to the Top End from Timor by European settlers in the first half of the 19th century, have been virtually eradicated because they were potential carriers of cattle disease and did much damage to the natural environment.

Fish You can't miss the silver barramundi, which creates a distinctive swirl near the water surface. It can grow to well over a metre long and changes its sex from male to female at the age of five or six years.

Rock Art

Kakadu is an important repository of rock art collections – there are over 5000 sites, which date from 20,000 years old right up to those from the 1960s. Two of the finest collections are at Ubirr and Nourlangie, and these have been opened to visitors. See the section on Aboriginal art for details of the various styles.

Orientation

From where the Arnhem Highway to Kakadu turns east off the Stuart Highway, it's 120 km to the park entrance and another 103 km east across the park to Jabiru; it's sealed all the way. The Kakadu Highway to Nourlangie Rock, Cooinda and Pine Creek turns south off the Arnhem Highway shortly before Jabiru.

A turn-off to the north, 18 km into the park along the Arnhem Highway, leads to camp sites at **Two Mile Water Hole** (eight km) and **Four Mile Water Hole** (38 km) on the Wildman River, which is popular for fishing. The track is not suitable for conventional

Mining

The Kakadu region contains nearly 10% of the world's known high-grade uranium ore. The national park surrounds three uranium-rich zones which are Aboriginal land, but which outside companies have the right to mine – Ranger, Jabiluka and Koongarra, all near the eastern border of the park. The Federal government currently maintains a three-mine limit on the number of working uranium mines in Australia, and only Ranger of the Kakadu sites is being worked. (The other two working mines are Nabarlek in Arnhem Land, which has been mined out and is now simply a shrinking stockpile, and Roxby Downs in South Australia.)

You can tour the Ranger mine, opened in 1981. Nearby Jabiru town was built for the mine workers. The highly dubious uses of uranium and its potential damage to the local environment were not the only sources of controversy surrounding the granting of permission for mining here in the 1970s. The Northern Territory land rights laws had just been passed, and Aborigines were given the right to say no to mining on their lands, but the Ranger area was excluded from this provision. The Aborigines could, however, still negotiate the terms on which the mine companies would lease the land from them. Under pressure from the Federal government and mine companies, the Aboriginal negotiators finally signed a deal in 1978, which brought them a decent share of the Ranger profits, but many felt that it didn't adequately protect their land or sacred sites.

By 1988 many of the Aboriginal owners of Jabiluka and Koongarra argued in favour of mining there, apparently impressed with the economic benefits brought by Ranger. It was estimated that the Aboriginal owners of the Ranger and Nabarlek mine sites had received about $100 million in royalties from the mine companies in less than a decade.

A large slice of Kakadu's Stage Three, declared national parkland in 1987, was temporarily set aside as a 'conservation zone', which means that the area was under national park protection except that mineral exploration was allowed. Mining companies were given five years to come to agreement with the Aboriginal landowners if they wanted to mine. In 1991, however, the Federal government refused permission for the Coronation Hill mine to go ahead, and Stage Three was given full national park status. ■

---

vehicles except in the Dry, and then only as far as Two Mile Water Hole.

About 35 km further east along the highway, a turn-off to the south, again impassable to conventional vehicles in the Wet, leads to camp sites at **Alligator** and **Red Lilly** billabongs, and on to the Kakadu Highway.

South Alligator River Crossing is on the highway 60 km into the park, about two km past the Kakadu Holiday Village. The cruises on the tidal river here are a good opportunity for crocodile-spotting. During the Dry there are daily two-hour tours at 10 am and 4 pm for $24.50. The schedule seems to vary throughout the season, so telephone ☎ (089) 41 0800 for details.

Seven km east of South Alligator a short side road to the south leads to **Mamukala**, with views over the South Alligator flood plain, an observation building, a three-km walking trail and bird-watching hides.

Information

The excellent Kakadu National Park Infor-

mation Centre (☎ (089) 79 2101), on the Kakadu Highway a couple of km south of the Arnhem Highway turn-off, is open daily from 8 am to 5 pm. Here you'll find informative displays, including a special building devoted to birds, a video room with several interesting films available, and details of guided art and wildlife walks. It's also where you pay the $10 entry fee (children under 16 free). This entitles you to stay in the park for 14 days. There are random ticket checks at various places throughout the park.

There's also an information centre at Jabiru Airport. In Darwin you can get information on Kakadu from the Australian Nature Conservation Agency. Top End tourist offices usually have copies of the *Kakadu Visitor Guide* leaflet, which includes a good map.

Fuel is available at Kakadu Holiday Village, Border Store (no unleaded petrol or diesel), Jabiru and Cooinda. Jabiru also has a supermarket, post office and a Westpac bank.

Walking

Kakadu is excellent but tough bushwalking country. Many people will be satisfied with the marked trails, which range from one km to 12 km long. For the more adventurous there are infinite possibilities, especially in the drier south and east of the park, but take great care and prepare well. Tell people where you're going and don't go alone. You need a permit from the park information centre to camp outside the established camp sites.

The Darwin Bushwalking Club (☎ (089) 85 1484) welcomes visitors and may be able to help with information too. It has walks most weekends, often in Kakadu. Or you could join a Willis's Walkabouts guided bushwalk (see Organised Tours in the Darwin Getting There & Around section).

Kakadu by Foot is a helpful guide to the marked walking trails in Kakadu. It is published by ANCA ($1.95) but seems to be in short supply.

Ubirr

This spectacular rock art site, also called Obiri Rock, lies 43 km north of the Arnhem Highway. The turn-off to Ubirr is 95 km from the park entrance and the road is sealed most of the way, but there are several creek crossings which make it impassable for a conventional vehicle for most of the wet season – sometimes for 4WD too. The rock art site is open daily from 8.30 am to sunset from June to November.

Shortly before Ubirr you pass the Border Store. Nearby are a couple of walking trails close to the East Alligator River, which forms the eastern boundary of the park here. There is a backpackers' hostel and camp site nearby.

An easily followed path from the Ubirr car park takes you through the main galleries and up to a lookout with superb views – a 1.5-km round trip. There are paintings on numerous rocks along the path, but the highlight is the main gallery with a large array of well-executed and preserved x-ray-style wallabies, possums, goannas, tortoises and fish, plus a couple of *balanda* (white men) with hands on hips.

The Ubirr paintings are in many different styles. They were painted during the period from over 20,000 years ago right up to the 20th century. Allow plenty of time to seek out and study them.

Jabiru (population 1730)

The township, built to accommodate the Ranger mine workers, has shops and a public swimming pool. Six km east is Jabiru Airport and the nearby **Ranger uranium mine**. Minibus tours of the mine ($10) are available three times a day through Kakadu Air (☎ (089) 79 2411).

Nourlangie Rock

The sight of this looming, mysterious, isolated outlier of the Arnhem Land escarpment makes it easy to understand why it has been important to Aborigines for so long. Its long, red, sandstone bulk – striped in places with orange, white and black – slopes up from surrounding woodland to fall away at one end in sheer, stepped cliffs, at the foot of which is Kakadu's best-known collection of rock art.

The name Nourlangie is a corruption of *nawulandja*, an Aboriginal word which refers to an area bigger than the rock itself. The Aboriginal name of the rock is Burrunggui. You reach it at the end of a 12-km sealed road which turns east off the Kakadu Highway, 22 km south of the Arnhem Highway. Other interesting spots nearby make it worth spending a whole day in this corner of Kakadu. The last few km of the road are closed from around 5 pm daily.

From the main car park a round-trip walk of about two km takes you first to the **Anbangbang shelter**, which was used for 20,000 years as a refuge from heat, rain and the area's frequent wet-season thunderstorms. From the gallery you can walk onto a lookout where you can see the distant Arnhem Land cliff line, which includes Lightning Dreaming (Namarrgon Djadjam), the home of Namarrgon. There's a 12-km marked walk all the way round the rock, for which the park information centre has a leaflet.

Heading back towards the highway you can take three turn-offs to further places of interest. The first, on the left about one km from the main car park, takes you to **Anbangbang Billabong**, with its picnic site and dense carpet of lilies. The second, also on the left, leads to a short walk up to **Nawulandja Lookout** with good views back over Nourlangie Rock.

The third turn-off, a dirt track on the right, takes you to another outstanding – but little visited – rock art gallery, **Nangaloar** or Nangaluwurr. A further six km along this road, followed by a three-km walk, brings you to **Gubara Pools**, an area of shaded pools set in monsoon forest.

Jim Jim & Twin Falls

These two spectacular waterfalls are along a 4WD dry-season track that turns south off the Kakadu Highway between the Nourlangie Rock and Cooinda turn-offs. It's about 60 km to Jim Jim Falls, with the last km on foot, and 70 km to Twin Falls, where the last few hundred metres are through the water up a snaking, forested gorge – great fun on an inflatable air bed. Jim Jim – a sheer 215-metre drop – is awesome after the rains, but its waters can shrink to nothing at the end of the Dry. Twin Falls doesn't dry up.

Yellow Water & Cooinda

The turn-off to the Cooinda accommodation complex and the superb Yellow Water wetlands, with their big water-bird population, is 48 km down the Kakadu Highway from its junction with the Arnhem Highway. It's then about four km to Cooinda, and a couple more km to the starting point for the boat trips on Yellow Water Billabong. These go three times daily year round and cost $22.50 ($11.50 for children) for two hours. There are also twice-daily tours of 1½ hours for $19.50 ($10.50). This trip is one of the highlights of most people's visit to Kakadu. Early morning is the best time to go as the bird life is most active. You're likely to see a saltwater crocodile or two. It's usually advisable to book your cruise the day before at Cooinda – particularly for the early departure.

Yellow Water is also an excellent place to watch the sunset, particularly in the dry season when the smoke from the many bushfires which burn in the Top End at this time of year turns bright red in the setting sun. Bring plenty of insect repellent as the mosquitoes are voracious.

Cooinda to Pine Creek

Just south of the Yellow Water and Cooinda turn-off the Kakadu Highway heads south-west out of the park to Pine Creek on the Stuart Highway, about 160 km from Cooinda. This stretch is often closed to normal traffic in the Wet. If you're travelling up the Stuart Highway from the south, ask the police at Pine Creek for information on this route into Kakadu. On the way there is a turn-off to the very scenic falls and plunge pool at **Waterfall Creek** (also called Gunlom) which featured in *Crocodile Dundee*. It's 37 km along a good dirt road.

Organised Tours

There are hosts of tours to Kakadu from Darwin and a few that start inside the park. Two-day tours typically take in Jim Jim Falls, Nourlangie Rock and the Yellow Water cruise, and cost from $170. Companies which aim at backpackers and seem to be popular include: Hunter Safaris (☎ (089) 81 272), $190 for two days; All Terrain (☎ (089) 41 0070); and Saratoga (☎ (089) 81 3521).

A one-day tour to Kakadu from Darwin is really too quick – but if you're short of time it's better than nothing. You could try Australian Kakadu Tours (☎ (089) 81 5144), which will whiz you to Yellow Water and Nourlangie Rock and back to Darwin for $88.

Longer tours usually cover most of the main sights plus a couple of extras. Some combine Kakadu with the Katherine Gorge.

Katherine Adventure Tours (☎ (089) 71 0246) is popular, charging $270 for three days (including Litchfield), or $450 for five days, from Katherine.

You can take 10-hour 4WD tours to Jim Jim and Twin Falls from Jabiru or Cooinda ($115, dry season) with Kakadu Gorge & Waterfall Tours (☎ (089) 79 2025).

Willis's Walkabouts (☎ (089) 85 2134) organises bushwalks guided by knowledgable Top End walkers following your own or preset routes of two days or more. Many of the walks are in Kakadu: prices vary, but $750 for a two-week trip, including evening meals and return transport from Darwin, is fairly typical.

Magela Tours (☎ (089) 79 2227), owned and run by Aborigines, offers day tours around Kakadu, concentrating on sites which are less frequented. The cost is $250 per person with pick-ups in Jabiru.

Northern Adventure Safaris (☎ (089) 81 3833) operates good two-day trips out of Jabiru for $195, and this includes the bus fare from Darwin.

Into Arnhem Land A couple of outfits offer trips into Arnhem Land from Kakadu. Kakadu Parklink (☎ (089) 79 2411) has weekday day tours from Jabiru or Cooinda into the Mikinj Valley for $135 ($108 children). The trips are usually accompanied by a local Aboriginal guide.

Scenic Flights Kakadu Air (☎ (089) 79 2411) does a number of flights over Kakadu. A half-hour flight from Jabiru costs $50, or it's $90 for an hour.

Places to Stay & Eat
Accommodation prices in Kakadu can vary tremendously depending on the season – dry-season prices (given here) are often as much as 50% above wet-season prices.

Camping There are National Parks sites, and also some (with power) attached to the resorts: *Kakadu Holiday Village*, South Alligator, $20 for two with power, $16 without; *Gagadju Lodge Cooinda*, $13 with power, $7 without; and *Kakadu Frontier Lodge*, Jabiru, $20 with power.

The three main National Parks camp sites are: *Merl*, near the Border Store; *Muirella*

Park, six km off the Kakadu Highway a few km south of the Nourlangie Rock turn-off; and *Mardugal*, just off the Kakadu Highway 1.5 km south of the Cooinda turn-off. Only the Mardugal site is open during the Wet. The camp sites have hot showers, flushing toilets, and drinking water and the fee is $7 per person.

The National Parks provide about 15 more basic camp sites around the park, and at these there is no fee. To camp away from these you need a permit from the park information centre.

South Alligator Just a couple of km west of the South Alligator River on the Arnhem Highway is the *Kakadu Holiday Village* (☎ (089) 79 0166), which has four-bed shared rooms for $28 per person, or singles/doubles for $110. The hotel has a restaurant and a basic shop.

Jabiru The *Gagadju Crocodile Hotel* (☎ (089) 79 2800) is probably most famous for its design – it's set out in the shape of a crocodile, although this is only apparent from the air. There's nothing very exotic about the hotel itself, although it is comfortable enough. Room prices start at $90/100.

The *Kakadu Frontier Lodge* (☎ (089) 79 2422) has four-bed rooms at $22 per person, or $80 for a whole room. The only cooking facilities are a few barbecues.

Apart from the restaurants at the two resorts, the licensed *Miners Hut* restaurant in the town has takeaway burgers and a more expensive eat-in section with meals from $10. There's also a bakery across the road.

Ubirr The basic *Hostel Kakadu* (☎ (089) 79 2333) has accommodation at $12 per person, and National Parks rangers put on a slide show each Thursday evening. The Border Store has snack food and is open daily until 5 pm.

Cooinda This is by far the most popular place to stay, mainly because of the proximity of the Yellow Water wetlands and the early-morning boat cruises. It gets mighty crowded at times, mainly with camping tours. The *Gagadju Lodge Cooinda* (☎ (089) 79 0145) has some comfortable units for $110 single or double, and much cheaper and more basic air-con 'budget rooms', which are just transportable huts of the type found on many building sites and more commonly known in the Territory as 'demountables' or 'dongas'. For $12 per person they are quite adequate, if a little cramped (two beds per room), although there are no cooking facilities.

The restaurant in the bar here serves unexciting but good-value meals, or there's the expensive *Mimi Restaurant*, with main courses at around $15.

Getting There & Around

Ideally, take your own 4WD. The Arnhem Highway is sealed all the way to Jabiru. The Kakadu Highway is sealed or gravel from its junction with the Arnhem Highway, near Jabiru, all the way to Pine Creek, with the exception of a 30-km stretch just inside the park's southern boundary. Sealed roads lead from the Kakadu Highway to Nourlangie Rock, the Muirella Park camping area and most of the way to Ubirr. Other roads are mostly dirt and blocked for varying periods during the Wet and early Dry.

Greyhound Pioneer runs daily buses from Darwin to Cooinda via Jabiru and back, with connections from Jabiru to Ubirr. The buses leave Darwin at 7 am and stop at Humpty Doo, the Bark Hut, Kakadu Holiday Village, Jabiru ($48, 3¼ hours), Nourlangie Rock and Cooinda ($52, five hours). The return service leaves Cooinda at 3 pm.

BATHURST & MELVILLE ISLANDS

These two large, flat islands about 80 km north of Darwin are the home of the Tiwi Aborigines. You need a permit to visit them and the only realistic option is to take a tour. Tiwi Tours (☎ (089) 81 5115), a company which employs many Tiwi among its staff, is the only operator, and its tours have been recommended.

The Tiwi people's island homes kept them fairly isolated from mainland developments until this century, and their culture has retained several unique features. Perhaps the best known are the *pukumani* burial poles, carved and painted with symbolic and mythological figures, which are erected around graves. More recently the Tiwi have turned their hand to art for sale – bark painting, textile screen printing, batik and pottery, using traditional designs and motifs.

The Tiwi had mixed relations with Macassan fisherpeople, who came in search of the trepang, or sea cucumber. A British settlement in the 1820s at Fort Dundas, near Pularumpi on Melville Island, failed partly because of poor relations with the locals. The main settlement on the islands is **Nguiu** in the south-east of Bathurst Island, which was founded in 1911 as a Catholic mission. On Melville Island the settlements are Pularumpi and Milikapiti.

Most Tiwi live on Bathurst Island and follow a nontraditional lifestyle. Some go back to their traditional lands on Melville Island for a few weeks each year. Melville

Figure carved in ironwood, Bathurst Island

Island also has descendants of the Japanese pearl divers who regularly visited here early this century, and people of mixed Aboriginal and European parentage who were gathered here from around the Territory under government policy half a century ago.

A full-day Tiwi Tours trip costs $230 and includes the necessary permit, a flight from Darwin to Nguiu, visits to the early Catholic mission buildings and craft workshops, a boat crossing of the narrow Apsley Strait to Melville Island, swimming at Turacumbie Falls, a trip to a pukumani burial site and the flight back to Darwin from Melville. This tour is available from April to October. Tiwi Tours also offers two- or three-day tours to the islands, staying at a tented camp, for $395 for a two-day trip or $545 for three days. There is sometimes a stand-by fare of $299 offered on the two-day trip if you book only 24 hours in advance.

COBOURG PENINSULA

This remote wilderness, 200 km north-east of Darwin, includes the Cobourg Marine Park and the Aboriginal-owned Gurig National Park. Entry to the latter is by permit only.

The ruins of the early British settlement at Victoria can be visited on **Port Essington**, a superb 30-km-long natural harbour on the northern side of the peninsula.

The track to Cobourg is accessible by 4WD vehicle only – and it's closed in the wet season. As you pass through part of Arnhem Land, and the Aboriginal owners there severely restrict the number of vehicles going through, you're advised to apply up to a year ahead for the necessary permit ($10 fee) from the Northern Territory Conservation Commission (☎ (089) 89 5511) at PO Box 496, Palmerston, NT. The drive from the East Alligator River takes about six hours and the track is in reasonable condition, the roughest part coming in the hour or so after the turn-off from Murgenella.

At **Black Point** there's a small store open daily, but only from 3 to 5 pm. It sells basic provisions, ice, camping gas and fuel (diesel, super, unleaded, outboard mix), and basic

mechanical repairs can be undertaken. Be warned that credit cards are not accepted here.

Places to Stay

There are 15 shady camp sites about 100 metres from the shore at the *Smith Point Camping Ground*. It's run by the Conservation Commission and facilities include a shower and toilet, and barbecue facilities. There's no electricity and generators are banned at night. The charge is $4 per site for three people, plus $1 for each extra person.

The fully equipped, four-bed *Cobourg Cottages* (☎ (089) 79 0263) at Smith Point cost $100 for the whole cottage, but you need to bring your own supplies. There's also a one-off $20 fee levied by the Aboriginal landowners for the use of the cottages, which goes to their funeral fund.

The only other accommodation option is the extremely luxurious, award-winning *Seven Spirit Bay Resort* (☎ toll-free 1800 891 189), set in secluded wilderness at Vashon Head and accessible only by air or boat. It charges a mere $399/698 for single/double accommodation, but this includes three gourmet meals, a day trip to Victoria Settlement, guided bushwalks and fishing. Accommodation is in individual open-sided, hexagonal 'habitats', each with their own partly outdoor, private bathroom! Return transfer by air from Darwin costs $270 per person.

Getting There & Away

There's an airstrip at Smith Point which is serviced by charter flights from Darwin.

Wimray (☎ (089) 45 2755) does a day tour from Darwin for $230, which includes a flight over Melville Island on the way, a cruise on Port Essington, visits to Aboriginal sacred sites, a tour of the Victoria ruins and game fishing.

ARNHEM LAND & GOVE

The entire eastern half of the Top End is the Arnhem Land Aboriginal Land, which is spectacular, sparsely populated and the source of some good Aboriginal art. It's vir-

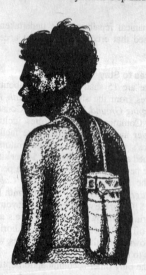

tually closed to independent travellers apart from Gove, the peninsula at the north-east corner.

At **Nhulunbuy** (population 3900), on the Gove Peninsula, there is a bauxite-mining centre with a deep-water export port. The Aborigines of nearby Yirrkala (population 580) made an important step in the land rights movement in 1963 when they protested at the plans for this mining on their traditional land. They failed to stop it, but forced a government inquiry and won compensation, and their case caught the public eye.

You don't have to have a permit to visit Nhulunbuy and you can fly there direct from Darwin for $227 or from Cairns for $315 with Qantas or Ansett. Travelling overland through Arnhem Land is not an option simply because permits are needed from the various communities and these are not issued unless you have a good reason for going there. Casual tourism is definitely not encouraged.

You can hire vehicles in Nhulunbuy to explore the coastline (there are some fine beaches, but beware of crocodiles) and the local area. You need to get a permit to do this from the Northern Land Council in Nhulunbuy (a formality).

Groote Eylandt, a large island off the east Arnhem Land coast, is also Aboriginal land, with a big manganese mining operation. The main settlement here is Alyangula (population 660).

Organised Tours

There are a number of tours into Arnhem Land, but these usually only visit the western part.

Umorrduk Aboriginal Safaris (☎ (089) 41 3882) has a one-day fly-in/fly-out tour from Darwin to Mudjeegarrdart airstrip in north-western Arnhem Land. The highlight of the trip is a visit to the 20,000-year-old Umorrduk rock art sites. The cost is $210 per person for two people, or $163 per person for three or four people. They also do two-day trips for $521 per person.

Another operator is Davidson's Arnhem-land Safaris (☎ (089) 27 5240). Max Davidson has been taking people into Arnhem Land for years and has a concession at Mt Borradaile, north of Gunbalanya (Oenpelli), where he has set up his safari camp. The cost of staying at the camp is $300 per person per day, which includes accommodation, all meals, guided tours and fishing; transfers from Darwin can be arranged.

AAT-Kings (☎ toll-free 1800 334 009) has two-day coach trips operating out of Darwin which take you through Kakadu and on to Davidson's Safari Camp. The cost of these trips is $449.

You can also visit the Injalak Arts & Crafts centre in Gunbalanya (Oenpelli); you must first get a permit from the Northern Land Council. Injalak is both a workplace and shopfront for artists and craftspeople who produce traditional paintings on bark and paper, dijeridus, pandanus weavings and baskets, and screenprinted fabrics. All sales benefit the community.

Other trips are available from Jabiru in Kakadu; see the Kakadu National Park section for details.

Down the Track

It's just over 1500 km south from Darwin to Alice Springs, and although at times it can be dreary there is an amazing variety of things to see or do along the road and nearby.

Until WW II the Track really was just that – a dirt track – connecting the Territory's two main towns, Darwin and 'the Alice'. The need to quickly supply Darwin, which was under attack by Japanese aircraft from Timor, led to a rapid upgrading of the road. Although it is now sealed and well kept all the way, short, sharp floods during the Wet can cut the road and stop all traffic for days at a time.

The Stuart Highway takes its name from John McDouall Stuart, who made the first crossing of Australia from south to north. Twice he turned back due to lack of supplies, ill health and hostile Aborigines, but finally completed his epic trek in 1862. Only 10 years later the telegraph line to Darwin was laid along the route he had followed, and today the Stuart Highway between Darwin and Alice Springs follows roughly the same path.

DARWIN TO KATHERINE

Some places along the Track south of Darwin (Howard Springs, Darwin Crocodile Farm and Litchfield Park) are covered in the Around Darwin section.

Lake Bennett

This is a popular camping, swimming, sailing and windsurfing spot among Darwinites. It's 80 km down the Track, then seven km east. You can rent canoes ($8), sailboards ($12.50), aquabikes ($10) and catamarans ($20) by the hour. Camping is available for $6, or there are on-site tents for $15/24. If you ring in advance (☎ (089) 76 0960) staff from the camp site will pick you up from the highway.

Batchelor (population 650)

This small town, 84 km down the Track from Darwin, then 13 km west, used to service the now-closed Rum Jungle uranium and copper mine nearby. In recent years it has received a boost from the growing popularity of nearby Litchfield National Park. Batchelor is the base for the Top End Gliding Club. It has a swimming pool open six days a week and an Aboriginal residential tertiary college.

About an hour's walk away, or a shorter drive, is **Rum Jungle Lake** where you can canoe or swim.

Places to Stay The *Batchelor Caravillage* (☎ (089) 76 0166) on Rum Jungle Rd has on-site vans for $42 a double, cabins for $60, or tent sites for $15. The *Rum Jungle Motor Inn* (☎ (089) 76 0123) has singles/doubles for $58/78.

Adelaide River (population 360)

Not to be confused with Adelaide River Crossing on the Arnhem Highway, this small settlement is on the Stuart Highway 111 km south of Darwin. It has a cemetery for those who died in the 1942-43 Japanese air raids. This whole stretch of the highway is dotted with a series of roadside WW II airstrips.

Adelaide River has a pub, an Aboriginal art shop, the *Shady River View Caravan Park* with tent sites ($6), and the *Adelaide River Motor Inn* with singles from $30 to $40, doubles $50 to $65 (☎ (089) 76 7047 for both of the above).

You can take tours from here or Batchelor to Litchfield Park, Daly River, Douglas Hot Springs and Butterfly Gorge – it's a bit cheaper than visiting the same places from Darwin.

Old Highway

South of Adelaide River a sealed section of the old Stuart Highway, makes a loop to the south before rejoining the main road 52 km on. It's a scenic trip and leads to a number of pleasant spots, but access to them is often cut in the wet season.

The beautiful 12-metre **Robin Falls** are a short walk off this road, 17 km along. The falls, set in a monsoon-forested gorge, dwindle to a trickle in the dry season, but are spectacular in the Wet.

The turn-off to **Daly River** is 14 km further on, and Daly River is 109 km from the Stuart Highway. There's a Catholic mission (the ruins of an 1886 Jesuit mission) and the Daly River Nature Park, where you can camp. Bird life is abundant at some times of the year, and quite a few saltwater and freshwater crocodiles inhabit the river. There's a couple of accommodation options here, including the *Woolianna on the Daly Tourist Park* (☎ (089) 78 2478), the *Daly River Roadside Inn* (☎ (089) 78 2418) and the *Mango Farm* (089) 78 2464.

To reach **Douglas Hot Springs**, turn south off the old highway just before it rejoins the Stuart Highway and continue on for about 35 km. The nature park here includes a section of the Douglas River, a pretty camping area and several hot springs – a bit hot for bathing at 40°C, but there are cooler pools.

Butterfly Gorge National Park is about 15 km beyond Douglas Hot Springs – you'll need a 4WD to get there. True to its name butterflies sometimes swarm in the gorge. Although it's generally safe to swim in these places, you should still watch out for crocs. There are camp sites with toilets and barbecues.

Pine Creek (population 440)

This small town, 245 km from Darwin, was the scene of a gold rush in the 1870s and some of the old timber and corrugated iron buildings survive. The Kakadu Highway goes north-east from Pine Creek to Kakadu National Park.

The old **railway station** has been restored and houses a visitors centre and a display on the Darwin to Pine Creek railway, which opened in 1889 but is now closed. **Pine Creek Museum** on Railway Parade near the post office has interesting displays on local history. The station and museum are usually open for an hour each morning and afternoon. **Ah Toys General Store** is a reminder of the gold-rush days when Pine Creek's

Chinese population heavily outnumbered the Europeans. In recent years gold mining has returned to Pine Creek with open-cut workings outside the town.

Places to Stay The town has an unattractive caravan park, and there's also the *Pine Creek Hotel/Motel* (☎ (089) 76 1288) with air-con singles/doubles at $60/70.

Around Pine Creek

A well-maintained dirt road follows the line of the old railway line east of the highway between Hayes Creek and Pine Creek. This is in fact the original 'north road', which was in use before the 'new road' (now the Old Stuart Highway!) was built. It's a worthwhile detour to see the 1930s corrugated-iron pub at **Grove Hill**, and the old tin-mine workings at **Mt Wells**, where there is also accommodation and camping.

About three km along the Stuart Highway south of Pine Creek is the turn-off to **Umbrawarra Gorge Nature Park**, about 30 km west along a dirt road (often impassable in the Wet). There's a camp site with pit toilets and barbecues, and you can swim in crocodile-free pools one km from the car park.

Edith Falls

At the 293-km mark you can turn off to the beautiful Edith Falls Nature Park, 19 km east of the road, where there's a free camp site with showers, pit toilets and barbecues. Swimming is possible in a clear, forest-surrounded pool at the bottom of the series of falls. You may see freshwater crocodiles (the inoffensive variety), but be careful. There's a good walk up to rapids and more pools above the falls. Edith Falls is part of Nitmiluk (Katherine Gorge) National Park.

KATHERINE (population 7100)

Apart from Tennant Creek, this is the only town of any size between Darwin and Alice Springs. It's a bustling little place where the Victoria Highway branches off to the Kimberley and Western Australia. It's scheduled to grow to about 10,000 people in the 1990s, partly because of the big, new air-force base at Tindal just south of town.

Katherine has long been an important stopping point, since the river it's built on and named after is the first permanent running water if you're coming north from Alice Springs. The town includes some historic old buildings, such as the Sportsman's Arms, featured in *We of the Never Never*, Jeannie Gunn's classic novel of turn-of-the-century outback life. The main interest here, however, is the spectacular Katherine Gorge 30 km to the north-east – a great place to camp, walk, swim, canoe, take a cruise or simply float along on an air mattress.

Orientation & Information

Katherine's main street, Katherine Terrace, is also the Stuart Highway as it runs through town. Coming from the north, you cross the Katherine River Bridge just before the town centre. The Victoria Highway to Western Australia branches off a further 300 metres on. After another 300 metres Giles St, the road to Katherine Gorge, branches off in the other direction.

At the end of the town centre is the Katherine Region Tourist Association office (☎ (089) 72 2650) which is open Monday to Friday from 8.45 am to 5 pm and weekends in the dry season from 10 am to 2.30 pm. The bus station is over the road from the tourist office. There's a Northern Territory Conservation Commission office (☎ (089) 73 8770) on Giles St.

Things to See

Katherine's old **railway station**, owned by the National Trust, houses a display on railway history and is open Monday to Friday from 10 am to noon and from 1 to 3 pm in the dry season. Mimi Arts & Crafts on Pearce St is an Aboriginal-owned and run shop, selling products made over a wide area – from the deserts in the west to the coast in the east.

The small **Katherine Museum** is in the old airport terminal building on Gorge Rd, about one km from the centre of town.

There's a good selection of old photos and other bits and pieces of interest, including the original Gypsy Moth biplane flown by Dr Clyde Fenton, the first Flying Doctor. It is open weekdays from 10 am to 4 pm, Saturday from 10 am to 2 pm and Sunday from 2 to 5 pm.

The **School of the Air** on Giles St offers an opportunity to see how remote outback kids are taught. There are guided tours on weekdays during the school term.

Katherine has a good public **swimming pool** beside the highway on the way out of town, about 750 metres past the bus station. There are also some pleasant **thermal pools** beside the river, about three km from town along the Victoria Highway.

Organised Tours

Tours are available from Katherine, taking in various combinations of the town and Springvale Homestead attractions, the Gorge, Cutta Cutta Caves, Mataranka and Kakadu. Most accommodation places can book you on these and you'll be picked up from where you're staying – or ask at the tourist office or Travel North in the bus station.

There are Aboriginal tours at Manyallaluk (Eva Valley; see the Around Katherine section for details) and Bill Harney's Jankanginya Tour's (☎ toll-free 1800 089 103). Bill Harney is one of the Wadaman people, and he takes tours out into their land, sometimes referred to as Lightning Brothers country. Here you learn about bush tucker, crafts and medicine, and hear some of the nonsecret stories associated with the rock art of the area. Accommodation is in a bush camp. The cost is $90 for a one-day trip, or $230 for two days.

Places to Stay

There are several camping possibilities. One of the nicest is *Springvale Homestead* (☎ (089) 72 1355), with shady sites for $11. It also has budget units at $39/46 for singles/doubles, and there is a licensed restaurant, and a kiosk for snacks. It's eight km out of Katherine; turn right off the Victoria Highway after four km and follow the signs.

On the road to Springvale, five km from town, is the *Katherine Low Level Caravan Park* (☎ (089) 72 1355), a good place close to the river. Tent sites are $12 for two, or $13 with power. Closer to town, on the Victoria Highway, is the *Riverview Caravan Park* (☎ (089) 72 1011), which has reasonably comfortable cabins for $35/40 singles/doubles and tent sites at $10 ($12 with power). The thermal pools are five minutes walk away.

The *Katherine Frontier Motor Inn* (☎ (089) 72 1744), four km south of town on the Stuart Highway, has camp sites at $16, plus a pool, barbecue area and restaurant. It also has rooms for $95.

Kookaburra Lodge Backpackers (☎ (089) 71 0257), on the corner of Lindsay and Third Sts, is just a few minutes walk from the transit centre. It consists of old motel units with between six and 10 beds and costs $12 a night, or there are some twin rooms for $36. With so many people in each unit the bathroom and cooking facilities can get overcrowded at times.

Just around the corner is the *Palm Court Backpackers* (☎ (089) 72 2722), on the corner of Third and Giles Sts. It's in the most horrendously tasteless building, but the air-con rooms are uncrowded and have their own TV, fridge and bathroom. The problem here is that the communal cooking facilities are inadequate. The cost is $11 per person, or $44 for a whole room (four beds). The Katherine YHA youth hostel (☎ (089) 72 2942) is two km along the Victoria Highway, on the right as you head out of town. It's a friendly place with 36 beds (no more than three in any room) and charges $9 a night, although the location is inconvenient.

The *Victoria Lodge* (☎ (089) 72 3464) is at 21 Victoria Highway, not far from the main street. It's a good place with six-bed rooms at $10 per person.

Among the motels, the *Beagle Motor Inn* (☎ (089) 72 3998) at the corner of Lindsay and Fourth Sts is probably the cheapest, with singles/doubles for $40/55, including a light breakfast.

Places to Eat

Basically, Katherine has one or two of each of the usual types of Aussie eatery. Over the road from the transit centre, which has a 24-hour cafe, there's a *Big Rooster* fast-food place. The *Katherine Hotel/Motel*, just up the main street, has counter meals as well as *Aussie's Bistro*, which is good value. Over the road there's the *Golden Bowl* Chinese restaurant. A block further up on the corner of Warburton St, the *Crossways Hotel* does good counter meals for around $7.

Alfie's Pizza and *Popeye's Pizza* (☎ (089) 72 3633) are both on the main street, and the latter does home deliveries. *Cafe Enio's* is a relaxed little place on the main street, serving mainly pasta dishes.

Getting There & Away

You can fly to Katherine on weekdays from Darwin ($144) and Alice Springs ($369) with Skyport. Darfield Travel (☎ (089) 72 1344), on the main street between Giles and Lindsay Sts, is the agent. Katherine Airport is eight km south of town, just off the Stuart Highway.

All buses between Darwin and Alice Springs, Queensland or Western Australia stop at Katherine, which means two or three daily to and from Western Australia, and usually four to and from Darwin, Alice Springs and Queensland. See the Darwin section for more details. Typical fares from Katherine are Darwin $49, Alice Springs $125, Tennant Creek $72 and Kununurra $47.

Avis, Budget, Hertz and Territory Rent-a-Car all have car-rental offices in town.

Getting Around

You can rent bicycles at the youth hostel or the other backpackers' hostels, or there's mopeds for hire at 67 Second St.

Travel North (☎ (089) 72 1044) has a six-times-daily bus service from the transit centre to the Gorge for $13 return, or Kookaburra Lodge has a daily return service for $12.

Northern Territory
Top: Jim Jim Falls, Kakadu National Park (RI)
Middle: The Ghan (NTTC)
Bottom: N'Dhala Gorge (TW)

Northern Territory
Top: Uluru (Ayers Rock) (MF)
Bottom: Kata Tjuta (The Olgas) (PS)

AROUND KATHERINE
Springvale Homestead

This homestead, eight km south-west of town (turn right off the Victoria Highway after 3.8 km), claims to be the oldest cattle station in the Northern Territory. Today it's also a tourist accommodation centre, and free half-hour tours around the old homestead are given once or twice daily. From May to September evening crocodile-spotting cruises ($31) are run from here, and three nights a week there are Aboriginal corroborees with demonstrations by the local Jawoyn people of fire making, traditional dance and spear throwing ($31 including barbecue). There's also horse riding ($30) and cattle musters by horseback ($40).

Nitmiluk (Katherine Gorge) National Park

Strictly speaking Katherine Gorge is 13 gorges, separated from each other by rapids of varying length. The gorge walls aren't high, but it is a remote, beautiful place. It is 12 km long and has been carved out by the Katherine River, which rises in Arnhem Land. Further downstream it becomes the Daly River before flowing into the Timor Sea 80 km south-west of Darwin. The difference in water levels between the Wet and Dry is staggering. During the dry season the gorge waters are calm, but from November to March they can become a raging torrent.

Swimming in the gorge is safe except when it's in flood. The only crocodiles around are the freshwater variety and they're more often seen in the cooler months. The country surrounding the gorge is excellent for walking.

Information It's 30 km by sealed road from Katherine to the visitors centre and the camp site, and nearly one km further to the car park where the gorge begins and cruises start. The visitors centre has displays and information on the national park, which spreads over 1800 sq km to include extensive back country and Edith Falls to the north-west, as well as Katherine Gorge. There are details of a wide range of marked walking tracks starting here that go through the picturesque country south of the gorge, descending to the river at various points. Notice the smooth-barked salmon gums. Some of the tracks pass Aboriginal rock paintings up to 7000 years old. You can walk to Edith Falls (76 km, five days) or points on the way. For the longer or more rugged walks you need a permit from the visitors centre. The Katherine Gorge Canoe Marathon, organised by the Red Cross, takes place in June.

There's a $6 entry fee to the park.

Activities & Cruises At the river you can rent canoes for one, two or three people (☎ (089) 72 3604 or call at the Kookaburra Backpackers). These cost $18/26/33 for a half-day, or $25/40/54 for a whole day. This is a great way of exploring the gorge. You can also be adventurous and take the canoes out overnight, but you must book in advance as only a limited number of people are allowed to camp out in the gorges. You get a map with your canoe showing things of interest along the gorge sides – Aboriginal rock paintings, waterfalls, plant life, and so on.

The alternative is a cruise. These depart daily: there's the choice of a two-hour run, which goes to the second gorge and includes a visit to some gorge-side rock paintings for $20 ($8 children); a four-hour trip to the third gorge for $35 ($18), including morning or afternoon tea; or an eight-hour trip to the fifth gorge (the most spectacular) for $60 (children full fare), including lunch and morning and afternoon tea. All involve some walking between gorges (four km on the longest trip). In the wet season there are no eight-hour cruises. Tickets for the gorge tours must be pre-booked on ☎ toll-free 1800 089 103.

You can also take light-aircraft ($47 for 30 minutes) and helicopter flights ($55 for 15 minutes) over the gorge.

Places to Stay The *Gorge Caravan Park* (☎ (089) 72 1253) has showers, toilets, barbecues and a store (open from 7 am to 7 pm) which also serves basic hot meals. Wallabies and goannas frequent the camp site. It costs $13 for a camp site ($17 with power) and there's plenty of grass and shade.

Getting There & Away The six-times-daily commuter bus costs $13 return, and it picks up from anywhere in town. Kookaburra also runs a daily bus for $12 return.

Cutta Cutta Caves

Guided tours of these limestone caverns, 24 km south-east of Katherine along the Stuart Highway, are led by park rangers six times a day in the dry season, and cost $6 ($3 children). Orange Horseshoe Bats, a rare and endangered species, roost in the main cave, about 15 metres below the ground. The rock formations outside the caves are impressive.

Manyallaluk (Eva Valley)

Manyallaluk is the former 3000-sq-km Eva Valley cattle station which abuts the eastern edge of the Nitmiluk (Katherine Gorge) National Park. These days it is owned by the Jawoyn Aboriginal people, some of whom now organise and lead tours.

Currently, one- and four-day tours are offered. The one-day trip includes transport to and from Katherine, lunch, billy tea and damper, and you learn about traditional bush tucker and medicine, spear throwing and playing a dijeridu. On the four-day trip you actually travel through Jawoyn land and on the last day join a trip up the gorge. The cost is $80 ($50 children) for the day trip, and $385 for the four-day trip. For bookings and enquiries phone ☎ (089) 75 4727.

The day trip operates on Monday, Wednesday and Saturday from Katherine, or with your own vehicle you can camp at Manyallaluk ($5 per person) and take the day tour from there, which costs $55. It is possible just to camp without taking the tour, but you are restricted to the camping area.

KATHERINE TO WESTERN AUSTRALIA

It's 513 km on the Victoria Highway from Katherine to Kununurra in Western Australia. The road is bitumen but still only one vehicle wide in places: whenever two vehicles approach they have to edge off the road and inevitably stones shower everywhere. To preserve your windscreen and headlights pull well off and slow down.

As you approach the Western Australian border you start to see the boab trees found in much of the north-west of Australia. There's a 1½-hour time change when you cross the border. There's also a quarantine inspection post, and all fruit and vegetables must be left here. This only applies when travelling from the Territory to Western Australia.

Victoria River Crossing

The highway is sometimes cut by floods – the wet season here is very wet. In the dry season, if you stand on the Victoria River Bridge by the Victoria River Inn at the crossing, it's hard to imagine that the wide river, flowing far below your feet, can actually flow over the top of the bridge!

Timber Creek

From April to October, daily boat trips are made on the river from Timber Creek, further west. Max, the boat operator, is a local character and you'll be shown fresh and saltwater crocodiles, fish and turtles being fed – try some real billy tea, play the dijeridu and light a fire using fire sticks. Max has good knowledge of the flora and fauna and local history. The cost of a 3½-hour morning tour is $25 ($12.50 children) and bookings can be made at Max's information centre in Timber Creek, or phone ☎ (089) 75 0850.

You can see a boab marked by an early explorer at Gregory's Tree Historical Reserve, west of Timber Creek.

Gregory National Park

This little-visited national park to the south and west of Timber Creek covers 10,500 sq km and offers good fishing, camping and bushwalking. There's also the 90-km 4WD **Bullita Stock Route** which takes eight hours, although it's better to break the journey at one of the three marked camp sites. For more details contact the Bullita ranger on ☎ (089) 75 0833.

Keep River National Park

Bordering Western Australia just off the Victoria Highway, the Keep River National Park is noted for its sandstone landforms and has some excellent walking trails. You can reach the main points in the park by conventional vehicle during the dry season. Aboriginal art can be seen near the car park at the end of the road.

There's a rangers' station (☎ (089) 67 8827) three km into the park from the main road, and there's camp sites with pit toilets at Gurrangalng (15 km into the park) and Jarrnarm (28 km).

MATARANKA

Mataranka is 103 km south-east of Katherine on the Stuart Highway. The attraction is **Mataranka Homestead**, seven km off the highway just south of the small town. The crystal-clear thermal pool here, in a pocket of rainforest, is a great place to wind down after a hot day on the road – though it can get crowded. There's no charge.

The pool is just a short walk from the homestead accommodation area, which includes a backpackers' hostel, camp site, motel rooms and restaurant – it's more relaxed than it sounds since you're a long way from anywhere else.

A couple of hundred metres away is the **Waterhouse River**, where you can walk along the banks, or rent canoes and rowing boats for $5 an hour. Outside the homestead entrance is a replica of the Elsey Station Homestead which was made for the filming of *We of the Never Never* (whose story is set near Mataranka). There are historical displays inside the replica.

Places to Stay & Eat

The backpackers' hostel at *Mataranka Homestead* (☎ (089) 75 4544) is quite comfortable and has some twin rooms, though the kitchen is small. It costs $15 per person or $30 for a twin room. Camping is $14 for a site ($18 with power), and air-con motel rooms with private bathroom are $59/74 for singles/doubles. In between there are self-contained budget cabins which cost $56 for two people, plus $9 for each extra adult ($5 per child), for up to six people, and three-bed units at $60, or with five beds for $70.

There's a store where you can get basic groceries, a bar with snacks and meals (not cheap), or you can use the camp-site barbecues.

In Mataranka town the atmospheric *Old Elsey Inn* (☎ (089) 75 4512) has a couple of rooms at $45/55, and the *Territory Manor Motel* (☎ (089) 75 4516) is a more luxurious place with a swimming pool, restaurant and motel rooms at $65/72 for singles/doubles; alternatively, you can camp for $14 ($18 with power). Hefty discounts are offered during the Wet.

Getting There & Around

Long-distance buses travelling up and down the Stuart Highway call at Mataranka and the homestead.

MATARANKA TO THREEWAYS

Not far south of the Mataranka Homestead turn-off, the Roper Highway branches east off the Stuart Highway. It leads about 200 km to **Roper Bar**, near the Roper River on the edge of Aboriginal land, where there's a store with a camp site and a few rooms – mainly visited by fishing enthusiasts. All but about 40 km of the road is sealed. About five km south of the Roper junction is the turn-off to the **Elsey Cemetery**, not far from the highway. Here are the graves of characters like 'the Fizzer' who came to life in *We of the Never Never*.

Larrimah

Continuing south from Mataranka you pass through Larrimah – at one time the railway line from Darwin came as far as here, but it was abandoned after Cyclone Tracy.

There are three camping grounds. The one on the highway at the southern end of town, *Green Park* (☎ (089) 75 9937), charges $8 per site ($12 with power). There's a swimming pool and a few crocodiles in fenced-off ponds. You can also camp at the *Larrimah Wayside Inn* (☎ (089) 75 9931), 100 metres or so off the highway opposite the Green Park. The Wayside has singles/doubles from $10/20, and camp sites for $10 with power;

it does counter meals and sells petrol several cents cheaper than the places on the highway.

Daly Waters

Further south again is Daly Waters, three km off the highway, an important staging post in the early days of aviation – Amy Johnson landed here. The *Daly Waters Pub* (☎ (089) 75 9927), with air-con double rooms at $40/50, is not surprisingly the focus of local life. It's an atmospheric place, dating from 1893 and said to be the oldest pub in the Territory, and there's good food available. The pub also has a caravan park with tent sites at $6/10 – and another WW II airstrip. The *Hi-Way Inn & Caravan Park* (☎ (089) 75 9925) has singles/doubles from $40/60 and camp sites at $3 per person.

Just south of Daly Waters the single-lane, sealed Carpentaria Highway heads off east to **Borroloola** (population 600), 378 km away near the Gulf of Carpentaria and one of the best barramundi fishing spots in the Territory. After 267 km the Carpentaria Highway meets the Tablelands Highway, also sealed, at Cape Crawford Roadhouse. The Tablelands Highway runs 404 km south to meet the Barkly Highway at Barkly Roadhouse and there's no petrol between the two roadhouses.

Daly Waters to Threeways

Back on the Stuart Highway, after Daly Waters, there's **Newcastle Waters** and **Elliott**, and the land just gets drier and drier. At Elliott, the *Midland Caravan Park* (☎ (089) 69 2037) has camp sites from $8 for two people. There's also the *Elliott Hotel* (☎ (089) 69 2069) and the *BP Roadhouse* (☎ (089) 69 2018), which both have single/double rooms from around $25/35. **Lake Woods**, 14 km west by dirt road, is a great spot for camping, though there are no facilities. Further south, a large rock known as **Lubra's Lookout** overlooks **Renner Springs**, and this is generally accepted as the dividing line between the seasonally wet Top End and the dry Centre.

About 50 km before Threeways and four

km off the road along the old Stuart Highway is **Churchill's Head**, a large rock said to look like Britain's wartime prime minister. Soon after, there's a memorial to Stuart at **Attack Creek**, where the explorer turned back on one of his attempts to cross Australia from south to north, reputedly after his party was attacked by a group of hostile Aborigines.

THREEWAYS

Threeways, 537 km north of the Alice, 988 km south of Darwin and 643 km west of Mt Isa, is basically a bloody long way from anywhere – apart from Tennant Creek, 26 km down the Track. This is a classic 'get stuck' point for hitchhikers – anybody who has hitched around Australia seems to have a tale about Threeways.

The *Threeways Roadhouse* (☎ (089) 62 2744) at the junction has air-con rooms at $45, or you can camp for $8 ($12 with power). The junction is marked by a memorial to John Flynn, the founder of the Royal Flying Doctor Service.

TENNANT CREEK (population 3500)

Apart from Katherine, this is the only town of any size between Darwin and Alice Springs. It's 26 km south of Threeways, 511 km north of Alice Springs. A lot of travellers spend a night here and there are one or two attractions, mainly related to gold mining, to tempt you to stay a bit longer.

There's a tale that Tennant Creek was first settled when a wagonload of beer broke down here in the early 1930s and the driver decided they might as well make themselves comfortable while they consumed the freight. Tennant Creek had a small gold rush around the same time. One of the major workings was **Nobles Nob**, 16 km east of the town along Peko Rd. It was discovered by a one-eyed man called John Noble who formed a surprisingly successful prospecting partnership with the blind William Weaber. This was the biggest open-cut gold mine in the country until mining ceased in 1985. Ore from other local mines is still processed and you can visit the open cut.

Information

The visitors centre (☎ (089) 62 3388) is located in the transit centre in the middle of town.

Anyinginyi is an interesting Aboriginal arts and crafts shop on the highway in the centre of town. Most of the stuff sold is made locally and prices are lower than in Alice Springs.

Things to See

Along Peko Rd you can visit the old **Tennant Creek Battery**, where gold-bearing ore was crushed and treated. The battery is still in working order and guided tours are given twice daily from April to October. Along the same road there is the **One Tank Hill lookout**. Nearby is the Argo mine, the main operation of the Peko company which used to mine at Warrego, north-west of Tennant Creek.

The **National Trust Museum**, on Schmidt St near the corner of Windley St, houses six rooms of local memorabilia and reconstructed mining scenes. It's open daily from 4 to 6 pm from May to October; admission is $2.

Organised Tours

An interesting diversion while in Tennant Creek is to take a morning Walala Bush Tucker Tour (☎ (089) 62 1353). These tours, which are led by local Aboriginal women, operate from March to November and delve into bush tucker and medicine. The cost is $25 ($15 children) for 2½ hours or $45 ($30) for four hours; bookings should be made one day in advance.

Places to Stay

Camping is the only cheap accommodation alternative. The *Outback Caravan Park* (☎ (089) 62 2459) is one km along Peko Rd, which runs east off the Stuart Highway opposite Windley St. It has a swimming pool, tent sites at $10 a double ($15 with power) and on-site vans or cabins (some air-on) for $25 to $45 double.

The basic youth hostel (☎ (089) 62 2719), at the corner of Leichhardt and Windley Sts,

has 24 beds. Windley St runs west off the Stuart Highway into the town centre, a block south of the visitors centre. A bed in the hostel costs $9.

Tennant Creek's motels aren't cheap. The *Safari Lodge Motel* (☎ (089) 62 2207) on the highway has singles/doubles for $59/69. It also has dormitory beds for $12. The *Gold-fields Hotel/Motel* (☎ (089) 62 2030), also on the highway, has singles/doubles for $55/65.

TENNANT CREEK TO ALICE SPRINGS

About 90 km south of Tennant Creek is the **Devil's Marbles Conservation Reserve**, a haphazard pile of giant spherical boulders scattered on both sides of the road. According to Aboriginal mythology they were laid by the Rainbow Serpent. The Rainbow Serpent obviously got around because there is a similar collection of boulders on a South Island beach in New Zealand, and the Devil's Pebbles are located 10 km north-west of Tennant Creek. At **Wauchope**, just to the south of the marbles, there's a pub and caravan park.

After the Devil's Marbles there are only a few places of interest to pause at on the trip south to the Alice. Near Barrow Creek the **Stuart Memorial** commemorates John McDouall Stuart. Visible to the east of the highway is Central Mt Stuart.

At **Barrow Creek** itself there is an old post-office telegraph repeater station. It was attacked by Aborigines in 1874 and the station master and linesman were killed – their graves are by the road. A great number of Aborigines died in the inevitable reprisals. The pub here is a real outback gem, and the Barrow Creek Races in August are a colourful event which draws people in from all over the area. The Thangkenharenge Resource Centre is a good outlet for local Aboriginal art. The *Barrow Creek Hotel & Caravan Park* (☎ (089) 56 9735) has single/double rooms and cabins for $20/35 and camp sites from $6.

The road continues through Ti Tree and finally Aileron, which is the last stop before the Alice.

Alice Springs

Population 20,500

The Alice, as it's usually known (never just Alice), was originally founded as a staging point for the overland telegraph line in the 1870s. A telegraph station was built near a permanent water hole in the bed of the dry Todd River. The river was named after Charles Todd, Superintendent of Telegraphs back in Adelaide, and a spring near the water hole was named after Alice, his wife.

A town, named Stuart, was first established in 1888, a few km south of the telegraph station as a railhead for a proposed railway line. Because the railway didn't materialise immediately, the town developed slowly. Not until 1933 did the town come to be known as Alice Springs.

The Overland Telegraph Line through the Centre was built to connect with the undersea line from Darwin to Java, which on its completion put Australia in direct contact with Europe for the first time. It was a monumental task, achieved in a remarkably short time.

Today, Alice Springs is a pleasant, modern town with good shops and restaurants. It is an access point for the many tourist attractions of central Australia. There is also a major and controversial US communications base, Pine Gap, nearby. The Alice Springs Peace Group (☎ (089) 52 1894) can tell you more about Pine Gap.

Alice Springs's growth to its present size has been recent and rapid. When the name was officially changed in 1933 the population had only just reached 200! Even in the 1950s Alice Springs was still a tiny town with a population in the hundreds. Until WW II there was no sealed road leading there and it was only in 1987 that the old road south to Port Augusta and Adelaide was finally replaced by a new, shorter and fully sealed highway.

Summer days in Alice Springs can get very hot (up to 45°C) and even winter days are pretty warm. However, winter nights car freeze and a lot of people get caught off guard. In winter (June and July), five minutes after the sun goes down you can fee the heat disappear, and the average minimum nightly temperature is 4°C. Despite the Alice's dry climate and low annual rainfall the occasional rains can be heavy and the Todd River may flood – as it did during the running of the 1993 Henley-on-Todd regatta and the races had to be abandoned!

Orientation

The centre of Alice Springs is a conveniently compact area just five streets wide, bounded by the dry Todd River on one side and the Stuart Highway on the other. Anzac Hill forms the northern boundary to the central area while Stuart Terrace is the southern end Many of the places to stay and virtually all of the places to eat are in this central rectangle.

Todd St is the main shopping street of the town; from Wills Terrace to Gregory Terrace it is a pedestrian mall. The bus centre i centrally located at the Melanka Lodge on Todd St, one block south of the mall.

Information

Tourist Office The Central Australian Tourism Industry Association office (☎ (089) 52 5199 is on the corner of Hartley St and Gregory Terrace in the centre of town. The staff here are helpful and they have a range of brochures and maps.

Post & Telecommunications The mai post office is on Hartley St, and there's a row of public phones outside.

Newspapers The *Centralian Advocate* i Alice Springs's twice-weekly newspaper.

Other Offices The Northern Territory Conservation Commission has a desk at th tourist office, with a comprehensive range o brochures on all the parks and reserves in th Centre. The main office (☎ (089) 51 8211) i just off the Stuart Highway, about five kr south of town.

The Department of Lands, Housing &

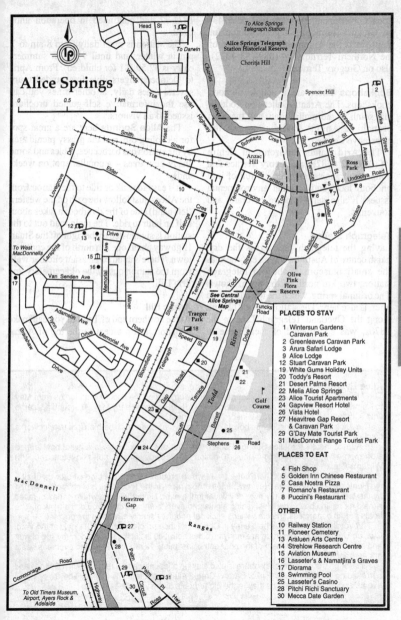

Alice Springs

0   0.5   1 km

To Darwin

Head St   1

To Alice Springs
Telegraph Station

Alice Springs Telegraph
Station Historical Reserve

Choritja Hill

Spencer Hill

Burke

Winnecke

Anzac
Hill

Schwartz   Cres

Wills Terrace

Parsons Street

Gregory Tce

Stott Terrace

Ross
Park

Chewings   St

Undoolya   Road

Olive
Pink
Flora
Reserve

Tuncks
Road

Traeger
Park

See Central
Alice Springs Map

Golf
Course

To West
MacDonnells

MacDonnell

Heavitree
Gap

Ranges

Commonage   Road

To Old Timers Museum,
Airport, Ayers Rock &
Adelaide

PLACES TO STAY

1 Wintersun Gardens
  Caravan Park
2 Greenleaves Caravan Park
3 Arura Safari Lodge
9 Alice Lodge
12 Stuart Caravan Park
18 White Gums Holiday Units
20 Toddy's Resort
21 Desert Palms Resort
22 Melia Alice Springs
23 Alice Tourist Apartments
24 Gapview Resort Hotel
26 Vista Hotel
27 Heavitree Gap Resort
  & Caravan Park
29 G'Day Mate Tourist Park
31 MacDonnell Range Tourist Park

PLACES TO EAT

4 Fish Shop
5 Golden Inn Chinese Restaurant
6 Casa Nostra Pizza
7 Romano's Restaurant
8 Puccini's Restaurant

OTHER

10 Railway Station
11 Pioneer Cemetery
13 Araluen Arts Centre
14 Strehlow Research Centre
15 Aviation Museum
16 Lasseter's & Namatjira's Graves
17 Diorama
18 Swimming Pool
25 Lasseter's Casino
28 Pitchi Richi Sanctuary
30 Mecca Date Garden

NORTHERN TERRITORY

Local Government office (☎ (089) 51 5743) on Gregory Terrace is a good source for maps, as is the Automobile Association of the Northern Territory (☎ (089) 53 1322), also on Gregory Terrace.

Bookshops There are a couple of good bookshops. The Aranta Gallery on Todd St just south of the mall is one, and there's a branch of Angus & Robertson in the Yeperenye Centre.

The Arid Lands Environment Centre (☎ (089) 52 6782) on Gregory Terrace is a nonprofit organisation which is full of info on both local and national environmental issues. It also sells a range of crafts and souvenirs.

Telegraph Station

Laying the telegraph line across the dry, harsh centre of Australia was no easy task, as the small museum at the old telegraph station, two km north of the town, shows. The original spring, which the town is named after, is also here. The station, one of 12 built along the Overland Telegraph Line in the 1870s, was constructed of local stone in 1871-72 and continued in operation until 1932.

The station is open daily from 8 am to 7 pm in winter, and until 9 pm in summer; entry is $2.50 ($1 for children). From April to October rangers give free guided tours several times daily; at other times you can use the informative self-guided brochure issued to all visitors.

The **Alice Springs** here are a great spot for a cooling dip, and the grassy picnic area by the station has barbecues, tables and some shady gum trees – a popular spot on weekends.

It's easy to walk or ride to the station from the Alice – just follow the path on the western (left hand) side of the riverbed; it takes about half an hour to ride. The main road out to the station is signposted to the right off the Stuart Highway about one km north of the centre of town. There's another pleasant circular walk from the station out by the old cemetery and Trig Hill.

Anzac Hill

At the northern end of Todd St you can make the short, sharp ascent to the top of Anzac

---

Alice Events

The Alice has a string of colourful activities, particularly during the cool tourist months from May to August. The Camel Cup, a series of camel races, takes place in early May. At around the same time, Chateau Hornsby, the local winery, has a beerfest.

The Alice Springs Agricultural show takes place in early July, and the highlight is a fireworks display.

In August there's the Alice Springs Rodeo, when for one week the town is full of bow-legged stockmen, swaggering around in their 10-gallon hats, cowboy shirts, moleskin jeans and R M Williams Cuban-heeled boots.

Finally in late September there's the event which probably draws the biggest crowds of all – the Henley-on-Todd Regatta. Having a series of boat races in the Todd River is slightly complicated by the fact that there is hardly ever any water in the river. Nevertheless a whole series of races is held for sailing boats, doubles, racing eights and every boat race class you could think of. The boats are all bottomless, the crews' legs stick out and they simply run down the course!

The Verdi Club Beerfest is held early in October, at the end of the regatta. It's held at the Verdi Club on Undoolya Rd and there are many frivolous activities including spit the dummy, tug of war, and stein-lifting competitions. For the beer enthusiast there's a range of local and overseas beers and a range of cuisines.

All through the cooler months there is also a string of country horse races at Alice Springs and surrounding outstations like Finke, Barrow Creek, Aileron or the Harts Range. They're colourful events and for the outstations they're the big turnouts of the year. ■

Hill (or you can drive there). From the top you have a fine view over modern Alice Springs and down to the MacDonnell Range that forms a southern boundary to the town. There are a number of other hills in and around Alice Springs which you can climb, but Anzac Hill is certainly the best known and most convenient.

Todd St Mall

Todd St is the main shopping street of the town and most of it is a pleasant pedestrian mall. Along the street you can see **Adelaide House**, built in the early 1920s and now preserved as the **John Flynn Memorial Museum**. Originally it was Alice Springs's first hospital. It's open from 10 am to 4 pm Monday to Friday, and from 10 am to 12.30 pm on Saturday. Admission is $2.50 (children $1) and includes a cup of tea or coffee. Flynn, who was the founding flying doctor, is also commemorated by the **John Flynn Memorial Church** next door.

Other Old Buildings

There are a number of interesting old buildings along Parsons St including the **Stuart Town Gaol** built in 1907-08. It's open Tuesday and Thursday from 10 am to 12.30 pm, and on Saturday between 9.30 and noon. The **Old Courthouse**, which was in use until 1980, is on the corner of Parsons and Hartley Sts.

Across the road is the **Residency** which dates from 1926-27. It's now used for historical exhibits and is open from 9 am to 4 pm weekdays and 10 am to 4 pm on weekends. Other old buildings include the **Hartley St School** beyond the post office and **Tunk's Store** on the corner of Hartley St and Stott Terrace.

Near the corner of Parsons St and Leichhardt Terrace, the old **Pioneer Theatre** is a former walk-in (rather than drive-in) cinema dating from 1944. These days it's a YHA hostel.

Spencer & Gillen Museum

Upstairs in Ford Plaza the Spencer & Gillen Museum of Central Australia has a fascinat-

ing collection, including some superb natural history displays. There's an interesting exhibition on meteors and meteorites (Henbury meteorites are on display). There are also exhibits on Aboriginal culture, some fine Papunya Tula sand paintings and displays of art of the Centre, including works by Albert Namatjira. Admission is $2 and it's open from 9 am to 5 pm on weekdays, and 10 am to 5 pm on weekends.

Royal Flying Doctor Service Base

The RFDS base is close to the town centre in Stuart Terrace. It's open from 9 am to 4 pm Monday to Saturday, and from 1 to 4 pm on Sunday. The tours last half an hour and cost $2.50 (children 50c). There's a small museum, and a souvenir shop.

School of the Air

The School of the Air, which broadcasts school lessons to children living on remote outback stations, is on Head St, about a km north of the centre. The school is open from 9 am to noon Monday to Friday during school terms.

Aviation Museum

Alice Springs has an interesting little aviation museum housed in the former Connellan hangar on Memorial Ave, where the town's airport used to be in the early days. The museum includes a couple of poignant exhibits which pinpoint the dangers of outback aviation.

The museum is not all tragedy – there are exhibits on pioneer aviation in the Territory and, of course, the famous Flying Doctor Service. The museum is open from Monday to Friday from 9 am to 4 pm, and Saturday and Sunday from 10 am to 2 pm; admission is free.

Strehlow Research Centre

This centre, on Larapinta Drive, commemorates the work of Professor Strehlow among the Arrernte people of the district (see the Hermannsburg Mission section). The main function of the building is to house the most comprehensive collection of Aboriginal

Charles Kingsford-Smith

In 1929 pioneer aviator Charles Kingsford-Smith went missing in the north-west in his aircraft *Southern Cross*. Two other aviators, Anderson and Hitchcock, set off to search for Kingsford-Smith in their tiny aircraft *Kookaburra*. North of Alice Springs they struck engine trouble and made an emergency landing. Despite not having any tools they managed to fix the fault, but repeated attempts to take off failed due to the sandy, rocky soil. They had foolishly left Alice Springs not only without tools, but with minimal water and food. By the time an aerial search had been organised and their plane located both had died. Their bodies were recovered but the aircraft, intact and undamaged, was left. Kingsford-Smith turned up unharmed a few days later.

The aircraft was accidentally rediscovered by a mining surveyor in 1961, and in the '70s it was decided to collect the remains and exhibit them. They proved strangely elusive, however, and it took several years to find them again. They were finally located in 1978 by Sydney electronics whiz Dick Smith. Fifty years of exposure and bushfires had reduced the aircraft to a crumbled wreck. It is now displayed only a few steps from where the aircraft took off on its ill-fated mission. A short film tells the sad story of this misadventure.

The museum also displays a Wackett, which went missing in 1961 on a flight from Ceduna in South Australia. The pilot strayed no less than 42° off course and put down when he ran out of fuel. An enormous search failed to find him because he was so far from his expected route. The aircraft was discovered, again completely by accident, in 1965. The museum has a small booklet on this bizarre mishap. ■

---

spirit items in the country. These were entrusted to Strehlow for safekeeping by the local Aborigines years ago when they realised their traditional life was under threat. Because the items are so important, and cannot be viewed by an uninitiated male or *any* female, they are kept in a vault in the centre. There is, however, a very good display on the works of Strehlow, and on the Arrernte people.

The building itself is something of a feature too – it has the largest rammed-earth wall in the southern hemisphere. The centre is open daily from 10 am to 5 pm (no entry after 4.30 pm); entry is $4.

Araluen Arts Centre

The Araluen Arts Centre on Larapinta Drive has a small gallery full of Namatjira paintings, and often has other displays as well. The stained-glass window in the foyer is the centrepiece of the centre.

Old Graves

Near the aviation museum there's a cemetery with a number of interesting graves including those of Albert Namatjira, and Harold Lasseter who perished while searching for the fabled gold of 'Lasseter's Reef'. Alice Springs has some pioneer graves in the small Stuart Memorial Cemetery on George Crescent, just across the railway lines.

Panorama Guth

Panorama Guth, at 65 Hartley St in the town centre, is a huge circular panorama which is viewed from an elevated, central observation point. It depicts almost all of the points of interest around the Centre with uncanny realism. Painted by a Dutch artist, Henk Guth, it measures about 20 metres in diameter and admission is $3 (children $1.50) – whether you think it's worth paying money to see a reproduction of what you may see for real is a different question! It's open from Monday to Saturday from 9 am to 5 pm Sunday from 2 to 5 pm, and is closed from December to February.

Diorama

On the outskirts of town on Larapinta Drive the diorama is open from 10 am to 5 pm daily Admission to this rather quirky collection of 3-D illustrations of various Aboriginal legends is $2. Children love it.

Olive Pink Flora Reserve

Just across the Todd River from the centre

off Tuncks Rd, the Olive Pink Flora Reserve has a collection of shrubs and trees which are typical of the 200-km area around Alice Springs. This arid-zone botanic garden is open from 10 am to 6 pm, and there's a visitors centre open between 10 am and 4 pm. There are some short walks in the reserve, including the climb to the top of the Saladeen Range, from where there's a fine view over the town.

Pitchi Richi Sanctuary
Just south of the Heavitree Gap causeway is Pitchi Richi (gap in the range), a miniature folk museum with a collection of sculptures by Victorian artist William Ricketts (you can see more of his interesting work in the William Ricketts Sanctuary in the Dandenongs near Melbourne) and an amazing range of various implements and other household items used by early pioneers. There's also billy tea and damper, and an interesting and lively chat on Arrernte Aboriginal lore and traditions.

The sanctuary itself doesn't look too promising, but it's well worth a visit. It's open daily from 9 am to 2 pm; entry is $8 (children $5).

Just a little further along from Pitchi Richi on Palm Circuit is the **Mecca Date Garden**. Entry is free and there are dates and date products for sale.

Frontier Camel Farm
A further five km along is the Frontier Camel Farm, where you have the chance to ride one of the beasts. These strange 'ships of the desert', guided by their Afghani masters, were the main form of transport before the railways were built. There's a museum with displays about camels, and a guided tour and camel ride is held daily at 10.30 am (and 2 pm April to October).

Also here is the **Arid Australian Reptile House**, which has an excellent collection of snakes and lizards.

The farm is open daily from 9 am to 5 pm. The cost of the camel tour is $8 (children $4), and it's $5 (children $2.50) to visit the reptile house.

The Old Ghan
At the MacDonnell Siding, off the Stuart Highway 10 km south of Alice Springs, a group of local railway enthusiasts have restored a collection of Ghan locomotives and carriages on a stretch of disused siding from the old narrow-gauge Ghan railway track. You can wander round the equipment, watch the restoration work and learn more about this extraordinary railway line at the information centre. It's open from 9 am to 5 pm daily and admission is $3 (children $1.50).

There are also trips on the old Ghan four days a week out to Mt Ertiva Siding, nine km south of town. The trip starts at 10 am, takes 1½ hours and costs $15 (children $7.50), and morning tea is available in the dining car. MacDonnell Siding is on the Alice Wanderer bus route (see Getting Around).

Chateau Hornsby
Alice Springs actually has a winery. It's 15 km out of town, five km off the road, before you get to the airport turn-off. The wine they produce here (moselle, riesling-semillon and shiraz) is not bad at all, although most of it gets sold to people intrigued at the novelty of a central Australian wine.

The pleasant restaurant here is open for lunch-time barbecues, and is a popular excursion from town. You can pedal out to Chateau Hornsby by bicycle – after tasting a little free wine the distance back seems much shorter. The easier option is to take the Alice Wanderer.

Organised Tours
The tourist office can tell you about all sorts of organised tours from Alice Springs. There are the usual big-name operators and a host of small local operators. There are bus tours, 4WD tours, even balloon tours.

Note that although many of the tours don't operate daily, there is at least one trip a day to one or more of the major attractions – Uluru (Ayers Rock) and Kata Tjuta (the Olgas), Kings Canyon, Palm Valley, both the Western and Eastern MacDonnell ranges, Simpson's Gap and Standley Chasm. Tours

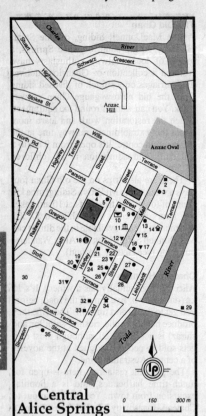

Central Alice Springs

0   150   300 m

PLACES TO STAY

2	Old Alice Inn
14	YHA Pioneer Hostel
21	Diplomat Motel
29	Alice Springs Pacific Resort
32	Melanka Backpackers
33	Melanka Lodge & Bus Centre
34	YHA Alice Springs Hostel

PLACES TO EAT

12	Joanne's Cafe & Le Cafeteriere
15	Flynn's on the Mall
17	Jolly Swagman
19	Overlander Steakhouse
22	La Casalinga
23	Eranova Cafeteria
26	Bojangles
31	Oriental Gourmet Chinese Restaurant

OTHER

1	Ford Plaza
3	Spring Plaza
4	Stuart Town Gaol
5	Old Courthouse
6	Yeperenye Shopping Centre
7	CAAMA
8	The Residency
9	Ansett Airlines
10	General Post Office
11	John Flynn Memorial Museum
13	Qantas & Gallery Gondwana
16	McCafferty's
18	Tourist Office
20	Hertz
24	Panorama Guth
25	Papunya Tula Artists & Avis
27	Automobile Association of the Northern Territory
28	Library & Civic Centre
30	Billy Goat Hill
35	Royal Flying Doctor Service Base

to less popular places – such as Rainbow Valley and Chambers Pillar – operate less frequently.

Most of the tours follow similar routes and you see much the same on them all, although the level of service and the degree of luxury will determine how much they cost. All the hostels can book tours, and they will also know exactly which company is offering the best deals.

Sahara Tours (☎ (089) 53 0881) offers very good daily camping trips to the Rock and elsewhere and these are popular with backpackers. It charges $185 for a two-day

trip to the Rock and Olgas, or you can pay an extra $80 and spend an extra day taking in Kings Canyon – well worthwhile if you have the time. AKT and Tracks are other cheaper operators.

Rod Steinert (☎ (089) 55 5000) operates a variety of tours, including the popular $42 Dreamtime & Bushtucker Tour. It's a half-day trip in which you meet some Aborigines and learn a little about their traditional life. There are demonstrations of weapons and foods and samples of barbecued witchetty grubs. AAT-Kings offers a similar trip.

Other tours include town tours, trips to the nearby gaps or longer day trips to Palm Valley, Chambers Pillar and other gorges. They start from $25 for the shorter half-day tours, and go up to $45 to $70 for longer day trips. Palm Valley is a popular day trip, as it requires a 4WD, and this tour costs around $65.

Camel treks are another central Australian attraction. You can have a short ride for a few dollars at the Frontier Camel Farm (☎ (089) 53 0444), or take longer overnight or two- to seven-day camel treks which cost from $385 to $800. Noel Fullerton's Camel Outback Safaris (☎ (089) 56 0925) also operates camel tours.

Sunrise balloon trips are also popular and cost from $88, which includes breakfast and the 30-minute flight. Operators include Outback Ballooning (☎ toll-free 1800 809 790) and Ballooning Downunder (☎ (089) 52 8816).

If your time is really limited, and your cash isn't, there are day trips to Uluru which involve flying between Alice and the Rock; the cost is typically $350.

Places to Stay
Camping Alice Springs's caravan parks and their rates are:

G'Day Mate Tourist Park (☎ (089) 52 9589), Palm Circuit, near the Mecca Date Garden and Pitchi Richi Sanctuary; camp sites ($12, $15 with power) and cabins ($45).

Greenleaves Tourist Park (☎ (089) 52 8645), two km east on Burke St; camp sites ($15, $17.50 with power) and on-site vans ($34).

Heavitree Gap Caravan Park (☎ (089) 52 2370), Palm Circuit, four km south of town; camp sites ($14, $16 with power) and on-site vans ($37).

MacDonnell Range Tourist Park (☎ (089) 52 6111), Palm Place, five km from town; camp sites ($13, $16 with power) and on-site cabins ($32 to $50).

Stuart Caravan Park (☎ (089) 52 2547), two km west on Larapinta Drive; camp sites ($12, $15 with power), on-site vans ($35) and cabins ($45).

Wintersun Gardens Caravan Park (☎ (089) 52 4080), two km north on the Stuart Highway; camp sites ($11, $15 with power), on-site vans ($30) and cabins ($38).

Hostels & Guesthouses There are plenty of hostels and guesthouses in Alice Springs. All the places catering to backpackers have the usual facilities and services – pool, courtesy bus, tour booking, bicycle hire, etc.

In the centre of town, on the corner of Leichhardt Terrace and Parsons St in the old Pioneer walk-in cinema, is the YHA *Pioneer Hostel* (☎ (089) 52 8855). It has 62 beds in air-con dorms, and charges $12. There's a swimming pool here, and bicycles for hire.

There's also the old 48-bed YHA *Alice Springs Hostel* (☎ (089) 52 5016) on the corner of Todd St and Stott Terrace. It is cheaper at $9, and is pretty quiet these days. It's a friendly and well-run place, and a good source of information on local activities. The office here is closed from 10 am to 5 pm.

Also central is the *Melanka Backpackers* (☎ toll-free 1800 815 066) at 94 Todd St, just a couple of steps from the bus station. This is a larger place with a variety of rooms, ranging from eight-bed dorms at $9 through to singles/doubles for $20/24. The adjacent *Melanka Lodge* has air-con, a swimming pool, cafeteria and restaurant, and all modern facilities. It's a popular place, if soulless.

Over the river and still just a short walk from the centre, is the relaxed *Alice Lodge* (☎ (089) 53 1975) at 4 Mueller St. This is a small, quiet and friendly hostel with a garden and pool. Nightly rates are $9 in the dorm, $23 for a single, $13 per person in a double, and $26 for an on-site van (prices include sheets; quilt hire is $1 with a $9 deposit). There's a small kitchen, and barbecue and laundry facilities.

Also on this side of the river at 18 Warburton St is *Ossie's Homestead* (☎ (089) 522 308), a VIP hostel. A bed in the 12-bed dorm is $10.50, in a four-bed room $12.50, and a double is $28. (VIP members get $1 off.) There's a swimming pool and the usual facilities, as well as a pet kangaroo called Boomer!

NORTHERN TERRITORY

Back on the other side of the river, at 41 Gap Rd, is *Toddy's Resort* (☎ (089) 52 1322). This complex has laundry facilities and a communal kitchen for those not in the self-contained units. There's a swimming pool, barbecue and small shop on the site. Prices are $10 for dorms with shared facilities, $12 with TV and bathroom, $28 for doubles, and $39 with bathroom.

Further along Gap Rd is the *Gapview Resort Hotel* (☎ (089) 52 6611). It's about one km from the centre, and charges $6.80 for a bed in an eight-bed room, $10.50 in a six-bed room, $12.60 in a four-bed room and $36.75 for a twin room. Each room has a bathroom, fridge and TV. Unfortunately, the kitchen is poorly equipped and the restaurant charges around $10 for a meal, but most people who stay here seem to enjoy it.

Hotels, Motels & Holiday Flats Right by the river at 1 Todd Mall is the *Old Alice Inn* (☎ (089) 52 1255). This pub gets noisy when there are bands playing on weekends, but it's otherwise quite a reasonable place to stay. Room rates are $40 for singles/doubles (some with bath).

At 67 Gap Rd there's the *Swagman's Rest Motel* (☎ (089) 53 1333) with singles/doubles for $52/62. The units are self-contained and there's a swimming pool.

The *Alice Tourist Apartments* (☎ (089) 52 2788) are on Gap Rd too and have one- and two-bedroom, self-contained, air-con apartments from $55 to $95. There's a communal laundry and the obligatory swimming pool. These are a good option for families.

There are plenty of motels, and prices range from around $50 to $100 for a double room. There are often lower prices and special deals during the hot summer months.

On Barrett Drive, next to the Melia Alice Springs, the *Desert Palms Resort* (☎ (089) 52 5977) has spacious rooms, each with a small kitchen, at $65. There's a swimming pool and if you've got a car this is one of the best value motels in the Alice.

Some of the better priced places, virtually all of them with swimming pools, include:

Alice Sundown Motel (☎ (089) 52 8422), 39 Gap Rd; self-contained rooms at $52/63 to $63/74 for singles/doubles.
Desert Rose Inn (☎ (089) 52 1411), 15 Railway Terrace; rooms at $71/79, or larger rooms at $95.
Larapinta Lodge (☎ (089) 52 7255), 3 Larapinta Drive; singles/doubles for $55/67, with communal kitchen and laundry.

At the top of the range there's the *Melia Alice Springs* (☎ (089) 52 8000), on Barrett Drive, with rooms from $205. A cheaper top-end option is the *Alice Springs Pacific Resort* (☎ (089) 52 6699) at 34 Stott Terrace right by the Todd River, not far from the centre of town. Rooms here go for $116/125.

Places to Eat
Snacks & Fast Food There are numerous places for a sandwich or light snack along Todd St Mall. Many of them put tables and chairs outside – ideal for breakfast in the cool morning air.

The *Jolly Swagman* in Todd Plaza off the mall is a pleasant place for sandwiches and light snacks. Also off the mall, but on the other side, *Joanne's Cafe* offers similar fare. *Le Cafeteriere* is at the southern end of the mall and is open for breakfast, burgers, sandwiches, etc.

The big Ford Plaza has a lunch-time cafeteria-style eating place called *Fawlty's* with snacks, light meals, sandwiches and a salad bar. Also here is *Doctor Lunch*, which is good for pancakes and coffee. Across the mall, the Springs Plaza has *Golly it's Good*, with more sandwiches and snacks.

In the Yeperenye shopping centre on Hartley St there's the *Boomerang Coffee Shop,* the *Bakery,* another *Fawlty's* outlet and a big Woolworth's supermarket.

Swingers' Cafe on Gregory Terrace has great coffee, foccacia and home-made vegetarian pasties. Delicious cakes and interesting salad sandwiches are $2.50. There is also a good notice board here.

Across the river on Lindsay St, near the corner of Undoolya Rd, the *Fish Shop* is a good and reasonably cheap fish & chip shop.

Pub Meals Far and away the most popular place is the *Todd Tavern* in the Old Alice Inn. The food is tasty and cheap, and there are special nights when you can get a meal for $5 to $8, including unlimited attacks on the vegetable bar. There's also the slightly more formal *Fishcaf* here, with meals in the $8 to $15 range.

Upstairs in the Ford Plaza on Todd St Mall the *Stuart Arms Bistro* does straightforward meals in the $7 to $12 bracket, and you can add a salad plate for a couple of dollars.

Restaurants The *Eranova Cafeteria*, at 70 Todd St, is one of the busiest eating spots in town and it's a comfortable place, with a good selection of excellent food. It's open for breakfast, lunch and dinner from Monday to Saturday. Meals range from $7 to $15.

Round the corner at 105 Gregory Terrace, *La Casalinga* has been serving up pasta and pizza for many years; it's open from 5 pm to 1 am every night. Meals cost $10 to $15 and it has a bar.

Also in the centre is the licensed *Flynn's on the Mall*, opposite the John Flynn Memorial Museum. It's a popular place, with meals in the $13 to $17 range. Meats such as crocodile and kangaroo are featured here, and indeed at quite a few restaurants around town.

Across the river from the centre, on the corner of Undoolya Rd and Sturt Terrace, the *Casa Nostra* is another pizza and pasta specialist. You can also get good pasta at *Al Fresco* at the northern end of the mall. *Rocky's* on the Stuart Highway is another pizza place.

There are a number of Chinese restaurants around the Alice. The *Oriental Gourmet* is on Hartley St, near the corner of Stott Terrace. *Chopsticks*, on Hartley St at the Yeperenye shopping centre, is said to be good, and so is the bright yellow *Golden Inn* on Undoolya Rd, just over the bridge from the centre. Aside from the usual items you can sample some Malaysian and Szechuan dishes.

Of course the Alice has to have a steakhouse, so you can try the *Overlander Steakhouse* at 72 Hartley St. It features 'Territory food' such as beef, buffalo, kangaroo and camel – a carnivore's delight! It's quite popular, but not that cheap with main courses in the $17 to $25 range.

For something a little different there's *Keller's Swiss & Indian Restaurant* on Gregory Terrace, which gives you the chance to try two vastly different cuisines at the one place. It's open for dinner nightly, and main courses start from around $10. *Puccini's* is an Italian restaurant in the Verdi Club on Undoolya Rd, across the Todd River from the centre of town.

Out-of-town dining possibilities include the daily barbecue lunches at the *Chateau Hornsby* winery, or a late breakfast, lunch or tea at the *White Gums Park* opposite the Simpson's Gap National Park turn-off.

Another interesting possibility is an evening meal combined with a ride on the Old Ghan train at MacDonnell Siding (☎ (089) 55 5047). It operates twice weekly from April to October, and weekly at other times. The cost is $49. The meal is actually provided by the *Camp Oven Kitchen* (☎ (089) 53 1411), and so consists of soup and damper, and a roast, all cooked in 'camp ovens' – cast-iron pots which are buried in hot coals. It's also possible to have the meal without the train ride for $45 on Monday, Wednesday and Saturday evenings.

Entertainment

The *Stuart Arms Bistro* in Ford Plaza has live music on Wednesday and Friday nights. At the Old Alice Inn, by the river on the corner of Wills and Leichhardt terraces, the *Jam Session* has live bands on Monday night, sometimes featuring better known bands.

Bojangles is a restaurant and nightclub on Todd St, and the *Alice Junction Tavern* off Ross Highway has a disco on Friday and Saturday nights. The *Overlander Steakhouse* is the home of a good local bush band – Bloodwood.

Outback 'character' Ted Egan puts on a performance of tall tales and outback songs three nights a week at *Chateau Hornsby* ($15, or $33 with dinner). If you want to watch the Australian gambling enthusiasm in a central Australian setting head for *Lasseter's Casino*, but dress up.

There are all sorts of events at the *Araluen Art Centre* on Larapinta Drive, including temporary art exhibits, theatre and music performances and regular films. Bookings can be made at the Araluen booking office (☎ (089) 52 5022).

Things to Buy

Alice Springs has a number of art galleries and craft centres. If you've got an interest in central Australian art or you're looking for a piece to buy, there's a couple of places where you can buy direct from the artists. The Papunya Tula Artists shop is on Todd St just south of the mall, or there's Jukurrpa Artists at 35 Gap Rd. Both of these places are owned and run by the art centres which produce the work.

The Central Australian Aboriginal Media Association (CAAMA) shop on Hartley St by the Yeperenye shopping centre is another very good place, and prices are reasonable.

There are plenty of other, generally more commercial outlets for Aboriginal art. Two of the better ones are Gallery Gondwana and the Original Aboriginal Dreamtime Gallery, both on the Todd St Mall.

Getting There & Away

Air You can fly to Alice Springs with Qantas (☎ 13 1313) or Ansett (☎ 13 1300). The two companies face each other across Todd St at the Parson St intersection.

Alice Springs to Adelaide costs $360, Darwin $440, Melbourne $500, Mt Isa $517, Perth $468 and Sydney $488. You can also fly direct to Uluru (Ayers Rock) from Adelaide, Sydney, Perth and Cairns. So if you're planning to fly to the Centre and visit Uluru it would be more economical to fly straight to Uluru, then continue to Alice Springs. See Getting There & Away under the Uluru & Kata Tjuta (the Olgas) section for more details.

Bus Greyhound Pioneer (☎ 13 2303) at the Melanka Lodge on Todd St has daily return

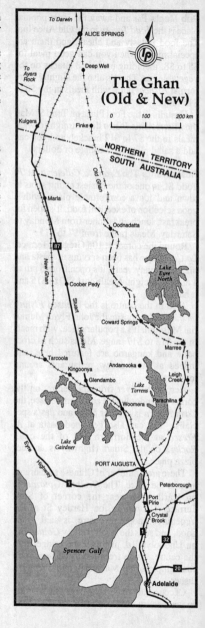

The Ghan
(Old & New)

0   100   200 km

The Ghan

Australia's great railway adventure would have to be the Ghan. The Ghan went through a major change in 1980 and although it's now a rather more modern and comfortable adventure, it's still a great trip.

The Ghan saga started in 1877 when it was decided to build a railway line from Adelaide to Darwin. It eventually took over 50 years to reach Alice Springs, and they're still thinking about the final 1500 km to Darwin more than a century later. The basic problem was that they made a big mistake right at the start, a mistake that wasn't finally sorted out until 1980. They built the line in the wrong place.

The grand error was a result of concluding that because all the creek beds north of Marree were bone dry, and because nobody had seen rain, there wasn't going to be rain in the future. In fact they laid the initial stretch of line right across a flood plain and when the rain came, even though it soon dried up, the line was simply washed away. In the century or so that the original Ghan line survived it was a regular occurrence for the tracks to be washed away.

The wrong route was only part of the Ghan's problems. At first it was built wide gauge to Marree, then extended narrow gauge to Oodnadatta in 1884. And what a jerry-built line it was – the foundations were flimsy, the sleepers were too light, the grading was too steep and it meandered hopelessly. It was hardly surprising that right up to the end the top speed of the old Ghan was a flat-out 30 km/h!

Early rail travellers went from Adelaide to Marree on the broad-gauge line, changed there to narrow gauge as far as Oodnadatta, then had to make the final journey to Alice Springs by camel train. The Afghani-led camel trains had pioneered transport through the outback and it was from these Afghanis that the Ghan took its name.

Finally in 1929 the line was extended from Oodnadatta to Alice Springs. Though the Ghan was a great adventure, it simply didn't work. At the best of times it was chronically slow and uncomfortable as it bounced and bucked its way down the badly laid line. Worse, it was unreliable and expensive to run. And worst of all, a heavy rainfall could strand it at either end or even in the middle. Parachute drops of supplies to stranded train travellers became part of outback lore and on one occasion the Ghan rolled in 10 days late!

By the early '70s the South Australian state railway system was taken over by the Federal government and a new line to Alice Springs was planned. The A$145 million line was to be standard gauge, laid from Tarcoola, north-west of Port Augusta on the transcontinental line, to Alice Springs – and it would be laid where rain would not wash it out. In 1980 the line was completed in circumstances that would be unusual for any major project today, let alone an Australian one – it was ahead of time and on budget.

In the late '80s the old Ghan made its last run and the old line was subsequently torn up. One of its last appearances was in the film *Mad Max III*.

Whereas the old train took 140 passengers and, under ideal conditions, made the trip in 50 hours, the new train takes twice as many passengers and does it in 24 hours. It's still the Ghan, but it's not the trip it once was. ■

services from Alice Springs to Uluru, Darwin and Adelaide. It takes about 20 hours from Alice Springs to Darwin (1481 km) or Alice Springs to Adelaide (1543 km). You can connect to other places at various points up and down the Track – Threeways for Mt Isa and the Queensland coast, Katherine for Western Australia, Erldunda for Uluru, Port Augusta for Perth. Alice Springs to Darwin is $135, Port Augusta or Adelaide is about $79, Uluru is $73, Coober Pedy is $79 and Katherine is $125.

McCafferty's (☎ (089) 52 3952) at 91

Gregory Terrace also has daily departures to Adelaide ($79), which can include a stop-over such as Coober Pedy for no extra cost. To Darwin it's $135, and you can stopover twice.

It's worth noting that McCafferty's has only just started services to the Alice and so there is something of a price war on. If this ceases, the normal fare of around $130 to Adelaide will probably be reintroduced.

Train The Ghan between Adelaide and Alice Springs costs $139 in coach class (no sleeper and no meals), $229 in holiday class (a sleeper with shared facilities and no meals) and $435 in 1st class (a self-contained sleeper and meals). Advance-purchase fares are available for 1st-class travel only and these cost $305. For bookings phone ☎ 13 2232 during office hours.

The train departs from Adelaide on Thursday at 2 pm, arriving in Alice Springs the next morning at 10.30 am. From Alice Springs the departure is on Friday at 2 pm, arriving in Adelaide the next day at 11 am. From April to December there's a second departure from Adelaide on Monday and Alice Springs on Tuesday.

You can also join the Ghan at Port Augusta, the connecting point on the Sydney to Perth route. Fares between Alice Springs and Port Augusta are $139 coach class, $180 holiday class and $310 1st-class sleeper.

You can transport cars between Alice Springs and Adelaide for $195, or between Alice Springs and Port Augusta for $185, but only between April and December. Double check the times by which you need to have your car at the terminal for loading: they must be there several hours prior to departure for the train to be 'made up'. Unloading at the Adelaide end is slow, so be prepared for a long wait.

Car The basic thing to remember about getting to Alice Springs is that it's a long way from anywhere, although at least roads to the north and south are sealed. Coming in from Queensland it's 1180 km from Mt Isa to Alice Springs or 529 km from Threeways, where the Mt Isa road meets the Darwin to Alice Springs road. Darwin to Alice Springs is 1481 km.

These are outback roads, but you're not yet in the *real* outer-outback, where a breakdown can mean big trouble. Nevertheless, it's wise to have your vehicle well prepared since getting someone to come out to fix it if it breaks down is likely to be very expensive.

Similarly, you are unlikely to die of thirst waiting for a vehicle to come by if you do break down, but it's still wise to carry quite a bit of water. Roads can sometimes be made

impassable by a short, sharp rainfall and you'll have to sit and wait for the water to recede. It usually won't take long on a sealed road, but you could have to sit and wait for a dirt road to dry out and become passable for rather a long time.

Fuel is readily available from stops along the road, but prices tend to be high. Some fuel stops are notorious for charging well over the odds, so carrying an extra can of fuel can save a few dollars by allowing you to go elsewhere.

Car Rental Avis, Budget, Hertz and Territory Rent-a-Car all have counters at Alice Springs Airport. In town, the Avis (☎ (089) 52 4366) office is at 78 Todd St, Hertz (☎ (089) 52 2644) is at 76 Hartley St, Budget (☎ (089) 52 8899) is at 10 Gap Rd, Thrifty (☎ (089) 52 2400) is at 94 Todd St and Territory Rent-a-Car (☎ (089) 52 9999) is on the corner of Stott Terrace and Hartley St.

Alice Springs is classified as a remote area, so car hire can be expensive, particularly if you want to drive down to Uluru or further afield. Territory, for instance, charges $28 per day plus 28c per km for its cheapest non-air-con vehicle.

Avis, Budget and Territory also have 4WDs for hire. You're looking at around $85 per day for a Suzuki, including insurance and 100 km free per day. For a Toyota Landcruiser or similar vehicle the price jumps to around $155 per day. Discounts apply for longer rentals (more than four to seven days, depending on the company).

Brits: Australia (☎ 52 8814) has 4WD campers for hire, and with offices in all the major cities one-way rentals become an option. The cost is around $180 per day for unlimited km, including a collision damage waiver.

Hitching Hitching to Alice is not the easiest trip in Australia since traffic is light. For those going south, Threeways is a notorious bottleneck where hitchers can spend a long time. The notice boards in the various Alice Springs hostels are good places to look for lifts.

Getting Around
Although there is a limited public bus system, Alice Springs is compact enough to get around on foot, and you can reach quite a few of the closer attractions by bicycle. If you want to go further afield you'll have to take a tour or rent a car.

To/From the Airport The Alice Springs airport is 14 km south of the town, about $20 by taxi.

There is an airport shuttle bus service (☎ (089) 53 0310) which meets flights and takes passengers to all city accommodation and to the railway station. It costs $9.

Bus Asbus buses leave from outside the Yeperenye shopping centre on Hartley St. The southern route (No 4) runs along Gap Rd to the southern outskirts of town – useful for Pitchi Richi and the Mecca Date Garden, or for hitching. The western route (No 1) goes out along Larapinta Drive, for the Strehlow Centre, Araluen Arts Centre and the Aviation Museum. Buses run approximately every 1½ hours from 7.45 am to 6 pm on weekdays and Saturday morning only. The fare for a short trip is 90c.

The Alice Wanderer bus does a loop around the major sights – Frontier Camel Farm, Mecca Date Garden, the Old Ghan, Flying Doctor Base, Strehlow Centre, Anzac Hill, School of the Air and the telegraph station. You can get on and off wherever you like, and it runs every 70 minutes from around 9 am to 3 pm. The cost is $15 for a full day, and $10 for half a day. If you phone ahead (☎ (089) 55 0099), you can be picked up from your accommodation prior to the 9 am departure. The most convenient pick-up point is the Melanka Lodge.

Bicycle Alice Springs has a number of bicycle tracks and a bike is a great way of getting around town and out to the closer attractions, particularly in winter. The best place to rent a bike is from the hostel you're staying at. Typical rates are $10 per day.

The MacDonnell Ranges

Outside Alice Springs there are a great number of places within day-trip distance or with overnight stops thrown in. Generally they're found by heading east or west along the roads running parallel to the MacDonnell Ranges, which are directly south of Alice Springs. Places further south are usually visited on the way to Uluru.

The scenery along the ranges is superb. There are many gorges that cut through the rocky cliffs and their sheer rock walls are spectacular. In the shaded gorges there are rocky water holes, a great deal of wildlife (which can be seen if you're quiet and observant) and wildflowers in the spring.

You can get out to these gorges on group tours or with your own wheels. Some of the closer ones are accessible by bicycle or on foot. By yourself the Centre's eerie emptiness and peace can get through to you in a way that is impossible in a big group.

Getting There & Away
Unfortunately, and somewhat surprisingly, there is no scheduled transport to either the Eastern or Western Macs, so without your own transport you're stuck with taking a tour. Virtually all places (with the exception of Ruby Gap in the Eastern Macs) are covered by tours from the Alice, so it's a matter of hunting around to find one which suits.

EASTERN MACDONNELL RANGES
Heading south from Alice Springs and just through the Heavitree Gap, a sign points out the road east – the Ross Highway. The highway is sealed all the way to Trephina Gorge, about 75 km from Alice Springs. It's in pretty good condition most of the way to Arltunga, about 100 km from Alice Springs. From here the road bends back west to rejoin the Stuart Highway 50 km north of Alice Springs, but this section is a much rougher road and sometimes requires a 4WD.

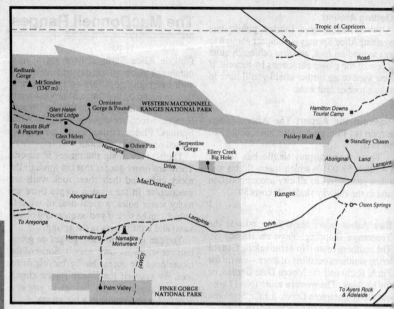

NORTHERN TERRITORY

Emily & Jessie Gap Conservation Reserve

Emily Gap, 16 km out of town, is the next gap through the ranges east of the Heavitree Gap – it's narrow and often has water running through it. The gap is registered as a sacred site and there are some well-preserved paintings on the eastern wall, although it often involves a swim to get to them.

Jessie Gap is only eight km further on and, like the previous gap, is a popular picnic and barbecue spot.

The two gaps are important to the Eastern Arrernte people as they are associated with the caterpillar Dreaming trail.

Corroboree Rock Conservation Reserve

Shortly after Jessie Gap there's the Undoolya Gap, another pass through the range, and the road continues 43 km to Corroboree Rock. There are many strangely shaped outcrops of rocks in the range and this one is said to have been used by Aborigines for their corroborees.

Trephina Gorge Nature Park

About 75 km out, and a few km north of the road, is Trephina Gorge. It's wider and longer than the other gaps in the range – here you are well north of the main MacDonnell Ranges and in a new ridge. There's a good walk along the edge of the gorge, and the trail then drops down to the sandy creek bed and loops back to the starting point.

Keen walkers can follow a longer trail (about five hours), which continues to the delightful **John Hayes Rockhole**, a few km west of Trephina Gorge. Here a sheltered section of a deep gorge provides a series of water holes which retain water long after the more exposed places have dried up. You can clamber around the rockholes or follow the 90-minute Chain of Ponds marked trail which takes you up to a lookout above the gorge and then back through the gorge –

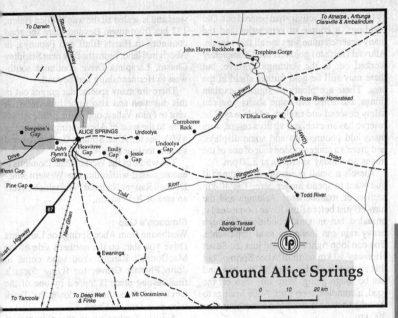

To Darwin

To Atnarpa , Arltunga
Claraville & Ambalindum

John Hayes Rockhole ● Trephina Gorge

Ross River Homestead ●

N'Dhala Gorge ●

Simpson's
Gap ●

ALICE SPRINGS

Undoolya

Corroboree
Rock

John
Flynn's
Grave

Heavitree Gap

Emily
Gap

Jessie
Gap

Undoolya
Gap

Fenn Gap ●

Pine Gap ●

Todd

River

Ringwood

Homestead

Road

Todd River ●

New Ghan

Santa Teresa
Aboriginal Land

Around Alice Springs

0   10   20 km

Ewaninga ●

To Tarcoola

To Deep Well
& Finke

▲ Mt Ooraminna

NORTHERN TERRITORY

perhaps you'll see why it is also called the Valley of the Eagles.

There's an excellent camp site at the gorge, and a smaller one (only two sites) at John Hayes Rockhole. There's a fee of $1 per adult for camping.

Ross River

Beyond Trephina Gorge it's another 10 km to the *Ross River Homestead* (☎ (089) 56 9711). It's much favoured by coach tours, but is an equally good place for independent visitors. It's a friendly sort of place and there's lots to do, including walks in the spectacular surrounding countryside, excursions to other attractions, short camel rides or safaris and horseback riding. Or simply lazing around with a cold one.

Units cost $90/100, and there are four-bed dorms for $12 per person, or you can camp for $15 for two. There's also a restaurant, which has good food, and the bar is very popular.

N'Dhala Gorge Nature Park

N'Dhala Gorge is about 10 km south of Ross River Homestead and has around 6000 ancient Aboriginal rock carvings, although they're generally not easy to spot. You may see rock wallabies. It's possible to turn off before the gorge and loop around it to return to Alice Springs by the Ringwood Homestead road, but this requires a 4WD. The track into N'Dhala from Ross River is marked as 4WD only but can be used with caution by conventional vehicles, in the dry season at least.

There's a small camp site here with a toilet, but you need to bring your own water and firewood. The flies are friendly, too.

Arltunga Historical Reserve

At the eastern end of the MacDonnell Ranges, 103 km north-east of Alice Springs, Arltunga is an old gold-mining ghost town. Gold was discovered here in 1887 and 10 years later reef gold was discovered, but by

1912 the mining activity had petered out. Old buildings, a couple of cemeteries and the many deserted mine sites are all that remain. Alluvial (surface) gold has been completely worked out in the Arltunga Reserve, but there may still be gold further afield in the area. There are plenty of signs to explain things and some old mine shafts you can safely descend and explore a little way. The reserve has an excellent visitors centre, with many old photographs and some displays, and there's a ranger-guided tour of one of the mines on Sunday afternoon at 2.30 pm.

There's a small camp site at Arltunga if you want to spend longer here. The 40-km section of road between Arltunga and the turn-off just before Ross River Homestead is unsealed but in good condition, although heavy rain can make the road impassable. You can loop right round and join the Stuart Highway 50 km north of Alice Springs, but this route is a graded track all the way and can be rough going. With side trips off the road, a complete loop from Alice Springs to Arltunga and back would be something over 300 km.

Ruby Gap Nature Park
Ruby Gap is a further 44 km to the east, and it's on a rough track which takes a good couple of hours to traverse – definitely 4WD only. The sandy bed of the Hale River is purple in places – due to the thousands of tiny garnets found here. The garnets were the cause of a 'ruby rush' to the area in the 19th century and a few miners did well out of it until the 'rubies' were discovered to be only garnets and virtually worthless. It's a remote and evocative place, and is well worth the effort involved in reaching it.

There's excellent bush camping along the riverbank in the park, and there are some beautiful spots. However, this is a remote area and you need to be well equipped – and bring your own water and firewood.

WESTERN MACDONNELL RANGES
Heading west from the Alice, Larapinta Drive divides just beyond Standley Chasm. Namatjira Drive continues slightly north-

west and is sealed all the way to Glen Helen, 132 km from town. Beyond there the road continues to Haasts Bluff and Papunya, in Aboriginal land. From the fork near Standley Chasm, Larapinta Drive continues south-west to Hermannsburg and beyond.

There are many spectacular gorges out in this direction and also some fine walks. A visit to Palm Valley, one of the prime attractions to the west of Alice Springs, requires a 4WD. See the Alice Springs Getting Around section for tour details.

The whole of the Western MacDonnells is encompassed within the new Western MacDonnell Ranges National Park, which covers an area of 2058 sq km.

Simpson's Gap
Westbound from Alice Springs on Larapinta Drive you start on the northern side of the MacDonnell Ranges. You soon come to **John Flynn's Grave**; the flying doctor's final resting place is topped by one of the Devil's Marbles, brought down the Track from near Tennant Creek.

A little further on is the picturesque Simpson's Gap, 22 km out. Like the other gaps it is a thought-provoking example of nature's power and patience – for a river to cut a path through solid rock is amazing, but for a river that rarely ever runs to cut such a path is positively mind-boggling. There are often rock wallabies in the jumble of rocks on either side of the gap.

Larapinta Trail
The Larapinta Trail is a new and extended walking track which, when finally completed in the next few years, will offer walkers a 220-km trail along the backbone of the Western MacDonnell Ranges, stretching from the telegraph station in Alice Springs to Mt Razorback, beyond Glen Helen. It will then be possible to choose anything from a two-day to a two-week trek, taking in a selection of the attractions in the Western MacDonnells. At the time of writing the route was complete as far as the Ochre Pits, 115 km west of Alice Springs.

Detailed trail notes and maps are available

from the Conservation Commission desk at the tourist office in Alice Springs, or contact the Northern Territory Conservation Commission (☎ (089) 50 8211) for further details.

Standley Chasm
Standley Chasm is 51 km out and is probably the most spectacular gap around Alice Springs. It is incredibly narrow – the near-vertical walls almost meet above you. Only for an instant each day does the noon sun illuminate the bottom of the gorge – at which moment the automatics click and a smile must appear on Mr Kodak's face! Entry is $2.50, and there is a cafe and toilet block by the car park.

Namatjira Drive
Not far beyond Standley Chasm you must choose whether to take the northerly Namatjira Drive or carry on along the more southerly Larapinta Drive. Further west along Namatjira Drive another series of gorges and gaps in the range awaits you. **Ellery Creek Big Hole** is 93 km from Alice Springs and has a large permanent water hole – just the place for a cooling dip, and there's a basic camp site close by. It's only 13 km further to **Serpentine Gorge**, a narrow gorge with a pleasant water hole at the entrance.

The **Ochre Pits**, just off the road 11 km west of Serpentine, were a source of painting material for the Aborigines. The various coloured ochres are weathered limestone, and the colouring is actually iron-oxide stains.

The large and rugged **Ormiston Gorge** also has a water hole and it leads to the enclosed valley of the Pound. When the water holes of the Pound dry up the fish that live there burrow into the sand, going into a sort of suspended animation and reappearing after rain. Ormiston has a camping area.

Only a couple of km further is the turn-off to the scenic **Glen Helen Gorge**, where the Finke River cuts through the MacDonnells. The road is worse beyond this point, but if you continue west you'll reach the red-walled **Redbank Gorge** with its permanent water, 161 km from Alice Springs. Also out this way is **Mt Sonder**, at 1347 metres the highest point in the Northern Territory.

Places to Stay & Eat There are basic camp sites at both Ellery Creek Big Hole and Ormiston Gorge.

At Glen Helen Gorge the *Glen Helen Lodge* (☎ (089) 56 7489) has camp sites and a variety of accommodation. Camping costs from $3 per person, and rooms are $24/34 for singles/doubles in the lodge section or $62/72 in the more luxurious motel section, plus there's a hostel with lots of beds at $10 in four-bed rooms. The restaurant here has a good reputation, although it's not particularly cheap.

Larapinta Drive
Taking the alternative road to the south from Standley Chasm, Larapinta Drive crosses the Hugh River, and then Ellery Creek before reaching the turn-off for **Wallace Rockhole**, 17 km off the main road and 117 km from Alice Springs. This is an Arrernte Aboriginal community (☎ (089) 56 7415) which offers camping and rock art tours (daily at 10 am and 4.30 pm; $4). Alcohol is prohibited here.

Back on Larapinta Drive, shortly before Hermannsburg, is the **Namatjira Monument**. Today the artistic skills of the central Australian Aborigines are widely known and appreciated. This certainly wasn't the case when the artist Albert Namatjira started to paint his central Australian landscapes in 1934.

In 1957 Namatjira was the first Aborigine to be granted Australian citizenship. Because of his fame, he was allowed to buy alcohol at a time when this was otherwise illegal for Aborigines, but in 1958 he was jailed for six months for supplying alcohol to Aborigines. He died the following year, aged only 57. (For further information on Namatjira see the Aboriginal art section.)

Hermannsburg (population 420)
Only eight km beyond the Namatjira monument you reach the Hermannsburg Aboriginal

NORTHERN TERRITORY

settlement, 125 km from Alice Springs. The **Hermannsburg Mission** here was established by German Lutheran missionaries in the middle of the last century. Many of the buildings are still intact, and it's well worth a stroll through. Not long after it was set up, Hermannsburg had a bigger population than Alice Springs.

There's a teahouse which serves excellent home-made pastries, and you can also get fuel (no plastics) and basic provisions at the settlement store. Although the town is restricted Aboriginal land, permits are not required to visit the mission or store, or to travel through.

Hermannsburg's most famous resident was Professor Ted Strehlow. He was born on the mission and spent more than 40 years studying the Arrernte people. His books about them are still widely read. The Arrernte people entrusted him with many items of huge spiritual and symbolic importance when they realised their traditional lifestyle was under threat. These items are now held in a vault in the Strehlow Research Centre in Alice Springs.

Finke Gorge National Park

From Hermannsburg the trail follows the Finke River south to the Finke Gorge National Park, only 12 km further on.

In the park, **Palm Valley** is a gorge filled with a variety of palm tree unique to this part of the MacDonnell Ranges – the central Australian cabbage palm (*Livistonia mariae*). This strangely tropical find in the dry Centre makes Palm Valley a popular day-trip destination.

The track to the park crosses the sandy bed of the Finke a number of times and you need a 4WD to get through, not so much because of the risk of getting bogged, but because of the high ground-clearance needed to negotiate the numerous bars of rock on the track to the gorge.

There's a beautiful shady camping area ($10) with some long-drop toilets, and a couple of signposted walks.

If you are travelling by 4WD there's a track which traverses the full length of the picturesque Finke Gorge, much of the time along the bed of the (usually) dry Finke River. It's a rough but worthwhile trip, and the camp sites at Boggy Hole, about 2½ hours from Hermannsburg, make an excellent overnight stop, although if you are in a hurry you can get from Palm Valley all the way to Kings Canyon (Watarrka National Park) in less than eight hours via this route. Ask the rangers at Palm Valley or Kings Canyon for details.

Ipolera

Continuing west from Hermannsburg along the road to Areyonga, there's a turn-off to the Arrernte Aboriginal community of Ipolera. Here it's possible to stay with the Malbunka family who offer excellent two-hour cultural tours. Male and female visitors are taken on separate tours to help preserve and maintain the unique laws which apply to the two sexes. The tours take place from February to November on Monday, Wednesday and Friday at 10 am and cost $25. There's also basic camping at $5 per person.

Permits are not required to visit Ipolera, but bookings for either camping or the tours are obligatory (☎ (089) 56 7466); alcohol is prohibited. The turn-off for Ipolera is 45 km west of Hermannsburg, and it's then 13 km along a dirt road.

Mereenie Loop Road

From the Ipolera turn-off you can continue west to the Areyonga turn-off (no visitors), and then take the newly opened Mereenie Loop Road to Kings Canyon. This dirt road is suitable for conventional vehicles and offers an excellent alternative to the Ernest Giles Road as a way of reaching Kings Canyon.

The Mereenie Loop Road was opened in June 1994. You need a permit from the Central Land Council to travel along it, as it passes through Aboriginal land. The permit includes the informative *Mereenie Tour Pass* booklet, which provides details about the local Aboriginal culture and has a route map.

South to Uluru (Ayers Rock)

You can make some interesting diversions off the road south to Uluru. The Henbury Meteorite Craters are only a few km off the road, but you've got further to go to get to Chambers Pillar, Finke or Kings Canyon.

The Old Ghan Road

Following the 'old south road' which runs close to the old Ghan railway line, it's only 35 km from Alice Springs to **Ewaninga**, with its prehistoric Aboriginal rock carvings. The carvings found here and at N'Dhala Gorge are thought to have been made by Aboriginal tribes who lived here earlier than the current tribes of the Centre.

Chambers Pillar, an eerie sandstone pillar, is carved with the names and visit dates of early explorers – and, unfortunately, some much less worthy modern-day graffiti artists. To the Aborigines of the area Chambers Pillar is the remains of Itirkawara, a gecko ancestor of great strength. It's 160 km from Alice Springs and a 4WD is required for the last 44 km from the turn-off at Maryvale station. There's a basic camp site but you need to bring water and firewood.

Back on the main track south, you eventually arrive at **Finke**, a small Aputula Aboriginal settlement 230 km south of Alice Springs. When the old Ghan was running, Finke was a thriving little town; these days it seems to have drifted into a permanent torpor. There's a basic community store, which is also the outlet for the Aputula Arts Centre, and fuel is available on weekdays. Alcohol is prohibited.

From Finke you can turn west to join the Stuart Highway at Kulgera (150 km), or east to Old Andado station on the edge of the Simpson Desert (120 km). Just 21 km west of Finke, and 13 km north of the road along an unmarked track, stands a five-metre-high replica of the flagpole found on top of Parliament House in Canberra. The reason? This point has been determined as Australia's centre of gravity!

Rainbow Valley Nature Park

The sandstone bluffs of the James Range are the main attraction of this small park, which lies 22 km off the Stuart Highway along a signposted rough track 75 km south of Alice Springs. There's a basic camping site but you will need to bring your own firewood and water.

Camel Outback Safaris

This camel farm, 90 km south of Alice, is run by Noel Fullerton, the 'camel king', who started the annual Camel Cup and has won it four times. For a few dollars you can try your hand at camel riding and there are one- and two-week safaris into Rainbow Valley and the outback. The farm exports camels to places around the world, including the Arab nations of the Gulf and Sahara.

It has been estimated that the central deserts are home to about 15,000 wild camels. (For inspiration read Robyn Davidson's bestselling book *Tracks*, an account of her trek by camel from the Alice to Port Hedland.)

Ernest Giles Road

The Ernest Giles Road heads off to the west of the Stuart Highway about 140 km south of the Alice. This is the route to Kings Canyon, and is an alternative route between Uluru and the Alice. You'll also find the Henbury Meteorite Craters just off it, a few km west of the Stuart Highway.

The 100-km stretch to the Luritja Rd (the turn-off to the south and Uluru) is still unsurfaced and often impassable after heavy rain; at other times it's fine for non-4WD vehicles. The section from the turn-off to the canyon is sealed. To go to Uluru via this route adds about 170 km to the Alice Springs to Uluru distance, but it's a worthwhile detour.

The Luritja Rd itself is 100 km long, 49 of which are gravel, although this stretch should be sealed by now.

Henbury Meteorite Craters

A few km along Ernest Giles Road, west of

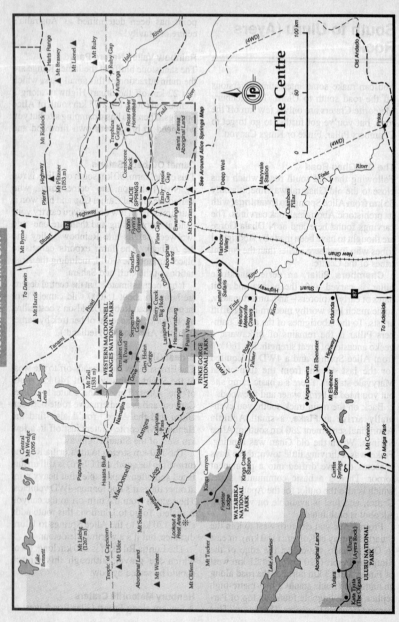

The Centre

the Stuart Highway, a turn-off to the north leads a few km to the Henbury Meteorite Craters, a cluster of 12 craters which are amongst the largest in the world. The biggest of the craters is 180 metres across and 15 metres deep. From the car park by the site there's a walking trail around the craters with signposted features.

There are no longer any fragments of the meteorites at the site, but the Spencer & Gillen Museum in Alice Springs has a small chunk which weighs in at a surprisingly heavy 46.5 kg. It is illegal to fossick for or remove any fragments.

The site is administered by the Conservation Commission and you are supposed to have a permit before staying at the basic camp site there ($1 per person).

Watarrka National Park

From the meteorite craters the road continues west to Kings Canyon, in the Watarrka National Park, 323 km from Alice Springs.

This is an alternative, and rougher, route to Uluru (Ayers Rock) although you have to backtrack the 105 km between the Luritja Rd and the canyon.

Kings Canyon is a spectacular gorge with natural features such as the Lost City, with its strange building-like outcrops, and the lush palms of the narrow gorge called the Garden of Eden. There are fine views and the walking trails are not too difficult. The walls of the canyon soar over 200 metres high, and the trail to the Lost City and Garden of Eden offers breathtaking views, although it is not for those who suffer from vertigo. There's a rangers' station just a few km before you reach the canyon.

Organised Tours Kurkara Tours (☎ toll-free 1800 891 101) is an Aboriginal-owned and run tour company which has a variety of trips from the Frontier Lodge (see below). There's the Mungartji (Sunset) Tour ($17), the 2½-hour Willy Wagtail Tour ($25) and

NORTHERN TERRITORY

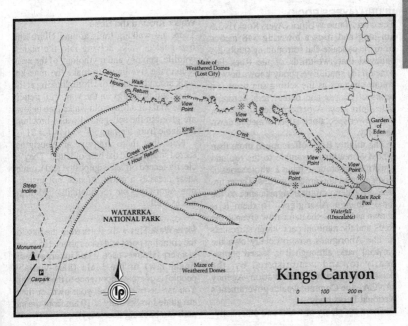

Kings Canyon

the Traditional Arts Tour ($33). All delve into various cultural aspects of the local Luritja people and are good fun.

Places to Stay & Eat The closest accommodation available is at the *Kings Canyon Frontier Lodge* (☎ (089) 56 7442), six km beyond the canyon. Camping sites cost $18, or $22 with power. There's a backpackers' bunk house with beds in four-bed rooms at $22 each, or more luxurious motel-type accommodation for $113/144. The resort has a swimming pool, bar, cafe, restaurant, shop and (expensive) fuel.

Otherwise, there's the basic but friendly *Kings Creek Station Camping Ground* about 35 km before the canyon, where camping costs $5 per person. Basic supplies and fuel (no credit cards) are also available here.

Uluru National Park

ULURU (AYERS ROCK)
The world-famous Uluru (Ayers Rock) is 3.6 km long and rises a towering 348 metres from the pancake-flat surrounding scrub. It's believed that two-thirds of the Rock lies beneath the sand. Everybody knows how its colour changes as the setting sun turns it a series of deeper and darker reds before it fades into grey. A performance in reverse, with fewer spectators, is performed at dawn each day.

The mighty Rock offers much more than a heavy-breathing scramble to the top and some pretty colours – it has a whole series of strange caves and eroded gullies. The entire area is of deep cultural significance to the local Anangu Aborigines. To them it is known as Uluru – the name now given to the Rock and the national park which surrounds it. The Aborigines now officially own the national park, although it is leased permanently to, and administered by, the Australian Nature Conservation Agency (ANCA), the Commonwealth government's National Parks body.

There are plenty of walks and other activities happening around Uluru and the township of Yulara, and it is not at all difficult to spend several days here.

Information
There is a rangers' station, information centre and Aboriginal-owned Maruku Art & Crafts shop a few km before the Rock on the road from Yulara. There are some interesting displays here, as well as the usual souvenirs. It's about the cheapest place in the Centre to buy souvenirs (carvings, etc) and you're buying direct from the artists. There's also the Aboriginal-run Ininti Store, which sells snacks, and a picnic area with gas barbecues.

Entry to the national park costs $10 (free for children under 16), and this is good for a five-day visit. Entry permits can be bought from the visitors centre at Yulara, or from the park entry gate on the road between Yulara and Uluru.

The park is open daily from half an hour before sunrise to sunset.

Walks Around the Base
There are walking trails around Uluru and free guided walks delving into the plants, wildlife, geology and mythology of the area. It can take five hours to make the nine-km walk around the base of Uluru, looking at the caves and paintings on the way. Full details of the Mala and Mutitjulu walks (see below) are given in the self-guided walks brochure available from the rangers' station for $1.

Note that there are several Aboriginal sacred sites around the base of Uluru. They're clearly fenced off and signposted and to enter these areas is a grave offence, not just for non-Aborigines but for 'ineligible' Aborigines as well.

Mala Walk This walk starts from the base of the climbing point and takes about 1½ hours at a very leisurely pace. The Tjukurpa (traditional law) of the Mala (hare-wallaby people) is of great importance to the Anangu. You can do this walk on your own, or there are guided walks daily at 10 am from the car park (no booking necessary).

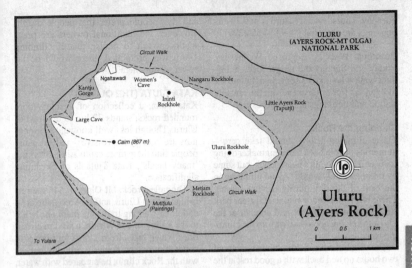

Uluru
(Ayers Rock)

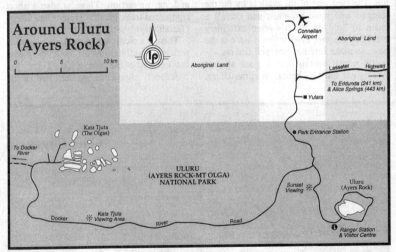

Around Uluru
(Ayers Rock)

Mutitjulu Walk Mutitjulu is a permanent water hole on the southern side of Uluru. The Tjukurpa tells of the clash between two snakes, Kaniya and Liru. The water hole is just a short walk from the car park on the southern side.

Liru Walk The Liru Walk starts from the rangers' station and gives an insight into the way the local Anangu people made use of the various shrubs and bush materials found in the area. It is a two-hour guided walk with Aboriginal guides, and it only operates on

Tuesday, Thursday and Saturday at 9.30 am; bookings are essential (☎ (089) 56 2299).

Botanical Walk At 3 pm on Wednesday, Friday and Sunday the ranger leads a 1½-hour walk which gives some insight into the indigenous flora. It leaves from the rangers' station and bookings are not necessary.

Climbing the Rock

Those climbing Uluru should take care – numerous people have met their maker doing so, usually by having a heart attack, but some by taking a fatal tumble. Avoid climbing in the heat of the day during the hot season. There is an emergency phone at the car park at the base of the climb, and another at the top of the chain, about halfway up the climbing route.

The climb itself is 1.6 km and takes about two hours up and back with a good rest at the top. The first part of the walk is by far the steepest and most arduous, and there's a chain to hold on to. It's often extremely windy at the top, even when it isn't at the base, so make sure hats are well tied on.

It's worth noting that it goes against Aboriginal spiritual beliefs to climb Uluru, and they would prefer that people didn't. However, the traditional owners are pragmatic enough to realise that if climbing Uluru was prohibited, there would be far fewer visitors here.

KATA TJUTA (THE OLGAS)

Kata Tjuta, a collection of smaller, more rounded rocks, stands 32 km to the west of Uluru. Though less well known, the monoliths are equally impressive – indeed many people find them more captivating. Meaning 'many heads', Kata Tjuta is of Dreaming significance.

The tallest rock, **Mt Olga**, at 546 metres, is higher than Uluru, and here too there are a couple of walking trails, the main one being to the **Valley of the Winds**, a six-km circuit track which takes from 2½ to four hours to cover. It's not particularly arduous but, as with the Rock climb, be prepared with water, and sun protection. There is also a short signposted track into the pretty Olga Gorge (Tatintjawiya).

There's a picnic and sunset-viewing area with toilet facilities just off the access road a few km west of the base of Kata Tjuta.

A lonely sign at the western end of the

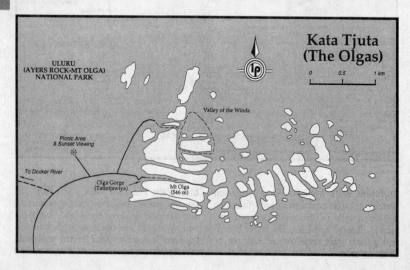

Kata Tjuta
(The Olgas)

access road points out that there is a hell of a lot of nothing if you travel west – although, suitably equipped, you can travel all the way to Kalgoorlie and on to Perth in Western Australia. It's 200 km to Docker River, an Aboriginal settlement on the road west, and about 1500 km all the way to Kalgoorlie. See the Warburton Road information in the Getting Around chapter. The *Perth to Alice Springs via Gunbarrel Highway or Warburton Road* map, published by the RAC of Western Australia, is interesting and informative.

YULARA (population 2200)

Yulara, the service village for the national park, has effectively turned one of the world's least hospitable regions into an easy and comfortable place for outsiders to visit. Lying just outside the national park, 20 km from Uluru and 53 km from Kata Tjuta (the Olgas), the \$260-million complex, administered by the Northern Territory government Ayers Rock Corporation, makes an excellent and surprisingly democratic base for exploring the area's renowned attractions. Opened in 1984, it supplies the only accommodation, food outlets and other services available in the region. The village incorporates the Ayers Rock Resort, and it combines futuristic flair with low, earth-toned foundations, fitting unobtrusively into the dunes.

By the 1970s it was clear that planning was required for the development of the area. Between 1931 and 1946 only 22 people were known to have climbed Uluru. In 1969 about 23,000 people visited the area. Ten years later the figure was 65,000 and now the annual visitor figures are approaching 300,000!

It was intended when Yulara was built that the ugly cluster of motels, restaurants and other commercial enterprises at the eastern base of Uluru would be demolished, leaving the prime attraction pleasingly alone in its age-old setting. Some of the original buildings are still there because they were turned over to the local Aborigines; they are not so obvious now because all access to Uluru is from the west and the Aboriginal community is off limits to the public.

Orientation & Information

In the spacious village area, where everything is within 15 minutes walk, there is a visitors centre, four hotels, apartments, a backpackers' lodge, two camp sites, a bank, post office, petrol station, newsagency, numerous restaurants, a Royal Flying Doctor Service medical centre, supermarket, craft gallery, pub (of course) and even a pink police station!

The visitors centre (open 8 am to 10 pm daily) contains good displays on the geography, flora and fauna and history of the region. You can also buy park entry permits here, and book tours with the only two operators licensed to run tours from Yulara (all other tours originate in Alice Springs). Information is also available at the rangers' station at Uluru.

The shopping square complex includes a supermarket, newsagency, post office and travel agency. You can get colour film processed at Territory Colour's same-day service. The only bank at Yulara is ANZ, but for \$2 you can use the electronic funds transfer (EFTPOS) facility in the pub to withdraw up to \$100 with most credit and bank cards. There's a childcare centre in the village for children aged between three months and eight years, which operates from 8 am to 5.30 pm daily. The cost is \$16.50 for half a day or \$27.50 for a full day. Bookings can be made on ☎ (089) 56 2097.

Please be aware that alcohol (grog) is a problem amongst the local Mutitjulu Aboriginal people living near Uluru. It is a 'dry' community and, at the request of the Aboriginal leaders, the liquor outlets have agreed not to sell it to Aborigines. For this reason you may be approached in the car park at Yulara by Aborigines who want you to buy grog on their behalf. The community leaders appeal to you not to do so.

Walks & Talks

There are a number of activities in the village, some conducted by the rangers and others organised by the resort.

The **Uluru – Heart of Australia** slide show and talk takes place at 2 pm daily in the

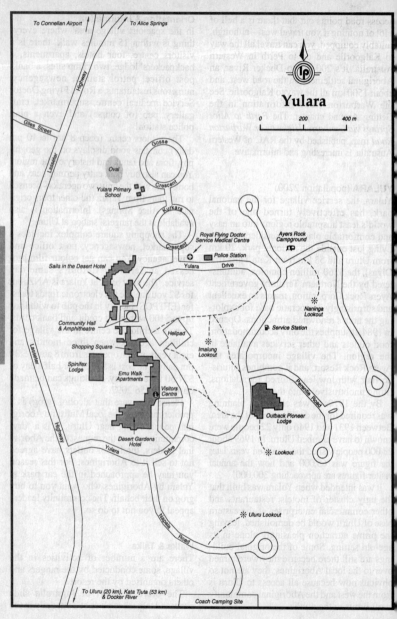

Yulara

0   200   400 m

To Connellan Airport
To Alice Springs

Highway

Giles Street

Lasseter Highway

Gosse Crescent

Oval

Yulara Primary School

Kurkara Crescent

Royal Flying Doctor Service Medical Centre

Ayers Rock Campground

Sails in the Desert Hotel

Police Station

Yulara Drive

Naninga Lookout

Community Hall & Amphitheatre

Helipad

Service Station

Imalung Lookout

Shopping Square

Spinifex Lodge

Emu Walk Apartments

Visitors Centre

Outback Pioneer Lodge

Perente Road

Desert Gardens Hotel

Yulara Drive

Lookout

Lasseter Highway

Nagala Road

Uluru Lookout

To Uluru (20 km), Kata Tjuta (53 km) & Docker River

Coach Camping Site

auditorium. It's free and you don't need to book.

The **Garden Walk** is a guided tour through the native garden of the Sails in the Desert Hotel. It takes place daily (except Sunday) at 7.30 am and is led by the hotel's resident gardener. This tour is also free and there's no need to book.

Each evening there's the **Night Time Sky Show**, which is an informative look into local and Greek astrological legends. Trips in English are at 8.15 and 10.15 pm, and bookings are required (☎ toll-free 1800 803 174). The cost is $15 and you are picked up from your accommodation.

Flights & Organised Tours

Flights While the enjoyment of those on the ground may be diminished by the constant buzz of light aircraft and helicopters overhead, for those actually up there it's an unforgettable – and very popular – trip.

Two companies operate the trips and they collect you from wherever you're staying.

Rockayer (☎ (089) 56 2345) charges $55 for a 30-minute flight over the Rock and Kata Tjuta, or $130 for a 35-minute helicopter flight. For a 15-minute helicopter flight over the Rock only it's $60.

The other operator is Skyport (☎ (089) 56 2093) and its charges are similar.

Organised Tours Only two companies, AAT-Kings and Uluru Experience, operate tours out of Yulara itself. If you arrive here from anywhere other than Alice Springs without a tour booked then you're pretty much limited to these two.

Uluru Experience (☎ toll-free 1800 803 174) has so-called 24- or 48-hour passes ($75 and $145 respectively). The 24-hour pass gives you sunrise at the Rock and a tour of Kata Tjuta, while the 48-hour pass includes an Edible Desert bush tucker tour, a Champagne Sunset and the Night Sky Show. Other tours offered include Valley of the Winds ($45), Mt Conner ($89), Edible Desert ($35) and Champagne Sunset ($25).

AAT-Kings (☎ (089) 56 2171) has a three-day Rock Pass which includes base, sunset,

climb, sunrise and Kata Tjuta (Olga Gorge only) tours for $94, or a Super Pass, which also includes Valley of the Winds, for $110. All these activities are also available on a one-off basis: base tour ($29.50), sunrise tour ($28), climb ($28), sunset ($17), base and sunset ($40), sunrise and climb ($44), climb and base ($52), sunrise and base ($45) and sunrise, climb and base ($62).

Entry fees to the national park are not included in any of these prices.

Tours to Uluru by private operators start at about $130 for a two-day trip, or $155 including dormitory accommodation at the Outback Pioneer Lodge and meals. For an extra $80 you can take a three-day trip which includes Kings Canyon

You have to shop around a bit because the tours run on different days and you may not want to wait for a particular one. Other things to check for include the time it gets to the Rock and Kata Tjuta, whether the return is done early or late in the day and how fast the bus is. Prices can vary with the season and demand, sometimes there may be cheaper 'stand-by' fares available. Bus-pass travellers should note that the bus service to the Rock is often heavily booked – if your schedule is tight it's best to plan ahead.

Places to Stay

Yulara has something for every budget, from a camping ground up to a five-star hotel.

The *Ayers Rock Campground* (☎ (089) 56 2055) costs $18 for two people on an unpowered site, or $24 with power. There are four-berth on-site vans for $60 for two, and $9 for each additional adult. The camp sites all have beautifully manicured patches of green grass and there's quite a bit of shade. There's also a swimming pool and the reception kiosk sells basic food supplies.

For backpackers the place to head is the well-equipped *Outback Pioneer Lodge* (☎ (089) 56 2170), with beds in 20-bed dorms for $18 for the first night, dropping to $10 on subsequent nights. There's excellent communal cooking facilities, and baggage storage lockers are available for $1. There are also cabin-type rooms with either two

NORTHERN TERRITORY

bunk beds or a double bed and one bunk, costing $80 for two, and $20 for each extra person up to four people, including bedding. The rooms have fridges and tea- and coffee-making facilities, but bathrooms are communal. Part of the same complex is known as the *Outback Pioneer Hotel* and this has expensive units with bathroom for $185. All buildings are air-con in summer and heated in winter and there's a swimming pool. Out the back is a good lookout point for sunset views of Uluru.

Next up is the *Spinifex Lodge* (☎ (089) 56 2131) which has 68 one-bedroom units which accommodate from two to four people at a cost of $85 for a double. These are quite good value, the main drawback being that the cooking facilities are pretty limited.

Probably the best deal at Yulara is offered by the *Emu Walk Apartments* (☎ (089) 56 2100). There are one- and two-bedroom flats which accommodate four and six people respectively. They have a lounge room with TV, a fully equipped kitchen and there's a communal laundry. They are also very central, being right between the visitors centre and the shopping square. The cost is $130 for the small apartments and $150 for the larger ones. Reservations and check-in are handled by the Desert Gardens Hotel.

Beyond this you're looking at the 'very expensive' category. The *Desert Gardens Hotel* (☎ (089) 56 2100) has 100 rooms with TV, phone, minibar and room service, and these cost $200 for a double. The hotel has a pool and a restaurant.

At the top of the range is the *Sails in the Desert Hotel* (☎ (089) 56 2200), which has all the facilities you'd expect in a top-class hotel. The cost is $245 for a double.

Places to Eat
The range of eating options is equally varied. At the shopping centre the *Yulara Take-Away* does pretty reasonable fast food which you can take back to eat wherever you are staying, or you can eat at the tables in the shopping area. It's open daily from 7.30 am to 9.30 pm.

The *Outback Pioneer Lodge* also has a couple of choices. The kiosk here offers light meals and snacks and is open from early in the morning until early evening. One of the best deals at Yulara is the 'Self-Cook Barbecue' which takes place here every night. For $6 to $9.80 you get meat (beef, chicken, sausages, hamburger or fish) which you then barbecue yourself, and there's a range of salads which you can help yourself to. There's also a vegetarian dish offered ($6), or for $5.50 you can just have the salads. It's a popular place to eat, probably made more so by the fact that 'exotic' meats such as kangaroo, buffalo and crocodile are often available. For more conventional dining the hotel also has the *Rocks Bistro*, which is open daily from 6 am.

For an interesting snack you can try the kangaroo, beef or chicken sticks which are offered each night at the *Taste of the Territory* stall during the entertainment at the Amphitheatre. The cost is $3 for two sticks. Still on the subject of cooked meat (this is the Territory after all!), the *Outback Barbecue* at the Tavern in the shopping square is yet another option. In the *Tavern* itself you can get good-value buffet meals for around $10.

The Desert Gardens Hotel has the *Rock View* restaurant for casual dining and the more formal *White Gums*, which is open only in the evening. Main courses here are in the $17 to $22 range.

Finally there's the Sails in the Desert Hotel which has the *Rock Pool* outdoor restaurant, the *Desert Rose Brasserie*, which features buffet meals, and the more sophisticated *Kunia Room* for up-market dining.

Entertainment
Each evening at the *Amphitheatre* there's free live entertainment. The current resident band is Indiginy, and they play an interesting range of music on a variety of instruments, the focus being on the dijeridu – and there's some fun audience participation too.

The *Tavern* has a disco or live bands on Wednesday and Saturday nights, and these go until 2 am.

Or if you are really bored you could see a

movie at the *Auditorium*. Recent releases are screened most nights.

Getting There & Away

Air Connellan Airport is about five km from Yulara. You can fly directly to Uluru from various major centres as well as from Alice Springs, which remains the popular starting point for Uluru. Ansett has at least two flights daily for the 45-minute, $173 hop from Alice to the Rock; Qantas has one.

The numerous flights direct to Uluru can be money-savers. If, for example, you were intending to fly to the Centre from Adelaide, it makes a lot more sense to go Adelaide-Uluru-Alice Springs rather than Adelaide-Alice Springs-Uluru-Alice Springs. You can fly direct between Uluru and Perth ($437), Adelaide ($506), Cairns ($453), Melbourne ($548), Sydney ($488) and Darwin ($474) with Qantas or Ansett, and to Coober Pedy ($200) with Kendell. Day trips to Uluru by air from Alice Springs cost from about $260.

Bus Apart from hitching, the cheapest way to get to the Rock is to take a bus or tour. Greyhound Pioneer has regular services between Alice Springs and Uluru for $73. The 441-km trip takes about 6½ hours. There are also direct services between Adelaide and Uluru, although this actually means connecting with another bus at Erldunda, the turn-off from the Stuart Highway. Adelaide to Uluru takes about 22 hours for the 1720-km trip and costs $224. It's cheaper, although much longer, to go direct to Alice Springs from Adelaide ($79) and then catch another bus from there to Uluru.

If you have an Aussiepass the cheapest way to visit the Rock is take the Greyhound Pioneer two-day tour package. This includes transport to and from Alice Springs, Kata Tjuta (Olga Gorge only) and a climb of the Rock. The cost is $40, or $123 if you don't have a bus pass. Accommodation and park entry are not included.

Car Rental If you haven't got your own wheels, renting a car in Alice Springs to go down to Uluru and back can be expensive.

You're looking at $70 to $100 a day for a car from the big operators, and this only includes 100 km a day, each extra km costing 25c. So if you spent three days and covered 1000 km (the bare minimum) you'd be up for around $450, including insurance and petrol costs. Still, between four people that's not much worse than taking a bus there and back. Cheaper deals are available from the smaller Alice Springs rent-a-car operators.

The road from Alice to Yulara is sealed and there are regular food and petrol stops along the way. Yulara is 441 km from Alice, 241 km west of Erldunda on the Stuart Highway, and the whole journey takes about six to seven hours. Mt Connor, which is seen on the left shortly before Curtin Springs, is often mistaken for the Rock itself. Along the way you might see kangaroos and dingoes or, at night, cows fast asleep on the warm bitumen.

Avis, Budget, Territory and Hertz are all represented at Yulara.

Getting Around

To/From the Airport AAT-Kings runs an airport shuttle bus for $7. It picks up from all accommodation points and can be booked on ☎ (089) 56 2171.

Around Yulara The village sprawls a bit, but it's not too large to get around on foot, and there's a free shuttle bus which runs between all accommodation points every 15 minutes from 7.30 am to 12.30 at night, except Wednesday and Saturday nights when it runs until 2 am. Walking trails lead across the dunes to little lookouts overlooking the village and surrounding terrain.

Bicycles can be rented by the day ($18) from the Mobil station in the village, but if you are on a bike don't underestimate the time and effort required to cycle out to the Rock – and back.

Around Uluru National Park Several options are available if you want to go further afield from the Yulara resort to Uluru or Kata Tjuta in the Uluru National Park. AAT-Kings offers transport from Yulara to the Rock and

NORTHERN TERRITORY

Kata Tjuta, but this is all in the form of tours. See the Tours section earlier for full details.

There are taxis at Yulara which operate on a multiple-hire basis. Costs include Yulara to Uluru and return for $20 per person, to Kata Tjuta and return $35, sunset $10, sunrise and climb $25, or to the airport $5. The operator is Sunworth (☎ (089) 56 2152).

Queensland

Area	1,727,000 sq km
Population	3,095,000

☎ From July 1995, Brisbane's existing phone numbers will be prefixed by the additional digit 3 (for example, ☎ 123 4567 becomes ☎ 3123 4567). From April 1998, Cairns's phone numbers will be prefixed by the additional digits 40. The area code for the state will be (07). ■

Queensland is Australia's holiday state. You're certain to find something to suit whether you prefer neon-lit Surfers Paradise, or long, deserted beaches, or the island resorts of the Great Barrier Reef, or the wild, remote national parks.

Brisbane, the state capital, is an increasingly lively city and the third biggest in Australia. In the north, Cairns is a busy travellers' centre and the base for a whole range of side trips and activities. Between Brisbane and Cairns a string of towns and islands offer virtually every maritime pastime you can imagine. Inland, several spectacular national parks are scattered over the ranges and between the isolated towns and cattle stations. In the far south-west corner of the state you'll find one of the most isolated towns of all, Birdsville, with its famous Birdsville Track.

North of Cairns, the Cape York Peninsula remains a wilderness against which people still test themselves. You can get an easy taste of this frontier in Cooktown, Australia's first British settlement and once a riotous gold-rush town. Just inland from Cairns is the lush Atherton Tableland with its countless beautiful waterfalls and scenic spots. Further inland, on the main route across Queensland to the Northern Territory, is the outback mining town of Mt Isa and, south-east of here, the town of Longreach with its Stockman's Hall of Fame.

Queensland started as yet another penal colony in 1824. As usual, the free settlers soon followed and Queensland became a separate colony independent of New South Wales in 1859. Queensland's early White settlers indulged in one of the greatest land grabs of all time and encountered fiercer Aboriginal opposition than in other states. For much of the 19th century, what amounted to a guerrilla war took place along the frontiers of the White advance. A good book on the experience of the White pioneers is *Queensland Frontier* (Aussie Books, Brisbane, 1988) by Glenville Pike.

Traditionally, agriculture and mining have been the backbone of the Queensland economy: the state contains a substantial chunk of Australia's mineral wealth. More recently, vast amounts of money have been invested in tourism, which is on the verge of becoming the state's leading money earner.

For many years, Queensland also had Australia's most controversial state government. The right-wing National Party was led by Sir Johannes Bjelke-Petersen (universally known as Joh) until 1987, when even Joh's own party decided he was a liability and replaced him. Whether it was views on rainforests, Aboriginal land rights, or even whether condom machines should be allowed in universities, you could count on the Queensland government to take the opposite stand to just about everybody else. Under the Nationals, the state also had more than its fair share of corruption scandals. Since the defeat of the Nationals in the 1990

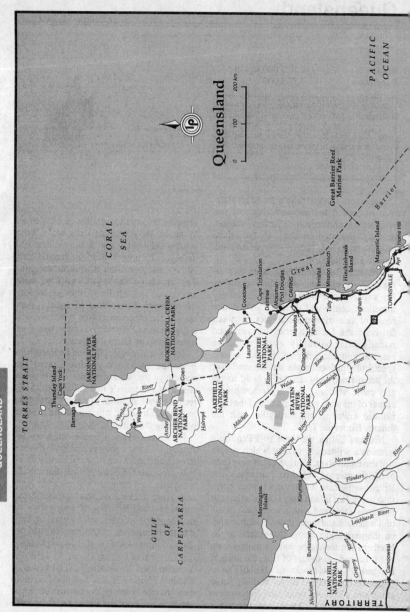

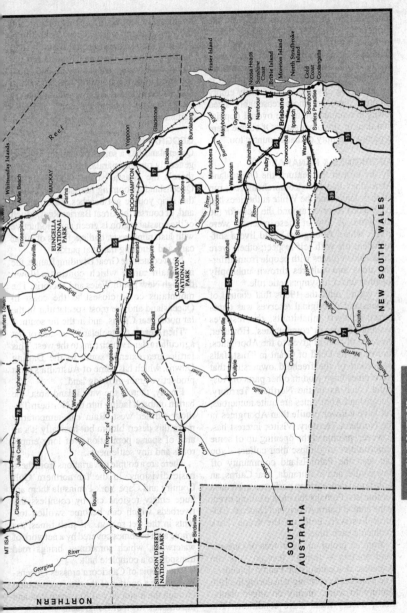

state election, it seems everyone from the former Commissioner of Queensland Police to Joh himself has appeared in court on charges relating to some sort of shady deal. Today, Queensland has a Labor government.

Unlike some other states, Queensland is not just a big city and a lot of fairly empty country; there are more reasonably sized towns in comparison to the overall population than in any other state. Of course there is plenty of empty outback country too.

ABORIGINES & KANAKAS

By the turn of the century, the Queensland Aborigines had been comprehensively run off their lands, and the White authorities had established reserves around the state for the survivors. A few of these reserves were places where Aborigines could live a self-sufficient life with self-respect; others were strife-ridden places with people from different areas and cultures thrown unhappily together under unsympathetic rule.

It wasn't until the 1980s that control of Queensland Aboriginal reserves was transferred to their inhabitants, the reserves becoming known as 'communities'. However, the form of control given to the Aborigines, known as the Deed of Grant in Trust, falls well short of the freehold ownership that Aborigines have won in other parts of Australia, such as in the Northern Territory. Queensland Aborigines are quite numerous, but have a lower profile than Aborigines in the Northern Territory. Visitor interest has, however, prompted the opening up of some opportunities to glimpse their culture – you can visit the Palm Island community off Townsville, and in Kuranda, near Cairns, an Aboriginal dance group performs most days for tourists. Perhaps the most exciting event is the annual Laura Aboriginal Dance & Cultural Festival, held on the Cape York Peninsula each June.

Another group on the fringes of Queensland society – though less so – is the Kanakas, descendants of Pacific Islanders. The Kanakas were brought in during the 19th century to work, mainly on sugar plantations, under virtual slave conditions. The business of collecting, transporting and delivering them was called blackbirding. The first Kanakas were brought over in 1863 for Robert Towns, the man whose money got Townsville going, and about 60,000 more followed until blackbirding was stopped in 1905. Today the Kanakas live predominantly in the coastal areas to the north of Rockhampton.

GEOGRAPHY

Queensland has a series of distinct regions, generally running parallel to the coast. First there's the coastal strip – the basis for Queensland's booming tourist trade. Along this strip you've got beaches, bays, islands and, of course, the Great Barrier Reef. Much of the coastal region is green and productive with lush rainforests, endless fields of sugar cane and stunning national parks.

Next comes the Great Dividing Range, the mountain range which continues down through New South Wales and Victoria. The mountains come closest to the coast in Queensland and are most spectacular in the far north near Cairns, and in the far south.

Then there is the tableland – an area of flat agricultural land which runs to the west. This fertile area extends south to the Darling Downs, which has some of Australia's most productive grain-growing land.

Finally, there's the vast inland area, the barren outback fading into the Northern Territory further west. Rain can temporarily make this desert bloom but basically it's an area of sparse population – of long empty roads and tiny settlements.

There are a couple of variations from these basic divisions. In the far northern Gulf Country and Cape York Peninsula there are huge empty regions cut by countless dry riverbeds which can become swollen torrents in the wet season. At such times, the whole area becomes covered by a network of waterways, which sometimes brings road transport to a complete halt.

The Tropic of Capricorn crosses Queensland about a quarter of the way up, running through the major city of Rockhampton and the outback town of Longreach.

CLIMATE

The Queensland seasons are more a case of hotter and wetter or cooler and drier than of summer or winter. November/December to April/May is the wetter, hotter half of the year, while the real Wet, particularly affecting northern coastal areas, is January to March. Cairns usually gets about 1300 mm of rain in these three months, with daily temperatures in the high 30s. This is also the season for cyclones, and if one hits, the main road north, the Bruce Highway, can be blocked by the ensuing floods.

In the south, Brisbane and Rockhampton both get about 450 mm of rain from January to March, and temperatures in Brisbane rarely drop below 20°C. Queensland doesn't really get 'cold weather', except at night inland or upland from about May to September. Inland, of course, there's also a lot less rain than near the coast.

INFORMATION

Queensland has none of the state-run tourist information offices that you find in some other states. Instead there are tourism offices, often privately run, which act as booking agents for the various hotels, tour companies and so on that sponsor them.

The Queensland Government Travel Centres are primarily booking offices, not information centres, but may prove useful. It's a good idea to check with these offices when planning a trip to Queensland as the cost of food and accommodation can vary greatly with the season, and high and low seasons often differ from one part of the coast to another. The interstate travel centre offices are:

Australian Capital Territory
  25 Garema Place, Canberra City 2601 (☎ (06) 248 8411)
New South Wales
  75 Castlereagh St, Sydney 2000 (☎ (02) 232 1788)
  Shop 2, 376 Victoria Ave, Chatswood 2067 (☎ (02) 412 3000)
  Shop 11, Mayfair Mall, St George St, Parramatta 2150 (☎ (02) 891 1966)
  Shop 1110, Lower Level, Westfield Shopping Town, Miranda 2228 (☎ (02) 526 1088)

Shop 3, 133-135 King St, Newcastle 2300 (☎ (049) 26 2800)
South Australia
  10 Grenfell St, Adelaide 5000 (☎ (08) 212 2399)
Victoria
  257 Collins St, Melbourne 3000 (☎ (03) 654 3866)
Western Australia
  55 St George's Terrace, Perth 6000 (☎ (09) 325 1600)
  Shop 6, 777 Hay St, Perth 6000 (☎ (09) 322 1777)

The Royal Automobile Club of Queensland (RACQ) has a series of excellent, detailed road maps covering the whole state, region by region. RACQ offices are a very helpful source of information about road and weather conditions, and they can also book accommodation and tours. Also good is the Sunmap series of area maps, published by the state government. There are Sunmap shops in most big towns.

NATIONAL PARKS

Queensland has more than 300 national parks, and while some just cover a single hill or lake, others are major wilderness areas. Many islands and stretches of coast are national parks, while inland three of the most spectacular are Lamington, on the forested rim of an ancient volcano on the New South Wales border; Carnarvon, with its 30-km gorge south-west of Rockhampton; and rainforested Eungella, near Mackay, which is swarming with wildlife. Many parks have camping grounds with water, toilets and showers and there are often privately run camping grounds, motels or lodges on the park fringes. Sizable parks usually have a network of walking tracks.

The Queensland National Parks & Wildlife Service operates five main information centres: Gold Coast Highway, Burleigh Heads (☎ (075) 35 3032); 160 Ann St, Brisbane (☎ (07) 227 8185); Bruce Highway, Monkland in Gympie (☎ (074) 82 4189); at the Great Barrier Reef Wonderland in Townsville (☎ (077) 21 2399); and Shute Harbour Rd, Airlie Beach (☎ (079) 46 7022). It's worth calling at one of these to find out what's where, and to get the rundown on camping in the national parks. You can also get info from the National Parks offices in most major towns, and from the park rangers.

To camp in a national park – whether in a fixed camping ground or in the bush – you need a permit which you can either get in advance by writing or calling in at the appropriate National Parks office, or from the ranger at the park itself. Camping in national parks costs up to $7.50 a night for a site for up to six people. Some camping grounds fill up at holiday times, so you may need to book well ahead; you can usually book sites six to 12 weeks ahead by writing to the appropriate office. Lists of camping grounds are available from National Parks offices. The handy *Discover National Parks* booklets ($2.50) also have useful information about Queensland's national parks and state forests, including things to do, camping details and how to get there. They're available from bookshops and National Parks offices.

STATE FORESTS

There are also camping areas, walking trails and scenic drives in some state forests which can be just as scenic and wild as national parks. You can get information on state forest camping sites and facilities from tourist offices or from the Forest Services section of the Department of Primary Industry (☎ (07) 234 0158), on the 5th floor at 160 Mary St, Brisbane. Some other forestry offices are at Fraser Rd, Two Mile, near Gympie; 52 McIllwraith St, Ingham; Gregory St, Cardwell; and at Atherton.

ACTIVITIES
Bushwalking

This is a popular activity in Queensland year round. There are bushwalking clubs in the state and several useful guidebooks. Lonely Planet's *Bushwalking in Australia* includes three walks in Queensland, which range between two and five days in length. National parks and state forests are some of the best places for walking, and they often have marked trails. You can get full information on walking in national parks and state forests from their respective offices.

There are excellent bushwalking possibilities in many parts of the state, including on several of the larger coastal islands such as Fraser and Hinchinbrook. National parks on the mainland favoured by bushwalkers include Lamington in the southern Border Ranges, Main Range in the Great Dividing Range, Cooloola just north of the Sunshine Coast, and Bellenden Ker south of Cairns, which contains Queensland's highest peak, Mt Bartle Frere (1657 metres).

Water Sports
Diving & Snorkelling The Great Barrier Reef provides some of the world's best diving and there's ample opportunity to learn and pursue this activity. The Queensland coast is probably the world's cheapest place to learn to scuba dive in tropical water – a five-day course leading to a recognised open-water certificate usually costs somewhere between $250 and $400 and you almost always do a good part of your learning out on the Barrier Reef itself. These courses are now very popular and almost every town along the coast has one or more diving schools. The three most popular places are Airlie Beach, Townsville and Cairns.

Important factors to consider when choosing a course include the school's reputation, the relative amounts of time spent on pool/classroom training and out in the ocean, and whether your open-water time is spent on the outer reef as opposed to reefs around islands or even just off the mainland. The outer reef is usually more spectacular. Normally you have to show you can tread water for 10 minutes and swim 200 metres before you can start a course. Some schools also require a medical which will usually cost extra.

For certified divers, trips and equipment hire are available just about everywhere. You usually have to show evidence of qualifications. You can snorkel just about everywhere too. There are coral reefs off some mainland beaches and around several of the islands, and many day trips out to the Barrier Reef provide snorkelling gear free.

During the wet season, usually January to March, floods can wash a lot of mud out into the ocean and visibility for divers and snorkellers is sometimes affected.

White-Water Rafting & Canoeing The Tully and North Johnstone rivers between Townsville and Cairns are the big ones for white-water rafting. You can do day trips for about $100 to $120, or longer expeditions.

Coastal Queensland is full of waterways and lakes so there's no shortage of canoeing territory. You can rent canoes or join canoe tours in several places – among them Noosa, Townsville and Cairns.

Swimming & Surfing There are plenty of swimming beaches close to Brisbane on sheltered Moreton Bay. Popular surfing beaches are south of the capital on the Gold Coast and north on the Sunshine Coast. North of Fraser Island the beaches are sheltered by the Great Barrier Reef so they're great for swimming but no good for surf. The clear, sheltered waters of the reef hardly need to be mentioned. There are also innumerable, good freshwater swimming spots around the state.

Other Water Sports Sailing enthusiasts will also find plenty of opportunities to practise their sport and many places which hire boats, both along the coast and inland. Airlie Beach and the Whitsunday Islands are probably the biggest centres and you can find almost any type of boating or sailing you want there. Fishing is probably Queensland's biggest participant sport and you can rent gear or boats for this in many places. Sailboards can also be hired in many spots along the coast.

Warning From around November to April, avoid swimming on unprotected northern beaches where deadly box jellyfish (also known as sea wasps or stingers) may lurk. If in any doubt, check with a local. If you're still in doubt, don't swim – their sting can be fatal. Great Keppel Island is usually the most northerly safe place in the box-jellyfish season. Also in northern waters, saltwater crocodiles are a hazard. They may be found

in the open sea or near creeks and rivers – especially tidal ones – sometimes surprising distances inland.

Fossicking
There are lots of good fossicking areas in Queensland – see the *Gem Field* brochure, published by the Queensland Government Travel Centre. It tells you the places where you have a fair chance of finding gems and the types you'll find. You'll need a 'miners right' before you set out.

GETTING AROUND
The peak tourist seasons are from mid-December to late January, 10 days either side of Easter, and mid-June to mid-October. The low season is February and March.

Air
Ansett and Qantas both fly to Queensland's major cities, connecting them to the southern states and across to the Northern Territory. Eastwest flies to Brisbane, the Gold and Sunshine coasts and Cairns. There's also a multitude of smaller airlines operating up and down the coast, across the Cape York Peninsula and into the outback. During the wet season, such flights are often the only means of getting around the Gulf of Carpentaria or the Cape York Peninsula. These smaller airlines include Sunstate, Queensland Regional (both closely linked to Qantas) and Flight West.

Bus
There are numerous bus services up the coast to Cairns and inland from Townsville through Mt Isa to the Northern Territory. The main companies on these routes are Greyhound Pioneer and McCafferty's. Prices are fairly similar, although McCafferty's tends to be a dollar or two cheaper. There's also a range of stopover deals.

You can catch a Greyhound Pioneer bus inland from Brisbane to Roma, Charleville, Longreach and up to Mt Isa, or you can go with McCafferty's from Rockhampton to Longreach. Alternatively, there are many

QUEENSLAND

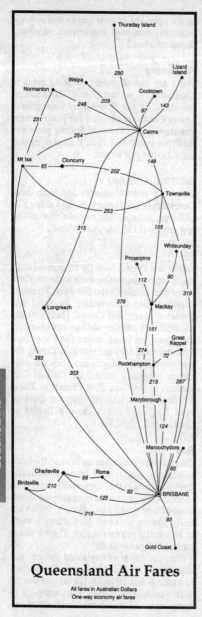

Queensland Air Fares

All fares in Australian Dollars
One-way economy air fares

local services like Cairns to Cooktown or Brisbane to the Gold Coast.

Train

There are four major rail routes in Queensland. The main one is Brisbane to Cairns, with a local extension on the scenic route into the Atherton Tableland. Inland from Brisbane, a service runs to Roma, Charleville and Quilpie; from Rockhampton you can go to Emerald, Longreach and Winton; and from Townsville there is a service to Mt Isa. There are other local and outback lines too. The Sunshine Rail Pass provides unlimited travel on all services in Queensland. Fares in economy/1st class are: 14 days for $254/370, 21 days for $294/454, and one month for $374/554.

Queensland trains are slower than buses but are similarly priced if you travel economy class. They're almost all air-con and you can get sleeping berths on most trains for $30 extra a night in economy, $50 in 1st class. You can break your journey on most services for no extra cost provided you complete the trip within 14 days. The only interstate rail connection from Queensland is between Brisbane and Sydney.

For rail bookings phone ☎ 13 2232 during office hours.

Boat

It's possible to make your way along the coast or even over to Papua New Guinea or Darwin by crewing on the numerous yachts and cruisers that sail Queensland waters. Ask at harbours, marinas and yacht or sailing clubs. Great Keppel Island, Airlie Beach, Townsville and Cairns are good places to try. Sometimes you'll get a free ride in exchange for your help, but it's more common for owners to ask $10 to $15 a day for food etc.

Brisbane

Population 1,334,000

When Sydney and the colony of New South Wales needed a better place to store its more recalcitrant 'cons', the tropical country further north seemed a good place to drop them. Accordingly, in 1824, a penal settlement was established at Redcliffe on Moreton Bay, but was soon abandoned due to lack of water and the presence of hostile Aborigines. The settlement was moved south and inland to Brisbane, a town grew up, and although the penal settlement was abandoned in 1839, Brisbane's future was assured when the area was thrown open to free settlers in 1842. As Queensland's huge agricultural potential and then its mineral riches were developed, Brisbane grew to be a city, and today it is the third largest in Australia.

For years it was considered to be a bit backward by its larger southern cousins, but since hosting several major international events in the 1980s, including the 1982 Commonwealth Games and Expo '88, Brisbane has developed into a modern and cosmopolitan city.

Although it's close to the coast, it is very much a river city. It's a scenic place, surrounded by hills and fine lookouts, with several impressive bridges spanning the Brisbane River. It is compact and easy to explore, and enjoys an excellent climate. Architecturally, as in the rest of the state, the city is dominated by 'Queenslanders' – sprawling, verandahed timber houses on stilts.

Several of Queensland's major attractions can be reached on day trips from Brisbane. The Gold and Sunshine coasts and their mountainous hinterlands are easy drives from the city, and you can also visit the islands of Moreton Bay or head inland towards the Great Dividing Range and the Darling Downs.

Orientation

Brisbane is built along and between the looping meanders of the Brisbane River, about 25 km upstream from the river mouth. The Brisbane transit centre, where you'll arrive if you're coming by bus or train, is on Roma St about half a km west of the city centre. Head left as you leave the centre's main entrance and you'll find King George Square, the large open area in front of City Hall; it's a popular place to sit and watch the world pass by.

You'll find most of the accommodation and eating options clustered in the suburbs surrounding the city. Just west of the centre is Paddington, which is quite trendy and has good restaurants. South-west of the centre and across the river are South Bank and the Queensland Cultural Centre, and the suburbs of South Brisbane, West End and Highgate Hill. North-east up Ann St from the city will take you to Fortitude Valley, one of the more cosmopolitan suburbs with lots of nightclubs, restaurants and a large ethnic population. To the east of the Valley is New Farm, which also has quite a few eating and accommodation options.

Information

Tourist Offices The Queen St Mall Information Centre (☎ 229 5918), on the corner of Queen and Albert Sts, is open Monday to Thursday from 9 am to 5.30 pm, Friday from 9 am to 9 pm, Saturday from 9 am to 4 pm and Sunday from 10 am to 4 pm.

The Greater Brisbane Tourist Association (☎ 236 2020) has a helpful information office on level 2 of the transit centre and an accommodation booking office on level 3; both are open weekdays from 8 am to 6 pm and weekends from 9 am to 1 pm. There's also the Tourism Brisbane information desk (☎ 221 8411) in the City Hall; it's open weekdays from 8.30 am to 5 pm.

The Queensland Government Travel Centre (☎ 221 6111), on the corner of Adelaide and Edward Sts, is more a booking office than an information centre but they may be able to answer some queries. It's open Monday to Friday from 8.30 am to 5 pm and Saturday from 9.30 am to 12.30 pm.

The Brisbane City Council runs an information service for disabled people – phone ☎ 225 4416 or ☎ 224 8031.

There are a number of free information guides circulated in Brisbane including *Tourism Brisbane*, which has a useful information directory at the back including a list

of foreign consulates in the city, and *This Week in Brisbane*. There are also two free entertainment guides, *Time Off* and *Rave*.

Post & Telecommunications The GPO is on Queen St. The STD telephone area code for Brisbane is 07.

Other Offices The RACQ (☎ 361 2444) is beside the GPO at 261 Queen St. The National Parks & Wildlife Service's Naturally Queensland office (☎ 227 8185), at 160 Ann St, is open on weekdays from 8.30 am to 5 pm.

The Queensland Conservation Council Environment Centre (☎ 221 0188), with a library and information desk open to the public on weekdays from 9 am to 5 pm, is on the 2nd floor of the School of Arts building at 166 Ann St.

The YHA membership office (☎ 236 1680) is at 154 Roma St, opposite the transit centre.

Bookshops Brisbane's largest bookshops include Dymocks, with several city shops including one in the Queen St Mall, and Angus & Robertson Bookworld, whose

PLACES TO STAY		28	Somewhere to Stay	24	Qan Heng's Restaurant
		29	Durham Villa	25	Cafe Tempo & Wholly
2	Powerhouse Hotel	31	Courtney Place		Munchies
	& Kingsford Hall		Backpackers	26	King Ahiram's
	Private Hotel				
7	Globe Trekkers Hostel	**PLACES TO EAT**		**OTHER**	
8	Homestead				
9	Atoa House	1	Breakfast Creek Hotel	4	Newstead House
12	Backpackers	3	Breakfast Creek Wharf	5	Valley Swimming Pool
	Paddington	6	Famish	16	Lang Park
14	Aussie Way	10	King Tut's & Red Chair	17	Museum of
	Backpackers		Cafe		Contemporary Art
15	Banana Benders	11	Masakan Indonesia	18	The Underground
	Backpackers	13	Sultan's Kitchen	20	William Jolly Bridge
19	Brisbane City Youth	22	Squirrels	21	Brewery
	Hostel	23	Three Monkeys Coffee	30	Brisbane Cricket
27	Swagman's Rest		House		Ground (the Gabba)

three city shops include one in Adelaide St under Post Office Square. Other good ones include the American Bookstore at 173 Elizabeth St, the Queensland Book Depot on Adelaide St opposite the City Hall and the Billabong Bookshop immediately east of Victoria Bridge, which is good for environmental and 'green' books and also has a good selection of Aboriginal books. Hema Maps, at 239 George St, specialises in travel books and maps.

Medical Services The Travellers Medical & Vaccination Centre (☎ 221 9066) is on the 6th floor, 247 Adelaide St. The Brisbane Sexual Health Clinic (☎ 227 7091) is at 484 Adelaide St.

City Hall

Brisbane's City Hall, on the corner of Adelaide and Albert Sts, has gradually been surrounded by skyscrapers but the observation platform still provides one of the best views across the city. There's a lift to the observation deck, which runs Monday to Friday from 9 am to 3.30 pm. The City Hall also houses a museum and art gallery on the ground floor; it's open daily from 10 am to 5 pm, except on public holidays, and admission is free.

Queen St Mall

Running two blocks from Edward St to

George St, this attractive mall is the shopping hub of the city. In addition to the hundreds of shops, there's an underground bus interchange, a Hilton Hotel, eight cinemas and even an indoor funfair in the Myer Centre.

City Hall, Brisbane

QUEENSLAND

The mall is bustling and alive, and quite often there are buskers and bands performing here. At night it's a popular promenading spot.

Early Buildings – city centre
The Brisbane City Council publishes a series of *Heritage Trail* brochures which guide you around the city's most interesting old buildings. The National Trust has its headquarters in **Old Government House** (1862), the former state governor's residence at the southern end of George St. Nearby, **Parliament House**, overlooking the Botanic Gardens, dates from 1868, and was built in French Renaissance style; the roof is made from Mt Isa copper. Free tours are given four times a day Monday to Friday (except when Parliament is sitting).

More of Brisbane's best old buildings line George St – notably the **Mansions** and **Harris Terrace**, Victorian terrace houses on the Margaret St corner, and the old **Treasury Buildings** between Queen and Elizabeth Sts, which are currently being restored and converted into a casino.

On Elizabeth St, the Gothic-style **Old St Stephen's** (1850) is the oldest church in Brisbane. The **GPO** is an impressive neoclassical edifice dating from the 1870s. Across Queen St and on the corner of Creek St, the **National Bank building** (1885) is reckoned to be one of the finest examples of the Italian Renaissance style in Australia. Its front doors were made from a single Queensland cedar log.

St John's Cathedral, between Ann and Adelaide Sts, is still under construction – work started in 1901. Guided tours are conducted at 10 am from Monday to Saturday. Queensland's first **Government House**, built in 1853, is now the deanery for the cathedral. The declaration of Queensland's separation from the colony of New South Wales was read here in 1859.

The 1828 **Commissariat Stores** building, at 115 William St, was used as a government store right up until 1962. Today it houses the Royal Historical Society of Queensland's library and museum, and can

be visited for $1, Tuesday to Friday from 11 am to 2 pm, and Sunday from 11 am to 4 pm.

The **Old Windmill & Observatory** on Wickham Terrace, just north of the city centre, is one of Brisbane's earliest buildings, dating from 1828. It was intended to grind grain for the early convict colony but, due to a fundamental design error, it did not work properly. In 1837 it was made to work as originally intended but the building was then converted to a signal post and later a meteorological observatory.

Early Buildings – suburbs
There are a number of interesting old houses and period re-creations around Brisbane. **Newstead House**, four km north-east of the centre on Breakfast Creek Rd in Newstead, is the oldest surviving home in Brisbane. Built in 1846, overlooking the river, it is a stately mansion fully fitted with Victorian furnishings. The house and its gardens are open from 10 am to 4 pm on weekdays and from 2 to 5 pm on Sundays and public holidays; entry costs $3. You can get there on bus No 160, 171 or 190 from the yellow stop on Edward St between Adelaide and Queen Sts.

Earlystreet Historical Village is on McIlwraith Ave, off Bennetts Rd in Norman Park, four km east of the centre. It's a re-creation of early Queensland colonial life with genuine old buildings in a garden setting. Entry is $6 and it's open daily from 10 am to 4.30 pm. You can get there on bus No 125, 145, 155 or 255 from Ann St by King George Square, or by train to Norman Park.

Miegunyah Folk Museum, at 35 Jordan Terrace in Bowen Hills, just north of Fortitude Valley, is housed in an 1884 building, a fine example of early Brisbane architecture. It's been furnished and decorated in period style as a memorial to the pioneer women of Queensland and is open from 10.30 am to 3 pm on Wednesdays and 10.30 am to 4 pm on weekends. To get there, take an airport bus No 160 or Toombul bus No 170, 171 or 190.

Queensland Cultural Centre
This superb complex (☎ 840 7208) spans two blocks either side of Melbourne St in

Northern Territory
Top: Devil's Marbles, Stuart Highway (RI)
Bottom: Glen Helen Gorge, MacDonnell Ranges (RI)

Northern Territory
Top: Ormiston Gorge (JC)
Left: Garden of Eden, Kings Canyon (TW)
Right: Palm Valley (TW)

South Brisbane, just across Victoria Bridge from the city centre. It houses the Queensland Art Gallery, the Queensland Museum and the State Library, all on the northern side of Melbourne St, and, to the south, the Performing Arts Complex.

Within the **Performing Arts Complex** are the Lyric Theatre, the Concert Hall and a small studio theatre, as well as a restaurant and cafes. There are free guided tours every weekday at midday.

The **Queensland Museum** is well worth a visit. Its large collection features a dinosaur garden and a new exhibition on whales. The aviation section includes the *Avian Cirrus*, in which Queensland's Bert Hinkler made the first England to Australia solo flight in 1928, as well as the wreck of Bill Lancaster's plane and the script of his poignant final message to his family. The museum is open daily from 9 am to 5 pm and on Wednesdays till 8 pm, except on Good Friday and Christmas day. Admission is free.

The **Queensland Art Gallery** has an impressive permanent collection and also features visiting exhibitions. Australian artists in the collection include Sir Sidney Nolan, William Dobell, Charles Blackman, Margaret Preston and Fred Williams. It's open daily from 10 am to 5 pm and on Wednesdays till 8 pm, again except for Good Friday and Christmas. Admission is free (except for special exhibitions). There are free guided tours daily at 10 am, 1 and 2 pm. The gallery's courtyard cafe is a good spot for lunch or a snack, and is reasonably priced.

The **State Library's** excellent facilities include newspaper and magazine sections, audiovisual programs, videos, music and of course plenty of books, as well as a great cafe (see Places to Eat). The library is open Monday to Thursday from 10 am to 8 pm and Friday to Sunday from 10 am to 5 pm.

Other Museums

At 102 George St in the city, there's the **Sciencentre**, a hands-on science museum with interactive displays, optical illusions and a regular 20-minute show in the theatre. It's open daily from 10 am to 5 pm, except for Christmas Day and Good Friday, and costs $5.

The **Museum of Contemporary Art**, on Petrie Terrace in Paddington, is in a converted grain silo. It's open Monday to Saturday from noon to 6 pm; admission is by $2 donation.

The **Queensland Maritime Museum**, on Sidon St in South Brisbane, has an 1881 dry dock, working models, and the WW II frigate HMAS *Diamantina*. It's open from 10 am to 5 pm daily; admission is $4.

Postal enthusiasts could try the **GPO Museum** at 261-285 Queen St. It's open Tuesday to Friday from 9.30 am to 3.30 pm and admission is free. Out in St Lucia on Sir Fred Schonell Drive, the **University of Queensland** has anthropology, antiquities and art museums.

Brisbane's trams no longer operate, but you can ride some early examples at the **Tramway Museum** at 2 McGinn Rd, Ferny Grove. The museum is 11 km north-west of the city centre, and is open from 12.30 to 4 pm Sundays and most public holidays; admission is $4.

The **Sir Charles Kingsford Smith Memorial**, featuring his famous *Southern Cross* plane under a giant dome, is beside the airport freeway just south of the domestic airlines terminal.

Casino Site

Brisbane's magnificent old Treasury Buildings, overlooking the Brisbane River from the block bordered by Queen, George, Elizabeth and William Sts, are currently being restored and converted into a casino, due to open in 1995.

South Bank Parklands

Brisbane's South Bank, formerly the site of Expo '88, has been extensively redeveloped and is now one of the city's liveliest and most interesting areas. Covering 16 hectares, its attractions include restaurants and cafes, parklands and bike paths, a rainforest sanctuary and butterfly house, market stalls and even a sandy swimming beach.

The **Gondwana Rainforest Sanctuary** is

a quite amazing re-creation of a rainforest environment. Set inside and around a massive synthetic rock, it's populated by native birds, mammals and reptiles including crocodiles, koalas, possums, lorikeets and snakes. An elevated boardwalk winds through the sanctuary. Gondwana is open daily from 10 am to 5.30 pm; entry costs $7.50.

The **Butterfly House** is a glass-enclosed tropical conservatorium that is home to hundreds of Australian butterflies, as well as a large collection of exotic insects and spiders. It's open daily from 10 am to 4 pm and entry costs $6. **Our World Environment** has a range of displays that feature different aspects of the environment. It's open daily from 9 am to 5 pm and admission costs $7.

The South Bank also includes a beautiful **Nepalese Pagoda** that took 160 craftspeople two years to make; boat trips through the park on canals; a **swimming beach and lagoon** patrolled by lifesavers; and a large craft and clothing **market** at the Stanley St Plaza which runs on Friday nights from 5 to 10.30 pm, on Saturdays from 11 am to 5 pm and on Sundays from 9 am to 5 pm. The picnic areas, with free gas barbecues, are also very popular day and night. The **Suncorp Piazza**, an outdoor entertainment venue, has regular concerts and performances, many of which are free. The South Bank Information Centre (☎ 867 2051) is located at the main entrance court.

Markets

The popular South Bank Markets, which feature craft and clothing stalls, are open every Friday evening, Saturday and Sunday. Every Sunday, the carnival-style Riverside Centre and Eagle St Pier Markets have 150 stalls, including glass blowing, weaving, leather work and children's activities. On Saturdays, the Fortitude Valley Market, with a diverse collection of crafts, clothes and junk, is held in the Brunswick St Mall.

Popular permanent markets include McWhirter's, on the corner of Brunswick and Wickham Sts in Fortitude Valley, and the West End Market, on the corner of Melbourne and Boundary Sts in the West End.

City Parks & Gardens

Brisbane's **Botanic Gardens** were establ lished in 1855 on a loop of the Brisban River, almost in the centre of the city. Th park occupies 18 hectares, is open 24 hour a day (and lit at night) and is a good spot fc strolling and bike riding. There's also a ver pleasant cafe at the southern end and fre tours (☎ 221 4528) Tuesday to Friday at 1 am and 1 pm.

There are good views from **Wickhan Park** and **Albert Park** on the hill just nort of the city centre. **New Farm Park**, by th river at the southern end of Brunswick St, i noted for its rose displays, jacaranda tree and Devonshire teas. **Captain John Burk Park** is a nice little place underneath th towering Story Bridge at the top of Kangaro Point.

Mt Coot-tha Park

This large park has a lookout and an excel lent botanic garden, and is just eight km we of the city centre. The views from the top ar superb. On a clear day you can see the distar line of Moreton and Stradbroke islands, th Glasshouse Mountains to the north, th mountains behind the Gold Coast to th south and Brisbane, with the river windin through, at your feet. The Summit (☎ 36 9922) restaurant is expensive but the view are sensational; it also serves Devonshir teas and has a kiosk.

There are some good walks around N Coot-tha and its foothills, like the one to J Slaughter Falls on Simpsons Rd.

The **Mt Coot-tha Botanic Gardens**, the foot of the mountain, are open daily fro 8.30 am to 5 pm. The gardens include a enclosed tropical dome, an arid zon rainforests and a Japanese garden, plus library and a teahouse. There are free guide walks through the gardens at 11 am and 1 p daily except Monday. You'll also find the S **Thomas Brisbane Planetarium** here; it the largest in Australia. Admission is $7 an there are shows at 3.30 and 7.30 pm Wedne day to Friday; 1.30, 3.30 and 7.30 p Saturday; and 1.30 and 3.30 pm Sunday.

There are buses to the lookout and botan

gardens at Mt Coot-tha. Bus No 37A to the gardens leaves from Ann St at King George Square.

Brisbane Forest Park

The Brisbane Forest Park is a 26,500-hectare natural bushland reserve in the D'Aguilar Range. The park starts on the outskirts of Brisbane and stretches for more than 50 km to the north and west. It's a great area for bushwalks, cycling, horse riding, camping and scenic drives.

There's an information centre (☎ 300 4855) in the Gap, at the start of the park. It's open on weekdays from 8.30 am to 4.30 pm and on weekends from 10 am to 5 pm, and the rangers run regular guided bushwalks and tours – ring for details.

In the same spot is **Walk-About Creek**, a freshwater study centre where you can see fish, lizards, pythons and turtles at close quarters. It's open daily from 9 am to 4.30 pm (weekends from 10 am); entry costs $3.50. Upstairs, there's an excellent cafe/restaurant.

To get to the park from the city, follow Musgrave, Waterworks and Mt Nebo Rds. By public transport, you can take a bus to the Gap – it's about a 700-metre walk to the info centre.

Wildlife Sanctuaries

The **Alma Park Zoo** at Kallangur, 28 km north of the city centre, is an excellent zoo in a subtropical garden setting of palm trees, ferns and native flora. It has a large collection of Australian and exotic wildlife including wallabies, koalas, emus, grizzly bears, monkeys and deer. It's open daily from 9 am to 5 pm except Christmas Day and admission costs $13.

The **Lone Pine Koala Sanctuary** at Fig Tree Pocket, 11 km south-west of the centre, has more than 100 koalas plus a variety of other Australian fauna including kangaroos, emus, lyrebirds and wombats. Visitors can feed and touch many of the animals. Lone Pine is open from 8.45 am to 5 pm daily and entry costs $10. You can get to the sanctuary by bus, river cruise or bus tour. Cityxpress

bus No 518 leaves from the Koala platform at the Queen St underground bus station hourly between 8.35 am and 3.35 pm, every day. Mirimar (☎ 221 0300) runs a daily river cruise to the sanctuary which costs $15.

Bunya Park, on Bunya Park Drive, Eatons Hill, 16 km north of the city, has more koalas to cuddle and plenty more native flora and fauna, including kangaroos and crocodiles. It's open daily from 9 am to 5 pm and costs $9.50.

Australian Woolshed

This attraction is at 148 Stamford Rd, Ferny Hills, 15 km north-west of the centre. Entry into the Ram Show, which features trained sheep, shearing demonstrations and other activities, costs $9, and there's also a water slide ($3 for 30 minutes) and a restaurant which has dinner dances on Friday and Saturday nights ($26).

Activities

For information about bushwalking near Brisbane, contact the Brisbane Bushwalkers Club on ☎ 856 4050. If you feel like jumping out of a plane, the Ramblers Parachute Club (☎ 399 6400) organises skydives and tandem jumps. There are a few horse-riding schools on the outskirts of Brisbane, including Silverado (☎ 890 2280) and Samford Valley (☎ 289 1046). And if you want some war action, Top Gun Paintball (☎ 395 7264) has a battlefield close to town.

Swimming Pools The Valley Pool, home to some champion Aussie swimmers, is open all year; on weekdays from 5.30 am to 8 pm, Saturday from 5.30 am to 6 pm and Sunday from 7.30 am to 6 pm. It's on the corner of Wickham and East Sts in Fortitude Valley.

The Spring Hill Baths in Torrington St are amongst the oldest in the southern hemisphere. The swimming pool is surrounded by colourfully painted, old-style changing cubicles, and is open from 6 am to 7 pm on weekdays and from 8 am to 6 pm on weekends. Centenary Pool, nearby on Gregory Terrace, is open daily from 6 am to 6 or 8.30

QUEENSLAND

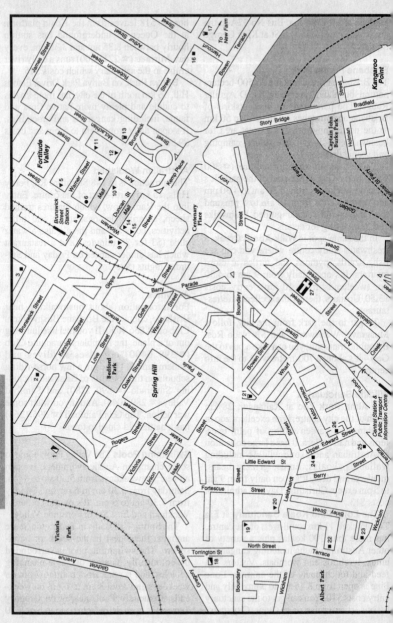

QUEENSLAND

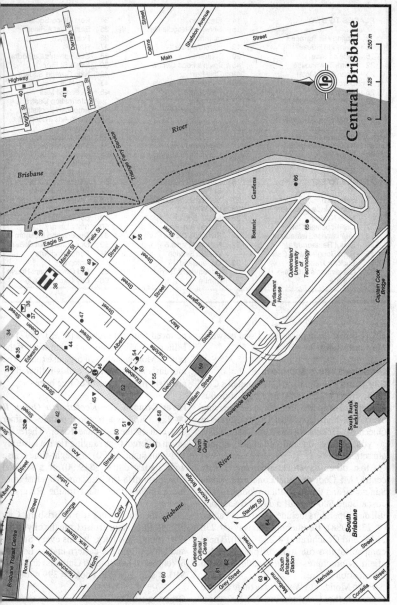

Central Brisbane

PLACES TO STAY

2   Spring Hill Terraces
3   Balmoral House
16 Pete's Place
22 Marrs Townhouse
23 Soho Club Motel
24 Dorchester Inn
25 Astor Motel
26 Annie's Shandon Inn
    & Yale Inner-City Inn
40 Story Bridge Hotel &
    Backpackers
    Brisbane Central
41 Ryan Lodge Motel
44 Hilton Hotel
63 Sly Fox

PLACES TO EAT

4   Sala Thai
5   Home Made Chinese
    Meal Kitchen
7   Cosmopolitan Cafe
8   Vietnamese Restaurant
9   Seoul Restaurant
10 Rum Boogie Bar & Cafe
11 Lucky's Trattoria
12 Giardinetto's & Cafe
    Europe

14 Enjoy Inn
15 Universal Noodle Res-
    taurant
19 Harold's Cafe
20 Tonton's
45 Jo Jo's Food Centre
49 Chill Bar
53 Parrots & Govinda's
    Restaurant
55 Sennari
56 Port Office Hotel

OTHER

1   Centenary Pool
6   McWhirter's Market
13 Dooley's Hotel
17 Brunswick Hotel
18 Spring Hill Baths
21 St Paul's Tavern
27 St John's Cathedral
28 Old Windmill
29 Anzac Square
30 Qantas Airlines
31 Riverside Centre
32 National Parks &
    Wildlife Service
33 Queensland
    Government Tourist
    Centre

34 Post Office Square
35 East-West Airlines
36 Post Office
37 RACQ
38 St Stephen's Cathedral
39 Eagle St Pier
42 King George Square
43 City Hall
46 Queen St Mall
    Information Centre
47 American Bookstore
48 Metro Arts Theatre &
    Cinema
50 Hema Maps
51 Ansett Airlines
52 Myer Centre &
    Underground
    Bus Station
54 Elizabeth Arcade
57 Billabong Bookshop
58 Treasury Build-
    ings/Casino Site
59 Sciencentre
60 State Library
61 Queensland Museum
62 Queensland Art Gallery
64 Performing Arts
    Complex
65 Old Government House
66 City Gardens Club

pm. (Both of these pools are closed between May and August.)

Organised Tours & Cruises

City Tours The Brisbane City Council's City Sights tour (☎ 225 4444) on a tram-style bus makes a 20-stop trip around the city, leaving every half-hour from Post Office Square in Queen St. Tickets cost $10 and last all day, so you can get on and off at the various attractions.

Most other day tours take in the city centre, Mt Coot-tha, the Lone Pine Koala Sanctuary and the Australian Woolshed, and cost around $20 for half a day and $35 for a full day. Operators include Australian Pacific (☎ 236 4088), Boomerang Baxway (☎ 236 3614) and Coachtrans (☎ 236 1000). These companies also run tours to places further afield – brochures are available from all information centres.

From Monday to Wednesday there are free tours of the Castlemaine XXXX (pro-nounced four-ex) brewery (☎ 361 7597) on Milton Rd, Milton, about 1.5 km west of the centre. Most hostels will organise tours. The tour lasts about an hour, and is followed by about 40 minutes worth of free beer.

River Cruises The *Kookaburra Queen II* (☎ 221 1300) is a restored paddle-steamer that cruises the Brisbane River. There are seven different trips ranging from a leisurely 1½-hour jaunt ($9.90) to a night-time cruise with a roast dinner ($19.90) or a seafood smorgasbord ($46). The cruises operate from the Eagle St Pier, next to the Riverside Centre.

Another interesting trip is Brisbane City Ferries' three-hour cruise from the city to the river mouth and back. It runs every Sunday and leaves from the eastern end of Edward St (corner of the Botanic Gardens) and costs $10. It's advisable to book (☎ 399 4768).

Other tours Some of the best day trips for

backpackers are run by Far Horizons (☎ 284 5475). They take small groups to Lamington and Noosa national parks, the Glasshouse Mountains and the Springbrook Plateau; day trips normally cost $45, $30 for backpackers and YHA members.

For a day trip to the Gold Coast, the High Roller bus (☎ 222 4067) to Jupiters Casino is good value. It leaves from the transit centre daily at 9 am and costs $10 return, which includes a $5 meal voucher and a $5 gaming voucher.

Aus-Trail (☎ 285 1711) offers a range of eight- to 10-day trips designed for budget travellers, to places including a cattle station near Roma, Carnarvon Gorge National Park, the Anakie gem fields and Noosa. The $500 cost includes food and camping equipment.

Festivals

Brisbane's major festival of the arts, the outdoor Warana Festival, is held over two weeks from mid-September. The Royal National Exhibition (the Ekka) is held at the exhibition grounds in mid-August. There's also a 12-day international film festival that starts in late August, an international comedy festival in April and a biennial music festival every second June.

Places to Stay

Brisbane has plenty of hostels and backpackers, and there are also quite a few well-priced hotels, motels and self-contained apartment blocks within easy reach of the centre.

Camping There are no caravan parks or camping grounds close to the city centre, and in any case many of the caravan parks are full with permanent residents. You could try the following:

Aspley Acres Caravan Park (☎ 263 2668), 13 km north at 1420 Gympie Rd, Aspley; tent sites from $12, on-site vans from $25.

Dress Circle Village (☎ 341 6133), 14 km south at 10 Holmead Rd, Eight Mile Plain; tent sites $10, on-site vans $40.

Gateway Junction Village (☎ 341 6333), 19 km south at 200 School Rd, Rochedale; powered tent sites $17, cabins from $45.

Springtime Gardens Caravan Park (☎ 208 8184), 24 km south on the corner of the Pacific Highway and Old Chatswood Rd, Springwood; tent sites from $10, on-site vans from $25.

Hostels Brisbane has a wide range of hostels, with everything from large modern places to small intimate ones, and from quiet, cosy hostels to full-on party places. It's a competitive market, and many places have touts at the bus and train stations. Most of the hostels have courtesy buses and do pick-ups on request.

The hostels are concentrated in four areas: Paddington, just west of the city centre; Fortitude Valley/New Farm, north-east of the city; south of the city in South Brisbane/West End; and east across the river in Kangaroo Point.

Paddington The first offering here is the *Brisbane City Youth Hostel* (☎ 236 1004) at 56 Quay St, just south of Upper Roma St. The facilities are excellent, although it's still very much a youth hostel. The cost for YHA members is $13 per person in a four- to six-bed dorm, or $32 for a twin room. Non-members pay a once-only temporary membership fee of $3 plus an extra $1 on the nightly rates. The hostel has a restaurant which serves good breakfasts, and dinner for $6.50.

Banana Benders Backpackers (☎ 367 1157) is a short walk north, on the corner of Petrie Terrace and Jessie St. The outside is painted bright yellow and blue, so you can't miss it. This is a small place with the usual facilities, and it has good views over to the west. Dorm beds are $12, doubles $28. The only hassle here is that Petrie Terrace can get noisy during peak hours.

Down the side street past Banana Benders is the small *Aussie Way Backpackers* (☎ 369 0711) at 34 Cricket St. It's in a rambling old house in a residential area. Each four-bed dorm has its own kitchenette, and a bed costs $12.

Moving west of the city, the long-running *Backpackers Paddington* (☎ 368 1047) is at 175 Given Terrace, the continuation of

QUEENSLAND

Caxton St. This is a very relaxed, old-style hostel, with a cosy atmosphere, though it's a bit rough around the edges these days. Dorm beds are $12, doubles $28.

Fortitude Valley & New Farm The YHA-associated *Balmoral House* (☎ 252 1397), at 33 Amelia St in Fortitude Valley, is a short walk from the Brunswick St train station. The building has recently been renovated and the facilities are excellent. This place is clean, modern and quiet, but it's not the place to stay if you're planning to party, as it's not really a backpackers' place. A bed in a three- or four-bed dorm costs $13, singles/doubles with shared bathrooms cost $28/32, and rooms with private bathrooms cost $45, or $48 for four.

Moving east into New Farm, you'll find four more hostels in and around Brunswick St. *Pete's Place* (☎ 254 1984) at 515 Brunswick St is in a rambling old timber house with a somewhat chequered history. It has adequate facilities and is quite clean and charges $12 for a dorm bed and $24 for a double.

A bit further along is the *Globe Trekkers Hostel* (☎ 358 1251) at 35 Balfour St. This is a friendly and quiet hostel in a renovated house, and the good atmosphere and small size make it quite popular. Dorm beds are $12.

The *Homestead* (☎ 358 3538), at 57 Annie St, has recently had a new section built at the rear. It's a large, modern place with good facilities including a small pool and various games. A bed in a six- or eight-bed dorm costs $12; doubles cost $28, or $39 with a private bathroom.

Further along Annie St, at No 95, is *Atoa House* (☎ 358 4507), a small travellers' hostel. A bed in a four-bunk self-contained dorm costs $13; singles/doubles cost $22/28; and you can camp in the back yard for $6.50.

South Brisbane & West End The *Sly Fox* (☎ 844 0022), on the corner of Melbourne and Hope Sts in South Brisbane, is a relaxed place with plenty of action; the staff organise regular nights out. It's in the top three storeys

of a pub and has good facilities including a rooftop sundeck and pool tables, although the kitchen is very small. The pub downstairs has live music, so it can be noisy. Dorm beds cost $12, twin rooms $28, and a double with a brass bed and private bathroom $35.

The *Somewhere to Stay* hostel (☎ 846 2858), at 45 Brighton Rd in the West End, is the biggest and one of the best in the city. It's one of the newer places, with a wide range of accommodation, although because of its size it can seem a bit impersonal. There's a pool, a garden and an outdoor area. Dorm beds range from $10 to $14, the more expensive ones having a TV, fridge, private bathroom and balcony. Single rooms cost $20 to $25, doubles $28 to $35, and doubles/twins with TV, fridge and private bathroom $45. The hostel runs a regular bus service to the transit centre, or you can get there on bus No 178 from Adelaide St, opposite Anzac Square.

A short distance away is the family-run *Durham Villa* (☎ 844 6853) at 17 Laura St. It's a smaller hostel and also has a pool and spacious gardens; dorm beds are $12, and singles/doubles cost $24/26.

The *Swagman's Rest* (☎ 844 9956) at 145 Vulture St is another West End option. It's on a busy road but has reasonably good facilities including access to a pool and regular barbecues. Dorm beds cost $10, twins/doubles $25.

Kangaroo Point Just over the Story Bridge from Fortitude Valley is *Backpackers Brisbane Central* (☎ 891 1434), in a de-licensed section of the Story Bridge Hotel at 200 Main St. This place has recently been renovated and has dorm beds from $11.

Further from the centre in a quiet suburban street is *Courtney Place Backpackers* (☎ 89 5166) at 50 Geelong St. This family-run place is in a two-storey house built many years ago by a dentist with 18 children! A bed in a four- or eight-bed dorm costs $12 doubles are $30, and each bed has its own security locker. This place has an in-house travel agent. It also has a couple of good self-contained two-bedroom flats down the road, which cost $45 a double or $55 a triple

Hotels & Motels Brisbane's range of centrally located hotel, motel and unit accommodation includes the following:

City *Annie's Shandon Inn* (☎ 831 8684), at 405 Upper Edward St, is a charming and friendly small hotel. It's a 10-minute walk uphill from the city centre. Singles/doubles are $36/46 including a light breakfast and free tea and coffee throughout the day – there are also a few rooms with private bathroom for $46/56. The hotel has laundry facilities, a TV room and a small car park at the rear.

Another good option in the same area is the *Dorchester Inn* (☎ 831 2967) at 484 Upper Edward St. This place has been fully renovated and has spacious units with modern cooking facilities and private bathrooms from $55/65 for singles/doubles, and four-bed units for $85.

The *Yale Inner-City Inn* (☎ 832 1663), next to Annie's at 413 Upper Edward St, has singles/doubles at $32/42 and a few rooms with private bathrooms at $52. The tariff includes a light breakfast. Rooms are small and the facilities are quite old, but it's clean and has a laundry, TV room and car park.

There are several motels around the corner in Wickham Terrace, some decently priced. The *Astor Motel* (☎ 831 9522), at No 193, has good air-con singles/doubles with private bathrooms from $45/50. Rooms have tea- and coffee-making facilities and breakfast is available.

Marrs Townhouse (☎ 831 5388), at 391 Wickham Terrace, has singles/doubles with shared bathrooms for $40/50, or from $55/65 with private bathrooms. The management is helpful and there are good views, but the rooms facing the road can be noisy.

Back at No 333, the budget *Soho Club Motel* (☎ 831 7722) charges $46/49 for singles/doubles.

Another very good option if you're looking for somewhere self-contained is *Spring Hill Terraces* (☎ 854 1048) at 260 Water St in Spring Hill, about 1.5 km north of the city centre. It's an attractive, modern place and offers two-bedroom apartments with all the mod-cons for $68 a double, plus $6 for each additional person. There are also good budget rooms at $40 a single/double.

Suburbs Just past Breakfast Creek on the way to the airport, the *Kingsford Hall Private Hotel* (☎ 862 1317), at 144 Kingsford Smith Drive in Hamilton (on the corner of Cooksley St), charges $34/37 for singles/doubles with shared bathroom, or $14 for backpackers in a twin room. It has a guest kitchen.

If you're looking for a bit of affordable luxury, the *Powerhouse Hotel* (☎ 862 1800), nearby and also on Kingsford Smith Drive, is a top-class boutique hotel. Double rooms start from $160 on weekdays, but on weekends the rate drops to $95 which is very good value for this standard of accommodation.

There's a string of motels in Kangaroo Point along Main St (the continuation of the Story Bridge). One of the best is the *Ryan Lodge Motel* (☎ 391 1011) at 269 Main St, which has singles/doubles from $65/75. Further south are a couple of cheaper options: the *Kangaroo Motel* (☎ 391 1145), at 624 Main St, and the *Southern Cross Motel* (☎ 391 2881), at 721 Main St, both have budget rooms for $40/45.

In Highgate Hill, about two km south of the city centre, the *Ambassador Brisbane Motel* (☎ 844 5661) at 180 Gladstone Rd has rooms at $49/55.

Colleges *International House* (☎ 870 9593) at 5 Rock St, St Lucia, offers B&B for $39/65 during the university vacation periods. Other colleges offer similar deals.

Places to Eat
Brisbane's restaurant and cafe scene has blossomed in recent years, and you'll find that there's no shortage of good eateries in the city and surrounding areas. Many of these places have taken advantage of the balmy climate and provide outdoor eating areas.

Apart from the city centre, the major clusters of eateries are in Paddington, Fortitude Valley and New Farm, on the South Bank and in the West End.

QUEENSLAND

City You'll find a bit of everything around the central area, including plenty of cafes and fast-food places, and a few good restaurants, especially in the Riverside Centre and Eagle St Pier complexes.

Queen St Mall teems with possibilities. *Jo Jo's*, a very popular food centre upstairs at 130 Queen St, has Greek/Mediterranean, Thai, European and Middle Eastern counters, and a bar. Tables are scattered about and prices range from $8 to $13. It's open daily until midnight. There are more possibilities in the ritzy *Myer Centre* on the mall. The lower level has a number of fast-food outlets and sandwich bars.

A Kabab, just around the corner from the mall at 227 Albert St, makes very good kebabs – beef, lamb, chicken, felafel or salad – from $3.30 to $4.20.

Jimmy's on the Mall has three excellent open-air, licensed cafes – one at the Edward St end of the mall, one in the middle (both open 24 hours) and the other near the Albert St corner. Coffee is expensive but there are plenty of reasonably priced snacks, meals and desserts.

Towards the Edward St end of the mall, on the 3rd level of the Wintergarden shopping complex, the *New Orleans Restaurant*, an up-market international food hall, is open from 10 am until 12.30 am (2 am on weekends). Most meals cost upwards of $10 and often there's live music.

For a good, cheap vegetarian feed, *Govinda's Restaurant*, upstairs at 99 Elizabeth St, offers filling all-you-can-eat meals for $5. It's run by the Hare Krishnas, and opens weekdays for lunch and Friday and Sunday for dinner. Nearby is *Parrots*, a stylish, licensed gourmet burger restaurant, open daily from 11.30 am to 11 pm. McDonald's certainly wouldn't recognise the fare that's dished up in this popular place. The various burgers cost from $8.50 to $10.50. *Sennari*, upstairs at 85 Elizabeth St, serves good Japanese food with mains from $12 to $18, set menus from $25 and a four-course lunch for $17.

The *Chill Bar*, a very hip and stylish basement bar on the corner of Edward and Mary Sts, has good music, pasta for $8 and other mains around $13.

The busy *Cafe d'Art*, in the basement of the Metro Arts building at 109 Edward St, is open daily for breakfast, lunch and dinner and offers good, cheap, wholesome food. The *Port Office Hotel* at 38 Edward St, on the Margaret St corner, is popular with office workers for lunch on weekdays, and meals range from $6 to $13.

The Riverside Centre, at the north-eastern end of Elizabeth St, has several restaurants that enjoy terrific river views, including the award-winning *Michael's* (☎ 832 5522), one of Brisbane's best restaurants. Main meals are in the $21 to $26 range. Next door, *Marco's* is a classy Italian bistro with mains from $15 to $18. For an inexpensive lunch try *On the Deck*, another international food hall with a good range of choices. It's in the next building to the south.

Further south again, the Eagle St Pier complex also has several excellent restaurants, including *Compadre's Bar & Grill* up on the 1st floor. It's a lively Mexican restaurant with a fun atmosphere and good food, with mains from $13 to $18. *Il Centro* (☎ 221 6090) is one of Brisbane's best and most impressive Italian restaurants, and has main courses from $15 to $19.

South Bank There are about a dozen restaurants and cafes in the South Bank Parklands, as well as the usual fast-food outlets. *Captain Snapper*, a very large seafood and steak restaurant just south of the Stanley St Plaza, has a good selection of meals at around $5 to $6, and for another $2.95 you can attack the all-you-can-eat salad and fresh-fruit bar. Other main meals range up to around $15, and it also has a takeaway section with tables by the canal.

The Riverside Restaurants building, on the riverfront near the Gondwana Rainforest Sanctuary, houses three places. *Cafe San Marco* is a casual cafe that serves everything from sandwiches to sirloin steaks, but the coffee is expensive. Next door, the *Wang Dynasty* restaurant serves Thai, Malaysian and Chinese food, which includes a range of kangaroo and crocodile meat dishes. It has a $7.50 lunch special. Upstairs, *Io Ti Amo* is a stylish Italian restaurant with main meals in the $15 to $18 range.

Sirocco, in the Waterway Cafes complex, is a large Mediterranean cafe/restaurant with Spanish, Italian and Greek food, with main meals around $15. On the Boardwalk, *Ned Kelly's* bush-tucker restaurant has outdoor tables, a bar and live music on weekend afternoons and at night in the warm weather.

One of the best value eateries on the riverfront is the simple *Riverfront Cafe* at the State Library. It has great rolls and sandwiches, coffee and snacks, and the tables on the outdoor courtyard overlook the river.

Spring Hill The *Spring Hill Hotel*, on the corner of Upper Edward and Leichhardt Sts, has good, cheap pub food ($2.50 lunches!) and a backyard barbecue.

At 48 Leichhardt St, *Tonton's* (☎ 831 1363) is highly recommended. Set in a wonderfully converted chapel, it's bright and spacious and has great French food and service to match. Mains are around $16. *Harold's Cafe*, at 466 Boundary St, has a good gourmet takeaway section, open from 10 am to 10 pm Monday to Saturday. In the restaurant section, meals start at $12.

Fortitude Valley Known simply as the Valley, this is one of Brisbane's liveliest and most exotic inner suburbs, and has a fascinating blend of residents; punks and drunks, yuppies and backpackers, prostitutes and transvestites. It also has plenty of interesting cafes and restaurants around Brunswick, Ann and Wickham Sts. (At night it's quite a rough area, so stick to the main streets and avoid walking alone.)

Duncan St, between Ann and Wickham Sts, has been transformed into Brisbane's Chinatown and there are lots of Chinese, Thai, Vietnamese and Korean restaurants in the area. The excellent *Enjoy Inn*, on the corner of Wickham and Duncan Sts, is open daily until midnight. It's quite up-market but its banquets (around $16.50 to $20) are a bargain. A good cheaper option is the *Uni-*

versal Noodle Restaurant at 145 Wickham St. It's not flash but has plenty of dishes for $5 and $6. Opposite Duncan St at 194 Wickham St, the *Vietnamese Restaurant* is also pretty basic but very popular, with most main dishes between $7 and $9. The *Seoul Restaurant*, at 178 Wickham St, serves fairly authentic Korean dishes ranging from $6 to $10.

The popular *Home Made Chinese Meal Kitchen*, at 257 Wickham St, has good food at moderate prices; main meals are mostly from $7 to $9, with seafood dishes around $12. *Sala Thai*, across the road at No 262, is a good, reasonably priced Thai restaurant with main meals from $10 to $16.

Brunswick St has plenty of good choices on either side of the Ann St corner and many of them have tables outside on the footpath. The *Rum Boogie Bar & Cafe* in Brunswick St Mall is very popular and has gourmet pizzas from $10 and other mains around $15. Opposite, the *Cosmopolitan Cafe* has inexpensive pastas, sandwiches, snacks and coffee. Up the road at 360 Brunswick St, *Cafe Europe* is a fun and hectic French cafe/restaurant with good pastas for $9 and other mains from $13 to $15. The popular *Giardinetto's*, next door at No 366, is a small, pleasant Italian place, which does pastas and pizzas for $10 to $12 and other Italian dishes for around $15. You can eat indoors or outside, and it's open for lunch and dinner. The buffet dinner for $12.50 on Sunday nights is very good value. Around the corner at 683 Ann St, the atmosphere is equally pleasant in *Lucky's Trattoria*, another good Italian restaurant with similar prices.

New Farm A bit further down Brunswick St at No 630, *Baan Thai* is a reasonably priced Thai restaurant, with mains between $8 and $12. At *Famish*, at No 640, you can get a very substantial hot roast meal – pork, chicken, lamb or beef with vegies – for around $10. *Cafe Lunar* at No 681 is a good deli with focaccias, salads and delicious cakes; it's open day and night. Further on at No 878, *Cafe Le Mer* is an inexpensive place that does burgers, pasta and fish & chips.

Breakfast Creek At the Breakfast Creek Wharf there's a riverfront boardwalk with several restaurants overlooking the river, including a *Taco Bill* Mexican restaurant and the *Breakfast Creek Wharf* seafood restaurant, which has very good food with mains around $15 to $19.

Across the river, the famous *Breakfast Creek Hotel*, a great rambling building dating from 1889, is a real Brisbane institution. It's long been a Labor Party and trade-union hang-out. In the public bar, the beer is still drawn from a wooden keg. The pub's *Spanish Garden Steak House* is renowned for its steaks, and a huge feed will set you back between $12.50 and $18.

Paddington Paddington also has plenty of interesting cafes, restaurants, pubs and bars, mostly scattered along the winding route of Caxton St/Given Terrace.

The *Sultan's Kitchen* (☎ 368 2194), at 163 Given Terrace, is an excellent Indian restaurant with great curries. It's open for lunch and dinner daily (except Saturday lunch), but it's pretty popular so book on weekends. The lunch-time smorgasbord is $12.95, and at dinner mains are around $14.

Masakan Indonesia is a reasonably priced Indonesian restaurant at 215 Given Terrace. Rice, noodle and vegetarian dishes are around $8 and seafood and meat dishes are from $11 to $13.

Further west along Given Terrace, at No 235, the *Red Chair Cafe* has a good atmosphere. It does excellent gourmet burgers ($9 to $12), plus pies, pastries, pastas and sandwiches.

A little further on, at No 267, is the very popular *King Tut's Wah Wah Hut*. This outdoor cafe is a great spot for breakfast, lunch or dinner, and has good salads, pastas, burgers, juices and sandwiches, all reasonably priced.

West End The West End is another good eating area, with Vietnamese, Italian and Lebanese restaurants and some good cafes. Boundary St, from the roundabout down to Vulture St, is an interesting little shopping centre, with good delis, fruit shops, cafes, a health-food shop, and a couple of good second-hand bookshops around the corner in Vulture St.

The *Three Monkeys Coffee House*, at 58 Mollison St near the Melbourne and Boundary Sts roundabout, is a great place – if you can get in! It's relaxed and casual and has good coffee, amazing cakes and a wide range of inexpensive meals. It opens daily from 10.30 am until midnight.

Qan Heng's, at 151 Boundary St, is very popular and inexpensive, with good Chinese and Vietnamese meals from $5.50 to $9. Further down at No 171, *Wholly Munchies* is a great wholefoods cafe and takeaway, with healthy sandwiches, juices and home-cooked goodies. It's open during the day only. *Cafe Tempo*, at No 181, is a busy and trendy Italian cafe with good coffee and excellent pastas from $6.50 to $8.50. It also has gourmet pizzas and focaccias, and is open day and night.

Around the corner at 88 Vulture St is *King Ahiram's*, a Lebanese place with good cheap takeaways like chicken or felafel rolls from $2.50 to $3. There's also an eat-in section, with mains from $7.50 to $10 and a banquet menu for $15.

On the corner of Melbourne and Edmondstone Sts in South Brisbane, *Squirrels* is a good vegetarian restaurant open daily for lunch and dinner. From the buffet, a small plateful is $7.90, a large one $9.90. It also has burgers, pies and pastries, as well as $8 all-you-can-eat nights – pasta on Thursdays and curries on Sundays.

Entertainment

The Courier Mail has daily arts and entertainment listings, and a 'What's On In Town' section each Thursday. For gig guides, concert calendars and info on pubs, clubs and music, see the free entertainment papers *Time Off* and *Rave*.

Pubs & Live Music Brisbane's rock pubs generally stay open until midnight, or 1 am on the weekends; cover charges for local bands are around $5 and for touring bands you can pay up to $15.

Probably the best live-music venue in the city is *Metropolis*, in the basement of the Myer Centre in the Queen St Mall, which features both local and international bands. Other good live-music venues in the city include the *Big Kahuna*, in the Majestic Hotel on the corner of George and Turbot Sts (beach-party surf scene and live bands most nights); *Club Afro Carib*, at the Brisbane Tavern on the corner of Wharf and Ann Sts (good Black African music, both local and international); the *Port Office Hotel*, on the corner of Edward and Margaret Sts (bands on Friday and Saturday nights and Sunday afternoons); and the *City Gardens Club* at the Queensland University of Technology in George St (a good live venue, and very good value if you have a student card). Many of the nightclubs also feature live bands (see below).

Quite a few pubs now put on special nights for backpackers, with drinking competitions, giveaways, cheap drinks and music. The *Brunswick Hotel*, in Brunswick St in New Farm, has backpacker nights on Tuesday and Friday. The *Story Bridge Hotel*, at 200 Main St in Kangaroo Point, is big on a Monday with Monday Madness – and it usually lives up to its name. It has live music most other nights of the week and jazz on Sunday afternoons. The *Plough Inn* and the *Ship Inn*, both at South Bank, are also popular and offer discounted drinks.

Other good rock pubs include *St Paul's Tavern*, on the corner of Leichhardt and Wharf Sts in Spring Hill (live alternative music); the *Pineapple Hotel* at 706 Main St in Kangaroo Point (with bands most nights); and *Jahmeyka*, at the Sly Fox Hotel in Melbourne St, South Brisbane (a weekly reggae and soul venue). *Dooley's Hotel*, on the corner of Brunswick and McLachlan Sts in Fortitude Valley, is a large Irish pub that has live music from Wednesday to Sunday nights. The upstairs bar has six pool tables. Three popular pubs in Paddington are the *Barracks Hotel*, on the corner of Petrie Terrace and Caxton St (live bands on week-

ends); the *Caxton Hotel*, further east along Caxton St (a large disco and beer garden, with bands on Saturday nights); and the *Paddo Tavern*, about a km further east on Given Terrace (a huge western-style saloon bar, with live music from Thursday to Saturday).

Nightclubs Brisbane has a lively nightclub scene, especially if you know where to look. The mainstream clubs are mostly based in and around the city, and the alternative scene is centred in Fortitude Valley. Most clubs stay open until 3 am, some until 5 am; cover charges vary from around $4 to $8.

The *Underground*, in the impressively converted former police barracks on Petrie Terrace in Paddington, is Brisbane's most popular mainstream nightclub. City nightclubs include *Club LQ's*, in Albert St just off the mall (more a disco than a nightclub); *Her Majesty's Bar* in the basement of the Hilton Hotel on Queen St (live local music); *Transformers*, at 127 Charlotte St (a stylish, more alternative club and band venue); *Mass*, in the Lands Office Hotel on the corner of George and Mary Sts (alternative/underground); and *Someplace Else* in the Sheraton Hotel at 249 Turbot St (mainstream).

Brisbane's alternative scene is based in the Valley, and there are some fairly wild clubs here including *Site*, at 201 Brunswick St, which is the biggest dance venue and often has dance parties; the *Beat*, at 677 Ann St, which has cheap drinks and opens until after sunrise but can be rough; and *Studio 694*, at 694 Ann St.

Jazz & Blues The *Jazz & Blues Club*, on the ground floor of the Travelodge in Roma St in the city, is the city's major jazz and soul venue and has good local and international acts. The *Brisbane Jazz Club*, at 1 Annie St, Kangaroo Point, is where the jazz purists head, and has live jazz most nights. For a Sunday afternoon jazz fix, check out the *Brunswick St Mall* or the *Story Bridge Hotel*.

The *Orient Hotel*, at the top end of Ann St in the city, has a long rock & roll history but is now a blues venue. The *Gabba Hotel* in

Woolloongabba has three blues bands on Sunday afternoons for $2, which includes lunch.

Theatre The *Performing Arts Complex*, in the Queensland Cultural Centre in South Brisbane, has a constant flow of events in its three venues, including concerts, plays, dance performances and film screenings.

Brisbane's other main theatres include the *Suncorp Piazza* at South Bank (with regular concerts and performances, many of them free); the *Rialto*, at 59 Hardgrave Rd, West End (with an interesting array of concerts, gigs and comedy shows); *Metro Arts*, at 109 Edward St in the city (community arts centre and 'alternative' theatre/dance); and the *Brisbane Arts Theatre*, at 210 Petrie Terrace (amateur productions). Brisbane's main professional theatre companies are *La Boite*, based at 57 Hale St in the city, and the *Queensland Theatre Company*, based at the Cultural Centre.

Cinemas There are plenty of mainstream cinemas in the city centre. The *Village Twin* in Brunswick St, New Farm, has $4 nights on Tuesdays, Wednesdays and Thursdays.

For alternative/art-house cinema, you have three choices: the *Schonell* (☎ 371 1879), at the University of Queensland in St Lucia; the *Classic* (☎ 393 1066), at 963 Stanley St, East Brisbane; and the *Metro Arts Cinema* (☎ 221 3505), at 109 Edward St.

Comedy *Snug Harbour* (☎ 391 2045), at the Dockside complex in Kangaroo Point, is one of Brisbane's best intimate venues and has regular stand-up comedy and karaoke nights. *Crazies* (☎ 369 0555), on the corner of Caxton and Judge Sts in Paddington, is a good comedy theatre-restaurant.

Spectator Sports You can see interstate cricket matches and international Test cricket at the Brisbane Cricket Ground (the Gabba) in Woolloongabba, just south of Kangaroo Point. Rugby league is the big winter spectator sport. Local heroes Brisbane Broncos play their home games at the ANZ/QE2 Stadium in Upper Mt Gravatt. Brisbane also has an Australian Rules football club, the Brisbane Bears, based at the Gabba. Like every other town and city in Australia, Brisbane has horse racing; the major tracks are at Doomben and Eagle Farm.

Getting There & Away

Arriving in and leaving Brisbane has been simplified by the transit centre on Roma St, about half a km west of the central King George Square. The transit centre is the main terminus and booking point for all long-distance buses and trains, as well as the airport bus. The centre has shops, banks, a post office, and plenty of places to eat and drink. There's also a foreign exchange counter, open on weekdays from 7.30 am to 9.30 am and on Saturdays from 8 am to 1 pm, and a tourist information office on level 2. Left-luggage lockers are on level 3: they cost $2 but you have to remove your gear by 9 pm each day.

Air There are frequent Ansett and Qantas flights from the southern capitals and north to the main Queensland centres like Rockhampton, Mackay, Townsville and Cairns. Eastwest also flies from Sydney and Cairns. Air NSW flies daily from Sydney.

Standard one-way fares include Sydney ($254), Melbourne ($371), Adelaide ($470), Darwin ($595) and Perth ($620). Within Queensland, one-way fares include Townsville ($319), Rockhampton ($215), Mackay ($274), Cairns ($379) and Mt Isa (Ansett only – $393).

There are numerous connections to smaller centres by smaller airlines, which include Eastwest, Air NSW, Oxley, Hazelton and Sunstate Airlines. The little outback airline Flight West goes to Roma ($93 one way), Charleville ($125), Quilpie and Barcaldine ($154), Blackall ($147), Longreach ($167), Winton and Windorah ($187) and Birdsville ($216).

Brisbane is also a busy international arrival and departure point with frequent flights to Asia, Europe, the Pacific islands, North America, New Zealand and Papua New Guinea.

Airline booking numbers include Qantas, Airlink and Sunstate (☎ 13 1313); Ansett, Skywest, Oxley and Hazelton (☎ 13 1300); Eastwest (☎ 13 1711); and Flight West (☎ 229 1177).

Bus The major bus companies all have booking offices at the Brisbane transit centre. Their booking numbers and opening hours are: Greyhound Pioneer (☎ 13 2030), open 6 am to 8 pm daily; McCafferty's (☎ 236 3033), open 5.30 am to 8.30 pm daily; and Kirklands (☎ 236 4444), Sunshine Coast (☎ 236 1901), Border Coaches (☎ 236 4189) and Baxway (☎ 236 4163), all open 7 am to 6 pm. Dial-a-Coach (☎ 221 2225), a bus-fare broker, is also worth calling.

Greyhound Pioneer and McCafferty's both run from Sydney to Brisbane. You can go inland via the New England Highway, or along the coast via the Pacific Highway; both ways take 15 to 16 hours. The usual fare is around $60, but Border Coaches does the inland route for $48 for YHA members and backpackers.

Between Brisbane and Melbourne, the most direct route is the Newell Highway which takes around 24 hours. Again, Greyhound Pioneer and McCafferty's follow this route daily. The fare between Brisbane and Melbourne is $122.

Between Adelaide and Brisbane, Greyhound Pioneer has a direct trip which takes around 29 hours; the fare is $146. McCafferty's can get you there via either Sydney or Melbourne; it takes longer, but it's also a little cheaper.

Border Coaches do a $10 backpackers' fare to Surfers Paradise and Coolangatta, and Baxter has a similar deal to Byron Bay for $18.

North to Cairns, Greyhound Pioneer and McCafferty's run five buses a day. The approximate fares and journey times to places along the coast are as follows:

Destination	Time	Cost
Noosa Heads	3 hours	$15
Hervey Bay	4 hours	$35
Rockhampton	9 hours	$65
Mackay	13 hours	$90
Townsville	19 hours	$118
Cairns	24 hours	$133

McCafferty's and Greyhound Pioneer also run daily services to the Northern Territory via Longreach (17 hours, $85) and Mt Isa (24 hours, $130).

Train – interstate You can reach Brisbane by rail from Sydney and continue north to Cairns or inland to Roma and Charleville. The daily XPT takes 14 hours between Sydney and Brisbane. Fares are $137 in 1st class, $95 in economy, and sleepers are an extra $80 in each class.

A Caper (Customer Advance Purchase Excursion Rail) ticket, which you have to buy at least seven days in advance, cuts about 30% off the price. As on all major interstate trains, you can break the journey anywhere provided you arrange it in advance and complete the journey within a specified period of time – two months with a one-way ticket or six months with a return ticket.

Train – within Queensland North from Brisbane, the Spirit of Capricorn runs the 639 km to Rockhampton daily (9½ hours; $103 1st class, $64 economy). The Capricornian covers the same route twice a week, but travels through the night. Sleepers cost an extra $50 in 1st class, $30 in economy.

The Sunlander departs three days a week for the 1631-km journey to Cairns (33 hours; $234 1st-class sleeper, $153 economy sleeper, $123 economy seat), via Mackay (18 hours; $192/125/95), and Townsville (26 hours; $218/152/112).

On Sundays only, a motorail service (the Queenslander) runs to Cairns. Passengers travelling 1st class have a special bar, and the cost of sleeping berths and all meals is included in the fare, which is nearly twice the usual 1st-class fare. You can travel economy on the Queenslander but there are no

QUEENSLAND

economy-class sleepers. To Mackay, the 1st-class/economy fares are $377/95; to Townsville $433/112; and to Cairns $489/123.

The Westlander runs on the inland route to Roma, Charleville and Cunnamulla twice a week.

Main-line departures from Brisbane leave from the Brisbane transit centre. For reservations, telephone ☎ 13 2232, or call into the Railway Travel Centre at Central Station, on the corner of Ann and Edward Sts.

Car Rental If you have a car, beware of the two-hour parking limit in the city and inner suburbs – there are no signs, and the parking inspectors are merciless!

The big rental firms have offices in Brisbane and there are a number of smaller operators, including Cut Rate Rentals (☎ 854 1809), Crown Rent a Car (☎ 854 1848), Dollar (☎ 854 1848), Low Price Hire Cars (☎ 891 1799), Penny Wise (☎ 252 3333), Dam Cheap (☎ 252 1177) and National (☎ 854 1499). Some companies do one-way rentals to Cairns and southern capitals, depending on availability, the season, and the hire period – it's best to ring around and haggle.

You can hire 4WDs from around $100 a day, usually with a three-day minimum. Operators include 4WD Hire Service (☎ 357 9077) and Allterrain (☎ 257 1101).

Getting Around
For bus, train and ferry transport information, ring the Trans-Info Service on ☎ 13 1230; it operates daily from 6 am to 10 pm. The Public Transport Information Centre in Central Station also covers local trains, ferries and buses. It's open Monday to Friday from 8.15 am to 4.30 pm.

To/From the Airport Brisbane's Eagle Farm Airport is north-east of the city, with the international terminal 13 km from the centre and the domestic terminal 17 km away. Coachtrans (☎ 236 1000) runs a shuttle bus from the transit centre to both terminals and back. Services run daily at 5, 6, 6.30 and 7 am, then every 20 minutes till 4 pm, then

every half-hour till 8.30 pm. The buses will also stop at various points in the city centre and Fortitude Valley. The fare is $5.40. There are also a few daily direct buses between the airport and the Gold and Sunshine coasts.

A taxi to the centre costs about $12 from the international terminal, $15 from the domestic. Avis, Budget, Hertz and Thrifty have car-rental desks at the airport.

Bus There is a Bus info centre in the underground bus station beneath the Myer Centre in the Queen St Mall; it opens on weekdays from 8.30 am to 5 pm.

In addition to the normal city buses, there are Cityxpress services, which run between the suburbs and the centre, and Rockets, which are fast peak-hour commuter buses. From the transit centre, you need to walk into the city centre to pick up some buses. Most above-ground bus stops in the city are colour coded to help you find the right one. The underground bus station beneath the Myer Centre is used mainly by Cityxpresses and buses to and from the south of the city. There is a map of the station, above ground in the mall on the corner of Queen and Albert Sts.

In the city centre, buses cost just 50c a trip. Other fares are on a zone system costing $1, $1.60, $2.20 or $2.60 for zones 1, 2, 3 or 4 respectively. Special deals include the unlimited-travel Day Rover ($5.50 from newsagents or shops with a yellow 'fare deal' sign in their window). The RoverLink is a one-day ticket providing unlimited travel on any buses or trains for $8. There are also cheaper off-peak ticket deals.

Buses run every 10 to 20 minutes Monday to Friday till about 6 pm, and on Saturday mornings. Services are less frequent on weekday evenings, Saturday afternoons and evenings, and Sundays. Buses stop at 7 pm on Sundays, and on other days at 11 pm. City Circle bus No 333 does a clockwise loop round the area along George, Adelaide, Wharf, Eagle, Mary, Albert and Alice Sts every five minutes until 5.45 pm Monday to Friday.

Useful buses from the city centre include Nos 177 and 178 to Fortitude Valley and

New Farm (from the brown stops on Adelaide St between King George Square and Edward St). Bardon bus No 144 to Paddington leaves from the red stops opposite the transit centre or from outside the Coles store on Adelaide St.

Bus Nos 160, 180 and 190 to Fortitude Valley, Newstead House and Breakfast Creek leave from the yellow stops on Edward St between Adelaide and Queen Sts. Bus No 177 to West End leaves from the brown stop on Edward St, opposite Anzac Square.

Bayside Buslines (☎ 245 3333) run between Brisbane and the southern Bayside (Capalaba Park, Wellington Point, Cleveland, Koala Park and Redland Bay). Hornibrook Bus Lines (☎ 284 1622) run between Brisbane and the northern Bayside (Sandgate, Clontarf, Redcliffe and Scarborough).

Train The fast Citytrain network has seven lines, out to Ipswich, Beenleigh and Cleveland in the south and Pinkenba, Shorncliffe, Caboolture and Ferny Grove in the north. You can buy Day Rover tickets ($8.50) a day ahead, from any station. These give you unlimited train travel for one day (after 9 am on weekdays).

All trains go through Roma St, Central and Brunswick St stations, and a journey in the city central area is $1.20.

Boat Brisbane has a fast, efficient ferry service along and across the Brisbane River. Cross-river ferries cost $1 one way and generally run every 10 to 15 minutes from around dawn until after 11 pm Monday to Saturday; there are shorter hours on Sunday. You can take a bicycle on the ferry for free (60c during peak hours).

The most central ferry stops are the Riverside Centre/Eagle St Pier; Edward St (on the corner of the Botanic Gardens); Thornton St, Holman St and Dockside, all on Kangaroo Point; the South Bank Parklands; the River Plaza Hotel in South Brisbane; the QUT Gardens Point; and New Farm. Maps

of the ferry routes are available at all the stops, as well as from information centres.

Bicycle A good way to spend a day is to ride the riverside bicycle track from the city Botanic Gardens out to the University of Queensland. It's about seven km one way: you can stop for a beer at the Regatta pub in Toowong, use the cheap swimming pool or hire a tennis court at the university, and have a meal in one of the reasonably priced eateries in Toowong on the way back.

At 87 Albert St, Brisbane Bicycle Sales (☎ 229 2433) hire mountain bikes for $9 an hour or $20 a day; it's open daily.

Moreton Bay

Moreton Bay, at the mouth of the Brisbane River, is said to have 365 islands. The larger islands shelter a long stretch of coast: South Stradbroke Island is only just north of the Gold Coast, while Bribie Island is only just south of the Sunshine Coast. In between are North Stradbroke and Moreton islands.

THE BAYSIDE
Situated 35 km north of Brisbane is **Redcliffe**, the first White settlement in Queensland. The Aborigines called the place Humpybong or 'Dead Houses' and the name is still applied to the peninsula. Redcliffe is now an outer suburb of Brisbane and a popular retirement place. South of Redcliffe, **Sandgate** is another long-running seaside resort, now more of an outer suburb.

Coastal towns south of the Brisbane River mouth include **Wynnum**, **Ormiston**, **Cleveland** and **Redland Bay**. Cleveland is the main access point for North Stradbroke Island. The Redland Bay area is a fertile market garden for Brisbane and a Strawberry Festival is held on the first weekend in September. There's an 1864 lighthouse at Cleveland Point and the 1853 Cleveland Courthouse is now a restaurant.

Ormiston House in Wellington St, Ormiston, is a very fine home built in 1862

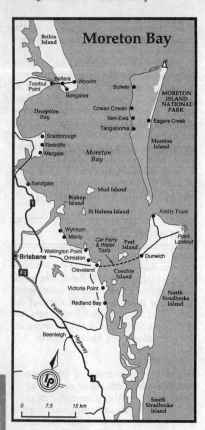

Moreton Bay

Bribie Island

Toorbul Point
Bellara
Bongaree
Woorim
Bulwer

Deception Bay

Cowan Cowan
Ben-Ewa
Tangalooma

MORETON ISLAND NATIONAL PARK

Eagers Creek

Moreton Island

Scarborough
Redcliffe
Margate

Moreton Bay

Sandgate

Mud Island

Bishop Island
St Helena Island

Amity Point

Wynnum
Manly

Car Ferry & Water Taxis
Peel Island

Point Lookout

Brisbane
Wellington Point
Ormiston
Cleveland
Coochie Island
Dunwich

Victoria Point

North Stradbroke Island

Redland Bay

Beenleigh
Pacific
Highway

South Stradbroke Island

0 7.5 15 km

and open for inspection Sunday afternoons between March and November. The first commercially grown sugar cane in Queensland came from this site. Whepstead on Main Rd, Wellington Point, is another early home, built in 1874; it's now a restaurant.

NORTH STRADBROKE ISLAND
(population 2290)
Until 1896, the two Stradbroke islands were one but in that year a storm cut the sand spit joining the two at Jumpinpin. Today, South Stradbroke is virtually uninhabited but it's a popular day trip from the Gold Coast.

North Stradbroke is the larger island and it has a permanent population. Although it's a popular escape from Brisbane it's still relatively unspoilt (although the Christmas and Easter holidays can get pretty hectic). 'Straddie' is a sand island, and despite the sand-mining operations in the south, there's plenty of vegetation and beautiful scenery in the north.

In 1828, Dunwich was established on the west coast of the island as a quarantine station for immigrants but in 1850 a ship brought cholera and the cemetery tells the sad story of the 28 victims of the outbreak that followed. Dunwich, Amity Point and Point Lookout, the three small centres on the island, are all in the north and connected by paved roads. Most of the southern part of the island is closed to visitors due to ongoing sand mining; the only road into this swampy, more remote area is a private mining company road.

Activities
Straddie's best beaches are around Point Lookout, where there's a series of points and bays around the headland, and then the endless white sand stretch of Main Beach. There are some excellent surfing breaks here, and you can hire surfboards and boogie boards from various places. A surf-lifesaving club overlooks Main Beach. The island is also famous for its fishing, and the annual Straddie Classic, held in August, is one of Australia's richest and best-known competitions.

On the ocean side you may even spot a humpback whale or two on their northward migration to the Great Barrier Reef where they breed during the winter months. Dolphins and porpoises are common.

Apart from beach activities, there's the island to explore. A sealed road runs across from Dunwich to **Blue Lake** in the centre of the island; a 2.7-km walking track leads from the road to the lake. You can swim in the freshwater lake or nearby **Tortoise Lagoon**, or walk along the track and watch for snakes, goannas, golden wallabies and birds. **Brown Lake**, about three km along the Blue Lake

QUEENSLAND

road from Dunwich, also offers deep fresh-water swimming, and is more easily accessible.

Alternatively, you could walk from Point Lookout south along Main Beach then 2.5 km inland to Blue Lake – 11 km one way in all. There's also a shorter beach walk to **Keyhole Lake**.

If you want to hike the 20 km across the island from Dunwich to Point Lookout, a number of dirt track loops break the monot-ony of the bitumen road. A pleasant diversion is to **Myora Springs**, surrounded by lush vegetation and walking tracks, near the coast about four km north of Dunwich.

Organised Tours

Stradbroke Island Tours (☎ (07) 409 8051) runs good 4WD tours of the island. Prices range from $25 for a fishing trip or half-day tour, $12 for a night tour, to $50 for a full day.

Straddie Experience Canoe Trips (☎ (07) 409 8279) offers several day trips to the island's mangrove creeks and freshwater lakes. The $35 cost includes transport and a picnic lunch.

Places to Stay

Dunwich, Amity Point and Point Lookout all have caravan and camping parks, although Dunwich and Amity Point are mainly resi-dential towns. Foreshore camping is allowed at designated areas (only accessible by 4WD). Sites cost $8 – ring ☎ (07) 409 8192 to book.

Point Lookout is the main town and has the best beaches, facilities and accommoda-tion, including three budget-priced hostels. The town itself is small but dispersed; it's about three km from one end to the other.

There are several caravan and camping grounds at Point Lookout. The *Thankful Rest Camping Ground* (☎ (07) 409 8192) and the *Adder Rock Camping Area* (☎ (07) 409 8125), both opposite Cylinder Beach, have tent sites from $8 and on-site vans from $22 a double. The *Stradbroke Island Carapark* (☎ (07) 409 8127) also has tent sites from $8

and fully self-contained cabins from $38 a double.

The *Stradbroke Island Guesthouse* (☎ (07) 409 8888), at 1 East Coast Rd, is the first place on the left as you come into Point Lookout. This is an impressive new guest-house with excellent, modern facilities. It costs $15 for a bed in a four-bed dorm, singles/doubles $35, and tariffs include the use of a surf ski and sand sailer (wind and tide permitting). The guesthouse runs a pick-up bus from Brisbane, which leaves from opposite the transit centre every Monday, Wednesday and Friday at 2.30 pm, and also stops at hostels; you need to book, and it costs $5.

The next place is also on the main road, on the left just after the Stradbroke Hotel (the only pub on the island). The *Straddie Hostel* (☎ (07) 409 8679) (formerly Point Lookout Backpackers) is in a two-storey beach-house. It has recently been renovated and has good facilities. The large dorms each have their own kitchen and bathroom, and beds cost $12 a night.

A little further up the road on the right-hand side, the *Headland Chalet* (☎ (07) 409 8252) is an old-style holiday village, with a collection of cabins scattered across a hill-side overlooking beautiful Main Beach. It doesn't look much from the outside, but it's an interesting, arty place. The rooms have a fridge, tea- and coffee-making gear, great views and a maximum of four beds and cost $12.50 per person, or $30 a double. There's a pool, a games and TV room, free washing machines and a small kitchen.

If you're thinking of staying awhile, a holiday flat or house can be good value, especially outside the holiday seasons. There are several real estate agents, including the Accommodation Centre (☎ (07) 409 8255).

Places to Eat

At Point Lookout, the *Stradbroke Hotel* has meal specials for $5 to $6 and a carvery with main courses from $9 to $12. It also has a great beer garden with an ocean outlook, and live music on Saturday nights and Sunday afternoons.

QUEENSLAND

Pasta Fino, in the Point Lookout Shopping Village in Endeavour St, is a modern, beachy cafe with pastas and pizzas from $9 and a Mexican menu on Friday nights. The *Masonic Club* on East Coast Rd has good meals from $3.50 to $9; it's open for lunch and dinner Wednesday to Sunday. The *Quarterdeck* at the Anchorage Village Resort is a bit more up-market; it has mains for around $16.

There are several general stores in Point Lookout that have some supplies and do takeaway food. If you're fixing your own meals bring basic supplies as the mark-up on the island is significant.

Getting There & Away

Cleveland, on the southern Bayside, is the departure point from the mainland and there are numerous ways of getting from central Brisbane to the island: a train or bus and water taxi or ferry; a through bus; or your own vehicle.

Bus or Train Stradbroke Island Coaches (☎ (07) 807 4299) runs daily services from Brisbane to the island, leaving at 9.30 am and 3 pm on weekdays and 7.45 am on weekends; the trip takes about 2½ hours all up. Buses leave Brisbane from stop 1 outside the transit centre, and stop at various other places (including hostels if you book). On weekends, the fare from Brisbane to Point Lookout is $9.50 ($18 return); you stay on the bus from start to finish. During the week, you take a bus to Cleveland, water taxi to the island and another bus to Point Lookout, and the combined fare is $7 ($14 return). Going back to Brisbane, buses leave Point Lookout at 6.50 and 11.35 am and 4 pm on weekdays and at 2 pm on weekends.

If you're going independently, trains leave Brisbane for Cleveland about every half-hour from 5 am. The journey takes about an hour. Bayside Buslines (☎ (07) 245 3333) runs a weekday 40-minute service between Brisbane and Cleveland on the Bayside Bullet as well as a regular service (Nos 621 and 622), which takes about an hour. Both cost $3.50 and depart about every half-hour (less frequently at weekends) from Elizabeth St in central Brisbane. In Cleveland, the buses stop at the railway station. A free bus service covers the km or so from the station to the ferry terminals, leaving about 15 minutes before the water taxis are due to depart for Straddie.

Water Taxi Two water-taxi companies operate between Cleveland and Dunwich. Stradbroke Ferries (☎ (07) 286 2666) have three boats – the *Spirit*, the *Pride* and the *Gateway* – and charge $9 return. There's also the *Stradbroke Flyer* (☎ (07) 286 1964), which costs between $7.50 and $10, depending on the season. The trip takes 20 minutes and boats depart hourly from 6 am to 7 pm weekdays, to 6 pm Saturdays and to 6.30 pm Sundays.

Car Ferry Stradbroke Ferries also runs the vehicle ferry from Cleveland to Dunwich about 12 times a day. It costs $63 return for a vehicle plus passengers, and $7 return for pedestrians. Last departures from Cleveland are normally at 6 pm but there are late ferries at 7.15 and 8 pm on Friday.

Getting Around

Stradbroke Island Coaches (☎ (07) 807 4299) runs 10 services a day between the three main centres; Dunwich to Point Lookout costs $3.50, and short trips around Point Lookout cost 50c to $1. The Stradbroke Island Taxi Service (☎ (07) 409 9124) charges about $25 from Dunwich to Point Lookout.

You can rent a 4WD for $100 a day ($60 a half-day) from Point Lookout Hire (☎ (07) 409 8353). The Stradbroke Island Guesthouse rents out motor scooters for $15 an hour or $70 a day (less for guests).

MORETON ISLAND (population 200)

North of Stradbroke, Moreton Island is less visited and still almost a wilderness. Apart from a few rocky headlands, it's all sand, with Mt Tempest, towering to 280 metres, the highest coastal sand hill in the world. It's a strange landscape, alternating between bare sand, forest, lakes and swamps, with a 30-km surf beach along the eastern side. The island's bird life is prolific, and at its northern tip is a **lighthouse**, built in 1857. Sand-mining leases on the island have been cancelled and 96% of the island is now a national park. There are several shipwrecks off the west coast.

Moreton Island has no paved roads but 4WD vehicles can travel along beaches and a few cross-island tracks – seek local advice about tides and creek crossings. The National Parks & Wildlife Service publishes a map of the island, which you can get on the ferry or from the National Parks office at False Patch Wrecks. The Sunmap Tourist Map, also available on the ferries, is very good.

Tangalooma, halfway down the western side of the island, is a popular tourist resort sited at an old whaling station. The only other settlements, all on the west coast, are **Bulwer** near the north-western tip, **Cowan Cowan** between Bulwer and Tangalooma, and **Kooringal** near the southern tip. The shops at Kooringal and Bulwer are expensive, so bring what you can from the mainland. For a bit of shark spotting, go to the Tangalooma Resort at 5 pm, when resort staff dump garbage off the end of the jetty.

Without your own vehicle, walking is the only way to get around the island, and you'll need several days to explore it. There are some trails around the resort area, and there are quite a few decommissioned 4WD roads with good walks. It's about 14 km from Tangalooma or the Ben-Ewa camping ground on the western side to Eagers Creek camping ground on the east, then seven km up the beach to Blue Lagoon and a further six to Cape Moreton at the north-eastern tip. There's a strenuous track to the summit of **Mt Tempest**, about three km inland from Eagers Creek; the views at the top are worth the effort.

About three km south and inland from Tangalooma is an area of bare sand known as the **Desert**, while the **Big Sandhills** and the **Little Sandhills** are towards the narrow southern end of the island. The biggest lakes and some swamps are in the north-east, and

the west coast from Cowan Cowan past Bulwer is also swampy.

Organised Tours
Several companies offer 4WD tours of the island, including Moreton Island Tourist Services (☎ (07) 203 6399). They leave from Scarborough every Sunday, Monday and Wednesday; the cost is $45 per person, which includes a barbecue lunch and the ferry trip across.

Places to Stay
National Parks camping sites, with water, toilets and cold showers, are at Ben-Ewa and False Patch Wrecks, both between Cowan Cowan and Tangalooma, and at Eagers Creek and Blue Lagoon on the northern half of the ocean coast. A site costs $7.50 a night for up to six people. Camping is allowed behind coastal dunes in many places. For information and camping permits, contact the National Parks & Wildlife Service (☎ (07) 227 8185) at 160 Ann St in Brisbane, or the ranger at False Patch Wrecks (☎ (07) 408 2710). It's also possible to pitch a tent under the trees by the beach at Reeders Point.

A twin room at the *Tangalooma Resort* (☎ (07) 268 6333) costs from $135 per night. There are a few holiday flats or houses for rent at Kooringal, Cowan Cowan and Bulwer.

Getting There & Away
The *Tangalooma Flyer* (☎ (07) 268 6333), a fast catamaran operated by the resort, leaves from Brisbane every day except Monday. You can use it for a day trip to the island or as a ferry if you're going to camp. A day trip from Brisbane costs $25 return; for any trip, it's advisable to book a day in advance. In Brisbane, the dock is at Holt St, off Kingsford Smith Drive in Eagle Farm.

The *Moreton Venture* (☎ (07) 895 1000) is a vehicle ferry which runs five to six days a week to Tangalooma or to Short Point. The ferry leaves from Whyte Island, which is joined to the mainland by road, at the southern side of the Brisbane River mouth. You can take your own 4WD across for $95 return (including passengers); pedestrians are charged $18 return.

Another ferry to the island is the *Combie Trader* (☎ (07) 203 6399), with daily services between Scarborough and Bulwer (except Tuesday). Fares are $50 one way and $85 return for a 4WD and four people, and $15 one way and $20 return for pedestrians. The ferry also does day trips on Monday, Wednesday, Saturday and Sunday for $18 return.

ST HELENA ISLAND

Just six km from the mouth of the Brisbane River, little St Helena Island was used as a high-security prison from 1867 to 1932. The island is now a national park. There are remains of several prison buildings on the island, plus the first passenger tramway in Brisbane which, when built in 1884, had horse-drawn cars. Sandy beaches and mangroves alternate around the island's coast.

Several outfits run day trips to St Helena, including guided tours on the island. Adai Cruises (☎ (07) 262 6978) leaves from the BP Marina on Kingsford Smith Drive, Breakfast Creek, at 9 am every Sunday and two or three other days each week, returning at 5 pm. The $25 price includes lunch. St Helena Ferries (☎ (07) 393 3726) runs two to three trips a week, leaving from Manly Harbour, opposite Cardigan Parade, on the southern Bayside. The $17 return fare includes a one-hour tour and entry to the national park. You can reach Manly from central Brisbane in about 35 minutes by train.

OTHER ISLANDS
Coochiemudlo Island

Coochiemudlo (or Coochie) Island is a 10-minute ferry ride from Victoria Point on the southern Bayside. It's a popular outing from the mainland, with good beaches, although it's more built-up than most other Moreton Bay islands you can visit. You can rent bicycles, boats, catamarans and surf skis on the island. The ferry runs continuously from 8 am to 5.30 or 6 pm on weekends and holidays, less often on other days.

Bay Isles

The Bay Isles, made up of **Russell, Lamb, Karragarra** and **Macleay** islands, are between the southern end of North Stradbroke and the mainland. At about seven km long, Russell is the largest; it features the interesting Green Dragon Museum in the north-west of the island. Bay Islands Ferries (☎ (07) 286 2666), operating from the Banana St ramp in Redland Bay, does a loop around the islands three or four times a day; fares are $32 return for a car and passengers, or $2 each way for pedestrians.

Bribie Island

Bribie Island, at the northern end of Moreton Bay, is 31 km long but apart from the southern end, where there are a couple of small towns, the island is largely untouched. There's a bridge across Pumicestone Passage from the mainland to Bellara on the southwest coast. Bongaree, just south of Bellara, is the main town. Buses run there from Caboolture and Brisbane. There's good surfing on the ocean side and a calm channel towards the mainland. Bongaree and Bellara, and Woorim on the south-east coast, have a few motels and holiday flats from about $50 a double, and there are some restaurants too.

Gold Coast

Population 310,000

The Gold Coast is a 35-km strip of beaches running north from the New South Wales-Queensland border. It's the most thoroughly commercialised resort in Australia and is virtually one continuous development culminating in the high-rise splendour of Surfers Paradise.

This coast has been a holiday spot since the 1880s but only after WW II did developers start taking serious notice of Surfers. More than two million visitors a year come to the Gold Coast. Japanese companies own a large slice of the coast's prime real estate.

You can stay on the Gold Coast pretty

cheaply, and there's quite a range of things to do – good surf beaches, excellent eating and entertainment possibilities and a hinterland with some fine natural features. There's also a huge variety of artificial 'attractions' and theme parks, although most are very commercial and fairly expensive.

Orientation

The whole coast from Tweed Heads in New South Wales up to Main Beach, north of Surfers Paradise, is developed, but most of the real action is around Surfers itself. Tweed Heads and Coolangatta at the southern end are older, quieter, cheaper resorts. Moving north from there you pass through Kirra, Bilinga, Tugun, Currumbin, Palm Beach, Burleigh Heads, Miami, Nobby Beach, Mermaid Beach and Broadbeach – all lower key resorts.

Southport, the oldest town in the area, is north and just inland from Surfers, behind the sheltered expanse of the Broadwater which is fed by the Nerang and Coomera rivers. The Gold Coast Highway runs right along the coastal strip, leaving the Pacific Highway just north of Tugun and rejoining it inland from Southport.

The Gold Coast airport is at Coolangatta. Most buses to the Gold Coast travel the full length of the strip.

Information

The Gold Coast Tourism Bureau (☎ (075) 38 4419), on Cavill Ave Mall in the heart of Surfers Paradise, is open from 8 am to 5 pm Monday to Friday, 9 am to 5 pm Saturday and 9 am to 3.30 pm Sunday. There are other tourist information offices in the Beach House Plaza (☎ (075) 36 7765) on the corner of Marine Parade and McLean St in Coolangatta, and on Wharf St in Tweed Heads; both are open daily except Sundays.

At Burleigh Heads, on the Gold Coast Highway, there's a National Parks information centre (☎ (075) 35 3032), a useful place to call in if you're planning to visit some of the state's national parks. It's open daily.

There are at least four free glossy booklets available, including *Wot's On*, *Today* and

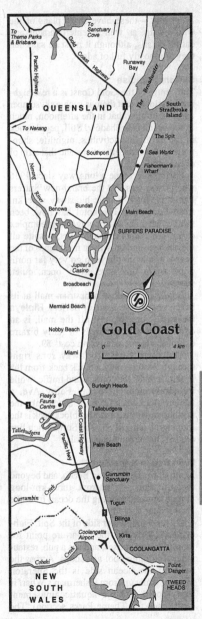

Point Out – these have street plans of the whole strip, as well as entertainment and eating details, although it must be said that they are mostly full of ads.

Surfers Paradise

The centre of the Gold Coast is a real high-rise jungle; in fact there is such a skyscraper conglomeration that in the afternoon, much of the beach is in shadow! Still, people pack in for the lights, activities, nightlife, shopping, restaurants, attractions and that strip of ocean sand.

Surfers has come a long way since 1936 when there was just the brand-new Surfers Paradise Hotel, a little hideaway nine km from Southport. The hotel has now been swallowed up by a shopping/eating complex called the Paradise Centre. Yet, despite all the changes and growth, at most times of the year you may not have to go very far north or south to find a relatively open, quiet, sunny beach.

Cavill Ave, with a pedestrian mall at its beach end, is the heart of Surfers. **Ripleys Believe It or Not**, just off the mall, is an odditorium with hundreds of fairly bizarre exhibits; it's open daily and costs $9.

The Gold Coast Highway runs right through Surfers, only a block back from the beach. It takes the southbound traffic, while Remembrance Drive and Ferny Ave, a further block back from the beach, take the northbound traffic. Another block back is the looping Nerang River. The Surfers rich live around the surrounding canals.

Main Beach & the Spit

North of Surfers is Main Beach, and beyond that the Spit – a narrow, three-km-long tongue of sand dividing the ocean from the Broadwater.

On the Broadwater side of the Spit, **Fisherman's Wharf** is the departure point for most pleasure cruises, and has a pub, restaurant, swimming pool and shops. Across the road on the ocean side is the Sheraton Mirage, while up from Fisherman's Wharf is **Sea World**, a huge aquatic amusement centre (see the Theme Parks section). The

beach at the northern end of the Spit is not developed and is good for relatively secluded sunbathing.

Southport & North

Sheltered from the ocean by the Spit, Southport was the original town on the Gold Coast but it's now modern, residential and rather nondescript. The built-up area continues north of Southport through Labrador, Anglers Paradise and Runaway Bay to Paradise Point. Sanctuary Cove, about 10 km north of Southport on Hope Island, is an up-market resort with a Hyatt hotel, two golf courses, a marina, flats and houses.

Southern Gold Coast

Just south of Surfers at Broadbeach, **Jupiter's Casino** is a Gold Coast landmark – it was Queensland's first legal casino and is open 24 hours a day. The **Burleigh Heads National Park**, on the northern side of the mouth of Tallebudgera Creek, is a small but diverse forest reserve with walking trails around and through the rocky headland, a lookout and picnic area. On the northern side is one of Australia's most famous surfing breaks.

There are three excellent wildlife sanctuaries in this area. **Fleay's Fauna Centre**, just back along the Tallebudgera Creek in West Burleigh, has an excellent collection of native wildlife and four km of walking tracks through mangroves and rainforest. The platypus was first bred in captivity here. The centre is open daily from 9 am to 5 pm and costs $7.50.

Back towards the coast, flocks of technicoloured lorikeets and other birds flutter in for morning and afternoon feeds at the **Currumbin Sanctuary**. Within the large bushland park there are also tree kangaroos, koalas, emus and lots more Australian fauna, plus a two-km miniature railway, an Australian botanical garden and wildlife presentations. The sanctuary is half a km south of Currumbin Creek, on both sides of the Gold Coast Highway; it opens daily from 8 am to 5 pm, and entry costs $13. If you're travelling by the Surfside bus, get off at stop No 20.

About eight km inland along Currumbin

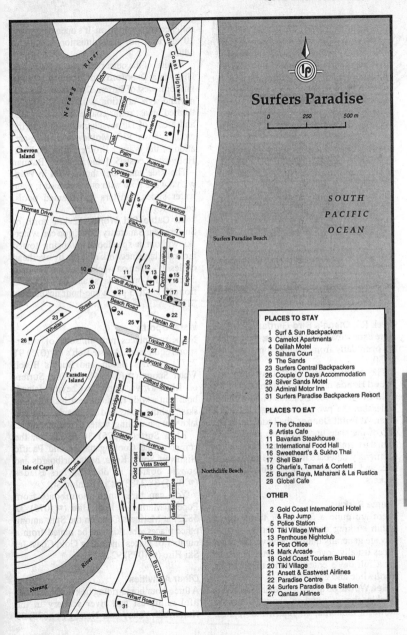

Surfers Paradise

SOUTH
PACIFIC
OCEAN

Surfers Paradise Beach

Northcliffe Beach

PLACES TO STAY

1 Surf & Sun Backpackers
3 Camelot Apartments
4 Delilah Motel
6 Sahara Court
9 The Sands
23 Surfers Central Backpackers
26 Couple O' Days Accommodation
29 Silver Sands Motel
30 Admiral Motor Inn
31 Surfers Paradise Backpackers Resort

PLACES TO EAT

7 The Chateau
8 Artists Cafe
11 Bavarian Steakhouse
12 International Food Hall
16 Sweetheart's & Sukho Thai
17 Shell Bar
18 Charlie's, Tamari & Confetti
25 Bunga Raya, Maharani & La Rustica
28 Global Cafe

OTHER

2 Gold Coast International Hotel
 & Rap Jump
5 Police Station
10 Tiki Village Wharf
13 Penthouse Nightclub
14 Post Office
15 Mark Arcade
18 Gold Coast Tourism Bureau
20 Tiki Village
21 Ansett & Eastwest Airlines
22 Paradise Centre
24 Surfers Paradise Bus Station
27 Qantas Airlines

Rainbow lorikeet

Creek Rd, **Olson's Bird Gardens** have yet more exotic feathered creatures; the gardens are open daily from 9 am to 5 pm and cost $8.50.

The 'twin towns' of **Coolangatta** and **Tweed Heads** mark the southern end of the Gold Coast. Tweed Heads is in New South Wales but the two places merge into each other. At **Point Danger**, the headland at the end of the state line, there are good views from the Captain Cook memorial. Coolangatta is a friendly, laid-back little place, the beach is fine, and it's a very popular stop for backpackers.

Theme Parks

There are quite a few major theme parks within striking distance of Surfers. While they are generally quite expensive, the ticket prices usually cover all rides and shows, so for a full day's entertainment they can be worthwhile and good fun.

Sea World, on the Spit in Main Beach, has dolphin shows, sea lion shows, water-ski shows, a monorail, an *Endeavour* replica, roller coasters and so on. It's open daily from 10 am to 5 pm and admission is $30 for adults.

Several of the other parks are on the Pacific Highway at **Oxenford** and **Coomera**, about 20 km north-west of Surfers. **Dreamworld**, a Disneyland-style creation with nine different themed areas, roller coasters, a water slide and a cast of Disney characters wandering around, costs $30. **Movieworld**, a re-creation of the Warner Brothers film studio in Hollywood, costs $31 and includes 'Batman – The Ride' and stunt shows. **Wet 'n Wild**, with a wave pool with one-metre surf, giant water slides, twisters and themed pools, costs $15.

At **Cable Ski World**, 12 km north of Surfers near Sanctuary Cove, you can water-ski without a speedboat, by being towed around a large network of lakes by overhead cables. It's open on weekdays from 11 am to 5 pm (till 9 pm Fridays) and on weekends from 10 am to 5 pm; a one-hour ticket costs $15.

Water Sports

Numerous places rent all sorts of watersports equipment. Aussie Bob's (☎ (075) 91 7577) at Main Beach, and Budd's Beach Water Sportz (☎ (075) 92 0644) at Surfers on River Drive, opposite Chevron Island, both rent a wide range of gear including jet skis, fishing boats and sailboards, and can take you parasailing, water-skiing and more.

Kirra Surf (☎ (075) 36 3922), on the corner of the Coolangatta Rd and Pacific Highway, South Kirra, rents surfboards and boogie boards, as does Surfers Blades (☎ (075) 38 3483) at 10 Hanlon St.

You can hire small motorboats from Popeye Marine & Boat Hire (☎ (075) 32 5822) at Mariners Cove on the Spit, among other places. Jet skis can be rented from a number of places, including Gold Coast Jet Ski Hire (☎ (075) 92 2415).

Other Activities

A three-hour horse-riding trek through beautiful rainforest and river scenery in the **Numinbah Valley** near Nerang (☎ (075) 33

4137) will cost you $25. The staff do pick-ups from the Gold Coast. The Gold Coast Riding Ranch (☎ (075) 94 4255), on the Broadbeach to Nerang road next to the Surfers Raceway, does trail rides from $20 an hour, and at Gum Nuts Horse Riding Resort (☎ (075) 43 0191) half a day costs $35 and a full day $60.

Bungee jumpers are catered for at Bungee Down Under, on the Spit by Sea World. First-time jumpers pay $69, while for experienced jumpers it's $50. There's another bungee jump at Cable Ski World.

The Gold Coast's latest adventure challenge is Rap Jumping (☎ 018 450 120). You get to abseil forwards off the top of the 80-metre high Gold Coast International Hotel for $50, or for $80 with a T-shirt and photo thrown in.

Organised Tours & Cruises

Tours run by some of the hostels are probably the best value. Otherwise, bus trips up into the mountains behind the coast cost $25 to Tamborine Mountain and $30 to Lamington National Park. River or canal cruises may include refreshments only, or lunch plus a floating floor show. In the evening you'll probably get music, dancing and dinner. A straight couple of hours along the inland waterways costs $22, while an evening dinner cruise will be around $50. Cruises to South Stradbroke Island usually include lunch and some form of entertainment for around $45.

Cruises leave from Fisherman's Wharf, or from the Tiki Village Wharf at the river end of Cavill Ave.

Places to Stay

Hostels and backpackers' places apart, accommodation prices are extremely variable according to the season. They rise severely during the school holidays and some motels push prices higher over Christmas than at other holiday peaks, although they may not rise at all if there's a cold snap.

All types of accommodation are cheaper outside Surfers. You'll find a selection of cheap motels at the southern end of the coast

at places like Mermaid Beach, Palm Beach and Coolangatta.

The holiday flats which are found all along the coast can be better bargains than motels, especially for a group of three or four. In peak seasons especially, flats will be rented on a weekly rather than overnight basis, but don't let that frighten you off. Even if they won't negotiate a daily rate, a decent $225-a-week, two-bedroom flat is still cheaper than two $30-a-night motel rooms, even for just four days.

The tourist information offices can provide you with lists of accommodation in every price bracket, including backpackers' places, but they can't hope to be comprehensive since there are so many possibilities – an estimated 3000 in all.

If you have a vehicle, one of the easiest ways to find a place to stay is simply to cruise along the Gold Coast Highway or the Esplanade and try a few places that have 'vacancy' signs out.

Camping There are caravan parks all the way along the Gold Coast from Main Beach to Coolangatta. Those close to the centre include the *Main Beach Caravan Park* (☎ (075) 81 7722) on Main Beach Parade, which has on-site cabins for $35 but no tent sites, and the *Loders Creek Tourist Park* (☎ (075) 81 7733) on the Gold Coast Highway in Southport, with tent sites at $10 and on-site cabins at $35.

To the south, the *Miami Caravan Park* (☎ (075) 72 7533), at 2200 Gold Coast Highway, charges $13.50 for tent sites and $25 for on-site units, and the excellent *Tallebudgera Creek Tourist Park* (☎ (075) 81 7700) at 1544 Gold Coast Highway in Palm Beach has tent sites from $10.

At Coolangatta/Tweed Heads, the *Border Caravan Park* (☎ (075) 36 3134) has tent sites at $11 and on-site vans from $32.

Hostels There are quite a few backpackers' hostels in and around Surfers, and others in Southport and Labrador to the north and Broadbeach and Coolangatta to the south; the places out of the centre all provide regular courtesy buses into Surfers. Prices are generally a couple of dollars higher during December and January.

Note that a few of the older hostels may not survive the tough new regulations currently being enforced.

Surfers Paradise The most impressive of the hostels here is the *Surfers Paradise Backpackers Resort* (☎ (075) 92 4677) at 2835 Gold Coast Highway, about a km south of the centre. It's clean and modern and has good facilities including a pool, a small gym and basement parking. There are two sections, one with four-bed dorms and another with excellent self-contained apartments, mostly accommodating four or five people in two bedrooms. A dorm or unit bed costs $14, doubles $28. The hostel also runs tours to various places.

A block south of the bus stop, at 40 Whelan St, is *Surfers Central Backpackers* (☎ (075) 38 4344) which has bunk rooms and a few doubles. There are two sections – one has 18 units (with private bathrooms) taking up to four people; the other has larger dorms. The communal kitchen is small, but there's a good pool with plenty of space for sunbathing and outdoor eating. Dorm beds cost $14, doubles $30.

At 18 Whelan St, *Couple O' Days Accommodation* (☎ (075) 92 4200) is a converted old apartment block, and looks a bit worn around the edges these days. A bed in a large dorm is $12, in a smaller dorm $14.

North of the town centre, at 3323 Gold Coast Highway, *Surf & Sun Backpackers* (☎ (075) 92 2363) is a converted motel with four-bed units with private bathroom, TV and fridge. It's a good place if you're in party mode. There's a pool, and this is the closest hostel to the beach. Dorm beds are $14, doubles $30 (low season only).

Southport & Labrador Southport has one of the nicest hostels on the south coast – the *Trekkers Guest House* (☎ (075) 91 5616) at 22 White St, about four km north of Surfers. It's in an old house which has been well renovated and furnished, and has all the usual facilities – laundry, kitchens, pool, TV lounge, courtesy bus – and accommodation is in three- or four-bed rooms, most with bathroom. The atmosphere is very appealing and the staff organise trips to nightclubs and other events most evenings. The twice-weekly $5 barbecues are also popular. The nightly cost is $14 and doubles are $30.

The *Gold Coast Backpackers Resort* (☎ (075) 31 2004) is nearby at 44 Queen St. It's a modern, purpose-built hostel but lacks atmosphere; dorm beds are $12.

At Labrador, a km further north again, is the family-run *Broadwater Backpackers* (☎ (075) 91 6743) at 2 Frank St. It's a large former convalescence home, and has good facilities but there's an institutional feel to the place. Large dorms cost $10, smaller rooms $12 and doubles $24.

Broadbeach At 2623 Gold Coast Highway, the *Big Backpackers* (☎ (075) 38 4633) certainly lives up to its name – it's so big even the staff get lost. This converted nursing home is clean and spacious but it feels a bit clinical. Dorms are $10, rooms with private bathrooms $14, and singles/doubles $19/28; there's a $3 linen fee.

Coolangatta The popular *Backpackers Inn* (☎ (075) 36 2422), at 45 McLean St, is a short walk from the post office end of Griffith St. It's in a comfortable old guesthouse, and has a bar, a restaurant serving dinner and breakfast, barbecues twice a week, and a small kitchenette. A bed in a two- or four-bed room costs $14, while single/double rooms are $19/28. There's a pool, and the management organises beach parties and trips to the hinterland mountains.

The *Gold Coast Youth Hostel* (☎ (075) 36 7644) is on Coolangatta Rd, Bilinga, just north of the airport and about three km from central Coolangatta. A bed in a six- or eight-bed dorm costs $11 for members; nonmembers pay an extra $1 plus an 'introductory fee' of $3. It's a newish building, with good facilities including a pool, but it's not really in a convenient location for anything except the airport.

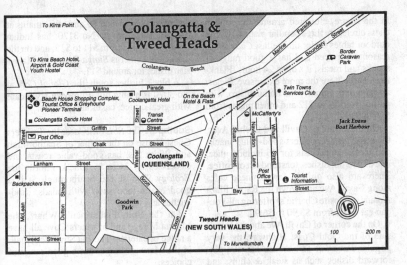

Motels & Flats As you might imagine, there are dozens of motels and holiday flats up and down the coast, and these are usually quite good value in the low season.

Surfers Paradise Close to the centre and on the waterfront, the *Sands* (☎ (075) 39 8433), a huge complex at 40 The Esplanade, has one-bedroom flats from $50 and two-bedroom flats from $90 for four people. One block north, *Sahara Court* (☎ (075) 39 8544) at 56 The Esplanade also has good self-contained units from $50 for one-bedroom or $70 for two-bedrooms.

A little way out of the centre, the *Delilah Motel* (☎ (075) 38 1722) on the corner of Ferny and Cypress Aves has motel rooms from $40/45 for singles/doubles. *Camelot Holiday Apartments* (☎ (075) 39 9380), nearby at 33 Cypress Ave, has self-contained four-bed units at $40 a double and $54 for four, including linen. There's a minimum stay of three days.

At 2985 Gold Coast Highway, the *Silver Sands Motel* (☎ (075) 38 6041) has singles/doubles from $45/55. Close by at No 2965, the *Admiral Motor Inn* (☎ (075) 39 8759) has rooms from $48.

Southern Gold Coast In Broadbeach, the *Motel Casa Blanca* (☎ (075) 70 3511), at 2649 Gold Coast Highway, has units from $55.

There are quite a few good cheap motels along the Gold Coast Highway at Mermaid Beach. The *Red Emu Motel* (☎ (075) 75 2748) at No 2583 has doubles from $28 in the low season. The *Mermaid Beach Motel* (☎ (075) 75 1577) at No 2395 is good value with clean units from $25, and at No 2267 the small *Van Diemen Motel* (☎ (075) 72 7611) has units from $28 a night.

In Burleigh Heads, the *Casino Motel* (☎ (075) 35 7133) at 1761 Gold Coast Highway has rooms from $30 a double.

In Coolangatta, the old *Coolangatta Sands Hotel* (☎ (075) 36 3066), on the corner of Griffith and McLean Sts, has rooms from $25/35. There are several motels along the beachfront, including *On the Beach Motel & Holiday Flats* (☎ (075) 36 3624) at 118 Marine Parade, with good motel units from $40 and self-contained units from $55.

Places to Eat
Surfers Paradise There are plenty of choices in and around the Cavill Ave Mall.

QUEENSLAND

In the centre, clustered around the sunken chess circle, are three popular places, all with outdoor tables under umbrellas. *Charlie's* is reasonably priced and has a good range of snacks and meals; it's open 24 hours. Flanking Charlie's are the more expensive *Tamari* and *Confetti*. Tamari is an Italian bistro, with pastas from $9 to $12 and other mains from $16 to $19.

On the corner of Cavill and Orchid Aves, the busy *Shell Bar* offers good-value snacks and meals. Breakfasts for $6 include juice, one of five hot dishes, toast and tea or coffee. There are also quite a few Chinese cafes along Cavill Ave and down the Raptis Plaza Arcade (opposite Charlie's) offering all-you-can-eat deals from $3.90 to $6.90.

On the corner of Cavill Ave and the inland side of the Gold Coast Highway, the very popular *Bavarian Steakhouse* has straightforward dishes such as steak & chips, and also a soup, pasta and salad buffet bar for $10 at lunch time and $13 at night. In the centre of the Dolphin Arcade, which runs between Orchid Ave and the Gold Coast Highway, there's a small international food hall.

Orchid Ave also has some good eateries. In the Mark shopping complex, at shop 38, *Sukho Thai* is a small place with good Thai food; mains range from $10 to $14. Two shops south is the excellent and popular *Sweetheart's*, which offers healthy rolls, burgers, salads and juices. It's open daily from 8.30 am to 8 pm. The *Shooters Bar*, in the Mark Arcade, has pool tables and inexpensive light meals. Further along Orchid Ave, the *Artists Cafe* is a casual place with outdoor tables; it serves breakfasts, sandwiches and snacks.

On the corner of Elkhorn Ave and the Esplanade, the *Montmartre French Patisserie* is good for breakfasts and lunches. On the adjacent corner, the *Chateau* has an all-you-can-eat breakfast buffet for $7.

On the Gold Coast Highway, in the block south of Beach Rd, are six restaurants side-by-side, and you can choose from Malaysian, French, Chinese, Italian and Indian food. At No 3118, *La Rustica* is a small and popular Italian bistro with pastas and pizzas for around $9 and other mains at $15.50; *Maharani*, at No 3120, has Indian food with mains from $11 to $15; and on the Trickett St corner is *Bunga Raya* with Malaysian dishes for around $11.

A block further south, the *Global Cafe* at No 3070 is a tiny, hip, European-style cafe with great coffee, cakes and pastries.

Southport The *RSL Club*, near the Trekkers Guest House on the corner of Scarborough and White Sts, has good-value roasts and casseroles for $4 to $5. One km north, the *Ecology Shop* at 116 Scarborough St is a good health-food shop with salads, sandwiches and juices.

On the Spit, Fisherman's Wharf, the Marina Mirage and Mariners Cove all have a range of eateries. The Eat Street food hall, in the Marina Mirage, has a good range of choices.

Southern Gold Coast There are heaps of places along the highway between Surfers and Burleigh Heads. *Sizzler*, on the Gold Coast Highway at Mermaid Beach, is a very popular place; meals cost around $10, and you can attack the salad bar for an extra $4.

The *Pizza Hut*, on the highway at Miami Beach, has all-you-can-eat pizza and pasta specials on Tuesday and Wednesday nights for $5.95.

In Burleigh Heads, the *Masakan Indonesia*, at 1837 Gold Coast Highway, has good Indonesian dishes with mains from $9 to $12. Around the corner, facing the beach, the Burleigh Hotel has the *Four Seasons Bistro*, with good pub fare. A block south of the pub, the Old Burleigh Theatre Arcade on Goodwin Terrace has several good restaurants including *Montezuma's* Mexican and *Tim's Malaysian Hut*.

Coolangatta The huge *Twin Towers Services Club* has a Snack Bar on the 2nd floor, which has good meals for $4 to $6 and $2.50 lunches on weekdays.

On the corner of McLean St and Marine Parade, the Beach House shopping complex has a number of eateries: *Farley's Coffee*

Lounge and the *Aussie Eatery* both have reasonably priced breakfasts and lunches. Also here is the *Jungle*, a Mexican cantina, *Little Malaya* with Malaysian and Chinese dishes, and *Casa Mia Piccola* with Italian food.

The *Coolangatta Sands Hotel* does cheap meals, and the *Coolangatta Hotel* on Marine Parade has a popular pub bistro. The famous *Coolangatta Pie Shop*, at 50 Griffith St, has good pies, pastries and fresh bread.

Entertainment

With more than 30 nightclubs around Surfers alone, entertainment is what it's all about on the Gold Coast. In addition, there's Jupiter's Casino, live-music venues, plenty of cinemas, and even a cultural centre. Most places have reasonably strict dress codes. Lots of the nightclubs give away free entry passes, both at their doors and on the streets. Some of the hostels organise nights out at clubs, with cheap drink nights and free entry.

The most popular backpackers' nightclubs are *Cocktails & Dreams*, the *Party*, and *Crazy Horse*, all in the Mark shopping complex off Orchid Ave. Cocktails & Dreams is big on Monday and Wednesday nights, the Party on Tuesdays, and Crazy Horse on Thursdays.

Benson's Nite Club, across the road at 22 Orchid Ave, is popular with travellers on Friday nights, and the *Penthouse*, also on Orchid Ave, which has four floors of nightlife with a piano bar, an over-25's disco and more, is good on Saturdays. The *Tunnel* is another Orchid Ave club.

The *Rose & Crown Hotel*, off Cavill Ave in the Raptis Plaza, is a good pub to head for early in the night, before the nightclubs fire up.

The *Surfers Beergarden*, upstairs off Cavill Ave, has a surf theme with old boards and surfing photos, and live bands on some nights. There's also live music at *Fisherman's Wharf* most days; Sunday afternoons (from 2 pm onwards) are popular. The long-running *Playroom*, on the Gold Coast Highway in Tallebudgera, often has big-name bands.

Quite a few restaurants also provide music or entertainment during meals. A popular cabaret restaurant is *Dracula's* (☎ (075) 75 1000) on Hooker Blvd in Broadbeach. Dracula's offers a four-course meal served by waiters and waitresses who throw themselves into the Dracula theme. The night climaxes in a disco. Jupiter's Casino, also in Broadbeach, has a restaurant and a good disco called *Fortunes*, with mixed music and age groups. Another more up-market nightspot is *Rolls*, in the Sheraton Hotel on the Spit.

In Coolangatta, the *Hill St Nightclub* (on Hill St!) is open most nights with a variety of entertainment. *Premieres*, on Warner St, is a fun nightclub/disco, and the *Patch* in the Queensland Hotel on Hill St (at the end of Marine Parade) is a good live-music venue. The *Coolangatta Sands Hotel* also has live bands. Much of the entertainment on the southern Gold Coast revolves around the clubs and pokies in Tweed Heads.

After all this, it may be a relief to know that there is the *Centre*, the Gold Coast's arts complex, beside the Nerang River at Bundall. It houses theatres, galleries, a restaurant and bar. Shows include musicals, concerts, plays, dance performances, and exhibitions, which are listed under Entertainment in some of the Gold Coast tourist publications.

Getting There & Away

Air The Gold Coast is only a couple of hours by road from the centre of Brisbane but has its own busy airport at Coolangatta.

Ansett and Qantas fly direct from the southern capitals. Standard fares include Sydney $254, Melbourne $371, Adelaide $422 and Perth $655. Eastwest also flies daily from Albury, Brisbane, Cairns, Hobart and Sydney, while Eastern Australia flies daily from Brisbane ($93) and several New South Wales coastal towns.

Booking numbers for the airlines include Ansett and Eastwest (☎ 13 1300), Qantas (☎ 13 1313) and Eastern Australia (☎ (075) 38 1188).

Bus The new Surfers Paradise bus station, on the corner of Beach and Cambridge Rds, is where you'll arrive if you're coming by bus. Inside the terminal are the booking desks of the bus companies, a cafeteria, and a backpackers' accommodation desk run by four of the local hostels. Opposite this desk are left-luggage lockers, costing $2 for six hours.

The main bus companies and their booking numbers are McCafferty's (☎ (075) 38 2700), Kirklands (☎ (075) 31 7145) and Greyhound Pioneer (☎ 13 2030). Most companies will allow you a free stopover on the Gold Coast if you have a through ticket.

Between Brisbane, Surfers and Coolangatta, Coachtrans (☎ (075) 38 9944) operates buses almost every half-hour from around 6.40 am to 8.15 pm. The trip from Brisbane takes about 1½ hours to Surfers and just over two hours to Coolangatta, and costs $12. Coachtrans also have frequent services from the Brisbane airport to the Gold Coast; the fare is $24.

There are three different bus stops in Coolangatta: the transit centre on the corner of Griffith and Warner Sts is the Coachtrans terminal; the Greyhound Pioneer terminal is in the Beach House on McLean St; and the McCafferty's terminal is on Boundary St in Tweed Heads.

Train There's no railway station on the Gold Coast but there are connecting bus services once daily to Murwillumbah (one hour) and Casino (three hours) in northern New South Wales; from there you can take a train to Sydney. There's a Queensland Rail booking office (☎ (075) 39 9088) in the Cavill Park building on the corner of Beach Rd and the Gold Coast Highway in Surfers Paradise.

Getting Around

To/From the Airport Coolangatta Airport is the seventh busiest in Australia. Several different bus companies run airport shuttle buses. Gold Coast Airport Transit (☎ (075) 36 6841) from Surfers Paradise meets every Qantas arrival and departure. It costs $8 between the airport and Surfers and $4 to Coolangatta, and they will do pick-ups or drop-offs from your accommodation. Airport & Charter Services (☎ (075) 76 4000) meets all Ansett and Eastwest arrivals

and departures, leaving Surfers 75 minutes before takeoff. If there are three or more of you it's cheaper to take a taxi.

Bus Surfside Buslines (☎ (075) 36 7666) runs a frequent 24-hour service up and down the Gold Coast Highway between Southport and Tweed Heads and beyond. You can buy individual fares, get a Day Rover ticket for $6.55, or buy a weekly one for $23.85.

Car & Moped Rental There are stacks of car-rental firms along the Gold Coast, particularly in Surfers – pick up any of the free Gold Coast guides or scan the Yellow Pages. All the big companies are represented, plus a host of local operators in the small car and rent-a-wreck categories. Rent-a-Bomb (☎ (075) 38 8222), at 8 Beach Rd, is one of the cheapest, and has cars, mokes and mopeds. Another cheapie is Red Rocket (☎ (075) 38 9074) at Shop 9 in the Mark shopping complex in Orchid Ave.

For mopeds, try Red Back Rentals (☎ 018 754 211) at 3 Beach Rd, opposite the bus station; or Surfers Blades (☎ (075) 38 3483) in Hanlon St behind Grundy's. They start from $25 a day.

Bicycle For bikes, try Surfers Blades (see above) or Green Bicycle Rentals (☎ 018 766 880), who have mountain bikes and do deliveries.

GOLD COAST HINTERLAND

The mountains of the **McPherson Range**, about 20 km inland from Coolangatta and stretching about 60 km back along the New South Wales border to meet the Great Dividing Range, are a paradise for walkers. The great views and beautiful natural features are easily accessible by car, and there are plenty of wonderfully scenic drives. Otherwise, there are several places offering tours and day trips from the coast. Expect a lot of rain in the mountains from December to March, and in winter the nights can be cold.

Tamborine Mountain

Just 45 km north-west of the Gold Coast, this

600-metre-high plateau is on a northern spur of the McPherson Range. Patches of the area's original forests remain in nine small national parks. There are gorges, spectacular waterfalls like Witches Falls and Cedar Creek Falls, great views inland or over the coast, and walking tracks. There's a visitor information centre (☎ (075) 45 1171) at Doughty Park, North Tamborine.

The main turn-off to the mountain is at Oxenford on the Pacific Highway. Some of the best lookouts are in **Witches Falls National Park**, south-west of North Tamborine, and at **Cameron Falls**, north-west of North Tamborine. **Macrozamia Grove National Park**, near Mt Tamborine township, has some extremely old macrozamia palms. At **Thunderbird Park**, near the Cedar Creek Falls, you can ride horses or fossick for thunder eggs.

There's a handful of reasonably priced motels and guesthouses in Mt Tamborine township and Eagle Heights, and a camping ground with on-site vans at *Thunderbird Park* (☎ (075) 45 1468) in Mt Tamborine.

Thunder Eggs
Thunder eggs are spherical rocks of volcanic origin which contain quartz crystals or semi-precious gems such as agate. The 'eggs', which range in size from a cm in diameter to about the size of a cricket ball, were formed when gas cavities in hardened lava filled with mineral deposits or crystal, and weathering of the rock created the smooth, rounded shape. ■

Springbrook Plateau
This forested 900-metre-high plateau, like the rest of the McPherson Range, is a remnant of the huge volcano which used to be centred on Mt Warning in New South Wales. It's a lovely drive from the Gold Coast, reached by paved road via Mudgeeraba.

Springbrook National Park has three sections: Springbrook, Mt Cougal and Natural Bridge. The vegetation is temperate rainforest and eucalypt forest, with gorges, cliffs, forests, waterfalls, an extensive network of walking tracks, and several picnic areas.

At the **Gwongorella picnic area**, just off the Springbrook road, the lovely Purling Brook Falls drop 109 metres into rainforest. Downstream, Waringa Pool is a beautiful summer swimming hole. There's a good camping ground beside the picnic area.

The **Natural Bridge section**, off the Nerang to Murwillumbah road, has a one-km walking circuit leading to a rock arch spanning a water-formed cave which is home to a huge colony of glow-worms.

There are ranger's offices and information centres at Natural Bridge and Springbrook. Pick up a copy of the National Parks walking tracks leaflet. Camping permits for Gwongorella are available from the ranger at Springbrook (☎ (075) 33 5147, between 3 and 4 pm weekdays only). Springbrook village itself has a general store, tearooms and craft shops, and several guesthouses.

Lamington National Park
West of Springbrook, this 200-sq-km park covers more of the McPherson Range and adjoins the Border Ranges National Park in New South Wales. It includes thickly wooded valleys, 1100-metre-high ranges, plus most of the Lamington Plateau. Much of the vegetation is subtropical rainforest. There are beautiful gorges, caves, superb views, a great many waterfalls and pools, and lots of wildlife. Bower birds are quite common and pademelons, a type of small wallaby, can be seen on the grassy forest verges in late afternoon.

The two most popular and accessible sections are **Binna Burra** and **Green Mountains**, both reached via paved roads from Canungra. The 24-km Border Trail walk links the two.

The park has 160 km of walking tracks ranging from a 'senses trail' for the blind at Binna Burra to a tree-top canopy walk along a series of suspension bridges at Green Mountains. Walking trail guides are available from National Parks offices.

Places to Stay The *Binna Burra Mountain Lodge* (☎ (075) 33 3622) has a good but

QUEENSLAND

small camping ground, with sites at $7 per person and on-site tents from $35 a double. It's advisable to book. The lodge has rustic log cabins which cost from $98 per person per night, but that includes all meals, free hiking and climbing gear, and activities like guided walks, bus trips and abseiling. There's a kiosk and tearooms near the camping ground.

The famous O'Reilly's Guesthouse (☎ (075) 44 0644), at Green Mountains, has similar prices and facilities to Binna Burra. There's also a kiosk, and a National Parks camping ground about 600 metres away with sites for $7.

You can bush camp in Lamington, but only a limited number of permits are issued. You can get information from the National Parks offices at Burleigh Heads or Brisbane, but camping permits must be obtained from the ranger at Green Mountains (☎ (075) 44 0634).

The Crash of the Stinson
On 19 February 1937, a Stinson airliner carrying seven people crashed in the thick, impenetrable forests of the McPherson mountain range. Four passengers were killed instantly, and another died after falling over a cliff when he went for help. The plane had been missing for nine days and search parties had almost given up when Bernard O'Reilly, owner of the Lamington Guesthouse, found the wreck and its two survivors. O'Reilly later said that one of the first questions the two men asked was 'What's the cricket score?'. Apparently, they were considerably cheered to hear that Don Bradman was 165 not out.

Parts of the wrecked plane, and photographs of the rescue, are on display at O'Reilly's Guesthouse. ■

Getting There & Away The Binna Burra bus service (☎ (075) 33 3622) operates daily between Surfers and Binna Burra. The trip takes one hour and costs $16. The bus leaves Surfers from the Coachtrans terminal at the bus station at 1.15 pm; departures from Binna Burra are at 10.30 am daily. Bookings are essential.

Allstate Scenic Tours (☎ (07) 285 1777) runs a bus service six times a week between the Brisbane transit centre and Green Mountains (O'Reilly's). The one-way trip takes about three hours and costs $16, or it's $32 for a day trip including lunch.

Holiday Service (☎ (075) 92 1066) has a daily service from the Gold Coast to Green Mountains via Mt Tamborine, costing $30 return. It does pick-ups from your accommodation.

Mt Lindesay Highway
This road runs south from Brisbane, across the Great Dividing Range west of Lamington, and into New South Wales at Woodenbong. **Beaudesert**, in cattle country 66 km from Brisbane, is just 20 km south-west of Tamborine Mountain. It has a pioneer museum and tourist information centre on Jane St.

West of Beaudesert is the stretch of the Great Dividing Range known as the **Scenic Rim** (see the Darling Downs section). Further south, **Mt Barney National Park** is undeveloped but popular with bushwalkers and climbers. It's in the Great Dividing Range just north of the state border. You reach it from the Rathdowney to Boonah road. There's a tourist information office (☎ (075) 44 1222) on the highway at Rathdowney.

Sunshine Coast

The stretch of coast from the top of Bribie Island to just north of Noosa is known as the Sunshine Coast. It's a popular holiday area, renowned for fine beaches, good surfing and fishing. Although it doesn't have the high-rise jungle and neon-lit strips of the Gold Coast, the coast is still quite commercial and has been heavily developed, especially in the last decade.

Noosa Heads is the most fashionable and exclusive town on the coast, but it also has a good range of budget accommodation, an excellent national park and great beaches. Maroochydore is also quite popular. North of Noosa is the Cooloola National Park and Rainbow Beach, an access point for Fraser Island. The inland Bruce Highway (the main road north) has a series of artificial tourist attractions, such as the rather large Pineapple and Cow.

Getting There & Away

Air The Sunshine Coast Airport is on the coast road at Mudjimba, about 10 km north of Maroochydore. Sunstate flies from Brisbane ($85), Eastwest/Ansett and Qantas from Sydney.

Bus Sunshine Coast Coaches (☎ (07) 236 1901) runs about 10 buses daily connecting Brisbane with the Sunshine Coast and its hinterland towns. It's about two hours from Brisbane to Maroochydore and three hours to Noosa. In Brisbane the buses leave from the transit centre.

Greyhound Pioneer and McCafferty's buses travel along the Bruce Highway, but not across to the coast. To head north from the Sunshine Coast, you need to take a bus to Nambour or Cooroy on the highway. Tewantin Bus Services (☎ (074) 49 7422) operate to and from Noosa; the last bus to Cooroy leaves around 5.45 pm, and from Cooroy to Noosa at around 6.45 pm.

Train The most convenient stations for the Sunshine Coast are Nambour and Cooroy. There are daily services to these places from Brisbane and from the north.

CABOOLTURE (population 12,700)

This region, 49 km north of Brisbane, once had a large Aboriginal population. Nowadays, it's a prosperous dairy centre famous for its yoghurt. It also has two interesting historical attractions, and a tourist information centre (☎ (074) 95 3122).

The **Abbey Museum**, on Old Toorbul Point Rd, is a world social history museum with a monastic curatorship. It's open on Tuesdays, Thursdays, Fridays and Saturdays

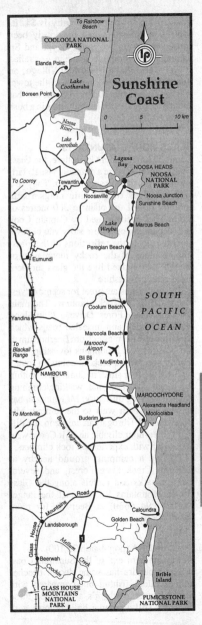

QUEENSLAND

from 10 am to 4 pm, and entry is $4. Its 4500-item collection had previously been housed in London, Cyprus, Egypt and Sri Lanka before finding its home in Australia.

The **Caboolture Historical Village**, on Beerburrum Rd, two km north of the town, is open daily from 10 am to 3 pm and has about 30 early Australian buildings in a bush setting; entry is $5.

GLASS HOUSE MOUNTAINS

About 20 km north of Caboolture, the Glass House Mountains are a dramatic visual starting point for the Sunshine Coast. They're a bizarre series of volcanic crags rising abruptly out of the plain to 300 metres or more. They were named by Captain Cook and, depending on whose story you believe, he either noted the reflections of the glass-smooth sides of the rocky mountains, or thought they looked like the glass furnaces in his native Yorkshire.

The mountains are great for scenic drives, bushwalking and rock climbing. The main access is via the Forest Drive, a 22 km-long series of sealed and unsealed roads which wind through the ranges from Beerburrum to the Glass House Mountains township, with several spectacular lookout points en route.

There are four small national parks within the range, and each has walking/climbing trails of varying difficulty: Mt Ngungun has an easy two-hour walk to the summit; Mts Beerwah and Tibrogargan are steep and difficult three-hour climbs; and Mt Coonowrin is popular with experienced rock climbers.

There's a camping ground nearby at Coochin Creek State Forest, and several caravan parks and motels along the Glass House Mountains Rd. Contact the ranger (☎ (074) 94 6630) at Beerwah for more information.

CALOUNDRA (population 22,100)

At the southern end of the Sunshine Coast strip, Caloundra has some decent beaches and excellent fishing but compared with places further north, it's a bit faded these days. It's still a popular holiday town with

families, but doesn't have much in the way of budget accommodation. Bulcock Beach, good for windsurfing, is just down from the main street, overlooking the northern end of Bribie Island.

Points of interest include the **Queensland Air Museum** at Caloundra Aerodrome, which is open Wednesday, Saturday and Sunday from 10 am to 4 pm and costs $3, and the **Ettamogah Pub** on the Bruce Highway, just north of the Caloundra turn-off. You can take cruises around the channels and to Bribie Island from Caloundra.

There's a tourist information office (☎ (074) 91 0202) on Caloundra Rd, just west of the town centre.

Places to Stay

Caloundra has more than eight caravan parks. The *Shelly Beach Holiday Village* (☎ (074) 91 6923) in William St is close to the beach and has tent sites from $10 and on-site cabins from $40. The *Caloundra Holiday Resort* (☎ (074) 91 3342) at Dicky Beach also has on-site cabins from $35.

There are plenty of motels and holiday units; the *Caloundra Motel* (☎ (074) 91 1411), at 30 Bowman Rd, is one of the cheapest with doubles from $30.

MAROOCHYDORE (population 28,500)

North of Caloundra, the coast is built up most of the way to the triple towns of Mooloolaba, Alexandra Headland and Maroochydore.

Maroochydore, the main town, is a busy commercial centre and popular tourist spot, with both an ocean beach and the Maroochy River, which has lots of pelicans and a few islands. Nearby, **Alexandra Headland** has a pleasant beach and good surfing off a rocky point.

Mooloolaba has the brightest atmosphere, with a long sandy beach and a strip of shops along the beachfront, including cafes, restaurants and the odd nightspot. Also at Mooloolaba is the **Wharf**, an impressive riverfront development with shops, eateries, a tavern, a marina and the excellent **Underwater World**, the largest oceanarium in the southern hemisphere. A transparent tunnel takes you underneath the oceanarium, and there's also a performing seals show. It's open daily from 9 am; entry costs $13.50.

Information

Tourist information in Maroochydore is available from the Maroochy Tourist Information Centre (☎ (074) 79 1566), near the corner of Aerodrome Rd (the main road connecting Maroochydore and Mooloolaba) and Sixth Ave.

Activities

Adventure Tours Sunshine Coast (☎ (074) 44 8824) offers four different one-day treks including a climb at the Glass House Mountains. Commando Adventures (☎ (074) 93 1445) also offers adventure tours and weekends, including a Fraser Island trip.

Places to Stay

There's the usual selection of caravan parks. One of the most popular with travellers is the *Cotton Tree Caravan Park* (☎ (074) 43 1253) on the Esplanade beside the river. Close to the beach in Mooloolaba there's the *Parkyn Parade Caravan Park* (☎ (074) 44 1201). Neither place has on-site vans. For these try the *Alexandra Gardens Caravan Park* (☎ (074) 43 2356) on Okinja Rd, Maroochydore.

Zords Backpackers (☎ (074) 43 1755), at 15 The Esplanade, is a friendly hostel in an old timber guesthouse overlooking the river. Dorm beds cost $10 and doubles $24. At 50 Parker St, the *Suncoast Backpackers Lodge* (☎ (074) 43 7544) is a modern, purpose-built hostel and has dorms and doubles at the same prices. The YHA *Holiday Hostel* (☎ (074) 43 3151) is at 24 Schirrmann Drive, a couple of streets off Bradman Ave. The nightly cost is $11 in a dorm and $24 for a double; nonmembers pay $1 more.

Motels are generally rather expensive. The small *Kyamba Court Motel* (☎ (074) 44 0202) at 94 Brisbane Rd, Mooloolaba, is one of the cheapest and has doubles from $40.

Getting There & Around

The long-distance bus stop is in the centre of Maroochydore, just off Aerodrome Rd (near KFC).

You can hire boats at several places in Maroochydore and Mooloolaba, or take river cruises from The Wharf in Mooloolaba. Beetles and motor scooters can be hired from Bugs Convertible (☎ (074) 43 7555) on Aerodrome Rd, near the info centre. Can Do Rentals (☎ (074) 43 8101) at 71 Aerodrome Rd also hire cars.

NOOSA (population 8062)

A surfers' Mecca since the early 1960s, Noosa has become a resort for the fashionable – with beaches, good restaurants, the fine coastal Noosa National Park and, just to the north, the walks, waterways and beaches of the Cooloola National Park. Noosa remains a far cry from the hype of the Gold Coast, and has more character than the rest of the Sunshine Coast.

Orientation

Noosa is actually a string of small linked centres – with confusingly similar names – stretching back from the mouth of the Noosa River and along its maze of tributary creeks and lakes. The slickest resort area is Noosa Heads, on the coast between the river mouth and rocky Noosa Head. From Noosa Heads two roads lead back to Noosaville, about three km away. One goes across an island known as Noosa Sound, the other circles round to the south through Noosa Junction. Noosaville is the departure point for most river cruises.

Further inland, beyond Noosaville, you reach Tewantin, six km from Noosa Heads. Sunshine Beach, which is about three km south of the centre, has long sandy surf beaches.

Information

The Hastings St Tourist Information Centre (☎ (074) 47 4988) in Noosa Heads is open daily from 9 am to 5 pm. There are also a number of privately run tourist information

QUEENSLAND

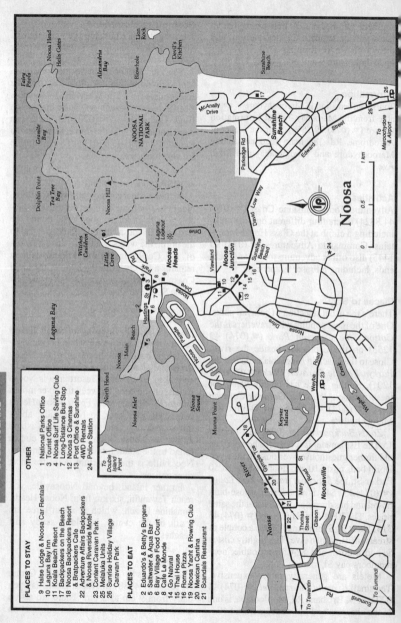

PLACES TO STAY

9 Halse Lodge & Noosa Car Rentals
10 Laguna Bay Inn
11 Koala Beach Resort
17 Backpackers on the Beach
18 Noosa Backpackers Resort
    & Bratpacks Cafe
22 Adventure Affairs Backpackers
    & Noosa Riverside Motel
23 Content Caravan Park
25 Melaluka Units
26 Sunrise Holiday Village
    Caravan Park

PLACES TO EAT

2 Eduardo's & Betty's Burgers
6 Saltwater & Aqua Bar
8 Bay Village Food Court
14 Go Natural
15 Thai House
16 Roma Pizza
19 Noosa Yacht & Rowing Club
20 Mexican Cantina
21 Scandals Restaurant

OTHER

1 National Parks Office
3 Tourist Office
4 Noosa Surf Life Saving Club
7 Long-Distance Bus Stop
12 Noosa 3 Cinemas
13 Post Office & Sunshine
    4WD Rentals
24 Police Station

Noosa

offices which double as booking agents for accommodation, trips, tours and so on.

Written Dimension, near the cinemas on Sunshine Beach Rd in Noosa Junction, is a good bookshop.

Noosa National Park

The spectacular cape at Noosa Head marks the northern end of the Sunshine Coast. This small but lovely national park extends for about two km in each direction from the headland, and has fine walks, great coastal scenery and a string of bays on the northern side which draw surfers from all over. Alexandria Bay on the eastern side is the best sandy beach.

The main entrance, at the end of Park Rd, has a car park, information centre and picnic areas, and is also the starting point for five great walking tracks, which range from one to four km in length. You can also drive up to the **Laguna Lookout** from Viewland Drive in Noosa Junction, or walk into the park from McAnally Drive or Parkedge Rd in Sunshine Beach.

Activities

Noosa Sea Sports (☎ (074) 47 3426) in Noosa Sound shopping centre rents surfboards, boogie boards, fishing and snorkelling gear, and also books tours and cruises. Catamarans and surf skis can be hired from the Noosa Main Beach. Most of the surf shops rent boards, including Ozmosis (☎ (074) 47 3300) in Hastings St.

Several places along the river in Gympie Terrace in Noosaville rent out boats and fishing gear, catamarans and surf skis.

Organised Tours & Cruises

You can do all sorts of boat cruises from Noosa, including trips up the Noosa River to the Cooloola National Park and dolphin-spotting ocean trips. Brochures and booking agents are everywhere.

There are also 4WD trips along the beaches of the national park and up to Fraser Island, with day trips costing between $65 and $90. All of the hostels organise or book three-day 4WD camping trips to Fraser

Island, which cost around $80 BYO food or $110 with food supplied.

Places to Stay

Except for hostels, accommodation prices can rise by 50% in quite busy times and by 100% in the December to January peak season. If you're going to stay a few days, it's worth asking at information offices and estate agents about holiday flats or units. These can be economical, especially for a group. In the off season, some estate agents rent private holiday homes at bargain rates, or advertise for caretakers – look on Sunshine Beach Rd in Noosa Junction or Hastings St in Noosa Heads.

Camping The *Content Caravan Park* (☎ (074) 49 7746), on Weyba Rd in Noosaville, and the *Sunrise Holiday Village* (☎ (074) 47 3294), on the beach in Sunshine Beach, both have tent sites, as well as on-site vans and cabins – book ahead in peak times.

Hostels All of Noosa's hostels have courtesy buses and do pick-ups from the bus stop.

The *Noosa Backpackers Resort* (☎ (074) 49 8151) at 9 William St, Munna Point, Noosaville, is a popular hostel with good cooking and sitting areas, a pool and a cafe (see places to eat). The owners can also organise river cruises or trips to the Cooloola area or Fraser Island. Dorm beds are $12, doubles $26 and a cooked breakfast costs $2.

Also in Noosaville is *Adventure Affairs Backpackers* (☎ (074) 49 8055) at 173 Gympie Terrace. The facilities are good, and include a pool, free bikes and a free light breakfast. Beds in the large dorm are $10, small dorms $12 and doubles $26.

In Sunshine Beach, *Backpackers on the Beach* (☎ (074) 47 4739), at 26 Stevens St, is close to the beach and has good two-bedroom self-contained units. Beds cost $13 a night, and bikes, surfboards and laundry are free.

Another good option in Sunshine Beach is the *Melaluka Units* (☎ (074) 47 3663) at 7 Selene St. It's also close to the beach, and has two- and three-bedroom holiday units with beds costing $13 per person. It has a pool, sauna and free laundry.

The new *Koala Beach Resort* (☎ (074) 47 3355), at 44 Noosa Drive in Noosa Junction, is a converted motel with good facilities including a pool, cafe, bikes and surfboards. A bed in a four-bed unit costs $12, doubles are $28 and there are family units available. This place is very central, and about 750 metres from the bus stop.

In Noosa Heads itself, *Halse Lodge* (☎ (074) 47 3254) is an immaculately kept place, run by the Anglican Church. It's housed in a beautiful 100-year-old guest-house, complete with polished wooden floors and great views over the town and sea. The staff are friendly, and although the lodge has an institutional air, it's excellent value at $18 for B&B, $6 more if you need linen.

Motels & Holiday Units One of the best areas for cheaper accommodation is along Gympie Terrace, the main road through Noosaville. The *River Palms* (☎ (074) 49 7318) at No 137 has holiday units from $40 a double. The *Noosa Riverside Motel* (☎ (074) 49 7551), at 175 Gympie Terrace, has singles/doubles from $35/40 in rooms with their own well-equipped kitchens. At No 281, *Noosa River Beach* (☎ (074) 49 7873) has a few budget holiday units from $35 a double.

The *Laguna Bay Inn* (☎ (074) 49 2873), at 2 Viewland Drive in Noosa Junction, is quite central and has four excellent self-contained units in a shady garden setting, costing from $60 a double. Most of the places around Hastings St and the beachfront in Noosa Heads are expensive. Cheapest of the bunch are *Tingirana* (☎ (074) 47 3274) at 25 Hastings St, with units from $60, and *Jacaranda* (☎ (074) 47 4011), also in Hastings St, with units from $70.

There are quite a few accommodation booking agents in Noosa, including Accom Noosa (☎ (074) 47 2224) and Holiday Noosa (☎ (074) 47 4011).

Places to Eat

Noosa has three main eating centres: Sun-shine Beach Rd in Noosa Junction, Gympie Terrace in Noosaville and Hastings St in Noosa Heads. Hastings St has the most glamorous (and most expensive) restaurants and cafes.

In Sunshine Beach Rd, *Roma Pizza*, at the southern end, has pastas and pizzas for around $9 and other main dishes from $12 to $15. On Monday, Tuesday and Wednesday nights there's an all-you-can-eat pasta or pizza special for $6. *Thai House*, upstairs at the Sunshine Centre opposite the cinemas, has main courses at $12.50. *Go Natural*, a health-food shop on the corner of Arcadia St, is a good spot for lunches.

In Noosaville there are several choices. *Scandals* is a good little BYO place on the corner of Thomas St and Gympie Terrace, while a little further along, at 247 Gympie Terrace, the *Mexican Cantina* is another BYO place with good food at reasonable prices. Across the road and overlooking the river, the *Noosa Yacht & Rowing Club* does carvery roasts for $5 and desserts for $2 four nights a week, and Sunday lunches. The *Bratpackers Cafe*, beside the Noosa Back-packers Resort, is very popular with locals and travellers, and has a good range of meals for around $9.

In Noosa Heads, trendy Hastings St is lined with restaurants and cafes, many with candle-lit outdoor tables under umbrellas or canopies. There are some great restaurants here – some very expensive, others quite affordable. *Eduardo's* (☎ (074) 47 5875) has excellent food and a great setting right on the beach; ask for a table on the beachfront deck. It serves breakfast, lunch and dinner. In the walkway leading to Eduardo's is *Betty's Burgers*, a small takeaway with a sensational range of burgers from $1 to $3.50. Back on Hastings St, the *Bay Village Food Court* has a selection of lunch-time stalls serving good food.

At the western end of Hastings St is the Mediterranean-style *Aqua Bar*, and *Saltwater* (☎ (074) 47 2234) has great takeaway fish & chips and a very good seafood restaurant upstairs – you'll need to book. Up the other end past the roundabout, *Cafe Le*

Monde is one of the most popular Hastings St restaurants, with reasonably priced pastas, salads and sandwiches, and sometimes live music.

Entertainment

Montana's, opposite Coles supermarket on Lanyana Way in Noosa Junction, and the *Rolling Rock* in Hastings St are the most popular nightclubs. The *Beach Chalet* in Sunshine Beach has a good reggae night every Monday, and the *Royal Mail Hotel* in Tewantin is popular with backpackers.

The *Noosa 3 Cinemas* (☎ (074) 47 5300) on Sunshine Beach Rd, Noosa Junction, show mainstream movies.

Getting Around

Tewantin Bus Services (☎ (074) 49 7422) runs daily services up and down the coast between Noosa, Sunshine Beach and Peregian Beach, and inland to Tewantin, Cooroy and Nambour. It also runs a local service linking Noosa Heads, Noosaville, Noosa Junction, etc.

Mokes are available from Noosa Car Rental (☎ (074) 47 3777), right opposite the bus stop in Noosa Heads. There are a number of other local operators, plus national firms like Avis and Thrifty.

If you want to drive up the Cooloola Coast beach to the wreck of the *Cherry Venture*, Rainbow Beach or Fraser Island, Sunshine 4WD Rentals (☎ (074) 47 3702), beside the Noosa Junction post office, rent 4WDs for $100 to $150 a day.

Noosa Sea Sports (☎ (074) 47 3426) in Noosa Sound rents bikes and mopeds.

COOLOOLA COAST

Just north of Noosa, the **Cooloola National Park** covers over 54,000 hectares and stretches around 50 km north to Rainbow Beach (see the later Rainbow Beach section). A couple of km upstream from Noosaville, the Noosa River takes a northward bend and widens out into Lake Cooroibah then Lake Cootharaba, which is at the southern end of the national park. It's a varied wilderness area with long sandy beaches, mangrove-lined waterways, forest, heath land and lakes, all of it featuring plentiful bird life and lots of wildflowers in spring.

There are various ways of accessing the coast and the park. The best way to see Cooloola is by boat from the Noosa River. From Tewantin, you can take a vehicle ferry across the Noosa River and drive to Lake Cooroibah and the beaches of Laguna Bay. Ferries operate daily from 6 am to 9 pm (till midnight on Fridays and Saturdays) and cost $4 per car. If you have a 4WD, you can drive right up this beach to Rainbow Bay, and from there cross to Fraser Island. On the way you'll pass the Teewah coloured sand cliffs and the rusting *Cherry Venture*, a 3000-tonne freighter swept ashore by a cyclone in 1973.

Another access road from the south is from Tewantin to Boreen Point, on the shores of Lake Cootharaba. The historic *Apollonian Hotel* (☎ (074) 85 3100) is worth a visit for a cold beer or a meal and it also has rooms with shared bathrooms for $30 a double. The *Jetty* restaurant (☎ (074) 85 3167) has good meals and a lovely setting overlooking the lake. There's also a caravan park, a motel and holiday units in the town.

From Boreen Point, the road continues five km north to Elanda Point where there's a lakeside camping ground and a ranger's office (☎ (074) 85 3245). Several walking trails start here including the 46-km Cooloola Wilderness Trail and a seven-km trail to the National Parks visitors centre (☎ (074) 49 7364) at Kinaba Island. Cooloola Way is a gravel road through the west of the park, between Kin Kin and Rainbow Beach.

There are around 10 camping grounds in the park, many of them alongside the river. The main ones are Fig Tree Point at the north of Lake Cootharaba and Harry's Hut about four km upstream. Freshwater is the main camp on the coast; it's about six km south of Double Island Point. For site bookings and info, contact one of the ranger's offices.

Northern Cooloola

The easiest way to reach this part of the national park is from the Rainbow Beach area. Northern Cooloola has camping grounds between Freshwater Lake and the eastern beach, and near Double Island Point on the north-facing beach (both 4WD or foot access only). There are several walking tracks, and the main vehicle access is from the Gympie to Rainbow Beach road, four km south of Rainbow Beach. You can get information and camping permits for northern Cooloola from the National Parks information centre in Rainbow Beach (☎ (074) 86 3160).

NAMBOUR (population 10,350)

At harvest time, you often see sugar-cane trains passing through this sugar-growing town. Pineapples and other tropical fruits are also grown in the area, and the 'Big Pineapple', one of Queensland's superbly kitsch 'big' creations, is just off the Bruce Highway about six km south of Nambour. You can climb up inside this 15-metre fibreglass wonder to see the full story of pineapple cultivation. As if that wasn't enough, six km north at Yandina, the 'Big Cow' stands on the side of the highway.

Further up the highway at Eumundi, you can fossick for thunder eggs at Thunder Egg Farm, or you could try the locally brewed beer of the same name.

SUNSHINE COAST HINTERLAND
Blackall Range

The mountains rise fairly close behind the coast, and west of Nambour or Landsborough you can take the scenic Mapleton to Maleny road right along the ridge line of the Blackall Range. **Mapleton Falls National Park** is four km west of Mapleton and **Kondalilla National Park** is three km off the Mapleton to Montville stretch of the road. Both have rainforest, and the Kondalilla Falls drop 80 metres into a rainforest valley, while at Mapleton Falls, Pencil Creek plunges 120 metres. This is a great area for exploring – there's lots of bird life and several walking tracks in the parks. The *Mapleton Tavern* has great views and is a good place for a counter meal or a cold beer.

Midway between Mapleton and Maleny,

the mountain village of **Montville** is a very popular tourist spot, with lots of craft shops and restaurants.

South Burnett

Further inland, the South Burnett region includes Australia's most important peanut-growing area. **Kingaroy** almost means 'peanuts' in Australia, not least because the well-known ex-premier of Queensland, Joh Bjelke-Petersen, hails from here. There's a tourist office (☎ (071) 62 3199) at 128 Haly St, Kingaroy. Next door, the Heritage Museum is open daily from 10 am to 2 pm.

South-east of Kingaroy, **Nanango** is another peanut town but with an earlier history of gold mining. You can fossick for gold at **Seven Mile Diggings**, 11 km from Nanango. **Murgon** is the main town of the region north of Kingaroy. It has the Queensland Dairy Industry Museum, on Gayndah Rd. Six km south of Murgon the **Cherbourg** Aboriginal community runs a pottery and craft shop, open from Monday to Friday.

The **Bunya Mountains**, isolated outliers of the Great Dividing Range, rise abruptly to over 1000 metres, and are accessible by sealed road about 50 km south-west of Kingaroy. The mountains are a national park, with a variety of vegetation from rainforest to heath land. There are three camping grounds in the park, plus a network of walking tracks to numerous waterfalls and lookouts. The ranger (☎ (076) 68 3127) is at Dalby.

Darling Downs

West of the Great Dividing Range in southern Queensland stretch the rolling plains of the Darling Downs, some of the most fertile and productive agricultural land in Australia. In the state's early history, the Darling Downs were something of a back door into the region. Nobody was allowed within an 80-km radius of the penal colony of Brisbane but settlers gradually pushed their way north from New South Wales through this area.

West of the Darling Downs, the population becomes more scattered as you move out of the crop-producing area into sheep and cattle country centred on towns like Roma, Charleville and Cunnamulla.

From Ipswich, just inland from Brisbane, there are two main routes west: a southern one through Warwick and Goondiwindi to Cunnamulla, and a northern one through Toowoomba and Roma to Charleville. From Charleville you can continue west to the Channel Country or turn north for Longreach (see the Outback Queensland section).

The Darling Downs region is linked to New South Wales by two main roads: the New England Highway from Warwick down to Tamworth and the Newell Highway from Goondiwindi to Dubbo. Further west, the Mitchell Highway from Charleville and Cunnamulla is the region's main road into New South Wales.

Getting There & Away

Air Eastland Air and Sabair both fly between Brisbane and Toowoomba at least once daily; tickets can be booked on ☎ (076) 38 1199 in Toowoomba. Flight West (☎ (07) 229 1177) flies Brisbane to Charleville and back six days a week, with stops at Roma five days a week.

Bus Many long-distance buses between Brisbane and Sydney or destinations in Victoria go through the Darling Downs. Ipswich, Toowoomba and Warwick are on the New England Highway route; Ipswich, Toowoomba and Goondiwindi are on the Newell Highway route.

Greyhound Pioneer runs a variety of buses west into Queensland from Brisbane: to Mt Isa daily (24½ hours, $129) through Ipswich, Toowoomba (2½ hours, $14), Roma (seven hours, $41), Charleville (11 hours, $52) and Longreach (17 hours, $83).

McCafferty's runs a bus service between Ipswich and Toowoomba several times a day to co-ordinate with the suburban trains between Brisbane and Ipswich. There are also McCafferty's buses between Toowoomba and the Gold Coast, Toowoomba and Mt Isa,

and between Brisbane and Rockhampton via Ipswich, Toowoomba and Miles.

Train The air-con Westlander runs twice a week from Brisbane to Cunnamulla and Quilpie, through Ipswich, Toowoomba, Roma and Charleville. The 777-km journey from Brisbane to Charleville takes about 17 hours.

Trains without air-conditioning run twice weekly between Brisbane and Dirranbandi, through Ipswich, Toowoomba, Warwick and Goondiwindi. Returning to Brisbane you have to change to a co-ordinated bus service between Toowoomba and Ipswich and then board a suburban train from Ipswich.

IPSWICH (population 73,310)

Now virtually an outer suburb of Brisbane, Ipswich was originally established as a convict settlement as early as 1827 and was one of the most important early Queensland towns. It's the main gateway to the Darling Downs. On the way from Brisbane to Ipswich, **Wolston House** at Grindle Rd, Wacol, 18 km west of Brisbane, is an early colonial country residence, built in 1852 of local materials. It's open from 9 am to 5 pm, Wednesday to Sunday and costs $3.

Ipswich has many fine old houses and public buildings: if you're interested in Queensland's distinctive architecture, pick up the excellent *Ipswich City Heritage Trails* leaflet which will guide you around a great diversity of buildings. There's a tourist information office (☎ (07) 281 0555) on the corner of D'Arcy Place and Brisbane St.

IPSWICH TO WARWICK

South-west of Ipswich, the Cunningham Highway to Warwick crosses the Great Dividing Range at **Cunningham's Gap**, with 1100-metre mountains rising either side of the road. **Main Range National Park**, which covers the Great Dividing Range for about 20 km north and south of Cunningham's Gap, is great walking country, with a variety of walks starting from the car park at the crest of Cunningham's Gap. Much of the range is covered in rainforest. There's a camping area by the road on the western side of the gap: contact the ranger (☎ (076) 66 1133) for permits. **Spicer's Gap**, in the range south of Cunningham's Gap, has excellent views and another camping area. To reach it you turn off the highway five km west of Aratula, back towards Ipswich.

WARWICK AREA

South-west of Brisbane, 162 km inland and near the New South Wales border, Warwick is the oldest town in Queensland after Brisbane. It's a busy Darling Downs farming centre noted for its roses, and for its rodeo on the last weekend in October. **Pringle Cottage** on Dragon St dates from 1863 and is now a museum, open daily except Tuesdays. There's a tourist office (☎ (076) 61 3122) on Albion St (the main highway). The *Warwick Youth Hostel* (☎ (076) 61 3660), with 18 beds at $9.50 a night ($10.50 nonmembers), is at 6 Palmerin St.

Killarney, south-east of Warwick near the New South Wales border, is a pretty little town in an area of fine mountain scenery. Among the many lovely waterfalls nearby is Queen Mary Falls, tumbling 40 metres into a rainforested gorge 10 km east of Killarney. There's a caravan park (☎ (076) 64 7151) on the road near the falls.

South of Warwick on the New England Highway is **Stanthorpe**, near the New South Wales border. At 915 metres it's the coolest town in the state and a centre for fruit and vegetable production and wine making, with more than 20 vineyards, some of which you can tour. There's a tourist office (☎ (076) 81 2057) at 61 Marsh St. Twelve km north at Thulimbah, *Summit Lodge* (☎ (071) 83 2599) on the New England Highway has dorm beds for $12.50 per person, and they can often help find harvest work for travellers. *Arcot Homestead* (☎ (076) 53 1360), 70 km west of Stanthorpe, is a host farm offering a number of station activities. The charge is $20 for self-catered accommodation in the shearers' quarters, $10 to camp or $80 for full board. Phone ahead for directions.

From the highway 26 km south of Stanthorpe, a paved road leads nine km east up to **Girraween National Park**, an area of 1000-metre-high hills, valleys and huge granite outcrops. The park has a visitor centre (☎ (076) 84 5157), two camping grounds with hot showers, and several walking tracks of varying length. Girraween adjoins Bald Rock National Park over the border in New South Wales. It can fall below freezing on winter nights here, but summer days are warm. Call the park's visitor centre to book camping sites.

GOONDIWINDI & FURTHER WEST

West of Warwick, **Goondiwindi** is on the New South Wales border and the Macintyre River. It's a popular stop on the Newell Highway between Melbourne and Brisbane. There's a small museum in the old customs house and a wildlife sanctuary at the Boobera Lagoon. If you continue inland from Goondiwindi you reach **St George**, where cotton is grown on irrigated land.

Much further west is **Cunnamulla**, 254 km north of Bourke in New South Wales and very definitely in the outback. This is another sheep-raising centre, noted for its wildflowers. The **Yowah** opal fields are about 150 km further west.

TOOWOOMBA (population 76,000)

On the edge of the Great Dividing Range and the Darling Downs, 138 km inland from Brisbane, this is the largest city in the region. It's a gracious city with parks, tree-lined streets, several art galleries and many early buildings.

The old **Bull's Head Inn** on Brisbane St, Drayton, six km west, dates from 1847 and you can visit it from 10 am to 4 pm, Thursday to Monday, for $2.50. In Toowoomba itself there's the **Cobb & Co Museum** at 27 Lindsay St, and the **Botanical Gardens** in Queens Park on the corner of Margaret and Lindsay Sts.

The tourist information centre (☎ (076) 39 3797) is at 541 Ruthven St.

Places to Stay

The two cheapest hotels in town are the

Ruthven Hotel, near the information centre, and the *Law Courts Hotel*, on the corner of Margaret and Neil Sts. Both are pretty basic.

Three km south of Jondaryan, which is about 45 km out of Toowoomba, there's a YHA-associated youth hostel in the 1859 *Jondaryan Woolshed* (☎ (076) 92 2229). The building is also a wool pioneer complex with museums, and daily shearing and black-smithing demonstrations. The nightly cost in the hostel is $5.

ROMA (population 5700)

An early Queensland settlement, and now the centre for a huge sheep- and cattle-raising district, Roma also has some curious small industries. There's enough oil in the area to support a small refinery, which produces just enough petroleum for local use. Gas deposits are rather larger, and Roma supplies Brisbane through a 450-km pipeline. There's also the small Romavilla Winery which is open daily; a wine festival is held in November.

Hervey Bay Area

North of the Sunshine and Cooloola coasts is 120-km-long Fraser Island. The two mainland departure points for the island are Rainbow Beach in the south and Hervey Bay opposite Fraser's west coast. Inland on the Bruce Highway are Gympie, where you turn off for Rainbow Beach, and Maryborough, where you turn off for Hervey Bay.

GYMPIE (population 10,800)

Gympie came into existence with an 1867 gold rush, and gold continued to be mined here right up to 1920. A week-long Gold Rush Festival is held in Gympie every October.

One of Queensland's four main National Parks information centres is on the Bruce Highway as you enter Gympie from the south (☎ (074) 82 4189). In the same building there's a tourist information office (☎ (074) 82 5444), open daily from 8.30 am

to 3.30 pm, and nearby is the interesting **Gympie Gold Mining & Historical Museum**.

A few km north of Two Mile, on Fraser Rd, is a second museum devoted to another source of Queensland's early wealth – the timber industry. The **Woodworks Forestry & Timber Museum** is open Monday to Friday from 10 am to 4 pm. You can get information on camping in nearby state forests here.

Gympie has several motels and caravan parks, and it's on the main bus and train routes north from Brisbane.

RAINBOW BEACH (population 726)

This little town, on the coast 70 km from Gympie, is an access point for Fraser Island and a base for visiting the northern part of Cooloola National Park.

From Rainbow Beach it's a 13-km drive north along the beach to Inskip Point, where ferries leave for Fraser Island. South-east of the town, the beach curves away 13 km to Double Island Point at the top of the Cooloola coast. One km along this beach is the 120-metre-high **Carlo sand blow**, and beyond it are the coloured sand cliffs which gave the town its name. You can walk behind or along the beach all the way from the town and up to the lighthouse on Double Island Point.

The privately run Rainbow Beach Tourist Information Centre (☎ (074) 86 3227) at 8 Rainbow Beach Rd has a list of other walks in the area. In a 4WD it's possible to drive to Noosa, 70 km south, along the beach most of the way. (See the earlier Cooloola National Park section.)

The National Parks office for obtaining Fraser Island vehicle and camping permits and northern Cooloola National Park camping permits is beside the main road as you enter Rainbow Beach; it's open daily from 7 am to 4 pm (☎ (074) 86 3160).

Places to Stay

The Rainbow Beach Holiday Village (☎ (074) 86 3222), on Rainbow Beach Rd and opposite the beach, has a backpackers' section with three-bed tents and basic

QUEENSLAND

cooking facilities for $7.50 per person. There's also tent sites for $10 and on-site vans from $25.

Rainbow Beach Backpackers (☎ (074) 86 3288), at 66 Rainbow Beach Rd, charges $11 per person. It's a small, clean place with a kitchenette, pool and restaurant next door (but no laundry).

The *Rainbow Beach Hotel/Motel* (☎ (074) 86 3125), near the beachfront, has rooms from $38/45, and the new *Rainbow Sands* (☎ (074) 86 3400) on Rainbow Beach Rd has good self-contained units from $49 a double.

Getting There & Away

A school bus (☎ (074) 82 2700) leaves Polley's Depot in Gympie at 6 am and 3 pm for Rainbow Beach, and heads back from Rainbow Beach at 7.20 am and 4.45 pm. It's open to all comers, runs Monday to Friday, and costs $8.95 one way. During school holidays, only the 6 am and 4.45 pm services run.

Another way to Rainbow Beach is to hitch along the beaches up from Noosa or on to Fraser Island. If you have a 4WD vehicle you can drive this way too.

Getting Around

In Rainbow Beach, the tourist information centre and Jeep City (☎ (074) 86 3223), at 10 Karounda Court, both rent 4WDs from around $90 a day with a two-day minimum hire.

There are also tours to Fraser Island, plus half-day trips to combinations of places like the Carlo sand blow, the coloured sand cliffs, Double Island Point, Lake Freshwater, Cooloola rainforest and the *Cherry Venture* wreck.

MARYBOROUGH (population 20,800)

Today, timber and sugar are Maryborough's major industries, but the town's earlier importance as an industrial centre and port on the Mary River led to the construction of a series of imposing Victorian buildings.

The greatest concentration of old buildings is on Wharf St. The **post office**, built in 1869, is just one of the many buildings which reflect Maryborough's early prosperity; some of the old hotels are also fine examples of Victoriana. A street market is held every Thursday in the town centre. Maryborough also has a **railway museum** in the old railway station on Lennox St.

There are several motels and caravan parks in the town, plus budget accommodation in some of the old hotels, such as the *Criterion Hotel* (☎ (071) 21 3043) at 98 Wharf St, with rooms for $12.50 per person.

HERVEY BAY (population 22,200)

The once-sleepy settlement of Hervey Bay has grown at an astronomical rate in the last decade, and it's now a major stopover on the backpacker circuit. The main attractions are Fraser Island, for which Hervey Bay is the main access point, and whale-watching trips in the bay.

The five small settlements which make up the town are popular family holiday spots with safe beaches and a huge number of caravan parks. There's no surf here, and the best beach is at Torquay.

Orientation

The five suburbs of Hervey Bay are strung along a 10-km-long, north-facing stretch of coast. From west to east they are Point Vernon, Pialba, Scarness, Torquay and Urangan. Pialba is the main business and shopping centre, although Torquay is where most of the action is. Fraser Island is 12 km across the Great Sandy Strait from Urangan, with Woody Island in between. River Heads, the departure point for the main Fraser Island ferries, is 15 km south of Urangan.

Information

There are numerous privately run information centres and tour booking offices, including the Hervey Bay Tourist & Visitors Centre (☎ (071) 24 4050) at 63 Old Maryborough Rd in Pialba.

Things to See

Situated on the corner of Maryborough Rd and Fairway Drive in Pialba, **Hervey Bay**

QUEENSLAND

Hervey Bay

PLACES TO STAY

1 Pialba Caravan & Camping Park
5 Mango Tourist Hostel
7 Scarness Caravan & Camping Park
9 Friendly Hostel
10 Hervey Bay Backpackers
11 Koala Backpackers & Willy's Restaurant
14 Torquay Caravan & Camping Park
19 Colonial Log Cabin & Backpackers Resort
21 Magnolia Caravan Park

PLACES TO EAT

2 Pialba Hotel
3 RSL Club
4 Scarborough Hotel
6 Brollies Deli Cafe
12 Torquay Hotel
13 Toto's Restaurant
22 Last Resort Tavern

OTHER

15 Vic Hislop's Shark Show
16 Neptune's Coral Cave
17 Matthew Flinders & Z Force Memorials
18 Urangan Harbour
20 Tourist & Visitors Centre
23 Bus Terminal
24 Hervey Bay Natureworld
25 Hervey Bay City Council

Point Vernon

Hervey Bay

Great Sandy Strait

Urangan Pier

Dayman Point

Urangan

Kent St
Dayman St
Pulgul St

Booral Road

To Airport & River Heads

Elizabeth St
Botanic Gardens

Shelly Beach
Esplanade
Charlton Street
Cypress Street
Truro Street
Dayman Street

Torquay

Boat Harbour Drive
Urangan Street
Robert St
Boundary St

Scarness

Tavistock St
Denman Camp Road
Bideford St

Queens Rd
Torquay Rd

Taylor St
Main Street
Doolong Road

Pialba

Old Maryborough Road
Central Avenue

Golf Course

To Maryborough

Boat Harbour Drive
Fairway Dr

Esplanade
Long Street
Charlton Street

Pulgul Ck

0   1   2 km

Natureworld has native fauna ranging from wedge-tailed eagles to koalas, as well as introduced species such as camels and water buffaloes. Crocodiles are fed at 11.30 am and lorikeets at 3.30 pm; entry costs $7.

Vic Hislop's Shark Show, on the corner of Charlton Esplanade and Elizabeth St in Urangan, has a collection of photos, articles, jaw bones and a great white shark, plus shark documentaries. It's open daily from 8 am to 6 pm and costs $8 ($6 for backpackers).

Urangan Pier, a little further along Charlton Esplanade, is 1.4 km long. Once used for sugar and oil handling, it's now a popular fishing spot, since the far end stands in 25 to 30 metres of water.

One km east of the pier, at **Dayman Point**, is **Neptune's Coral Cave**, an aquarium with coral displays, fish, seals, turtles and a croc. It opens daily from 9 am and costs $7. From the point itself, there are good views over to Woody and Fraser islands, and there are monuments to Matthew Flinders and the Z Force WW II commandos who sank Japanese ships in Singapore Harbour in 1943.

Organised Tours

At last count there were 19 different boats running whale-watching tours from Hervey Bay and from the tip of Fraser Island. There are half-day tours (from $42 to $54) and full-day tours (from $40 to $60 including lunch) between August and mid-October. There are also half a dozen companies running cruises and day trips to Fraser Island – see that section for details. Tours can be booked through the information centres or hostels.

Places to Stay

Camping There are at least a dozen caravan parks in Hervey Bay. Some of the best are the council-run parks along Charlton Esplanade at Scarness (☎ (071) 28 1274), Torquay (☎ (071) 25 1578) and Pialba (☎ (071) 28 1399). These parks have tent sites for $9.50 and on-site vans for around $25 – book ahead.

The *Magnolia Caravan Park* (☎ (071) 28 1700), on the corner of Boat Harbour Drive

and Taylor St, has tent sites for $13 and on-site cabins for $45.

Hostels Hervey Bay has five hostels, spread between Scarness and Urangan. All do pickups from the main bus stop, and all organise trips to Fraser Island.

First up is the very friendly *Mango Tourist Hostel* (☎ (071) 24 2832) at 110 Torquay Rd, Scarness. It's a small, relaxed place, with bunks at $11 and one double at $25, and the young couple running it really look after you. This is also a good place for getting info about Fraser Island and alternative ways of getting there and seeing it.

The impressive *Koala Backpackers* (☎ (071) 25 3601) is at 408 Charlton Esplanade, Torquay. It's a large place with excellent facilities including a good pool and recreation room, and the beach is just across the road. Accommodation is in either two-bedroom units with their own kitchen and bathroom ($13) or dorms with good communal facilities ($12); doubles cost $28.

The *Hervey Bay Backpackers* (☎ (071) 24 1322) is at 195 Torquay Terrace in Scarness. It has the usual hostel facilities and a pool. There are two sections, one with dorms and one with rooms with private bathroom and TV; the nightly cost is $12 per person.

At Urangan, the *Colonial Log Cabin & Backpackers Resort* (☎ (071) 25 1844), on the corner of Boat Harbour Drive and Pulgul St, is very well set up. It's a few km out of the centre, but it's quiet and spacious and backs onto bushland. The two- and three-bed dorms cost $13, self-contained cabins cost $13 to $15 per person, and twin rooms are $26. Visitors have free use of bicycles, and there's a good pool and tennis court.

Another option is the newly established *Friendly Hostel* (☎ (071) 24 4107) at 182 Torquay Rd, Scarness. It's a small place with three units (each with three bedrooms and their own TV lounge, kitchen and bathroom); beds are $10 per person.

Motels & Holiday Flats There are plenty of these too. The *Bay View Motel* (☎ (071) 28 1134), at 399 Charlton Esplanade, Torquay,

QUEENSLAND

has units from $30/35. *Calypso Holiday Units* (☎ (071) 25 2688), at 480 Charlton Esplanade in Torquay, has self-contained units from $45 for up to four people.

Places to Eat

Despite being the 'business' centre, Pialba has few places to eat. The *Pialba Hotel* has excellent meals for around $10, and also has live music some nights. The *RSL Club* on Torquay Rd is slightly cheaper.

Charlton Esplanade in Torquay is the food focus in Hervey Bay. *Willy's*, next to Koala Backpackers, has always been popular with backpackers (although a recent fire has put its future in doubt). *Toto's*, on Fraser St, has good pizza and pasta, while *Gringo's Mexican Cantina*, at 449 Charlton Esplanade, needs no explanation. *Raw Energy*, next door, is a takeaway place with good burgers, juices and healthy meals. The pub in Torquay has the *China Garden* restaurant and a good beer garden – you can sit outside to eat, often with musical accompaniment. *Brollies Deli Cafe*, at 353 Charlton Esplanade in Scarness, is a good place for breakfast or lunch and has real coffee and excellent sandwiches.

The *Last Resort Tavern*, near the bus terminal on Boat Harbour Drive, is a popular beer barn with live music and good meals between $3.50 and $9.

Getting There & Away

Sunstate flies to and from Brisbane six or seven days a week. Hervey Bay Airport is off Booral Rd, Urangan.

Hervey Bay is on the major bus route. It's about 4½ hours from Brisbane (around $30), and about 5½ hours from Rockhampton ($55).

Hervey Bay's main bus stop is Geldard's Coach Terminal (☎ (071) 24 4000) in Central Ave, off Boat Harbour Drive in Pialba.

Getting Around

Maryborough-Hervey Bay Coaches (☎ (071) 1 3719) runs a service between the two centres, with nine trips every weekday and three on Saturdays.

There are several good 4WD hire places.

Fraser Coast 4x4 Rentals (☎ (071) 24 2488) at 196 Old Maryborough Rd in Pialba, Bay 4WD Centre (☎ (071) 28 2981) at 54 Boat Harbour Drive in Pialba and Allterrain (bookings through Koala Backpackers) all have good, reliable vehicles ranging from about $80 a day for a Suzuki Sierra to $120 for a Toyota Landcruiser, usually with a two-day minimum. Aussie Trax (☎ (071) 24 4433) at 56 Boat Harbour Drive has old ex-army jeeps for $69 a day.

FRASER ISLAND

Fraser Island, the world's largest sand island, was inscribed on the World Heritage List in 1993. The island is 120 km long by about 15 km wide and rises to 200 metres above sea level in places. Apart from three or four small rock outcrops, it's all sand – mostly covered in vegetation. Here and there the cover is broken by sand blows – dunes that grow, shrink or move as the wind pushes them. The island also has about 200 lakes, some of them superb for swimming. Almost half of the island forms the Great Sandy National Park.

Fraser Island is a delight for those who love fishing, walking, exploring by 4WD or trail bike, and for those who simply enjoy nature. There are superb beaches (though swimming in the ocean can be dangerous due to severe undertows and the odd shark or ten!), towering dunes, thick forests, walking tracks, interesting wildlife and clear fresh-water lakes and streams for swimming. You can camp or stay in accommodation. The island is sparsely populated and although more than 20,000 vehicles a year pile on to it, it remains wild. A network of sandy tracks crisscrosses the island and you can drive along great stretches of beach – but it's 4WD or trail bike only; there are no paved roads.

History

The island takes its name from Eliza Fraser, the wife of the captain of a ship which was wrecked further north in 1836. Making their way south to look for help, a group from the ship fell among Aborigines on Fraser Island. Some of the group died during their two-

Fraser Island

sand-mining company. The decision went to the conservationists.

Information

There's a visitor centre on the east coast of the island at Eurong (☎ (071) 27 9128), and ranger's offices at Dundubura and Waddy Point. These places all have plenty of leaflets detailing walking trails and the flora and fauna found on the island.

At Central Station (the old forestry depot) there's a small display on the history of exploration and logging on the island.

A good map is essential if you will be spending a few days exploring. The Sunmap 1:140,000 ($6) provides all the detail you need, and is widely available in Hervey Bay

General supplies are available from stores at Eurong, Happy Valley and Cathedral Beach, but as you might expect, prices are high. There are also public telephones at these sites.

It's possible to leave your car at the River Heads general store for $2 per day.

Permits You'll need a permit to take a vehicle onto the island, and to camp. The most convenient place to get permits is the River Heads general store, just half a km from the ferry to Wanggoolba Creek. Vehicles cost $15, and camping costs $7.50 per site per night. If you're staying in cabin accommodation, or camping in one of the island's private camping grounds, there's no need to pay the $7.50.

Permits can also be obtained from any of the National Parks offices in the area, or from the Hervey Bay City Council (☎ (071) 2: 0222) in Tavistock St.

Driving on the Island The only thing stopping you taking a conventional (non-4WD) vehicle onto the island is the fact that you probably won't get more than half a km before you get bogged in sand. Small 4WD sedans are OK, but you may have ground-clearance problems on some of the inland tracks – a 'proper' 4WD gives maximum mobility.

Ask on the mainland about island driving conditions before renting a 4WD vehicle

month wait for rescue, but others, including Eliza Fraser, survived with Aboriginal help.

The Butchulla Aborigines who used Fraser Island as a seasonal home were driven out onto missions when timber cutters moved on to the island in the 1860s. The cutters were after satinay, a rainforest tree almost unique to Fraser Island which is highly resistant to marine borer; this timber was used to line the Suez Canal. It was not until 1991 that logging on the island ceased.

In the mid-1970s, Fraser Island was the subject of a bitter struggle between conservationists and industry – in this case a

ometimes rain and storms can make
eaches and tracks very heavy going, if not
npassable. The best sources of such infor-
ation are probably the offices issuing the
ehicle permits.

Driving on the island requires a good deal
f care, to protect not only yourself but the
ragile environment. Apart from the beaches,
here you are free to drive at will, all tracks
re obvious and you should stick to them.
lost major junctions are signposted, but
nly the two dedicated 'scenic routes' are
ignposted along their length. When driving,
ou should have 4WD engaged at all times,
ot so much because of the danger of getting
tuck, but because your wheels are less likely
» spin and damage the sandy tracks.

When driving on the beaches, keep an eye
ut for washouts at the many creek outlets,
specially after heavy rain. Use your indica-
ors to show oncoming vehicles which side
ou intend passing on. Low tide is the best
me to travel as large expanses of smooth
ard sand are exposed. An additional hazard
. that the beach directly outside the resorts
. used as a landing strip for small aircraft.
.t high tide it is much more difficult, and
uite slow going. The speed limit on the
eaches is 80 km/h, and on the inland tracks
's 35 km/h, although there's little opportu-
ity to reach that speed.

Drive slowly when passing walkers and
eople fishing, as they probably won't hear
ou coming above the roar of the surf!

Driving on the eastern beach is fairly
raightforward; the western beach is more
eacherous and has swamps and holes –
void it.

round the Island

tarting from the south at Hook Point, you
ross a number of creeks and get to Dilli
illage, the former sand-mining centre.
fter the settlements of Eurong and Happy
'alley, you cross Eli Creek, the largest
ream on the east coast. About 65 km from
'ook Point are the remains of the *Maheno*,
former passenger liner which was wrecked
ere in 1935 as it was being towed to a
apanese scrap yard.

Four km beyond Eurong is a signposted
walking trail to the beautiful **Lake Wabby**,
which is being slowly filled by a massive
sand blow that advances about three metres
a year. It's a 45-minute walk (rewarded by a
swim in the lake), or you can drive a further
2.6 km north along the beach to take a scenic
route to a lookout on the inland side of the
lake. *Don't* dive into the lake after running
down the steep sand dunes – in the last few
years, five people have suffered spinal injuries doing just that.

A popular inland area for visitors is the
south-central lake and rainforest country
around Central Station and McKenzie, Jen-
nings, Birrabeen and Boomanjin lakes. **Lake
McKenzie** is unbelievably clear. Known as
a 'window' lake, the water here is actually
part of the water table, and so has not flowed
anywhere over land.

Two marked vehicle tracks lead inland
from Happy Valley: one goes to **Lake Garawongera**, then south to the beach again at
Poyungan Valley (15 km); the other heads to
Yidney Scrub and a number of lakes before
returning to the ocean beach north of the
wreck of the *Maheno* (45 km). The latter
route will take you to some fine lakes and
good lookout points among the highest
dunes on the island.

Not far north of Happy Valley you enter
the national park and pass the *Maheno* and
the **Cathedrals**, 25 km of coloured sand
cliffs. Dundubara has a ranger's hut, and
probably the best camping ground on the
island. Then there's a 20-km stretch of beach
before you come to the rock outcrops of
Indian Head, Middle Rocks and Waddy
Point. Just past here is **Orchid Beach**, and
it's a further 30 km of beach up to **Sandy
Cape**, the northern tip, with its lighthouse a
few more km to the west.

Walking Tracks There are a number of
'walkers-only' tracks, ranging from the one-
km Wungul Sand Blow Track at Dundubara
to the 13-km trail between Wabby and
McKenzie lakes. The useful *Fraser Island
Recreation Area* leaflet put out by the National
Parks & Wildlife Service lists several more.

QUEENSLAND

Organised Tours

Most day tours to Fraser Island allow you to split the trip and stay a few days on the island before coming back.

There are several 4WD bus tour operators in Rainbow Beach and Hervey Bay. Prices for day tours range upwards from $50. Each outfit follows a different route but a typical tour might take in a trip up the east coast to the *Maheno* wreck and the Cathedrals, plus Central Station and a couple of the lakes in the centre of the island. The Kingfisher Bay Resort (☎ (071) 25 5511) offers ranger-guided ecotours for $56 including lunch.

Self-drive tours organised from the hostels are popular, and currently cost around $80 per person for a three-day trip. This doesn't include food or fuel but all the gear is organised for you. These trips are an affordable and (usually) fun way to see the island, but you'll probably be in a group of nine, and, like relatives, you can't choose who you go with. There are alternative ways to see the island – like walking.

Places to Stay & Eat

Come well equipped since supplies on the island are limited and only available in a few places. And be prepared for mosquitoes and horseflies.

Camping This is the cheapest way to stay on the island and gives you the chance to get closer to Fraser Island's unique natural environment. The National Parks service and forestry department operate 11 camping areas on the island, some accessible only by boat or on foot. Those in the north at Dundubara, Waddy Point and Wathumba and in the south at Central Station, Lake Boomanjin and Lake McKenzie all have toilets and showers. You can also camp on some stretches of beach. To camp in any of these public areas you need a permit.

A word of warning: backpackers' tours have a bad reputation amongst the rangers here, and they will quite happily throw you off the island and/or fine you if they find you drunk and disorderly or disturbing other campers.

There's also the privately run *Cathedra Beach Resort & Camping Park* (☎ (071) 2 4988), 34 km north of Eurong. Tent sites cos $14 and on-site vans $50 a night, but they'r not too keen on backpackers here.

Other Accommodation *Dilli Village Recre ation Camp* (☎ (071) 27 9130) is 200 metre from the east coast, 24 km from Hook Poi and nine km from Eurong. A four-bed cabi with shower and equipped kitchen costs $4 per night and sleeps up to four people. Yo can camp here for $3 per person, but thi place doesn't take backpacker groups.

The *Eurong Beach Resort* (☎ (071) 2 9122), 35 km north of Hook Point on the ea coast, has several sections ranging from motel rooms with kitchenettes for $65 double to two-bedroom apartments for $15(The resort also has a general store, bar an bistro.

Just south of Happy Valley, the low-ke *Yidney Rocks Cabins* (☎ (071) 27 9167) a right on the edge of the beach. They're ol but comfortable; the nightly rate is $65 an they sleep from six to eight people.

The *Happy Valley Resort* (☎ (071) 2 9144) has good self-contained timber lodge for $100 a double, and older units at $350 week for four people. The resort also has bar, bistro and shop.

The impressive and luxurious *Kingfishe Bay Resort* (☎ 1800 072 555) on the we coast has hotel rooms from $170 a night an two-bedroom villas from $570 for thre nights. The resort has restaurants, bars an shops, and, architecturally, it's worth a loc even if you're not staying here. There's als a day-trippers' section near the jetty, with th *Sandbar* bar and brasserie.

Getting There & Around

See the Hervey Bay and Rainbow Beac sections for details of 4WD hire from th mainland. On the island, vehicles are avai able through Kingfisher Bay 4WD Hi (☎ (071) 20 3366) at $130 a day, ar Shorty's Car Hire at Eurong has a couple Suzukis for $90 per day.

On the island you can get fuel at Eurong, Happy Valley, Cathedral Beach and King-fisher Bay.

Vehicle ferries (known locally as barges) operate to the southern end of Fraser Island from Inskip Point near Rainbow Beach, and to the west coast of the island from River Heads, south of Urangan. The barges take walk-on passengers for $10 return. There's also a ferry, the *Fraser II*, from Urangan to Moon Point on the island, but this is an inconvenient place to land as it's a long drive across to the other side.

The *Rainbow Venture* (☎ (074) 86 3154) operates the 10-minute crossing from Inskip Point to Hook Point on Fraser Island. It makes this crossing regularly from about 7 am to 5 pm daily. The price is $35 return for a vehicle and passengers, and you can get tickets on board the ferry.

The *Fraser Venture* (☎ (071) 24 1900) makes the 30-minute crossing from River Heads to Wanggoolba Creek (also called Woongoolber Creek) on the west coast of Fraser Island. It departs from River Heads at 9 am and 3.30 pm, and returns from the island at 9.30, 10.15 am and 4 pm. The barge takes 27 vehicles but it's still advisable to book. The return fare for vehicle and driver is $40, plus $3 for each extra passenger.

The Kingfisher Bay Resort (☎ (071) 25 5155) also operates two boats: the *Major Dundee* does the 25-minute crossing from River Heads to Kingfisher Bay daily. Departures from River Heads are at 7 and 11 am and 2 pm, and from the island at 9.45 am, 2.45 and 4.30 pm. The return fare is $40 for a vehicle and driver, plus $3 for extras. The *Kingfisher 1* is a passenger catamaran that crosses from the Urangan Boat Harbour to Kingfisher Bay, leaving from Urangan at 8.30 and 11 am and 4 pm and returning at 9.30 am, 1 and 5 pm. The fare is $18 return and the trip takes 30 minutes.

It's quite possible to make your own way around the island, and hitching along the main tracks and beaches is pretty common practice. River Heads is probably the best place to try your luck, as this is where most of the island's traffic starts its journey.

CHILDERS (population 1470)

Childers, a historic township inland on the Bruce Highway, has quite a few buildings from the Victorian era, and is the turn-off for lovely beachside **Woodgate** and **Woodgate National Park**.

The *Palace Backpackers Hostel* (☎ (071) 26 2244) is right in the centre of Childers at 72 Churchill St. It's in a restored old hotel, and has excellent facilities and four- and six-bed dorms for $11 per person. It's mainly a workers' hostel, and the owners can often find harvest work for travellers.

BUNDABERG (population 38,000)

At the northern end of Hervey Bay and on the southern edge of the Capricorn Coast, Bundaberg is a major sugar-growing, pro-cessing and exporting centre. Some of the sugar ends up in the famous Bundaberg Rum. The town is 50 km off the Bruce Highway and 15 km inland from the coast on the Burnett River. It's the southernmost access point for the Great Barrier Reef and the departure point for Lady Elliot and Lady Musgrave islands.

Bundaberg attracts a steady stream of trav-ellers looking for harvest work picking everything from avocados to zucchinis, and the hostels here can often help you find work – but be wary of promises for work which doesn't exist. It's worth ringing a few of the hostel managers and enquiring before you come.

Orientation & Information

The Bundaberg Tourist Information Centre (☎ (071) 52 2333) is on the corner of Isis Highway, the main road as you enter the town from the south, and Bourbong St. It's open daily from 9 am to 5 pm. The town centre and post office are about a km east along Bourbong St from the tourist office.

Things to See

You can tour the **Bundaberg Rum distillery** on Avenue St in East Bundaberg at 10 and 11 am and 1, 2 and 3 pm on weekdays, and at 10 and 11 am, noon and 1 pm on weekends.

QUEENSLAND

The tour costs $3, including a drink, and the distillery is not far off the eastern end of Bourbong St.

The **Hinkler House Museum** is dedicated to the life and times of the aviator Bert Hinkler, who was born in Bundaberg and in 1928 made the first solo flight between England and Australia. The house in which he lived his final years was transported from Southampton, England, to the corner of Young St and Perry Rd in North Bundaberg, and is open daily from 10 am to 4 pm.

Back on the Bruce Highway, 50 km west of Bundaberg, Gin Gin is an old pastoral town. The strange **Mystery Craters** – 35 small craters in a big sandstone slab said to be at least 25 million years old – are 17 km along the Bundaberg road from Gin Gin.

Beaches

The beaches of **Moore Park**, 20 km north, and **Bargara**, 13 km east, are popular with families. Local buses go to Bargara and Moore Park a few times on weekdays from Bundaberg post office.

There's a **turtle rookery** at Mon Repos Beach, 15 km north-east of Bundaberg. Four types of turtle – loggerhead, green, flatback and leatherback – have been known to nest here from late November to January, but it's predominantly the loggerhead which lays its eggs here. The rookery is unusual, since

turtles generally prefer sandy islands off the coast. The young emerge and quickly make their way to the sea from mid-January to March. You're most likely to see the turtles laying their eggs around midnight when the tide is high. Observation of the turtles is controlled by National Parks staff.

Places to Stay

The *Bundaberg Backpackers & Traveller Lodge* (☎ (071) 52 2080) is diagonally oppo site the bus terminal, on the corner of Targo and Crofton Sts. Dorm beds are $10, double $22. The very well set up *City Centre Back packers* (☎ (071) 51 3501), in the Grosveno Hotel at 216 Bourbong St, has two section six-bed motel units cost $12 per person dorm beds cost $11 and doubles $24.

The *Royal Motel* (☎ (071) 51 2201), o the corner of Barolin and Bourbong Sts, ha singles/doubles for $28/35. The town als has plenty of other motels and caravan park

At Bargara Beach, the *Linksview Mote* (☎ (071) 59 2295), 13 See St, has backpackers units at $11 per person or $26 a double.

Getting There & Away

Air services are by Sunstate (from Brisban Gladstone, Rockhampton, Mackay an Townsville daily) and Flight West (dail from Brisbane and Gladstone). All the mai bus companies serve Bundaberg on the mai north-south route. The main stop is Stewart Coach Terminal (☎ (071) 52 9700) at 6 Targo St. Bundaberg is also a stop for train between Brisbane and Rockhampton o Cairns.

Capricorn Coast

This central coastal area of Queensland take its name from its position straddling th Tropic of Capricorn. Rockhampton is th major population centre in the area, and ju off the coast lies Great Keppel Island (popular island getaway) and the Capricorn Marine Park, the southernmost part of th Great Barrier Reef.

There are some good beaches on the coast itself, and a few small towns, most of them minor resorts with a variety of accommodation.

SOUTHERN REEF ISLANDS

The Capricornia section of the Great Barrier Reef begins 80 km north-east of Bundaberg around Lady Elliot Island. The coral reefs and cays in this group dot the ocean for about 140 km up to Tryon Island east of Rockhampton.

Several cays in this part of the reef are excellent for reef walking, snorkelling, diving and just getting back to nature – though reaching them is generally more expensive than reaching islands nearer the coast. Access is from Bundaberg, Gladstone or Rosslyn Bay near Yeppoon. A few of the islands are important breeding grounds for turtles and sea birds.

Camping is allowed on the Lady Musgrave, Masthead, Tryon and North West national park islands, and campers must be totally self-sufficient. Numbers of campers are limited so it's advisable to apply well ahead for a camping permit. You can book six months ahead for these islands instead of the usual six to 12 weeks for other Queensland national parks. Contact the Queensland National Parks & Wildlife Service (☎ (079) 72 6055) on the corner of Goondoon and Tank Sts in Gladstone. If you get a permit you'll also receive information on any rules, such as restrictions on the use of generators, and on how not to harm the wildlife.

Lady Elliot Island

Eighty km north-east of Bundaberg, this 0.4-sq-km resort island is not a national park. The only accommodation is at the *Lady Elliot Island Resort* (☎ (071) 53 2485), which charges $199 per person for the first night and $99 for subsequent nights, including return flights and meals. The resort has good diving facilities and you can take certificate courses there. It also offers day trips by plane from Bundaberg for $105, or from Hervey Bay for $109. For bookings contact Sunstate Travel (☎ 1800 072 200) at 167 Bourbong St, Bundaberg.

Lady Musgrave Island

This 0.15-sq-km cay in the Bunker Group is an uninhabited national park about 100 km north-east of Bundaberg. You can make day trips to Lady Musgrave by fast catamaran or seaplane from Bundaberg and you can also camp there with a National Parks permit. Campers must be totally self-sufficient, and numbers are limited to 50.

Lady Musgrave Cruises (☎ (071) 52 9011), at 1 Quay St in Bundaberg, operates the *Lady Musgrave* fast catamaran. The day trip costs $92, including lunch, snorkelling gear and a glass-bottomed boat ride. You get about 3½ hours on the island. The boat leaves from Port Bundaberg at 8.30 am and returns at 5.30 pm. You can use it as a camping drop-off service for $180 return.

Heron Island

Only a km long and 0.17 sq km in area, Heron Island is 72 km east of Gladstone. *Heron Island Resort* (☎ (079) 78 1488), owned by P&O, covers the north-eastern third of the island; the rest is national park, but you can't camp there. The resort has room for more than 250 people, with normal nightly costs in the cheapest rooms of $140 per person including meals – though there are cheaper stand-by rates. Getting there, on the *Reef Adventurer* fast catamaran from Gladstone, costs $65 one way.

Although large sections of coral have been killed by silt as a result of dredging for a new, longer jetty at the island, Heron is still something of a Mecca for divers. The resort offers lots of diving facilities and trips and has its own diving school – a certificate course for guests is $350, and single dives are also available for certified divers.

Wilson Island

North of Heron, Wilson Island is a national park. You can make day trips from Gladstone on the *Reef Adventurer* fast cat via Heron Island, and P&O has a new resort on the island ($150 per day). However, not everyone enjoys the visitors. Apparently 300 nesting pairs of endangered roseate terns temporarily abandoned the island when

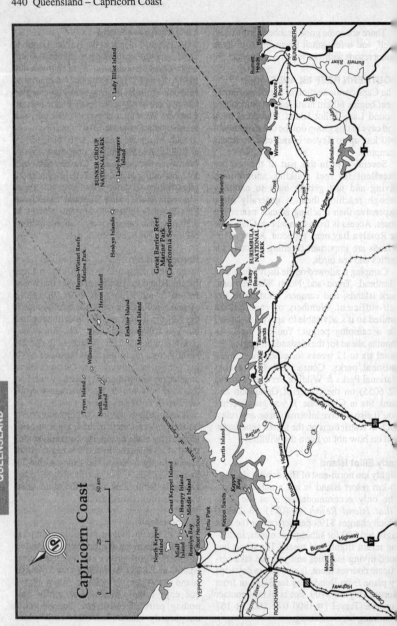

QUEENSLAND

egular visitors began turning up – it's mportant to avoid disturbing them.

North West Island

At 0.9 sq km, North West Island is the biggest ay on the Barrier Reef. It's all national park nd you can camp there independently with permit, but there's a limit of 150 people and ou must be totally self-sufficient. There are lso day trips from Rosslyn Bay near Rockampton and Yeppoon.

Day trips are on the *Capricorn Reefseeker* ast catamaran from Rosslyn Bay and Great Leppel Island, every Saturday. The $100 are includes lunch, a ride in a glass-botomed boat and snorkelling gear. Bus ansport to and from accommodation in ockhampton or on the coast costs an extra 10. For information contact Capricorn 'ruises (☎ (079) 33 6744) at Rosslyn Bay Harbour. If you're camping, the *Capricorn eefseeker* will drop you off and pick you up n the following Saturday for $160 per erson.

ryon Island

here's a limit of 30 campers on this tiny, x-hectare national park island, north of orth West Island. Again, you must be tally self-sufficient. Although there is no egular access to the island, the *Capricorn eefseeker* will drop off a group of 20 or ore people for $160 per head.

GLADSTONE (population 23,500)

wenty km off the highway, Gladstone is one f the busiest ports in Australia. It handles gricultural, mineral and coal exports from entral Queensland, plus the alumina which processed in Gladstone from bauxite ore nipped from Weipa on the Cape York Pennsula.

Gladstone is the main departure point for oats to Heron, Masthead and Wilson islands n the Barrier Reef. Its own harbour, Port urtis, has many islands. It has plenty of otels and caravan parks, and the *Harbour odge* (☎ (079) 72 6463) is a basic hostel at 6 Roseberry St with single rooms for $15.

There's a tourist information office (☎ (079) 72 4000) at 56 Goondoon St.

Most coast buses stop at Gladstone and it's also on the Brisbane to Rockhampton rail route. Air services include Sunstate's daily coastal hop and daily flights by Lloyd Air from Bundaberg and Brisbane. Flight West flies from Brisbane once a week.

ROCKHAMPTON (population 55,800)

Australia's 'beef capital' sits astride the Tropic of Capricorn. First settled by Europeans in 1855, Rockhampton had a relatively small, early gold rush but cattle soon became the big industry.

Rockhampton is an access point for Great Keppel and other islands. The boats leave from Rosslyn Bay on the coast about 50 km away near Yeppoon, but transport from Rocky is easy. There's also plenty of accommodation on the coast itself.

Orientation

Rockhampton is located about 40 km from the coast, along the Fitzroy River. The long Fitzroy Bridge connects the old central part of Rockhampton with the newer suburbs on the northern side of the river.

The Bruce Highway skirts the town centre and crosses the river upstream of the Fitzroy Bridge. Coming from the south, turn right up Denham or Fitzroy Sts to reach the centre of town.

Information

The Capricorn Information Centre (☎ (079) 27 2055), on the highway as you enter Rocky from the south, is beside the Tropic of Capricorn marker and three km from the town centre.

There's also the Riverside Information Centre (☎ (079) 22 5339) in a riverfront rotunda on the Quay St, and a small info kiosk on the East St Mall. The RACQ (☎ (079) 27 2255) is at 134 William St.

The National Parks district office (☎ (079) 36 0511) is on the corner of Norman and Yeppoon Rds, just after the turn-off to Yeppoon.

QUEENSLAND

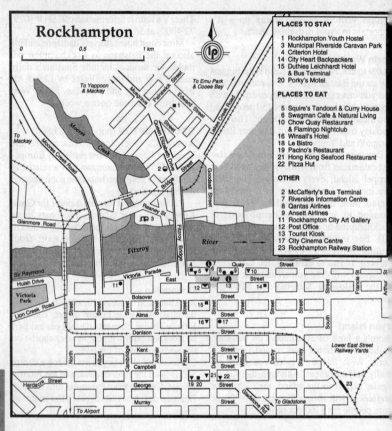

Rockhampton

0   0.5   1 km

PLACES TO STAY

1 Rockhampton Youth Hostel
3 Municipal Riverside Caravan Park
4 Criterion Hotel
14 City Heart Backpackers
15 Duthies Leichhardt Hotel
   & Bus Terminal
20 Porky's Motel

PLACES TO EAT

5 Squire's Tandoori & Curry House
6 Swagman Cafe & Natural Living
10 Chow Quay Restaurant
   & Flamingo Nightclub
16 Winsall's Hotel
18 Le Bistro
19 Pacino's Restaurant
21 Hong Kong Seafood Restaurant
22 Pizza Hut

OTHER

2 McCafferty's Bus Terminal
7 Riverside Information Centre
8 Qantas Airlines
9 Ansett Airlines
11 Rockhampton City Art Gallery
12 Post Office
13 Tourist Kiosk
17 City Cinema Centre
23 Rockhampton Railway Station

Things to See

There are many fine buildings in the town, particularly on **Quay St**, which has a number of grand Victorian-era buildings which date back to the gold-rush days. You can pick up tourist leaflets and magazines which map out walking trails around the town.

The **Rockhampton City Art Gallery** on Victoria Parade is open on weekdays from 10 am to 4 pm and on Sundays from 2 to 4 pm; admission is free. On the Bruce Highway, six km north of the centre, is the **Dreamtime Cultural Centre**, an Aboriginal heritage display centre. It's open daily from 10 am to 5.30 pm, and tours are run daily at 11 am and 2 pm; admission is $8.

The **Botanic Gardens**, situated at the end of Spencer St in the south of the city, were established in 1869 and have an excellent tropical collection and a walk-through aviary.

Places to Stay

Camping There are several caravan parks in Rocky, including the *Municipal Riverside Caravan Park* (☎ (079) 22 3779), just across the bridge to the north of the city centre, with tent sites for $9 but no on-site vans. The

Southside Caravan Village (☎ (079) 27 8013), across the Bruce Highway from the Capricorn Information Centre, on the southern approach to Rocky, is a well-kept place with a backpackers' section at $11 per person in on-site vans, tent sites at $10 and cabins for $38. You can get buses to the town centre.

Hostels The *Rockhampton Youth Hostel* ☎ (079) 27 5288), over the river at 60 Macfarlane St, has dorms at $12 ($13 for nonmembers) and twin rooms at $28/30. It's a spacious hostel with good facilities, and is a 20-minute walk north of the centre. Except on weekends, you can get there on a High St bus. The hostel is five minutes walk from McCafferty's terminal, and the other bus companies will drop you nearby on request. This is a good place to organise trips to Great Keppel Island, and to make bookings for the popular YHA hostel there.

City Heart Backpackers (☎ (079) 22 2414) at 170 East St is clean and central with all the usual facilities, although the sleeping areas are huge and lack privacy. Dorms are $12 a night.

Hotels & Motels There are plenty of old-fashioned hotels around the centre. On Quay St, the old *Criterion Hotel* (☎ (079) 22 1225) is one of Rockhampton's most magnificent old buildings. It has budget rooms with shared bathrooms at $15 a single, hotel rooms with private bathrooms for $30 a double and motel units from $40.

Duthies Leichhardt Hotel (☎ (079) 27 7733) on the corner of Denham and Bolsover Sts also has backpackers' accommodation, with three beds in a motel unit at $15 per person. Motel rooms are $40/48 for singles/doubles.

Porky's Motel (☎ (079) 27 8100) at 141 George St is quite central and affordable, and despite the dodgy name has respectable rooms at $35/40. You'll find lots of other motels on the Bruce Highway as you come into Rockhampton from both the north and south.

Places to Eat
The *Criterion Hotel* has bar meals from $3.50, bistro meals from $9.50 and a seafood and steak restaurant where main meals are around $12. It also has a smorgasbord lunch in the bistro on Friday ($10) and Saturday ($12). *Chow Quay*, in the *Heritage Tavern* on the corner of Quay and William Sts, has two-course Chinese lunches for $5.50 and smorgasbord dinners. *Winsall's Hotel* on the corner of Denham and Alma Sts has a reasonably priced bistro.

The *Swagman Cafe*, at 8 Denham St, is good for cooked breakfasts at $5 to $7, and, two shops north, *Natural Living* has healthy lunches and salads. The *Tropical Fruit & Juice Bar*, on the mall across from the post office, has good fruit salads and smoothies.

The *Pizza Hut* on the corner of George and Denham Sts has an all-you-can-eat pizza and pasta special for $5.95 every Tuesday and Wednesday night. Across the road, the *Hong Kong Seafood Restaurant* has Chinese food with most mains around $9.

Pacino's, on the corner of Fitzroy and George Sts, about a km south of the Fitzroy Bridge, is a good Italian restaurant if you're in the mood for a minor splash-out. For French food, there's *Le Bistro* at 120 William St. *Squire's Tandoori & Curry House* at 39 East St has Indian food with main meals around $10.

Entertainment
The Criterion Hotel has a busy but relaxed scene in its little *Newsroom Bar* where local musicians and groups play from Wednesday to Saturday nights. Rockhampton has several nightclubs, including the *Flamingo*, on Quay St between William and Derby Sts, which opens from Wednesday to Sunday. The *City Cinema Centre* (☎ (079) 22 1511) is on Denham St.

Getting There & Away
Air You can fly to Rocky from all the usual places along the coast with Ansett or Qantas. Sunstate does a daily coastal hop from Brisbane to Rockhampton ($215), Rockhampton to Mackay ($151), and back. Qantas also has flights between Rockhampton, Mackay and Proserpine.

QUEENSLAND

Qantas and Sunstate are on the mall at 107 East St, and Ansett is nearby at 137 East St.

Bus The major bus companies all pass through Rockhampton on the coastal route. McCafferty's also runs to Longreach ($51) via Emerald ($28) three times a week. From Rockhampton to Cairns is 13 hours ($90); to Mackay, four hours ($40); and to Brisbane, 10 hours ($65).

McCafferty's (☎ (079) 27 2844) terminal is just north of the bridge off Queen Elizabeth Drive. Greyhound Pioneer buses all stop outside Duthies Leichhardt Hotel on the corner of Bolsover and Denham Sts.

Duthies Travel (☎ (079) 27 6288), on Denham St opposite the hotel, handles tickets for most destinations.

Train Both the Sunlander (three times a week) and Queenslander (once a week) travel between Brisbane and Cairns, stopping in Rockhampton. The Spirit of Capricorn travels between Rockhampton and Brisbane daily. Twice weekly, the Spirit of the Outback runs between Brisbane, Rockhampton, Emerald and Longreach. For more information, contact the Queensland Rail Travel Centre at the station (☎ (079) 32 0297).

Getting Around
Rockhampton Airport is five km south of the centre. The Rockhampton railway station is about one km from the centre.

There's a reasonably comprehensive city bus network from Monday to Friday. Young's Bus Service (☎ (079) 22 3813) runs day trips to Mt Morgan, and Rothery's Coaches (☎ (079) 22 4320) do various trips to Koorana Crocodile Farm and the Capricorn Coast, the town sights and the Capricorn caves.

AROUND ROCKHAMPTON
Berserker Range
This rugged range, which starts 26 km north of Rocky, is noted for its spectacular limestone caves and passages. Several tours a day are taken through **Olsen's Capricorn Caverns**

and **Cammoo Caves**, near the Caves township, east off the Bruce Highway.

Mt Morgan (population 2800)
The open-cut gold and copper mine at Mt Morgan, 38 km south-west of Rockhampton on the Burnett Highway, was worked (off and on) from the 1880s until 1981. You can still visit the 325-metre-deep mine – tours (☎ (079) 38 1550) leave from the museum every weekday at 1 pm – and some of the town buildings are reminders of its more exciting past. There's quite a good museum on the corner of Morgan and East Sts (open daily) and a tourist information centre in the library on Morgan St.

Young's Bus Service (☎ (079) 22 3813) operates a regular bus from Rockhampton to Mt Morgan three times daily on weekdays, twice on Saturdays. In Rockhampton, the buses leave from the corner of East and William Sts.

YEPPOON (population 7000)
This small seaside resort, on the coast 43 km north-east of Rockhampton, is much cooler than Rocky in summer. It's also where you come to catch ferries to Great Keppel Island. If you can't afford to stay at Great Keppel there's a good hostel in Yeppoon, and the beaches in the area are quite good, too.

The Capricorn Coast Information Centre (☎ (079) 39 4888) is at the Ross Creek Roundabout at the entrance to the town.

Places to Stay
Up on the hill behind the town, *Barrier Reef Backpackers* (☎ (079) 39 4702), at 30 Queen St, is a relaxed place in a comfortable old timber house. It has all the usual facilities, large back yard and good views of the town. Four-bed dorms cost $12, doubles $26, and the staff do pick-ups from Rockhampton and will drop you at the Rosslyn Bay Boat Harbour if you're going to Great Keppel.

The pleasant *Surfside Motel* (☎ (079) 3 1272), opposite the beach at 30 Anzac Parade, has units with kitchenettes from $35/40.

Places to Eat

Sandy's Cafe, at 16 Normanby St, does breakfasts, burgers, sandwiches and the like. Across the road is *Castro's*, a small Mexican cafe. The *Galaxy* Chinese restaurant at 26 James St has a smorgasbord for $9.80 eat in or $6 takeaway.

Entertainment

The *Strand Hotel*, on the corner of Anzac Parade and Normanby St, is a popular pub with live bands on Friday and Saturday nights. Back on Hill St is the flashier *Bonkers* disco/nightspot. The *Yeppoon Cinema* (☎ (079) 39 5411) is upstairs on the corner of Normanby and Hill Sts.

Getting There & Away

If you're heading for Great Keppel or the reef, some of the cruise and ferry operators will transport you between your accommodation and Rosslyn Bay Harbour. Otherwise, Young's Bus Service (☎ (079) 22 3813) and Rothery's (☎ (079) 22 4320) both run buses from Rockhampton to Yeppoon ($10 return) and the rest of the Capricorn Coast, departing from Duthies Hotel on the corner of Denham and Bolsover Sts in Rocky.

If you're driving to Rosslyn Bay there's a free day car park at the harbour, and the Kempsea lock-up car park (on the main road just north of the harbour turn-off) charges $6 a day ($2 for motorbikes) and runs a free bus to and from the harbour.

YEPPOON TO EMU PARK

There are beaches dotted all along the 19-km coast running south from Yeppoon to Emu Park. At **Cooee Bay**, a couple of km from Yeppoon, the annual Australian 'Cooee' Championships are held each August.

Rosslyn Bay Harbour, reached by a short side road about seven km south of Yeppoon, is the departure point for trips to the Keppel Bay islands and North West Island.

South of Rosslyn Bay are three fine headlands with good views – **Double Head**, **Bluff Point** and **Pinnacle Point**. After Pinnacle Point the road crosses **Causeway Lake**, a saltwater inlet where you can rent canoes and

sailboards. Further south at **Emu Park** there are more good views and the 'Singing Ship' memorial to Captain Cook – a series of drilled tubes and pipes which emit whistling or moaning sounds when there's a breeze blowing. Emu Park also has a museum which doubles as a tourist information centre.

Koorana Crocodile Farm is five km off the Emu Park to Rockhampton road. The turn-off is 15 km from Emu Park. The farm has hundreds of crocs, and is open daily from 11.30 am, with $9 tours between 1 and 2.30 pm.

Places to Stay

There are many possibilities along this stretch of coast, including several caravan parks. At Cooee Bay, the *Poinciana Tourist Park* (☎ (079) 39 1601) has tent sites at $8 and cabins for $20. Further along, at Lammermoor Beach just before the turn-off to Rosslyn Bay Harbour, *Golden Sands* (☎ (079) 33 6193) has two-bedroom holiday flats opposite the beach from $45.

A couple of km south of the Rosslyn Bay turn-off, *Capricorn Palms Caravan Park* (☎ (079) 33 6144) is a modern, well-kept place with tent sites for $12 and on-site cabins for $30. Further south, the *Coolwaters Holiday Village* (☎ (079) 39 6102) at Kinka Beach and the *Bell Park Caravan Park* (☎ (079) 39 6202) at Emu Park also have tent sites and on-site vans at similar prices.

GREAT KEPPEL ISLAND

Although it's not actually on the reef, Great Keppel is the equal of most islands up the coast. It's 13 km offshore, and big enough to take a few days to explore. It covers 14 sq km and boasts 18 km of very fine beaches.

The good news about Great Keppel is that, unlike many of the resort islands, there are some good budget accommodation alternatives, and it's also one of the cheapest and easiest Queensland islands to reach. Day-trippers to the resort have access to outdoor tables and umbrellas, a pool, bar and restaurant, and they can hire all sorts of water-sports gear.

The Great Keppel Island Resort, owned

by Qantas Airlines, was given a $14 million facelift in 1991 and is now a very popular resort, especially among young families and couples. The airline has a variety of package tours to Great Keppel: depending on your departure point, seven days there will cost you around $1000 per person including air fares, food and facilities.

Things to See & Do

It only takes a short stroll from the main resort area to find your own deserted stretch of white, sandy beach. The water's clear, warm and beautiful. There is good coral at many points around the island, especially between Great Keppel and Humpy Island to the south. A 30-minute walk around the headland south of the resort brings you to **Monkey Beach** where there's good snorkelling.

There are a number of bushwalking tracks from **Fishermans Beach**, the main beach. The longest, and one of the more difficult, goes across to the lighthouse near **Bald Rock Point** on the far side of the island (2½ hours one way). Some beaches, like **Red Beach** near the lighthouse, are only accessible by boat.

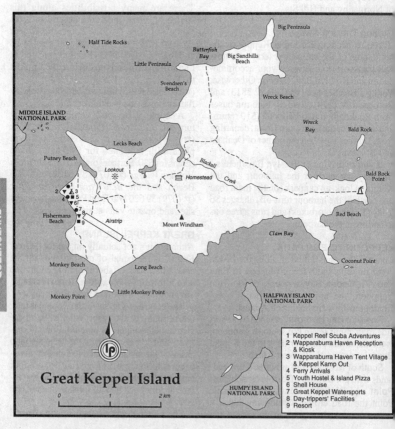

Great Keppel Island

0   1   2 km

1 Keppel Reef Scuba Adventures
2 Wapparaburra Haven Reception & Kiosk
3 Wapparaburra Haven Tent Village & Keppel Kamp Out
4 Ferry Arrivals
5 Youth Hostel & Island Pizza
6 Shell House
7 Great Keppel Watersports
8 Day-trippers' Facilities
9 Resort

There's a fine **underwater observatory** by Middle Island, close to Great Keppel. A confiscated Taiwanese fishing junk was sunk next to the observatory to provide a haven for fish.

Several outfits offer **water sports** activities. The Beach Shed on Putney Beach and Great Keppel Watersports on Fishermans Beach both hire out sailboards, catamarans, motorboats, fishing tackle and snorkelling gear, and they can also take you parasailing or water-skiing. Keppel Reef Scuba Adventures (☎ (079) 39 5022) on Putney Beach offers introductory dives for $60, or, if you're qualified, two dives with all gear supplied for $50. You can also do a five-day diving course for $385.

Organised Cruises
The *Capricat*, a sailing catamaran, does a morning snorkelling cruise for $20 on Wednesday, Friday and Sunday, and a sunset 'booze cruise' for $28 on Wednesday, Thursday, Friday and Sunday from 4 to 6 pm.

Capricorn Cruises (☎ (079) 33 6744) also runs various cruises, mainly aboard the *Reefseeker*. The island cruise departs daily from Rosslyn Bay at 9 am and Fishermans Beach at 10 am, and continues on a three-hour cruise around the island, which includes boom netting, snorkelling and an optional visit to the underwater observatory ($10 extra). You then have the afternoon on the island before returning at 4.30 pm; the cruise costs $32 from Rosslyn Bay. If you're already on the island, you can join the cruise at Fishermans Beach for $10.

The *Reefseeker* also does inner reef trips on Tuesdays and Thursdays ($65) and an outer reef trip on Saturdays ($100); the cost includes a smorgasbord lunch.

Places to Stay
Most people take package tours, but there are terrific alternatives for the budget traveller. The *Great Keppel Youth Hostel* (☎ (079) 39 4341) has dorms at $12 and four-bunk cabins at $14; nonmembers pay $1 extra. The hostel rents snorkelling gear and organises bushwalks and other activities. Book through the Rockhamp-

ton Youth Hostel or well ahead through the Brisbane YHA.

At *Wapparaburra Haven* (☎ (079) 39 1907) you can camp close to the beach for $8 per person or rent a bed in a four-bed tent for $15. The communal facilities in the tent village include fridges, barbecues and basic kitchen equipment. There are also cabins at $75 for singles/doubles plus $15 for each extra person.

Next door to Wapparaburra Haven is *Keppel Kamp Out* (☎ (079) 39 2131), which is geared to the 18 to 35 age bracket, and has organised activities. The cost – from $49 per person per day – includes twin-share tents, three meals and activities like water sports, parties and video nights.

Places to Eat
If you want to cook it's best to bring a few basic supplies. Fruit, vegetables, groceries and dairy foods are sold at the reasonably pricey *Wapparaburra Kiosk*, which also does breakfasts and takeaways. Next door, the *Reef Bar & Bistro* does lunches and evening meals from $10 (and a fairly mean cocktail). Next to the hostel, the friendly

QUEENSLAND

GREAT BARRIER REEF
Facts & Figures
The Great Barrier Reef is 2000 km in length. It starts slightly south of the Tropic of Capricorn, somewhere out from Bundaberg or Gladstone, and ends in the Torres Strait, just south of Papua New Guinea. This huge length makes it not only the most extensive reef system in the world, but also the biggest structure made by living organisms. At its southern end, the reef is up to 300 km from the mainland, while at the northern end it runs nearer to the coast, is much less broken and can be up to 80 km wide. In the 'lagoon' between the outer reef and the coast, the waters are dotted with smaller reefs, cays and islands. Drilling on the reef has indicated that the coral can be more than 500 metres thick. Most of the reef is around two million years old, but there are sections dating back 18 million years.

What is It?
Coral is formed by a small, primitive animal, a marine polyp of the family *Coelenterata*. Some polyps, known as hard corals, form a hard surface by excreting lime. When they die, the hard 'skeletons' remain and these gradually build up the reef. New polyps grow on their dead predecessors and continually add to the reef. The skeletons of hard corals are white and the colours of reefs come from living polyps.

Coral needs a number of preconditions for healthy growth. First the water temperature must not drop below 17.5°C – thus the Barrier Reef does not continue further south into cooler waters. The water must be clear to allow sunlight to penetrate, and it must be salty. Coral will not grow below depths of 30 metres because the sunlight does not penetrate sufficiently, nor does it grow around river mouths. The Barrier Reef ends near Papua New Guinea because the Fly River's enormous water flow is both fresh and muddy.

One of the most spectacular sights of the Barrier Reef occurs for a few nights after a full moon in late spring or early summer each year, when vast numbers of corals spawn at the same time. The tiny bundles of sperm and eggs are visible to the naked eye and the event has been likened to a gigantic underwater snowstorm.

Reef Types
What's known as the Great Barrier Reef is not one reef but about 2600 separate ones. Basically, reefs are either fringing or barrier. You will find fringing reefs off sloping sides of islands or the mainland coast. Barrier reefs are further out to sea: the 'real' Great Barrier Reef, or outer reef, is at the edge of the Australian continental shelf, and the channel between the reef and the coast can be 60 metres deep. In places, the reef rises straight up from that depth. This raises the question of how the reef built up from that depth when coral cannot survive below 30 metres? One theory is that the reef gradually grew as the sea bed subsided, implying that the reef was able to keep pace with the rate of subsidence. Another theory is that the sea level gradually rose, and again the coral growth was able to keep pace.

Reef Inhabitants
There are about 400 different types of coral on the Great Barrier Reef. Equally colourful are the many clams which appear to be embedded in the coral. Other reef inhabitants include about 1500 species of fish, 4000 types of mollusc (clams, snails, etc), 350 echinoderms (sea urchins, starfish, sea cucumbers and so on, all with a five-arm body plan), and countless thousands of species of crustaceans (crabs, shrimps and their relatives), sponges and worms.

Reef waters are also home to dugong (the sea cows which gave rise to the mermaid myth) and breeding grounds for humpback whales, which migrate every winter from Antarctica. The reef's islands form important nesting colonies for many types of sea bird, and six of the world's seven species of sea turtle lay eggs on the islands' sandy beaches in spring or summer.

Crown-of-Thorns Starfish One reef inhabitant which has enjoyed enormous publicity is the crown-of-thorns starfish – notorious because it appeared to be chewing through large areas of the Great Barrier Reef. It's thought that the crown-of-thorns develops a taste for coral when the reef ecology is upset – as, for example, when the supply of bivalves (oysters, clams), which comprise its normal diet, is diminished.

Dangerous Creatures Hungry sharks are the usual idea of an aquatic nasty but the Barrier Reef's most unpleasant creatures are generally less dramatic. For a start, there are scorpion fish with highly venomous spines. The butterfly cod is a very beautiful scorpion fish and relies on its colourful, slow-moving appearance to warn off possible enemies. In contrast, the stonefish lies hidden on the bottom, looking just like a rock, and is very dangerous to step on. Although they're rather rare, it's a good idea to wear shoes when walking on the reef – this is sensible anyway to protect yourself against sharp coral and rocks.

Stinging jellyfish are a danger only in coastal waters and only in certain seasons. The deadly 'sea wasp' is in fact a box jellyfish (see the Warning at the beginning of this chapter). As for sharks, there has been no recorded case of a visitor to the reef islands meeting a hungry one.

Viewing the Reef
The best way of seeing the reef is by diving or snorkelling in it. Otherwise you can walk on it, view it through the floor of glass-bottomed boats or the windows of semisubmersibles, or descend below the ocean surface inside 'underwater observatories'. You can also see a living coral reef and its accompanying life forms without leaving dry land, at the Great Barrier Reef Wonderland aquarium in Townsville.

Innumerable tour operators run day trips to the outer reef and to coral-fringed islands from towns on the Queensland coast. The cost depends on how much reef-viewing paraphernalia is used, how far the reef is from the coast, how luxurious the vessel that takes you there is, and whether lunch is included. Usually, free use of snorkelling gear is part of the package. Some islands have good reefs too: they're usually cheaper to reach and you can stay on quite a few of them.

The Great Barrier Reef Marine Park Authority (GBRMPA) is the body looking after the welfare of most of the reef. Its address is PO Box 1379, Townsville, Queensland 4810 (☎ (077) 81 8811). It also has an office in Great Barrier Reef Wonderland in Townsville.

Islands
There are three types of island off the Queensland coast. In the south, before you reach the Barrier Reef, are several large vegetated sand islands like North Stradbroke, Moreton and Fraser islands. These are interesting to visit for a variety of reasons but not for coral. Strung along the whole coast, mostly close inshore, are continental islands like Great Keppel, most of the Whitsundays, Hinchinbrook and Dunk. At one time, these would have been the peaks of coastal ranges, but rising sea levels submerged the mountains. The islands' vegetation is similar to that of the adjacent mainland.

The true coral islands, or cays, may be on the outer reef, or may be isolated between it and the mainland. Green Island near Cairns, the Low Isles near Port Douglas and Heron Island off Gladstone are all cays. Cays are formed when a reef is above sea level, even at high tide. Dead coral is ground down by water action to form sand and, in some cases, eventually vegetation takes root. Coral cays are low-lying, unlike the often hilly islands closer to the coast. There are about 300 cays on the reef, 69 of them vegetated.

The Queensland islands are extremely variable so don't let the catchword 'reef island' suck you in. Most of the popular resort islands are actually continental islands and some are well south of the Great Barrier Reef. Being a reef island is not necessarily important, since many continental islands will still have fringing reefs as well as other attractions that a tiny dot-on-the-map coral cay is simply too small for – like hills to climb, bushwalks, and secluded beaches where you can get away from other island lovers.

The islands also vary considerably in their accessibility – Lady Elliot for instance is a $170 return flight, others are just a few dollars by ferry. If you want to stay on an island rather than make a day trip from the mainland, this too can vary widely in cost. Accommodation is generally in the form of expensive resorts, where most visitors will be on an all-inclusive package holiday. But there are a few exceptions to this rule, plus on some islands it's possible to camp. A few islands have proper camping areas with toilets and fresh water on tap while, at the other extreme, on some you'll even have to bring drinking water with you.

For more information on individual islands, see under the Capricorn Coast, Whitsunday Coast, North Coast and Far North Queensland sections of this chapter. Lonely Planet's *Islands of Australia's Great Barrier Reef* is also a good reference. ■

QUEENSLAND

Island Pizza makes good pizzas, pastas and submarines, eat in or takeaway.

The resort has day-trippers' facilities plus the *Keppel Cafe* with burgers from $3.50, meat pies, etc. There's also a bar and the *Anchorage Char Grill* with steaks, salad and chips for $10.50.

Halfway along Fishermans Beach, the *Shell House* not only has a shell or two, but also does excellent Devonshire teas. The friendly owner has lived on Keppel for many years. His tropical garden offers a pleasant break from the sun.

Getting There & Away
Air Qantas flies at least twice daily between Rockhampton and Great Keppel ($72 one way).

Boat Ferries for Great Keppel leave from Rosslyn Bay Harbour on the Capricorn Coast. You can book the ferries through your accommodation or agents in Rockhampton and on the Capricorn Coast. If you're staying at the hostel, the youth hostel in Rockhampton has a special deal of $32 for the bus trip, the ferry across and a three-hour island cruise.

Capricorn Cruises (☎ (079) 33 6744) operate two boats, the *Reefseeker* and the *Spirit of Keppel*. The *Reefseeker* leaves Rosslyn Bay at 9 am and returns from Great Keppel at 4.30 pm, and the $32 return fare includes an island cruise (see Organised Cruises earlier). The *Spirit of Keppel* leaves Rosslyn Bay at 9.15 and 11 am and 3.30 pm, and returns from Great Keppel at 10 am and 2 and 4.15 pm; it costs $24 return.

Another boat, the *Australis* (☎ (079) 33 6865), leaves Rosslyn Bay at 9 and 11 am and returns from Great Keppel at 9.45 am and 4 pm, and costs $20 return.

OTHER KEPPEL BAY ISLANDS
Great Keppel is only the biggest of the 18 continental islands which are dotted around Keppel Bay, all within 20 km of the coast. It's possible to visit **Middle Island**, with its underwater observatory, or **Halfway** and **Humpy** islands if you're staying on Great Keppel. Most of the islands have clean, white beaches and several, notably Halfway, have excellent fringing coral reefs. Some, including Middle and **Miall**, are national parks where you can maroon yourself for a few days camping.

To camp on a national park island, you need to take all your own supplies including water. Numbers of campers allowed on each island are restricted – for example, eight on Middle and six on Miall. You can get information and permits from the National Parks regional office in Rockhampton (☎ (079) 36 0511) or the ranger's office at Rosslyn Bay Harbour (☎ (079) 33 6608).

North Keppel Island is the second largest of the group and one of the most northerly. It covers six sq km and is a national park. The most popular camping spot is Considine Beach on the north-west coast, which has well water for washing, and toilets. Take insect repellent.

Just south of North Keppel, tiny **Pumpkin Island** has five cabins (☎ (079) 39 2431) which accommodate five or six people at a cost of $90 to $110 per cabin. There's water and solar electricity, and each cabin has a stove, fridge and bathroom with shower. Bedding is provided.

For information about getting to any of these islands, ring Capricorn Cruises (☎ (079) 33 6744) or Island Taxis (☎ (079) 39 5095), both based at Rosslyn Bay.

CAPRICORN HINTERLAND
The Capricorn Highway runs inland from Rockhampton, virtually along the Tropic and across the central Queensland highlands to Barcaldine, from where you can continue west and north-west along the Landsborough Highway to meet the Townsville to Mt Isa road.

The area was first opened up by miners chasing gold and copper around Emerald, and sapphires around Anakie, but cattle, grain crops and coal provide its main living today. Carnarvon, south of Emerald, is one of Australia's most spectacular and interesting national parks.

Getting There & Away
Sunstate (☎ (07) 860 4577) links Brisbane

with Blackwater and Emerald. Flight West (☎ (07) 229 1177) has flights from Brisbane to Townsville, Rockhampton and Mackay; and from Mt Isa to Blackall, Longreach, Winton and Barcaldine.

McCafferty's has a Rockhampton to Longreach service three times a week which calls at all towns along the Capricorn Highway. The twice-weekly Spirit of the Outback train runs between Rockhampton and Longreach, following the same route as the highway.

Blackdown Tableland National Park

On the way to Emerald from Rocky you pass through the coal-mining centre of **Blackwater**. About 30 km before Blackwater and 11 km west of Dingo is the turn-off for Blackdown Tableland National Park. The tableland is around 800 metres high, with spectacular sandstone scenery plus some unique fauna and plant species. The 20-km gravel road leading on to the tableland can be unsafe in wet weather, and is not suitable for caravans at any time.

In the park, you can bushwalk to waterfalls and lookout points, study Aboriginal rock art, and swim. There's a camping area at **Mimosa Creek**, about 10 km into the park. Camping permits for the park are available from the ranger at Blackdown (☎ (079) 86 1964). Bring a gas stove for cooking.

Coal Mines

About 200 km inland from Rockhampton and Mackay, several of the area's massive open-cut coal mines give free tours lasting about 1½ hours; book ahead. The tour of the Blackwater Mine (☎ (079) 82 5166) leaves the mine's main office, off the Rockhampton to Emerald road, on Wednesdays at 10 am. For the Goonyella (☎ (079) 41 3333) and Peak Downs (☎ (079) 41 6233) mines near Moranbah, buses depart from Moranbah's town square at 10 am on Tuesdays and Thursdays. Tours of the Blair Athol Mine (☎ (079) 83 1866) near Clermont are on Tuesdays at 9 am.

Gem Fields

West of Emerald, about 270 km inland from Rockhampton, the gem fields around Anakie, Sapphire, Rubyvale and Willows Gemfield are known for their sapphires, zircons, amethysts, rubies, topaz, jasper, and even diamonds and gold. To go fossicking, you need a 'fossicking licence', sold from the Emerald Courthouse or on the gem field. There are also quite a few tourist mines which you can visit and explore.

Anakie, 42 km west of Emerald on the Capricorn Highway, has the Gemfields Information Centre where you can find out how to go fossicking and pick up maps of the fossicking areas. **Sapphire** is 10 km north of Anakie on a sealed road. There's large-scale open-cut mining between here and **Rubyvale**, seven km further north, but plenty of room for fossickers as well. About a km out of Sapphire, on the road to Rubyvale, *Sunrise Cabins & Camping* (☎ (079) 85 4281) has camp sites at \$9 for doubles or rustic stone cabins at \$12/25, with communal kitchen facilities. You can get information, licences and maps, and hire fossicking gear here. There are also caravan parks at Anakie, Rubyvale and Willows Gemfield.

Sapphires are found close to the surface at **Willows Gemfield**, 38 km west of Anakie.

Clermont (population 2700)

North of Emerald is Clermont, and the huge Blair Athol open-cut coal mine. Clermont is Queensland's oldest tropical inland town, founded on copper, gold, timber and cattle. It was the scene of gold-field race riots in the 1880s, and a military takeover of the town occurred in 1891 after a confrontation between striking sheep shearers and non-union labour. The town has a couple of pubs and a caravan park with on-site vans.

Springsure (population 730)

Springsure, south of Emerald, has an attractive setting with a backdrop of granite mountains and surrounding sunflower fields (the sunflowers are used to produce oil and seed). There's a small **historical museum** by the windmill as you enter town from the south. The **Virgin Rock**, an outcrop of Mt

QUEENSLAND

Zamia on the northern outskirts, was named after early settlers claimed to have seen the image of the Virgin Mary in the rock face.

Ten km south-west at Burnside is the **Old Rainworth Fort**, built following the Wills Massacre of 1861 when Aborigines killed 19 Whites on Cullin-La-Ringo Station north-west of Springsure.

For accommodation you have the choice of a motel and a caravan park.

Carnarvon National Park

Rugged Carnarvon National Park, in the middle of the Great Dividing Range, features dramatic gorge scenery and many Aboriginal rock paintings and carvings. The national park has several sections, but the impressive Carnarvon Gorge is the one that most people see as the others are pretty inaccessible.

Carnarvon Gorge is stunning, partly because it's an oasis surrounded by drier plains and partly due to its scenic variety, which includes sandstone cliffs, moss gardens, deep pools, and rare palms and ferns. There's also lots of fauna. Aboriginal art can be viewed at three main sites – **Baloon Cave**, the **Art Gallery**, and **Cathedral Cave**.

From Rolleston to Carnarvon Gorge, the road is bitumen for 20 km and unsealed for 75 km. From Roma via Injune and Wyseby, the road is good bitumen for about 200 km then unsealed and fairly rough for the last 45 km. After rain, both roads become impassable.

Three km into the Carnarvon Gorge section, there's an information centre and a scenic camping ground. The main walking track starts beside the information centre and follows the Carnarvon Creek through the gorge, with detours to various points of interest such as the Moss Garden (3.6 km from the camping ground), Ward's Canyon (4.8 km), the Art Gallery (5.6 km) and Cathedral Cave (9.3 km). You should allow *at least* half a day for a visit here, and you must bring lunch and water with you as there are no shops!

To get into the more westerly and rugged Mt Moffatt section of Carnarvon National Park, there are two unsealed roads from Injune: one through Womblebank Station, the other via Westgrove Station. There are no through roads from Mt Moffatt to Carnarvon Gorge or to the other remote sections of the park – Salvator Rosa and Ka Ka Mundi. Mt Moffatt has some beautiful scenery, diverse vegetation and fauna, and **Kenniff Cave**, an important Aboriginal archaeological site. It's believed Aborigines lived here as long as 19,000 years ago.

Places to Stay You need a permit to camp at the National Parks camping ground, and it's advisable to book by phoning the Carnarvon Gorge rangers (☎ (079) 84 4505). Sites cost $7.50, or you can bush camp for $2 per night. Wood for cooking is scarce, so bring your own gas cooking equipment.

You can also camp at Big Ben camping area, 500 metres upstream from Cathedral Cave – a 10-km walk up the gorge. Again, permits are required.

In the Mt Moffatt section, camping with a permit is allowed at six sites but you need to be completely self-sufficient, and a 4WD is advisable; phone the Mt Moffatt rangers for details (☎ (076) 26 3581).

The *Oasis Lodge* (☎ (079) 84 4503), near the entrance to the Carnarvon Gorge section of the park, offers safari cabins from $150 a night per person, including full board and organised activities. From December to March, the cost is $80 per person, not including activities. There's a general store with fuel.

Whitsunday Coast

The Whitsunday Islands, which lie just off the coast between Mackay and Bowen, are famous for their clear aqua-blue waters and forests. This is one of the most beautiful parts of the coast, and there's an extensive range of activities to choose from, including dive courses, cruises to and around the islands, snorkelling, fishing and sailing.

Mackay itself is a major regional centre

while the main access point for the islands themselves is Airlie Beach (Shute Harbour). Airlie Beach is a very popular travellers' hang-out, mainly because many companies offering diving courses and boat trips to the islands operate from here.

MACKAY (population 40,250)

Mackay is surrounded by sugar cane – a third of Australia's sugar crop is processed here. The sugar, loaded at the world's largest sugar-loading terminal at Port Mackay, has been grown here since 1865.

Mackay is nothing special, although its town centre is attractively planted, and there are some good beaches a bus ride away. It's also an access point for the national parks at Cape Hillsborough and Eungella, and for the Great Barrier Reef; there are some interesting islands just an hour or two away.

Orientation

Mackay is on the Pioneer River and its main streets are laid out in a simple grid on the southern side of the river. The main intersecting streets are Wood and Victoria. The railway and bus stations are only a few blocks from the centre and the airport is also fairly close. The newer suburbs are north of the river, and most of the popular beaches are further on again to the north.

Information

Mackay's tourist information centre (☎ (079) 52 2677) is about three km south of the centre on Nebo Rd (the Bruce Highway). It's open from 9 am to 5 pm Monday to Friday, and from 9 am to 4 pm on Saturday and Sunday. The building is a replica of the old Richmond Sugar Mill. While you're here, pick up a copy of the very handy *Things to See & Do in Mackay* brochure.

The RACQ (☎ (079) 57 2918) is at 214 Victoria St, and the National Parks district office (☎ (079) 51 8788) is on the corner of Wood and River Sts.

Things to See & Do

There are botanic gardens and an orchid house in **Queen's Park**, towards the eastern end of Gordon St. There are good views over the harbour from **Mt Basset**, and at **Rotary Lookout** on Mt Oscar in North Mackay. The tourism office has a **heritage walk** brochure to guide you around Mackay's older buildings.

Town Beach is situated at the eastern end of Shakespeare St, two km from the centre. Other beaches include **Far Beach**, six km south of the river mouth; **Harbour Beach**, just south of the harbour wall to the north; and **Lamberts Beach**, north of the harbour. But the best beaches are about 16 km north of Mackay at **Blacks Beach**, **Eimeo** and **Bucasia**. You turn right at the 'Northern Beaches' sign four km north of town on the Bruce Highway to reach them. Back in town, the **Memorial Swimming Pool** on Milton St is open from August till May.

In the cane-crushing season (July to mid-November), you can visit the **Racecourse Sugar Mill** (☎ (079) 57 4727) at 1.30 pm on weekdays for a tour. Polstone Sugar Farm gives tours for $12.50 at 1.30 pm on weekdays. The 19th-century home of Mackay's founder, John Mackay, is at **Greenmount Homestead**, 20 km from town along the Peak Downs Highway towards Clermont. It's open to visitors from 9.30 am to 12.30 pm Monday to Friday, and from 10 am to 3.30 pm on Sundays.

Organised Tours

Roylen Cruises (☎ (079) 55 3066) runs fast catamaran day trips from Mackay Harbour to Brampton Island, Credlin Reef on the Barrier Reef, and Lindeman and Hamilton islands in the Whitsundays, costing from $40 to $85. The Credlin trip, every Monday, Wednesday and Friday, takes you to a pontoon on the reef with an underwater observatory and costs $85. It includes a semisubmersible ride and lunch, and you can hire snorkelling or diving gear.

The tourist office has details of other trips including Fredrickson's and Air Pioneer's flights out to the Barrier Reef for snorkelling and reef walking.

Day trips by various operators go to the town sights, the sugar terminal, Cape Hillsborough,

QUEENSLAND

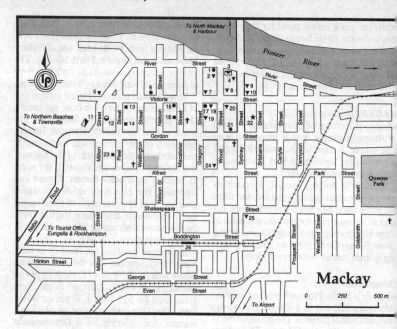

Mackay

0   250   500 m

PLACES TO STAY

13 Austral Hotel
14 Backpackers
   Retreat &
   Paradise
   Lodge Motel
16 International
   Lodge
23 Larrikin Lodge

PLACES TO EAT

2 Woody's
  Bakehouse
4 Toong Tong
5 Pizza Hut
7 Wilkinson's Hotel
8 Gourmet Deli &
  Picnic Basket
9 Rajput
10 Tropical Salad
   Bar

18 Col's Place
19 Creperie
20 Hog's Breath
   Cafe
24 Taylor's Hotel
25 Classics Rock
   Cafe

OTHER

1 National Parks
  Office

3 Post Office
6 RACQ
11 Memorial
   Swimming Pool
12 Mackay Bus
   Terminal
15 Ansett Airlines
17 Qantas
   Airlines
21 City Cinema
22 Police Station
26 Railway Station

Greenmount Homestead, Eungella National Park, the southern beaches and Hay Point coal terminal; try Coastal Explorer (☎ (079) 56 4606), SBS Tours (☎ (079) 57 7277) or Reeforest Tours (☎ (079) 53 1000).

Places to Stay

Camping The *Beach Caravan Park* (☎ (079) 57 4021), on Petrie St at Illawong Beach, about three km south of the centre, has tent sites at

$12 and on-site vans from $28. The *Central Caravan Park* (☎ (079) 57 6141), at 15 Malcomson St in North Mackay, costs $10 and there are cabins for $20 a double. There are more camping grounds at the northern beaches.

Hostels *Larrikin Lodge* (☎ (079) 51 3728) at 32 Peel St is a small associate-YHA hostel in an airy timber house. It's clean and comfortable, and there's a small pool. A bed costs $12 a night. The hostel can book various trips and tours.

Behind the bus station, *Backpackers Retreat* (☎ (079) 51 1115) is at 21 Peel St. Accommodation is in six-bed units, each with its own kitchen and bathroom facilities; a bed costs $12. This place looks good from the outside, but inside it's a bit dingy and could use a good clean. There's a small pool and a good notice board.

Unless you're just passing through Mackay, a great place to stay is *Beachcomber Backpackers* (☎ (079) 54 6204) at Eimeo Beach, about 15 km north. The small hostel is fairly basic but the setting is great, overlooking a lovely beach, and you can often see dolphins here in the mornings. A lot of travellers have good things to say about this place. The staff do pick-ups from Mackay, and beds cost $12 per night.

Hotels & Motels The friendly *International Lodge* (☎ (079) 51 1022) at 40 Macalister St is quite central and has good, clean motel rooms at $36/38 for singles/doubles.

The *Austral Hotel* (☎ (079) 51 3288) on the corner of Victoria and Peel Sts has rooms with shared bathrooms for $35. The *Paradise Lodge Motel* (☎ (079) 51 3644), next to the Backpackers Retreat at 19 Peel St, costs $42/48 for singles/doubles. There's a whole string of motels south along Nebo Rd (the Bruce Highway). *Cool Palms* (☎ (079) 57 5477), at 4 Nebo Rd, is still fairly close to the centre, and charges from $36 a room.

Places to Eat

Mackay seems to have a pub on every corner in the city centre, so finding a counter meal is not a problem. Wilkinson's Hotel on the corner of Victoria and Gregory Sts has the up-market *Wilkie's Balcony Restaurant* upstairs, with lunch and dinner mains for around $10; bar meals are available downstairs from $3 to $5.

The friendly *Austral Hotel*, on the corner of Victoria and Peel Sts, also has a good restaurant, and cheap meals are available in the corner bar. *Taylor's Hotel*, on the corner

of Wood and Alfred Sts, is another pub with good food.

At 23 Wood St, the narrow and popular *Gourmet Deli* has very cheap and fresh sandwiches, salads and cakes, and is great for lunch. A few doors south, the *Picnic Basket* is a gourmet takeaway and another good lunch option, but a bit more expensive. The *Tropical Salad Bar*, on the corner of Victoria and Sydney Sts, serves fresh juices and salads.

Col's Place, at 91 Victoria St, does breakfasts and other meals and takeaways from early till very late. *Woody's Bakehouse*, in an arcade off Wood St, has home-made pies, cakes and breads.

At 10 Sydney St, the well-presented *Toong Tong* Thai restaurant has mains for around $10. Across the road at No 27, Rajput has good Indian curries at similar prices. The *Creperie*, on Gregory St, serves excellent savoury pancakes for around $10, and there are cheaper sweet ones as well.

The *Hog's Breath Cafe*, on Wood St just south of Victoria St, is a saloon-style bar and grill with burgers and snacks around $8 and steaks and grills around $16. *Classics Rock Cafe*, on the corner of Shakespeare and Sydney Sts, is an interesting place with a '60s and '70s rock-music theme; steaks and other meals are around $12.

Entertainment

The *Blue Moose* nightclub, upstairs at Wilkinson's Hotel, is said to be the best in town. The *Austral Hotel* has live entertainment every Friday and Saturday nights, and a great jazz night on the first Thursday of each month. Plenty of other pubs have live bands on the weekends, including the *Prince of Wales* on River St. Other nightclubs include *Legends*, at 99 Victoria St, and *Paradise Nights* in Toucan's Arcade at 85 Victoria St.

The *City Cinema* (☎ (079) 57 3515) is at 30 Gordon St.

Getting There & Away

Air Ansett has direct flights most days between Mackay and Brisbane ($274),

Sugar Growing

Sugar is easily the most visible crop in the area north of Mackay, past Cairns and up the Queensland coast. Sugar was a success almost from the day it was introduced to the region back in 1865, but its early days had a distinctly unsavoury air as the plantations were worked by Pacific Islanders who were often forced from their homes to come and work on Australian cane fields. 'Blackbirding', as this virtual slave trading was known, took a long time to be stamped out.

Today, cane growing is a highly mechanised business and visitors are welcome to inspect the crushing plants during the harvesting season from about August to December. The most spectacular part of the operation is the firing of the cane fields, when rubbish is burnt off by night fires. Mechanical harvesters cut and gather the cane which is then transported to the sugar mills, often on narrow-gauge railway lines laid through the cane fields. These lines are a familiar sight throughout cane country. The cane is then shredded and passed through a series of crushers. The extracted juice is heated and cleaned of impurities and then evaporated to form a syrup. The next process reduces the syrup to molasses and low-grade sugar. Further refining stages end with the sugar loaded into bulk containers for export.

Sugar production is a remarkably efficient process. The crushed fibres, known as bagasse, are burnt as fuel; impurities separated from the juice are used as fertilisers; and the molasses is used either to produce ethanol or as stock feed. ■

Cairns, Hamilton Island, Rockhampton ($151) and Sydney. Qantas has direct daily flights between Brisbane and Rockhampton.

Queensland Regional Airlines flies to and from Rockhampton, Proserpine and Brampton Island; Helijet Air Services flies to and from Lindeman Island, Hamilton Island and Whitsunday Airport; and Sunstate flies to and from Townsville, Rockhampton, Gladstone, Bundaberg and Brisbane.

In Mackay, Ansett's offices are on the corner of Victoria and Macalister Sts; Qantas, Sunstate and Queensland Regional (☎ (079) 57 1411) are at 105 Victoria St.

Bus All buses travelling along the coast stop at Mackay. The bus station is on Milton St, about a 10-minute walk west of the town centre. Average journey times and typical fares are: Cairns, 10½ hours ($70); Townsville, four hours ($48); Airlie Beach, two hours ($26); and Brisbane, 14 hours ($90).

Train The Sunlander and Queenslander (both from Brisbane to Cairns) stop at Mackay. The Sunlander costs $95 in economy and $142 in 1st class from Brisbane, while the Queenslander only has 1st class at $379. Mackay railway station is on

Boddington St; bookings are handled at the Mackay bus terminal (☎ (079) 51 3088).

Getting Around

Count on about $8 for a taxi from Mackay Airport to the city. Avis, Budget and Hertz have counters at the airport.

Transit Coaches runs the bus service to the northern beaches twice daily on weekdays. Buses leave from outside the RSL on Sydney St. It's about an hour from Mackay to most of the northern beaches, and the fare is $2.75.

AROUND MACKAY
Eungella National Park

Most days of the year you can be pretty sure to see platypuses in the pools near the Broken River bridge and camping ground in this large national park, 74 km west of Mackay. The best times to see the creatures are the hours immediately after dawn and before dark; you must remain patiently silent and still.

Eungella (pronounced Young-ulla, meaning Land of Clouds) covers nearly 500 sq km of the Clarke Range, climbing to 1280 metres at Mt Dalrymple. The area has been cut off from other rainforest areas for probably 30,000 years and has at least six life forms which exist nowhere else: the Eungella honeyeater (a bird), the orange-sided skink (a lizard), the Mackay tulip oak (a tall buttressed rainforest tree) and three species of frog, one of which – the Eungella gastric brooding frog – has a highly unusual habit of incubating its eggs in its stomach and then giving birth by spitting out the tadpoles!

There's a ranger's office, camping ground, picnic area and kiosk near the bridge over **Broken River**, five km south of the Eungella township. Several walking tracks start from the bridge, and a short walk downstream there's a good swimming hole. Near the bridge colourful birds are prolific, while at night the rufous bettong, a small kangaroo, is quite common. You might also see two types of brush-tailed possum and two species of glider. Park rangers sometimes lead wildlife-watching sessions, or night spotlighting trips to pick up nocturnal animals.

At the **Finch Hatton Gorge** section of the park, two walking tracks lead from the picnic ground to spectacular waterfalls and swimming holes. The last two or three km of the 12-km drive from the main road are quite rough and involve several creek crossings.

Places to Stay There are three National Parks camping grounds. You'll need to get camping permits ($7.50) from the ranger at Broken River (☎ (079) 58 4552). During school holiday periods it's advisable to book.

Also beside the bridge here, the *Broken River Mountain Retreat* (☎ (079) 58 4528) has motel rooms from $48 and self-contained units from $62.

In Eungella township there's the old *Eungella Chalet* (☎ (079) 58 4509); it's fairly basic but it has spectacular views and is understandably popular with the hang-gliding fraternity. It has a small backpackers' section at $12 per person, guesthouse rooms from $20/35, motel rooms for $50 and self-contained cabins for $70. There's also a bar and restaurant here. Nearby, the *Valley View Caravan Park* has tent sites.

Just a couple of km from the Finch Hatton Gorge is the *Platypus Bush Camp* (☎ (079) 58 3204). It's a beautiful retreat, with camping sites ($10) and bush huts with cooking facilities

($45 for up to three people). You need to bring all your own food, and bookings are advised. If you phone from Finch Hatton village, someone will pick you up.

Getting There & Away There are no buses to Eungella, but hitching is quite possible. Reeforest Adventure Tours (☎ (079) 53 1000) runs day trips from Mackay, plus a drop-off service, for $30 return.

Cape Hillsborough National Park

This small coastal park, 54 km north of Mackay, takes in the rocky, 300-metre-high Cape Hillsborough and nearby Andrews Point and Wedge Island, which are joined by a causeway at low tide. There are beaches and several walking tracks and the scenery ranges from cliffs, rocky coast, dunes and scrub to rainforest and woodland. Kangaroos, wallabies, sugar gliders and turtles are quite common. There's a visitors information centre at the cape, and a good foreshore picnic and barbecue area nearby.

Places to Stay Situated at the end of Cape Hillsborough Rd, the *Cape Hillsborough Resort* (☎ (079) 59 0152) has tent sites for $6, on-site vans and cabins from $20, and some motel rooms.

There's a small National Parks camping ground at Smalleys Beach; you'll need a permit (☎ (079) 59 0410). At Halliday Bay, the *Halliday Bay Resort* (☎ (079) 59 0121) has self-contained rooms from $52; the resort's facilities include a shop, pool, tennis court and restaurant.

Getting There & Away A school bus, which anyone can take, leaves Mackay post office at 2.45 pm Monday to Friday during the school term. It only goes to Seaforth, but if you're staying at Cape Hillsborough Resort, the driver might drop you there.

Brampton & Carlisle Islands

These two mountainous national park islands are in the Cumberland Group, 32 km north-east of Mackay. Both are about five sq km in area, and are joined by a sand bank which you can walk across at low tide. Carlisle's highest point is the 389-metre Skiddaw Peak; Brampton's is the 219-metre Brampton Peak. Both islands have forested slopes, sandy beaches, good walks and fringing coral reefs with good snorkelling.

The Qantas-owned *Brampton Island Resort* (☎ (079) 51 4499) is on its north-east coast, opposite Carlisle Island. Accommodation starts at $80/130 a night for singles/doubles, or there are five-night package deals from $700, including air fares. Carlisle Island is uninhabited; you can camp but there are no facilities and you must bring everything, including water.

The *Spirit of Roylen* (☎ (079) 55 3066) fast catamaran leaves Mackay Harbour daily for Brampton Island ($40 return), and you can use it for a day trip. You can also fly daily from Mackay ($70 one way with Queensland Regional).

Most other islands in the Cumberland Group and the Sir James Smith Group to the north are also national parks; if you fancy a spot of Robinson Crusoeing and can afford to charter a boat or seaplane, Goldsmith and Scawfell are good bets. Contact the National Parks offices in Mackay (☎ (079) 51 8788) or Seaforth (☎ (079) 59 0410) for all camping permits and information.

Newry & Rabbit Islands

These small, little-known tropical islands are two of a cluster of tiny islands just off the coast about 40 km north-west of Mackay. Newry Island, one km long, has a small resort (☎ (079) 59 0214) where camping is $7 per site, and a bunk is $12. There are also cabins which sleep up to five and have their own bathrooms and cooking facilities. The cabins cost $20 per person with a maximum charge of $60. All guests can use the resort restaurant and bar.

Rabbit Island, the largest of the group at 4.5 sq km, has a National Parks camping ground with toilets and a rainwater tank which can be empty in dry times. It also has the only sandy beaches in the group. From November to January sea turtles nest here. Contact the Mackay (☎ (079) 51 8788) or

Seaforth (☎ (079) 59 0410) National Parks offices for permits and information.

The Newry resort picks up guests from Victor Creek, four km west of Seaforth, for $15 return.

AIRLIE BEACH & SHUTE HARBOUR

It's 25 km from the Bruce Highway at Proserpine to Airlie Beach, which is the main accommodation centre opposite the Whitsunday Islands. Most boats to the islands leave from Shute Harbour, eight km east of Airlie Beach, or from the Abel Point Marina, one km west.

Airlie Beach has grown phenomenally over the past 10 years or so and it's now a bustling place, with a huge range of budget accommodation, good eateries, and a lively night life. The area is one of the pleasure-boating capitals of Australia. Apart from Shute Harbour itself, which is packed with craft, lots of boats anchor in Airlie Bay and at the Abel Point Marina.

Airlie Beach also has a reputation as a centre for learning to scuba dive. Whale-watching boat trips, between July and September, are another attraction. Yet, despite all of this development, it's still a small place which has managed to retain its relaxed air.

The road between Airlie Beach and Shute Harbour passes through **Conway National Park** which stretches away north and south along the coast. The southern end of the park separates the Whitsunday Passage from Repulse Bay, named by Captain Cook who strayed into it thinking it was the main passage. Most of the park is composed of rugged ranges and valleys covered in rainforest, but there is a camping ground and picnic area off the main road, and a few walking tracks in the surrounding area. The two-km walk up to Mt Rooper lookout, north of the road, gives good views of the Whitsunday Passage and islands.

Another pleasant walk is along Mandalay Rd, about three km east of Airlie Beach, up to **Mandalay Point**.

To reach the beautiful **Cedar Creek Falls**, turn off the Proserpine to Airlie Beach road

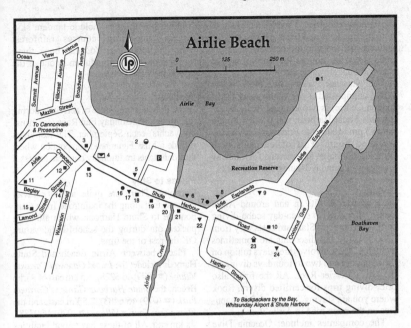

Airlie Beach

PLACES TO STAY

3 Colonial Court Motel
10 Airlie Beach Hotel
11 Sunlit Waters Holiday Flats
12 Club 13 Begley Street
13 Whitsunday Wanderers Resort
15 Airlie Beach Motor Lodge
18 Beaches Backpackers
19 Hibiscus Backpackers
21 Whitsunday Village Resort
23 Club Habitat YHA

PLACES TO EAT

5 Cafe Le Mignon
6 Hog's Breath Cafe
8 Pinky's
9 Airlie's Own & Chompin' Charlie's
17 Beaches Bar & Grill
20 Magnums Bar & Grill
22 KC's Char Grill
24 JJ's Cafe

OTHER

1 Whitsunday Sailing Club
2 Long-distance Bus Stop
4 Post Office
7 Mandy's Mine of Information
14 Market Cars and Scooters
16 Newsagent & Notice Board

on to Conway Rd, eight km from Proserpine. It's then about 15 km to the falls – the roads are well signposted. At the end of Conway Rd, 27 km from the turn-off, is the small settlement of **Conway** with a beach, the Black Stump Caravan Park and a pleasant pub.

Information

Nearly everything of importance in Airlie Beach is on the main road, Shute Harbour Rd.

The Whitsunday Visitors Bureau (☎ (079) 46 6673), in an arcade off Coral Ave, is mainly a marketing body but can answer most phone enquiries. There's also a host of booking agencies and ticket offices, and the notice board outside the newsagent on the main street has notices for work, rooms to rent and boat crews needed.

The National Parks office (☎ (079) 46 7022) (signposted as the Whitsunday Information Centre) is two km past Airlie Beach towards Shute Harbour, and is open from 8 am to 5 pm Monday to Friday and at varying weekend hours. This office deals with camping bookings and permits for Conway and the Whitsunday Islands national parks.

Diving
At least four outfits in and around Airlie Beach offer five- to seven-day scuba-diving certificate courses. Standard costs vary from $250 to $420 but discounts are sometimes available. Most involve three days tuition on the mainland and two to four days diving on the Great Barrier Reef. All the firms also offer diving trips for certified divers. Book where you are staying, or at one of the agencies on the main road in Airlie Beach.

The companies include: Oceania Dive (☎ (079) 46 6032), Reef Enterprise Dive Services (☎ (079) 46 7228) and Pro-Dive (☎ (079) 46 6508), all on Shute Harbour Rd; and Barrier Reef Diving Services (☎ (079) 46 6204) on Airlie Esplanade.

Other Activities
The 25-metre freshwater pool at the Coral Sea Resort on Ocean View Ave is open to the public daily from 8 am to 6 pm.

You can take half-day horseback trail rides ($30) with Brandy Creek Trail Rides (☎ (079) 46 6665), 12 km from Airlie Beach back towards Proserpine. They can pick you up from your accommodation.

The Wildlife Park has a large collection of Australian mammals, birds and reptiles, with various shows each day such as crocodile feeding, koala feeding and snake handling. The park opens daily from 8.30 am to 5.30 pm and entry costs $12. It's 8 km west of Airlie Beach, and a courtesy bus does pick-ups and drop-offs from wherever you're staying.

Other possibilities include tandem sky-diving, hang-gliding courses, rainforest tours and kayaking. You can book these through your accommodation or one of the agents in Airlie Beach.

Festivals
Airlie Beach is the centre of activities during the annual Whitsunday Fun Race (for cruising yachts) each September. The festivities include a Miss Figurehead competition where the contestants traditionally compete topless.

Places to Stay
Camping There are quite a few caravan parks strung along the main road from Cannonvale to Shute Harbour, which although packed out during the school holidays are OK the rest of the time.

Places between Airlie Beach and Shute Harbour include: the *Island Gateway Caravan Village* (☎ (079) 46 6228), 1.5 km east of Airlie Beach; the *Shute Harbour Gardens Caravan Park* (☎ (079) 46 6483), 2.5 km east; and the *Flame Tree Tourist Village* (☎ (079) 46 9388), six km east. All of these have good facilities including a pool, and tent sites from $9, on-site vans from $25 and on-site cabins from $35.

A tent site at the Conway National Park camping ground, midway between Airlie Beach and Shute Harbour, is $7.50 a night for up to six people; there's a maximum stay of two weeks. There are a couple more sites at Swamp Bay, reached by a 4.5-km walking track. For camping permits and bookings, contact the National Parks office (☎ (079) 46 7022) on Shute Harbour Rd, two km from Airlie Beach.

Hostels There's been such a proliferation of hostels in recent years that the competition to get bodies on beds is fierce. At the time of writing there was a no-holds-barred price war on, with some places offering beds for $6, but these prices are unlikely to last. The standard price for a dorm bed is usually around $12. At the main bus stop there's a row of booths where the hostel reps tout for trade when the buses arrive. All the places out of the centre run courtesy buses to and from Airlie Beach.

Right in the centre, the *Whitsunday Village Resort* (☎ (079) 46 6266) is a huge place, set out in a very pleasant tropical garden with two pools. The emphasis here is on partying, with a restaurant and bar next door which has activities each night. The standard of accommodation varies, with a range of four- to six-bed units and cabins. Some have limited cooking equipment, and there are no communal facilities. Dorms are $10 to $12 and doubles from $30 to $45.

Also in the centre is *Beaches Backpackers* (☎ (079) 46 6244), another big place with a party attitude and its own bar and restaurant. The rooms and facilities in this converted motel are good, with five-bed (not bunk) units with their own bathroom and balcony, TV and air-con, a pool and a good kitchen. Beds cost $12, and there are a few doubles at $30.

Sandwiched between these two places is *Hibiscus Backpackers* (☎ (079) 46 6105), another converted old motel. This place isn't as flash, with eight-bed units and limited cooking facilities, but it's a good cheap option at $8 a bed.

A little further along Shute Harbour Rd is *Club Habitat YHA* (☎ (079) 46 6312), yet another motel converted to backpackers' accommodation. A night in a four- to six-bed unit with bathroom costs $12, and twin rooms cost $32; nonmembers pay an extra $1. There's a pool, good communal kitchen and lounge, and the atmosphere is friendly. *Club 13 Begley St* (☎ (079) 46 7376) overlooks the bay from the hill just above the centre. This modern multilevel place consists of five three-bedroom apartments. Each apartment has two bathrooms (some with spa), its own cooking and laundry facilities, and a balcony with tremendous views. Beds are $12, including breakfast.

Half a km out of town towards Shute Harbour is *Backpackers by the Bay* (☎ (079) 46 7267) at Lot 5, Hermitage Drive. It's a small, relaxed hostel with a good atmosphere, and is probably quieter than those in the centre. The nightly cost in a four-bed dorm is $12 and doubles are $29.

Back the other way from the centre is the *Beach House* (☎ (079) 46 6306), overlooking Shingley Beach. It's about 1.5 km from Airlie Beach – take the Abel Point Marina turn-off and turn left. There are 10 fan-cooled units, each with a kitchenette, bathroom and TV; there's also a pool. The nightly cost in a four-bed unit is $12.

Further along towards Cannonvale, just under two km from Airlie Beach, is the *Bush Village Backpackers Resort* (☎ (079) 46 6177) in St Martin's Lane. It's a family-run place, with clean and simple four-bed cabins at $12 per person, which includes breakfast. Each cabin has cooking facilities, fridge, bathroom and TV. There's also a pool, and the owners are very helpful.

Hotels & Motels The *Airlie Beach Hotel* (☎ (079) 46 6233), on Shute Harbour Rd, has motel units at $30/40 for singles/doubles.

Motels are pretty expensive: about the cheapest is the *Airlie Beach Motor Lodge* (☎ (079) 46 6418) on Lamond St which has motel rooms from $44/48. It also has two-bedroom self-contained units. The *Colonial Court Motel* (☎ (079) 46 6180), on the corner of Shute Harbour Rd and Broadwater Ave, has units with kitchenettes from $40/50.

Resorts & Holiday Flats Outside the peak seasons, some of the resorts are much cheaper. *Whitsunday Wanderers* (☎ (079) 46 6446), on Shute Harbour Rd in Airlie Beach, costs from $90 a double but it has stand-by rooms from $60. There are four pools, tennis, landscaped gardens, a bar, restaurant and nightly live entertainment. You might have to stay a few nights to qualify for these offers. *Club Crocodile* (☎ (079) 46 7155) at Cannonvale, two km west of Airlie Beach, has similar prices and facilities.

Generally, you'll find better value in some of the holiday flats. Four people sharing a flat will pay $17 each or less in these places; all bed linen and cooking equipment is supplied. *Sunlit Waters* (☎ (079) 46 6352), at the corner of Begley St and Airlie Crescent in Airlie Beach, has a pool and good views and charges $30 to $38 for two people, $8 for each extra person.

Other holiday flats in Airlie Beach include *Roger's* (☎ (079) 46 6224), at 265 Shute Harbour Rd, with doubles from $40; and *McDowall's* (☎ (079) 46 6176), at 32 Airlie Crescent, which has similar prices. Neither of these places has a pool, however.

Places to Eat

Most of the eating possibilities are on, or just off, Shute Harbour Rd in Airlie Beach. If you're preparing your own food, there's a small supermarket on the main street near the car park entrance.

The *Airlie Beach Hotel* has a bistro with pub meals from $8 to $10. On Airlie Esplanade, *Airlie's Own* is a budget-priced eatery serving hamburgers and other snacks. Next door, the tiny *Chompin' Charlie's* has good breakfasts and very tasty beef, chicken, lentil and fish burgers, all around the $3.50 mark. It's open from early until very late. *Pinky's*, near the corner of Shute Harbour Rd, has a varied menu with breakfasts from $4, sandwiches from $3 and meals from $7.

JJ's Cafe, opposite the pub, has friendly owners and fresh, natural and healthy tucker – sandwiches, salads and juices – at good prices. Just by the main car park, the small *Cafe Le Mignon* is a popular, reasonably priced place with breakfasts, sandwiches and croissants with fancy fillings from $5 upwards.

Beaches Bar & Grill, in the Beaches Backpackers complex, is popular with both travellers and locals. The bar has various happy hours and specials and plays good music. Meals range from burgers at $4.50, pastas for $5 to $6 and other mains around $8.50, and there's a Mexican buffet on Tuesdays. *Magnums Bar & Grill*, at the Whitsunday Village Resort, is equally popular and has a similar approach to Beaches', with pool tables and a video screen. All meals are $6, or $4 or if you're staying there.

KC's Char Grill is a bit more up-market, and good for a splurge. It has a rustic, lively atmosphere and excellent food, with char-grilled steaks and seafood in the $16 to $22

range. Across the road is the *Hog's Breath Cafe*, another bar & grill place with lunches from $6 to $8 and dinners from $13 to 17.

Entertainment

The *Airlie Beach Hotel* has toad races on Tuesday, Wednesday and Thursday nights at 7.30 pm. There are good prizes for the winners of each race (usually boat cruises), and all proceeds go to charity. You can rent a steed for $3 and the whole evening is a rowdy, fun event. This pub is also the place to go for live rock music, and there's a disco most nights, as well as Saturday and Sunday afternoons.

There are a couple of nightclubs on Shute Harbour Rd: *Tricks*, next to the newsagent, and *Mainstreet* upstairs in an arcade near the post office.

You can also try night party cruises to a couple of resort islands.

Getting There & Away

Air The Whitsunday Airport is about six km past Airlie Beach towards Shute Harbour. Helijet Air Services (☎ (079) 46 9133) can fly you to Hamilton Island for $35 one way or Lindeman Island for $45.

Bus All the main bus companies make detours to Airlie Beach. There are buses to and from Brisbane (18 hours, $105), Mackay (two hours, $26), Rockhampton (six hours, $57), Townsville (four hours, $40) and Cairns (nine hours, $63).

Unless you have a pass with a major bus company, to travel between Proserpine and Airlie Beach or Shute Harbour you have to get a Sampsons bus (☎ (079) 45 2377); these run several times daily between Proserpine Airport, Mill St in Proserpine, Airlie Beach and Shute Harbour. The one-way fare is $6.50.

None of the main bus companies have offices in Airlie Beach, but any booking agency along Shute Harbour Rd can help. The main bus stop is in the car park behind the shops, about halfway along Shute Harbour Rd.

Boat The sailing club is at the end of Airlie Esplanade. There are notice boards at the newsagent in Airlie Beach and at Abel Point Marina showing when rides or crewing are available. Ask around Airlie Beach or Shute Harbour.

Getting Around
Several car-rental agencies operate locally; Avis, Budget and National all have agencies on Shute Harbour Rd. Market Cars & Scooters (☎ (079) 46 6110), one block back from the main street, has scooters and cars for rent. Whitsunday Taxis can be booked on (☎ 1800 811 388).

WHITSUNDAY ISLANDS
The 74 Whitsunday Islands are probably the best-known Queensland islands. The group was named by Captain Cook, who sailed through here on 3 July 1770. They're scattered on both sides of the Whitsunday Passage and are all within 50 km of Shute Harbour. The Whitsundays are mostly continental islands, the tips of underwater mountains, but many of them have fringing coral reefs. The actual Barrier Reef is at least 60 km out from Shute Harbour; Hook Reef is the nearest part of it.

The islands – mostly hilly and wooded – and the passages between them are simply beautiful, and while a few are developed with tourist resorts, most are uninhabited and several offer the chance of some back-to-nature beach camping and bushwalking. All but four of the Whitsundays are predominantly or completely national park. The exceptions are Dent Island, and the resort islands of Hamilton, Daydream and Hayman.

The other main resorts are on South Molle, Lindeman, Long and Hook islands.

Most people stay in the resorts on package holidays and, with the exceptions of some cabins and resort camping on Long and Hook islands, resort accommodation is beyond the reach of the budget traveller.

Camping on the Islands
Although accommodation in the island resorts is mostly expensive, it's possible to camp on several islands. Hook Island has a privately run camping ground, and on North Molle, Whitsunday, Henning, Border, Haslewood, Shaw, Thomas, Repulse and Hook islands you can camp cheaply at National Parks sites. Self-sufficiency is the key to camping in National Parks sites; some have toilets, but only a few have drinking water, and then not always year round. You're advised to take five litres of water per person per day, plus three days extra supply in case you get stuck. You should also have a fuel stove – wood fires are banned on some islands and unwelcome on the others. There's a National Parks leaflet which describes the various sites, and provides detailed information on what to take and do. The National Parks district office (☎ (079) 46 7022) is two km east of Airlie Beach, on Shute Harbour Rd.

For information on boat transport to and from the islands, contact one of the many booking agencies in Airlie Beach. For $40 to $65 return per person, a number of the regular day-trip boats will drop you off at the end of a cruise and pick you up again on an agreed date. Generally the day-tour boats are better for this than the island resort boats.

QUEENSLAND

The Whitsundays
Curiously, the Whitsundays are misnamed – Captain Cook didn't really sail through them on Whit Sunday. When he got back to England, his meticulously kept log was a day out because he had not allowed for crossing the international date line! As he sailed through the Whitsundays and further north, Cook was also unaware of the existence of the Barrier Reef, although he realised there was something to the east of his ship making the water unusually calm. It wasn't until he ran aground on the Endeavour Reef, near Cooktown, that he finally found out about the Great Barrier Reef. ■

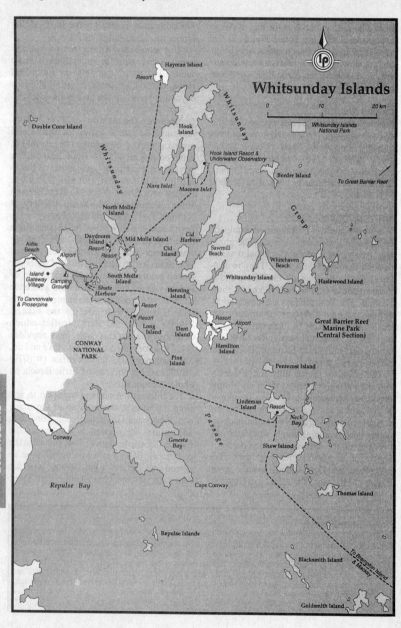

Whitsunday Islands

Hayman Island
Resort

Double Cone Island

Hook
Island

Whitsunday

Hook Island Resort &
Underwater Observatory

Nara Inlet

Macona Inlet

Border Island

To Great Barrier Reef

Whitsunday

North Molle
Island

Daydream
Island
Resort
Resort

Mid Molle Island

Cid
Harbour

Cid
Island

Sawmill
Beach

Whitehaven
Beach

Group

Airlie
Beach

Island
Gateway
Village

Airport

Camping
Ground

South Molle
Island

Shute
Harbour

Henning
Island

Whitsunday Island

Haslewood Island

To Cannonvale
& Proserpine

Resort

Resort

Long Island

Dent
Island

Resort

Airport

Great Barrier Reef
Marine Park
(Central Section)

CONWAY
NATIONAL
PARK

Hamilton
Island

Pine
Island

Pentecost Island

Conway

passage

Genesta
Bay

Lindeman
Island

Resort

Neck
Bay

Shaw Island

Repulse Bay

Cape Conway

Thomas Island

Repulse Islands

To Brampton Island
& Mackay

Blacksmith Island

Goldsmith Island

QUEENSLAND

Some boat operators will rent you water containers or help you organise other gear.

Contact the National Parks office to arrange a camping permit ($2 per person per night); sites take up to six people and numbers are limited for each camping area.

The possibilities for camping in national parks in the Whitsundays are summarised in the table.

Island	Location	Sites	Drinking Water
Shute	northern end	2	no
North Molle	Cockatoo Beach	5	seasonal
Whitsunday	Whitehaven Beach (southern end)	10	no
	Scrub Hen Beach	3	no
	Dugong Beach	7	yes, but may be seasonal
	Sawmill Beach	5	seasonal
	Joe's Beach	4	no
Hook	Curlew Beach	4	no
Thomas	Sea Eagle Beach	3	no
Shaw	Neck Bay Beach	3	no
South Repulse	western beach	3	no
Gloucester*	Bona Bay	7	no
Armit*	western beach	5	no
Saddleback*	western side	3	no
Grassy	south-west point	2	no

* Northern islands like Armit, Gloucester and Saddleback are harder to reach since the water taxi and cruises from Shute Harbour don't usually go there. Gloucester and Saddleback are best reached from Earlando, Dingo Beach or Bowen.

Long Island

The closest of the resort islands to the coast, Long Island has two active resorts and is nearly all national park. The 16.5-sq-km island has lots of rainforest, 13 km of walking tracks and some fine lookouts.

The *Club Crocodile Resort* (☎ (079) 46 9400), where the cruise boats stop, has a long expanse of genuine tropical island beach. The resort has two pools, tennis, archery, water sports and so on, as well as the obligatory disco. The resort has four styles of accommodation, ranging from bunk-style lodge units at $30 per person per night to beachfront units at $75 per person per night.

Palm Bay Island Resort (☎ (079) 46 9233), about two km south of Happy Bay, is one of the most relaxed and old-fashioned of the island resorts. There are eight simple huts and six more-elaborate cabins, with cooking facilities and fridges; you can get supplies here or bring them over from the mainland. Prices range from $117/186 for singles/doubles, plus another $48 for three meals a day. There's good snorkelling, and dinghies, catamarans and sailboards can be hired.

Hook Island

Second largest of the Whitsundays, Hook Island is 53 sq km and rises to 450 metres at Hook Peak. There are a number of beaches dotted around the island and there's also an underwater observatory ($8.50). It's mainly national park, with a camping area at Curlew Beach in the southern Macona Inlet. There's also the *Hook Island Resort* (☎ 018 775 142) facing Whitsunday Island in the south. The low-key resort is popular with backpackers, and has tent sites at $10 per person and an accommodation block with 12 adjoining bunk units at $20 per person. There's also a very casual restaurant with cheap lunches and dinners, or you can use the barbecues or communal kitchen area.

The beautiful, fjord-like Nara Inlet on Hook Island is a very popular deep-water anchorage for visiting yachts.

Daydream Island

This small, two-km-long island is only a couple of hundred metres across at its widest point. It's the nearest resort island to Shute Harbour and has one of the best swimming pools. The totally rebuilt resort (☎ (079) 48 8488) mainly caters for families and honeymooners. Accommodation starts at $170 a night for singles/doubles, including non-powered water activities and tennis, but cheaper stand-by rates are often available from Shute Harbour. You can spend the day on Daydream for $20 return.

South Molle Island

Largest of the Molle group of islands at four sq km, South Molle is virtually joined to Mid Molle and North Molle islands. It has long stretches of beach and is crisscrossed by walking tracks. The highest point is 198-metre Mt Jeffreys, but the climb up Spion Kop is also worthwhile. You can spend a day walking on the island for the cost of the $25 ferry trip.

Most of South Molle is national park but there's the *South Molle Island Resort* (☎ (079) 46 9433) in the north, where the boats come in, with nightly costs from $140 per person including all meals. Stand-by rates of $80 are offered out of peak season. The resort has a big pool, a small golf course and a gym, and offers tennis, squash, archery, snorkelling and windsurfing, all included in the price. Hundreds of rainbow lorikeets fly in to feed every day at 3 pm.

Hamilton Island

The most heavily developed resort island in the Whitsundays, Hamilton has its own jet airport, a 400-boat marina and accommodation for more than 2000, including three high-rise tower blocks. The range of entertainment possibilities, not surprisingly, is extensive (and expensive): helicopter joy rides, game fishing, parasailing, cruising, scuba diving, nine restaurants, shops, squash courts and even a hill-top fauna reserve with wombats, crocodiles and koalas. The cheapest double room costs $200, but stand-by rates cut about one-third off this price. Hamilton is more like a small town than a resort,

so there are a variety of restaurants and takeaways and even a small supermarket.

Hamilton is about five sq km in area and rises to 200 metres at Passage Peak. It can make an interesting day trip from Shute Harbour ($20 return for the launch only), and you can use all of the resort facilities.

The airport is used mainly by people jetting between resort islands, with launches and helicopters laid on to whisk them off to their chosen spots. Ansett flies nonstop to Hamilton from Brisbane ($289 one way), Cairns ($230), Melbourne ($485) and Sydney ($407).

Hayman Island

Owned by Ansett, Hayman is an exclusive resort – no day trips here. The nearest you'll probably get is to some of the reefs or small islands nearby such as Black Island (also called Bali Hai) or Arkhurst, Langford or Bird islands.

The most northerly of the Whitsunday Group, Hayman has an area of four sq km, and rises to 250 metres above sea level. It has forested hills, valleys and beaches. The resort, in the south, is fronted by a wide, shallow reef which emerges from the water at low tide. Rooms range from $350 to $2800 a night, and food is equally expensive.

Lindeman Island

One of the most southerly of the Whitsundays,

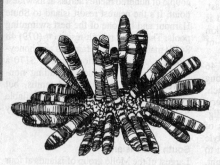
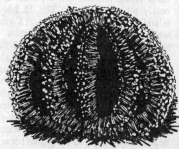

Sea urchins

Lindeman covers eight sq km, most of which is national park. The island has 20 km of walking trails and the highest point is 210-metre Mt Oldfield.

The *Club Med* (☎ (079) 46 9333) resort, in the south, has a golf course, tennis and lots of water-based activities. Nightly rates range from $175 to $250 per person, including meals, drinks, activities and entertainment, and there are launches from Shute Harbour. Lindeman also has its own airstrip: Helijet (☎ (079) 46 9133) flies from Mackay ($65), Whitsunday Airport near Shute Harbour ($45) and Hamilton Island ($35).

With plenty of little beaches and secluded bays on Lindeman it's no hassle at all to find one to yourself. There are also a lot of small islands dotted around, some of which are easy to get across to.

Whitsunday Island

The largest of the Whitsunday Group, this island covers 109 sq km and rises to 438 metres at Whitsunday Peak. There's no resort, but six-km Whitehaven Beach on the south-east coast is the longest and finest beach in the group (some say in the country!), with good snorkelling off its southern end. There are National Parks camping areas at Whitehaven Beach, Scrub Hen Beach in the north-west, Dugong and Sawmill beaches on the west, and Joe's Beach.

Cid Harbour

Between Cid and Whitsunday islands, Cid Harbour was the anchorage for part of the US Navy before the Battle of the Coral Sea, the turning point in the Pacific theatre of WW II. Today, visiting ocean cruise liners anchor here.

Getting Around

Air Helijet Air Services (☎ (079) 46 9133), based at Whitsunday Airport, near Shute Harbour, makes scenic flights over the islands and/or reef (minimum two adults) from $40 for 15 minutes to $100 for an hour. It will also land seaplanes on the reef for semisubmersible rides, glass-bottomed boating, reef walking or snorkelling; prices start at $100.

Boat There's a bamboozling array of boat trips, and all the hostels and agencies have dozens of brochures. Mandy's Mine of Information (☎ (079) 46 6848), on Shute Harbour Rd in Airlie Beach, prints a useful list dividing the trips into manageable categories, and a visit here can be quite an entertaining experience. You can make bookings at Mandy's or any of the other agents in Airlie Beach.

Most boats depart from Shute Harbour or the Abel Point Marina, although a few leave from the Airlie Bay beach. Most of the cruise operators do coach pick-ups from Airlie Beach. You can take a bus to Shute Harbour – or you can leave your car in the Shute Harbour car park for $7 for 24 hours. There's a lock-up car park a few hundred metres back along the road by the Shell service station, costing $5 from 8 am to 5 pm or $8 for 24 hours.

Depending on how much time and money you have, you can choose from the following: day trips to the islands or reefs from $40 to $50; overnight cruises from $120; two-night/three-day trips from $200, or $225 for three nights/four days; four-night/five-day camping trips from $200; or self-skippered charter yachts for around $210 per person for three nights/four days. There are motor cruisers and sailing ships, and most trips include activities like snorkelling and boom netting, with scuba diving as an optional extra. It's worth asking how many people will be on your boat.

BOWEN (population 8300)

Bowen, founded in 1861, was the first coastal settlement to be established north of Rockhampton. Although soon overshadowed by Mackay to the south and Townsville to the north, Bowen survived, and today it's a thriving fruit- and vegetable-growing centre which attracts hundreds of people for seasonal picking work.

The Bowen Historical Museum, at 22 Gordon St, has displays relating to the town's early history. It's open weekdays and Sunday mornings. Just north of Bowen several sandy beaches, some of them quite secluded, dot the coast around the cape.

Places to Stay

Barnacles Backpackers (☎ (077) 86 1245), at 16 Gordon St, is a workers' hostel with a relaxed atmosphere and good facilities. The owner can often find seasonal work for travellers. Ring from the bus stop for a pick-up or directions. Dorm beds are $10, doubles $24.

Bowen Backpackers (☎ (077) 86 3433) is nearby at 56 Herbert St (the main road). It's a long-running workers' hostel with a good reputation for finding fruit-picking work, although the hostel itself is fairly basic. The owners will also get very annoyed if they find you work and you subsequently move somewhere else, like the (cheaper) caravan park. The nightly cost is $12 in four- to eight-bed dorms.

Another alternative is the *Whitsunday North Resort* (☎ (077) 86 1101) on Stone Island, four km south-east of Bowen. The island itself is small, barren and rocky, and home to hundreds of wallabies. The resort is well set up and has a pool, a bar and a restaurant with dinners from $3 to $5, and the rooms have their own bathrooms. Dorm beds are $12, doubles $32 or you can camp for $7 a night. There's a regular ferry service across, and if you're working, the ferry and van to work will cost you another $3.

Places to Eat

On Herbert St, the *Club Hotel*, one block down from the backpackers' hostel, and the *Grandview Hotel* further down, both do counter meals. The *Denison Hotel* on Powell St is also good.

On Gregory St (parallel with Herbert St), try *Fellows Fish Bar* for takeaway fish & chips, or the *Hot Wok* nearby for cheap Chinese takeaways. There's also the *Blue Bird Cafe* in William St, next to the bus stop.

Getting There & Away

The long-distance bus stop is outside the travel centre (☎ (077) 86 2835) on William St, near the city centre.

There are buses to and from Rockhampton (6½ hours, $71), Airlie Beach (two hours, $22) and Townsville (2½ hours, $31). The Sunlander and Queenslander trains also stop at Bowen. The economy fare from Brisbane is $104. If you're sick of driving, there's also a motorail service between Bowen and Townsville.

North Coast

AYR (population 8600)

This sugar town is on the delta of one of the biggest rivers in Queensland, the Burdekin. Rice is also grown in the area. On Wilmington St, the **Ayr Nature Display** has displays of orchids, butterflies and other Australian animals; it's open from 8 am to 5 pm daily.

Across the Burdekin River to the south is **Home Hill**, which has a historical museum. To the north, between Ayr and Townsville, you pass the **Australian Institute of Marine Science** on Cape Ferguson. You can visit it from 8 am to 4 pm Monday to Friday, with guided tours on Fridays.

Twenty-eight km south of Townsville, or 72 km north of Ayr, along the Bruce Highway, then six km south by paved road, there's a good camping ground by Alligator Creek in the big **Bowling Green Bay National Park**. Swimming holes in the creek are good during the wet season and some walking tracks start from the camping ground. Alligator Creek tumbles down between two rugged ranges which rise steeply from the coastal plains. The taller range peaks in Mt Elliot (1234 metres), whose higher slopes harbour some of Queensland's most southerly tropical rainforest. There's no public transport to the park.

TOWNSVILLE (population 87,000)

The third largest city in Queensland and the main centre in the north of the state, Townsville is the port city for the agricultural and mining production of the vast inland region of northern Queensland. Founded in 1864 by the efforts of a Scot, John Melton Black, and the money of Robert Towns, a Sydney-based sea captain and financier, Townsville developed mainly on the back of Chinese and Kanaka labour.

Today Townsville is a working city, a major armed forces base, and the site of James Cook University. It's the start of the main route from Queensland to the Northern Territory. It's the only departure point for Magnetic Island (20 minutes away by ferry), while the Barrier Reef is about 1¾ hours away by fast catamaran.

In recent years, millions of dollars have been spent in an effort to encourage more visitors to stop in Townsville, rather than going straight through to Cairns. A Sheraton hotel-casino and a marina have been built on Townsville's oceanfront, and the Flinders St East and Palmer St areas on opposite sides of Ross Creek are being redeveloped. The centrepiece here is the Great Barrier Reef Wonderland complex. Along with these big money efforts, there's been a boom in budget accommodation and in the eating and entertainment scene; yet the visitors are still staying away in droves. Apart from a few attractions, such as the Great Barrier Reef Wonderland, and as an access point for Magnetic Island, Townsville still hasn't really got a lot going for it from a budget traveller's point of view.

Orientation

Townsville centres on Ross Creek and is dominated by 290-metre Castle Hill, which has a lookout perched on top. The city sprawls a long way, but the centre's a fairly compact area that you can easily get around on foot.

Most of the accommodation is in the centre. The transit centre, the arrival and departure point for long-distance buses, is on the corner of Palmer and Plume Sts, just south of Ross Creek. The city centre is immediately to the north of the creek, over the Dean St bridge. Flinders St Mall stretches to the left from the northern side of the bridge, towards the railway station. To the right of the bridge is the Flinders St East area, which contains many of the town's oldest buildings, cafes and restaurants, the Great Barrier Reef Wonderland and the ferry terminal.

Information

Townsville Enterprises' main tourist information office (☎ (077) 78 3555) is on the Bruce Highway, eight km south of the city centre. There's also a more convenient information booth (☎ (077) 21 3660) in the middle of Flinders St Mall, between Stokes and Denham Sts. It's open Monday to Friday from 9 am to 5 pm, and Saturdays and Sundays from 9 am to noon. The RACQ (☎ (077) 75 3999) is at 202 Ross River Rd, in the suburb of Aitkenvale.

Apart from the main post office on Flinders St, there's a branch in the Barrier Reef Wonderland which is open weekends as well as weekdays. There's also a National Parks information office (☎ (077) 21 2399) at the Wonderland, open from Monday to Saturday between 9 am and 5 pm.

There are a lot of rodeos in Queensland, a number of them in the small towns inland from Townsville. The season is May to October and the tourist office should have details.

Great Barrier Reef Wonderland

Townsville's top attraction is at the end of Flinders St East beside Ross Creek. While its impressive aquarium is the highlight, there are several other sections including a theatre, a museum, shops, a good National Parks information office, the Great Barrier Reef Marine Park Authority office and a terminal for ferries to Magnetic Island.

A combined ticket to the aquarium, theatre and museum costs $18, or you can pay for each individually.

Aquarium The huge main tank has a living coral reef and hundreds of reef fish, sharks, rays and other life, and you can walk beneath the tank through a transparent tunnel. To

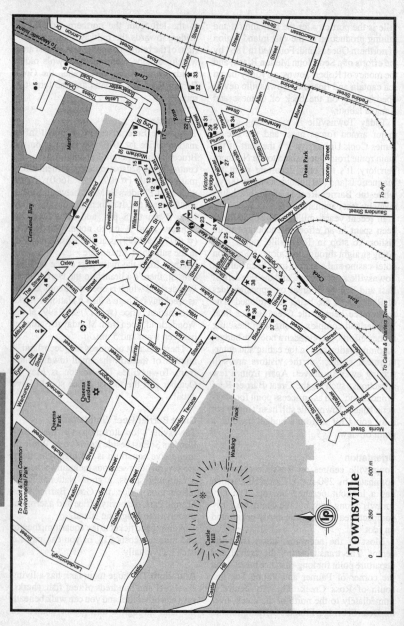

QUEENSLAND

Townsville

PLACES TO STAY		PLACES TO EAT		8	Tobruk Olympic Swimming Pool
4	Strand Motel	1	Rasa Pinang & El Charro	12	Bank Nightclub
9	Yongala Lodge & Restaurant	2	Hotel Allen	16	Criterion Tavern
11	Backpackers International & Luvits Cafe	3	Seaview Hotel	17	Great Barrier Reef Wonderland & Ferry Terminal
15	Reef Lodge	10	Thai International Restaurant	18	Perc Tucker Regional Gallery
28	Shamrock Hotel	13	Exchange Hotel	19	Townsville Museum
30	Andy's Backpackers	14	A Kabab	20	Tourist Office Kiosk
31	Globetrotters Hostel	24	Fisherman's Wharf	21	Post Office
		26	Australian Hotel	22	Maritime Museum
33	Adventurers Resort YHA	27	Cactus Jack's Bar & Grill	23	Qantas Airlines
		41	Jun Japanese Restaurant	25	Ansett Airlines
34	Southbank Village Backpackers	43	Cafe Nova	29	Bus Transit Centre
36	Civic House Backpackers Inn			32	Crown Tavern
		OTHER		35	Mike Ball Watersports
37	Sunseeker Private Hotel	5	Sheraton Breakwater Casino	38	Police Station
				39	Townsville Cinema Centre
42	Great Northern Hotel	6	Ferry Terminal	40	STA Travel
		7	Hospital	44	Railway Station

maintain the natural conditions needed to keep this community alive, a wave machine simulates the ebb and flow of the ocean, circular currents keep the water in motion and marine algae are used in the purification system. The aquarium also has several smaller tanks, extensive displays on the history and life of the reef, and a theatrette where slide-shows on the reef are shown, plus regular guided tours. It's open daily from 9.30 am to 5 pm and admission is $10.

Omnimax Theatre This cinema has angled seating and a dome-shaped screen to create a 3-D effect. Hour-long films on the reef and various other topics, such as outer space, alternate through the day from 9.30 am till 5.30 pm. Admission to one film is $9.50.

Museum of Tropical Queensland This small museum has two sections, with one display focusing on the Age of Reptiles and the other half devoted to the natural history of north Queensland, including wetland birds and other fauna, rainforest, ocean wrecks and Aboriginal artefacts. The museum is open daily from 9 am to 5 pm and admission is $2.50.

Other Museums & Galleries
The **Townsville Museum** on the corner of Sturt and Stokes Sts has a permanent display on early Townsville and the North Queensland independence campaigns, as well as temporary exhibitions. It's open daily from 10 am to 3 pm (to 1 pm on weekends).

The **Jezzine Military Museum** is just off the northern end of the Strand. There's also a **Maritime Museum** on Palmer St, beside Ross Creek in South Townsville, open on weekdays from 10 am to 4 pm and weekends from 1 to 4 pm ($2). The **Perc Tucker Gallery**, at the Denham St end of the Flinders St Mall, is a good regional art gallery and admission is free. It's open on Tuesdays, Thursdays and Saturdays from 10 am to 5 pm, Fridays from 2 to 9 pm, and Sundays from 10 am to 1 pm.

Parks, Gardens & Sanctuaries
The **Queens Gardens** on Gregory St, a km from the town centre, contain sports playing fields, tennis courts and Townsville's original **Botanic Gardens**, dating from 1878. The entrance to these lovely gardens is on Paxton St. The new botanic gardens, **Anderson Park**, are six km south-west of the centre on Gulliver St, Mundingburra.

For a chance to see some wildlife, make your way out to the **Town Common Environmental Park**, five km north of the centre, just off Cape Pallarenda Rd. This 32-sq-km area ranges from mangrove swamps and salt marsh to dry grassland and pockets of woodland and forest. The common is best known for water birds such as magpie geese, which herald the start of the wet season, and stately brolgas, which gather in the Dry. Early morning is the best time to see them.

The **Billabong Sanctuary**, 17 km south on the Bruce Highway, is a zoo of Australian animals. It's open daily from 9 am to 5 pm, with various shows (including crocodile, koala and giant eel feeding) throughout each day. Admission costs $12.

The **Palmetum**, about 15 km south-west of the centre off University Rd, is a 25-hectare botanic garden devoted to native palms in their natural environments, ranging from desert to rainforest species.

Other Attractions

The **Flinders St Mall** is the retail heart of the city. It's bright, breezy and full of interest, with fountains, plantations and crowds of shoppers. Every Sunday morning, the busy **Cotters Market** is held in the mall, with a wide range of crafts and local produce on offer. A block south of the mall is **Fisherman's Wharf**, a collection of riverfront eateries with open-air tables and live music most nights.

East of the mall you can stroll along **Flinders St East** beside the creek. Many of the best 19th-century buildings are in this part of town, while further out on a breakwater at the mouth of Ross Creek, the casino, entertainment centre and a couple of up-market seafood restaurants are located on the waterfront. A more pleasant walk is north along **the Strand**, a long beachfront drive with a marina, gardens, some awesome banyan trees, the Tobruk swimming pool and a big artificial waterfall.

There's a road up to the top of **Castle Hill**, where there are very good views over the town and coast, and you can also walk up from Stanton Terrace.

Diving

Townsville has four or five diving schools, including one of Australia's best – Mike Ball Watersports (☎ (077) 72 3022), at 252 Walker St. Five-day certificate courses start twice a week and cost around $360 with five trips to the reef – plus two nights there on the more expensive option. You have to take a $40 medical before you start the course.

Pro-Dive, another well-regarded diving school, also runs courses in Townsville. Its office (☎ (077) 21 1760) is in the Great Barrier Reef Wonderland. Pro-Dive's five-day certificate course costs $395, starts twice a week, and includes two nights and three days on the reef, with a total of eight dives.

You can get cheap or free accommodation at some hostels if you book a diving course from that hostel.

For experienced divers, the wreck of the *Yongala*, a passenger liner which sank off Cape Bowling Green in 1911 with 122 lives lost, is more of an attraction than the John Brewer Reef, the destination for many day trips. The *Yongala* has huge numbers of fish and large marine life like turtles and rays. John Brewer Reef has been damaged by cyclones and the crown-of-thorns starfish, and parts of the reef have little live coral. Mike Ball and Pro-Dive both run trips out to the *Yongala*.

Organised Tours

Two companies, Pure Pleasure Tours & Cruises (☎ (077) 21 3555) and Detours Coaches (☎ (077) 21 5977), offer a variety of tours in and around Townsville, including city sights tours, bus trips to the Billabong Sanctuary or Charters Towers, and cruises to Magnetic Island and the outer reef.

Places to Stay

Camping There are two caravan parks which are only about two km from town. *Rowes Bay Caravan Park* (☎ (077) 71 3576), just over the road from the beach on Heatley Parade, Rowes Bay, has tent sites for $12 and on-site cabins for $34; and the *Showground Caravan Park* (☎ (077) 72 1487), at 16 Kings Rd, West End, has tent sites for $10 and on-site vans for $25.

Hostels Townsville's hostel scene is probably the best example of large operators jumping on the budget accommodation bandwagon. Two huge hostels in Townsville is *at least* one too many, and the resulting oversupply of beds means that the general standard of hostels here is not as good as in many other towns along the coast.

Palmer St, in the area of the transit centre, has four hostels. The huge *Adventurers Resort YHA* (☎ (077) 21 1522), at 79 Palmer St, is a modern multilevel complex with over 300 beds, a shop, a licensed budget restaurant and a swimming pool. The kitchen, laundry and other facilities are very good, although because the place is so large it can feel a bit anonymous. Accommodation in a four-bunk dorm costs $12 for YHA members, $13 for nonmembers; singles cost $20/22 and doubles $28/30.

Townsville's other huge offering is *Andy's Backpackers* (☎ (077) 21 2322), which is upstairs on top of the transit centre. Although convenient for bus departures, the place lacks atmosphere. Dorm beds are $13 and doubles are $30.

Between these two places is the smaller *Globetrotters Hostel* (☎ (077) 71 3242), behind a house at 45 Palmer St. This relaxed hostel has all the usual facilities – kitchen area, lounge, pool, laundry – and it's clean and well run. Six-bed dorms cost $11 per night, singles cost $22, and a twin room is $28. Also on this side of the river is *Southbank Village Backpackers* (☎ (077) 72 2122), at 33 Plume St. It's an old, rambling hostel spread over several buildings and, although it's pretty run down and disorganised, it's cheap at $10 a bed.

There are more places north of Ross Creek, in and around the city centre. The pick of this bunch is probably *Civic House Backpackers Inn* (☎ (077) 71 5381) at 262 Walker St. This easy-going hostel has three- or four-bed dorms for $11 or six-bed dorms with bathroom and air-con for $12. It also has very pleasant twin and double rooms at $28,

or $35 with a private bathroom. On Friday nights there's a free barbecue for guests.

Next up is *Backpackers International* (☎ (077) 72 4340), which occupies the two levels above a cafe at 205 Flinders St East. There are two dorms on the 2nd floor and a kitchen and lounge on the 1st floor. This place is central and has two broad balconies looking out over the river, although the dorms are quite large and it's a bit run down. Dorm beds are $10.

The *Reef Lodge* (☎ (077) 21 1112), at 4 Wickham St, has dorm beds for $12, or there are singles/doubles for $26/32 with coin-in-the-slot air-con. It's another small, old-style place with the usual facilities, although the stoves in the kitchen also require coins (20c).

Hotels & Guesthouses A number of Townsville's traditional old hotels offer accommodation. The *Great Northern Hotel* (☎ (077) 71 6191), at 500 Flinders St down by the railway station, is a good old-fashioned pub with clean, simple rooms opening out onto a broad verandah. Nightly cost is $18/30; some doubles have private bathrooms for an extra $5, and the food downstairs is good.

The *Seaview Hotel* (☎ (077) 71 5005), at 56 The Strand, has singles/doubles at $22/30, and the *Shamrock Hotel* (☎ (077) 71 4351) opposite the transit centre also has a few pub rooms upstairs at similar prices.

The *Sunseeker Private Hotel* (☎ (077) 71 3409), situated at 10 Blackwood St, has small singles/doubles with shared bathrooms at $25/28 and triples at $33, but it's a pretty gloomy and cheerless place. There's a communal kitchen downstairs.

Motels Cheaper motels include the *Tropical Hideaway Motel* (☎ (077) 71 4355) at 74 The Strand, with rooms from $42; the central *Rex City Motel* (☎ (077) 71 6048) at 143 Wills St, with singles/doubles from $46/50; and the *Strand Motel* (☎ (077) 72 1977) at 51 The Strand, with rooms at $46/49.

Yongala Lodge (☎ (070) 72 4633), at 11 Fryer St, has both heritage-style motel units and self-contained rooms at $59, or two-bedroom flats with fully equipped kitchenette, sitting area and balcony at $89 for up to four people. At the front, in a lovely 19th-century building, is a Greek restaurant (see Places to Eat). Numerous other motels are on the two roads leading into Townsville from the Bruce Highway to the south.

Some holiday flats offer similar prices to the cheaper motels. *A&A Holiday Apartments* (☎ (077) 21 1990), about 1.5 km north of the centre at 80 Mitchell St, has good one- and two-bedroom units from $45 a double or $70 for four.

Places to Eat

Flinders St East is the main area for eateries, and offers plenty of choices. The *Thai International Restaurant*, upstairs at 235 Flinders St East, has fine soups for $6 and imaginative main courses for $10 to $14.

Further along, *Luvits Cafe* is a good spot for breakfast or brunch, and it also does filled savoury pancakes and Indian meals at night, with mains around $10. At No 179, the licensed *Capitol* Chinese restaurant has two sections: a seafood smorgasbord at $29.50 a head, or an à la carte restaurant with mains around $10.

Flinders St East also has *A Kabab* up past the Exchange Hotel, with chicken, beef and lamb kebabs for $4.20, as well as the *Hog's Breath Cafe*, one of a chain of saloon-style bar & grills, near the Denham St corner.

Fisherman's Wharf, overlooking Ross Creek from near the western end of Victoria Bridge, has an inviting collection of food stalls and open-air tables. Cuisines featured include Italian, seafood, Mexican, health food and more, all at reasonable prices, and there's also a bar and live entertainment from Wednesday to Sunday nights.

Many of the pubs do decent counter meals. The *Exchange Hotel* on Flinders St has a wine-bar restaurant with meals from $8 to $10, and the Melton Blacks Bistro upstairs has a pleasant balcony, live music and more-expensive food. The *Great Northern Hotel*, on the corner of Flinders and Blackwood Sts, has an excellent bistro with mains from $10 to $12 and good bar meals from $4 to $7. The

Australian Hotel on Palmer St also has good pub food, and features live jazz on Friday nights and Sunday afternoons. The *Seaview Hotel* on the Strand and the *Hotel Allen*, around the corner on Gregory St, are also popular places to eat, and both have pleasant beer gardens.

Over on Palmer St is *Cactus Jack's Bar & Grill*, a lively licensed Mexican place with main courses in the $8 to $12 range; you'll need to book on weekends. The cafe in the transit centre serves quite substantial meals and is open from 5 am to 11 pm. At the front of the centre, *Andy's Bistro* has a bar and a range of meals from $4 to $8.

Back on Flinders St, past the southern end of the mall, is the *Jun Japanese Restaurant*, which is nothing special but is moderately priced at $12 to $15 for main courses. The reasonably priced *Cafe Nova*, on Blackwood St near the corner of Flinders St, is open from 6 pm till late every night except Monday; it has snacks, light meals including vegetarian dishes, and good desserts and coffee. On the corner of Blackwood and Sturt Sts, *Admiral's Seafood Restaurant* serves good seafood in a nautical-style setting.

Just off the Strand, near the Seaview Hotel, is the small *Rasa Pinang* Malaysian restaurant. All the dishes on the menu are less than $10, and the $5 takeaway dishes are very good value. Next door is *El Charro*, another lively and popular Mexican restaurant.

Historic *Yongala Lodge* has a Greek restaurant in a lovely old building, with displays of period furniture, memorabilia, and finds from the *Yongala* wreck. Main meals are in the $16 to $20 range, or there's a banquet menu at $30 a head.

Entertainment

Townsville's nightlife is almost as lively as Cairns' and ranges from pub bands to flashy clubs and, of course, the casino. Much of the action is along Flinders St and the Strand.

The big and colourful *Criterion Tavern*, on the corner of the Strand and King St, is very popular. It has a beer garden, nightclub, restaurant and several bars, and live bands in its outdoor section. Moving along the Strand, the *Seaview Hotel* has rock music in its large beer garden on Fridays, Saturdays and Sundays, plus an over-25's nightclub upstairs.

The *Australian Hotel*, south of the river on Palmer St, is a relaxed, old-fashioned pub with live jazz sessions on Friday nights and Sunday afternoons.

The *Tavern*, at 237 Flinders St East, has rock & roll bands every night except Tuesday. *Portraits Wine Bar*, at the Exchange Hotel on Flinders St, attracts a more sophisticated (older) crowd. Nearby is the *Bank*, at 169 Flinders St East, the city's most up-market nightclub; it's open nightly till late, with a $3 to $5 cover charge and dress regulations.

The *Townsville Cinema Centre* (☎ (077) 71 4101), on the corner of Sturt and Blackwood Sts, has five cinemas showing mainstream current releases.

The *Civic Theatre* (☎ (077) 72 2677), on Boundary St in South Townsville, is the regional centre for performing arts and varied cultural pursuits. If you have the right clothes and fancy trying your luck on the spin of the wheel, the *Sheraton Breakwater Casino* is down at the end of Sir Leslie Thiess Drive, beyond Flinders St East.

Getting There & Away

Air You can fly to Townsville from Cairns ($148), Brisbane ($319), Sydney or Melbourne several times a day with Ansett or Qantas – and from other major centres usually once or twice a day. You can also get to Perth, Darwin or Alice Springs from Townsville with either airline. Ansett and Qantas both have offices in the Flinders St Mall.

Sunstate Airlines has services to Cairns, Dunk Island, Mackay, Proserpine, Rockhampton, Gladstone and Bundaberg.

Flight West (☎ (077) 25 1622) has flights to Mt Isa ($253) at least once a day, often with stops at smaller places on the way. It also flies to Cairns ($148), Mackay ($155) and Rockhampton ($223).

Bus Greyhound Pioneer and McCafferty's

(☎ (077) 72 5100) have daily services between Brisbane and Cairns. Fares and times from Townsville include Brisbane (18 to 21 hours, $118), Rockhampton (11 hours, $76), Mackay (six hours, $48), Airlie Beach (3½ hours, $40), Mission Beach (three hours, $38) and Cairns (4½ hours, $40). To Mt Isa the trip takes 11 hours and costs $84.

All the bus companies use the Townsville transit centre on Palmer St.

Train The Brisbane to Cairns Sunlander travels through Townsville three times a week. The trip from Brisbane to Townsville takes 25 hours ($112 in economy, $168 in 1st class). From Townsville, Proserpine is a five-hour journey, Rockhampton is 14½ hours and Cairns seven hours. The Queenslander does the same Brisbane to Cairns run once a week (leaving Brisbane on Sunday mornings and Cairns on Tuesday mornings). It's a bit faster than the Sunlander and has a special bar for 1st-class passengers, where movies are shown. Economy fares are the same as on the Sunlander: 1st class from Brisbane to Townsville is $433 which includes all meals and a sleeping compartment.

The Inlander operates twice weekly from Townsville to Mt Isa (18 hours; $95 in economy, $192 in 1st-class sleeper). Townsville to Charters Towers takes three hours ($20 in economy only).

Car Rental The larger car-rental agencies are all represented in Townsville. Smaller operators include Rent-a-Rocket (☎ (077) 72 6880) at 14 Dean St, South Townsville; Sunrunner Moke Hire (☎ (077) 21 5038) on Palmer St opposite the transit centre; and Townsville Limousine Hire (☎ (077) 72 1093) also on Palmer St, opposite the Australian Hotel.

Getting Around

To/From the Airport Townsville Airport is five km north-west of the city at Garbutt; a taxi to the centre costs $9. The City-Airport Express bus (☎ (077) 75 7333) services all main arrivals and departures. It costs $5 one way and will drop off or pick up almost anywhere fairly central.

Bus A free tourist bus operates daily from a number of the accommodation places to the casino and ferry terminals – timetables for this bus are available at information centres and wherever you're staying.

Taxi For a taxi in Townsville, call Standard White Cabs (☎ (077) 72 1555).

MAGNETIC ISLAND (population 2500)

Magnetic is one of the most popular islands for travellers because it's so cheap and convenient to get to. It's big enough to offer plenty of things to see and do, including some fine bushwalks.

Only eight km offshore from Townsville, Magnetic Island was named by Captain Cook, who thought his ship's compass went funny when he sailed by in 1770. The island has some fine beaches, lots of bird life, bushwalking tracks, a koala sanctuary and an aquarium. It's dominated by 500-metre Mt Cook.

There are several small towns along the coast and the island has quite a different atmosphere to the purely resort islands along the reef. Magnetic is one of the larger reef islands (52 sq km) and about 70% of it is national park.

Orientation & Information

Magnetic Island is roughly triangular in shape with Picnic Bay, the main town and ferry destination, at the southern corner. There's a road up the eastern side of the island to Horseshoe Bay and a rough track along the west coast. Along the north coast it's walking only.

The Island Travel Centre (☎ (077) 78 5155) has an information centre and booking office between the end of the pier and Picnic Bay Mall. You can book local tours and accommodation here, and they can also handle domestic and international travel arrangements.

Walks

The National Parks service produces a leaflet for Magnetic Island's excellent bushwalking tracks. Possible walks, with distances and one-way travel times, include:

Nelly Bay to Arcadia	6 km	2 hours
Picnic Bay to West Point	8 km	2½ hours
Horseshoe Bay road to Arthur Bay	2 km	½ hour
Horseshoe Bay to Florence Bay	2.5 km	1 hour
Horseshoe Bay to the Forts	2 km	¾ hour
Horseshoe Bay to Balding Bay	3 km	¾ hour
Horseshoe Bay to Radical Bay	3 km	¾ hour
Mt Cook ascent	8 km	all day

Picnic Bay

Picnic Bay is the main settlement on the island, and the first stop for the ferries. The new mall along the waterfront has a good selection of shops and eateries, and you can hire bikes, mokes and scooters here. Picnic Bay also has quite a few places to stay, and the main beach has a stinger-free enclosure and is patrolled by a lifesaving club.

There's a lookout above the town and just to the west of Picnic Bay is **Cockle Bay** with the wreck of the *City of Adelaide*. Heading around the coast in the other direction is **Rocky Bay** where there's a short, steep walk down to its beautiful beach.

Nelly Bay

Next around the coast is Nelly Bay, which has a good beach with shade, and a reef at low tide. At the far end of the bay there are some pioneer graves. Nelly Bay also has the **Shark World** aquarium, which has coral displays, tropical fish aquariums, tortoises and sharks. Admission costs $5, and the sharks are fed daily at 11.30 am and 2.15 pm. There's also a snack bar, and a licensed restaurant, open from 8 am to 7.30 pm.

Arcadia

Round the next headland you come to **Geoffrey Bay**, a marine park area which has an interesting 400-metre low-tide reef walk over the fringing coral reef from the southern

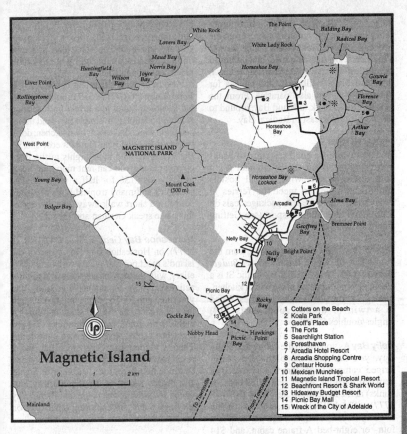

Magnetic Island

1 Cotters on the Beach
2 Koala Park
3 Geoff's Place
4 The Forts
5 Searchlight Station
6 Foresthaven
7 Arcadia Hotel Resort
8 Arcadia Shopping Centre
9 Centaur House
10 Mexican Munchies
11 Magnetic Island Tropical Resort
12 Beachfront Resort & Shark World
13 Hideaway Budget Resort
14 Picnic Bay Mall
15 Wreck of the City of Adelaide

end of the beach; a board indicates the start of the trail. Some of Magnetic Marine's ferries also stop at the jetty on Geoffrey Bay.

Overlooking the bay is the town of Arcadia, with shops, more places to stay and the Arcadia Hotel Resort (where there are live bands at weekends and the pool is open to the public). Just around the next headland is the very pleasant Alma Bay beach.

Radical Bay & the Forts
The road runs back from the coast until you reach the junction of the road to Radical Bay. You can go straight to Horseshoe Bay, take

the central track via the Forts, or turn right to Radical Bay, with tracks leading off to secluded Arthur and Florence bays and the old **Searchlight Station** on the headland between the two.

At Radical Bay you can hire kayaks, catamarans, windsurfers and jet skis. From here you can walk across the headland to the beautiful **Balding Bay** (an unofficial nude bathing beach) and Horseshoe Bay.

Horseshoe Bay
Horseshoe Bay, on the north coast of the island, has a few shops, some accommodation and a

long stretch of beach. There's a **bird sanctuary** lagoon a few hundred metres from the beach, a desolate **Koala Park** which is quite a long drive off the main road, and a **mango plantation** which you can visit. At the beach there are boats, sailboards and canoes for hire and you can also parasail. From the beach you can walk to Maud Bay, around to the west, or back east to Radical Bay.

Places to Stay

Hostels There's a good selection of backpackers' hostels on the island and it's a competitive scene, with several hostels sending vehicles to meet the ferries at Picnic Bay. There are also package deals on accommodation and transport (see Getting There & Away).

Picnic Bay Only a minute's walk from the Picnic Bay ferry pier, the *Hideaway Budget Resort* (☎ (077) 78 5110) at 32 Picnic St is a clean, newly renovated place with a kitchen, pool, TV room and laundry facilities. A bed in a twin or double room costs $14, singles/doubles $22/28.

Nelly Bay As you round the corner into Nelly Bay, you'll notice the blue- and-white-striped 'camp-o-tel' accommodation (a cross between a cabin and a tent with beds or bunks) at the *Beachfront Resort* (☎ (077) 78 5777) at Shark World. It costs $7 per person to camp in your own tent, $12 per head in a four- or eight-bed A-frame cabin, and $14 per head in the camp-o-tels (which apparently get unbearably hot in summer).

The *Magnetic Island Tropical Resort* (☎ (077) 78 5955), on Yates St off the main road, is the island's newest budget resort and has accommodation in spacious A-frame cabins, each with six beds and its own bathroom. Dorm beds cost $12, doubles with en-suites cost $40, or you can rent a whole four-bed cabin for $38. This place is good if you're after somewhere quiet, and it has a pool and an inexpensive restaurant.

Arcadia The popular *Centaur House* (☎ (077) 78 5668), at 27 Marine Parade, is a rambling, old-style hostel opposite the beach. The atmosphere is relaxed, there's a pleasant garden, and a bed in the clean spacious dorms costs $14; double rooms are $34. This place is quiet and friendly.

Also in Arcadia, situated at 11 Cook Rd, is *Foresthaven* (☎ (077) 78 5153), another small, old-fashioned hostel in a lovely bush setting. Accommodation is in simple two- and three-bed units which have their own kitchen; dorm beds cost $12 and twins/doubles cost $26/30. Barbecues are held most nights in the large courtyard, and you can rent mountain bikes at $10 a day ($6 for half a day). Koalas, wallabies and many tropical birds are often seen just a short walk away. The owners of this place speak German and French.

Horseshoe Bay *Geoff's Place* (☎ (077) 78 5577), on Horseshoe Bay Rd, is one of the island's most popular places for young travellers, with its party atmosphere and nightly activities. There are extensive grounds, and you can camp for $6 per person, take a bunk in a marquee for $8 or share a four- or eight-bed A-frame cedar cabin for $12. (The eight-bed cabins have their own bathroom.) There's a communal kitchen, a bar and a restaurant with meals from $4 to $7. You can hire mountain bikes from $10 a day, ride horses at a nearby ranch, or use the courtesy bus, which shuttles between here and Picnic Bay six times a day, for exploring other bays on the island.

Hotels & Holiday Flats There are hotels, motels, resorts and more than a dozen holiday flats on the island. These can get very busy, especially during school holiday periods, so it's wise to phone ahead and book if necessary.

The *Picnic Bay Holiday Hotel* (☎ (077) 78 5166) on the Esplanade in Picnic Bay has motel rooms from $40. In Arcadia, the *Arcadia Hotel Resort* (☎ (077) 78 5177) has poolside motel-style units for $35/55, or terrace rooms for $40/65.

Prices for holiday flats vary with demand – one-bedroom flats are around $250 to $350 per week, two-bedroom flats $300 to $450.

Among the cheapest is *Ti-Tree Lodge* (☎ (077) 78 5499), at 20 Barbara St in Picnic Bay, ranging from $200 to $280 a week for up to six people. On Hayles Ave, also in Arcadia, the *Magnetic Retreat* (☎ (077) 78 5357) has modern, fully equipped one- and two-bedroom flats from $65 to $75 a night.

Places to Eat

Picnic Bay The Picnic Bay Mall, along the waterfront, has a good selection of eating places. The *Picnic Bay Pub* has counter meals from $6 to $10, and there are cheaper snacks. Further along, *Crusoe's* is a straightforward restaurant with evening meals from $6 to $12. The *Green Frog Cafe* is good for breakfasts or light lunches.

The licensed *Max's*, at the far end of the Esplanade, is a bit more up-market. It's open seven days and has meals from $10 to $14.

Nelly Bay *Mexican Munchies* runs the gamut from enchiladas to tacos, and is open daily from 6 pm. There's a blackboard outside where you can chalk up your reservation during the day. Nearby, in the small shopping centre on the main road, is *Possum's Cafe*, good for snacks and takeaways. There's also a good supermarket in this centre.

Arcadia The *Arcadia Hotel Resort* has a number of eating possibilities; bistro meals range from $4.50 to $12, and you can eat outdoors by the pool. *Gatsby's* has more-expensive meals.

Alla Capri on Hayles Ave is a licensed Italian place with pizzas and pastas from $7.50, and a pleasant outdoor eating area with visiting possums for entertainment.

In the small Arcadia shopping centre, the *Bakehouse* opens early and is a good place for a coffee and croissant breakfast. Next door is *Banister's Seafood*, which is a good fish & chips place with an open-air BYO dining area. Nearby, the *Blue Waters Cafe & Restaurant* has some of the best food on the island, with inexpensive lunches, a dinner menu with mains from $8 to $14, and a nightly backpackers' special for $4.50. There's a pleasant courtyard out the back.

Horseshoe Bay *Cotters on the Beach* is a relaxed licensed restaurant with steak, chicken and seafood mains from $10 to $14, and breakfast and lunch specials. Next door, the *Bounty Snack Bar* has takeaways. There's also a small general store if you're preparing your own food.

Getting There & Away

Two companies, Magnetic Marine (☎ (077) 72 7122) and Magnetic Link (☎ (077) 21 1913), both run 10 or 11 ferries a day to and from Townsville for $15 return ($12 with a student card). All ferries go to Picnic Bay (a 20-minute ride) and some of Magnetic Marine's continue on to Arcadia.

Both companies' ferries depart from the Great Barrier Reef Wonderland; Magnetic Marine also has a terminal on the breakwater on Sir Leslie Thiess Drive, near the Sheraton Casino.

Ferries operate from 6.15 am on weekdays and from 7.15 am on weekends. The last ferry leaves Townsville at 9.30 pm Monday to Thursday, at 11.30 pm on Friday, just after midnight on Saturday and around 6 pm on Sunday.

Both companies offer package deals which include return ferry tickets and accommodation; one-night packages start at $23.

The Capricorn Barge Company (☎ (077) 72 5422) runs a vehicle ferry to Arcadia from the southern side of Ross Creek three times a day during the week and twice a day on weekends. It's $85 return for a car and up to six passengers.

Getting Around

Bus The Magnetic Island Bus Service operates between Picnic Bay and Horseshoe Bay 12 to 18 times a day, meeting all ferries and dropping off at all accommodation places. Some bus trips include Radical Bay, others the Koala Park. You can either get individual tickets ($1.20 to $3) or a full-day pass ($6).

Car & Moke Rental Magnetic Island Rent-a-Moke (☎ (077) 78 5377) on the Esplanade in Picnic Bay has mokes from $27 a day plus 30c per km, or Suzuki Sierras from $30 a day.

Holiday Moke Hire (☎ (077) 78 5703) has similar vehicles and prices; its office is in the Jetty Cafe in the Picnic Bay Mall.

Moped Rental Roadrunner Scooter Hire (☎ (077) 78 5222) has an office in an arcade just off the Picnic Bay Mall. Day hire is $25, half-day hire $19, and 24-hour hire $35.

Bicycle Magnetic Island is ideal for cycling, and there are mountain bikes available for rent at various places including the Esplanade in Picnic Bay, Foresthaven resort in Arcadia and Geoff's Place in Horseshoe Bay. Bikes cost $10 for a day, $6 for half a day.

TOWNSVILLE TO MISSION BEACH
Mt Spec National Park
This rainforested national park straddles the 1000-metre-plus Paluma Range, west of the Bruce Highway.

To get there, turn off the Bruce Highway 61 km north of Townsville. There are two access routes: one road winds up along the southern edge of the park, passing **Little Crystal Creek** (with good swimming and a picnic area) and **McClelland's Lookout** (which also has a picnic area) on the way to the small village of Paluma. The second road leads to **Big Crystal Creek** in the centre of the park, which is another good place to swim. There's another barbecue area here, plus a camp site – to book, contact the park ranger (☎ (077) 70 8526). Bower birds are relatively common in the park. Detours Coaches runs day trips from Townsville ($48).

Jourama Falls National Park
Jourama Falls National Park is six unpaved km off the highway, 91 km north of Townsville. Centred around the Waterview Creek, this small but beautiful park has good swimming holes, several lookouts, a picnic area and a camping ground (bookings and permits as for Big Crystal Creek). From the end of the access road, a 1.5-km walking track leads to the waterfalls.

Ingham (population 5100)
The Spanish and Italian influences of its Mediterranean settlers are noticeable in this sugar-producing town. **Lucinda**, a port town 24 km from Ingham, has a six-km jetty used for shipping the huge amount of sugar produced in the area. Lucinda is also the access point for the southern end of Hinchinbrook Island.

In Ingham, there's a good tourist information centre (☎ (077) 76 5211) on the corner of Lannercost St and Townsville Rd. The *Hinchinbrook Hotel* (☎ (077) 76 2227), at 83 Lannercost St, offers beds to backpackers at $10 each in a twin room. This is also a good place for a meal, with bistro mains from $6 to $9 and more-expensive meals in the restaurant. The National Parks district office (☎ (077) 76 1700), at the end of an arcade at 11 Lannercost St, deals with information for Mt Spec, Wallaman Falls and Jourama Falls national parks and Orpheus Island.

There are a number of places to visit around Ingham including **Wallaman Falls National Park**, 48 km inland, where a tributary of the Herbert River cascades for 305 metres, the longest single-drop falls in Australia. The falls are much more spectacular in the wet season. You can normally reach them by conventional vehicle along an unpaved road; there's a National Parks camping area with a swimming hole nearby.

Only seven km east of Ingham is the **Victoria Mill**, the largest sugar mill in the southern hemisphere. Free tours are given in the crushing season.

Orpheus Island
Lying off the coast between Townsville and Ingham, Orpheus is a narrow 14-sq-km granite island surrounded by coral reefs. One of the Palm Group, it's a quiet, secluded island which is good for camping, snorkelling and diving. Orpheus is mostly national park and is heavily forested, with lots of bird life; turtles also nest here. Camping is allowed in two places (permits from Ingham) but you must take your own water. Also on the island are a giant clam research station

and a small resort with rooms at $340-plus per person.

If you want to camp, you can get there by charter boat from Lucinda or Taylor's Beach (25 km from Ingham), or the MV *Scuba Doo* (☎ (077) 77 8220) can take you from Dungeness (north of Lucinda) for $120 return.

Cardwell (population 1300)

South of Cardwell, the Bruce Highway climbs high above the coast with tremendous views down across the winding, mangrove-lined waterways known as the Everglades, which separate Hinchinbrook Island from the coast.

Cardwell is one of north Queensland's very earliest towns, dating from 1864, and is the only town on the highway between Brisbane and Cairns which is actually right on the coast. It's more or less a one-street place and is the departure point for Hinchinbrook and other continental islands. It also has a National Parks information office (☎ (070) 66 8601) (signposted as the Rainforest & Reef Centre) on the highway in the middle of town. The office is open Monday to Thursday from 8 am to noon and on Fridays from 8 am to 4 pm.

Things to See & Do The **Cardwell Forest Drive** starts from the centre of town and is a 26-km round trip, taking you to some excellent lookouts, swimming holes, walking tracks and picnic areas.

Most of the coastal forest north of Cardwell is protected as the **Edmund Kennedy National Park**, named after the ill-fated explorer who was killed by Aborigines at Cape York. At the southern end of the park, there's a camp site close to the beach and some walking tracks – turn off the highway four km north of Cardwell to reach them. Don't swim or cross any of the creeks in the park – the mangroves here are home to estuarine crocodiles.

The **Murray Falls** have fine rock pools for swimming, a walking track and a barbecue area. They're 22 km west of the highway – turn off at the 'Murray Upper Road' sign about 27 km north of Cardwell.

Cardwell Day Tours (☎ (070) 66 8741) takes small groups on eco-style tours to several of the area's natural attractions.

Places to Stay The *Kookaburra Holiday Park* (☎ (070) 66 8648), which includes the YHA *Hinchinbrook Hostel*, is at 175 Bruce Highway roughly in the middle of town. The hostel section has dorm beds at $11 and doubles at $25; nonmembers pay another $1. You can also camp here for $6 per person, or there are on-site vans from $26, on-site cabins from $32 and self-contained units. This place is very well set up, with good facilities including a pool and free use of mountain bikes and fishing gear. It's also a good source of info about Hinchinbrook Island and other attractions in the area.

Across the highway, the *Pacific Palms Caravan Park* (☎ (070) 66 8671) has a backpackers' section at $10 a bed. There are also several motels and holiday units in the town.

Getting There & Away All buses between Townsville and Cairns stop at Cardwell. The fare is around $20 from either place. Cardwell is also on the main Brisbane to Cairns railway.

Hinchinbrook Island

Hinchinbrook Island is a spectacular and unspoiled wilderness area, with granite mountains rising dramatically from the sea and a varied terrain – lush tropical forest on the mainland side, thick mangroves lining the shores, towering mountains in the middle and long sandy beaches and secluded bays on the eastern side. All 635 sq km of the island is a national park and rugged Mt Bowen, at 1142 metres, is the highest peak. There's plenty of wildlife, especially pretty-faced wallabies and the iridescent blue Ulysses butterfly.

Hinchinbrook Island is very popular with bushwalkers and naturalists and has some excellent walking tracks. The highlight is the East Coast Trail, a 32-km walking track from Ramsay Bay to Zoe Bay and on to George

Point at the southern tip; allow three to five days for the walk. Zoë Bay, with its beautiful waterfall, is one of the most scenic spots on the island. Walkers are warned to take plenty of insect repellent – the sandflies and mosquitoes on Hinchinbrook can be a real pest. You'll also have to learn how to protect your food from the native bush rats, and, again, there are estuarine crocodiles in the mangroves!

There's a low-key resort (☎ (070) 66 8585) on the northern peninsula, Cape Richards, with rooms for around 60 people, but it's not cheap at around $200 a day per person, including meals.

There are also 12 National Parks camping grounds, including ones at Macushla on Missionary Bay in the north (bring drinking water with you) and at nine spots along the east coast (water available at most). The East Coast Trail camping areas include Nina Bay, Little Ramsay Bay, Zoe Bay, Mulligan Bay and George Point. Numbers for each camping area are limited (anywhere from 10 to 35) and depend on the total number of walkers on the island. For camping permits and detailed trail information, contact the National Parks office in Cardwell (☎ (070) 66 8601).

An excellent way of seeing the island is by boat. Hinchinbrook Sail Safaris (☎ (070) 66 8143) have day trips for $48 including lunch and snorkelling, or two- and three-day safaris for $65 a day including all meals. R'n'R (☎ toll-free 1800 079 039) also operate four-day sea-kayaking expeditions along the east coast of Hinchinbrook from Lucinda every two weeks. The $480 cost includes all meals and equipment.

Getting There & Away There are two ferry services from Cardwell to the northern end of Hinchinbrook Island. Hinchinbrook Travel & Booking Office (☎ (070) 66 8539) at 131 Bruce Highway, Cardwell, operates the *Hinchinbrook Explorer*, departing daily at 9 am and returning at 4 pm. Hinchinbrook Adventures (☎ (070) 66 8270) at 135 Bruce Highway operates the *Reef Cat*, departing daily at 9.30 am and returning around 4 pm.

Both boats can drop you at Cape Richards, Macushla or Ramsay Bay, and both charge around $40 return or $25 one way. Services are less frequent during the wet season (January to March).

Hinchinbrook Wilderness Safaris (☎ (070) 77 8307) operates a transfer service between Lucinda and the southern end of the island. The boat departs at different times each day depending on the tides – ring to find out – and the cost is $17 one way or $27 return. Pick-ups from Ingham and Cardwell can also be arranged.

Tully (population 2700)

The wettest place in Australia, Tully gets a drenching average of 440 cm of rain a year. It's the cheapest place to start from if you're doing a white-water rafting trip on the Tully River. The town is a regular stop for buses and trains between Townsville and Cairns, and it has a couple of caravan parks and a motel. Nearby Mission Beach, however, is a much more appealing place to stay, and the rafting operators will pick you up from there.

MISSION BEACH (population 810)

This small stretch of coast has become an increasingly popular stopover on the backpackers' circuit. The name Mission Beach actually covers a string of small settlements along a 14-km coastal strip east of Tully. Mission Beach, where the buses stop, is in the centre; Wongaling Beach and South Mission Beach are to the south, and Bingil Bay and Garners Beach are to the north.

There are three very good hostels in the area, and it's a good base for a number of activities: visits to Dunk Island and the Reef, white-water rafting trips on the Tully River, boat trips out to the reef or walks through the rainforest.

Mission Beach is named after an Aboriginal mission which was founded here in 1914 but destroyed by a cyclone in 1918. Tam O'Shanter Point, beyond South Mission Beach, was the starting point for the ill-fated 1848 overland expedition to Cape York led by 30-year-old Edmund Kennedy. All but three of the party's 13 members, including Kennedy, died. There's a memorial to the expedition at Tam O'Shanter Point.

Information
The new tourist information centre (☎ (070) 68 7099) is on Porters Promenade in Mission Beach. It's open from 9 am to 5 pm seven days a week. Right next door is the Visitor Interpretation Centre, which has information on cassowary conservation.

Walks
The rainforest around Mission Beach is a haunt of cassowaries but unfortunately the population has been depleted by road accidents and the destruction of rainforest by logging and cyclones. The rainforest comes right down to the coast in places, and there are some impressive walks including the **Licuala Walking Track** (two hours), **Laceys Creek Walk** (half-hour), the **Bicton Hill Lookout** (1½ hours) and the **Edmund Kennedy Walking Track** (three hours).

Mission Beach Rainforest Treks (☎ (070) 68 7500) take guided walks through the forests – the morning walk costs $24 and the night walk is $14.

White-Water Rafting
Raging Thunder (☎ (070) 51 4911) and R'n'R (☎ toll-free 1800 079 039) charge around $110 from Mission Beach for trips on the Tully River. These are the same as the trips on offer in Cairns, but you'll save about $10 and several hours travel time by doing them from here. See the Cairns section for more details on white-water rafting trips.

Raging Thunder also offers three-day sea-kayaking expeditions to Dunk Island and the Family Islands for $375 including meals and equipment (but not sleeping bags). R'n'R runs three-day sea-kayaking trips from Kurrimine Beach, 10 km north of Mission Beach, to the Barnard Islands for $360.

Organised Cruises
There are three cruise companies based at the Clump Point jetty just north of Mission Beach. Friendship Cruises take day trips out to the reef, with snorkelling and a ride in a glass-bottomed boat, for $49. On the *Quick Cat* you can do a similar trip for $105, or a day trip to Dunk Island for $23. The MV *Lawrence Kavanagh* also does day trips to Dunk ($18) and Bedarra ($16) islands or a combined trip for $39.

River Rat Wildlife Cruises (☎ (070) 68 7250) runs cruises with mud-crabbing, fishing and crocodile-watching along the Hull River from South Mission Beach. Half-day trips cost $28 and night cruises $36 with a barbecue dinner.

Places to Stay
Camping The *Hideaway Caravan Park* (☎ (070) 68 7104), in the centre of Mission Beach, has tent sites from $11 and on-site cabins from $36. At South Mission Beach, the *Beachcomber Coconut Village* (☎ (070) 68 8129) has tent sites from $11.50, camp-o-tels from $13/18 and a range of on-site cabins from $29.

Hostels All three hostels have courtesy buses and do pick-ups from the bus stop in Mission Beach proper.

Two of the hostels are at Wongaling Beach, five km south of the bus stop. *Mission Beach Backpackers Lodge* (☎ (070) 68 8317), at 28 Wongaling Beach Rd, is a modern, well-equipped place with a pool and garden. There are two buildings, one with spacious dorms at $12 a bed, the other with very good double rooms priced from $28 to $33. This easy-going hostel is a five-minute walk from the beach.

Scotty's Mission Beach House (☎ (070) 68 8676) is at 167 Reid Rd, also at Wongaling Beach. This friendly and fun-oriented place is right opposite the beach. Dorm beds range from $12 to $15 and doubles are from $28 to $43, with the more expensive rooms having their own bathrooms and air-con. There's a pool, evening meals from $4 to $6, and barbecues on the beach every Wednesday and Saturday night.

The *Treehouse* (☎ (070) 68 7137), an associate-YHA hostel, is at Bingil Bay, six km north of Mission Beach. It's a quiet,

484 Queensland – North Coast

relaxed place in an impressive timber stilt house with a pool and good views over the surrounding rainforest and the coast. A bed in a six-bed dorm costs $13, or you can camp here for $9.

Motels & Holiday Units *Watersedge* (☎ (070) 68 8479), at 32 Wongaling Rd, Wongaling Beach, has good, simple, self-contained holiday units on the waterfront. There's also a small pool. The one-bedroom flats sleep up to six and cost from $39 a double, plus $5 for each extra person; the two-bedroom flats sleep up to eight and start at $55 a double.

There's a scattering of other units, motels and resorts along the coast. The *Mission Beach Village Motel* (☎ (070) 68 7212), at 7 Porter Promenade in Mission Beach, has rooms from $50, and, if you're feeling flush, the *Point Resort* (☎ (070) 68 8154) at South Mission Beach is very stylish with rooms for $138 a double.

Places to Eat
Mission Beach proper has a good selection of eateries. The tiny *PC's Cafe*, beside the bus stop, has breakfasts, home-made meals and good coffee. In the arcade just across Campbell St is *On the Bite*, a seafood cafe with excellent takeaway fish & chips and burgers, and eat-in meals from $8 to $10.

Across the road on opposite corners of David St are *Butterflies*, a casual Mexican place with main courses from $9 to $13, and *Friends*, a popular and stylish open-air BYO restaurant with meals around $17. Further down David St is an Italian bistro called *Piccolo Paradiso*, with pizzas and pastas from $8.

The *Mission Beach Hotel*, in Wongaling Beach, has a bistro with main meals in the $8 to $16 range or meals in the public bar from $4 to $7. If you're preparing your own food, there are supermarkets at Mission Beach and Wongaling Beach.

Getting There & Around
Around five buses a day make the detour here off the Bruce Highway, stopping outside

Harvey World Travel (☎ (070) 68 7187) in Mission Beach. The average fare is $16 from Cairns and $38 from Townsville.

Most of the tour and cruise companies have courtesy buses, and you can hire good bikes from Outpack Rentals in Mission Beach. Baz's Bus Service (☎ (070) 68 8707) operates regular daily services from Tully to Mission Beach and along the coastal strip.

DUNK ISLAND & THE FAMILY ISLANDS
Dunk Island is an easy and affordable day trip from Mission Beach. It's 4.5 km off the coast, and has walking tracks through rainforest and good beaches.

From 1897 to 1923 E J Banfield lived on Dunk and wrote his book *The Confessions of a Beachcomber*; the island is remarkably little changed from his early description. Today it has a small artist colony centred around Bruce Arthur, a tapestry maker and former Olympic wrestler. Dunk is noted for its prolific bird life (nearly 150 species) and many butterflies. There are superb views over the entrances to the Hinchinbrook Channel from the top of 271-metre Mt Kootaloo. Thirteen km of walking tracks lead from the camping ground area to headlands and beaches.

There's a Qantas-owned resort (☎ (070) 68 8199) at Brammo Bay on the northern end of the island, with rooms from upwards of $150 per person. There's also a National Parks camping ground close to the resort, as well as a takeaway food kiosk and a watersports place that hires out catamarans, sailboards and snorkelling gear. Camping permits are booked through the resort's water-sports office (☎ (070) 68 8199). You can rent camping gear from Outpack Rentals (☎ (070) 68 7220) in Mission Beach.

South of Dunk are the seven tiny Family Islands. One of them, Bedarra, has a very exclusive resort, where costs start at around $500 a day per person. Five of the other Family Islands are national parks and you can bush camp on Wheeler and Combe (permits from Cardwell; take your own water).

Getting There & Away

Dowd's Water Taxis (☎ (070) 68 8310) has about six daily services from Wongaling Beach to Dunk and back, and Mission Beach-Dunk Island Water Taxis (☎ (070) 68 8333) has similar services from South Mission Beach. Both companies charge $18 return, although the hostels can usually get you across for less.

You can fly to Dunk with Qantas Regional Airlines from Townsville ($107) or Cairns ($97).

MISSION BEACH TO CAIRNS

Innisfail (population 8500)

Innisfail is at the junction of the North and South Johnstone rivers. The North Johnstone, flowing down from the Atherton Tableland, is good for white-water rafting and canoeing.

Innisfail has been a sugar city for over a century. It's a busy place, with a large Italian population, and on Owen St you can also find a Chinese temple (open daily from 7 am to 5 pm). The Italians first arrived early this century to work the cane fields: some became plantation owners themselves and in the 1930s there was even a local branch of the Mafia, called the Black Hand!

At **Mourilyan**, seven km south of Innisfail, there's the Australian Sugar Museum, open from 9 am to 4.30 pm daily. An export terminal on the coast east of Mourilyan handles the sugar produced in Innisfail, Tully and Mourilyan.

At Mena Creek, twenty km south-west of Innisfail, is **Paronella Park** (☎ (070) 65 3225), a rambling tropical garden set amongst the ruins of a Spanish castle built in the 1930s. This place is quite bizarre and well worth a visit – it's open daily from 9 am to 5 pm and costs $5. There's also camping and caravan facilities (with 24-hour access to the park) – $10 for an unpowered site, $12 for a powered site.

Twenty-eight km west of Innisfail at **Nerada** is one of Australia's few tea plantations and factories (☎ (070) 64 5177). It's open daily from 9 am to 4.30 pm. The Palmerston Highway winds up to the Atherton Tableland, passing through the rainforest of

the **Palmerston National Park**, which has a number of creeks, waterfalls, scenic walking tracks and a camping ground at Henrietta Creek just off the road. The ranger's office (☎ (070) 64 5115) is at the eastern entrance to the park, 33 km from Innisfail.

Places to Stay

Backpackers Innisfail (☎ (070) 61 2284), at 73 Rankin St, has dorm beds at $12 a night. There are also a few reasonably priced motels and a handful of caravan parks. Flying Fish Point, on the northern side of the Johnstone River mouth, is reportedly a good camping spot.

Babinda

Babinda is the next place on the Bruce Highway north of Innisfail, but before you reach it there's a turning to **Josephine Falls**, a popular picnic spot eight km inland from the highway. The falls are at the foot of the Bellenden Ker Range which includes Queensland's highest peak, **Mt Bartle Frere** (1657 metres). A trail leads to the Bartle Frere summit from the ranger's hut near Josephine Falls. The ascent is for fit and experienced walkers only – it's a 15-km, two-day return trip, and rain and cloud can close in suddenly.

Babinda Boulders, where a creek rushes between enormous rocks, is another good picnic place, seven km inland from Babinda. From the boulders you can walk the **Goldfield Track** – first opened up in the 1930s when there was a minor gold rush. It leads 10 km to the Goldsborough Valley, across a saddle in the Bellenden Ker Range. The track ends at a causeway on the Mulgrave River, from where a forestry road leads eight km to a camping ground in the **Goldsborough Valley State Forest Park**. From there it's 15 km on to the Gillies Highway between Gordonvale and Atherton.

Gordonvale (population 2660)

Back on the Bruce Highway, Gordonvale is almost at Cairns. It has two Sikh gurdwaras (places of worship). The winding Gillies

Highway leads from here up onto the Atherton Tableland.

Also at Gordonvale is the **Mulgrave Rambler** (☎ (070) 56 3300), a steam train which runs through sugar country along the course of the Little Mulgrave River. The $5 cost includes a sugar mill tour; departures are every weekday at 10 am, 1.30 and 3 pm.

NORTH COAST HINTERLAND

The Flinders Highway heads inland from Townsville and runs virtually due west for its entire length – almost 800 km from Townsville to Cloncurry.

Ravenswood

At Mingela, 83 km from Townsville, a paved road leads 40 km south to Ravenswood, once a gold-rush centre. Two pubs, a church, a school and a couple of hundred people linger on amid the old mines and near-abandoned streets.

Situated a further 80 km down the road past Ravenswood, the big **Burdekin Falls Dam**, completed in 1987, holds back more than 200 sq km of water.

Charters Towers (population 9000)

This busy town, 130 km inland from Townsville, was Queensland's fabulously rich second city in the gold-rush days. Many old houses, with classic verandahs and lace work, and imposing public buildings and mining structures remain. It's possible to make a day trip here from Townsville and get a glimpse of outback Queensland on the way.

At 336 metres above sea level, the dry air of Charters Towers makes a welcome change from the humid coast. The gleam of gold was first spotted in 1871, in a creek bed at the foot of Towers Hill, by an Aboriginal boy called Jupiter Mosman. Within a few years, the surrounding area was peppered with diggings and a large town had grown. In its heyday (around the turn of the century), Charters Towers had a population of 30,000, nearly 100 mines, and even its own stock exchange. It attracted wealth seekers from far and wide and came to be known as 'the

World'. Mosman St, the main street in those days, had 25 pubs.

When the gold ran out in the 1920s, the city shrank, but survived as a centre for the beef industry. Since the mid-1980s, Charters Towers has seen a bit of a gold revival as modern processes have enabled companies to work deposits in previously uneconomical areas.

Orientation & Information Central Charters Towers is basically two streets, Gill St and Mosman St, which meet at right angles. Towers Hill stands over the town to the south. Buses arrive at and depart from the Goldfield Star service station on the corner of Gill and Church Sts. The railway station (☎ (077) 87 3521) is on Enterprise Rd, 2.5 km east along Gill St from the centre.

The National Trust of Queensland (☎ (077) 87 2374) has an office in the Stock Exchange Arcade on Mosman St, which doubles as a tourist information office. Pick up the free *Guide to Charters Towers* booklet and a copy of the National Trust's walking tour leaflet.

Things to See On Mosman St a few metres up the hill from the corner of Gill St is the picturesque **Stock Exchange Arcade**, built in 1887 and restored in 1972. Today it houses the National Trust office, a couple of galleries and shops and a poorly displayed mining museum.

At 62 Mosman St there's the **Zara Clark Museum**, with an interesting collection focusing on transport and lifestyles in early Charters Towers. It's open daily from 10 am to 3 pm.

There are a number of other interesting old buildings on Gill St. **Stan Pollard's Store** (1906), near the Mosman St end, has an ancient 'flying fox' – a sort of aerial runway which transports cash from the counters to the central till. There's also a great selection of country hats.

Probably the finest of the town's old houses is Frederick Pfeiffer's, on Paull St. It's now a Mormon chapel, but you can walk

QUEENSLAND

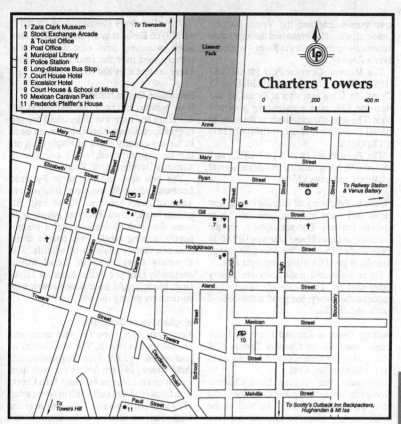

1 Zara Clark Museum
2 Stock Exchange Arcade
& Tourist Office
3 Post Office
4 Municipal Library
5 Police Station
6 Long-distance Bus Stop
7 Court House Hotel
8 Excelsior Hotel
9 Court House & School of Mines
10 Mexican Caravan Park
11 Frederick Pfeiffer's House

To Townsville

Lissner
Park

Charters Towers

0   200   400 m

Anne   Street

Mary   Street

Mary   Street

Ryan   Street

Hospital

To Railway Station
& Venus Battery

Elizabeth   Street

Gill   Street

Hodgkinson   Street

Aland   Street

Mexican   Street

Towers   Street

Melville   Street

To Scotty's Outback Inn Backpackers,
Hughenden & Mt Isa

To
Towers Hill

Paull   Street

around the outside. Pfeiffer was a gold-miner who became Queensland's first millionaire.

Five km from town is the **Venus Battery**, where gold-bearing ore was crushed and processed from 1872 until as recently as 1972. The battery has been restored to working order and is open from 9 am to 5 pm daily, with guided tours at 10 am and 2 pm; entry is $3.

Festivals During the Australia Day weekend in late January, more than 100 cricket teams and their supporters converge on Charters Towers for a competition known as the Gold-field Ashes. The town also hosts one of Australia's biggest annual country music festivals on the May Day weekend each year.

Places to Stay The excellent *Scotty's Outback Inn Backpackers* (☎ (077) 87 1028) is at 58 York St, 1.4 km south of the town centre. The owner will pick you up from the bus stop if you ring. It's a renovated timber house built in the 1880s, with pleasant breezy verandahs and sitting areas. The cost is $11 a night and you can rent bedding for $1. There are bikes for rent and you can get a cheap combined ticket for some of the town's museums and the Venus Battery. Canoe trips are also organised through cattle stations along the Burdekin River – when the river's flowing.

The *Mexican Caravan Park* (☎ (077) 87 1161) is fairly central, south of Gill St at 75 Church St. It has tent sites at $9 and on-site vans for $24, plus a swimming pool and store. The next cheapest beds in town are in the old *Court House Hotel* (☎ (077) 87 1187) at 120 Gill St.

The *Park Motel* (☎ (077) 87 1022), at 1 Mosman St, has pleasant grounds and a good restaurant and costs $55/63.

Places to Eat Nearly all the pubs have decent meals and most of them have hot 'daily special' lunches. For atmosphere, try the *Excelsior* or *Court House* hotels on Gill St. *Ye Olde Coffee Shop*, at the Stock Exchange Arcade, is good for drinks and light eats.

Other cafes and restaurants are mainly along Gill St. The *Naturally Good Cafe*, opposite the library, has good home-cooked meals and snacks.

Getting There & Around There are buses from Townsville to Charters Towers (1¾ hours, $18) and from Charters Towers on to Mt Isa (nine hours, $78).

By train, the journey from Charters Towers to Townsville takes three hours and costs $20, economy only. As well as the twice-weekly Inlander running between Townsville and Mt Isa, there's a once-weekly motorail service from Charters Towers to Townsville. You can make transport bookings and enquiries at Harvey World Travel (☎ (077) 87 1546) at 114 Gill St.

Scotty's Backpackers hires bikes, and Gold Nugget Scenic Tours (☎ (077) 87 1568) runs city tours most weekdays.

Charters Towers to Hughenden

There are a few small towns, mostly with caravan parks and a single motel, along this 243-km easterly stretch. Around Hughenden, sheep begin to take over from cattle on the stations, although grass seed, which is abundant to the east, can ruin the wool.

The *Allan Terry Caravan Park* (☎ (077) 41 119) on Resolution St, Hughenden, has a large swimming pool next door but the railway yard over the road is a bit noisy. There are tent sites and on-site vans.

Porcupine Gorge National Park

If the weather has been dry, and you're not in a hurry and have a vehicle, take a trip out to Porcupine Gorge National Park, an oasis in the dry country north of Hughenden off the mostly unpaved, often corrugated Kennedy Developmental Road.

The best spot to drive to is **Pyramid Lookout**, about 80 km from Hughenden. You can camp here and it's an easy 30-minute walk down into the gorge, with some fine rock formations and a permanently running creek. Few people come here and there's a fair bit of wildlife. The Kennedy Developmental Road would eventually take you to the Atherton Tableland, but it would be a pretty rough trip, particularly during the wet season.

Hughenden to Cloncurry

Keep your eyes open for wild emus and brolgas on this stretch. The small towns of **Richmond**, 112 km from Hughenden, and **Julia Creek**, 144 km further on, both have motels and caravan parks. From Julia Creek, a surfaced road turns off north to Normanton (420 km) and Karumba (494 km) near the Gulf. You can also reach Burketown (467 km) this way; see the Cape York and the Gulf section for more information on these towns.

Far North Queensland

Queensland's far north is one of the most popular tourist destinations in the country, especially in winter when sun-starved southerners flock here in droves.

Cairns, with its international airport, is the major centre for the region. It's a place where most travellers spend a few days before heading off – north to the superb rainforests of Daintree and Cape Tribulation and the historic town of Cooktown; west to the cool air of the Atherton Tableland; or east to the islands and the Barrier Reef.

CAIRNS (population 64,500)

The 'capital' of the far north and perhaps the best-known city on the Queensland coast, Cairns is now firmly established as one of Australia's top travellers' destinations.

Cairns is a centre for a whole host of activities – not just scuba diving but also white-water rafting, canoeing, horse riding and, of course, the latest lunatic crazes like bungee jumping and sky diving. On the debit side, Cairns's rapid tourist growth has destroyed much of its laid-back tropical atmosphere. It also lacks a beach, but there are some good ones not far north.

Cairns marks the end of the Bruce Highway and the railway line from Brisbane. The town came into existence in 1876 as a beachhead in the mangroves, intended as a port for the Hodgkinson River gold field 100 km inland. Initially, it struggled under rivalry from Smithfield 12 km north, a rowdy frontier town that was washed away by a flood in 1879 (it's now an outer Cairns suburb), then from Port Douglas, founded in 1877 after Christie Palmerston discovered an easier route from there to the gold field. What saved Cairns was the Atherton Tableland 'tin rush' from 1880. Cairns became the starting point of the railway to the tableland, built a few years later.

Cairns is at its climatic best – and busiest – from May to October; in summer it gets rather sticky (to put it mildly!).

Orientation

The centre of Cairns is a relatively compact area running back from the Esplanade. Off Wharf St (the southern continuation of the Esplanade), you'll find Great Adventures Wharf, Marlin Jetty and the Pier – the main departure points for reef trips. Further round is Trinity Wharf (a cruise-liner dock with shops and cafes) and the transit centre, where long-distance buses arrive and depart.

Back from the waterfront is City Place, a pedestrian mall at the meeting of Shields and Lake Sts.

Cairns is surrounded to the south and north by mangrove swamps, and the shallow sea in front of the town becomes a long sweep of mud at low tide, although it does attract lots of interesting water birds.

Information

Tourist Offices There's no shortage of tourist information in Cairns – if anything, it's the opposite. The Far North Queensland Promotion Bureau (☎ (070) 51 3588) has a good information centre on the corner of Grafton and Hartley Sts; it's open on weekdays from 9 am to 5 pm and on Saturdays from 9 am to 1 pm.

There are dozens of privately run information centres in Cairns, such as the Cairns Tourist Information Centre (☎ (070) 31 1751) at 99 The Esplanade. These places are basically booking offices for tours. Also good for information are the various backpackers' hostels, as most have a separate tour-booking service. The only problem here is that each booking agent and hostel will be selling different tours, depending on the commission deal they have with the tour companies – so shop around.

The Community Information Service (☎ (070) 51 4953) in Tropical Arcade off Shields St, half a block back from the Esplanade, is good for some tourist information plus more offbeat things like where you can play croquet or do t'ai chi. It also has details on foreign consulates in Cairns and health services.

Post & Telecommunications The GPO, on the corner of Grafton and Hartley Sts, has a poste restante service. For general business (stamps etc), there's also an Australia Post shop in the Orchid Plaza on Lake St.

Other Offices The RACQ office (☎ (070) 51 4788), at 112 Sheridan St, is a good place to get information on road conditions, especially if you're driving up to Cooktown or the Cape York Peninsula, or across to the Gulf of Carpentaria.

The National Parks & Wildlife Service

QUEENSLAND

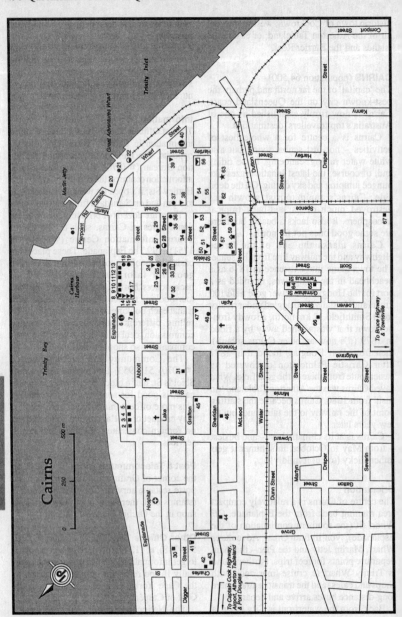

QUEENSLAND

Cairns

0   250   500 m

Trinity Bay

PLACES TO STAY		66	Gone Walkabout Hostel	18	Johno's Blues
		67	Up Top Down Under		Bar
2	Bel-Air Backpackers			19	Air Nuigini
3	Rosie's Backpackers	**PLACES TO EAT**		21	Great Adventures
4	Silver Palm				Office
	Guesthouse	14	Greens	22	Trinity Wharf &
5	Caravella's 149 Hostel	15	Meeting Place		Transit Centre
7	Wintersun Apartments	16	End of the World	25	Qantas & Sunstate
8	YHA on the Esplanade		Nightclub		Airlines
9	Hostel 89	17	Pumphouse Bar &	26	City Place
10	Bellview		Restaurant		Amphitheatre
11	Jimmy's on the	23	Fiesta Cantina	27	Ansett & Eastwest
	Esplanade	24	Base Rock Cafe & Bar		Airlines
12	Caravella's Hostel 77	32	Galloping Gourmet	28	Lake St Transit
13	International Hostel	38	Blue Moon Cafe		Bus Stop
20	Hilton Hotel	39	Samuel's Saloon &	29	Orchid Plaza &
30	Cairns Backpackers Inn		Playpen Nightclub		Australia Post Shop
31	Parkview Backpackers	47	George's Greek	33	Cairns Museum &
34	Aussie II Hostel		Taverna		Swagman's
42	City Court Garden	50	La Fettucine		Restaurant
	Apartments	51	Continental Shelf Deli	35	STA Travel
43	Captain Cook	53	Mozart's Pastry	36	Central Arcade,
	Backpackers	54	Tiny's Juice Bar		Fox & Firkin Hotel
44	Castaways	55	Taj Indian Restaurant		& Tropo's Nightclub
45	Tracks Hostel	57	John & Diana's	37	Tropical Paradise
46	Inn the Tropics		Breakfast &		Travel
49	Pacific Coast Budget		Burger House	40	Far North
	Accommodation	61	Bangkok Room Thai		Queensland
58	Grand Hotel		Restaurant		Promotion Bureau
59	YHA McLeod St		& Hog's Breath Cafe	41	Cock & Bull Hotel
	Hostel			48	RACQ
62	Coconut Palms	**OTHER**		52	Rusty's Pub &
	Hostel				Bazaar
64	Dreamtime Travellers	1	The Pier & Radisson	56	Post Office
	Rest		Plaza Hotel	60	National Parks &
65	Ryan's Rest	6	Cairns Tourist		Wildlife Service
	Guesthouse		Information Centre	63	Police Station

(☎ (070) 52 3096), at 10 McLeod St, is open on weekdays from 8.30 am to 4.30 pm and deals with camping permits for Davies Creek, the Frankland Islands, Lizard Island and Jardine River.

Bookshops Proudmans, in the Pier complex, and Walkers Bookshop, at 96 Lake St, both have a good range. The Green Possum Environmental Bookshop, in an arcade off Grafton St right by Rusty's Bazaar, is also interesting. For maps, check out Sunmap at 15 Lake St.

Things to See
A walk around the town centre turns up a few points of historical interest, although with the spate of recent development, the older

buildings are now few and far between. The oldest part of town is the **Trinity Wharf** area, but even this has been redeveloped. There are still some imposing neoclassical buildings from the 1920s on Abbott St, and the frontages around the corner of Spence and Lake Sts date from 1909 to 1926. A walk along the **Esplanade**, with views over to rainforested mountains across the estuary and cool evening breezes, is very agreeable.

The **Pier** is an impressive up-market shopping plaza with expensive boutiques and souvenir shops downstairs, and some interesting eating possibilities upstairs. On Saturday mornings there's a food market inside, and on Sundays there's a craft market. These are known as the Mud Markets. The up-market Radisson Plaza Hotel, also in the complex, has the most amazing lobby – it's a mock-up of some north Queensland rainforest, but the effect is like something straight out of Disneyland!

Right in the centre of town, on the corner of Lake and Shields Sts, the **Cairns Museum** is housed in the 1907 School of Arts building, a fine example of early Cairns architecture. It has Aboriginal artefacts, a display on the construction of the Cairns to Kuranda railway, the contents of a now demolished Grafton St joss house, exhibits on the old Palmer River and Hodgkinson gold fields, and material on the early timber industry. It's open daily (except Sundays) from 10 am to 3 pm and entry costs $2.

A colourful part of town on weekends is the **Rusty's Bazaar** area bounded by Grafton, Spence, Sheridan and Shields Sts. The bustling weekend markets held here are great for people-watching and for browsing among the dozens of stalls, which sell produce, arts and crafts, clothes and lots of food. The markets are held on Friday nights and Saturday and Sunday mornings; Saturdays are the busiest and best. This part of Grafton St used to be the Cairns Chinatown and red-light district.

North-west of town, in Edge Hill, are the **Flecker Botanic Gardens** on Collins Ave. A boardwalk leads through a patch of rainforest to **Saltwater Creek** and the two small **Centenary Lakes**. Collins Ave turns west off Sheridan St (the Cook Highway) three km from the centre of Cairns, and the gardens are 700 metres from the turning. Just before the gardens is the entrance to the **Whitfield Range Environmental Park**, with walking tracks which give good views over the city and coast. You can get there with Cairns Trans Buses or the Red Explorer.

Also in Edge Hill, the **Royal Flying Doctor Service** regional office, at 1 Junction St, is open to visitors daily from 9 am to 4.30 pm; entry is $5.

Diving & Snorkelling

Cairns is one of the scuba-diving capitals of the Barrier Reef, which is closer to the coast here than it is further south. The competition

is cutthroat – and the company offering the cheapest deal one week may be old news the next.

Most people look for a course which takes them to the outer Barrier Reef rather than the reefs around Green or Fitzroy islands. Some places give you more time on the reef than others – but you may prefer an extra day in the pool and classroom before venturing out. A chat with people who have already done a course can tell you some of the pros and cons. A good teacher can make all the difference to your confidence and the amount of fun you have. Another factor is how big the groups are – the smaller the better if you want personal attention.

Two schools with good reputations are Deep Sea Divers Den (☎ (070) 31 2223) at 319 Draper St, and Pro-Dive (☎ (070) 31 5255) at Marlin Jetty. But that's not to dismiss the others, which include Down Under Dive (☎ (070) 31 1288) at 155 Sheridan St, Peter Tibbs Scuba School (☎ (070) 51 2604) at 370 Sheridan St and Cairns Dive Centre (☎ (070) 51 0294) at 135 Abbott St. Most of these places can be booked through the hostels.

If you want to learn about the reef before you dive, an entertaining and educational lecture is given at the Cairns Library at 117 Lake St every night (except Sunday) from 6.15 to 8.30 pm. The cost is $10 – for more details ring Reef Teach (☎ (070) 51 6882).

Prices differ quite a bit between schools but usually one or other of them has a discount going. Expect to pay around $350 to $400 for two days in the pool and classroom, one day trip to the reef and back, and two more days on the reef with an overnight stay on board.

White-Water Rafting & Kayaking

Three of the rivers flowing down from the Atherton Tableland make for some excellent white-water rafting. Most popular is a day in the rainforested gorges of the Tully River, 150 km south of Cairns. So many people do this trip that there can be 20 or more craft on the river at once, meaning you may have to queue up to shoot each section of rapids – yet despite this, most people are exhilarated at the end of the day. The Tully day trips leave daily year round. Two companies running them from Cairns are Raging Thunder (☎ (070) 31 1466) at 111 Spence St, and R'n'R (☎ (070) 51 7777 or toll-free 1800 079 039) at 74 Abbott St. Day trips on the Tully cost around $120 from Cairns. There are cheaper half-day trips on the Barron River ($65), not far inland from Cairns, or you can make two-day ($360) or five-day ($750) expeditions on the remote North Johnstone River which rises near Malanda and enters the sea at Innisfail.

Foaming Fury (☎ (070) 32 1460) offers white-water rafting for $99 on the Russell River, south of Bellenden Ker National Park, half-day trips on the Barron River for $64 and two-day trips on the North Johnstone River for $220.

Peregrine Adventures (☎ (070) 35 4004) offers pleasant canoe trips along the Mulgrave River, costing $80 for a day trip.

Raging Thunder and R'n'R also offer a range of sea-kayaking expeditions from Cairns. R'n'R runs a day trip from Palm Cove, just north of Cairns to Double Island for $85.

Other Activities

There are two A J Hackett (☎ (070) 31 1119) bungee-jumping sites near Cairns. The closest is 15 km north on the Cook Highway, just past the Kuranda turn-off, where for $89 you can take the plunge from a steel tower with sensational views. A courtesy bus does pick-ups from hostels. There's another within the markets at Kuranda where, for $70, you can fling yourself from a cage suspended from a crane.

Tandem skydiving (☎ (070) 31 5899), the latest craze for adrenalin junkies, will set you back about $270.

For something a bit more sedate, but equally expensive, try a chopper ride over the reef (☎ (070) 35 9002).

Reef Air Tours (☎ (070) 53 7936) offers a wide range of aerial tours in light planes, ranging from a 35-minute flight over the reef ($90) to a day's excursion to Green Island and the Daintree ($240).

Balloon Experience (☎ (070) 95 3899) offers one-hour hot-air balloon flights over the tableland for just $135 including champagne breakfast. For a bit of airborne nostalgia, DC3 Australia has daily DC3 flights to Cooktown from $140 return, while Cairns Tiger Moth Scenic Flights (☎ (070) 35 9400) start at $75.

Brumby Bob's (☎ (070) 59 1730) offers two-hour horse rides through the forests around Palm Cove, north of Cairns, for $45. Transport from Cairns costs another $5. Dan's Tours (☎ (070) 32 1460) has various mountain-bike tours including a half-day ride to Port Douglas ($49).

Organised Tours & Cruises

Most of the following and abovementioned courses and trips can be booked through your accommodation or through a variety of agents, as well as via the operators themselves.

As you'd expect, there are hundreds of tours available from Cairns. Some are specially aimed at backpackers and many of these are pretty good value. Agencies include Tropical Paradise Travel (☎ (070) 51 9533), at 25 Spence St, and Going Places (☎ (070) 51 4055) at 26 Abbott St.

Cairns Half-day trips around the city sights, or two-hour cruises from Marlin Jetty up along Trinity Inlet and around Admiralty Island, cost around $20.

Atherton Tableland Day trips to the Atherton Tableland with the conventional tour companies will cost anywhere from $60 to $80, and usually include the waterfalls and lakes circuit and a trip on the Kuranda Scenic Railway to the Kuranda markets. The cheaper tour companies, such as Jungle Tours, KCT and Tropics Explorer, offer similar trips for $35 to $45.

The On the Wallaby hotel offers an overnight trip to the tableland for $25 including meals and activities – see the Yungaburra section for details.

Daintree, Cape Tribulation & Cooktown Jungle Tours, KCT and Tropics Explorer all offer good-value and fun-oriented trips north from Cairns.

A day trip to Mossman Gorge and the Daintree River, including a cruise, will cost $48. There are day trips to Cape Tribulation, but you'd be better off taking one of the overnight or longer packages, which cost around $69 for two days, $79 for three days or $92 for five days, and include Mossman Gorge, the Daintree River and accommodation at Crocodylus Village and/or Jungle Lodge and/or PK's Jungle Village. Mountain Bike & Rainforest (☎ (070) 55 3089) has day trips from around $80.

Barrier Reef There are dozens of options available for day trips to the reef. It's worth asking a few questions before you book, such as how many passengers the boat takes, what's included in the price and how much the extras (such as wetsuit hire and introductory dives) cost, and exactly where the boat is going. Some companies have a dubious definition of outer reef; as a general rule, the further out you go, the better the diving.

Great Adventures (☎ (070) 51 0455) does a nine-hour, $120 outer-reef trip which includes a two-hour stop on Green Island. You get three hours on the reef itself, lunch, snorkelling gear, and a semisubmersible and glass-bottomed boat ride. Great Adventures does day trips to Michaelmas Cay for $95, including two hours on Green Island, and a nine-hour cruise to Fitzroy Island and Moore Reef for $85 with free use of snorkelling gear. Great Adventures has its own wharf.

The MV *Seastar II* (☎ (070) 31 2336), *Compass* (☎ (070) 35 4354) and Noah's Ark Cruises (☎ (070) 51 7777) all offer day trips to Hastings Reef and Michaelmas Cay for around $40, including boom netting, snorkelling gear and lunch. Certified divers can take two dives for an extra $40.

Ocean Free (☎ (070) 31 6601), *Falla* (☎ (070) 31 3488) and *Passions of Paradise* (☎ (070) 31 6465) are all ocean-going yachts which sail out to Upolo Cay, Green Island and Paradise Reef daily for around $40, which again includes lunch and snorkelling gear.

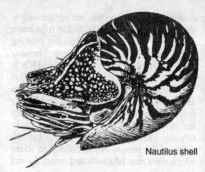

Nautilus shell

There are many, many other boats and operators, so shop around.

Outback There are a number of companies which operate 4WD trips between Cairns, Alice Springs and Darwin, via the Gulf Country and Kakadu. Frontier Safaris (☎ (070) 31 6711) has a three-day camping trip from Cairns to Alice for $99, a six-day trip to Alice and Uluru (Ayers Rock) for $278 and a nine-day round trip for $350. Costs don't include meals.

K'Gari Expeditions (☎ 018 184 961) offers a 12-day expedition from Cairns to Darwin via Normanton, Lawn Hill National Park, the Katherine Gorge and Kakadu for $828, including all meals and camping gear. It also has a 12-day trip to Uluru (Ayers Rock) via Lawn Hill, the MacDonnell Ranges and Kings Canyon for the same price. Both tours are available as 16-day round trips for $944.

For something completely different, Cape York Air Services (☎ (070) 35 9399), the local mail contractor, does mail runs to remote outback stations on weekdays. Space permitting, you can go along on these runs, but it's not cheap at $140 to $275, depending on the length of the trip.

Places to Stay
Cairns has hostels and cheap guesthouses galore, as well as plenty of reasonably priced motels and holiday flats. The accommodation business is extremely competitive and prices go up and down with the seasons.

Lower weekly rates are par for the course. Prices given here for the more expensive places can rise by 30% or 40% in the peak season, and some of the hostels will charge $1 or $2 less in the quiet times.

Camping There are about a dozen caravan parks in and around Cairns, though none of them are really central. Almost without exception they take campers as well as caravans. The closest one to the centre is the *City Caravan Park* (☎ (070) 51 1467), about two km north-west on the corner of Little and James Sts, with tent sites for $12 and on-site vans for $28.

Out on the Bruce Highway, about eight km south of the centre, is the excellent *Cairns Coconut Caravan Village* (☎ (070) 54 6644), with camp sites for $13.50, camp-o-tel units for $18 a double and cabin vans from $32.

Hostels The Cairns hostel scene is constantly changing as new places open up, old ones change hands and others rise and fall in quality and popularity. The type of accommodation is pretty standard – fan-cooled bunk rooms with shared kitchen and bathroom, usually also with sitting areas, laundry facilities and a swimming pool. Cairns has had a reputation for fairly dodgy accommodation, but recent changes in council regulations and increased competition has forced many places to decrease the number of beds in dorms and upgrade their facilities. Unfortunately, you still have to beware of theft in some places – use lock-up rooms and safes if they're available.

The Esplanade has the greatest concentration of hostels, and is a lively part of town. The hostels here tend to pack them in, and have very little outside space – any outdoor area is usually cramped with a swimming pool. On the plus side, these hostels are ideally located. The hostels away from the centre offer much more breathing space and are generally quieter, and the inconvenience of being out of the centre is minimal as there are courtesy buses which make regular runs into town.

Esplanade Starting from the corner of Shields St and heading along the Esplanade, the *International Hostel* (☎ (070) 31 1424) at No 67 is a big, old, multilevel place with about 200 beds. The accommodation is fairly basic, with fan-cooled four- to eight-bed dorms for $11 or twin rooms for $24. There are also doubles for $26, or $28 with either air-con and TV or a private bathroom.

Caravella's Hostel 77 (☎ 51 2159), at 77 The Esplanade, is another big, rambling place with about 150 beds. It's one of the longest established Cairns hostels and has old-fashioned but clean rooms, all with air-con. The cost in four- to six-bunk dorms is $10, or $11 with a bathroom. Doubles range from $25 to $27, or $35 with private bathroom.

Jimmy's on the Esplanade (☎ (070) 31 6884), at No 83, is a recently renovated place with 46 beds in six-bed air-con units with their own bathrooms. There's a new pool and kitchen, and the cost here is $12 a night.

Bellview (☎ (070) 31 4377), at No 85, is a good, quiet hostel with clean and comfortable four-bed dorms at $14 per person, singles at $27 and twin rooms at $32. All rooms are air-conditioned, the kitchen facilities are good, and there's a small pool and outdoor tables. There are also motel-style units at $49 a double, and two smaller units at $42.

Hostel 89 (☎ (070) 31 7477 or toll-free 1800 061 712), at No 89, is one of the best kept hostels on the Esplanade. It's a smallish and helpful place, with twin and double rooms and a few three- or four-bed dorms, all air-conditioned. Nightly costs are from $15 per person, with singles/doubles at $25/30. Security is good, with a locked grille at the street entrance.

At No 93 is *YHA on the Esplanade* (☎ (070) 31 1919). There are two blocks, one with spacious, airy five-bed dorms with their own bathroom, the other with small twins and doubles. Some rooms have air-con. Dorm beds cost $14 and doubles $32; nonmembers pay an extra $1.

Three blocks further along the Esplanade at No 149 is another bigger hostel, *Caravella's*

149 (☎ (070) 51 2431). Its popularity means that even the big cooking/recreation area at the back can get pretty busy. You pay $9 in a 14-bed dorm or $11 in a four- or six-bunk room, a few of which have air-con and bathroom. Doubles cost $24, or $26 with air-con.

Rosie's Backpackers (☎ (070) 51 0235), at No 155, has several buildings with either spacious dorms or six-bed flats at $12 per person. This place is helpful and well run. It has a small pool and a popular Saturday night barbecue.

Next door at No 157, *Bel-Air Backpackers* (☎ (070) 31 4790) is a newly renovated place, with doubles and twins downstairs for $24 and spacious dorms upstairs for $12.

Around Town Close to the centre, *Parkview Backpackers* (☎ (070) 51 3700) is at 174 Grafton St, three blocks back from the Esplanade. This is a very laid-back place where you can relax by the pool and listen to reggae music. It's in a rambling old timber building with a large tropical garden, and four- to eight-bed dorms cost $12 per person.

Tracks Hostel (☎ (070) 31 1474), on the corner of Grafton and Minnie Sts, spans three old timber houses and so has a number of kitchens and plenty of other facilities. Costs are $10 per person in four-bed dorms or twin rooms, or $22 a double, and there's a free evening meal.

Over at 255 Lake St, *Cairns Backpackers Inn* (☎ (070) 51 9166) occupies three houses. The dorms are big and roomy, and there are spacious gardens and living areas. You pay $10 in dorms, some of which have air-con, or there are twins/doubles for $24. The courtesy bus goes to the town centre 16 times a day.

City Court Garden Apartments (☎ (070) 51 7642), at 13 Charles St, has two sections, one with self-contained apartments, the other with four-bed dorms. Although small, this place has a spacious feel. There's also a pool. Dorm beds are $10, doubles $28, and there's a one-bedroom apartment for $40.

Captain Cook Backpackers Hostel (☎ (070) 51 6811), at 204 Sheridan St, is a huge place with over 300 beds. It's a converted old motel, with good facilities including two pools, a bar, bikes for hire and a restaurant with free evening meals, but there are no kitchen facilities. The six- to eight-bed units, with either a kitchen or air-con, cost $10 per person, and doubles range from $30 to $35.

At 207 Sheridan St is *Castaways* (☎ (070) 51 1238), a quiet and smallish place with mostly double and twin rooms costing $24, or $28 with air-con. All rooms are fan-cooled and have a fridge, and there's a pool and courtesy bus.

At 72 Grafton St, the *Aussie II Hostel* (☎ (070) 51 7620) is clean and roomy with space for about 60 people. You pay $10 for a dorm bed, with four to seven people in each room. There are also singles at $15 and twin and double rooms at $24. The hostel has two kitchens and a TV room. There's no pool but you can use the pools at the two Caravella hostels.

Two blocks west of the station at 274 Draper St, *Gone Walkabout Hostel* (☎ (070) 51 6160) is one of the best in Cairns. It's small, simple and well run, with a friendly atmosphere. Rooms are mostly twins and doubles, with a few four-bed dorms, and there's a tiny pool. You pay $10 in a dorm, $22 for a twin room and $24 for a double. It's not a place for late partying, however.

The YHA *McLeod St Youth Hostel* (☎ (070) 51 0772), at 20-24 McLeod St, has dorm beds for $12 and singles/doubles for $20/30; nonmembers pay $1 extra. The facilities are good and the hostel has car parking spaces.

On the corner of Spence and Sheridan Sts, the *Coconut Palms Hostel* (☎ (070) 51 6946) has dorm beds for $10, twin rooms at $22 and doubles at $24. It's a clean, simple place in an old timber house, with a nice garden and a pool.

The *Up Top Down Under Holiday Lodge* (☎ (070) 51 3636) at 164-170 Spence St, 1.5 km from the town centre, is a spacious and quiet place with a large, well-equipped kitchen, two TV lounges and a pool. Dorm beds are $12 and singles/doubles $25/27, all with shared bathroom.

Guesthouses A couple of places in this bracket are in the hostel price range, the difference being that their emphasis is on rooms rather than dorms.

Dreamtime Travellers Rest (☎ (070) 31 6753), at 4 Terminus St, is a small guesthouse run by a friendly and enthusiastic young Irish/English couple. It's in a brightly renovated timber Queenslander and has a good pool, double rooms at $28 to $30 and three- or four-bed (no bunks) rooms at $12 per person.

Another good guesthouse with a similar approach is *Ryan's Rest* (☎ (070) 51 4734), down the road at 18 Terminus St. It's a cosy and quiet family-run place with three good double rooms upstairs at $30, and two self-contained flats downstairs with twins/doubles at $25, and a four-bed dorm at $12.50 per person. Cooked and tropical breakfasts are available for $5 and $4 respectively.

At 153 The Esplanade, the spotless *Silver Palm Guesthouse* (☎ (070) 31 6099) has singles/doubles from $27.50/32.50, including the use of a kitchen, laundry, pool and TV room.

The recently opened *No Worries* (☎ (070) 31 6380) at 323 Draper St is a small B&B place with just eight beds. Twins and doubles cost $12 per person.

At 100 Sheridan St is *Pacific Coast Budget Accommodation* (☎ (070) 51 1264), an old guesthouse with basic rooms with shared bathrooms from $29/39 for singles/doubles.

Motels & Holiday Flats Holiday flats are well worth considering, especially for a group of three or four people who are staying a few days or more. Expect pools, air-con and laundry facilities in this category. Holiday flats generally supply all bedding, cooking utensils, etc.

Wintersun Motel Holiday Apartments (☎ (070) 51 2933), at 84 Abbott St, is quite a good place. Large, fully equipped, one-bedroom flats with immaculate '60s decor and air-con cost $45/55. At 209 Lake St is *Castle Holiday Flats* (☎ (070) 31 2229), one of the city's cheapest places. There's a small

pool, and it has rooms with shared facilities at $25/30 for singles/doubles, one-bedroom flats from $45 and two-bedroom flats from $60.

There's a string of motels and holiday units along Sheridan St, including the *Pacific Cay* (☎ (070) 51 0151) at No 193, with one-bedroom holiday units from $50 and two-bedrooms units from $75, and the *Concord Holiday Units* (☎ (070) 31 4522) at No 183, with one-bedroom units from $50.

Inn the Tropics (☎ (070) 31 1088), at 141 Sheridan St, is a relatively new place with a good pool, a small guests' kitchen and an open-air courtyard with tables. Clean and modern motel-style rooms with shared bathrooms cost $30/35, or $40/45 with an en-suite.

The *Poinsietta Motel* (☎ (070) 51 2144) at 169 Lake St is one of the cheapest central motels, with clean budget rooms for $42/46.

Places to Eat

For a town of its size, Cairns has quite an amazing number and variety of restaurants. Opening hours are long, and quite a few places take advantage of the climate by providing open-air dining.

Cafes & Takeaways The Esplanade has a large collection of fast-food joints and restaurants – the stretch between Shields and Aplin Sts is virtually wall-to-wall eateries, where you'll find Italian and Chinese food, burgers, kebabs, pizzas, seafood and ice cream – at all hours.

There's also the *International Foodhall* at No 67, but it's a bit grotty nowadays. The *Meeting Place*, around the corner on Aplin St, is a much better food hall and you can choose between Japanese, Thai, Chinese, steak and seafood meals in the $7.50 to $12 range. *Greens*, also on Aplin St near the Esplanade corner, is a popular (although pricey) vegetarian and health-food takeaway – the $3.95 vegie burgers should keep you going for a while.

The *Galloping Gourmet Takeaway* offers a full breakfast for $5, and has a lunch deal for $4 – both good value. *Mozart's Pastry,* on the corner of Grafton and Spence Sts, is good for a breakfast croissant and coffee, and also has a range of pastries, cakes and sandwiches. *John & Diana's Breakfast & Burger House*, at 35 Sheridan St, has virtually every combination of cooked breakfast imaginable for $5 or less. Across the road is the *Continental Shelf*, an excellent eat-in deli with gourmet meals and snacks.

Tiny's Juice Bar, on Grafton St near the Spence St corner, has a great range of fruit and vegetable juices as well as filled rolls and lentil and tofu burgers at good prices. The *Blue Moon Cafe*, nearby at 45 Spence St, is a friendly little place open for lunch and dinner, with Chinese and vegetarian dishes, sandwiches and soups at reasonable prices.

Central Arcade, on the Lake and Spence Sts corner, has several good eateries including the hip and trendy *Glass Onion*, which has good coffee and a range of cakes, pastries and sandwiches.

Nightclubs & Bars Most of the hostels have vouchers for cheap meals at various nightclubs, pubs and bars around town, often with free or discounted drinks thrown in. *Samuel's Saloon*, near the corner of Hartley and Lake Sts, is one of the most popular places, with roasts, pastas and stews for $3.50. It even has a bus that collects hungry travellers from the hostels!

The *End of the World*, a nightclub on the corner of Abbott and Aplin Sts, has very basic food, but it's cheap and a lot of people seem to eat here, again with hostel meal vouchers. Next door on Abbott St is the *Pumphouse*, a lively bar with a good range of $3, $4 and $5 meals. The *Fox & Firkin Hotel*, an English-style tavern on the corner of Spence and Lake Sts, also has cheap meals; the $1 Sunday barbecue is fairly hectic!

The *Base Rock Cafe & Bar* on Shields St is a bit more up-market than the other places, with both live music and DJs, and it has a wide range of meals priced from $4 to $16. It opens daily from noon until late.

Restaurants The *Bangkok Room Thai Restaurant*, at 62 Spence St, has a pleasant setting and friendly service, with tasty Thai dishes for around $12. Next door is the popular *Hog's Breath Cafe*, a saloon-style bar & grill. Further along Spence St, the *Taj* serves pretty good Indian food.

La Fettucine, at 62 Spence St, is a narrow and stylish little BYO place with excellent home-made pastas for $9.90 and Italian mains for $14. *George's Greek Taverna*, on the corner of Grafton and Aplin Sts, is a fairly up-market place with Greek and seafood dishes at around $16. For Mexican food, try the *Fiesta Cantina*, in an arcade at 96-98 Lake St; it's a bright new place with main meals ranging from $7 to $12.

The Pier plaza has a couple of good eating options. The *Pier Tavern* is a popular pub with several bars and outdoor decking overlooking Trinity Bay and the Esplanade. Bistro meals in the Boat Bar are all $9.90, and there are live bands from Wednesday to Sunday. Up on the first level of the shopping plaza is *Donninis*, a smart but casual licensed restaurant with some of the best Italian food (and service) in town: gourmet pizzas from $9 to $15, pastas from $8 to $10 and Italian mains around $14.

Entertainment
Johno's Blues Bar, above McDonald's on the corner of Shields St and the Esplanade, is a big, lively place with blues, rock and R&B bands every night until late. There's a cover charge of $5 on Friday and Saturday nights.

On Abbott St near the Aplin St corner, the *Pumphouse* is another backpackers' favourite, with a rowdy bar atmosphere and cheap meals. It's a good pre-nightclub option, and stays open until 2 am.

The *Fox & Firkin Hotel*, on the corner of Spence and Lake Sts, and the *Cock & Bull*, on the corner of Grafton and Grove Sts, are both English-style taverns with good atmosphere and affordable meals. Quite a few pubs in Cairns have regular live bands, including the Fox & Firkin, the *Pier Tavern*, *Rusty's Pub* on the corner of Spence and Sheridan Sts, and the *Big O* on Wharf St opposite the transit centre.

Cairns's nightclub scene is notoriously

wild, especially in the early hours of the morning. A huge complex on the corner of Lake and Hartley Sts houses three places: *Samuel's Saloon*, a backpackers' bar and eatery; the *Playpen International*, a huge nightclub which often has big-name bands, stays open until sunrise and charges from $2 to $5 entry; and the more up-market *Court Jester* bar. The *End of the World* nightclub, on the corner of Abbott and Aplin Sts, is another popular place for a drink and a bop, with a huge video screen, low lighting, loud music and cheap drinks deals. *Tropo's*, next to the Fox & Firkin, has live bands, a disco and a $5 cover charge.

If you want to catch a movie, there's the *Cairns 5 Cinemas* (☎ (070) 31 1077) at 108 Grafton St, the art-house *Cinema Capri* (☎ (070) 51 3817) at 88 Lake St, or the *Coral Twin Drive-in* on the Bruce Highway on the southern edge of town.

Free lunch-time concerts are held at the *City Place Amphitheatre*, in the mall on the corner of Lake and Shields Sts.

Things to Buy

Many artists live in the Cairns region, so there's a wide range of local handicrafts available – pottery, clothing, stained glass, jewellery, leather work and so on. Aboriginal art is also for sale in a few places, as are crafts from Papua New Guinea and places further afield in the Pacific. Apart from the many souvenir shops dotted around the town centre, the weekend markets at Rusty's Bazaar and the Pier are all worth a visit.

Getting There & Away

Air In Cairns, Qantas and Sunstate Airlines are on the corner of Shields and Lake Sts, and Ansett and Eastwest are at 84 Lake St.

Domestic Flights Airlines serving Cairns include Ansett, Qantas, Flight West and Eastwest. Regular one-way fares to the major destinations are Melbourne $567, Sydney $491, Brisbane $379, Townsville $148, Darwin $404, Alice Springs $377, Perth $621 and Adelaide $579. You can get

cheaper advance-purchase fares – the further ahead you book, the cheaper the fare.

Flights inland and up the Cape York Peninsula from Cairns are shared amongst a number of small feeder airlines. Sunstate flies to Bamaga ($261), Lizard Island ($143) and Thursday Island ($290). Ansett flies to Weipa ($209) and Mt Isa ($254). Flight West (☎ (070) 35 9511 or through Ansett) operates a service through the Gulf, the Cape York Peninsula and to Bamaga and the Torres Strait Islands.

International Flights Cairns International Airport has regular flights to and from North America, Papua New Guinea and Asia. Air Niugini (☎ (070) 51 4177) is at 4 Shields St; the Port Moresby flight costs $378 one way and goes daily except Sunday. Qantas also flies to Port Moresby (daily except Wednesday and Sunday), as well as direct to the US west coast (daily except Tuesday) and to Hong Kong every Thursday.

Bus All the bus companies operate from the transit centre at Trinity Wharf.

Greyhound Pioneer and McCafferty's (☎ (070) 51 5899) both run at least five buses a day up the coast from Brisbane and Townsville to Cairns. Journey times and fares are: Brisbane, 23 to 27 hours ($133); Rockhampton, 14 to 16 hours ($90); Mackay, 10 to 12 hours ($70); and Townsville, 4½ hours ($40).

Train The Sunlander between Brisbane and Cairns runs three times a week, and the Queenslander motorail service goes once a week (leaving Brisbane on Sunday and Cairns on Tuesday). The 1681-km trip from Brisbane takes 32 hours. The economy fare from Brisbane is $123 on both trains, while 1st-class fares are $234 on the Sunlander and $489 (including sleeping berth and all meals) on the Queenslander. Call Queensland Rail in Cairns for bookings (☎ 13 2232) and information (☎ (070) 52 6249).

Car Rental It's well worth considering renting a car. There's plenty to see and do on land

QUEENSLAND

around Cairns, whether it's making the beach crawl up to Port Douglas or exploring the Atherton Tableland. Mokes are about the cheapest cars to rent and are ideal for relaxed, open-air sightseeing; most of the car-rental firms in Cairns have them. While the major firms are along Lake St, local firms have mushroomed all over Cairns and some of them offer good deals, particularly for weekly rental. However, don't be taken in by cut-rates advertising – once you add in all the hidden costs, prices are fairly similar everywhere. Shop around and find the deal that suits. Generally, mokes are around $45 per day, VW convertibles $55, and regular cars from $50 up. It's also possible to rent 4WDs from around $110.

Note that the majority of Cairns's rental firms specifically prohibit you from taking most of their cars up the Cape Tribulation road, on the road to Cooktown, or on the Chillagoe Caves road. A sign in the car will usually announce this prohibition and the contract will threaten dire unhappiness if you do so. Of course, lots of people ignore these prohibitions, but if you get stuck in the mud halfway to Cape Tribulation, it could be a little embarrassing. Be warned that these roads are fairly rough and sometimes impassable in conventional vehicles. Also note that a sizable deposit is generally required for car rental, anything from $100 to $250 in Cairns, although this is waived if you're paying with a credit card.

Getting Around

To/From the Airport The airport in Cairns has two sections, both off the Captain Cook Highway north of the town. The main domestic and international airlines use the new section, officially called Cairns International Airport. This is reached by an approach road that turns off the highway about 3.5 km from central Cairns. The other part of the airport, which some people still call Cairns Airport, is reached from a second turning off the highway, 1.5 km north of the main one.

The Australia Coach shuttle bus (☎ (070) 35 9555) from the main terminal costs $4 and will drop you almost anywhere in central Cairns; ring when you're leaving. A taxi is about $9. Avis, Budget, Hertz and Thrifty have desks at the international terminal.

Bus There are a number of local bus services in and around Cairns. Schedules for most of them are posted at the main city stop (known as the Lake St Transit) in City Place. Buses on most routes leave hourly from around 7 am to 6 pm from Monday to Friday, and less frequently on Saturday mornings. Most routes close down from Saturday lunch time to Monday morning.

The Beach Bus (No 208) run by Marlin Coast Buslines (☎ (070) 57 7411) goes up to Trinity and Clifton beaches, Wild World, Palm Cove and Ellis Beach. The last buses back to Cairns leave Ellis Beach at 4.40 pm Monday to Friday and at 4 pm on weekends.

Cairns Trans (☎ (070) 35 2600) operates the local bus services including buses to Yorkey's Knob and Holloways Beach, with last buses leaving Yorkey's Knob at 6.15 pm Monday to Friday and 1.10 pm on Saturday. From Holloways Beach, last buses are at 5.55 pm on weekdays and 12.50 pm on Saturdays; there are no services on Sundays. Southern Cross Bus Services (☎ (070) 55 1240), which runs to Machans Beach, has last buses to Cairns at 4.50 pm Monday to Friday and 10 am Saturday; there's no service on Sunday.

The Cairns Red Explorer (☎ (070) 55 1240) is an air-con service which plies a circular route around the city, and you can get on or off at any of the nine stops. It departs every hour from 9 am to 4 pm daily (Sundays May to October only) from the Lake St Transit Mall; a day ticket costs a hefty $20. The main stops of interest are No 4 (Freshwater Creek swimming hole), No 5 (Freshwater Connection), No 6 (Mangrove Boardwalk near the airport), No 7 (Botanic Gardens) and No 8 (Royal Flying Doctor Complex).

Bicycle & Motorcycle Most of the hostels and car-hire firms, plus quite a few other places, have bikes for hire so you'll have no trouble tracking one down. Expect to pay around $10 a day. Jolly Frog (☎ (070) 31 2379) at 101 The Esplanade has scooters from $25 and larger bikes from $55 per day.

ISLANDS OFF CAIRNS

Green and Fitzroy are wooded islands off Cairns which attract hordes of day-trippers. Resorts on both islands are owned by the same company, and they operate a scam whereby you have to exchange your money for souvenir money before you can buy anything on either island. Don't fall for the trick of keeping this stuff as a souvenir or forgetting to exchange it for real dollars on the way back.

North of Green Island and 40 km from Cairns, tiny **Michaelmas Cay** is a national park and home to thousands of sea birds. During the peak nesting season in summer, 30,000 or more birds cram on to the cay; some day trips from Cairns call here.

Getting There & Away

Great Adventures (☎ (070) 51 0455) is one of a number of outfits running ferries from Cairns to Green and Fitzroy islands. It has its own wharf in Cairns, near Trinity Wharf, and offers a wide choice of services. The high-speed cats cost $22 return to Fitzroy or $44 return to Green. You can visit both for $49. Other operators include the Big Cat (☎ (070) 51 0444), which offers a return trip to Green Island for $28 taking 80 minutes. The *Reef Jet* (☎ (070) 31 5559) does the journey in half that time, and a half-day trip costs $28, a full day $33.

Green Island

Green Island, 27 km north-east of Cairns, is a true coral cay, 660 metres long by 260 metres wide. The beautiful island and its surrounding reef are all national park. A multimillion-dollar luxury resort is under construction and due to open in August 1994. Nevertheless, a 10-minute stroll from the resort to the far end of the island will remind you that the beach is beautiful, the water fine, the snorkelling good and the fish prolific.

The artificial attractions start at the end of the pier with the underwater observatory. Glass-bottomed boats go from the pier too, while on the island there's Marineland Melanesia with fish and corals in tanks, larger creatures (sharks, turtles, crocodiles) in pools or enclosures, and a display of art from South-East Asia and the South Pacific. The more expensive day trips to Green Island include entry to all these 'wonders'. You can hire sailboards or canoes.

Places to Stay & Eat The new five-star *Green Island Reef Resort* (☎ (070) 31 3300) is very exclusive and equally expensive.

Fitzroy Island

Six km off the coast and 26 km south-east of Cairns, Fitzroy is a larger continental island with coral-covered beaches which are good for snorkelling, but not ideal for swimming and sunbaking, although Nudey Beach is quite pleasant. Snorkellers will find good coral only 50 metres off the beach in the resort area, and the island has its own diving school. There are some fine walks, including one to the island's highest point.

Places to Stay & Eat Unlike Green Island, Fitzroy's resort (☎ (070) 51 9588) has a variety of accommodation. There are hostel-style units accommodating four people in bunks at $24 each, with shared kitchen and bathroom. The 'villa units' cost $208/290 for single/double, including activities and breakfast and dinner. If all that's beyond your budget, you can camp at the National Parks camping grounds (permits and bookings through Great Adventures). Sites cost $10 a night, and campers can use *most* of the resort's facilities. There's a pool, snack bar with fish & chips and pizza, a bar, a couple of shops and also a laundromat.

ATHERTON TABLELAND

Inland from the coast between Innisfail and Cairns, the land rises sharply then rolls gently across the lush Atherton Tableland towards the Great Dividing Range. The tableland's altitude, more than 900 metres in places, tempers the tropical heat, and the

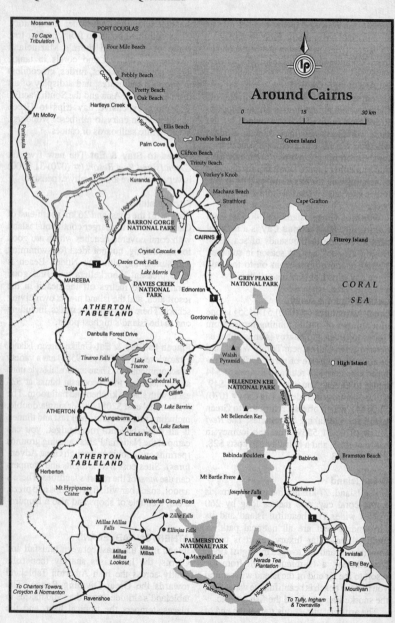

Around Cairns

0   15   30 km

QUEENSLAND

abundant rainfall and rich volcanic soil combine to make this one of the greenest places in Queensland. In the south are Queensland's two highest mountains – Bartle Frere (1657 metres) and Bellenden Ker (1591 metres).

Little more than a century ago, this peaceful, pastoral region was still wild jungle. The first pioneers came in the 1870s, looking for a repeat of the Palmer River gold rush, further north. As elsewhere in Queensland, the Aboriginal population was violently opposed to this intrusion but was soon overrun. Some gold was found and rather more tin, but although mining spurred the development of roads and railways through the rugged, difficult land of the plateau, farming and timber soon became the chief activities.

Getting There & Around

The train ride from Cairns to Kuranda is a major tableland attraction – but without a car the rest of the tableland can be hard to reach. From south to north, the four good roads from the coast are: the Palmerston Highway from Innisfail to Millaa Millaa and Ravenshoe; the Gillies Highway from Gordonvale past Lakes Tinaroo, Barrine and Eacham to Yungaburra and Atherton; the Kennedy Highway from Cairns to Kuranda and Mareeba; and the Peninsula Developmental Road from Mareeba through Mt Molloy to Mossman.

Kuranda (population 620)

Famed for its markets, this beautiful mountain village is surrounded by spectacular tropical scenery. Unfortunately, Kuranda's charms have long been discovered by the masses, and the place is flooded with busloads and trainloads of tourists on market days. Many of the stalls and shops sell mainly trashy souvenirs, although there are still quite a few good art, craft and produce stalls.

There are also two good places to stay here; one old and full of character, the other modern and stylish.

Things to See The **Kuranda markets** are held every Wednesday, Thursday, Friday and Sunday, although things quieten after about 2 pm. On other days, Kuranda reverts to its normal sleepy character.

Near the market area, the **Australian Butterfly Sanctuary** ($9.50) is open daily from 10 am to 3 pm and has regular guided tours. On Coondoo St, the **Kuranda Wildlife Noctarium** ($8), where you can see nocturnal rainforest animals like gliders, fruit bats and echidnas, is open from 10 am to 4 pm daily.

Also on Coondoo St, the award-winning **Tjapukai Dance Theatre**, a local Aboriginal dance troupe, goes through its paces daily at 11 am and 1.30 pm, and at 12.15 pm on market days ($16). The hour-long performance tells you a few basic things about Aboriginal culture with song, dance and humour and features dijeridu playing and dancing. Almost across the road is the **Jilli Binna Aboriginal Crafts & Museum**; there's a small display (admission free) on Aboriginal culture and the old Mona Mona mission near Kuranda, many of whose people and their descendants live on in the area.

Over the footbridge behind the railway station you can hire canoes on the Barron River, take a one-hour river cruise ($8) or a forest walking tour daily at 10.15 am ($9).

There are several picturesque walks starting with short signed tracks down through the market. **Jumrum Creek Environmental Park**, off Barron Falls Rd, 700 metres from the bottom of Thongon St, has a short walking track and a big population of fruit bats. Further down, Barron Falls Rd divides: the left fork takes you to a lookout over the falls, while a further 1.5 km along the right fork brings you to Wrights Lookout where you can see back down the Barron Gorge to Cairns.

Places to Stay The *Kuranda Van Park* (☎ (070) 93 7316) is a few km out of town, up the road directly opposite the Kuranda turn-off on the Kennedy Highway. It has camp sites for $11 or on-site cabins at $32.

The friendly and atmospheric *Kuranda*

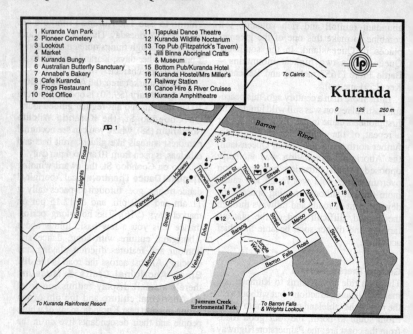

1 Kuranda Van Park
2 Pioneer Cemetery
3 Lookout
4 Market
5 Kuranda Bungy
6 Australian Butterfly Sanctuary
7 Annabel's Bakery
8 Cafe Kuranda
9 Frogs Restaurant
10 Post Office
11 Tjapukai Dance Theatre
12 Kuranda Wildlife Noctarium
13 Top Pub (Fitzpatrick's Tavern)
14 Jilli Binna Aboriginal Crafts
    & Museum
15 Bottom Pub/Kuranda Hotel
16 Kuranda Hostel/Mrs Miller's
17 Railway Station
18 Canoe Hire & River Cruises
19 Kuranda Amphitheatre

Kuranda

To Cairns

0   125   250 m

Barron River

To Kuranda Rainforest Resort

Jumrum Creek
Enviromental Park

To Barron Falls
& Wrights Lookout

Hostel (☎ (070) 93 7355), also known as *Mrs Miller's*, is at 6 Arara St, near the railway station. It's a rambling old place with a huge garden, a small salt-water pool, a sitting/video room, an enlightening graffiti room and a separate TV room. Dorm accommodation is $12 (plus $1.50 extra the first night for a sheet) and there are double rooms for $30 (sheets provided). Hostel guests can get worthwhile discounts on most Kuranda attractions, and the $28 day tour of the tableland is particularly popular.

A couple of km out of town, back on the Kennedy Highway towards Mareeba, the modern and up-market *Kuranda Rainforest Resort* (☎ (070) 93 7555) no longer has a backpackers' section, but it does have excellent facilities, including a bar, restaurant, swimming pool and tennis courts; note, however, that this isn't a party place. Regular motel rooms are $85 and two-bedroom serviced units (some with cooking facilities) start at $140. The resort has a free courtesy

bus which picks up three times daily from Trinity Wharf in Cairns and also does airport transfers.

The *Bottom Pub/Kuranda Hotel* (☎ (070) 93 7206) at the corner of Coondoo and Arara Sts, has a pool and 12 motel-style rooms at $28/38.

Places to Eat The Bottom Pub has the *Garden Bar & Grill*, with burgers for $4 and other grills for $8. The *Top Pub* has lunch and dinner, from $4 for burgers to $8 for chicken, fish or steak dishes.

Next to the Tjapukai Theatre on Coondoo St, the *Kuranda Village Bistro* is a popular spot, although it's not particularly cheap. A better bet is the licensed *Frogs Restaurant*, a bit further along. It serves full breakfasts for $7, burgers and sandwiches around $6 and main meals from $10. *Cafe Kuranda*, with two sections on the corner of Coondoo and Therwine Sts, does sandwiches, snacks and takeaways. And just a few doors along, the excellent *Annabel's Bakery* has a large range of pastries.

Getting There & Away White Car Coaches (☎ (070) 51 9533) has buses three or four times daily (twice on weekends), leaving from outside Tropical Paradise Travel at 25 Spence St in Cairns. The fare is $7 one way, $14 return.

The best and most popular way of getting to Kuranda is on the appropriately named Kuranda Scenic Railway that winds 34 km from Cairns to Kuranda. This line, which took five years to build, was opened in 1891 and goes through 15 tunnels, climbing more than 300 metres in the last 21 km. Kuranda's railway station, decked out in tropical flowers and ferns, is justly famous.

The historic steam trains operate daily and cost $20 one way, $34 return. There are uniformed hostesses, free orange juice, and a commentary. You also get a booklet on the line's history and a photo stop at the 260-metre Barron Falls. The train has its own ticket office at Cairns railway station (☎ (070) 52 6249) – or you can board at Freshwater Connection (☎ (070) 55 2222), 10 km out of Cairns.

Mareeba (population 6800)
From Kuranda, the Kennedy Highway runs west across the tableland to Mareeba, the centre of a tobacco- and rice-growing area, then continues south to Atherton in the centre of the tableland. From Mareeba, the Peninsula Developmental Road heads 40 km north to Mt Molloy, where it forks for Mossman and the coast one way, Cooktown and Cape York the other. This is the main road from Cairns to the north. Mareeba has a range of accommodation and in July the town hosts one of Australia's biggest rodeos.

Chillagoe (population 500)
From Mareeba, you can continue 140 km west to Chillagoe. After Dimbulah (42 km) the road is gravel; although it may be impassable in the Wet, for most of the year you can make this interesting trip in a conventional vehicle. At Chillagoe you can visit impressive limestone caves and rock pinnacles, Aboriginal rock-art galleries, ruins of smelters from early this century, a working mine and a museum.

The caves are a national park and there are guided tours of some of them, usually given at 9 am and 1.30 pm. For more information, phone the ranger (☎ (070) 94 7163) on Queen St in the town, or contact the Cairns National Parks office. The rangers can also tell you about other caves with self-guiding trails, for which you'll need a torch.

Places to Stay There's a small National Parks camping ground at Chillagoe, and the *Chillagoe Caravan Park* (☎ (070) 94 7177) on Queen St has tent sites. *Chillagoe Caves Lodge* (☎ (070) 94 7106), at 7 King St, has a few backpackers' beds at $8, budget rooms with shared bathrooms at $25 a double and motel units at $45. You can also camp here for $5, and there's an inexpensive restaurant.

Getting There & Away White Car Coaches runs buses to Chillagoe twice a week – one from Cairns, one from Atherton, and both travel via Mareeba. Cairns to Chillagoe takes about four hours and costs around $40 return. There are day tours from Cairns for about $90.

Atherton (population 5200)
Although it's a pleasant, prosperous town, Atherton has little of interest in its own right. On the Herberton road, about a km from the centre, is Atherton's old post office, now an art gallery and information office, and a restored Chinese joss house. *Atherton Backpackers* (☎ (070) 91 3552) at 37 Alice St, not far from the centre of town, is quite a good place and has dorm beds for $13 and doubles for $27.

Lake Tinaroo
From Atherton or nearby Tolga it's a short drive to this large lake created for the Barron River hydroelectric power scheme. Tinaroo Falls, at the north-western corner of the lake,

QUEENSLAND

has a motel and a caravan park which offers tent sites, self-contained cabins and motel rooms. You can rent sailboards over the road from the caravan park. A restaurant and kiosk overlook the dam.

The road continues around the dam as a gravel track which does a 31-km circuit of the lake, finally emerging on the Gillies Highway at Boar Pocket Rd, four km north of Lake Barrine. This is called the **Danbulla Forest Drive** and it's a pleasant trip – though sometimes impassable for conventional vehicles after heavy rain. It passes several free lakeside camping grounds, run by the Queensland forestry department (there are showers and toilets). **Lake Euramoo**, about halfway along, is in a double volcanic crater; there's a short botanical walk around the lake. There is another crater at **Mobo Creek**, a short walk off the drive. Then, 25 km from the dam, it's a short walk to the **Cathedral Fig**, a truly gigantic strangler fig tree.

Yungaburra (population 770)

This pretty village is 13 km east of Atherton along the Gillies Highway. It's right in the centre of the tableland, and if you have transport it's a good base from which to explore the lakes, waterfalls and national parks nearby. The central streets of the town have been classified by the National Trust and are quite atmospheric.

Three km out of Yungaburra on the Malanda road is the **Curtain Fig**, a strangler fig named for its aerial roots which form a 15-metre-high hanging screen.

Places to Stay & Eat The excellent *On the Wallaby* (☎ (070) 51 0889), at 37 Eacham Rd, is a small place sleeping 15, with double and twin rooms upstairs and good living areas downstairs. There's a free pick-up bus from Cairns and the nightly cost is $15 per person including breakfast, or you can camp in the back yard for $7.50. This place also runs overnight trips from Cairns every Monday, Wednesday and Friday for $25, which includes accommodation, transport,

all meals, and activities such as rainforest walks, canoeing and platypus spotting.

The *Lake Eacham Hotel* (☎ (070) 95 3515), in Yungaburra, is a fine old village pub with rooms at $35/40. Or there's the *Kookaburra Lodge* (☎ (070) 95 3222) on the corner of Oak St and Eacham Rd, with bright modern units from $40 a double. There's a pool and tiny dining room with three-course meals for $17.

The *Burra Inn* is a charming little gourmet restaurant opposite the pub. The country-style food is excellent, with main meals for around $18.

Lakes Eacham & Barrine

These two lovely crater lakes are off the Gillies Highway just east of Yungaburra. Both are reached by paved roads, and are great swimming spots. There are rainforest walking tracks around their perimeters – 6.5 km around Lake Barrine, four km around Lake Eacham.

At Lake Barrine there's a restaurant and most of the year you can take a 45-minute cruise (twice a day). Lake Eacham is quieter and more beautiful – an excellent place for a picnic or a swim, and there's a small kids' pool.

Both lakes are national parks and camping is not allowed. However, there are camp sites at *Lake Eacham Tourist Park* (☎ (070) 95 3730), two km down the Malanda road from Lake Eacham. *Chambers Rainforest Holiday Apartments* (☎ (070) 95 3754) has self-contained one-bedroom apartments sleeping one to four people at $240 for three nights.

Malanda (population 900)

About 15 km south of Lake Eacham, Malanda is one of the most pleasant spots to stay on the tableland – a small town with some old buildings in its centre, a couple of pubs and some good places to eat and stay. Malanda also has a huge dairy and claims to have the longest milk run in Australia since it supplies milk all the way to Darwin and the north of Western Australia.

Places to Stay The *Malanda Falls Caravan Park* (☎ (070) 96 5314) is at 38 Park Ave, beside the Atherton road on the edge of town. It's spacious and next to a swimming hole where the upper waters of the North Johnstone River tumble over Malanda Falls. There are tent sites, cabins and on-site vans.

Millaa Millaa (population 330)

The 16-km 'waterfall circuit' road near this small town, 24 km south of Malanda, passes some of the most picturesque falls on the tableland. You enter the circuit by taking Theresa Creek Rd, one km east of Millaa Millaa on the Palmerston Highway. **Millaa Millaa Falls**, the first you reach, are the most spectacular, and have the best swimming hole.

Continuing around the circuit, you reach **Zillie Falls** and then **Ellinjaa Falls** before returning to the Palmerston Highway just 2.5 km out of Millaa Millaa. A further 5.5 km down the Palmerston Highway there's a turning to **Mungalli Falls**, five km off the highway, with a teahouse/restaurant and a few self-contained units (☎ (070) 97 2358). The Palmerston Highway continues through Palmerston National Park to Innisfail.

Millaa Millaa itself has a caravan park with tent sites and cabins, and the *Millaa Millaa Hotel* has accommodation and meals. The **Eacham Historical Society Museum** is on the main street.

A few km west of Millaa Millaa, the East Evelyn road passes the **Millaa Millaa Lookout** with its superb panoramic view.

Mt Hypipamee

The Kennedy Highway between Atherton and Ravenshoe passes the eerie Mt Hypipamee crater. It's a scenic 400-metre walk from the picnic area, past **Dinner Falls**, to this narrow, 138-metre-deep crater with its spooky, evil-looking lake far below. You can camp at the picnic area – permits are available from the National Parks office in Lake Eacham (☎ (070) 95 3768).

Herberton (population 950)

On a slightly longer alternative route between Atherton and Ravenshoe, this old tin-mining town holds a colourful Tin Festival each September. On Holdcroft Drive is the **Herberton Historical Village**, made up of about 30 old buildings which have been transported here from around the tableland.

Ravenshoe (population 880)

At an altitude of 915 metres, Ravenshoe is a forestry centre on the western edge of the tableland. It has the usual caravan/camping park and a couple of pubs and motels.

Little Millstream Falls are a few km south of Ravenshoe on the Tully Gorge road.

The Kennedy Highway continues southwest from Ravenshoe for 114 km, from where you can head south to Charters Towers by paved road all the way, or west by the Gulf Developmental Road to Croydon and Normanton.

Six km past Ravenshoe and one km off the road are the **Millstream Falls**, the widest in Australia although only 13 metres high. You can camp here, but you must get a permit from the National Parks office at Yungaburra (☎ (070) 95 3768).

The small mining town of **Mt Garnet**, 47 km west of Ravenshoe, comes alive one weekend every May when it hosts one of Queensland's top outback race meetings. About 60 km past Mt Garnet, the road passes through **Forty Mile Scrub National Park**, where the semi-evergreen vine thicket is a descendant of the vegetation that covered much of the Gondwana supercontinent 300 million years ago – before Australia, South America, India, Africa and Antarctica drifted apart.

Gulf Developmental Road

From the Kennedy Highway to Normanton, the 460-km road is mostly paved, but some rough stretches west of Georgetown make it a dry-weather route only. The road passes through Mt Surprise, Georgetown and Croydon. There are hotels or motels and caravan/camping parks at Mt Surprise, Georgetown, Einasleigh and Forsayth. The region crossed by the road has many ruined

QUEENSLAND

gold mines and settlements, and attracts some gem fossickers.

The **Elizabeth Creek** gem field, 42 km west of Mt Surprise and accessible by conventional vehicle in the Dry, is Australia's best topaz field. Information on the field is available at the Mt Surprise service station (☎ (070) 62 3153). Between Mt Surprise and Georgetown, an unpaved road leads south to tiny **Einasleigh**, from where you can reach Kidston, Australia's richest gold mine. Einasleigh Gorge, good for swimming, is just across the road from the Einasleigh pub.

CAIRNS TO PORT DOUGLAS

The Bruce Highway, which runs nearly 2000 km north from Brisbane, ends in Cairns, but the surfaced coastal road continues another 110 km north to Mossman and Daintree. This final stretch, the Cook Highway, is a treat because it often runs right along the shore and there are some superb beaches.

Heading out of Cairns, towards the airport, you'll find an interesting and informative elevated **mangrove boardwalk** off Airport Ave, a couple of hundred metres before you reach the airport. There are explanatory signs at regular intervals, and these give some insight into the surprising ecological complexities of swamp vegetation. There's also a small observation platform.

Kamerunga Rd, off the Cook Highway just north of the airport turning, leads inland to the **Freshwater Connection**, a railway museum complex where you can also catch the Kuranda Commentary Train. It's 10 km from the centre of town. Just beyond Freshwater is the turning south along Redlynch Intake Rd to **Crystal Cascades**, a popular outing with waterfalls and swimming holes 22 km from Cairns.

North along the Cook Highway are the Cairns northern beaches, which are really a string of suburbs. In order, these are **Machans, Holloways, Yorkey's Knob, Trinity, Kewarra** and **Clifton** beaches and **Palm Cove**. Holloways and Trinity are the best for a short beach trip from Cairns. At Palm Cove, 22 km from Cairns, **Wild World** has lots of croco-

diles and snakes, tame kangaroos and Australian birds; there are shows daily.

Round the headland past Palm Cove and Double Island, **Ellis Beach** is a lovely spot. Its southern end is an unofficial nude bathing beach and the central part of the beach has a good camping ground.

Soon after Ellis Beach and 40 km from Cairns, **Hartleys Creek Crocodile Farm** has a collection of Australian wildlife typical of the far north. Most of the enclosures are a bit shoddy but showmanship makes it one of the most interesting 'animal places' in Australia. When they feed Charlie the crocodile in the 'Crocodile Attack Show' you know for certain why it's not wise to get bitten by one! And you've never seen anything eat apples until you've seen a cassowary knock back a dozen of them. The park is open daily and there's a park tour at 11 am and a snake show at 2 pm, but make sure you're there at crocodile feeding time which is at 3 pm; entry is $10.

Shortly before Mossman there's a turn-off to fashionable Port Douglas, the departure point for the delightful Low Isles. Then just before Daintree village is the gravel turn-off to the Cape Tribulation rainforests. From Cape Tribulation, it's possible to continue up to historic Cooktown by 4WD along the Bloomfield Track, a road-building enterprise which was rigorously opposed by environmentalists during its construction in 1984. Alternatively, there's the partly surfaced inland road from Cairns, but both roads to Cooktown can be cut after periods of heavy rain.

PORT DOUGLAS (population 3670)

In the early days of far north Queensland's development, Port Douglas was a rival for Cairns, but when Cairns eventually got the upper hand, Port Douglas became a sleepy little backwater. In the mid-1980s, however, people began to realise what a delightful place it was, and up went the multimillion-dollar Sheraton Mirage and Radisson Royal Palms resorts. These were quickly followed by a golf course, a heliport, hovercraft services from Cairns, a marina and shopping complex, and an avenue of palms lining the road from the Cook Highway to Port Douglas – all the ingredients of a retreat for the rich and fashionable. Yet, despite all this development, 'Port' has managed to keep most of its original charm and there is still cheap accommodation. Many travellers arrive here and soon wonder why they spent so long in Cairns – Port is much more relaxed, and there's plenty to do.

The little town has a couple of good central pubs with outdoor sitting areas, and a string of interesting little shops and restaurants to wander around when the beach, the boats and the lookout get dull. You can make trips to the Low Isles, the Barrier Reef, the Mossman Gorge and Cape Tribulation.

Orientation & Information
It's six km from the highway along a long, low spit of land to Port Douglas. The Sheraton Mirage resort occupies a long stretch of Four Mile Beach. The main road in, Davidson St, ends in a T-intersection with Macrossan St; the beach is to the right, and to the left there's the town centre with most of the shops and restaurants. There's a fine view over the coastline and sea from Flagstaff Hill lookout.

There are several tour booking agents along Macrossan St, including the helpful Port Douglas Tourist Information Centre (☎ (070) 99 5599) at No 23.

Things to See
On the pier off Anzac Park, Ben Cropp's **Shipwreck Museum** is quite interesting and open from 9 am to 5 pm daily; admission is $4. The **Rainforest Habitat**, where the Port Douglas road leaves the main highway, is a new and very impressive eco-attraction – a huge enclosed canopy forms an artificial rainforest environment with elevated timber boardwalks, home to at least 30 species of birds and as many of butterflies. It's all very wonderful, but a bit over the top at $14 per person.

Diving
The Port Douglas Dive Centre (☎ (070) 99 5327), with a shop down near the public wharf at the end of Anzac Park, runs open-water diving certificate courses. Other diving companies here include Haba Dive (☎ (070) 99 5254) in the marina, and the Outer Edge (☎ (070) 99 4544) at 30A Wharf St.

Reef Trips Quicksilver's 300-passenger fast cats do daily trips to Agincourt Reef on the outer reef for $108, which includes snorkelling gear, a semisubmersible ride, underwater observatory viewing and lunch. For certified divers, two 40-minute dives will cost an extra $65 with all gear provided. If you'd rather go in a smaller group, there are quite a few smaller boats, including *Wavelength*, *Impulse*, MV *Freestyle* and MV *Outer Edge*, which offer similar but much more personalised reef, snorkelling and diving trips starting at $80.

Low Isles There are also cruises out to the Low Isles, a fine little coral cay surrounded by a lagoon and topped by an old lighthouse. Several of the smaller boats, such as *Sail Away*, *Willow*, *Shaolin* and *Aurora*, offer good day trips for around $70, which generally includes lunch, snorkelling gear and boom netting. Quicksilver also runs trips to the Low Isles for $90. All boats operate from the marina, and you can book with one of the agents along Macrossan St.

Organised Tours
There are day trips to Cape Tribulation from $75, or to Daintree and the Mossman Gorge from $45. A two-day 4WD Cooktown loop – up via the inland road, back by the Bloomfield Track – is $199 with Strikie's Safaris (☎ (070) 99 5599). During crushing season (June to November), Bally Hooley Rail Tours (☎ (070) 98 5899) at the marina runs trips in a miniature steam train to Mossman sugar mill and Drumsara sugar plantation beyond Mossman.

QUEENSLAND

Places to Stay

Port Douglas has a number of caravan parks. The *Kulau Caravan Park* (☎ (070) 99 5449) at 28 Davidson St is central and close to the beach, and has tent sites from $12.50 and on-site cabins from $45. About a km further out, the *Pandanus Van Park* (☎ (070) 99 5944) at 111 Davidson St has tent sites and cabins at similar prices as well as guesthouse units from $35 a double.

The only backpackers' accommodation in Port is the excellent *Port o' Call Lodge* (☎ (070) 99 5422), in Port St about one km from the centre – signposted off the main road (Davidson St) as the Port o' Call Motel. It's a YHA associate and has modern four-bed units with private bathrooms at $15 per person for YHA members or $16 for non-members. Private rooms are available; rates vary seasonally. There's a pool, cooking facilities, a licensed restaurant and a free courtesy coach to and from Cairns. You can also hook up with a couple of the tours which operate between Cairns and Cape Trib from here.

Most of the motels, holiday flats and resorts are fairly expensive. You can expect to pay anywhere from $80 or $400 a night for a double room, although there are a few affordable exceptions. *Hibiscus Lodge* (☎ (070) 99 5315), on the corner of Mowbray and Owen Sts, has good one-bedroom holiday units ranging from $45 to $65 a double. This place is very central and has a pool, but there are only three units so you'll probably need to book.

The *Archipelago Motel & Holiday Apartments* (☎ (070) 99 5387) at 72 Macrossan St also has self-contained studio units from $60, although they go up to $85 in the peak seasons. The *Coconut Grove Motel* (☎ (070) 99 5124), on Macrossan St near the corner of Davidson St, has singles/doubles from $55/65.

At the top of the range are the *Sheraton Mirage* resort (☎ (070) 99 5888), with an amazing swimming pool and five-star hotel units from $400 a night, and the *Radisson Royal Palms* (☎ (070) 99 5577), which seems relatively affordable at a mere $150 a night.

Places to Eat

Port Douglas has a surprisingly good array of cafes and restaurants for such a small town. Most of the eateries are along Macrossan St.

For breakfast, try *Namaste Cafe* at No 43. Choices include muesli with fruit, croissants, or eggs on toast, all from $3 to $6. It's also a good place for lunch, with gourmet sandwiches, salads and burgers around $5. Further down and across the road, *Ada's Gourmet* also does good breakfasts and excellent sandwiches.

For takeaways, there's a good range of choices side-by-side near the corner of Macrossan and Grant Sts: *Sunshine Health Foods*, *EJ's Takeaway* with fish & chips and burgers, and the *Port Douglas Bakery*. The *Court House Hotel* on the corner of Macrossan and Wharf Sts has an outdoor eating area with meals ranging from $7 to $10.

In the centre of Macrossan St, opposite the Central Hotel, *Thai By Night* has excellent curries, salads and seafood dishes ranging from $12 to $16, and a takeaway menu with main dishes from $7 to $12. On the same side of the road, *Bandito's* is a casual Mexican cafe with main meals around $15. Across the road at No 25 is the *Jade Inn*, a good place for takeaway Chinese tucker.

The restaurant at the *Coconut Grove Motel*, near the intersection of Davidson and Macrossan Sts, is popular with the locals and said to be good value. The dinner menu offers steaks, seafood, pasta, curries and Tex-Mex meals for around $12.

Port's best-known restaurant is the bizarre *Going Bananas* (☎ (070) 99 5400) at 87 Davidson St. The decor is almost beyond description – a sort of post-cyclone tropical forest look – and the service is often equally strange. It's quite expensive, with main meals from $16 to $25, but well worth the splurge.

Entertainment

On Macrossan St, there's the *Courthouse Hotel*, with live bands at weekends (more often during the peak tourist season), and the *Wave Bar & Nightclub*, with a variety of ntertainment. In the marina, there's *FJ's Nightspot*, a disco/bar which is open until 3 m, and the *Tide Tavern*, which also has ands three nights a week. The *Combines Club* on the waterfront is a good spot for a drink.

Getting There & Away
Bus Coral Coaches (☎ (070) 98 2600) is a Mossman-based bus company which covers the Cairns to Cooktown coastal route, travelling via Port Douglas, Mossman, Daintree, Cape Tribulation and Bloomfield. Bookings and departures in Cairns are made from the transit centre at Trinity Wharf (☎ (070) 31 1577).

Coral Coaches runs several buses daily between Cairns and Port Douglas (1¼ hours, $13.80), Mossman ($15.10), and on to Daintree village ($17.80). From Mossman you can get connections to Mossman Gorge ($5 return). Road conditions permitting, services from Cairns to Cape Tribulation go twice daily ($24.40). They also operate to Cooktown via the inland road every Wednesday, Friday and Sunday ($43.40) and via the Bloomfield Track on Tuesday, Thursday and Saturday ($47.90).

Coral Coaches usually lets you stop over as often as you like along the route, so the trip can be as good as any tour. Owing to the ruggedness of some of the roads, the possibility of delays, and the frequent hopping in and out of the variety of vehicles which cover different sections of the route, riding with Coral Coaches is about as close as Australia comes to travelling in the Third World – and it's fun.

Boat Apart from the Coral Coaches buses, there's the daily Quicksilver fast catamaran service from Port Douglas to Cairns and back. It's $16 one way, $26 return. The Quicksilver booking office (☎ (070) 99 5500) in Port Douglas is in the Marina Mirage complex.

Getting Around
Avis, National and Budget all have offices on Macrossan St. Cheaper local car-rental

operators include Network (☎ (070) 99 5111) and Crocodile (☎ (070) 99 5555).

Port is very compact, and the best way to get around is by bike. Both Port Douglas Bike Hire at 40 Macrossan St and the Port o' Call Lodge hire good bikes for $10 a day.

MOSSMAN (population 1800)
Mossman, the most northerly sugar town and a centre for tropical-fruit growing, has a couple of accommodation places but is of little interest in its own right. At beautiful **Mossman Gorge**, five km west, there are some excellent swimming holes and rapids and a three-km circuit walking track through rainforest. Coral Coaches runs buses up to the gorge from Mossman, or you can take one of the hostel tours from Port Douglas.

Places to Stay & Eat
You can't camp at the Gorge, but there's a creekside caravan park next to the swimming pool at the northern end of Mossman. The old green and cream *Exchange Hotel* in the centre of town has basic but clean pub rooms at $10/20 for singles/doubles, or there's the *Demi-View Motel* (☎ (070) 98 1277) at 41 Front St (the main street) with rooms at $45/50.

The best place for lunch is *Who's Who Coffee Lounge*, in Mill St opposite the Exchange Hotel, with excellent sandwiches and cakes.

DAINTREE
The highway continues 35 km beyond Mossman to the tiny village of Daintree, passing the turn-off to the Daintree River ferry after 24 km. In Daintree village, the **Butterfly Farm** at Barratt Creek is open daily from 10 am to 4 pm. The small **Timber Museum** is worth a look, although the pieces for sale carry quite astronomical price tags.

Five km beyond Daintree village, along Stewarts Creek Rd, is a coffee plantation which, apart from coffee, also has an extensive range of exotic fruit and nut trees, and a signposted rainforest walk. Owned by a very friendly old hippie, it's open daily from 10 am to 4.30 pm; entry is $4.50.

Daintree River Tours

A number of operators offer river trips on the Daintree from various points between the ferry and Daintree village. It's certainly a worthwhile activity. Bird life is prolific, and in the colder months (April to September) croc sightings are common, especially on sunny days when the tide is low, as they love to sun themselves on the exposed banks.

Many of the tours which depart from the ferry crossing are very much in it for the quick buck, and their boats reflect this – gimmicky colours, and one even calls itself a 'train'. The more low-key Daintree River & Cruise Centre, four km beyond the ferry turn-off on the Mossman to Daintree road, has three boats taking from 30 to 52 passengers. The trips take one hour, cost $10 and depart daily at 9.50 am and 1.10, 2.15 and 3.30 pm. A longer tour (1½ hours) departs daily at 11.10 am and costs $15.

There are several smaller operators. Chris Dahlberg's Specialised River Tours (☎ (070) 98 6169), based at Daintree village, takes groups of six people on early-morning river trips; Chris is an enthusiastic bird-watcher and a knowledgeable guide. The two-hour trips depart at 6 and 8.15 am and cost $22. Big River Cruises (☎ (070) 90 7515), between the Cape Trib turn-off and the ferry crossing, also take small groups, with 2½-hour tours at 10.30 am and 1.30 pm at $22, and a night cruise at $55.

Places to Stay

The Daintree Riverview Caravan Park has tent sites for $12 and there are on-site vans for $32.

There are several B&Bs in Daintree. The excellent Red Mill House (☎ (070) 98 6169) in the centre of town has two comfortable twin rooms, lovely spacious gardens and a pool. The cost is from $50 a double and includes a full breakfast on the balcony. Views of the Daintree (☎ (070) 98 6118), on Stewart Creek Rd, is a modern homestead with great views over the big river. There are

two separate double rooms with en-suites $95, including breakfast.

There's also the new Daintree Ecotouri Lodge (☎ (070) 98 6100), with classy timb lodges starting at $285 a double.

Places to Eat

Barney's Place, a casual cafe in the centre Daintree, has lunches from $7 to $12 ar dinners at $14. Across the road, the B Barramundi at the Timber Museum has ai outdoor eating area and serves sandwiche burgers and, of course, barramundi. There also the restaurant at the Daintree Ecotouri Lodge, which is quite expensive but ver good. Nearby, the Daintree Tea House boas barramundi with trimmings for $9.50

CAPE TRIBULATION AREA

After crossing the Daintree River by ferr it's another 34 km of alternating paved ar unpaved road, with a few hills and cree crossings, to Cape Tribulation. The road quite good and, unless there has been excep tionally heavy rain, conventional vehicle can easily make it, with care, to Cape Tribu lation.

Cape Tribulation was named by Captai Cook, since it was a little north of here th his troubles started when his ship ran on t the Endeavour Reef. Mt Sorrow was als named by Cook.

In the '70s, much of this coast was seldom-visited hippie outpost, with settle ments like Cedar Bay, north of Cape Tri between Bloomfield and Cooktown. Thes days, Cape Tribulation is becoming mor and more popular with visitors. It's a incredibly beautiful stretch of coast, and i one of the few places in Australia wher tropical rainforest meets the sea.

Remember, however, that this is rainfore: – you'll need to take mosquito repellent wit you. Approaching Cape Trib from the soutt the last bank is at Mossman. You can ge petrol at two or three places between Mossma and Cooktown by this coastal route.

Getting There & Away

See the Port Douglas section for details o

To Bloomfield River (22 km),
Wujal Wujal Aboriginal community,
Bloomfield & Cooktown

Mt Halcyon
(874 m)

Pilgrim Sands
Holiday Park

Mt Pieter Botte
(928 m)

Mt Sorrow

Cape
Tribulation

PK's Jungle Village
Jungle Lodge

Shop & Petrol

Myall   Creek

CAPE TRIBULATION
NATIONAL PARK

Mt Hemmant

Noah   Creek

National Park
Camping Ground

Noah Beach

Marrdja Botanical Walk

Thornton Peak
(1375 m)

Table
Mountain

Thornton Beach Kiosk

Heritage Lodge

Turpentine   Road

Thornton Beach

Inn the Rainforest

Lync-Haven

Mt
Hutchinson

Alexandra
Bay

Hutchinson

Bailey Hill

Crocodylus
Village

Floraville Tea Garden
Cow Bay Hotel
Rainforest Retreat

Matt
Lock's

Buchanan   Creek Rd

Cow Bay

Daintree Rainforest
Environmental Centre

Cable Ferry

Mt Alexander

Club
Daintree

Cape   Kimberley   Road

Daintree   River

Cape
Kimberley

To
Daintree

Snapper
Island

Trinity
Bay

**Around Cape
Tribulation**

To Mossman

0   3   6 km

QUEENSLAND

the buses between Cairns, Port Douglas and
Cape Trib.

Some excellent deals can be found at most
of the hostels in Cairns combining tours and
transport to Cape Tribulation with hostel
accommodation – for instance $69 including
one night's accommodation or $79 including
two nights.

It's quite easy to hitch, since beyond the
Daintree ferry all vehicles *have* to head to
Cape Trib – there's nowhere else to go!

Daintree River to Cape Tribulation

Ten km back from Daintree village, on the
Mossman to Daintree road, is the five-km
road to the Daintree River ferry and Cape
Trib. Ferries operate every few minutes from
6 am to midnight and charge $5 for a car, $3
for a motorbike and $1 for a pedestrian.

Three km beyond the ferry, Cape Kimberley Rd leads down to Cape Kimberley beach,
five km away. About nine km from the ferry,
just after you cross the spectacular Heights
of Alexandra range, is the **Daintree Rainforest Environmental Centre** – an excellent
information centre with rainforest displays,
a self-guided forest boardwalk and an audiovisual show. It's open daily from 9 am to 5
pm; entry is $8.

About 12 km from the ferry you reach
Buchanan Creek Rd, which is the turn-off for
Cow Bay (5.5 km) and Crocodylus Village.

Further on, the road strikes the shore at
Thornton Beach. The **Marrdja Botanical
Walk**, at Noah Creek, is an interesting 800-
metre boardwalk through rainforest and
mangroves. **Noah Beach**, with a National
Parks camping ground, is eight km before
Cape Trib.

Places to Stay & Eat At Cape Kimberley
beach, *Club Daintree* (☎ (070) 90 7500) is a
secluded beachfront camping park with
camp sites for $5 per person, tent-cabins for
$8 per person and four-share cabins for $12
per person.

Crocodylus Village (☎ (070) 98 9166) is
an associate-YHA hostel 2.5 km off the main
Cape Trib road, down Buchanan Creek Rd.
It is set in the rainforest and has spacious,

Rainforest

Nearly all of Australia was covered in rainforest 50 million years ago, but by the time Europeans arrived, only about 1% of the rainforest was left. Today, logging and clearing for farms have reduced that to less than 0.3% – about 20,000 sq km. More than half of this, and nearly all the *tropical* rainforest, is in Queensland.

The biggest area of surviving virgin rainforest covers the ranges from south of Mossman up to Cooktown. It's called the Greater Daintree. This is one of the few places on earth where evolution has continued, virtually uninterrupted, since flowering plants first appeared about 130 million years ago.

Throughout the 1980s, a series of battles over the future of the forests was waged between conservationists, the timber industry and the Queensland government. The conservationists argued that apart from the normal reasons for saving rainforests – such as combating the greenhouse effect and preserving species' habitats – this forest region has special value because it's such a diverse genetic storehouse. The timber industry's case, aside from job losses, was that only a small percentage of the rainforest was used for timber – and then not destructively, since cutting is selective and time is left for the forest to regenerate before being logged again.

In 1983, the local Douglas Shire Council decided to bulldoze a gravel road 22 km through the forest from just north of Cape Tribulation to the Bloomfield River. Cape Trib became the scene of a classic 'greenies versus bulldozers' blockade. Several months and numerous arrests later, the road builders won and the Bloomfield Track was opened, despite serious concerns that soil run-off from the track would wash into the ocean and damage the Great Barrier Reef.

The greenies may have lost that battle but the national exposure of the blockade indirectly led to the Federal government's moves in 1987 to nominate Queensland's wet tropical rainforests for World Heritage listing. Despite strenuous resistance by the Queensland timber industry and state government, the area was listed in 1988, with one of the key outcomes being a total ban on commercial logging in the area.

Stretching from Townsville to Cooktown, the Wet Tropics World Heritage Area covers 900,000 hectares of the coast and hinterland and includes the Atherton Tableland, Mission Beach, Mossman Gorge, Jourama Falls, Mt Spec and the Daintree-Cape Tribulation area. The scenery is diverse and spectacular, ranging from coastal mangroves and eucalypt forests to some of the oldest rainforests in the world.

Despite the recent discord, a 1993 survey found that 80% of north Queenslanders now support the wet tropics area. Part of the reason for the turnaround has been the buzzword of the 1990s – ecotourism – north Queensland's green gold. With reef- and rainforest-related tourism easily eclipsing sugar production to become the far north's biggest industry, the rainforest has become a vital part of the north's livelihood. The challenge now is to learn how to manage and minimise the environmental impact of the recent enormous growth in tourism and population. ■

elevated canvas cabins. There's a pool, small store, cafe and bar. Nightly costs in the 16- to 20-bed dorms are $13 ($14 nonmembers). There are also cabins with a double bed, six bunks and bathrooms – these cost $45 a double, plus $10 for each extra person. You can hire bikes and the hostel vehicle runs guests to and from Cow Bay beach. The hostel also organises quite a few activities, including informative guided walks through the forests each morning and evening, half-day horse rides ($35), a three-hour sunrise paddle trek ($30 with breakfast) and a two-day sea-kayaking trip to Snapper Island ($129 with everything supplied).

Matt Lock's service station on Buchanan Creek Rd has petrol and food. Back on the Cape Trib road, close to the Buchanan Creek Rd turn-off, are the *Floravilla Tea Garden* and the new *Cow Bay Hotel* (☎ (070) 98 9011), which has motel units at $55/60 and bistro meals. Across the road there's also the *Rainforest Retreat* (☎ (070) 98 9101), with self-contained motel-style units at $40/60, family units at $80 and a 20-bed bunk house at $13 per person. Next door is the *Tropica Palms Restaurant*.

About three km south of Cooper Creek is *Lync-Haven* (☎ (070) 98 9155), a 40-acre property with walking trails and plenty of wildlife. There are individual tent sites at $8.50, on-site vans at $30 and self-contained six-berth cabins from $65 a double. One km north, *Inn the Rainforest* (☎ (070) 98 9162) has three comfortable self-contained units in a serene setting. The spacious family unit costs $75 a night, and the double and twin units are $50.

On Turpentine Rd, which runs inland of Cooper Creek near Thornton Beach, the secluded *Heritage Lodge* (☎ (070) 98 9138) has excellent facilities and motel-style units from $99 a double.

At Thornton Beach, the *Thornton Beach Kiosk* is a laid-back beachfront eatery, with takeaways and a bar/cafe with good meals from $5 to $10. Further north at Noah Beach there's a National Parks camping ground with toilets and water – it's a self-registration site, and permits can be booked through the rangers at Cape Trib (☎ (070) 98 0052).

Cape Tribulation

Cape Tribulation is famed for its superb scenery, with long beaches stretching north and south from the low, forest-covered cape. If you want to do more than relax on the beach, PK's Jungle Village organises a good range of activities including reef-snorkelling trips ($69), fishing, paddle trekking ($35 for half a day), horse riding ($39 for half a day), night walks ($16.80) and half-day guided bushwalks ($15.80); there are also plans afoot for a sea-kayaking trip (around $80). The walks are great value, and for the really energetic, there are also mountain bikes for hire.

The **Bat House**, opposite PK's, is a small rainforest information and education centre, open daily from 10 am to 4 pm.

Places to Stay & Eat Cape Tribulation has a well-appointed hostel, *PK's Jungle Village* (☎ (070) 98 0040). It's a fun-oriented place with a strong party atmosphere, so if you're looking for peace and quiet you'll be better off down at Crocodylus Village or at the more up-market Jungle Lodge. PK's Jungle Village has comfortable log cabins, a pool and bar and a restaurant which serves break-

fasts for $4 and evening meals from $8. The nightly cost in an eight-bed cabin is $14 per person. There are also double rooms for $44, or you can camp in the grounds for $7 per person.

The *Jungle Lodge* (☎ (070) 98 0086), off the road just before the cape, has up-market motel-style accommodation, some self-contained with aircon and all with en-suites. Prices range from $80 to $120, shared among one to four people. The lodge has a pool and a restaurant.

Opposite PK's, the *Boardwalk Takeaway* opens from 8 am to 7 pm and serves good breakfasts, burgers and sandwiches at very reasonable prices.

Just off the road, three km north of PK's, the *Pilgrim Sands Holiday Park* (☎ (070) 98 0030) has camp sites for $10.50, one self-contained cabin for $43 (with four beds), and two-bedroom units (with five beds and bathroom) for $58. Bed linen can be supplied for a small charge. The Pilgrim Sands closes for the Wet, from November until Easter.

Three km south of the cape, the *Coconut Beach Rainforest Resort* (☎ (070) 98 0033) has timber lodges with all the mod-cons at $165/230 for singles/doubles, including breakfast.

CAPE TRIBULATION TO COOKTOWN

Just north of Cape Tribulation, the Bloomfield Track (4WD only) heads through the forest as far as **Wujal Wujal** Aboriginal community 22 km north, on the far side of the Bloomfield River crossing. Even for 4WD vehicles, the Bloomfield River and some of the track are impassable after heavy rain.

From Wujal Wujal another dirt road – rough but usually passable in a conventional vehicle in the Dry – heads 46 km north through the tiny settlements of **Bloomfield**, **Rossville** and **Helenvale** to meet the main Cairns to Cooktown road (also dirt) 28 km before Cooktown.

Places to Stay & Eat

At Helenvale, the *Lion's Den* is a good place to halt – it's a colourful 1875 bush pub. You can camp beside the river and the pub has a few rooms.

The *Home Rule Rainforest Lodge* (☎ (070) 60 3925) is a couple of km towards the coast from Rossville, 43 km south of Cooktown. It has cheap share accommodation ($12) and cooking facilities, or you can buy meals for $8. The lodge also has cheap packages from Cairns.

The *Bloomfield Wilderness Lodge* (☎ (070) 35 9166) is close to the mouth of the Bloomfield River and aims to make holes in fat wallets – $885/1260 for a single/double for three all-inclusive nights (minimum stay), and children are 'not encouraged'.

The *Bloomfield Beach Resort* (☎ (070) 60 8207), 11 km north of the Bloomfield River, is a little more affordable, with tent sites for $8 ($14 with tent supplied) and cabins at $15 per person on a share basis or $60 for the whole cabin. It also offers tours and river cruises.

CAIRNS TO COOKTOWN – THE INLAND ROAD

The 'main' road up from Cairns loops through Kuranda, Mareeba, Mt Molloy, the wolfram-mining town of Mt Carbine, Palmer River crossing and Lakeland, where the road up to the Cape York Peninsula splits off. Most of the second half of this 341-km road is unpaved, and often corrugated.

In **Mt Molloy**, the *National Hotel* (☎ (070) 94 1133) has cheap accommodation. James Venture Mulligan, the man who started both the Palmer River and Hodgkinson River gold rushes, is buried in the Mt Molloy cemetery. At the **Palmer River** crossing there's a cafe/service station and a camping ground. The 1873 to 1883 gold rush, for which the Palmer River is famous, happened in very remote country about 70 km west of here. Its main towns were Palmerville and Maytown, of which very little is left today.

Shortly before Cooktown, the road passes **Black Mountain**, a pile of thousands of granite boulders. It's said there are ways between the huge rocks which will take you under the hill

from one side to the other, but people have died trying to find them. Black Mountain is known to the Aborigines as Kalcajagga – 'Place of the Spears'. The colour comes not from the rocks themselves, but from the lichen which grows on them.

COOKTOWN (population 1340)

Cooktown can claim to have been Australia's first British settlement. From June to August 1770, Captain Cook beached his barque *Endeavour* there and, during that time, Joseph Banks, the chief naturalist, took the chance to study Australian flora and fauna along the banks of the Endeavour River. Banks collected 186 plant species and wrote the first European description of a kangaroo. The northern side of the river has scarcely changed since that first visit.

The explorers had amicable contacts with the local Aborigines, but race relations in the area turned sour a century later when Cooktown was founded as the unruly port for the 1873 to 1883 Palmer River gold rush 140 km south-west. Hell's Gate, a narrow pass on the track between Cooktown and the Palmer River, was the scene of frequent ambushes as Aborigines tried to stop their lands being overrun. Battle Camp, about 60 km inland from Cooktown, was the site of a major battle between Whites and Cape York Aborigines.

In 1874, before Cairns was even thought of, Cooktown was the second biggest town in Queensland. At its peak there were no less than 94 pubs, almost as many brothels, and the population was over 30,000! As many as half of these were Chinese, whose industrious presence led to some wild race riots.

After the gold rush ended, cyclones and a WW II evacuation came close to killing Cooktown. The opening of the excellent James Cook Historical Museum in 1970 started to bring in some visitor dollars, although Cooktown's population is still only around 1300 and just three pubs remain.

The effort of getting to Cooktown is rewarded not just by the atmosphere but by some fascinating reminders of the area's

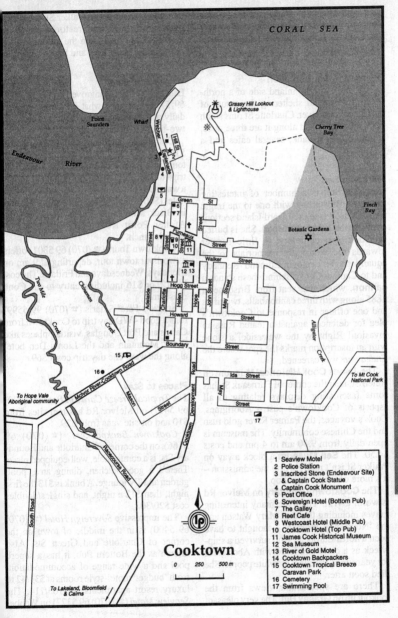

Cooktown

0   250   500 m

1 Seaview Motel
2 Police Station
3 Inscribed Stone (Endeavour Site) & Captain Cook Statue
4 Captain Cook Monument
5 Post Office
6 Sovereign Hotel (Bottom Pub)
7 The Galley
8 Reef Cafe
9 Westcoast Hotel (Middle Pub)
10 Cooktown Hotel (Top Pub)
11 James Cook Historical Museum
12 Sea Museum
13 River of Gold Motel
14 Cooktown Backpackers
15 Cooktown Tropical Breeze Caravan Park
16 Cemetery
17 Swimming Pool

CORAL SEA

Endeavour River

Point Saunders

Wharf

Grassy Hill Lookout & Lighthouse

Cherry Tree Bay

Finch Bay

Botanic Gardens

Two Mile Creek

Chinaman Creek

Alligator Creek

Hall St
Webber
Esplanade
Green St
Furneaux Street
Street
Walker Street
Hogg Street
Howard Street
Boundary Street
Ida Street
Adelaide Street
Charlotte Street
Helen Street
Hope Street
John Street
May Street
May Street
Street

To Mt Cook National Park

To Hope Vale Aboriginal community

McIvor River-Cooktown Road

Mason Street

Cooktown Development Road

Racecourse Road

South Road

To Lakeland, Bloomfield & Cairns

QUEENSLAND

past. With a vehicle, you can use the town as a base for visiting the Quinkan rock art near Laura or even for travelling as far as Lakefield National Park.

Orientation & Information

Cooktown is on the inland side of a north-pointing headland sheltering the mouth of the Endeavour River. Charlotte St runs south from the wharf, and along it are three pubs, a post office, a bank, several cafes and a restaurant.

Things to See

Charlotte St has a number of interesting monuments starting with one to the tragic Mary Watson (see the Lizard Island section) opposite the Sovereign Hotel. She is buried in Cooktown cemetery. A little further towards the wharf are memorials to the equally tragic explorer Edmund Kennedy and to Captain Cook. Behind these stands a cannon, which was sent from Brisbane in 1885 along with three cannonballs, two rifles and one officer in response to Cooktown's plea for defences against a feared Russian invasion! Right by the waterside, a stone with an inscription marks the spot where the *Endeavour* was careened.

The **James Cook Historical Museum** on Helen St, near the corner of Furneaux St, has some fascinating displays relating to all aspects of Cooktown's past – Aborigines, Cook's voyages, the Palmer River gold rush and the Chinese community. The museum is open daily from 9.30 am to 4 pm and costs $4.50. The **Sea Museum** a block away on Walker St isn't really worth the admission – it's more of a souvenir shop.

The **Cooktown Cemetery** on McIvor Rd is worth a visit. There are many interesting graves including those of Mary Watson and the 'Normanby Woman' – thought to have been a north European who survived a shipwreck as a child and lived with Aborigines for years until 'rescued' by white people. She died soon after.

There are spectacular views from the lookout up on **Grassy Hill**. The very pleasant

Botanic Gardens, off Walker St, were first planted in 1886 and restored in 1984. Walking trails lead from the gardens to the beaches at Cherry Tree and Finch bays.

Organised Tours

Endeavour River Mangrove Cruises (☎ (070) 69 5712) does just what its name suggests daily at 2 pm (and some days at 9 am); the two-hour scenic cruise costs $18.

Cooktown Destinations (☎ (070) 69 5166), operated by the hostel, offers various tours in a seven-seater 4WD, including day trips to the Split Rock Aboriginal site ($70), a waterfalls tour with a visit to the Lion's Den hotel ($60), and a sightseeing tour that takes in Black Mountain, Annan Gorge and the Archer Point Roadhouse ($55). Costs include lunch.

Cooktown Tours (☎ (070) 69 5301) offers a two-hour town tour, departing at 9 am on Mondays, Wednesdays and Fridays. The cost is $12, or $16 including entry to the Cook museum.

Strikie's Feral Safaris (☎ (070) 99 5599) runs a good 4WD day trip to Cooktown from Cairns and Port Douglas, visiting places like Black Mountain and the Lion's Den hotel along the way. The day trip costs $69.

Places to Stay

The *Tropical Breeze Caravan Park* (☎ (070) 69 5417) on McIvor Rd has tent sites from $10 and on-site vans from $29.

Cooktown Backpackers (☎ (070) 69 5166), on the corner of Charlotte and Boundary Sts, is a comfortable, well-equipped place. There's a good kitchen, dining area, pool, garden and TV lounge. A bunk is $13 the first night, then $12 a night, and singles/doubles cost $20/30.

The impressive *Sovereign Hotel* (☎ (070) 69 5400) is in the middle of town on the corner of Charlotte and Green Sts. Also known as the Bottom Pub, it has a superb pool and a wide range of accommodation, from 'budget' motel-style rooms at $31/42 to luxury resort apartments at $103/114. The *Seaview Motel* (☎ (070) 69 5377) on Webber

...splanade has good units from $55 a double,
...r the modern *River of Gold Motel* (☎ (070)
...9 5222) on the corner of Hope and Walker
...ts has rooms from $53/64.

Places to Eat

...he *Cooktown Hotel* (Top Pub) has inexpen-
...ive bar meals, and its tavern has excellent
...teaks for around $11; it also has a great beer
...arden. The *Sovereign Hotel* also has reason-
...bly priced meals in the bar downstairs, and
... very pleasant balcony restaurant upstairs
...vith excellent meals ranging from $8 to $16.

The *Galley*, next to the Sovereign Hotel,
...as a variety of good-value food including
...izzas, salads and curries; a large pizza is
...bout $12. The *Reef Cafe*, on Charlotte St,
...lso has a wide range of takeaway or eat-in
...meals and sandwiches.

The *Endeavour Inn*, just beyond the Reef
...Cafe, is a more up-market licensed restau-
...ant, with seafood mains around $18.

Getting There & Away

Air Flight West (☎ (070) 51 0718) operates
...lights between Cairns and Cooktown twice
...a day on weekdays and once on Saturdays
...and Sundays, costing $97 one way. Hinter-
...and Aviation in Cairns (☎ (070) 35 9323)
...operates scenic flights between Cairns and
...Cooktown, with drop-offs at Cow Bay. You
...need at least four people, but the price per
...head is a worthwhile saving on the scheduled
...flights.

Bus Coral Coaches (☎ (070) 98 2600) travels
...from Cairns to Cooktown via the inland road
...on Wednesdays, Fridays and Sundays
...($43.40, 6½ hours) and via the Bloomfield
...Track on Tuesdays, Thursdays and Satur-
...days ($47.90, 8½ hours

Getting Around

The Hire Shop (☎ (070) 69 5601), on
...Webber Esplanade just north of the Sover-
...eign Hotel, has mokes, scooters, cars and
...boats for hire.

LIZARD ISLAND

Lizard Island, the furthest north of the
Barrier Reef resort islands, is about 100 km
from Cooktown. It was named by Joseph
Banks after Captain Cook spent a day there,
trying to find a way out through the reef to
the open sea.

A Queensland tragedy took place here in
1881 when a settler's wife, Mary Watson,
took to sea in a large metal pot with her son
and a Chinese servant, after Aborigines
killed her other servant while her husband
was away fishing. The three eventually died of
thirst on a barren island to the north, Mary
leaving a diary of their terrible last days. Their
tragic story is told at the Cooktown museum.

The island has superb beaches, great
swimming and snorkelling, the remains of
the Watsons' cottage, a pricey resort and a
National Parks camping ground. There are
plenty of bushwalks and bird life, and great
views from Cook's Look, the highest point
on the island, from where Captain Cook
surveyed the area in search of a passage
through the reef.

Places to Stay

There is a small National Parks camping
ground at Watson's Bay. It has a fireplace, pit
toilet, picnic table and a hand-pumped water
supply 250 metres away. Camping permits
are available from the National Parks office
(☎ (070) 52 3096) at 10 McLeod St in Cairns,
and you must take all supplies with you as the
resort won't sell you any. You'll also need
charcoal for the barbecues as all timber on
the island, including driftwood, is protected.

In the resort, accommodation including all
meals and use of the facilities costs from a
mere $437 per day. As the island is relatively
isolated, it's been a favourite retreat for
celebrities, and a popular stop for yachties,
for many years.

Getting There & Away

Sunstate (☎ (070) 50 4000) flies from Cairns
for $143 one way.

QUEENSLAND

Cape York & the Gulf

CAPE YORK PENINSULA

The Cape York Peninsula is one of the wildest and least populated parts of Australia. The Tip, as it is called, is the most northerly point on the mainland of Australia, and between here and Papua New Guinea, just 150 km away, scattered islands dot the Torres Strait.

Getting up to the north along the rough and rugged Peninsula Developmental Road is still one of Australia's great road adventures. It's a trip for the tough and experienced since the roads are *all* dirt, and even at the height of the Dry there are some difficult river crossings. In the last few years, several tour operators have sprung up to offer this adventure to those who can't or don't want to go it alone.

Ron and Viv Moon's book *Cape York, An Adventurer's Guide* provides all the necessary detail. It costs about $20 and is available from many Queensland bookshops.

Getting There & Away

Air Sunstate Airlines (☎ (070) 50 4000) flies daily from Cairns to Bamaga ($261), Lizard Island ($143) and Thursday Island ($290). Ansett flies to Weipa ($209). Flight West (☎ (070) 35 9511 or through Ansett) also operates a daily service through the Gulf and the Cape York Peninsula, and to Bamaga and the Torres Strait Islands.

The airborne Peninsula Mail Run, claimed to be the longest in the world, flies to remote cattle stations along the peninsula every weekday. They also take passengers along, with round trips costing from $140 to $275, depending on the length of the trip. For more details, contact Cape York Air Services (☎ (070) 35 9399).

Driving to the Top Every year, more and more hardy travellers, equipped with their own 4WD vehicles or trail bikes, make the long haul up to the top of Cape York. Apart from being able to say you have been as far

north as you can get in Australia, you als[o] test yourself against some pretty hard goin[g] and see some wild and wonderful countr[y] into the bargain. It's no easy trip, and durin[g] the wet season nothing moves by road at al[l].

The travelling season is from mid-May t[o] mid-November but the beginning and end o[f] that period are borderline, depending on ho[w] late or early the wet season is. The best tim[e] is June to September. Conventional vehicle[s] can usually reach Coen and even, with car[e] and skill, get across to Weipa on the Gulf o[f] Carpentaria but it's *very* rough going. If yo[u] want to continue north from the Weipa turn[-] off to Cape York, you'll need 4WD, a winc[h] and plenty of strong steel wire.

The major problem is the many rive[r] crossings; even as late as June or July the[y] will still be swift-flowing and frequentl[y] alter their course. The rivers often have ver[y] steep banks. The Great Dividing Range run[s] right up the spine of the peninsula and river[s] run east and west off it. Although the river[s] in the south of the peninsula only flow in th[e] wet season, those further north flow yea[r] round.

The ideal set-up for a Cape York expedi[-] tion is two 4WD vehicles travelling togethe[r] – one can haul the other out where necessary. You can also make it to the top on motorcy[-] cles, floating the machines across the wide[r] rivers. There are usually large truck inne[r] tubes left at the river crossings for this purpose. Beware of crocodiles!

After the Archer River Roadhouse, 65 km beyond Coen, Weipa (on the west coast) and usually Bamaga (just south of the Tip) are the only places for a regular supply of petro[l] and mechanical repairs. Visits to the RACQ and the National Parks office in Cairns are well worthwhile before you head north.

You don't need a permit to visit Aboriginal communities on the peninsula or traverse their land, but it's advisable to make contact beforehand by letter or radio phone. The same applies to Torres Strait Islander communities. Apart from Bamaga, most of the mainland Aboriginal communities are well off the main track north, and do not have any facilities or accommodation for travellers.

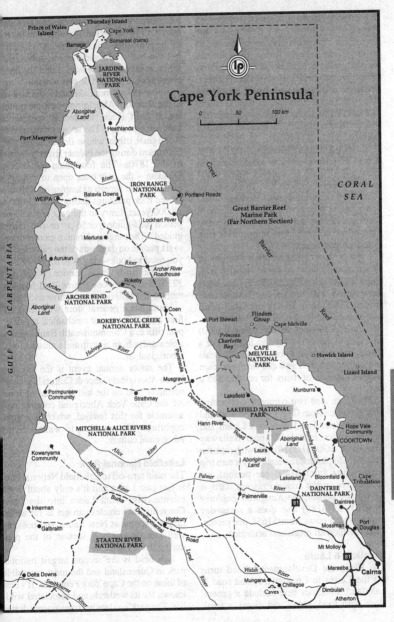

Cape York Peninsula

0   50   100 km

QUEENSLAND

Organised Tours A host of companies operate 4WD tours from Cairns to Cape York. The trips generally range from six to 16 days, and take in Laura, the Quinkan rock-art galleries, Lakefield National Park, Coen, Weipa, Indian Head Falls, Bamaga, Somerset and Cape York itself. Most trips also visit Thursday Island, as well as taking in Cape Tribulation, Cooktown and/or the Palmer River gold fields at the start or end of the odyssey.

Travel on standard tours is in 4WDs with five to 12 passengers, accommodation is in tents and all food is supplied. Some 4WD tour companies include Oz Tours Safaris, Australian Outback Travel, Heritage 4WD Tours, New Look Adventures and Wild Track Adventure Safaris, the last two being among the most experienced operators with excellent reputations.

Most of the companies offer a variety of alternatives, such as to fly or sail one way, and travel overland the other. Typical costs are around $1200 for a six-day fly/drive tour, around $1800 for a 16-day overland safari, and over $2000 for a 12-day sail/drive tour.

Cape York Motorcycle Adventures (☎ (070) 58 1148) offers a five-day trip for $700 or a 10-day trip for $1450. Prices include all meals and equipment, and you can ride your own bike or hire one of theirs for another $85 a day.

There are also two companies operating luxury cruises from Cairns to Cape York and Thursday Island and back, via Lizard and several other islands. Clipper Sailaway Cruises (☎ (070) 31 2516) has two boats: the *Atlantic Clipper* does an eight-day return trip which costs from $1400 per person, and seven days on the *Island Princess* starts at $1000 per person; the *Kangaroo Explorer* (☎ (070) 55 8188) also does a seven-day cruise which costs from $1655 per person. Costs include all meals and activities.

Lakeland & Laura

The Peninsula Developmental Road turns off the Cairns to Cooktown inland road at Lakeland. Facilities here include a general store with food, petrol and diesel, a small caravan park and a hotel/motel. From Lakeland it's 734 km to Bamaga, almost at the top of the peninsula. The first stretch to Laura not too bad – just some corrugations, potholes, grids and causeways – and the creek crossings are bridged. It gets worse.

About 48 km from Lakeland is the turn-off to the **Quinkan Aboriginal rock-art galleries** at Split Rock, located in spectacular sandstone country. The art was executed by Aboriginal tribes whose descendants were decimated during the Palmer River gold rush of the 1870s. The four main galleries at Quinkan – the only ones open to visitors contain some superb examples of well-preserved rock paintings dating back 13,000 to 14,000 years. Entry to the park costs $3 per person (self-guided) or $6 per person (ranger guided). The rangers also take groups of one to six people on day tours of the galleries, but you need to book – ring ☎ (070) 60 3214.

Trezise Bush Guide Service (☎ (070) 60 3236) also offers one-, three- and four-day tours to the galleries from Cairns and Laura.

Laura has a general store with food and fuel, a place for minor mechanical repairs, a post office, a Commonwealth Bank agency, a pleasant pub, an airstrip and a museum with Aboriginal art.

The major annual event is the two-day Laura Aboriginal Dance & Cultural Festival, normally held on the last weekend of June. All the Cape York Aboriginal communities assemble for this festival, which is a great opportunity for outsiders to witness living Aboriginal culture.

Lakefield National Park

The main turn-off to Lakefield National Park is just past Laura and it's only about a 45 minute drive from Laura into the park. Conventional vehicles can get as far as the ranger's station at New Laura, and possibly well into the northern section of the park during the dry season.

Lakefield is the second largest national park in Queensland and the most accessible of those on the Cape York Peninsula. It's best known for its wetlands and associated wildlife. The park's extensive river system drains into Princess Charlotte Bay on its northern perimeter. This is the only national park on the peninsula where fishing is permitted, and a canoe is a good way to investigate the park. Watch out for crocs! You can bush camp at a number of sites – get permits from the rangers at New Laura (☎ (070) 60 3260) or Lakefield (☎ (070) 60 3271), further north in the park.

The wide sweep of Princess Charlotte Bay, which includes the coastal section of Lakefield National Park, is the site of some of Australia's biggest rock-art galleries. Unfortunately, this stretch of coast is extremely hard to reach except from the sea.

Laura to Archer River Roadhouse
It's 135 km from Laura to **Musgrave** with its historic fortress telegraph station, built in 1887. Before Musgrave, there's the Hann River crossing and a roadhouse at the 75-km mark. Musgrave itself has petrol, diesel, food, beer, an STD phone, a cafe and an airstrip.

Coen, 245 km north of Laura, is virtually the capital of the peninsula with a pub, general store, hospital, school and police station. You can get mechanical repairs done here. Coen has an airstrip and a racecourse where picnic races are held each August. The whole peninsula closes down for this event, even the mining town of Weipa. There are a few free camp sites both in and around town.

Apart from a few telegraph stations, the only habitation on the 402-km stretch from Coen to Bamaga is the **Archer River Roadhouse**, 65 km north of Coen. This is the final stop for regular petrol and mechanical repairs; you can also camp and get a hot shower and buy your last supplies before Bamaga.

Northern National Parks
Four national parks can be reached from the main track north of Coen. To stay at any of them, you must be totally self-sufficient. Only a few km north of Coen, before Archer River Roadhouse, you can turn west to **Rokeby-Croll Creek National Park** and **Archer Bend National Park** – the ranger station is in Rokeby, about 45 km off the main track. Access is for 4WD only.

These little-visited parks cover a large area including the McIlwraith Range in Rokeby and, in the west of very remote Archer Bend, the junction of the Coen and Archer rivers. There are no facilities but bush camping is permitted at a number of river sites in Rokeby. These parks are best explored by bushwalkers.

Around 21 km north of the Archer River Roadhouse is the turn-off to Portland Roads, the Lockhart River Aboriginal community and **Iron Range National Park**. The 150-km road into the tiny coastal settlement of Portland Roads passes through the national park. While still pretty rough, this track has been improved. If you visit the national park, register with the ranger on arrival. It has the rugged hills of the Janet and Tozer ranges, beautiful coastal scenery and Australia's largest area of lowland rainforest, plus some animals which are also found in New Guinea but no further south in Australia. Bush camping is permitted.

The fourth of the northern national parks is the **Jardine River**.

Weipa (population 2500)
Weipa is 135 km from the main track. The southern turn-off to it is about 20 km north of the Iron Range turn-off, and this road has recently been upgraded – you can cover the distance in just a couple of hours. You can also get to Weipa from Batavia Downs, which is a little further up the main track and has a 19th-century homestead. The two approaches converge about halfway along.

Weipa is a modern mining town which works the world's largest deposits of bauxite (the ore from which aluminium is processed). The mining company, Comalco, runs regular tours of its operations from May to December. The town has a wide range of facilities including a motel, hotel and camping ground.

In the vicinity, there's interesting country to explore, good fishing and some pleasant camp sites.

North to the Jardine
Back on the main track, after Batavia Downs there are almost 200 km of rough road and

numerous river crossings (the Wenlock and the Dulhunty being the two major ones) before you reach the Jardine River ferry crossing. Between the Wenlock River and the Jardine ferry there are two possible routes: the more direct but rougher old route (116 km), and the more circuitous but quicker new route (159 km), which branches off the old route about one km past the South Alice Creek crossing.

If you intend camping further north, you'll need to get a permit from the ranger at **Heathlands**, about 80 km north of the Wenlock and about 12 km from both the old and new roads.

The **Jardine River National Park** stretches east to the coast from the main track. The Jardine River spills more fresh water into the sea than any other river in Australia. It's wild, impenetrable country. There's a good camping spot on the banks of the Jardine at the crossing, and permits must be obtained from the ranger at Heathlands.

The Top

The first settlement north of the Jardine River is the mainly Torres Strait Islander community of **Bamaga**. There's a motel (advance bookings required) and camping grounds at nearby Seisa and Cowral Creek. The town has postal facilities, STD phones, a hospital, Commonwealth Bank agency, supermarket and some petrol (closed Saturday afternoon and Sunday). It's only about 40 km from Bamaga to the very northern tip. Daily ferries run between Bamaga and Thursday Island.

Beyond Bamaga, off the Cape York track but only about 11 km south-east of the cape, is **Somerset** which was established in 1863 as a haven for shipwrecked sailors and to signal to the rest of the world that this was British territory. It was hoped at one time that it might become a major trading centre, a sort of Singapore of north Queensland, but it was closed in 1879 when its functions were moved to Thursday Island, which was also thought more suitable for a pearling industry. The story of Somerset is inextricably linked with the adventurous Jardine family, one of whom stayed on after Somerset was officially closed to run his own cattle stations, coconut plantation and pearling business. He married a Samoan princess and entertained passing British dignitaries. He and his wife are buried at Somerset. Sadly, apart from a few of Jardine's coconut trees, there's nothing much left at Somerset now, but the fishing is good and there are lovely views.

At **Cape York** itself there are two resorts. *Pajinka Wilderness Lodge* (☎ (070) 69 1444), 400 metres from the Tip, is a luxury resort costing from $150/220 per night for singles/doubles. It also has a small camping ground with a kiosk, toilets and showers. *Punsand Bay Private Reserve* (☎ (070) 69 1722) provides more-modest accommodation on the western side of the cape. There are cabins and permanent tents or you can pitch your own in the camping ground. Between June and September, a ferry runs from Punsand Bay to Thursday Island daily (except Sunday) at 7.30 am.

Torres Strait Islands (population 5000)

The Torres Strait Islands have been a part of Queensland since 1879, the best known of them being Thursday Island. The 70 other islands are sprinkled from Cape York in the south almost to New Guinea in the north but only 17 of them are inhabited, and all but three are set aside for islanders. Most visitors to Cape York take a look at Thursday Island or the nearby islands.

Torres Strait Islanders came from Melanesia and Polynesia about 2000 years ago, bringing with them a more material culture than that of the mainland Aborigines. The strait has witnessed violence from the early days right through to WW II, including headhunters, marauding pirates, greedy men in pursuit of pearls, 'blackbirders' and Japanese bombs. Christianity, replacing warlike islander cults, has done well this century. **Possession Island**, an uninhabited national park close to Cape York, was where Captain Cook 'claimed' all the east coast of Australia for England in 1770.

The islands' economy is based on fishing but it's hard to compete with the technology used by outfits on Australia's east coast. There is high islander unemployment and economic difficulties have led to cries for compensation, even independence. In the past, the islanders have not been allowed to share in managing the area's few resources, nor have they been provided with adequate education. The cries for secession will probably bring more autonomy, but not independence.

Thursday Island is hilly, just over three sq km in area and 39 km off Cape York. At one time, it was a major pearling centre and the pearlers' cemeteries tell the tragic tale of what a dangerous occupation it was. Some pearls are still produced here from seeded 'culture farms' which don't offer much employment to the locals. The island has also lost its importance as a halt for vessels but it's still a popular pause for passing yachties.

Thursday Island is an attractive, easygoing place and its main appeal is its cultural mix – Asians, Europeans and Pacific Islanders have all contributed to its history.

Places to Stay & Eat Accommodation and food are available at Thursday Island's one motel and four hotels. The airport is on nearby Horn Island and a ferry links the two islands. There's a camping ground near the wharf on Horn Island, but none on Thursday Island. You can hire boats for fishing trips and cruises. You might be able to find accommodation on other islands by asking around.

Getting There & Around Sunstate and Flight West Airlines fly to most of the inhabited islands. At least two ferry services operate from Bamaga and Punsand Bay to Thursday Island, both taking roughly an hour one way and costing about $50 return.

GULF OF CARPENTARIA

North of Mt Isa and Cloncurry, the Gulf is a sparsely populated region cut by a great number of rivers. During the Wet, the dirt roads turn to mud and even the surfaced roads can be flooded, so June to September is the safest time to visit this area.

Although Burke and Wills were the first Europeans to pass through the Gulf Country, the coast of the Gulf of Carpentaria had been charted by Dutch explorers even before Captain Cook's visit to Australia. The actual coastline of the Gulf is mainly mangrove swamps which is why there is little habitation there.

Two of the settlements in the region, Burketown and Normanton, were founded in the 1860s, before better-known places on the Pacific coast like Cairns and Cooktown came into existence. Europeans settled the area as sheep and cattle country, also in the hope of providing a western port for produce from further east and south in Queensland.

Today the Gulf Country is mainly cattle country. It's a remote, hot, tough region with excellent fishing and a large crocodile population. Mornington Island, in the Gulf itself 120 km north of Burketown, is an Aboriginal community.

The main road into the Gulf region is from Cloncurry to Normanton (378 km, surfaced all the way), with a turn-off to Burketown at the Burke & Wills Roadhouse, which is also the junction of the surfaced road from Julia Creek. Between Cloncurry and Normanton, the flat plain is interrupted by a solitary hill beside the road – Bang Bang Jump-up. There's also an unpaved 332-km road from Camooweal, west of Mt Isa, to Burketown, with a turn-off at the Gregory Downs supply stop for **Lawn Hill National Park**. If you're driving any of these roads, make sure to ask about fuel stops and carry water with you.

For tourist information, advice on road conditions and general enquiries, contact the Gulf Local Authorities Development Association, 55 McLeod St, Cairns (☎ (070) 31 1631).

Fishing

A number of places have been set up especially to cater for people who have become addicted to barramundi fishing, and other cheaper places where the fishing is good. These include: *Sweers Island Resort* (☎ (077) 48 5544), which charges $150 per person per day all inclusive; *Sweers Island Houseboats* (☎ (077) 43 9690), $80; *Birri Fishing Resort* (☎ (077) 45 7277) on Mornington Island, which costs $210 per day including meals, accommodation, all tackle and boat hire; and *Hell's Gate Roadhouse* (☎ (077) 45 8258), 50 km east of the Northern Territory border, which has B&B for $25.

Savannah Guides

The Savannah Guides (☎ (070) 31 7933 in Cairns) are a network of professionals who staff guide posts at strategic locations throughout the Gulf. They are people with good local knowledge, and have access to points of interest, many of which are on private property and would be difficult to visit unaccompanied. For more information, phone the guides or write to PO Box 6268, Cairns.

Getting There & Away

Air Flight West Airlines (☎ (077) 43 9333) flies a few times a week between Mt Isa and Cairns ($253) as well as various places in the Gulf Country, including Normanton ($248), Karumba ($271), Julia Creek ($283), Burketown ($329) and Mornington Island ($339).

Bus Campbell's Coaches (☎ (077) 43 2006) has a weekly bus service between Mt Isa, Normanton and Karumba. Karumba Coachline (☎ (070) 35 1853) has a service three times a week from Cairns to Karumba ($116), via Georgetown ($61) and Normanton ($105).

Train From the Atherton Tableland, the Gulf Developmental Road runs to Normanton through Georgetown and Croydon. The last stretch into Normanton on this route can be made on the famous Gulflander train which runs just once weekly in each direction between Croydon and Normanton. The 151-km trip, in a very vintage-looking train, is made from Croydon on Thursday and from Normanton on Wednesday (four hours, $32).

It's also possible to travel by train from Cairns to Forsayth, about 50 km south of Georgetown, every Wednesday.

Burketown (population 200)

This tiny town is probably best known for its isolation. In the centre of a cattle-raising area, Burketown is 25 km south of the Gulf and can be reached by road from Cloncurry, Julia Creek or Camooweal. You've got to cover at least 150 km of unpaved road to reach it, whichever direction you come from. Some of Nevil Shute's famous novel *A Town Like Alice* is set here.

Burketown is an excellent place for bird-watching, and is also one of the places to view the phenomenon known as 'Morning Glory' – weird tubular cloud formations, extending the full length of the horizon, which roll out of the Gulf in the early morning, often in lines of three or four. This only happens from September to November.

The Gregory Downs Hotel, 117 km south of town, is the focal point of the annual North-West Canoe Race in May; the swimming hole in Gregory Downs is superb.

The town has a caravan park (no on-site vans) or you can get rooms in the *Albert Hotel* (☎ (077) 45 5104) for $50/70. *Escott Lodge* (☎ (077) 48 5577), 17 km west of Burketown, has singles/doubles for $45/75 and a camping ground; meals are available.

Normanton (population 1190)

Normanton was first established as a port for the Cloncurry copper fields but then became Croydon's gold-rush port, its population peaking at 3000 in 1891. The huge railway station on the edge of town, a monument to the gold era, still functions twice a week. The centre of town life today is the Albion Hotel, especially on Friday nights when people crowd in from the surrounding area.

You can get rooms in the *Albion Hotel* (☎ (077) 45 1218) for $45/50; there's also a motel, and a caravan park with on-site vans.

Karumba (population 710)

Karumba, 69 km from Normanton by paved

oad and actually on the Gulf at the mangrove-fringed mouth of the **Norman River**, s a centre for prawn, barramundi and crab ishing. It's possible to charter boats for ishing trips from here, and there's a regular vehicle barge between Karumba and Weipa.

The town has quite an interesting history. At one time it was a refuelling station for the flying boats which used to connect Sydney and the UK. The RAAF has also had Catalina flying boats based here.

The *Karumba Lodge Hotel/Motel* (☎ (077) 45 9143) charges $55/66 for singles/doubles, and the *Gulf Country Caravan Park* (☎ (077) 45 9148) has cabins.

Croydon (population 220)

Connected to Normanton by the curious-looking Gulflander train, this old gold-mining town was once the biggest in the Gulf and today it still has some interesting buildings. It's reckoned there were once 50,000 gold mines in the area and reminders of them is scattered all around the countryside. Such was the prosperity of the town that it had its own aerated water factory, gas street lamps, a foundry and coach builders.

The **courthouse** and **Mining Warden's Office** have their original furnishings, while the **Club Hotel** also dates back to the mining days. There's a bit of a resurgence of gold mining in the area again today, with new technology making it feasible to rework the old diggings.

The Croydon General Store has a small museum, and there's an open-air display of old mining and steam equipment.

For accommodation, the town has the *Club Hotel* (☎ (077) 45 6184) with pub rooms at $20/30 and motel units at $25/40; meals are available and it's also possible to camp. The *Gulf Gate Roadhouse* (☎ (077) 45 6169) has air-con motel units at $25/30.

Other Gulf Towns

There are accommodation possibilities in other Gulf towns, including: Georgetown; Mt Surprise; Tallaroo Station (☎ (070) 62 1221), 50 km west of Georgetown; Dorunda

Station (☎ (077) 45 3477), 200 km northeast of Normanton; Forsayth; Einasleigh; and the *Heartbreak Hotel* (☎ (089) 75 9928) at Cape Crawford, 110 km south-west of Borroloola at the junction of the Carpentaria and Tableland highways (actually in the Northern Territory).

At Lawn Hill National Park, off the road between Camooweal and Burketown, there are camp sites for $7.50; contact the National Parks office at the park (☎ (077) 48 5572) or in Mt Isa (☎ (077) 43 2055) for permits. The *Burke & Wills Roadhouse* (☎ (077) 42 5909), on the Cloncurry to Normanton road, has four air-con rooms at $30/40 and a few camp sites which cost $3.50 per person.

Outback

Heading west from the Queensland coast across the Great Dividing Range, the land soon starts to become drier, and the towns smaller and further apart.

The area, although sparsely settled, is well serviced by major roads – the Flinders Highway connects northern Queensland with the Northern Territory, meeting the Barkly Highway at the mining town of Mt Isa, while the Landsborough and Mitchell highways run from the New South Wales border south of Cunnamulla right up to Mt Isa. Longreach, with its Stockman's Hall of Fame, is a major destination for trips through outback Queensland.

Once off these major arteries, however, road conditions deteriorate rapidly, services are virtually nonexistent and you need to be fully self-sufficient, carrying spare parts, fuel and water. With the correct preparation, it's possible to make the great outback journeys down the tracks which connect Queensland with South Australia – the Strzelecki and Birdsville tracks.

CLONCURRY (population 2310)

The centre for a copper boom in the last century, Cloncurry was the largest copper producer in the British empire in 1916. Today it's a pastoral centre.

The town's major claim to fame is as the birthplace of the Royal Flying Doctor Service, and the **John Flynn Place Museum** in Daintree St houses exhibits on the Flying Doctor Service, the School of the Air and mining.

Cloncurry's **Mary Kathleen Park & Museum**, just off the highway on the eastern side of town, is partly housed in buildings transported from Mary Kathleen. The collection includes relics of the Burke and Wills expedition and a big collection of local rocks and minerals. You can see steam engines outside for free.

The Burke Developmental Road, north of Cloncurry, is paved all the way to Normanton (375 km) and Karumba (449 km) near the Gulf of Carpentaria. Burketown is 443 km from Cloncurry.

Places to Stay

You can camp in the *Cloncurry Caravan Park* opposite the museum or take an on-site van. The cheapest motel in Cloncurry is the historic *Wagon Wheel Motel* (☎ (077) 42 1866) at 54 Ramsay St, with budget singles/doubles at $32/45 and newer units at $55.

CLONCURRY TO MT ISA

This 124-km stretch of the Flinders Highway has a number of interesting stops. At **Corella River**, 41 km west of Cloncurry, there's a memorial cairn to the Burke and Wills expedition, which passed here in 1861. Ten km beyond this is the site of **Mary Kathleen**, a uranium-mining town from the 1950s to 1982. It has been completely demolished.

The turning to **Lake Julius**, Mt Isa's reserve water supply, is 36 km beyond Mary Kathleen. There's a camping ground at the lake and **Battle Mountain**, north of the Lake Julius dam wall, was the scene of the last stand of the Kalkadoon people in 1884, a rare pitched battle between Aborigines and Europeans.

MT ISA (population 23,400)

The mining town of Mt Isa owes its existence to an immensely rich copper, silver, lead and zinc mine, and the skyline is dominated by the massive 270-metre-high exhaust stack from the lead smelter. 'The Isa', as the town is known locally, also lays claim to being the largest city in the world – it covers an area of 41,255 sq km!

It's a rough-and-ready though prosperous town, and the job opportunities here have attracted people from about 60 different ethnic groups. There's plenty of low-cost accommodation for travellers stopping over, and you can tour the mine.

The first Mt Isa deposits were discovered in 1923 by a prospector called John Campbell Miles who gave Mt Isa its name – a corruption of Mt Ida, a gold field in Western Australia. Since the ore deposits were large and low grade, working them required the sort of investment only a company could make. Mt Isa Mines was founded in 1924 but it was during and after WW II that Mt Isa really took off and today it's the Western world's biggest silver and lead producer. Virtually the whole town is run by Mt Isa Mines, and the ore is railed 900 km to Townsville on the coast.

Orientation & Information

The town centre, a fairly compact area, is immediately east of the Leichhardt River which separates it from the mining area. Greyhound Pioneer buses stop right in the centre on Miles St, while McCafferty's use the Campbell's Coaches depot on the Barkly Highway.

There's a tourist office (☎ (077) 43 7966) on Marian St between Corbould and Mullan Sts. It's open Monday to Friday from 8 am to 5 pm, plus Saturdays and Sundays (between April and September) from 8.30 am to 1.30 pm.

The Crusade Bookshop, at 11 Simpson St, is the best between Townsville and Darwin.

The Mine

The mine is the town's major attraction and there are two tours available.

The three-hour underground tour, for which you don a hard hat and miner's suit, takes you down into some of the 4600 km of

Queensland
Top: Brisbane River at Pier Nine, Brisbane (RI)
Middle: Brisbane city by night (PS)
Bottom: Aerial view of Surfers Paradise, Gold Coast (PS)

Queensland
Top: Mt Warning, Lamington National Park (JC)
Bottom: Coloured sands, Fraser Island (MA)

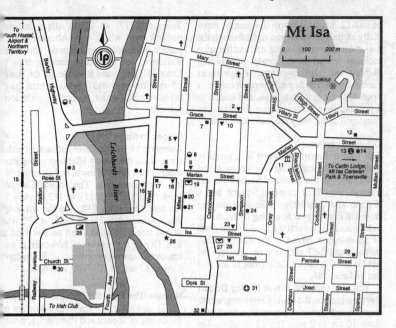

Mt Isa

0   100   200 m

To
Youth Hostel,
Airport &
Northern
Territory

Lookout

Mary   Street

Grace   Street

Marian   Street

Isa   Street

Ian   Street

Dora St

Leichhardt River

Rose St

Church St

To Irish Club

Railway   Avenue

Fourth   Ave

Hilary St   Hilary   Street

Street

To Carlin Lodge,
Mt Isa Caravan
Park & Townsville

Pamela   Street

Joan   Street

Deighton   Street

Stanley   Street

Spence   Street

PLACES TO STAY			18	Mt Isa Hotel		13	Tourist Office
			23	Red Lantern Chinese		14	Kalkadoon Tribal
7	Burke & Wills Isa			Restaurant			Centre
	Resort		28	The Tavern		15	Railway Station
12	Budget					19	Old Post Office
	Accommodation		**OTHER**			20	Flight West Airlines
17	Boyd Hotel					21	Ansett Airlines
29	Travellers Haven		1	Campbell's Coaches &		22	Crusade
32	Walton's Motel			McCafferty's			Bookshop
				Terminal		24	Curly Dan's Outdoor
PLACES TO EAT			3	Royal Flying Doctor			World
				Service		25	Swimming Pool
2	Pizza Hut		4	Civic Centre		26	Police Station
5	Bazza's Cafe		6	Cinema Mt Isa		27	New Post Office
9	Flamenco Cafe		8	Greyhound Pioneer		30	Mining Display &
10	Buffalo Club			Bus Terminal			Visitors Centre
16	Clicks Cafe		11	Frank Aston Museum		31	Hospital

unnels. Since only nine people are allowed on each tour, it's advisable to book as far ahead as possible by phoning the visitors centre (☎ (077) 44 2104). Tours leave at 8 and 11.45 am Monday to Friday and cost $20.

The two-hour surface tours (by bus) leave daily Monday to Friday year round, and on Saturday and Sunday mornings from April to September. Book through Campbell's Coaches (☎ (077) 43 2006) – they pick up from various places on request and the tour costs $12. It's well worth the money, especially as the bus takes you right through the major workshops and mine site, and the price includes a visit to the company's mining display and visitors centre. The visitors centre, on Church St near the town centre, is open daily from 9 am to noon and from 1 to 4 pm, and from 10 am to 2 pm Saturday and Sunday. The $2 entry fee includes a film.

Other Attractions

The **Frank Aston Museum** is a partially underground complex on a hill close to the town centre at the corner of Shackleton and Marian Sts. This rambling place has a diverse and interesting collection ranging from old mining gear to ageing flying doctor radios, and displays on the Lardil Aborigines of Mornington Island in the Gulf of Carpentaria and the Kalkadoon people from the Mt Isa area. It's open daily from 10 am to 3 pm and costs $4.

You can visit the **Royal Flying Doctor Service** base on the Barkly Highway, weekdays from 9 am to 5 pm and on weekends from 10 am to 2 pm. The $2.50 admission includes a film.

The **School of the Air**, which brings education by radio to children in remote places, is at the Kalkadoon High School on Abel Smith Parade. It's open for public tours at 10 and 11 am on school days; the tours cost $2.

The National-Trust-classified **Tent House**, at 16 Fourth Ave, is one of the last surviving houses typical of the early days of Mt Isa. It is open weekdays from 9 am to 3 pm.

The **Kalkadoon Tribal Centre & Culture-Keeping Place**, on Marian St next to the tourist office, is open most weekdays (admission $1). It's partly a museum and you can see some artefacts.

Mt Isa has a big, clean **swimming pool** on Isa St, just over the river and next to the tennis courts. Entry costs $1, and the pool opens daily from 8 am (noon on Mondays).

Mt Isa's August rodeo is the biggest in Australia.

Organised Tours

Between April and September, Copper City Tours (☎ (077) 44 2006) offers full-day outback trips which visit Aboriginal rock paintings, an old copper mine and Mary Kathleen; and three-day camping trips to Lawn Hill gorge and Riversleigh, the site of 15-million-year-old fossils which have revealed much about Australia's prehistoric animals.

Places to Stay

Camping Mt Isa has a string of caravan parks, some along the Barkly Highway going east, others in the north of town, and all about two km from the centre. The *Mt Isa Caravan Park* (☎ (077) 43 3252), at 112 Marion St, has tent sites from $10, and the *Riverside Tourist Park* (☎ (077) 43 3904) at 195 West St has tent sites at $11 and on-site vans at $28. One of the best spots, however, is four km out of town going west, at *Moondarra Caravan Park* (☎ (077) 43 9780).

Hostels The *Travellers Haven* (☎ (077) 43 0313), about a half a km from the centre on the corner of Spence and Pamela Sts, is well set up with bunk beds from $11 and singles/doubles from $22/26. It's fully air-con, has a pool and good bikes for hire ($1 a day), and its courtesy coach does pick-ups.

Mt Isa's 28-bed youth hostel (☎ (077) 43 5557), in the shadow of the mines at Wellington Park Rd, costs $10 ($11 nonmembers). It's very basic, and unless Travellers Haven is full it's hard to think of any good reason for walking the two km.

Hotels & Motels The *Boyd Hotel* (☎ (077) 43 3000), on the corner of West and Marian Sts, has basic pub rooms at $20 per person. *Budget Accommodation* (☎ (077) 43 4004), an old and dim boarding house opposite the tourist office, charges $15 per person, but it's more for permanent residents.

At 23 Camooweal St, *Walton's Motel* (☎ (077) 43 2377) is one of the cheapest central motels, with air-con singles/doubles at $40/50 and a small pool. *Carlin Lodge* (☎ (077) 43 2019), at 11 Boyd Parade, has clean motel units with kitchenettes and air-con from $40 a double. It's hard to find – ring for directions.

If you're looking for something more expensive, the three-star *Burke & Wills Isa Resort* (☎ (077) 43 8000) on the corner of Grace and Camooweal Sts can accommodate you with singles/doubles from $79/89.

Other motels include the *Inland Oasis Motel* (☎ (077) 43 3433) at 195 Barkly Highway, with rooms at $49/57, and the *Copper Gate Motel* (☎ (077) 43 3233) at 97 Marian St, which costs $40/53.

Places to Eat

Mt Isa's clubs are amongst the best places to eat. In the south of town, the *Irish Club* (☎ (077) 43 2577) on the corner of Buckley and Nineteenth Aves serves good-value meals, with smorgasbords at $6.50 for lunch and $12.50 for dinner. On the corner of Camooweal and Grace Sts, the *Buffalo Club* also has good bistro meals ranging from $7 to $12. Visitors to the clubs sign in as honorary buffaloes or Irish persons, and dress regulations apply.

The *Tavern*, on Isa St, has excellent counter meals at lunch times and evenings. You'll pay about $5 to $10 in the public bar, and meals in the bistro range upwards from $10. At the Boyd Hotel, *Boydie's Fair Dinkum Steakhouse* serves good grills from $7 to $13 and has daily backpacker specials for $4 or $5 – usually a rice or pasta dish.

There are a number of centrally located pizzerias, cafes and snack bars, including *Clicks* on West St and *Bazza's* on Miles St, which both offer a variety of burgers and sandwiches. *Flamenco*, on Marian St near the corner of Miles St, also has burgers, sandwiches and 20 flavours of ice cream.

If you've just stepped off an early morning bus, the *Mt Isa Hotel*, on the corner of Marian and Miles Sts, serves good breakfasts from to 9 am, which cost from $4 to $10.

Entertainment

There are bands in the *Boyd Hotel* on weekend evenings. Also popular are the *Cave* nightclub in the Mt Isa Hotel and the *Buffalo Club* on Grace St. The *Irish Club* has a good entertainment program, with free video nights on Monday and Tuesday, live rock & roll on Friday nights and a disco on Saturday.

The *Cinema Mt Isa* is on Marion St, between West and Miles Sts.

Getting There & Away

Air Ansett and Flight West Airlines (☎ (077) 43 9333) are both on Miles St, half a block south of Marian St.

Ansett has nonstop flights daily to Brisbane ($393), on Sundays to Alice Springs ($227) and on Saturdays and Sundays to Cairns ($254).

Flight West also flies daily to Cairns ($254), as well as to Townsville ($253), Normanton ($231), Karumba ($226) and various places along the Flinders Highway.

Bus Greyhound Pioneer is at 24 Miles St, near the corner of Marian St. McCafferty's operates from the Campbell's Coaches terminal (☎ (077) 43 3685) at 27 Barkly Highway.

Greyhound Pioneer and McCafferty's run daily services between Townsville and Tennant Creek, passing through Mt Isa. Townsville to Mt Isa takes 11 hours ($84), while the trip on to Tennant Creek takes another six or seven hours ($68). Both companies have connections at Tennant Creek for Alice Springs ($120) and Darwin ($130).

Greyhound Pioneer and McCafferty's operate daily to Brisbane ($129, about 24 hours) by the inland route through Winton ($46) and Longreach ($53).

Campbell's Coaches go to Normanton ($64) and Karumba ($70) once a week.

Train The air-con Inlander operates twice weekly between Townsville and Mt Isa, via Charters Towers, Hughenden and Cloncurry. The full journey takes about 18 hours and costs $192 in a 1st-class sleeper, $95 in economy.

MT ISA TO THREEWAYS

There's nothing much for the whole 650 km to the Threeways junction in the Northern

Territory. Camooweal is 188 km from Mt Isa, just before the Queensland-Northern Territory border and it's the only place of any size at all. West of Camooweal, the next service station (and the most expensive petrol anywhere between Townsville and Darwin) is 270 km along at *Barkly Homestead* (☎ (089) 64 4549). You can camp here for $3.50 per person. Motel rooms are $62/72.

Lawn Hill National Park
Amid arid country 400 km from Mt Isa and 100 km west of Gregory Downs and the Camooweal to Burketown road, the Lawn Hill gorge is an oasis of gorges, creeks, ponds and tropical vegetation which the Aborigines have enjoyed for perhaps 30,000 years. Their paintings and old camping sites abound. Two rock-art sites have been made accessible to visitors. There are freshwater crocodiles – the inoffensive variety – in the creek. Also in the park are extensive and virtually unexplored limestone formations.

Getting there is the problem – it's a beautiful, pristine place that's miles from anywhere or anybody. The last 300 km or so from Mt Isa – after you leave the Barkly Highway – are unsealed and often impassable after rain. Four-wheel-drive vehicles are recommended, though they are not always necessary in the dry season. There's a camping ground with showers and toilets in the park, and 17 km of walking tracks. The nearest place to buy petrol is at Gregory Downs. There's accommodation at the *Gregory Downs Hotel* and you can camp beside the Gregory River.

MT ISA TO LONGREACH
Fourteen km east of Cloncurry, the narrow Landsborough Highway turns off south-east to McKinlay (91 km), Kynuna (165 km), Winton (328 km) and Longreach (501 km).

McKinlay is a tiny settlement which would probably have been doomed to eternal insignificance were it not for the fact this is the location of the *Walkabout Creek Hotel* (☎ (077) 46 8424), which featured in the amazingly successful movie *Crocodile Dundee*. Photos from the film and other memorabilia clutter the walls of the pub. Greyhound Pioneer buses travelling between Mt Isa and Brisbane via Longreach make refreshment stop here, and if you want to hang around there are rooms at $30/40 and tent sites at $10. The *Blue Heeler* at **Kynuna** is another renowned old outback pub, which for some reason has its own surf-lifesaving club!

Winton (population 1160)
Winton is a sheep-raising centre and also the railhead from which cattle are transported after being brought from the Channel Country by road train. The road north to Cloncurry is fully paved, but still gets washed out during a really bad wet season.

On the main street, there's a *Jolly Swagman* statue and the **Qantilda Museum** which commemorates two local claims to fame: the founding of Qantas airlines at Winton in 1920 and the regionally inspired poetry of Australia's most famous poet/songwriter, Banjo Paterson. The *North Gregory Hotel* (☎ (076) 57 1375) at 67 Elderslie St has clean budget rooms with air-con at $2? a head.

Around Winton
At **Combo Waterhole** on Dagworth Station between Winton and Kynuna, Banjo Paterson is said to have written 'Waltzing Matilda' way back in 1895.

The country around Winton is rough and rugged, with much wildlife, notably brolgas. There are also Aboriginal sites with paintings, carvings and artefacts.

At **Lark Quarry Environmental Park** 120 km south-west of Winton, dinosaur footprints 100 million years old have been perfectly preserved in limestone. It takes around two hours to drive from Winton to Lark Quarry in a conventional vehicle but the dirt road is impassable in wet weather. You can get directions at the Winton Shire Council offices (☎ (076) 57 1188) at 7? Vindex St. There's no water at the site or along the road from Winton, so take your own.

LONGREACH (population 3610)

This prosperous outback town was the home of Qantas earlier this century, but these days it's just as famous for the Australian Stockman's Hall of Fame & Outback Heritage Centre, probably the biggest attraction in outback Queensland.

Longreach's human population is vastly outnumbered by the sheep, which number over a million; there are a fair few cattle too.

It was here that the Queensland & Northern Territory Aerial Service, better known as Qantas, was based in its early days in the 1920s. The original Qantas hangar, which still stands at Longreach Airport (almost opposite the Hall of Fame), was also the first aircraft 'factory' in Australia – six DH-50 biplanes were assembled here in 1926. There are plans to build an aviation museum alongside the original hangar, but in the meantime there's a 'preview' display housed in the Longreach tourist office, itself a replica of the first Qantas booking office. It's on the corner of Duck and Eagle Sts, and is open daily.

Longreach was also the starting point for one of Queensland's most colourful early crimes when, in 1870, a bushranger sporting the title 'Captain Starlight' stole 1000 head of cattle and trotted them 2400 km south to South Australia where he sold them. He then made his way back to Queensland, where he was arrested and, unbelievably, acquitted.

Stockman's Hall of Fame

The centre is housed in a beautifully conceived building, two km east of town along the road to Barcaldine. The excellent displays are divided into periods from the first White settlement through to today; and these deal with all aspects of the pioneering pastoral days. The centre was built as a tribute to the early explorers and stockmen, and it also commemorates the crucial roles played by the pioneer women, Aboriginal stockmen and Aboriginal women.

It's well worth visiting the Hall of Fame, as it gives a fascinating insight into this side of the European development of Australia. Admission is $15 ($10 concession), and the centre is open daily from 9 am to 5 pm. Allow yourself half a day to take it all in. Greyhound Pioneer and McCafferty's both operate daily services from the terminal on Eagle St for $3 (free with Greyhound Pioneer if you have an Aussie Pass). Otherwise it's a half-hour walk.

Organised Tours

The number of tours available is surprising, and most of them can be booked through the Outback Travel Centre (☎ (076) 58 1776) at 115 Eagle St. They offer a one-day tour of the town which takes in the Hall of Fame, a river cruise, an outback station and the Qantas hangar for $50 including lunch. Yellowbelly Express (☎ (076) 58 1919) does popular river trips on the nearby Thomson River.

You can also make a visit to one or more of the sheep stations in the area. They include: Toobrack (☎ (076) 58 9158), 68 km south; Oakley (☎ Outback Travel Centre); Longway (☎ (076) 58 2191), 17 km north; Lorraine (☎ (076) 57 1693), between Longreach and Winton; and Avington (☎ (076) 57 5952), 75 km west of Blackall. Some of these places are only open for day trips while others offer accommodation and a range of activities. Avington, for example, has beds in its shearers' quarters for $15 as well as rooms in its homestead for $50/90, including B&B and dinner. Activities include horse riding, trail-bike riding, canoeing and barge cruises. For any visit to a sheep station you'll need to ring before you arrive.

You can also take a scenic flight in either a Cessna or a helicopter for $20.

Places to Stay & Eat

The *Longreach Swaggies Backpackers* (☎ (076) 58 2777) is on the corner of Womproo and Thrush Rds, about one km east of the centre. It's pretty basic but quite well set up, with cooking and laundry facilities and a TV lounge. Dorm beds cost $12, and it does pick-ups from the train and bus terminals if you ring.

QUEENSLAND

The *Gunnadoo Caravan Park* (☎ (076) 58 1781), east of town on the corner of the highway and Thrush Rd, has tent sites at $10 and self-contained cabins at $45. There's a choice of at least four pubs on Eagle St, including the *Welcome Home Hotel* (☎ (076) 58 1361) with air-con pub rooms for $20/35.

At 84 Galah St, the *Longreach Motor Inn* (☎ (076) 58 2322) has good motel rooms from $58/68.

There are several cafes and takeaways, and a bakery, along Eagle St. *Starlight's Tavern*, also on Eagle St, has good bistro meals under $10. Out on the road towards the Hall of Fame, *Squatters* (☎ (076) 58 3215) is a good homestead-style restaurant with Aussie tucker. It's open for lunch and dinner, and main courses range from $10 to $15. It also has a few basic rooms out the back with shared bathroom and kitchen; singles/doubles cost $35/50.

Getting There & Away

Flight West has daily flights from Longreach to Brisbane ($303), and also flies twice a week to Winton ($85) and Townsville ($216).

Long-distance buses stop at the Outback Travel Centre (☎ (076) 58 1776) in Eagle St. Greyhound Pioneer and McCafferty's both have daily services to Mt Isa (7½ hours, $53) and Brisbane (17 hours, $83). McCafferty's also operates three times a week to Rockhampton (nine hours, $51).

The twice-weekly Spirit of the Outback train connects Longreach with Rockhampton (14 hours, $69 in economy, $160 for a 1st-class sleeper).

LONGREACH TO CHARLEVILLE

Barcaldine (population 1530)

Barcaldine, between Emerald and Longreach, is another sheep and cattle centre. It was the scene of a major step towards the 1902 formation of the Australian Labor Party when, in 1891, striking shearers met under a ghost-gum tree, before marching to Clermont to continue their struggle. At the same time dock workers in Sydney rioted, refusing to handle bales of wool sheared by nonunion labour.

The tree is now called the Tree of Knowledge, and still stands in the centre of town. The Australian Workers Heritage Centre, built to commemorate the role played by workers in the formation of Australian social, political and industrial movements, was opened during the Labor Party's centenary celebrations in Barcaldine in 1991. The centre includes an impressive circular theatre-tent, museum, gallery and garden, and an accommodation complex is on the drawing board. The centre is open daily from 9 am to 5 pm (from 10 am on weekends).

South of Barcaldine is Blackall, supposedly the site of the mythical Black Stump. Not far from here is **Black's Palace**, an Aboriginal site with burial caves and impressive rock paintings. It's on private property but can be visited with the permission of the warden (☎ (076) 57 4455/4663).

Charleville (population 3510)

About 800 km from the coast, Charleville marks the end of the Warrego Highway and is the centre of another huge cattle- and sheep-raising region. This was an important centre for early explorers and, being on the Warrego River, is something of an oasis in the outback. Around the town there are various reminders of the early explorers, and there's a historical museum in the 1880 Queensland National Bank building on Albert St.

The observatory four km from town has high-powered telescopes which you can gaze through in the evenings for $8.

THE CHANNEL COUNTRY

The remote and sparsely populated south-western corner of Queensland, bordering the Northern Territory, South Australia and New South Wales, takes its name from the myriad channels which crisscross the area. In this inhospitable region it hardly ever rains, but water from the summer monsoons further north pours into the Channel Country along the Georgina, Hamilton and Diamantina rivers and Cooper Creek. Flooding towards the great depression of Lake Eyre in South Australia, the mass of water arrives on this huge plain, eventually drying up in water holes or salt pans.

Only on rare occasions (the early '70s and 1989 during this century) does the vast amount of water actually reach Lake Eyre and fill it. For a short period after each wet season, however, the Channel Country does become fertile, and cattle are grazed here.

Getting There & Around

Some roads from the east and north to the fringes of the Channel Country are paved, but during the October to May wet season even these can be cut – and the dirt roads become quagmires. In addition, the summer heat is unbearable so a visit is best made in the cooler winter from May to September. Visiting this area requires a sturdy vehicle (4WD if you want to get off the beaten track) and some experience of outback driving. If you're travelling anywhere west of Cunnamulla or Quilpie, always carry plenty of petrol and drinking water and notify the police, so that if you don't turn up at the next town, the necessary steps can be taken.

You can reach Quilpie on the Westlander train from Brisbane twice a week. Flight West Airlines (☎ (07) 229 1177 in Brisbane) flies twice weekly from Brisbane to Birdsville ($392) and back, via Charleville, Quilpie and Windorah. Augusta Airways flies from Port Augusta in South Australia to Birdsville, Bedourie and Boulia on Saturdays, and back on Sundays.

Diamantina Developmental Road

The main road through the Channel Country is the Diamantina Developmental Road that runs south from Mt Isa through Boulia to Bedourie and then turns east through Windorah and Quilpie to Charleville. In all, it's a long and lonely 1340 km, a little over half of which is surfaced.

Boulia is the 'capital' of the Channel Country. Burke and Wills passed through here on their long trek, and there's a museum in a restored 1888 stone house in the little town. Near Boulia, the mysterious Min Min Light, a sort of earthbound UFO, is sometimes seen. It's said to resemble the headlights of a car and can hover a metre or two above the ground before vanishing and reappearing in a different place.

Boulia has the *Australian Motel/Hotel* (☎ (077) 46 3144) with singles/doubles at $27/32, or $40/50 with private bathroom. There's also a caravan park (no on-site vans) and a couple of cafes.

Windorah is either very dry or very wet and has a pub and a caravan park. **Quilpie** is an opal-mining town and the railhead from which cattle, grazed here during the fertile wet season, are railed to the coast. It has two pubs with rooms, and a motel.

Other Routes The Kennedy Developmental Road runs from Winton to Boulia and is mostly surfaced with a couple of fuel and accommodation stops, at **Middleton** and **Hamilton**, on the way.

From Quilpie to Birdsville you follow the Diamantina road through Windorah but then branch off south to Betoota. It's 394 dull km from Windorah to Birdsville. **Betoota**, with one store and one pub, is all there is along the way.

South of Quilpie and west of Cunnamulla is **Thargomindah**, with a pub and a motel. From here camel trains used to cross to Bourke in New South Wales. **Noccundra**, further west, was once a busy little community. It now has just a hotel (with fuel, food and accommodation) and a population of three!

Birdsville

This tiny settlement, with a population of about 30, is the most remote place in Queensland and possesses one of Australia's most famous pubs – the *Birdsville Hotel* (☎ (076) 56 3244), which dates from 1884. You can stay there for $42/64 for a single/double. There's also a caravan park with camp sites.

Birdsville, only 12 km from the South Australian border, is at the northern end of the 481-km Birdsville Track which leads down to Marree in South Australia. In the late 19th century, Birdsville was quite a busy place as cattle were driven south to South Australia and a customs charge was made on each head of cattle leaving Queensland. With Federation, the charge was abolished, and as cattle are now moved by rail and road, Birdsville has become almost ghost-like. Its big moment today is the annual Birdsville Races on the first weekend in September, when as many as 3000 racing and boozing enthusiasts make the trip to Birdsville.

Birdsville gets its water from a 1219-metre-deep artesian well which delivers the water at 65°C.

Birdsville Track

To the south, the Birdsville Track passes between the Simpson Desert to the west and Sturt Stony Desert to the east. The first stretch from Birdsville has two alternative routes. Ask local advice about which is better. The Inner Track – marked 'not recommended' on most maps – crosses the Goyder Lagoon (the 'end' of the Diamantina River) and a big Wet will sometimes cut this

route. The longer, more easterly Outside Track crosses sandy country at the edge of the desert where it is sometimes difficult to find the track. Travellers driving the Birdsville Track must fill in a 'destination' card with Birdsville police and then report to the police at the other end of the track.

Simpson Desert National Park

West of Birdsville, the waterless Simpson Desert National Park is Queensland's biggest at 5000 sq km. Conventional cars can tackle the Birdsville Track quite easily but the Simpson requires far more preparation. Official advice is that crossings should only be tackled by parties of at least three 4WD vehicles and that you should have an HF radio to call for help if necessary. Permits are required before you can traverse the park, and you should advise the Birdsville police of your intended movements. For permits, contact National Parks offices in Longreach (☎ (076) 58 1761), Emerald (☎ (079) 82 4555) or Charleville (☎ (076) 54 1255).

South Australia

Area 984,277 sq km
Population 1,459,000

☎ From August 1996, Adelaide's existing seven-digit phone numbers will be prefixed by the additional digit 8 (for example, ☎ 123 4567 becomes ☎ 8123 4567). Also from that date, Adelaide's existing six-digit numbers beginning with 3 will be prefixed by the additional digits 83; existing six-digit numbers beginning with 4 will be prefixed by the additional digits 84. From February 1997, in regional areas, the last two digits of the current area code will be added to the existing number (for example, ☎ (012) 123 456 becomes ☎ 1212 3456). The area code for the state will be (08). ■

South Australia is the driest of the states – even Western Australia doesn't have such a large proportion of desert. It is also the most urbanised. Adelaide, the capital, once had a reputation as the wowsers' capital and is often referred to as 'the city of churches'. The churches may still be there, but otherwise times have changed.

Today the city's cultural spirit is epitomised by the biennial Adelaide Arts Festival, while the death of wowserism is nowhere better seen than in the Barossa Valley Vintage Festival held every two years. Another example of South Australia's relatively liberal attitude is that it was the first Australian state to have a legal nudist beach – Maslin Beach, just a short drive south of Adelaide.

South Australia is renowned for its vineyards and wineries. The Barossa Valley is probably the best-known wine-producing area in the country, but there are also the fine Clare and Coonawarra valleys, and the wineries of McLaren Vale, only a short drive from the city.

Further north, the rugged Flinders Ranges offer spectacular scenery and superb bushwalking, while the far north and west of the state have some of the most inhospitable land in Australia. The long drive west across the Nullarbor Plain starts in South Australia: the road runs close to dramatic cliffs along the Great Australian Bight.

That still leaves the Murray River, the interesting coast towards the Victorian border, fascinating Kangaroo Island and the Eyre, Yorke and Fleurieu peninsulas.

Colonel William Light landed at Holdfast Bay (today Glenelg) in 1836, proclaimed the area a British colony and chose a site about 10 km inland for the capital. Light designed and surveyed the city, but he did not name it. The colony's first governor, Captain John Hindmarsh, named the city after the wife of the then reigning British monarch, William IV. At first, progress in the colony was slow and only British-government funds saved the independently managed colony from bankruptcy. The colony was self-supporting by the mid-1840s and self-governing by 1856. Steamers on the Murray River linked the state with the east, and agricultural and pastoral activity became the main industry.

SOUTH AUSTRALIAN ABORIGINES

It is estimated that there were 12,000 Aborigines in South Australia at the beginning of the 19th century. Many were killed by the White settlers or died from introduced diseases; the survivors were pushed off their lands to the more barren and inhospitable parts of the state.

Today, however, most of the state's 14,000 Aborigines live in urban centres such as

537

SOUTH AUSTRALIA

WESTERN AUSTRALIA

NORTHERN TERRITORY

QUEENSLAND

ALICE SPRINGS

Kulgera

Great Victoria Desert

Aboriginal Land

WITJIRA NATIONAL PARK

Simpson Desert

Simpson Desert Cons Park

Simpson Desert Regional Reserve

Birdsville

Sturt Stony Desert

Innamincka Regional Reserve

Marla

Oodnadatta

LAKE EYRE NATIONAL PARK

Lake Eyre North

Innamincka

Namungarintja Conservation Park

Coober Pedy

Oodnadatta Track

Stuart Highway

Woomera Prohibited Area

Lake Eyre South

Marree

Birdsville Track

Strzelecki Track

Aboriginal Land

Maralinga

Roxby Downs

Andamooka

Leigh Creek

Lake Frome

Nullarbor Plain

Tarcoola

Glendambo

Lake Torrens

Flinders Ranges

Nullarbor

Trans-Australia Railway

Nullarbor Regional Reserve

Yellabinna Regional Reserve

Woomera

Wilpena

FLINDERS RANGES NATIONAL PARK

Hawker

Broken Hill

Nullarbor Roadhouse

Eucla

Yalata

Penong

Yumbarra Cons Park

Lake Gairdner

Cockburn

NEW SOUTH WALES

NULLARBOR NATIONAL PARK

Aboriginal Land

CEDUNA

Streaky Bay

Flinders Hwy

Eyre Hwy

Pinkawillinie Cons Pk

WHYALLA

PORT AUGUSTA

Quorn

Barrier Hwy

Peterborough

Great Australian Bight

Elliston

Cleve

Cowell

PORT PIRIE

Burra

Clare

Morgan

Murray River

Eyre Peninsula

Lincoln Hwy

Spencer Gulf

Tumby Bay

Kapunda

Waikerie

Renmark

Loxton

PORT LINCOLN

LINCOLN NATIONAL PARK

Yorke Peninsula

GAWLER

Mannum

Barossa Valley

Adelaide

MURRAY BRIDGE

Kingscote

Victor Harbor

Fleurieu Peninsula

Tailem Bend

VICTORIA

Kangaroo Island

The Coorong

Dukes Hwy

Bordertown

Naracoorte

Kingston SE

Robe

Penola

Beachport

Princes Hwy

Millicent

MT GAMBIER

Portland

South Australia

0   100   200 km

SOUTHERN

OCEAN

Heysen Trail
Destined to become one of the world's great long-distance walks, the extraordinary Heysen Trail extends over 1500 km from Cape Jervis at the tip of the Fleurieu Peninsula to Parachilna Gorge in the northern Flinders Ranges. En route it passes over the Mt Lofty Ranges, through the Barossa Valley wine region and the fascinating old copper town of Burra in the mid-north and into the Flinders Ranges, scaling Mt Remarkable and Mt Brown, then on to Wilpena Pound.

For the truly intrepid, the Heysen Trail presents a remarkable challenge, but it is also possible to follow short sections of the trail on day trips or over a few days. Fifteen maps detailing all the sections of the route are available for $5.50 each from the Recreation & Sport Resource Centre (☎ (08) 226 7373), Shop 20, City Centre Arcade, 11 Hindmarsh Square, Adelaide (or write to GPO Box 1865, Adelaide). Due to fire restrictions, the trail is closed between December and April. ■

Adelaide and Port Augusta. *Survival in Our Own Land* (Hodder & Stoughton, 1992), edited by Christobel Mattingley & Ken Hampton, has been exhaustively researched and has beautifully written individual and historical accounts by Nungas (South Australian Aborigines). It is available for $34.95 from good bookshops in Adelaide, such as Imprints in Hindley St.

GEOGRAPHY
South Australia is sparsely settled. Adelaide, the Fleurieu Peninsula to the south, and the area to the north of the capital with the wine-producing Barossa and Clare valleys are green and fairly fertile, but much of the rest of the state is far more barren. As you travel further north or west the terrain becomes drier and more inhospitable; most of the north is a vast area of desert and dry salt lakes with only scattered tiny settlements.

South Australia is also known for its scenic coastline and peninsulas. Starting from the Victorian border, there's the south-east region with Mt Gambier, the wine-producing Coonawarra area and the long, coastal lake of the Coorong. Then there's the Fleurieu Peninsula and nearby Kangaroo Island, the Yorke Peninsula, the remote Eyre Peninsula merging into the Great Australian Bight, and the Nullarbor Plain, which extends into Western Australia.

INFORMATION
Tourism South Australia (TSA) produces a good series of regional brochures. TSA travel centres can also supply leaflets on travel details, accommodation costs and so

on. TSA also produces a range of booklets on areas of interest, such as the wineries, for a nominal cost. Offices include:

New South Wales
143 King St, Sydney 2000 (☎ (02) 232 8388)
South Australia
1 King William St, Adelaide 5000 (☎ (08) 212 1505)
Victoria
25 Elizabeth St, Melbourne 3000 (☎ (03) 614 6522)
Western Australia
13/14 Mezzanine floor, Wesley Centre, 93 William St, Perth 6000 (☎ (09) 481 1268)

The State Information Centre (☎ (08) 204 1900), at 77 Grenfell St, Adelaide, is a handy resource centre on features of interest in the state, including cycling and trekking routes. It has a vast range of brochures on South Australian sights, including national parks, museums, etc, and sells maps of the Heysen Trail.

NATIONAL PARKS
For information on national parks, contact the Department of Environment & Natural Resources Information Centre (☎ (08) 204 1910), which is also at 77 Grenfell St.

ACTIVITIES
Bushwalking
A good general guide to bushwalks in South Australia is Tyrone T Thomas's *Fifty Walks in South Australia* (Hill of Content Publishing Company, 1992, $15.95). Close to Adelaide there are many walks in the Mt Lofty Ranges, including those at Belair

National Park, Cleland Park, Morialta Park, Deep Creek Park, Bridgewater-Aldgate, Barossa Reservoir and Para Wirra Park. In the Flinders Ranges there are excellent walks in the Wilpena Pound area, further south in the Mt Remarkable National Park and further north in the Arkaroola-Mt Painter Sanctuary area. Some walks in the Flinders Ranges are for more experienced walkers, as conditions can be extreme. Get a copy of *Flinders Ranges Walks* ($4.95), produced by the Conservation Council of South Australia.

There are several bushwalking clubs in the Adelaide area which organise weekend walks in the Mt Lofty and Flinders ranges. Information can be obtained from bush-gear shops like Paddy Pallin and Thor Adventure Equipment (☎ (08) 232 3155), which share a shop at 228 Rundle St, Adelaide. You can also hire gear there.

Women of the Wilderness takes walks through the Adelaide Hills and environs on the first Sunday of each month. The group also runs courses and workshops for women in a range of outdoor activities; phone ☎ (085) 56 3586 for details.

Water Sports
Canoeing & Sailing The Murray River and the Coorong are popular for canoeing trips, and visitors can hire equipment and join in canoe trips organised by canoeing associations in South Australia. There is good sailing all along the Adelaide shoreline of Gulf St Vincent and there are lots of sailing clubs.

Scuba Diving There are good diving possibilities around Adelaide. Several shipwrecks off Kangaroo Island are easily accessible to scuba divers. Port Noarlunga Reef Marine Reserve (18 km south of Adelaide) and Aldinga (43 km south) are good centres for diving from boats. The reefs around Snapper Point (42 km south) are suitable for snorkelling.

At Rapid Bay (88 km south of Adelaide), there's abundant marine life; you can dive from the jetty. Wallaroo on the Yorke Peninsula, Port Lincoln on the Eyre Peninsula and Second Valley (65 km south of Adelaide) are other good areas.

Swimming & Surfing Seacliff, Brighton, Somerton, Glenelg, West Beach, Henley Beach, Grange, West Lake, Semaphore, Glanville and Largs Bay are all popular city beaches. Further south there are plenty of beaches with good surf. Skinny dipping is permitted at Maslin Beach, 40 km south of the city.

You have to get over to Pondalowie on the Yorke Peninsula for the state's best waves. Other good surf areas can be found along the Eyre Peninsula: close to Adelaide at Boomer and Chiton, between Victor Harbor and Port Elliot, and near Goolwa. Cactus Beach, on remote Point Sinclair west of Ceduna, is famous for its surf.

GETTING THERE & AWAY
See the Adelaide Getting There & Away section for details on transport to South Australia. It is worth noting that if you're travelling to Western Australia you can't take honey, plants, fruit or vegetables past the Norseman checkpoint; travelling into South Australia from Victoria between Mildura and Renmark you'll come across a similar checkpoint.

GETTING AROUND
Air
Kendell Airlines (book through Ansett on ☎ 13 1300) is the main regional operator with flights fanning out from Adelaide to Mt Gambier, Kangaroo Island, Port Lincoln, Ceduna, Coober Pedy and Broken Hill (in New South Wales). There are a number of smaller operators, including Southern Australia Airlines (book through Qantas on ☎ 13 1313) and Lincoln Airlines (☎ toll-free 1800 018 234). See the South Australian air-fare chart for prices.

Bus
As well as the major interstate companies, services within the state include Stateline (the main operator) and Premier (☎ (08) 41

South Australian Air Fares

All fares in Australian Dollars
One-way economy air fares

(Map showing air fare routes from Adelaide to:)
Ceduna, Coober Pedy 238, Woomera, To Broken Hill, Port Augusta 170, Streaky Bay 185, Whyalla, Renmark 98, 135, 110, 104, 155, Port Lincoln, 109, ADELAIDE, Kangaroo Island 58, 140, Mt Gambier

5555 for both), Yorke Peninsula (☎ (08) 391 2977) and smaller local companies.

Train

Apart from suburban trains and a couple of tourist steam trains, South Australia does not have any intrastate passenger trains. You can, however, travel within the state on interstate trains – the Indian Pacific (Sydney to Perth), the Ghan (Adelaide to Alice Springs) and the Overland (Adelaide to Melbourne).

Adelaide

Population 957,000

Adelaide is a solid, dare I say gracious, city: when the early colonists built they generally built with stone. The solidity goes further than architecture, for despite all the liberalism of the years of Don Dunstan (a flamboyant former premier), Adelaide has not lost its conservatism entirely: it's still an 'old money' place.

Adelaide is civilised and calm in a way no other Australian capital city can match.

What's more, it has a superb setting, for the city centre is surrounded by green parkland while the metropolitan area is bounded by a range of hills, the Mt Lofty Ranges, which crowds it against the sea.

Orientation

The city centre is laid out on a clear grid pattern, with several squares. The main street is King William St, with Victoria Square at the geographical centre of the city. Continue north up King William St and you'll come to the TSA travel centre on the corner of North Terrace. Most cross streets change their name at King William St.

Rundle Mall is colourful – always a hive of activity – and most of the big shops are here. Just across King William St, Rundle Mall becomes Hindley St. Here there are plenty of reasonably priced restaurants and snack bars, and a number of glitzy bars and dance clubs. These days, however, Hindley St is looking decidedly weary, and Rundle St (the eastern extension of Rundle Mall) is Adelaide's cosmopolitan heart and avant-garde artists' quarter. Here you'll find the best in alfresco dining, retro clothing and *haute d'grunge*.

The next street north of Hindley St is North Terrace, with the casino and suburban railway station just to the west of King William St, and a string of magnificent public buildings, including the art gallery, museum, state library and university to the east.

Continue north and you're in the North Parkland, with the Festival Centre; then it's across the Torrens River and into North Adelaide.

Information

Tourist Offices The Tourism South Australia (TSA) travel centre (☎ 212 1505; toll-free 1800 882 092) is at 1 King William St. It's open from 8.45 am to 5 pm on weekdays and from 9 am to 2 pm on weekends and public holidays. There's a recorded information service on ☎ 212 1505.

SA-FM, a local radio station, has a 'community switchboard' which provides current information on forthcoming concerts and festivals, as well as prevailing surfing conditions and a beach report; phone ☎ 271 1277.

The Women's Information Switchboard (☎ 223 1244) operates from 9 am to 9 pm daily except public holidays. Gayline (☎ 362 3223) operates between 7 and 10 pm nightly and from 2 to 5 pm on weekends.

Post & Telecommunications The GPO is in the city centre on King William St. The STD telephone code for Adelaide is 08.

Other Offices The Royal Automobile Association of South Australia (RAA) (☎ 202 4500) is central at 41 Hindmarsh Square. The YHA office (☎ 231 5583) is at 38 Sturt St, and the Department of Environment & Natural Resources (☎ 204 1910) is at 77 Grenfell St. Information and maps can also be obtained from the Division of Recreation, Sport & Racing's Resource Centre (☎ 226 7373), at Shop 20, City Centre Arcade, 11 Hindmarsh Square.

The Disability Information Centre (☎ 223 7522) is at 195 Gilles St. The centre can provide advice on areas around the state which cater for people with disabilities; it can also direct you to travel agencies experienced and knowledgeable about mobility-restricted travel.

Bookshops Try the excellent Europa Bookshop at 16 Pulteney St for its selection of foreign-language books. Both the university and the State Library on North Terrace have good bookshops.

There are a couple of good bookshops on Hindley St, including Imprint Booksellers, at 80 Hindley St, which has quality literature and a good gay and lesbian section. Mary Martin's Bookshop, an Adelaide institution, is at 12 Pirie St. The Conservation Council has a shop at 120 Wakefield St. This is a very good environmental resource centre, and also has a reference library.

Murphy Sisters Bookshop, at 240 The Parade, Norwood, specialises in feminist and lesbian works. The sisters have also opened a new shop at Semaphore: Sisters by the Sea, Shop 1, 14 Semaphore Rd.

A good range of second-hand books can be found at the Central and Orange Lane markets (see the following Markets section for details).

Maps Mapland (☎ (08) 226 3895), at the Department of Environment & Natural Resources, 282 Richmond Rd, Netley, has a good range of maps. Maps are also sold at the department's Survey Records office, in the Treasury building, on the corner of Flinders and King William Sts.

South Australian Museum

On North Terrace, the South Australian Museum is an Adelaide landmark with huge whale skeletons in the front window. The museum has a very good collection of Aboriginal artefacts, as well as Ngurenderi, an Aboriginal Dreamtime exhibition. Open between 10 am and 5 pm daily, it's a fine museum and should not be missed; admission is free.

Other Museums

On North Terrace by the casino and local railway station, the old **Parliament House** is open for inspection weekdays and public holidays from 10 am to 5 pm and weekends from noon to 5 pm; admission is $4. For some free entertainment, head to nearby **Speaker's Corner** and hear various versions of how to improve the world.

The excellent **Migration Museum**, at 82 Kintore Ave, next to the State Library, tells the story of immigration to Australia. It is open weekdays from 10 am to 5 pm, and weekends and public holidays from 1 to 5 pm; admission is free. As you're leaving this museum, turn left and walk along the lane and turn right at the double-storey building where the free **Police Museum** can be found on the 1st floor. It's open on weekends and public holidays from 1 to 5 pm.

The **Museum of Classical Archaeology**, on the 1st floor of the Mitchell Building (in the university grounds on North Terrace) has a good collection of antiquities. It's open

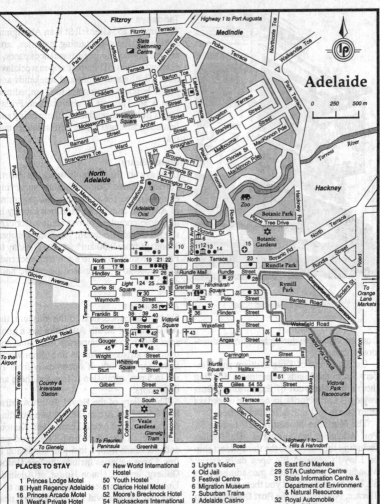

Adelaide

0   250   500 m

PLACES TO STAY
1 Princes Lodge Motel
8 Hyatt Regency Adelaide
16 Princes Arcade Motel
18 West's Private Hotel
19 Festival Lodge
21 The Terrace
24 Hindley Parkroyal
25 City Central Motel
27 Austral Hotel
34 Cannon St Lodge
36 Earl of Zetland Hotel
37 YMCA
38 Sunny's Backpackers Hostel
40 Metropolitan Hotel
41 Backpack Australia
44 East Park Lodge
47 New World International Hostel
50 Youth Hostel
51 Clarice Hotel Motel
52 Moore's Brecknock Hotel
54 Rucksackers International
55 Backpackers Adelaide Hostel

PLACES TO EAT
30 Taj Tandoor
45 Ming's Palace
46 Red Ochre Grill
48 Paul's Cafe

OTHER
2 St Peter's Cathedral
3 Light's Vision
4 Old Jail
5 Festival Centre
6 Migration Museum
7 Suburban Trains
9 Adelaide Casino
10 Government House
11 State Library
12 South Australian Museum
13 Art Gallery of South Australia
14 University of Adelaide
15 Royal Adelaide Hospital
17 Lion Arts Centre
20 Qantas & Ansett Airlines
22 Tourism South Australia Travel Centre
23 Ayers House
26 Edmund Wright House
28 East End Markets
29 STA Customer Centre
31 State Information Centre & Department of Environment & Natural Resources
32 Royal Automobile Association
33 Tandanya
35 General Post Office
39 Central Bus Station
42 Central Market
43 St Francis Xavier Cathedral
49 YHA Office
53 Disability Information Centre

SOUTH AUSTRALIA

One of Adelaide's old pubs

from noon to 3 pm during term time; admission is free.

On the corner of King William and Flinders Sts in the Lands Department Building there's the **Museum of Exploration, Surveying & Land Heritage**, open on weekdays from 10 am to 4 pm; admission is free.

The **Maritime Museum**, 126 Lipson St, Port Adelaide, has a number of old ships, including the *Nelcebee*, the third-oldest ship on Lloyd's register. It's open daily except Monday from 10 am to 5 pm; admission is $7. Bus No 153 will get you there from North Terrace. Next door is the **Port Dock Station Museum**, open Sunday to Friday from 10 am to 5 pm and Saturdays from noon to 5 pm; admission is $6.

Other museums include the free **Postal Museum**, at 2 Franklin St (open weekdays from 11 am to 2 pm), and the **Historical Museum** at Hindmarsh Place, Hindmarsh (open on the first and third Sundays of each month from 2 to 5 pm; admission is free).

Tandanya

Tandanya at 253 Grenfell St is an Aboriginal cultural institute containing galleries, arts and crafts workshops, performance spaces, a cafe and a good gift shop. It's open weekdays from 10.30 am to 5 pm and weekends and public holidays from noon to 5 pm; admission is $4. The cafe is also open on Friday nights from 8 pm until late in the evening and features traditional music performances and plays.

State Library

Displays at the State Library on North Terrace include Colonel Light's surveying equipment, an 1865 photographic panorama of Adelaide and, in the Mortlock Library in the same complex, memorabilia of cricket star Sir Donald Bradman. The library is open Mondays from 9.30 am to 6 pm, Tuesday to Friday from 9.30 am to 8 pm and weekends from noon to 5 pm (closed on public holidays).

Art Galleries

On North Terrace, next to the museum, the **Art Gallery of South Australia** has a good selection from contemporary Australian and overseas artists, as well as fine minor works from many periods. It's open daily from 10 am to 5 pm, admission is free and there are daily tours.

The gallery of the **Royal South Australian Society of Art**, in the Institute Building on the corner of North Terrace and Kintore Ave, is open weekdays from 11 am to 5 pm and weekends from 2 to 5 pm; admission is free. Other galleries include the free **Union Gallery**, level 6, Union House, at Adelaide University (open weekdays from 10 am to 5 pm) and the **Festival Centre Gallery** near the Playhouse in the Festival Centre.

Ayers House & Edmund Wright House

Ayers House is at 288 North Terrace, close to the city centre. This fine old mansion was originally constructed in 1846 but was added to over the next 30 years. Now completely restored, it houses two restaurants and is open to visitors Tuesday to Friday between

10 am and 4 pm and on weekends and public holidays between 2 and 4 pm. Admission is $2 and on weekdays there are tours ($4). The elegant bluestone building serves as the headquarters of the South Australian branch of the National Trust (☎ 223 1655). One of the restaurants has regular Murder Mystery dinners. They cost about $37, including a four-course meal.

At 59 King William St, Edmund Wright House, built in 1876, was originally constructed in an elaborate Renaissance style with intricate decoration for the Bishop of South Australia. It is open daily from 9 am to 4.30 pm; admission is free. On Wednesdays from noon to 2 pm there are lunch-time concerts here.

Other City Buildings

The imposing **town hall**, built between 1863 and 1866 in 16th-century Renaissance style, looks out on to King William St between Flinders and Pirie Sts. The faces of Queen Victoria and Prince Albert are carved into the facade. The **GPO** across the road is almost as impressive.

On North Terrace, **Government House** was built between 1838 and 1840, with further additions in 1855. The earliest section is one of the oldest buildings in Adelaide. **Parliament House** on North Terrace has a facade with 10 marble Corinthian columns. Building commenced in 1883 but was not completed until 1939.

Holy Trinity Church, also on North Terrace, was the first Anglican church in the state; it was built in 1838. Other early churches are **St Francis Xavier Cathedral** on Wakefield St (built around 1856) and **St Peter's Cathedral** in Pennington Terrace, North Adelaide (built between 1869 and 1876). St Francis Xavier Cathedral is beside Victoria Square, where you will also find a number of other important early buildings: the **Magistrate's Court** (built between 1847 and 1850); the 1869 **Supreme Court**; and the **Treasury building**.

Festival Centre

The Adelaide Festival Centre, completed in 1977, is close to the Torrens River. Looking uncannily like a squared-off version of the vastly more expensive Sydney Opera House, it performs a similar function with its variety of auditoriums and theatres.

One of the most pleasant aspects of the Festival Theatre is its riverside setting; people picnic on the grass in front of the theatre and there are several places to eat. You can also hire pedal boats nearby or enjoy free concerts (see the following Entertainment section) and exhibitions here.

Lion Arts Centre

On the corner of Morphett St and North Terrace, the Lion Arts Centre, with galleries, stage areas, artists' studios, and craft workshops, is the home of the Fringe Festival administration (☎ 231 7760) and a broad spectrum of arts-related activities. The **Mercury Theatre** here has a film festival and shows art-house films.

Botanic Gardens & Other Parks

The central city is completely surrounded by green parkland, and the Torrens River, itself bordered by park, separates Adelaide from North Adelaide, which is also surrounded by parkland.

On North Terrace, the Botanic Gardens have pleasant artificial lakes and are only a short stroll from the city centre. Every Tuesday and Friday at 10.30 am, free guided tours of the gardens, taking about 1½ hours, leave from the kiosk. The gardens are open weekdays from 7 am to sunset, and on weekends and public holidays from 9 am to sunset. The stunning conservatory in the gardens recreates a tropical rainforest environment. It is open between 10 am and 4 pm; admission is $2.50.

Rymill Park in the East Parkland has a boating lake and a 600-metre-long jogging track. The South Parkland contains **Veale Gardens**, with streams and flower beds. To the west are a number of sports grounds, while the **North Parkland** borders the Torrens and surrounds North Adelaide. The **Adelaide Oval**, the site of interstate and

SOUTH AUSTRALIA

Grand Prix

The Australian Formula One Grand Prix is the final race of the international Grand Prix season. Held in Adelaide since 1985, a shock statement in late 1993 announced that the race will take place in Melbourne from 1996. This has further exacerbated the rivalry between South Australia and Victoria, which was fuelled by Adelaide's nominal success in the 1993 Australian Rules football season. The Adelaide 'Crows' team was eliminated during the semifinals. Needless to say, with both a Grand Final victory and now the Grand Prix whisked out of their grasp by those wretched Victorians, many South Australians are not impressed!

Adelaide has set Victoria quite a challenge – the Adelaide Grand Prix must be one of the easiest Grands Prix in the world to get to, as you can easily find a place to park (if you don't mind a 10-minute walk to the track), and there's plenty of public transport. The track is along city streets immediately to the east of the city centre, and the cars reach 300 km/h down Dequetteville Terrace.

With practice sessions and supporting races, the event continues for five days. For Grand Prix information (year round) phone ☎ 22 3111. Grand Prix Event Management (☎ toll-free 1800 818 484) can help with tickets for events. It also has a home hosting scheme, with listings of houses available for rental, or it can arrange accommodation with host families. ∎

---

international cricket matches, is north of the Torrens River in this part of the park.

Light's Vision

On Montefiore Hill, north of the city centre across the Torrens River, stands the statue of Light's Vision. Adelaide's founder is said to have stood here and mapped out his plan for the city. It is a good place to start your exploration of the city centre because you get a bird's-eye view of the modern city, with green parkland and the gleaming white Festival Centre at your feet.

Adelaide Zoo

On Frome Rd, the zoo has a noted collection of Australian birds as well as other important exhibits, including sloths, giant anteaters, spider monkeys and ring-tailed lemurs. It is open daily from 9.30 am to 5 pm; admission is $8. The best way of getting there is to take a cruise on the *Popeye* ($4), which departs from Elder Park in front of the Festival Centre (summer only, according to weather conditions). You can also catch bus No 272 or 273 from Currie St.

Markets

The **East End Markets** near Rundle St are open Fridays from 8 am to 9 pm and weekends and public holidays from 8 am to 5 pm. This is the place to head for alternative gear, clothes and jewellery.

The **Orange Lane Market** is Adelaide's answer to Petticoat Lane, with Indian fabrics, second-hand clothes, tarot readings, antiques and even massages on offer. It's on the corner of Edward St and Orange Lane (off Norwood Parade) on weekends from 10 am to 6 pm.

In town, the **Central Market** on Victoria Square, Grote St, is a great place for self-catering travellers. It sells a wide range of produce and a huge variety of fresh Asian foods and takeaways. It's open Tuesdays and Thursdays from 7.30 am to 5.30 pm, Fridays from 7 am to 9 pm and Saturdays from 7 am to 1 pm.

Glenelg

Glenelg, one of the most popular of the beaches stretching in a long chain south of Adelaide, is an excellent place to stay – there are many guesthouses, hotels and holiday flats here if you can't find something suitable in the city.

This is one of the oldest parts of Adelaide – the first South Australian colonists actually landed in Glenelg – so there are a number of places of historic interest. Glenelg is exceptionally easy to get to. A vintage tram runs from Victoria Square in the city centre right to Glenelg Beach, taking about 30 minutes (see the following Getting Around section for details).

At the jetty in front of the town hall and

y the beach is Bay World, a tourist information centre and souvenir shop. Next door, Beach Hire (☎ 294 1477) can arrange parasailing for $40 a flight. It's open from September to April only; the opening times vary, but if it's sunny, it'll be open.

Holdfast Cycles, at 768 Anzac Highway, hires excellently maintained mountain bikes for the serious touring cyclist. It provides maps for self-guided tours to points of interest, and helmets are included in the rates ($7.50 an hour; $30 a day). The shop is open from 9 am to 5.30 pm weekdays and 10 am to 3 pm on weekends.

On MacFarlane St, the **Old Gum Tree** marks the spot where the proclamation of South Australia was read in 1836. Governor Hindmarsh and the first colonists landed on the beach nearby and bus Nos 167 and 168 can take you there.

The boat harbour shelters a large number of yachts and Glenelg's premier attraction, a reproduction of **HMS Buffalo**, the original settlers' conveyance. The original *Buffalo* was built in 1813 in India. You'll find one of Adelaide's best seafood restaurants here (☎ 294 7000). The ship and a museum are open to visitors for $2.50 from 10 am to 5 pm daily.

Other Attractions

In Jetty St, Grange (west of the city centre), is **Sturt's Cottage**, the home of the famous early Australian explorer. It's open Wednesday to Sunday and public holidays from noon to 5 pm; admission is $2.50. Take bus No 112 from Grenfell St and get off at stop 29A. In Semaphore (north-west of the city centre), there's **Fort Glanville**, at 359 Military Rd, Semaphore Park. The fort was built in 1878, when Australia was having its phase of Russophobia as a result of the Crimean War. It's open from 1 to 5 pm on the third Sunday of each month; admission is $3.

In Springfield (south-east of the city), **Carrick Hill**, at 46 Carrick Hill Drive, is built in the style of an Elizabethan manor house set in an English-style garden. It's open Wednesday to Sunday and public holidays from 10 am to 5 pm, and there are daily

guided tours ($6). Catch bus No 171 from King William St and get off at stop 16.

Ice Skating

Adelaide's ice-skating rink (☎ 352 7977), at 23 East Terrace in Thebarton, is open daily. It also has an artificial indoor snow-skiing centre, with a 150-metre-long slope. You can get there on bus Nos 110 to 118 from Currie St.

Organised Tours & Cruises

Half-day city tours with Premier (☎ 415 5555) cost $24. You can go further afield to Hahndorf in the Adelaide Hills, or to the Mt Lofty Ranges and the Cleland Reserve (where there's a koala cuddlery) for $25. Tour Delights (☎ 373 1134) has an excellent Clare Valley wine tour ($47) and a Barossa winery tour ($40).

For $18 you can get a day pass on the Adelaide Explorer ('Adelaide's only road registered tram replica') which does a continuous circuit of a number of attractions, including Glenelg. The only problem is that it's a long circuit and you have to wait over two hours for the next 'tram' to come past. Daily departures are at 9.15 am and 12.25 and 2.55 pm, and leave from 10 King William St.

E&K Mini-Tours (☎ 337 8739) is popular with travellers. It has a Barossa day tour for $24, including lunch, and a two-hour Adelaide by Night tour for $10.

You can take a day trip to Kangaroo Island with Kendell Airlines (book through Ansett on ☎ 13 1300), but you'd have to be pretty short of time and long on cash for it to be an option. It costs $195, including air fares, a tour, all entrance fees and a barbecue lunch. There are numerous trips to the Flinders Ranges – True Blue (☎ 296 0938) has a fully inclusive three-day package for $410. Freewheelin' Cycle Tours (☎ 232 6860) has a variety of rides, including the McLaren Vale and Barossa wineries (both $39). You can also hire bicycles from Freewheelin' at 237 Hutt St.

In Port Adelaide (north-west of the city), you can take a cruise on the *Jessica Lauren*

(☎ 341 5666) from North Parade Wharf any Sunday except in July. Bookings are essential.

Adelaide Arts Festival

The Adelaide Arts Festival takes place in February and/or March of even-numbered years. The three-week festival of the arts attracts culture vultures from all over Australia to drama, dance, music and other live performances. It also includes a writers' week, art exhibitions, poetry readings and other activities with guest speakers and performers from all over the world.

The Fringe Festival, which takes place at the same time as the main festival, features alternative contemporary performance art and music.

Places to Stay

Many motel and some hotel prices rise between Christmas and the end of January, and almost all are higher during the Grand Prix, when accommodation is extremely scarce.

Camping There are quite a few caravan parks around Adelaide. The following are within 10 km of the city centre – check the tourist office for others. All prices given are for two people; prices rise around Christmas and during the Grand Prix, when most places are booked out.

Adelaide Caravan Park (☎ 363 1566), two km north-east of the city centre at Bruton St, Hackney; on-site vans from $34, cabins $53 and camp sites $15.

Windsor Gardens Caravan Park (☎ 261 1091), seven km north-east at 78 Windsor Grove, Windsor Gardens; camp sites $10 and single/double cabins $25/40.

West Beach Caravan Park (☎ 356 7654), eight km west of the city at Military Rd, West Beach; camp sites $12, on-site vans $41 and cabins $59. This park is close to the beach and only a couple of km from Glenelg.

Marine Land Village (☎ 353 2655), also at Military Rd, West Beach; two-bedroom villas for $80 (the longer you stay, the cheaper it gets), self-contained cabins for $55 and on-site vans for $40. There are no camp sites.

Hostels – city There are a couple of hostels near the bus station. When you leave the terminal, turn left onto Franklin St and on the next corner you'll find *Sunny's Backpacker Hostel* (☎ 231 2430). Second-hand books are available in the foyer and there's a licensed travel agent on the premises (open at 5.30 am). Dorm beds are priced from $1 and mountain bikes are available for hire for $15 per day.

At 11 Cannon St, a lane running off Franklin St opposite the bus station, the *Cannon St Lodge* (☎ 410 1218) has dorm beds from $1 ($13 in four-bed rooms), singles/twins for $16/28 and double-bed rooms for $38. You can hire bicycles here for $12 a day. This is a spartan, gloomy, cavernous place, but it's handy to the central bus station. *Backpac Australia* (☎ 231 0639) is at 128 Grote St opposite the Central Market. Beds cost from $10 to $15 and meals are available.

A new hostel on the scene is *New World International Hostel* (☎ 212 6888; toll-free 1800 807 367), at 29-31 Compton St, near the Central Market. This spotless place (there are even boxes provided under the bunks to put your smelly shoes in) is light and airy and has a security safe, TV, video and air-con. Dorm beds cost $12, and someone will pick you up if you ring.

Most of the other hostels are clustered in the south-eastern corner of the city centre. You can get there on bus No 191 or 192 from Pulteney St or take any bus going to the South Terrace area (Nos 171 and 172 to Hutt St; 201 to 203 to the King William St and South Terrace corner), although it's not really that far to walk.

The youth hostel (☎ 223 6007) is at 290 Gilles St. Beds for members cost $11, and nonmembers can purchase an introductory pass for an additional $6 which is valid for three consecutive nights in YHA hostels around the state. The hostel is closed between 10 am and 1 pm from Monday to Saturday, and from 10 am to 5.30 pm on Sundays.

Nearby is the *Backpackers Adelaide Hostel* (☎ 223 5680) at 263 Gilles St, with another house a few doors along. It has pleasant, casual atmosphere, and there are lots of travel brochures and information to help you work out where you're headed next. Dorm beds cost from $11, and double-bed rooms are $25. Bicycle hire is available at $8 for half a day. At 257 Gilles St, *Rucksackers International* (☎ 232 0823) is of a similar standard; it has dorm beds from $10, and a double-bed room with en-suite for $10 per person.

Two streets closer to the city centre on Carrington St, there are a few other hostels. *Adelaide City Backpackers* (☎ 232 5330) has dorm beds for $13 and doubles for $15. There's some off-street parking. Nearby at 112 Carrington St, *Adelaide Backpackers Inn* (☎ 223 6635) is a converted pub with dorm beds from $13 and doubles from $32. It has coin-operated laundry facilities, and the licensed travel agent on the premises can arrange tours and tickets.

At the eastern end of Angas St, *East Park Lodge* (☎ 223 1228) at No 341 is in a grand old building. It's clean and well run and there's a magnificent view of the city and the Adelaide Hills from the rooftop. Dorm beds cost $13, (small) single rooms $16, twin bunk-bed rooms $14 per person, and double-bed rooms $15 per person. It's close to parkland and the Grand Prix circuit.

The large *YMCA* (☎ 223 1611) at 76 Flinders St is central and takes guests of either sex. Dorms cost $11 and singles/twins are $18/30. Office hours are 8.30 am to 8.30 pm daily, but you can enter dorms at all hours.

Hostels – Glenelg There's a lot of accommodation in Glenelg. *Glenelg Beach Headquarters* (☎ 376 0007) at 7 Mosely St is around the corner from the tram terminus. It has a pool room and an inexpensive restaurant. Comfortable beds (not bunks) are $13 in dorms and $16 per person in smaller shared rooms. There's a book exchange opposite the hostel.

Further south of the tram line but on the sea at 16 South Esplanade is the wonderful *Albert Hall* (☎ 294 1966), a beautifully restored mansion. Charlie the cocky does free-range flights around the common room,

where you'll find fish in a bathtub and other exotica. Dorm beds cost from $13 and there are some private rooms for around $32.

Hotels – bottom end Unless otherwise stated, the following provide basic pub-style accommodation with common facilities. The *Metropolitan Hotel* (☎ 231 5471) at 46 Grote St is opposite the Central Market and next to Her Majesty's Theatre. It has singles/doubles for $20/28 plus a $10 key deposit.

If you want to be handy to Hindley St, you won't get any closer than *West's Private Hotel* (☎ 231 7575), smack in the middle of the mayhem at 110B Hindley St. Rooms are clean but basic, and each has its own basin. Dorm beds are priced from $15 ($10 for subsequent nights), and singles/doubles are $20/30. At 205 Rundle St the *Austral Hotel* (☎ 223 4660) has singles/doubles for $25/35. There's an up-market bar downstairs.

Moore's Brecknock Hotel (☎ 231 5467), at 410 King William St, has singles/doubles for $30/40, including a light breakfast. This is a popular Irish pub, and Irish bands play on Friday and Saturday nights.

At 44 Flinders St, near the bus station, the *Earl of Zetland Hotel* (☎ 223 5500) has large single/double self-contained rooms for $45/59.

The *St Vincent Hotel* (☎ 294 4377) at 28 Jetty Rd in Glenelg has single/twin rooms for $30/50, or self-contained singles/doubles for $40/60 – all with a light breakfast.

There are many holiday flats and serviced apartments; most quote weekly rather than daily rates. The friendly *Glenelg Seaway Apartments* (☎ 295 8503) at 18 Durham St offers accommodation for backpackers at $15 year round; its self-contained apartments are $45 a couple. It's a very plain and down-to-earth place, but the manager is friendly and makes his guests very welcome.

Hotels & Motels – middle The *City Central Motel* (☎ 231 4049), at 23 Hindley St, is a good place as long as you can cope with the bright-orange bedspreads. Singles/doubles cost $49/54.

At 262-266 Hindley St, the *Princes Arcade Motel* (☎ 231 9524) has motel rooms from $52/68, and off-street parking is available.

The *Clarice Hotel/Motel* (☎ 223 3560) is at 220 Hutt St, around the corner from the youth hostel. There are budget rooms with shared facilities from $25, doubles/triples with private toilets for $45/55, and a motel-style double for $59. All tariffs include a light breakfast. The *Princes Lodge Motel* (☎ 267 5566), 73 Lefevre Terrace, North Adelaide, has friendly management and is handy to a number of restaurants. It's within walking distance of the city, and budget singles/doubles with a light breakfast cost $25/45.

Festival Lodge (☎ 212 7877), 140 North Terrace, is opposite the casino and has rooms from $69/80. There's no on-site parking, but the motel negotiates reduced rates in nearby car parks.

Although there are motels all over Adelaide, it's worth noting that there's a 'motel alley' along Glen Osmond Rd, the road that leads into the city centre from the south-east. This is quite a busy road so some places are a bit noisy. *Powell's Court* (☎ 271 7033) is two km south of the city centre at 2 Glen Osmond Rd, Parkside. Double/triple rooms here cost from $55/65, and all rooms have kitchens.

The *Princes Highway* (☎ 379 9253), at 199 Glen Osmond Rd, Frewville, has rooms from $42/46.

Hotels – top end The *Hindley Parkroyal* (☎ 231 5552), 65 Hindley St, offers luxury accommodation from $120. Opposite the casino, and with panoramic views, the *Terrace* (☎ 217 7552), 150 North Terrace, has luxuriously appointed rooms from $210. With a handsome pile of chips from the casino you could indulge yourself at the *Hyatt Regency Adelaide* (☎ 231 1234), North Terrace, where rooms start at $260.

Colleges At Adelaide University, *St Ann's College* (☎ 267 1478) operates as a hostel from the second week in December through to the end of January; beds are around $15. At other colleges, accommodation generally includes meals and is much more expensive.

Places to Eat

Adelaide has more restaurants per head of population than any other city in Australia and its huge variety of cuisines makes dining here a culinary adventure. Licensing laws are liberal in South Australia so a high proportion of restaurants are licensed.

For $12.95, the *Advertiser Good Food Guide* is a good guide to the constantly changing food scene.

Rundle St At the eastern extension of the Rundle Mall, Rundle St has evolved into Adelaide's Bohemian quarter, with shops specialising in Art Deco artefacts and a swag of restaurants and cafes.

Tapas at No 242 is a wonderful Spanish bar – if you're perplexed by the menu, ask the friendly staff for suggestions. *Amalfi*, at 29 Frome St, just off Rundle St, has excellent Italian cuisine. It's difficult to get into on Friday nights, but is worth the wait.

The *Alfresco Gelateria* at 260 Rundle St is a good place for a gelati, cappuccino or a variety of sweets. *Scoozi*, at No 272, is a huge cosmopolitan cafe that's popular on Friday and Saturday nights. *Marconi's* and *Cafe Italia* are adjacent, and on balmy nights the tables out the front of these three places merge and it's impossible to tell who's eating where.

Mezes is a small, casual Greek place at No 287 with an open-view kitchen and tables on the street. *Mecca*, at 290 Rundle St, is open until midnight from Sunday to Thursday, and until 1.30 am on Fridays and Saturdays. There's live jazz here on Sundays. It has an interesting menu, with specialities such as char-grilled kangaroo with spiced couscous and a lime and ginger glaze – sort of an Australian/Moroccan/Caribbean conglomeration.

The new *Terrace Eatery* is a pleasant and casual dining area in the Myer Centre

Rundle Mall. There are many other interesting eateries – half the fun is checking the menus out the front and embarking on your own culinary exploration.

Hindley St & North Terrace Hindley St has become a tad passé, with its glittery bars and discos; however, if you're feeling nostalgic, the old favourites still persevere, and the quality and variety of food is still good.

Cafe Boulevard at 15 Hindley is a pleasant coffee lounge with hot meals for under $7 and cheap and delicious sweets on display. The licensed *Cafe Macchiato* at No 21 has good meals for under $9 with daily specials. It has tempting cakes and is open 24 hours a day.

Signatures Cafe Pizzeria, at No 53, has main meals for under $10. There are two restaurants at the Hindley Parkroyal, 65 Hindley St. *Cafe Mo* has international cuisine. Lunch-time buffets on weekdays are $15.50 and the evening buffet is $21. There are lots of dark-suited businesspeople here wielding mobile phones. Also at the Park Royal is *Oliphants*, with imaginative main courses from $17. Upstairs at No 79, *Food for Life*, a Hare Krishna restaurant, has vegetarian food (all you can eat) for $4, including dessert. It's open for lunch on weekdays from noon to 3 pm, and evenings from 5 to 8 pm.

Abdul and Jamil's friendly *Quiet Waters* downstairs at No 75 is a pleasant Lebanese coffee lounge serving predominantly vegetarian dishes. Takeaways are also available. Garlic is a favourite ingredient, and there's a belly dancer on Wednesday nights.

Pagana's at 101 Hindley St does main-course pastas from $8. It has good authentic Italian food and wine by the glass. There is a string of Middle Eastern takeaways, most with yiros at about $4.50. *Mekong Thai*, at No 106, specialises in Cambodian, Thai and Malaysian dishes.

Tung Sing, at No 149, is open every day except Monday from 6 pm to 2 am. Traditional Chinese dishes are between $9 and $12, and entrées are around $3.50.

Still on Hindley St but across Morphett St, the *Peaceful Vegetarian Restaurant* at No

167 serves healthy Asian dishes. Originally run by a Buddhist nun, it serves meals that are strictly vegetarian.

Cafe Vego & Loven'it, upstairs at 240 Hindley St, is a great little vegetarian discovery. You can eat in and enjoy your tofu-tempeh burger ($4) to the mellow sounds of Frank Sinatra; takeaways are also available. *Zorbas by Night* is an authentic Greek place with a wonderful atmosphere and delicious food. It has live entertainment, and even plate smashing when things really liven up. Takeaway meals are also available. At 273 Hindley St *Marcellina* is a favourite with people from the restaurant trade. This place comes alive after 2 am. It has Italian food and all-you-can-eat pizza deals for $5, or pizza and pasta for $7.50.

On Gilbert Place, which dog-legs between Hindley St and King William St, the *Pancake Kitchen* is open 24 hours a day and has main-course specials for under $7. Next door the *Penang Chinese Coffee Shop* is open Monday to Saturday until 10 pm and has main courses for under $5.

The *Ceylon Hut*, just off Hindley St at 27 Bank St, has tasty curries from $3.50.

Also close to Hindley St one of the best Indian restaurants would have to be *Taj Tandoor* at 76 Light Square.

The *City Cross Arcade*, off Grenfell St, has European and Asian food, as does *Food Affair* at the Gallerie Shopping Centre, which runs from North Terrace through to Gawler Place. On the corner of Hindley and Leigh Sts, the *Underground Diner* has mainly Asian stalls; dishes start at $4.50 and there's a bar.

At 199 North Terrace, *La Luna* is a popular place for a tasty snack. *Billy Baxters*, on the corner of North Terrace and Austin St, has the best pancakes in town. *Parlimento*, on the corner of North Terrace and Bank St, has chef's specials for under $9 and great coffee.

Around the City Gouger St is another street of restaurants with some long-standing fish and seafood places. Try *Paul's*, at 79 Gouger St, for probably the best fish & chips in town.

In the same area, the *Rock Lobster Cafe*, at 108 Gouger St, is a great place for fresh rock lobster (in season) and oysters.

The award-winning *Star of Siam* at No 67 serves good Thai food; a seven-course luncheon banquet costs $16, and evening banquets start at $20. The popular *Mamma Getta Restaurant* at No 55 is an authentic Italian place and most dishes are around $6.50. *Ming's Palace* is an unpretentious Chinese restaurant serving good food at 201 Gouger St. It's open daily and is renowned for its yum cha.

The *Red Ochre Grill*, at 129 Gouger St, is Australian bush tucker gone gourmet. It's open for lunch and dinner, and the menu reads like an internal memo at the National Parks & Wildlife Service. Meals are superb, and you may never again get to sample emu or possum, followed by wattle-seed ice cream. It's not cheap – an average of $14 for a main course – but is worth the splurge.

Spices Restaurant in the Terrace Hotel, 150 North Terrace, has just about every Oriental cuisine represented. Wonderfully aromatic main courses start at around $12.80.

Himeiji, at 61 O'Connell St, is a brand-new Japanese restaurant, with Adelaide's best sushi chef preparing reasonably priced Japanese fare. It's about five minutes drive from the city centre.

Adelaide University's union building is close to the city centre – try the *Bistro* there. It's open Monday to Friday from noon to 2.30 pm and from 5.30 to 8.30 pm. Its main courses start from just $5 and the coffee is unlimited. The *Union Cafeteria* on the ground floor is cheaper, and there are other cafes and eating areas.

The *Central Market* between Gouger and Grote Sts near Victoria Square is good value for all types of food, fruit, vegetables and bread. *Venezia*, an Italian restaurant at 121 Pirie St, has pastas from $5.80 and steaks from $12.

On Grote St, a block south of the bus station, the *Chinatown* centre has a good collection of Asian-style food centres (where a group of kitchens share a communal eating area), an excellent and inexpensive way to eat. Also good is the *Hawker's Corner* on the corner of West Terrace and Wright St. It's open for lunch and dinner daily except Monday and has Chinese, Vietnamese, Thai and Indian food.

The *Volga*, upstairs at 116 Flinders St, is Adelaide's only Russian restaurant. It's quite a formal place, with gypsy violinists (Friday and Saturday nights) and beluga caviar for those with expensive palates. Main meals (without the caviar) range from $11.50 to $19. Nearby, at 63 Hyde St, *Seoul* is a Korean restaurant open for lunch and dinner. Meals cooked at your table are around $13, or fresh from the kitchen, they're about $8. The *Pullman Adelaide Casino Restaurant* has a smorgasbord, with lunch at $20.30 ($22.30 on weekends) and dinner from $25.30 ($27.30 on weekends). The *Witches Brew* on the corner of Sturt St and Whitmore Square has cheap main courses – the entertainment is psychic readings.

Adelaide is very well supplied with hotels offering counter meals, particularly at lunch time. Just look for those telltale blackboards standing outside. You don't have to search for long to find one with meals under $5. Across in North Adelaide, the *British*, at 58 Finniss St, has a pleasant beer garden where you can grill the food yourself at the barbecue. Main courses are about $11 ($1 less if you cook your own).

Pie Floaters

If you're after late-night eats, then look for the pie carts which appear every night from 6 pm till the early hours; they're an institution. If a pie floater (the great Australian meat pie floating on a thick pea soup, completely covered in tomato sauce) is your thing then look for the vans on the corner by the GPO (the original and best) and on North Terrace near the railway station. Floaters cost $2.80. They look as bad as they sound, but evidently taste better than they look, given the numbers of diners who can be seen enjoying this culinary abomination. There are also more straightforward pies, as well as tea and coffee. ■

Hindmarsh Square is a good place to start looking for lunch in the sun. On the north Pulteney St corner, *Carrots* is a long-running health-food place. It has a nice, airy position from which to look out over the square, and is open weekdays from 10 am to 4 pm.

Further north, is the *Festival Bistro*, in the Festival Centre, overlooking the Torrens River. It has sandwiches and snacks and is open late into the evenings (closed on Sundays).

Entertainment

Bookings for performances at the Festival Centre and other Adelaide venues can be made through Bass on ☎ 13 1246. There is a Bass outlet at the centre (open 9 am to 8.30 pm Monday to Saturday) and another on the 5th floor of the Myer department store in Rundle Mall.

Casino The Adelaide Casino is housed in the old railway station on North Terrace. Apart from gambling facilities (including a two-up game, of course) there are three bars and two restaurants. It's open Monday to Thursday from 10 am to 4 am, and 24 hours a day from Friday to Sunday and on public holidays. Smart casual dress is required.

Cinemas There are a number of commercial cinemas around town, particularly on Hindley St; phone ☎ 0055 14632 for a recorded listing of films currently showing.

The *Mercury Theatre* (☎ 410 1934), at 13 Morphett St, is the home of the biennial Frames Festival of Film & Video. This festival features recent short Australian films and videos, and is usually held in September (even-numbered years).

Other alternative cinemas are the *Picca-dilly* (☎ 267 1500), at 181 O'Connell St, North Adelaide, and the *Capri Theatre* (☎ 272 1177), at 141 Goodwood Rd, Good-wood, which shows foreign films and has live performances, including an organist on Tuesdays, Fridays and Saturdays. There are free lunch-time films at the *State Film & Video Library* (☎ 348 9355) at various times of the year.

Pubs & Music There are lots of pubs with entertainment. Check the *Gig Guide* in Thursday's *Advertiser* newspaper or phone the radio station SA-FM (☎ 272 1990) for a recorded rundown of who's playing what where around town. The free music paper *Rip it Up* is worth picking up for its listings. For theatre and gallery reviews check the free monthly paper *Adelaide Review*. You'll find both these publications at most record shops, hotels, cafes and night spots around town.

Several pubs brew their own beer. The best of these is the *Port Dock Brewery Hotel* at 10 Todd St in Port Adelaide. It produces four distinctively different brews, the whole process is overseen by a German brew specialist.

The *Earl of Aberdeen*, on Hurtle Square, is a more up-market place which brews good beer. It's handy to the backpackers' hostels in the south-east of the city centre.

There's the usual rock pub circuit. Better pubs include the *Austral* and the *Exeter* in Rundle St at Nos 205 and 246 respectively. The Exeter is an art students' hang-out, and is a good place to go for a drink before heading out to eat.

The *Universal Wine Bar* at 285 Rundle St has gone overboard with the iron filigree. The doors fold back on summer nights so you can catch the breeze while sipping a designer ale.

The Commercial Hotel on the corner of Morphett and Hindley Sts is known as *Nixon's*. This place has up-market aspirations, but the heavy-duty bouncers are an incongruous element. *Jules* in Hindley St has a younger clientele, but if disco's your thing, this is the place to head. It's open 24 hours a day.

Le Rox, on Light Square, looks like a set from the Poseidon Adventure – no, that's not due to your last gin sling – the furniture really is attached to the ceiling. This is one of the city's most popular live-band venues for interstate and international groups. If there are no international acts in town, there's a disco at Le Rox on Friday and Saturday nights.

Adelaide University often has big-name rock bands on at the union (☎ 303 5927). Every Friday lunch time during term, there is a free band playing upstairs in the union bar or on the Barr-Smith lawns from 1 to 2 pm. The union bar is also an excellent venue for social, cultural and avant-garde performances and activities. There's always something interesting taking place, and visitors are welcome.

There are often free concerts in the amphitheatre at the *Adelaide Festival Centre* on alternate Sundays during summer, and in the centre's foyer every Sunday during winter. On Saturday nights between 10 pm and 1 am, the *Hot Club*, at the centre, is a good jazz venue; admission is $5.

Every Friday night the *Irish Club* at 11 Carrington St has live music. The bar at the *Earl of Zetland* pub on Flinders St near the YMCA claims to have the world's largest collection of malt whiskies, with over 275 varieties available by the nip.

Things to Buy
Rundle St is the place to head for retro clothes and gear. If you simply can't leave town without a synthetic leopard skin lamp shade, Port O' Call, at No 281, is sure to please. See under the earlier Markets section for more shopping details.

Tandanya, the large centre run by the Aboriginal Cultural Institute at 253 Grenfell St, includes a crafts and souvenir shop; it is open daily and there's also a cafe. Craftwork is produced and sold at the Jam Factory Craft & Design Centre, in the Lion Arts Centre on the corner of Morphett St and North Terrace.

Getting There & Away
Air Many flights from Melbourne and Sydney to the Northern Territory go via Adelaide, and the Darwin route is often heavily booked. Qantas (☎ 13 1313) is at 144 North Terrace and Ansett (☎ 13 1300) is at 142 North Terrace.

Standard one-way fares from Adelaide include: to Brisbane $470, to Sydney $324, to Melbourne $225, to Perth $482, to Alice Springs $360 and to Darwin $518. Remember that there are almost always cheaper fares available.

For air fares within the state, refer to the air-fares chart in the introductory Getting Around section in this chapter.

Bus Adelaide's central bus station is at 101-111 Franklin St. Greyhound Pioneer and Stateliner have their offices here. Left-luggage lockers are available. Greyhound Pioneer (☎ 13 2030) has services between Adelaide and all major cities. The fare to Melbourne is $50 (10 hours), to Sydney $90 (22 hours), to Perth $180 (34 hours), and to Alice Springs $79 (20 hours).

McCafferty's (☎ 212 5066), at 220 Morphett St, offers backpackers' discounts on some routes. A sample of its fares is Melbourne $40; Sydney $75 via Melbourne and $90 direct ($70 for backpackers); Alice Springs $79; Darwin $187; Brisbane $127 ($120 for backpackers); and Cairns $180 ($170 for backpackers).

Firefly Express (☎ 231 1488) is at 185 Victoria Square, near the corner of Franklin St. It runs to Melbourne every evening from Victoria Square at 8.30 pm ($45) and on to Sydney for $50 (day service) and $45 (overnight service). There are various other bus operators, particularly on the Perth route, and there are frequent special deals on offer.

If you're going to Melbourne, a popular alternative to the major bus lines is to spend three days and two nights on the trip with the Wayward Bus Company (☎ 232 6646; toll-free 1800 882 823), which has a 22-seat bus which deviates from the main highways, taking in Victoria's spectacular Great Ocean Road, the Coorong wetlands and a winery or two along the way. The $125 fare (10% off for students and YHA members) includes lunches but not accommodation or other meals. Departures from Adelaide are on Wednesday at 8 am; from Melbourne they depart on Saturday at 8 am. Wayward also has a similar 10-day Adelaide to Alice Springs trip. Departures are monthly from March to early December, and take in the

Barossa and Clare valleys, the Flinders Ranges, the Oodnadatta track, Coober Pedy and Uluru (Ayers Rock). The $540 cost includes admission to all national parks, all meals and camping or bunkhouse accommodation en route.

Stateliner, Premier (☎ 415 5555 for both) and other South Australian operators are at the central bus station. Stateliner has services to Wilpena Pound, the Eyre Peninsula, Ceduna, Arkaroola, Roxby Downs and the Riverland area. Premier goes to Goolwa, Victor Harbor, Moonta and Murray Bridge. See the appropriate Getting There & Away sections in this chapter for details.

Yorke Peninsula bus service (☎ 391 2977), at the central bus station, has services to the east coast and the centre of the Yorke Peninsula. Mt Barker bus service (☎ (08) 391 2977) runs from the same depot and has frequent buses going to Hahndorf ($3.90) and Mt Barker ($4.10).

Train There are two stations in Adelaide: the large one on North Terrace, for suburban trains; and the interstate terminal (☎ 231 7699 for information; 13 2232 for bookings) on Railway Terrace, Keswick, just south-west of the city centre. It's wise to book ahead, particularly on the very popular Ghan.

Caper fares are considerably cheaper than standard fares. They can be purchased (according to availability) any day prior to travel, but there are no refunds if the ticket is cancelled within seven days of travel. Caper discounts are only available on the more expensive fares.

Adelaide is connected by rail with Sydney, Melbourne, Perth, Broken Hill, Alice Springs and other centres. To Melbourne the daily overnight Overland takes about 12 hours and costs $45 in economy, or $89 ($60 Caper) in 1st class and $149 with sleeper ($99 Caper).

You can travel daily between Sydney and Adelaide via Melbourne on the Melbourne Express (Sydney to Melbourne) and Overland (Melbourne to Adelaide). The connection is poor in Melbourne – you will need to spend the day there.

The Indian Pacific travels via Broken Hill twice weekly. Via Melbourne it's $94 economy, $158 for a 1st-class seat ($139 Caper) and $284 for a 1st-class sleeper ($234 Caper). Via Broken Hill it's $105 economy, $199 for a holiday-class economy sleeper ($139 Caper) and $317 for a 1st-class sleeper ($272 Caper).

There's also the Speedlink – a daily bus and train connection which is not only cheaper but five or six hours faster. You travel from Sydney to Albury on the XPT train, and from Albury to Adelaide on a V/Line bus. Travel time is under 20 hours. An economy/1st-class seat is $99/109 (no Capers).

Between Adelaide and Perth there is the Indian Pacific which runs twice weekly (Tuesdays and Fridays). The trip takes about 36 hours. Fares are $170 for an economy seat, $399 for a holiday-class sleeper (no meals; $279 Caper), and $566 for a 1st-class sleeping berth with meals ($397 Caper).

The Ghan between Adelaide and Alice Springs runs weekly throughout the year (departing Thursdays) and twice weekly from April to October (Mondays and Thursdays). The fare is $139 in economy; $229 in a holiday-class sleeper (no meals; $160 Caper); and $435 in a 1st-class sleeper with meals ($305 Caper).

Boat The MV *Island Seaway* runs a passenger service from Port Adelaide to Kingscote (Kangaroo Island). See the Kangaroo Island section for details.

Car & Motorbike Rental The major companies are represented in Adelaide. Those with cheap rates include Access Rent-a-Car (☎ 223 7466), Smile Rent-a-Car (☎ 234 0655) and Action Rent-a-Car (☎ 352 7044). Access is one of the few companies that will allow its cars to be taken over to Kangaroo Island.

Show & Go (☎ 376 0333), at 236 Brighton Rd, Brighton, has motorscooters for $49 per day (car licence required) and 250 cc motorbikes for $59 (full bike licence required).

Getting Around

To/From the Airport Adelaide's modern international airport is conveniently located eight km west of the city centre. There's an airport bus service (☎ 381 5311) operating between hotels at least half-hourly from around 7 am to 9 pm on weekdays and hourly on weekends and public holidays for $4.

From Victoria Square to the domestic terminal the trip takes about 35 minutes; slightly less to the international terminal. If you're catching a flight on one of the smaller airlines (eg to Kangaroo Island) let the driver know, as the drop-off point is different. A taxi costs about $12. You can travel between the city and the airport entrance on bus Nos 276, 277 and 278.

Budget, Hertz, Avis and Thrifty have hire-car desks at the airport.

Public Transport Adelaide has an integrated local transport system operated by the State Transport Authority (STA) (☎ 210 1000). The STA Customer Centre, where you can get timetables and buy a transport map for 60c, is on the corner of King William and Currie Sts.

The system covers metropolitan buses and trains, as well as Adelaide's vintage tram which operates to Glenelg, and the O-Bahn Busway, which runs on concrete tracks between the city centre and Tea Tree Plaza, home of the huge Westfield Shopping Centre & Cinema Complex. Tickets purchased on board the buses are $2.70 before 9 am, after 3 pm on weekends and $1.60 between 9 am and 3 pm weekdays. They are valid for two hours from the commencement of the first journey. (Tickets cannot be purchased on board trains.) For travellers, the best deal is the day-trip ticket, which permits unlimited travel for the whole day and costs $4.40.

The free Bee Line bus service runs down King William St from the Glenelg tram terminus at Victoria Square and round the corner to the railway station. It operates every five to eight minutes from 8 am to 6 pm weekdays, and every 15 minutes to 7 pm on Fridays and from 8 am to 5 pm on Saturdays.

The airport to city bus service calls into the interstate train station (Keswick) on its regular run between the airport and the city ($2.50 from the station to the city centre).

There's a solitary vintage tram service which will whisk you out to Glenelg from Victoria Square.

Moped & Bicycle Hire-Mate (☎ 264 2400), 754 North East Rd, Holden Hill, rents mopeds during the Grand Prix and over the Christmas period.

Adelaide is a relatively cyclist-friendly city, with good cycling tracks and bicycle lanes on many city streets. Linear Park Mountain Bike Hire (☎ 223 6953) is at Elder Park, next to the Festival Theatre, and conveniently located near the Linear Park Bike & Walking Track, a 40-km track which wends its way from the beach to the foot of the Adelaide Hills. Bicycles are $8 per hour or $20 for the day. Several of the hostels around the city rent bicycles. Pulteney City Cycles (☎ (08) 223 6678) at No 309 rents mountain and racing bicycles from $15 per day or $90 for a week.

Freewheelin' (☎ 232 6860), at 237 Hutt St, has bicycles from $15 to $20 per day, and offers a pick-up and drop-off service. It also has entire touring outfits, including panniers etc.

Adelaide Hills

Only 30 minutes drive from the city centre, the scenic Adelaide Hills, part of the Mt Lofty Ranges, encompass the region bordered by the towns of Meadows and Strathalbyn to the south, Mt Barker and Nairne to the east, and Mt Pleasant and Springton to the north. Apart from the beauty of the hills themselves, the opportunities for bushwalking (over 1000 km of trails crisscross the hills), the range of conservation parks in the hills precincts, and historic townships such as Clarendon, Hahndorf and Strathalbyn make this region a popular daytrip destination from Adelaide.

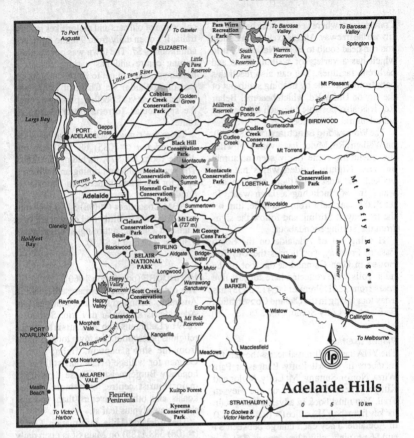

Adelaide Hills

0   5   10 km

The RAA produces a touring booklet of the Adelaide Hills region ($3). The Adelaide Hills Information Centre is in Hahndorf.

NATIONAL PARKS & SCENIC DRIVES

To visit the northern hills area, leave the city via Payneham Rd and continue onto Torrens Gorge Rd. This route takes you through Birdwood and north to the Barossa Valley. However, you might prefer to head south at Birdwood and travel through Hahndorf, returning to Adelaide via the South Eastern Freeway. Alternatively, leave Payneham Rd and take McGill Rd through **Morialta Con-**servation Park, near Rostrevor, which has walking trails, barbecues, waterfalls and a rugged gorge. Continue south via Norton Summit and Summertown to the **Cleland Conservation Park**. There's a wide variety of wildlife in the park, and it's open from 9 am to 5 pm daily. Buses run to the park; contact the TSA in Adelaide for details.

A slight detour will take you to **Mt Lofty Summit**, with impressive views back over the city (particularly at night). From the summit you can continue about three km to the **Mt Lofty Botanical Gardens** (open daily from 10 am to 4 pm). Further south is

Crafers, from where you can head back to the city via the freeway. Alternatively, from Crafers you can head south to **Belair National Park**, which has a variety of walking trails and barbecue facilities. You can also reach this park from Adelaide by heading south out of the city on Unley Rd, which becomes Belair Rd. It is also possible to reach the park by suburban train from Adelaide.

The **Warrawong Sanctuary** (☎ 388 5380), on Williams Rd, Mylor, has a variety of wildlife, including some rarely seen nocturnal animals. Nightly guided walks must be booked and cost $10; there are also day walks for $6, including a dawn walk. To reach the sanctuary from Adelaide, turn off the freeway at Stirling and follow the signs from the Stirling roundabout.

Heading out of Adelaide on the South Eastern Freeway, you'll pass the **Old Toll House** in Glen Osmond at the foot of the hills. Tolls were collected here for just five years from 1841. Premier (☎ 415 5555) has a day tour taking in the Cleland Conservation Park and Mt Lofty Summit for $25.

Places to Stay

The YHA has five 'limited access' hostels for members in the Mt Lofty Ranges at Para Wirra, Norton Summit, Mt Lofty, Mylor and Kuitpo. These hostels are on the Heysen Trail. You must book in advance and obtain the key from the YHA office (☎ (08) 231 5583) in Adelaide. They each charge between $4 and $6 per night, plus a key deposit ($5).

The friendly *Fuzzies Farm* (☎ (08) 390 1111) at Norton Summit is a developing 'eco-village' on 17 hectares next to the Morialta Conservation Park, about 15 km east of Adelaide. There are various farm animals, vegetable gardens and craft studios, as well as a restaurant, spa and pool. A one-night introduction to Fuzzies is available for $19, including a tour of the farm, an evening meal and accommodation. If you decide to stay on, a six-night deal is available.

BIRDWOOD (population 580)

The **Birdwood Hill Museum** has the largest collection of old cars and motorbikes in Australia. It's open daily from 9 am to 5 pm and admission is $7. The town was once a gold-mining centre and has various other old buildings. You can get to Birdwood (50 km east of Adelaide) via Chain of Ponds and Gumeracha or via Lobethal, passing through the spectacular **Torrens River Gorge** en route.

There isn't much accommodation – the *Birdwood Inn* (☎ (085) 68 212) has one double room for $75, including breakfast. The inn has a pleasant dining area which is open for lunch and dinner from Thursday to Sunday.

ABM Coachlines (☎ (08) 347 3336) runs from Adelaide to Birdwood on weekdays at 7 am and 3.45 pm, returning on weekdays at 3.30 pm. The cost is $7.10.

HAHNDORF (population 1660)

The oldest surviving German settlement in Australia, Hahndorf, 29 km south-east of Adelaide, is a popular day trip. Settled in 1839 by Lutherans who left Prussia to escape religious persecution, the town took its name from the ship's captain, Hahn; *dorf* is German for 'village'. Hahndorf still has an honorary Burgermeister. These days it's a major tourist centre, with more stuffed koalas and other souvenirs than you can shake a eucalyptus leaf at.

The Adelaide Hills Information Centre (☎ (08) 388 1185) on Main St is open daily from 10 am to 4 pm. Various German festivals are held in the town, and on Foundation Day long weekend in January, there are street parades and wine tastings, and all the local eateries peddle their wares from tables outside their premises.

The **German Arms Hotel** at 50 Main St dates from 1834. The **Hahndorf Academy**, next to the information centre, was established in 1857, and houses an art gallery featuring the work of the 19th-century artist Sir Hans Heysen. Guided tours through Sir Hans's studio and house, the Cedars, are conducted every Tuesday at 11.30 am and 2.30 pm ($5). The **Antique Clock Museum** at 91 Main St has a fine collection of time-pieces, including a very large cuckoo clock; admission is $3.

Places to Stay & Eat
Höchstens Convention & Tourist Centre (☎ (08) 388 7921) has a motel, caravan park and camp sites. It's 1.5 km out of town on Main St. Camp sites are $10, cabins $36 and motel rooms $75/79 for singles/doubles. Other than this and a couple of expensive motels, the only option is to take up the offer of 'emergency accommodation for stuck backpackers' (☎ (08) 388 7079), at 54 English St – it's very cheap but there's only one room, so don't rely on it.

Hahndorf restaurants have good, solid German food, of course; they include the *German Arms* and the *Cottage Kitchen* on Main St. *Karl's German Cafe*, at 17 Main St, is recommended by locals for authentic German cuisine.

A great place to purchase German, Swiss and Dutch foods, including bockwurst, brat-wurst and other gourmet delights, is the *Hahndorf Wursthaus*, at 76 Main St.

Getting There & Away
Mt Barker bus service (☎ (08) 391 2977) runs several times daily from the central bus station in Adelaide ($3.90).

Getting Around
A pleasant way to amble around the town is in the horse-drawn carriage which leaves regularly from in front of the German Arms. If that's a little too sedate for you, Original Harley Tours (☎ (08) 370 3348) has rides on Harley-Davidson motorcycles starting from $15 (weekends and public holidays).

STRATHALBYN (population 2600)
On the Angas River, this picturesque town was settled in 1839 by Scottish immigrants. The tourist office (☎ (085) 36 3212) is on South Terrace. Among the many interesting old buildings in this classified 'heritage town' is St Andrew's Church, one of the best-known country churches in Australia.

Pick up a walking-tour pamphlet from the tourist office ($1.20) which lists buildings and sites of interest in the township. Strathalbyn has an annual **Penny Farthing Bicycle Challenge**, which takes place in March and is a must for vintage bicycle buffs; phone the tourist office for exact dates.

Places to Stay
The council caravan park (☎ (085) 36 3681), on Coronation Rd, is a basic, shady place with on-site vans from $20. The *Terminus Hotel* (☎ (085) 36 2026) on Rankine St has singles/doubles for $25/45, including break-fast.

Getting There & Away
Mt Barker bus service (☎ (08) 391 2977) runs from Adelaide (changing at Mt Barker) to Strathalbyn on weekdays for $5.70.

CLARENDON
Beautiful Clarendon, 28 km south of Ade-laide, has inspiring views and heritage buildings. The *Old Clarendon Winery Complex* (☎ (08) 383 6166) has cellar-door sales and tastings, as well as a gallery and bakery. You can also stay here – the rooms have breathtaking views over the township. Singles/doubles are $60/70, including a light breakfast.

Fleurieu Peninsula

South of Adelaide is the Fleurieu Peninsula, so close that most places can be visited on day trips from the city. The Gulf St Vincent has a series of fine beaches down to Cape Jervis.

The peninsula was named by Frenchman Nicholas Baudin after Napoleon's minister for the navy, who financed Baudin's expedition to Australia. In the early days, settlers on the peninsula ran a busy smuggling business, but in 1837 the first whaling station was established at Encounter Bay. This grew to become the colony's first successful industry.

There are good surfing beaches along this

Fleurieu Peninsula

rugged coastline. Inland there's rolling countryside and the vineyards of the McLaren Vale area.

Getting There & Away

Premier (☎ (08) 415 5555) has up to three services daily on the two-hour Adelaide to McLaren Vale ($4.50), Port Elliot ($10.50), Goolwa ($10.50) and Victor Harbor ($10.50) route.

The Kangaroo Island Connection (☎ (08) 384 6860) runs twice a day to Cape Jervis from Adelaide. The fare to Yankalilla is $8.90 and to Cape Jervis $13.

A steam train operates between Adelaide and Victor Harbor at selected periods throughout the year. The Cockle Train is a smaller version which travels between Victor Harbor and Goolwa. See the Victor Harbor section for details.

GULF ST VINCENT BEACHES

There is a string of fine beaches south of Adelaide along the Gulf St Vincent coast of the peninsula. The beaches extend from **Christie's Beach** through **Port Noarlunga**, **Seaford Beach** and **Moana Beach** to **Maslin Beach**, the southern end of which became the first legal nudist beach in Australia.

Further south, beyond **Aldinga Beach** and **Sellicks Beach**, the coastline is rockier but there are still good swimming beaches at **Myponga**, **Normanville** and several other places. The coast road ends at **Cape Jervis** at the tip of the peninsula. From here you can look across the narrow Backstairs Passage to Kangaroo Island, 13 km away. Near Cape Jervis there's a 12-hectare fauna park. The cape is a popular spot for hang-gliding.

The picturesque **Inman Valley** is only 16 km from Victor Harbor and is a prime dairy and grazing area. It is an access point for the Heysen Trail.

Places to Stay

The *Cape Jervis Tavern* (☎ (085) 98 0276),

the only place to stay in Cape Jervis, has rooms for $45/55 and also serves meals.

There are two caravan parks in Normanville with on-site vans, and the *Yankalilla Hotel* (☎ (085) 58 2011), in Yankalilla, four km east of Normanville, has a cottage for $50.

The youth hostel (☎ (085) 58 8277), in Inman Valley near Glacier Rock, 16 km west of Victor Harbor, is in a lovely tranquil setting. Beds are $7, and maps of the Heysen Trail are available from the hostel manager.

SOUTHERN VALES

Adelaide has sprawled so far that the small town of **Morphett Vale** is now an outer suburb. Amongst its historic buildings is St Mary's (1846), the first Roman Catholic church in the state. **Old Noarlunga** is a tiny old township only 10 minutes drive from McLaren Vale. Heritage walks are conducted at 2 pm on the first and third Sundays of each month, leaving from the Market Reserve; phone ☎ (08) 384 7918 for details.

The Fleurieu Peninsula has a string of wineries, centred predominantly around **McLaren Vale** (population 1470), but also encompassing **Reynella, Willunga** and **Langhorne Creek**. The area is particularly well suited to red wines, but a trend towards white wine consumption in the 1970s prompted growers to diversify. There are over two dozen wineries in the McLaren Vale area alone and about 50 in the whole region.

The first winery in the area was established in Reynella in 1838, and some of the wineries still in existence date back to the last century and have fine old buildings. Most of them are open to the public from Monday to Saturday, and many are open on Sunday as well. Some have picnic or barbecue areas close to the cellar-door sales area.

Each winery has its own appeal, whether it be a superb setting or just a good full-bodied drop of the home product. The following are suggestions to help with your explorations.

Chapel Hill, Chapel Hill Rd, McLaren Vale south, has a magnificent hill-top location with views over the Gulf St Vincent. This is a small vineyard producing sophisticated whites and reds.

Noon's, Rifle Range Rd, McLaren Vale south, specialises in full-bodied reds. This winery is in a pleasant rural setting beside a small creek, and there are barbecue facilities.

d'Arenburg, Osborne Rd, McLaren Vale, has produced consistently good wines since 1928. There is nothing highbrow about this place – the tasting room is very informal and the staff are friendly and helpful.

Woodstock, Douglas Gully Rd, McLaren Flat, is another small winery in a tranquil garden setting.

The McLaren Vale Wine Bushing Festival takes place over a week in late October and/or early November each year. It's a busy time of wine tastings and tours, and the whole thing is topped by a grand feast.

Guided bicycle tours of the wineries are a pleasant way to amble around this scenic area. Tours take two hours and include afternoon tea. They leave every Tuesday, Thursday and Sunday, and cost $20; phone ☎ 018 083 801 for details. If you want to head off on your own, mountain bikes are available for $20, including helmet (or $15 for two or more people) from the same crowd. There's a walking/bicycle track along the old railway line from McLaren Vale to Willunga, six km to the south.

A great way to visit a few wineries is on a camel with the Outback Camel Co (☎ (085) 567 236). A one-day trek costs $75, and overnight trips are also available.

Willunga, in the south of the Southern Vales winery area, has a long history and a collection of fine buildings from the colonial era. It is the centre for Australian almond growing, and the Almond Blossom Festival is held in July.

There's an information centre at the coffee shop in the magnificent Hardy's Tintara complex (open 10 am to 4 pm), in McLaren Vale. During the Bushing Festival, a safe way to ensure you get to sample all the offerings of the McLaren Vale wineries is on the winery bus service, which chortles around the wineries, picking up and dropping off imbibers en route. At the **Mt Magnificent Conservation Park**, 12 km east of Willunga, you can see kangaroos and take pleasant walks.

Places to Stay & Eat

The *McLaren Vale Lakeside Caravan Park* (☎ (085) 323 9255), set amidst vineyards on Field St, has camp sites and on-site vans, and the friendly owners are very knowledgeable about the McLaren Vale area. *Southern Vales* (☎ (085) 323 8144), Chalk Hill Rd, is a friendly place with rates of $70 per double for B&B. The *Hotel McLaren* has singles/doubles for $30/45.

The wine-tasters' lunches can be a good deal: the *Oliverhill Winery* (☎ (08) 323 8922) on Seaview Rd has main courses for $9 or less, but *Haselgrove Wines* (☎ (08) 323 8706) on the corner of Kangarilla and Foggo Rds has the best meals from $11. In Willunga, the *Willunga Hotel* (☎ (085) 56 2135) has rooms from $25 per person.

PORT ELLIOT (population 1200)

On Horseshoe Bay, a smaller part of Encounter Bay, Port Elliot was established in 1854 as the seaport for the Murray River trade and was the first town on Encounter Bay. **Horseshoe Bay** has a sheltered, safe swimming beach with a good cliff-top walk above it. Nearby surf beaches include **Boomer Beach**, on the western edge of town, and **Middleton Beach**, to the east of town. The Southern Surf Shop, a few doors down from the Royal Family Hotel, hires surfing gear and can provide information on prevailing surfing conditions.

Places to Stay & Eat

You can camp or stay in on-site vans at the *Port Elliot Caravan Park* in Horseshoe Bay. The *Royal Family Hotel* (☎ (085) 54 2219) at 32 North Terrace has singles/doubles for $20/30. Counter meals start from $6, and there's a bakery across the road.

VICTOR HARBOR (population 5900)

The main town on the peninsula, 84 km south of Adelaide, Victor Harbor looks out on to Encounter Bay where Flinders and Baudin had their historic meeting in 1802. Up on the headland known as the Bluff, there's a memorial to the 'encounter' which took place on the bay below. It's a steep climb up to the Bluff for the fine views.

The town was founded early in South Australia's history as a sealing and whaling centre. South of the town at Rosetta Bay, below the Bluff, is **Whaler's Haven** with many interesting reminders of those early whaling days and a restaurant and coffee shop. The first whaling station was estab-

---

Southern Right Whales

Southern right whales, so called because they were considered by whalers to be the 'right' whales to harpoon because of their fine whalebone and quantity of oil, used to roam the seas in prolific numbers; however, due to the unrestricted slaying of these magnificent creatures by whalers last century, their numbers dwindled from 100,000 to an estimated 3000 today. They are now considered endangered, but are fighting their way back from the brink of extinction. During recent years southern right whales have migrated during the winter months (June to September) to Encounter Bay, near Victor Harbor. A 'whale siren' is sounded whenever a whale is sighted in Encounter Bay.

The large number of visitors endeavouring to catch a glimpse of these mighty sea creatures has placed pressure on the coastal environment, particularly the fragile sand dunes. In an attempt to minimise this pressure, a 'whale watchers kit' has been compiled which details whale behaviour and ways in which whale watchers can reduce their impact on the fragile coastal ecosystem. It is available from petrol stations in the Victor Harbor region or from the Department of Environment & Natural Resources Information Centre (☎ (08) 204 1910), 77 Grenfell St, Adelaide, and the Fleurieu district office at 57 Ocean St, Victor Harbor. A whale information hotline has reports on whale sightings (☎ 0055 31636), and during the winter period, Whale Information Centres are operated at 2 Ocean St, Victor Harbor (☎ (085) 52 1022), and at the Hotel Victor (☎ (085) 52 1288), and provide up-to-the-minute information on sightings, as well as literature on the southern right whale. ■

lished here in 1837 and another followed soon after on Granite Island, but whaling ceased in 1864.

Historic buildings include **St Augustine's Church of England** (1869), the **Telegraph Station** (1869), the **Fountain Inn** (1840) and the **Old Station Master's Residence** (1866), now administered as a museum by the National Trust (open Sundays from 11 am to 4 pm). The Telegraph Station houses an art gallery.

The tourist office (☎ (085) 52 4255) is on Torrens St, diagonally opposite the police station. It's open every day from 10 am to 4 pm (9 am to 4.30 pm during summer).

The port is protected from the high southern seas by **Granite Island**, a small island connected to the mainland by a causeway. You can ride out there on a double-decker tram pulled by Clydesdale draught horses ($3). On the island there are good views across the bay, and if you're feeling lazy you can ride to the top of the hill on a chair lift.

The National Parks & Wildlife Service operates one-hour **Little Penguin Sunset Walks** at 8.30 pm nightly during summer (check frequency and times in winter). They cost $5 and leave from the information bay on Granite Island, near the end of the causeway. There are also guided walks of Granite Island, focusing on the island's Aboriginal and European history; phone ☎ (085) 52 3677 for details of both walks.

Places to Stay

The council caravan park (☎ (085) 52 1142) has camp sites and on-site vans. The *Warringa Hostel* (☎ (085) 52 5970) is part of the Anchorage Guest House complex, at 16 Flinders Parade, near the railway station. Beds in very basic dorms are $10 for YHA members and $15 for nonmembers. Single/double guesthouse rooms start from $35/60. Arrangements can be made for transfers to Cape Jervis to catch the ferry to Kangaroo Island, and bicycles are available for hire.

The *Grosvenor Hotel* (☎ (085) 52 1011), a block away on Ocean St, is reasonable at $25/35. The *City Motel* (☎ (085) 52 2455) is centrally located next to the post office on Ocean St, and has singles/doubles from $40/50.

Places to Eat

The *Original Fish & Chip Shop* on Ocean St is popular, although prices for sit-down meals are high. The *Hotel Victor* has tasty counter meals from about $3.50, and a more formal dining room. Locals recommend the *Emerald Restaurant*, on Port Elliot Rd, for good-value Chinese cuisine.

Getting There & Away

The Southern Encounter steam train runs between Adelaide and Victor Harbor via Goolwa on Sundays from September to November and May to mid-June. The fare is $39, and bookings are essential. Contact the SteamRanger (☎ (08) 231 1707), 6th floor, 38 Currie St, Adelaide. Premier buses to/from Adelaide's central bus station leave daily and cost $10.50.

The Cockle Train travels daily on the scenic Encounter Coast between Goolwa and Victor Harbor over Easter and during school holidays, with selected Sunday trips at other times. The return fare is $12, and tickets can be purchased at the station in Victor Harbor.

Getting Around

Mopeds can be hired during the summer holiday season from two Shell service stations: 105 Victoria St, near the Inman River bridge; and 165 Hindmarsh Rd.

GOOLWA (population 3000)

On Lake Alexandrina near the mouth of the Murray River, Goolwa initially grew with the developing trade along the mighty Murray. The Murray mouth silted up and large ships were unable to get up to Goolwa, so a railway line, the first in the state, was built from Goolwa to nearby Port Elliot. In the 1880s a new railway line to Adelaide spelt the end for Goolwa as a port town.

The **museum** on Porter St ($1 admission) is open every afternoon except on Mondays and Fridays. The **art gallery**, next door (free), is housed in the old superintendent's cottage. Two km away at the **Malleebaa Woolshed**, you can see 18 breeds of sheep and other sheep-related displays – it's only open on long weekends and during school holidays.

The **Sir Richard Peninsula** is a long stretch of beach leading to the mouth of the Murray. You can drive along it (4WD only), but there's no way across to the similar beaches of the Coorong which begin on the other side of the Murray River mouth.

There are cruises on Lake Alexandrina on the MV *Aroona* or PS *Mundoo* from $15. Possibly more amusing is a trip with the Coorong Pirate (☎ (085) 52 1221), a large and irredeemably ocker gentleman who runs fun trips from about $5.

Milang on Lake Alexandrina was a centre for the river trade even before Goolwa. In the early days of the river shipping business, bullock wagons carried goods overland between here and Adelaide.

The tourist office (☎ (085) 55 1144), open from 10 am to 4 pm, is in the centre of Goolwa near Signal Point. The **Signal Point River Murray Interpretive Centre** (open 10 am to 5 pm) is on the waterfront and contains interesting exhibits on the early history of life on the river ($5). Self-guided walking-tour pamphlets of Goolwa are available from the interpretive centre and the tourist office.

A free vehicle ferry over to **Hindmarsh Island** operates 24 hours a day.

Places to Stay

The *Camping & Tourist Park* (☎ (085) 55 2144) on Kessell Rd has camp sites ($8) and on-site vans ($20 to $30). The *Corio Hotel* (☎ (085) 55 1136) on Railway Terrace has rooms for $25, including a cooked breakfast.

On Hindmarsh Island, *Narnu Farm* (☎ (085) 55 2002) has cottages from $60. The farm is in a rural setting, and has free-range domestic animals and poultry. Visitors are encouraged to take part in farm activities.

Graham's Castle (☎ 085) 55 2182), a rambling old home built in 1868, is about two km from the town centre, on Castle St, about

500 metres from the beach. Dormitory accommodation is available for $12 (linen hire extra). There's a pool and games room, and the owners will pick you up from the town centre if you give them a ring on arrival.

Getting There & Away

Daily buses to Adelaide cost $10.50. See the earlier Victor Harbor section for details of steam trains which pass through Goolwa.

Kangaroo Island

Separated from the mainland over 10,000 years ago, Kangaroo Island is the third-largest island in Australia (after Tasmania, and Melville Island off Darwin). About 150 km long and 30 km wide, the island is sparsely populated and offers superb scenery, pleasant sheltered beaches along the north coast, a rugged and wave-swept south coast, plus lots of native wildlife and excellent fishing.

It was not until early this century that evidence was found of Aboriginal habitation on Kangaroo Island – prehistoric stone implements have since been discovered scattered across many areas, suggesting human occupation over 11,000 years ago. Archaeologists are uncertain as to what caused the demise of these early inhabitants.

Like other islands off the south coast of Australia, Kangaroo Island had a rough-and-ready early European history with sealers, whalers and escaped convicts all playing their often ruthless part. Many of the place names on the island have a French flavour, as it was first charted by the French explorer Nicholas Baudin.

Kangaroo Island's geographical isolation from the mainland has been a boon to the native wildlife, as the island is free of introduced pests such as rabbits and foxes. In fact, a number of threatened native Australian animals, such as the koala and platypus, have been introduced to the island where conditions are considered more conducive to their survival. The main threat is of the vehicular

Kangaroo Island

INVESTIGATOR STRAIT

0   10   20 km

SOUTHERN   OCEAN

form, as the numbers of furry corpses on the roadsides attest: reducing your driving speed, which is a good idea anyway due to the island's many unsealed roads, may help to increase the animals' chances of survival.

Apart from beaches, bushwalks and wildlife, there are also a number of shipwrecks off the coast, many of which are of interest to scuba divers.

Information

The main National Parks office (which doubles as the tourist office) is at 37 Dauncey St in Kingscote (☎ (0848) 22 381). It is open from 8.45 am to 5 pm Monday to Friday. Camping permits can be obtained here ($2 per site per day), or you can purchase an Island Pass, valid for one year, which covers all entry and camping fees for the whole island (passes can only be purchased on the island). The pass also entitles holders to free National Parks tours (see under Organised Tours). Permits and passes can be obtained from any of the island's seven National Parks offices, as well as at other selected outlets; contact the Kingscote office for details.

During summer months, fire restrictions are in force. Only gas fires may be lit in

national parks, and on days of total fire ban, no fires may be lit (including gas fires). Penalties for lighting a fire illegally are severe. Contact district council offices, the Country Fire Service or park rangers for further information.

If you intend walking in remote areas, advise rangers of your plans. It is essential to carry food and water.

Organised Tours

The National Parks & Wildlife Service operates a range of economical guided tours and walks for visitors to areas of conservation and historical significance, and these are free for Island Pass holders.

At **Seal Bay**, 55 km south of Kingscote, 45-minute guided tours to the seal colonies are conducted regularly between 9 am and 4.30 pm daily. Tours at the **Kelly Hill Caves Conservation Park**, 79 km from Kingscote, take place daily between 10 am and 4 pm (3 pm in winter).

At **Cape Borda**, 103 km from Kingscote on the western extremity of the island, tours of historic buildings and talks on the history of the Cape Borda Lighthouse are conducted about six times daily.

All of these tours cost $3.50 for adults (concessions are available). Unless you form part of a large group, bookings are not required. Half-day and full-day tours are also available.

There are a number of package tours designed for backpackers. The Penneshaw Youth Hostel (☎ (0848) 31 173) has three-day tours ex-Adelaide starting from $115. Australian Odysseys (☎ (0848) 31 294) operates 4WD tours ranging from one to six days. Many of the Adelaide hostels run trips to Kangaroo Island.

Places to Stay

Individual establishments are listed under the major towns. The National Parks & Wildlife Service can arrange budget-priced wilderness accommodation in historic cottages in the national parks, including the lightkeepers' cottages at Cape Willoughby. Contact the service's office in Kingscote for details. The *Valerie Jane* ferry booking office in Penneshaw (☎ (0848) 31 233; toll-free 1800 018 484) has a range of combined accommodation and car-hire packages. Staff can book self-contained properties around the island starting at $40 for a double (car hire extra). Sealink (☎ 13 1301) has similar combined ferry and accommodation packages.

In addition to those at the main townships, caravan parks are located at Emu Bay, Stokes Bay, Vivonne Bay and Tandanya.

Getting There & Away

Air Air Kangaroo Island (☎ (08) 234 4177) has daily services from Adelaide to American River ($56 one way), Parndana ($58) and Kingscote ($58.50); there are reduced advance-purchase return fares available on application. If you fly into American River you must arrange a transfer into town. Albatross Airlines (☎ (0848) 22 296) flies from Adelaide to Kingscote three times daily ($60 one way). Its free courtesy bus transfers passengers between the airport and the town.

Kendell Airlines (☎ 13 1300) services Kingscote from Adelaide. Fares are $72 or there's an advance-purchase Saver fare for

$45. Emu Air (☎ toll-free 1800 182 353) has a twice-daily service to Penneshaw and Kingscote from Adelaide; the fare is $58 one way.

Ferry The *Island Seaway* (☎ (0848) 22 273) crosses to Kingscote from Port Adelaide every Monday. The crossing takes 7½ hours and costs $25 one way. Accompanied bicycles cost $4.80, motorbikes $22.40 and cars $61. The service between Kingscote and Port Lincoln has been discontinued but might recommence. Contact the agents, R W Miller (☎ (08) 47 5577), 3 Todd St, Port Adelaide, for more information. In Kingscote contact Patrick Sleigh Shipping (☎ (0848) 22 273) on Commercial St.

Most people cross from Cape Jervis, opposite Kangaroo Island on the end of the Fleurieu Peninsula. The *Valerie Jane* (☎ (0848) 31 233; toll-free 1800 018 484) is a passenger-only ferry which runs to Penneshaw twice daily for $27, taking 30 minutes – during either July or August the service takes a break. For an extra $7, you can travel by bus from Adelaide to Cape Jervis to connect with the ferry. Contact the *Valerie Jane* booking office for details.

Sealink (☎ 13 1301) operates two vehicle ferries which run all year, taking an hour to Penneshaw. There are at least a couple of sailings each day, with more in January. One-way fares are $29 for passengers, $5 for bicycles, $20 for motorbikes and $58 for cars.

A bus service from Adelaide to Port Jervis which connects with ferry departures costs $13 one way. It departs from the central bus station. Bookings are essential; phone ☎ 13 1301.

Getting Around

To/From the Airport There's an airport bus running from the Kangaroo Island Airport to Kingscote for about $6. The airport is 14 km from the town centre. Kingscote Taxi & Tours provides a service on request between American River, Kingscote (town and airport) and Penneshaw. Fares aren't cheap (approximately $70 from Kingscote to Penneshaw). Contact Explorer Tours (☎ 22 640), Dauncey St, Kingscote.

To/From the Ferry Landings The *Valerie Jane* has a shuttle link from Penneshaw to American River; if you require this service, advise when booking the ferry. The Sealink Shuttle (☎ 13 1301) connects with ferries and links Penneshaw with Kingscote ($10) and American River ($6). You have to book.

Car & Moped Rental Kangaroo Island Rental Cars (☎ (0848) 22 390) in Kingscote has rates starting at $69 with 200 free km. The same crowd owns Kingscote Car Hire, which has cars from $45 per day. Budget (☎ (0848) 23 133) rates are comparable with Kangaroo Island Rental Cars. Very few car-rental outlets on the mainland will allow their vehicles to be taken across to Kangaroo Island. One exception is Access Rent-a-Car (☎ (08) 223 7466), 122 Angas St, Adelaide. Rates start at $69 per day plus a $10 per day Kangaroo Island surcharge (the surcharge applies only for the days the vehicle is on Kangaroo Island).

You can hire mopeds at the Country Cottage Shop (☎ (0848) 22 148), Centenary Rd, in Kingscote, and at Island Bike Hire (☎ (0848) 22 148), in Penneshaw. You can't take them on unsealed roads.

Bicycle Due to the number of unsealed roads and the relatively long distances between settlements, bicycling is hard work and the rigours of the roads prove detrimental to the bicycles themselves. If you're still game, bicycles (including tandems) can be hired from Jackie's Toybox (☎ (0848) 23 151), on Commercial St, opposite the Ozone Hotel in Kingscote. The Mobil service station, next to Muggleton's shop in Penneshaw, has mountain bikes.

KINGSCOTE (population 1440)
Kingscote, the main town on the island, was the first White settlement in South Australia. Although there had been other Europeans on the island many years earlier, Kingscote was only formally settled in 1836 and was all but abandoned just a few years later.

There is an ANZ bank branch in town, and an EFTPOS cash-withdrawal facility at Turner Fuel, 21 Murray St.

Things to See & Do
The rock pool and **Brownlow Beach** are good places for swimming. **Hope Cottage**, on Centenary Ave, was built in 1857. It is now a museum ($2), and has a variety of old colonial implements and memorabilia.

Every evening at 4 pm there's **bird feeding** at the Bay of Shoals boat ramp, about two km west of the town centre. Those wonderful beaked battleships, pelicans, turn up for the free tucker, but of course the greedy gulls usually get the lion's share. Each evening at 8.30 pm rangers take visitors on a **'Discovering Penguins' walk**. They leave from the reception area of the Ozone Hotel on the Esplanade and cost $3.50 – wear sturdy footwear.

Places to Stay & Eat
The *Kingscote Caravan Park* (☎ (0848) 22 394) is on the foreshore. The *Kingscote Budget Hostel* (☎ (0848) 22 711) is at 19 Murray St. Dorm beds are $12.

The *Queenscliffe Family Hotel* (☎ (0848) 22 254) has comfortable singles/doubles (some with four-poster beds) for $43/53. It can be a bit rowdy before midnight, when the noise from the public bar downstairs filters up to the rooms. Reasonably priced meals are available in the hotel's restaurant.

The *Ozone Hotel* (☎ (0848) 22 011), situated on the seafront, has singles/doubles from $52/66, and there's a restaurant in the complex.

AMERICAN RIVER (population 120)
Between Kingscote and Penneshaw, the small settlement of American River takes its name from the American sealers who built a boat here from 1803 to 1804. The town is on a small peninsula and shelters an inner bay, named **Pelican Lagoon** by Flinders, which is now a bird sanctuary.

Every afternoon at 4.30 pm you can watch the **pelican feeding** down on the wharf.

Places to Stay & Eat

Linnetts Island Club (☎ (0848) 33 053) has rooms from $40. It also offers cheap hostel beds. The same people manage the *American River Caravan Park*.

At *Casuarina Holiday Units* (☎ (0848) 33 020), next to the post office, self-contained units are priced from $35.

PENNESHAW

Looking across the narrow Backstairs Passage to the Fleurieu Peninsula, Penneshaw is a quiet little resort town with a pleasant beach at **Hog's Bay** and the tiny inlet of **Christmas Cove**, which is used as a boat harbour. It is also the arrival point for ferries from Cape Jervis.

The council offices on Middle Terrace issue camping permits. Outside business hours, try Muggleton's shop. There's no bank in town, but the post office is an agent for the Commonwealth Bank, there's an ANZ agency at the council offices on Mondays and Thursdays from 10 to 11 am, and the Serv-Wel supermarket has an EFTPOS cash-withdrawal facility.

Things to See & Do

In the evenings rangers take visitors to view the penguins that nest in the sand dunes and cliffs near the township. In summer the tours depart at 8.30 and 9.30 pm, in winter at 7 and 8 pm, and the price is $3.50. The **Penneshaw Maritime & Folk Museum** is worth a look.

Penneshaw is situated on Dudley Peninsula, a knob of land at the eastern end of the island, and this peninsula has several points of interest outside the town itself: **Pennington Bay** has surf; the sheltered waters of **Chapman River** are popular for canoeing; and the **Cape Willoughby Lighthouse**, the oldest lighthouse in the state – it was first operated in 1852 – has half-hour tours every 30 minutes between 10 am and 4 pm daily.

Adventureland Diving (☎ (0848) 31 072), 10 km from Penneshaw on the Kingscote road, runs three-day diving courses ($440 fully inclusive, including the ferry fare from Cape Jervis). It also offers abseiling, canoeing and rock climbing for beginners, as well as dive charter (licensed divers only).

Places to Stay

The *Penneshaw Youth Hostel* (☎ (0848) 31 173), on North Terrace, has dorm rooms for $10, or twin rooms for $12 per person. The *Penguin Hostel* (☎ (0848) 31 018) has beds in self-contained units for $12; doubles cost about $35. It also operates Kangaroo Island Explorer Tours, and has a range of tours, including a popular $99 camping package ex-Adelaide (ferry fare included). *Coranda Farm* (☎ (0848) 31 019), seven km from Penneshaw on the Willoughby road, has a 'tent city' and charges $6 per person in two-person tents. The *Sorrento Resort Motel* (☎ (0848) 31 028), on North Terrace, has singles/doubles from $55/88.

NORTH COAST

There are several fine, sheltered beaches along the north coast. Near Kingscote, **Emu Bay** has a beautiful, long sweep of sand. Other good beaches include **Stokes Bay**, **Snelling Beach** and the sandy stretch of **Snug Cove**.

FLINDERS CHASE NATIONAL PARK

Occupying the western end of the island, Flinders Chase is South Australia's largest national park. It has beautiful eucalyptus forests with koalas, wild pigs and possums, as well as kangaroos and emus which have become so fearless of humans that they'll brazenly badger you for food – the picnic and barbecue area at Rocky River Homestead is fenced off to protect visitors from these free-loaders.

On the north-western corner of the island, **Cape Borda** has a lighthouse built in 1858. There are guided tours Monday to Friday from 2 to 4 pm. There's also an interesting little cemetery nearby at **Harvey's Return**.

In the southern corner of the park, **Cape du Couedic** is wild and remote. An extremely picturesque lighthouse built in 1906 tops the cape; you can follow the path from the car park down to Admirals Arch – a natural archway pounded by towering seas. You can often see seals and penguins here.

At Kirkpatrick Point, a couple of km east of Cape du Couedic, the **Remarkable Rocks** are a series of bizarre granite rocks on a huge dome stretching 75 metres down to the sea.

Places to Stay

In Flinders Chase you can camp at the Rocky River park headquarters and in other designated areas with a permit. Watch out for kangaroos if you are camping at Flinders Chase. They get into tents looking for food and can cause a lot of damage.

Flinders Keep, at the north-western tip of Flinders Chase, and the *Old Rocky River Homestead* are administered by the National Parks & Wildlife Service. See Places to Stay at the beginning of the Kangaroo Island section for details on these and other National Parks cottages.

SOUTH COAST

The south coast is rough and wave-swept compared with the north coast. At **Hanson Bay**, close to Cape du Couedic at the western end of the coast, there's a colony of fairy penguins. A little further east you come to **Kelly Hill Caves**, a series of limestone caves 'discovered' by a horse named Kelly in the 1880s, who fell into them through a hole in the ground, much to the disquiet of his owner.

Vivonne Bay has a long and beautiful sweep of beach. There is excellent fishing but bathers should take great care; the undertows are fierce and swimmers are advised to stick close to the jetty or the river mouth. **Seal Bay** is another sweeping beach, with plenty of resident seals. They can only be visited with a park ranger.

Nearby and close to the south coast road is **Little Sahara**, a series of enormous, spectacular white sand dunes.

Places to Stay & Eat

Eleanor River Holiday Cabins (☎ (0848) 94 250) are in Vivonne Bay. *Parndana &*

Karatta Lodge, at Cape du Couedic, is another residence administered by National Parks. See Places to Stay at the beginning of the Kangaroo Island section for details. The historic *Kaiwarra Cottage* on the south coast road near the Seal Bay turn-off has light meals and Devonshire teas.

Barossa Valley

South Australia's famous valley, about 50 km north-east of Adelaide, vies with the Hunter Valley in New South Wales for the title of best-known wine-producing area in Australia. The gently sloping valley is about 40 km long and five to 11 km wide.

The Barossa still has some of the German flavour from its original settlement in 1842. Fleeing religious persecution in Prussia and Silesia, those first settlers weren't wine makers, but fortunately someone soon came along and recognised the valley's potential. The name is actually a misspelling of Barrosa in Spain, close to where Spanish sherry comes from. Prior to WW I place names in the Barossa probably sounded even more Germanic, but during the war many German names were patriotically anglicised. When the fervour died down some were changed back.

You must get off the main road to begin to appreciate the Barossa Valley. Take the scenic drive between Angaston and Tanunda, the palm-fringed road to Seppeltsfield and Marananga or wander through the sleepy historic settlement of Bethany.

The Barossa Valley Visitors Centre (☎ toll-free 1800 812 662) is at 66-68 Murray St, Tanunda. It's open from 9 am to 5 pm Monday to Friday and 10 am to 4 pm on weekends and holidays.

Wineries

The Barossa has over 50 wineries; many of them are open to the public and offer guided tours or free wine tastings. Get a copy of TSA's Barossa leaflet for full details of locations and opening hours.

Barossa Valley

1	Stockwell Wines	11 Hardy's Siegersdorf	20	Bethany Wines
2	Wolf Blass	12 Tolley Pedare Wine	21	Rockford Wines
3	The Willows Vineyard	13 Leo Buring	22	Grant Burge Wines
4	Greenock Creek Vineyard	14 Peter Lehmann	23	Charles Melton Wines
5	Seppelts	15 Veritas	24	Krondorf
6	Penfolds	16 Old Barn Wines	25	Orlando
7	Kaesler Farm	17 Basedow Wines	26	Rovalley
8	Bunkhaus Travellers Hostel	18 Barossa Valley Visitors	27	Jenke Vineyards
9	Saltram Wine Estate	Centre	28	Chateau Yaldara
10	Yalumba	19 St Hallett Wines	29	Kies Estate Cellars

Following are some well-known and some not so well-known wineries.

Chateau Yaldara at Lyndoch was established in 1947 in the ruins of a 19th-century winery and flour mill. It has a notable antique collection which can be seen on conducted tours ($2).

St Hallett at Tanunda is a small winery well known for its fortified wines. There is a keg factory opposite where you can watch kegs being made.

Orlando, at Rowland Flat, between Lyndoch and Tanunda, was established in 1847 and is one of the oldest wineries in the valley.

Saltram Wine Estate in Angaston is another old winery. Established in 1859, it has friendly and informative staff, and is set in beautiful gardens.

Seppelts in Seppeltsfield was founded in 1852; the old bluestone buildings are surrounded by gardens and date palms. The extensive complex includes a picnic area with gas barbecues. There is also a family mausoleum. Daily tours cost $2.

Wolf Blass out beyond Nuriootpa was only founded in 1973, but by a combination of excellent wines and clever marketing it has quickly become one of the better known wine makers in Australia.

Yalumba in Angaston was founded way back in 1849. The blue-marble winery, topped by a clock tower and surrounded by gardens, is the largest family-owned winery in the valley.

Bethany Wines, Bethany Rd, Bethany, is a small family-operated winery in a scenic location. Its white port is highly recommended.

Grant Burge Wines, Jacobs Creek, Barossa Valley Highway, Tanunda, is a relative newcomer but is attaining a reputation for consistently good wines.

Barossa Events

The **Vintage Festival** is the Barossa's big event, taking place over seven days starting on Easter Monday in odd-numbered years. The colourful festival features processions, brass bands, tug-of-war contests between the wineries, maypole dancing and, of course, a lot of wine tasting.

Other festive occasions include the **Oom Pah Fest** in January; **Essenfest** in March; the **Hot Air Balloon Regatta** in May; the **Classic Gourmet Weekend** in August; and a **Brass Band Competition** in November.

The main events in the Barossa move with the grape-growing seasons. It takes four to five years for grape vines to reach maturity after they are first planted in September and October. Their useful life is usually around

40 years. The vines are pruned back heavily during the winter months (July to August) and grow and produce fruit over the summer. The busiest months in the valley are from March to early May when the grapes are harvested.

Getting There & Away

There are several routes from Adelaide to the valley; the most direct is via the main north road through Elizabeth and Gawler. More picturesque routes go through the Torrens Gorge, Chain of Ponds and Williamstown or via Chain of Ponds and Birdwood. If you're coming from the east and want to tour the wineries before hitting Adelaide, the scenic route via Springton and Eden Valley to Angaston is the best bet.

The Barossa to Adelaide Passenger Service (☎ (085) 62 3277) has three services daily between the valley and Adelaide. Fares from Adelaide are Lyndoch $6.20, Tanunda $7.60, Nuriootpa $8.30 and Angaston $9. There are no services on public holidays. Greyhound Pioneer passes through Nuriootpa twice daily (on request) on its Adelaide to Sydney run ($9).

Getting Around

Valley Tours (☎ (085) 62 1524) has a good day tour of the Barossa for $30; a three-course lunch is included. A helicopter flight over the valley costs from $30 (☎ (085) 24 4209), while a hot-air balloon flight (☎ (08) 389 3195) costs about $185.

The Zinfandel Tea Rooms in Tanunda, the Nuriootpa Caravan Park and the Bunkhaus Travellers Cottage in Nuriootpa rent bicycles. There's a bicycle path between Nuriootpa and Tanunda, which runs past the Bunkhaus Travellers Cottage.

LYNDOCH (population 960)

Coming up from Adelaide, Lyndoch, at the foot of the low Barossa Range, is the first valley town. The fine old **Pewsey Vale Homestead** is near Lyndoch. The Original Aboriginal Art Gallery (☎ (08) 24 4522) is at 28 Barossa Valley Highway. South of town on the Gawler road is the **Museum of Mechanical Music** (☎ (085) 24 4014), with some fascinating old pieces and a knowledgeable owner; admission is $5 – less if you're in a group. A few km further south, the **Barossa Reservoir** has a 'whispering wall'.

Places to Stay

The *Barossa Caravan Park* (☎ (085) 24 4262), Barossa Valley Highway, Lyndoch, has camp sites from $10, on-site vans from $25 and cabins from $40.

The *Kersbrook Youth Hostel* (☎ (08) 389 3185), 20 km south of Lyndoch, is in the grounds of a National Trust property called Roachdale. Beds cost $6 and due to the hostel's distance from the main Barossa towns, you'll need your own transport to get around.

Places to Eat

The valley's only true German-style bakery is the *Lyndoch Bakery & Restaurant* in Lyndoch. According to locals, *Errigo's Italian Restaurant* makes a mean pizza, but there's nothing mean about the friendly Italian woman behind the counter.

TANUNDA (population 3100)

In the centre of the valley is Tanunda, the most Germanic of the towns. You can still see early cottages around **Goat Square**, the site of the original Ziegenmarkt.

At 47 Murray St the **Barossa Valley Historical Museum** has exhibits on the valley's early settlement; it's open daily from 10 am to 5 pm.

Three km from Tanunda on the Gomersal road, trained sheepdogs go through their paces at the **Breezy Gully** property on Mondays, Wednesdays and Saturdays at 2 pm ($6).

There are fine old churches in all the valley towns but Tanunda has some of the most interesting. The Lutheran **Tabor Church** dates from 1849, and the 1868 Lutheran **St John's Church** has life-size wooden statues

of Christ, Moses, and the apostles Peter, Paul and John.

From Tanunda, turn off the main road and take the scenic drive through Bethany and via Mengler Hill to Angaston. It runs through beautiful, peaceful country; the view over the valley from Mengler Hill is especially good.

Places to Stay

The *Tanunda Caravan Park* (☎ (085) 63 2784), on the Barossa Valley Highway, has camp sites for $10, on-site vans from $27 and air-con cabins from $33.

There's also the reasonable *Tanunda Hotel* (☎ (085) 63 2030) at 51 Murray St with singles/doubles from $38/44 and the *Valley Hotel* (☎ (085) 63 2039), also on Murray St, which has rooms from $25/35.

Places to Eat

Crackers Restaurant has very good meals. The *Zinfandel Tea Rooms* at 58 Murray St specialises in light lunches and continental cakes. *Giovannis* at the Barossa Junction Resort has reasonably priced Italian food.

NURIOOTPA (population 3300)

At the northern end of the valley Nuriootpa is the commercial centre of the Barossa Valley. There are several pleasant picnic grounds and a swimming pool in the park, as well as some excellent wineries in the area.

Places to Stay

The *Barossa Valley Tourist Park* (☎ (085) 62 1404), on Penrice Rd in Nuriootpa, has camp sites from $10 and cabins from $30.

The *Bunkhaus Travellers Cottage* (☎ (085) 62 2260) is set on a family vineyard, one km outside Nuriootpa on the main highway between Nuriootpa and Tanunda (look for the keg on the corner). It's a friendly place with dorm beds for $11 plus a cottage for two to four people for $30, and mountain bikes can be hired here.

The *Angas Park Hotel* (☎ (085) 62 1050) at 22 Murray St has rooms for $15. The nearby *Vine Inn Hotel/Motel* (☎ (085) 62 2133) has motel units from $60/75.

ANGASTON (population 1800)
On the eastern side of the valley, this town was named after George Fife Angas, one of the area's pioneers. **Collingrove Homestead**, built by his son in 1856, is owned by the National Trust; it's open from 1 to 4.30 pm weekdays and 11 am to 4.30 pm on weekends and during festivals ($3). There's a local tourist office in the Angaston Galleria, Murray St.

Places to Stay
Angaston has the *Barossa Brauhaus* (☎ (085) 64 2014) at 41 Murray St, a fine hotel with B&B rates of $18 per person. Just down the street at No 59 is the *Angaston Hotel* (☎ (085) 64 2428). Rooms are $25 per person for B&B. Good for a splurge in Angaston is the National Trust's 1856 *Collingrove Homestead* (☎ (085) 64 2061). The four rooms are part of the old servants' quarters and cost $75/100, including breakfast.

OTHER BAROSSA VALLEY TOWNS
Near Tanunda, **Bethany** was the first German settlement in the valley. There's a gallery in a restored cottage featuring arts and crafts. Old cottages still stand around the Bethany reserve, while the Landhaus is claimed to be the smallest hotel in the world.

Springton, in the south-east of the valley, has the Herbig Tree – an enormous hollow gum tree where a pioneer settler lived with his family from 1855 to 1860.

Mid-North

The area between Adelaide and Port Augusta is generally known as the mid-north. Two main routes run north of Adelaide through the area. The first runs to Gawler where you can turn east to the Barossa Valley and the Riverland area, or continue north through Burra to Peterborough. From there you have the option of turning north-west to the Flinders Ranges or continuing on the Barrier Highway to the north-east for the long run to Broken Hill in New South Wales.

The second route heads off slightly north-west through Wakefield and then to Port Pirie and Port Augusta on Spencer Gulf. You can then travel to the Flinders Ranges or the Eyre Peninsula or head west towards the Nullarbor and Western Australia.

The mid-north area includes some of the most fertile land in the state. Sunshine, rainfall and excellent soil combine to make this a prosperous agricultural region with excellent wine-making areas like the Clare Valley.

KAPUNDA (population 2000)
About 80 km north of Adelaide and a little north of the Barossa Valley, Kapunda is off the main roads which head north, but you can take a pleasant back route from the valley through the town and join the Barrier Highway a little further north. Copper was found at Kapunda in 1842 and it became the first mining town in Australia – for a while it was the biggest country town in the state. At its peak, it had a population of 10,000 and 22 hotels, but the mines closed in 1888.

There's a **lookout point** in the town with views over the old open-cut mines and mine chimneys. There's a **historical museum**, and an eight-metre-high bronze statue of 'Map Kernow' (the 'Son of Cornwall' in old Cornish) stands at the Adelaide end of town as a tribute to pioneer miners.

AUBURN (population 330)
The township of Auburn, about 32 km south of Clare, has some beautifully preserved historic buildings, particularly on St Vincent St. Auburn was the birthplace of C J Dennis, one of Australia's best-known colonial authors, but unfortunately the hotel where he was born is no longer standing.

The Auburn Gallery has some fine local work and interesting crafts, and there is a swag of antique shops in which to browse.

CLARE (population 2570)

At the heart of the Clare Valley wine region, this pleasant little town 135 km north of Adelaide has eschewed many of the tourist trappings characteristic of some of South Australia's larger wine-producing centres. It was settled in 1842 and named after County Clare in Ireland.

The tourist office (☎ (088) 42 2131) is in the town hall on the main street. Day tours of the district can be arranged through this office.

The first vines were planted in 1848 by Jesuit priests and communion wine is still produced. The Jesuit **St Aloysius Church** dates from 1875 and the adjoining Sevenhill Cellars produces some fine wines. There are many other wineries in the valley, including the Leasingham Winery (formerly the Stanley Wine Company), dating from 1894. Winery opening times vary, but the *Clare Valley Wine Region Visitor's Guide*, available at the tourist office, has all the relevant details.

The town has a number of interesting buildings, including an impressive Catholic church and a police station and courthouse dating from 1850 which are preserved as a **museum**. The **Wolta Wolta Homestead** dates from 1864 and is open on Sundays from 10 am to 1 pm; admission is $3.

Bungaree Station (☎ (088) 42 2677), a working property 12 km north of Clare, has many historical exhibits. Self-conducted cassette tours are possible between 9 am and sundown ($4).

Mintaro, a small town 18 km south-east of Clare, has many architectural gems, including **Martindale Hall**.

Places to Stay

The *Christison Park Caravan Park* (☎ (088) 42 2724) is the closest camping ground to town and has sites for $10 (or $5 if you're travelling solo), on-site vans for $28.50 and cabins for $44.

On Main St, the *Taminga Hotel* (☎ (088) 42 2808) has basic singles/doubles for $15/30. The *Clare Hotel* (☎ (088) 42 2816)

has one-bed rooms for $14 or single/double motel rooms for $35/40. *Bentley's Hotel/Motel* (☎ (088) 42 2815) on the main street has backpackers' accommodation for $10.

Bungaree Station (☎ (088) 42 2677) has accommodation in the shearers' quarters for about $15 a bed, but groups have precedence. *Geralka Farm* (☎ (088) 45 8081), 25 km north of Clare, is another working farm which caters for visitors. You can camp ($11 for a powered site) or stay in on-site vans (from $25).

In Mintaro, *Martindale Hall* (☎ (088) 43 9088) is an imposing mansion that offers accommodation at imposing prices (from $60 per person for B&B).

Getting There & Away

The daily (except Saturday) Stateliner bus to Adelaide costs $13.70.

BURRA (population 1200)

This pretty little town was a copper-mining centre from 1847 to 1877, with various British ethnic groups forming their own communities (the Cornish being the most numerous). The district, Burra Burra, takes its name from the Hindi word for 'great' by one account, and from the Aboriginal name of the creek by another.

Information

The tourist office (☎ (088) 92 2154) in Market Square is open from 10 am to 4 pm daily. Here you can purchase *Discovering Historic Burra* ($4.95), a booklet outlining all of the town's interesting sites on its 11-km heritage trail. The *Burra Passport* includes this booklet, as well as giving you a key to gain access to some buildings. The basic passport costs $15 (per car), while the *Burra Museum Passport* costs $25 and covers the same sites but also includes a couple of the museums. The tourist office also has the *Burra Historic Tour* booklet for $12.50.

Things to See

There are many solid, old stone buildings, tiny Cornish cottages and numerous remind-

1	Hampton (Ruins of English Village)
2	Redruth Gaol
3	Miss Mabel Cottage
4	Royal Exchange Hotel
5	Bon Accord Mining Museum
6	Powder Magazine
7	Peacock's Chimney
8	Burra Motor Inn
9	Caravan Park
10	Cornish Cottages
11	Kooringa Hotel
12	Market Square Museum
13	Burra Hotel
14	Tourist Office
15	Dugouts
16	Post Office
17	Commercial Hotel
18	Polly's Tea Room
19	Lookout
20	Morphetts Enginehouse & Shaft
21	Burra Mine Museum

Burra

ers of the mining days. The **Market Square Museum** (admission $2) is across from the tourist office.

The 33 cottages at **Paxton Square** were built for Cornish miners in the 1850s; one of the cottages, **Malowen Lowarth**, has been furnished in 1850s style. It's open Saturdays from 1 to 3 pm and Sundays and public holidays from 10.30 am to 12.30 pm; admission is $3. The others are available for accommodation (see Places to Stay & Eat). In Burra's early days nearly 1500 people lived in **dugouts** by the creek and a couple of the miners' dugouts have been preserved.

The historic tour booklet describes many other interesting old buildings, including **Redruth Gaol** and more **Cornish cottages** on Truro St, north of the town centre.

The **Burra Mine & Enginehouse Museum** is on the site of an original mine. The **Bon Accord Complex** ($3) was a Scottish mining enterprise; however instead of ore, an underground water source was discovered. Not to be deterred, the canny Scots sold the site to the town, and the property supplied Burra's water until as recently as 1966. The site is now an interpretive centre, and is open weekdays from 12.30 to 2.30 pm.

SOUTH AUSTRALIA

There's a lookout over the town at the old mine site, near the powder magazine and Morphett's engine house and mine shaft.

Places to Stay & Eat

You can stay at the historic *Paxton Square Cottages* (☎ (088) 92 2622). Prices range from $40 to $50. There's quite a lot of pub accommodation, including the grand old *Burra Hotel* (☎ (088) 92 2389) on Market Square which has singles/doubles for $26/46 for B&B.

The *Burra Motor Inn* (☎ (088) 92 2777) has large rooms overlooking the creek. Singles/doubles cost $50/55, and the restaurant at this motel has very good, reasonably priced meals.

There are also several B&B places. One is *Miss Mabel Cottage* (☎ (08) 362 2206), which offers self-catering B&B for $95. The cottage has homely touches like freshly ground coffee and fresh eggs, and 19th-century romantic novels by the bed! There is also a small caravan park in the town.

The *Burra Hotel* has good counter meals and a more formal dining room. You can get a good lunch at *Polly's Tea Rooms*.

Getting There & Away

Greyhound Pioneer's Adelaide to Sydney service passes through Burra daily, and it's $16 to Adelaide. The Mobil service station is the agency. ABM Coaches (☎ (08) 347 3336) has a service three times weekly which passes through Burra ($13.60) on its Adelaide to Orroroo run.

PORT PIRIE (population 14,100)

Port Pirie, 84 km south of Port Augusta, is an industrial centre with lead smelters that handle the output from Broken Hill. There are smelter tours on Wednesdays and Saturdays which depart at 10 am – contact the tourist office (☎ (086) 33 0439) in the Tourism/Art Centre in the former railway station on Mary Ellie St, opposite the silos. Don't confuse this with the *older* railway station, on Ellen St, which houses a **National Trust museum** (admission $2).

Carn Brae at 32 Florence St is the home of the gracious Mr and Mrs Young. It has a phenomenal collection of furniture from the turn of the century, in addition to paintings and memorabilia, and Mrs Young will take you on an extensive tour of the house, describing the function and history of the exhibits; admission is $5, and is well worth it.

There's a new **Mangrove Interpretive Trail** near the Port Pirie Caravan Park. **Nalshaby Reserve** is at the foot of the southern Flinders Ranges, 10 minutes by car from Port Pirie. A walking and wheelchair trail meanders through the reserve to a bird hide on the reservoir and beyond.

Places to Stay & Eat

The *Port Pirie Caravan Park* (☎ (086) 32 4275) has sites from $81 and on-site vans from $25. The friendly *Family Hotel* (☎ (086) 32 1382) at 134 Ellen St has rooms for $15 per person. Counter meals are available and there's an à la carte restaurant on Friday and Saturday nights. Check out the pub's foundation stone, on the side of the building in the lane adjacent to the hotel: the contractors who built the pub in 1904 were named Scotcher & Beer! The *Abaccy Motel* (☎ (086) 32 3701) on Florence St charges $40/45.

If you're hungry in the evening try any of the pubs or the *Three Plenties Palace* Chinese restaurant, next to the Abaccy Motel. There's often a pie cart parked near the post office at night.

OTHER MID-NORTH TOWNS

North of the Clare Valley on the southern edge of the Flinders Ranges, **Jamestown** is a country town with a Railway Station Museum.

Tiny **Terowie** (population 200), 23 km south of Peterborough, is definitely worth the short detour off the Barrier Highway. The town was originally linked by broad-gauge train line to Adelaide, and narrow-gauge to Peterborough, and the town's railway yards provided hundreds of jobs, as goods had to be transferred from carriages on one line to

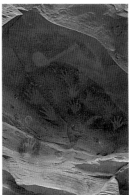

Queensland

A Moored boats, Port Douglas (RI)
B Cape Tribulation (VT)
C Baloon Cave, Carnarvon Gorge (MA)
D Goanna, Cape Kimberley (MA)
E Barron River, near Cairns (MA)

A
B	C	D
E

Queensland

A Hinchinbrook Island (TW)

B Pisonias, Lady Musgrave Island (TW)

C Heron Island (TW)

D Watson's Bay,
Lizard Island (TW)

E South Molle Island (TW)

the other. At its peak, the population exceeded 2000 people. In 1967 the broad-gauge line was extended to Peterborough, sounding the death knell for Terowie. The town is worth a visit as much for its lingering air of a bygone age, as for its wonderful, though sadly deteriorating, historic street-scape.

Peterborough (population 2100) is another gateway town to the Flinders Ranges. Steamtown is a working railway museum – on holiday weekends between April and October and some school holidays, narrow-gauge steam trains run between Peterborough and **Orroroo** to the north-west; phone ☎ (086) 51 2106 for details (bookings are sometimes necessary). There's a number of museums in the town – ask at the tourist office (☎ (086) 51 2708), which is located in an old railway carriage near the town hall.

The *Budget Travellers' Backpackers Hostel* (☎ (086) 51 2711) has beds from $10, or there are camp sites and on-site vans at the *Peterborough Caravan Park* (☎ (086) 512 545).

South-East

The Western and Dukes highways form the most direct route between Melbourne and Adelaide (729 km). Although the South Australian stretch is not terribly exciting, south of this route there is more interesting country and you can take detours. The Princes Highway along the coast is of greater interest. Along this road you pass through Mt Gambier with its impressive crater lakes and then along the Coorong, an extensive coastal lagoon system.

Getting There & Away

Air Kendell Airlines flies from Melbourne to Mt Gambier and on to Adelaide most days. The fare from Mt Gambier to either city is $140. O'Connors Air Services (☎ (087) 23 9666) also flies between Mt Gambier and both Adelaide and Melbourne.

Bus Bonds Mt Gambier Motor Service (☎ (08) 231 9090 in Adelaide; (087) 25 5037 in Mt Gambier) runs from the central bus station in Adelaide to Mt Gambier daily (six hours) for $36.10. You can travel either along the coast via the spectacular Coorong, stopping at Meningie ($17.50), Kingston SE ($28.10) and Robe ($31.60); or inland via Bordertown ($26.90), Naracoorte ($33.30) and Coonawarra/Penola ($34.30).

The Victorian government's V/Line bus runs to Melbourne from Mt Gambier daily (six hours, $46.20).

THE COORONG

The Coorong is a unique national park – a long, narrow strip curving along the coast for 145 km. The northern end is at Lake Alexandrina where the Murray River reaches the sea; the southern end is at Kingston SE. It's a narrow, shallow lagoon and a complex series of salt pans, separated from the sea by the huge sand dunes of the Younghusband Peninsula, more commonly known as the Hummocks.

The area is a superb natural bird sanctuary with vast numbers of water birds. *Storm Boy*, a film about a young boy's friendship with a pelican, based on the novel by Australian author Colin Thiele, was shot on the Coorong, and these wonderful birds are evident in the park. At Salt Creek you can take the nature trail turn-off from the Princes Highway and follow the old road which runs along the shore of the Coorong for some distance.

Places to Stay

Camping is permitted in most areas of the park, but you need a prior permit ($3 for up to five people per night) from the National Parks office (☎ (085) 75 7014) at Salt Creek or Noonameena. The Coorong National Park headquarters (☎ (085) 75 1200) is on the Princes Highway in Meningie. Camping permits are issued and information on tours can be obtained here.

Camp Coorong (☎ (085) 75 1557), 10 km south of Meningie on the Princes Highway, is run by the Ngarrindjeri Lands & Progress

Association. The **Cultural Museum** here has information about the Ngarrindjeri people. Visitors can listen to Dreamtime stories about traditional lifestyle, visit a midden site and talk to Ngarrindjeri Aborigines. Self-contained units are available ($35; bring your own bedding and food), and there's also accommodation in the bunkhouse ($10). Bookings are necessary.

KINGSTON SE (population 1400)
At the southern end of the Coorong, Kingston is a small beach resort and a good base for visiting the Coorong.

Attractions in town include the **Pioneer Museum** and the nearby **Cape Jaffa Lighthouse**. Kingston is a centre for rock-lobster fishing, and the annual Lobsterfest, held in the second week of January, is celebrated with live bands and exhibitions. This is the only time that the historic lighthouse is activated. The Australian obsession with gigantic fauna and flora is apparent in **Larry the Big Lobster**, which looms over the highway on the Adelaide approach to town. Larry fronts a tourist centre and cafe. You can buy rock lobster, freshly cooked, at the jetty.

The **Jip Jip National Park**, 45 km northeast of Kingston, features huge granite outcrops in the bush. From Kingston conventional vehicles can drive 16 km along the beach to the **Granites**, while with 4WD you can continue right along the beach to the mouth of the Murray River.

In Kingston the *Backpackers Hostel* (☎ (087) 67 2185) at 21 Holland St has spartan dorm accommodation for $10. Clean but basic singles/doubles without private facilities are available at the *Crown Inn* (☎ (087) 67 2005), on Agnes St, for $16/28.

There's a daily bus to Adelaide ($28.10) and Mt Gambier ($19).

ROBE (population 730)
Robe, a small port dating from 1845, was one of the state's first settlements. Its citizens made a fortune in the late 1850s as a result of the Victorian gold rush. The Victorian government instituted a £10 head tax on

Chinese gold miners, and many Chinese circumvented the tax by getting to Victoria via Robe; 10,000 arrived in 1857 alone. The **Chinamen's Wells** in the region are a reminder of that time.

Early buildings include the 1863 **Customs House**, on Royal Circus, which is now a nautical museum. The amiable curator has a wealth of knowledge on local history, and will spin you some yarns which you won't find in history texts.

The tourist information office (☎ (087) 68 2465) is in the library on the Smillie and Victoria Sts intersection. Nearby **Long Beach** is good for windsurfing.

Places to Stay
The *Lakeside Caravan Park* is in a beautiful setting with resident ducks and peacocks. On-site vans cost from $28, camp sites $6.

Robe Backpackers (☎ (087) 68 2445), at 39 Victoria St, offers beds in spotless dorms for $10, and there's bicycle hire.

The *Caledonian Inn* (☎ (087) 68 2029) on Victoria St, has basic but clean rooms for $30/50 with a full breakfast, and self-contained cottages within a stone's throw of the beach for $60/80.

BEACHPORT (population 440)
If you have a yen for peace and solitude you'll love this quiet little seaside town south of Robe with its aquamarine sea and historic buildings. The **Old Wool & Grain Store Museum** ($2) is located in a National Trust building. The interesting **Aboriginal Artefacts Museum**, housed in the former primary school in McCourt St, has an extensive collection. It is open from 2 to 4 pm daily in January, or by appointment (☎ (087) 35 8140), and admission is $1.

There's good surfing at the local surf beach, and windsurfing is popular at Lake George, five km north of the township.

The *Beachport Caravan Park* (☎ (087) 35 8128) has on-site vans from $30. The *Beachport Youth Hostel* (☎ (087) 35 8197) is in the old harbour master's house, on the foreshore at the end of Railway Terrace.

Dormitory rooms are $7 for members. The hostel closes for one month in winter (June or July).

MILLICENT (population 5120)
At Millicent, 47 km from Mt Gambier, the 'Alternative 1' route through Robe and Beachport rejoins the main road. The town has a central swimming lake, and on George St the local tourist information centre has a National Trust **museum** (open Monday to Saturday from 10 am to 4 pm and Sundays from 1 to 4 pm; $2.50). The centre also contains the **Admella Craft Gallery**. The **Canunda National Park** with its giant sand dunes is 13 km west of town. You can camp near Southend – contact the ranger (☎ (087) 35 6053) for details. New walking trails have been established in the area.

In **Tantanoola**, 21 km to the south-east, the stuffed 'Tantanoola Tiger' is on display at the Tantanoola Tiger Hotel. This beast, actually an Assyrian wolf, was shot in 1895 after a lot of publicity. It was presumed to have escaped from a shipwreck, but quite why a ship would have a wolf on board is not clear!

The **Tantanoola Caves** are nearby. The caves' visitor centre (☎ (087) 34 4153) runs tours daily, including adventure caving tours (minimum of four people – $18 per person; sturdy footwear is essential). The Tourist Cave is the only cave in South Australia with wheelchair access. Tours must be booked at least one day in advance.

MT GAMBIER (population 21,150)
The major town and commercial centre of the south-east, Mt Gambier is 486 km from Adelaide. It is built on the slopes of the volcano from which the town takes its name.

There are three craters, each with its own lake – the beautiful **Blue Lake** is the best known, although from about March to November the lake is more grey than blue. In November it mysteriously changes back to blue again, just in time for the Blue Lake Festival, which is celebrated with exhibitions and concerts. A recent innovation is a

Blues Festival, run concurrently with the Blue Lake Festival, when musicians from South Australia and interstate perform at local hotels.

The lake is 70 metres deep and there's a five-km scenic drive around it. Boardwalks have been erected over the Valley Lake, and a wildlife park established. There are picnic areas, barbecues and signposted walking trails. Contact the Lady Nelson Tourist Information & Interpretive Centre (☎ (087) 24 1730), on Jubilee Highway East.

Places to Stay & Eat
The *Blue Lake Motel* (☎ (087) 25 5211), at 1 Kennedy Ave, just off the highway, has dorm rooms for $12 per person.

The *Commercial Hotel* (☎ (087) 25 3006), a grand old pub on Commercial St in the city centre, welcomes backpackers with rates of $15/25 for singles/doubles. Live bands play here on Friday nights.

Also on Commercial St, the *Mt Gambier Hotel* (☎ (087) 25 0611) has large rooms with spas for $55/65.

The grand old *Jens Hotel* (☎ (087) 25 0188) on Commercial St was originally a boarding house run by the ignominious Ginger Beer Jack. The present building was constructed in 1884 after battles with local temperance groups. Whopping counter meals are available.

Further west on Commercial St, *Squiggles*, a licensed bistro and coffee shop in the art gallery foyer, has a wicked Mississippi mud cake and other tempting offerings.

Getting There & Away
Bonds Mt Gambier Motor Service (☎ (087) 25 5037) buses depart daily for Adelaide (six hours; $36.10).

PORT MACDONNELL (population 680)
South of Mt Gambier, this quiet fishing port was once a busy shipping port, hence the surprisingly big 1863 **customs house**. There's a **Maritime Museum**, and the poet Adam Lindsay Gordon's home, **Dingley**

Dell, set in a conservation park, is now a museum ($3).

There are some fine walks in the area, including the path to the top of **Mt Schank**, an extinct volcano crater. Closer to town, the rugged coastline to the west is worth a visit.

ALONG THE DUKES HIGHWAY

The first town on the South Australian side of the border is **Bordertown** (population 2230). The town is the birthplace of former Australian prime minister Bob Hawke, and there's a bust of Bob outside the town hall. On the left as you enter the town from Victoria there is a wildlife observatory, with various species of Australian fauna, including a rare white kangaroo, in various states of marsupial torpor, visible behind a wire fence.

Keith (population 1180) is another farming town; it has a small museum and the **Mt Rescue Conservation Park** 16 km north.

Tintinara (population 320) is the only other town of any size; it's also an access point to the Mt Rescue park. The tiny township of **Coonalpyn** is an access point to the **Mt Boothby Conservation Park**.

NARACOORTE (population 4710)

Settled in the 1840s, Naracoorte is one of the oldest towns in the state and one of the largest in the south-east. The tourist office (☎ (087) 62 1518) is at the **Sheep's Back Wool Museum** on MacDonnell St. The museum, housed in a former flour mill, has an interesting display of Australiana, including a stuffed dog with its tail caught mid-wag. Admission to the museum is $3, and the centre is open from 10 am to 4 pm daily. On Jenkins Terrace, the **Home of a Hundred Collections** museum has an eclectic and interesting collection and a $5 entry fee.

The **Naracoorte Caves** (open daily; ☎ (087) 62 2340) are 12 km south-east of Naracoorte on the road to Penola. These extraordinary caves featured in David Attenborough's *Life on Earth* series, and the Victoria Fossil Cave has been nominated for World Heritage listing due to the significance of its fossils.

There are three other caves with stalactites and stalagmites. **Bat Cave**, from which bats make a spectacular departure on summer evenings, is 17 km out of town. There are adventure tours to undeveloped caves in the area, involving climbing and crawling (wear sneakers or sandshoes), and there is a camp site with powered and unpowered sites nearby. Guided tours of the caves run from 9.30 am to 3.30 pm, and prices start from $4. It is also possible to take self-guided tours through the recently opened **Wet Cave**.

There are some 75 species of birds at the **Bool Lagoon Reserve**, 24 km to the south, which, with Hacks Lagoon, is the largest wetland in the south-east. The self-guided 1.5-km walk is a must for twitchers, and guided tours are also available. There's a camp site near the park office in the Hacks Lagoon area, but you have to take your own water.

Places to Stay & Eat

The classic old *Naracoorte Hotel* (☎ (087) 62 2400), 73 Ormerod St, has motel-style rooms for $42/55, and backpackers' accommodation for $10 per person.

The *Old Aussie Eatery*, at 190 Smith St, has an interesting menu including a stockman's challenge and a drover's delight. If you haven't yet tried 'roo steak, this is the place to head for.

COONAWARRA & PENOLA

This very compact (only 12 km by two km) wine-producing area, renowned for the quality of its red wine, is 10 km north of Penola. Wynn's Coonawarra Estate is the area's best-known winery and there are about 18 others which offer cellar-door sales daily from 10 am to 4 pm.

The historic town of **Penola** has obtained recent fame as the site of the Sisters of S Joseph of the Sacred Heart, the order which Mary MacKillop, who may be canonised as Australia's first saint, co-founded in 1866 Penola has been named as one of three sig nificant MacKillop pilgrimage sites (the others are in Adelaide).

The **Woods/MacKillop Schoolhouse**, built in 1867, houses memorabilia associated with Mother Mary MacKillop and Father Julian Tenison Woods, who founded the school, the first in Australia to welcome children from lower socioeconomic backgrounds. Opening times vary; check with the helpful people at the tourist information centre, on Arthur St (open 10 am to 4 pm daily).

If you would like to wend your way around the wineries, bicycles can be hired at Coonawarra Bike Hire. Bookings can be made at Chardonnay Lodge (☎ (087) 36 3309), on the Naracoorte road, three km north of Penola. After your cycling exertions, tasty victuals can be found at the *Sweet Grape*, in the town centre.

Over 20 restored historic cottages in the Penola district offer accommodation, with prices starting at around $50 for twin share. For further information, or to make a reservation, contact TSA.

Buses depart daily (except Saturday) for Adelaide ($34.30) and Mt Gambier ($7.30) from the tourist information centre.

Murray River

Australia's greatest river starts in the Snowy Mountains in the Australian Alps and for most of its length forms the boundary between New South Wales and Victoria. However, it's in South Australia that the Murray comes into its own.

First, it flows west through the Riverland area where irrigation has turned unproductive land into an important wine-making and fruit-growing region.

Then at Morgan the river turns sharply south and flows through the Lower Murray region to the sea. In all, the river flows 650 km from the border of South Australia with New South Wales and Victoria to the sea.

The Murray has lots of water-sport possibilities, plenty of wildlife (particularly water

birds), and in the Riverland section a number of wineries to visit.

This is also a river with a history. Before the advent of the railways, the Murray was the Mississippi of Australia, with paddle-steamers carrying trade from the interior down to the coast.

The Murray River region has plenty of conventional accommodation, including a hostel in Berri, but a very pleasant way to explore the Murray is to rent a houseboat and set off along the river. Houseboats can be hired in Morgan, Waikerie, Loxton, Berri, Renmark and other river centres, but they are popular so it's wise to book well ahead. Contact TSA or the Riverland Holiday Booking Centre (☎ (085) 86 4444) in Renmark. Typical prices are around $600 a week for a four-berth houseboat, and around $950 for eight or 10-berth boats. These costs can drop in winter.

For the well heeled there are the trips on riverboats such as the huge paddle-steamer PS *Murray River Queen*, which makes its stately way up and down the river from Murray Bridge. The MV *Barrangul* also has cruises from Murray Bridge and the PS *Murray River Princess* is based in Mannum; see entries for these towns for details.

Getting There & Away

Air Southern Australia Airlines flights can be booked through Qantas (☎ 13 1313). It flies to Renmark from Adelaide ($104) twice daily on weekdays and once on Sundays.

Bus Stateliner (☎ (08) 415 5555) has daily services to the Riverland towns. The fare to Berri, Loxton and Renmark is $25.40. Greyhound Pioneer passes through the Riverland region several times daily on its Adelaide to Sydney journey.

Getting Around

Riverland Bike Hire (☎ (085) 82 2929) has mopeds for hire at selected outlets in Barmera, Renmark, Morgan, Waikerie, Berri and (possibly) Loxton. Bicycles cost $12.50 per hour and can only be hired in pairs.

RENMARK (population 4250)

In the centre of the Riverland irrigation area and 254 km east of Adelaide, Renmark was a starting point for the great irrigation projects that revolutionised the area, and was the first of the river towns.

You can visit the 1911 paddle-steamer *Industry*, now restored and with various components working. The *Waterway Safari* has hour-long cruises ($8) departing from the Riverbend Caravan Park (☎ (085) 85 5131). There are several art galleries in town, and koalas and other wildlife on **Goat Island**, which also has a number of walking trails. The **Angoves** and **Renmano wineries** have cellar-door sales and tastings.

The tourist office (☎ (085) 86 6703) is on Murray Ave.

Places to Stay & Eat

Grays Caravan Village (☎ (085) 86 6522) is close to the town centre and has on-site vans for $23 (no camp sites). About a km to the east is the *Renmark Caravan Park* (☎ (085) 86 6315), idyllically situated on a bend in the river. Camp sites cost $11.50 and on-site vans range from $27. Further along the river, the *Riverbend Caravan Park* (☎ (085) 85 5131) has cabins for $39 and hires canoes and bicycles.

The *Renmark Hotel/Motel* (☎ (085) 86 6755) has rooms in the hotel for $45/50 and motel units from $55/60.

Sophia's Restaurant has good Greek food and a takeaway service downstairs. *Snoopy's*, on Renmark Ave, has a tempting range of ice creams.

BERRI (population 3730)

At one time a refuelling stop for the wood-burning paddle-steamers, the town takes its name from the Aboriginal words *berri berri*, meaning 'big bend in the river'. **Berri Estates winery** at Glossop, 13 km west of Berri, is one of the biggest wineries in Australia, if not the whole southern hemisphere. It's open for tastings and cellar-door sales from Monday to Saturday from 9 am to 5 pm.

The tourist office (☎ (085) 82 1655) is on Vaughan Terrace.

In town, the lookout on Fiedler St has views over the town and river. Near the ferry wharf there's a **monument** to Jimmy James, an Aboriginal tracker, with some interesting information on tracking. There's also a **koala sanctuary** near the Martins Bend recreation area on the river.

The **Willabalangaloo Reserve** is a flora and fauna reserve with walking trails and a museum. It's open Thursday to Monday from 10 am to 4 pm (daily during school holidays).

Punts still cross the river to Loxton from opposite the Berri Hotel on Riverside Ave.

Places to Stay

The *Berri Riverside Caravan Park* (☎ (085) 82 3723) has camp sites and on-site vans. The *Berri Backpackers* (☎ (085) 82 3144), on the Sturt Highway, must be one of the best equipped hostels anywhere. There's a pool, games room and bicycles for guests' use, and canoes are available for hire. You can ask here about fruit-picking work. Beds are $12 ($75 per week).

At the *Berri Hotel/Motel* (☎ (085) 82 1411) on Riverview Drive, singles/doubles cost from $34/38 in the pub, and from $54/62 in the motel.

LOXTON (population 3320)

From Berri the Murray makes a large loop south of the Sturt Highway. At the base of this loop is Loxton. The **Katarapko Game Reserve** occupies much of the area within the loop; you can camp here with a permit ($2 per night per adult). Contact the National Parks office (☎ (085) 85 2177) in Berri.

The tourist office (☎ (085) 84 7919) is in front of the Loxton Hotel on East Terrace. Loxton's major attraction is the riverside **Historical Village**; it's open from 10 am to 4 pm on weekdays and to 5 pm on weekends; admission is $4.

There are two-hour river cruises on the MV *River Rambler* (☎ (085) 84 6359) for $8.50, and the **Australian Vintage** (formerly

Penfolds) winery is open daily except Sundays. Riverland Canoeing Adventures (☎ (085) 84 1494) on Alamein Ave rents one-person kayaks for $12 per day and double kayaks and canoes for $20 a day.

Places to Stay & Eat
The *Loxton Riverfront Caravan Park* (☎ (085) 84 7862) has camp sites for $9.50 and on-site vans for $25. Cabins start at $30.

The *Loxton Hotel/Motel* (☎ (085) 84 7266) on East Terrace has basic pub rooms from $16/24, or $32/37 with attached bath. Motel units cost from $46/50. The hotel has a couple of dining rooms, plus counter meals. Otherwise there's the *Loxton Palace Chinese Restaurant* and several coffee shops and takeaways.

BARMERA (population 1860)
On the shores of Lake Bonney, Barmera was once on the overland stock route along which cattle were driven from New South Wales.

The ruins of **Napper's Old Accommodation House**, built in 1850 at the mouth of Chambers Creek, are a reminder of that era, as is the **Overland Corner Historic Hotel** on the Morgan road, 19 km out of town. It takes its name from a bend in the Murray River where overlanders, travellers and explorers once stopped. Later, drovers paused here, and the hotel (built in 1859) has a number of interesting historical exhibits. You can also stay here – see under Places to Stay. There's also an **art gallery** and **museum** in the town.

Lake Bonney, which has sandy beaches, is popular for swimming and water sports. There's a nudist beach at **Pelican Point**. At **Moorook** there's a conservation reserve, or there's the **Loch Luna Game Reserve**, near the Overland Corner Historic Hotel. Both reserves have nature trails and are good spots for bird-watching. For camping permits, contact the Berri National Parks office (☎ (085) 85 2177).

Riverland Safaris (☎ (085) 88 2869) offers various guided trips ranging in duration from two hours ($11) to five days ($300). Fishing and yabbying trips cost about $15 per person a day (based on a minimum of eight people). Contact the tourist office (☎ (085) 88 2289) for details – it's at the top of the main street next to the roundabout, and is open weekdays from 8.30 am to 5.30 pm.

Places to Stay
There are several caravan parks, including *Lake Bonney* (☎ (085) 88 2234), which has camp sites for $10, on-site vans for $26, cabins from $28 to $36 and cottages from $44 to $46. Double rooms at the *Overland Corner Historic Hotel* (☎ (085) 88 7021) cost $50 and include breakfast.

WAIKERIE (population 1750)
The town takes its name from the Aboriginal word for 'anything that flies', after the teeming bird life on the lagoons and river around Waikerie. Curiously, Waikerie also has the most active gliding centre in Australia (☎ (085) 41 2644).

Other attractions in and around the town are the **Eremophila Park**, off the Sturt Highway, which has Mallee fowl, abundant native bird life and nature walks, the **Kangaroo Park** and **Holder Bend Reserve**.

Bush camping is possible at *Eremophila Park* – there's no power, but other amenities are available; phone ☎ (086) 89 3023 for details. There is a tourist centre (☎ (085) 41 2295) at 20 McCoy St, or you can obtain information from the big **Orange Tree** (☎ (085) 41 2332), another gargantuan creation in fibreglass, which is open daily from 9 am to 5.30 pm. The *Waikerie Hotel* (☎ (085) 41 2999) has pub rooms for $37/44 and motel rooms for $40/49.

MORGAN (population 450)
In its prime this was the busiest river port in Australia, with wharves towering 12 metres high. There's a car ferry across the Murray here. Most businesses around town will give you a leaflet detailing a historic walk (50c). The **Morgan Museum** has exhibits on the paddle-steamer trade; it opens according to demand.

The *Morgan Riverside Caravan Park* (☎ (085) 40 2207) has camp sites for $9, on-site vans for $25 and cabins for $35. It also hires mopeds and canoes. The *Commercial Hotel* (☎ (085) 40 2107) has rooms from $15.

SWAN REACH (population 230)
This sleepy old town, 70 km south-west of Waikerie, has picturesque river scenery and, hardly surprisingly, lots of swans. Just downstream the Murray makes a long, gentle curve for 11 km in all. The bend is appropriately known as Big Bend; there's a picnic reserve here and many sulphur-crested cockatoos.

MANNUM (population 2030)
The *Mary Ann*, Australia's first riverboat, was built here and made the first paddle-steamer trip up the Murray from Mannum in 1853. The river is very wide here and there are many relics of the pioneering days, including the 1898 paddle-steamer *Marion*, now a floating museum ($2.50).

The tourist information centre (☎ (085) 69 1303) is at the entrance to the museum, and is open daily from 10 am to 4 pm. You can see relics of the *Mary Ann* in the town's recreation ground.

The **Purnong Rd Bird Sanctuary** has a variety of water birds. A 12-km tourist drive which takes in the sanctuary can be taken from Mannum. The **Cascade Waterfalls**, 11 km from Mannum on Reedy Creek, are also worth a visit. Although the falls only flow during winter, the scenery is spectacular, and can be enjoyed at any time. Off Purnong Rd there's a lookout tower.

River Cruises
The grand paddle-steamer *Murray River Princess* now operates from Mannum. Five-night cruises range upward in price from $560 per person. Three-night cruises start at $335, while selected weekend cruises are priced from $210. Contact Murray River Cruises (☎ toll-free 1800 804 843) for more details.

Sulphur-crested cockatoo

MURRAY BRIDGE (population 12,500)
South Australia's largest river town, only 82 km south-east of Adelaide, is named for the long 1879 bridge, reputedly the first to span the Murray. It's a popular area for fishing, swimming, water-skiing and barbecues.

Tourist information can be obtained from the very helpful information centre (☎ (085) 32 6660) on South Terrace, parallel to the main shopping strip. Chocaholics will enjoy viewing chocolate manufacturing in the old town pump house, between the vehicle and railway bridges on the town side of the river.

Near Murray Bridge is **Monarto**, 20 km to the west – the town that never was. A grandiose plan was drawn up to build a second major city for South Australia by the turn of the century. This site was chosen and land purchased in the early 1970s, but nothing further happened and the project was totally abandoned. The Monarto Zoo has a range of both Australian and international exhibits.

River Cruises
The MV *Barrangul* operates day cruises and there's a restaurant on board. The PS *Proud*

Mary departs from Murray Bridge – two-night cruises start at $290 (triple share), and five-night cruises start at $725. Contact Proud Australia Holidays (☎ (08) 231 9472) in Adelaide.

The grand old PS *Murray River Queen* is also based in Murray Bridge and has three-night cruises from $275 and six-night cruises from $550. Contact Murray River Cruises (☎ toll-free 1800 804 843) for more details.

Places to Stay & Eat

The *Avoca Dell Caravan Park* (☎ (085) 32 2095) has camp sites and on-site vans. The *Balcony Private Hotel* (☎ (085) 32 3830) is right in the centre of town and costs $22/35 for singles/doubles.

You can eat at the *Oriental Garden* or the *Murray Bridge Hotel*, which has good counter meals. The *Italian Club* on Lincoln Rd serves dinner from Thursday to Sunday. Thursday is pasta night – all you can eat for $6.

Getting There & Away

Buses to Adelaide cost $9.50 with the Murray Bridge Passenger Service (☎ (085) 32 6660); they leave daily from outside the tourist office, where tickets can be purchased. If you are travelling from Adelaide, bookings need to be made with Premier on ☎ (08) 415 5555.

You can pick up a Greyhound Pioneer bus to Melbourne ($50) or Sydney ($100). Tickets to Mt Gambier ($30.20) with Bonds Mt Gambier Motor Service (☎ (08) 231 9090) must be booked at the central bus station in Adelaide.

TAILEM BEND (population 1500)

At a sharp bend in the river, Tailem Bend is near the mouth of the Murray River. **Old Tailem Town** is a re-creation of a pioneer village; it's open daily and costs $5. After Wellington, south of Tailem Bend, the Murray opens into huge **Lake Alexandrina**; there are lots of water birds, but sometimes boating is tricky due to the vagaries of the currents. You can take a ferry (free) across the river to Jervois from where it's 11 km to

the interesting old town of Wellington, where you'll find the **Old Wellington Court House Museum** (open daily). Aboriginal middens can be seen two km south-east of the township.

There are two hotels, a motel and two caravan parks.

Yorke Peninsula

The Yorke Peninsula is a popular holiday area within easy driving distance of Adelaide. There are pleasant beaches along both sides, the Innes National Park on the tip of the peninsula and plenty of opportunities for fishing. The area's economy was originally based on the copper mines of Little Cornwall (the name given to the copper mining areas of Yorke Peninsula). As the mines declined, agriculture developed and much of the land now grows barley and other grains.

The innovative inhabitants of the Yorke Peninsula have developed the Creative Activities Network, a range of workshops, bush walks, heritage tours – even farm visits – run by local Yorke Peninsula artisans and residents. A range of 'personalised learning experiences' are available, from spending a day on a sheep farm to attending a bush painting workshop with a local artist. For more details, contact TSA.

Cornwall & Copper Mines

In the early 1860s, copper was discovered in the Moonta-Kadina-Wallaroo area (known as the Copper Triangle) and within a few years a full-scale copper rush was on. Most of the miners were from Cornwall in England, and the area still has a strong Cornish influence. The boom peaked around the turn of the century, but in the early 1920s a slump in copper prices and rising labour costs closed all the peninsula's mines.

Over a long weekend in May of odd-numbered years, the Kernewek Lowender Festival is held in Australia's Little Cornwall. It's a chance to try Cornish pasties or watch a wheelbarrow race – you may even see a piskey – a mischievous sprite believed by the Cornish people to bring good fortune.

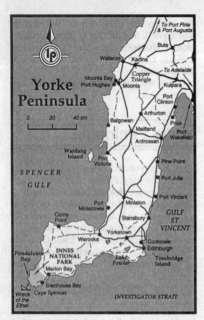

Getting There & Away

Premier (☎ (08) 415 5555) operates a daily bus from Adelaide to Kadina, Wallaroo, Moonta, Port Hughes and Moonta Bay. It takes about three hours to Moonta and costs $13.90.

Yorke Peninsula bus service (☎ (08) 391 2977) runs from Adelaide's central bus station to Yorketown daily. The route alternates daily between the east coast and down the centre of the peninsula. Fares from Adelaide are: Yorketown $23.60, Edithburgh $23.60 and Port Vincent $22.50.

WEST COAST

The west coast, looking out onto the Spencer Gulf, has plenty of beaches, but the road generally runs inland.

Kadina (population 3530)

The largest town on the peninsula, Kadina was once the centre of copper mining. The **Kadina Museum** ($3) includes a number of buildings, one of which – Matta House – was the home of the Matta Matta mine manager. There are other displays here and the Matta Matta mine. It's open from 2 to 4.30 pm on Wednesdays, weekends and holidays.

The **Wallaroo Mines** are one km west of the town on the Wallaroo road. It takes half an hour to stroll around the complex, including the impressive ruins of the engine building.

The main tourist office (☎ (088) 21 1600) for the Copper Triangle is in the town hall.

Places to Stay & Eat The *Kadina Caravan Park* (☎ (088) 21 2259) has camp sites and on-site vans. The *Wombat Hotel* (☎ (088) 21 1108), on Taylor St, charges $19 per person, while the *Kadina Hotel* (☎ (088) 21 2008), a block away, has singles/doubles/triples for $35/52/67. The *Royal Exchange Hotel* (☎ (088) 21 1084) has single rooms only, including a light breakfast, for $20.

Cornish pasties are found in many shops; *Prices Bakery* has excellent ones. *Sarah's Place* is good for pancakes, and the *Dynasty Room* is a Chinese place on Goyder St; it has lunch specials, as do the pubs.

Wallaroo (population 2465)

This port town was a major centre during the copper boom, and is the second point of the Copper Triangle. The 'big stack', one of the great chimneys from the copper smelters (built in 1861), still stands, but today the port's main function is exporting agricultural products, and the grain terminal dwarfs the town. In the old post office there's the **Maritime Museum**, open on Wednesdays, weekends and school holidays; admission is $3.

A map detailing a heritage walk around the town can be obtained from the tourist information desk (☎ (088) 23 2020) in the post office, on the corner of Irwin St and Owen Terrace.

Places to Stay & Eat On the beach near the grain terminal, the *Office Beach Caravan Park* (☎ (088) 23 2722) has camp sites for

$12 and on-site vans for $30. The *Weerona Hotel* (☎ (088) 23 2008) on John Terrace has singles/doubles for $22/32.

Some of the hotels have counter meals and you can get snacks from *Prices Bakery* or more substantial meals in the restaurant in the old railway station.

Moonta (population 2700)

At Moonta, 18 km south of Wallaroo, the copper mine was once said to be the richest mine in Australia. The town grew so fast that its school once had over 1000 students; the building now houses an excellent museum (admission $2.50). It's part of the collection of mine-works ruins at the **Moonta Heritage Site** which you can explore with a self-guiding map from the museum or from the tourist office in Kadina. On weekends and public holidays, the tourist railway will take you around the **Moonta Mines Complex** ($2).

Tandem bicycles can be obtained from the friendly 'I'm not flippin' Cornish' *Scottish* gentleman at Needles & Pins (☎ (088) 25 3392), 47 George St. The shop is generally open daily from 9 am to 5 pm.

Places to Stay Right on the beach three km away, the *Moonta Bay Caravan Park* (☎ (088) 25 2406) has powered camp sites for $14 and cabins for $46. The *Cornwall Hotel* (☎ (088) 25 2304) on Ryan St has rooms for $27.50/40; at the *Royal* (☎ (088) 25 2108) nearby they're $25/40.

EAST COAST

The east-coast road from the top of Gulf St Vincent down to Stenhouse Bay near Cape Spencer closely follows the coast. There are many sandy beaches and secluded coves. **Port Clinton** is the northernmost beach resort. A little south is **Price**, where salt is produced at salt pans just outside town. **Ardrossan** is the largest port on this coast. There's a museum (open Sundays from 2.30 to 4.30 pm and public holidays) on Fifth St.

Continuing south, in the next 50 km the road runs through **Pine Point**, **Black Point**,

Port Julia and **Port Vincent** (each has a sandy beach). Port Vincent has the *Tuckerway Youth Hostel* (☎ (088) 53 7285) which costs $7.50, and there are two caravan parks in the town.

The road continues to hug the coast through **Stansbury** (with a museum set in a pretty cottage garden), **Wool Bay**, **Port Giles** and **Coobowie** to Edithburgh.

Edithburgh has a tidal swimming pool in a small cove; from the cliff tops you can look across to **Troubridge Island**. A 2½-hour tour, including a historical commentary, can be taken to the island, and there is also accommodation available; phone ☎ (088) 52 6290 for details.

In the town there is a small maritime museum, and nearby Sultana Point is a good spot for swimming. The road from Edithburgh to Stenhouse Bay is very scenic.

Near Marion Bay is *Hillocks Drive* (☎ (088) 54 4002), a private property where you can camp or stay in on-site vans. There's superb scenery, native wildlife and wildflowers. Bush camping is $5 per car, and on-site vans are $22 to $25. For visitors there's a $3 entry fee.

Yorketown is the region's business and administrative town. The salt lakes around the town mysteriously turn pink whenever there is going to be a change in the weather.

INNES NATIONAL PARK

The southern tip of the peninsula, marked by Cape Spencer, is part of the Innes National Park. There's a $3 entry fee per vehicle. **Stenhouse Bay**, just outside the park, and **Pondalowie Bay**, within the park, are the principal settlements. The park has fine coastal scenery, good fishing and reef diving.

Pondalowie Bay is the base for a large lobster-fishing fleet and also has a fine surf beach. All the other beaches, except for Browns Beach, are dangerous for swimming.

In the park is the wreck of the barque *Ethel*, a 711-tonne ship which ran ashore in 1904. All that remains are the ribs of the hull rising forlornly from the sands. Her anchor

SOUTH AUSTRALIA

is mounted in a memorial on the cliff top above the beach.

Just past the Cape Spencer turn-off is a marker which directs you to the six ruined buildings at the **Inneston Historic Site**.

Places to Stay

With a permit ($3 per group per night), you can camp in most places in the park; phone the National Parks office in Stenhouse Bay (☎ (088) 54 4040) for more details.

Getting There & Away

There is no public transport to the end of the peninsula. Yorke Peninsula bus service will take you as far as Warooka ($23.60) or Yorketown ($23.60) and then you can try to hitch, but traffic is light.

Eyre Peninsula

The wide Eyre Peninsula points south between Spencer Gulf and the Great Australian Bight. It's bordered on the northern side by the Eyre Highway from Port Augusta to Ceduna. The coastal run along the peninsula is in two parts: the Lincoln Highway southwest from Port Augusta to Port Lincoln; and the Flinders Highway north-west to Ceduna. It's 468 km from Port Augusta direct to Ceduna via the Eyre Highway; via the loop south it's 763 km.

This is a resort area with many good beaches, sheltered bays and pleasant little port towns. On the west coast there are superb surf beaches and spectacular coastal scenery. The area offshore further west is home to the great white shark. This is a favourite locale for making shark films – some scenes for *Jaws* were filmed here.

The Eyre Peninsula also has a flourishing agricultural sector, while the iron-ore deposits at Iron Knob and Iron Baron are processed and shipped from the busy port of Whyalla. The peninsula takes its name from Edward John Eyre, the hardy explorer who made the first recorded east to west crossing of the continent in 1841.

Getting There & Away

Air Kendell Airlines flies to Port Lincoln ($109), Whyalla ($110) and Ceduna ($185) on the Eyre Peninsula. Lincoln Airlines (☎ (086) 82 5688) flies between Port Lincoln and Adelaide for $85. Whyalla Airlines (☎ toll-free 1800 088 858) flies to Streaky Bay ($135) and Whyalla ($90).

Bus Stateliner (☎ (08) 415 5555) has daily services to Port Augusta ($26.10), Whyalla ($29.90), Port Lincoln ($52.50), Ceduna ($61.50) and Streaky Bay ($55). You can also travel to Port Augusta and Ceduna with the major companies on their Adelaide to Perth run. It takes about 11½ hours from Adelaide to Ceduna.

Boat There are plans to commence a ferry service between Wallaroo, on the Yorke Peninsula, and Cowell, on the east coast of the Eyre Peninsula. It's at the drawing-board stage at present. Check with TSA.

PORT AUGUSTA (population 14,500)

Matthew Flinders was the first European to set foot in the area, but the town was not established until 1854. Today, this busy port city is the gateway to the outback region of South Australia. It's also a major crossroads for travellers.

From here, roads head west across the Nullarbor to Western Australia, north to Alice Springs and Darwin in the Northern Territory, south to Adelaide and east to Broken Hill and Sydney in New South Wales. The main railway line between the east and west coasts and the Adelaide to Alice Springs route both pass through Port Augusta.

Information

The Wadlata Outback Centre (☎ (086) 42 4511) at 41 Flinders Terrace is the tourist information centre; it also has an interpretive centre ($6), with exhibits tracing the Aboriginal and European history of the outback. The centre is open weekdays from 9 am to 5.30 pm and weekends from 10 am to 4 pm.

Things to See & Do

There are tours of the **School of the Air**, at the southern end of Commercial Rd, at 10 am and 2 pm on weekdays (admission by donation). The School of the Air may be relocating – check at the Wadlata Outback Centre.

Other attractions include the **Curdnatta Art & Pottery Gallery**, in Port Augusta's first railway station, and the **Homestead Park Pioneer Museum**, Elsie St, open daily from 10 am to 5 pm ($2.50). Pick up a brochure from the Wadlata Outback Centre detailing a **heritage walk** around the town.

Places to Stay

The *Fauna Caravan Park* (☎ (086) 42 2974) has camp sites for $12, on-site vans for $28 and cabins for $45. It also has a bunkhouse for backpackers ($10) with an adjacent campers' kitchen.

Port Augusta Backpackers (☎ (086) 41 1063) at 17 Trent Rd is a friendly place with beds for $12. You can arrange Flinders Ranges tours here. The hostel is just off Highway 1, and if you let the bus drivers know, they'll let you off near the hostel.

The *Flinders Hotel* (☎ (086) 42 2522), at 39 Commercial Rd, has backpackers' accommodation for $12, single/double pub-style rooms for $38/48 and motel-style rooms for $44/55.

Getting There & Away

Air Augusta Airways (☎ (086) 42 3100) flies to Adelaide on weekdays for $98. On Saturday you can take the mail plane to Boulia in outback Queensland, stopping in Birdsville and Innamincka on the way, for $325.

Bus The bus station (☎ (086) 42 5055) is at 23 Mackay St. Stateliner runs to Adelaide ($26.10), Coober Pedy ($56.70), Wilpena Pound ($22.90), Whyalla ($10.50), Port Lincoln ($37), Ceduna ($48.60) and other places on the Eyre Peninsula. Greyhound Pioneer travels to Perth ($180) and Alice Springs ($134).

Train By train Sydney is 32 hours away and a standard economy ticket costs $133. An economy/1st-class sleeper is $227/345. It takes 33 hours to Perth; an economy seat is $170; an economy/1st-class sleeper is $337/556.50. It's four hours to Adelaide ($28). In Port Augusta, phone ☎ (086) 41 8111 for enquiries and bookings.

WHYALLA (population 25,500)

The largest city in the state after Adelaide, Whyalla is a major steel-producing centre with a busy deep-water port. There are tours of the **BHP steel works** at 9.30 am on Mondays, Wednesdays and Saturdays. They start from the tourist centre and cost $5. The tourist centre (☎ (086) 45 7900) is on the Lincoln Highway, near BHP. Next to the tourist centre is the **Maritime Museum**; admission is $4.

Ore comes to Whyalla from Iron Knob, Iron Monarch and Iron Baron. **Iron Knob** was the first iron-ore deposit in Australia to be exploited; there are tours ($3) of the mine at 10 am and 2 pm on weekdays and at 2 pm on Saturdays. Sturdy footwear is required.

Whyalla also has fine beaches, and the **Wildlife & Reptile Sanctuary** on the Lincoln Highway near the airport; admission to the latter is $4.50. On Ekblom St, there are historical exhibits in the **Mt Laura Homestead Museum** (☎ (086) 45 9319), which is open Sundays, Mondays and Wednesdays from 2 to 4 pm and Fridays from 10 am to noon; admission is $1.

Places to Stay & Eat

The *Whyalla Foreshore Caravan Park* (☎ (086) 45 7474) has camp sites for $9.50, on-site vans for $24 and cabins from $26.

Backpackers' accommodation is available at the *Bushman's Rest* (☎ (086) 44 0620), 46 Aikman Crescent. Beds start from $8. The *Hotel Whyalla* (☎ (086) 45 7411), on Darling Terrace opposite the police station, is a pub in the grand old style, with a long, cool bar and a wonderful verandah. It has self-contained singles/doubles from $20/30.

The *Oriental Inn* Chinese restaurant on Essington Lewis Ave has been recommended.

Next door is *Spaggs Italian Restaurant*, with main meals from $9.

WHYALLA TO PORT LINCOLN
Cowell (population 700)
Cowell is a pleasant little town near a large jade deposit. You can see cutting and polishing at the **Cowell Jade Factory** on Second St. There's a small **museum** in the old post office (next door to the operating post office) and an **agricultural museum** on the Lincoln Highway. Oysters are farmed locally, and you can buy them cheaply just about everywhere in the town.

Places to Stay The *Cowell Foreshore Caravan Park* (☎ (086) 29 2307) has camp sites and on-site vans. The impressive *Franklin Harbour Hotel* (☎ (086) 29 2015) has rooms for $15/25. *Schultz Farm* (☎ (086) 29 2194) has rooms for $25 per person including a cooked breakfast.

Further South
The first tiny township heading south from Cowell is **Elbow Hill** (15 km down the Lincoln Highway). There's not much here, but the beaches at nearby **Point Gibbon** (six km) are magnificent – huge white sand dunes and a beautiful coastline. The very hospitable *Elbow Hill Inn* (☎ (086) 28 5012) provides morning and afternoon tea, counter meals and evening dining. They also have two rooms with en-suites ($30/60 for singles/doubles), and a pool.

Cleve is 43 km inland from Cowell, and although it's just a quiet country town, the drive there is pleasant. There's a fauna park with a nocturnal house, and the *Cleve Hotel/Motel* (☎ (086) 28 2011), Fourth St, has pub rooms for $20/30 and motel rooms for $40/50. Back on the coast, **Arno Bay** is another small beach resort.

South again is **Port Neill**, a pleasant seaside town with a vintage vehicle museum. Further south is **Tumby Bay**, with its long, curving white-sand beach, a National Trust museum and a number of interesting old buildings around the town. Hales Mini Mart

(☎ (086) 88 2584) has tourist information and also hires tandem bicycles ($3 per hour).

The **Sir Joseph Banks Islands** are 15 km offshore, and form a marine conservation park. A couple of islands in this group have sea-lion colonies, and there are many attractive bays and reefs plus a wide variety of sea birds, including Cape Barren Geese, which nest on the islands. Cruises and bareboat charter can be arranged; contact Hales Mini Mart in Tumby Bay or the tourist office in Port Lincoln for details.

North Shields is a very small settlement 13 km north of Port Lincoln on the shore of Boston Bay. The Karlinda Collection here has over 10,000 shells, rocks and examples of marine life.

PORT LINCOLN (population 11,500)
Port Lincoln, at the southern end of the Eyre Peninsula, is 662 km from Adelaide by road but only 250 km as the crow flies. The first settlers arrived in 1839 and the town has grown to become the tuna-fishing capital of Australia; the annual Tunarama Festival, which runs over the Australia Day weekend in January, signals the start of the tuna-fishing season with boisterous merriment.

Information
The tourist office (☎ (086) 82 6666) is at the Eyre Travel Centre on Tasman Terrace (the foreshore). Contact the ranger at the National Parks & Wildlife Service (☎ (086) 88 3177) for permits to visit Lincoln National Park (see Around Port Lincoln).

There is excellent surf around the coast; for information about the best areas for skin diving and surfing, contact the Port Lincoln Skin-Diving & Surf shop (☎ (086) 82 4428), at 73 Mortlock Terrace. You can also hire gear here.

Things to See & Do
Port Lincoln is pleasantly situated on Boston Bay. There are a number of historic buildings, including the **Old Mill** on Dorset Place which has a lookout which affords good views out over the bay. The **Lincoln Hotel**

dates from 1840, making it the oldest hotel on the peninsula. On the Flinders Highway, **Mill Cottage** is a historic homestead built in 1866. The **Axel Stenross Maritime Museum** is a memorial to a local boat-building identity and includes his workshop.

Fourteen km offshore is **Dangerous Reef**, the world's largest breeding area for the white pointer shark, although sightings are rare. Cruises to the reef can be arranged through Eyre Travel (☎ (086) 82 6666) or Westward Ho holiday flats (☎ (086) 822425). Prices start at $40, which includes a visit to the underwater viewing platform moored near Boston Island to view southern bluefin tuna.

Places to Stay & Eat

The *Kirton Point Caravan Park* (☎ (086) 82 2537) has camp sites for $5 and cabins from $27. The *Boston Hotel* (☎ (086) 82 1311) on King St has singles/doubles for $20/30. The *Pier Hotel* (☎ (086) 82 1322), at 33 Tasman Terrace, has rooms at $26/35 with bathrooms. *Westward Ho* holiday flats (☎ (086) 82 2425) has flats from $45.

Bugs Restaurant on Eyre St has very good pasta and seafood from $5 to $10. Counter meals at the *Lincoln*, *Tasman* and *Pier* hotels are good value.

Getting There & Away

Daily Stateliner buses run from Adelaide via Cummins (about 11 hours) or Tumby Bay (about 9½ hours) for $52.50, but there is no public transport between here and Streaky Bay.

Getting Around

There are various tours, including town tours ($15), a day tour including the town and Whalers Way ($40) and a day tour incorporating the lower Eyre Peninsula and Coffin Bay ($45). For details see the tourist office.

AROUND PORT LINCOLN

Cape Carnot, better known as Whalers Way, is 32 km south of Port Lincoln. Although it is privately owned, it is possible to visit by obtaining a permit ($15 plus key deposit),

which is valid for 24 hours and enables you to camp at Redbanks or Groper Bay. Permits can be obtained from most petrol stations or from the tourist office in Port Lincoln. You can also buy permits ($5) to visit **Mikkira Koala Sanctuary** (closed November to February) from most petrol stations in Port Lincoln or at the tourist office.

There are beautiful beaches at **Sleaford Bay**, a three-km detour off the road to Whalers Way. Cabins are available for overnight or weekly stays at the *Sleaford Bay Holiday Park* (☎ (086) 88 3177).

Also south of Port Lincoln is the **Lincoln National Park**, again with a magnificent coastline. There are camp sites in the park, and caravan access, but you'll need to obtain a permit ($6 for two adults) from the National Parks & Wildlife Service (see Information in the earlier Port Lincoln section). Over 90% of the tracks in the park can be visited in a conventional vehicle.

You can visit offshore islands such as **Boston Island**; the tourist office in Port Lincoln will help you find a boat to get you out to them. It is also possible to stay in a historic homestead on Boston Island; enquire at the tourist office or phone ☎ (086) 82 1741.

PORT LINCOLN TO STREAKY BAY
Coffin Bay

Despite its ominous name, Coffin Bay is a sheltered stretch of water with some fine beaches and Coffin Bay township (population 340). The town was named by Matthew Flinders in honour of Sir Isaac Coffin. From here you can find spectacular coastal scenery at **Point Avoid**, **Almonta Beach** and **Yangie Bay**. Coffin Bay Peninsula is a national park. There's a 25-km trail to Yangie Bay, but you'll need a 4WD to get from there to Point Sir Isaac on the tip of the peninsula. The prolific bird life is a feature of the **Kellidie Bay Conservation Park**.

Places to Stay The *Coffin Bay Caravan Park* (☎ (086) 85 4170) is the only place in the nearby area where you can camp; it also has on-site vans. There are motel units at the

Coffin Bay Hotel (☎ (086) 85 4111) from $45/52.

Bush camping (difficult access) is allowed at a few places on the peninsula. Contact the ranger at Coffin Bay township (☎ (086) 85 4047).

Coffin Bay to Point Labatt

Just past **Coulta**, 40 km north of Coffin Bay, there's good surfing at **Greenly Beach**. About 15 km south of **Elliston**, a small resort and fishing town with a nice bay, **Locks Bay** is a good area for salmon fishing.

Just north of Elliston, take the seven-km detour to **Anxious Bay** and **Salmon Point** for some great ocean scenery. There's accommodation on **Flinders Island**; phone ☎ (086) 26 1403 for details.

There are good swimming beaches around **Waterloo Bay**, while **Blackfellows** has fine surf. **Talia**, further up the coast, has impressive granite rock faces and the limestone **Talia Caves**.

At **Port Kenny** on Venus Bay, there are more beaches, and southern right whales are often seen off the coast when they come to breed in October.

Shortly before Streaky Bay, the turn-off to **Point Labatt** takes you to the only permanent colony of sea lions on the Australian mainland. You look down on their rocks from the cliff top, 50 metres above.

STREAKY BAY (population 960)

This little town takes its name from the 'streaky' water, caused by seaweed in the bay. A museum containing the **Keish Pioneer Hut** and other exhibits is open on Fridays from 2 to 4 pm and at other times by prior arrangement. There's also the **Powerhouse Museum** which contains restored engines.

Curious granite outcrops known as inselbergs are found at numerous places around the Eyre Peninsula. You can see a good group known as **Murphy's Haystacks** near the highway about 20 km south-east of Streaky Bay. The back beach, four km west of Streaky Bay, is good for surfing.

Places to Stay

The *Foreshore Tourist Park* (☎ (086) 26 1666) has camp sites for $9.25 and on-site cabins from $31. The *Streaky Bay Community Hotel* (☎ (086) 26 1008) has singles/doubles for $25/30 and motel units for $44/52.

SMOKY BAY (population 100)

Since the annual rodeo left town, this little settlement has reverted back into a quiet area where the fishing is good and there's plenty of time to relax – there's not much else to do! The friendly caravan park (☎ (086) 25 7030) has cabins from $25, and camp sites for $6.

CEDUNA (population 2750)

Just past the junction of the Flinders and Eyre highways, Ceduna marks the end of the Eyre Peninsula area and the start of the long, empty stretch of highway across the Nullarbor Plain into Western Australia. The town was founded in 1896, although a whaling station had existed on St Peter Island, off nearby Cape Thevenard, back in 1850.

There's a friendly tourist office (☎ (086) 25 2972) in the main street. It's also a travel agency, and you might find yourself visiting to buy a bus ticket to Western Australia after a few days waiting for a lift. Greyhound Pioneer charges $180 to Perth and $139 to Noseman.

The **Old Schoolhouse Museum** has pioneer exhibits and artefacts from the British atomic weapons program at Maralinga. It is possible to visit TESTRA, an overseas telecommunications earth station 34 km north of Ceduna where microwave communications are bounced off satellites. Contact the Ceduna tourist office.

There are many beaches and sheltered coves around Ceduna, while 13 km out of town, you can see the old **McKenzie Ruin** at the earlier township site of Denial Bay. **Laura Bay**, off the road to Smoky Bay 20 km south-west of Ceduna, is a small conservation park that contains many species of bird.

Turn off the highway at **Penong** (famous for its numerous windmills), about 75 km west of Ceduna, and a 20-km dirt track gets you to **Point Sinclair**. Here you'll find **Cactus Beach** and some of Australia's best surf, as well as more sheltered beaches. The whole point is private property but you can camp for $4 – fees are collected daily. Bring your own water.

Places to Stay

There are a number of caravan parks with on-site vans and cabins, including the *Ceduna Foreshore* (☎ (086) 25 2290), which has camp sites from $10 and cabins from $30. The *Ceduna Community Hotel* (☎ (086) 25 2008) has pub rooms from $25/29 and motel units from $58/63.

Flinders Ranges

Rising from the northern end of Gulf St Vincent and running north for 800 km into the arid outback, the Flinders Ranges offer some of the most spectacular scenery in Australia. It's a superb area for bushwalks, wildlife or taking in the ever-changing colours of the outback. In the far north of the Flinders region, the mountains are hemmed in by barren salt lakes.

As in other dry regions of Australia, the vegetation here is surprisingly diverse and colourful. In the spring, when rain is most likely, the country is at its greenest and carpeted with wildflowers. In summer the nights are cool but the days can be searingly hot. Winter is probably the best time to visit, although there are attractions at any time of year.

In 1802, when Flinders first set foot in the ranges, there were a number of Aboriginal tribes in the region. You can visit some of their sites: the rock paintings at Yourambulla (near Hawker) and Arkaroo (near Wilpena); and the rock-cut patterns at Sacred Canyon (near Wilpena) and Chambers Gorge.

Bushwalking is one of the main attractions of the area. Campers can generally find water

in rock pools during cooler months, but this is wild, rugged country and care should be taken before setting out. Wilpena Pound, the Arkaroola-Mt Painter Sanctuary and Mt Remarkable National Park all have excellent walks, many of them along marked trails.

In the early mornings and evenings, you've got a good chance of spotting wildlife, including emus, a variety of kangaroos and many different lizards. The bird life is especially prolific, with colourful parrots, galahs, rosellas and many others – often in great numbers.

Information

The main National Parks office for the Flinders Ranges and the far north is at Hawker (☎ (086) 48 4244), in the same building as the post office. There's another office at Wilpena (☎ (086) 48 0048) which has information on display 24 hours a day and is staffed from 8 am to 5.30 pm daily. It's definitely worth getting a good map of the area, as there are many back roads and a variety of road surfaces. The Flinders Outback Regional Tourism Association's visitor booklet is quite good, and the RAA, TSA and the National Parks office all put out maps of the ranges area and Wilpena Pound. *Touring in the Flinders Ranges* is a good little book produced by the RAA and available from its offices. If you're planning on doing more than just the standard walks in the Flinders, look for a copy of the Adrian Heard's *Walking Guide to the North Flinders Ranges* (State Publishing, 1990, $14.95). Tyrone T Thomas's *Fifty Walks in South Australia* (Hill of Content Publishing Company, 1992, $15.95) has a good section on the Flinders Ranges.

Organised Tours

There are plenty of tours from Adelaide to the ranges and also tours out from Wilpena Pound and Arkaroola. A few cater for backpackers – see hostel notice boards for current fares and itineraries.

The major bus companies also do tours and there are plenty of companies offering more adventurous 4WD tours, including

SOUTH AUSTRALIA

Flinders Ranges

Flinders Ranges

0   25   50 km

To Oodnadatta
& Alice Springs

Marree

Birdsville Track
to Birdsville

Strzelecki Track

To Innamincka

Mt Hopeless

Talc Mine

Paralana
Springs

Mt Painter
(790 m) ▲

Arkaroola

GAMMON RANGES
NATIONAL PARK

Lyndhurst

Copley

Leigh Creek

Balcanoona
National Park
Headquarters

Puttapa

Italowie
Gorge

Sliding Rock

Moro
Gorge

Beltana

Lake Frome
(Salt)

Lake Torrens
(Salt)

Parachilna
Gorge

Glass's
Gorge

Eregunda
Valley

Chambers
Gorge

Parachilna

Blinman

Angorichina
Village

South
Blinman

Wirrealpa Homestead

Great Wall
of China

FLINDERS RANGES
NATIONAL PARK

Brachina
Gorge

Bunker Hills

Frome Downs
(Private Homestead)

Barytes
Mine

Bunyeroo
Gorge

Oraparinna
Homestead

Wilpena

Moralana
Scenic
Route

Sacred
Canyon

Arkaroo
Rock Shelter

Rawnsley
Park

To Coober Pedy
& Alice Springs

Yourambulla
Rock Shelter

Hawker

47

Kanyaka
(Ruins)

Buckaringa
Gorge

Cradock

Warren
Gorge

Quorn

Belton

To Broken Hill (195 km)

Stuart Highway

87

PORT
AUGUSTA

Pichi
Richi
Pass

Bruce

Carrieton

Hammond

Mannahill

To Perth

1

Alligator
Gorge

Wilmington

Willowie

Orroroo

Yunta

32

Barrier Highway

ALT 1

Hancocks
Lookout

S6

Willowie

Mambray
Creek

Mt
Remarkable
(963 m) ▲

Melrose

Pekina

Black
Rock

Booleroo
Centre

S6

WHYALLA

Port
Germein

Germein
Gorge

Murray
Town

Wirrabara

Peterborough

83

SPENCER
GULF

To Adelaide

To Burra & Adelaide

MT REMARKABLE
NATIONAL PARK

SOUTH AUSTRALIA

Treckabout Australia (☎ (08) 396 2833), based in Adelaide; Intrepid Tours (☎ (086) 48 6277), in Quorn; and Sambells Scenic Tours (☎ (085) 22 2871) and Gawler Outback Tours (☎ (085) 22 2149), both in Gawler. Horse-riding treks are also available at the Pichi Richi Holiday Camp (☎ (086) 48 6075), 14 km south of Quorn in the Pichi Richi Pass, which leads to Stirling North. Closer to Wilpena Pound, Ngarri Mudlanha Horse Tours has treks to the ABC Range, just north of the Pound. These include an informative cultural commentary, and can be booked through the Wilpena Pound Motel (☎ toll-free 1800 805 802). The cost is $20 for one hour or $35 for two hours.

There are camel treks from Blinman, ranging from 1½-hour rides ($25) to week-long treks ($730); phone ☎ (086) 48 4874 for details.

At Wilpena you can take a scenic flight for $32 (15 minutes) or $47 (30 minutes). Costs increase if there are less than three people on the flight. Bookings can be made through the Wilpena Pound Motel.

Places to Stay

There are hotels and caravan parks as well as many cottages and farms offering all sorts of accommodation in the Flinders Ranges, but there is no hostel accommodation at Wilpena Pound itself. To stay here, you will need either your own camping gear or to be prepared to fork out for the relatively expensive, but very comfortable, *Wilpena Pound Motel*. The closest budget accommodation is at Rawnsley Park, 10 km south of Wilpena, just outside the walls of the Pound, where on-site vans are available. See under Wilpena Pound. Contact the TSA travel centre in Adelaide (☎ toll-free 1800 882 092) for further details.

In Quorn, Quornucopia (☎ (086) 486 282), at 17 Railway Terrace, can arrange accommodation. Costs range from $29 per night in a basic hut to $69 per night in a self-contained cottage.

To camp in the national park (except at the private camping ground at Wilpena Pound) you need a permit from a National Parks office for $3 per night, valid for up to five people.

Getting There & Away

Bus Stateliner has four services a week to Wilpena Pound (7½ hours, $47.30). All services are via Quorn ($33.50), Hawker ($44) and Parachilna ($50.40). Twice a week the service continues to Arkaroola (13 hours, $70.30).

Car There are good bitumen roads all the way north to Wilpena Pound. From there the roads are gravel, and although these are quite good when they're dry, they can be closed by heavy rain. Check with National Parks offices for current information. The Marree road skirting the western edge of the Flinders Ranges is surfaced up to Lyndhurst.

Probably the most interesting way to get to Arkaroola is to go to Wilpena Pound and on to South Blinman, then head east to Wirrealpa Homestead, where you head north via Chambers Gorge to meet the Frome Downs road south of Balcanoona. All these roads tend to be difficult after heavy rain.

For recorded information on road conditions in the Flinders Ranges region and other outback regions of South Australia, phone ☎ (08) 11 633.

Getting Around

If you have a vehicle you can make a loop that takes you around an interesting section of the southern part of the ranges. From Port Augusta go through the Pichi Richi Pass to Quorn and Hawker and on up to Wilpena Pound. Continue north through the Flinders Ranges National Park past the Oraparinna Homestead, then veer west through the Brachina Gorge to the main Leigh Creek to Hawker road. From this junction you can either head straight back to Hawker, or make a detour off the main Leigh Creek to Hawker road and travel to Hawker via the Moralana Scenic Route. The section via the Brachina Gorge has a self-guided geology trail, with interpretive signs posted en route. Pick up a leaflet describing the trail from the National Parks office at Wilpena.

From Wilpena Pound, you can also loop north into the Flinders Ranges National Park through Bunyeroo Gorge, meeting up with the Brachina Gorge road. From here you can either head back to Wilpena via the Oraparinna Homestead, or head west to the Leigh Creek to Hawker road and travel back to Hawker.

MT REMARKABLE NATIONAL PARK

South-east of Port Augusta, and in the southern stretch of the Flinders Ranges, between Melrose and Wilmington, is the Mt Remarkable National Park. From **Wilmington** (population 250) you can drive into the park and walk through narrow **Alligator Gorge**; in places the walls of this spectacularly beautiful gorge are only two metres apart. The Wilmington Deli is a good place to go for information on walks in the region, and you can obtain a copy of the locally produced *Mt Remarkable District Visitor Directory* here for $2.50. Pub-style accommodation is available at the *Wilmington Hotel* (☎ (086) 67 5154). The town also has two caravan parks.

Hancocks Lookout, just north of the park near Horrocks Pass, offers excellent views of Spencer Gulf. There is a camping ground in the Mambray Creek section, and bush camping is permitted in some areas. The ranger's office (☎ (086) 34 7068), where you can get camping permits, is at Mambray Creek. The entry fee for the Mt Remarkable National Park is $3 for a group of five, and there's a camp site with facilities at Mambray ($6 per site).

MELROSE (population 200)

This tiny town is the oldest settlement in the Flinders Ranges. It's in a beautiful setting, on the southern edge of the Mt Remarkable National Park, at the foot of Mt Remarkable (956 metres). There's a walking trail to the top of the mountain. The old police station and courthouse now houses a museum. The **Mt Remarkable Hotel** was built in 1846 and its exterior has scarcely changed since (apart from the colour – it's now an alarming shade of green).

Places to Stay

The *Melrose Caravan Park* (☎ (086) 66 2060) has camp sites for $11, on-site vans for $24 and cabins for $35. The *Mt Remarkable Hotel* (☎ (086) 66 2119) has motel accommodation for $27/35. The *North Star Hotel* (☎ 66 2110) has singles/doubles for $15/25.

SOUTH OF THE FLINDERS RANGES

Other towns in the south of the Flinders Ranges include **Carrieton**, where a major rodeo is held each October, **Bruce** and **Hammond** – railheads which have faded away to ghost towns – and **Orroroo**, an agricultural centre. Nearby **Black Rock Peak** has good bushwalks and terrific views. You can see Aboriginal **rock carvings** at Pekina Creek, and the nearby ruins of the **Pekina Station Homestead** are worth a visit.

Between Melrose and Port Germein you pass through the scenic **Germein Gorge**, while **Bangor** has the ruins of the Gorge Hotel. At **Port Germein** the *Casual Affair* (☎ (086) 34 5242) is a coffee shop, gallery and craft centre where there's some backpackers' accommodation. Dorm beds are in a tranquil, Japanese-style room, and cost about $9. Further south at **Wirrabara** there's a youth hostel (☎ (086) 68 4158) with beds for $12.

QUORN (population 1050)

The 'gateway to the Flinders' is about 330 km north of Adelaide and 41 km north-east of Port Augusta. It became an important railway town after the completion of the Great Northern Railway in 1878, and it still has some flavour of the pioneering days.

The railway was closed in 1957, but some of the line has reopened as a tourist railway. A vintage steam engine makes a 32-km round trip from Quorn to the scenic Pichi Richi Pass for $16. It runs on some weekends and public holidays between March and mid-November (☎ (08) 276 6232).

The town, picturesquely sited in a valley, has a couple of art galleries. **Quornucopia** offers a range of unusual crafts and gifts, and there's a restaurant in the small **Quorn Mill**, an old flour mill.

From Quorn you can make 4WD trips into the Flinders Ranges and visit the nearby **Warren Gorge** (which has good rock climbing and is a pleasant picnic site) and the **Waukarie Creek Trail** which runs from Woolshed Flat to Waukarie Creek. **Buckaringa Sanctuary**, encompassing the Buckaringa Gorge, lies 30 km north of Quorn. An ecotourism venture is planned for the sanctuary, including self-contained cabins and a restaurant. Contact TSA for details.

Places to Stay

The *Quorn Caravan Park* (☎ (086) 48 6206) has camp sites and on-site vans. The *Transcontinental Hotel* (☎ (086) 48 6076) on Railway Terrace is a friendly place with backpackers' beds at $10 a night and cooking facilities. There are also singles/doubles for $22/32.

The *Pichi Richi Holiday Camp* (☎ (086) 48 6075), 14 km south of Quorn in the Pichi Richi Pass, has a self-contained cottage for $80 per night (for up to six people; $10 each extra person). It also has horse treks ranging in duration from two hours to seven days.

KANYAKA

About 40 km north of Quorn, on the way to Hawker, are the ruins of the old Kanyaka settlement, founded in 1851. Up to 70 families lived here, tending the settlement's 50,000 sheep, but it was abandoned in the 1870s following devastating droughts. The epitaphs on the headstones in the tiny graveyard reflect the courage of these early pioneers.

From the homestead ruins, you can take a 10-minute walk to the old woolshed. The track continues about 1.5 km to a picturesque permanent water hole, overlooked by the **Kanyaka Rock**.

If you are coming from Wilpena Pound, don't be confused by the sign which indicates when the Kanyaka area was first surveyed – the clearly marked turn-off for the ruins is about 10 km further on.

HAWKER (population 350)

Hawker is 55 km south of Wilpena Pound. The National Parks office for the Flinders Ranges and Far North is in the same building as the post office, on the corner of Wilpena Rd and Elder Terrace. For tourist information, chat with the helpful staff at the Mobil service station on Wilpena Rd.

There are Aboriginal rock paintings 12 km south of Hawker at the **Yourambulla Rock Shelter**, a hollow in the rocks high up on the side of Yourambulla Peak, a half-hour walk from the road. The **Jarvis Hill Lookout** is about six km south-west of Hawker and affords magnificent views.

The Moralana Scenic Route is a round-trip drive from Hawker, taking in the magnificent scenery between the Elders and Wilpena

Legends

The 'spirit of place', almost palpable, which inhabits the Flinders Ranges, has inspired a rich heritage of dreaming stories. Known by the Adnyamathanha ('hill people') as Ikara, Wilpena Pound was an important ceremonial site, and many of these legends – many secret, but some related by Adnyamathanha elders – explain creation, the extraordinary geological features of the pound, and the native birds and animals which inhabit it.

One Adnyamathanha story describes Akurra, a giant snake who carved out gorges on his quest to find water. The rumblings from his giant belly can be heard resounding around the walls of Ikara.

Another story relates that the walls of the pound are the bodies of two Akurra, who coiled around Ikara during an initiation ceremony, creating a whirlwind during which they devoured most of the participants.

In another story, the bossy eagle Wildu sought revenge on his nephews, who had tried to kill him, by building a great fire. All birds were caught in the flames, and, originally white, they emerged blackened and burnt. The magpies and willie wagtails were partially blackened, but the crows were entirely blackened, and have remained so until this day. ■

ranges. It is about 19 km to the Moralana turn-off, and 28 km along an unsealed road that joins up with the sealed Hawker to Leigh Creek road, from where it is 40 km back to Hawker.

Places to Stay & Eat
The *Hawker Caravan Park* in town has sites for $10 and on-site vans for $30. The *Hawker Hotel* (☎ (086) 48 4102) costs $25/35 for pub-style singles/doubles. Motel units are $50/60. The *Outback Motel* (☎ (086) 48 4100) has singles/doubles for $65/75.

The *Sightseers Cafe* has reasonably priced meals, or there's the more up-market *Old Ghan Restaurant* in the disused railway station.

Getting There & Away
There are four services a week to Wilpena Pound with Stateliner ($8.60).

WILPENA POUND
The best-known feature of the ranges is the huge natural basin known as Wilpena Pound. Covering about 80 sq km, it is ringed by cliffs and is accessible only by the narrow opening at Sliding Rock through which Wilpena Creek sometimes flows. From outside Wilpena Pound, the cliff face is almost sheer – soaring to 1000 metres – but inside, the basin floor slopes gently away from the peaks.

There is plenty of wildlife in Wilpena Pound, particularly birds – everything from rosellas, galahs and budgerigars to emus and wedge-tailed eagles. You can make scenic flights over Wilpena Pound from $32 (book at the Wilpena Pound Motel) or excursions to other places of interest in the vicinity. **Sacred Canyon**, with rock-cut patterns, is off to the east. North of Wilpena Pound is the **Flinders Ranges National Park** where scenic attractions include the Bunyeroo and Brachina gorges and the Aroona Valley.

Bushwalks
If you're planning to walk for more than about three hours, fill in the log book at the ranger's office – and don't forget to 'sign off' when you return.

There is a series of bushwalks in the park, clearly marked by blue triangles along the tracks. (Sections which incorporate parts of the Heysen Trail are indicated by red markers.) Pick up a copy of the Wilpena leaflet issued by the National Parks & Wildlife Service ($1.50). Topographical maps (scale 1:50,000) are available from the National Parks office in the Pound for $7 each.

It is recommended that you do not walk solo and that you are adequately equipped – particularly with drinking water and sun protection, especially during the summer months.

Most of the walks start from the camping ground and the walking times indicated are for a reasonably easy pace. The St Mary Peak walk is probably the most interesting, but there are plenty of others worth considering. They vary from short walks, suitable for those with small children, to longer ones taking more than a day.

You can take an excellent day-long walk from the camp site in Wilpena Pound to **St Mary Peak** and back – either as an up-and-down or a round-trip expedition. Up and back, it's faster and more interesting to take the route outside Wilpena Pound and then up to the Tanderra Saddle, as the scenery this way is much more spectacular.

The final climb up to the saddle is fairly steep and the stretch to the top of the peak is a real scramble. The views are superb from the saddle and the peak; the white glimmer of Lake Torrens is visible off to the west and the long Aroona Valley stretches off to the north.

Descending from the peak to the saddle you can then head back down on the same direct route or take the longer round-trip walk through Wilpena Pound via the old homestead and Sliding Rock. This is the same track you take to get to Edeowie Gorge. Alternatively, you can take your time and stay at the Cooinda bush-camping site.

Arkaroo Rock is at the base of the Wilpena Range, about 10 km south of Wilpena off the

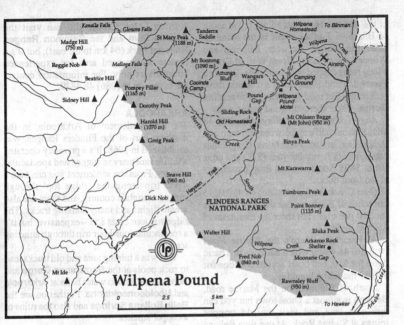

Wilpena Pound

0   2.5   5 km

Hawker road. From the car park it takes about an hour at a moderate pace to reach the rock shelter, where there are Aboriginal depictions of emu and bird tracks in red ochre.

Places to Stay & Eat

Unless you've got a tent there is no cheap accommodation at Wilpena Pound. There's a camping ground with facilities including a well-stocked store. Permits for this site can be purchased at the store ($8). Otherwise, the *Wilpena Pound Motel* (☎ toll-free 1800 805 802) has all mod cons including a restaurant and swimming pool but it costs $74/79 a night for singles/doubles, including a light breakfast (during December and January, rates are $64/69). You can get pies, pasties, groceries and last-minute camping requirements at the general store. Counter lunches are available in the motel bar, and there's also a very good restaurant.

Off the Hawker road, about 10 km south of Wilpena and close to the Pound's outer edge, *Rawnsley Park* (☎ (086) 48 0030) has camp sites for $8.50, on-site vans for $32 and cabins from $48. The Stateliner bus will drop you at the turn-off and from there it's a four-km walk. If you have booked an on-site van or cabin and let the park know which bus you will be on, they'll collect you from the turn-off. You can also make horse treks and guided 4WD treks from here.

BLINMAN (population 100)

From the 1860s to the 1890s this was a busy copper town but today it's just a tiny country town on the circular route around Wilpena Pound. It's a useful starting point for visits to many of the scenic attractions in the area. The delightful *Blinman Hotel* (☎ (086) 48 4867) has a real outback pub flavour – rooms cost $20 per person or $25 with bathroom.

AROUND BLINMAN

The beautiful **Aroona Valley** and the ruins

of the **Aroona Homestead** are to the south of Blinman. Further south is the stunning **Brachina Gorge**. Between Blinman and Wilpena Pound is the **Great Wall of China**, a long ridge capped with ironstone. Between Parachilna and Blinman, it's a scenic drive on a rough dirt road through the **Parachilna Gorge**, where there are good picnic areas.

Angorichina Tourist Village (☎ (086) 48 4842), about halfway between Blinman and Parachilna in the Parachilna Gorge, has camp sites ($7), on-site vans ($12) and units (from $42). Stateliner will drop passengers at the front door.

Gum Creek Station (☎ (086) 48 4883), 15 km south of Blinman, has shearers' quarters for $10 per adult, but there's a minimum of $50 per night.

At Parachilna there's the *Prairie Hotel* (☎ (086) 48 4895) which has beds in a basic dorm for $10, and hotel accommodation for $30/50 including breakfast.

North of Blinman, on the Marree road, **Beltana** is almost a ghost town but you can turn east here and visit the **old copper mines** at Sliding Rock. At one time Beltana was a major camel-breeding station and much of the town is being restored. The roadhouse (☎ (086) 75 2744) is a good source of information about the area. The *Old School House* (☎ (086) 75 2280), in Old Beltana, has bunks. It can accommodate up to eight people for $40.

It's a long drive from anywhere to **Chambers Gorge**, well to the north-east towards Lake Frome. The deep gorge has rock carvings and from Mt Chambers you can see Lake Frome and the Flinders Ranges all the way from Mt Painter to Wilpena.

LEIGH CREEK (population 1400)

North of Beltana, Leigh Creek's huge open-cut coal mine supplies the Port Augusta Power Station. Tree planting has transformed this once barren town; you can do a drive-yourself tour of the coal works by following the green-arrow signs. In 1982 the whole town was shifted south a few km to allow mining on the site.

From Leigh Creek, you can visit the **Aroona Dam** and the **Gammon Ranges National Park** (64 km to the east), but it's a remote and rugged area for experienced bushwalkers only. For information contact the ranger on ☎ (086) 48 4829.

ARKAROOLA

The tiny settlement of Arkaroola, in the northern part of the Flinders Ranges, was established in 1968. It's a privately operated wildlife sanctuary in rugged and spectacular country. From the settlement you can take a 4WD trip along the 'ridge top' through rugged mountain country, and there are also scenic flights and many walking tracks. The ridge-top tour costs $55 – expensive, but it's a spectacular four-hour trip through amazing scenery.

This was a mining area and old tracks lead to rock pools at the **Barraranna Gorge** and **Echo Camp**, and to water holes at **Arkaroola** and **Nooldoonooldoona**. Further on are the **Bolla Bollana Springs** and also the ruins of a copper smelter.

Mt Painter is a very scenic landmark, and there are fine views from **Freeling Heights** across Yudnamutana Gorge or from **Siller's Lookout**, from where you can see the salt flats of Lake Frome. This is real red outback country and Mt Painter is a spectacular example of that landscape. **Paralana Hot Springs** is believed to be the site of the last geyser activity to have taken place in Australia.

Places to Stay & Eat

The resort camp site (☎ (086) 48 4848) costs $10 for two and there is a variety of other accommodation. Bunk beds are $10 but you have to book these in advance. Units cost $39 for twin rooms with shared facilities, or there are motel units from $59 a double. There's a small shop where you can buy basic supplies, and a restaurant.

Getting There & Away

Stateliner buses run twice a week from Adelaide (around 13 hours; $70.30).

Outback

The area north of the Eyre Peninsula and the Flinders Ranges stretches into the vast, empty area of South Australia's far north. Although sparsely populated and difficult to travel through, it has much of interest. Large parts of the far north are prohibited areas (either Aboriginal land or the Woomera restricted area) and without 4WD or camels it's not possible to stray far from the main roads as there are virtually no other surfaced roads.

National Park Permits

To visit the national parks up here (and much of the far north is national park) you need a Desert Parks Permit which costs $50 per vehicle. It's valid for a year and includes an excellent information book and detailed route and area maps.

Permits are available in many towns (although not from most National Parks offices, strangely) including: Adelaide (RAA and others), Alice Springs (Shell Todd service station), Birdsville Track (Mungerannie Roadhouse), Broken Hill (RAA), Coober Pedy (Underground Books), Hawker (Hawker Motors), Innamincka (Trading Post), Marree (Khans General Store, Oasis Cafe), Mt Dare Homestead, Oodnadatta (Pink Roadhouse), Port Augusta (Wadlata Outback Centre) and William Creek (William Creek Hotel).

If you want to visit the **Dalhousie Mound Springs** in the Witjira National Park north of Oodnadatta, you need only buy a $15 day/night permit, available from the Pink Roadhouse in Oodnadatta or Mt Dare Homestead.

ROUTES NORTH

The Stuart Highway is a smooth bitumen road all the way from Adelaide to Alice Springs. It's a long way – 933 km from Port Augusta to the Northern Territory border. The temptation to rush along that smooth road has resulted in more than a few high-speed meetings between cars and cattle. Take care.

For those who want to travel to the Northern Territory the hard way, there is still the **Oodnadatta Track**. This old road runs from Port Augusta through the Flinders Ranges to Leigh Creek, Lyndhurst, Marree and Oodnadatta and eventually joins the Stuart Highway not far south of the Territory border. For most of the way it runs close to the old railway-line route. The road is surfaced as far as Lyndhurst, after which it's a typical outback track. There are a number of routes across from Oodnadatta to the Stuart Highway.

The two other routes of interest in the far north are the famous **Birdsville Track** and the **Strzelecki Track** – see the relevant sections later in this chapter. These days the tracks have been so much improved that during the winter season it's quite feasible to do them in any car that's in good condition – a 4WD is not necessary.

For more information on these outback routes check with the state automobile associations. *Outback Central & South Australia*, published by the South Australian Department of Lands, is an excellent tourist map with a lot of interesting information. Algona Publications (16 Charles St, Northcote, Victoria 3070) does a good *Simpson Desert South-Lake Eyre* map which covers all three tracks. For more detail on outback travel, see Lonely Planet's *Outback Australia*.

The South Australian outback includes much of the **Simpson Desert** and the harsh, rocky land of **Sturt Stony Desert**. There are also huge salt lakes which every once in a long while fill with water. **Lake Eyre**, used by Donald Campbell for his attempt on the world's land-speed record in the '60s, filled up for a time in the '70s. It filled up again in 1989, only the third occasion since Europeans first reached this area.

When the infrequent rains do reach this dry land the effect is amazing – flowers bloom and plants grow at a breakneck pace in order to complete their life cycles before the dry returns. There is even a species of frog that goes into a sort of suspended animation, remaining in the ground for years on end, only to pop up with the first sign of rain.

On a much more mundane level, roads can be washed out and the surface turned into a sticky glue. Vehicles are often stuck for days – or even weeks.

WOOMERA (population 1600)

During the '50s and '60s Woomera was used to launch experimental British rockets and conduct tests in an abortive European project to send a satellite into orbit. The Woomera Prohibited Area occupies a vast stretch of land in the centre of the state. The town of Woomera, in the south-eastern corner of the Prohibited Area, is now an 'open town' but it is just a shadow of its former self. These days its main role is as a service town for the mostly US personnel working at the so-called Joint Facility at Nurrungar, a short distance south of Woomera near Island Lagoon. About 1600 people live here today, as against 5000 at the town's peak.

A small **heritage centre** in the centre of town has various local oddments and a collection of old aircraft and missiles. The museum tells you something about the missile testing in the past but little about what goes on today. The centre is open from 9.45 am to 5 pm daily from March to November, and is closed over the summer.

Places to Stay & Eat

The *Woomera Travellers' Village* (☎ (086) 73 7800), near the entrance to the town, has backpackers' accommodation for $12 a bed, camp sites for $5 per person (although the ground is like concrete) and on-site vans from $25 a double. There's also a very basic kiosk here.

The only alternative is the *Eldo Hotel* (☎ (086) 73 7867) in town on Kotana Ave. It has singles/doubles for $32.50/45 ('Eldo' is the acronym for the European Launcher Development Organisation).

The small shopping centre has a snack bar with the usual takeaway fare; for something better you'll have to try the restaurant in the *Eldo Hotel*. It serves reasonable but unexciting pub-type meals for around $8 for a main course. The Eldo also has poker machines for those who feel like a flutter.

Getting There & Away

Air Kendell Airlines (book through Ansett on ☎ (08) 13 1300) flies from Adelaide to Woomera most days of the week for $131.

Bus Woomera is seven km off the Stuart Highway from the tiny and scruffy little settlement of Pimba, 175 km north of Port Augusta. Stateliner and the long-distance bus lines pass through Woomera daily. It's about $40 to Adelaide and $120 to Alice Springs.

ANDAMOOKA (population 470)

Off the Stuart Highway, north of Woomera and west of Lake Torrens, Andamooka is a rough-and-ready little opal-mining town. Many residents live underground to avoid the temperature extremes. From Pimba, Andamooka is about 115 km north along a good road.

Olympic Dam is a huge uranium, gold, silver and copper mine on Roxby Downs Station near Andamooka. Tours of the mine run daily at 9.45 am from the BP service station at Roxby Downs town (population 2000); phone ☎ (086) 71 0788 for details.

Places to Stay

You can camp or stay in an on-site van ($24) at the caravan park (☎ (086) 72 7117), and the *Tuckerbox* there does good meals. The *Andamooka Motel* (☎ (086) 72 7186) has rooms for about $35/45 (less in summer).

At Roxby Downs, the caravan park (☎ (086) 71 1000) has camp sites for $4.50, while the motor inn (☎ (086) 71 0311) charges $83 for rooms.

Getting There & Away

Stateliner has three buses a week from Adelaide to Roxby Downs (7½ hours, $67), and these go on to Andamooka (30 minutes, $18).

GLENDAMBO

Glendambo is 113 km north of Pimba and 252 km south of Coober Pedy. It has a store, pub, motel and caravan park, all developed since the completion of the new Stuart Highway – an indication of the increased traffic since the road was sealed.

The *Glendambo Tourist Centre Caravan Park* (☎ (086) 72 1035) and motel (☎ (086) 72 1030) has camp sites from $12.50 for two people, on-site vans from $30 a double and bunk-house accommodation for $15. The motel has singles/doubles for $75/85.

COOBER PEDY (population 2500)

On the Stuart Highway, 860 km north of Adelaide, Coober Pedy is one of Australia's best-known outback towns. The name is Aboriginal and means 'white fellow's hole in the ground'. This aptly describes the place, as a large proportion of the population lives in dugouts to shelter from the extreme climate: daytime summer temperatures can soar to over 50°C and the winter nights are cold. Apart from the dugouts, there are over 250,000 mine shafts in the area!

Coober Pedy is in an extremely inhospitable area and the town reflects this; even in the middle of winter it looks dried out and dusty, with piles of junk everywhere. This is no attractive little settlement; in fact it's hardly surprising that much of *Mad Max III* was filmed here – the town looks like the end of the world!

Coober Pedy has a very mixed population – 53 nationalities are represented. It also has a reputation for being pretty volatile: since 1987 the police station has been bombed twice, the courthouse has been bombed once, the most successful restaurant (the Acropolis) has been demolished by a blast and hundreds of thousands of dollars worth of mining equipment has gone the same way.

To state the obvious, while it should be perfectly safe for visitors, it would be unwise for lone females to wander around unaccompanied late at night or accept invitations from unfamiliar men to visit mines or opal collections.

Information

The tourist office (☎ (086) 72 5298) is in the council offices, opposite the Opal Inn as you enter the town. It is open weekdays and sometimes weekends. The Underground Bookshop is very good for information on the local area and the outback in general. It also sells second-hand books.

Buses leave from the new service station opposite the council offices.

Dugout Homes

Many of the early dugout homes were simply worked-out mines; now, however, they're often cut specifically as residences. Several homes are open to visitors – all you have to do is create an eccentric enough abode and you can charge admission!

Other Attractions

Coober Pedy has a number of other attractions worth a look. The most dominant of these is the **Big Winch**, which is a lookout over the town and an extensive display of cut and uncut opal.

The **Old Timers Mine** is an old mine and underground home which is well worth the $3 entry fee.

The **Umoona Mine & Museum** is right in the centre of town; opal was still being pulled out of here until mining within the town limits was banned some years ago. Informative tours of the mine ($2) are given twice daily,

A couple of km out of town to the north you can find the **Underground Potteries**, where you can buy some nice pottery. A couple of km further on is **Crocodile Harry's** ($2), a dugout home which has featured in a number of documentaries, the movies *Mad Max III* and *Ground Zero*, and the miniseries *Stark*. Harry is an interesting character who spent 13 years in far north Queensland and the Northern Territory hunting crocodiles. His wrecked cars out the front of his dugout make novel vegetable beds!

Opal Mining

The town survives from opals, which were

North West
Ridge

North West Ridge Road

German Hill Road

To Oodnadatta

Catacomb Road

To Crocodile
Harry's &
Underground
Potteries

17 Mile Road

Russell St

Oodnadatta St

Hutchison Street

O'Neil Road

Umoona Road

Old Water Tank Road

Post
Office
Hill

Post Office Road

Mile Road

Alp Street

17

Hill Road

5

6

Brewster Street

Crowders Gully Rd

※ 3

4

Public
Noodling
Area

7

▼ 8

Hill Road

10 ▼

11 ▼

12 ▼

13 ▼
14 ●

Cameron Dr

Paxton Road

Oliver St

9

Club Road

Willcox Street

Bean Street

St Nicholas Street

Water
Conservation
Reserve

Van Brugge Street

Flat Hill Road

Wilke Pde

Brady Street

Reilly Street

Kent Street

Grund Street

▼ 15 16

● 17

18

Hocking St

Robins

Giles Street

Eyre Street

Ward Street

Hutchison Street

Burke Street

Bartum Street

Wrights Street

Stuart Street

Flinders Street

To Wind Generator &
William Creek

Stuart Highway

PLACES TO STAY

2 Oasis Caravan Park
6 Umoona Mine & Museum
7 Opal Cave & Bedrock
9 Desert Cave Motel
16 Opal Inn Hotel/Motel
19 Stuart Ranges Caravan Park

PLACES TO EAT

8 Last Resort Cafe
  & Underground Bookshop
10 Underground Dugout Restaurant
11 Old Miners Cafe
12 Traces
13 The Taverna
15 Chinese Restaurant

OTHER

1 Catacomb Church
3 Big Winch
4 Old Timers Mine
5 Supermarket
14 Miners Store
17 Council Offices
18 Service Station & Bus Station

19

Stuart Highway

To Rudy's
Camel Mine

SOUTH AUSTRALIA

LP

Coober Pedy

0   50   100 m

Opals

Australia is the opal-producing centre of the world and South Australia is where most of Australia's opals come from. Opals are hardened from silica suspended in water, and the colour is produced by light being split and reflected by the silica molecules. Valuable opals are cut in three different fashions: solid opals can be cut out of the rough into cabochons (domed-top stones); triplets consist of a layer of opal sandwiched between an opaque backing layer and a transparent cap; and doublets are simply an opal layer with an opaque backing. In addition, some opals from Queensland are found embedded in rock; these are sometimes polished while still incorporated in the surrounding rock.

An opal's value is determined by its colour and clarity – the brighter and clearer the colour the better. Brilliance of colour is more important than the colour itself. The type of opal is also a determinant of value – black and crystal opals are the most valuable, semiblack and semicrystal are in the middle, and milk opal at the bottom. The bigger the pattern the better, and visible flaws (like cracks) also affect the value.

Shape is also important – a high dome is better than a flat opal. Finally, given equality of other aspects, the size is important. As with the purchase of any sort of gemstone, don't expect to find great bargains unless you clearly know and understand what you are buying. ∎

first discovered in 1911. Keen fossickers can have a go themselves after acquiring a prospecting permit from the Mines Department in Adelaide. Fossicking through the outcasts is known as noodling. There are literally hundreds of mines around Coober Pedy but there are no big operators. When somebody makes a find, dozens of others head off to the same area.

There are many migrants in Coober Pedy, and while Greeks, Yugoslavs and Italians form the biggest groups, the gem buyers are usually from Hong Kong. They stay in the Opal Inn and when one heads back to base (often the Hong Kong travellers' centre Chungking Mansions in Kowloon) another Hong Konger takes over the room.

Organised Tours

There are several tours, most taking three hours and costing around $15, which cover the sights and take you into an opal mine, underground home and a working opal field. Joe's Tours (book at the Budget Motel) include Crocodile Harry's.

On Mondays and Thursdays you can travel with the mail truck along 600 km of dirt roads as it does the trip round Coober Pedy, Oodnadatta and William Creek. There's a backpackers' special price of $49, or the standard fare including lunch is $59. This is a great way to get off the beaten track.

You can stay at Oodnadatta or William Creek and return to Coober Pedy on the next mail truck (☎ toll-free 1800 802 074, or contact the Underground Bookshop).

Places to Stay

Camping There are two caravan parks in town itself and another further out. The *Oasis Caravan Park* (☎ (086) 72 5169) is good and has camp sites (hard gravel) and on-site vans. It also shows an informative video on the town and opal mining in general each evening.

The *Stuart Range Caravan Park* (☎ (086) 72 5179) has less shade and is also less central. Even further out (about five km along the William Creek road), *Rudy's Camel Mine* (☎ (086) 72 5614) charges $4 per person.

Hostels The *Backpackers' Inn* at Radeka's Dugout Motel (☎ (086) 72 5223) offers underground dormitories at $10.

Tom's Backpackers (☎ (086) 72 5333) on the main street opposite the Desert Cave Motel is the most popular and has underground accommodation at $10 for 24 hours, or above-ground rooms for $8.

The *Bedrock* is another place popular with travellers, and the *Opal Cave* also has backpackers' accommodation.

Hotels & Motels There are a number of hotels and motels, some underground, some with big air-cons! Listed here are some of the cheaper places. The *Umoona Opal Mine* (☎ (086) 72 5288) on Hutchison St has singles/doubles for $15/25. Bathrooms are communal but there are kitchen facilities. The *Budget Motel* (☎ (086) 72 5163) has rooms from $16/26 or from $40 with bathrooms. The *Opal Inn Hotel/Motel* (☎ (086) 72 5054) has pub rooms for $25/35, or motel rooms for $65/70. *Radeka's Dugout Motel* (☎ (086) 72 5223) costs from $55/65 for singles/doubles.

Places to Eat

The *Last Resort Cafe*, next to the Underground Bookshop, does a good line in drinks and desserts as well as meals, including breakfast – easily the best place in town. Unfortunately it's open only during the day.

Sergio's has Italian food, including spaghetti from $6, and the servings are enormous.

There are a couple of Greek places, the *Taverna* and *Traces*, and these are both popular in the evenings. (Traces stays open until 4 am.) There are also a couple of pizza places, and the *Opal Inn* does counter meals. The *Miners' Store*, next to the post office, is the best of the supermarkets.

The *Underground Dugout Restaurant* is indeed underground and has a few interesting menu items, including kangaroo fillets. It's not all that cheap, however, and the service can be brusque.

Entertainment

Playing pool at the Oasis Inn seems to be the main form of entertainment in town.

Getting There & Away

Air Kendell Airlines (book through Ansett on ☎ (08) 13 1300) flies from Adelaide to Coober Pedy most days of the week ($238), and from Coober Pedy to Uluru (Ayers Rock) once a week ($200). The Desert Cave Motel handles reservations.

Bus It's 413 km from Coober Pedy to Kulgera, just across the border into the Northern Territory, and from there it's another 280 km to Alice Springs. Greyhound Pioneer buses pass through on the Adelaide to Alice Springs route. It's about $68 from Adelaide and $79 from Alice Springs.

AROUND COOBER PEDY
Breakaways

Breakaway Reserve is an area of low hills about 30 km from Coober Pedy which have 'broken away' from the Stuart Range. You can drive to the lookout in a conventional vehicle and see the natural formation known as the **Castle**, which featured in *Mad Max III*.

With a 4WD you can make a 65-km loop from Coober Pedy, following the Dogproof Fence back to the road from Coober Pedy to Oodnadatta. The Underground Bookshop in Coober Pedy has a leaflet and 'mud map'.

MARLA (population 250)

Not far south of the Northern Territory border, Marla is a small settlement where the Ghan railway line crosses the Stuart Highway. The opal-mine fields of **Mintabie** are 35 km west (permit required). Fuel, supplies, etc are available in Marla 24 hours a day. The *Marla Travellers Rest* (☎ (086) 70 7001) has camp sites at $4 per person, air-con on-site cabins for $25/36, and motel rooms from $49/59.

On the Stuart Highway 83 km south of Marla, *Cadney Homestead* (☎ (086) 70 7994) has camp sites for $6 per person and on-site cabins for $35, or there are motel rooms for $65/72. If you're heading for Oodnadatta, turning off the highway here gives you a shorter run on dirt roads than going via Marla or Coober Pedy, and you pass through the **Painted Desert** on the way.

MARREE (population 400)

On the rugged alternative road north through Oodnadatta, Marree is a tiny township once used as a staging post for the Afghani-led camel trains of the last century. There are still a few old date palms here, and an incongruously large pub. Marree is also the southern end of the Birdsville track. Six km east of town is **Frome Creek**, a dry creek bed that can fill when it rains and cut the track for weeks on end.

Places to Stay

The *Marree Tourist Park* (☎ (086) 75 8371) has camp sites ($2.50 per person) and on-site vans ($25 a double). The only alternative is the *Great Northern Hotel* (☎ (086) 75 8344), with rooms for $25 per person, or $35 with breakfast.

Getting There & Away

Stateliner has a weekly service between Adelaide and Marree. The trip takes 12 hours and costs $70.

OODNADATTA (population 200)

The tiny town of Oodnadatta (like Marree, it got even tinier with the old Ghan track's closure) is at the point where the road and the old railway lines diverged. It was an important staging post during the construction of the overland telegraph line and later was the railhead for the line from Adelaide, from its original extension to Oodnadatta in 1884 until it finally reached Alice Springs in 1929.

Today the town's most distinctive feature is the Pink Roadhouse, which is an excellent place to ask advice about track conditions in any direction. The owners, Adam and Lynnie Plate, have spent a great deal of time and effort putting in road signs and km pegs over a huge area in this district – even in the Simpson Desert you'll come across signs erected by this dedicated pair! They have no doubt saved many a 4WD traveller hours of searching for the right track. The roadhouse is also the place to buy a permit if you intend camping at Dalhousie Springs.

The old railway station has been converted into an interesting little **museum**. It is kept locked but pick up the key from the pub, store or roadhouse.

The local Aboriginal community owns the town's only pub and the general store.

Places to Stay

The *Oodnadatta Caravan Park* (☎ (086) 70 7822), attached to the Pink Roadhouse, has camp sites for $10.50 ($13.50 with power), one on-site van for $25/30 a single/double and units for $40. Or there's the *Transcontinental Hotel* (☎ (086) 70 7804), which charges $30/55.

BIRDSVILLE TRACK

Years ago cattle from the south-west of Queensland were driven down the Birdsville Track to Marree where they were loaded onto trains – these days they're trucked out on the 'beef roads'. It's 520 km between Marree and Birdsville, just across the border.

Although non-4WD vehicles can manage the track without difficulty, it's worth bearing in mind that it's a long way to push if you break down – and that traffic along the road isn't exactly heavy. Petrol is available at Mungeranie, about 220 km north of Marree and 300 km south of Birdsville. The track is more or less at the meeting point between the sand dunes of the Simpson Desert to the west and the desolate wastes of Sturt Stony Desert to the east. There are ruins of a couple of homesteads along the track and artesian bores gush out boiling-hot salty water at many places. At **Clifton Hill**, about 200 km south of Birdsville, the track splits and the main route goes round the eastern side of Goyders Lagoon. The last travellers to die on the track took the wrong turning, got lost, ran out of petrol and died before they were discovered.

STRZELECKI TRACK

These days the Strzelecki Track can be handled by regular vehicles. It starts at Lyndhurst, about 80 km south of Marree, and runs 460 km to the tiny outpost of Innamincka. The discovery of natural gas deposits near Moomba has brought a great deal of development and improvement to the track. The new Moomba-Strzelecki Track is better kept but longer and less interesting than the old track, which follows the Strzelecki Creek. Fuel is available at Moomba in emergencies.

SOUTH AUSTRALIA

INNAMINCKA

At the northern end of the Strzelecki Track, Innamincka is on Cooper Creek, where the Burke and Wills expedition of 1860 came to its end. Near here is the Burke and Wills 'dig' tree, the memorials and markers where their bodies were found and the marker where King, the sole survivor, was found. He was cared for by Aborigines until his rescue.

There is also a memorial where Howitt, who led the rescue party, set up his depot on the creek. The dig tree is actually across the border in Queensland. The word 'dig' is no longer visible, but the expedition's camp number can still be made out.

Cooper Creek only flows during floods, but there are permanent water holes, so the area was important to Aborigines and was a base for the European explorers of the 1800s.

Algona Publications' *Innamincka-Coongie Lakes* map is a good source of information on the Innamincka area. For a moving account of the bumbling, foolhardy and tragic Burke and Wills expedition, read Alan Moorehead's *Cooper's Creek*.

Places to Stay

The *Innamincka Hotel* (☎ (086) 75 9901) has just four motel-style rooms at $30/50/75 for singles/doubles/triples. The *Innamincka Trading Post* (☎ (086) 75 9900) has three cabins at $25 per person. There are plenty of places to camp along the creek.

THE GHAN

See the Northern Territory chapter for details of the famous train line from Adelaide to Alice Springs.

Tasmania

Area   67,800 sq km
Population   453,000

☎ From November 1996, Hobart's existing phone numbers will be prefixed by the additional digits 62 (for example, ☎ 12 3456 becomes ☎ 6212 3456). Launceston's additional digits will be 63, and Burnie's 64. The area code for the state will be (03). ∎

Tasmania is Australia's only island state and this has been a major influence on its historical, cultural and geographical development. Being an island, it was considered an ideal location for penal settlements, and convicts who re-offended on the Australian mainland were shipped there. Its isolation has also helped preserve its rich colonial heritage, and ensured that most of the state's wilderness areas (with a few notable exceptions) have remained relatively unspoiled.

The first European to see Tasmania was the famous Dutch navigator Abel Tasman, who arrived in 1642 and called it Van Diemen's Land, after the Governor of the Dutch East Indies. In the 18th century, Tasmania was sighted and visited by a series of famous European sailors, including captains Tobias Furneaux, James Cook and William Bligh, all of whom believed it to be part of the Australian mainland.

European contact with the Tasmanian coast became more frequent after the soldiers and convicts of the First Fleet settled at Sydney Cove in 1788, mainly because ships heading to the colony of New South Wales from the west had to sail around the island.

In 1798 Lieutenant Matthew Flinders circumnavigated Van Diemen's Land and proved that it was an island. He named the rough stretch of sea between the island and the mainland Bass Strait, after George Bass, the ship's surgeon. The discovery of Bass Strait shortened the journey to Sydney from India or the Cape of Good Hope by a week.

In the late 1790s Governor King of New South Wales decided to establish a second colony in Australia, south of Sydney Cove. Port Phillip Bay in Victoria was considered, but a site on the Derwent River in Tasmania was finally chosen, and in 1804 Hobart Town was established. Although convicts were sent with the first settlers, penal settlements were not built until later: at Macquarie Harbour in 1821, at Maria Island in 1825 and at Port Arthur in 1832. For more than three decades, Van Diemen's Land was the most feared destination for British convicts.

In 1856 transportation to Van Diemen's Land was abolished and its first parliament was elected. Also in 1856, in an effort to escape the stigma of its dreadful penal reputation, Van Diemen's Land became officially known as Tasmania, after its first European discoverer.

Reminders of the island's convict days and early history are everywhere. There are the penal settlement ruins at Port Arthur, many convict-built bridges, a host of beautifully preserved Georgian sandstone buildings and more than 20 historic towns or villages classified by the National Trust.

Tasmania is also renowned world wide for its pristine wilderness areas and, during the last 20 or so years, for the essential role it has played in world environmental and conservation issues.

In the 1989 state elections, Tasmania's

TASMANIA

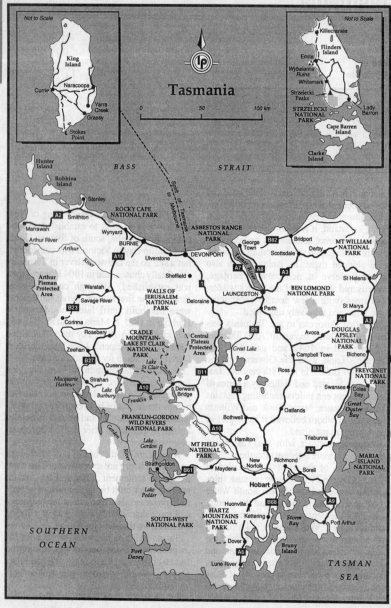

Tasmania

0   50   100 km

Not to Scale

King
Island

Currie

Naracoopa

Yarra
Creek

Grassy

Stokes
Point

Not to Scale

Killiecrankie

Flinders
Island

Emita

Wybalenna
Ruins   Whitemark

Strzelecki
Peaks

STRZELECKI
NATIONAL
PARK

Cape Barren
Island

Clarke
Island

Lady
Barron

Hunter
Island

BASS   STRAIT

Robbins
Island

Stanley

ROCKY CAPE
NATIONAL PARK

A2   Smithton

ASBESTOS RANGE
NATIONAL
PARK

George
Town   B82   Bridport

MT WILLIAM
NATIONAL
PARK

Marrawah

Wynyard

BURNIE

A10

Ulverstone

DEVONPORT

Scottsdale

Derby

Arthur River

Arthur
River

A7   A8

Sheffield

1

St Helens

Arthur
Pieman
Protected
Area

Waratah

WALLS OF
JERUSALEM
NATIONAL
PARK

LAUNCESTON

BEN LOMOND
NATIONAL PARK

St Marys

Savage River

B23

Corinna

Deloraine

Perth

A4   A3

Rosebery

CRADLE
MOUNTAIN-
LAKE ST CLAIR
NATIONAL
PARK

Central
Plateau
Protected
Area

B5

1

Avoca

DOUGLAS
APSLEY
NATIONAL
PARK

Bicheno

Zeehan

B27

Queenstown

Lake
St Clair

Great Lake

Campbell Town

FREYCINET
NATIONAL
PARK

Macquarie
Harbour

Strahan

A10

Lake
Burbury

Derwent
Bridge

B11

A5

Ross

B34

Swansea

Coles
Bay

Franklin R

Great
Oyster
Bay

FRANKLIN-GORDON
WILD RIVERS
NATIONAL PARK

Gordon
River

Lake
Gordon

MT FIELD
NATIONAL
PARK

Bothwell

Oatlands

Hamilton

A10

Derwent River

1

Triabunna

A3

MARIA
ISLAND
NATIONAL
PARK

Strathgordon

B61

Maydena

New
Norfolk

Richmond

Sorell

Lake
Pedder

SOUTH-WEST
NATIONAL
PARK

Hobart

HARTZ
MOUNTAINS
NATIONAL
PARK

Huonville

Kettering

B68

A9

SOUTHERN

OCEAN

Port
Davey

Dover

A6

Lune River

Storm
Bay

Bruny
Island

Port Arthur

TASMAN

SEA

Green Independents gained 18% of the vote and held the balance of power in parliament until the 1992 election. For more information, read *The Rest of the World is Watching - Tasmania and the Greens* (Pan Macmillan, Australia), edited by C Pybus & R Flanagan.

TASMANIAN ABORIGINES

Since European settlement, the story of Australia's Aborigines has not been a happy one, and nowhere has it been more tragic than in Tasmania.

Tasmania's Aborigines became separated from the mainland over 10,000 years ago when rising ocean levels, caused by the thawing of the last ice age, cut the state off from the rest of the country. From that time on their culture diverged from that of the mainland population. They lived by hunting, fishing and gathering, sheltered in bark lean-tos and, despite Tasmania's cold weather, went naked apart from a coating of grease and charcoal. Their society was based on sharing and exchange – a concept the European invaders failed to come to terms with.

European settlers found Tasmania fertile and fenced it off to make farms. As the Aborigines lost more and more of their traditional hunting grounds, they realised that the Europeans had come to steal their land, not share it, and began to fight for what was rightfully theirs. By 1806 the killing on both sides was out of control. The Aborigines speared shepherds and their stock, and, in turn, were hunted and shot. Europeans abducted Aboriginal children to use as forced labour, raped and tortured Aboriginal women, gave poisoned flour to friendly tribes, and laid steel traps in the bush.

In 1828 martial law was proclaimed by Governor Arthur, giving soldiers the right to arrest or shoot on sight any Aborigine found in an area of European settlement. Finally, in an attempt to flush out all Aborigines and corner them on the Tasman Peninsula, a human chain, known as the Black Line, was formed by the settlers, and this moved for three weeks through the state. Ultimately unsuccessful, it did, however, manage to clear the tribes from settled districts.

Between 1829 and 1834 the remnants of this once proud and peaceful race were collected from all over the island and resettled in a reserve on Flinders Island – to be 'civilised' and Christianised. With nothing to do but exist, most of them died of despair, homesickness, poor food or respiratory disease. Of the 135 who went to the island, only 47 survived to be transferred to Oyster Cove in 1847. It's hard to believe, but during those first 35 years of European settlement, 183 Europeans and nearly 4000 Aborigines were killed.

European sealers had been working in Bass Strait since 1798, and although they occasionally raided tribes along the coast, on the whole their contact with the Aborigines was based on trade. Aboriginal women were also traded and many sealers settled down on the Bass Strait islands with these women and had families.

By 1847 a new Aboriginal community, with a lifestyle based on both Aboriginal and European ways, had emerged on the Furneaux group of islands, saving the Tasmanian Aborigines from total extinction. Today there are more than 6500 of their descendants still living in Tasmania.

GEOGRAPHY

Although Tasmania is a small state, its geographical diversity ensures that it has something for everyone.

Tasmania's population is concentrated mainly on the north and south-east coasts, where the undulating countryside is rich and fertile. The coast and its bays are accessible and inviting, with attractive coves and beaches. In winter, the midlands region is almost a re-creation of the green England so beloved of early settlers, and the sparsely populated lakes country in the central highlands is serenely beautiful.

By contrast, the south-west and west coasts are amazingly wild and virtually untouched. For much of the year, raging seas batter the length of the west coast, and rainfall is high. Inland, the forests and mountains of Tasmania's west and south-west form one of the world's last great wilderness areas, almost all of it made up of national parks which have been listed as World Heritage regions.

INFORMATION
Tourist Offices

There are privately run Tasmanian Travel & Information Centres in Hobart, Launceston, Devonport and Burnie. On the mainland there are government-run branches in:

Australian Capital Territory
165 City Walk, Canberra 2601 (☎ (06) 209 2122)
New South Wales
149 King St, Sydney 2000 (☎ (02) 202 2022)
Queensland
40 Queen St, Brisbane 4000 (☎ (07) 405 4122)
South Australia
32 King William St, Adelaide 5000 (☎ (08) 400 5522)
Victoria
256 Collins St, Melbourne 3000 (☎ (03) 206 7922)

These travel centres have information on just about everything you need to know about Tasmania and are also able to book accommodation, tours and even airline, boat and bus tickets. The Department of Tourism publishes an invaluable bimonthly free newspaper called *Tasmanian Travelways* which, along with feature articles, has comprehensive listings of accommodation, visitor activities, public transport, connecting transport facilities and vehicle hire, all with an indication of current costs throughout the state.

The travel centres also stock a host of free tourist literature, including the monthly magazine *This Week in Tasmania* and the excellent *Let's Talk About* ... leaflets, which provide in-depth information about particular towns or areas. The annual *Tasmania Visitors Guide*, which has a good fold-out touring map of Tasmania, is particularly useful.

One of the best maps of the island is produced by the Royal Automobile Club of Tasmania (RACT) and costs $3. It's available from any Tasmanian Travel & Information Centre or RACT office.

Accommodation

There's a good choice of accommodation in Tasmania, including youth hostels in most of the major towns and plenty of caravan parks most of which have camp sites as well as on-site vans and cabins. Tasmania also has a wide selection of colonial accommodation – that is, places built prior to 1901 which have been decorated in a colonial style. Although a bit pricey (typically $60 to $100 for double B&B), colonial accommodation is a great way to savour Tasmania's history, and can be a real treat for a couple of nights.

Despite the variety of places to stay, Tasmania's major tourist centres are often fully booked in summer, so it's wise to make reservations. Accommodation also cost more in summer.

Money

Banks are not abundant in Tasmania outside Hobart and Launceston, and those that do exist in the smaller towns are often only open one or two days a week. Automatic teller machines (ATMs) are even more difficult to find: it can sometimes be hundreds of km between one ATM and another, so do not rely on them for funds in an emergency in any but the two main centres.

NATIONAL PARKS

Tasmania has set aside a greater percentage of its land as national park or scenic reserve than any other Australian state. In 1982 Tasmania's three largest national parks, Cradle Mountain-Lake St Clair, Franklin-Gordon Wild Rivers and South-West, were declared among the last great temperate wilderness areas in the world and placed on the UNESCO World Heritage List. Since then several other parks and reserves have been added to the list. Today, about 20% of Tasmania is World Heritage area, protected from logging, hydroelectric power schemes and with a few simple rules, ourselves.

An entry fee is charged for all 14 of Tassie's national parks, and there are a number of passes available. A one-day pass to any number of parks costs $5 per person; a three-day pass costs $8, a 14-day pass costs $20, a

ne-month pass costs $30 and a one-year
ass costs $40. There is no charge for chil-
ren under 18 years old.

ACTIVITIES

Bushwalking

Tasmania, with its many national parks, has
some of the finest bushwalks in Australia, the
most famous of which is the superb Cradle
Mountain-Lake St Clair Overland Track.
(See the Cradle Mountain-Lake St Clair
section for details of this walk.)

Good books on the subject include *100
Walks in Tasmania* by Tyrone T Thomas,
South West Tasmania by John Chapman, and
Lonely Planet's *Bushwalking in Australia* by
John & Monica Chapman, which has a large
section on some of Tasmania's best walks.

The Department of Parks, Wildlife & Heritage (☎ (002) 33 8011) has a great deal of
informative literature about the state's
national parks and reserves, as well as
several leaflets on particular aspects of
bushwalking.

On long walks, it's important to remember
that in any season a fine day can quickly
become cold and stormy, so warm clothing,
waterproof gear, a tent and a compass are
vital. The Department of Parks, Wildlife &
Heritage publishes a booklet called *Welcome
to the Wilderness – Bushwalking Trip Planner
for Tasmania's World Heritage Area*, which
has sections on planning, minimal-impact
bushwalking and wilderness survival. Also
included is a very useful equipment check
list which is essential reading for bushwalkers who are unfamiliar with Tasmania's
notoriously changeable weather. If you write
to the department at GPO Box 44A, Hobart,
you'll be sent this booklet and other leaflets
free of charge. You can also pick up all the
department's literature from its head office
at 134 Macquarie St, Hobart; from its office
at Henty House, Civic Square, Launceston;
or from any ranger station in the national
parks.

The department also produces an excellent series of maps; again, these can be sent
for or can be picked up at most bush outdoor-
equipment stores, Wilderness Society shops

and newsagencies throughout the state. The
Tasmap Centre (☎ (002) 33 3382) is on the
ground floor of the department's head office.

As bushwalking is so popular in Tasmania, there are many excellent shops selling
bush gear, as well as several youth hostels
which hire out equipment or take bushwalking tours. In the former category, Paddy
Pallin in Hobart and Launceston, Allgoods
in Launceston and the Backpackers' Barn in
Devonport all have a very good range of
bushwalking gear and plenty of invaluable
advice.

See the sections on individual national
parks for more information on Tasmania's
walks.

Water Sports

Swimming The north and east coasts have
plenty of sheltered white-sand beaches
which are excellent for swimming. Although
there are some pleasant beaches near Hobart,
such as Bellerive and Sandy Bay, these tend
to be polluted so it's better to head towards
Kingston, Blackmans Bay or Seven Mile
Beach for safe swimming. On the west coast
there's some pretty ferocious surf but the
beaches are unpatrolled.

Surfing Tasmania has plenty of good surf
beaches, particularly on the east coast north
of Bicheno. Closer to Hobart, Clifton Beach
and the surf beach en route to South Arm are
popular surfing spots. The southern beaches
of Bruny Island, particularly Cloudy Bay, are
also good.

Scuba Diving On the east coast and around
King and Flinders islands there are some
excellent scuba-diving opportunities. Equipment can be rented in Hobart, Launceston or
on the east coast, and dive courses in Tasmania are considerably cheaper than those on
the mainland.

Rafting & Canoeing With so many rivers
and lakes, rafting, rowing and canoeing are
all popular pastimes in Tasmania. The most
challenging of rivers to raft is probably the
Franklin (see the Franklin-Gordon Wild

Rivers National Park section), although rafting trips are also organised on the Picton, upper Huon, Weld and Leven rivers. For information about tour operators etc, contact the Department of Parks, Wildlife & Heritage (☎ (002) 33 8011) in Hobart.

Fishing Fishing is another popular activity. Many of the rivers offer superb trout fishing, and the coastal waters are also popular. Note that a licence is required to fish in Tasmania's rivers, and there are bag, season and size limits on a number of fish. Licences cost $38 for the full season (see the next paragraph for dates), $20 for 14 days and $12 for one day, and are available from sports stores, police stations and Tasmanian Travel & Information Centres.

Most inland waters open for fishing on the Saturday closest to 1 August and close on the Sunday nearest 30 April. The lakes in the centre of the state are some of the best-known spots for both brown and rainbow trout – Arthurs Lake, Great Lake, Little Pine Lagoon (fly fishing only), Western Lakes (including Lake St Clair), Lake Sorell and Lake Pedder. For more information contact the Tasmanian Inland Fisheries Commission (☎ (002) 33 8305), 127 Davey St, Hobart.

Caving

Tasmania's caves are regarded as being some of the most impressive in Australia. The caves at Mole Creek and Hastings are open daily to the public but gems such as the Kubla Khan and Croesus caves (near Mole Creek) are only accessible to experienced cavers.

Skiing

There are two minor ski resorts in Tasmania: Ben Lomond, 60 km from Launceston; and Mt Mawson, in Mt Field National Park. Both offer cheaper, although less-developed, ski facilities than the major resorts in Victoria and New South Wales, but despite the state's southerly latitude, snowfalls tend to be fairly light and unreliable. For more information see the sections on the Ben Lomond and Mt Field national parks.

GETTING THERE & AWAY
Air

The airlines that fly to Tassie are Ansett (☎ 13 1300), Qantas (☎ 13 1313), Eastwest (☎ 13 1711), Kendell (☎ toll-free 1800 338 894), Phillip Island Air Services (☎ (059) 56 7316), King Island Airlines (☎ (03) 580 3777), Airlines of Tasmania (☎ toll-free 1800 030 550), Aus-Air (☎ toll-free 1800 338 894), Promair (☎ (056) 88 1487) and Hazelton Air Service (☎ (02) 235 1411).

Ansett and Qantas have flights to Tasmania from most Australian state capitals, while the other airlines operate from various airports in Victoria. Most flights are to Hobart, Launceston, Devonport, Wynyard (Burnie), Smithton, Flinders Island or King Island, although Airlines of Tasmania also has flights from Melbourne to Queenstown and Strahan.

Air fares to Tasmania are constantly changing, but because of the number of operators, prices are competitive and you can get some good deals – especially if you book well in advance or if you are planning a trip in the winter months. In addition, students under 25 years can get some good discounts on fares with the larger airlines.

To/From Hobart The standard one-way economy fare with Ansett and Qantas from Melbourne is $216, although much cheaper fares are often available (about $220 return). From Sydney, fares are slightly more expensive, and an advance-purchase return ticket from Brisbane is around $440.

There's also a weekly Qantas/Air New Zealand flight between Christchurch, New Zealand and Hobart.

To/From Launceston Ansett and Qantas fly from Melbourne for $187 one way, but it's around $200 return if you book far enough in advance. The smaller airlines flying out of Melbourne generally use the city's second-string airports of Essendon (Airlines of Tasmania, $169 one way) or Moorabbin (Aus-Air, $160). Promair flies from Welshpool in eastern Victoria ($130), Hazelton from Sale ($169).

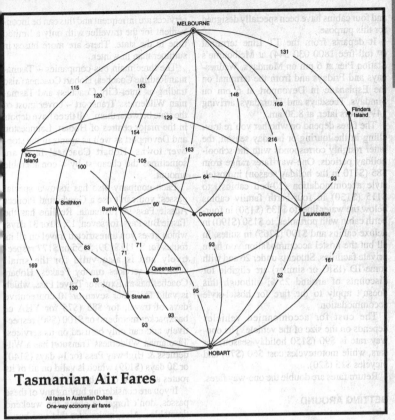

MELBOURNE
131
115
120
163
148
169
Flinders Island
129
154
216
King Island
163
100
105
93
Smithton
64
60
Burnie
Devonport
Launceston
83
93
71
71
169
Queenstown
161
130
83
52
Strahan
95
93
93
93
HOBART

Tasmanian Air Fares

All fares in Australian Dollars
One-way economy air fares

To/From Devonport & Wynyard (Burnie)

There are flights from Melbourne to Devonport and Burnie by Kendell Airlines ($148 and $158 respectively) and Aus-Air ($136 and $148). Airlines of Tasmania also flies from Melbourne to Burnie for $154. Phillip Island Air Services flies to Burnie for $105 one way.

To/From Other Destinations

Airlines of Tasmania (from Essendon) and Aus-Air (from Moorabbin) fly to Smithton for $120 one way and to Flinders Island for $130 one way, while Aus-Air and Kendell Airlines

(from Melbourne Airport) fly to King Island for $110 one way. King Island Airlines also flies from Moorabbin to King Island and is cheaper, at $95 one way.

Boat

The *Spirit of Tasmania*, which operates between Melbourne and Devonport, can accommodate 1300 passengers and over 600 vehicles. It has four decks and, with its swimming pool, saunas, restaurant, gaming machines and bars, is more like a cruise ship than a ferry. The public areas of the ship have been designed to cater for wheelchair access, and four cabins have been specially designed for this purpose.

It departs from the TT Line terminal (☎ toll-free 1800 030 344) at Melbourne's Station Pier at 6 pm on Mondays, Wednesdays and Fridays and from the terminal on the Esplanade in Devonport at 6 pm on Sundays, Tuesdays and Thursdays, arriving 14½ hours later, at 8.30 am.

The fares depend on whether you're travelling in the touring or holiday season; the latter roughly corresponds with the school-holiday periods. One-way fares range from $85 ($110 in the holiday season) in hostel-style accommodation (20-bed cabins), to $115 ($130) in four-berth family cabins below the water line, to $135 ($150) in four-berth cabin with portholes, to $150 ($190) in deluxe cabins and $190 ($265) in suites. In all but the hostel accommodation you have private facilities. Students under 26 and with some ID (ISIC or similar) are eligible for discounts of around 25%, although this doesn't apply to the fare for hostel-style accommodation.

The cost for accompanied vehicles depends on the size of the vehicle. The one-way rate is $90 ($150 holiday season) for cars, while motorcycles cost $60 ($70) and bicycles $15 ($20).

Return fares are double the one-way fares.

GETTING AROUND
Air
Airlines of Tasmania (☎ toll-free 1800 030 550) operates a fairly extensive network of flights around the island which can be booked at most travel agencies and any Tasmanian Travel & Information Centre. The chart shows all their routes and prices. It's worth noting that the airline also has flights between Melbourne and Launceston via Flinders Island which are only a little more expensive than flying direct; these give you the option of a stopover on Flinders, more or less free.

Bus
Tasmania has a good bus network connecting all major towns and centres, but weekend services are infrequent and this can be inconvenient for the traveller with only a limited time in the state. There are more buses in summer than in winter.

The three main bus companies – Tasmanian Redline Coaches, Hobart Coaches (also trading as Inter-City Coaches) and Tasmanian Wilderness Transport – cover most of the state between them. All three have depots in the major centres of Hobart, Launceston and Devonport as well as agents in the stop-over towns. Hobart Coaches' fares are sometimes the cheapest by a considerable amount.

Each company also has its own special passes; you can't use a Greyhound Pioneer Aussie Pass in Tasmania. Redline has the Tassie Bus Pass, for seven, 15, 20 or 31 days, which gives you unrestricted travel on all its routes for $111, $139, $155 or $177 respectively and is also valid for the small east-coast services run by Peakes. Hobart Coaches has an Explorer Travel Pass, which is valid for either seven or 10 consecutive days of travel, for $85 ($75 for YHA or backpacker members) or $100 ($90) respectively and can only be used on its services. Tasmanian Wilderness Transport has a Wilderness & Highway Pass for 14 days ($140) or 30 days ($179) which is valid on all of its routes and those of Hobart Coaches.

If you are considering buying any of these passes, don't forget to check the weekend timetables. Also, make sure that you buy a pass with a company that has services to the areas that you want to visit; *Tasmanian Travelways* has details of timetables and fares for major routes. These passes can also be bought in advance on the mainland from Greyhound Pioneer, but generally it's cheaper to buy them in Tasmania. To give you some idea of the costs, a one-way trip between Hobart and Launceston costs about $17, between Hobart and Queenstown $29 and between Launceston and Bicheno $18.

Train
For economic reasons there are no longer any passenger rail services in Tasmania, which probably accounts for the number of

railway models, displays and exhibitions in the state!

Car & Campervan

Although you can bring cars from the mainland to Tasmania, it might work out cheaper to rent one for your visit, particularly if your stay is a short one. Tasmania has a wide range of national and local car-rental agencies, and the rates (along with parking fines) are considerably lower than they are on the mainland.

Tasmanian Travelways lists many of the rental options, but before you decide on a company, don't forget to ask about any km limitations and what the insurance covers and ensure that there are no hidden seasonal adjustments. It is, however, quite normal for smaller rental companies to ask for a bond of around $200.

If you arrange your car rental with one of the large national firms like Budget, Hertz or Avis you should, with a bit of bargaining, be able to get a rate of around $60 a day for a small car (Corolla, Laser, Pulsar). Although this is more expensive than rates offered by many smaller companies, there's no bond and you get unlimited km, comprehensive insurance and reliable cars. While many of the larger firms have offices at airports or docks, the smaller ones can often arrange for your car to be picked up at your point of arrival.

Small local firms like Advance Car Rentals, which has offices in Hobart, Launceston and Devonport, charge around $44 a day ($264 a week) for the same type of cars, but with varied conditions. Tasmania also has a number of companies renting older cars like VW beetles for around $20 a day. In this bracket Rent-a-Bug, with offices in Hobart and Devonport, has a good reputation. See the individual Getting There & Away entries for specific locations for more information.

Tasmanian Travelways also has a listing of campervan rental companies. All the larger national firms have campervans for around $800 a week, but by far the cheapest and most popular is Touring Motor Homes

(☎ (003) 95 1366) at 21 Glen Dhu St, Launceston, near the youth hostel.

While you're driving around the state, watch out for the wildlife which, all too often, ends up flattened on the roadside.

Hitching

Travel by thumb in Tassie is generally good but wrap up in winter and keep a raincoat handy. A good number of the state's roads are still unsurfaced and the traffic can be light, so although these roads often lead to interesting waterfalls etc, you might have to give them a miss if you're hitching.

Bicycle

Tasmania is a good size for exploring by bicycle and you can hire bikes throughout the state. If you plan to cycle between Hobart and Launceston via either coast, count on it taking around 10 to 14 days. For a full circuit of the island, you should allow 14 to 28 days.

Rent-a-Cycle at the Launceston City Youth Hostel has a good variety of touring and mountain bikes plus all the equipment you'll need for short or long trips. You should be able to hire a bike for between $10 and $15 a day or $60 and $70 a week. If you're planning on an extended ride it's worth considering buying a bike and reselling it at the end.

If you bring a bike over on the *Spirit of Tasmania* it will cost you $15 to $20 each way, depending on the season. By air, Ansett charges $15 to carry a bicycle one way to Hobart or Launceston, while Qantas charges $10. It's easier to get your bike over to Tassie on flights to Hobart or Launceston than on those to smaller airports such as Burnie or Devonport.

Hobart

Population 127,000

Hobart is Australia's second-oldest capital city and also the smallest and most southerly. Straddling the mouth of the Derwent River and backed by mountains which offer fine views over the city, Hobart has managed to combine the progress and the benefits of a modern city with the rich heritage of its colonial past. The beautiful Georgian buildings, the busy harbour and the easy-going atmosphere all make Hobart one of the most enjoyable and engaging of Australia's cities.

Tasmania's first colony was founded in 1803 at Risdon Cove, but a year later Lieutenant-Colonel David Collins, governor of the new settlement in Van Diemen's Land, sailed down the Derwent River and decided that a cove about 10 km below Risdon and on the opposite shore was a better place to settle. This became the site of Tasmania's future capital city, which began as a village of tents and wattle-and-daub huts with a population of 178 convicts, 25 marines, 15 women, 21 children, 13 free settlers and 10 civil officers.

Hobart Town, as it was known until 1881, was proclaimed a city in 1842. Very important to its development was the Derwent River estuary, one of the world's finest deepwater harbours, and many merchants made their fortunes from the whaling trade, shipbuilding and the export of products like corn and merino wool.

Orientation

Being fairly small and simply laid out, Hobart is an easy city to find your way around. The streets in the city centre, many of which are one way, are arranged in a grid pattern around the Elizabeth St Mall. The Tasmanian Travel & Information Centre, Ansett Airlines, Qantas and the GPO are all in Elizabeth St. The Cat & Fiddle Arcade is another central shopping area.

Salamanca Place, the famous row of Georgian warehouses, is along the waterfront, while just south of this is Battery Point, Hobart's delightful, well-preserved early colonial district. If you follow the river around from Battery Point you'll come to Sandy Bay, the site of Hobart's university and the Wrest Point Hotel Casino – one of Hobart's main landmarks.

The northern side of the centre is bounded by the recreation area known locally as the Domain (short for the Queen's Domain), which includes the Royal Tasmanian Botanical Gardens and the Derwent River. From here the Tasman Bridge crosses the river to the eastern suburbs and the airport.

Information

Tourist Office The Tasmanian Travel & Information Centre (☎ 30 8233) on the corner of Davey and Elizabeth Sts is open weekdays from 8.30 am to 5.15 pm, and from 9 am to 4 pm at weekends and on holidays. You can also get tourist information from the travel section of Mures Fish Centre, Victoria Dock.

If you have an FM radio, you can pick up tourist information broadcast on 88 MHz within a six-km radius of the city centre.

Post & Telecommunications The GPO is in the centre of the city, on the corner of Elizabeth and Macquarie Sts. Hobart's STD area telephone code is 002.

Other Offices The Tasmanian YHA (☎ 34 9617) is at 28 Criterion St and is open Monday to Friday from 9 am to 4.30 pm. The RACT (☎ 38 2200) is on the corner of Murray and Patrick Sts. Paddy Pallin (☎ 31 0777) is at 76 Elizabeth St. The Wilderness Society's head office (☎ 34 9366) is at 130 Davey St and its shop is in the Galleria, Salamanca Place; the National Trust shop is in the same arcade.

For information about the Department of Parks, Wildlife & Heritage and the Tasmap Centre, see the earlier Bushwalking section under Activities.

Historic Buildings

One of the things that makes Hobart so unusual among Australian cities is its wealth of old and remarkably well-preserved buildings. There are more than 90 buildings in Hobart that are classified by the National Trust and 60 of these, featuring some of Hobart's best Georgian architecture, are in Macquarie and Davey Sts. An excellent booklet on the subject, *An Architectural*

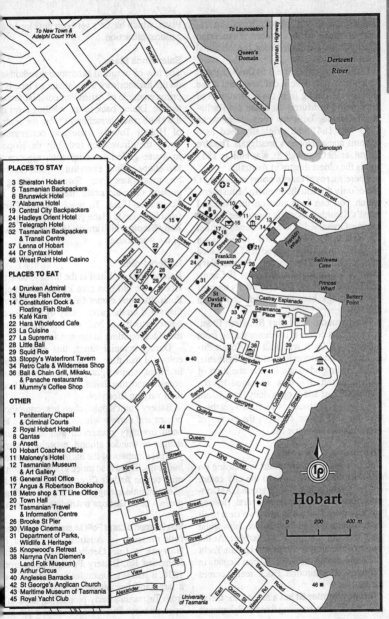

PLACES TO STAY
3 Sheraton Hobart
5 Tasmanian Backpackers
6 Brunswick Hotel
7 Alabama Hotel
19 Central City Backpackers
24 Hadleys Orient Hotel
25 Telegraph Hotel
32 Tasmanian Backpackers
  & Transit Centre
37 Lenna of Hobart
44 Dr Syntax Hotel
46 Wrest Point Hotel Casino

PLACES TO EAT
4 Drunken Admiral
13 Mures Fish Centre
14 Constitution Dock &
  Floating Fish Stalls
15 Kafé Kara
22 Hara Wholefood Cafe
23 La Cuisine
27 La Suprema
28 Little Bali
29 Squid Roe
33 Stoppy's Waterfront Tavern
34 Retro Cafe & Wilderness Shop
36 Ball & Chain Grill, Mikaku,
  & Panache restaurants
41 Mummy's Coffee Shop

OTHER
1 Penitentiary Chapel
  & Criminal Courts
2 Royal Hobart Hospital
8 Qantas
9 Ansett
10 Hobart Coaches Office
11 Maloney's Hotel
12 Tasmanian Museum
  & Art Gallery
16 General Post Office
17 Angus & Robertson Bookshop
18 Metro shop & TT Line Office
20 Town Hall
21 Tasmanian Travel
  & Information Centre
26 Brooke St Pier
30 Village Cinema
31 Department of Parks,
  Wildlife & Heritage
35 Knopwood's Retreat
38 Narryna (Van Diemen's
  Land Folk Museum)
39 Arthur Circus
40 Anglesea Barracks
42 St George's Anglican Church
43 Maritime Museum of Tasmania
45 Royal Yacht Club

Hobart

0   200   400 m

Guide to the City of Hobart (Royal Australian Institute of Architects, Tasmanian Chapter), is available from the National Trust for $3.15.

Close to the city centre is **St David's Park**, which has some lovely old trees, and some gravestones dating from the earliest days of the colony. In Murray St is the old **Parliament House**, built by convicts between 1835 and 1841 and originally used as a customs house. Hobart's prestigious **Theatre Royal**, at 29 Campbell St, was built in 1837 and is the oldest theatre in Australia.

There's a **royal tennis court** in Davey St, one of only three in the southern hemisphere, which you can look into on the National Trust's Saturday-morning tour – see the following Organised Tours & Cruises section for details. (Royal or 'real' tennis is an ancient form of tennis played in a four-walled indoor court.) The historic **Penitentiary Chapel & Criminal Courts** are at 28 Campbell St; the National Trust runs daily tours of the buildings between 10 am and 2 pm ($2.50).

Runnymede, at 61 Bay Rd, New Town, is a gracious colonial residence dating from the early 1830s. It was built for Robert Pitcairn, the first lawyer to qualify in Tasmania, and a leading advocate for the abolition of transportation. It's now managed by the National Trust and is open daily from 10 am to 4.30 pm; admission is $3.50. To get there take bus No 15 or 16 from the corner of Argyle and Macquarie Sts.

Waterfront

Hobart's busy waterfront area, focusing on **Franklin Wharf**, is close to the city centre and very interesting to walk around. At **Constitution Dock** there are several floating takeaway seafood stalls and it's a treat to sit in the sun munching fresh fish & chips while watching the activity in the harbour. At the finish of the annual Sydney to Hobart Yacht Race and during the Royal Hobart Regatta in February, Constitution Dock really comes alive.

Nearby **Hunter St** has a row of fine Georgian warehouses, rivalling those of Salamanca Place, which haven't yet been developed as a tourist attraction.

Salamanca Place

The row of beautiful sandstone warehouses on the harbourfront at Salamanca Place is prime example of Australian colonial architecture. Dating back to the whaling days of the 1830s, these warehouses were the centre of Hobart Town's trade and commerce. Today they have been tastefully developed to house galleries, restaurants, nightspots and shops selling everything from vegetables to antiques. Every Saturday morning popular open-air **craft market** is held at Salamanca Place. To reach Battery Point from Salamanca Place you can climb up the **Kelly Steps**, which are wedged between two of the warehouses.

Battery Point

Behind Princes Wharf is the historic core of Hobart, the old port area known as Battery Point. Its name comes from the gun battery that stood on the promontory by the guard house, which was built in 1818 and is now the oldest building in the district.

During colonial times, this area was a colourful maritime village, home to master mariners, shipwrights, sailors, fishermen, coopers and merchants. The houses reflect their varying lifestyles.

Battery Point's pubs, churches, conjoined houses and narrow winding streets have all been lovingly preserved and are a real delight to wander around, especially when you get glimpses of the harbour between the buildings. There is so much to see here; don't miss out on **Arthur Circus** – a small circle of quaint little cottages built around a village green – or **St George's Anglican Church**.

Van Diemen's Land Folk Museum The oldest folk museum in Australia is housed in Narryna, a fine Georgian home at 103 Hampden Rd, Battery Point. Dating from 1836, it stands in beautiful grounds and has a large and fascinating collection of relics from Tasmania's early pioneering days. It's open on weekdays from 10 am to 5 pm and

Battery Point, Hobart

at weekends from 2 to 5 pm; admission is $4 ($2 for children).

Maritime Museum of Tasmania Secheron House, in Secheron Rd, Battery Point, was built in 1831 and is classified by the National Trust. It also houses the fascinating Maritime Museum, which has an extensive collection of photos, paintings, models and relics depicting Tasmania's, and particularly Hobart's, colourful shipping history. Admission is $2 and it's open daily from 1 to 4.30 pm except Saturdays, when it's open from 10 am to 5 pm.

Tasmanian Museum & Art Gallery
The excellent Tasmanian Museum & Art Gallery, at 5 Argyle St (enter via Macquarie St), incorporates Hobart's oldest building, the Commissariat Store, built in 1808. The museum section features a Tasmanian Aboriginal display and relics from the state's colonial heritage, while the gallery has a good collection of Tasmanian colonial art. It's open daily from 10 am to 5 pm and admission is free.

Anglesea Barracks
Built in 1811, this is the oldest military establishment in Australia still used by the army. There's no admission fee to the museum, which is open weekdays from 9 am to 3.30 pm, and there are guided tours of the restored buildings and grounds on Tuesdays at 11 am.

Cascade Brewery
Australia's oldest brewery, on Cascade Rd close to the city centre, is still in use and produces some of the finest beer in the country – although no doubt others would argue differently! There are two-hour tours daily ($7) at 9.30 am and 1 pm, and bookings are essential (☎ 24 1144). The brewery is on the south-western edge of the city centre; bus Nos 44, 46 and 49 go right by it – alight at stop 18.

Other Museums
The **Allport Museum & Library of Fine Arts** is based in the State Library at 91 Murray St. It has a collection of rare books on Australasia and the Pacific region and you

can visit free on weekdays from 9 am to 5 pm.

Other museums include the **John Elliott Classics Museum** at the University of Tasmania, the **Tasmanian Transport Museum** in Glenorchy, and Australia's first public museum, the **Lady Franklin Gallery**, in Lenah Valley Rd.

Other Attractions

Just by the Tasman Bridge are the **Royal Tasmanian Botanical Gardens**, which are very pleasant and definitely worth a visit, and the recreation area called the **Queen's Domain**.

Hobart is dominated by 1270-metre-high **Mt Wellington**, and there are many fine views and interesting walking tracks in the mountain area. There are also good views from the **Old Signal Station** on Mt Nelson, above Sandy Bay.

Organised Tours & Cruises

Several boat cruise companies operate from the Brooke St Pier and Franklin Wharf and offer a variety of cruises in and around the harbour. One of the most popular is the four-hour Cadbury's Cruise, run by the Cruise Company (☎ 30 8233), which costs $28 ($13 for children). You do a slow return cruise to the Cadbury Schweppes factory in Claremont where you disembark and tour the premises (this is a good place to stock up on chocolate if you are planning on any bushwalking). The cruise timetables are pretty changeable so it is best to book. Harbour cruises are also available, and these typically last one ($10) or two hours ($16).

One of the best ways to get a feel for Hobart's colonial history is to take the Saturday morning walking tour organised by the National Trust. The tour concentrates on the historic Battery Point area and departs at 9.30 am from the wishing well in Franklin Square – you don't have to book, just turn up. The walk costs $5 and takes 2½ hours. You could do a similar tour on your own with the help of a *Historic Village Battery Point* leaflet available from the National Trust shop (80c).

Day and half-day bus tours in and around Hobart are operated by Redline and Hobart Coaches. Typical half-day tours include trips to Richmond ($15), the City Sights and Mt Wellington ($15). Full-day tour destinations include Port Arthur ($32), the Huon Valley ($48), Maria Island ($38), Bruny Island ($50) and Ross ($25). Tasmanian Wilderness Transport also runs day and two-day excursions to places like Mt Field National Park, Cradle Mountain and Strahan.

Scenic flights are offered by Par Avion (☎ 48 5390).

Festivals

From 29 December to 2 January, Hobart's waterfront area is alive with spectators and celebrating yachties at the finish of the annual New Year Sydney to Hobart Yacht Race. The Royal Hobart Regatta, in February, is a major aquatic carnival with boat races and other activities.

Places to Stay

Camping The handiest camping ground is the *Sandy Bay Caravan Park* (☎ 25 1264), which is less than four km from the city, at 1 Peel St, Sandy Bay. It charges $10 a double for a camp site ($12 with power), while on-site vans are $32 a double and cabins $42. To get there, take Metro bus No 54, 55 or 56 from stop D in Elizabeth St near the GPO. There are also parks a little further out at Elwick and Berriedale (north of the city) and at Mornington (in the eastern suburbs).

Hostels Right in the centre of town is the *Central City Backpackers* (☎ toll-free 1800 811 507) at 138 Collins St. It's a rambling place with excellent facilities and a friendly couple in charge. There are good and spacious communal areas, as well as a laundry and individual safe-deposit boxes. The cost is $12 for a bed in a four-bed dorm, or there are twin-share rooms for $16 per person, and singles/doubles for $28/35. Security is good here and it's clean and quiet.

On the 1st floor of the New Sydney Hotel at 87 Bathurst St is *Tasmanian Backpackers* (☎ 34 4516). Although the facilities are quite adequate, the pub can get noisy at times when there's a band on, making sleep difficult. The hostel charges $12 per night.

At the Transit Centre at 199 Collins St is the *Tasmanian Backpackers Transit Centre* (☎ 34 7874). It has beds for the usual $12 per night and has all the facilities, but the communal area is a bit cavernous and lacks atmosphere.

Hobart also has three YHA hostels. The main one, *Adelphi Court* (☎ 28 4829), is 2.5 km from the city at 17 Stoke St, New Town. It's an excellent hostel with good facilities and charges $12 for a dorm bed, or $16 each for a twin room. To get there take Metro bus No 15 or 16 from Argyle St to stop 8A, or any one of bus Nos 25 to 42, 100 and 105 to 128 to stop 13. Redline also runs a daily drop-off and pick-up service between here and the airport.

The peaceful *Bellerive Hostel* (☎ 44 2552) is on the other side of the Derwent River at 52 King St, Bellerive, and charges $9 a night. The lovely, old stone building used to be a schoolhouse and dates from 1869. To get there at the weekends, when the ferry doesn't run, you can catch any of the Bellerive buses (Nos 83 to 87) from stop C or D near the GPO in Elizabeth St.

The *Woodlands Hostel* (☎ 28 6720), at 7 Woodlands Ave, New Town, is a superb building and one of New Town's original homes, but it is only used as an overflow hostel when Adelphi Court is full. It's best to turn up at nearby Adelphi first, and if there isn't any room you'll be directed here. A dorm bed costs $10.

Guesthouses In addition to its hostel, *Adelphi Court* (☎ 28 4829), at 17 Stoke St, New Town, also has guesthouse accommodation at $35/40, or $40/50 including a cooked breakfast.

In Sandy Bay there's *Red Chapel House* (☎ 25 2273) at 27 Red Chapel Ave, past the casino. Singles/doubles in this smoke-free establishment cost $48/60 including a cooked breakfast, and the place has a friendly, family-run atmosphere.

If you have the money, in Battery Point

you can stay in some beautiful colonial guesthouses and cottages. *Barton Cottage* (☎ 24 1606), at 72 Hampden Rd, is a two-storey building which dates back to 1837 and is classified by the National Trust. B&B accommodation costs $70/90. *Colville Cottage* (☎ 23 6968), at 32 Mona St, is more recent, dating from the 1870s. It has six rooms, an extensive garden and some tasteful antiques. The cost here is also $70/90. Another worth considering is *Cromwell Cottage* (☎ 23 6734) at 6 Cromwell St. This two-storey townhouse dates from the late 1880s and is in a beautiful position overlooking the Derwent River. Each of the five rooms costs $70/90 for B&B.

Other places in Battery Point include the *Battery Point Guest House* (☎ 24 2111) at 7 McGregor St ($65/85); *Portsea Terrace* (☎ 34 1616) at 62 Montpelier Retreat, just behind Salamanca Place and dating back to 1850 ($70 for a one-bedroom unit); and the *Colonial Battery Point Manor* (☎ 24 0888) at 13 Cromwell St ($75/95 B&B).

An interesting option is the *Signalman's Cottage* (☎ 23 1215) on the top of Mt Nelson at 685 Nelson Rd. There's just the single self-contained one-bedroom unit and the cost is $45/55. You'd need your own transport for this one to be convenient.

Hotels At 67 Liverpool St, near the mall, the *Brunswick Hotel* (☎ 34 4981) is pretty central and has average rooms costing $30/45 with a continental breakfast. Across the road, at 72 Liverpool St, the *Alabama Hotel* (☎ 34 3737) is a little more comfortable and charges $30/48 for singles/doubles.

Two blocks up from the mall, at 145 Elizabeth St, is the *Black Prince* (☎ 34 3501), which has large, modern rooms with bathroom and TV for $38/48.

If you want to stay by the waterfront, the *Telegraph Hotel* (☎ 34 6254), at 19 Morrison St, is in the heart of Franklin Wharf and good value at $30/40 with a continental breakfast. A few doors away, the *Customs House Hotel* (☎ 34 6645), at 1 Murray St, has even better views of the waterfront and charges $30/50 with a continental breakfast.

There are also a couple of moderately priced hotels in Sandy Bay. The *Dr Syntax Hotel* (☎ 23 6258), at 139 Sandy Bay Rd, is very close to Battery Point. It has comfortable singles/doubles with TV for $32/45. The *Beach House Hotel* (☎ 25 1161), at 646 Sandy Bay Rd, is two km past the casino and has good rooms with TV and continental breakfast for $38/49.

Hadleys Orient Hotel (☎ 23 4355), at 34 Murray St, is one of Hobart's best older style hotels. Compared to the large hotel chains, this hotel has a lot more charm and, at $75/90, is considerably cheaper.

Top-end, international-standard accommodation is available at the *Sheraton Hobart* (☎ 35 4535), the ugly blot on the skyline right in the heart of the city at 1 Davey St, which charges from $210; or the *Wrest Point Hotel Casino* (☎ 25 0112) at 410 Sandy Bay Rd, five km south of the city centre. Rooms here start at $198.

If none of these appeal, there's always the wonderful *Lenna of Hobart* (☎ 23 2911), an old mansion at 20 Runnymede St, Battery Point, which is steeped in history and luxury and charges from $125 for a single/double room.

Motels & Holiday Flats There are plenty of motels in Hobart but some are rather a long way out. The cheapest include the *Shoreline Motor Motel* (☎ 47 9504) on the corner of Rokeby Rd and Shoreline Drive, Howrah, which charges $45 for a double with continental breakfast; the *Marina Motel* (☎ 28 4748) at 153 Risdon Rd, New Town, where singles/doubles cost $45/55; and the *Highway Village Motor Inn* (☎ 72 6721) at 897 Brooker Ave, Berriedale, which charges $44/52. For a motel closer to the city centre, you could try the *Mayfair Motel* (☎ 31 1188) at 17 Cavell St, West Hobart, which has rooms for $60/65.

Hobart has a number of self-contained holiday flats with fully equipped kitchens. Fairly close to town, the *Domain View Apartments* (☎ 34 1181) at 352 Argyle St, North Hobart, charges $46 a double and $6 for each extra person, with a one-night surcharge. The

Knopwood Apartment (☎ 23 2290), at 6 Knopwood St, Battery Point, is a three-bedroom upstairs flat overlooking Salamanca Place. It costs $57 a double and $12 for each extra person, and has a one-night surcharge.

Places to Eat
Cafes & Light Meals Hobart has plenty of straightforward street cafes such as the *Carlton Restaurant*, at 50 Liverpool St. The *Criterion Coffee Lounge*, at 10 Criterion St, is recommended for an excellent cheap breakfast, while *Kafé Kara*, at 119 Liverpool St, has good food, real cappuccinos (not too common in Hobart) and great decor.

A good lunch-time cafe is *La Cuisine* at 85 Bathurst St and 79 Harrington St. There's a good selection of croissants, quiches and patés and you can get a quick, light meal for around $6.

A couple of fun places are the *Belfry* at 171 Elizabeth St, which is open until midnight on Saturdays, and the *Retro Cafe* on the corner of Salamanca Place and Montpelier Retreat, which is open until midnight on Fridays.

If you're looking for a snack late at night, you could also try *Mummy's Coffee Shop* at 38 Waterloo Crescent, just off Hampden Rd, Battery Point. It's open from 10 am to midnight Sunday to Thursday and from 10 am to 2 am Fridays and Saturdays.

Constitution Dock has a number of floating takeaway seafood stalls such as *Mako Quality Seafoods* and *Flippers*. Close by is *Mures Fish Centre*, where you can get excellent fish & chips and other fishy fare at the bistro on Lower Deck, or an ice cream in the Polar Parlour.

A little more difficult to get to, but well worth the effort, is the historic *Mount Nelson Signal Station Tea House*, on the summit of Mt Nelson, which has spectacular 180° panoramic views of Hobart and the surrounding area.

Pub Meals For $6 you can get a very filling meal at the *New Sydney Hotel*, below Tasmanian Backpackers, at 87 Bathurst St. Many other hotels serve good counter meals and those in the $7 to $9 range include the *Bruns-*

South Australia
Top: Rotunda, Adelaide (PS)
Bottom: Sign on the Eyre Highway, Nullarbor Plain (RN)

	A	
B	C	D
	E	

South Australia

A Wilpena Pound, Flinders Ranges (TW)
B Local personality, Moonta (MC)
C Wildflowers, Flinders Ranges (MC)

D Old farm, Flinders Ranges (PS)
E Dwelling in Coober Pedy (MK)

wick at 67 Liverpool St; the *Wheatsheaf Hotel* at 314 Macquarie St; and the *Telegraph Hotel* at 19 Morrison St.

Stoppy's Waterfront Tavern, on Salamanca Place, is a little trendier and has good counter meals for around $8 as well as bands from Thursday to Sunday nights.

Restaurants The licensed *Aegean* (☎ 31 1000), at 121 Collins St in the city, is a Greek restaurant which serves excellent food and often provides entertainment such as belly dancing, Greek music and the traditional smashing of plates. Main courses are in the $15 to $18 range, or there's a banquet for $30.

At 84A Harrington St, the *Little Bali* (☎ 34 3426) is tiny but has cheap, good-value Indonesian food to eat in or take away. It is only open for dinner on Saturdays and Sundays but does lunch from Monday to Friday.

The licensed *Hara Wholefood Cafe* (☎ 34 1457) at 181 Liverpool St has an extensive range of mouth-watering vegetarian dishes and is open from 10 am until late evening Monday to Saturday. For delicious homemade pasta dishes try *La Suprema* at 255 Liverpool St.

Also worth trying in town is *Squid Roe* (☎ 34 7978), at 210 Liverpool St, a relaxed BYO restaurant serving seafood and pasta.

Elizabeth St in North Hobart has a reputation for good-value, interesting places to eat. At 321 Elizabeth St is *Ali Akbar* (☎ 31 1770), a popular BYO Lebanese restaurant. *Marti Zucco* (☎ 34 9611), at 364 Elizabeth St, has a great atmosphere, good food and is a deservedly popular BYO Italian restaurant. Also worth checking out is the *Street Cafe* (☎ 34 3336), at 340 Elizabeth St, which is both BYO and licensed.

North Hobart also has plenty of Asian restaurants. *Vanidols* (☎ 34 9307), at 353 Elizabeth St, is a comfortable BYO restaurant specialising in Thai, Indian and Indonesian cuisine. Just down the street is another BYO Asian restaurant, *Dede* (☎ 31 1068), which has good food but can feel a bit cramped on a busy night. There is a BYO

Chinese restaurant, the *Kan Wan Cafe* (☎ 34 6650), at 404 Elizabeth St, while at 333 Elizabeth St there's the BYO *Everest* Indian restaurant (☎ 34 8113), which has a good-value banquet for $16.

At Salamanca Place, *Mr Wooby's* (☎ 34 3466), in a side lane, is a pleasant licensed eatery where you can get a three-course meal for under $20 or snacks for $5; it's open until quite late. Nearby, at 87 Salamanca Place, is the licensed *Ball & Chain Grill* (☎ 23 2655), which has a good reputation for grilled steaks; main courses are around $13. At No 39 there is *Cutty's Cafe*, a trendy bar which also has good meals, while at No 89 there's *Panache* (☎ 24 2929), a licensed cafe/restaurant which has an outdoor eating area by the adjoining rock walls. For excellent Japanese food, try the licensed *Mikaku* (☎ 24 0882) at 85 Salamanca Place. Good Japanese fare is also to be found at the licensed *Orizuru Sushi Bar* (☎ 31 1790), at Mures Fish Centre on Victoria Dock.

At 31 Campbell St there's the *Theatre Royal Hotel* (☎ 34 6925), with its recently renovated bistro and atrium bar. It's right next door to the Theatre Royal, Australia's oldest functioning performing-arts theatre.

In South Hobart there are two popular French BYO restaurants: the *Paris Restaurant* (☎ 24 2200), at 356 Macquarie St; and *Le Provençal* (☎ 24 2526), across the road at 417 Macquarie St. At 182 Goulburn St in nearby West Hobart is *Round Asia* (☎ 34 9385), a little suburban BYO restaurant with lots of atmosphere.

In Hampden Rd, Battery Point, is the very popular *Brasserie*, which has a reputation for excellent food at moderate prices.

In Sandy Bay the licensed Italian restaurant *Don Camillo* (☎ 34 1006), in the shopping centre, has an excellent reputation, and *Tarantella* (☎ 23 6652) at 16A Princes St has also been recommended for Italian food.

In the more expensive bracket is the famous *Upper Deck* licensed restaurant (☎ 31 2121) with the spectacular harbour view at Mures Fish Centre, Victoria Dock, and *Prossers on the Beach* (☎ 23 2646), a licensed seafood restaurant in Beach Rd, Long Point, off Sandy Bay Rd, Lower Sandy Bay.

Also on the waterfront, the licensed *Drunken Admiral* (☎ 34 1903) at 17 Hunter St has been highly recommended for good seafood and a great atmosphere. Right next door is the *Riviera Ristorante* (34 3230), a popular Italian restaurant. Although it is licensed, you can bring your own bottled wine if you prefer.

Entertainment

The *Mercury* newspaper has details on most of Hobart's entertainment.

There are cover bands most nights of the week at the *Duke of Wellington*, 192 Macquarie St. The *New Sydney Hotel* at 87 Bathurst St is Hobart's Irish pub and there is live music there most nights.

For jazz, blues and rock & roll, both the *St Ives Hotel* at 86 Sandy Bay Rd and the *Travellers Rest*, 394 Sandy Bay Rd, have bands from Wednesday to Sunday nights.

There is always a good scene to be found at *Maloney's Hotel* on the corner of Macquarie and Argyle Sts; there are bands on Friday and Saturday nights and a nightclub upstairs. Another recommended nightclub is *Round Midnight* at 39 Salamanca Place, which is open until 4 am Tuesday to Saturday. Round Midnight is on the top floor of the building which houses the bars *Knopwood's Retreat* and *Cutty's Cafe*.

There are 17 bars at the Wrest Point Hotel Casino; and some, like the *Birdcage*, need to be seen to be believed. The casino also has a disco every night with a cover charge on Fridays and Saturdays only.

At 375 Elizabeth St, North Hobart, you'll find the *State Cinema* (☎ 34 6318), which screens alternative/offbeat films, while at 181 Collins St there's a large *Village* complex (☎ 34 7288) which shows the mainstream releases.

Getting There & Away

Air For information on international and domestic flights to and from Hobart see the Getting There & Away section at the begin-

ning of this chapter. Ansett (☎ 13 1300) has an office in the Elizabeth St Mall, as does Qantas (☎ 13 1313). Airlines of Tasmania (☎ 48 5030) has an office at Hobart Airport.

Bus The main bus companies operating from Hobart are Redline Coaches (☎ 31 3233) at the Transit Centre, 199 Collins St; Hobart Coaches (☎ 34 4077) at 60 Collins St; and Tasmanian Wilderness Transport & Tours (☎ 34 2226), also operating out of 60 Collins St. Hobart Coaches has additional departure points at St David's Cathedral, on the corner of Macquarie and Murray Sts, and outside the Treasury Building in Murray St.

Hobart Coaches' destinations include New Norfolk ($3.40), Woodbridge, Cygnet, Geeveston ($8.70), Dover ($11), and Port Arthur ($11). Both Redline and Hobart Coaches run to Bicheno ($18), Swansea ($15), St Marys, St Helens (Hobart Coaches $26/Redline $28.80), Oatlands, Ross, Campbell Town, Launceston ($17), Deloraine, Devonport ($28) and Burnie. Redline also runs to Wynyard, Stanley and Smithton; and both Redline and Tasmanian Wilderness Transport run to Queenstown ($29.40) and Strahan ($34.20).

Car Rental There are more than 20 car-rental firms in Hobart. Some of the cheaper ones include Rent-a-Bug (☎ 31 0300) at 105 Murray St; Advance Car Rentals (☎ toll-free 1800 030 118) at 277 Macquarie St; Bargain Car Rentals (☎ 34 6959) at 189A Harrington St; and Statewide Rent-a-Car (☎ 25 1204) at 388 Sandy Bay Rd, Sandy Bay.

Hitching To start hitching north, take a Bridgewater or Brighton bus from opposite the GPO in Elizabeth St. To hitch along the east coast, take a bus to Sorell first.

Getting Around

To/From the Airport The airport is in Hobart's eastern suburbs, 26 km from the city centre. Redline runs a pick-up and dropoff shuttle service between the city centre (via Adelphi YHA on request) and the airport for $6.

Bus The local bus service is run by Metro. The main office (☎ 33 4223) is at 18 Elizabeth St, opposite the GPO. Most buses leave from this area of Elizabeth St, known as the Metro City Bus Station.

If you're planning to bus around Hobart, it's worth buying Metro's user-friendly timetable, which only costs $1.50. For $2.60, you can get a Day Rover ticket which can be used all day at weekends and between 9 am and 4.30 pm and after 6 pm on weekdays.

If you want to go to Mt Wellington without taking a tour, take bus No 48 from Franklin Square in Macquarie St; it will get you to Fern Tree at the base of the mountain, but from there it's a 13-km walk to the top!

Bicycle The Backpackers Transit Centre has mountain bikes for $15 per day, or regular 10-speed road bikes for $5. Brake Out (☎ 34 7632) is a company which has rentals and bicycle tours.

Boat On weekdays the ferry MV *Emmalisa* operates between Franklin Wharf and Bellerive Wharf and is a very pleasant way to cross the Derwent River. It departs Hobart at 6.55, 7.40 and 8.15 am and 4.35, 5.15 and 5.55 pm. From Bellerive there are services at 7.25, 8 and 8.35 am and at 4.50, 5.30 and 5.10 pm. A one-way ticket costs $1.50. There is no weekend service.

Around Hobart

TAROONA

Ten km from Hobart, on the Channel Highway, is Taroona's famous **Shot Tower**, completed in 1870. From the top of the 48-metre-high tower there are fine views over the Derwent River estuary. Lead shot was once produced in high towers like this by dropping molten lead from the top which, on its way down, formed a perfect sphere, before solidifying when it hit water at the bottom.

The tower, small museum, craft shop and beautiful grounds are open daily from 9 am to 5 pm and admission is $3 ($1.50 for children). There is also a tearoom which advertises 'convictshire' teas. Take bus No 60 from Franklin Square near Elizabeth St and get off at stop 45.

From Taroona Beach, you can walk around to Kingston Beach (about three km) along the Alum Cliffs Track; at some points the track runs close to rock cliffs and you get good views of the Derwent across to Opossum Bay.

KINGSTON

The town of Kingston, 11 km south of Hobart, is the headquarters of the Commonwealth Antarctic Division. The centre is open weekdays from 9 am to 5 pm and admission is free. There's a pleasant picnic area along Browns River at the eastern end of Kingston Beach.

Close by there are also some pleasant beaches, including **Blackmans Bay**, which has a blowhole; **Tinderbox**, where you can go snorkelling along an underwater trail marked with submerged information plates; and **Howden**. There are views across to Bruny Island from Piersons Point, near Tinderbox.

BRIDGEWATER

This town, 19 km north of Hobart, is so named because of the causeway built here by convicts in the 1830s. More than 150 convicts laboured in chains (moving two million tonnes of stone and clay) to build this main north-south crossing of the Derwent River. The old **watch house**, on the other side of the river from the town, was built by convicts in 1838 to guard the causeway and is now a museum housing relics from the convict days. Admission is $1.50.

PONTVILLE

Further north, on the Midland Highway, is the historic town of Pontville, which has a number of interesting buildings dating from the 1830s. Much of the freestone used in Tasmania's early buildings was supplied from quarries at Pontville.

In nearby Brighton, on Briggs Rd, is the

very good **Bonorong Park Wildlife Centre**, which is open daily from 8 am to 5 pm; Admission is $5.

NEW NORFOLK (population 5800)

Set in the lush, rolling countryside of the Derwent Valley, New Norfolk is an interesting historical town. It was first settled in 1803 and became an important hop-growing centre, which is why the area is dotted with old oast houses used in the drying of hops. Also distinctive are the rows of tall poplars planted to protect crops from the wind.

Originally called Elizabeth Town, New Norfolk was renamed after the arrival of settlers (1807 onwards) from the abandoned Pacific Ocean colony on Norfolk Island.

Things to See & Do

The **Visitors Historical & Information Centre**, next to the council chambers in Circle St, has an interesting photographic and memorabilia display. The key to the centre can be obtained from the council office during working hours.

The **Oast House** on Hobart Rd is a unique museum devoted to the history of the hop industry, a tearoom and a fine-arts gallery. It's open daily from 10 am to 5 pm and admission is $3.50. The building itself has been classified by the National Trust and is worth seeing from the outside, even if you don't go in.

Also interesting to visit are **St Matthew's Church of England**, built in 1823, which is Tasmania's oldest existing church, and the **Bush Inn**, claimed to be the oldest continuously licensed hotel in Australia. The **Old Colony Inn**, at 21 Montagu St, is a wonderful museum of colonial furnishings and artefacts; there's also a tearoom where you can get some great home-made snacks. The inn is open from 9 am to 5 pm and admission is $1.50.

Australian Newsprint Mills (☎ (002) 61 0433) is one of the area's major industries and tours can be arranged Tuesday to Friday if you give at least 24 hours notice.

For $30 ($17 for children) you can also take a **jet-boat ride** on the Derwent River rapids. The 30-minute ride can be booked at the Devil Jet office (☎ (002) 61 3460), behind the Bush Inn.

In 1864, the first rainbow and brown trout in the southern hemisphere were bred in the **Salmon Ponds** at Plenty, 11 km west of New Norfolk. The ponds and museum on Lower Bushy Park Rd are open daily and there's also a restaurant. (If you're ordering the fish you'll know it's fresh!)

Places to Stay

Camp sites and on-site vans and cabins are available at the *New Norfolk Caravan Park* (☎ (002) 61 1268), on the Esplanade, 1.5 km north of town.

The hotel choices here are pretty limited. The *Bush Inn* (☎ (002) 61 2011), in Montagu St, was built in 1815 and has singles/doubles for $28/48 including a cooked breakfast, but there's a one-night surcharge. The *Old Colony Inn* (☎ (002) 61 2731), also in Montagu St, has just one double room for $70.

Probably the nicest place is *Tynwald* (☎ (002) 61 2667), overlooking the river by the Oast House. It's a three-storey house which dates back to the 1830s and is oozing character. The rooms are well furnished, and it has a heated swimming pool and a tennis court for the energetic. The cost is $88/100 which includes a light breakfast.

Getting There & Away

Hobart Coaches (☎ (002) 34 4077) is the main operator between Hobart and New Norfolk and on weekdays there are eight or nine buses in both directions. At weekends there's a limited service: a one-way/return fare costs $3.40/6.80. In New Norfolk, the buses leave from 15 Stephen St.

MT FIELD NATIONAL PARK

Mt Field, only 80 km from Hobart, was declared a national park in 1916, which makes it one of Australia's oldest. The park is well known for its spectacular mountain scenery, alpine moorland, dense rainforest, lakes, abundant wildlife and spectacular waterfalls. The magnificent **40-metre Russell**

Falls is an easy 15-minute walk (the path is suitable for wheelchairs), and there are also easy walks to Lady Barron, Horseshoe and Marriotts falls as well as eight-hour bushwalks. With sufficient snow, there's cross-country and limited downhill skiing at **Mt Mawson**. For more information, contact the park ranger (☎ (002) 88 1149).

Places to Stay
Lake Dobson Cabins, 15 km into the park, has three very basic six-bunk cabins. The cost per cabin is $10 a night, regardless of numbers, and you must book at the ranger's office. There's also a camping ground in the park run by the rangers; a site (for two) costs $10.

The smoke-free *National Park Youth Hostel* (☎ (002) 88 1369) is in the township of National Park, on the main road between Strathgordon and New Norfolk. The hostel is 200 metres past the turn-off to the park and charges $10 a night. The nearby *Russell Falls Holiday Cottages* (☎ (002) 88 1198) consists of four one- or two-bedroom fully equipped cottages, which cost $50 a double, plus $5 for each extra person.

Getting There & Away
On weekdays, the 4 pm Hobart Coaches bus from Hobart to New Norfolk continues on to Mt Field. There is a return service to Hobart on weekdays at 7.55 am. Tasmanian Wilderness Transport also runs one bus to and from Scotts Peak via the park and Maydena (twice weekly and at weekends).

RICHMOND (population 750)
Richmond is just 24 km from Hobart and, with more than 50 buildings dating from the 19th century, is Tasmania's premier historic town. Straddling the Coal River, on the old route between Hobart and Port Arthur, Richmond was a strategic military post and convict station. The famous and much-photographed **Richmond Bridge**, built by convicts in 1823, is the oldest road bridge in Australia.

With the completion of the Sorell Cause-

way in 1872, traffic travelling to the Tasman Peninsula and the east coast bypassed Richmond, which is why the village is so well preserved today.

Things to See & Do
The northern wing of **Richmond Gaol** was built in 1825, five years before the settlement at Port Arthur, and is the best preserved convict jail in Australia. It features detailed records of the old penal system and convicts who were confined there, and is open daily from 10 am to 5 pm; admission is $2.50 ($1.50 for children).

Other places of interest include **St John's Church** (1836), the oldest Catholic church in Australia; **St Luke's Church of England** (1834); the **courthouse** (1825); the **old post office** (1826); the **Bridge Inn** (1817); the **granary** (1829); and the **Richmond Arms Hotel** (1888). There's also a model village (designed from original plans) of Hobart Town as it was in the 1820s. It's open daily from 9 am to 5 pm and admission is $4.50 ($2.50 for children). The maze, on the main street, is quite fun but is only made of wooden divides, not hedges; admission is $2.50 ($1.50).

Places to Stay & Eat
Accommodation in Richmond is mostly of the 'colonial cottage' type and is therefore not particularly cheap. Cheapest of all is the *Richmond Cabin & Tourist Park* (☎ (002) 60 2192), on Middle Tea Tree Rd. It has camp sites ($12 for two people), on-site vans ($32) and cabins ($35).

The cheapest place in town is the *Richmond Country Guest House* (☎ (002) 60 4238), on Prossers Rd, six km north of town, which charges $35/50 for singles/doubles including breakfast. Right in town is the *Dispensary* (☎ (002) 60 2226) in Edward St. This 1830s cottage has just one bedroom and costs $95 for a double with a two-night minimum.

Prospect House (☎ (002) 60 2207) is a superb two-storey Georgian country mansion set in 10 hectares of grounds. It's just outside Richmond, on the Hobart road. Accommodation costs \$86/96, or \$10 more if breakfast is included.

You can get something to eat and drink at *Ashmore* or at the maze tearooms, which are both in Bridge St, Richmond's main street.

Getting There & Away

If you have your own car, Richmond is an easy day trip from Hobart. If you don't, both Redline and Hobart Coaches have bus tours to Richmond. Hobart Coaches runs four buses a day on weekdays to and from Richmond (\$6 return). The Hobart Coaches agent in Richmond is the Richmond Store on the main street. There are no weekend services.

South-East Coast

South of Hobart are the scenic fruit-growing and timber areas of the Huon Peninsula, D'Entrecasteaux Channel and Esperance, as well as beautiful Bruny Island and the Hartz Mountains National Park. The area is known for its spectacular rainbows, which probably occur frequently here due to the southern latitude.

In the 1960s, it was fruit growing (particularly apple growing) in the Huon Valley that put Tasmania on the international export map. Today, however, far less fruit is grown, and most of that is for the domestic market. Around the end of February and during March there is sometimes fruit-picking work, but competition for jobs is stiff.

KETTERING (population 295)

The small port of Kettering, on a sheltered bay 34 km south of Hobart, is the terminal for the Bruny Island car ferry. The nearby town of **Snug** has a walking track to Snug Falls, and you can visit the Channel Historical & Folk Museum. Just south of Snug there is a good swimming beach at **Coningham**.

On weekdays, Hobart Coaches has about four buses a day to Woodbridge via Kingston, Margate, Snug and Kettering.

BRUNY ISLAND (population 450)

Bruny Island is almost two islands, joined by an isthmus where mutton birds and other waterfowl breed, and is a peaceful and beautiful retreat. The sparsely populated island has five state reserves and is renowned for its varied wildlife, including fairy penguins and many species of reptile. The island's coastal scenery is superb and there are plenty of fine swimming and surf beaches, as well as good sea and freshwater fishing. There are a number of signposted walking tracks within the reserves, especially the southern Labillardiere State Reserve.

The island was sighted by Abel Tasman in 1642 and later visited by Furneaux, Cook, Bligh and Cox between 1770 and 1790, but was named after Rear-Admiral Bruny D'Entrecasteaux, who explored and surveyed the area in 1792. Truganini, the last full-blooded Tasmanian Aborigine, was a member of Bruny Island's south-east tribe.

The island's history is recorded in the **Bligh Museum of Pacific Exploration** at Adventure Bay, South Bruny, which is open daily, except Wednesday, from 10 am to 3 pm; admission is \$2.50 (\$1.50 for children). Also of historical interest is South Bruny's lighthouse, which was built in 1836 and is the second oldest in Australia. The lighthouse reserve is open to the public.

There's a small information centre (☎ (002) 93 1137) at Alonnah.

Places to Stay

Adventure Bay on the north-eastern shore of the southern part of the island is the main accommodation area, but there are places dotted throughout the island. Alonnah is the main settlement, and Lunawanna the only other one; both are on the southern part of the island.

The *Adventure Bay Caravan Park* (☎ (002) 93 1270) has cosy little three-bed cabins for \$40, or on-site vans for \$30 and camp sites at \$10. The *Captain James Cook Caravan Park* (☎ (002) 93 1128) also has on-site vans.

There are bush camp sites in a couple of

the reserves. The one at Jetty Beach near the lighthouse on the south of the island is on a beautiful sheltered cove. There's another near the isthmus.

On Lighthouse Rd, Lunawanna, South Bruny, the *Whaler's Inn Holiday Village* (☎ (002) 93 1271) has cheap backpacker accommodation. This place has a very good reputation and some wonderful views over the D'Entrecasteaux Channel to the Hartz Mountains.

In Adventure Bay there is the *Lumeah Hostel* (☎ (002) 93 1265), which has dormitory beds for $13, or there's a number of cottages, such as *Rosebud Cottage* (☎ (002) 93 1325) and *Mavista Cottage* (☎ (002) 93 1347), offering B&B for around $60 a double.

On North Bruny the *Channel View Guest House* (☎ (002) 60 6266) has good-value accommodation at $30/45 for singles/doubles with breakfast. Also, at Dennes Point, there is *House Sofia Holiday Accommodation* (☎ (002) 60 6277), which charges $35/50, which includes a cooked breakfast.

Getting There & Away

On weekdays there are nine daily ferry services between Kettering and Roberts Point, on Bruny Island. On Fridays there is an extra crossing, and the weekend schedule can vary, so check the times in Hobart's *Mercury* newspaper. There's no charge for foot passengers, but if you have a car it will cost $17 return from Monday to Thursday, and $22 on Friday afternoons and at weekends. Cycles cost $2. Hobart Coaches has two buses on most days which connect with the ferry.

CYGNET (population 920)

This small township was originally named 'Port de Cygne Noir' (Port of the Black Swan) by the Frenchman Rear-Admiral D'Entrecasteaux because of the many swans seen on the bay. Now known as Cygnet, the town and surrounding area have many apple and other fruit orchards and offer excellent fishing, plenty of bushwalks and some fine beaches, particularly further south at Verona

Sands. Close to Cygnet is the **Talune Wildlife Park & Koala Garden**, the **Elsewhere Vineyard** and the **Deepings** wood-turning workshop, which can all be visited.

Places to Stay

Balfes Hill Youth Hostel (☎ (002) 95 1551) is on the Channel Highway, about five km from town. It charges $10 a night and can get crowded during the fruit-picking season. From December to April the manager organises rafting trips on the Huon River which are good fun and cost around $65 a day, including lunch. You can explore the area on the mountain bikes which are available for rent from the hostel at $12 per day.

The *Cygnet Hotel* (☎ (002) 95 1267) has singles/doubles for $25/50 with a cooked breakfast, while at 22 Channel Highway the *Wilfrid Lodge* (☎ (002) 95 1604) charges $30/50 including a cooked breakfast. There's also a basic camping ground. If you are fruit picking, many of the hotels in Cygnet will rent you a room at a reasonable weekly rate.

Getting There & Away

Hobart Coaches has a once-daily weekday service to Gordon ($6.20 one way) and Cygnet ($5.90).

GROVE

On the Huon Highway, about six km north of Huonville, is the **Huon Valley Apple & Heritage Museum**, which is crammed with displays and machinery that take you back 100 years. It's open daily from 9 am to 5 pm and the $2.50 admission fee includes an apple prepared on the antique apple corer and peeler.

HUONVILLE (population 1550)

Named after Huon D'Kermandec, who was second in command to D'Entrecasteaux, this busy, small town on the picturesque Huon River is another apple-growing centre. The valuable softwood Huon pine was also first discovered here, though large stands are now found only around the Gordon River. For the visitor, one of Huonville's main attractions these days is a jet-boat ride on the river. You can also hire pedal boats and aqua bikes from the office (☎ (002) 64 1838) on the Esplanade.

Places to Stay
Huonville has a couple of good guesthouses. The *Osborne Park* (☎ (002) 64 22772), a couple of km north of town, has a couple of rooms at $40/55 for B&B. The other place is the *Budget Holiday Villas* (☎ (002) 64 1847) at 183 Main Rd. Here there are two self-contained units at $65 for a double.

GEEVESTON (population 830)
Geeveston, 31 km south of Huonville, is the administrative centre for Esperance, Australia's most southerly municipality, and also the gateway to the wild Hartz Mountains National Park.

The town's main attraction is the **Esperance Forest & Heritage Centre** in Church St. It has comprehensive displays on all aspects of forests and of logging and forest management. From here there are a number of walks to take in the area, including the West Creek Lookout Walk, which gives you a canopy view of some rainforest. The centre also incorporates the South-West Visitor Centre (☎ (002) 97 1836) and is open daily from 10 am to 4 pm; admission is $4 ($2 for children).

Hobart Coaches runs four buses a day between Hobart and Geeveston ($8.70 one way) via Huonville ($5.60 one way), but there are no weekend services.

HARTZ MOUNTAINS NATIONAL PARK
This national park, classified as a World Heritage area, is very popular with weekend walkers and day-trippers as it's only 84 km from Hobart. The park is renowned for its snow-capped, rugged mountains, glacial lakes, deep gorges, alpine moorlands and dense rainforest. Being on the edge of the South-West National Park, it is subject to vicious changes in weather, so even on a day

walk take waterproof gear and warm clothing.

There are some great views from the **Waratah Lookout** (24 km from Geeveston) – look for the jagged peaks of the Snowy Range and the Devils Backbone. There are good walks in the park, including tracks to Hartz Peak (1255 metres), Mt Picton (1327 metres) and the Arthur Range, near Federation Peak (1224 metres). For information about walking in the area, visit the Wilderness Society or Paddy Pallin in Hobart; the Lune River Youth Hostel also has plenty of advice and information, as does the park ranger (☎ (002) 98 3198).

DOVER (population 520)
This picturesque fishing port, 21 km south of Geeveston on the Huon Highway, has some fine beaches and excellent bushwalks; the three small islands in the bay are known as Faith, Hope and Charity. Last century, the processing and exporting of Huon pine was Dover's major industry, and sleepers made here and in the nearby timber towns of Strathblane and Raminea were shipped to China, India and Germany. If you have your own car and are heading further south, it's a good idea to buy petrol and food supplies here.

Places to Stay
The *Dover Beachside Caravan Park* (☎ (002) 98 1301), on Kent Beach Rd, has camp sites ($8), on-site vans ($28) and one cabin ($25). The *Dover Hotel* (☎ (002) 98 1210), on the Huon Highway, charges $28 per person for B&B in the hotel, or there are more expensive motel rooms. *Three Island Holiday Apartments* (☎ (002) 98 1396), on Station Rd, charges $50 a double.

Getting There & Away
Hobart Coaches runs one bus a day to and from Dover on weekdays; the fare is $11 one way.

HASTINGS
Today, it's the spectacular **Hastings Cave &**

Thermal Pool that attract visitors to the once thriving logging and wharf town of Hastings, 21 km south of Dover. The cave is found among the lush vegetation of the **Hastings Caves State Reserve**, 10 km inland from Hastings and well signposted from the Huon Highway. Daily tours of the cave ($8; $1 for children) leave promptly at 11.15 am and 1.15, 2.15 and 3.15 pm, with an extra tour at 4.15 pm from December to April. It's best to allow about 10 minutes for the delightful rainforest walk to the cave entrance.

About five km from the cave is a thermal swimming pool ($2.50; $1.50 for children), filled daily with warm water from a thermal spring. Near the pool there is a kiosk and a restaurant.

For those interested in a more adventurous exploration of the 20-km cave system at Hastings, Exit Cave Adventure Tours (☎ (002) 43 0546) runs a 4½-hour expedition ($80 per person including transport from Hobart) which is suitable for beginners.

LUNE RIVER
A few km south-west of Hastings is Lune River, a haven for gem collectors and the site of Australia's most southerly post office and youth hostel. From here you can also take a scenic 16-km ride on the **Ida Bay Railway** to the lovely beach at Deep Hole Bay. The train departs daily at 11.30 am and 1 and 3 pm (in summer and at weekends there are more services) and costs $9 ($5 for children).

The most southerly drive you can make in Australia is along the secondary road from Lune River to **Cockle Creek** and beautiful **Recherche Bay**. This is an area of spectacular mountain peaks, endless beaches and secluded coves – ideal for camping and bushwalking. This is also the start (or end) of the challenging South Coast Track, which, with the right preparation and a week or so to spare, will take you all the way to Port Davey in the south-west.

Places to Stay
The *Lune River Youth Hostel* (☎ (002) 98 3163), also known as the Doing Place, charges $10 a night. It's a cosy hostel and

there's certainly plenty to do – ask the managers about hiring mountain bikes or kayaks, or about bushwalking, fishing and caving. Don't forget to bring plenty of food with you as the hostel only has basic supplies.

About half a km further south, *Ida Bay Holiday Units* (☎ (002) 98 3110) offers backpackers' accommodation for $10 a night, but you need all your own bedding. The *Lune River Cottage* (☎ (002) 98 3107) has three rooms at $28/50, but no cooking facilities.

Getting There & Away
The Lune River Hostel also runs a shuttle service every Tuesday from the Adelphi Court Youth Hostel in Hobart to Lune River. The cost is $16, which includes your first night's accommodation at the hostel. A return trip leaves Lune River for Adelphi Court every Monday ($10).

Tasman Peninsula

The Arthur Highway runs from Hobart through Sorell and Copping to Port Arthur, 100 km away. As there is no bank on the Tasman Peninsula and the supermarkets are quite expensive, it's a good idea to take advantage of both the banking and shopping facilities at Sorell. And to get you into the convict mood, there's an excellent **colonial convict exhibition** at Copping, which features many objects once used at Port Arthur.

PORT ARTHUR
In 1830, Governor Arthur chose the Tasman Peninsula as the place to confine prisoners who had committed further crimes in the colony. He called the peninsula a 'natural penitentiary' because it was only connected to the mainland by a narrow strip of land, less than 100 metres wide, called Eaglehawk Neck. To deter convicts from escaping, ferocious guard dogs were chained in a line across the isthmus and a rumour circulated that the waters on either side were infested with sharks.

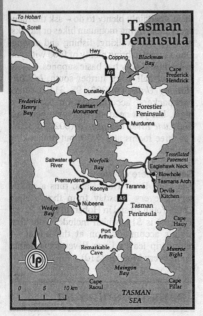

Tasman Peninsula

Between 1830 and 1877, about 12,500 convicts served sentences at Port Arthur, and for most of them it was a living hell. With its Model Prison, featuring a new system of solitary confinement, which replaced brutal beatings, Port Arthur was seen as an advancement in prison reform. In reality, however, the punishment of total isolation and sensory deprivation sent the convicts mad.

The township of Port Arthur became the centre of a network of penal stations on the peninsula and was, itself, much more than just a prison town. It had fine buildings and thriving industries including timber milling, shipbuilding, coal mining, brick and nail production and shoemaking. Australia's first railway literally 'ran' the seven km between Norfolk Bay and Long Bay: convicts pushed the carriages along the tracks. A semaphore telegraph system allowed instant communication between Port Arthur, the penal outstations and Hobart. Convict farms pro-

vided fresh vegetables, a boys' prison was built at Point Puer to reform and educate juvenile convicts, and a church, one of the most readily recognised tourist sights in Australia, was erected.

The Isle of the Dead, in the middle of Carnarvon Bay, was the cemetery for 1769 convicts and 180 free settlers and officers. Convicts were buried six or seven to a grave with no headstones, their bodies wrapped in sailcloth and covered with quicklime.

Today, the well-presented historic site of Port Arthur is Tasmania's premier tourist attraction. For a fee of $12 ($5 for children) you can visit all the restored buildings including the Lunatic Asylum (now a museum) and the Model Prison. The ticket is valid for 24 hours and entitles you to free admission to the museum and a guided tour of the settlement. The tours are well worthwhile and leave hourly from the car park in front of the information office (☎ (002) 50 2363) between 9.30 am and 3.30 pm. Once you've entered the site you can also take a cruise to the Isle of the Dead, or a historic tour in a horse-drawn carriage, but both cost extra. The site is open daily from 9 am to 5 pm, and there's nothing to stop you from wandering around outside those hours without paying the entry fee, although the museum and tours are closed.

Activities

Ghostly apparitions, poltergeists and unexplained happenings have been recorded at Port Arthur since the 1870s, and nightly lantern-lit walking 'Ghost Tours' of the buildings and ruins are fun but also pretty spooky. From December to April, two-hour Ghost Tours leave from outside the information office at 9.30 pm, and are well worth the $6.

Places to Stay

The *Port Arthur Garden Point Caravan Park* (☎ (002) 50 2340) is two km before Port Arthur and has good cooking shelters and a laundry. It costs $9 for two people to camp and $45 a double for a cabin. The *Stewart*

Bay beach is accessible by a short walking track.

The *Port Arthur Youth Hostel* (☎ (002) 50 2311) is very well positioned on the edge of the historic site and charges $10 a night. To get there, continue half a km past the Port Arthur turn-off and turn left at the sign for the hostel and the Port Arthur Motor Inn. You can buy your historic-site entry ticket at the hostel.

Apart from this, most of Port Arthur's accommodation is pricey. The *Port Arthur Motor Inn* (☎ (002) 50 2101) also overlooks the site and has rooms from $68/80. In this same area, but without views of the ruins, are the *Port Arthur Villas* (☎ (002) 50 2239). These self-contained units sleep four to six people and cost $60 per double plus $12 for each extra adult.

Port Arthur Holiday World (☎ (002) 50 2262) is a somewhat grandiose name for a group of pleasant log cabins, on the highway about 500 metres before the turn-off to the historic site. The cabins can accommodate up to eight people and cost $60 for a double plus $10 for each extra adult. There's a licensed restaurant here, and the sheltered swimming beach of Stewart Bay is just a few minutes walk away.

Places to Eat

The licensed *Frances Langford Tea Rooms*, in the restored policemen's quarters inside the settlement, is a good place for a cuppa or for a light lunch, and is open from 10 am to 5 pm. Also at the historic site is the *Parsonage Restaurant*, housed (strangely enough) in the old parsonage. It offers more formal dining and is open daily from noon until 8.30 pm. The *Broad Arrow* cafeteria is next to the information office and is open from 9 am to 6 pm (5 pm in the low season).

The *Port Arthur Motor Inn*, next to the youth hostel, often has cheap specials on the menu.

Entertainment

During the high season there is some unique entertainment at Port Arthur. From October to May at 7.45 pm every evening the classic 1926 silent movie *For the Term of His Natural Life* is screened at the Broad Arrow cafeteria. This film, based on the Marcus Clarke novel about convict life and filmed on location in Port Arthur, costs $5 and finishes just in time for the Port Arthur Ghost Tour.

Getting There & Away

If you don't have your own transport, the only way to take a day trip to Port Arthur from Hobart is on an organised tour; if you want to use public transport, you'll have to stay the night.

Hobart Coaches has a weekday service once a day which travels via most towns on the Tasman Peninsula and costs $11 one way. The Peninsula Coach Service (☎ (002) 50 3186) also runs one service a day on weekdays, and visits many of the sights on the Peninsula ($9 one way). It operates from the Transit Centre in Hobart and will pick you up or drop you off at the youth hostel in Port Arthur.

To get to the east coast from Port Arthur, take the morning Hobart Coaches bus (7 am) as far as Sorell, and ask the bus driver to radio ahead to ensure that the connecting Hobart Coaches bus to Bicheno waits for you.

AROUND THE PENINSULA

The Tasman Peninsula has many bushwalks, superb scenery, delightful stretches of beach and beautiful bays. Near Eaglehawk Neck there are the incredible coastal formations of the **Tessellated Pavement**, the **Devils Kitchen**, the **Blowhole** and **Tasmans Arch**.

South of Port Arthur is **Remarkable Cave**, which you can walk through when the tide is out. You can also visit the remains of the penal outstations at **Koonya**, **Premaydena** and **Saltwater River**, and the ruins of the dreaded **Coal Mines Station**. The **Tasmanian Devil Park** at Taranna is open daily and admission is $6. The **Bush Mill**, on the Arthur Highway, features a steam railway and pioneer settlement; admission here is $12 ($7 for children).

Organised Tours

Remarkable Tours (☎ (002) 50 2359) runs

Tasmanian devil track pattern

one trip a day ($5) to Remarkable Cave as well as twilight tours of the peninsula's other attractions, and bookings are essential. Tours leave from the car park in front of Port Arthur's information office.

Places to Stay & Eat

At Eaglehawk Neck, 20 km before the penal settlement, is the *Eaglehawk Neck Backpackers* (☎ (002) 50 3248), on Old Jetty Rd. It's a small, friendly, smoke-free hostel charging $10 a night, and a good base from which to do the many hikes in the area. Delicious home-grown vegetables are available from the hostel managers.

In the pleasant seaside town of Nubeena, 11 km beyond Port Arthur, the *White Beach Caravan Park* (☎ (002) 50 2142) has camp sites ($10), on-site vans ($28) and cabins ($40). Also worth checking out is *Parker's Holiday Cottages* (☎ (002) 50 2138), where self-contained five-bed units cost $45 for a double and $6 for each additional person. The *Nubeena Tavern* does good counter meals.

At Koonya, originally an outstation of Port Arthur, there's colonial-style accommodation at the *Cascades* (☎ (002) 50 3121). The Officers' Quarters are one-bedroom units which cost $75 for a double, while the Overseers Cottage accommodates three and also costs $75.

There are also free but basic camping facilities at Lime Bay and White Beach run by the Department of Parks, Wildlife & Heritage. At Fortescue Bay there are two camping grounds – Banksia and Mill Creek – run by the Forestry Commission of Tasmania (☎ (002) 50 2433). There's no power, but cold showers and firewood are available. The charge is $6 per person.

East Coast & North-East

Tasmania's scenic east coast, with its long sandy beaches, fine fishing and rare peacefulness, is known as the 'sun coast' because of its mild climate. The area boasts more than 2250 hours of sunshine a year.

Exploration and settlement of the region, which was found to be most suitable for grazing, proceeded rapidly after the establishment of Hobart in 1803. Offshore fishing and particularly whaling also became important, as did tin mining and timber cutting. Many of the convicts who served out their terms in the area stayed on to help the settlers lay the foundations of the fishing, wool, beef and grain industries which are still important today.

The largest town on the coast is St Helens, with a population of only 1000, and a leisurely trip up the Tasman Highway to this north-eastern town is highly recommended. The spectacular scenery around Coles Bay is not to be missed, and Bicheno and Swansea are pleasant seaside towns in which to spend a few restful days.

Banking facilities on the east coast are very limited and in some towns the banks are only open one or two days a week. There are agencies for the Commonwealth Bank at all post offices. If you get stuck for money at a weekend, the only key-card facility on the coast is at the 4-Square store in Bicheno.

Getting There & Around

Bus Redline and Hobart Coaches are the main bus companies operating on the east coast, but a couple of smaller companies – Peakes Coach Service (☎ (003) 72 2390), Bicheno Coach Services (☎ (003) 75 1461) and Suncoast Bus Service (☎ (003) 76 1807) – also do runs between Swansea, Coles Bay, Bicheno, St Marys, St Helens and Derby. With all of these you can buy your tickets when boarding. The Redline Tassie Bus Pass can be used on services run by Peakes.

Bus services are limited at weekends, so it might take a little longer to travel between towns than you anticipate.

Bicycle Cycling along the east coast is one of the most pleasant ways of appreciating this part of Tasmania. If you are planning to cycle between Swansea and Coles Bay, there's an informal boat service for cyclists and hikers which operates between the eastern end of Nine Mile Beach and Swanwick, just north of Coles Bay. The 10-minute trip costs $8 and you need to phone ahead (☎ (002) 57 0239). The service only runs from October to mid-May, but will save you a 65-km ride.

BUCKLAND

This tiny township, 61 km from Hobart, was once a staging post for coaches. Ye Olde Buckland Inn, at 5 Kent St, welcomed coach drivers and travellers a century ago and today offers a good counter lunch from Thursday to Sunday.

The stone **Church of St John the Baptist**, dating from 1846, is worth a visit. It has a stained-glass window which was rescued from a 14th-century abbey in England just before Cromwell sacked the building.

ORFORD (population 500)

Orford is a popular little seaside resort on the Prosser River (named after an escaped prisoner who was caught on its banks). The area has good fishing, swimming and some excellent walks.

Places to Stay

There's plenty of accommodation in Orford, although the cheapest is probably the *Sea Breeze Holiday Cabins* (☎ (002) 57 1375). It is on the corner of Rudd Ave and Walpole St and charges $35 a double. On the Tasman Highway, the *Blue Waters Motor Hotel* (☎ (002) 57 1102) has singles/doubles for

$35/45, while the *Island View Motel* (☎ (002) 57 1114) has them for $42/50.

More lavish, and expensive, is the *Eastcoaster Resort*, on Louisville Point Rd, four km north of the post office. (You can catch the catamaran to Maria Island here.)

TRIABUNNA (population 830)

The larger town of Triabunna, a little further north, was a whaling station and garrison town when nearby Maria Island was a penal settlement. Today its main industries are fishing and woodchip processing.

There's a small Pioneer & Working Horse Museum on the main street, which is open daily from 9 am to 5 pm; admission is $4 ($2 for children).

You can also charter boats for fishing and cruising and go bushwalking or horse riding at popular Woodstock Farm (☎ (002) 57 3186). The ferry to Maria Island leaves from the jetty at Triabunna.

Places to Stay & Eat

The *Triabunna Caravan Park* (☎ (002) 57 3575), on the corner of Vicary and Melbourne Sts, has camp sites ($7) and on-site vans ($23 double). The *Triabunna Youth Hostel* (☎ (002) 57 3439), in Spencer St, is a comfortable and quiet place to stay for $9 a night. It's set in farmland, across the bridge from the main part of town. The *Spring Bay Hotel* in Charles St by the jetty has rooms at $30/50 and good cheap counter meals.

MARIA ISLAND NATIONAL PARK

In 1971 Maria Island was declared a wildlife sanctuary and a year later became a national park. It's popular with bird-watchers, being the only national park in Tasmania where you can see 11 of the state's native bird species. Forester kangaroos, Cape Barren geese and emus are a common sight during the day.

This peaceful island features some magnificent scenery, including fossil-studded sandstone and limestone cliffs, beautiful white, sandy beaches, forests and fern gullies. There are some lovely walks on the island, including the Bishop & Clerk Mountain Walk and the historical Fossil Cliffs Nature Walk; brochures are available for both. The marine life around the island is also diverse and plentiful, and for those with the equipment, the scuba diving is spectacular.

Historically, Maria Island is also very interesting – from 1825 to 1832, the settlement of Darlington was Tasmania's second penal colony (the first was Sarah Island near Strahan). The remains of the penal village, including the commissariat store (1825) and the mill house (1846), are remarkably well preserved and easy to visit; in fact, you'll probably end up staying in one of the old buildings. There are no shops on the island so don't forget to bring your own supplies.

Places to Stay
The rooms in the penitentiary at Darlington and some of the other buildings have been converted into bunkhouses for visitors. These are called the *Parks, Wildlife & Heritage Penitentiary Units* (☎ (002) 57 1420) and cost $8 a night, but it's wise to book, as the beds are sometimes taken by school groups. There is also a camping ground on the island.

Getting There & Away
The ferry MV *Maria Lady* (☎ (002) 57 3264) operates once a day between the Triabunna Jetty and Darlington, on Maria Island. The return fare is $16 for day visitors ($10 for children) and $19 ($12) for campers. There are two extra trips each day in the summer months. Bad weather can sometimes delay the service so be prepared to stay a day or so longer on the island if necessary.

Another service, the Catamaran Express (☎ (002) 57 1172), is operated by the Eastcoaster Resort, Louisville Point Rd, four km north of the Orford post office. It has up to four services a day, departing from the resort jetty. Fares are the same as for the ferry.

SWANSEA (population 420)
On the shores of Great Oyster Bay, with superb views across to the Freycinet Peninsula, Swansea is a popular place for camping, boating, fishing and surfing. It was first settled in the 1820s and is the administrative centre for Glamorgan, Australia's oldest rural municipality.

Swansea has a number of interesting historic buildings including the original council chambers, which are still in use, and the lovely red-brick Morris's General Store, built in 1838. The **community centre** dates from 1860 and houses a museum of local history and the only oversized billiard table in Australia. The museum is open from Monday to Saturday and admission is $2.

The **Swansea Bark Mill & East Coast Museum**, at 96 Tasman Highway, is also worth a look. In one section, the processing of black-wattle bark, a basic ingredient used in the tanning of heavy leathers, is demonstrated while the adjoining museum features displays of Swansea's early history, including some superb old photographs. It's open daily from 9 am to 5 pm and admission is $4.50 ($2.25 for children).

Places to Stay & Eat
The *Swansea Caravan Park* (☎ (002) 57 8177) in Shaw St, just by the beach, is very clean and has camp sites ($11) and cabins ($30).

The *Swansea Youth Hostel* (☎ (002) 57 8367), at 5 Franklin St, is in a lovely spot right by the sea, although it's not a particularly attractive building. It charges $9 a night, and in the busy summer season priority is given to YHA members.

More appealing is the smoke-free *Central Swansea Backpackers* (☎ (002) 57 8399), at 20 Franklin St. It's in an attractive old house in the main street, and the charge is $12 per person.

Also in Franklin St, almost opposite the youth hostel, is the *Oyster Bay Guest House* (☎ (002) 57 8110), which was built in 1836 and offers friendly colonial accommodation at $35/55 for singles/doubles with a cooked breakfast.

Just Maggies, at 26 Franklin St, has coffee, cakes and light lunches, but for breakfast go to the *Swansea Pier Milk Bar*, just along the road. The *Swan Inn* does counter meals, or for something special try the licensed *Shy Albatross Restaurant* in the Oyster Bay Guest House.

Getting There & Away
Hobart Coaches has at least one morning and afternoon service between Hobart and Bicheno ($17.90 one way) via Swansea ($14.60) on most days except Saturday. The Hobart Coaches agent in Swansea is the Shell service station in Franklin St.

On weekdays only, Redline has one service between Launceston and Bicheno ($18) via Swansea ($14.40). The route runs through Campbell Town and past the Lake Leake turn-off. There's also a daily service between Hobart and Bicheno ($25.80) via Swansea ($22.40) from Monday to Friday. The Redline agent in Swansea is the Food Store at 8 Franklin St.

Peakes Coach Service runs a daily bus on weekdays between Swansea and St Marys ($8) via Bicheno ($4). The buses depart from Morris's General Store in Franklin St.

COLES BAY & FREYCINET NATIONAL PARK
The tiny township of Coles Bay is both dominated and sheltered by the spectacular 300-metre-high, pink granite mountains known as the Hazards. It's the gateway to many white-sand beaches, secluded coves, rocky cliffs and excellent bushwalks in the Freycinet National Park.

The park, incorporating Freycinet Peninsula, beautiful Schouten Island and the Friendly Beaches (on the east coast north of Coles Bay), is noted for its coastal heaths, orchids and other wildflowers and for its wildlife, including black cockatoos, yellow wattlebirds, yellow-throated honeyeaters and Bennetts wallabies. Walks include a 27-km circuit of the peninsula plus many other shorter tracks, one of the most beautiful being the return walk to **Wineglass Bay**, which takes from 2½ to three hours. On any walk remember to sign in (and sign out) at the registration booth at the car park. For

more information contact the ranger station on ☎ (002) 57 0107.

There is one general store in Coles Bay which sells groceries, basic supplies and petrol, and hires out small motor boats, a large speed boat (for which you need a licence) and scuba-diving tanks.

On the road in to Coles Bay, look out for **Moulting Lagoon**, which is a breeding ground for black swans.

Places to Stay
The *Iluka Holiday Centre* (☎ (002) 57 0115) on Muirs Beach has the cheapest accommodation in Coles Bay itself. This place is not as well kept as it might be and is definitely a bit rough around the edges. There's a variety of on-site vans ($30) and cabins ($45). The *Coles Bay Caravan Park* (☎ (002) 57 0100) also has on-site vans at $30, but it's four km from the town, on the Bicheno road.

The *Coles Bay Youth Hostel*, actually in the national park, is mainly used by groups, and must be booked at the YHA state office in Hobart (☎ (002) 34 9617).

There are a number of private shacks and cabins for rent, and these are probably the best deal for a group of people. *Pine Lodge Cabins* (☎ (002) 57 0113) in Harold St has two cabins which sleep four to five and these are good value at $45 per cabin, even with a one-night surcharge. *Jessie's Cottage* (☎ (002) 57 0143) right on the Esplanade by the general store is neat and cosy. It sleeps four and costs $60 for a double.

Actually in the national park is the recently refurbished *Freycinet Lodge* (☎ (002) 57 0101), a group of cabins leading down to the water's edge. Prices start at $45 per person, and there's a variety of rooms – including some with spas, which unfortunately only exacerbate the town's chronic water problems.

Sites at the main national park camping ground (☎ (002) 57 0107) cost $10 a double. Facilities are basic – pit toilets and cold water. During school holidays and at Easter and Christmas it is essential to book.

The scenery at the free camp sites of Wineglass Bay (one to 1½ hours), Hazards Beach (two to three hours) and Cooks Beach (about 4½ hours) is well worth the walk. There's no reliable drinking water at any of these sites, and little elsewhere on the peninsula, so you'll need to carry your own.

Places to Eat

Eating options are limited. The only eatery is at the *Freycinet Lodge*, and it's not that cheap, but the views across the bay are superb. Other than that it's a matter of putting your own food together. The general store is pretty well stocked, and the kiosk at Iluka also has some supplies.

Getting There & Away

Redline and Hobart Coaches can drop you at the Coles Bay turn-off en route to Bicheno and you can hitch the 28 km from there, but traffic may be light. Bicheno Coach Services (☎ (002) 57 0293) runs at least two buses each weekday between Coles Bay and Bicheno, and one on Saturdays. In Bicheno, buses depart from the newsagency in Foster St, and in Coles Bay, from the general store; tickets are $5 per person and $2.50 for a bicycle.

It is more than five km from the town to the national park walking-tracks car park, and Bicheno Coach Services has a weekday shuttle bus. You must book, however. The cost is $2 return. It leaves the general store at 9.40 am, and departs the car park for the return trip at 10 am.

BICHENO (population 700)

In the early 1800s, whalers and sealers used Bicheno's tiny, picturesque harbour, called the Gulch, to shelter their boats. They also built lookouts in the hills to watch for passing whales. These days, fishing is still one of the town's major occupations, and if you are down at the Gulch around lunch time, when all the fishing boats return, you can buy fresh crayfish, abalone, oysters or anything else caught that night straight from the boats. Tourism is also very important to Bicheno; it's a lovely spot to visit for a few days.

Things to See & Do

An interesting three-km **foreshore walkway** from Redbill Point to the blowhole continues south around the beach to Courlands Bay. For the views, you can also walk up to the **Whalers Lookout** and the **Freycinet Lookout**.

At nightfall you may be lucky enough to see the fairy penguins at the northern end of Redbill Beach and at low tide you can walk out to **Diamond Island**, opposite the youth hostel.

The Dive Centre (☎ (003) 75 1138), opposite the Sea Life Centre on the foreshore, runs courses which are more reasonably priced than those in warmer waters, and you can also hire or buy diving equipment from its shop.

The **Sea Life Centre** is open daily from 9 am to 5 pm and features Tasmanian marine life swimming behind glass windows. There's also a restored trading ketch, but at $4 for admission, the centre is rather over-priced and a bit depressing. Seven km north of town is the 32-hectare **East Coast Birdlife & Animal Park**, which is open daily from 9 am to 5.30 pm; admission is $6.

Just a couple of km north of the animal park is the turn-off to the **Douglas-Apsley National Park**. The park was proclaimed in 1989 and protects a large and undisturbed sclerophyll forest. It has a number of water-falls and gorges, and birds and animals are prolific. There's road access to the **Apsley Gorge** in the south of the park, where there's a waterhole with excellent swimming. You can walk the north-south trail through the park in a couple of days.

Places to Stay

The *Bicheno Cabin & Tourist Park* (☎ (003) 75 1117), in Champ St, has camp sites ($10) and expensive on-site vans ($40). The *Bicheno Campervan Park* (☎ (003) 75 1280), on the corner of Burgess and Tribe Sts, charges $8 a double for a camp site and $28 a double for an on-site van.

Three km north of town, on the beach opposite Diamond Island, is the *Bicheno Youth Hostel* (☎ (003) 75 1293). It charges

$9 a night and may be booked out in summer. The *Bicheno Dive Centre* (☎ (003) 75 1138) has three self-contained cabins, each with six bunks. Although these are used mainly by divers, anyone can stay in them. At $12 per person, they are good value, especially if you get a cabin to yourself. *Camp Seaview* (☎ (003) 75 1247) in Banksia St has dormitory accommodation for $10.

The *Wintersun Lodge Motel* (☎ (003) 75 1225), on the northern outskirts of town at 35 Gordon St, is a friendly place with singles/doubles at $45/50. The *Silver Sands Resort* (☎ (003) 75 1266) has rooms with good views of the bay, and these cost $60/65.

Places to Eat

On the Tasman Highway, the *Longboat Tavern* has good counter meals and seafood. Also on the highway is *Waubs Bay House*, which does eat-in or takeaway pizzas. For lunch you can try the bistro at the *Sea Life Centre*, which specialises in seafood but could give better value for money. In the main shopping centre there's the *Galleon Coffee Shop*, which has reasonably priced meals (and bicycle hire and fishing trips). *Cyrano* is a small seafood restaurant.

About 30 km north of Bicheno is the Chain of Lagoons, where you can buy reasonably priced fresh crayfish from a roadside stand called *Wardlaw's Picnic Crays*.

Getting There & Away

For information on the Bicheno services run by Redline, Hobart Coaches and Peakes Coach Service, see the Getting There & Away section for Swansea. The agent for Redline in Bicheno is Sam's Cut Price Store, 39 Foster St; for Hobart Coaches it's the Mobil service station on the Tasman Highway. The Peakes bus to Swansea and St Marys leaves from the BP service station in Foster St. The Bicheno Coach Services bus to Coles Bay leaves from the newsagency in Foster St.

ST MARYS (population 630)

St Marys is a charming little town, 10 km inland from the coast, near the Mt Nicholas range. There's not much to do there except enjoy the peacefulness of the countryside, visit a number of waterfalls in the area, and take walks in the state forest. St Marys is also an important road junction, as this is where the Tasman Highway meets the A4 which heads west through Fingal and Avoca to the Midland Highway.

Seventeen km north of St Marys is the resort town of **Scamander**, which has excellent beaches for swimming and surfing, and is a popular fishing spot.

Places to Stay & Eat

The superbly positioned *St Marys Youth Hostel* (☎ (003) 72 2341), on a working sheep farm called Seaview, is surrounded by state forest. It's at the end of a dirt track, eight km from St Marys on German Town Rd, and commands magnificent views of the coast, ocean and mountains. It costs $8 a night to stay in the hostel and $20 a double in units. The hostel is a great place to stay and you can either hitch up there or the warden will pick you up from the post office between 10 and 11 am any day except Sunday.

Accommodation is also available in the *St Marys Hotel* (☎ (003) 72 2181), where singles/doubles cost $18/32. The pub also has counter meals, or there's the *Coach House Restaurant* in the main street, which has pizzas and takeaways.

Getting There & Away

The Peakes bus between St Marys and Swansea ($8) via Bicheno ($4) departs from the newsagency on Gray Rd.

Redline has one service from Launceston ($13.40), and another from Hobart ($25.20) every day except Saturday – both continuing on to St Helens. The Redline agent in St Marys is the newsagency on Gray Rd.

ST HELENS (population 1150)

St Helens, on Georges Bay, is the largest town on the east coast and a popular holiday destination. First settled in 1830, this old whaling town has an interesting and varied history which is recorded in the **History Room**, at 59 Cecilia St, adjacent to the town's library. The room is open weekdays from 9 am to 4 pm and admission is $2.

Today, St Helens is Tasmania's largest fishing port, with a big fleet based in the bay. Visitors can charter boats for offshore game fishing or just a lazy cruise.

While the beaches in town are not particularly good for swimming, there are excellent scenic beaches at **Binalong Bay** (10 km from St Helens), **Sloop Rock** (12 km) and **Stieglitz** (seven km), as well as at St Helens and Humbug points. You can also visit **St Columba Falls**, near Pyengana, 24 km away.

The town's only bank, Westpac, is open only on Thursdays all year round, except during January and February, when it is also open on Tuesdays.

Places to Stay

The *St Helens Caravan Park* (☎ (003) 76 1290), in Penelope St, is a little way out of town, along the road to St Marys. There are camp sites ($10), on-site vans ($30) and cabins ($38).

The *St Helens Youth Hostel* (☎ (003) 76 1661), at 5 Cameron St, is in a lovely, quiet spot by the beach and charges $10 a night. The *St Helens Hotel Motel* (☎ (003) 76 1133), at 49 Cecilia St, has quite adequate rooms at $20/45. There are also more up-market rooms at $40/60 for singles/doubles, and reasonably priced counter meals.

The *Artnor Lodge* (☎ (003) 76 1234) is a comfortable guesthouse on the main street in the middle of town. Rooms cost $35/45 with a continental breakfast. For self-catering accommodation, try the *Queechy Cottages* (☎ (003) 76 1321), on the highway about a km south of the centre. The units here sleep four to six people and cost $44 for a double, plus $12 for each extra adult.

Places to Eat

Trimbole's Italian Restaurant on the main street does good pizza and pasta, or there are takeaways such as *Deano's*. If you are doing your own cooking, *Ripples* sells fresh seafood.

Getting There & Away

Redline has daily (except Saturday) connections to Launceston ($16.60) and Hobart ($28.80). The Redline agent in St Helens is the newsagency in Cecilia St. During the week you can get to St Marys or Derby (to connect with the Redline bus to Launceston) with Suncoast Bus Service.

WELDBOROUGH

The Weldborough Pass, with its mountain scenery and dense rainforests, is quite spectacular. During the tin-mining boom last century, hundreds of Chinese migrated to Tasmania and many made Weldborough their base. The famous Joss House, now in Launceston's Queen Victoria Museum & Art Gallery, was built in Weldborough.

The *Weldborough Hotel*, the town's only pub, also calls itself the Worst Little Pub in Tassie and has, among other things, 'leprechaun pea soup' and 'blowfly sponge' on the menu, but don't be put off – it's quite a nice place to stop for a drink.

GLADSTONE

About 25 km off the Tasman Highway, between St Helens and Scottsdale, is the tiny town of Gladstone. The town was one of the last tin-mining centres in north-eastern Tasmania, until the mine closed in 1982. At one time, the area had a number of mining communities and a large Chinese population. Today, many of the old mining settlements are just ghost towns, and Gladstone shows signs of heading that way too.

Twelve km from Gladstone is the popular **Mt William National Park**, where you can see large numbers of Forester kangaroos. The park also has some excellent beaches – Picnic Rocks is a good surf beach – and there are good bushwalking opportunities along the beaches and fire trails. There are three bush camp sites with pit toilets and bore water, so you need to carry drinking water. The **Eddystone Lighthouse**, built in 1887, is within the park boundary. For more information, phone the ranger station on ☎ (003) 57 2108.

You can get to Gladstone on the mail run,

which departs daily from outside the post office in Derby.

DERBY

In 1874, tin was discovered in Derby, and due mainly to the famous Briseis Tin Mine, this little township flourished throughout the late 19th century. Today Derby is a classified historic town, and some of the old mine buildings are now part of the excellent **Tin Mine Centre**, which features a mine museum of old photographs and mining implements, and a re-creation of an old mining shanty town. The centre is open from 10 am to 4 pm and admission is $4 ($1.50 for children).

Places to Stay & Eat

The *Dorset Hotel* (☎ (003) 54 2360) has singles/doubles for $28/45 with breakfast, and also does good counter meals. The *Crib Shed Tea Rooms* (part of the mine museum) specialises in country cooking and serves delicious scones.

Six km from Winnaleah, near Derby, is the peaceful *Merlinkei Home Hostel* (☎ (003) 54 2152), which charges $9 a night. If you are hitching, most vehicles will give you a lift, or if you ring from Winnaleah, the manager will pick you up. Being a dairy farm, it has an unlimited supply of fresh milk, and hostellers can help around the farm and even earn a 'milking certificate'.

Getting There & Away

On weekdays, Redline has a daily service between Launceston and Winnaleah ($12.40) via Derby ($11) and Scottsdale. There's only one service on Sundays, and none on Saturdays. The Redline agent is the general store in Derby's main street. On weekdays, you can get to St Helens and Winnaleah on the Suncoast bus.

SCOTTSDALE (population 2000)

Scottsdale, the major town in the north-east, serves some of Tasmania's richest agricultural and forestry country, and its setting is consequently quite beautiful. A camp site at the nearby *Scottsdale Camping Ground*

(☎ (003) 52 2176) costs $5. Of the two hotels in town, accommodation is cheapest at *Lords Hotel* (☎ (003) 52 2319), at 2 King St.

At Nabowla, 21 km west of Scottsdale, is the **Bridestowe Lavender Farm**. It's open daily during the spectacular flowering season from Boxing Day until the third week in January, and admission is $3. At other times it is open on weekdays only, and entry is free. Twenty-one km north of Scottsdale is the popular beach resort of **Bridport**, where there's plenty of accommodation. From there, it's another 45 km to the unspoiled beaches and great diving and snorkelling at **Tomahawk**.

For bus services to Scottsdale, see the Getting There & Away section for Derby. To get to Bridport, you can take a local bus from Scottsdale; buses depart twice daily on weekdays from the Redline stop in Scottsdale. You'll need your own transport to visit Tomahawk.

BEN LOMOND NATIONAL PARK

This 165-sq-km park, 50 km south-east of Launceston, includes the entire Ben Lomond Range and is best known for its good snow coverage and skiing facilities. During the ski season, a kiosk, tavern and restaurant are open in the alpine village and there's accommodation at the *Creek Inn* (☎ (003) 72 2444) for $78 a double for B&B. To check conditions for downhill or cross-country skiing, ring Ben Lomond Ski Rentals (☎ (003) 31 1312) or listen to 7LA radio for snow reports. Lift tickets and all ski equipment hire here cost about half what they do on the mainland.

The scenery at Ben Lomond is magnificent all year round and the park is particularly noted for its alpine wildflowers which run riot in spring and summer. The park's highest point is Legges Tor (1573 metres), which is also the second highest peak in Tasmania. It can be reached via a good walking track from Carr Villa, on the slopes of Ben Lomond. The ranger's telephone number is ☎ (003) 90 6279.

Getting There & Away

During the ski season, Tasmanian Wilderness Transport has a daily return service ($25) between the ski fields and the rear entrance of Paddy Pallin at 59 Brisbane St, Launceston. Tasmanian Wilderness Transport also runs a shuttle service from the bottom of Jacobs Ladder to the alpine village ($6 one way).

Midlands

Tasmania's midlands region has a definite English feel, due to the diligent efforts of early settlers who planted English trees and hedgerows. The agricultural potential of the area contributed to Tasmania's rapid settlement, and coach stations, garrison towns, stone villages and pastoral properties soon sprang up as convict gangs constructed the main road between Hobart and Launceston. Fine wool, beef cattle and timber milling put the midlands on the map and these, along with tourism, are still the main industries.

The course of the Midland Highway has changed slightly from its original route and many of the historic towns are now bypassed, but it's definitely worth making a few detours to see them.

Getting There & Away
Both Redline and Hobart Coaches have several daily services up and down the Midland Highway which can drop you off at any of the towns mentioned in this section. Fares from Hobart include Oatlands $9.40, Ross $12.60, Campbell Town $14.20 and Launceston $16.80.

OATLANDS (population 520)
With the largest collection of colonial architecture in Australia, and the largest number of buildings dating from before 1837, the town of Oatlands is not to be missed. In the main street alone, there are 87 historic buildings and the oldest is the 1829 convict-built **courthouse**. Much of the sandstone for these early buildings came from the shores

of **Lake Dulverton**, now a wildlife sanctuary, which is beside the town.

Today, one of Oatlands's main attractions is **Callington Mill**, the restoration of which was Tasmania's main Bicentennial project. The mill features a faithfully restored cap with a fantail attachment that automatically turns its sails into the wind, and you can climb up the middle. It's open on weekdays and admission is free.

An unusual way of seeing Oatlands's sights is to go on one of Peter Fielding's historical tours (☎ (002) 54 1135). The Ghost Tour is a candlelight inspection of historic buildings starting at 8 pm from Callington Mill ($6, or $3 for children); the Convict Tour leaves at 5 pm from the mill and costs $4 ($2 for children).

Places to Stay & Eat
There's plenty of accommodation in Oatlands, although much of it is of the more expensive colonial type. The *Oatlands Youth Hostel* (☎ (002) 54 1320), at 9 Wellington St, is a couple of hundred metres off the main street and charges $10 a night. The *Midlands Hotel* (☎ (002) 54 1103), at 91 High St, charges $30/45 for singles/doubles; the price includes a cooked breakfast. The *Oatlands Lodge* (☎ (002) 54 1444) on the main street has four rooms with attached bath at $65/80 including breakfast.

Holyrood House, on the main street, dates from 1840. It's a good place for meals, which are served by staff in colonial dress.

ROSS (population 280)
This ex-garrison town, 120 km from Hobart, is steeped in colonial charm and history. It was established in 1812 to protect travellers on the main north-south road and was an important coach staging post.

Things to See
The town is famous for the unique convict-built **Ross Bridge**, the third oldest bridge in Australia. Daniel Herbert, a convict stonemason, was granted a pardon for his detailed

work on the 184 panels which decorate the arches.

In the heart of town is a crossroads which can lead you in one of four directions – 'temptation' (represented by the Man-O'-Ross Hotel), 'salvation' (the Catholic church), 'recreation' (the town hall) and 'damnation' (the old jail).

Other interesting historic buildings include the **Scotch Thistle Inn**, first licensed in 1840 as a coaching inn and now a licensed restaurant; the **old barracks**, restored by the National Trust; the **Uniting Church** (1885); **St John's Church of England** (1868); and the **post office** (1896).

The **Tasmanian Wool Centre**, a museum and craft shop in Church St, is open daily from 9.30 am to 5.30 pm; entry to the shop is free, to the museum $4 ($2 for children). Also in Church St is a small **militaria museum**, open from Saturday to Thursday.

Places to Stay

Adjacent to the Ross Bridge is the *Ross Caravan Park* (☎ (003) 81 5462), which has cheap camp sites ($5) and good-value on-site cabins ($25). The *Man-O'-Ross Hotel* (☎ (003) 81 5240), in Church St, has singles/doubles for $30/48. If you want to treat yourself, then stay in either *Apple Dumpling Cottage* (1880) or *Hudson Cottage* (1850). Both cost $75 a double including a light breakfast and need to be booked (☎ (003) 81 5354).

CAMPBELL TOWN (population 820)

Twelve km from Ross is Campbell Town, another former garrison settlement which boasts plenty of examples of early colonial architecture. These include the convict-built **Red Bridge** (1836), the **Grange** (1847), **St Luke's Church of England** (1835), the **Campbell Town Inn** (1840), the building known as the **Fox Hunters Return** (1829), and the **old school** (1878).

There's a secondary road from Campbell Town, through the excellent fishing and bushwalking area around **Lake Leake** (32 km), to Swansea on the east coast. The daily

Redline bus from Hobart to Bicheno travels via this route and can drop you at the Lake Leake turn-off, four km from the lake. From Conara Junction, 11 km north of Campbell Town, the A4 heads east from the Midland Highway to St Marys.

Launceston

Population 66,750

Officially founded by Lieutenant-Colonel William Paterson in 1805, Launceston is Australia's third oldest city and the commercial centre of northern Tasmania.

The Tamar River estuary was discovered in 1798 by Bass and Flinders, who were attempting to circumnavigate Van Diemen's Land to show that it was not joined to the rest of Australia. Launceston was the third attempt at a settlement on the river and was originally called Patersonia, after its founder. In 1907, the city was renamed in honour of Governor King, who was born in Launceston, England, a town settled 1000 years before on the Tamar River in the county of Cornwall.

Orientation

The city centre is arranged in a grid pattern around the Brisbane St Mall, between Charles and St John Sts. Two blocks north, in Cameron St, there's another pedestrian mall called the Civic Square. To the east of both malls is Yorktown Square, a charming and lively area of restored buildings which have been turned into shops and restaurants.

Although Launceston suffers from a lack of street signs, it's not difficult to find your way around. Launceston's main attractions are all within walking distance of the centre.

Information

The Tasmanian Travel & Information Centre (☎ (003) 36 3119), on the corner of St John and Paterson Sts, is open weekdays from 9 am to 5 pm, and on Saturdays and public holidays (and Sundays during the high season) between 9 am and noon. You can

TASMANIA

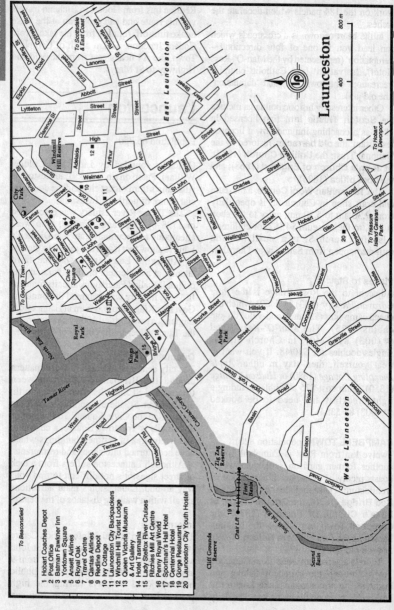

Launceston

800 m

400

0

To Scottsdale
& East Coast

To George Town

To Beaconsfield

To Hobart
& Devonport

To Treasure
Island Caravan Park

East Launceston

West Launceston

Tamar River
North Esk River
South Esk River
Cataract Gorge
First Basin
Second Basin

Zig Zag
Reserve

Cliff Grounds
Reserve

Chair Lift

Royal Park
Kings Park
Civic Square
City Park
Windmill Hill Reserve
Arbor Park

1 Hobart Coaches Depot
2 Post Office
3 Batman Fawkner Inn
4 Yorktown Square
5 Ansett Airlines
6 Royal Oak
7 Travel Centre
8 Qantas Airlines
9 Redline Depot
10 Ivy Cottage
11 Launceston City Backpackers
12 Windmill Hill Tourist Lodge
13 Queen Victoria Museum
   & Art Gallery
14 Hotel Tasmania
15 Lady Stelfox River Cruises
16 Ritchies Mill Art Centre
17 Penny Royal World
18 Sportman's Hall Hotel
19 Gorge Restaurant
20 Launceston City Youth Hostel

also get tourist information from the Wilderness Shop (☎ (003) 34 2499) at 174 Charles St, and there's a Tasmap Centre at Henty House in the Civic Square.

For camping gear try Paddy Pallin, at 59 Brisbane St, and Allgoods, at 60 Elizabeth St – both are excellent. If you're in town at the weekend, there's a craft market in Yorktown Square.

Cataract Gorge

Only a 10-minute walk from the city centre is the magnificent Cataract Gorge. Here, almost vertical cliffs line the banks of the South Esk River as it enters the Tamar. The area around the gorge has been made a reserve for native wildlife and is one of Launceston's most popular tourist attractions.

Two walking tracks, one on either side of the gorge, lead up to **First Basin**, which is filled with water from the South Esk River (the northern trail is easier than the southern). The waters of First Basin are cold and very deep, so you may feel safer swimming in the concrete pool. The landscaped area around the basin features picnic spots, the Gorge Restaurant and a cafe. There's also a chair lift, which crosses the basin to the reserve on the other side; the six-minute ride costs $4 one way or return. A good walking track leads further up the gorge to **Second Basin** and Duck Reach. A little further on is the Trevallyn Dam quarry where you can do some 'simulated' hang-gliding for $7 (open daily in summer, weekends only in winter).

Penny Royal World

The Penny Royal entertainment complex, which claims to take you back to a 'world of yesteryear', has exhibits including working 19th-century water mills and windmills, gunpowder mills and model boats. You can take a ride on a barge or a restored city tram, or, best of all, take a 45-minute cruise up the gorge on the *Lady Stelfox* paddle-steamer. Although some parts of the Penny Royal complex are interesting, overall it's not worth the $19.50 ($9.50 for children) admission. You can, however, just pay for one of the attractions; the cruise, for instance, only costs $6.50 ($3.50 for children).

Queen Victoria Museum & Art Gallery

The Queen Victoria Museum & Art Gallery was built late last century and displays the splendour of the period both inside and out. It has a unique collection of Tasmanian fauna, Aboriginal artefacts, penal-settlement relics and colonial paintings. A major attraction is the splendid joss house, donated by the descendants of Chinese settlers. The museum's planetarium is also popular. The centre is open Monday to Saturday from 10 am to 5 pm, and from 2 to 5 pm on Sundays. The gallery and museum are free, but it costs $1.50 to visit the planetarium, which is open for inspection at 2 pm and 3 pm Tuesday to Saturday.

Community History Museum

The historic Johnstone & Wilmot warehouse, on the corner of Cimitiere and St John Sts, dates from 1842 and holds the Community History Museum. The museum houses the city's local-history archives. It is open from 10 am to 4 pm Monday to Saturday and from 2 to 4 pm on Sundays; admission is $1.

Historic Buildings

In the Civic Square is **Macquarie House**, built in 1830 as a warehouse but later used as a military barracks and office building. It now houses part of the Queen Victoria Museum & Art Gallery and is open from 10 am to 4 pm Monday to Saturday, and on Sunday afternoons.

The **Old Umbrella Shop**, at 60 George St, was built in the 1860s and still houses a selection of umbrellas. Classified by the National Trust, it is the last genuine period shop in the state. The interior is lined with Tasmanian blackwood timber, and the shop sells a good range of National Trust items. It's open from 9 am to 5 pm on weekdays and from 9 am to noon on Saturdays.

On weekdays at 9.45 am there's a one-hour guided historic walk around the city centre. The tours leave from the Tasmanian Travel & Information Centre and cost $10.

If you don't want the tour, pick up a copy of the *Historic Walks* brochure and do it yourself.

On the Midland Highway, six km from the city, is **Franklin House**, one of Launceston's most attractive Georgian homes. It was built in 1838 and has been beautifully restored and furnished by the National Trust. An outstanding feature of its interior is the woodwork, which has been carved from New South Wales cedar. The house is open daily from 9 am to 5 pm (4 pm in winter) and admission is $4.50.

Parks & Gardens

Launceston is sometimes referred to as 'the garden city', and with so many beautiful public squares, parks and reserves, it's easy to understand why.

The 13-hectare **City Park** is a fine example of a Victorian garden and features an elegant fountain, a bandstand, a monkey and wallaby enclosure and a conservatory. **Princes Square**, between Charles and St John Sts, features a bronze fountain bought at the 1858 Paris Exhibition.

Other public parks and gardens include **Royal Park**, near the junction between the North Esk and Tamar rivers; the **Punchbowl Reserve**, with its magnificent rhododendron garden; **Windmill Hill Reserve**; and the **Trevallyn Recreation Area**.

Other Attractions

On Bridge Rd near the Penny Royal is **Ritchies Mill Art Centre**, housed in a restored 1834 flour mill and miller's cottage. As the mill stands by the river in pleasant leafy grounds and has a good restaurant, it's a nice place to spend an hour or two.

The **Design Centre of Tasmania**, on the corner of Brisbane and Tamar Sts, is a retail outlet displaying work by the state's top artists and craftspeople.

The **Waverley Woollen Mills & National Automobile Museum** are on Waverley Rd, five km from the city centre. The mills were established in 1874 and are the oldest operating woollen mills in Australia. The mills are open daily from 9 am to 4 pm, and the

museum until 5 pm; admission is $3 and $4 respectively.

The **Tamar Knitting Mills**, founded in 1926, are at 21 Hobart Rd and can also be inspected. They are open daily from 9 am to 4 pm, and admission is $1.

Organised Tours

Redline Coaches (☎ (003) 31 3233) in George St has half and full-day tours of Launceston ($23), the Tamar Valley ($26), the north-west coast ($32), the north-east ($40) and Cradle Mountain ($47). Tasmanian Wilderness Transport has tours to wilderness areas like Cradle Mountain and Lake St Clair that take between one and four days.

Places to Stay

Camping The *Treasure Island Caravan Park* (☎ (003) 44 2600) is in Glen Dhu St, past the Launceston City Youth Hostel. It has camp sites ($9), on-site vans ($32) and cabins ($42). As this is the only caravan park in Launceston, it can get crowded at times, and being right next to the highway is quite noisy.

Hostels Conveniently located in the centre of town is the smoke-free *Launceston City Backpackers*, signposted back from the road at 139 George St. It's an old house which has been thoughtfully renovated, and the cost is $14 per person in four-bed rooms. The hostel is not on the phone, but the owners can be contacted on (003) 34 2327.

The *Launceston City Youth Hostel* (☎ (003) 44 9779), which is not a YHA hostel, is at 36 Thistle St, two km from the centre of town. It has dorm beds and family rooms for $12 a night. The building dates from the 1940s and used to be the canteen for the Coats Patons woollen mill. The hostel has mountain and touring bikes for hire as well as a comprehensive selection of bushwalking gear.

Guesthouses The cosy *Ashton Gate Tourist Lodge* (☎ (003) 31 6180) is at 32 High St, and charges $45/55 for singles/doubles with breakfast. A few doors away, at 22 High St, the *Windmill Hill Tourist Lodge* (☎ (003) 31 9337) charges $40/50. The lodge also has self-contained holiday flats at $55 a double.

If you can afford the extra, there are some great guesthouses offering rather luxurious colonial accommodation, such as *Airlie Dorset Terrace* (☎ (003) 34 2162), at 138 St John St, where singles/doubles cost $57/70, including a cooked breakfast.

For something really special, you could try renting your own fully furnished two-bedroom colonial cottage. The wonderful *Ivy Cottage* and *Alice's Place* (☎ (003) 34 2231 for both) are next door to each other at 17 York St. Both are only a short stroll from the city centre and have their own small gardens. They each cost $115 for two people, and $25 for each additional person.

Another place with a history is the *Old Bakery Inn* (☎ (003) 31 7900) on the corner of York and Margaret Sts. It dates back to 1870, has 26 rooms and charges $68/87. The *Antiquity Lodge* (☎ (003) 31 5651) at 45 Elizabeth St also has atmosphere. The two self-contained units cost $85 for a double plus $20 for each extra person.

Hotels Launceston has a good selection of hotels for a town of its size. One of the cheapest and quietest is the *Sportsman's Hall Hotel* (☎ (003) 31 3968), at 252 Charles St, where singles/doubles cost $28/40, which includes breakfast.

Close by, at 191 Charles St, is the *Hotel Tasmania* (☎ (003) 31 7355), which has rooms with a fridge, tea- and coffee-making facilities and telephone for $40/56; the price includes breakfast.

The *TRC Hotel* (☎ (003) 31 3424), adjacent to the Penny Royal Windmill at 131 Paterson St, has good, clean rooms with bathroom for $28/46, including a cooked breakfast; the staff here are very friendly.

Motels & Holiday Flats Although fairly close to the city centre, the *Mews Mini Motel* (☎ (003) 31 2861), at 89 Margaret St, is in a quiet part of town. Rooms cost $60 a double, which includes breakfast. The *Motel Maldon*

(☎ (003) 31 3211), at 32 Brisbane St, is a two-minute walk from the city centre and charges $50/60, which includes breakfast.

Although a little difficult to find, *Clarke Holiday House* (☎ (003) 34 2237) at 19 Neika Ave, near the corner of Basin Rd and Brougham St, is good value at $35 a double.

Places to Eat
Banjo's bakes all its own breads, pizzas, cakes, etc, and has two shops, one in Yorktown Square and one at 98 Brisbane St; both are open daily from 6 am to 6 pm. At Yorktown Square, you can also dine alfresco at *Molly York's Coffee Shoppe*.

The *Deli*, at the rear of the Identity Store, 40 St John St, is popular with shoppers and has good coffee and quality cakes and snacks. The *Konditorei Cafe Manfred* has delicious, inexpensive home-made German rolls and pastries. It's at 95 George St, near the Redline depot, and a good place to sit while waiting for a bus. *Ripples Restaurant*, in the Ritchies Mill Art Centre, specialises in light meals such as crepes and pancakes, and there's a lovely view of the boats on the Tamar River from the outdoor tables.

Most of Launceston's many hotels have filling, reasonably priced counter meals but you probably won't get cheaper than the $7 specials at the *Royal Oak*, on the corner of Brisbane and Tamar Sts.

There are a few good restaurants in Launceston charging $9 to $13 for a main meal. One of the most popular is *Calabrisella Pizza* (☎ (003) 31 1958), at 56 Wellington St, which serves excellent Italian food and is often packed, so bookings are advisable. It's open until the early hours on Fridays and Saturdays, and until midnight on other nights except Tuesdays. You can also get takeaway pizza.

The *Pasta House*, in Yorktown Square, is a licensed restaurant with pasta dishes for around $8.50; it's open until 9.30 pm Monday to Saturday. *Arpar's Thai Restaurant* on the corner of Charles and Paterson Sts is well worth a try, and main courses cost around $12.

For Chinese food try the *Canton*, at 201

Charles St; it's one of the best moderately priced Chinese restaurants in town. *Bailey's BYO* at 150 George St specialises in Tasmanian produce – local seafoods and King Island beef all feature on the menu. The *Aristocrat* on the corner of Paterson and Charles Sts is a family restaurant featuring Australian and Greek dishes.

For $13 or more, there's the *Satay House* out at Kingscourt Shopping Centre, Kings Meadows, which serves excellent Indonesian fare. The award-winning *Fee & Me* licensed brasserie at 36 the Kingsway has excellent food and a good selection of Tasmanian wines. Also good for Tasmanian wines (and excellent meals) is the *Owl's Nest* at 147 Paterson St, next to the Penny Royal complex.

Shrimps, at 72 George St, is a good up-market choice for seafood and an intimate atmosphere, and *Dicky Whites*, at 107 Brisbane St, is a good family steakhouse. For French dining in style try the *Elm Cottage* at 168 Charles St. Launceston's only Japanese restaurant is the *Tairyo* at Yorktown Square.

The *Gorge Restaurant*, at Cataract Gorge, has fairly good food and undoubtedly the best setting in Launceston.

Entertainment

There's quite a good choice of evening entertainment in Launceston, most of which is advertised either in the free *Launceston Week* newspaper or in *This Week in Tasmania*.

The *Batman Fawkner Inn*, at 35-39 Cameron St, has live music nightly (except Tuesdays), a disco on Friday and Saturday nights, free films every Wednesday night and a monthly Friday-night showing of the film *The Blues Brothers*.

The *Pavilion Tavern* in Yorktown Square also has music Tuesday to Saturday nights and a cabaret-style nightclub called Twains. *Rosies Tavern*, at 158 George St, has music every night except Tuesdays and Sundays and nice comfy couches to lounge in. The *Royal Hotel*, also in George St, is another popular venue for live bands from Wednesday to Saturday nights. *Alfresco's* is a wine bar in the Victoria Hotel, 211 Brisbane St,

which is also becoming quite a popular venue.

In the disco department, *Hot Gossip*, in the Launceston Hotel (107 Brisbane St), is open Wednesdays to Saturdays, while upstairs, Slates is a historic pool room, which is worth seeing.

If you want to risk a few dollars, or just observe how the rich play, check out the *Launceston Federal Country Club Casino* at Prospect, 10 km from the city centre. Any big-name bands touring from the mainland usually perform here. You don't have to pay to get in and about the only article of clothing disapproved of these days is track shoes. The disco at the casino, *Regines*, is also free, and the drinks are not as expensive as you might expect.

Getting There & Away

Air For information on domestic flights to and from Launceston, see the Getting There & Away section at the beginning of this chapter. Ansett Airlines is at 54 Brisbane St, Qantas is based on the corner of Brisbane and George Sts, and Airlines of Tasmania has an office at the airport.

Bus The main bus companies operating out of Launceston are Redline (☎ (003) 31 3233), 112 George St; Hobart Coaches (☎ (003) 34 3600), 83 Cimitiere St; Tasmanian Wilderness Transport (☎ (003) 34 4442), 101 George St; and Tamar Valley Coaches (☎ (003) 34 0828), 26 Wellington St.

Both Redline and Hobart Coaches run buses to Deloraine ($6), Launceston ($17), Devonport ($11.80) and Burnie ($15.80) (fares quoted are Redline's). Redline also has services to Wynyard, Stanley, Smithton ($25.80), George Town ($6), St Marys ($13.40), St Helens ($16.60), Bicheno ($18) and Swansea ($14.40). Tasmanian Wilderness Transport has services to Ben Lomond during the ski season ($25) and to Cradle Mountain ($35).

Car Rental There are plenty of car-rental firms in Launceston. Some of the cheaper ones are Apple Car Rentals (☎ (003) 43

3780), 192 Wellington St; Advance Car Rentals (☎ (003) 44 2164), 32 Cameron St; and Aberdeen Car Rentals (☎ (003) 44 5811), 35 Punchbowl Rd.

Hitching To start hitching to Devonport and the north-west, catch the Prospect Casino bus from stop C in St John St. For Hobart and the east coast, catch a Franklin House bus from the same stop. For the Tasman Highway route to the east coast catch a Waverley bus from stop G in St John St.

Getting Around
To/From the Airport Redline operates an airport shuttle service which meets all incoming flights and picks up passengers an hour or so before all departures. The fare is $6. By taxi it costs about $16 to get into the city.

Bus The local bus service is run by Metro, and the main departure point is at Metro Central, in St John St, between Paterson and York Sts. For $2.50 you can buy an unlimited-travel Day Rover ticket which can be used all day at weekends and between 9 am and 4.30 pm and after 6 pm on weekdays. Most routes, however, do not operate in the evenings, and Sunday services are limited.

Bicycle Rent-a-Cycle, at the Launceston City Youth Hostel (☎ (003) 44 9779), has a good range of 10-speed tourers and mountain bikes. The tourers cost $10 a day or $65 a week, including helmet and panniers; and the mountain bikes cost $90 a week. There's a reducing rate for each additional week, and a bond of $50 applies to all rentals. You can leave your luggage at the hostel, and it's also possible to do a one-way rental and send the bicycle back by bus.

Around Launceston

HADSPEN (population 1330)
Eighteen km from Launceston and just west of Hadspen is **Entally House**, one of Tasmania's best-known historic homes. It was built in 1819 by Thomas Haydock Reibey but is now owned by the National Trust. Set in beautiful grounds, it creates a vivid picture of what life must have been like for the well-to-do on an early farming property. The home, its stables, church, coach house and grounds are open daily from 10 am to 12.30 pm and from 1 to 5 pm and admission is $4.50 ($2.50 for children). The Reibeys have quite an interesting family history which you can read about in a brochure on sale at the property ($1.50).

On the roadside two km west of Hadspen is **Carrick Mill**, a lovely, ivy-covered bluestone mill, which dates from 1810 and has been well restored.

Places to Stay & Eat
In Hadspen, on the corner of the Bass Highway and Main Rd, is the *Launceston Cabin & Tourist Park* (☎ (003) 93 6391).

Around Launceston

The park has good facilities and charges $9 for a camp site, $30 a double for an on-site van and $45 a double for well-equipped cabins.

The *Red Feather Inn* (☎ (003) 93 6331), built in 1844, has a good restaurant with main meals for around $14.

LIFFEY VALLEY

The Liffey Valley State Reserve protects the beautiful rainforested valley at the foot of the Great Western Tiers and features the impressive **Liffey Valley Falls**. It's a popular destination for fishing or bushwalking, and day-trippers are also attracted by an amazing fernery which has for sale the largest variety of native ferns in the whole state.

The fernery, tearooms and gallery were built from wattle and pine. You can sit in the tearooms, enjoy freshly made scones and take in the view of Drys Bluff, which, at 1297 metres, is the highest peak in the Great Western Tiers. The fernery and tearooms are open from Wednesday to Sunday between 11 am and 5 pm but are closed during July. Liffey is 34 km south of Carrick, via Bracknell, and is a good day trip from Launceston.

EVANDALE (population 770)

Evandale, 19 km south of Launceston in the South Esk Valley, is another town classified by the National Trust. Many of its 19th-century buildings are in excellent condition. In keeping with its olde-worlde atmosphere, Evandale hosts the National Penny Farthing Championships in February each year, which attract national and international competitors.

Eight km south of Evandale is the National Trust property of **Clarendon**, which was completed in 1838 and is one of the grandest Georgian mansions in Australia. The house and its formal gardens are open daily from 10 am to 5 pm (closing an hour earlier in June, July and August) and admission is $5 ($2.50 for children).

The **Clarendon Arms Hotel** has been licensed since 1847 and there are some inter-esting murals in the hall depicting the area's history. The locals may encourage you to see if you can spot the well-concealed rabbit in the stagecoach mural; have a go – it really is there!

Places to Stay & Eat

The unexciting *Prince of Wales Hotel* (☎ (003) 91 8381) has rooms from $25/40. Much more interesting is the 1836 *Solomon Cottage* (☎ (003) 91 8331), which can sleep four people. The cost is $85 for a double, plus $25 for each extra person; the price includes a light breakfast.

There are a number of the ubiquitous tea-rooms-cum-galleries, and counter meals are available at the pubs.

LONGFORD (population 2600)

Longford, also classified by the National Trust, is 27 km from Launceston, in the rich pastoral area watered by the South Esk and Macquarie rivers.

One of the best ways to explore this historic town is to follow the National Trust's *Longford Walkabout* brochure, which will take you past many colonial buildings, such as **Christ Church**, **Jessen Lodge** and **Noake's Cottages**.

If you want to stay overnight, the *Riverside Caravan Park* (☎ (003) 91 1470), on the banks of the Macquarie River, has camp sites and on-site vans.

The **Longford Wildlife Park**, on Pateena Rd, about 14 km from the town, provides a permanent conservation area for native Tasmanian wildlife. The 70 hectares of bush and pasture has kangaroos, wallabies, echidnas, Cape Barren geese, wild ducks and native birds. It's open Tuesdays to Thursdays and at the weekends from 10 am to 5 pm; admission is $4 ($2 for children).

About eight km from Longford is the historic town of **Perth**, which has a number of noteworthy buildings. The distinctive octagonal Baptist Tabernacle, in Clarence St, was built in 1889 and is definitely well worth a look.

Tamar Valley

The Tamar River separates the east and west Tamar districts and links Launceston with its ocean port of Bell Bay. Crossing the river near Deviot is Batman Bridge, the only bridge on the lower reaches of the Tamar. The river is tidal for the 64 km to Launceston and wends its way through some lovely orchards, pastures, forests and vineyards. Black swans are seen here.

The Tamar Valley and nearby Pipers River are among Tasmania's main wine-producing areas, and the tasty, dry premium wines produced here are starting to achieve world recognition.

European history in the region dates from 1798, when Bass and Flinders discovered the estuary. The valley then slowly developed, first as a port of call for sailors and sealers from the Bass Strait islands and then as a sanctuary for some of the desperate characters who took to the bush during the convict days.

In the late 1870s gold was discovered at Cabbage Tree Hill – now Beaconsfield – and the fortunes of the valley took a new turn. The region boomed and for a time Cabbage Tree Hill was the third largest town in Tasmania, with over six million dollars worth of gold being extracted before water seepage forced the mines to close in 1914.

Getting There & Away

On weekdays Tamar Valley Coaches (☎ (003) 34 0828) has at least one bus a day running up and down the West Tamar Valley, but there are no services at the weekends. A one-way ticket to Beaconsfield costs $5.10.

On most weekdays Redline has four buses a day that run up the East Tamar Valley between Launceston and George Town. At weekends there is one service a day.

NOTLEY GORGE STATE RESERVE

This reserve, opened in 1940, is the last remnant of the dense rainforest that once blanketed the western side of the Tamar Valley. Originally saved from the settlers' axes because of its inaccessibility, the 10 hectares of ferns, trees and shrubs are also a wildlife sanctuary. Early last century the notorious bushranger Matthew Brady and his gang eluded capture for some time by hiding in the forests here. Notley Gorge is 23 km from Launceston via Legana, and being so wild is an exciting place for a picnic.

DEVIOT

Many of the Tamar Valley's vineyards are based in and around Deviot and are open to the public for tasting sessions. One that you can visit is Marion's Vineyard, Foreshore Drive, where a tasting fee of $3.50 is charged only if you don't buy any wine. **Batman Bridge**, with its 100-metre-high steel A-frame tower, spans the river just north of Deviot.

BEACONSFIELD

The once-thriving gold-mining town of Beaconsfield is still dominated by the ruins of its three original mine buildings. One of these houses is the **Grubb Shaft Museum** complex, which is open daily from 10 am to 4 pm ($2). It has interesting displays of local memorabilia, and a reconstruction of a miner's cottage and old school. Beaconsfield Gold Mines has opened up the old Hart shaft next to the museum, and with today's technology overcoming the water-seepage problem is hoping to strike some of the town's still plentiful gold reserves.

Further north is picturesque **Beauty Point** and, at the mouth of the Tamar River, the holiday and fishing resorts of **Greens Beach** and **Kelso**, where there are good beaches and caravan parks.

LOW HEAD

It is notoriously difficult to navigate up the Tamar River, and the **Pilot Station** at Low Head, on the eastern shore, guides vessels safely through the waters. This convict-built station, dating from 1835, is the oldest in Australia and houses an interesting **maritime museum**, and a good cafe which is open daily; admission is $1. There are

TASMANIA

several navigational lead lights around town which date from 1881, and on Tuesdays and Thursdays, the **lighthouse** (built in 1888) can be inspected. There is good surf at **East Beach**, on Bass Strait, and safe swimming at **Lagoon Bay**, on the river.

The *Beach Pines Holiday Park* (☎ (003) 82 2602) is right by the sea and has cabins for $40 a double, and camp sites for $8. The other alternative is the very pleasant *Belfont Cottages* (☎ (003) 82 1841), which are self-contained and cost $80 for two people.

GEORGE TOWN (population 5030)

George Town is best known as the site where Colonel Paterson landed in 1804, leading to the settlement of northern Tasmania. Although these days the town gets relatively few visitors, there are some interesting attractions in George Town and the surrounding area.

In Cimitiere St, the **Grove** is a lovely Georgian stone residence dating from the 1830s which has been classified by the National Trust. It's open daily from 10 am to 5 pm, and admission is $2.50. Refreshments are available and lunch is served by staff in period costume.

The **Old Watch House** in Macquarie St dates from 1843 and has been turned into a museum; it's open on weekdays from 8 am to 5 pm and it costs nothing to look around. Also of interest is the **St Mary Magdalen Anglican Church** in Anne St.

Places to Stay

The *Travellers Hostel* (☎ (003) 82 1399) at 4 Elizabeth St is a smoke-free YHA hostel in a restored house which dates back to 1891. It has beds for $12 and family rooms for $40. *Gray's Hotel* (☎ (003) 82 2655), at 77 Macquarie St, charges $70 a double and the *Pier Hotel Motel* (☎ (003) 82 1300), at 3 Elizabeth St, has similar prices.

HILLWOOD

Further south is the attractive rural area of Hillwood, where from November to April you can pick your own strawberries, raspber-

ries and apples and sample some Tasmanian fruit wines at the **Hillwood Strawberry Farm**. The village is also noted for its fishing and lovely river views.

LILYDALE

The small town of Lilydale, 27 km from Launceston, stands at the foot of Mt Arthur and is a convenient base for bushwalkers heading for the mountain or other scenic trails in the area. Three km from the town is the **Lilydale Falls Reserve**, which has camping facilities and two easily accessible waterfalls. At the nearby town of Lalla, there's the century-old **Rhododendron Gardens**, which are spectacular in season.

North-Central

Between the northern coastal strip and the Great Western Tiers (which rise up to Tasmania's central plateau), there are some interesting towns and scenic spots. The Bass Highway continues west from Launceston to Deloraine, on the edge of the north-western region.

Getting There & Away

Redline has daily buses from Launceston, through Westbury and Deloraine to Smithton, as well as a service from Deloraine to Mole Creek; Hobart Coaches has services between Hobart, Launceston, Deloraine and Burnie; while Tasmanian Wilderness Transport buses run between Launceston, Devonport, Sheffield, Lake St Clair and Cradle Mountain.

WESTBURY (population 1290)

The historic town of Westbury, 28 km west of Launceston, is best known for its **White House**, a property built in 1841 and now managed by the National Trust. The house features colonial furnishings and a collection of 19th-century toys, and is open from 10 am to 4 pm on Tuesdays, Thursdays and weekends; admission is $4.

The **Westbury Gemstone, Mineral & Mural Display**, on the Bass Highway, is open daily from 9.30 am to 4.30 pm; admission is $2. Next door is **Pearn's Steam World**, which is open from 9 am to 5 pm; it costs $3 to inspect a wide range of steam engines.

DELORAINE (population 2100)

Deloraine is Tasmania's largest inland town and, with its lovely riverside picnic area, superb setting at the foot of the Great Western Tiers and good amenities, makes a great base from which to explore the surrounding area. Being so close to the Cradle Mountain area, and even closer to a number of impressive waterfalls and shorter walking tracks, Deloraine is fast becoming a major bushwalking centre. You'll find a visitor information centre at 29 West Church St.

The town itself has a lot of charm, as many of its Georgian and Victorian buildings have been faithfully restored. Places of interest include the **Folk Museum**, **St Mark's Church of England**, and **Bonney's Inn**, which serves lunches and Devonshire teas. Two km out of town is the **Bowerbank Mill**, which is classified by the National Trust; these days it offers accommodation and a gallery.

Places to Stay & Eat

The *Highview Lodge Youth Hostel* (☎ (003) 62 2996), perched on the hillside at 8 Blake St, has magnificent views of the Great Western Tiers and charges $10 a night. The managers are experienced bushwalkers and organise reasonably priced and well-equipped trips to Cradle Mountain, the Walls of Jerusalem and other destinations. The hostel also offers bush transport, and rents mountain or touring bikes to guests. This hostel receives excellent reports from many travellers.

The *Backpackers Modern Hotel* (☎ (003) 62 3408) is a backpackers' hostel at 24 Bass Highway, across the river from the main part of town. It's clean and modern and charges $10 a night. Almost opposite is the *Bush Inn*

(☎ (003) 62 2365), which also offers good backpackers' accommodation at $13 a night with breakfast.

The *Deloraine Hotel* (☎ (003) 62 2022), near the river on the main street, is a beautiful old-fashioned hotel with singles/doubles for $20/35, or $25/40 including a cooked breakfast. There is also the *Apex Caravan Park* (☎ (003) 62 2345) in West Parade, half a km from the town centre. There are camp sites ($7) and on-site vans ($25).

The previously mentioned *Bowerbank Mill* (☎ (003) 62 2628) on the Bass Highway has cottages with one or two bedrooms and limited cooking facilities from $60/85.

One of the best places to eat in Deloraine is *Reuben's Restaurant*, in the main street, which is open daily from 8 am onwards. The atmosphere is relaxed and the cooking, whether you order a filling home-made soup for $4 or a more-expensive meal, is delicious.

Getting There & Away

See under Getting There & Away at the beginning of the North-Central section. Redline's agent in Deloraine is the visitor information centre at 29 West Church St; the Hobart Coaches agent is Sam's Supermarket at 1 Emu Bay Rd; and Tasmanian Wilderness Transport's agent is Sullivans Restaurant at 17 West Parade.

MOLE CREEK (population 250)

About 25 km west of Deloraine is Mole Creek, in the vicinity of which you'll find spectacular limestone caves, leatherwood honey and one of Tasmania's best wildlife parks.

Marakoopa Cave, from the Aboriginal word meaning 'handsome', is a wet cave 14 km from Mole Creek which features an incredible glow-worm display. In summer, one-hour tours leave at 10 and 11.15 am and 2.30 and 4 pm. **King Solomon Cave** is a dry cave with amazing calcite crystals that reflect light. In summer, 45-minute tours leave at 10.30 and 11.30 am and 12.30, 2, 3 and 4 pm. It costs $8 ($4 for children) to visit either cave, or you can buy a combined ticket for $12 ($6). If you're visiting in winter, ring the ranger (☎ (003) 63 5182) to find out the tour times.

The leatherwood tree only grows in the damp western part of Tasmania, so honey made from its flower is unique to this state. From January to April, when the honey is being extracted, you can visit the **Stephens Leatherwood Honey Factory** and learn all about this fascinating industry. The factory is open during weekdays from 8 am to 4 pm, and admission is free.

Two km from Chudleigh, east of Mole Creek, is the **Tasmanian Wildlife Park & Koala Village**, which is worth a visit. It's open daily from 9 am to 5 pm, and admission is $6.50 ($2.50 for children).

Places to Stay

Two km west of town, at the turn-off to the caves and Cradle Mountain, is the *Mole Creek Camping Ground* (☎ (003) 63 1150). It has basic facilities and charges $4.

The *Mole Creek Hotel* (☎ (003) 63 1102), in the main street, has rooms for $20/35. The *Mole Creek Guest House* (☎ (003) 63 1313), also in the main street, is a small place with rooms for $45 a double for B&B.

SHEFFIELD (population 990)

Sheffield is either referred to as 'the town of murals' or 'the outdoor art gallery'. Since 1986, 23 murals depicting the history of the area have been painted in and around this little town, and these have become a major tourist attraction. At the **Diversity Murals Theatrette**, in the main street, you can see an interesting documentary explaining the history and meaning of the individual paintings. The theatrette is open all day from Monday to Saturday, and weekend afternoons; admission is $1.50.

The scenery around Sheffield is also impressive, with **Mt Roland** (1231 metres) dominating the peaceful farmlands, thick forests, and rivers brimming with fish. Nearby is beautiful **Lake Barrington**, part of the Mersey-Forth hydroelectric scheme and

a major rowing venue and state recreation reserve.

Places to Stay

Paradise Cottage (☎ (004) 91 1613), five km from town and owned by the Diversity Theatrette, charges $30/40 a night and is a great out-of-the-way place to stay. A similar place, but a good deal more expensive, is the *Carinya Host Farm* (☎ (004) 91 1593) at Roland, nine km west of Sheffield. The cost here is $55/65, and meals can be supplied on request.

In town itself, the *Sheffield Hotel* (☎ (004) 91 1130) has rooms for $30/45 with a light breakfast. The town also has a motel, and a caravan park with on-site vans.

DEVONPORT (population 22,750)

Nestled behind the dramatic lighthouse-topped Mersey Bluff, Devonport is the terminal for the *Spirit of Tasmania*, the vehicular ferry between Victoria and Tasmania.

The Bluff Lighthouse was built in 1889 to direct the colony's rapidly growing sea traffic, and its light can be seen from up to 27 km out to sea. Today, the port is still very important and handles much of the export produce from the rich agricultural areas around Devonport.

Devonport tries hard to attract tourists but its visitors are usually arriving or departing rather than actually staying. Indeed, the city is often referred to as the 'gateway to Tasmania'.

Information

The Tasmanian Travel & Information Centre at 18 Rooke St (☎ (004) 21 6226) in the city centre is a good place for tourist information.

For any information about Devonport and Tasmania in general, head for the Backpackers' Barn (☎ (004) 24 3628) at 12 Edward St. The Barn is open daily from 8 am to 6 pm, and the staff can arrange transport, car rental, help organise itineraries or look after your backpack. It has a cafe, an excellent bushwalking shop, and a rest room with

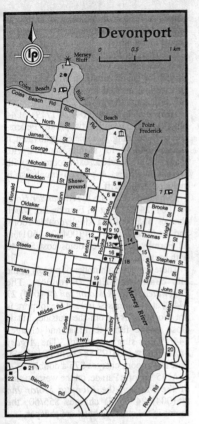

Devonport

0   0.5   1 km

PLACES TO STAY

3   Mersey Bluff Caravan Park
5   River View Lodge
6   Elimatta Motor Inn
7   Abel Tasman Caravan Park
11 Edgewater Hotel & Motor Inn
16 Alexander & Formby hotels
19 Wenvoe Heights
20 Argosy Motor Inn
22 MacWright House Youth Hostel

PLACES TO EAT

8   Tamahere Hotel
12 Backpackers' Barn

OTHER

1   Mersey Light
2   Tiagarra
4   Maritime & Folk Museum
9   Hobart Coaches, Wilderness
    Transport
10 Devonport Showcase
13 Post Office
14 Mersey River Ferry Service
15 Spirit of Tasmania Ferry Terminal
17 Tasmanian Travel Centre
18 Railway Station
21 Home Hill

the Tasmanian Aboriginal word for 'keep', and was set up to preserve the art and culture of the Tasmanian Aborigines. The centre has a rare collection of more than 250 rock engravings, and is open daily from 9 am to 4.30 pm; it's well worth the $2.50 admission fee.

Museums

The **Tasmanian Maritime & Folk Museum**, at 47 Victoria Parade, has a display of model sailing ships based on the vessels which visited Tasmania in the early days. It's open Tuesday to Sunday from 2 to 4 pm and admission is $1.

Taswegia, in the lovely old building at 55-57 Formby Rd, is a commercial printing house with an interesting and historic printing museum. It's open daily from 10 am to 5 pm, and admission is $2.

The **Don River Railway & Museum**, out of town on the Bass Highway towards Ulverstone, features a collection of steam

showers which travellers can use for $3 a day.

The Devonport Showcase (☎ (004) 24 8176), at 5 Best St, also has a complete range of tourist information with displays and workshop demonstrations of arts and crafts. The centre is open daily from 9 am to 5 pm. The Wilderness Shop (☎ (004) 24 7393) is at 27 Stewart St.

Tiagarra

The Tasmanian Aboriginal Culture & Art Centre is at Mersey Bluff, on the road to the lighthouse. It's known as Tiagarra, which is

locomotives and passenger carriages, and you can take a ride on a vintage train along the banks of the Don River. It's open daily from 11 am to 4 pm and admission is $6.

Other Attractions

The **Devonport Gallery & Art Centre**, at 45-47 Stewart St, is open from 10 am to 5 pm Monday to Friday and on Sunday afternoons.

At 77 Middle Rd, not far from the youth hostel, is **Home Hill**, which used to be the residence of Joseph and Dame Enid Lyons. The house was built by them in 1916 and is now administered by the National Trust. Joseph Lyons is the only Australian to have been both the premier of his state and prime minister of Australia, and Dame Enid Lyons was the first woman to become a member of the House of Representatives. Home Hill is open Tuesday to Thursday and at weekends from 2 to 4 pm; admission is $4.50.

Organised Tours

Most of the tours operating out of Devonport are to Tasmania's wilderness areas and they vary from one-day trips to four-day tours. The two main operators are Tasmanian Wilderness Transport and Maxwell's Charter Tour Coach & Taxi Service, whose agent is the Backpackers' Barn.

Places to Stay

East Devonport has two caravan parks for visitors, both of which are close to the beach and have good reputations. The *Abel Tasman Caravan Park* (☎ (004) 27 8794), at 6 Wright St, has camp sites ($7), bunkhouse accommodation ($11), on-site vans ($28) and cabins ($35). *Devonport's Vacation Village* (☎ (004) 27 8886), in North Caroline St, has similar facilities and prices.

The *Mersey Bluff Caravan Park* (☎ (004) 24 8655) is 2.5 km from town, near Tiagarra. It's a pleasant place with some good beaches nearby. It has camp sites only.

MacWright House (☎ (004) 24 5696), 400 metres past Home Hill at 155 Middle Rd, is Devonport's YHA hostel; it charges $9 a night. It's a 40-minute walk from the town

centre. A Tasmanian Wilderness Transport bus can take you from the ferry terminal or airport to the hostel.

The friendly *River View Lodge* (☎ (004) 24 7357), at 18 Victoria Parade, charges $40/50 for singles/doubles, which includes an excellent cooked breakfast; it's deservedly popular with travellers.

Wenvoe Heights (☎ (004) 24 1719), at 44 MacFie St, is a beautiful two-storey Federation brick building. Completely renovated, it charges $44/54 for singles/doubles with shared facilities and $15 extra for rooms with private facilities. A cooked breakfast is included in the tariff.

Two good hotels are the *Alexander Hotel* (☎ (004) 24 2252), at 78 Formby Rd, which charges $35/50 for a single/double room; and the *Hotel Formby* (☎ (004) 24 1601), at 82 Formby Rd, where rooms cost $30/40 with breakfast.

There are quite a number of motels in the city centre and East Devonport. The *Edgewater Hotel & Motor Inn* (☎ (004) 27 8441), at 2 Thomas St in East Devonport, is not too attractive from the outside, but is close to the ferry terminal and charges $44/49 for singles/doubles. The *Argosy Motor Inn* (☎ (004) 27 8872), in Tarleton St, East Devonport, charges $75 a double.

At 15 Victoria Parade, on the western side of the Mersey, the *Elimatta Motor Inn* (☎ (004) 24 6555) charges $55/60; the rooms in the attached hotel are cheaper.

Places to Eat

There are plenty of coffee lounges and takeaways in the mall, but for a good atmosphere and great snacks try *Billy N Damper*, the cafe at the front of the Backpackers' Barn, 12 Edward St. It's open daily from 8 am to 6 pm, and will take party bookings in the evenings. The *Coffee Shop* in the Devonport Showcase is also open daily and is good for a drink or a snack. In the Devonport Central shopping centre in King St the *Natural Tucker* cafe has interesting snacks.

Most hotels have good counter meals from around $7; try the *Tamahere* at 34 Best St, the *Alexander* at 78 Formby Rd, or the *Formby* at 82 Formby Rd. In East Devonport, the *Edgewater Hotel*, at 2 Thomas St, has cheap counter meals for around $6.

Devonport has a good selection of moderately priced restaurants. *Greex*, at 159 Rooke St, has Greek and Lebanese food for around $13 a main dish, and good light-lunch specials from $7. For Italian food, try *Il Mondo Antico* at 142A William St, and for Chinese food, try the *Silky Apple* at 33 King St, the *Chinese Chef* at 4b Kempling St, the *Golden Panda* at 38 Formby Rd or the *Mandarin Inn* at 156 William St. On Sundays the smoke-free *Old Rectory*, at 71 Wright St, does a good, filling Sunday roast, and it has excellent evenings meals from Thursday to Saturday.

Carnivores might like the *Raging Bull Steakhouse* at 93 Oldaker St, in the Four Ways shopping centre about half a km west of the city centre.

Entertainment

Check the *Advocate* newspaper for Devonport's entertainment details. The *Warehouse Nightclub* and *Spurs Saloon* are in King St. The *Elimatta Motor Inn*, at 15 Victoria Parade, occasionally has weekend bands, and on Wednesday, Friday and Saturday nights, a nightclub called *Steps*. At the Tamahere Hotel, there's a nightclub called *Club One*, while *City Limits*, at 18 King St, is also a popular nightspot.

Getting There & Away

Air For information on domestic flights to and from Devonport, see the Getting There & Away section at the beginning of this chapter.

Bus Redline's agent is the Backpackers' Barn (☎ (004) 24 3628) at 12 Edward St, although the depot (☎ (004) 24 5100) is right across the road at No 9. All buses also stop at the ferry terminal. Redline has daily buses from Devonport to Hobart ($28.60), Queenstown ($31.70), Strahan ($36.50), Launceston ($11.80), Burnie ($6.20) and Smithton ($10.50).

The Hobart Coaches office (☎ (004) 24 6599) is at the Devonport Central shopping centre in King St. Hobart Coaches has daily buses to Launceston, Hobart and Burnie, and all towns en route.

The majority of Tasmanian Wilderness Transport's wilderness services depart daily from Devonport. Most days their buses can take you to Sheffield, Cradle Mountain ($30), Strahan ($50), Zeehan, Derwent Bridge, Lake St Clair ($45) or, in summer only, the Walls of Jerusalem. Their depot (☎ (004) 34 4442) is at 14 King St.

If none of the scheduled wilderness services suit your particular needs, then you can charter a minibus from either Tasmanian Wilderness Transport or the Backpackers' Barn. For example, a bus from Devonport to Cradle Mountain costs $120 or, if there are five people or more, $30 each.

Car Rental There are plenty of cheap car-rental firms including Range/Rent-a-Bug (☎ (004) 27 9034), at 5 Murray St, East Devonport; and Advance Car Rentals (☎ (004) 24 8885) on the corner of William and Oldaker Sts. The major companies all have desks at the *Spirit of Tasmania* terminal.

Boat See the Getting There & Away section at the beginning of this chapter for details on the *Spirit of Tasmania* ferry service between Melbourne and Devonport. The TT Line terminal (☎ toll-free 1800 030 344) is on the Esplanade, East Devonport.

Getting Around

There's no shuttle bus to the airport, so the only option is a taxi (about $10).

South of Best St, local buses are run by Tasmanian Wilderness Transport, while north of Best St and East Devonport is covered by Hobart Coaches. If this is confusing don't worry; most places in Devonport are within easy walking distance.

There's also a Mersey River ferry service linking central Devonport with East Devonport, which operates seven days a week. The one-way adult fare is $1.20 and bicycles cost 50c.

You can hire bicycles at the Backpackers' Barn or from Trevor Goss (☎ (004) 24 3889) at 51 Raymond Ave.

AROUND DEVONPORT
Port Sorell

Port Sorell is a low-key beach and holiday town at the mouth of the Rubicon River, 19 km east of Devonport. There's not a great deal to do in town except laze on the beach, although it is a good base for excursions to the Asbestos Range National Park on the eastern side of the Rubicon River.

Places to Stay The *Moomba Holiday Park* (☎ (004) 28 6140) has cabins at $29 or camp sites for $6.50. There's a couple of small guesthouses, such as the *Newcroft* (☎ (004) 28 6835), which charges $30/55 for B&B, or there's the more up-market *Shearwater Country Club* (☎ (004) 28 6205), which has rooms for $80/95 and self-contained units for $135. Facilities include a heated pool, sauna, tennis court and golf course.

Asbestos Range National Park

This former farm was declared a national park in 1976 and was named for the mineral once found in the area. Animals and birds are prolific, and there are a number of signed walking tracks through the park. The **Springlawn Nature Walk** takes about an hour from the car park and includes a board-walk over a wetland to a bird hide.

There are three camp sites in the park with pit toilets, bore water and firewood provided. For more information, contact the park ranger on ☎ (004) 28 6277.

North-West

Tasmania's magnificent north-west coast is a land as rich in history as it is diverse in scenery. Its story goes back 37,000 years to a time when giant kangaroos and wombats roamed the area. Aboriginal tribes once took

shelter in the caves along the coast, leaving a legacy of rock engravings and middens.

Europeans quickly realised the potential of the region and settlers moved further and further west, building towns along the coast and inland on the many rivers. The area was soon transformed into a vital part of the young colony's developing economy.

ULVERSTONE (population 9920)

Ulverstone, at the mouth of the Leven River, is a pleasant town with some fine beaches and good amenities; it's a good base from which to explore the surrounding area.

Just 30 km south is the **Gunns Plains Cave Reserve**; daily guided tours of the spectacular wet cave leave hourly from 10 am to 4 pm and cost $4. Nearby is **Leven Canyon**, a magnificent gorge with a number of walking tracks. If you have your own transport, you can combine visits to both attractions in a 105-km round trip from Ulverstone through Sprent, Central Castra and Nietta to Leven Canyon, near Black Bluff (1339 metres), and back via Preston, Gunns Plains and North Motton.

If you're driving between Ulverstone and Penguin, consider taking the old Bass Highway, which runs closer to the coast than the new one and offers some fine views of three small islands known as the **Three Sisters**.

Places to Stay & Eat

There are plenty of camping grounds in Ulverstone, including the *Apex Caravan Park* (☎ (004) 25 2935) in Queen St in West Ulverstone and the *Ulverstone Caravan Park* (☎ (004) 25 2624) in Water St, which also has on-site vans ($29 double), cabins ($39) and units ($49).

For a great location try the *Ocean View Guest House* (☎ (004) 25 5401) at 1 Victoria St, 100 metres from the beach. It's a lovely old house where singles/doubles with a continental breakfast cost $35/55. At 42 Reibey St, in the centre of town, there's the Federation-style *Furner's Hotel* (☎ (004) 25 1488), which charges $35/50.

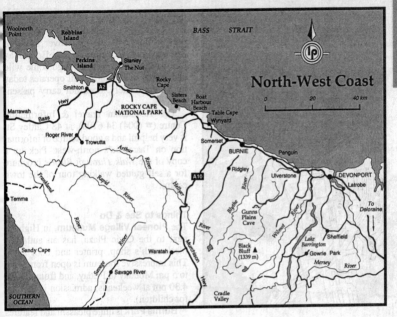

North-West Coast

Pedro the Fisherman, down by the wharf, does extremely cheap but filling takeaway fish & chips or seafood & chips – and if you can't finish the packet there are plenty of obliging seagulls around!

In Reibey St there's the *Jade Willow* Chinese restaurant, or in West Ulverstone you could try *Midnight Express*, a restaurant in Queen St which combines Chinese, Indian and Italian cuisines!

Getting There & Away

See the Burnie Getting There & Away section for details of transport to and from Ulverstone.

PENGUIN (population 2880)

At the foot of the Dial Range State Forest and on three lovely bays, the township of Penguin takes its name from the colonies of fairy penguins which used to be found along the coast. The penguins are rare these days but can be seen, if you're lucky, from

November to March around Johnsons Beach, near the caravan park. If you miss out, there's a much larger model one on the Esplanade, which can be viewed any time.

See the Getting There & Away section under Burnie for information on transport to Penguin.

BURNIE (population 20,500)

Although Burnie sits on the shores of Emu Bay and is backed by rich farming land, it's factory smoke, not the views, which usually welcomes the visitor to Tasmania's fourth largest city. One of Burnie's main assets is its deep-water port, which has always made cargo shipping an important industry. Another major employer is Amcor, which now owns Associated Pulp & Paper Mills, which began producing paper in 1938.

The town (named after William Burnie, a director of the Van Diemen's Land Company) started life quietly until the discovery of tin at Mt Bischoff in Waratah. In

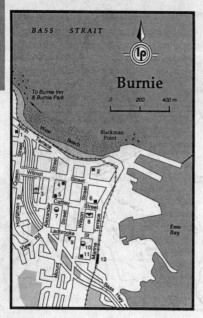

PLACES TO STAY

1   Regent Hotel
2   Beach Hotel
4   Club Hotel
6   Bay View Hotel
11   Burnie Town House

PLACES TO EAT

9   Renusha's Indian Restaurant,
     Kasbah Pizza Bar & Li Yin

OTHER

3   Pioneer Village Museum
5   Tasmanian Travel Centre
7   Hobart Coaches Depot
8   Post Office
10   Redline Depot
12   Railway Station

1878, the Van Diemen's Land Company opened a wooden tramway between the mine at Waratah and the port of Burnie. This was

the humble beginning of the important Emu Bay Railway, which, in the 1900s, linked the port of Burnie to the rich silver fields of Zeehan and Rosebery. The Emu Bay Railway, which travels through some wild and impressive country, still operates today but, unfortunately, does not carry passengers.

The Tasmanian Travel & Information Centre (☎ (004) 34 6105), at 48 Cattley St, is very helpful and a good source of information on Tasmania's north-west. Pick up a copy of the *Walk Through Burnie* brochure for a self-guided walking tour of the town centre.

Things to See & Do

The **Pioneer Village Museum**, in High St, next to the Civic Plaza, has an authentic blacksmith's shop, printer and boot shop. This impressive museum is open from 9 am to 5 pm Monday to Friday, and from 1.30 to 4.30 pm at weekends; admission is $3 (50c for children).

Burnie Park is quite pleasant and features an animal sanctuary and the oldest building in town, the Burnie Inn. The Inn was built in 1847 and moved from its original site to the park in 1973. It's classified by the National Trust and is open at weekends.

From Monday to Thursday, at 2 pm, you can take a free tour of the Amcor complex. On weekdays you can also visit the Lactos cheese factory, on Old Surrey Rd, where you can taste and purchase the products. The **Burnie Regional Art Gallery**, in Wilmot St, is open daily and is also worth a look.

There are a number of waterfalls and viewpoints in the Burnie area, including **Roundhill Lookout** and **Fern Glade**, just three km from the centre, and the impressive **Guide Falls** at Ridgley, 16 km away.

Places to Stay

At Cooee, three km west of Burnie on the Bass Highway, the *Treasure Island Caravan Park* (☎ (004) 31 1925) has camp sites ($13), cabins ($44 double) and on-site vans ($32). There's no budget accommodation in

Burnie and the nearest youth hostel is at Wynyard, 19 km away.

Cheapest of the hotels is the *Regent* (☎ (004) 31 1933), at 26 North Terrace, which charges $20/30 for singles/doubles. *Glen Osborne House* (☎ (004) 31 9866) at 9 Aileen Crescent, about a km from the town centre, has rooms with their own facilities for $60/75. Closer to the centre is the *Burnie Town House* (☎ (004) 31 4455) at 139 Wilson St, which charges a fairly steep $80/90 for rooms with their own facilities.

Places to Eat

There are plenty of cafes along Mount, Wilmot, Wilson and Cattley Sts. For cheap lunches try the *Zodiac* in Cattley St or the *Napoli* cafe above Fitzgerald's department store on the corner of Wilson and Cattley Sts.

Most hotels have reasonably priced counter meals from Monday to Saturday. The *Beach Hotel* at 1 Wilson St, on the waterfront, always has a good spread.

Ladbrooke St, between Mount and Wilson Sts, is the area to go when you're hungry. *Renusha's Indian Restaurant* serves cheap and tasty food, and is BYO. Next door is the *Kasbah Pizza Bar*, and opposite is the *Li Yin*, which has good Chinese food and an all-you-can-eat three-course meal for $12.

Not far away, at 104 Wilson St, the *Burnie Steak House* has meals for around $15. The *Rialto Gallery Restaurant*, at 46 Wilmot St, serves good Italian food and is open for dinner on Sunday nights.

Entertainment

Check the *Advocate* newspaper for entertainment listings. On Friday and Saturday nights there are discos at the *Bay View Hotel* and the *Club Hotel*. On Friday nights, the *Beach Hotel* is a popular place for a drink.

Getting There & Away

Air The nearest airport is at Wynyard, 20 km from Burnie. North West Travel (☎ (004) 31 2166), on the corner of Wilmot and Mount Sts in Burnie, is the agent for Kendell and Ansett Airlines.

Bus Redline has daily services to and from Smithton, Wynyard, Devonport, Launceston and Hobart. During the week, two of these services make the detour to Stanley. Redline also has at least one service between Burnie and Strahan ($30.40) via Devonport, Deloraine, Cradle Mountain and Queenstown ($25.60). The Redline agent in Burnie is at 117 Wilson St.

Hobart Coaches has daily services between Hobart and Burnie via Launceston, Deloraine, Devonport, Ulverstone and Penguin. Its buses leave from outside the Tasmanian Travel & Information Centre in Cattley St.

During the week, Metro Burnie (☎ (004) 31 3822), at 30 Strahan St, also has regular buses to Ulverstone, Penguin and Wynyard which depart from various stops in Cattley St.

WYNYARD (population 4680)

Sheltered by the impressive Table Cape and geologically fascinating Fossil Bluff, Wynyard sits both on the seafront and on the banks of the Inglis River. The town is surrounded by beautiful patchwork farmland, which is best appreciated by flying into Wynyard airport.

Although there's not much to see in the town itself, Wynyard is a good base from which to explore the many attractions in the area. Good sources of tourist information include the council chambers in Saunders St, and most hotels and restaurants.

Places to Stay & Eat

Close to town, on the Esplanade, is the *Wynyard Caravan Park* (☎ (004) 42 2740). East of Wynyard, on the scenic road to Burnie, the *Leisure Ville Caravan Park* (☎ (004) 42 2291) has camp sites ($10), cabins ($42) and on-site vans ($30).

The *Wynyard Youth Hostel* (☎ (004) 42 2013) is at 36 Dodgin St, one block south of the main shopping centre, and charges $10 a night. If you've arrived by air, take the airport road and turn right into Dodgin St – it's only a five-minute walk. The *Federal Hotel*

(☎ (004) 42 2056) at 82 Goldie St, in the middle of town, charges $30/50 for singles/doubles for B&B and also has good counter meals seven days a week.

Getting There & Away

For information on domestic flights to and from Wynyard, see the Getting There & Away section at the beginning of this chapter.

See the Burnie section for details on Redline and Metro Burnie bus services to Wynyard. The Redline agent is the BP service station next to the post office, and Metro Burnie buses depart from outside the St Vincent de Paul shop in Jackson St.

AROUND WYNYARD

Seven km from Wynyard, beyond the golf course, is **Fossil Bluff**, where the oldest marsupial fossil found in Australia was unearthed. The soft sandstone here features numerous shell fossils deposited when the level of Bass Strait was much higher.

Other attractions in the area include the unforgettable views from **Table Cape** and its lighthouse. At **Boat Harbour Beach**, 14 km from Wynyard, there's a beautiful bay with white sand and crystal-blue water – a lovely spot for rock-pool exploring and snorkelling. If you want to stay the night, try the *Boat Harbour Beach Backpackers* (☎ (004) 45 1273), set on four hectares of land not far from the beach. The town also has a caravan park and other motel-style accommodation.

Nearby, in the **Rocky Cape National Park**, is Sisters Beach, an eight-km expanse of glistening white sand, safe swimming and good fishing. Also in the park is the 10-hectare **Birdland Native Gardens**, which has information on more than 60 species of birds native to the area. You can also visit a number of waterfalls, including **Detention Falls**, three km south of Myalla, and **Dip Falls**, near Mawbanna.

Unless you have your own transport, you will have to hitch to get to most of these places. Redline Coaches will drop you at the turn-off to Boat Harbour (three km) and Sisters Beach (nine km). Boat Harbour

Beach Backpackers also does pick-ups from the highway.

STANLEY (population 580)

Nestled at the foot of the extraordinary Circular Head (better known as the Nut), Stanley is a very appealing historic village which has changed little since its early days. In 1826 it became the headquarters of the London-based Van Diemen's Land Company, which was granted a charter to settle and cultivate the Circular Head region.

The area really prospered when it began shipping large quantities of mutton, beef and potatoes to Victoria's goldfields, and it continued to do well when settlers discovered the rich dairying land behind Sisters Hills and the tin reserves at Mt Bischoff.

Today, Stanley is a charming fishing village with many historic buildings and great seascapes. To better appreciate Stanley's charm, pick up a walking-tour map from De Jonge's Souvenirs or the Discovery Centre, both in Church St. The Plough Inn also has tourist information and rents bicycles for local use.

The Nut

This striking 152-metre-high basalt formation, thought to be 12½ million years old, can be seen for many km around Stanley. It's a hard 10-minute climb to the top, but the view is definitely worth it. For the less energetic, a chairlift operates from 9.30 am to 4.30 pm; rides cost $5.50 ($3.50 for children).

Other Attractions

The old bluestone building on the seafront is the **Van Diemen's Land Company Store**, which was designed by John Lee Archer, Tasmania's famous colonial architect, and dates from 1844. The company's actual headquarters were at Highfield, to the east of Stanley, and these are currently being restored.

Also near the wharf is a particularly fine old bluestone building which used to be a grain store and was built in 1843 from stones brought to Stanley as ship's ballast.

The **Plough Inn** (1840), in Church St, has been fully restored and furnished with period furniture. Next door is a little folk museum called the **Discovery Centre**, which is open daily from 10 am to 4.30 pm; admission is $2.

Other buildings of historical interest include **Lyons Cottage**, in Church St, which was the birthplace of former Prime Minister Joseph Lyons and is open from 10 am to 4 pm; the **Union Hotel**, also in Church St, which dates from 1849; and the **Presbyterian Church**, which was probably Australia's first prefabricated building, bought in England and transported to Stanley in 1853.

Places to Stay

Stanley has a wide selection of accommodation. The *Stanley Youth Hostel* (☎ (004) 58 1266) is near the beach in the *Wharf Rd Caravan Park* and charges $10 a night. The caravan park has camp sites ($10) and on-site vans ($30) and cabins ($45).

Pol & Pen (☎ (004) 58 1334) are a pair of two-bedroom self-contained cottages, which are good value at $55 a double and $10 for each additional person. The *Union Hotel* (☎ (004) 58 1161), situated in Church St, has singles/doubles for $25/35. Also in Church St is *Touchwood Cottage* (☎ (004) 58 1348), a lovely colonial guesthouse which charges $50/60, which includes a cooked breakfast.

Places to Eat

Julie & Patrick's Seafood Restaurant is next door to Hursey Seafoods (where live crays, crabs and fish are kept in tanks in the shop). Both places are owned by the same people, which means that the food served in the restaurant couldn't be fresher.

Sullivans, a licensed restaurant at 25 Church St, is open daily and serves light lunches, teas and dinner. At the Nut there is the *Nut Shop Tearooms*, and the *Union Hotel* has quite good counter meals.

Getting There & Away

Redline has two services a day on weekdays which run from Hobart to Smithton via Stanley, and three running via Stanley in the other direction. The Redline agent is the BP service station on the corner of Wharf Rd and Marine Esplanade.

AROUND STANLEY

Twenty-two km from Stanley, **Smithton** serves one of Tasmania's greatest forestry areas and is also the administrative centre for Circular Head. There's not much to see or do in the town itself, but the town's airport makes it an arrival point for some light aircraft flights from the mainland.

Woolnorth, on the north-western tip of Tasmania, near Cape Grim, is a 220-sq-km cattle and sheep property which is the only remaining holding of the Van Diemen's Land Company. Unfortunately, tours of the property are now only available to members of bus tours.

Allendale Gardens, on the B22 road to Edith Creek, is a good place to walk around or relax in; the two-hectare property includes impressive botanical gardens, a rainforest walk, a wild-flower section and a cafe serving Devonshire teas. The centre is open daily from 10 am to 6 pm (closed June to August) and admission is $5 ($2.50 for children).

Massive ferns, myrtles, fungi and lichens are all found at **Milkshake Forest Reserve**, 45 km south of Smithton. A little further west of the reserve, set in beautiful rainforest, is tranquil **Lake Chisholm**.

MARRAWAH

Marrawah, at the end of the Bass Highway, is where the wild Indian Ocean occasionally throws up the remains of ships wrecked on the dangerous and rugged west coast. To visit Marrawah, the most westerly town in Tasmania, it is best to have your own vehicle, but from Monday to Saturday you can get a lift on the mail run from Smithton.

This part of the coast was once home to Tasmanian Aborigines, and particular areas have been proclaimed reserves to protect the environment and remaining relics, including rock carvings, middens and hut depressions. The main Aboriginal sites are at **Mt Cameron**

West, near Green Point, at **West Point** and at **Sundown Point**.

The township of Marrawah consists of a hotel and a general store selling petrol and supplies. The hotel has meals, and no accommodation, but there is a basic camp site at Green Point, two km from Marrawah. This region is good for fishing, camping and bushwalking, or just for getting away from it all. Marrawah's main attraction, however, is its enormous surf: the state's surfing championships are held here every year around Easter.

ARTHUR RIVER

The sleepy town of Arthur River, 14 km south of Marrawah, is mainly a collection of holiday houses for people who come here to fish. There is one kiosk with basic supplies, no public transport and, apart from a camp site (with no facilities), only one place to stay. The *Arthur River Holiday Units* (☎ (004) 57 1288), in Gardiner St, has singles/doubles for $40/55.

Apart from the fishing, visitors come here to explore the **Arthur Pieman Protected Area** and to take a cruise on the Arthur River. The attractions of the Protected Area include magnificent ocean beaches, waterfalls on the Nelson River, Rebecca Lagoon, Temma Harbour, the old mining town of Balfour, the Pieman River and the Norfolk Ranges.

If you are exploring south of Temma Harbour, you really need a 4WD, and if you are going south of Greens Creek you need to get a permit from the Arthur River Base Office (☎ (004) 57 1225) in Arthur River.

Arthur River Cruise

Paddy and Turk Porteous operate scenic day cruises on the Arthur River (☎ (004) 57 1158) which depart at 10 am and return at 3 pm. You sail up the river, feeding sea eagles on the way, to the confluence of the Arthur and Frankland rivers. Here you have lunch, with billy tea, in a rainforest clearing which took Turk almost five years to clear. After lunch there is a one-hour guided walking tour through the dense vegetation. The cruise runs most days in summer, but as a minimum

of eight people is required, it's best to book you can do this at any Tasmanian Travel & Information Centre. The cost is $35 ($12 for children).

HELLYER GORGE

It's about 150 km on the Murchison Highway between Somerset, on the north coast, to Zeehan, close to the west coast Hellyer Gorge is a serene myrtle forest reserve on the banks of the Hellyer River halfway between Somerset and the turn-off to Waratah, Savage River and Corinna. The highway winds precariously through the impressive gorge, and there are plenty of rest and picnic areas.

The new Guildford Junction Highway between Hampshire and Guildford, was built to shorten the trip from the north coast to the west, but it's also had the effect of diverting traffic from the peaceful recreational reserve at Hellyer Gorge. The new road follows part of the Emu Bay Railway route and links up with Burnie.

SAVAGE RIVER

The Mt Bischoff mine, near Waratah, was once the world's richest tin mine, but these days it is the iron ore of Savage River that keeps mining alive in the region. The ore, once mined, is pumped as a slurry 85 km to Port Latta on the north coast.

There are mine tours on Tuesdays and Thursdays at 9 am and 2 pm, but these have to be booked (☎ (004) 43 4105).

Accommodation is available only at the *Savage River Motor Inn* (☎ (004) 46 1177), where rooms cost $40/50.

CORINNA

Corinna, 28 km south-west of Savage River, was once a thriving gold-mining settlement but is now little more than a ghost town. These days it's the scenery and the Pieman River Cruises (☎ (004) 46 1170) that attract the visitors. The cruise takes you through impressive forests of eucalypts, ferns and Huon pines to the Pieman Heads. Costing $28 ($14 for children), which includes morning tea, the tours on the MV *Arcadia II* depart daily at 10.30 am and return at 2.30 pm. It's definitely best to book during the summer months.

The only accommodation is at the *Pieman Retreat Cabins* (☎ (004) 46 1170). Each cabin can sleep up to six people and costs $80 regardless of numbers. The cabins are self-contained and linen is available at extra cost.

ROSEBERY (population 1640)

Mining began in Rosebery in 1900 with the completion of the Emu Bay Railway between Burnie and Zeehan, but when the Zeehan lead smelters closed in 1913 operations also shut here. The Electrolytic Zinc Company then bought and reopened the mine in 1936 and it has operated ever since. There's not much to see in Rosebery, but if you want to stay overnight, the *Plandome Hotel* (☎ (004) 73 1351) has accommodation, and there's a caravan park.

West Coast

Nature at its most awe-inspiring is the attraction of Tasmania's rugged and magnificent west coast. Formidable mountains, buttongrass plains, ancient rivers, tranquil lakes, dense rainforests and a treacherous coast are all features of this compelling and beautiful region, much of which is now World Heritage area.

Centuries before the arrival of Europeans, this part of Tasmania was home to many of the state's Aborigines, and plenty of archaeological evidence, some of it more than 20,000 years old, has been found of these original inhabitants. Indeed, were it not for its vast mineral reserves and rich stands of Huon pine, this region would probably have remained the domain of the Aborigines.

Prior to 1932, when the road from Hobart to Queenstown was built, the only way into the area was by sea, through the dangerously narrow Macquarie Harbour to Strahan. Despite such inaccessibility, early European

settlement brought explorers, convicts, soldiers, loggers, prospectors, railway gangs and fishermen, while the 20th century has brought outdoor adventurers, naturalists and environmental crusaders.

It was over the wild rivers, beautiful lakes and lonely valleys of Tasmania's south-west that the battles between environmentalists and big business raged. This is the area that saw the flooding of Lake Pedder and the creation of a system of lakes on the upper reaches of the Pieman River to feed massive hydroelectric schemes. It was here, over the proposed damming of the Franklin and

Lower Gordon rivers, that the greatest and longest environmental debate in Australia's history, culminating in an 11-week river blockade, took place.

While debate continues on questions of wilderness versus electricity and World Heritage area versus woodchip, nature herself has begun to reclaim what is hers. The rusting railways, abandoned mines and deserted towns of the early west-coast mining days are becoming mere spectres in the regeneration of the bush.

ZEEHAN (population 1130)
In 1882, rich deposits of silver and lead were discovered in the quiet little town of Zeehan, and by the turn of the century, it had become a booming mining centre with a population that peaked at nearly 10,000. In its heyday, Zeehan had 26 hotels, and its Gaiety Theatre was the largest in Australia. In 1908, however, the mines began to fail and the town declined.

With the reopening of the Renison Tin Mine at Renison Bell in the 1970s, the town experienced a revival, but today, with the low price of tin, its future does not look bright.

Things to See
Buildings that remain from the early boom days include the once famous **Grand Hotel**, the **Gaiety Theatre**, the **post office**, the **bank** and **St Luke's Church**.

For an excellent insight into the workings of a mine, visit the **West Coast Pioneers' Memorial Museum** in Main St. It's open daily from 8.30 am to 5 pm and is free (donations welcome). The museum also features an interesting mineral collection and an exhibit of steam locomotives and carriages used on the early west-coast railways.

The only bank with a branch here is the ANZ, and there is no ATM.

Places to Stay
At the *Treasure Island West Coast Caravan Park* (☎ (004) 71 6633) in Hurst St there are camp sites ($10), cabins ($44) and on-site vans ($35). The *Heemskirk Motel* (☎ (004)

71 6107) offers backpackers' accommodation in its old holiday lodge section for $12 per person. It also has motel rooms from $68.

The old *Hotel Cecil* (☎ (004) 71 6221) in Main St has singles/doubles for $30/50, or self-contained holiday units with cooking facilities for $68/70.

Getting There & Away
On most days (except Sundays) there's at least one Redline service from Burnie to Strahan via Zeehan; the return bus travels from Strahan to Devonport via Zeehan. The Redline agent in Zeehan is Maines Milk Bar in Main St. Tasmanian Wilderness Transport's Strahan to Devonport service also stops in Zeehan.

QUEENSTOWN (population 3370)
The final, winding descent into Queenstown from the Lyell Highway is an unforgettable experience. With deep, eroded gullies and naked, multicoloured hills, there is no escaping the fact that this is a mining town, and that the destruction of the surrounding area is a direct result of this industry.

In 1881, the discovery of alluvial gold in the Queen River valley first brought prospectors to the area. Two years later, mining began on the rich Mt Lyell deposits, and for nearly a decade miners extracted a few ounces of gold a day and ignored the mountain's rich copper reserves. In 1891, however, the Mt Lyell Mining Company began to concentrate on the copper and it soon became the most profitable mineral on the west coast.

In 1899, the company built a 35-km railway between Queenstown and Strahan to transport copper, and passengers, to the coast. It traversed spectacular terrain (48 bridges were built) and was so steep in some sections that the rack and pinion system had to be used to assist the two steam engines hauling the train.

At the turn of the century, Queenstown had a population of 5051 and was the third largest town in Tasmania. It had 14 hotels, there were 28 mining companies working the

Mt Lyell deposits, and 11 furnaces were involved in the smelting process. The Mt Lyell Mining & Railway Company eventually acquired most of the mines or leases, and since 1933 has worked the area without a rival.

After 20 years of mining, the rainforested hills around Queenstown had been stripped bare: three million tonnes of timber had been felled to feed the furnaces. By 1900, uncontrolled pollution from the copper smelters was killing any vegetation that had not already been cut down, and bushfires raged through the hills every summer, fuelled by the sulphur-impregnated soils and dead stumps, until there was no regrowth left at all.

With the closure of the Mt Lyell mine in late 1994, Queenstown's future does not look bright. Tourism is now the town's major industry.

Information

The RACT (☎ (004) 71 1974), at 18 Orr St, has plenty of tourist brochures and the staff are very helpful. You can also get visitor information at the Galley Museum (☎ (004) 71 1758) on the corner of Sticht and Driffield Sts.

The only bank is the Trust Bank, and there is also a credit union branch here.

Things to See

The **Galley Museum** started life as the Imperial Hotel and was the first brick hotel in Queenstown. The building has since served many purposes, including a period as the single men's quarters for the Mt Lyell Company. The museum features a good collection of old photographs (recording the history of Queenstown and the west coast), as well as a display of early mining equipment, personal effects and household goods from the town's pioneering days. The museum is open from 10 am to 12.30 pm and from 1.30 to 4.30 pm Monday to Friday, and from 1.30 to 4.30 pm at weekends; admission is $2. It might be worth enquiring here to see if there are still tours of the mine site.

There are good views from **Spion Kop Lookout**, in the centre of town (follow

Bowes St). If you are wondering why the football oval on your left is brown instead of green, Queenstown's footy team is tough – they play on silica, not grass, and this is the only silica oval in the world.

Queenstown has a good *Historic Walk* brochure which guides you around the town from the Galley Museum to Spion Kop Lookout. You can pick up the leaflet and map in any shop or hotel and it is an excellent way to see all the sights.

The **Miner's Siding**, in Driffield St, is a public park featuring a restored ABT steam locomotive and a rock sculpture which tells the history of the Queenstown to Strahan railway.

At **Newell Creek**, nine km south of Queenstown on the Mt Jukes Rd, a platform for visitors gives access to a patch of superb King Billy and Huon pine rainforest.

Places to Stay & Eat

The *Queenstown Cabin & Tourist Park* (☎ (004) 71 1332), at 17 Grafton St, about half a km from the town centre, has bunkhouse accommodation for $17 a double plus $6 for each extra person. There are also on-site vans ($30) and cabins ($43).

At 1 Penghana Rd, just over the bridge on the way to Strahan, is the *Mountain View Holiday Lodge* (☎ (004) 71 1163), which is the old single men's quarters for the Mt Lyell Mining Company. The hostel section is pretty basic, but for $8 a night you get your own room and there are cooking facilities. Many of the rooms have been renovated as motel-style units and cost $50 a double.

The *Empire Hotel* (☎ (004) 71 1699), at 2 Orr St, is a lovely old hotel with an imposing staircase classified by the National Trust. Clean and pleasant singles/doubles cost $20/35 and, for a little extra, you can get breakfast. *Hunter's Hotel* (☎ (004) 71 1531), further up Orr St, is not as attractive and charges $20 per person.

The *Mount Lyell Motor Inn* (☎ (004) 71 1888), at 1 Orr St, has motel suites for $40/50; the staff are friendly.

Apart from counter meals, which are pretty good at the *Mount Lyell Motor Inn*,

Queenstown has little to offer in the way of places to eat. In Orr St, *Axel's* has good cakes and light snacks, and nearby you'll find the *Chester the Chick* chicken shop and *Filis Pizza*.

Getting There & Away

See the Air Fares chart in the Getting Around section at the start of this chapter for air fares to and from Queenstown.

Redline has daily bus services (Monday to Saturday) between Queenstown and Strahan ($4.80), Hobart ($29.40), Burnie ($25.56) and Devonport ($31.70). The Redline agent is in Orr St.

If you are hitching, it can be a long wait between vehicles on both the Lyell and Murchison highways, and in winter it gets pretty bloody cold.

STRAHAN (population 600)

Strahan, 40 km from Queenstown on Macquarie Harbour, is the only town on this rugged and dangerous coast. Though only a shadow of its former self, the town is rich in convict, logging and mining history.

Treacherous seas, the lack of natural harbours and high rainfall discouraged early settlement of the region until Macquarie Harbour was discovered by sailors searching for the source of the Huon pine that frequently washed up on the southern beaches.

In those days, the area was totally inaccessible by land and very difficult to reach by sea, and in 1821 these dubious assets prompted the establishment of a penal settlement on Sarah Island, in the middle of the harbour. Its main function was to isolate the worst of the colony's convicts and to use their muscle to harvest the huge stands of Huon pine. The convicts worked upriver 12 hours a day, often in leg irons, felling the pines and rafting them back to the island's saw-pits, where they were used to build ships and furniture.

With its barbaric treatment of prisoners, Sarah Island became one of Australia's most notorious penal settlements. The most dreaded punishment was confinement on tiny Grummet Island, where up to 40 convicts at a time were held in appalling conditions on what was little more than a windswept rock – for some, death was a welcome release.

Sarah Island appeared in Marcus Clarke's graphic novel about convict life *For the Term of his Natural Life*. In 1834, however, after the establishment of the 'escape-proof' penal settlement at Port Arthur, Sarah Island was abandoned.

As the port for Queenstown, Strahan reached its peak of prosperity with the west-coast mining boom, and the completion of the Mt Lyell Mining Company's railway line in the 1890s. At the turn of the century, it was a bustling centre with a population of 2000. Steamers operated regularly between Strahan and Hobart, Launceston and Melbourne carrying copper, gold, silver, lead, timber and passengers. The closure of many of the west-coast mines and the opening of the Emu Bay Railway from Zeehan to Burnie led to the decline of Strahan as a port.

These days, Strahan is a charming seaside town which draws visitors in droves for cruises on the Gordon River and scenic flights over the area.

Information

The architecturally unusual and innovative Strahan Visitor Centre (☎ (004) 71 7488) on the waterfront is almost a tourist attraction in its own right. The foyer information area has a river-gravel floor and a superb reception desk built out of Huon pine. Beyond this is the museum section, which presents all aspects of the history of the south-west in a way that really captures the imagination. The centre is open daily from 10 am to 6 pm; entry to the museum section is $4.50.

There is an office of the Department of Parks, Wildlife & Heritage (☎ (004) 71 7122) in the old Customs House building close to the town centre. This building also houses the post office. There is no bank in Strahan.

Things to See

Probably the finest building on the west

coast is Strahan's imposing **Customs House**.

Hogarth Falls is a pleasant 20-minute walk through the rainforest from Peoples Park, which is just a few minutes walk around the bay from the town centre.

The **lighthouse** at Cape Sorell, on the south head of the harbour, is the third largest in Tasmania. Opposite the caravan park is a **gemstone & mineral museum**.

Six km from the town is the impressive 33-km **Ocean Beach**, where the sunsets have to be seen to be believed. In October, when the birds return from their winter migration, the beach is also a mutton-bird rookery.

Twenty km along the road from Strahan to Zeehan are the **Henty Dunes**, some spectacular sand dunes, many of which are more than 30 metres in height.

Organised Tours & Cruises

Gordon River Cruise A traditional way of experiencing the beauty of the Gordon River is on one of the cruises which operate out of Strahan.

Gordon River Cruises (☎ (004) 71 7317) has half-day trips (9 am to 2 pm) for $40 ($20 for children), including morning tea, or full-day trips (9 am to 4 pm) for $55 ($25 for children), including a smorgasbord lunch.

World Heritage Tours (☎ (004) 71 7174) has the MV *Heritage Wanderer*, which charges $32 ($15 for children) for a trip from 9 am to 2 pm; lunch is available on board.

All cruises include visits to Sarah Island, Heritage Rainforest Walk and Hells Gates (the narrow entrance to Macquarie Harbour).

Seaplane Tour A highly recommended way to see the river and surrounding World Heritage area is on a seaplane tour with Wilderness Air (☎ (004) 71 7280). The planes take off from Strahan's wharf every 1½ hours from 9 am onwards and fly up the river to Sir John Falls, where they land so that you can take a walk in the rainforest, before flying back via Sarah Island, Cape Sorell, Hells Gates and Ocean Beach. The 80-minute flight is well worth the $90. Demand

for flights is heavy, so it's good to book if possible.

Jet-Boat Ride Wild Rivers Jet (☎ (004) 71 7174), also at the Wilderness Air office on the wharf, operates 40-minute jet-boat rides up the King River for $30 ($20 for children).

4WD Wilderness Trips Strahan Wilderness Tours (☎ (004) 71 7401) offers 4WD trips to and along Ocean Beach for $40, to nearby Teepookana Forest for $30, or for sunset at Ocean Beach for $20.

Places to Stay

Although Strahan has a range of accommodation, places are often full, so it's best to book.

There's the *West Strahan Caravan Park* (☎ (004) 71 7239), which charges $8 for a double camp site, and there's also a camping ground with basic facilities 15 km away at Macquarie Heads.

At $12 a night, the *Strahan Youth Hostel* (☎ (004) 71 7255) in Harvey St is the cheapest accommodation in town. It is about a 10-minute walk from the town centre. There are also cabins available at $35/45 a double/triple.

Three km from town, on Ocean Beach Rd, is the historic *Strahan Lodge* (☎ (004) 71 7142), where singles/doubles with a continental breakfast cost $30/40. Unless you have your own transport, it may be a bit inconvenient.

Hamer's Hotel (☎ (004) 71 7191) is opposite the wharf right in the middle of town and has passable rooms in the old section of the pub for $35/50, including a continental breakfast. They also have a group of somewhat twee, self-contained cottages built in various colonial styles, and these are also on the waterfront. They cost $95 for two, and $120 with a spa.

For a memorable stay you could try the historic *Franklin Manor* (☎ (004) 71 7311), on the Esplanade just around the bay from the town centre. The cost to stay in one of the 12 self-contained suites is $105/112 for B&B.

At *Azza's* (☎ (004) 71 7253), a general store near the youth hostel, there are a number of self-contained cabins at $45 for a double.

If you're stuck for somewhere to stay, ring Mrs Abel (☎ (004) 71 7271); she charges $36 for a double B&B.

Places to Eat

At the magnificent *Franklin Manor* (☎ (004) 71 7311) you can get an excellent three-course meal for $26 but it's best to book. *Hamer's Hotel*, *Regatta Point Tavern*, on the Esplanade, and the *Strahan Inn*, Jolly St, all have good meals. The *Harbour Cafe* has takeaways, but it's pleasant to eat on the premises as there are great views across the wharf.

Getting There & Away

See the Getting Around section at the beginning of this chapter for information on flights to Strahan.

Redline has daily (except Sunday) services from Hobart ($34.20), Burnie ($30.40) and Devonport ($36.50). The Redline agent is the newsagency in the main street.

Tasmanian Wilderness Transport also runs buses between Strahan and Hobart ($55) and Devonport ($50); its agent is the Harbour Cafe in the main street.

FRANKLIN-GORDON WILD RIVERS NATIONAL PARK

This World-Heritage-listed park includes the catchment areas of the Franklin and Olga rivers and part of the Gordon River, as well as the excellent bushwalking region known as **Frenchmans Cap**. It has a number of unique plant species and a major Aboriginal archaeological site at **Kutikina Cave**.

Much of the park is impenetrable rainforest, but the Lyell Highway traverses its northern end and there are a few short walks which you can do from the road. These include hikes to **Donaghys Hill**, from which you can see the Franklin River and the magnificent white quartzite dome of Frenchmans

Cap, a walk to **Nelson Falls** and several short walks around the Collingwood River area.

The walk to Frenchmans Cap, which takes three to five days and features a ride across the Franklin River on a pulley contraption called the Flying Fox, is probably the park's best-known bushwalk. The best way, however, to see this magnificent park is not to cross the Franklin River but to raft down it.

Rafting the Franklin

The Franklin is a very wild river and rafting it can be a hazardous journey. Experienced rafters can tackle it if they are fully equipped and prepared, or there are tour companies who offer complete rafting packages. Whether you go with an independent group or a tour operator, it's a good idea to contact the Queenstown office of the Department of Parks, Wildlife & Heritage (☎ (004) 71 2511; PO Box 21, Queenstown) for a copy of their excellent and up-to-date notes on the trip. Also worth contacting is the South Australian company Wilderness Guides (☎ (08) 296 7093), at 60 Holder Rd, North Brighton, which publishes laminated, spiral-bound rafting maps of the Franklin River.

All expeditions should register at the booth at the junction between the Lyell Highway and the Collingwood River, 49 km west of Derwent Bridge. The trip, starting at Collingwood River and ending at Heritage Landing, on the Franklin, takes about 14 days (you can do a shorter eight-day one) and there are camp sites along the way. From your exit point, you can be picked up by a Gordon River Cruise boat or a Wilderness Air seaplane.

Tour companies that arrange complete rafting packages include Peregrine Adventures (☎ (03) 663 8611), 258 Lonsdale St, Melbourne; World Expeditions (☎ (02) 264 3366), 3rd floor, 441 Kent St, Sydney; and Rafting Tasmania (☎ (002) 27 8293), 63 Channel Highway, Taroona. An all-inclusive rafting package, including transport from Hobart, costs around $180 a day. Departures are mainly from December to March.

A	
B	C	D
E	

Tasmania

A Georgian warehouses, Hobart (GB)
B Salamanca Place, Hobart (HF)
C Arts and crafts shop, Richmond (HF)
D Port Arthur, Tasman Peninsula (PS)
E Mt Field National Park (PS)

A	
B	C	D
E	

Tasmania

A Eroded hills near Queenstown (HF)

B Mt Hyperion, Cradle Mountain-
Lake St Clair (JC)

C Cradle Mountain (PS)

D Coastal scenery near Swansea (P

E Ross Bridge (c1836), Ross (GB)

SOUTH-WEST NATIONAL PARK

There are few places left in the world as isolated and untouched as Tasmania's south-west wilderness, the state's largest national park. It is the home of some of the world's last tracts of virgin temperate rainforest, and these contribute much to the grandeur and extraordinary diversity of this ancient area.

The south-west is the habitat of the endemic Huon pine, which lives for more than 3000 years, and of the swamp gum, the world's tallest hardwood and flowering plant. About 300 species of lichen, moss and fern, some rare and endangered, festoon the dense rainforest; superb glacial tarns decorate the jagged mountains; and in summer, the delicate alpine meadows are ablaze with wildflowers and flowering shrubs. Through it all are the wild rivers, with rapids tearing through deep gorges and waterfalls plunging over cliffs. Each year more and more people venture into the heart of this incredible part of Tasmania's World Heritage area, seeking the peace, isolation and challenge of a region as old as the last ice age.

The best-known walk in the park is the **South Coast Track** between Port Davey and Cockle Creek, near Recherche Bay. This takes about 10 days and should only be tackled by experienced hikers, well prepared for the often vicious weather conditions. Light planes are used to airlift bushwalkers into the south-west and there is vehicle access to Cockle Creek. A whole range of escorted wilderness adventures are possible, involving flying, hiking, rafting, canoeing, mountaineering, caving and camping; more information on these can be obtained from any Tasmanian Travel & Information Centre or from the Wilderness Society. The ranger's telephone number is ☎ (002) 88 1283.

LAKE PEDDER

At the edge of the south-west wilderness lies Lake Pedder, once a spectacularly beautiful natural lake considered the crown jewel of the region. In 1972, however, it was flooded beyond all recognition to become part of the Hydro-Electric Commission's (HEC's) Gordon River power development, although its original name was retained. Together with nearby Lake Gordon, Pedder now holds 27 times the volume of water in Sydney Harbour and is the largest inland freshwater catchment in Australia. The underground Gordon Power Station is the largest in Tasmania and the HEC conducts daily tours around it. The visitors centre at the Gordon Dam site has plenty of information about the scheme.

> **Lake Pedder**
> The flooding of Lake Pedder was, and still is, very controversial. The beauty of the original lake was such that many are still campaigning to see the lake returned to its natural state, and in 1974 Edward St John, the QC on the National Lake Pedder Committee of Inquiry, voiced the opinion that they may be successful: 'Our children will undo what we so foolishly have done'. ■

STRATHGORDON

Built to service HEC employees, the township of Strathgordon is the base from which to visit lakes Pedder and Gordon, the Gordon Dam and the power station. Strathgordon is also becoming a popular bushwalking, trout fishing, boating and water-skiing resort. There's a camping ground, and accommodation is available at the *Lake Pedder Motor Inn* (☎ (002) 80 1166), where singles/doubles cost $50/60.

Cradle Mountain-Lake St Clair

Tasmania's best-known national park is the superb 1262-sq-km World Heritage area of Cradle Mountain-Lake St Clair. The spectacular mountain peaks, deep gorges, lakes, tarns, wild open moorlands, and the reserve's incredible variety of wildlife, extend from the Great Western Tiers in Tasmania's north to Derwent Bridge, on the Lyell Highway in

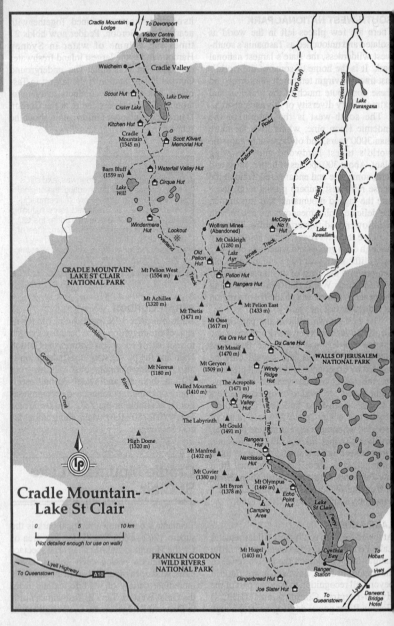

Cradle Mountain Lodge

To Devonport

Visitor Centre & Ranger Station

Waldheim

Cradle Valley

Scout Hut

Lake Dove

Crater Lake

Kitchen Hut

Cradle Mountain (1545 m)

Scott Kilvert Memorial Hut

Barn Bluff (1559 m)

Waterfall Valley Hut

Lake Will

Cirque Hut

Windermere Hut

Lookout

Wolfram Mines (Abandoned)

Old Pelion Hut

Mt Oakleigh (1280 m)

Lake Ayr

McCoys No 1 Hut

Lake Rowallan

CRADLE MOUNTAIN-LAKE ST CLAIR NATIONAL PARK

Mt Pelion West (1554 m)

Pelion Hut

Rangers Hut

Mt Achilles (1320 m)

Mt Thetis (1471 m)

Mt Pelion East (1433 m)

Mt Ossa (1617 m)

Kia Ora Hut

Du Cane Hut

Mt Massif (1470 m)

WALLS OF JERUSALEM NATIONAL PARK

Mt Nereus (1180 m)

Mt Geryon (1509 m)

Windy Ridge Hut

Walled Mountain (1410 m)

The Acropolis (1471 m)

Pine Valley Hut

The Labyrinth

Mt Gould (1491 m)

High Dome (1320 m)

Rangers Hut

Mt Manfred (1402 m)

Narcissus Hut

Mt Cuvier (1380 m)

Mt Olympus (1449 m)

Mt Byron (1378 m)

Echo Point Hut

Lake St Clair

Camping Area

Cradle Mountain-Lake St Clair

0   5   10 km

(Not detailed enough for use on walk)

Mt Hugel (1403 m)

Cynthia Bay

To Hobart

FRANKLIN GORDON WILD RIVERS NATIONAL PARK

Gingerbread Hut

Ranger Station

Joe Slater Hut

Lyell Highway

To Queenstown

A10

To Queenstown

Derwent Bridge Hotel

Lyell Hwy

Murchison

Gorge River

Gell Creek

Patons Road

Arm Road

Meago Road

Mersey Road

Forest Road

Lake Parangana

Lake Rowallan

Innes Track

Overland Track

Ferry

4 WD only

the south. It is one of the most glaciated areas in Australia and includes Mt Ossa (1617 metres), Tasmania's highest mountain, and Lake St Clair, Australia's deepest natural freshwater lake.

The preservation of this region as a national park is due, in part, to the Austrian Gustav Weindorfer, who fell in love with the area and claimed, 'This must be a national park for all time. It is magnificent. Everyone should know about it, and come and enjoy it'. In 1912 he built a chalet out of King Billy pine called Waldheim ('Forest Home' in German), and from 1916 he lived there permanently. Today, eight bushwalkers' huts have been constructed near his original chalet, at the northern end of the park, and the area is named Waldheim, after his chalet.

There are plenty of day walks in both the Cradle Valley and Cynthia Bay (Lake St Clair) regions, but it is the spectacular 80-km walk between the two that has turned this park into a bushwalkers' Mecca. The Overland Track is one of the finest bushwalks in Australia, and in summer up to 100 people a day can set off on it. The track can be walked in either direction, but most people walk from north to south, from Cradle Valley to Cynthia Bay.

Information

Cradle Valley At the northern park boundary, and built on the verge of an amazing rainforest, the visitor centre and ranger station (☎ (004) 92 1133) is open year round from 8 am to 5 pm. The centre is staffed by rangers who can advise you about weather conditions, walking gear, maximum and minimum walking groups, bush safety, and bush etiquette. The centre also has plenty of leaflets and videos for hikers on all aspects of walking, from the dangers of hypothermia to the skills of minimal-impact bushwalking.

For visitors in wheelchairs, or with youngsters in prams, the centre also features an easy, but quite spectacular, 500-metre circular boardwalk through the adjacent rainforest called the **Rainforest-Pencil Pine Falls Walking Track**.

Cradle Mountain Scenic Flights (☎ (004) 92 1132), which operates from the Cradle View Restaurant, offers a much less energetic way to see all the sights. A 25-minute trip costs $130 for two or $55 each for three or more people.

Whatever time of the year you visit, be prepared for shitty weather in the Cradle Valley area – on average it rains on seven days out of 10, it is cloudy on eight days out of 10, the sun shines all day only one day in 10, and it snows on 54 days each year!

Cynthia Bay Cynthia Bay, near the southern park boundary, also has an informative ranger station (☎ (002) 89 1115) where you register to walk the Overland Track in the opposite direction. At the nearby kiosk (☎ (002) 89 1137) you can book a seat on the small *Idaclair!* ferry. The boat does a $13 one-way or $16 return trip to Narcissus Hut at the northern end of Lake St Clair ($20 if you break the trip for a couple of hours, $26 if you return on a different day) departing at 9 am and 12.30 and 3 pm. The boat is available for charter. From the same kiosk you can also hire dinghies for a spot of fishing or relaxing on the lake, but don't fall in – it's freezing!

The Overland Track

The best time to walk the Overland Track is during summer, when the flowering plants are most prolific, although spring and autumn also have their attractions. You can walk the track in winter, but only if you're very experienced.

The trail is well marked for its entire length and, at an easy pace, takes around five or six days to walk. En route, however, there are many secondary paths leading up to mountains like Mt Ossa (only three km off the track) or other natural features, making it a great temptation to take a few more days to explore the region fully. In fact, the length of time you take is only limited by the amount of supplies you can carry. There are 12 unattended huts along the track which you can use for overnight accommodation, but in summer they can get full.

A detailed description of the walk is given

in Lonely Planet's *Bushwalking in Australia*. The most dangerous part of the walk is the exposed high plateau between Waldheim and Pelion Creek, near Mt Pelion West. The south-west wind that blows across here can be bitterly cold and sometimes strong enough to knock you off your feet.

If you are walking from Cradle Valley to Cynthia Bay, you have the option of radioing from Narcissus Hut for the *Idaclair!* ferry to come and pick you up. This trip costs $13 and will save you a 5½-hour walk. The *Idaclair!* can also take you from Cynthia Bay to the hut if you are walking in the other direction.

Places to Stay & Eat
Cradle Valley Region The cheapest place in this area is the *Cradle Mountain Camping Ground* (☎ (004) 92 1395), 2.5 km outside the national park; it costs $14 a double to camp here or $20 per person to stay in the bunkhouse.

At Waldheim, about 10 km into the national park, there are eight basic huts sleeping four, six or eight people, all containing gas stoves, cooking utensils and wood heaters but no bedding. The minimum fees for these cabins are $55, $65 or $75, or if all the beds are occupied, $20 each a night. Check-in and bookings for the huts are handled by the camping ground.

Just on the national-park boundary is the luxurious *Cradle Mountain Lodge* (☎ (004) 92 1303), where singles/doubles in the main chalet cost $80/100, self-contained cabins are $129 a double, and a deluxe spa cabin costs $169 a double. The lodge has good facilities for its guests and anyone is welcome to eat at the excellent restaurant (make sure you book first), visit the Tavern Bar or buy basic groceries and unleaded petrol at the lodge's general store.

The *Cradle View Restaurant*, near the camping ground, serves reasonably priced home-made meals; you can also buy leaded petrol and diesel from outside the restaurant.

Cynthia Bay Region At the southern end of Lake St Clair, *Lake St Clair Holidays*

(☎ (002) 89 1137) has five huts (one 16-bed, one four-bed and three nine-bed), plenty of camp sites and a kiosk that sells basic food supplies. It costs $8 for two to camp and $6 per person a night to stay at *Milligania*, the 16-bed dormitory-style hut. The other huts contain a stove, fridge, cooking utensils and a wood heater but no bedding and cost $8 per person, with a minimum of $30 for the one-bedroom and $60 for the two-bedroom huts; they're mainly used by groups.

At Derwent Bridge, five km away, there's accommodation at the wooden chalet-style *Derwent Bridge Hotel* (☎ (002) 89 1144). Rooms in transportable huts cost $15 per person, and rooms in the hotel are $45/65, including a continental breakfast. The hotel does good, hearty meals and, with its open fire and friendly staff, is a good place to spend an evening. You can also buy food, basic supplies and maps, and rent fishing or bushwalking gear from here.

Getting There & Away
Cradle Valley Region From Tuesday to Saturday Redline has a service from Burnie to the Cradle Mountain Lodge ($26.20, via Devonport). This bus goes on to Queenstown and Strahan.

Tasmanian Wilderness Transport has buses three days a week from Launceston ($35) and from Devonport to Cradle Mountain ($30) – on Saturdays these go on to Strahan ($35). In the opposite direction they run from Strahan to Cradle Mountain on Sundays.

Cynthia Bay Region Redline has services five days a week between Hobart and Strahan via Derwent Bridge. One-way fares from Hobart to Derwent Bridge are $20, and from there to Strahan are $16. Redline's agent is the Road House on the Lyell Highway.

Tasmanian Wilderness Transport has return trips to Lake St Clair from Devonport, Launceston and Hobart; its agent is the kiosk at Lake St Clair.

Getting Around
Cradle Valley Region Every day except

Sundays, Tasmanian Wilderness Transport runs a local bus service between Dove Lake, Waldheim, the visitor centre, Cradle Mountain Lodge, Cradle Mountain Camping Ground and Leary's Corner (the Cradle Valley turn-off); one-way fares range from $2 to $6.

Cynthia Bay Region Maxwell's Coach & Taxi Service runs an informal taxi to and from Cynthia Bay and Derwent Bridge for $4. Maxwell's also meets the Redline buses at Derwent Bridge, on the Lyell Highway, which are heading to Hobart or Strahan.

Lake Country

The sparsely populated lake country of Tasmania's central plateau is a region of breathtaking scenery, with steep mountains, hundreds of glacial lakes, crystal-clear streams, waterfalls and a good variety of wildlife. It's also known for its fine trout fishing, and for its ambitious hydroelectric schemes, which have seen the damming of rivers, the creation of artificial lakes, the building of power stations, both above and below ground, and the construction of km of massive pipelines over the rough terrain.

Tasmania has the largest hydroelectric power system in Australia, generating 95% of its own and 8% of Australia's total electricity output. The first dam was constructed on Great Lake in 1911. Subsequently, the Derwent, Mersey, South Esk, Forth, Gordon, King, Anthony and Pieman rivers were also dammed.

If you want to inspect the developments, go along to the Tungatinah, Tarraleah and Liapootah power stations on the extensive Derwent scheme between Queenstown and Hobart.

Just south-east of Cradle Mountain is the **Walls of Jerusalem National Park**, which is a focal point for mountaineers, bushwalkers and cross-country skiers. There's excellent fishing at **Lake King William**, on the Derwent River, south of the Lyell

---

Tasmania's Dams
Over the years, dam building for the hydroelectric power stations has been a subject of considerable controversy. While conservationists have been greatly concerned over the dams' potential to harm the environment, many Tasmanians have seen the dams and power stations as a welcome source of employment. The first public outcry against the uncontrolled damming of Tasmania's magnificent rivers was brought about by the flooding of Lake Pedder in the mid 1970s. The most famous dispute was, of course, over the proposed damming of the Franklin and Lower Gordon rivers, which was won, after seven long years, by the environmentalists. With the completion of the schemes on the King and Anthony rivers, however, the era of large dam building in Tasmania will be just about over. Any other suitable sites are in World Heritage areas and cannot be touched. ∎

Highway, as well as at **Lake Sorell, Lake Crescent, Arthurs Lake** and **Little Pine Lagoon**.

At Waddamana, on the road which loops off the Lake Highway between Bothwell and Great Lake, there's the HEC's **Waddamana Power Museum**. It's an interesting display of the state's early hydro history, and it's open weekdays from 10 am to 4 pm, and weekends from noon to 2 pm; admission is free.

Bothwell (population 400)
Bothwell, in the beautiful Clyde River valley, is a charming and historic town, with 53 buildings recognised or classified by the National Trust. Places of particular interest include the beautifully restored **Slate Cottage** (☎ (002) 59 5554) of 1835; a **bootmaker's shop** (☎ (002) 59 5736), fitted out as it would have been in the 1890s; **Thorpe Mill** (☎ (002) 59 5580), a flour mill from the 1820s; the delightful **St Luke's Church** (1821); and the **Castle Hotel**, first licensed in 1821. Note that the places with telephone numbers must be rung in advance to arrange a visit.

Although Bothwell is probably best known for its great trout fishing, it also has

Australia's oldest golf course. This is still in use today and is open to members of any golf club.

Places to Stay

Accommodation in Bothwell can be expensive, but *Mrs Wood's Farmhouse* (☎ (002) 59 5612), at Dennistoun, eight km from town, is highly recommended at $65 a double. Otherwise, you can try either *Whites Cottage* (☎ (002) 59 5651), at $85 a double including a continental breakfast, or *Bothwell Grange* (☎ (002) 59 5556), at $55 for B&B. Both are in town.

The *Bronte Park Highland Village* (☎ (002) 89 1126) at Bronte Park, six km north of the Lyell Highway, has a pleasant hostel which charges $10 a night; cottages from $60 a double; chalet rooms at $40/55 for singles/doubles; and camp sites for $9 a double.

At Swan Bay, near Miena, the *Great Lake Hotel* (☎ (002) 59 8163) has singles/doubles for $35/55 including a continental breakfast, cabins for $15 each, and camp sites for $8.

At Tarraleah the *Tarraleah Chalet* (☎ (002) 89 3128) has rooms for $27/45.

The *Lachlan Hotel* (☎ (002) 87 1215) in Ouse has rooms for $25/40 including a cooked breakfast.

Getting There & Away

Public transport to this area is not good (and neither is the hitching). Tasmanian Wilderness Transport's services between Lake St Clair and Launceston or Devonport go via Bronte Park and Miena. Its agent is the Bronte Park Highland Village. Tasmanian Wilderness Transport also runs a limited return service to the Walls of Jerusalem from either Devonport or Launceston via Deloraine.

Bass Strait Islands

Tasmania has two main islands guarding the eastern and western entrances to Bass Strait.

Once the temporary and sometimes violent home of sealers, sailors and prospectors, King and Flinders islands are now retreats of unspoiled natural beauty, rich in marine life and other wildlife.

KING ISLAND (population 2750)

At the western end of Bass Strait, this rugged island is 64 km across at its widest point, and has more than 145 km of unspoiled coastline, with beautiful beaches and quiet lagoons.

Discovered in 1798, and named after Governor King of New South Wales, King Island quickly gained a reputation as a home and breeding ground for seals and sea elephants. Just as quickly, however, these animals were hunted close to extinction by brutal sealers and sailors known as the Straitsmen.

Over the years, the stormy seas of Bass Strait have claimed many ships, and there are at least 57 wrecks in the coastal waters around King Island. The island's worst shipwreck occurred in 1845 when the *Cataraqui*, an immigrant ship, went down with 399 people aboard.

King Island is probably best known for its dairy produce (particularly its rich Brie cheese and cream), although kelp and large crayfish are other valuable exports. Its other main industry was the production of scheelite (used in the manufacture of armaments) until the mine and factory at Grassy closed in December 1990.

Visitors can swim at one of King Island's long, deserted beaches or scuba dive amongst its exotic marine life and accessible shipwrecks. Because of the treacherous seas, the island has four lighthouses; the one at Currie is open to visitors between 2 and 4 pm at weekends. About half the island is native bush harbouring a wide variety of wildlife, including Bennetts wallabies, pheasants, platypuses, echidnas, turkeys, sea eagles and fairy penguins. Near **Surprise Bay**, in the south, an amazing calcified forest has the experts puzzling over whether the formations are of wood, coral or even kelp roots. There is excellent bushwalking on the island, particularly on the unpopulated north coast.

Cycling is also popular because of the island's size and relative flatness.

King Island's main town is Currie, on the west coast. Top Tours, in Main St, conducts full-day and half-day tours around the island; it's also a good place for tourist information. Currie's **King Island Museum** has some interesting historic artefacts; admission is $2.

Places to Stay & Eat

Currie *King Island A-Frame Holiday Homes* (☎ (004) 62 1260), in North Rd, charges $60 for a double in a fully self-contained unit. The *Bass Caravan Park* is part of the same place and has on-site vans at $40 a double. *Top Tours & Accommodation* (☎ (004) 62 1245), at 13 Main St, has good accommodation with singles/doubles for $40/50, including a continental breakfast.

The *Boomerang Motel* (☎ (004) 62 1288) is more expensive at $65/75, including a continental breakfast, and its restaurant has a good reputation.

Naracoopa In Naracoopa, on the east coast, the *Naracoopa Lodge* (☎ (004) 61 1294) has good hostel-style accommodation at $15 a night. The *Naracoopa Holiday Units* (☎ (004) 61 1326) in Beach Rd charges $45 a double.

Further south, in Yarra Creek Rd, the *Yarra Creek Host Farm* (☎ (004) 61 1276) has singles/doubles for $30/45, including a cooked breakfast. Note, however, that the road from Currie to Naracoopa is only partly sealed, and that it's really only feasible to stay in this part of the island if you have a car.

Getting There & Around

See the Getting There & Away section at the beginning of this chapter for information on flights to and from King Island.

In Currie, you can rent cars from King Island Auto Rentals (☎ (004) 62 1297) from about $45 a day plus insurance, or from Howell's Auto Rent (☎ (004) 62 1282) from about $65. Be warned that some King Island roads are extremely rough, so unless you

have a 4WD you might need some digging gear.

You can also hire mountain bikes from Top Tours (☎ (004) 62 1245) for about $8 a day or $40 a week.

FLINDERS ISLAND (population 980)

Flinders Island is the largest of the Furneaux Group, a collection of islands which cover an area of 1969 sq km off the north-eastern tip of Tasmania. Flinders is approximately 60 km long and 20 km wide and is followed in size by Cape Barren and Clarke islands.

First charted in 1798 by the navigator Matthew Flinders, the Furneaux Group became a base for the Straitsmen, who not only slaughtered seals in their tens of thousands but also indulged in a little piracy. Of the 120 or so ships wrecked on the islands' rocks, it is thought that quite a number were purposely lured there by sealers displaying false lights.

The most tragic part of Flinders Island's history, however, was the role it played in the virtual annihilation of Tasmania's Aborigines. Between 1829 and 1834, those Aborigines who had survived the state's martial law (which gave soldiers the right to arrest or shoot any Aborigine found in a settled area) were brought to the island to be resettled. Of the 135 survivors who were transported to Wybalenna (an Aboriginal word meaning 'Black man's house') to be 'civilised' and educated, only 47 survived to make their final journey to Oyster Cove in 1847.

On a brighter note, Flinders Island has many attractions for the visitor. Its beaches, especially on the western side, are beautiful, and the fishing and scuba diving are also good. There is no shortage of shipwrecks around the islands, some of which are clearly visible from shore. A more unusual pastime is fossicking for 'diamonds' (which are actually fragments of white topaz) on the beach and creek at **Killiecrankie Bay**. At one time there were plenty of stones to be found, but there are fewer now, and the locals have actually started to dive for them using special equipment.

Flinders Island has some great bushwalks, the most popular being the five-hour return walk to the granite peaks of **Mt Strzelecki** which affords some great views of the surrounding area. There's also a number of lookouts on the island, including **Furneaux Lookout**, almost in the centre of the island, **Walkers Hill** and **Mt Tanner**.

The island's abundant vegetation supports a wide variety of wildlife, including more than 150 species of bird, the most well known being the Cape Barren goose (now protected) and the mutton bird.

The main industries on Flinders Island are farming, fishing and seasonal mutton-birding. The main administrative centre is Whitemark, and Lady Barron in the south is the main fishing area and deep-water port.

Wybalenna

Today, all that remains of this unfortunate settlement is the **cemetery**, which tells the tragic story, and the **chapel**, which has been restored by the National Trust and is open to visitors. Because of its historical significance it is rated as the third most important historic building in the state. Nearby, there's also the **Emita Museum**, which displays a variety of Aboriginal artefacts as well as old sealing and sailing relics. It is open on weekend afternoons only.

Places to Stay

On Bluff Rd, the *Flinders Island Cabin Park* (☎ (003) 59 2188) has cabins for $20/35. At Pats River, Whitemark, *Bluff House* (☎ (003) 59 2034) has singles/doubles with a cooked breakfast for $29 per person, while in the centre of town the *Interstate Hotel* (☎ (003) 59 2114) has rooms for $20/35.

At Emita, on Fairhaven Rd, the *Green-*

Mutton Birds

Each September, the mutton birds return to Flinders and other Bass Strait islands, after a summer in the northern hemisphere, to clean out and repair their burrows from the previous year. They then head out to sea again before returning in November for the breeding season, which lasts until April. Eggs are then laid in one three-day period, and the parents take it in turns, two weeks at a time, to incubate them.

Once their single chick has hatched, both parents feed the fledgling until mid-April, when all the adult birds depart, leaving the young to fend for themselves and hopefully to follow their parents north.

Unfortunately for the well-fed little mutton birds, they make good eating, and once the adult birds leave the nests the 'birders', or mutton-bird hunters, move in. ■

glades Host Farm (☎ (003) 59 8506) offers three cooked meals a day plus lodging for $45 per person.

The rather luxurious *Furneaux Tavern* (☎ (003) 59 3521) at Lady Barron, has rooms for $70/95, including continental breakfast.

For longer stays, there's also a good selection of reasonable holiday houses and flats on the island.

Getting There & Around

For information on flights to and from Flinders Island see the Getting There & Away section at the beginning of this chapter.

In Whitemark, Bowman Transport (☎ (003) 59 2014) has cars from around $45 a day, while both Flinders Island Car Rentals (☎ (003) 59 2168) and Flinders Island Transport Services (☎ (003) 59 2060) rent cars from $50 a day.

Victoria

VICTORIA

Area   228,000 sq km
Population   4,460,000

☎ From May 1995, Melbourne's existing phone numbers will be prefixed by the additional digit 9 (for example, ☎ 123 4567 becomes ☎ 9123 4567). From 1997, in regional areas, the last two digits of the current area code will be added to the existing number (for example, ☎ (012) 123 456 becomes ☎ 1212 3456). The area code for the state will be (03). ■

When White Australia's founders up in Sydney decided it was time to get a foothold on some other part of the continent, they had a go at establishing a settlement on Port Phillip Bay in 1803. A combination of bad luck and bad management soon persuaded them that it was a lousy place to live and the settlers moved down to Tasmania. So it is not surprising that when Melbourne did become established, a long-lasting rivalry with Sydney began.

In 1835 the first permanent European settlement was made at the present site of Melbourne, although whalers and sealers had used the Victorian coast for a number of years. The earliest settlers, John Batman and John Pascoe Fawkner, came to Melbourne in search of the land they had been unable to obtain in Tasmania. Not until 1837, by which time several hundred settlers had moved in, was the town named Melbourne and given an official seal of approval.

Their free-enterprise spirit naturally led to clashes with the staid powers of Sydney. The settlers were not interested in the convict system, for example, and on a number of occasions turned convict ships away. They wanted to form a breakaway colony, and their PR efforts included naming it after the Queen and the capital city after her Prime Minister, Lord Melbourne.

Finally, in 1851, the colony of Victoria was formed and separated from New South

Wales. At about the same time gold was discovered, and the population doubled in little more than a year. As with a number of other Australian gold rushes, few people made fortunes but many stayed on to establish new settlements and work the land. Some of the most interesting historical areas in Victoria are associated with those gold-rush days.

Melbourne, as Australia's second city, is naturally the state's prime attraction. Although it is not as intrinsically appealing as Sydney, it does lay claim to being the fashion, food and cultural capital of Australia. For many years it was also considered to be Australia's financial and business capital, but it now shares this role with Sydney. Victoria is the most densely populated of the Australian states and also the most industrialised.

Of course Victoria is much more than its capital city. The Great Ocean Road runs south-west towards South Australia; it has some of the most spectacular coastal scenery in the world and evocative reminders of the whaling days in some of the small port towns that predate Melbourne. To the south-east of the capital is Phillip Island with its nightly penguin parade. Further south is Wilsons Promontory – the southernmost point on the Australian mainland and also one of the best loved national parks, with excellent scenery and bushwalks. Continuing east towards the

VICTORIA

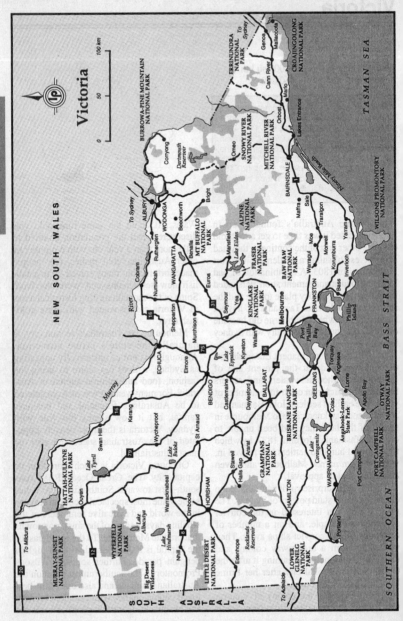

Victoria

New South Wales border there's more great coast and superb rainforests in the East Gippsland region.

Victoria's stretch of the Great Dividing Range includes the Victorian Alps, which have some of the best ski fields in Australia and are much closer to Melbourne than the New South Wales fields are to Sydney. Skiing on weekends is easy for Melburnians, while in summer the mountains are popular for camping, walking and a whole host of outdoor activities. Of course you don't have to go all the way to the Alps to get into the hills; the ever-popular Dandenongs are less than an hour from the centre of Melbourne, while the spectacular Grampians, another popular mountain area, are further to the west.

Finally, there's the Murray River region in the north, which has many historic river towns, such as Swan Hill and Echuca. Victoria also has its wine-growing areas, particularly in the north on the slopes of the Great Dividing Range. And the gold country certainly shouldn't be forgotten – towns like Bendigo and Ballarat still have a strong flavour of those heady gold-rush days, and lucky prospectors are still finding gold today.

GEOGRAPHY

Victoria's geography is probably more diverse than that of any other Australian state, as it includes both the final stretch of the Great Dividing Range and associated outcrops plus a swath of flatter country to the west. The Great Dividing Range reaches its greatest altitude across the Victoria-New South Wales border. The mountains run south-west from the New South Wales border, then bend around to run more directly west as the range crosses north of Melbourne and finally fades out before the South Australian border.

The Victorian coast is particularly varied. On the eastern side is the mountain-backed Gippsland region while to the west is spectacular coastline running to South Australia.

The north-west of the state, beyond the Great Dividing Range, is flat plains. It is especially dry and empty in the extreme north-west of the state, where you'll find the eerie Sunset Country. For most of the length of the border between New South Wales and Victoria, the mighty Murray River forms the actual boundary.

CLIMATE

Victoria, and Melbourne in particular, has a single major drawback – the climate. Statistically it's not that bad; the average temperature summer or winter is only a few degrees less than Sydney's and it's certainly far less humid than Sydney or Brisbane. The annual rainfall is also less than in either of those damp cities. The trouble with Melbourne's climate is that it's totally unpredictable; the old joke is that if you don't like the weather, just wait a minute. Melbourne does have four distinct seasons, although sometimes it seems like they all come on the same day. A good guiding principle is to expect the unexpected.

Although the weather is basically somewhat cooler in Melbourne than elsewhere in continental Australia, you'll rarely need more than a light overcoat or jacket even in the depths of winter. Inland, however, in places like Ballarat or in the Alps, it can get really cold.

INFORMATION

The Victorian Tourism Commission operates the following offices around Australia:

New South Wales
    403 George St, Sydney 2000 (☎ (02) 299 2088)
Queensland
    45 Queen St, Brisbane 4000 (☎ (07) 221 4500)
South Australia
    16 Grenfell St, Adelaide 5000 (☎ (08) 231 4129)

Remarkably, there is no office in Melbourne. Tourism information is handled by the RACV (☎ (03) 650 1522) at 230 Collins St.

Information Victoria, the state government's information centre, is at 318 Little Bourke St. The information desk downstairs supplies free sketch maps of national parks, and the Government Map Shop at the next

VICTORIA

desk sells maps both of Victoria and of other parts of Australia.

NATIONAL & STATE PARKS

Victoria has 31 national parks, 46 state parks and a wide range of other protected areas, including coastal and marine reserves and historic areas. These parks are managed by the Department of Conservation & Natural Resources, which has offices in Melbourne and throughout the state, and also publishes handouts to virtually every park in Victoria. The DC&NR's head office (☎ (03) 412 4011), at 240 Victoria Parade in East Melbourne, has a bookshop and information centre where you can get maps, leaflets, books and colour posters on the state's parks, animals and native plants. The office is open on weekdays from 10 am to 5 pm.

ACTIVITIES

Bushwalking

Victoria has some great bushwalking areas and a number of very active clubs. Check the bush-gear shops around Hardware and Little Bourke Sts in Melbourne for local club news and magazines. For more information about bushwalking in Victoria look for the handy walking guides *50 Bush Walks in Victoria* and *50 Day Walks Near Melbourne*, both by Sandra Bardwell and published by Anne O'Donovan.

Walking areas close to the city include the You Yangs, 56 km to the south-west, with a wide variety of bird life; and the Dandenongs right on the eastern edge of the metropolitan area. Wilsons Promontory is to the south-east in Gippsland. 'The Prom' has many marked trails from Tidal River and from Telegraph Bay – walks that can take from a few hours to a couple of days. The Alpine Walking Track starts near Walhalla, at Mt Erica, 144 km east of Melbourne, and ends at Tom Groggin on the New South Wales border. This very long trail is for the experienced walker. There are other popular marked trails in the Bright and Mt Buffalo areas of the Alps.

The Grampians, 250 km to the west, are where Victoria's only remaining red roos

hang out. Mallacoota Inlet in East Gippsland is equally rugged inland but the coastal walks are easier.

You can have backpacks and camping equipment repaired by Aiking Repairs at 377 Little Bourke St, above the Mountain Designs shop.

Rock Climbing

Again, the Hardware St bush-gear shops are good info sources. Mt Arapiles, in the Western District 330 km north-west of Melbourne near Natimuk, is famous among rock climbers from around the world as it has a huge variety of climbs for all levels of skill.

If you just want to scramble around in rather crowded conditions there is Hanging Rock (of *Picnic at Hanging Rock* fame) 72 km north-west of Melbourne. Sugarloaf and Jawbones are 112 km north-east of Melbourne in the Cathedral Range State Park, a popular weekend spot. The Grampians, 250 km west of Melbourne, have a wide variety of climbs. At Mt Buffalo, 369 km north in the alpine area, the hardest climb is Buffalo Gorge.

Water Sports

Swimming & Surfing Although there is reasonably good swimming on the eastern side of Port Phillip Bay, you have to get outside the bay to find surf. Some of the bay beaches close to the city are not too special but as you get further round the bay they get a lot better. Along the Mornington Peninsula you have the choice between sheltered bay beaches on one side and the open ocean beaches, only a short distance away on the other side of the peninsula.

Further out there are excellent beaches at Phillip Island and right along the Gippsland coast. Similarly, on the western side of the state, the coast from Point Lonsdale to Apollo Bay is popular for surfing.

Scuba Diving Flinders, Portland, Kilcunda, Torquay, Anglesea, Lorne, Apollo Bay, Mallacoota, Portsea, Sorrento and Wilsons Prom are all popular diving areas. In Melbourne there are clubs and organisations renting equipment.

Boats & Sailing There are many sailing clubs all around Port Phillip Bay and on Albert Park Lake in Melbourne. Elsewhere around the state there are many lakes popular for sailing. On the large Gippsland Lakes system you can hire yachts and launches, which work out to be quite economical among a few people.

At Studley Park, in the Melbourne suburb of Kew, you can hire a whole selection of rowing boats, canoes and kayaks by the hour – good fun, although a fair few people seem to find themselves upside down in the muddy Yarra!

Further upstream at Fairfield Park there is another boathouse, restored to its original Edwardian elegance, offering Devonshire teas and other snacks, and boats and canoes for hire. You might catch a performance in the outdoor amphitheatre on a bend in the river in the natural bushland.

Canoes can also be rented at Como Park, further down the Yarra towards the city. At Albert Park Lake you can hire rowing boats and sailing boats.

Houseboat holidays are also popular, and these can be arranged on Lake Eildon or on the Murray River at Echuca or Mildura.

Running & Cycling

The four-km jogging track (popularly known as 'the Tan') around the Kings Domain and the Royal Botanic Gardens in central Melbourne is one of the most popular running circuits in Australia. Albert Park Lake is also busy. With its relatively flat terrain, Melbourne is very popular with bike riders – quite a few of us at Lonely Planet ride bicycles to work.

It's easy to hire bicycles on the popular Yarra-side bicycle track but not so easy to find them for longer term hire in Melbourne. Contact Bicycle Victoria (☎ (03) 328 3000) for information on tours and organised rides in Victoria. They also run the Great Victorian Bike Ride, held annually around November, in which thousands of cyclists take part.

They may be able to tell you where you can hire a touring bike.

GETTING THERE & AWAY
See the Melbourne section for details of transport into Victoria.

GETTING AROUND
V/Line (☎ 13 2232) has a fairly comprehensive rail network of metropolitan and country services. The rail services are supplemented by connecting V/Line buses. The principal rail routes radiating from Melbourne are:

West to Geelong then inland to Warrnambool; a bus runs along the Great Ocean Road from Geelong through Lorne and Apollo Bay.

North-west to Ballarat and on through Horsham in the central west to Adelaide in South Australia; buses connect from Stawell south-west to Halls Gap in the Grampians or north-west towards the Mallee.

North-west through Ballarat and then to Mildura on the Murray River.

North through Bendigo and the central highlands to Swan Hill on the Murray.

North to Shepparton, Numurkah and Cobram along the Goulburn Valley.

North along the Hume Highway route to Albury-Wodonga on the route to Sydney; buses run from Wangaratta to Beechworth and Bright or north to Corowa.

East through Traralgon and Sale to Bairnsdale in Gippsland; a branch line runs to Leongatha near Wilsons Prom. Buses connect from Bairnsdale to Lakes Entrance, Orbost, Cann River and Merimbula.

V/Line has four regional timetables with details of all its services, and these are available from station bookstalls.

Melbourne

Population 2,900,000

Melbourne has always had a fierce rivalry with Sydney. It goes right back to their founding; Sydney had nearly 50 years head start on its southern sister and even then the foundation of Melbourne was a rather haphazard affair. Not until 1835, following

VICTORIA

exploratory trips from Tasmania, was the Melbourne area eventually settled by a group of Tasmanian entrepreneurs.

In 1851 the colony of Victoria became independent of New South Wales and almost immediately the small town of Melbourne became the centre for Australia's biggest and most prolonged gold rush. In just a few years Melbourne suddenly became a real place on the map, and the city's solid, substantial appearance essentially dates from those heady days. For a while last century Melbourne was the larger and more exciting city, known as 'Marvellous Melbourne', but Sydney gradually pulled ahead and Melbourne now ranks number two to its more glamorous northern sister.

In population there's little between them; they're both large cities in the three million bracket, but Sydney is more the metropolis than Melbourne. These days Melbourne is a big Australian city; Sydney's a big world one. This doesn't stop people from liking Melbourne more, and many visitors find it to be the more easygoing and friendly of the two.

Orientation

Melbourne's city centre is apparently simple, with its grid of wide boulevards. However, these are interspersed with narrow streets and alleys, giving the otherwise overpoweringly orderly and planned centre a little human chaos. The main streets are Collins and Bourke Sts (south-west to north-east) crossed by Swanston and Elizabeth Sts (south-east to north-west).

Swanston St crosses straight over the river to the south and runs right out of the city into Carlton to the north. Most traffic coming into the city from the south used to enter by Swanston St, but this all came to a stop early in 1992 when the street was closed to traffic and converted into a pedestrian mall, known as Swanston Walk. The result has been great for pedestrians and terrible for car users. Most traffic from the north comes in on parallel Elizabeth St, since this is the direct route in from the airport and from Sydney.

The Yarra River forms a southern bound-

ary to the city area, with railway lines running between the river and Flinders St (the city-centre street running closest to the river bank). Right beside the river on the corner of Swanston and Flinders Sts is the ornate Flinders St Station. This is the main railway station for suburban railway services, and 'under the clocks' at the station entrance is a favourite Melbourne meeting place. Princes Bridge Station is opposite. The other main Melbourne station, for country and interstate services, is Spencer St Station, and next to it you have the Spencer St bus terminal, from which V/Line and the interstate companies operate.

The Collins and Bourke St blocks between Swanston and Elizabeth Sts are Melbourne's shopping centre, the Bourke St block also being a pedestrian and tram mall – watch out for trams! On the mall you'll find Myer (the biggest department-store chain in Australia) and right next door on the Bourke and Elizabeth Sts corner is the GPO.

Most travellers will arrive in Melbourne at either the Spencer St bus station in the city's west (Skybus, McCafferty's, Firefly and V/Line buses and trains) or at the Franklin St terminal (Greyhound Pioneer buses) on the northern side of the city.

Information

Tourist Offices In the city, the best places for information are the on-street information booths run by the city council – one in the Bourke St Mall and one in Collins St beside the city square. Both are open Monday to Thursday from 9 am to 5 pm, Friday from 9 am to 7 pm, Saturday from 10 am to 4 pm and Sunday from 11 am to 4 pm.

The RACV (Royal Automobile Club of Victoria) (☎ 650 1522) has a tourist information and accommodation booking office at 230 Collins St.

The Federal Airports Corporation has a tourist information booth (☎ 339 1805) in the international terminal at Melbourne Airport (at Tullamarine).

Post & Telecommunications The Melbourne GPO is on the corner of Bourke and

Elizabeth Sts. There's an efficient poste restante and phones for interstate and international calls. Phone centres can also be found behind the GPO on Little Bourke St and across the road on Elizabeth St.

The STD telephone area code for Melbourne is 03.

Other Offices The National Trust (☎ 654 4711) is on Tasma Terrace, 6 Parliament Place, where it has a bookshop.

The YHA (☎ 670 7991) has its helpful Melbourne office at 205 King St, on the corner of Little Bourke St. The Travellers Aid Society (☎ 654 2600), on the 2nd floor at 169 Swanston St, offers assistance in emergencies.

Foreign Embassies Quite a number of countries have diplomatic representation in Melbourne. Look up Consulates & Legations in the Yellow Pages for details.

Bookshops Melbourne has a lot of excellent bookshops including a big Angus & Robertson on Elizabeth St, several Dymocks and Collins branches around the city, and the agreeably chaotic McGills on Elizabeth St opposite the GPO (good for interstate and overseas newspapers).

Information Victoria (☎ 651 4100) at 318 Little Bourke St has a good range of local maps and guidebooks, and Bowyangs Travel Books at 372 Little Bourke St has a more extensive range of travel publications. Readings on Lygon St in Carlton is more literary and has an excellent window notice board where you'll find all sorts of offers to share accommodation or rides. There are several good bookshops on Brunswick St, Fitzroy, and Acland St, St Kilda.

Although not strictly a bookshop, the Environment Centre (☎ 654 4833) at 247 Flinders Lane has a wide variety of books, calendars, posters and magazines and is a good place for information about activities in the environment and conservation movements.

Publications Among the many guides to Melbourne, the National Trust's *Walking Melbourne* is especially useful.

Medical Services The Travellers' Medical Clinic (☎ 602 5788) is at Level 2, 393 Little Bourke St in the city. It is open weekdays from 8.30 am to 5.30 pm, and Saturdays from 9 am to noon, and has excellent information on the latest vaccinations needed for most countries. The Fairfield Infectious Diseases Hospital also has a travellers' advice line (☎ 0055 15676).

Dangers & Annoyances

Melbourne trams should be treated with some caution by car drivers. You can only overtake a tram on the left and must always stop behind one when it halts to drop or collect passengers (except where there are central 'islands' for passengers). In the city centre at most junctions a peculiar left-hand path must be followed to make right-hand turns, in order to accommodate the trams. Note that in rainy weather tram tracks are extremely slippery; motorcyclists should take special care. Cyclists must beware of tram tracks at all times; if you get a wheel into the track you're flat on your face immediately, and painfully.

Tram passengers should be cautious when stepping on and off – a lot of people have been hit by passing cars, so don't step off without looking both ways. Pedestrians in Bourke St Mall and Swanston Walk should watch for passing trams too.

City Centre

Swanston St runs through the heart of the city. Formerly a major traffic artery, it was closed to traffic in early 1992 to create Swanston Walk, a boulevard lined with trees and street cafes and shared by pedestrians, trams and commercial vehicles.

At the intersection of Flinders and Swanston Sts are three of Melbourne's best-known landmarks. The grand old **Flinders St Station** is the main railway station for suburban trains. Across the road from the station is one of Melbourne's best-known pubs, **Young & Jackson's**, which is famed

VICTORIA

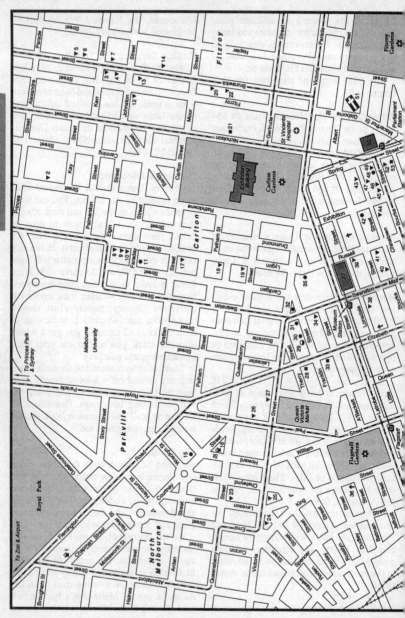

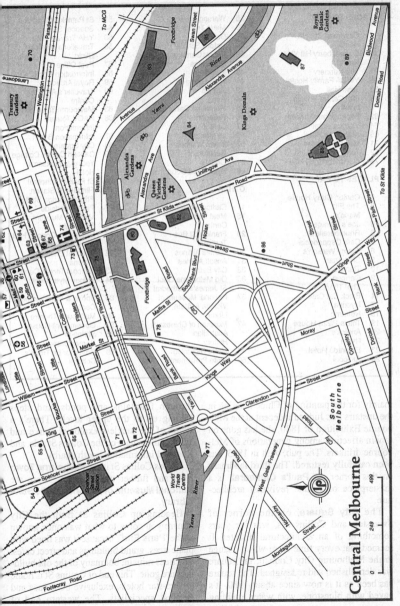

VICTORIA

Central Melbourne

0   249   499

PLACES TO STAY		25	Warung Agus	51	St Patrick's Cathedral
		26	Maria Trattoria	54	Spencer St Bus Station
1	Chapman St YHA Hostel	27	Dalat's	55	YHA Travel Office
		34	Oxford Scholar Hotel	56	Traveller's Medical Clinic
16	Queensberry Hill YHA Hostel	38	Peony Gardens		
		39	Stalactites	57	Post Office
21	The Nunnery	40	Kunming	58	Information Booth
28	YWCA Family Hostel	41	Nam Loong	59	Royal Arcade
33	Toad Hall	43	Jan Bo	60	Traveller's Aid Support Centre
53	City Centre Private Hotel	44	Ronz		
		45	Florentino Cellar Bar	63	Melbourne Town Hall
62	Backpackers City Inn	46	Pellegrini's	66	RACV Tourist Information
64	Victoria Hotel	47	Cafe K		
65	Kingsgate Hotel	49	Le Monde	67	Information Booth
71	Hotel Enterprise	52	Italian Waiter's Restaurant	68	City Square
72	Terrace Pacific Inn			70	Captain Cook's Cottage
78	Queensbridge Hotel	61	Gopal's	73	Young & Jackson's Hotel
		69	Hyatt Food Court		
PLACES TO EAT				74	St Paul's Cathedral
		OTHER		75	Flinders St Station
2	Carlton Curry House			76	Princes Bridge Station
3	The Fitz	11	Carlton Moviehouse	77	Polly Woodside Maritime Museum
4	Mario's	15	Meat Market Craft Centre		
5	Joe's Garage			79	Southgate
6	Rhumbarella's	29	Franklin St Bus Terminal	80	Melbourne Concert Hall
7	Cafe Cappadocia			81	Theatres Building
8	Jimmy Watson's	30	Qantas Airlines	82	National Gallery of Victoria
9	Shakahari	31	Ansett Airlines		
10	Tiamo's	32	City Baths	83	National Tennis Centre
12	Carmen	35	Old Melbourne Gaol	84	Sidney Myer Music Bowl
13	Thai Thani	36	St James's Cathedral		
14	Black Cat Cafe	37	National Museum of Victoria & State Library	85	Sports & Entertainment Centre
17	Nyonya				
18	Notturno			86	Malthouse Theatre
19	Toto's Pizza House	42	Museum of Chinese & Australian History	87	Government House
20	Annick's			88	Shrine of Remembrance
22	Nyala	48	Metro Nightclub		
23	Eldorado Hotel	50	State Parliament	89	Governor La Trobe's Cottage
24	Amiconi				

mainly for the painting of Chloe hanging in the upstairs bar. Judged indecent at the Melbourne Exhibition of 1880, she has gone on to win affection among generations of Melbourne drinkers. The pub, built in 1853, has been carefully restored. The third landmark on this corner, **St Paul's Cathedral**, is a masterpiece of Gothic revivalist architecture.

The **City Square**, on the corner of Swanston and Collins Sts, was for years something of an architectural disaster. It seemed that every time there was a change in the Melbourne City Council, the square was demolished and redesigned. The square has been as it is now since about 1980. It's paved with bluestone, with water tumbling through fountains and ponds, and steps leading up to the upper levels. There's a statue of the luckless explorers Burke and Wills in the square on the Collins St side, and a helpful information booth nearby.

Across Collins St is the **Melbourne Town Hall**, and further up Swanston St are the **National Museum of Victoria** and the **State Library**.

Heading up Collins St from the City Square you come to what was once known as the **'Paris End'**, because it was lined with plane trees, grand buildings and street cafes. The trees remain, but many of the old buildings are gone. This end of Collins St is home to five-star hotels, exclusive boutiques and medical specialists. The western end of

Collins St, from Elizabeth St down, is the financial end, home to bankers and brokers. The three old bank buildings on the corner of Collins and Queen Sts are fine examples of the extravagance of late Victorian architecture during Melbourne's land boom period.

Bourke St has more shops but less style than Collins St. In the '70s, when every Australian city had to have a pedestrian mall, Melbourne got one too: the **Bourke St Mall**. It's difficult for a pedestrian mall to work with 30-tonne trams barrelling through the middle of it every few minutes. However, after several multimillion-dollar rearrangements of the potted plants and the benches, the mall has emerged as something of a focus for city shoppers, with its buskers, missionaries and big department stores.

Half a block up from Bourke St is **Chinatown** on Little Bourke St. This narrow lane was a thronging Chinese quarter even back in the gold-rush days and it's now a busy, crowded couple of blocks of often excellent Chinese restaurants, Asian supermarkets and shops. The successful touch here was the addition of decorative street lamps and Chinese tiled arches over the lane. Yes, I know they're artificial and garish but they look great. Lonsdale St, between Russell and Swanston Sts, is the central city's Greek quarter – a good place to have a coffee at an outdoor table and watch the world pass by.

City Buildings

Melbourne is an intriguing blend of the soaring new and the stately old. Carrying the 'new' banner are buildings like the **Melbourne Central** shopping and office complex on the corner of Latrobe and Elizabeth Sts. It was opened amid much fanfare in late 1991, and the centrepiece of the complex is the old **Shot Tower**, which still stands on its original site but is now enclosed within the new building. The **Rialto** on Collins St is another architectural landmark. Its semireflective glass looks stunningly different under varying light – it's something of a city Ayers Rock! When it was finished the

Rialto building, Collins St, Melbourne

Rialto was the tallest office building in Australia. Beside it is the imaginative Le Meridien Hotel which uses the facades of two old buildings and cleverly incorporates an old stone paved alleyway which used to run between them.

Or there's **Nauru House** on Exhibition St. Nauru is a tiny Pacific island whose entire population could comfortably be housed in this big office block. It is an extremely wealthy island since it's basically solid phosphate, hence the building's nickname of 'Birdshit House'. Only a sparrow hop away is the equally soaring **Regent Hotel**, with its 15-storey central atrium starting on the 35th floor. It's a great place to stay if you can stretch to $200 a night.

On Spring St is a hotel of quite another era: the gracious old **Windsor Hotel**. Across the road from this is the imposing **State Parliament House**, a relic of Melbourne's gold-rush wealth. It served as the national parliament while Canberra was under construction. There are free tours of both houses, when parliament is in recess, every weekday at 10 and 11 am, noon, and 2, 3 and 3.45 pm.

Other old buildings in the centre include the 1853 **Treasury Building** in the Treasury Gardens and, beside Flagstaff Gardens, the 1872 **Old Royal Mint** and the 1842 **St James's Cathedral** (Melbourne's oldest surviving building). Victoriana enthusiasts may also find some very small Melbourne buildings of interest – scattered around the city are a number of very fine cast-iron men's **urinals** (like French *pissoirs*). They mainly date from 1903 to 1914, and one on the corner of Exhibition and Lonsdale St is classified by the National Trust. Other good examples include one outside the North Melbourne Town Hall where there is also a very fine drinking fountain.

The **Melbourne Club**, pillar of the Melbourne establishment, is off Spring St up at the Treasury Gardens end of town. This end block of Bourke St is popular and has some good restaurants, bookshops and record shops. **St Patrick's Cathedral**, one of the city's most imposing churches, is also at this end of town.

National Museum & State Library

Extending for a block between Swanston St and Russell St beside Latrobe St is the National Museum plus the State Library and La Trobe Library. The State Library has a gracious, octagonal, domed reading room and any book lover will enjoy its atmosphere. Its collection of more than a million books and other reference material is particularly notable for its coverage of the humanities and social sciences, as well as art, music, performing arts, Australiana and rare books, including a 4000-year-old Mesopotamian tablet.

Exhibits at the museum range from the first car and aircraft in Australia to the stuffed remains of Phar Lap, the legendary racehorse which nearly disrupted Australian-American relations when it died a suspicious death in the USA. The complex also includes a planetarium.

The museum is open from 10 am to 5 pm every day and admission costs $5 for adults and $2.50 for children – special exhibits are more expensive. Some time in the future the museum is scheduled to move to a new home in the Exhibition Gardens near the Exhibition Building just north of the city centre, but until that is finished (some time in the next century, perhaps?) the museum stays where it is.

Old Melbourne Gaol

A block further up Russell St is this gruesome old prison and penal museum. It was built of bluestone in 1841 and was used right up to 1929. In all, over 100 prisoners were hanged there. It's a dark, dank, spooky place. The museum displays include death masks of noted bushrangers and convicts, Ned Kelly's armour, the very scaffold from which Ned took his fatal plunge and some fascinating records of early 'transported' convicts, indicating just what flimsy excuses could be used to pack people off to Australia's unwelcoming shores. It's an unpleasant reminder of the brutality of Australia's early convict days. It is open from 9.30 am to 4.30 pm daily, and admission is $6 (children $3, family $16, students $4).

The Yarra River

Melbourne's prime natural feature, the Yarra, is a surprisingly pleasant river, enhanced by the parks, walks and bike tracks that have been built along its banks. Despite the cracks about it 'running upside down', it's just muddy, not particularly dirty.

When the racing rowing boats are gliding down the river on a sunny day, or you're driving along Alexandra Ave towards the city on a clear night, the Yarra can really look quite magical. Best of all you can bike it for several km along the riverside without risking being wiped out by some nut in a Holden. The bike tracks have been gradually extended further upstream and hopefully will eventually start to move further downstream as well. On weekends you can hire bicycles – see Getting Around.

There are also barbecues beside the river and near **Como Park** in South Yarra, and you can hire canoes, kayaks and rowing boats further upstream. **Studley Park** in Kew is the most popular place for boating.

A more leisurely way to boat down the river is on one of the tour boats which operate on the river from Princes Walk beside Princes Bridge (across from Flinders St Station).

There are some really beautiful old bridges across the Yarra, and Alexandra Parade, the riverside boulevard on the southern side, provides delightful views of Melbourne by day or night. A stylish pedestrian bridge crosses the Yarra from behind Flinders St Station, linking the city with the new Southgate development, the Victorian Arts Centre and the National Gallery of Victoria.

Southbank

The area opposite the city centre on the southern side of the Yarra has recently been given a major facelift. This former industrial wasteland has been impressively redeveloped and features three levels of riverside cafes, restaurants, an international food hall and an up-market shopping galleria with some exclusive and interesting specialty boutiques. There's also an aquarium, the five-star Sheraton Towers Hotel and some specially commissioned sculptures and other art works.

It's a great area for shopping, eating, drinking or just browsing, and of course the major theatres and galleries are nearby. See Places to Eat for details of some of Southbank's eateries.

Polly Woodside Maritime Museum

Close to Spencer St Bridge, immediately south of the city centre, is the *Polly Woodside*. Built in Belfast, Northern Ireland, in 1885, it's an old iron-hulled sailing ship which carried freight in the dying years of the sailing era. The *Polly Woodside* is the centrepiece of the maritime museum, which

opens from 10 am to 4 pm daily; admission is $7 ($4 for children). Across the river stands the World Trade Centre.

Queen Victoria Market

Over on the northern side of the city, the Queen Victoria Market is on the corner of Peel and Victoria Sts. It's the city's main retail produce centre – a popular multicultural scene on Tuesdays, Thursdays, Fridays and Saturday mornings, when the stall operators shout, yell and generally go all out to move the goods. On Sundays the fruit and vegies give way to general goods, which sell everything from cut-price jeans to secondhand records.

Royal Melbourne Zoo

Just north of the city centre in Parkville is Melbourne's excellent zoo. There are numerous walk-through enclosures in this well-planned zoo. You walk through the aviary, around the monkey enclosures and even over the lions' park on a bridge. The new butterfly enclosure and the gorilla forest are both excellent. This is the oldest zoo in Australia and one of the oldest in the world.

The zoo is open from 9 am to 5 pm every day of the week and admission is $9 (children $4.50, family $25). You can get to it on tram No 55 from William St in the city. The zoo is in Royal Park; a marker in the park indicates where the Burke and Wills expedition set off on its ill-fated journey in 1860.

Science Works Museum

Opened in mid-1992, this is Melbourne's newest museum. It's the science and technology section of the Museum of Victoria, and has a huge and fascinating array of tactile displays. Many of the exhibits were mothballed for years as there was no room in the National Museum in Swanston St. It's at 2 Booker St, Spotswood, about 15 minutes walk from Spotswood Station, or just over the West Gate Bridge if you're driving. It's open daily and costs $6 for adults, $3 for children.

The Melbourne Cup

If you happen to be in Melbourne in November you can catch the greatest horse race in Australia, the prestigious Melbourne Cup. Although its position as the bearer of the largest prize for an Australian horse race is constantly under challenge, no other race can bring the country to a standstill.

For about an hour during the lead-up to the race on the first Tuesday in November, a public holiday in the city's metropolitan area, people all over the country get touched by Melbourne's spring racing fever.

Serious punters and fashion-conscious racegoers pack the grandstand and lawns of the Victoria Racing Club's beautiful Flemington Racecourse, once-a-year betters make their choice or organise Cup syndicates with friends, and the race is watched or listened to on TVs and radios in hotels, clubs and houses across the land. Australia virtually comes to a halt for the three or so minutes during which the race is actually run.

The two-mile (3.2 km) flat race has in recent years attracted horses and owners from Europe and the Middle East, breaking the stranglehold that New Zealand horses and trainers had on the coveted gold cup for many years.

Many people say that to be in Melbourne in November and not go to the Cup is like going to Paris and skipping the Louvre, or turning your back on the bulls in Pamplona!

Melbourne Cricket Ground

The MCG is one of Australia's biggest sporting stadiums and was the central stadium for the 1956 Melbourne Olympics. Set in Yarra Park, which stretches from the city and East Melbourne to Richmond, the huge stadium can accommodate over 100,000 spectators, and does so at least once a year. The big occasion is the annual Australian Rules football Grand Final in October. This is Australia's biggest sporting event and brings Melbourne, which engages in a winter of Aussie Rules football mania each year, to a fever pitch. The only other sporting event which generates the same sort of national interest in Australia is the Melbourne Cup horse race each November.

Cricket is, of course, the other major sport played in the MCG; international Test and one-day matches as well as interstate Sheffield Shield and other local district games take place here over the summer months, and draw big crowds.

On the city side of the stadium there's the **Australian Gallery of Sport & Olympic Museum**, a museum dedicated to Australia's sporting passions. It's open from 10 am to 4 pm every day and admission is $6 (children $3).

Victorian Arts Centre

As you cross the river to the south of the city, Swanston St becomes St Kilda Rd, a very fine boulevard which runs straight out of the city towards the war memorial, takes a kink around the shrine and then continues to St Kilda. Beyond the memorial it's ad agency alley, with many office blocks lining the road.

Right by the river is Melbourne's large arts precinct. The building closest to the Yarra is the **Melbourne Concert Hall**, the main performance venue for major artists and companies, and the base for the Melbourne Symphony Orchestra. The next building, with the distinctive spire of scaffolding, combines with the Concert Hall to form the Victorian Arts Centre. This **theatres building** houses the State Theatre, the Playhouse and the George Fairfax Studio. The Westpac Gallery and the Vic Walk Gallery are also found in the theatres building. There are one-hour tours of the complex ($8) Monday to Friday at noon and 2.30 pm, and on Sunday there are 1½-hour backstage tours ($10) at 12.15 and 2.15 pm; it's best to book (☎ 684 8152).

The next building along, the **National Gallery**, was the first part of the complex to be completed, back in 1968, and it houses a very fine collection of art. The gallery has outstanding local and overseas collections, an excellent photography collection and many fascinating temporary exhibits from all over the world. There is usually a good display of Aboriginal art, and the 19th-century gallery is really worth a visit. The stained-glass ceiling in the Great Hall is superb – best viewed from a supine position. The gallery is open from 10 am to 5 pm and the admission is $6 (students and children $3). On Mondays admission is free, although only the ground floor is open. There are additional charges for some special exhibits.

The **Performing Arts Museum** is located at ground level in the Concert Hall building, facing the river. The museum has changing exhibits on all aspects of the performing arts: it might be a display of rock musicians' outfits or an exhibit on horror in the theatre! Opening hours are weekdays 11 am to 5 pm and weekends noon to 5 pm; admission is $5 (children $3.50).

Parks & Gardens

Victoria has dubbed itself 'the garden state' and it's certainly true in Melbourne; the city has many swaths of green all around the central area. They're varied and delightful – formal central gardens like the Treasury and Flagstaff gardens, wide empty parklands like Royal Park, the particularly fine Botanic Gardens, and many others.

Royal Botanic Gardens Certainly the finest botanic garden in Australia and arguably among the finest in the world, this is one of the nicest spots in Melbourne. There's nothing more genteel to do in Melbourne than to have scones and cream by the lake on a Sunday afternoon. The beautifully laid out gardens are right beside the Yarra River; indeed the river once actually ran through the gardens and the lakes are the remains of curves of the river, cut off when the river was straightened out to lessen the annual flood damage. The garden site was chosen in 1845 but the real development took place when Baron Sir Ferdinand von Mueller took charge in 1852.

There's a surprising amount of fauna as well as flora in the gardens. Apart from the many water fowl and the frequent visits from cockatoos you may also see rabbits and possums if you're lucky. In all, more than 50 varieties of birds can be seen in the gardens. A large contingent of fruit bats, usually found in the warmer climes of north Queensland, has taken up residence for the last ten summers or so – look for them high up the trees of the fern gully.

You can pick up guide-yourself leaflets at the park entrances; these are changed with the seasons and tell you what to look out for at the different times of year. The gardens are open daily from sunrise to sunset.

Kings Domain The Botanic Gardens form a corner of the Kings Domain, a park which also contains the Shrine of Remembrance, Governor La Trobe's Cottage and the Sidney Myer Music Bowl. It's flanked by St Kilda Rd. The whole park is encircled by the Tan Track, a four-km running track which is probably Melbourne's favourite venue for joggers. The track has an amusing variety of exercise points – a mixture of the stations of the cross and miniature golf, someone once said.

Beside St Kilda Rd stands the massive **Shrine of Remembrance**, a WW I war memorial which took so long to build that WW II was well under way when it eventually opened. Huge though it is, the shrine somehow manages to look completely anonymous; you could almost forget it was there. It's worth climbing up to the top as there are fine views to the city along St Kilda Rd. The shrine's big day of the year is Anzac Day. Back during the Vietnam era some enterprising individuals managed to sneak up to the well-guarded shrine on the night before Anzac Day and paint 'PEACE' across the front in large letters. The shrine is open to visitors daily, except Sunday, from 10 am to 5 pm.

Across from the shrine is **Governor La Trobe's Cottage**, the original Victorian government house sent out from the UK in prefabricated form in 1840. It was originally sited in Jolimont, near the MCG, and was moved here when the decision was made to preserve this interesting piece of Melbourne's early history. The simple little cottage is open Monday and Wednesday from 10 am to 4 pm, and weekends from 11 am to 4 pm; admission is $3.50 (children $1.80, family $8).

The cottage is flanked by the **Old Observatory** and the **National Herbarium**. On some nights the observatory is open to the public for a free view of the heavens between 8 and 10 pm, but it is usually booked out months in advance. Phone the National Museum of Victoria (☎ 669 9942) for details. Amongst other things the herbarium tests suspected marijuana samples to decide if they really are the dreaded weed.

The imposing building overlooking the Botanic Gardens is **Government House** where Victoria's governor resides. It's a copy of Queen Victoria's palace on England's Isle of Wight. There are guided tours on Monday, Wednesday and Saturday for $5 per person (☎ 654 4562).

Across the road from the herbarium on Dallas Brooks Drive is the **Australian Centre for Contemporary Art** which is open Tuesday to Friday from 11 am to 5 pm, weekends from 2 to 5 pm; admission is free. It shows mainly the work of Australian artists. Up at the city end of the park is the **Sidney Myer Music Bowl**, an outdoor performance area in a natural bowl. It's used for concerts in the summer months but not rock concerts, due to trouble in the past from some younger members of the audience! In winter it turns into a skating rink.

Treasury & Fitzroy Gardens These two popular formal parks lie immediately to the east of the city centre, overshadowed by the Hilton Hotel. The Fitzroy Gardens, with its stately avenues lined with English elms, is a popular spot for wedding photographs; on virtually every Saturday afternoon there's a continuous procession of wedding cars pulling up for the participants to be snapped. The pathways in the park are actually laid out in the form of a Union Jack!

The gardens contain several points of interest including **Captain Cook's Cottage**, which was uprooted from its native Yorkshire and reassembled in the park in 1934. Actually it's not certain that the good captain

ever did live in this house, but never mind, it looks very picturesque. The house is furnished in period style and has an interesting Captain Cook exhibit. It's open from 9 am to 5 pm daily and admission is $2.50 (children $1.20).

In the centre of the gardens, by the kiosk, is a miniature Tudor village and a carved fairy-tale tree. Off in the north-western corner of the park is the people's pathway – a circular path paved with individually engraved bricks. Anybody who dropped by here on 5 February 1978 got to produce their own little bit of art for posterity and it's quite intriguing to wander around.

The two gardens have a large resident population of possums; you may see them in the early evening or at night.

Other Parks The central **Flagstaff Gardens** were the first public gardens in Melbourne. From a lookout point here, ships arriving at the city were sighted in the early colonial days. A plaque in the gardens describes how the site was used for this purpose. Closer to the seafront is **Albert Park Lake**, a shallow lake created from a swamp area. The lake is popular for boating and there's another popular jogging track around the perimeter. The Jolly Roger Boathouse is at the city end of the lake and rents rowing and sailing boats. On Saturday the two sailing clubs here have races on the lake.

On the northern side of the city, the **Exhibition Gardens** are the site of the Exhibition Building, a wonder of the southern hemisphere when it was built for the Great Exhibition of 1880. Later it was used by the Victorian parliament for 27 years, while the Victorian parliament building was used by the national legislature until Canberra's parliament building was finally completed. It's still a major exhibition centre today and a new extension is one of the few successful uses of the 'mirror building' architectural craze which gripped Melbourne for a spell. There are some fine old fountains around the building, one of them well reflected in the mirror building.

To the north-east of the city, the Yarra is

bordered by parkland, much loved by runners, rowers and cyclists. Rowing boats can be hired from the **Studley Park & Fairfield boathouses** – you can dawdle down the river with cockatoos screeching on the banks and the rush-hour traffic roaring along the Eastern Freeway overhead. In parts of Studley Park you could be out in the bush; it's hard to believe the city's all around you. The birds here are sometimes spectacular.

At 7 Templestowe Rd in the Melbourne suburb of Bulleen, **Heide Park & Gallery** is the former home of two prominent Australian artists, John and Sunday Reed, and houses an impressive collection of 20th-century Australian art. The sprawling park is an informal combination of deciduous and native trees, with a carefully tended kitchen garden and scattered sculpture gardens running right down to the banks of the Yarra. Heide is open from Tuesday to Friday between 10 am and 5 pm, and on Saturdays and Sundays between noon and 5 pm. Bus No 203 goes to Bulleen, and the Yarra bike path goes close by.

Other Old Buildings

Como Overlooking the Yarra River from Como Park in South Yarra, Como was built between 1840 and 1859. The home with its extensive grounds has been authentically restored and furnished and is operated by the National Trust. Aboriginal rites and feasts were still being held on the banks of the Yarra when the house was first built, and an early occupant writes of seeing a cannibal rite from her bedroom window.

Como is open from 10 am to 5 pm every day and admission is $6.60 (students $4.40, children $3.30) and you can get there on tram No 8 from the city.

Ripponlea Ripponlea is at 192 Hotham St, Elsternwick, close to St Kilda. It's another fine old mansion with elegant gardens inhabited by peacocks. Ripponlea is open 10 am to 5 pm daily (8 pm in summer) and admission is $6.60 (students $4.40, children $3.30, family $16.50).

Montsalvat In Eltham, the mud-brick and alternative lifestylers' suburb, Montsalvat on Hillcrest Ave (26 km out) is Justus Jorgensen's eclectic re-creation of a European artists' colony which today houses all manner of artists and artisans. It's open dawn to dusk daily; admission costs $5 for adults and $2.50 for kids. It's also the venue for Australia's biggest jazz festival, every January. It's a two-km walk from Eltham Station.

Other Museums

There are a number of smaller museums around Melbourne. In Chinatown in the city centre the **Museum of Chinese Australian History** is on Cohen Place, close to the corner of Lonsdale and Exhibition Sts. Housed in an 1890s Victorian warehouse, the museum traces the history of the Chinese in Australia. It's open daily from 10 am to 4.30 pm, except Saturdays when it's open from noon to 5 pm; admission is $3 (children $1.50). The museum also conducts two-hour walking tours around Chinatown every morning, and these cost $9, or $22 including lunch at a Chinatown restaurant. Phone ☎ 662 2888 for bookings.

The **Melbourne Fire Brigade Museum** is at 8 Gisborne St, East Melbourne, and is open Fridays from 9 am to 3 pm and Sundays from 10 am to 4 pm; admission is $3 (children $1).

On Latrobe St near the corner of Russell St in the city is a small **Police Museum**, open weekdays from 10 am to 4 pm; admission is free.

Out at Moorabbin Airport, Cheltenham, the **Moorabbin Air Museum** has a collection of old aircraft including a number from WW II. It's open daily from 10 am to 5 pm.

Trams

If Melbourne has a symbol then it's a movable one – trams. Not those horrible, plastic-looking modern ones either; real Melbourne trams are green and yellow, ancient-looking and half the weight of an ocean liner. Trams are the standard means of public transport and they work remarkably well. More than a few cities which once had trams wish they still did today.

The old trams are gradually being replaced by new ones and some of the older trams have been turned into mobile works of art, painted from front to back by local artists. If you like old trams then watch out for them on weekends when some delightful vintage examples are rolled out on summer Sundays and used in place of the modern ones on the Hawthorn run from Princes Gate.

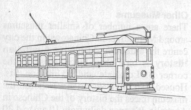

A W-class Melbourne tram

A free city-circle tram has been introduced, designed primarily for tourists and passing many city sights on its route. The trams are the nice older ones, but painted a deep burgundy and gold. They travel on a fixed route along Flinders, Spring and Nicholson Sts to Victoria Parade and then back along La Trobe and Spencer Sts. They run daily every 10 minutes, from 10 am to 6 pm.

To really come to grips with Melbourne and its trams try a ride on tram No 8. It starts off along Swanston St in the city, rolls down St Kilda Rd beside the Kings Domain, turns round by the war memorial and continues on to Toorak Rd through South Yarra and Toorak. Another popular tram ride is on Nos 15 and 16 which cruise right down St Kilda Rd to St Kilda.

Trams are such a part of Melbourne life they've even been used for a play – Act One of *Storming Mont Albert by Tram* took place from Mont Albert to the city, Act Two on the way back. The passengers were the audience, the actors got on and off along the way. It wasn't a bad play! There's even a tram restaurant: the *Colonial Tramcar Restaurant*

cruises Melbourne every night and you can have dinner on the move for $50 to $85 including drinks, depending on the time and the night (☎ 696 4000 for reservations).

Melbourne Suburbs

Melbourne's inner-city suburbs have gone through the same 'trendification' process that has hit Sydney suburbs like Paddington and Balmain. Carlton is the most obvious example of this activity, but Parkville, Fitzroy, South Melbourne, Albert Park, Richmond and Hawthorn are other popular inner-city suburbs with a strong Victorian flavour.

Carlton & Fitzroy Carlton is one of Melbourne's most interesting inner-city suburbs – partly because here you'll find probably the most attractive collection of Victorian architecture, partly because the University of Melbourne is here and partly because Carlton is also the Italian quarter of Melbourne with the biggest collection of Italian restaurants in Australia.

Lygon St is the backbone of Carlton and along here you'll find enough Italian restaurants, coffee houses, pizzerias and gelaterias to satisfy the most rabid pasta and cappuccino freak. The Lygon St Festa is held annually in November and always gets a good turn-out. The greasy-pole-climbing competition is popular.

Carlton is flanked by gracious Parkville and the seedy/trendy mixture of Fitzroy. Fitzroy's **Brunswick St** displays the liveliest array of cafes, restaurants, young designer clothes shops and bookshops to be found in Melbourne – an essential place on any itinerary. **Johnston St**, Fitzroy, is Melbourne's Spanish quarter and the home of the annual Hispanic Festival, held every November.

South Yarra & Toorak South of the Yarra River (as the name indicates) South Yarra is one of the more frenetic Melbourne suburbs, Toorak one of the most exclusive. The two roads to remember here are Toorak Rd and Chapel St. **Toorak Rd** is one of Australia's classiest shopping streets, frequented by

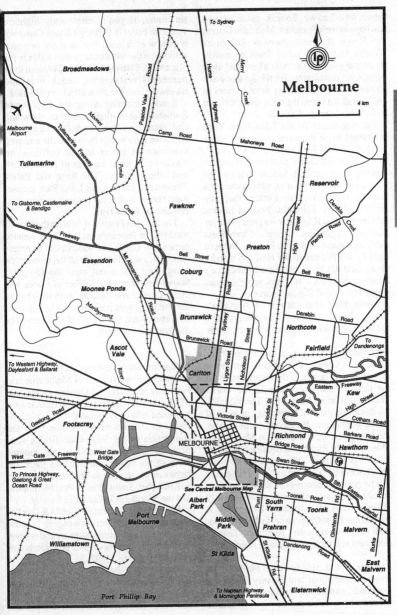

Melbourne

VICTORIA

0   2   4 km

To Sydney

Broadmeadows

Melbourne
Airport

Tullamarine

To Gisborne, Castlemaine
& Bendigo

Calder   Freeway

Essendon

Moonee Ponds

Ascot
Vale

To Western Highway,
Daylesford & Ballarat

Footscray

West   Gate   Freeway

West Gate
Bridge

To Princes Highway,
Geelong & Great
Ocean Road

Port
Melbourne

Williamstown

Port Phillip Bay

Fawkner

Preston

Coburg

Brunswick

Carlton

Pascoe Vale   Road

Hume   Highway

Merri   Creek

Camp   Road

Mahoneys   Road

Reservoir

Moonee   Ponds   Creek

Mt   Alexander   Road

Bell   Street

Bell   Street

Sydney   Road

Darebin   Creek

High   Street

Plenty   Road

Northcote

Darebin   Road

To
Dandenongs

Fairfield

Brunswick   Road

Maribyrnong   River

Lygon Street

Nicholson   Street

Hoddle St

Victoria   Street

MELBOURNE

See Central Melbourne Map

Albert
Park

Middle
Park

St Kilda

Yarra   River

Eastern   Freeway

Kew

Cotham   Road

Barkers   Road

Richmond

Bridge Road

Hawthorn

Swan   Street

Sth   Eastern   Road

South
Yarra

Prahran

Toorak   Road

Punt   Road

Glenferrie   Rd

Toorak

Dandenong   Road

St   Kilda   Rd

Malvern

Burke   Road

East
Malvern

Elsternwick

To Nepean Highway
& Mornington Peninsula

those well-known Toorak matrons and cowboys in their Porsches, Mercedes Benzes and Range Rovers (otherwise known as 'Toorak tractors'). Apart from expensive shops and some of Australia's best (and most expensive) restaurants, Toorak Rd also has a number of very reasonably priced places to eat. Toorak Rd forms the main artery through both South Yarra and Toorak.

Running across Toorak Rd in South Yarra is **Chapel St**; if the word for Toorak Rd is 'exclusive' then for Chapel St it's 'trendy'. The street is virtually wall-to-wall boutiques ranging from punk to Indian bangles and beads, op-shop to antique, plus restaurants and the imaginative Jam Factory shopping centre, with the delightful Prahran Market off Commercial Rd nearby – a great place for fruit and vegetables. Chapel St trendiness fades as it gets further into Prahran, but turn right by the Prahran Town Hall and wander along Greville St, at one time Melbourne's freak street, which still has some curious shops and a good Sunday market.

South Yarra also has one of Australia's finest colonial mansions, Como House, and the Royal Botanic Gardens flank the suburb.

Richmond As Carlton is to Italy so Richmond is to Greece; this suburb, just to the east of the city centre, is the Greek centre for the third largest Greek city in the world. That's right, after Athens and Thessaloniki, Melbourne is the next largest city in terms of Greek population. Richmond is, of course, the best place for a souvlaki in Melbourne! More recently Richmond became the centre for a huge influx of Vietnamese, and colourful **Victoria St** is known as 'Little Saigon'.

The suburb is another centre for Victorian architecture, much of it restored or currently in the process of restoration. **Bridge Rd** is something of a Melbourne fashion centre, with shops where many Australian fashion designers sell their seconds and rejects.

St Kilda This seaside suburb is Melbourne's most cosmopolitan and is very lively on weekends, particularly on Sundays. It's also the somewhat feeble excuse for a Melbourne

sin centre; if you're after seedy nightlife you'll do better in Sydney's Kings Cross but if you want a meal late at night or some activity on the weekends then St Kilda is the place to be. **Fitzroy & Acland Sts**, with their numerous restaurants, snack bars and takeaways, are the main streets in St Kilda.

Sunday morning along the **Esplanade** features an interesting amateur art show and craft market, while along Acland St gluttons will have their minds blown by the amazing selection of cakes in the coffee-shop windows. St Kilda has lots of local Jewish and ethnic colour. The huge old Palais Theatre and the raucous Luna Park amusement centre, with roller coasters and the like, can also be found here.

The St Kilda Festival is held on the second weekend in February. Acland St is usually turned into a mall with food stalls and entertainment, and in Fitzroy St all the restaurants bring their tables out onto the footpath. Stages are set up in a number of places and there is music and dancing, with rock bands and ethnic groups performing. The finale of the festival and the weekend is a fireworks display over the beach.

Williamstown At the mouth of the Yarra, this is one of the oldest parts of Melbourne and has many interesting old buildings and lots of waterside activity. Williamstown remained relatively isolated from developments in the rest of Melbourne until the completion of the West Gate Bridge suddenly brought it to within a few minutes drive of the centre. On Sundays there are ferries across the bay to Williamstown from St Kilda Pier, Station Pier in Port Melbourne and the World Trade Centre in the city.

Moored in Williamstown, **HMAS Castlemaine**, a WW II minesweeper, is now preserved as a maritime museum and is open on weekends from noon to 5 pm; admission is $2.50 (children $1.50).

The **Railway Museum** on Champion Rd, North Williamstown, has a fine collection of old steam locomotives. It's open weekends and public holidays from noon to 5 pm and also on Wednesdays during school holidays. Admission is $3 (children $1).

Other Suburbs South of the centre are other Victorian inner suburbs with many finely restored old homes, particularly in the bayside suburbs of **South Melbourne**, **Middle Park** and **Albert Park**. Emerald Hill in South Melbourne is a whole section of 1880s Melbourne, still in relatively authentic shape. **Port Melbourne** is the latest suburb to become the target of yuppies. Wealthier inner suburbs to the east, also popular shopping centres, include **Armadale**, **Malvern**, **Hawthorn** and **Camberwell**.

Sandwiched between the city and Richmond is the compact area of **East Melbourne**; like Parkville it's one of the most concentrated areas of old Victorian buildings around the city with numerous excellent examples of early architecture.

Beaches

Melbourne hasn't got fine surf beaches like Sydney, at least not close to the city, but it still has some that are reasonable for swimming and you can find surf further out on the Mornington Peninsula. Starting from the city end, **Albert Park** and **Middle Park** are the most popular city beaches – local meeting places and spots to observe Aussie beach kulcha in a Melbourne setting.

Further along there's **St Kilda** and then **Elwood**, **Brighton** and **Sandringham**, which are quite pleasant beaches. For a city beach **Half Moon Bay** is very good indeed. Beyond here you have to get right round to the Mornington Peninsula before you find the really excellent beaches.

Organised Tours

Several companies, including Melbourne Sightseeing (☎ 670 9706), Australian Pacific (☎ 650 1511) and AAT Kings (☎ 650 1244), run conventional city bus tours, as well as trips to the most popular tourist destinations like Sovereign Hill, Healesville Sanctuary, Phillip Island and the Great Ocean Road. Brochures are available at hostels and information centres.

Autopia Tours (☎ 326 5536) runs fun-oriented bus tours for backpackers and hostellers, with a maximum of 19 people. A day trip to Hanging Rock and a local winery costs $30; along the Great Ocean Road costs $49; and a visit to the Phillip Island penguin parade and fauna park costs $40. Its two-day tours to Phillip Island and Wilsons Prom cost $58; two days along the Great Ocean Road is also $58.

Mac's Backpacker Tours (☎ (052) 41 3180) also takes small groups along the Great Ocean Road (one day $49), to Phillip Island and the Great Ocean Road (two days, $79) and to both the Grampians National Park and the Great Ocean Road (three days, $89). Both Mac's and Autopia close down over winter.

Melbourne Backpacker Sightseeing (☎ 650 0088) has a wide range of day trips to Phillip Island, the Great Ocean Road and other destinations around Victoria, and offers special discounts for YHA members.

Some interesting smaller tour operators include Lancefield Bush Rides & Tucker (☎ (054) 29 1627), which offers a day trip to Hanging Rock, with horse riding and bush tucker, for $55; Echidna Walkabout (☎ 646 8249), an ecotourism company which offers three walkabout tours with bushwalking and wildlife-watching; Club Ned (☎ 570 1651), with rock-climbing and abseiling weekends to the Grampians for $135; and Polperro Dolphin Swims (☎ (059) 88 8437), which can take you for a swim with dolphins in Port Phillip Bay, leaving from Sorrento on the Mornington Peninsula. Bogong Jack Adventures (☎ (057) 27 3382) has a wide range of cycling, bushwalking, skiing and canoeing tours through the Victorian Alps.

The recently established Australian Backpacker Airlines (☎ 587 2696) offers flights and tours to Echuca, Phillip Island, the Great Ocean Road and around Port Phillip Bay, costing from $25 to $57 per person.

Festivals

Moomba is Melbourne's major annual festival, held around the beginning of March. The weather is usually good and Melburnians let their hair down.

VICTORIA

The Melbourne Film Festival is one of the world's oldest and best, although the catch is that it's held in June, the depths of winter.

Melbourne is Australia's comedy capital, and the Comedy Festival in April is an exciting time, with local acts (often en route to the Edinburgh Fringe) and international guests.

The Melbourne International Festival of the Arts is an excellent arts festival with many and varied events, including the concurrently run and popular Fringe Festival. Both festivals are held in October. The world-famous Melbourne Cup is run on the first Tuesday in November each year.

Places to Stay

Melbourne has a fairly wide range of accommodation, with everything from backpackers' hostels to five-star hotels. The tricky part is deciding which area to stay in. The city centre is convenient and close to things like theatres, restaurants, museums and the train and bus terminals, although it can be a little lifeless at night. The alternative is to stay in one of the inner suburbs that ring the city, each of which has its own distinct flavour and characteristics.

If you decide to stay longer, look in the *Age* classifieds on Wednesdays and Saturdays under share accommodation. You could also try the notice boards in the hostels, or places like the universities, Readings bookshop in Carlton, Cosmos Books & Music and the Galleon restaurant in St Kilda, or the Black Cat cafe in Fitzroy. Several of the hostels can also organise long-term flats.

Camping Melbourne has a few caravan and camping sites in the metropolitan area, although none of them are very close to the centre. The most convenient place is probably the comprehensive Melbourne Caravan & Tourist Park in Coburg East, 10 km north of the city. (From the city, take tram No 19 or 20 from Elizabeth St then bus No 526; the bus doesn't run on Sundays!) The Footscray site is also convenient but has on-site vans only. The following are some of Melbourne's closer sites:

Melbourne Caravan & Tourist Park (☎ 354 3533), 10 km north at 265 Elizabeth St, Coburg East; camping $16, on-site vans $34.50, cabins from $39.50.

Northside Caravan Park (☎ 305 3614), 14 km north on the corner of the Hume Highway and Coopers Rd, Campbellfield; camping $14, cabin vans $40.

Crystal Brook Holiday Centre (☎ 844 3637), 21 km north-east on the corner of Warrandyte and Andersons Creek Rds, Doncaster East; camping $16, on-site vans $30, on-site cabins $60.

Footscray Caravan Park (☎ 314 6646), eight km west at 163 Somerville Rd, West Footscray; no camping, on-site vans $35.

Hobsons Bay Caravan Park (☎ 397 2395), 17 km south at 158 Kororoit Creek Rd, Williamstown; camping $14, cabins $30/35.

Hostels There are quite a few backpackers' hostels in and around the city centre and two good YHA hostels in North Melbourne, although the seaside suburb of St Kilda has the widest range of budget options, with at least half a dozen hostels. The hostel scene is fairly competitive, and it can be hard to find a bed in one of the better places over summer, whereas prices often drop by a few dollars when things are quieter. Several of the larger hostels have courtesy buses that do pick-ups from the bus and train terminals.

City Centre The best of the city bunch is *Toad Hall* (☎ 600 9010) at 441 Elizabeth St, within easy walking distance of the bus terminals. It's been recently upgraded and is well equipped and comfortable, with a pleasant courtyard and off-street parking ($5). A bed in a four- or six-bed dorm costs from $12; single/double rooms cost from $25/45.

The *City Centre Private Hotel* (☎ 654 5401) at 22 Little Collins St is clean and quiet. All rooms have shared bathrooms and there's a TV lounge and kitchen on each floor. Backpackers' rooms cost $15 in a three- or four-bed room and doubles are $34; serviced singles/doubles are $34/50.

The *Backpackers City Inn* (☎ 650 4379) is upstairs in the Carlton Hotel at 197 Bourke St. There are cheap bistro meals and a bar, although both the pub and the accommoda-

...ion are pretty rough around the edges. Dorm beds cost $14, twins and doubles $32.

Fitzroy Well located on the fringe of the city at 116 Nicholson St is the *Nunnery* (☎ 419 8637), one of the best budget accommodation options in Melbourne. It's a converted Victorian building with comfortable lounges, good facilities and a friendly atmosphere. The rooms are small but clean and centrally heated. Costs range from $13 in a twelve-bed dorm to $16 in a three-bed dorm; singles are $39 and twins/doubles $49/$54. Take tram No 96 heading east along Bourke St, and get off at stop No 11.

North Melbourne There are two YHA hostels in North Melbourne, which is about three km from the city centre. Both offer discounts for a four-day or longer stay. From the airport you can ask the Skybus to drop you at the North Melbourne hostels.

The YHA showpiece is the *Queensberry Hill Hostel* (☎ 329 8599) at 78 Howard St. This huge 348-bed place was only completed in mid-1991 and so has excellent facilities. Four- or six-bed dorms cost $16 for YHA members ($3 more for nonmembers); singles/doubles are $36/44, or $46/54 with private bathroom. There's a breakfast and dinner service available, and office hours are 7.30 am to 10.30 pm, although there is 24-hour access once you have checked in. Catch tram No 55 from William St and get off at stop No 15, or any tram north up Elizabeth St to stop No 13.

The YHA's *Chapman St Hostel* (☎ 328 3595), at 76 Chapman St, is smaller and older but can be a bit more intimate than Queensberry Hill. Dorms here cost $13, twin rooms $32 and doubles $36. Both hostels have good notice boards if you're looking for people to travel or share lifts with, cheap airline tickets or just general information. There are a number of very good tours which operate out of the hostels, and destinations include Phillip Island, Wilsons Prom, the Great Ocean Road and the Grampians.

St Kilda St Kilda is one of Melbourne's most interesting and cosmopolitan suburbs, with a good range of budget accommodation as well as plenty of restaurants and entertainment possibilities. From Swanston St in the city, tram No 15 or 16 will take you down St Kilda Rd to Fitzroy St, or there's the faster light-rail service (No 96 from Spencer St and Bourke St) to the old St Kilda railway station and along Fitzroy and Acland Sts.

Enfield House Backpackers (☎ 534 8159), at 2 Enfield St, is the original and probably the most popular of St Kilda's hostels. It's a rambling old Victorian boarding house with over 100 beds, mostly four-bunk dorms at $14 per person, but also singles at $25 and twin rooms from $32 to $36. The facilities are good and the staff can help organise tours, nights out and activities. There is a courtesy van which picks up travellers from the bus terminals, and from Station Pier for the Tasmanian ferries. There are also some nearby flats managed by the hostel which are good if you're intending to stay longer in Melbourne, costing $160 a week for up to four people.

At 169 Fitzroy St, the *Ritz* (☎ 525 3501) is the newest hostel in St Kilda. It's upstairs from a restaurant/bar and is quite stylish, with comfortable lounges and sitting rooms, although the kitchen is pretty small. Four- to eight-bunk dorms cost $12, twin rooms $30 and doubles $35.

The excellent *Olembia Bed & Breakfast* (☎ toll-free 1800 032 635) at 96 Barkly St is a warm and intimate guesthouse. The facilities are better here than at most places, and there's a cosy guest lounge, central heating, a courtyard and off-street parking. Dorm beds cost $14, singles are $38, doubles/twins are $52, and breakfast is available for $5. Linen hire is $2.

The *St Kilda Backpackers Inn* (☎ 534 5283), also known as the Coffee Palace, is at 24 Grey St. It's big and basic but otherwise OK, and cheap at $10 for a dorm bed and $20/26 for singles/doubles. Around the corner at 56 Jackson St is *Kookaburra Cottage* (☎ 534 5457), a smaller hostel which has been recently renovated. It's quite comfortable and has all the usual facilities;

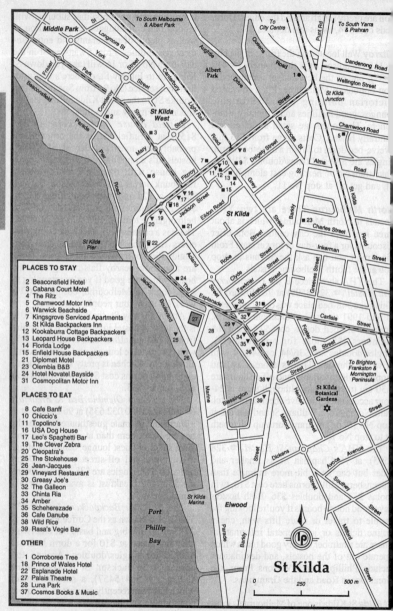

PLACES TO STAY

2 Beaconsfield Hotel
3 Cabana Court Motel
4 The Ritz
5 Charnwood Motor Inn
6 Warwick Beachside
7 Kingsgrove Serviced Apartments
9 St Kilda Backpackers Inn
12 Kookaburra Cottage Backpackers
13 Leopard House Backpackers
14 Florida Lodge
15 Enfield House Backpackers
21 Diplomat Motel
23 Olembia B&B
24 Hotel Novatel Bayside
31 Cosmopolitan Motor Inn

PLACES TO EAT

8 Cafe Banff
10 Chiccio's
11 Topolino's
11 USA Dog House
16 Leo's Spaghetti Bar
19 The Clever Zebra
20 Cleopatra's
25 The Stokehouse
26 Jean-Jacques
29 Vineyard Restaurant
30 Greasy Joe's
32 The Galleon
33 Chinta Ria
34 Amber
35 Scheherezade
36 Cafe Danube
38 Wild Rice
39 Rasa's Vegie Bar

OTHER

1 Corroboree Tree
18 Prince of Wales Hotel
22 Esplanade Hotel
27 Palais Theatre
28 Luna Park
37 Cosmos Books & Music

St Kilda

0   250   500 m

orm beds are $10 and there are a couple of ood twin rooms at $24.

On the corner of Grey St and Jackson St *Leopard House* (☎ 534 1200), an old and oomy two-storey Edwardian house with ostly four-bed dorms at $10. Further up rey St at No 37, *Florida Lodge* (☎ 525 048) is a converted block of bland 1950s ats. At $50, the standard is pretty basic, but ach flat has its own facilities.

Another option is the *Beaconsfield Hotel* ☎ 534 0225), opposite the beach at 341 Beaconsfield Parade, with a few bunk beds pstairs at $12.50 per person. The facilities ren't great, but there's always the bar and istro downstairs.

South Yarra *Lord's Lodge Backpackers* ☎ 510 5658) is at 204 Punt Rd, which is a airly hectic main road. This is a large, two-torey place with a range of accommodation, ncluding six-bed dorms with their own itchens and three small bungalows in the ack yard. Beds here cost $12.

Richmond The *Richmond Hill Guesthouse* ☎ 428 6501), well located at 353 Church St, s another recent addition to the hostel scene. 's a big old Victorian building with spa-ious living areas and clean rooms. A four-r six-bed dorm costs $15 and singles/doubles re $25/40. Also in Richmond, although not s well located, is *Central House* (☎ 427 826), a small and modern hostel at 337 Highett St. Dorm beds here cost from $11 nd there are also twins and doubles from 24.

Preston The *Terrace Travellers Hostel* (☎ 470 006) is at 418 Murray Rd, Preston – take ram No 10 or 11 and get off at stop No 48. Although the facilities here are as good as at ny of the other hostels, it is a long way from he centre of things, and it lacks atmosphere. Dorm beds are $12.

Hotels, Motels, B&Bs & Serviced Apart-ments As with cheaper accommodation, you ave a choice between the convenience of he city centre and the often more pleasant surroundings of the inner suburbs. You can generally find a reasonable double room from around $40, or from $50 with a private bathroom.

City Centre The *Terrace Pacific Inn* (☎ 621 3333) is at 16 Spencer St, a five-minute walk south from the Spencer St bus and train terminals. It's a newly opened hotel with simple but good rooms from $39 a double, or from $67 with a private bathroom. The tariff includes a light breakfast. Nearby at 44 Spencer St, the *Hotel Enterprise* (previously the John Spencer Hotel) (☎ 629 6991) is another refurbished hotel, with budget rooms from $39/49 for singles/doubles, or from $78/88 with a private bathroom.

At 131 King St, the *Kingsgate Hotel* (☎ 629 4171) is a private hotel that has been repainted and cleaned up. It's a big old place, with budget rooms with shared bathrooms from $30/50 or en-suite rooms from $42/58, and breakfast is available in the dining room for $6.

The *YWCA Family Hotel* (☎ 329 5188) is conveniently central at 489 Elizabeth St, also close to the bus terminals. It has singles/doubles at $48/58 and share rooms at $20 per person (when available). All rooms have shower and toilet, air-con and tea-making facilities. This place is well worn but comfortable, and it's well maintained and secure.

The *Victoria Hotel* (☎ 653 0441) at 215 Little Collins St is a notch up from the cheapest city hotels, and a bit of a Melbourne institution. There are 520 rooms in three categories: budget rooms with shared facilities at $46/59, standard rooms with en-suite and TV at $74/95, and executive rooms at $82/110. The Victoria is one of the most convenient hotels in Melbourne – you could hardly ask to be more central.

Just south of the city centre is the *Queensbridge Hotel* (☎ 686 3117), at 1 Queensbridge St. It's a cosy old pub with clean and simple rooms upstairs costing $35/55, which includes a cooked breakfast.

West Melbourne Although located in a

VICTORIA

fairly uninspiring part of town, the *Miami Motel* (☎ 329 8499) at 13 Hawke St is simple, well kept, and an easy walk from the centre. All rooms have shared bathrooms, and the tariff of $34/48 includes breakfast.

East Melbourne East Melbourne is a much more pleasant area. It's close to the city, yet has a residential feel with its tree-lined streets and grand old Victorian terrace houses. The *Georgian Court Guesthouse* (☎ 419 6353), at 21 George St, is an elegant and homely B&B with singles/doubles with shared bathrooms at $55/65, or a room with an en-suite at $75/85; prices include a buffet breakfast.

At 101 George St the *George Street Apartments* (☎ 419 1333) is a secure and friendly place with serviced apartments, all with bathroom, fridge and cooking facilities, at $70 a double. At 25 Hotham St, the *East Melbourne Studio Apartments* (☎ 412 2555) are also good but a bit more stylish, and accordingly more expensive at $95 a night.

Parkville The *Parkville Park Inn* (☎ 387 8300), at 825 Park St, is close to the Melbourne Zoo and has a 24-hour pick-up service from the airport. This place is very well run and popular with international visitors, and has spacious and modern motel-style rooms from $70 and apartments with kitchenettes from $100.

Another good option north of the city is the *Royal Park Inn* (☎ 380 5599) on the corner of Park St and Royal Parade. It's an Edwardian-style guesthouse with communal kitchen, laundry and lounge, and en-suite rooms from $70/75.

South Yarra Tram No 8 from Swanston St in the city takes you along Toorak Rd into the heart of South Yarra. the *Tilba* (☎ 867 8844), on the corner of Toorak Rd West and Domain St, is an elegant boutique hotel with gracious Victorian-era rooms costing from $125 to $170 a double, depending on size – expensive, but well worth it.

A cheaper option is the *West End Private Hotel* (☎ 866 5375), at 76 Toorak Rd, with

singles/doubles at $40/48, although it's old fashioned and a bit run down now. In th same area, the *Albany Motel* (☎ 866 4485 on the corner of Toorak Rd and Millswyn S has good rooms at $70/75. The *Domair Motel* at 52 Darling St is an older motel bu well located, with budget rooms at $55/62.

South Yarra is the serviced-apartmen capital of Melbourne. These are mostly con verted blocks of flats, fully self-containe and regularly serviced – they can be rente overnight, weekly or long-term. Some o them are quite expensive but cheaper one include the *Manor House Apartment* (☎ 867 1266) at 23 Avoca St, with studi apartments from $70 a night; *South Yarr Place* (☎ 867 6595) at 41 Margaret St, wit one-bedrooms flats from $65 ($75 for courtyard unit); *Darling Towers* (☎ 86 5200) at 32 Darling St, with studios from $6 and two-bedroom apartments from $158; o the *Aston Apartments* (☎ 866 2953) at 4 Powell St, with one-bedroom units at $85.

St Kilda St Kilda also has some good, afford able serviced apartments. One of the bes places is *Kingsgrove* (☎ 536 3000), right i the heart of the action at 44 Fitzroy St. Thi place has secure and modern apartment from $78 for a studio, $130 for an apartmen that sleeps four or $175 for the two-bedroon model. In a quieter, more suburban part of S Kilda, *Maxim's Redan Apartments* (☎ 52 5000) at 25 Redan St are also good, and star from $75 a night.

Opposite St Kilda beach at 363 Beacons field Parade, *Warwick Beachside* (☎ 52 4800) has 1950s-style holiday flats. They aren't glamorous, but they're clean, comfort able and well equipped, and cost from $5 for three people or from $79 for five. There'. a laundry and off-street parking here. Th modern high-rise *Novatel Bayside* (☎ 52 5522), overlooking the bay from 14-16 Th Esplanade, has four-star hotel rooms starting at $120 a double.

St Kilda has plenty of motels, but th standard varies enormously. Some of th more respectable places are the *Cabanz Court Motel* (☎ 534 0771), at 46 Park St (on

...lock back from Fitzroy St), which has self-contained units from $71/80 for singles/doubles; the *Cosmopolitan Motor Inn* (☎ 534 0781) at 6 Carlisle St (close to Acland St, Luna Park and the beach), with singles/doubles from $69 and family units with kitchenettes from $109; the *Diplomat Motel* (☎ 534 4003) at 12 Acland St, with well-worn 1970s-style rooms at $60/65; and the very pleasant *Charnwood Motor Inn* ☎ 525 4199), in a quieter part of St Kilda at 8 Charnwood St, with rooms at $69/74.

Albert Park The *Hotel Victoria* (☎ 690 8666), which overlooks the bay from 123 Beaconsfield Parade, is a restored 1888 hotel. It's in a great location and has simple pension-style rooms with shared bathrooms at $45/50, or spacious corner suites which are worth the $150 a night just for the views.

Colleges Melbourne has three universities: the long-established University of Melbourne and two newer 'bush universities' – La Trobe and Monash. Visitors would probably find La Trobe and Monash too far away from the centre to be worth considering.

The University of Melbourne is just to the north of the city centre in Parkville. The following colleges have accommodation in the vacation period from late November to mid-February; B&B ranges from $25 to $45 per night, and there's a minimum stay of three nights: *International House* (☎ 347 5655); *Medley Hall* (☎ 663 5847); *Ridley College* (☎ 387 7555); *Ormond College* ☎ 348 1688); *Queen's College* (☎ 349 9500); *Trinity College* (☎ 347 1044); *University College* (☎ 347 3533); and *Whitley College* (☎ 347 8388). There are cheaper rates for students at all these colleges.

Places to Eat

Melbourne is a wonderful place to have an appetite – and a terrible place to start a diet. Everywhere you go, there are restaurants, cafes, delicatessens, markets, bistros, brasseries and takeaways. Gastronomically, you can travel the world here – go to Lygon St, Carlton, for Italian food; Swan St, Rich-

mond, for Greek food; Victoria St, Richmond, for (very cheap) Vietnamese; Sydney Rd, Brunswick, for Turkish; Little Bourke St in the city for Chinese; Johnston St, Fitzroy, for Spanish; or for sheer variety go to Brunswick St in Fitzroy or Acland St in St Kilda.

The restaurants listed are just a small selection of favourites which are in the main areas where travellers may be staying or visiting. If you want to make a more in-depth study of food in Melbourne, pick up a copy of *The Age Good Food Guide* or *The Age Cheap Eats in Melbourne*.

Most of Melbourne's restaurants are either licensed to sell alcohol or BYO, meaning you can bring your own booze, but some places are a bit of both. Some BYO places charge a small fee for corkage.

City Centre The centre of town has a variety of cuisines and price ranges, and some particularly good Chinese and Italian places.

Chinatown The area in and around Chinatown, which follows Little Bourke St from Spring St to Swanston St, is one of the best and most diverse food precincts, with great Chinese restaurants as well as Italian, Malaysian, Thai and others.

Starting from the top end, *Jan Bo* at 40 Little Bourke St has reasonably priced and authentic Chinese food, and serves great yum cha daily from 11 am to 3 pm. Further down at No 50, the *Shark Finn Inn* is also very popular for lunch or dinner, and stays open until 1.30 am. *Cafe K*, in Little Bourke St, is a classy European bistro with main meals in the $7 to $13 range.

Ronz, at 105 Little Bourke St, has great Malaysian food and a pleasant ambience, with main courses around $6 to $10. The highly acclaimed and impressive *Flower Drum* (☎ 662 3655), at 17 Market Lane, is very expensive but has some of the best Cantonese food (and service) this side of Hong Kong. *Yamato* is a tiny Japanese restaurant at 28 Corrs Lane, hidden away off Little Bourke St. It's been around for years and turns out excellent food at reasonable prices. Main courses cost from $9 and the banana tempura is definitely worth a try.

At *Nam Loong*, 223 Russell St, even the blackboard menu is in Chinese. You almost feel like they're being condescending when they produce an English menu and you can certainly expect nothing but chopsticks. The prices are, however, something to smile about, with main dishes from $4 to $8. You need to eat early though, as Nam Loong closes at 9.30 pm. *King of Kings*, nearby at 209 Russell St, also has very good and cheap food, and stays open until 2 am.

The crowded *Kunming Restaurant* at 212 Little Bourke St combines straightforward, no-frills decor with excellent, cheap food. Authentic noodle and rice dishes cost about $6.

Peony Gardens at 283 Little Lonsdale St is a busy cafeteria-style place that also does takeaways. Most dishes are $2.50 to $4 and at that price you really can't complain about plastic plates and utensils or having to clear the table after you've eaten. It's open for lunch and early dinner Monday to Friday.

Bourke St *Le Monde*, next to the Metro nightclub at 18 Bourke St, is a narrow and trendy bar which serves snacks and meals until very early in the morning. Across the road and hidden away at 20 Myers Place is the *Italian Waiter's Restaurant*, one of Melbourne's favourite institutions. It serves good, cheap Italian food in unglamorous but cosy surrounds – if you can't find it, just ask someone on the street.

Back on Bourke St at No 66 is another Melbourne institution – *Pellegrini's*. It's a bohemian Italian bar with great apple strudel, pasta and risotto, and long, strong coffees. It's also a popular meeting place. The *Florentino Cellar Bar*, at No 80, looks expensive and up-market but is actually very reasonable. Pastas are $7, and they also serve soup, focaccia and antipasto.

Other Areas The cheapest place to eat in town is *Gopal's*, at 139 Swanston St, a vegetarian cafe run by the Hare Krishna sect. It's open for lunch and dinner and has dishes from $1 to $3, three courses for $5.50 or all you can eat for $8.50.

There's a small Greek enclave in the city along Lonsdale St between Russell and Swanston Sts. *Stalactites*, on the corner of Lonsdale and Russell Sts, is the best known mainly for its bizarre stalactite decor and the fact that it's open 24 hours. *Electra* at 195 Lonsdale St is more elegant than the average run of cheap Greek places, with main courses at around $12, and there's also the pleasant *Tsindos the Greek's Restaurant* at 197 Lonsdale.

Campari Bistro at 25 Hardware St, a hop, step and jump from the GPO, is a busy little Italian bistro which can get very crowded at lunch time; main courses are around $9.

There's a good choice of pub food around the city. The *Sherlock Holmes*, an English style pub at 415 Collins St, is popular with travellers and has authentic English ales, snacks and meals. The *Oxford Scholar Hotel* opposite RMIT at the top end of Swanston St, is always full of students and has meals from $4 to $7.

Food Courts & Emporiums The *Hyatt Food Court* on the corner of Russell and Collins St is a spacious and stylish international food court with a wide range of cuisines to choose from, plus a bar. Another good food court is the *Sportsgirl Centre*, on Collins St just down from Swanston St. For Asian food, go to the *Ong International Food Court*, in the basement at 265 Little Bourke St.

Melbourne's major department stores also have great food emporiums. *Cooks World* at Daimaru features an excellent Japanese food bar; Myer's *Wonderful World of Food*, on the ground floor at Little Bourke St, and David Jones's *Food Glorious Food*, in the basement of the Bourke St store, both have a selection of goodies to satisfy even the most obscure craving.

Southgate Southgate, a new development on the southern side of the Yarra River beside the Concert Hall, is now one of the best and most popular eating centres in Melbourne. The setting is great, there's a good range of styles and prices, and you can either eat ndoors or outside overlooking the river and the city.

In the centre of the ground floor is the *Wharf Food Market*, where you have a choice of Japanese, Malaysian or Thai food, fish & chips, a salad and fruit-juice bar, delicatessen or an ice-cream parlour. On the same level are *Egusto*, a stylish Italian bistro with main courses from $8 to $15, and *Bistro Vite*, a simple French bistro with excellent food.

On the mid-level, the casual *Blue Train Cafe* serves breakfasts, pastas and risottos, wood-fired pizzas and salads, all at very reasonable prices. *Scusa Mi* is a more up-market Italian bistro and bar with great food and smart service. *Simply French*, on the upper level, is a bar, coffee shop and patisserie with a mouth-watering selection of pastries.

St Kilda St Kilda has everything from hamburger joints and felafel bars to stylish cafes, bars and restaurants. Most of the eating places are along Fitzroy and Acland Sts.

Starting from the seaside end of Fitzroy St, *Cleopatra's* is a tiny takeaway Lebanese place with excellent and cheap Middle Eastern food. At No 19, the *Clever Zebra* is a good place for breakfast or lunch, with dishes like gado gado, stir-fries and burgers around $6.50 to $8.50.

At 55 Fitzroy St *Leo's Spaghetti Bar* is something of a St Kilda institution, with pastas around $6 to $8, excellent coffee and late opening hours. Leo's is divided into three parts – coffee bar, bistro and restaurant. The *USA Dog House Cafe* at No 63 serves hot-dogs, burgers and sandwiches.

Topolino's at 87 Fitzroy St is the place to go for a pizza or a big bowl of pasta – it's usually packed late at night and stays open until sunrise. *Chiccio's*, at No 109, is another pizza/pasta place and offers meals for two people for $5.50 each, including a drink, bread and salad. Further up Fitzroy St at No 145 is the relaxed *Cafe Banff*, with curries, pastas, casseroles and pizzas from $7 to $10.

Further south near Acland St, the *Galleon*, at 9 Carlisle St, is a quirky and casual cafe where you can have home-cooked meals like soup or apple crumble for $3.80, chicken and leek pie for $4.50 or pasta for $6 – great value and great fun. On the corner of Carlisle and Acland Sts, *Greasy Joe's* is a loud and lively grill bar with most meals under $10.

If you're craving a big juicy steak, head for the *Vineyard Restaurant* at 71a Acland St. The decor ain't great but the steaks are huge and cost around $12 – another $3.60 with salad. *Amber* at No 73 is an Indian place with excellent food and reasonable prices. Across the road at No 94, *Chinta Ria* combines wonderful Malaysian food with jazz and soul; curries, laksas and satays are between $6 and $10.

Cafe Danube at No 107 and *Scheherezade* at No 99 also do good, plain Central European food in large quantities. Acland St's crowning glory is its orgiastic cake shops. The displays in the shop windows emanate so many calories you're in danger of putting on kg just walking by them!

Wild Rice, round the corner at 211 Barkly St, is a very good little cafe where the emphasis is on macrobiotic and other interesting snack food; the variety is excellent, the prices low, and the rear courtyard very pleasant. Round the next corner is *Rasa's Vegie Bar* at 5 Blessington St, with good-value vegetarian dishes; tofu or lentil burgers are $4.50 and most mains $8.50.

Jean-Jacques by the Sea, at 40 Jacka Blvd, is a classy seafood restaurant perched on the foreshore. While it's pretty expensive inside, for those of us without American Express gold cards there's a takeaway section with great fish & chips and outdoor tables. Nearby, the *Stokehouse* has an equally good foreshore position. There's a formal (and expensive) restaurant upstairs, and a spacious casual section downstairs with a good range of meals under $10.

Last but by no means least is the wonderful *Kitchen* way up the back of the Esplanade Hotel, at 11 Upper Esplanade. It's always busy, the food is great and inexpensive, and after you've eaten you can play pool or check out one of the (usually free) live bands.

South Melbourne There are plenty of eating options along Clarendon St. At No 331 is the *Chinese Noodle Shop*, with excellent authentic noodle dishes at around $7 to $10. Further down, *Taco Bill* at No 375 has good value Mexican food and a fun atmosphere (and is much better than the American chain Taco Bells!).

The *Last Aussie Fishcaf* (☎ 699 1942), just off Clarendon St at 256 Park St, is a sort of movie musical vision of a '50s fish & chips cafe, complete with jukebox and bobbysoxers. It's a fun place with a party attitude and good seafood. Main meals are $13 to $18, and cost less at lunch – you'll need to book.

North Melbourne Home to the YHA hostels, North Melbourne has some good possibilities if you're prepared to search a little. The *Eldorado Hotel* at 46 Leveson St is a bustling pub with a menu that covers lots of territory – burgers, grills, chillies, pastas – all from $7 to $10.

Amiconi (☎ 328 3710), at 359 Victoria St, is a traditional Italian bistro and a local favourite – you may need to book. Also in Victoria St is *Warung Agus* at No 305, which has superb Balinese food, with main meals starting at $8.

For Vietnamese food, head down towards the market to either *My Tien* at 284 Victoria St or *Dalat's* at No 270. For good and inexpensive pasta around here, the locals head to *Maria Trattoria* at 122 Peel St.

Carlton Lygon St, Melbourne's Italian centre, is all bright lights, big restaurants and flashy boutiques – a local writer calls it an antipodean Via Veneto. Still, there are some pleasant surprises scattered amongst the more up-market places. Tram No 1 or 21 along Swanston St will get you there, or it's a pleasant stroll up Russell St.

Toto's Pizza House at No 101 claims to be the first pizzeria in Australia. Pizzas are cheap and good, it's licensed and it stays open till after midnight. Head on up Lygon St after your pizza for an excellent coffee and cake at *Notturno* at No 177. There are tables out on the pavement and it's open 24 hours a day.

Nyonya, at No 191, has excellent Malaysian/Chinese food. It's a bright and cheerful place to eat; main courses are mostly $7 to $10 – try the superb curry laksa. At No 303 *Tiamo's* is a popular, straightforward Italian bistro with pastas from $6 and great breakfasts just like mama used to cook. Nearby at No 329 *Shakahari* is one of Melbourne's longest running and most popular vegetarian restaurants, with a really interesting menu with main dishes around $10. Across the road, *Trotters* at No 400 is a popular little bistro serving good breakfasts and hearty Italian fare in the $6 to $9 range.

Further down at 333 Lygon St, *Jimmy Watson's* is a famous Melbourne institution. Wine and talk are the order of the day at this wine bar but the food is good too. There are hot meals or you can make up a plate of excellent cold food for around $8. This place is open Saturday mornings and weekdays until 6 pm.

Head a block over from Lygon St to Rathdowne St where there are several interesting places to choose from. At 154 Rathdowne St the *Carlton Chinese Noodle Cafe* does a whole bunch of noodle dishes and some good curries. It's basically a takeaway place but you can eat there too. The *Carlton Curry House* (☎ 347 9632) at 204 Rathdowne St is plain and simple, but the curries are excellent and main courses are around $7 – you'll probably need to book.

Much further up Rathdowne St is the *Paragon Cafe* at No 651. The food's excellent from breakfast to dinner, there are lots of vegetarian dishes on the menu and come dessert time the trifle is a knockout. A block north is *La Porchetta* at No 392, with some of the cheapest pizzas and pastas in town – that's why it's always full of uni students!

Fitzroy Brunswick St can't be beaten for sheer variety. It's one of the funkiest and most fascinating streets in Melbourne, and has just about everything – casual cafes, bars, Thai, Indian, African, Turkish, Italian, rench, Malaysian – even Ethiopian and fghan restaurants!

At the city end at 113 Brunswick St, *Nyala* oes Ethiopian and other African food. The ombination plate gives you an interesting ariety of dishes to try, and you scoop them p with the spongy bread known as injera. Mains range from $10 to $13. *Annick's* (☎ 419 3007) at No 153 is a popular and omfortable little restaurant with excellent rench food in the $15 to $17 range – you must book.

Further up towards Johnston St is the amous *Black Cat Cafe* at No 252, an arty-rendy 1950s-style cafe, ideal for coffee and ake or snacks at late hours. *Thai Thani* at No 293 is an excellent place for lovers of hot nd spicy Thai food.

Across Johnston St you'll find *Mario's* at No 303, which is highly favoured by the ocals. It's a fairly hip cafe with great Italian-ased food that's good for any time of the ay or night. *Cafe Cappadocia*, across the oad at No 324, is an unpretentious Turkish estaurant with honest, affordable food. Another good option is the *Fitz* at No 347, which has a delicious range of meals leaping ff the whiteboard – you won't go home ungry.

Afghanistan is not a place noted for its uisine, but if you want to give it a go (steaks, ebabs, curries) then head for the *Afghan Gallery Restaurant* at No 327. *Rhum-parella's*, at No 342, is an arty, barn-sized place with an art gallery upstairs and a great deli section next door. Also good is *Joe's Garage* up at No 366.

Round the corner on Johnston St you'll find Melbourne's Spanish quarter with places like *Carmen* at No 74, with authentic Spanish food, an outdoor barbecue, fla-menco and live music most nights; *Bolero*, upstairs at No 50, a wild and lively bar/night-club; and small Spanish tapas bars such as *La Tasca* at No 42 and *La Sangria* at No 46. At 15 Johnston St, near the corner of Nich-olson St, *Chishti's* is well known for its excellent Indian food, good vegetarian meals and friendly service. Main courses are around $12 to $15.

Sydney Rd, Brunswick Head north of the city centre along tree-lined Royal Parade and you suddenly find yourself in congested Sydney Rd. As well as being the main route to Sydney, it's a great area for cheap eating, especially in the many Turkish restaurants, most of which bake their own delicious bread (pide) on the premises. From the city, take tram No 18, 19 or 20 from Elizabeth St.

At *Alasya* at No 555, you can choose from the menu or opt for a fixed-price meal ($14 to $20 a head) which gets you dips, a mixture of main courses, a selection of desserts, heaps of freshly baked bread and coffee.

Further up at No 803, the *Golden Terrace* is very good value, with mains from $5 to $7 or a $12 banquet. Also good is the *Sultan Ahmet* at No 835, which is slightly more expensive – both of these places feature belly dancers on Friday and Saturday nights. *Pasa*, at No 528, is a little more stylish and intimate than its neighbours, but still cheap with main courses mostly $8 to $9.

Sydney Rd isn't all Turkish however; at No 217 you can head for Spain at *La Paella*, with superb paella and a flamenco floor-show on Friday and Saturday nights. Opposite at No 246 is a large, popular Italian restaurant called *La Nostalgia*.

Richmond Victoria St in Richmond, known as Little Saigon, is Melbourne's Vietnamese centre and is packed with Vietnamese busi-nesses, shops and dozens of bargain-priced restaurants. Tram No 23 (peak hours only) or 42 will get you there from Victoria Parade, north of the city centre.

Don't expect vogue decor, but the food will be fresh, cheap and lightning fast. You can have a huge steaming bowl of soup that will be a meal in itself for around $4, and main courses are generally $4 to $8, so you can afford to be adventurous. The very basic *Thy Thy 1* is probably the best-known and most popular place, hidden away upstairs at No 142. *Thy Thy 2* at No 116 is a bit more up-market – try the pork, chicken, prawn or vegetable spring rolls.

Vao Doi at No 120 is another good place to try, as is *Victoria* across the road at No 311.

The menu here also offers Thai and Chinese food. Down the city end at No 66 is the ultra-modern *Tho Tho* – incredibly stylish but still pretty cheap.

Victoria St isn't all Vietnamese food. Have a beer in the *Bakers Arms Hotel* at No 355, an old pub converted into a cross between an arty cafe and your grandmother's lounge room – the food is pretty good too. *Pamukkale* at No 375 has excellent authentic Turkish food, while *El Rincon* on the next corner is the place to go for a huge feed of South American or Mexican food.

If it's good Greek food you're after, take tram No 70 from Batman Ave, by the river in the city, and get off on Swan St at the Church St intersection. You'll find half a dozen Greek restaurants in the next 100 metres or so.

Kaliva at No 256 is an old favourite. The decor is fairly plain but the food is good, with main dishes from $10 to $15, and you can dine to background bouzouki music Thursday to Sunday nights. The tiny *Salona* at No 260a has the standard Greek menu, but also has some excellent and affordable seafood dishes.

Laikon at No 272 is plain and simple and the food straightforward and tasty. There's no menu so just go to the counter and order. *Agapi* at No 262 also has the usual Greek offerings, plus a few Aussie dishes like steak and chips.

Bridge Rd, the road out from the city midway between Swan and Victoria Sts, also has some great food possibilities. Take tram No 48 or 75 (or 24 during rush hours) from Flinders St in the city to these restaurants. Starting at the city end of Bridge Rd there's the elegant *Chilli Padi* at 18 Bridge Rd, which serves an excellent variety of Malaysian/Chinese dishes. At 78 Bridge Rd, the *Tofu Shop* is definitely one for those on a vegetarian/health kick. It can be a squeeze finding a stool at the counter at lunch time but never mind, the salads, vegetables, filled filo pastries and soyalaki (great invention) are tasty.

Rajdoot is at 142 Bridge Rd; if you've travelled in India you'll remember the name as a popular Indian motorcycle brand! It's small place with excellent Indian foo including some great tandoori dishes. If yo want something fancier (and more expen sive) head for *Cafe Kanis* at No 138, wher the food is rather like what Californian would call California Cuisine. Bridge R also has one of the best pizzerias in Mel bourne – *Silvio's* at No 270.

The *All Nations Hotel*, at 64 Lennox S can be hard to find but it's a great old plac with some of the best pub food in Melbourne It's only open for lunch, and meals ar mostly between $5 and $10.

South Yarra Take tram No 8 from Swanston St in the city to South Yarra. Along Tooral Rd you'll find some of Melbourne's mos expensive restaurants – fortunately there are some more affordable places in between *Cafe Ramblas* at No 37 is a sparse and stylish Spanish cafe serving a wide variety o dishes, mostly around $5 to $8, and goo paellas at $13. *Barolo's*, at No 74, is a narrow Italian bistro with a rear courtyard and goo food; it has pastas for $10 and other mai dishes $13 to $15.

At No 156 is *Tamani's*, Italian once again and something of a Melbourne institution It's a popular, friendly and cheap bistro with good pasta dishes and salads. The *Come Centre*, on the corner of Toorak Rd and Chapel St, has a very up-market internationa food hall with plenty of choices; most meals are in the $6 to $9 range.

Head down Chapel St for an eclectic blend of cafes and bars, open-air eating and expen sive restaurants – scattered in amongst all the shops and boutiques. *Caffe e Cucina*, at N 581, is one of the smallest, coolest and best cafes in town, with great food in the $6 to $10 range – if you can get a table. Down a No 571 is *Chapellis*, where the people are friendly, the pasta is quite good and, mos importantly, it's open round the clock. Righ next door at No 569 is *Kanpai*, a neat little Japanese restaurant with surprisingly modestly priced dishes.

Prahran The Prahran Market, on Commerial Rd, is a wonderful place to shop or just wander, with fresh fruit, vegetables, fish, and plenty of little delis to explore. There are also some great eateries in the area. Right opposite the market at 176 Commercial Rd, *China Ria* has good Malaysian meals ranging from $6 to $10, and next door the stylish *Betelnut Cafe* serves excellent Indo-Javanese food with main courses at similar prices and seafood dishes for $13.

Back on Chapel St, the *Ankara Restaurant* at No 310 does good fixed-price Turkish meals and has a belly dancer on Friday and Saturday nights. Further down at 68 Chapel St, Windsor, the *Marmara* is even better with great marinated kebabs and delicious thick Turkish bread.

Greville St, which runs off Chapel St beside the Prahran Town Hall, has an eclectic collection of recycled and designer clothes shops, book and record shops, junk shops and eateries. Beside the railway tracks at No 95 is the ever-popular *Feedwell Cafe*, an earthy vegetarian cafe serving interesting and wholesome food like satays, pizzas, curries and sandwiches from $5 to $10. The *Continental Cafe* at No 132 is a fun, friendly and up-market cafe open from 7 am until midnight, with a wide range of excellent food and a great jazz-and-blues club upstairs.

Entertainment

The best source of 'what's on' info in Melbourne is the *Entertainment Guide* (*EG*) which comes out every Friday with the *Age* newspaper. *Beat* and *Inpress* are free music and entertainment magazines that have reviews, interviews, dates of gigs, movie guides and more.

Bass Victoria (☎ 11 566) is the main booking agency for theatre, concerts, sports and other events. If you're looking for cheap tickets, the Half-Tix booth (☎ 650 9420) in the Bourke St Mall sells half-price tickets on the day of the event.

During the summer months watch out for the FEIPP (Fantastic Entertainment In Public Places) program with all sorts of free activities in city parks and public places – ring ☎ 663 8307 for info.

Melbourne's major venues include the Victorian Arts Centre, the National Tennis Centre, the outdoor Sidney Myer Music Bowl in the Kings Domain and the Sports & Entertainment Centre.

Rock Music Melbourne has always enjoyed a thriving pub-rock scene and is widely acknowledged as the country's rock capital. The sweaty grind around Melbourne's pubs has been the proving ground for many of Australia's best outfits. To find out who's playing where, look in the *EG*, *Beat* or *Inpress*, or listen to the gig guides on FM radio stations like 3MMM (105.1), 3RRR (102.7), 3PBS (106.7) or 3JJJ (107.5) – these last three are excellent alternative stations. Cover charges at the pubs vary widely; some gigs are free, but most are generally from $6 to $10.

In St Kilda is the well-known *Esplanade Hotel*, on the Esplanade of course, which has live music every night and Sunday afternoons, free of charge. It's also a great place just to sit with a beer and watch the sun set over the pier, or have a meal in the Kitchen out the back. You can't leave Melbourne without visiting the Espie. Also in St Kilda are the *Prince of Wales Hotel* at 29 Fitzroy St, and the *Palace* beside the Palais Theatre on the Lower Esplanade.

The *Station Hotel* on Greville St, Prahran is one of the longest running of the rock pubs, a place with a bit of Melbourne rock history. The sculpture of the locomotive crashing through the house next door is quite arresting. The *Club* at 132 Smith St, Collingwood, is a small and intimate live music club that has been around for ever. Some of the other good inner-city music venues are: in Richmond, the *Central Club Hotel* at 293 Swan St, the *Cherry Tree Hotel* at 53 Balmain St, the *Great Britain Hotel* at 447 Church St and the *Corner Hotel* at 57 Swan St; in the city, the *Grainstore Tavern* at 46 King St and the *Lounge* at 243 Swanston St; in Collingwood, the *Prince Patrick Hotel* at 135 Victoria Parade; and in Brunswick St, Fitzroy, the *Evelyn Hotel* at No 351, the *Punters Club* at No 376 and the *Royal Derby Hotel* at No 446.

Folk & Acoustic Music The *EG* has an acoustic and folk music listing. One of the main venues is the *Dan O'Connell Hotel*, on the corner of Princes and Canning Sts in Carlton. Usually it's folk music on Wednesday and Thursday, Irish music on Friday and sometimes Saturday.

O'Sullivan's Hotel at 442 Nicholson St in North Fitzroy often has good bands and performers. *Molly Bloom's* in Bay St, Port Melbourne, is also popular (though it can get a bit rough at times). The Melbourne Folk Club headquarters is the *Brunswick East Club Hotel* at 280 Lygon St.

Jazz Popular jazz joints include *Ruby Red* in Drewery Lane, near the corner of Swanston and Lonsdale Sts in the city; the cabaret-style *Continental Cafe*, upstairs at 132 Greville St in Prahran; the *Fountain Inn Hotel* in Bay St, Port Melbourne; the *Limerick Arms* in Clarendon St, South Melbourne; *Bell's Hotel & Brewery* at Moray St, South Melbourne; and the *Beaconsfield Hotel* in St Kilda.

Nightclubs & Discos Melbourne has an awesome collection of nightclubs and discos, ranging from small and exclusive club-style places to huge barn-sized discos. Cover charges range from around $6 to $12.

The sophisticated *Metro* nightclub at 20 Bourke St has no less than eight bars, in what used to be the Metro Theatre. The place was given a high-tech multimillion-dollar renovation in '87 to become the biggest disco in the southern hemisphere. Also worth a visit are the *Colosseum* at 60 King St, the *Grainstore* next door, the *Sugar Shack* in Banana Alley off Flinders St and the *Tunnel* at 590 Little Bourke St.

Some good places outside the city centre are *Chasers* at 386 Chapel St in South Yarra; the *Chevron* at 519 St Kilda Rd in Prahran; the Latin-style *Bolero* in Johnston St, Fitzroy; and the new *Circus* in Fitzroy St, St Kilda.

Hotels, Brewery Pubs & Wine Bars Apart from the music pubs there are quite a few other popular pubs and wine bars. Top of the

wine-bar list would have to be *Jimm Watson's* on Lygon St, Carlton – very muc a place to see and be seen, especially aroun lunch time Saturday, but a good place for glass of wine anytime. It has a delightfu (when the sun is shining) open courtyard ou the back.

Also in Carlton, the *Lemon Tree Hotel* a 10 Grattan St, by the Exhibition Gardens, i another popular gathering place with a pleas ant courtyard and good food. In Nort Fitzroy the *Lord Newry Hotel* at 543 Bruns wick St, *Lord Jim's Hotel* at 36 St George Rd and the *Standard Hotel* at 293 Fitzroy S are all popular hang-outs.

On Smith St in Collingwood you'll fine the *Smith St Bar & Bistro* at No 14, and th *Grace Darling* on the corner of Smith an Peel Sts – both well worth a visit. In Nort Melbourne, the *Eldorado* at 46 Leveson S is a great place for a beer or a bite. The *Redback Brewery*, at 75 Flemington Rd, is another good North Melbourne pub. At the *Limerick Arms*, 364 Clarendon St in Sout Melbourne, you can play chess or cards and listen to music.

The *Sydney Liars Club*, 337 Racecourse Rd, Flemington, is a fun place to visit. The walls are covered in photos, bizarre stories anecdotes and quotes – lies, all of it! They also have live acoustic music and good bistro meals.

In the city, have a beer with the famous Chloe upstairs at *Young & Jackson's Hotel* on the corner of Swanston and Flinders Sts. The *Sherlock Holmes* at 415 Collins St and the converted *Sheeps Back* at 120 King St are other good watering holes.

In South Yarra, the *Botanical Hotel* in Domain Rd and the *Fawkner Club Hotel* in Toorak Rd are two of Melbourne's more stylish pubs. For something a little more low-key, try the *New Argo Inn* at 64 Argo St.

Bars & Cafes Melbourne has a fairly new generation of European-style bars, mostly small and stylish places that feature strong coffee and booze and good food, and generally attract a fairly funky clientele.

The following are all worth a visit: in the

city, *Le Monde* at 18 Bourke St, and the American-styled *95th & Queen* at 95 Queen St; in St Kilda, the *Dogs Bar* at 54 Acland St, the *George Hotel* on the corner of Grey and Fitzroy Sts, and *Catani Bar* at 42 Fitzroy St; in Fitzroy, the *Gypsy Bar* at 334 Brunswick St, or any of the tapas bars along Johnston St; and in Chapel St, Prahran, the *Iguana Bar* at No 564, the *Limbo Bar* at No 382 or way down near Dandenong Rd at No 20, *Cha Chas*, just a short walk from the wonderful Art-Deco Astor Cinema.

Comedy Melbourne celebrates its place as Australia's comedy capital with the annual International Comedy Festival, held for 17 days from 1 April. At other times of the year, several places feature comedy acts on a fairly regular basis – check the *EG* for specific shows.

The *Last Laugh* (☎ 419 8600), on the corner of Smith and Gertrude Sts in Collingwood, is the granddaddy of Melbourne's comedy venues. It's an old cinema/dole office, done up in a dazzling mishmash of styles with room for 200 people to have a good time. The food is reasonably good (vegetarians are catered for) and there's a bar. Dinner and show tickets cost from $28 to $40, and for show only it's $15 to $22. *Le Joke*, a smaller stand-up comedy venue upstairs, has dinner and show tickets from $26 to $32 or show only for around $10.

The *Prince Patrick Hotel* at 135 Victoria Parade in Collingwood, the *Waiting Room* at the Esplanade Hotel in St Kilda and the *Star & Garter Hotel* in Nelson Rd in South Melbourne are other regular comedy venues.

Cinemas Most of the mainstream cinemas in the city are found on Bourke and Russell Sts, around where those streets intersect. Tickets cost from $7.50.

Melbourne also has an excellent collection of independent cinemas that feature art-house, classic and alternative films – tickets cost $6 to $11, and many places have half-price nights on Monday. They include the wonderfully Art-Deco *Astor Cinema* on the corner of Chapel St and Dandenong Rd

in St Kilda; the off-beat home of cult films, the *Valhalla* at 89 High St in Northcote; the *Carlton Moviehouse* at 235 Faraday St; *Cinema Nova* at 380 Lygon St in Carlton; the twin *Kino* complex at Collins Place in the city; the *Longford* at 59 Toorak Rd in South Yarra; and the *Trak* at 445 Toorak Rd in Toorak. Check the *EG* or newspapers for screenings and times.

Theatre The *Victorian Arts Centre* (☎ 684 8484) is the city's major arts venue. Flanked by the Yarra River on one side and the National Gallery on the other (also part of the arts complex), the two buildings house four theatres – the Melbourne Concert Hall, the State Theatre, the Playhouse and the George Fairfax Studio.

The Melbourne Theatre Company is the major theatrical company. Its headquarters are at the *Russell St Theatre*, although its larger performances are held at the Arts Centre. *La Mama* at 205 Faraday St in Carlton is a tiny, long-running experimental theatre and a great forum for new Australian works. The Playbox company, based at the *Malthouse* in Sturt St, South Melbourne, also stages predominantly Australian works. Anthill, at the *Gasworks Theatre* in Graham St, Albert Park, stages innovative reinterpretations of classic European works. The *Universal Theatre* at 13 Victoria St, Fitzroy, manages to pack them in with productions which may only appeal to a minority but are always adventurous and interesting.

Commercial theatres, the places you go to see the major productions, include the *Athenaeum* at 188 Collins St, the *Comedy Theatre* at 240 Exhibition St, *Her Majesty's Theatre* at 219 Exhibition St and the *Princess Theatre* at 163 Spring St.

The Footy Despite the heretical moves to a national competition, Melbourne is still very much the stronghold of Aussie Rules football. If you're here between April and October you won't be able to avoid the Footy. Although it's no longer a daring innovation for a TV station not to show match replays on Saturday nights, there's still an

VICTORIA

awful lot of media coverage of topics such as Plugger's hammie or Dermie's hip.

You should try to see a match, as much for the crowds as the game. Footy is one of those satisfying games in which the umpire's interpretation of some pretty convoluted rules plays a big part. This gives the fans something to agree on – the umpire is blind or biased. Other than this, the fans don't agree on much at all, and the sheer energy of the barracking at a big game is exhilarating. Despite the fervour of the fans, crowd violence is almost unknown.

Big matches are often scheduled at the vast MCG. Collingwood, a mighty club with a fanatical following, always provides excited crowds. Its home ground, Victoria Park, is in Johnston St, Collingwood. Carlton is another team worth seeing, and its ground at Princes Park, on Sydney Rd north of the University of Melbourne, is also close to the city. You can book seats through Bass, but you usually won't need to.

Things to Buy

Although Melbourne is far from the main centres for Aboriginal crafts there are some interesting places to look. Aboriginal Handcrafts is on the 9th floor of Century House at 125 Swanston St and is open weekdays from 10 am to 4.30 pm. It sells bark paintings and handicrafts from all over the country. The Gallery Gabrielle Pizzi at 141 Flinders Lane, just round the corner from the Hyatt Hotel, specialises in Aboriginal art; expensive but interesting to see. The Aboriginal Gallery of Dreamings, 73-77 Bourke St, has good and affordable crafts.

Art galleries and craft centres can be found all over Melbourne; check the weekly *Entertainment Guide* in the *Age* for what's on.

The local craft scene is especially strong in the fields of ceramics, jewellery, stained glass and leathercraft. Go to the Meat Market Craft Centre (☎ 329 9966) at 42 Courtney St, North Melbourne, near the youth hostels, to see the best of local crafts and other exhibitions. It's at the corner of Courtney and Blackwood Sts, North Melbourne, and open daily from 10 am to 5 pm; get there on any

of the Flemington Rd trams (Nos 49, 55 and 59).

Another craft gallery worth a visit is Distelfink (☎ 818 2555), 432 Burwood Rd, Hawthorn; or just take a walk along the St Kilda Esplanade any Sunday, where there is a street craft market of varying styles and quality.

There are numerous craft shops in the inner suburbs, usually selling an eclectic mix of local and imported crafts. One of the longest running is Ishka Handcrafts at 409 Chapel St, South Yarra, and also at South Melbourne, Kew, Camberwell and elsewhere.

In many suburbs there are weekend craft markets, and further out there are craft places in Warrandyte and the small towns in the Dandenongs. Several country cities and towns have interesting craft outlets, notably Geelong and Lorne to the south-west, Castlemaine, Maldon and Beechworth to the north, and at Red Hill and other locations on the Mornington Peninsula.

For more details, pick up a copy of the Victorian Craft Association's *Craft Outlets in Victoria*, available at the Meat Market, Ishka and other craft places.

Melbourne claims to be the fashion capital of Australia – judge for yourself in the small shops along Swan St and Bridge Rd in Richmond (where the larger shops' seconds outlets are also located), and Chapel St, Prahran. The best shoe shops are in Sydney Rd, Brunswick – Italian designs at reasonable prices. The youngest fashion designers have toeholds in Brunswick St, Fitzroy. The best bargains are to be found at the Queen Victoria Market, especially on Sundays.

For general shopping in the city there are a number of intimate and elegant little shopping arcades apart from the glossier modern affairs. The Royal Arcade off Bourke St Mall is noted for its figures of Gog and Magog which strike the hours. The two big old-established department stores are Myer and David Jones in the Bourke St Mall. They have recently been joined by the glossy new Melbourne Central complex, further up Swanston St, which includes the Daimaru department store.

You'll find local products at the Queen Victoria Market on Sundays, including superb sheepskins for around $50 and a range of sheepskin goods.

Getting There & Away

Air Melbourne Airport at Tullamarine services both domestic and international flights. It's more spacious than Sydney's airport and also gets fewer flights, so if you make this your Australian arrival point you may get through immigration and customs a little more speedily.

There are frequent connections between Melbourne and other state capitals – Melbourne to Sydney flights depart hourly during the airport operating hours. Standard one-way economy fares include Adelaide $223, Brisbane $371, Canberra $193, Perth $539 and Sydney $239. Connections to Alice Springs are mostly via Adelaide ($500). As a matter of course the airlines offer heavy discounts off their standard fares for advance bookings – the further ahead you book, the cheaper the fare. Ring around for the best price, which will depend on when and where you're flying.

Melbourne is the main departure point from the mainland to Tasmania. Flights to Hobart with Ansett or Qantas cost $216, and to Launceston they cost $187. Flights to Devonport cost $151 and are operated by Kendell Airlines.

The Qantas office (☎ 13 1313) is at 50 Franklin St while Ansett's (☎ 13 1300) is at 501 Swanston St. Both have smaller offices dotted around the city. Eastwest (☎ 13 1711) is at 465 Swanston St. Kendell Airlines (book through Ansett) operates the main flights within Victoria.

Bus The major bus companies that operate in Melbourne are Greyhound Pioneer and McCafferty's. Fares are similar, although McCafferty's are generally a few dollars cheaper. Firefly also operates services from Melbourne to Sydney and Adelaide.

The Greyhound Pioneer office and terminal (☎ 13 2030) is in Franklin St in the city centre. Firefly (☎ 670 7500) and McCafferty's

(☎ 670 2533) buses both operate out of the Spencer St bus station.

V/Line buses also operate from the Spencer St Bus Station, and go to all parts of Victoria (☎ 619 5000). See the towns in this chapter for the appropriate fares.

The Greyhound Pioneer network is the most extensive, with buses from Melbourne to Adelaide (10 hours, $50), Perth (48 hours, $230), Brisbane (24 hours, $122), Canberra (nine hours, $52), and Sydney (direct, 12 hours, $58, or $50 overnight; or via the Princes Highway, 15 hours, $58).

Firefly has services to Adelaide ($40) and Sydney ($45) only. McCafferty's has services to Sydney ($45), Brisbane ($115) and throughout Queensland; and to Adelaide ($40) continuing up through the centre to Darwin.

There are two fun and scenic alternatives if you're travelling to Sydney or Adelaide. The Wayward Bus (☎ toll-free 1800 882 823) takes three days exploring the Great Ocean Road and coastal route to Adelaide, and costs $125 including three lunches – you pay for hostel (or other) accommodation and other meals. The Straycat Bus (☎ toll-free 1800 800 840) operates on a similar principle, taking three days to get to Sydney via the High Country, and also costs $125 including all meals.

Train Rail tickets for interstate services can be booked by phoning ☎ 13 2232 (you may be on hold for 10 or 20 minutes at busy times!), or bought at most suburban stations and at Spencer St railway station in Melbourne, from where the interstate services depart.

Interstate Melbourne to Sydney takes 12½ to 13 hours by train. The overnight Sydney Express from Melbourne and Melbourne Express from Sydney operate every night. The fare is $49 in economy and $79 in 1st class; a 1st-class sleeper costs $135 (there are no economy sleepers).

To get to Canberra by rail you take the daily Canberra Link which involves a train to Wodonga on the Victoria-New South

Wales border and then a bus from there. This takes about eight hours and costs $45 ($59 1st class).

To or from Adelaide the Overland operates overnight every day of the week. The trip takes 12 hours and costs $45 (economy), $89 (1st) or $149 (1st-class sleeper). The Daylink involves a train to Dimboola near the border and a bus from there. This trip is about an hour faster than the through train and costs $45 in economy, $75 in 1st class. You can transport a car to or from Adelaide for $75.

To get to Perth by rail from Melbourne you take the Overland to Adelaide and then the Trans Australian (which originates in Adelaide) or the Indian-Pacific (which comes through Adelaide from Sydney). The Melbourne to Perth fare is $215 for a seat in economy. Including meals a sleeping berth costs $488 in economy, $715 in 1st class. The trip from Melbourne to Perth takes two days and three nights. If you're travelling to or from any of the major cities, you can save up to 30% with a Caper fare (Customer Advance Purchase Excursion Rail – would you believe).

Within Victoria For V/Line services within Victoria there are a number of special fares available. Super Saver fares give you a 30% discount for travelling at off-peak times. Basically this means travelling on Tuesday, Wednesday or Thursday, arriving in Melbourne after 9.30 am, and leaving Melbourne at any time except between 4 and 6 pm.

A Victoria Pass gives you two weeks unlimited travel on V/Line trains and buses within the state for $130.

See the relevant country towns for information on V/Line train, bus or bus/train travel from Melbourne.

Car Rental All the big car-rental firms operate in Melbourne. Avis, Budget, Hertz and Thrifty have desks at the airport and you can find plenty of others in the city. The offices tend to be at the northern end of the city or in Carlton or North Melbourne.

Melbourne also has a number of rent-a-

wreck-style operators, renting older vehicles at lower rates. Their costs and conditions vary widely so it's worth making a few enquiries before going for one firm over another. You can take the 'from $18 a day' line with a pinch of salt because the rates soon start to rise with insurance, km charges and so on. Beware of distance restrictions; many companies only allow you to travel within a certain distance of the city, typically 100 km.

Some places worth trying are Delta (☎ 359 2222), Dollar (☎ 662 1188) and Dan Cheap (☎ 428 3487), all of which have branches around Melbourne. Other operators are Rent-a-Bomb (☎ 429 4003) in Richmond and Y-Not (☎ 525 5900) in St Kilda. The Yellow Pages lists lots of other firms including some reputable local operators who rent newer cars but don't have the nationwide network (and overheads) of the big operators.

Getting Around

To/From the Airport Although Melbourne Airport (Tullamarine) is 22 km from the city it's quite easy to get to since the Tullamarine Freeway runs almost into the centre. A taxi between the airport and city centre costs about $25 but there's the regular Skybus (☎ 335 2811) service which costs $9 (children $4.50). In the city the Skybus departs from Bay 30 at the Spencer St bus terminal. There are buses about every half-hour, sometimes even more frequently, between 6 am and 8.30 pm.

There is also a fairly frequent bus by Gull Bus Lines (☎ (052) 21 1185) between the airport and Geelong. It costs $20 one way. The Geelong terminus is at 45 McKillop St.

Melbourne Airport is modern, with a single terminal: Qantas at one end, Ansett at the other, international in the middle. There's an information desk upstairs in the international departure area. It's one of the most spacious airports in Australia and doesn't suffer the night flight restrictions which apply to some other Australian airports. There are reasonable snack bars and cafeteria sections in the terminal.

Public Transport Melbourne's public transport system, the Met, is based on buses, suburban railways and the famous trams. The trams are the real cornerstone of the system; in all there are about 750 of them and they operate as far as 20 km out from the centre. They're frequent and fun.

Buses are the secondary form of public transport, taking routes where the trams do not go, and replacing them at quiet weekend periods. There is also a host of private bus services, some of which operate using the public buses! The train services provide a third link for Melbourne's outer suburbs. The underground city loop, which was completed in 1985, drops passengers at both Spencer and Flinders St stations, as well as at Flagstaff, Museum and Parliament stops.

For information on Melbourne transport phone the Transport Information Centre (☎ 617 0900). It operates 7.30 am to 8.30 pm Monday to Saturday, and from 9.15 am to 8.30 pm on Sunday. The Met Shop at 103 Elizabeth St in the city also has transport information and sells souvenirs and some tickets. It also has a 'Discover Melbourne' kit. If you're in the city it's probably a better bet for information than the telephone service, which is always busy. Railway stations also have some information.

There's quite an array of tickets, and the Met has a glossy brochure which describes them all. Basically you've got a choice in Melbourne of paying a straight fare for a short trip, getting a time ticket for either two hours or one day (which allows you unlimited travel during that period and within the purchased zone), or buying a weekly or monthly season ticket. The short trip ticket allows you two tram or bus sections, while a 'rail plus two' ticket is for a one- or two-station train trip. Further afield you need a time ticket with which you can chop and change your transport.

The metropolitan area is divided into three zones, and the price of tickets depends on which zone/s you will be travelling in and across. Zone 1 is big enough for most purposes. You'll only need zone 3 if you're going right out of town – on a trip to the Healesville Sanctuary, for example, or down the Mornington Peninsula. The fares are as follows:

Zones	2 Hours	All Day	Weekly
1	$2.10	$4	$17.30
2 or 3	$1.40	$2.70	$11.80
1 & 2	$3.50	$6.70	$29
1, 2 & 3	$4.90	$8.80	$35.20

A straightforward one-way 'short trip' within zone 1 will cost you $1.40. If you've got lots of travelling to do within the central business district you can get a 10-trip City Saver ticket which costs $11. Coming from outside the inner neighbourhood, train travellers can get off-peak tickets for use after 9.30 am which take you into the city and then allow unlimited travel within the City Saver area. If you buy a weekly season ticket, you can travel in any zone at the weekend. There are numerous other deals but we don't want to make this too complicated, do we!

Bicycle Melbourne's a great city for cycling – there are long bicycle tracks along the Yarra, the Maribyrnong, the Merri Creek and other rivers, as well as bicycle tracks and lanes around the city. Plus it's reasonably flat so you're not pushing and panting up hills too often.

Unfortunately, up-to-date maps of bicycle tracks and routes are hard to find. The best guide is the hefty *Melway Greater Melbourne* – you should be able to buy last year's edition at under half-price. Most bike shops stock whatever maps are available. Look for a copy of *Weekend Bicycle Rides* for a pleasant introduction to bike rides around Melbourne. There are quite a few journeys you can make in the surrounding country by taking one train out of Melbourne then riding across to a different line to get the train back. An example is to take the train out to Gisborne and ride the ridge down to Bacchus Marsh from where you can get another train back in to the city.

A couple of companies hire bikes specifically for leisurely rides along the Yarra: Bicycle Rental (☎ 801 2156), below Princes

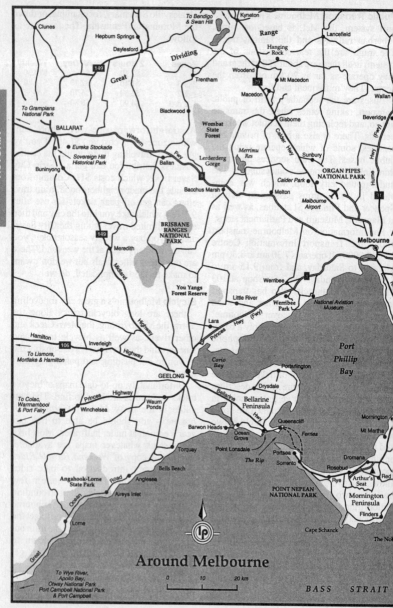

Around Melbourne

0   10   20 km

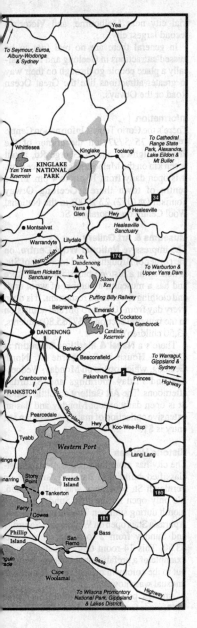

Bridge on the gallery side of the Yarra, and Bicycle Now (☎ 826 8877), on the corner of Chapel St and Alexandra Ave in South Yarra. For more serious riding, many bike shops will hire second-hand bikes if they have any – look under Bicycles & Accessories in the Yellow Pages, or try St Kilda Cycles (☎ 534 3074) or the Melbourne Bicycle Centre (☎ 489 1334).

Phone Bicycle Victoria (☎ 328 3000) for more information or drop into their shop at 19 O'Connell St, North Melbourne. They'll be able to put you onto local clubs and tours.

Around Melbourne

You don't have to travel far from Melbourne to find places worth visiting. There are the beaches and towns around Port Phillip Bay, the old gold towns to the north and west, and the hills to the east which give a good introduction to the bush at its best.

SOUTH-WEST TO GEELONG

It's a quick trip down the Princes Highway to Geelong – it's freeway all the way. You can leave Melbourne quickly over the soaring West Gate Bridge and enjoy the fine views of the city on the way over. The rest of the highway trip, however, is pretty dull.

Werribee Park

Not far out of Melbourne is Werribee Park with its free-range zoological park and the huge Italianate **Werribee Park Mansion**, built between 1874 and 1877. The flamboyant building is surrounded by formal gardens and there are also picnic and barbecue areas.

Entrance to the park is free, but admission to the mansion costs $5 (children $1.80) and the safari bus tours cost $7 (children $4). Werribee Park is open on weekdays from 10 am to 3.45 pm, and on weekends from 10 am to 4.45 pm.

National Aviation Museum

Near Werribee is the National Aviation Museum at the RAAF base at Point Cook.

Displays include one on WW I German ace Baron von Richtofen. It's open Sundays to Thursdays from 10 am to 4 pm; admission costs $3.

You Yangs

You can also detour to the You Yangs, a picturesque range of volcanic hills just off the freeway. Walks in the You Yangs include the climb up **Flinders Peak**, the highest point in the park, with a plaque commemorating Matthew Flinders' scramble to the top in 1802. There are fine views from the top, down to Geelong and the coast.

Wineries

There are also a number of wineries in the Geelong area. The Idyll Vineyard at 265 Ballan Rd, Moorabool, is credited with re-establishing the area's name for wines after a lapse of many years. Other Geelong area wineries are the Mt Duneed Winery at Feehans Rd in Mt Duneed and the Tarcoola Estate Winery at Spiller Rd in Lethbridge.

Brisbane Ranges National Park

You can make an interesting loop from Melbourne out to the You Yangs and back through the Brisbane Ranges park and Bacchus Marsh. The scenic **Anakie Gorge** in the Brisbane Ranges is a popular short bushwalk and a good spot for barbecues. You may see koalas in the trees near the car park/picnic area.

Fairy Park, on the side of Mt Anakie at the southern edge of the Brisbane Ranges, has 100 clay fairy-tale figures.

GEELONG (population 126,000)

The city of Geelong began as a sheep-grazing area when the first White settlers arrived in 1836, and it initially served as a port for the dispatch of wool and wheat from the area. This function was overshadowed during the gold-rush era when it became important as a landing place for immigrants and for the export of gold. Around 1900, Geelong started to become industrialised and that's very much what it is today – an indus-trial city near Melbourne, and Victoria's second largest city.

In general there are no real 'not to be missed' attractions in Geelong and it is basically a place people go through on their way to greater attractions like the Great Ocean Road or the Otways.

Information

There's the Corio Tourist Information Centre (☎ (052) 75 5797) on the corner of the Princes Highway and St George Rd, about seven km on the Melbourne side of Geelong. It is open daily from 10 am to 4 pm. In the centre of town there's Geelong Otway Tourism (☎ (052) 22 2900) in the National Wool Centre on Moorabool St.

Museums & Art Gallery

The impressive **National Wool Centre**, on the corner of Brougham and Moorabool Sts, is housed in a historic bluestone wool store and has a museum, a number of wool craft and clothing shops and a restaurant. It is open every day from 10 am to 5 pm and admission to the museum section is $7 ($5.80 students, $3.50 children).

There's a **Naval & Maritime Museum** at Osborne House in Swinburne St, North Geelong, which opens on Monday, Wednesday and Friday mornings and Saturday afternoons. The **Art Gallery** on Little Malop St is open daily except Monday and has an extensive collection of mainly Australian art; entry is $1.

Historic Houses

The city has more than 100 National-Trust-classified buildings. **Barwon Grange** on Fernleigh St, Newtown, was built in 1856. It's only open on the first Sunday of each month during summer. The **Heights**, at 140 Aphrasia St, is open on Wednesday, Saturday and Sunday from 2 to 5 pm; entry costs $3.50. This 14-room timber mansion is an example of a prefabricated building brought out to the colony in pieces, and it features an unusual watchtower.

Another prefabricated building is **Corio Villa**, made from iron sheets in 1856. The bits

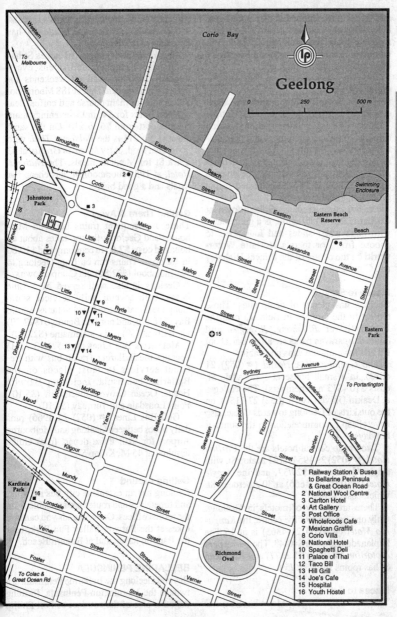

Geelong

Corio Bay

Swimming Enclosure

0   250   500 m

Johnstone Park

Eastern Beach Reserve

Eastern Park

Kardinia Park

Richmond Oval

To Melbourne

To Colac & Great Ocean Rd

To Portarlington

1 Railway Station & Buses
   to Bellarine Peninsula
   & Great Ocean Road
2 National Wool Centre
3 Carlton Hotel
4 Art Gallery
5 Post Office
6 Wholefoods Cafe
7 Mexican Graffiti
8 Corio Villa
9 National Hotel
10 Spaghetti Deli
11 Palace of Thai
12 Taco Bill
13 Hill Grill
14 Joe's Cafe
15 Hospital
16 Youth Hostel

and pieces were shipped out from Glasgow but nobody claimed them on arrival! It's now a private house, overlooking Eastern Beach. **Osborne House** and **Armytage House** are other fine old private buildings.

Other Attractions

Geelong's Botanical Gardens (part of Eastern Park) contain the **Customs House**, Victoria's oldest wooden building, which displays telegraph equipment and memorabilia. **Eastern Beach** is Geelong's popular swimming spot and promenade where boats and bicycles can be hired on weekends in summer. There is also a signposted scenic drive along the beachfront.

On hot summer days, **Splashdown** at Coppards Rd, Whittington, is a great place, with huge water slides and four pools to choose from, or there's **Norlane Waterworld** on the corner of the Princes Highway and Cox St.

Places to Stay

Geelong has plenty of camp sites. Those closest to the city are in Belmont near the Barwon River. *Billabong*, *Riverglen* and *Southside* caravan parks are all on Barrabool Rd and have on-site vans and cabins.

The *Geelong YHA Hostel* (☎ (052) 21 6583), in a small house at 1 Lonsdale St, costs $10 ($13 nonmembers). The colleges at Deakin University (☎ (052) 27 1158), on the outskirts of Geelong towards Colac, also have cheap accommodation in the summer holidays.

Two cheap central hotels are the *Carlton Hotel* (☎ (052) 29 1954) at 21 Malop St, with singles/doubles at $29/37, and the *Argyle Hotel* (☎ (052) 21 4666) at 30 Aberdeen St, which costs $28/40.

There are plenty of motels in Geelong. Only one km north of the centre, the *Kangaroo Motel* (☎ (052) 21 4365) is at 16 The Esplanade and costs $40/48. The *Innkeepers Motor Inn* (☎ (052) 21 2177) at 9 Aberdeen St has rooms from $52/59.

Places to Eat

The *Hill Grill*, at 228 Moorabool St, has burgers, pastas, souvlakis and grills from $4 to $10. Across the road, *Joe's Cafe* also has inexpensive meals.

The *Wholefoods Cafe* at 10 James St has good natural tucker, and opens every weekday for lunch and on weekends for dinner. The *Spaghetti Deli* at 188 Moorabool St has a good 'main course and coffee' deal at lunch times for $4; in the evenings main courses cost from $6 to $10. On the same street at No 211 is the *Palace of Thai*, with good Thai food, or try *Mexican Graffiti* at 43 Yarra St for Mexican meals. The *National Hotel*, at 195 Moorabool St, has cheap bar meals and a good bistro.

Getting There & Away

There are frequent trains between Melbourne and Geelong; the trip takes about an hour and costs $7.60 in economy and $10.60 in 1st class. Trains run on from Geelong to Warrnambool ($22.80) via Camperdown.

Geelong is also well served by V/Line buses, with several daily services south along the Great Ocean Road as far as Apollo Bay ($16.80), and north to Bendigo ($27.20) via Ballarat ($9) and Castlemaine ($22.80).

McHarry's Bus Lines (☎ (052) 23 2111) operates the Bellarine Transit bus with frequent services to most places on the Bellarine Peninsula, including Barwon Heads, Ocean Grove, Queenscliff ($5.10), Point Lonsdale and Torquay ($4.10).

Gull Bus Lines (☎ (052) 22 4966) runs daily buses between Geelong and Melbourne Airport for $20; these depart from Gull's terminal at 45 McKillop St.

Getting Around

Geelong has an extensive city bus network, and timetables and routes are available from the tourist offices. On weekends you can hire bikes at the Barwon Valley Fun Park, near the Barwon River, and at Eastern Beach.

BELLARINE PENINSULA

Beyond Geelong the Bellarine Peninsula is a twin to the Mornington Peninsula, forming the other side of the entrance to Port Phillip

Bay. Like the Mornington Peninsula this is a popular holiday resort and boating venue.

Round the peninsula in Port Phillip Bay is **Indented Head** where Flinders landed in 1802, one of the first visits to the area by a European. In 1835 John Batman landed at this same point, on his way to buy up Melbourne.

Portarlington

At Portarlington there's a fine example of an early steam-powered **flour mill**. Built around 1856, the massive, solid building is owned by the National Trust and is open from 2 to 5 pm on Sundays from September to May and on weekends and Wednesdays during January. Portarlington has an associate youth hostel (☎ (052) 59 2536) at 12 Grassy Point Rd, costing $10 a bed. **St Leonards** is a popular little resort just south of Indented Head.

Queenscliff (population 3700)

Queenscliff was established around 1838 as a pilot station to guide ships through the Rip at the entrance to Port Phillip Bay. **Fort Queenscliff** was built in 1882 to protect Melbourne from the perceived Russian threat and at the time it was the most heavily defended fort in the colony. Today it houses the Australian Army Command and the Fort Queenscliff Museum, and is open daily; entrance is $2.

In recent years, Queenscliff has been sand-blasted, paint-stripped and rediscovered by Melbourne's new gentry. There are some fine Victorian buildings, especially pubs, and these are popular for leisurely (and expensive) weekend lunches.

Railway enthusiasts will enjoy the **Bellarine Peninsula Railway** (☎ (052) 52 2069), which operates from the old Queenscliff Station with a fine collection of old steam trains. On Sundays, public holidays and most school holidays steam trains make the 16-km return trip to Drysdale or shorter runs to Laker's Siding. On days of total fire ban, diesel engines are used.

The **Marine Studies Centre** (☎ (052) 52 3344) next to the ferry pier has an aquarium displaying local marine life. It's open on weekdays (plus weekends during December and January), and also organises a range of trips: snorkelling tours, nocturnal beach walks and a bird-watchers' cruise to Mud Island. All trips are led by naturalists; ring to see what they have on offer. Next door, the **Queenscliff Maritime Museum** is open weekends and summer holidays; entry is $2.

Places to Stay Queenscliff has four caravan parks and three have on-site vans for around $25. The friendly and atmospheric *Queenscliff Inn* (☎ (052) 52 3737) at 59 Hesse St, is a fine old restored building right in the centre of town. There are bunk rooms for $15 per person, and a hearty breakfast is available for $8.50. There are also good singles/doubles upstairs from $40/65, which includes breakfast. There are communal washing and cooking facilities.

Nothing would be finer than to stay in one of the restored grand hotels. With rooms starting from $50 and going way up, you can stay at the *Royal*, *Ozone*, *Vue Grand* or *Queenscliff* hotels.

Getting There & Away McHarry's operates the Bellarine Transit bus service with regular connections between Geelong, Point Lonsdale and Queenscliff.

A passenger ferry and a car ferry operate between Queenscliff and Sorrento and Portsea on the Mornington Peninsula. See the Mornington Peninsula Getting There & Away section for details.

Point Lonsdale (population 3700)

Point Lonsdale and the Mornington Peninsula are geographically so close they're practically joined. The lighthouse and a fleet of pilot boats guide ships through the narrow and often turbulent Rip into the bay. You can view the Rip from a lookout and walk to the lighthouse. Below the lighthouse is **Buckley's Cave** where the 'wild White man', William Buckley, lived with Aborigines for 32 years after escaping from the settlement at

Sorrento on the Mornington Peninsula in 1803. Actually this area is dotted with 'Buckley Caves'!

Ocean Grove (population 7000)

This resort on the ocean side of the peninsula has good scuba diving on the rocky ledges of the Bluff, and further out there are wrecks of ships which failed to make the tricky entrance to Port Phillip Bay. Some of the wrecks are accessible to divers. The beach at the surf-lifesaving club is very popular with surfers. Ocean Grove is a real-estate agent's paradise and has grown to become the biggest town on the peninsula.

Places to Stay Ocean Grove has motels and holidays flats but there is no budget accommodation. There are plenty of caravan parks but even an on-site van will cost around $30.

The *Collendina Resort* (☎ (052) 55 1122) is the cheapest of the other possibilities, with rooms from $30/45, and more-expensive two-bedroom units.

Barwon Heads

Barwon Heads is a small resort just along from Ocean Grove. It has sheltered river beaches and surf beaches around the headland. The *Barwon Heads Hotel*, overlooking the river, is a popular place for a meal; there are also a few rooms at $30/50, although most cost $75. On-site vans and cabins are available at the *Rondor Caravan Park* (☎ (052) 54 2753), two km from the centre on Sheepwash Rd.

NORTH-WEST TO BENDIGO

It's about 160 km north-west of Melbourne along the Calder Highway to the old mining town of Bendigo and there are some interesting stops along the way.

You've hardly left the outskirts of Melbourne when you come to the turn-off to the surprisingly pretty and little-visited **Organ Pipes National Park** on the right and the amazingly ugly Calder Thunderdome Raceway on the left.

Gisborne & Mt Macedon

Next up is Gisborne, at one time a coach stop on the gold-fields route. Mt Macedon, a 1013-metre-high extinct volcano, then looms large on the right. The scenic route up Mt Macedon takes you past many impressive country mansions and some lovely gardens to a lookout point at the summit; the road then continues down to Woodend or Hanging Rock.

Hanging Rock

Just north of Mt Macedon is Hanging Rock, a popular picnic spot made famous by the book and later the film *Picnic at Hanging Rock*. At that mysterious picnic, three schoolgirls on a school trip to the rock disappeared without trace; in an equally mysterious way one of the girls reappeared a few days later. The rocks are fun to clamber over and there are superb views from higher up. The Hanging Rock Picnic Races, held on New Year's Day, are a great day out.

Woodend is another pleasant old town, and this is the closest you can get to Hanging Rock by public transport; the one-way train fare is $7.90. See Organised Tours in the Melbourne section for details of day trips to the Hanging Rock area.

Kyneton & Malmsbury

The road continues through Kyneton with its fine bluestone buildings. Piper St is a historic precinct, with antique shops, tearooms, and a **Historical Museum**, housed in a building dating from 1855 which was originally a two-storey bank.

A further 11 km brings you to Malmsbury with its historic bluestone **railway viaduct** and a magnificent ruined **grain mill**, which has been converted into a delightful restaurant and gallery.

HEALESVILLE & AROUND

You don't have to travel far to the east of Melbourne before you start getting into the foothills of the Great Dividing Range. In winter you can find snow within 100 km of the city centre.

Healesville is on the regular Melbourne suburban transport network; trains operate to

Lilydale from where connecting buses run to Healesville. McKenzie's Bus Lines (☎ (03) 853 6264) runs a weekday service from the Spencer St bus terminal through Healesville to Marysville, Alexandra and Lake Eildon.

Yarra Valley & the Wineries

With more than 30 wineries sprinkled through the Yarra Valley, this area is a popular, scenic and very pleasant day trip from Melbourne. Wineries open daily include Domaine Chandon, Lilydale Vineyards, De Bortoli, Fergussons, Kellybrook and Yarra Burn, and about 15 others are open on weekends and holidays.

Gulf Station, a couple of km north of Yarra Glen, is part of an old grazing run dating from the 1850s. Operated by the National Trust, it's open Wednesdays to Sundays and on public holidays from 10 am to 4 pm ($6). There is an interesting collection of rough old timber buildings plus the associated pastures and a homestead garden typical of the period.

Healesville (population 6200)

Healesville is on the outskirts of Melbourne, just where you start to climb up into the hills. There are some pleasant drives from Healesville, particularly the scenic route to Marysville, but the **Healesville Wildlife Sanctuary** is a prime attraction. This is one of the best places to see Australian wildlife in the whole country. Most of the enclosures are very natural, and some of the birds just pop in for the day.

Some enclosures are only open at certain times so you may want to plan your visit accordingly. The platypus, for example, is only on show in its glass-sided tank from 11.30 am to 1 pm and from 1.30 to 3.30 pm. The nocturnal house, where you can see many of the smaller bush dwellers which only come out at night, is open from 10 am to 4.30 pm, as is the reptile house. The whole park is open from 9 am to 5 pm and admission is $11 (children and students $5.50). There are barbecue and picnic facilities in the pleasantly wooded park.

Getting There & Away McKenzie's (☎ (03) 853 6264) runs a Monday to Friday service from Lilydale railway station at 9.40 and 11.40 am right to the sanctuary, leaving for the return trip at 3.40 and 5.30 pm.

Warburton (population 2500)

Beyond Healesville is Warburton, another pretty little hill town in the Great Dividing Range foothills. There are good views of the mountains from the Acheron Way nearby and you'll sometimes get snow on Mt Donna Buang, seven km from town.

There's a range of accommodation here; for example, the *Warburton Waters* (☎ (059) 66 9166) guesthouse is very pleasant and costs from $30/65.

Marysville (population 660)

This delightful little town is a very popular weekend escape from Melbourne, with lots of bush tracks to walk. Nicholl's Lookout, Keppel's Lookout, Mt Gordon and Steavenson Falls are good ones. **Cumberland Scenic Reserve**, with numerous walks and the Cumberland Falls, is 16 km east of Marysville. The cross-country skiing trails of **Lake Mountain Reserve** are only 10 km beyond Marysville.

The **Cathedral Range State Park** is about 10 km north-west of Marysville, and it offers excellent bushwalks and camping.

Places to Stay Much of the accommodation is in guesthouses which include all meals and tend to be expensive. A couple of these are the *Marylands* (☎ (059) 633 204) and the *Mountain Lodge* (☎ (059) 633 270).

Cheaper options include the *Scenic Motel* (☎ (059) 633 247) and the on-site vans at the *Marysville Caravan Park* (☎ (059) 633 433).

Getting There & Away McKenzie's operates buses from Marysville to Melbourne and Eildon.

THE DANDENONGS

The Dandenong Ranges to the east of Melbourne are one of the most popular day trips. In fact they're so popular with Melburnians that the city now laps at their edge. The Dandenongs are cool due to the altitude (Mt Dandenong is all of 633 metres tall) and lushly green due to the heavy rainfall. The area is dotted with fine old houses, classy restaurants, beautiful gardens and some fine short bushwalks. You can clearly see the Dandenongs from central Melbourne (on a smog-free day) and they're only about an hour's drive away.

The small **Ferntree Gully National Park** has pleasant strolls and lots of bird life. Unfortunately, the lyrebirds for which the Dandenongs were once famous are now very rare. The **Sherbrooke Forest Park** is similarly pleasant for walks and you'll see lots of rosellas. These parks, together with Doongalla Reserve, make up the Dandenong Ranges National Park, proclaimed in 1987.

The **William Ricketts Sanctuary**, on Olinda Rd, is set in fern gardens and features the work of the sculptor William Ricketts, who died in 1993 aged 94. His work was inspired by the Aboriginal people and their affinity with the land – the sculptures rise like spirits out of the ground. The forest sanctuary is open every day from 10 am to 4.30 pm and is well worth the $5 admission.

The only budget accommodation in this area is the *Emerald Backpackers* (☎ (059) 68 4086), a comfortable hostel with dorm beds for $11 – they can sometimes find work for travellers in the local nurseries and gardens.

Puffing Billy

One of the major attractions of the Dandenongs is Puffing Billy (☎ (03) 754 6800 for bookings; ☎ (03) 870 8411 for times) – a restored miniature steam train which runs along the 13-km track from Belgrave to Lakeside at the Emerald Lake Park. Puffing Billy was originally built in 1900 to bring farm produce to market.

Emerald is a pretty little town with many craft galleries and shops. At **Lakeside** there's a whole string of attractions from paddleboats, barbecues and water slides to a huge model railway with more than two km

of track! It's hard to drag kids away. At Menzies Creek beside the station there's a **Steam Museum** open on weekends and public holidays from 11 am to 5 pm. It houses a collection of early steam locomotives.

Puffing Billy runs every day except Christmas day and days of total fire ban; the round trip takes about 2½ hours and costs $14 for adults and $8.50 for children aged four to 14; family concessions are also available. You can get out to Puffing Billy on the regular suburban rail service to Belgrave.

MORNINGTON PENINSULA

The Mornington Peninsula is the spit of land down the eastern side of Port Phillip Bay, bordered on its eastern side by the waters of Western Port. The peninsula really starts at Frankston, 40 km from the centre of Melbourne, and from there it's almost a continuous beach strip, all the way to Portsea at the end of the peninsula, nearly 100 km from Melbourne. At the tip of the peninsula is a national park recently opened on the site of a military base. From here you can look out across the Rip, the narrow entrance to Port Phillip Bay.

This is a very popular Melbourne resort area with many holiday homes; in summer the accommodation and camp sites along the peninsula can be packed right out and traffic can be very heavy. In part this popularity is due to the peninsula's excellent beaches and the great variety they offer. On the northern side of the peninsula you've got calm water on the bay beaches (the front beaches) looking out onto Port Phillip Bay, while on the southern side there's crashing surf on the rugged and beautiful ocean beaches (the back beaches) which face Bass Strait.

Town development tends to be concentrated along the Port Phillip side; the Western Port and Bass Strait coasts are much less developed and you'll find pleasant bushwalking trails along the Cape Schank Coastal Park, a narrow coastal strip right along the Bass Strait coast from Portsea to Cape Schank.

There's a tourist information centre in Dromana (☎ (059) 87 3078) on the Nepean

Highway and the National Parks brochure *Discovering the Peninsula* ($3.50) tells you all you'll want to know about the peninsula's history, early architecture and walking tours.

Markets

The peninsula is an excellent place to check out craft and produce markets, as there's usually one each week somewhere in the area. The main ones are: Red Hill, 1st Saturday morning each month; Emu Plains Market, 3rd Saturday; Boneo Market, 3rd Saturday morning; Rosebud, 2nd Saturday; and Sorrento, last Sunday.

Getting There & Away

There's a regular V/Line bus service from Frankston through to Portsea (phone ☎ (03) 619 5000 for details) and suburban trains run from Melbourne to Frankston.

The *Peninsula Princess* (☎ (052) 52 3244) is a car and passenger ferry which links Sorrento with Queenscliff on the Bellarine Peninsula. It runs all year, departing Queenscliff every two hours from 7 am to 5 pm (with a 7 pm service from December to Easter) and returning from Sorrento every two hours from 8 am to 8 pm. A standard car costs $32 plus $3 per adult; a motorcycle and rider costs $16; and pedestrians cost $6 ($4 for kids).

A passenger ferry (☎ (059) 84 1602) also operates regular daily crossings from Sorrento and Portsea to Queenscliff between Christmas and Easter and during school holidays; the adult fare is $6 each way.

Frankston to Blairgowrie

Beyond Frankston you reach **Mornington** and **Mt Martha**, suburban settlements with some old buildings along the Mornington Esplanade and fine, secluded beaches in between. The **Briars** in Mt Martha is an 1840s homestead open to the public.

Also of interest in Mornington is the **Australian Museum of Modern Media**, which is full of memorabilia relating to TV, cinema and radio.

Dromana is the real start of the resort development and just inland a winding road

leads up to **Arthur's Seat** lookout at 305 metres; you can also reach it by a scenic chair lift (weekends and holidays in summer only). On the slopes of Arthur's Seat, in McCrae, the **McCrae Homestead** is a National Trust property, dating from 1843 and open daily from noon to 4.30 pm on weekends and public holidays. **Coolart** on Sandy Point Rd, Balnarring, on the other side of the peninsula, is another historic homestead, also noted for the wide variety of its bird life.

After McCrae there's **Rosebud, Rye** and **Blairgowrie** before you reach Sorrento.

Sorrento

Just as you enter Sorrento there's a small memorial and pioneer cemetery from the first Victorian settlement at pretty **Sullivan Bay**. The settlement party, consisting of 308 convicts, civil officers, marines and free settlers, arrived from England in October 1803, intending to forestall a feared French settlement on the bay. Less than a year later, in May 1804, the project was abandoned and transferred to Hobart, Tasmania. The main reason for the settlement's short life was the lack of water. They had simply chosen the wrong place; there was an adequate supply further round the bay. The settlement's numbers included an 11-year-old boy, John Pascoe Fawkner, who 31 years later would be one of the founders of Melbourne. It also included the convict William Buckley, who escaped soon after the landing in 1803.

Sorrento has a rather damp and cold little aquarium and an interesting small historical museum in the old **Mechanic's Institute** building on the Old Melbourne Rd. From the 1870s, paddle-steamers used to run between Melbourne and Sorrento. The largest, entering service in 1910, carried 2000 passengers. From 1890 through to 1921 there was a steam-powered tram operating from the Sorrento pier to the back beach. The magnificent hotels built of local limestone in this period still stand – the Sorrento (1871), Continental (1875) and Koonya (1878).

Places to Stay The YHA-affiliated *Bell's*

Hostel (☎ (059) 84 4323) in Sorrento is a very popular place to stay. The owners, Ian and Margaret, are friendly hosts and organise activities including dolphin swims, coastal walks and bird-watching. The nightly charge is $12 for YHA members and $13 for non-members.

Portsea

Portsea, at the end of the Nepean Highway, offers another choice between calm and surf beaches. At the Portsea back beach (the surf side) there's the impressive natural rock formation known as **London Bridge**, plus a cliff where hang-gliders make their leap into the void, and fine views across Portsea and back to Melbourne from **Mt Levy Lookout**. Portsea is a popular diving centre, and scuba-diving trips on the bay operate regularly from Portsea Pier.

Point Nepean National Park After being off limits to the general public for over 100 years, most of the tip of the peninsula was opened up in 1988 as a national park. There's an excellent visitor centre (☎ (059) 84 4276) where an entrance fee of $7 is payable. There are walking tracks through the area, or you can use the tractor-drawn Transporter. A booklet, *A Guide to Point Nepean's Past* ($5), is available from the visitor centre.

At the entrance to the park are two historic gun barrels which fired the first shots in WW I and WW II. In 1914 a German ship was on its way out from Melbourne to the heads when news of the declaration of war came through on the telegraph. A shot across its bows at Portsea resulted in its capture. The first shot in WW II was fired at an Australian ship!

Cheviot Beach, at the end of the peninsula, featured more recently in Australian history. In 1967, the then prime minister, Harold Holt, went for a swim here and was never seen again. The area was closed to the public for many years but has recently been reopened.

The Ocean Coast

The southern (or eastern) coast of the penin-sula faces Bass Strait and Western Port. A connected series of walking tracks has been developed all the way from London Bridge to Cape Schank and Bushrangers Bay. Some stretches of the Peninsula Coastal Walk are along the beach (some are actually cut by the high tide), but in its entirety the walk extends for more than 30 km and takes at least 12 hours to walk from end to end. The walks can easily be done in stages because the park is narrow and accessible at various points.

Cape Schank is marked by the 1859 lighthouse and there are good walking possibilities around the cape. The rugged coast further east towards **Flinders** and **West Head** has many natural features including a blowhole. Towns like Flinders and **Hastings** on this coast are not quite as popular and crowded in the summer as those on Port Phillip Bay. **Point Leo**, near Shoreham, has a good surf beach.

Off the coast in Western Port is **French Island**, once a prison farm, which is virtually undeveloped, although there are a few camp sites and a lodge. Koalas were introduced some years ago, and the thriving colony now provides top-ups for depleted areas elsewhere in Victoria. A daily ferry service operates between Stony Point and Tankerton Jetty on French Island (phone ☎ 018 553 136 for details).

PHILLIP ISLAND

At the entrance to Western Port, 137 km south-east of Melbourne, Phillip Island is a very popular holiday resort for the Melbourne area. Its main attractions are its excellent surf beaches and the incredibly popular and famous (although somewhat commercialised) fairy penguin parade. The island is joined to the mainland by a bridge from San Remo to Newhaven.

Orientation & Information

Cowes, the main town, is on the northern side of the island and has most facilities including banks plus a good range of eateries and accommodation. The southern side of the island has surf beaches like Woolamai,

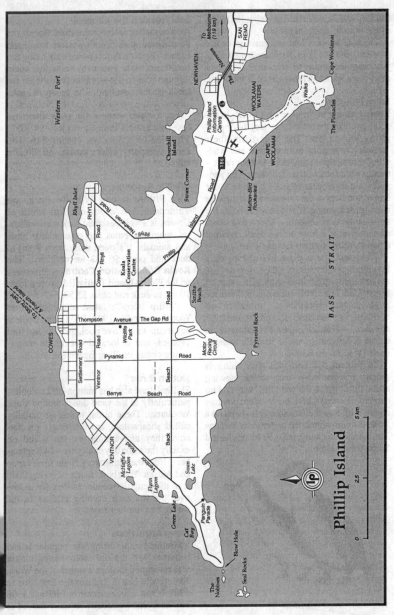

Phillip Island

Cat Bay and Summerland, which is the home of the famous penguin parade.

There is an excellent information centre (☎ (059) 56 7447) in Newhaven just after you cross the bridge to the island. It is open daily from 9 am to 5 pm (to 6 pm in summer).

Fairy Penguins

Every evening at Summerland Beach in the south-west of the island, the tiny fairy penguins which nest there perform their 'parade', emerging from the sea and waddling resolutely up the beach to their nests – totally oblivious of the sightseers. The penguins are there year round but arrive in far larger numbers in the summer when they are rearing their young. It's no easy life being the smallest type of penguin – after a few hours of shut-eye, it's down to the beach again at dawn to start another hard day's fishing.

The parade takes place like clockwork a few minutes after sunset each day and it is a major tourist attraction – Australia's second biggest, in fact. Not surprisingly there are huge crowds, especially on weekends and holidays, so bookings should be made in advance – contact either the information centre at Newhaven, or the Penguin Reserve itself (☎ (059) 56 8300).

To protect the penguins everything is strictly regimented – keep to the viewing areas, don't get in the penguins' way and no camera flashes. There's a modern visitors centre with an excellent souvenir shop and a walk-through simulated underwater display. The admission charge is $6.50 for adults and $2.50 for children.

Fairy penguins

Seal Rocks & the Nobbies

A colony of fur seals inhabits Seal Rocks, off Point Grant at the south-western tip of the island. There's a timber boardwalk along the foreshore, and you can view the seals through coin-in-the-slot binoculars from the kiosk on the headland. The group of rocks closest to the island is called the Nobbies.

For a closer view of the seals, there are two-hour cruises from Cowes jetty (☎ (059) 52 1014) on most days, costing $16. The same company offers cruises to French Island.

Wildlife Reserves

The **Phillip Island Wildlife Park**, on Thompson Ave about one km south of Cowes, is a well-designed park with wallabies, wombats, emus and other native birds and animals. It's open daily from 9 am to dusk and costs $6 ($3 for children). The **Koala Conservation Centre**, at Fiveways on the Phillip Island Tourist Rd, is open from 10 am to dusk and costs $2.50.

Phillip Island's latest attraction, **Reef World**, opened in 1994. It's a large tropical aquarium with a dive pool, gardens and bird aviaries, and is located beside the motor-racing circuit on Back Beach Rd.

Mutton Birds

Phillip Island also has mutton-bird colonies, particularly in the sand dunes around Cape Woolamai. These birds, which are actually called shearwaters, are amazingly predictable; they arrive back on the island on exactly the same day each year – 24 September – from their migratory flight from Japan and Alaska. Your best chance of seeing them is at the penguin parade, as they fly in low over the sea each evening at dusk in the spring and summer months.

Other Attractions

Swimming and surfing are popular island activities and the old motor-racing circuit was revamped to stage a round of the World Motorcycle Grand Prix for the first time in 1989. It was a huge success in 1989 and 1990 but the event was controversially moved to

Sydney in 1991, partly due to the then Victorian government's opposition to tobacco advertising.

Rugged **Cape Woolamai** with its walking track is particularly impressive. There's a great contrast between the high seas on this side of the island and the sheltered waters of the northern (Cowes) side. Access to the signposted walking trail is from the Woolamai surf beach. It's about a half-day walk.

Churchill Island is a small island with a restored house and beautiful gardens. It was here, in 1801, that the first building was constructed by White settlers in Victoria. The island is connected to Phillip Island by a footbridge and the turn-off is well signposted about one km out of Newhaven. It's open daily from 10 am to 5 pm and admission is $4.50.

Organised Tours

There are many, many tours of Phillip Island available, mostly day trips from Melbourne. Some of the most popular trips with backpackers are run by Autopia Tours (☎ (03) 326 5536); they have a one-day tour ($40) or a two-day tour ($58) that also takes in Wilsons Prom – see Organised Tours in the Melbourne section for more details.

Phillip Island Air Services (☎ (059) 56 7316) operates scenic flights ranging from a 10-minute zip around Cape Woolamai for $30 to a 40-minute loop around Western Port for $75.

Places to Stay

Phillip Island is a very popular escape from Melbourne so there are all sorts of hostels, guesthouses, motels, holiday flats and camp sites on the island. You should try to make a reservation in the peak periods – Christmas, Easter and school holidays.

Camping Apart from Amaroo Park (see Hostels below), there are about half a dozen caravan parks in the vicinity of Cowes. The *Kaloha Caravan Park* (☎ (059) 52 2179), on the corner of Chapel and Steele Sts, is about

200 metres from the beach and close to the centre of Cowes.

Hostels Far and away the best place in this range is the very friendly *Amaroo Park Backpackers Inn* (☎ (059) 52 2548) on the corner of Church and Osborne Sts in Cowes. It's a caravan park with an associate-YHA hostel, with six-bed dorms costing $10 ($13 for nonmembers), doubles at $24/30 and tent sites for $5/6.50. It's a friendly place with a small bar and cheap evening meals. They have bikes for hire and will organise trips out to the penguin parade and to Wilsons Prom. The V/Line drivers all know this place and will usually drop you off at the door.

Also YHA affiliated is the *Anchor Belle Caravan Park* (☎ (059) 52 2258) at 272 Church St, about 2.5 km further from the centre of Cowes. The small hostel section has 12 beds costing $10 ($13 nonmembers).

Hotels, Guesthouses & Flats The *Isle of Wight Hotel* (☎ (059) 52 2301), on the Esplanade in the centre of Cowes, has hotel rooms for $30/35 or motel units at $38/50. Not quite so central is the *Glen Isla Motel* (☎ (059) 52 2822) at 234 Church St (about two km from the main street), where double rooms start at $45. A more up-market option is the central *Continental Resort* (☎ (059) 52 2316) at 5 The Esplanade, where double rooms start at $60 ($75 with air-con).

Rhylston Park Historic Homestead (☎ (059) 52 2730), at 190 Thompson Ave about a km from the centre of Cowes, is a restored 1886 homestead with very good period-style guestrooms for $40/65.

Trenavin Park (☎ (059) 56 8230) is on a rise about nine km from the centre of Cowes, out along the road to the penguin parade. There are good views across to the back beaches of the Mornington Peninsula, and there's a pool and central heating. The B&B tariff at this small place is $45 per person or $95 on Saturdays including dinner.

Further along this road, only about a km from the Summerland Beach itself, is the *Flynns Reef Guest House* (☎ (059) 56 8673).

There are just four rooms, and these cost $25/40 for singles/doubles.

Places to Eat

Thompson Ave or the Esplanade in Cowes both have a good range of eateries. There are the usual takeaways, and at least three BYO pizza/pasta restaurants. The *Isola de Capri* has a good reputation, and offers a 10% discount to backpackers. *Fish Bizz*, on the Esplanade behind the Isola, has good souvlakis and fish & chips.

The *Isle of Wight Hotel* has good-value counter meals and a buffet restaurant upstairs. Better again is the *Jetty* on the corner of Thompson Ave and the Esplanade. This place is by no means cheap but the food is very good – especially the seafood.

Further along the Esplanade is the *Rusty Harpoon* which has grills, steaks and a few Chinese dishes. Main courses are in the range of $17 to $20. This place is popular with the bus tours from Melbourne which come down to the island for the penguin parade.

Back on Thompson Ave, the cosy *Rossi Restaurant*, next to the post office, has good Western tucker with the emphasis on fish and chicken in the $15 to $20 range.

Entertainment

During the high season the *Isle of Wight* and *San Remo* hotels both feature live bands, but otherwise things are pretty quiet.

Banfields Theatre Bar & Bistro (☎ (059) 52 2088) at 192 Thompson Ave has live music most Saturday nights, plus a cinema showing latest-release movies.

Getting There & Away

Air Phillip Island is a departure point for cheap flights to Tasmania. There are flights to Wynyard in Tasmania on Wednesday, Friday, Saturday and Sunday. The cost is $105 one way, or there's a $79 stand-by fare. Contact Phillip Island Air Services (☎ (059) 56 7316) for more information.

Bus V/Line has a daily train/bus service to Phillip Island via Dandenong. The trip takes

2¼ hours and costs $12.80, and the drivers will usually drop you off right where you want to stay. Return buses leave from the Esplanade, outside the Isle of Wight Hotel.

Amaroo Park Backpackers also have a free courtesy bus from Melbourne twice a week – ring them for details.

Getting Around

There is no public transport around the island. You can hire bikes from several places in Thompson Ave, or from Amaroo Park.

Phillip Island Bus Tours (☎ (059) 52 2642) operates an evening service out to the Penguin parade during the high season, and Amaroo Park also runs trips out there on most nights.

Great Ocean Road

For over 300 km, from Torquay (a short distance south of Geelong) almost to Warrnambool where the road joins the Princes Highway, the Great Ocean Road provides some of the most spectacular coastal scenery in Australia. For most of the distance the road hugs the coastline, passing some excellent surfing beaches, fine diving centres and even some hills from which hang-gliding enthusiasts launch themselves to catch the strong uplifts coming in from the sea in the evenings. Between Anglesea, Lorne and Apollo Bay the road features the beautiful contrast of the ocean beaches on one side and the forests and mountains of the Otway Ranges on the other. Further west is the famous Port Campbell National Park section, with its amazing collection of rock sculptures such as the Twelve Apostles and the Loch Ard Gorge.

The coast is well equipped with camp sites and other accommodation possibilities and if the seaside activities pall, you can always turn inland to the bushwalks, wildlife, scenery, waterfalls and lookouts of the Otway Ranges.

The Great Ocean Road was completed in

1932 as a works project during the Depression, and stretches of the country through which it runs are still relatively untouched.

Organised Tours

Autopia Tours (☎ (03) 326 5536) runs bus tours along the Great Ocean Road and to Port Campbell. There is a one-day tour ($49) on Sundays and Wednesdays and a two-day tour ($59) which leaves Melbourne on Mondays and Thursdays. Tours leave from the YHA hostels. Mac's Backpacker Tours (☎ (052) 41 3180) also runs small tours from hostels; the one-day tour costs $49 and there is also a two-day tour that takes in both Phillip Island and the Great Ocean Road.

Another popular trip with backpackers is the Wayward Bus (☎ toll-free 1800 882 823), which does a three-day ramble from Melbourne to Adelaide following the coast all the way. It costs $125, which includes lunches (but not accommodation). Kangavic (☎ (052) 57 1889) offers personalised tours for up to four people along the Great Ocean Road and to the Otways; it too receives good reports from travellers. Otway Bush Tours (☎ (052) 33 8395) is another company doing tours in this area.

Places to Stay

The whole coastal stretch is often heavily booked during the peak summer season and at Easter, when prices also jump dramatically. Accommodation is generally expensive, which only leaves camping or on-site vans for budget travellers, though there is an excellent backpackers' hostel at Lorne, and other associate-YHA hostels at Apollo Bay and Port Campbell.

Getting There & Away

V/Line has a bus service from Geelong railway station along the Great Ocean Road to Apollo Bay three times daily Monday to Friday, and twice daily on weekends. Bellarine Transit buses run more frequently from Geelong to Torquay and Jan Juc (see under Geelong). V/Line also has an extended service from Apollo Bay to Port Campbell and Warrnambool and vice versa on Fridays.

TORQUAY (population 4900)

This popular resort town marks the eastern end of the Great Ocean Road and is just 22 km south of Geelong. Some of the most popular surfing beaches are nearby, including **Jan Juc** and **Bell's Beach**. Bell's hosts an international surfing championship every Easter and waves can reach six metres or more. Around the town, **Fisherman's Beach** is the least crowded but is often windy; the front beach and back beach are the most popular and best for swimming. In the shopping complex on the Surfcoast Highway are huge surf shops such as Rip Curl and Quicksilver.

There are tennis courts and a golf course at the western end of town. Past the golf course and just out of Torquay along Duffields Rd is **Ocean Country Park** which has a grass ski slope and water slide.

The Surf Coast Walk follows the coastline from Jan Juc to Aireys Inlet. The full distance takes about 11 hours, but can be done in stages. The Shire of Barrabool puts out a useful leaflet, available from tourist offices in the area.

Places to Stay

There are three caravan parks, including the *Zeally Bay Caravan Park* (☎ (052) 61 2400) with tent sites from $12 and on-site vans from $32. The *Torquay Hotel/Motel* (☎ (052) 61 2001) at 36 Bell St costs $47/52, or the *Tropicana Motel* (☎ (052) 61 4399) on the Surfcoast Highway has rooms from $63/72.

Places to Eat

In Gilbert St (the main shopping centre), the *Tapas Cafe* at No 14 is a good place for coffee or a snack, or further down there's *Yummy Yoghurt*, a health-food cafe with good sandwiches, smoothies, felafels and cakes.

Micha's, at 23 The Esplanade, is a casual Mexican place with main dishes around $12. At 28 The Esplanade, *Ida's* is slightly more up-market but has good food, especially seafood. The *Green Oak*, at 45 Surfcoast

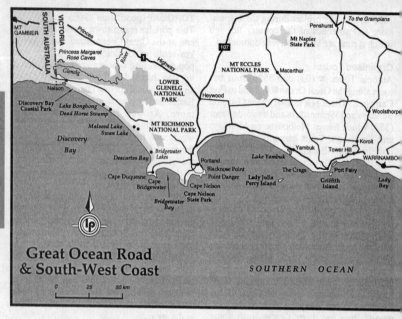

Great Ocean Road & South-West Coast

SOUTHERN OCEAN

0   25   50 km

Highway, has good Thai food with meals from $10 to $15.

ANGLESEA (population 1970)

Another popular seaside resort, Anglesea is 44 km from Geelong and apart from the usual beach activities it also offers the nearby **Ironbark Basin** nature reserve, off the Point Addis Rd, and the famous **Anglesea Golf Club**, with its large population of resident kangaroos. The course is open to the public.

Places to Stay & Eat

Anglesea has a number of caravan parks, with on-site vans for around $25, as well as motels and a hotel. The *Debonair* (☎ (052) 63 1440) has old-fashioned guesthouse rooms from $39/52, or motel rooms from $46/59, including breakfast.

Diana's Cafe Restaurant on the Great Ocean Road is expensive but worth a visit. There's also *Diggers*, a cheap pizza/pasta place behind the Shell service station.

ANGLESEA TO LORNE

Much of this section of the Great Ocean Road is wedged between the ocean and steep cliffs. At Aireys Inlet, midway between Anglesea and Lorne, there's the **Spit Point Lighthouse** as well as a pub, motel, caravan park, and two excellent restaurants, *Ernie's Cantina* and *Mark's*.

Aireys Inlet also marks the start of the **Angahook-Lorne State Park**, which covers 22,000 hectares of coastline, hills and beaches. Within the park are well-signposted walking trails, picnic and camping areas and an abundance of wildlife. For information, walking guides and camping permits, contact the Department of Conservation & Natural Resources (☎ (052) 89 1732) or the tourist information office in Lorne.

LORNE (population 1150)

The small town of Lorne, 73 km from Geelong, was a popular seaside resort even before the Great Ocean Road was built. The

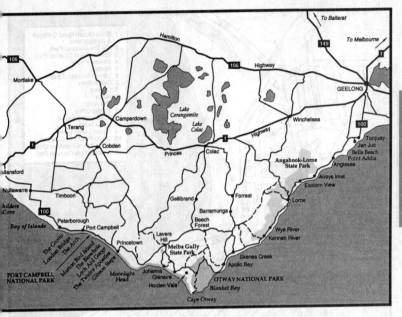

Labels on map: To Ballarat, To Melbourne, 149, Hamilton, Highway, 106, 106, Mortlake, 1, GEELONG, Lake Corangamite, Camperdown, Lake Colac, Winchelsea, 100, Terang, Torquay, Jan Juc, Bells Beach, Cobden, Princes, Colac, Point Addis, Anglesea, Angahook-Lorne State Park, Aireys Inlet, Eastern View, allansford, Nullawarre, Timboon, Gellibrand, Forrest, Lorne, hilders Cove, 100, Peterborough, Barramunga, Wye River, Bay of Islands, Port Campbell, Beech Forest, Kennett River, The Grotto, London Bridge, The Arch, Lavers Hill, Princetown, Mutton Bird Island, The Blowhole, Loch Ard Gorge, The Twelve Apostles, Gibson Steps, Melba Gully State Park, Skenes Creek, Apollo Bay, PORT CAMPBELL NATIONAL PARK, Moonlight Head, Johanna, Glenaire, Horden Vale, OTWAY NATIONAL PARK, Blanket Bay, Cape Otway

VICTORIA

mountains behind the town not only provide a spectacular backdrop but also give the town a mild, sheltered climate all year round. Lorne has good beaches, surfing and bushwalks in the vicinity, especially in the Angahook-Lorne State Park. It's also the most fashionable resort on the coast, which means it has some great restaurants and cafes plus a good range of accommodation, including camping grounds, a good backpackers' hostel, guesthouses, cottages and even a glossy resort hotel.

Climb up to **Teddy's Lookout** behind the town for fine views along the coast. The beautiful **Erskine Falls** are also close behind Lorne; you can drive there or follow the walking trail beside the river, passing Splitter's Falls and Straw Falls on the way. It's about a three-hour walk each way. There are numerous other short and long walks around Lorne.

There's a helpful tourist information centre (☎ (052) 89 1152) at 144 Mountjoy Parade, which opens Monday to Friday from 9.15 am to 5 pm and on weekends and public holidays from 10 am to 3 pm.

Places to Stay

Prices soar and the 'no vacancy' signs go out during the summer school holiday season when half of Melbourne seems to move down. Even pitching a tent in one of the camp sites could prove difficult at peak periods.

The Lorne Foreshore Committee (☎ (052) 89 1382) has four camping sites at Lorne. The *Erskine River Section* is pleasantly sited by the river and is right in the thick of things. The *Queens Park Section* is above it all, on the headland overlooking the pier. Site prices are in the $12 to $18 range and there are minimum booking requirements at peak periods.

The *Great Ocean Road Cottages & Backpackers* (☎ (052) 89 1809) is on Erskine Ave, just above the river. It's an associate-YHA

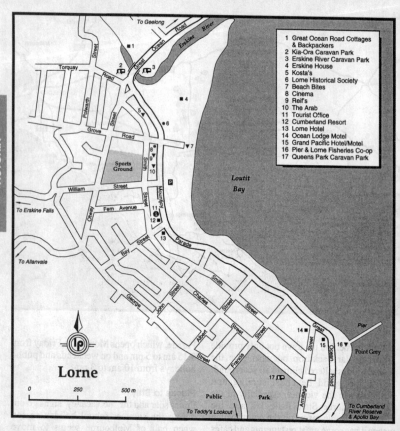

Lorne

1 Great Ocean Road Cottages & Backpackers
2 Kia-Ora Caravan Park
3 Erskine River Caravan Park
4 Erskine House
5 Kosta's
6 Lorne Historical Society
7 Beach Bites
8 Cinema
9 Reif's
10 The Arab
11 Tourist Office
12 Cumberland Resort
13 Lorne Hotel
14 Ocean Lodge Motel
15 Grand Pacific Hotel/Motel
16 Pier & Lorne Fisheries Co-op
17 Queens Park Caravan Park

0   250   500 m

hostel and is very well set up, with dorm beds at $17 ($15 for YHA members). There are also five-bed self-contained cottages which cost from $65 to $110, depending on the season. The hostel and cottages are just behind the supermarket, which is where the V/Line bus stops.

The *Lorne Hotel* (☎ (052) 89 1409) on the Great Ocean Road has motel-style rooms from $60 and self-contained units from $80. The *Pacific Hotel* (☎ (052) 89 1609), opposite the pier, has motel-style rooms from $50/60.

Lorne has a number of old-fashioned

guesthouses, including the 1930s-style *Erskine House* (☎ (052) 89 1209) on Mountjoy Parade, where B&B costs from $46/92, or $86/112 with a private bathroom. *Erskine Falls Cottages* (☎ (052) 89 1751) charge from $75 for a one-bedroom cottage.

Places to Eat

There's no chance of boredom when it comes to eating out in Lorne although at the fancier restaurants you should make sure you have a table booked during the peak season.

There are plenty of fast-food and takeaway places, including *Beach Bites* on the beach by the swimming pool (closed in winter) and *QS Fine Fast Food* on Mountjoy Parade. Next to QS there's the famous *Arab* which has been a Lorne institution since the mid-50s; main courses range from $13 to $16.

The popular and lively *Kosta's Tavern* (☎ (052) 89 1883), at 48 Mountjoy Parade, has good Mediterranean food with mains around $16; while at No 82, the casual *Reif's* cafe has an affordable range of meals and snacks. For seafood, try the *Pier*, with a great setting and mains from $16 to $25, or the fishing co-op next door, which sells fish fresh off the boats.

LORNE TO APOLLO BAY
This is one of the most spectacular sections of the Great Ocean Road, a narrow twisting roadway carved into sheer cliffs that drop away into the ocean. Along this section are the small towns of **Wye River**, **Kennett River** and **Skenes Creek**.

APOLLO BAY (population 890)
The pretty port of Apollo Bay, 118 km from Geelong, is a fishing town and popular resort (but more relaxed than Lorne). There is a small **historical museum** (open Sundays and holidays) and the Westcoast School of Hang-Gliding (☎ (052) 37 6486) is based nearby, but the real attractions are the beaches and the surrounding Otway Ranges. **Mariners Lookout** a few km from town provides excellent views along the coast. The tourist information centre (☎ (052) 37 6529), at 155 Great Ocean Road, opens daily from 10 am to 4 pm (9 am to 6 pm during summer).

Places to Stay
Two km north of the centre, the *Pisces Caravan Resort* (☎ (052) 37 6749) has a small and basic associate-YHA hostel with 10 bunks at $10 per night ($15 nonmembers). There are also tent sites for $13 and on-site vans for $30.

The *Apollo Bay Hotel* (☎ (052) 37 6250) in the centre of town has motel units from

$45/50, and *Bayside Gardens* (☎ (052) 37 6248) at 219 Great Ocean Road has comfortable self-contained units from $60.

Places to Eat
Most of Apollo Bay's eateries are along the Great Ocean Road. For a quick bite, try the *Wholefoods Deli*, a good health-food shop at No 61, or the *Bay Leaf*, a gourmet deli at No 131. The *Apollo Bay Hotel* has bistro meals from $11 to $15 or cheaper bar meals.

Buff's Bistro, at No 51, is a good BYO with a varied menu and meals in the $10 to $14 range. This place is open for breakfast, lunch and dinner and features live music on Friday nights.

OTWAY RANGES
From Apollo Bay the road temporarily leaves the coast to climb up and over Cape Otway. The coast is particularly beautiful and rugged on this stretch, but it is dangerous and there have been many shipwrecks. Cape Otway is covered in rainforest, much of it still relatively untouched, and although many of the roads through the cape are unsurfaced and winding, they present no problems for the average car.

There are a number of scenic lookouts and nature reserves along here but the **Melba Gully State Park** is probably the best, with the beautiful ferns and glow-worms for which the cape is noted. In this reserve is one of the area's last remaining giant gums – it's over 27 metres in circumference and more than 300 years old. Three km east of this small park is **Lavers Hill**, a tiny township which once had a thriving timber business. Waterfalls, such as **Hopetoun Falls** and **Beauchamps Falls**, and shipwrecks at **Moonlight Head** are other Otway attractions.

The 1848 convict-built **Cape Otway Lighthouse**, adjacent to the Otway National Park, is nearly 100 metres high and is 15 km off the main road. The lighthouse grounds are open Monday to Friday from 10 am to 4 pm. The **Otway National Park** has walking trails and picnic areas at Elliot River, Shelly Beach and Blanket Bay.

There are a number of other small picturesque settlements dotted throughout the Otways, such as **Beech Forest**. There is a good craft market at **Gellibrand** on the second Sunday of each month. There are some excellent bushwalking opportunities in the Otways, one of the most popular being along the old railway line which used to connect Beech Forest and Colac.

The Great Ocean Road continues from Lavers Hill past the turn-off to **Johanna**, which has camping and good surfing, to **Princetown**, which also has camping. At Princetown the road rejoins the coast and runs along it through the spectacular Port Campbell National Park.

Places to Stay

Bimbi Park (☎ (052) 37 9246) is an adventure camp, caravan park and horse-riding ranch that offers 1½-hour trail rides along the coast for $20. A bed in an on-site van costs $10, or one in an old army canvas tent costs $6; there are also camp sites from $7 and on-site vans for $25. Bimbi Park is off the Cape Otway lighthouse road, about 7 km after you turn off the Great Ocean Road.

At Blanket Bay, also off the lighthouse road, there's a National Parks camping ground with picnic and barbecue facilities; ring the Department of Conservation & Natural Resources (☎ (052) 37 6889) in Apollo Bay for more information.

There are a number of self-contained cottages along the coast and hidden away in the ranges. Some places include the *Cape Otway Cottages* (☎ (052) 37 9256) at Horden Vale, costing from $80 (minimum of two nights); the *Glenaire Log Cabins* (☎ (052) 37 9231), just past the lookout at Glenaire, from $75; and the *Red Johanna Holiday Cabins* (☎ (052) 37 4238) near Johanna beach.

PORT CAMPBELL NATIONAL PARK

If the Great Ocean Road offers some of the most dramatic coastal scenery in Australia, then the stretch on either side of Port Campbell is the most exciting part. The views are fantastic, with beautiful scenes like the rock formations known as the **Twelve Apostles** where huge stone pillars soar out of the pounding surf (only 10 pillars remain standing now, and only seven can be seen from the lookouts).

Loch Ard Gorge has a sad tale to tell: in 1878 the iron-hulled clipper *Loch Ard* was driven onto the rocks offshore at this point. Of the 50 or so on board only two were to survive: an apprentice officer and an Irish immigrant woman, both aged 18. They were swept into the narrow gorge now named after their ship. Although the papers of the time tried to inspire a romance between the two survivors, the woman, the sole survivor of a family of eight, soon made her way back to Ireland's safer climes. This was the last immigrant sailing ship to founder en route to Australia.

A little further along the coast is **Port Campbell** itself, the main town in the area and again sited on a spectacular gorge. Port Campbell has a pleasant beach and calm waters.

Beyond Port Campbell, **London Bridge**, a bridge-like promontory arching across a furious sea, was once a famous landmark along this coast but in 1990 it collapsed dramatically into the sea, stranding a handful of amazed – and extremely lucky – visitors at the far end. Other formations along here include the **Crown of Thorns** and the beautiful **Bay of Islands**. Soon after Peterborough the Great Ocean Road veers away from the coast and heads inland to Warrnambool, where it joins the Princes Highway.

Places to Stay & Eat

In Port Campbell township, the associate-YHA *Tregea Hostel* (☎ (055) 98 6379) is a pleasant, easy-going place overlooking the gorge. A dorm bed costs $10 and enquiries should be made at Nelson's general store. Port Campbell also has four motels and a caravan park, and for food there's the excellent *Boggy Creek Pub* nearby, on Curdievale Rd, Niranda.

Other accommodation possibilities include *Mackas Farm* (☎ (055) 98 8261), a working farm with B&B and self-contained units from $65 a double; and the *Apostles View Motel* (☎ (055) 98 8277), with units from $41/50. Both of these are close to the Twelve Apostles.

South-West

At Warrnambool the Great Ocean Road ends and you're on the final south-west coast stretch to South Australia on the Princes Highway. This stretch includes some of the earliest settlements in the state, and is promoted as the 'shipwreck coast'.

WARRNAMBOOL (population 24,000)
Warrnambool is 264 km from Melbourne and has sheltered beaches as well as surf beaches. Gun emplacements intended to repel the Russian invasion which Australia feared in the 1880s can be seen near the lighthouse. This is now the site of the excellent **Flagstaff Hill Maritime Village**, with a museum, restored sailing ships, maritime films and port buildings of the era. It's open daily from 9.30 am to 4.30 pm; entry is $9.50 (students $8, children $4.50).

Warrnambool's **art gallery**, on Timor St, has a good collection of Australian art and opens Tuesday to Sunday from 12 noon to 5 pm ($2). Other attractions include the **Botanic Gardens** on the corner of Queen and Cockman Sts; the **Lake Pertobe Adventure Playground** for the kids; a **Time & Tide**

Museum on Stanley St, which has a varied collection of bits and pieces of dubious merit – including over 5000 beer labels; and **History House** on Gilles St.

The tourist information centre (☎ (055) 64 7837) at 600 Raglan Parade opens daily from 9 am to 5 pm; you can pick up the useful *Warrnambool Visitors Handbook* and the three-km **Heritage Trail** brochure.

Southern Right Whales
The southern coast around Port Fairy and Warrnambool is where the southern right whale (*Baleana glacialis*) comes in large numbers every May or June, staying until around October. Whales have been sighted yearly off the Victorian coast since 1970, and at Logan's Beach since 1982. By 1940 it was estimated that there were fewer than 1000 southern right whales left. Although the species has been protected since 1935, today they still number only around 1200 to 1500.

Places to Stay
The *Surf Side One Caravan Park* (☎ (055) 61 2611) on Pertobe Rd is less than a km from the ocean and is right on the beach. Dorm beds cost $10 for YHA members, and there are on-site cabins at $40 and tent sites at $12.

There are a number of other caravan parks along Pertobe Rd, all with similar prices and facilities. The *Lady Bay Hotel* (☎ (055) 62 1544), also on Pertobe Rd, has single/double rooms for $30/40.

Shipwrecks
The Victorian coastline between Cape Otway and Port Fairy was a notoriously dangerous stretch of water in the days when sailing ships were the major form of transport. Navigation through the waters of Bass Strait was made exceptionally difficult due to numerous barely hidden reefs and the frequent, heavy fog. More than 80 vessels came to grief on this 120-km stretch in just 40 years.

The most famous wreck was probably that of the *Loch Ard* (described earlier). Another famous wreck was the *Falls of Halladale*, a Glasgow barque which ran aground in 1908 en route from New York to Melbourne. Although there were no casualties, it lay on the reef, still fully rigged and with sails set, for a couple of months.

Other vessels which came to grief include the *Newfield* in 1892 and the *La Bella* in 1905.

All these wrecks have been investigated by divers and relics are on display in the Flagstaff Hill Maritime Village in Warrnambool. ■

In the centre of town there are plenty of hotels and motels. The cheapest place is the *Royal Hotel* (☎ (055) 62 2063) on the corner of Timor and Fairy Sts, with basic pub rooms at $15 per person for B&B.

Of the motels, one of the cheapest is the *Riverside Gardens Motor Inn* (☎ (055) 62 1888) on the corner of Simpson and Verdon Sts. Units start at $40/50.

Places to Eat
Liebig St, which runs south off Raglan Parade, has most of the cafes and restaurants. At No 61, *Bojangles* is a good Italian bistro with pasta and pizza around $10. At No 69, *Malaysia* has Chinese and Malaysian food, or for Mexican food there's *Taco Bill* across the road at No 58.

Getting There & Away
There are three daily V/Line trains between Melbourne and Warrnambool ($31.80), via Geelong ($22.80). The trip takes around three hours.

Heading west from Warrnambool, daily V/Line buses continue on to Port Fairy ($3.60), Portland ($11.40) and Mt Gambier ($25). On Fridays only, a bus runs back along the Great Ocean Road to Apollo Bay ($19.40) and on to Geelong ($34).

TOWER HILL STATE GAME RESERVE
Midway between Warrnambool and Port Fairy, this 614-hectare reserve is the remains of an ancient crater, and after years of deforestation by White settlers from as long ago as the 1850s, the state government has set about the task of regenerating the natural bush and reintroducing wildlife to the area. There are emus, koalas, grey kangaroos, sugar gliders and peregrine falcons within the reserve, and you can drive around a ring road which circles the lake crater.

PORT FAIRY (population 2470)
This small fishing port 27 km west of Warrnambool was one of the first European settlements in the state, dating back to 1835, although there were temporary visitors right

back in 1826. These first arrivals were whalers and sealers seeking shelter along the coast, and Port Fairy is still the home port for one of Victoria's largest fishing fleets.

Port Fairy was originally known as Belfast and although the name was later changed there's still a Northern Irish flavour about the place and a Belfast Bakery on the main street.

A signposted **history walk** guides you around the many fine old buildings, 50 of which are classified by the National Trust. Also worth a look are the **historical centre** on Bank St, **Mott's Cottage** at 5 Sackville St, the **old fort and signal station** at the mouth of the river, and **Griffiths Island**, which is reached by a causeway from the town and has a lighthouse and a mutton-bird colony.

On the Labour Day long weekend in early March the Port Fairy Folk Festival is held. It's Australia's foremost folk festival, with the emphasis on Irish-Australian music, and it attracts top performers. The town's population swells by around 500% during the festival, and except for camping, accommodation is nonexistent.

There's an information centre (☎ (055) 68 2682) on Bank St, and this is also where the V/Line buses operate from.

Places to Stay
There are several caravan parks, the closest to the centre being the *Gardens Reserve* (☎ (055) 68 1060). Port Fairy's well-established youth hostel (☎ (055) 68 2468), housed in a historic building at 8 Cox St, has bunk rooms in the house, new units out the back, bikes and canoes for hire, and costs $10 ($13 nonmembers). Other budget possibilities include the *Star of the West Hotel* (☎ (055) 68 1715) on Bank St, at $20 including breakfast; and *Southcomb Park*, with bunks for $12.50 (book through the information centre).

There's also a good range of B&Bs, guesthouses, pubs and motels; the information centre has a list of places and can make bookings.

Places to Eat
Most of the eateries are along Bank St,

including *Lunch*, an excellent gourmet deli beside the information centre. For pub food, try the *Commercial Hotel* or the *Star of the West*. The expensive but well-regarded *Dublin House Inn* restaurant is at 57 Bank St.

Getting There & Away
Daily V/Line buses run to Warrnambool and Mt Gambier.

PORTLAND (population 10,000)
Continuing west 72 km from Port Fairy you reach Portland, just 75 km from the South Australian border. This is the oldest settlement in Victoria. Established in 1834, it predates Port Fairy by one year. It's an indication of the piecemeal development of Victoria that the first 'official' visitor, Major Thomas Mitchell, turned up here on an overland expedition from Sydney in 1836 and was surprised to find it had been settled two years earlier. Whalers knew this stretch of coast long before the first permanent settlement and there were even earlier short-term visitors.

Points of interest include **Burswood Homestead & Gardens**, at 15 Cape Nelson Rd; the **Botanic Gardens** in Cliff St; a **historical museum** in Charles St; and the **old watch house** in Cliff St, which is now the tourist information office (☎ (055) 23 2671).

The lighthouse at the tip of Cape Nelson, south of Portland, is also classified by the National Trust, although it is not open to the public. It is part of the **Cape Nelson State Park** which has some excellent walks and coastal views.

Places to Stay
Portland has numerous camp sites, guesthouses and motels. *Victoria House* (☎ (055) 21 7577), at 5 Tyers St, is an excellent B&B with rooms at $52/59.

PORTLAND TO THE SOUTH AUSTRALIAN BORDER
From Portland the Princes Highway turns inland before crossing the border to Mt Gambier in South Australia, but there is also a smaller road which runs closer to the coast, past the **Mt Richmond National Park** and the **Discovery Bay Coastal Park**. The road meets the coast just before the border at the little town (village even) of **Nelson**, a popular resort for Mt Gambier. It's right on the Glenelg River, and there are daily cruises up the river to the Princess Margaret Rose limestone caves for $15, and canoes and fishing boats for hire.

Nelson is also a good access point to the **Lower Glenelg National Park** with its deep gorges and brilliant wildflowers, and the information centre (☎ (087) 38 4051) is the place to make camping reservations. This park is very popular with canoeists and those who like dangling a line, and the **Princess Margaret Rose Caves**, just three km from the border, are worth a look – there are guided tours several times a day.

Along the south coast between Portland and the border, the 200-km **Great South West Walk** traverses the Discovery Bay Coastal Park. It's a very rewarding 10-day hike, or you can just walk stages of it.

Places to Stay
The *Nioka Farm Home Hostel* (☎ (055) 20 2233) is 40 km west of Portland, not far from the Mt Richmond National Park. Book ahead since there's only room for 10 at $16 per day for YHA members ($20 nonmembers), including breakfast and dinner. They will arrange to pick you up from Portland ($5). This is a good opportunity to stay on a working sheep farm.

Nelson has caravan parks and motels, and the *Nelson Hotel* (☎ (087) 38 4011) has a few rooms at $14 per person.

The Lower Glenelg National Park has a number of very pretty camp sites with minimal facilities. At the Princess Margaret Rose Caves there are camp sites and cabins – contact the ranger for bookings (☎ (087) 38 4171).

THE WESTERN DISTRICT
The south-west of the state, inland from the coast and stretching to the South Australian border, is particularly affluent sheep-raising

---

The Major Mitchell Trail

The Major Mitchell Trail is a 1700-km 'cultural trail' which follows as closely as possible the route taken by the New South Wales Surveyor General on his exploratory trip though Victoria in 1836.

He entered Victoria near present-day Swan Hill, and travelled south to the coast, before returning to New South Wales through Hamilton, Castlemaine, Benalla and Wodonga. On his trip he named many places along the way (and explored and discovered some previously little-known areas), including the Grampians, Mt Macedon and rivers such as the Loddon, Glenelg and Wimmera.

Mitchell was so pleasantly surprised with the lushness of the land he saw, in comparison with the dry expanses of New South Wales, that he named the area *Australia Felix* (Australia Fair).

The route today takes you along many back roads and is well signposted along its entire length with distinctive small brown and blue signs. An excellent descriptive handbook is available from the Department of Conservation & Natural Resources and local tourist offices for $10. ∎

---

and pastoral country. It's also said to be the third largest volcanic plain in the world, and the area is littered with craters, lakes, lava tubes and other signs of its volcanic past.

Melbourne to Hamilton

You can reach Hamilton, the 'capital' of the Western District, via Ballarat along the Glenelg Highway or via Geelong along the Hamilton Highway. On the Glenelg Highway the **Mooramong Homestead** at Skipton is owned by the National Trust and open by appointment. Further along the highway the small town of **Lake Bolac** is beside a large freshwater lake, popular for water sports. **Inverleigh** is an attractive little town along the Hamilton Highway.

The Princes Highway runs further south, reaching the coast at Warrnambool. **Winchelsea**, on the Princes Highway, has Barwon Park Homestead, a rambling bluestone National Trust property. The stone Barwon Bridge dates from 1867. You can reach the Grampians on a scenic route from **Dunkeld** on the Glenelg Highway.

Colac (population 10,000)

Colac lies on the eastern edge of the Western District, and there are many **volcanic lakes** in the vicinity of the town – a couple of lookouts give excellent views. There's also a **botanical garden**, a tourist information office (☎ (052) 31 3730) and the **Colac Historical Centre**.

Hamilton (population 9760)

The major town of the area, Hamilton is particularly known for its excellent **art gallery** on Brown St, which opens daily. The Hamilton Tourist Information Centre (☎ (055) 72 3746) is on Lonsdale St.

The **Hamilton & Western District Museum** on Gray St houses an Aboriginal 'keeping place' – the works of craft and art of the local tribes preserved by them as a means of maintaining their history and culture. The museum is open Wednesday to Friday from 1 to 4 pm ($1).

The **Big Woolbales** has displays devoted to promoting the wool industry and things woolly; it's open daily and is free. There's a flora and fauna nature trail at Hamilton's **Institute of Rural Learning**, which is also the last refuge of the endangered eastern barred bandicoot (*Perameles gunnii*), a small, ground-dwelling marsupial.

South of Hamilton are the **Mt Napier State Park** and the **Mt Eccles National Park**, where you can see some fascinating volcanic remnants including the lava tubes of Byaduk Caves and Tunnel Cave. There are also walking trails and lookouts, and camp sites at Mt Eccles. Contact the ranger (☎ (055) 76 1014) for more information.

Places to Stay The *Lake Hamilton Caravan park* (☎ (055) 72 3855) has tent sites at $7 and on-site vans from $24. The *Commercial Hotel* (☎ (055) 72 1078) at 145 Thompson

Ave has rooms at $15/25; breakfast is another $5.

Getting There & Away V/Line has daily buses to Melbourne ($36.40) and on to Mt Gambier ($16.80). There are also weekday services south to Warrnambool and north to Horsham.

Lake Condah

At **Lake Condah Aboriginal Mission**, about 45 km south of Hamilton on the Portland road, there is an important project tracing the history and culture of local tribes.

Most of Victoria's Koories suffered early and rapid detribalisation, especially in the Western District where the squatters (land-grabbers who became wealthy pastoralists – today's 'squattocracy') quickly cleared the land of its people in their hurry to begin intensive sheep farming.

Part of the legalistic argument against granting Aboriginal land claims in the '70s was that as they were a nomadic people who didn't work the land they couldn't be said to have ever 'owned' Australia. That argument was eventually thrown out of court, and the discovery of permanent stone dwellings and a complex system of stone canals and fish traps at Lake Condah should be enough to convince the most materialistic Aussie that by any criterion the Aborigines did indeed own Australia.

The original mission buildings have long since disintegrated, but it's still possible to get an idea of the place. The mission is now run by the Kerrup-jmara community. There are 4WD tours of Mt Eccles and Lake Condah, modern four-bed cabins which cost $40/50 a night, and also a couple of family units and larger units for groups (☎ (055) 78 4257).

The Wimmera

The Wimmera region, in Victoria's far west, is mostly endless expanses of wheat fields and sheep farms. In the south is one of Victoria's major attractions, the spectacularly scenic mountains of the Grampians National Park. The region's other main points of interest are the Little Desert National Park, and Mt Arapiles, Australia's most famous rock-climbing venue.

The main road through the Wimmera is the Western Highway, which is also the busiest route between Melbourne and Adelaide. It passes through Stawell, which is the turn-off point for the Grampians, and Horsham, the major town and commercial centre for the region.

ARARAT (population 7600)

After a brief flirtation with gold in 1857, Ararat settled down as a farming centre. Its features include the **Langi Morgala Museum** (open weekends 2 to 4 pm), the **Alexandra Gardens**, an **art gallery** and some fine old bluestone buildings. The tourist information centre (☎ (053) 52 2181) is on the corner of Barkly and Vincent Sts.

Fourteen km east, the **Langi Ghiran State Park** has good walking tracks and climbs, plus a winery.

Midway between Ararat and Stawell, **Great Western** is one of Australia's best-known champagne regions. You can tour the old underground cellars at Seppelt's Great Western, and also visit Best's and Garden Gully wineries.

Places to Stay

The *Ararat Hotel* (☎ (053) 52 2477) on Barkly St has B&B for $18/30, and the *Chalambar Motel* (☎ (053) 52 2430) on the Western Highway has singles/doubles from $25/34.

STAWELL (population 6340)

Stawell, another former gold town, is the turn-off for Halls Gap and the Grampians. There is a good tourist information office (☎ (053) 58 2314) on the Western Highway, just before the turn-off.

The town has a number of National-Trust-classified buildings, but it's best known as the home of the Stawell Gift, Australia's richest foot race, which attracts up to 20,000 visitors every Easter! The **Stawell Gift Hall of Fame** on Main St details the history of the event.

Bunjil's Cave, with Aboriginal rock paintings, is on the Pomonal road 11 km south.

Places to Stay

There are two caravan parks and plenty of motels in town and along the highway. The tourist office has an accommodation booking service.

The *Stawell Holiday Cottages* (☎ (053) 58 2868) cost from $45 a double and sleep up to six people.

Getting There & Away

Stawell is connected with Melbourne by daily trains ($29.40). There's also the daily bus link to the Grampians – see that section for details.

GRAMPIANS (GARIWERD) NATIONAL PARK

Named after the mountains of the same name in Scotland, the Grampians are the south-west tail end of the Great Dividing Range. The area is a large national park renowned for fine bushwalks, superb mountain lookouts, excellent rock-climbing opportunities, prolific wildlife and, in the spring, countless wildflowers.

The Grampians are at their best from August to November when the flowers are most colourful. On a weekend in early spring there's a wildflower exhibition in the Halls Gap Hall. There are also many Aboriginal rock paintings in the Grampians, as well as waterfalls such as the spectacular McKenzie Falls.

There are many fine bushwalks around the Grampians, some of them short strolls you can make from Halls Gap. Keep an eye out for koalas and kangaroos; you sometimes see koalas right in the middle of Halls Gap.

In 1991 the Grampians name was officially changed to include the Aboriginal name, Gariwerd, but it was changed back again when the Kennett government came into office.

Orientation & Information

The Grampians lie immediately west of Ararat and south of the Western Highway between Stawell and Horsham. The tiny town of **Halls Gap**, about 250 km from Melbourne, is right in the middle of the region and has camping and motel facilities. The closest railway station to Halls Gap is 25 km away at Stawell.

The National Park visitor centre (☎ (053) 56 4381), three km south of Halls Gap on the Dunkeld road, has excellent information, maps, walking guides and audiovisual displays – their *Highlights in One Day* brochure is handy for a short stay. The centre is open daily from 9 am to 4.45 pm.

There is no bank in Halls Gap, although

Koala

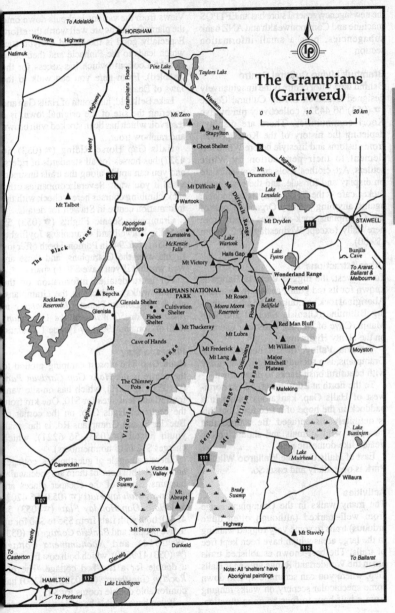

The Grampians (Gariwerd)

0   10   20 km

VICTORIA

To Adelaide

HORSHAM

Wimmera Highway

Natimuk

Pine Lake

Taylors Lake

Western Highway

Grampians Road

Henty Highway

107

Mt Zero

Mt Stapylton

Ghost Shelter

Mt Talbot

Mt Difficult

Wartook

Mt Difficult Range

Mt Drummond

Lake Lonsdale

Mt Dryden

STAWELL

111

Bunjils Cave

Aboriginal Paintings

The Black Range

Zumsteins

McKenzie Falls

Lake Wartook

Halls Gap

Lake Fyans

To Ararat, Ballarat & Melbourne

Mt Bepcha

Mt Victory

Wonderland Range

Rocklands Reservoir

Glenisla

Glenisla Shelter

GRAMPIANS NATIONAL PARK

Cultivation Shelter

Fishes Shelter

Cave of Hands

Mt Thackeray

Mt Rosea

Moora Moora Reservoir

Lake Bellfield

Pomonal

Mt Lubra

Mt Frederick

Mt Lang

Red Man Bluff

Mt William

Major Mitchell Plateau

124

Moyston

Grampians Road

The Chimney Pots

Mafeking

Lake Buninjon

Serra Range

Victoria Range

Mt William Range

107

Cavendish

Victoria Valley

Bryan Swamp

111

Mt Abrupt

Lake Muirhead

Brady Swamp

Highway

Willaura

Mt Sturgeon

Mt Stavely

112

To Ballarat

To Casterton

HAMILTON

Glenelg Highway

Dunkeld

Lake Linlithgow

112

To Portland

Note: All 'shelters' have Aboriginal paintings

the newsagency/general store has an EFTPOS machine and Commonwealth and ANZ bank subagencies, plus a small information section.

Brambuk Living Cultural Centre

Behind the visitor centre is the imaginatively designed Brambuk Living Cultural Centre (☎ (053) 56 4452), collectively run by five Koori communities. There are displays depicting the history of the Koori people, from customs and lifestyle before White settlement to their persecution by White settlers. Art, clothes, tools and souvenirs are on display and for sale, and there's a bush-tucker cafe – the $3.50 entry is refundable against anything you buy. Organised tours of the Grampians rock-art sites depart from here daily (except Wednesday) at 2.30 pm ($9.50).

Other Attractions

To the west, the rugged **Victoria Range** is known for its red gums, and there are many Aboriginal rock paintings in the area, including Billimina (Glenisla Shelter) and Wab Manja (Cave of Hands), both near Glenisla on the Henty Highway.

Victoria Valley, in the centre of the Grampians, is a secluded wildlife sanctuary with beautiful bush tracks to drive down.

To the north at **Zumsteins**, 22 km north-west of Halls Gap, kangaroos gather in a paddock in the hope of a free feed, but this is definitely discouraged. Be warned that these are wild animals and should not be treated like domestic pets.

East of Halls Gap, the **Wallaroo Wildlife Park** is open daily and costs $6.

Activities

The many walks in the Grampians range from well-marked (although often quite arduous) trails to some very rugged walking in the large areas which have been kept free of trails. The best-known established trails are in the Wonderland Range area near Halls Gap, where you can scramble up and down some spectacular scenery on walks ranging from a half-hour to four hours in duration.

Views from the various lookouts down onto the plains far below are well worth the effort. Especially good is the Grand Canyon trail which leads to the Pinnacle and then on to Boroka Lookout (which has access for the disabled). From here you can walk to the Jaws of Death!

Lake Bellfield, just south of Halls Gap and covering the site of the original town, is a reservoir which has been stocked with brown and rainbow trout.

Halls Gap Horse Riding (☎ (053) 56 4327) has horses for all standards of riders, and you can amble along the trails unsupervised if you want. Several companies offer rock-climbing courses here – check with the information centre in Stawell for details.

Grampians Scenic Flights (☎ (053) 58 2855) in Stawell and Grampians Joyflights (☎ (053) 56 6294) in Pomonal both offer joy flights over the Grampians, and these are well worth it if you have $30 to spare.

For more detailed information on the various walks available in the Grampians, check out Lonely Planet's *Bushwalking in Australia*, or *50 Walks in the Grampians* (Hill of Content, 1991) by Tyrone T Thomas.

Places to Stay

Halls Gap The closest camping ground to the centre is the *Halls Gap Caravan Park* (☎ (053) 56 4251), which has on-site vans for $30 and tent sites for $10. One km from the centre of Halls Gap, on the corner of Buckler St and Grampians Rd, is the small youth hostel (☎ (053) 56 6221), which charges $12 ($15 nonmembers).

There's a gaggle of guesthouses, cottages and motels, but none of them are spectacular bargains. Some of the cheaper places are *Kingsway Holiday Flats* (☎ (053) 56 4202) and *Halls Gap Holiday Flats* (☎ (053) 56 4304), both with flats from $35 to $60 for up to five people; and *Banksia Cottage* (☎ (053) 58 2314) and *Noonammena Cottage* (☎ (053) 41 7520), which both cost from $60 a double for a five-bed cottage. The old *Rocklyn Guesthouse* (☎ (053) 56 4250) has comfortable double rooms for $45.

If you have trouble booking accommodation in advance (which often happens in peak holiday periods – especially Easter), the Stawell & Grampians Information Centre in Stawell (☎ (053) 58 2314) operates an accommodation booking service.

In the Park There are more than 15 camp sites in the national park, all with toilets, picnic tables and fireplaces, and most with at least limited water. There's no booking system – it's first in, best site. Permits cost $6 from the visitors centre.

Bush camping is permitted anywhere outside the designated camp sites except in the Wonderland Range area and around Lake Wartook.

When camping in the park pay close attention to the fire restrictions – apart from the damage you could do to yourself and the bush, you stand a good chance of being arrested if you disobey them. Remember that you can be jailed for lighting *any* fire, including fuel stoves, on days of total fire ban, and the locals will be more than willing to dob you in.

Places to Eat
The general store in Halls Gap has a cafe and takeaway section, and there's a well-stocked supermarket next door. The *Flying Emu Cafe* is good for lunch or a snack.

The casual *Serra Range* restaurant at the front of the Mountain Grand guesthouse has home-style mains from $7 to $11, and the *Golden Phoenix* has reasonable Chinese food. The excellent *Kookaburra Restaurant* (☎ (053) 56 4222) has a menu based on fresh local produce with mains around $17.

Getting There & Away
V/Line has a daily bus between Halls Gap and Stawell ($6.30), and it connects with trains to and from Melbourne ($36.40). Trains should be booked in advance.

Grampians National Park Tours (☎ (053) 56 6221) (based at the YHA hostel) offers half-day tours for $28 and full-day tours for $48 ($35/60 for nonmembers), which includes return travel to and from Stawell.

You can stay as many days as you like before using the return sector to Stawell.

HORSHAM (population 12,500)
Horsham was first settled in 1842, and has grown to become the main commercial centre for the Wimmera. The town has an **art gallery**, **botanic gardens** and **'Olde Horsham'** with antique displays and a small fauna park. The **Wimmera Wool Factory**, out on the Golf Course Rd, is a community project which provides employment and skill development for handicapped people. There are daily tours and these give an insight into all aspects of the wool industry.

There's a tourist information centre (☎ (053) 82 1832) at 20 O'Callaghans Parade.

Places to Stay
The *Horsham Caravan Park* (☎ (053) 82 3476) is at the end of Firebrace St by the river and has on-site vans at $28 and tent sites at $8. The *Royal Hotel* (☎ (053) 82 1255) at 132 Firebrace St has B&B for $20/30, and there are at least a dozen motels in the area as well.

MT ARAPILES
Twelve km from Natimuk on the Wimmera Highway, Mt Arapiles (or more commonly the Piles) lures rock climbers from around the world. There are more than 2000 climbs for all levels of skill, with colourful names such as Violent Crumble, Punks in the Gym and Cruel Britannia. It's usually alive with climbers.

So great is its attraction that the sleepy town of Natimuk is now home to quite a few climbers who have moved into the area, bringing with them tastes and attitudes not usually associated with small rural towns in Australia – the Natimuk pub must be one of the few to boast vegetarian pancakes on its counter-meal menu, and the milkshakes at the local shops are famous.

Despite the mountain's climbing fame, there is a sealed road right to the top for those unable to haul themselves up the hard way, and there are excellent views from the lookout. Not far away is the lone rocky outcrop of Mitre Rock, near to its namesake lake, and the Wimmera stretches into the distance.

As might be expected, accommodation in Natimuk is tight, particularly for long-term stays. There is a camp site (known locally as 'the Pines') at Centenary Park at the base of the mountain and there's always an eclectic mix of people here. It must be one of the best-patronised camp sites in any of Victoria's state forests, although the facilities here are minimal: one washbasin.

DIMBOOLA (population 1600)

The name of this quiet, typically Australian country town on the Wimmera River is a Sinhalese word meaning 'Land of the Figs'. The **Pink Lake**, just south of the highway, is a little way beyond Dimboola. Beside the Wimmera River nearby you can see Aboriginal canoe trees; the red gums are scarred where canoes have been cut out in one piece from their bark.

The **Ebenezer Mission Station** was established in Antwerp, north of Dimboola, to tend to local Aborigines in 1859. The ruins, complete with its small cemetery, are signposted off the road, close to the banks of the Wimmera River.

LITTLE DESERT NATIONAL PARK

Just south of the Western Highway and reached from Dimboola or Nhill, the Little Desert National Park is noted for its brilliant display of wildflowers in the spring. The name is a bit of a misnomer because it isn't really a desert at all, nor is it that little. In fact with an area of 132,000 hectares it's Victoria's fifth largest national park, and the 'desert' extends well beyond the national park boundaries.

There are several introductory walks in the east block of the park: south of Dimboola is the **Pomponderoo Hill Nature Walk**; south of Nhill the **Stringybark Walk**; and south of Kiata there's the **Sanctuary Nature Walk**.

Places to Stay

You can camp in the park 10 km south of Kiata, just east of Nhill, or on the Wimmera River south of Dimboola. Ring the rangers at Dimboola (☎ (053) 89 1204) for more information about camping.

The *Little Desert Lodge* (☎ (053) 91 5232), in the park and 16 km south of Nhill, has units with B&B for $42/56 for singles/doubles, or you can camp for $9.50 per site. There's also an environmental study centre and the only aviary in the world to have the fascinating mallee fowl.

The Mallee

North of the Wimmera is the least populated part of Australia's most densely populated state. Forming a wedge between South Australia and New South Wales, this area even includes the one genuinely empty part of Victoria. The contrast between the wide, flat Mallee, with its sand dunes and dry lakes, and the lush alpine forests of East Gippsland is striking – despite being the smallest mainland state, Victoria really does manage to cram in a lot.

The Mallee takes its name from the mallee scrub which once covered the area. Mallee roots are hard, gnarled and slow-burning. Some great Aussie kitsch can still be found – mallee-root eggcups and ashtrays – although they may have crossed that thin line from being kitsch to being 'collectable'.

The Mallee region extends from around the Wyperfeld National Park in the south, all the way up to the irrigated oasis surrounding Mildura. Much of the northern area is encompassed in the recently proclaimed Murray-Sunset National Park.

The main town in the Mallee is Ouyen, at the junction of the Sunraysia, Calder and Mallee highways, although Mildura is by far the largest centre in the area. The north-west corner of the Mallee is known as 'Sunset Country' – a fine name for the edge of the arid wilderness that stretches right across the continent.

National Parks & Reserves

Murray-Sunset National Park This is the newest of the state's national parks, having been proclaimed in July 1991, and at 633,000 hectares it is the state's second largest, after the Alpine National Park.

Its creation was the subject of a good deal of controversy as much of the land it took over was good, although degraded, grazing and agricultural land. It was created to try to stop the eradication of much of the area's unique native fauna, which has suffered greatly as more than 65% of the mallee scrub has been cleared.

The park takes in the older Pink Lakes National Park, and is contiguous with the Hattah-Kulkyne National Park.

Wyperfeld National Park Best reached from Albacutya, north of Rainbow, this large park contains a chain of often-dry lakes, including Lake Albacutya. A combination of river gums on the flood plains, sandy mallee scrubland and treed plains supports a wide variety of wildlife, including emus and kangaroos. There are two six-km walking tracks, a 15-km nature drive, and some good longer walks. The park information centre can advise on these and it also has details on the area's flora and fauna, which of course includes the mallee fowl. There are four camping grounds with basic facilities.

Big Desert Wilderness This large wilderness area contains no roads, tracks or any other facilities, which makes it difficult and dangerous to travel in except for those with considerable wilderness experience. It consists of sand dunes and mallee scrub, and wildlife abounds.

If you aren't equipped to venture into the wilderness, you can get a tantalising glimpse of the Big Desert along the dry-weather road which runs from Nhill north to Murrayville on the Ouyen Highway. There are camp sites and bore water to be found at **Broken Bucket Reserve**, which is about 55 km north of Nhill.

Hattah-Kulkyne National Park With the near-desert of the mallee country, the wood-lands, gum-lined lakes and the Murray River, Hattah-Kulkyne is a diverse and beautiful park.

The park hit the headlines in 1990 when the state government decided to cull some of the 20,000-odd kangaroos which inhabit the park – it has been estimated that the park can only carry around 5000 roos without harming the fragile environment. Of course, any operation that involves killing kangaroos is going to be controversial, and this one was no exception.

The Hattah Lakes system fills when the Murray floods and supports many species of water birds. There is a good information centre (☎ (050) 29 3253) at Lake Hattah, a few km into the park from the small town of Hattah, on the Sunraysia Highway 35 km north of Ouyen. Check at the centre on the condition of tracks in the park – many are impassable after rain.

There are camping facilities at Lake Hattah and Lake Mournpall, but note that there is limited water and the lake water, when there is any, is muddy and unsuitable for drinking. Camping is also possible anywhere along the Murray River frontage, which is also the Murray-Kulkyne State Park.

Murray River

The mighty Murray River is Australia's most important inland waterway, flowing from the mountains of the Great Dividing Range in north-east Victoria to Encounter Bay in South Australia, a distance of some 2500 km. The river actually has its source in New South Wales, close to Mt Kosciusko, but soon after forms the border between the two states, and most of the places of interest are on the Victorian side.

The Murray is also a river with a history. It was travelled along by some of Australia's earliest explorers, including Mitchell, Sturt and Eyre, and later became a great trade artery and an important means of opening up the interior.

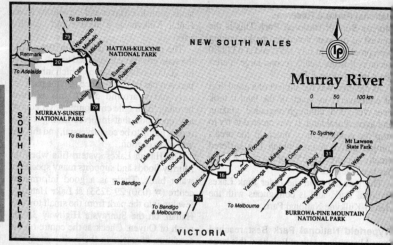

Long before roads and railways crossed the land the Murray was an antipodean Mississippi with paddle-steamers carrying supplies and carting wool to and from remote sheep stations and homesteads. The township of Echuca became Australia's leading inland port as boats traded for hundreds of km along the Murray's winding waterways, to other thriving river towns like Swan Hill and Mildura, as well as up and down the Murrumbidgee, Goulburn and Darling rivers.

Many of the river towns have good museums, old buildings from the riverboat era or well-preserved paddle-steamers that recall that colourful age.

The Murray is also of great economic importance as it supplies the vital water for the irrigation schemes of northern Victoria that have made huge areas of previously barren land agriculturally viable.

As early as the 1890s Victorian MP Alfred Deakin (later prime minister) recognised the agricultural potential of developing irrigation projects in the state's north. He encouraged the Chaffey brothers of California to design and install pumps and irrigation facilities using the waters of the Murray. The brothers also planned the township of Mildura which, together with the new farming possibilities, soon attracted settlers from all over the country and overseas. Deakin's vision proved to be correct and the extensive tracts of irrigated land around Mildura and down through South Australia all stem from the Chaffey brothers' early work.

The Murray and its irrigation projects now support prosperous dairy farms, vineyards, vegetables and the citrus orchards which provide fresh fruit and supply the thriving dried-fruit industry. In recent years, however, salinity in the soil after years of irrigation has become a major problem, one which poses a long-term threat to the viability of much of the irrigated land along both sides of the Murray.

The river is also famous for its magnificent forests of red gums, its plentiful wildlife and as a great place for adventurous canoe trips, relaxing riverboat cruises or leisurely river-bank camping.

In the north-west of Victoria, the Murray Valley Highway begins where it meets the Sunraysia Highway at a junction 69 km south of Mildura. From there it follows, for the most part, the course of the Murray River eastwards as far as Corryong, which is almost back to the river's source near Mt Kosciusko in New South Wales.

Getting There & Away

Bus & Train Greyhound Pioneer and McCafferty's both go through Mildura on the Sydney to Adelaide run.

V/Line has bus or combination bus/train services which connect Melbourne, Bendigo and Ballarat with the Murray River towns, and it also operates bus services running along the Murray between Albury and Mildura.

Boat Of course the most appropriate way to travel on the Murray is by boat. The paddle-steamers of Echuca, Mildura and Swan Hill provide day or overnight trips, and the same towns have numerous places that rent house-boats. Check with tourist information offices for details.

MILDURA (population 23,000)

Noted for its exceptional amount of sun-shine, Mildura was the site of the first Murray River irrigation projects. Today it's something of an oasis in this arid region, and a popular tourist town with quite a few worthwhile attractions.

Mildura's festivals include the Siesta Fiesta in January, Country Music Week in September and a Jazz & Wine Festival every Melbourne Cup weekend.

Information

The Sunraysia Tourism Office (☎ toll-free 1800 039 043), in the Mildura railway station on Seventh St, is open weekdays from 9 am to 5 pm and Saturdays from 9 am to noon. This place has a good range of information and can also book tours and accommodation.

The Department of Conservation & Natural Resources has an office (☎ (050) 23 2906) at 253 Eleventh St with good info on all the national and state parks in the area. The RACV (☎ (050) 21 3272) is at 82a Langtree Ave, in the mall.

Fruit Picking If you're looking for fruit-picking work, contact Mildura's Department of Employment, Education & Training (☎ (050) 21 9500) around the first week of February, when there's a good chance of getting a job as a grape picker or cart opera-tor. After a few days you'll get used to the backbreaking, 10-hour-a-day labour. Picking usually starts around February and lasts for around six weeks. It's hard work, but if you've done it before it can mean big bucks, like about $350 a week. Some farmers provide accommodation, but take a tent if you're not sure.

Things to See

The **Mildura Arts Centre & Rio Vista** complex is well worth a visit. There's an excellent collection of Australian and Euro-pean art and a historic homestead with interesting displays. It's on the corner of Chaffey and Curtin Aves, opens weekdays from 9 am to 5 pm and weekends from 2 to 5 pm, and costs $2.50.

The **Mildura Workingman's Club** is famous for having the longest bar in the world – visitors must sign in, and you can have a beer at the bar or a meal in the bistro.

Orange World, seven km north of town (in New South Wales), has one-hour tours ($5) on tractor trains around the property and is a fascinating introduction to how citrus fruit is produced. The **Golden River Zoo**, four km north-west, opens daily from 9 am to 5 pm and costs $7.50.

Lest you forget that this is riverboat country, you can take **paddle-steamer trips** from the Mildura wharf. The historic steam-powered PS *Melbourne* has two cruises daily ($15), and the PV *Rothbury* does day trips to the zoo ($30) and to Trentham winery ($32). The *Showboat Avoca* has two-hour lunch cruises ($23) and cabaret-dinner cruises by night (from $35).

Places to Stay

There are many caravan parks in the area. One of the most central is *Cross Roads Caravan Park* (☎ (050) 23 3239), three km south-west, on the corner of Deakin Ave and

Fifteenth St. Tent sites cost $12.50 and on-site vans are $26.

Rosemont Holiday House (☎ (050) 23 1535), at 154 Madden Ave, is an associate-YHA pastel with single/double rooms for $15 per person, or doubles with bathroom and TV for $38. A good breakfast is included and linen hire costs $2. The rooms are clean, there's a pool and all the usual facilities and the owners are very helpful and hospitable.

Mildura, especially along Deakin Ave, is overrun with motels, so prices are quite low with a lot of special deals. Two of the cheapest central places are the *Riviera Motel* (☎ (050) 23 3696), 157 Seventh St, with singles/doubles from $36/38; or the *Vineleaf Motel* (☎ (050) 23 1377), corner of Tenth St and Pine Ave, from $33/37.

There are around 20 operators renting houseboats here and costs range upwards from $500 a week for four people, usually with a three-night minimum. Contact the tourist office or the RACV for details.

Places to Eat
On the corner of Seventh St and Deakin Ave, *Jackie's Corner* is a Chinese cafe with an extensive menu and cheap takeaways. Next door, the *Souvlaki Inn* has burgers, souvlakis and a separate hot-dog and ice-cream section.

Bananas Vegetarian Restaurant on the corner of Seventh and Chaffey Sts has interesting and exotic main dishes from $10 to $12. On Langtree Ave, north of the mall, you'll find *Taco Bill* Mexican restaurant, the *Siam Palace* Thai restaurant, a ribs-and-steaks joint and several other choices. The *Sandbar*, on the corner of Langtree and Eighth Aves, is a good bar with live entertainment, a pleasant courtyard and meals from $8 to $12.

The gambling clubs across the river in New South Wales provide cheap meals, free movies and free transport to entice the Victorians across.

Getting There & Away
Air Southern Australia Airlines (☎ (050) 22 2444) fly to Melbourne ($162), Adelaide

($115), Broken Hill ($98) and Renmark ($76). Kendell Airlines (☎ 13 1300) also fly to Melbourne ($162).

Bus V/Line has an overnight bus service between Melbourne and Mildura ($50.60); this runs every night except Saturday. There's also a daily Melbourne-Mildura bus service via Bendigo ($50.60). The bus fare to Ballarat or Bendigo from Mildura is $44. V/Line also has a three-times-weekly bus service connecting all the towns along the Murray River between Mildura and Albury, including Swan Hill ($27.20), Echuca ($34.80) and Albury ($50.70).

Greyhound Pioneer and McCafferty's both have daily services from Mildura to Adelaide ($35) and Sydney ($70), and Greyhound Pioneer also has a thrice-weekly service to Broken Hill ($35).

Getting Around
Mildura Bus Lines provide a regular bus service around town from Monday to Saturday. You can get a timetable from the tourist office. Hodgson Cycles at 106 Pine Ave rent bikes for $10 a day.

AROUND MILDURA
Leaving Mildura you don't have to travel very far before you realise just how desolate the country around here can be. The Sturt Highway runs west arrow-straight and deadly dull to South Australia, about 130 km away.

Going the other way into New South Wales you follow the Murray another 32 km to **Wentworth**, one of the oldest river towns where you can visit the Old Wentworth Gaol and the Morrison Collection.

A popular excursion from Mildura is to **Mungo National Park** in New South Wales to see the strange natural formation known as the Walls of China. See the New South Wales chapter for more details.

Red Cliffs, 17 km south, is the home of **Big Lizzie**, a huge steam-engined tractor – a taped commentary tells her story.

There are also some good wineries to visit

around Mildura, such as Lindemans, Mildara Blass and Trentham Estate.

SWAN HILL (population 9400)

One of the most interesting and popular towns along the entire length of the Murray, Swan Hill was named by the early explorer Major Thomas Mitchell, who spent a sleepless night here within earshot of a large contingent of noisy black swans.

Swan Hill is 340 km from Melbourne and has a tourist information centre (☎ (050) 32 3033) at 306 Campbell St.

Pioneer Settlement

The major attraction is the Swan Hill Pioneer Settlement. The town is a re-creation of a riverside port town of the paddle-steamer era, and you enter through the old PS *Gem* riverboat.

The settlement has everything from an old locomotive to a working blacksmith's shop and an old newspaper office, plus free rides on horse-drawn vehicles. It's definitely worth a visit and is open daily from 8.30 am to 5 pm; admission is $9 for adults and $5 for children.

Each night at dusk there is a 45-minute sound and light show for $6, during which you are driven around the settlement. The paddle-steamer *Pyap* makes short trips from the pioneer settlement for $6.

Other Attractions

The town's **Military Museum**, at 400 Campbell St, has a rather fascinating collection of war memorabilia – you can even have your photo taken in the uniform of your fetish! It's open daily and costs $6.50. The MV *Kookaburra* (☎ (050) 32 0003) offers one-hour cruises along the Murray for $7, and also has a luncheon cruise for $20.

The historic **Murray Downs** sheep station is a fine example of a working property from the earliest days of European settlement along the Murray. The station is in New South Wales, two km across the river, and is open daily (except Mondays) from 9 am to 4.30 pm. Informative tours cost $6.90.

Tyntynder, 17 km north of the town, also has a small museum of pioneering and Aboriginal relics and many reminders of the hardships of colonial life, like the wine cellar! Admission is $6.50, which includes a rather rushed tour, and the homestead is open daily from 9 am to 4.30 pm.

Places to Stay

The *Riverside Caravan Park* (☎ (050) 32 1494) is next to the river and the Pioneer Settlement. There are on-site vans for $26 and tent sites for $10.

The *White Swan Hotel* (☎ (050) 32 2761) at 182 Campbell St has clean singles/doubles for $20/30, or $30/35 with bathroom. The cheapest central motel is the *Mallee Rest* (☎ (050) 32 4541) at 369 Campbell St, which costs $38/45.

Places to Eat

Campbell St has plenty of possibilities. One of the better ones is *Teller's*, on the corner of McCrae St. They have good burgers and sandwiches, plus pastas and other main courses for around $8 to $10.

For a counter meal, try the *White Swan Hotel* at 182 Campbell St. The PS *Gem* at the Pioneer Settlement has a licensed restaurant upstairs which is open in the evenings only. Expect to pay around $25 per person.

Getting There & Away

V/Line has daily trains from Melbourne ($40.60) via Bendigo ($21.60), and three-times-weekly buses from Swan Hill to Mildura ($27.20), Echuca ($21.80) and Albury-Wodonga ($46).

KERANG (population 4000)

Kerang is on the Murray Valley Highway about 25 km south of the river, and is best known for the huge flocks of ibis which breed on the 50 or so lakes found in the area. Middle Lake, nine km north of Kerang, is the best place to see the colonies, and there's a small hide here. The town itself has a small historical museum, caravan parks and motels.

GUNBOWER STATE FOREST

The superb Gunbower State Forest, which is actually on a long 'island' enclosed by the Murray River and Gunbower Creek, features magnificent river red gums, abundant wildlife and plenty of walking tracks.

Cohuna, 32 km east of Kerang, is the main access point to the forest, although there are numerous marked tracks in from the highway. The graded tracks (maintained dirt tracks) within the forest are all on old river mud, which turns impossibly slippery after rain – conventional vehicles will find them impassable in the wet, and 4WD will be necessary.

Ganawarra Wetlander Cruises (☎ (054) 53 2680) offer a variety of day and night cruises through the creeks and wetlands (August to May only); their two-hour cruise costs $15.

The Department of Conservation & Natural Resources (☎ (054) 56 2699) in Cohuna sells detailed maps of the park for $3.75. In the park there are over 100 numbered tent sites with fireplaces and picnic tables (all marked on the park map) right on the edge of the river.

There are caravan parks, motels and hotels in Cohuna.

ECHUCA (population 9500)

Strategically sited where the Goulburn and Campaspe rivers join the Murray, Echuca, which is an Aboriginal word meaning 'the meeting of the waters', was founded in 1853 by the enterprising ex-convict Henry Hopwood.

In the riverboat days this was the busiest inland port in Australia and the centre of the thriving river trade. In the 1880s the famous red-gum wharf was more than a km long and there were stores and hotels all along the waterfront. At its peak there were more than 300 steamers operating out of the port here.

Today tourism is the main money-spinner, and the attractions are, not surprisingly, centred around the old port. In mid-October Echuca hosts its annual Rich River Festival which is 10 days of entertainment and games.

Information

The Echuca tourist information centre (☎ (054) 80 7555), by the old port at 2 Leslie St, opens daily from 9 am to 5 pm.

Port of Echuca

The old port area now has numerous attractions along the riverfront. You start at the old Star Hotel (where you buy the tickets) with various old photographs on display, and the 1858 Bridge Hotel nearby, now a licensed restaurant.

Across the road at the wharf, there's a vintage train collection, a cargo shed with audiovisual displays, and the historic paddle-steamers PS *Pevensey* (which featured as the *Philadelphia* in the miniseries *All the Rivers Run*) and PS *Adelaide*. The port is open daily from 9.15 am to 5 pm, and Passport tickets cost $5.50 ($2.50 for children).

Other Attractions

In the same street as the wharf are various other attractions, including the **Red Gum Works**, where wood is still worked using traditional machinery; **Sharp's Magic Movie House** ($7), which has old penny arcade equipment, displays relating to Australia's cinema industry, and films projected on authentic equipment; and a **Coach House & Carriage Collection** ($3).

The **World in Wax Museum**, at 630 High St, features 60 gruesome and famous characters and opens daily from 9 am to 5 pm ($5). The **historical museum** ($1) in Dickson St is housed in the old National-Trust-classified police station and lock-up building (open weekends from 1 to 4 pm). There's also the **National Holden Museum** ($4) in Warren St, and the **Joalah Fauna Park** ($4.50) 3 km south of the town.

Activities

A **paddle-steamer cruise** is almost obligatory, so head down to the river north of the old port and check out the sailing times. The steam-driven PS *Emmylou* does one-hour cruises ($9) and overnight trips (from $15 for dinner B&B). PS *Canberra* and PS *Pride* *f the Murray* also have one-hour cruises $8), and the MV *Maryann* and PS *Captain Proud* both do two-hour lunch cruises ($20) nd dinner cruises.

Echuca Canoe & Boat Hire (☎ (054) 80 5208) has boats, kayaks and canoes for hire, nd it also runs canoe trips on the Murray River. Each canoe takes two people plus camping gear and supplies, and included in he price is land transport upstream.

Places to Stay
The *Echuca Caravan Park* (☎ (054) 82 2157) in Crofton St is the most central of the own's caravan parks, and has on-site vans at $28 and tent sites at $10.

The YHA *Echuca Riverboat Hostel* ☎ (054) 80 6522), a comfortable old house at 103 Mitchell St, has 16 beds at $12 ($15 nonmembers) – it's about a ten-minute walk from the town centre, and there are bikes for hire.

Of the pubs, the *Pastoral Hotel* (☎ (054) 82 1812) near the railway station has rooms from $26/40, although the central *American Hotel* (☎ (054) 82 5044) at 239 Hare St is a better choice with rooms at $25/35.

There's a stack of motels, the cheapest of which is the *Highstreet Motel* (☎ (054) 82 1013) at 439 High St, costing $41/46. The National-Trust-classified *Steam Packet Motel* (☎ (054) 82 3411) on Murray Esplanade has rooms from $46/56. *Murray House B&B* (☎ (054) 82 4944) at 55 Francis St has good rooms at $65/88.

Three companies have houseboats for hire: Rich River Houseboats (☎ (054) 82 2994), Magic Murray Houseboats (☎ (054) 80 6099) and Dinki-Di Holiday Houseboats ☎ (054) 82 5223).

Places to Eat
The *Taras Hall Hotel*, near the hostel at 130 Pakenham St, has good bar meals from $3 to $8, and the *Shamrock Hotel* at 583 High St has an excellent bistro. At 433 High St, the *Tangled Garden* is a good cafe/restaurant with light lunches, snacks and more substantial evening meals, and a lovely courtyard.

For a lunch with a view, the *Riverside Restaurant* is right by the old port and has a very pleasant outdoor terrace with a good outlook over the river. There's also the rustic and stylish *Echuca Cellar Door* at Tisdall's Winery on Radcliffe St, with charcoal grills from $11 to $15 and wines by the glass.

Getting There & Away
V/Line (☎ (054) 82 3589) has a daily service between Melbourne and Echuca ($25), changing from train to bus at Bendigo. There are also V/Line buses to Kyabram ($3.60), Wagga ($38) and Deniliquin ($7.60).

Three times a week there are V/Line buses connecting Echuca with Albury-Wodonga ($29.10), and down the Murray to Swan Hill ($21.80) and Mildura ($34.80).

BARMAH STATE FOREST
This beautiful wetland area, 34 km northeast of Echuca, centres around the flood plains of the Murray and is forested with old river red gums. A central feature is the **Dharnya Centre** – a visitor centre run by the local Yorta Yorta Koori community, with displays on Aboriginal heritage and the state park. It is open daily from 10 am to 5 pm.

There are good walking tracks, and track notes are available from the Dharnya Centre. Canoeing is also popular through here, and the *Kingfisher* (☎ (054) 82 6788) cruise boat offers two-hour discovery tours for $15.

Camping is available at the Barmah Lakes camping area (☎ (058) 69 3302) and there's a bunk house at the centre, although this is mainly used by school groups.

YARRAWONGA (population 3600)
About 40 km east of Cobram on the banks of Lake Mulwala, Yarrawonga is known for its fine and sunny weather, for a host of aquatic activities including windsurfing, swimming, power boating and water-skiing, and as a retirement centre.

Lake Mulwala was formed by the completion in 1939 of Yarrawonga Weir, which in turn was part of the massive Lake Hume project (near Albury) to harness the waters of the Murray for irrigation.

Victoria's Gold Rush

In May 1851 E H Hargraves discovered gold near Bathurst in New South Wales. It was not the first time the mineral had been found in Australia, but the sensational accounts of the potential wealth of the find caused an unprecedented rush as thousands of people dropped everything to try their luck.

The news of the discovery reached Melbourne at the same time as the accounts of its influence on the people of New South Wales. Sydney had been virtually denuded of workers and the same misfortune soon threatened Melbourne. Victoria was still in the process of being established as a separate colony so the loss of its workforce to the northern gold fields would have been disastrous.

A public meeting was called by the young city's businessmen and a reward was offered to anyone who could find gold within 300 km of Melbourne. In less than a week gold was rediscovered in the Yarra but the find was soon eclipsed by a more significant discovery at Clunes. Prospectors began heading to central Victoria and over the next few months the rush north across the Murray was reversed as fresh gold finds and new rushes became an almost weekly occurrence in Victoria.

Gold was found in the Pyrenees, the Loddon and Avoca rivers, at Warrandyte and Bunninyong. Then in September 1851 the biggest gold discovery was made at Ballarat, followed by others at Bendigo, Mt Alexander, Beechworth, Walhalla, Omeo and in the hills and creeks of the Great Dividing Range.

By the end of 1851 about 250,000 ounces of gold had already been claimed. Farms and businesses lost their workforce and in many cases were abandoned altogether as employers had no choice but to follow their workers. Hopeful miners began arriving from England, Ireland, Europe, China and the failing gold fields of California. During 1852 about 1800 people a week arrived in Melbourne.

The government introduced a licence fee of 30 shillings a month for all prospectors, whether they found gold or not. This entitled the miners to a claim, limited to eight feet square, in which to dig for gold and provided the means to govern and enforce the laws that were improvised for the gold fields.

The administration of each field was headed by a chief commissioner whose deputies, the state troopers, were empowered to organise licence hunts and to fine or imprison any miner who failed to produce the permit. Though this was later to cause serious unrest on the diggings, for the most part it successfully averted the complete lawlessness that had characterised the California rush.

There is a tourist information centre (☎ (057) 44 1989) on the corner of Belmore St and Irvine Parade.

Ninety-minute cruises of Lake Mulwala are available on the *Lady Murray* or the *Paradise Queen*, and you can hire small canoes.

Yarrawonga was first settled by Elizabeth Hume, sister-in-law of the early explorer Hamilton Hume, in about 1842. Her interesting octagonal-shaped home, **Byramine Homestead**, is 15 km west of the town and is open daily ($4).

Places to Stay & Eat

The *Yarrawonga Caravan Park* (☎ (057) 44 3420) on the Murray River has sites and on-site vans. The *Terminus* (☎ (057) 44 3025) and *Criterion* (☎ (057) 44 3839), both on Belmore St, are the cheapest hotels in town. *Yarrawonga Cottages* (☎ (057) 48 4265), 11 km west, are good value from $65 a double.

The *Left Bank* cafe in Belmore St is good for breakfast, lunch or dinner, or there's the more sophisticated *Shag's Nest* next door, with main meals around $14.

Gold Country

Goldfields Tourist Route

If you have transport, the well-signposted Goldfields Tourist Route takes in all the major centres involved in the rush of last century, and makes for an interesting excursion for a couple of days.

Ballarat and Bendigo are the two major towns on the route, but, in a clockwise direc-

There were, however, the classic features that seem to accompany gold fever, like the backbreaking work, the unwholesome food and hard drinking, and the primitive dwellings. There was the amazing wealth that was to be the luck of some, the elusive dream of others; and for every story of success there were hundreds more of hardship, despair and death.

In his book *Australia Illustrated*, published in 1873, Edwin Carton Booth wrote of the gold fields in the early 1850s:

...it may be fairly questioned whether in any community in the world there ever existed more of intense suffering, unbridled wickedness and positive want, than in Victoria at (that) time...To look at the thousands of people who in those years crowded Melbourne, and that most miserable adjunct of Melbourne, Canvas Town, induced the belief that sheer and absolute unfitness for a useful life in the colonies...had been deemed the only qualification requisite to make a fortunate digger.

While the gold rush certainly had its tragic side and its share of rogues, including the notorious bushrangers who regularly attacked the gold shipments being escorted to Melbourne, it also had its heroes who eventually forced a change in the political fabric of the colony. (See the Rebellion section, under Ballarat.)

Above all, perhaps, the gold rush ushered in a fantastic era of growth and material prosperity for Victoria and opened up vast areas of country previously unexplored by Whites.

In the first 12 years of the rush, Australia's population increased from 400,000 to well over a million, and in Victoria alone it rose from 77,000 to 540,000. To cope with the moving population and the tonnes of gold and supplies the development of roads and railways was accelerated.

The mining companies which followed the independent diggers invested heavily in the region over the next couple of decades. The huge shanty towns of tents, bark huts, raucous bars and police camps were eventually replaced by the timber and stone buildings that were the foundation of many of Victoria's modern provincial cities, most notably Ballarat, Bendigo, Maldon and Castlemaine.

It was in the 1880s that the gold towns reached their heights of splendour, but although gold production was gradually to lose its importance after that time, the towns of the region by then had stable populations, and agriculture and other activities steadily supplanted gold as the economic mainstay.

Gold also made Melbourne Australia's largest city and financial centre, a position it held for nearly half a century. ■

on from Ballarat, it goes through Linton, Beaufort, Ararat, Stawell, Avoca, Maryborough, Dunolly, Tarnagulla, Bendigo, Maldon, Castlemaine, Daylesford and Creswick.

BALLARAT (population 65,000)
The area around present-day Ballarat, which is the second largest inland city in Victoria, was first settled in 1838. When gold was discovered at the small township of Buninyong in 1851 the rush was on and within a couple of years the town that grew out of the Ballarat diggings had a population of 40,000.

Ballarat's fabulously rich quartz reefs were worked by the larger mining companies until 1918. About 28% of the gold unearthed in Victoria came from Ballarat.

Today there are still many reminders of this gold-mining past, although Ballarat doesn't have quite the historical flavour of Bendigo. Ballarat is 112 km from Melbourne on the main Western Highway to Adelaide.

Information
The helpful Ballarat Visitor Information Centre (☎ (053) 32 2694) is in a small building at the corner of Albert and Sturt Sts. It is open Monday to Friday from 9 am to 5 pm and on weekends from 10 am to 4 pm. The RACV (☎ (053) 32 1946) has an office at 20 Doveton St North.

Sovereign Hill
Ballarat's major tourist attraction is Sovereign Hill, a fascinating re-creation of a gold-mining township of the 1860s. It is probably the best attraction of its type in the

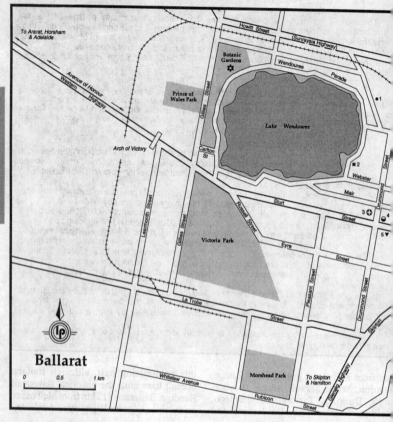

country, and has won numerous awards, so you should allow at least half a day for a visit.

The main street features a hotel, post office, blacksmith's shop, bakery and a Chinese joss house. It's a living history museum with people performing their chores dressed in costumes of the time. The site was actually mined back in the gold era so much of the equipment is authentic. There's a variety of above-ground and underground mining works, and you can pan for gold in the stream.

Sovereign Hill is open daily from 9.30 am to 5 pm and admission is $15.50 for adults

($11.50 for students, $8 for children, $42.50 for families), which includes entry into the nearby Gold Museum.

Also at Sovereign Hill is the new sound and light show Blood on the Southern Cross, a simulation of the Eureka Stockade battle. There are two shows nightly (except Sundays); tickets cost $17 ($8 for children) or $33/20 with dinner.

Gold Museum

Opposite Sovereign Hill, this museum has imaginative displays and samples from all the old mining areas in the Ballarat region.

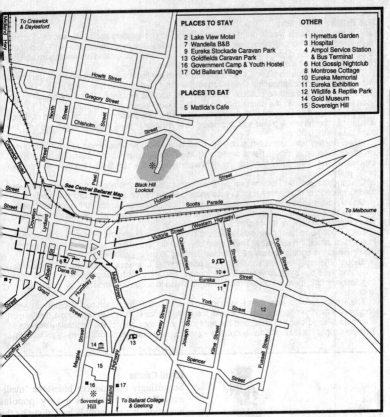

PLACES TO STAY
2 Lake View Motel
7 Wandella B&B
9 Eureka Stockade Caravan Park
13 Goldfields Caravan Park
16 Government Camp & Youth Hostel
17 Old Ballarat Village

PLACES TO EAT
5 Matilda's Cafe

OTHER
1 Hymettus Garden
3 Hospital
4 Ampol Service Station
   & Bus Terminal
6 Hot Gossip Nightclub
8 Montrose Cottage
10 Eureka Memorial
11 Eureka Exhibition
12 Wildlife & Reptile Park
14 Gold Museum
15 Sovereign Hill

t's open 9.30 am to 5.30 pm daily and is well worth the $4 admission.

Eureka Stockade Memorial & Exhibition
The site of the Eureka Stockade is now a park on the corner of Eureka and Stawell Sts. There's a monument to the miners and a coin-in-the-slot diorama gives you an action replay of the events and causes of this revolt against British rule.

Across the road, the Eureka Exhibition museum features a series of 'computer-controlled' scenes which depict various facets of the rebellion. It's open daily from 9 am to 5 pm but at $5 is overpriced (the diorama gives you much the same thing for 20c).

Botanic Gardens & Lake Wendouree
Ballarat's excellent 40-hectare Botanic Gardens are beside Lake Wendouree, which was used as the rowing course in the 1956 Olympics. A paddle-steamer makes tours of the lake on weekends. On weekends and holidays a tourist tramway operates around the gardens from a depot at the southern end.

VICTORIA

The Eureka Rebellion

Life on the gold fields was a great leveller, erasing all pre-existing social classes as doctors, merchants, ex-convicts and labourers toiled side by side in the mud. But as the easily-won gold began to run out, the diggers came to recognise the inequality that existed between them and the privileged few who held the land and government power.

The limited size of the claims, the inconvenience of the licence hunts coupled with the police brutality that often accompanied the searches, the very fact that while they were in effect paying taxes they were allowed no political representation, and the realisation that they could not get good farming land, fired the unrest that led to the Eureka Rebellion at Ballarat.

In September 1854 Governor Hotham ordered that the hated licence hunts be carried out twice a week. A month later a miner was murdered near a Ballarat hotel after an argument with the owner, James Bentley.

When Bentley was found not guilty, by a magistrate who just happened to be his business associate, a group of miners rioted over the injustice and burned his hotel down. Though Bentley was retried and found guilty, the rioting miners were also jailed, which fuelled the mounting distrust of the authorities.

Creating the Ballarat Reform League, the diggers called for the abolition of the licence fees, the introduction of the miners' right to vote and increased opportunities to purchase land.

On 29 November about 800 miners tossed their licences into a bonfire during a mass meeting and then set about building a stockade at Eureka where, led by an Irishman called Peter Lalor, they prepared to fight for their rights.

On 3 December, having already organised brutal licence hunts, the government ordered the troopers to attack the stockade. There were only 150 diggers within the makeshift barricades at the time and the fight lasted only 20 minutes, leaving 30 miners and five troopers dead.

Though the rebellion was short-lived the miners were ultimately successful in their protest. They had won the sympathy of most Victorians, and with the full support of the gold fields' population behind them the government deemed it wise to acquit the leaders of the charge of high treason.

The licence fee was abolished and replaced by a Miners' Right, which cost one pound a year. This gave them the right to search for gold; the right to fence in, cultivate and build a dwelling on a moderate-sized piece of land; and the right to vote for members of the Legislative Assembly. The rebel miner Peter Lalor actually became a member of parliament himself some years later. ∎

Lydiard St, Ballarat

Kryal Castle

Surprisingly this modern bluestone 'medieval English castle' is a very popular attraction. It's no doubt helped along by the daily hangings (volunteers called for) regular 'whipping of wenches' and a weekly jousting tournament – kids love it. The castle is eight km from Ballarat, towards Melbourne, and is open from 9.30 am to 5.30 pm daily; admission is $11 for adults ($8.50 for students).

Other Attractions

Lydiard St is one of the most impressive and intact streetscapes of Victorian architecture in the country, with many fine old buildings including Her Majesty's Theatre, the art gallery and Craig's Royal Hotel. The *Historic Lydiard Precinct* brochure is available from the info centre.

The **Ballarat Fine Art Gallery**, 40 Lydiard St North, is one of Australia's best provincial galleries and its Australian collection is particularly strong. You can also see the remnants of the original Eureka flag here. The gallery is open daily from 10.30 am to 4.30 pm; admission is $3 (students $1.50).

At 111 Eureka St, **Montrose Cottage & the Eureka Museum** is an early miner's cottage furnished in period style with a historical museum next door; it's open daily and costs $4.50.

There's also a **Wildlife & Reptile Park**, on the corner of York and Fussell Sts in East Ballarat, open daily from 9 am to 5.30 pm ($7). Other attractions include an **aviation museum** at the Ballarat Airport, and the lovely **Hymettus Garden** at 8 Cardigan St.

Festivals

In early March Ballarat holds its annual Begonia Festival which is 10 days of fun, flowers and the arts. Between August and November there's the Royal South Street Competitions, Australia's oldest eisteddfod.

Places to Stay

Convenient camping grounds include the

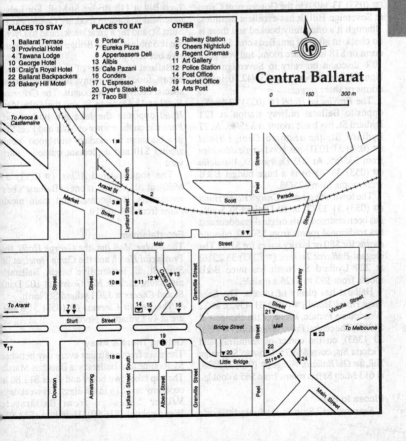

PLACES TO STAY
1 Ballarat Terrace
3 Provincial Hotel
4 Tawana Lodge
10 George Hotel
18 Craig's Royal Hotel
22 Ballarat Backpackers
23 Bakery Hill Motel

PLACES TO EAT
6 Porter's
7 Eureka Pizza
8 Apperteasers Deli
13 Alibis
15 Cafe Pazani
16 Conders
17 L'Espresso
20 Dyer's Steak Stable
21 Taco Bill

OTHER
2 Railway Station
5 Cheers Nightclub
9 Regent Cinemas
11 Art Gallery
12 Police Station
14 Post Office
19 Tourist Office
24 Arts Post

Central Ballarat

0   150   300 m

To Avoca & Castlemaine

To Ararat

To Melbourne

VICTORIA

Goldfields Caravan Park (☎ (053) 32 7888) at 108 Clayton St, 200 metres north of Sovereign Hill, with tent sites at $11 and on-site vans at $30; and the *Eureka Stockade Caravan Park* (☎ (053) 31 2281), right next to the Eureka Stockade Memorial, with tent sites at $7.50 and on-site vans for $20.

Ballarat Backpackers (☎ (053) 31 3132), 92 Little Bridge St, is upstairs in an old pub (the Bridge Mall Inn). Although pretty basic, it's central, has reasonably good facilities, and costs $13 in a two- or four-bunk room. Phone ahead and they'll pick you up from the bus or railway station.

There's an associate-YHA youth hostel (☎ (053) 33 3409) in the Government Camp at Sovereign Hill. It has excellent facilities, although it's often fully booked and there is no check-in after 10 pm. Beds cost $15 in a dorm or $18 in a share room, and you get a 10% discount on entry to Sovereign Hill. Non-YHA members pay $33/42.50 in the dorms or share rooms.

The *Provincial Hotel* (☎ (053) 32 1845), opposite Ballarat railway station at 121 Lydiard St, has basic rooms at $25/45. At 27 Lydiard St, the restored *George Hotel* (☎ (053) 31 1031) has good singles/doubles from $35/65. At 202 Dawson St, *Wandella* (☎ (053) 33 7046) is a huge budget B&B with rooms from $25/38.

The town's first hotel, *Craig's Royal Hotel* (☎ (053) 31 1377) at 10 Lydiard St South, has been restored to its original grandeur and has traditional rooms from $50/60, en-suite rooms for $80 or luxury suites for $120. The elegant *Ballarat Terrace* (☎ (053) 33 2216) at 229 Lydiard St North has three B&B rooms from $95 to $125 a double.

Ballarat has plenty of motels. The *Lake View Hotel/Motel* (☎ (053) 31 4592), at 22 Wendouree Parade, is one of the cheapest at $49/52. The central *Bakery Hill Motel* (☎ (053) 33 1363), on the corner of Humffray and Victoria Sts, costs $68/75. Close to Sovereign Hill, the *Old Ballarat Village* (☎ (053) 31 3588) at 613 Main St has rooms from $65 a double.

Places to Eat

L'Espresso, 417 Sturt St, is a funky little cafe with good food and coffee. They also sel (and play) a great selection of jazz, blues anc alternative music. *Apperteasers Deli*, 312 Sturt St, makes excellent sandwiches, salads and hot foods. Further up at 805 Sturt St *Matilda's Cafe*, run by a nondenominationa! Christian group, is a relaxed music venue with very cheap home-made meals anc snacks.

Eureka Pizza, at 316 Sturt St, is a casua! BYO with pastas, pizzas and other dishes from $7 to $10. At 102 Sturt St, *Cafe Pazan* is a stylish European bar/restaurant with meals in the $9 to $13 range.

For Mexican food and margaritas, head tc *Taco Bill* at 113 Bridge St Mall. For Lebanese/Middle Eastern food, try *Conders* at 12 Sturt St; and for a great steak, head to *Dyer's Steak Stable* in Little Bridge St – it's expensive but very good.

Ballarat has plenty of pubs with good. cheap food, and many places advertise special deals on blackboards. The *Criterion Hotel* at 18 Doveton St and the *Lake View Hotel* opposite the lake are both good. *Porter's*, on the corner of Mair and Peel Sts. is a bit more up-market, with good meals around $10 and a pleasant outdoor courtyard.

The sophisticated *Alibis* (☎ (053) 31 6680), at 10 Camp St, is one of Ballarat's best restaurants. It's licensed and main meals range from $15 to $19.

Entertainment

The *Bridge Mall Inn*, the *George Hotel*, the *Provincial Hotel*, and the *Camp Hotel*, at 36 Sturt St, all feature live bands. Ballarat's nightclubs include *Hot Gossip* at 102 Dana St and *Cheers* at 120 Lydiard St North.

The *Regent Cinemas* (☎ (053) 31 1399) are at 49 Lydiard St North.

Getting There & Away

There are frequent trains every day between Melbourne and Ballarat via Bacchus Marsh The trip takes two hours and costs $12.80 ir economy and $18 in 1st class. On weekdays V/Line buses go from Ballarat tc Warrnambool ($16.80), Hamilton ($22.80)

Mt Gambier ($40.60) and Bendigo ($16.80)
via Castlemaine ($12.80). There are also
regular buses to Geelong ($9) and trains to
Mildura ($44).

Greyhound Pioneer and McCafferty's
buses operate from the terminal at the Ampol
service station (☎ (053) 33 2706) on the
corner of Sturt and Ascot Sts.

Ballarat Coachlines (☎ (053) 33 4660)
have daily services to Melbourne Airport for
$20, leaving from the railway station.

Getting Around
The Begonia City Explorer (☎ (053) 39
4922) operates a one-hour guided sightseeing tour (adults $7, children $4) as well as an
all-day transfer service between the local
attractions ($10/5). The bus leaves from Sov-
ereign Hill, but will also pick you up from
wherever you're staying.

Timetables for the local Ballarat Transit
bus service are available from the railway
station or the tourist office. The two main
terminals are in Curtis St and Little Bridge
St, on either side of the Bridge St Mall. Take
bus No 9 to Sovereign Hill from the northern
side of Sturt St, between Armstrong and
Lydiard Sts. For the Botanic Gardens and
Lake Wendouree, catch bus No 15 from
Little Bridge St. Bus No 2 takes you to the
railway station.

CLUNES (population 840)
Clunes was the site of one of Victoria's very
first gold discoveries in June 1851. Although
other finds soon diverted interest, there are
still many fine buildings as reminders of the
former wealth of this charming little town.
The town has a small museum housed in a
double-storey bluestone building, but it is open
only on Saturdays and school holidays ($2).

The small hills around Clunes are extinct
volcanoes. Nearby **Mt Beckworth** is noted
for its orchids and bird life; you can visit the
old gold diggings of **Jerusalem** and **Ullina**;
and at **Smeaton**, between Clunes and
Daylesford, an impressive bluestone water-
driven mill has been restored (open Sunday
afternoons only).

Places to Stay
The *Clunes Caravan Park* (☎ (053) 45 3278)
on Purcell St has tent sites and on-site vans,
or the excellent *Keebles of Clunes* (☎ (053)
45 3220) guesthouse has B&B for $100 a
double.

MARYBOROUGH (population 7600)
The district around Charlotte Plains was
already an established sheep run, owned by
the Simson brothers, when gold was discovered at White Hills and Four Mile Flat in
1854. A police camp established at the diggings was named Maryborough and by 1854
the population had swelled to over 40,000.
Gold mining ceased to be economical in
1918 but Maryborough by then had a strong
manufacturing base and is still a busy town
today.

Its Victorian buildings include a magnificent railway station. In fact a century ago
Mark Twain described Maryborough as 'a
railway station with a town attached'.

Maryborough's Highland Gathering has
been held every year on New Year's Day
since 1857 and the annual 16-day Golden
Wattle Festival is celebrated in September
with literary events, music, the national
gumleaf-blowing and bird-call championships, and street parades.

There's a tourist information centre
(☎ (054) 61 2643) on the corner of Tuaggra
and Alma Sts.

Places to Stay & Eat
Apart from several motels, hotels and guesthouses there's the *Maryborough Caravan
Park* (☎ (054) 61 2864), Holyrood St, which
has tent sites for $9 and on-site vans for $20.

Twains, on the platform of the old railway
station, is an interesting restaurant with
meals under $10 and live (or other) entertain-
ment.

MOLIAGUL, TARNAGULLA & DUNOLLY
The rich alluvial gold fields of the Golden
Triangle produced more gold nuggets than
any other area in the country, including the
world's largest gold nugget, the 65-kg

Welcome Stranger. The Stranger was unearthed in Moliagul in 1869, then taken into Dunolly where it was cut into pieces because it was too big to fit on the scales!

At the height of the gold rush there were some 30,000 diggers fossicking in the area. Nowadays things are much quieter: Moliagul is a tiny, tumbledown village with a memorial commemorating the discovery of the Welcome Stranger. Tarnagulla is well worth a visit, with many historic houses and churches, a gemstone and minerals museum and the ghost town of **Wanyarra** nearby. At Dunolly, the largest of the three towns, there's the interesting **Goldfields Historical Arts Museum**, which opens on Sundays and public holidays from 1.30 to 5 pm.

Places to Stay

The *Progress Caravan Park* (☎ (054) 68 1262) on the corner of Thompson and Desmond Sts in Dunolly has tent sites and on-site vans. The *Tarnagulla B&B* (☎ (054) 38 7366), a restored bank building on Victoria St, has double rooms for $80.

DAYLESFORD (population 2500)

Originally called Wombat, after the pastoral run where gold was first discovered, Daylesford is a picturesque town set amongst lakes, hills and forests. It boasts more of that sturdy Victorian and Edwardian architecture and, along with nearby Hepburn Springs, is having a revival as the 'spa centre of Victoria'.

The well-preserved and restored buildings show the prosperity that visited this town during the gold rush as well as the lasting influence of the many Swiss-Italian miners who expertly worked the tunnel mines in the surrounding hills.

The health-giving properties of the town's mineral springs were known before gold was discovered in the area. By the 1870s Daylesford was a popular health resort, attracting droves of fashionable Melburnians. It was claimed that the waters, which were bottled and sold, could cure any complaint, and the spas and relaxed scenic environment of the town could rejuvenate even the most stressed turn-of-the-century city-dweller.

The current trend towards healthy lifestyles has prompted a revival of interest in Daylesford as a health resort, and the bath houses and charming guesthouses are again being used. There's a tourist information desk (☎ (053) 48 3707) in a shop at 49 Vincent St.

Things to See

There are some great **walking trails** around here; the information centre has maps. The huge 19th-century **Convent Gallery** has been brilliantly converted into an arts and crafts gallery and cafe; it's in Daly St and entry costs $2.

The excellent **Historical Museum** is worth visiting, as are the lovely **Wombat Hill Botanic Gardens. Lake Daylesford**, a popular fishing and picnic area, is close to the centre of town, and boats and kayaks are available for hire. There is also a **Sunday market** at Daylesford railway station.

The **Bin Billa Winery** is four km from Daylesford on the Ballan road. The volcanic crater of **Mt Franklin**, 10 km north, is visible from the lookout tower in the botanic gardens and has a beautiful camping and picnic area.

Places to Stay & Eat

The *Jubilee Lake Caravan Park* (☎ (053) 48 2186), three km south-east, has tent sites for $8 and on-site vans at $30.

B&Bs include *Ambleside B&B* (☎ (053) 48 2691) at 15 Leggatt St, costing $75 a double ($95 weekends); and *Hillsyde Cottage* (☎ (053) 48 1056) at 26 Millar St from $70 a double. *Lavender Cottage* (☎ (053) 48 1288), a self-contained cottage at 33 Vincent St North, sleeps up to four and costs from $75. The *Central Springs Inn* (☎ (053) 48 3134) on Wills Square has motel units from $50/65.

On Vincent St, *Daylesford Healthfood* has good pastries, pies and sandwiches, or there's *Sweet Decadence* next door, serving light meals, afternoon teas and home-made chocolates.

On Albert St, *David's Kitchen* is famous or its home-made muffins and shortcakes, while across the road at No 29, the laid-back *Harvest Cafe* has good lunches around \$7.50 and dinners from \$10 to \$13.

Daylesford's best restaurant is the wonderful *Lake House* (☎ (053) 48 3329); it's expensive but worth it!

Getting There & Away

There's a daily bus/train service to and from Melbourne (\$11.40) via Woodend (\$3.60). There are also V/Line buses every weekday to Ballarat (\$7.50), Castlemaine (\$3.60) and Bendigo (\$7.50).

HEPBURN SPRINGS (population 800)

At Hepburn Springs, a delightful little town just north of Daylesford, Hepburn's Mineral Springs Reserve has four main springs, of magnesium, iron, lime and sulphur, and the bubbling waters contain at least 10 different minerals.

The spa complex is a great relaxation and rejuvenation centre, and there's a good range of restored guesthouses and B&Bs to stay in although none are particularly cheap!).

Spa Complex

The refurbished Hepburn Springs Mineral Spa complex (☎ (053) 48 2034) boasts excellent facilities and is open weekdays from 10 am to 8 pm and weekends from 9 am to 8 pm. Services offered include an indoor pool and spa (\$7); aero spas with essential oils \$15/25 for singles/doubles); massage (\$30 for half an hour); floatation tanks (\$35 an hour); and sauna-spa couches (\$5).

Places to Stay & Eat

The *Springs Caravan Park* (☎ (053) 48 161), close to the Springs Reserve on Forest Ave, has camp sites for \$8 and a few on-site vans for \$25. The self-contained *Camp Hill Cottages* (☎ (053) 48 2111) are also close to the springs and cost from \$60. *Liberty House* (☎ (053) 48 2809), a cosy place right opposite the springs, has B&B from \$40/80.

The friendly *Mooltan Guest House* (☎ (053)

48 3555) overlooks the spa complex and costs \$50/75 – the breakfast is wonderful. The evocative *Villa Parma* (☎ (053) 48 3512) on Main Rd is a rambling Tuscan-style pensione, with B&B from \$60/100.

The *Cosy Corner Cafe* and the *Springs Hotel* both have good food.

Getting There & Away

A shuttle bus runs back and forth between Daylesford and Hepburn Springs eight times a day (weekdays only).

CASTLEMAINE (population 6800)

Settlement of this district dates back to the 1830s when most of the land was taken up for farming. The discovery of gold at Specimen Gully in 1851, however, radically altered the pastoral landscape as 30,000 diggers worked a number of gold fields known, collectively, as the Mt Alexander diggings.

The township that grew up around the Government Camp, at the junction of Barkers and Forest creeks, was named Castlemaine in 1853 and soon became the thriving marketplace for all the gold fields of central Victoria.

Castlemaine's importance was not to last, however, as the district did not have the rich quartz reefs that were found in Bendigo and Ballarat. The centre of the town has been virtually unaltered since the 1860s when the population began to decline as the surface gold was exhausted.

These days Castlemaine is a charming town where the legacy of its rapid rise to prosperity lies in the splendid architecture of its public buildings and private residences and in the design of its streets and many gardens.

The Castlemaine State Festival, one of Victoria's leading celebrations of the arts, is held every second October (even years) and features a host of home-grown and international music, theatre and art.

Information

There is a tourist office (☎ (054) 73 2222) in

a rotunda on Duke St (the Pyrenees Highway), opposite the Castle Motel. It's open on weekends and school and public holidays from 10 am to 4 pm.

Buda Historic Home & Gardens

Originally built by a retired Indian Army officer in 1857, this is a superb example of Victorian-era colonial architecture. The house and magnificent gardens were extended in the 1890s by a Hungarian gold and silversmith, Ernest Leviny. The house and gardens are now open to the public and provide an insight into the town's refined and gracious past. Buda is on the corner of Urquhart and Hunter Sts, and is open from 10 am to 5 pm daily; admission is $4.

Market Museum

Castlemaine's original market building, on Mostyn St, is now a museum with audiovisual displays and artefacts depicting the colourful history of the gold fields. It is open daily from 10 am to 5 pm.

Castlemaine Art Gallery

The Castlemaine Art Gallery, Lyttleton St, has an excellent collection of colonial and contemporary art, as well as a historical museum featuring photographs, relics and documents. It's open daily from 10 am to 5 pm; admission is $2.

Other Attractions

The beautiful **Botanic Gardens** on Walker St were designed in the 1860s by the director of Melbourne's Botanic Gardens, Baron von Mueller, and it's well worth taking the time for a picnic by the lake or just a stroll amongst the 'Significant Trees' registered by the National Trust.

Other places of interest include the **Camp Reserve**, the site of the original Government Camp of the gold rush; the **Burke & Wills Monument**, if you're into statues; a host of **gold-rush buildings**, such as the town hall, the sandstone jail, several hotels and the courthouse; and the **Kaweka Wildflower Reserve**.

Places to Stay

The *Botanic Gardens Caravan Park* (☎ (054) 72 1125), beside the gardens, has tent site for $9 and on-site vans for $26.

The *Cumberland Hotel* (☎ (054) 72 1052), on Barker St, has basic pub rooms fo $25/35. The *Midland Private Hotel* (☎ (054) 72 1085), opposite the railway station at ? Templeton St, is a fascinating blend o Victorian and Edwardian architecture, an has simple B&B rooms upstairs at $35 pe person. The *Colonial Motel* (☎ (054) 72 4000) at 252 Barker St has rooms from $58/68.

Ellimatta (☎ (054) 72 4454), a histori guesthouse and restaurant at 233 Barker St charges $60/70 for B&B. Behind th Castlemaine Bookshop at 242 Barker St, th charming and self-contained *Bookshop Cottage* (☎ (054) 72 1557) costs $70 double with breakfast.

Places to Eat

Bing's Cafe at 71 Mostyn St has a goo selection of interesting home-made meal and snacks, and *Tog's Place* at 58 Lyttleton St is another very good cafe. The *Stable. Tearooms*, Main Rd, Campbell's Creel (three km south of Castlemaine), is a grea setting for Devonshire teas.

The restaurant at *Ellimatta* has excellen food, as does the *Globe Garden* at 81 Fores St, with main meals from $11 to $19.

Entertainment

The historic *Theatre Royal* (☎ (054) 72 1196), at 30 Hargreaves St, is now a cinema licensed restaurant, nightclub, cabaret ... it' worth ringing to find out what's on.

Getting There & Away

There are daily trains between Castlemain and Melbourne ($14.20), and these als operate to Bendigo ($3.60) and Swan Hi ($25).

V/Line buses go through Castlemaine t Daylesford ($3.60), Ballarat ($12.80) Geelong ($21.60) and Maldon ($2.60).

VICTORIA

AROUND CASTLEMAINE

The area around Castlemaine holds enough attractions – most of them related to the gold fields – to keep you going for a couple of days. You can visit the remains of **Garfield's Water Wheel** and a **dingo farm**, both near Chewton; the **Heron's Reef Gold Diggings** at Fryerstown; the sombre **Pennyweight Children's Cemetery**, east of Castlemaine; the **Vaughan Springs** mineral springs and swimming hole; and the **Hilltop Cottage Garden** and **Tara Garden**, both at Guildford.

MALDON (population 1200)

The current population of Maldon is a scant reminder of the 20,000 who used to work the local gold fields but the whole town is a well-preserved relic of the era with many fine buildings constructed from local stone.

In 1966 the National Trust named Maldon the country's first 'notable town', an honour bestowed only on towns where the historic architecture was intact and valuable. Special planning regulations were introduced to preserve the town for posterity. It's a very popular tourist destination and so, as you might expect, has its share of trendy (and overpriced) antique shops. Its Spring Folk Festival takes place every November.

The tourist information centre (☎ (054) 75 2569) on High St opens daily.

Things to See

The interesting buildings around town and along the verandahed main street include **Dabb's General Store** (now the supermarket); the **Maldon**, **Kangaroo** and **Grand** hotels; the **Eaglehawk Gully Restaurant**; the 24-metre-high **Beehive Chimney**; and the **North British Mine & Kilns**. The tourist office has a brochure of a self-guided historical town walk.

Carman's Tunnel Goldmine is two km south of town, and the 570-metre-long tunnel was excavated in the 1880s. Candlelight tours through the mine take place on weekends and school and public holidays, from 1.30 to 4 pm; they cost $2.

On Sundays rail enthusiasts may like to ride the **steam train** which makes trips along the old line which used to connect Maldon with Castlemaine. Tickets cost $7 ($5 for students). The trains do not operate on days of total fire ban.

The **historical museum** on High St opens daily from 1.30 to 4 pm. **Porcupine Township**, a re-creation of an 1850s gold-rush town with timber-slab, mud-brick, tin and stone buildings, is open daily from 10 am to 5 pm and costs $6.

There are some good bushwalks around the town, and amateur gold hunters still scour the area with some success. From the top of nearby **Anzac Hill** there are excellent views over the town, and these are even better from the higher **Mt Tarrengower**.

Places to Stay

The *Maldon Caravan Park* (☎ (054) 75 2344), Hospital St, has tent sites at $10 and on-site vans from $29.

Most of the other accommodation is in up-market B&B-type places. The historic *Eaglehawk Restaurant & Accommodation* (☎ (054) 75 2750) at 35 Reef St has stylish B&B units for $75 a double ($90 on weekends). The *Derby Hill Lodge* (☎ (054) 75 2033), Phoenix St, has motel-style rooms at $30/50. Other accommodation possibilities include *Calder House* (☎ (054) 75 2912) at 44 High St, with B&B for $60 a double ($90 on weekends); and *Spring Cottage* (☎ (054) 46 9941), a fully self-contained miner's cottage costing $85 a double.

Places to Eat

The *Kangaroo Hotel* on High St has good meals from $10 to $14. For afternoon tea there's the *Cumquat Tree Tearooms*, while *McArthur's Restaurant* has affordable meals ranging from sandwiches to roasts.

For something more up-market, head for the excellent *Eaglehawk Restaurant & Accommodation*, which specialises in regional cuisine. *Ruby's at Calder House* is also good.

Getting There & Away

V/Line has a twice-daily bus service on

weekdays between Castlemaine and Maldon ($2.60), but there's nothing on weekends.

BENDIGO (population 70,000)

The solid, imposing and at times extravagant Victorian-era architecture of Bendigo is a testimony to the fact that this was one of Australia's richest gold-mining towns.

In the 1850s thousands upon thousands of diggers converged on the fantastically rich Bendigo Diggings, which covered more than 300 sq km, to claim the easily obtained surface gold. As this began to run out and diggers were no longer tripping over nuggets, they turned their pans and cradles to Bendigo Creek and other waterways around Sandhurst (as Bendigo was then known) in their quest for alluvial gold.

The arrival of thousands of Chinese miners caused a great deal of racial tension at the time, and had a lasting effect on the town.

By the 1860s the easily won ore was running out and the scene changed again as reef mining began in earnest. Independent miners were soon outclassed by the large and powerful mining companies, with their heavy machinery for digging and crushing, who poured money into the town as they extracted enormous wealth from their network of deep mine shafts. The last of these was worked until the 1950s.

Bendigo today is the second largest city in country Victoria, a busy market town with a number of local industries that makes the most of its gold-mining past to promote tourism. Its annual Easter Fair, first held in 1871 to aid local charities, features a procession with a Chinese dragon, a lantern parade, a jazz night and other entertainment.

Information

The Bendigo Regional Tourist Information Centre (☎ (054) 41 5244), on the Calder Highway four km south of the centre, is open Monday to Friday from 9 am to 5 pm and on weekends from 10 am to 4 pm.

The RACV (☎ (054) 43 9622) has an office at 112 Mitchell St, while the Department of Conservation & Natural Resources (☎ (054) 44 6666) is on the corner of Mundy and Hargreaves Sts.

The La Trobe Bookshop, at 271 Lyttleton Terrace, and Collins Booksellers, at 302 Hargreaves Mall, both have a good selection of books, and there's a book exchange in High St.

Central Deborah Mine

This 500-metre-deep mine, worked on 17 levels, became operational in the 1940s, and was connected to the two other shafts which date back to the early days of the gold fields. About 1000 kg of gold was removed before it closed in 1954 and it has now been restored and developed as a museum, with lots of interesting exhibits and photographs.

The mine is on Violet St – you can't miss it – and is open from 9 am to 5 pm daily. A surface tour costs $5.50 ($4.50 for students), an underground tour is $11 ($9.50), and a combined ticket for both the surface and underground tours and the 'talking tram' (see below) costs $18 ($16).

Chinese Joss House

This Chinese joss house on Finn St in North Bendigo is built of timber and hand-made bricks. Exhibits include embroidered and stone-rub banners, figures representing the 12 years of the Chinese solar cycle, commemorative tablets to the deceased, paintings and Chinese lanterns. It's open from 10 am to 5 pm daily and admission is $3 ($2 for students).

There's a Chinese section in the White Hills Cemetery on Killian St and also a prayer oven where paper money, and other goodies which you can't take with you, were burnt.

Bendigo Talking Tram

A vintage tram makes a regular tourist run from the Central Deborah Mine, through the centre of the city and out to the tramways museum (free if you have a tram ticket) and the joss house, with a commentary along the way. It departs daily at 9.30 and 11 am and 12.30, 2 and 3.30 pm from the Central

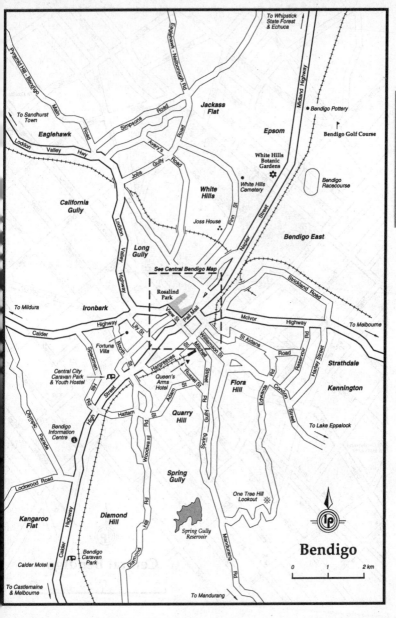

VICTORIA

Bendigo

0   1   2 km

VICTORIA

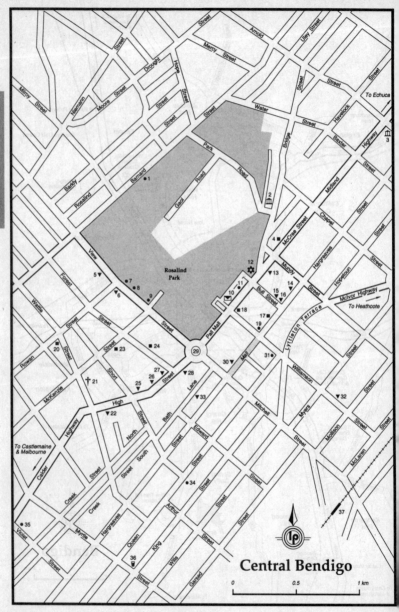

Rosalind
Park

To Echuca

To Heathcote

To Castlemaine
& Melbourne

Central Bendigo

0   0.5   1 km

PLACES TO STAY					
		15	Bar Black Sheep	7	Dudley House
		16	Metropolitan Hotel	8	Capitol Theatre
4	Universal Bar &	22	Dianne's Deli	9	Art Gallery
	Hotel	25	Rasoyee	10	Post Office
17	Old Crown Hotel	26	Mexican Kitchen	11	Law Courts Building
18	Shamrock Hotel	27	Jo Joe's	12	Conservatory
20	Marlborough House	28	City Family Hotel	19	Hot Gossip Nightclub
23	Villa Heidi	30	Lunchbox	21	Sacred Heart
24	City Centre Motel	32	Jolly Puddler		Cathedral
		33	Green Olive Deli	29	Alexandra Fountain
PLACES TO EAT				31	Abbey Road
		OTHER			Nightclub
5	Turkish Kitchen			34	Golden Twin Cinemas
6	Rifle Brigade	1	Aquatic Centre	35	Central Deborah Mine
	Pub-Brewery	2	Golden Dragon	36	Golden Vine Hotel
13	Clogs		Museum	37	Railway Station
14	House of Khong	3	Tram Museum		

VICTORIA

Deborah Mine, or five minutes later from the fountain. During holiday periods it runs more frequently; the fare is $6 ($5.50 for students).

Sacred Heart Cathedral

Construction of the massive Sacred Heart Cathedral, the largest Gothic-style building in Victoria outside Melbourne, was begun last century and completed in 1977. Angels poke out from the timber arches, there's a beautifully carved bishop's chair, and the stained-glass windows are lovely. The pews are magnificent Australian blackwood and the marble is Italian.

Bendigo Art Gallery

The Bendigo Art Gallery, 42 View St, was built in the 1880s and has an outstanding collection of Australian colonial and contemporary paintings and 19th century European art. It's open Monday to Friday from 10 am to 5 pm and on weekends from 2 to 5 pm; admission is $2.

The Shamrock Hotel

The third hotel of the name on the same site, this magnificent incarnation was built in 1897. It's a fully restored and very fine example of the hotel architecture of the period. Its size gives some indication of how prosperous the town was in the gold-mining era when, so the story goes, the floors were

regularly washed down to collect the gold dust brought in on miners' boots.

The Shamrock is on the corner of Pall Mall and Williamson St and is a good place for a drink in the bar or on the upstairs balcony; there are also gambling facilities in the hotel.

Golden Dragon Museum

On Bridge St, the Golden Dragon Museum houses Loong and Sun Loong, the Chinese dragons which are the centrepieces of the annual Easter Fair parade, plus a collection of Chinese heritage items and costumes. It is open daily from 9.30 am to 5 pm; entry is $5.

Other Attractions

There are some fine old buildings around Pall Mall and McCrae St, including the extremely elaborate **post office** and **law courts**, the **Alexandra Fountain** at Charing Cross, the **war memorial** and the **town hall** at the end of Bull St.

Dudley House, at 60 View St, is classified by the National Trust. It's a fine old residence with beautiful gardens and is open weekends and during school holidays from 2 to 5 pm. On Chum St the stately mansion **Fortuna Villa**, with its lake and Italian fountain, was once owned by George Lansell, the 'Quartz King'. It's now the Army Survey Regiment Headquarters and is only open to the public on Sundays for a three-hour tour ($3) at 1 pm.

North of Bendigo, Eaglehawk also has some impressive historic buildings. The *Eaglehawk Heritage Trail* brochure, available from the information office, guides you around many of them.

Rosalind Park, just north of Pall Mall, features open lawns and picnic tables, a lookout tower with sensational views, a fernery and the lovely **Conservatory Gardens**.

Perhaps Bendigo's most curious attraction is the annual 'Swap Meet', held in November. It draws thousands of enthusiasts from all over the country in search of that elusive vintage-car spare part.

Organised Tours
Barry Maggs runs Goldseeker Tours (☎ (054) 49 6346), taking people gold hunting in the Golden Triangle with metal detectors.

Places to Stay
There isn't a great range of budget accommodation in Bendigo. The *Central City Caravan Park* (☎ (054) 43 6937), at 362 High St, has an associate-YHA hostel with beds at $12 ($15 for nonmembers). It also has tent sites from $10 and on-site vans from $26, but it's about 2.5 km south of the town centre – you can get there on a Kangaroo Flat bus from Hargreaves St. There's also the *Bendigo Caravan Park* (☎ (054) 47 7733), 7 km south on the Calder Highway, with tent sites from $10 and on-site vans from $35.

The *Old Crown Hotel* (☎ (054) 41 6888) at 238 Hargreaves St has rooms with shared bathrooms at $25/40 for singles/doubles, which includes breakfast. The *Universal Bar & Hotel* (☎ (054) 43 7588), at 131 McCrae St, is another central pub with rooms upstairs at similar prices. Close to the railway station at 150 Williamson St, the *Brougham Arms Hotel* (☎ (054) 42 3555) has motel rooms at $40/50.

There are plenty of motels in town. Some of the cheaper places to consider include the *City Centre Motel* (☎ (054) 43 2077) at 26 Forest St, with rooms at $39/46; the *Oval Motel* (☎ (054) 43 7211) at 194 Barnard St at $40/46; and, out on the Calder Highway 7 km south of town, the *Calder Motel* (☎ (054) 47 7411) has rooms for $36/44.

The famous *Shamrock Hotel* (☎ (054) 43 0333) is a nice place for a splurge. Traditional rooms with shared bathrooms are $50 a double ($80 with en-suite) and the two-room suites start at $125. *Villa Heidi* (☎ (054) 41 4265), a small B&B at 35 McKenzie St, has good rooms at $60 a double. Also very good is the historic and elegant *Marlborough House* (☎ (054) 41 4142) on the corner of Rowan and Wattle Sts, with B&B from $55/90 for rooms with private bathrooms. There are quite a few other B&Bs in and around Bendigo – the information centre can make bookings.

Places to Eat
Many of the city's pubs have good meals at affordable prices. The *Rifle Brigade Pub-Brewery* at 137 View St is a shade more up-market than your average pub, and has bar meals for around $7 and a good bistro with a courtyard. They also brew their own beers, including Koala, Rifle Lager and Bendigo Best Bitter. Other good-food pubs include the *Metropolitan Hotel*, on the corner of Bull and Hargreaves St, the *City Family Hotel*, at 41 High St and the *Shamrock Hotel*. Try the *Queen's Arms* at 25 Russell St for cheap bar meals.

For lunch-time snacks, you can't go past *Gillies*, in the Hargreaves St Mall, whose pies are regarded, by connoisseurs, as amongst the best in Australia. A Bendigo institution, you queue at the little window, order one of their five or so varieties, then sit in the mall to eat it.

Bendigo has some good cafes including *Munchy's* and the *Lunchbox*, both in the mall; *Dianne's Deli*, opposite the cathedral in High St; or the *Green Olive Deli* in Bath Lane, which has great rolls, salads and a variety of patés and cheeses.

The licensed *Bar Black Sheep* on Bull St is an interesting bar/bistro in an old converted garage, with great grills and snacks – try the chicken-fillet burger at $7. Around the corner at 107 Pall Mall, *Clogs* is a stylish licensed eatery with pizzas, pastas and a wide range of other meals, and stays open until 1 am during the week and until 4 am on weekends. *Jo Joe's*, near the corner of High and Forest Sts, is another good pizza/pasta place.

The *Mexican Kitchen* at 28 High St, the *Turkish Kitchen* at 159 View St, and the *Rasoyee* Indian restaurant at 40 High St, all have filling main courses for around $10 or less and also do takeaways. The *House of Khong*, a Chinese and Siamese restaurant at 200 Hargreaves St, has a lunch smorgasbord for $8 and good evening meals; on Friday and Saturday nights it becomes a karaoke venue.

For a splurge, the *Jolly Puddler* at 101 William St is an excellent licensed restaurant with main meals from $14 to $18.

Entertainment

For live pub music one of the best places is the *Golden Vine Hotel* on the corner of King and Myrtle Sts. The *Universal Bar*, at 131 McCrae St, also has live bands, plus pool tables, a movie-theme room and a beach volleyball court.

Bendigo's nightclubs include *Hot Gossip*, on the corner of Williamson and Hargreaves Sts, and *Abbey Road* on the corner of Williamson and Queen Sts.

The *Golden Twin Cinemas* (☎ (054) 42 1666) are at 107 Queen St.

Getting There & Away

Trains from Melbourne to Bendigo take about two hours and cost $19.40 in economy, $27.20 in 1st class. The first train departs from Melbourne at 8.35 am and there are about half a dozen services a day on weekdays, fewer on weekends. One of these trains continues to Swan Hill ($21.60).

There's also a weekday V/Line bus service between Bendigo and Castlemaine ($3.60), Ballarat ($16.80) and Geelong ($27.20). Other destinations served by V/Line buses include Swan Hill ($21.60), Mildura ($44) and Echuca ($5.20).

Getting Around

Bendigo and its surrounding area is well served by public buses. Check the route map at the bus stop on Mitchell St, at the end of the mall, or pick up timetables and route maps from the tourist office or railway station. Tickets cost $1.20 and are valid for two hours.

AROUND BENDIGO
Sandhurst Town

Sandhurst Town is a re-created gold town at Myers Flats, 10 km along the Loddon Valley Highway, north-west of Bendigo. It includes a working 24-inch-gauge railway line, a eucalyptus distillery, colonial stores, and the chance to pan for gold. The town is open daily (except Fridays) from 10 am to 5 pm and admission is $9.50 ($7.50 students).

Bendigo Pottery

Bendigo Pottery, the oldest pottery works in Australia, is on the Calder Highway at Epsom, 12 km north of Bendigo. As well as roofing tiles and the like, which keep the works financial, the historic kilns are still used to produce fine pottery. There are guided tours of the works and you can buy finished pieces. It also houses the **Central Victorian Motor Museum**, which will be of interest to car buffs. It is open daily from 9 am to 5 pm. There's also a large undercover Sunday market at Epsom which attracts big crowds.

Whipstick State Forest

The 2300-hectare Whipstick State Forest, north of Bendigo, is a state park which was established to conserve the distinctive Whipstick mallee vegetation. There are picnic areas sited on old eucalyptus distilleries, and walking tracks. Holders of Miners' Rights can fossick for gold in designated areas. **Hartland's Eucalyptus Oil Factory** close to the Whipstick Forest was established in 1890 and the production process can be inspected on Sundays ($4).

Wineries

There are also several good wineries in the district which are open for tastings, and these include Château Leamon (10 km south of

Bendigo), Balgownie (eight km west) and Château Doré (eight km south-west).

Lake Eppalock & Heathcote

The large Lake Eppalock reservoir, about 30 km south-east of Bendigo, provides the town's water supply and is popular for all sorts of water sports.

There are some fine lookouts in the vicinity of Heathcote, a quiet little highway town with a gold-mining past and a wine-making present. The town, 47 km from Bendigo, is surrounded by some excellent wineries including Jasper Hill, McIvor Creek, Zuber, Heathcote Winery and Huntleigh.

ALONG THE CALDER HIGHWAY

From Bendigo it's 45 km along the Calder to **Inglewood**, another town with its roots firmly planted in the gold fields. Eucalyptus oil has been distilled here for over 100 years. There's an old distillery in town and many eucalyptus farms in the area.

West of Inglewood are the **Melville Caves**, named after the gentleman bushranger Captain Melville who used to hide out there. In 1980 the 27-kg Hand of Faith gold nugget was unearthed in the tiny town of **Kingower**, 11 km west of Inglewood. Kingower also has the Blanche Barkly and Passing Clouds wineries, both well worth a visit. *Passing Clouds* (☎ (054) 38 8287) has excellent B&B units at $90 a double.

Next up is **Wedderburn**, 35 km north-west of Inglewood, where small gold nuggets are still being found. You can visit the working **Christmas Reef Gold Mine**, five km east of the town. A tour of the mine costs $5. In the town there's also the cluttered but interesting **General Store Museum** at 51 High St.

RUSHWORTH (population 1000)

This historic town, 100 km north-east of Bendigo and 20 km west of the Goulburn Valley Highway, was once a busy gold-mining centre and now has a National Trust classification. Apparently it was so named because the (gold) rush was worth coming to.

Seven km south of town, in the Rushworth State Forest, is the gold-mining ghost town of **Whroo** (pronounced 'roo'). The small Balaclava open-cut mine here yielded huge amounts of ore. At its peak the town had over 130 buildings, although today ironbark trees and native scrub have largely reclaimed the site.

The old cemetery (also National-Trust-classified) is an evocative place, and the headstone inscriptions bear testimony to the hard life experienced by those who came in search of gold. There are a couple of signposted nature trails, one leading to a small rock water hole used by the Koories who inhabited this region. There's also a small mud-brick visitors centre and a camp site. Worth the detour.

North-East

LAKE EILDON

About 150 km north-east of Melbourne, via the hill towns of Healesville and Marysville, is Lake Eildon, a massive lake created for hydroelectric power and irrigation purposes. It's a popular holiday area and one of Victoria's favourite water sports play-grounds – water-skiing, fishing, sailing and houseboat trips are all popular here.

The township of **Eildon** is the main town on the southern end of the lake, and **Bonnie Doon** on one of the lake's northern arms also has some facilities. The main boat harbour is two km north of Eildon township.

The **Snob's Creek Visitors Centre**, six km south-west of Eildon, is a trout farm and hatchery and opens daily ($3.50). On the western shores of the lake, the **Fraser National Park** has some good short walks including an excellent guide-yourself nature walk. The 24,000-hectare **Eildon State Park** takes in the south-eastern shore area of the lake. On the eastern side of the lake is the old mining town of **Jamieson**.

Places to Stay

There's a stack of caravan parks in and around Eildon. There are also camp sites in the Fraser National Park (☎ (057) 72 1293) and in the Eildon State Park (phone the Fraser National Park number to book). You'll need to book during holiday periods.

In Eildon, the *Golden Trout Hotel/Motel* (☎ (057) 74 2508) has singles/doubles from $30/35. The *Lakeside Leisure Resort* (☎ (057) 78 7252) in Bonnie Doon has an associate-YHA hostel with bunks at $11 ($15 for nonmembers).

For houseboat hire, try *Lake Eildon Holiday Boats* (☎ (057) 74 2107) in Eildon or *Peppin Point Houseboats* (☎ (057) 78 7338), nine km south of Bonnie Doon. Costs range from $500 to $2800 a week for six to 10 people, usually with a three-day minimum.

Getting There & Away

McKenzie's (☎ (03) 853 6264) runs a daily service to Eildon ($16.80) via Marysville ($10.20) and Alexandra ($15).

MANSFIELD (population 2200)

Mansfield is one of the best base-towns for Victoria's alpine country, with a good range of accommodation and eateries. In winter it has easy access to the snowfields of Mt Buller and Mt Sterling, and at other times it's a good base for horse riding, bushwalks and water sports on Lake Eildon.

In late October, the Mansfield Mountain Country Festival features the Great Mountain Race, with the country's best brumbies and riders, and other activities.

The graves of three police officers killed by Ned Kelly at Tolmie in 1878 are in the Mansfield cemetery, and there's a monument to them in the town.

There's a tourist information centre (☎ (057) 75 1464) and accommodation booking office in High St.

Places to Stay & Eat

The *James Holiday Park* (☎ (057) 75 2705) on Ultimo St is the most convenient place to camp, with sites at $12 and on-site vans from $25.

The *Mansfield Backpackers Inn* (☎ (057) 75 1800), in a restored heritage building at 112 High St, has good facilities, and bunks at $15 per person ($20 on winter weekends) and doubles at $35.

The *Mansfield Hotel* (☎ (057) 75 2101), at 86 High St, and *Delatite Hotel* (☎ (057) 75 2004), at 95 High St, have B&B for $25 per person, and there are also a few motels.

Good eateries include the *Witch's Brew* cafe, *Mingo's Bar & Grill* and *Buckley's Chance*, all on High St.

Getting There & Away

V/Line buses operate daily from Melbourne for $25. In the ski season Mansfield-Mt Buller Bus Lines (☎ (057) 75 2606) have daily buses to Mt Buller ($16.50/27 one way/return) and Mt Stirling ($12.80/22).

GOULBURN VALLEY

The Goulburn Valley region runs in a wide band from Lake Eildon north-west across the Hume Highway and up to the New South Wales border. The Goulburn River joins the Murray just upstream of Echuca.

Seymour (population 6600)

Seymour is an industrial and agricultural centre situated on the Hume Highway and the Goulburn River. The army base of Puckapunyal, nine km west, has the **RAAC Tank Museum** with a large collection of tanks and armoured vehicles. It opens daily from 10 am to 4 pm and costs $3.

Nagambie (population 1200)

On the shores of Lake Nagambie (created by the construction of Goulburn Weir), Nagambie has some interesting old buildings, a historical society display and many good picnic spots.

About eight km south-west are two of the best-known wineries in Victoria: Chateau Tahbilk is in a beautiful old building with notable cellars dating back to 1860 and classified by the National Trust, while just a few km away the Mitchelton Winery is ultra-modern with a strange observation tower looming unexpectedly from the surrounding countryside.

Shepparton (population 30,500)

Shepparton and its adjoining centre of Mooroopna are in a prosperous fruit- and vegetable-growing area irrigated by the Goulburn River.

The **Shepparton City Historical Museum** on the corner of High and Welsford Sts has a great collection and is well worth a visit. It's only open Sunday afternoons, but the curator will happily show you through at other times – contact the tourist office. There's also an **art gallery** in Welsford St, a fairly tacky **International Village**, tours of the huge **Shepparton Preserving Company (SPC) cannery** (January to early April), and good views from the **telecommunications tower** (near the post office).

Most travellers come to Shepparton looking for casual fruit-picking work. The main season is January to April – contact the Department of Employment, Education & Training (☎ (058) 32 0300) for information.

There's a tourist information office (☎ (058) 32 9870) by the lake on Wyndham St, just south of the city centre.

Places to Stay & Eat The Shepparton area has six caravan parks. The *Victoria Hotel*

Kelly Country
In the north-east of the state en route to the New South Wales border you pass through the interesting 'Kelly Country', where Australia's most famous outlaw, Ned Kelly, had some of his most exciting brushes with the law. Kelly and his gang of bushrangers shot three police officers at Stringybark Creek in 1878, and robbed banks at Euroa and Jerilderie before their lives of crime ended in the siege at Glenrowan. Ned and members of his family were held and tried in Beechworth. Not far to the east of the Hume are the Victorian Alps – in winter you'll catch glimpses of their snow-capped peaks from the highway near Glenrowan. ■

(☎ (058) 21 9955), situated on the corner of Wyndham and Fryers Sts, charges $19/30 for singles/doubles.

The town's best restaurants are *Tuscany's*, in an old church at 127 Fryers St, and *Daiquiris* at 130 High St.

Getting There & Away Daily trains and buses from Melbourne run to Shepparton ($21.50) and these continue to the Murray at Cobram ($6.40). V/Line buses also connect Shepparton with Bendigo ($13.60), Albury ($25.40) and Wagga (NSW).

GLENROWAN (population 350)

In 1880, the Kelly gang's exploits finally came to an end in a bloody shoot-out here, 230 km north of Melbourne. Ned Kelly was captured alive and eventually hanged in Melbourne.

You can't drive through Glenrowan without being confronted by the commercialisation of the Kelly legend. The town has everything from a giant statue of Ned (complete with armoured helmet), colonial-style tearooms and souvenir shops, and 10-minute horse-drawn coach rides ($3), to an impressive animated computerised theatre, **Kelly's Last Stand** ($12).

The ruins of the Kelly family homestead can be seen a few km off the highway at Greta, though little remains of the slab bush hut.

WANGARATTA (population 16,000)

'Wang', as it is commonly known, is at the junction of the King and Ovens rivers; it's also the turn-off point for the Ovens Highway to Mt Buffalo, Bright and the north of the Victorian Alps. The town has some pleasant parks, and bushranger Mad Dog Morgan is buried in the local cemetery.

At Wangaratta Airport, four km east off the Hume Highway, **Airworld** has a collection of 40 vintage flying aircraft. It's open daily from 9 am to 5 pm and costs $6.

Wang has a visitors' information centre (☎ (057) 21 5711) on the corner of the Hume Highway and Handley St – don't miss **Mrs**

Stell's World in Miniature! The popular Wangaratta Jazz Festival is held on the weekend before the Melbourne Cup horse race.

Places to Stay

There are three caravan parks with on-site vans and cabins, and at least a dozen motels, ranging from $40 to $80 for a double.

Of the town's pubs, the *Pinsent* (☎ (057) 21 2183) at 30 Reid St has singles/doubles for $25/40.

Getting There & Away

Daily trains from Melbourne cost $27.20, and to Albury it's $9. There's also a daily (except Saturday) V/Line bus to Bright ($9) via Beechworth, and a three-times-weekly service to Rutherglen ($3.60) and Corowa ($4.20).

CHILTERN (population 1200)

Close to Beechworth and only one km west off the Hume Highway between Wangaratta and Wodonga, Chiltern once swarmed with gold-miners in search of their fortunes. It's now a charming and historic town and is worth a visit.

Author Henry Handel Richardson's home, **Lake View**, is preserved by the National Trust and is open from 10 am to 4 pm on weekends and school and public holidays.

RUTHERGLEN (population 1900)

Close to the Murray River and north of the Hume, Rutherglen is the centre of one of Victoria's major wine-growing areas and has long been famous for its fortified wines. This

is a great area for bike touring – bikes can be hired from Walkabout Cellars (☎ (060) 32 9784) at 84 Main St, which is also something of a local information centre. Bogong Jack's Adventures (☎ (057) 27 3382), in Oxley near Wangaratta, also offers winery tours by bicycle – ring for details.

The town boasts a small museum and, on the main street, **Jack O'Keeffe's Barber Shop** is a local attraction. Jack, a barber and historian, is a mine of information and something of a local celebrity. His shop is stacked full of bits and pieces of interest – and you can even have a haircut.

Festivals include the Winery Walkabout Weekend, held on the Queen's Birthday weekend, and the Tastes of Rutherglen Weekend held in June.

Wahgunyah, nine km north-west, was once a busy port for the Ovens Valley gold towns. Its Customs House is a relic of that era.

Wineries

An excellent (and free) map and brochure is available from Walkabout Cellars and the wineries. It guides you around the 15 or so wineries in the area, which include **All Saints**, which is classified by the National Trust and has a wine museum; **Chamber's Rosewood**, an old family-run winery close to Rutherglen; **Gherig's Winery**, set around the historic Barnawartha Homestead; **Mt Prior**, with luxurious (and expensive) accommodation and a highly regarded restaurant; and **St Leonard's**, with an excellent bistro and a very scenic picnic spot on a billabong by the Murray River. Several of the

Victorian Wineries

Victoria has a great climate for viticulture and has been producing excellent wines since the days of the gold rush. The local industry flourished from the 1850s until the turn of the century, and in the last 20 years things have taken off again to the extent that many of the producers are successfully exporting their wine to the competitive US and European markets.

The main local styles are shiraz, cabernet sauvignon, riesling, chardonnay and sparkling wines. Fortified ports and muscats are also prominent, especially in the north-east. There are more than 150 wineries scattered around Victoria, and the major wine areas are the Yarra Valley, the Mornington Peninsula, around Geelong, Great Western and the Pyrenees, Central Victoria, the Macedon Ranges and the north-east around Rutherglen, Wahgunyah and Milawa. ■

wineries charge a $2 or $5 tasting fee, refundable if you buy wine.

Places to Stay & Eat
The *Rutherglen Caravan Park* (☎ (060) 32 9577) has on-site vans at $22 and sites for $8. The *Victoria Hotel* (☎ (060) 32 9610), which is classified by the National Trust, charges $20/36 for its basic, old-fashioned rooms, and the *Star Hotel* (☎ (060) 32 9625) has similar rooms and prices. There are also at least three motels.

There are plenty of eating choices, including several tearooms and pubs with counter meals along Main St. *Chattler's*, on the highway west of town, doesn't look much but the food is wonderful – there's a three-course set menu for $24. The *Shamrock*, at 152 Main St, also has pretty good food.

Mrs Mouse's Pantry at Wahgunyah is a good place to eat. It's open for lunch and teas daily from 10 am to 5 pm, and for dinner from Thursday to Sunday.

Getting There & Away
V/Line buses from Wangaratta ($3.20) run three times a week.

WODONGA (population 23,500)
The Victorian half of Albury-Wodonga is on the Murray River, the border between Victoria and New South Wales. The combined cities form the main economic and industrial centre of this region.

For tourist info there's the Gateway Tourist Information Centre (☎ (060) 41 3875), on the Lincoln Causeway between Wodonga and the Murray. For more information, see the Albury section in the New South Wales chapter.

Places to Stay
The *Herb & Horse* (☎ (060) 72 9553), on the Murray River 60 km east of Wodonga, is a great place to stay. It's an 1890s homestead and farm, with home-cooked meals, good horse-riding and canoe trips. Beds cost from $12 to $18, doubles are $42 and linen hire is $3. The staff can usually arrange free transport from Albury-Wodonga if you ring in advance.

CORRYONG (population 1200)
Corryong, the Victorian gateway to the Snowy Mountains and Kosciusko National Park, is close to the source of the Murray River, which at this point is merely an alpine stream.

Corryong's main claim to fame, however, is as the last resting place of Jack Riley, 'the Man from Snowy River'. Though some people dispute that Banjo Patterson based his stockman hero on Riley, a tailor turned mountain man who worked this district, the 'man' is nevertheless well remembered in Corryong.

Jack Riley's grave is in the town cemetery and the **Man from Snowy River museum**, with local history exhibits, is open daily from 10 am to noon and 2 to 4 pm ($2).

Places to Stay
The town has two caravan parks (both with on-site vans and cabins), a pub and a couple of motels.

YACKANDANDAH (population 600)
There's a saying, around these parts, that 'all roads lead to Yackandandah'. If you *were* to get lost in the beautiful hills and valleys of this district you would find that most of the signposts do indeed point to this charming little town.

The pretty little 'strawberry capital', 32 km south of Wodonga, 23 km from Beechworth and always on the way to somewhere, has been classified by the National Trust; not just the odd building but the entire town.

Yackandandah was a prosperous gold town and, back then, a welcome stopover on the old main road between Sydney and Melbourne. It has many fine old buildings, including the 1850 **Bank of Victoria** which is now a museum. The well-preserved buildings along the main street now house a variety of local craft shops, antique stores, cafes and tearooms.

There are tent sites and on-site vans at the *Yackandandah Caravan Park* (☎ (060) 27 1380), on the Dederang Rd, close to some good bushwalks.

BEECHWORTH (population 3100)

This picturesque town set amid the rolling countryside of the Ovens Valley has been attracting tourists for a good many years. Way back in 1927 it won the Melbourne *Sun News Pictorial*'s 'ideal tourist town' competition.

It is still a pleasure to visit Beechworth and spend a few days enjoying its wide tree-lined streets with their fine and dignified gold-rush architecture, or exploring the surrounding forested valleys, waterfalls and rocky gorges. It's a perfect place for walking or cycling.

The town is 35 km east of Wangaratta, and if you're travelling between Wang and Wodonga the detour through Beechworth makes a worthwhile alternative to the frenetic pace of the Hume Highway.

Information

There's a visitors information centre in the Rock Cavern (☎ (057) 28 1374), which is a gemstone and mineral museum opposite the post office on Ford St. Don't waste your $2 on the displays, though.

Things to See

In the 1850s Beechworth was the very prosperous hub of the Ovens River gold-mining region. Signs of the gold wealth are still very much in evidence, reflected in the fact that 32 buildings are classified by the National Trust. They include **Tanswell's Hotel** with its magnificent old lacework, the **post office** with its clock tower, and the **training prison** where Ned Kelly and his mother were imprisoned for a while.

The five-km **Gorge Scenic Drive** takes you past the 1859 **powder magazine**, now a National Trust museum which is open 10 am to noon and 1 to 4 pm daily ($1). The National Trust's **Carriage Museum**, on Railway Ave, is open during the same hours

and has a collection of old carriages including a Cobb & Co coach ($1.50).

The very well presented and interesting **Burke Museum**, in Loch St, has an eclectic collection of relics from the gold rush and a replica of the main street a century ago, complete with 16 shopfronts – well worth the $3.50 entry. The hapless explorer Robert O'Hara Burke was the Superintendent of Police in Beechworth during the early days of the gold rush before he set off on his historic trek north with William Wills.

Other things of interest in and around Beechworth include the historic **Murray Brewery Cellars**, established in 1872, on the corner of William and Last Sts; the **historic courthouse** on Ford St, site of Ned Kelly's first court appearance; the **Chinese burning towers** and **Beechworth Cemetery**, where the towers, altar and many graves are all that remain of the town's huge Chinese population during the gold rush; and the **Golden Horseshoe Monument** to a local pioneer who made gold horseshoes for his friend who had won a seat in parliament to represent the local miners.

Woolshed Falls, just out of town on the Chiltern road, is a popular picnic area and the site of a major alluvial gold field which yielded over 85,000 kg of gold in 14 years. Further west at **Eldorado** a gigantic gold dredge still floats on the lake where it was installed in 1936. At the time it was the largest dredge in the southern hemisphere.

Places to Stay

The National-Trust-classified *Star Hotel* (☎ (057) 28 1425), at 59 Ford St, is a big old place with good facilities; backpackers' beds are $15 and doubles $30. Across the road at No 30, *Tanswell's Commercial Hotel* (☎ (057) 28 1480) has B&B singles/doubles for $25/40 ($35/55 weekends).

Beechworth has a great selection of B&Bs and cottages. One of the best is *Rose Cottage* (☎ (057) 28 1069) at 42 Camp St, costing $55/80 for B&B. *Burnbrae* (☎ (057) 28 1091) is a picturesque Victorian cottage on Gorge Rd on the edge of town, and costs from $65/82. For a splurge, *Finches of*

Beechworth (☎ (057) 28 2655) at 3 Finch St offers B&B at $140 a double ($210 with dinner) in a magnificent Victorian house.

Five km out of town towards Chiltern, the self-contained *Woolshed Cabins* (☎ (057) 28 1035) sleep up to five people, and cost from $48 for two plus $7 per extra person.

Places to Eat

Brambley Cottage, 32 Ford St, is a good BYO restaurant which specialises in home-made pasta, while the *Parlour & Pantry* on the same street is a gourmet deli and restaurant with a wide range of goodies. *Beechworth Provender* at 18 Camp St is another gourmet deli.

More up-market is the *Bank Restaurant*, housed in the historic Bank of Australasia building at 86 Ford St. It has pasta nights on Monday and Wednesday, and a carvery on Sundays.

Tanswell's Hotel does good counter meals, the *Hibernian Hotel* has an excellent bistro, and the *Beechworth Bakery* on Camp St has an irresistible selection of hot bread, cakes and home-made pies. On a sunny morning, the tables on the footpath are an excellent place for a coffee and fresh croissant breakfast.

Getting There & Away

V/Line has daily buses to both Wangaratta and Bright, with train connections from Wangaratta to Albury, Adelaide and Melbourne.

Golden Era Bus Lines on Ford St in Beechworth has daily buses to Albury-Wodonga.

BRIGHT (population 1800)

Deep in the Ovens Valley, Bright today is a focal point of the winter sports region and a summer bushwalking centre, and is renowned for its beautiful golden shades in autumn. In 1857 the notorious Buckland Valley riots took place near here; the diligent Chinese gold-miners were forced off their claims and given much less than a fair go. It is about an hour's scenic drive from town to the snowfields of Mt Hotham and Falls Creek, and a half-hour to Mt Buffalo. Snow chains must be carried in winter.

The tourist information centre (☎ (057) 55 2275) in Delany Ave is open daily from 10 am to 4 pm.

Activities

There are plenty of good walking trails and lookouts in the area – maps are available from the tourist office. There are also several horse-riding ranches, with everything from one-hour trots to overnight treks.

If you want to get airborne, Alpine Paragliding and the Eagle School of Hang-Gliding (at Porepunkah) both offer courses from here – check with the tourist office for details.

Places to Stay

The *Municipal Caravan Park* (☎ (057) 55 1141), close to the centre of town on Cherry Lane, has a very good associate-YHA hostel with beds at $15 ($18 nonmembers). There are also tent sites ($11) and on-site cabins ($33). This is only one of about a dozen caravan parks in the town.

There's a whole range of other accommodation, most of it holiday flats. During holidays and long weekends rooms are scarce. The best bet may be to phone the tourist office, which has an accommodation booking service.

The *Bright Alps Guest House* (☎ (057) 55 1197) at 83 Delany Ave has B&B from $25/48. The *Alpine Hotel* (☎ (057) 55 1366) at 7 Anderson St has singles/doubles for $30/40. The *Elm Lodge Motel* (☎ (057) 55 1144) at 2 Wood St is the best value at $30/35 (discounts for backpackers!).

Places to Eat

The *Liquid Am-Bar* on Anderson St is a fun cafe/bar with an interesting and affordable menu. *Alps Pasta & Pizza* on Gavan St has cheap pizzas, pastas and Mexican food.

Getting There & Away

V/Line has buses which run daily (except Saturday) between Bright and Wangaratta (via Beechworth), which connect with trains to and from Melbourne ($36.40).

The Alps

These mountains are the southern end of the Great Dividing Range, which runs all the way from Queensland down through the north-east of Victoria then south and west past Ballarat. The Dandenongs, just outside Melbourne, are a spur of the range.

The Victorian ski fields are at lower altitudes than those in New South Wales, but they receive as much snow and have similar conditions above and below the snow line. The two largest ski resorts are Mt Buller and Falls Creek. Mt Hotham is smaller, but has equally good skiing, while Mt Buffalo and Mt Baw Baw are smaller resorts which are popular with families and novice to intermediate skiers. Lake Mountain, Mt Stirling and Mt St Gwinear are all mainly cross-country skiing areas with no overnight accommodation. Dinner Plain, near Mt Hotham, is an architect-designed village above the snow line (and has a great pub!).

The roads are fully sealed to all ski resorts except Mt Baw Baw, Mt Sterling and Dinner Plain. In winter, snow chains must be carried to all ski resorts (you may be turned back if you haven't got them) and driving conditions can be hazardous. Other roads that crisscross the Great Dividing Range are unsealed for at least part of their way and only traversable in summer.

The skiing season officially commences on the first weekend of June, and ski-able snow usually arrives later in the month. Spring skiing can be good as it is sunny and warm with no crowds, and there's usually enough snow until the end of September.

In the summer months, especially from December to February, the area is ideal for bushwalking, rock climbing, fishing, camping, and observing the native flora and fauna. Other activities are canoeing, rafting, hang-gliding, horse trekking and paragliding.

Bushwalkers should be self-sufficient, with a tent, a fuel stove, warm clothes and sleeping bag, and plenty of water. In the height of summer, you can walk all day in the heat without finding water, and then face temperatures below freezing at night.

Places to Stay

There are many places to stay, especially in the ski resorts, which have lots of accommodation for the skiers. Overall, these are very expensive in winter and many people prefer to stay in towns below the snow line and drive up to the ski fields. In July and August it is advisable to book your accommodation, especially for weekends. In June or September it is usually possible to find something if you just turn up. Hotels, motels, chalets, self-contained flats and units, and caravan parks abound in the region. There are also youth hostels at Mt Buller and Mt Baw Baw, plus an associate hostel in Bright and a backpackers' in Mansfield.

Apart from these, the cheapest accommodation in the ski resorts is a bed in one of the club lodges, or it is possible to cut costs by cramming as many people as possible into a flat. The various accommodation booking services at the resorts should be able to help you find a place. In summer, bushwalkers may find bargain accommodation in the skiing areas.

ALPINE NATIONAL PARK

The 646,000-hectare Alpine National Park was proclaimed in 1989. Victoria's largest national park, it covers most of the state's prime 'high country' of the Great Dividing Range, from Mansfield north-east to the New South Wales border, and is contiguous with the Kosciusko National Park in New South Wales. Most of the ski resorts in the state fall within the park's boundaries, and access is possible from many points.

Bushwalking and, in winter, cross-country skiing are the main activities within the park as it is largely undeveloped, and plans are to keep it that way. Large areas which are now part of the park were used for

VICTORIA

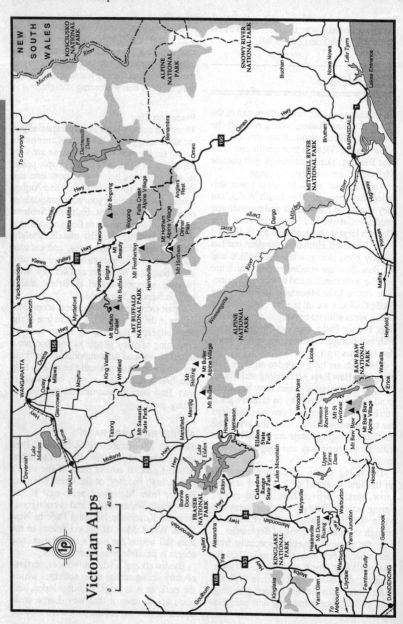

Victorian Alps

0   20   40 km

many years for cattle grazing, but this is now being restricted.

The Alpine Walking Track is a walking trail which runs for 400-km from Mt Erica, near Walhalla, to Tom Groggin on the New South Wales border. For more information, visit a Department of Conservation & Natural Resources office for a brochure. The department also publishes an excellent 70-page colour guidebook called *Into the High Country* ($17.95). The trail is also covered in Lonely Planet's *Bushwalking in Australia* by John & Monica Chapman.

MT BUFFALO NATIONAL PARK

Apart from Mt Buffalo itself, the park is noted for its many pleasant streams and fine walks. The mountain was named back in 1824 by explorers Hume and Hovell on their trek from Sydney to Port Phillip Bay.

The mountain is surrounded by huge granite tors – great blocks of granite broken off from the massif by the expansion and contraction of ice in winter and other weathering effects. There is abundant plant and animal life around the park, and over 140 km of walking tracks. Leaflets are available for the **Gorge Nature Walk, View Point Nature Walk** and the **Dicksons Falls Nature Walk**. A road leads up to just below the summit of the 1720-metre Horn, the highest point on the massif.

In summer Mt Buffalo is a hang-gliders' paradise (definitely not for beginners) and the near-vertical walls of the Gorge provide some of the most challenging rock climbs in Australia. **Lake Catani** is good for swimming, camping and canoeing, while in winter Mt Buffalo turns into a ski resort with downhill and cross-country skiing being the most popular activities – see the Ski Resorts section for more details.

An entry fee of $5 per car is charged ($9 in winter).

HARRIETVILLE (population 100)

This pretty little town sits in the valley at the fork of the eastern and western branches of the Ovens River, and is surrounded by the high Alps. Harrietville is well known for its beautiful natural surroundings and its proximity to the ski resort of Mt Hotham. During the ski season there is a shuttle bus which connects the town with Mt Hotham. Always check beforehand to find out if the road to Hotham is closed because of snow.

The town is also the usual finishing point for the Feathertop bushwalk, one of the most popular walks in Victoria, and so is busy on long weekends outside the ski season.

Places to Stay

The *Harrietville Caravan Park* (☎ (057) 59 2523) has sites and on-site vans. The rambling *Bon Accord* (057) 59 2530) isn't exactly flash, but it has the basic facilities and backpackers' beds for $12 ($17.50 with a bathroom). The *Snowline Hotel* (☎ (057) 59 2524) has a few pub rooms for $30/40, and motel rooms for $40/45 ($45/60 winter weekends), and the *Harrietville Alpine Lodge* (☎ (057) 59 2525) has motel-style B&B from $30/50.

OMEO (population 270)

This small town is on the Omeo Highway, the southern access route to the snowfields of Mt Hotham during winter. In summer it's a popular departure point for the Bogong High Plains. Rafting trips take place on the nearby Mitta Mitta River.

Omeo still has a handful of interesting old buildings despite the disastrous bushfire and two earthquakes which have occurred since 1885. Omeo's **log jail, courthouse** and **historical museum** are worth searching out. The town also had its own little gold rush.

Places to Stay

The *Holston Tourist Park* (☎ (051) 59 1351) has tent sites from $8 and on-site vans from $24. *Colonial Bank House* (☎ (051) 59 1388) has four small self-contained units at $30/40, and the *Golden Age Hotel* (☎ (051) 59 1344) has B&B for $22 per person.

Getting There & Away

There is a weekday bus between Omeo and

Bairnsdale ($22.20) operated by Omeo Buslines (☎ (051) 59 4231).

SKI RESORTS
Skiing in Victoria goes back to the 1860s when Norwegian gold-miners introduced it in Harrietville. It has grown into a multimillion dollar industry with three major ski resorts and six minor ski areas. None of these resorts is connected to another by a lift system, but it is possible for the experienced and well-equipped cross-country skier to go from Mt Hotham to Falls Creek across the Bogong High Plains. There is an annual race that covers this route.

The Alpine Resorts Commission (ARC) is responsible for managing the ski resorts and on-mountain information centres. Resort entry fees are between $8 and $15 per car per day in winter.

Falls Creek (1780 metres)
It sits at the edge of the Bogong High Plains overlooking the Kiewa Valley, a five-hour, 375-km drive from Melbourne. Falls Creek is one of the best resorts in Victoria and in the last few years has received the heaviest snow falls. It is the only ski village in Australia where everyone can ski directly from their lodge to the lifts and from the slopes back to their lodge.

The skiing is spread over two bowls with 30 km of trails, 22 lifts and a vertical drop of 267 metres. Runs are divided into 17% beginners, 53% intermediate and 30% advanced. A day ticket costs $47, a seven-day ticket costs $282 and a daily lift and lesson package costs $66. Entry fees are $15 per car, and the ARC (☎ (057) 58 3325) has an information office in the lower car park.

You'll find some of the best cross-country skiing in Australia here. A trail leads around Rocky Valley pondage to some old huts from the cattle days. The more adventurous can tour to the white summits of Nelse, Cope and Spion Kopje.

You can choose between ski skating on groomed trails; light touring with day packs; and general touring with heavier packs, usually involving an overnight stay in a tent. Cross-country downhill, the alternative to skiing on crowded, noisy slopes, is also becoming popular.

Mt Stirling has day facilities only for cross-country skiers at Windy Corner. At times, cheaper accommodation is available at the Department of Sport & Recreation (☎ (057) 58 3228) facility at Howman's Gap, although it's mainly for groups.

In summer there are plenty of opportunities for alpine walking to places like Ruined Castle, Ropers Lookout, Wallaces Hut and Mt Nelse, which is part of the Alpine Walking Track.

Places to Stay & Eat There is very little cheap accommodation in Falls Creek in winter. Where to Stay in Falls Creek (☎ (057) 58 3358) or Falls Creek Central Reservations (☎ (057) 57 2718) can help you find accommodation on the mountain.

A number of ski lodges offer B&B plus dinner packages per week or weekend. One of the best and cheapest is the *Silver Ski Lodge* (☎ (057) 58 3375), costing from $450 to $790 per person weekly, depending on the season; however, it's normally fully booked during peak seasons. The small *Four Seasons Lodge* (☎ (057) 58 3254) costs from $35 to $65 per person daily, or $250 to $430 weekly.

In summer, the *Attunga Lodge* (☎ (057) 58 3255) and the *Pretty Valley Alpine Lodge* (☎ (057) 58 3210) both cost around $65 per person daily for dinner B&B.

Cafe Max in the village bowl is a good bistro/bar, and *Winterhaven* is about the best restaurant. The *Man* is a fairly wild nightclub with live bands and other entertainment.

Getting There & Around During the ski season, Pyles Coaches (☎ (057) 57 2024) runs buses to and from Melbourne on Fridays to Sundays for $49/90 one way/return, and it also has daily services to and from Albury ($22/44) and Mt Beauty ($12/24). There is over-snow transport available from the car park to the lodges and back again.

Mt Baw Baw (1480 metres)

This is a small resort in the Baw Baw National Park, with eight lifts on the edge of the Baw Baw plateau. It is 173 km and an easy three-hour drive from Melbourne, via Noojee. It's popular with novices and families and is more relaxed and less crowded than the main resorts. Runs are 25% beginners, 64% intermediate and 11% advanced, with a vertical drop of 140 metres. There are plenty of cross-country trails, including one that connects to the Mt St Gwinear trails on the southern edge of the plateau.

Car entry fees are $14 and a day ticket costs $35; the ARC (☎ (051) 65 1136) office is in the village.

Places to Stay & Eat The only cheap place is the YHA *Baw Baw Youth Hostel* (☎ (051) 65 1129), which is in the village and close to all the facilities. During the ski season, members' costs are $80 per person for a weekend, $200 for Sunday to Thursday and $40 for one night; these prices include three meals a day. Bookings are essential. The hostel sometimes takes groups in summer ($15 per person).

The ARC (☎ (051) 65 1136) or Baw Baw Bookings (☎ (03) 879 7809) can advise you on other accommodation options.

Getting There & Away On winter weekends, Gippsland Mountain Travel (☎ (03) 830 1044) has buses to and from Melbourne for $45 return.

Mt Buffalo (1400 metres)

This is a magnificent national park, and apart from the two guesthouses there are no private lodges on the mountain. From Melbourne it is 333 km by road and takes about five hours. The entry fee is $9 per car.

It is another small place more suited to intermediate and beginner skiers, but again has more challenging cross-country skiing. Tatra is a picturesque and not overly expensive village, but the downhill skiing is not very good and the snow does not last as long as in some of the other resorts. There are a number of cross-country loops, and one of the trails goes to the base of the Horn, which skiers climb on foot.

The walks are also interesting and take the walker beneath towering granite monoliths.

Places to Stay & Eat The *Lake Catani Campground* (☎ (057) 55 1577) next to the lake has sites from $7 in winter or $11 in summer.

The *Mt Buffalo Chalet* (☎ (057) 55 1500) was the first place built on the mountain and still has the charm of the 1920s. The rooms are from $95 per person with all meals. The *Tatra Inn* (☎ (057) 55 1988) has bunk rooms with dinner B&B from $75 per person or motel units from $95. Both of these places have a restaurant and ski hire.

Getting There & Away There is no public transport to the village. The closest you can get is Porepunkah on the Ovens Highway.

Mt Buller (1600 metres)

Less than a three-hour drive from Melbourne and only 246 km away, Mt Buller is the most popular (and crowded) resort in Victoria, especially on the weekends. It has a large lift network with 24 lifts, including a chair lift which begins in the car park and ends in the middle of the ski runs. Runs are 25% beginners, 45% intermediate and 30% advanced, and there's even night skiing from Wednesday to Sunday until 10 pm.

In years of light snow cover, Buller is skied out much sooner than Falls Creek or Mt Hotham, though snow-making equipment now extends the season on the main beginners' area. Cross-country skiing is possible around Buller and there is access to Mt Stirling which has some good trails. A trail-use fee is payable ($5).

A day ticket costs $49, a seven-day ticket $283 and a daily lift and lesson package costs $70 ($49 for beginners). The entry fee is $15 per car, and the ARC (☎ (057) 77 6077) office is in the village.

Places to Stay There is plenty of accommodation. The youth hostel (☎ (057) 77 6181) is of course the cheapest on the mountain. During the ski season, the nightly rate is $37 for members, $41 for nonmembers. You'll need to book well in advance – ring or write to PO Box 23, Mt Buller 3723. In summer the rate is $12 per person per day (although it doesn't always open in summer).

Club lodges are again the best value, starting at about $32 per person per night, with mostly bunk accommodation and kitchen facilities; contact the Mt Buller Accommodation & Information office (☎ (057) 77 6280 or toll-free 1800 039 049).

Getting There & Around During winter only, there are daily V/Line buses from Melbourne to Mt Buller, via Mansfield, costing $38.50/77 one way/return. Mansfield-Mt Buller Buslines (057) 75 2606) travel where their name suggests daily during winter; fares are $16.50/27.

In winter, there is an over-snow transport shuttle service that moves people around the village and to and from the car park; fares range from $3 to $8. Day-trippers can take the quad chair lift from the car park into the skiing area and save time and money by bypassing the village. There are ski rental facilities in the car park. Cross-country skiers turn off for Mt Stirling at the Mt Buller entrance gate at the base of the mountain. There are day facilities and fast food available at Telephone Box Junction.

Mt Hotham (1750 metres)
Known as Australia's powder capital, Hotham does get the lightest snow in the country, but don't expect anything like Europe or North America. It's about a 5½-hour drive from Melbourne; you can take either the Hume Highway via Harrietville or the Princes Highway via Omeo.

The lift system here is not well integrated and some walking is necessary, even though the 'zoo cart' (see Getting There & Around) along the main road offers some relief. The skiing here is good: there are eight lifts and runs are 23% beginners, 37% intermediate and 40% advanced. This is a skiers' moun-

tain with a vertical drop of 428 metres and the nightlife mainly happening in ski lodges. There is some good off-piste skiing in steep and narrow valleys. A day ticket costs $45, a seven-day pass $242, and a lift and lesson package $64. Car entry costs $15. The ARC (☎ (057) 59 3550) has an information office in the village centre.

Cross-country skiing is good around Hotham and ski touring is very good on the Bogong High Plains which you can cross to Falls Creek. This is also the starting point for trips across the Razorback to beautiful Mt Feathertop. Below the village, on the eastern side, there is a series of trails which run as far as Dinner Plain. The biathlon (shooting and skiing) course between Mt Hotham and Dinner Plain is here at Wire Plain.

Places to Stay Most of the accommodation is in private and commercial lodges. It is possible to find beds in these or apartments through the Mt Hotham Accommodation Service (☎ (057) 59 3636) or Skicom (☎ (057) 59 3522).

The *Jack Frost Lodge* (☎ (057) 59 3586) has one- and two-bedroom apartments costing anywhere from $600 to $2300 per week, depending on the season and number of people. The huge *Arlberg Inn* (☎ (03) 809 2699) also has apartments sleeping from two to eight people; weekly costs start at $235 per person. *Zirky's* (☎ (057) 59 3518) has six double rooms at $90 per person nightly for B&B. There is very little accommodation at Hotham outside the ski season.

It is also possible to stay at Dinner Plain, 11 km from Mt Hotham Village, where there are cabins, lodges and B&Bs – ring one of the booking services on ☎ (051) 59 6426 or ☎ (051) 59 6451.

Getting There & Around In winter, Trekset Snow Services (☎ (03) 370 9055) have two buses from Melbourne to Mt Hotham on Fridays and Sundays, costing $65/85 one way/return. They also have daily services between Hotham and Myrtleford, Bright and Harrietville; fares range from $17 to $25, depending on when you're going.

The village was built on a ridge almost at the top of the mountain and is strung out along the road. Luckily, there are free shuttle buses that run frequently all the way along the ridge from 7.15 am to midnight ($1 after 4 pm), and the free 'zoo cart' takes skiers from their lodges to the lifts between 8.15 am and 5.45 pm. Another shuttle service operates to Dinner Plain.

Other Resorts

There are five other snowfields, although they're mainly for cross-country skiing or sightseeing and have no accommodation. For more information, contact their respective information offices on the numbers given below.

Lake Mountain (☎ (059) 63 3288) is 120 km from Melbourne via Marysville. The cross-country facility here is world class, with over 40 km of trails that are groomed daily.

Skiing for the experienced is found around the summit of Victoria's highest peak, **Mt Bogong**. Here, steep gullies tempt the cross-country downhill skier. Accommodation is in tents and in mountain huts. This area is not for beginners.

Mt St Gwinear (☎ (051) 65 3204) is 171 km from Melbourne via Moe and has connecting cross-country ski trails with Mt Baw Baw.

Mt Stirling (☎ (057) 77 5624/6077) is a few km from Mt Buller and is another cross-country ski area, with more than 60 km of mostly groomed trails.

Mt Donna Buang is the closest to Melbourne (95 km via Warburton), but is mainly for sightseeing or tobogganing.

Gippsland

The Gippsland region is the south-east slice of Victoria. It stretches from Western Port, near Melbourne, to the New South Wales border on the east coast, with the Great Dividing Range to the north.

Named in 1839 by the Polish explorer Count Paul Strzelecki after Sir George Gipps, the former governor of New South Wales, Gippsland was first settled by prospectors in the 1850s, then by farmers after the completion of the railway from Melbourne in 1887. Extremely fertile and well watered, Gippsland is now the focus of the state's dairy industry.

The region can be divided into four distinct sections: West Gippsland, which is dominated by Victoria's industrial heartland, the Latrobe Valley; South Gippsland, which includes the wonderful Wilsons Promontory National Park; the Gippsland Lakes, Australia's largest system of inland waterways; and East Gippsland, an area of often breathtaking beauty known as the Wilderness Coast.

Getting There & Away

Soon after leaving Dandenong the road divides. The Princes Highway continues east through the Latrobe Valley to Bairnsdale, near the coast, then on into New South Wales. Meanwhile the South Gippsland Highway heads off to the south-east to Phillip Island and Wilsons Promontory. For a slower but more scenic drive, you can follow the South Gippsland Highway, detour to visit the Prom, and then rejoin the Princes Highway at Sale, 214 km from Melbourne.

V/Line operates a regular daily Melbourne-Traralgon-Sale-Bairnsdale service, sometimes by bus from Sale onwards, with connections on to Lakes Entrance, Orbost, Cann River, Eden and Narooma (in New South Wales).

WEST GIPPSLAND & THE LATROBE VALLEY

The Latrobe Valley contains one of the world's largest deposits of brown coal, and its mines and power stations supply most of Victoria's electricity, while the offshore wells in Bass Strait provide most of Australia's petroleum and natural gas. While the major towns along the Princes Highway are predominantly residential and industrial centres for the various workforces, the regions surrounding this industrial land-

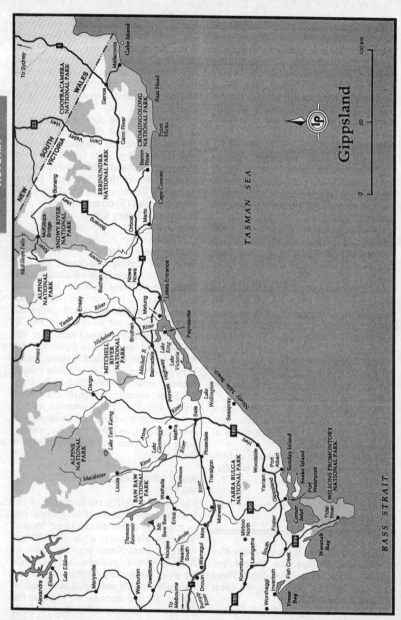

Gippsland

scape are surprisingly beautiful. The Princes Highway provides access to a number of very scenic areas, including the idyllic and historic former gold-mining township of Walhalla and the gourmet delights of the Neerim South region.

Warragul (population 9000)
A regional centre for the district's dairy farms which provide most of Melbourne's milk, Warragul is the first major town east of Dandenong. **Darnum Musical Village**, about eight km east of the centre of town, is an old church with a collection of old and modern musical instruments. It opens daily from 10 am to 4 pm and entry costs $8.

Places to Stay The *Warragul Caravan Park* (☎ (056) 23 2707) in Burke St has tent sites and on-site vans, and *Helen's B&B* (☎ (056) 23 1626), in an old pub at 73 Queen St, has B&B at $20/35.

Moe (population 18,000)
The main attraction of this coal-mining centre is the **Old Gippsland Pioneer Township**, on the Princes Highway, with a collection of 30 or more 19th-century buildings. The place has an authentic feel to it, and there are a number of working displays of old crafts, as well as rides in horse-drawn vehicles of varying descriptions. Old Gippsland is open daily from 9 am to 5 pm; entry is $6. Devonshire teas are served in the historic **Bushy Park Homestead** on Sundays.

You can visit **Yallourn Power Station** from Moe, and the former site of the township of Yallourn, which was moved lock, stock and barrel to provide access to the brown-coal deposits underneath. From the hill behind the town site there is a lookout with some information for visitors and views of the vast open-cut mine area.

There's a scenic road from Moe north to Walhalla, the Baw Baw National Park and Mt Erica, from where a secondary road continues north across the Victorian Alps. You can get onto the panoramic Grand Ridge Road across the Strzelecki Ranges easily

from either Trafalgar or Moe by turning south via the lovely little townships of Narracan or Thorpdale.

Morwell (population 15,500)
Founded in the 1880s as a supply centre for diggers and traders heading for the gold fields at Walhalla, these days Morwell is basically an industrial town servicing the massive open-cut mine, Hazelwood Power Station, the APM pulp mills and the local briquette works.

The SEC's visitors centre (☎ (051) 35 3415), signposted off Commercial Rd, houses models and displays of the Latrobe Valley's coal-mining and power-generating activities. There are also guided tours of the Morwell open cut and Hazelwood Power Station. The small Morwell National Park is 15 km south of town.

Places to Stay *Morwell Caravan Park* (☎ (051) 34 3507) is on Maryvale Crescent, and the *Hazelwood Motor Inn* (☎ (051) 34 4222) at 259 Princes Highway has good rooms at $59/66.

Traralgon (population 20,000)
The original township was a rest stop and supply base for miners and drovers heading further into the gold and farming country of Gippsland. It is now the centre of the state's paper and pulp industry and a major Latrobe Valley electricity centre. Its future is assured by the colossal Loy Yang Power Station, six km to the south. The SEC is so proud of this incredible construction that there is a tourist road right through the middle of the complex.

Places to Stay There's the *Park Lane Caravan Park* (☎ (051) 74 6749) on Park Lane, or the *Grand Junction Hotel* (☎ (051) 74 6011), Franklin St, which has singles/doubles for $27.50/40.

Walhalla (population 30)
At the end of 1862 Edward Stringer, one of a small party of prospectors who had made

it over the mountains, found gold in a creek running through a deep wooded valley north of Moe. The payable gold in Stringer's Creek attracted about 200 miners but it was the later discovery of Cohen's Reef, the outcrop of a reef almost two miles long, that put the growing township of Walhalla on the map.

Work began on the Long Tunnel Mine, the single most profitable mine in Victoria, in 1865 and continued for 49 years. Walhalla reached its peak between 1885 and 1890 when there were over 4000 people living in and around the town.

The railway line from Moe, incorporating a truly amazing section of tunnels and trestle bridges between Erica and Walhalla, was finally completed in 1910 just as the town's fortunes began to decline.

Though the population is tiny these days, there's plenty to see in Walhalla and the area is quite beautiful. There are a number of old buildings (some of which are classified by the National Trust), a museum and a very interesting cemetery. The **Long Tunnel Extended Gold Mine** is open for tours on weekends and public holidays; entrance is $4.

South of Walhalla, there is a car park and marked trail to the summit of Mt Erica, the start of the Alpine Walking Track, which offers a good taste of Victoria's alpine bushland.

Places to Stay There are a couple of camp sites along the creek, and the *Old Hospital* (☎ (051) 65 6246) is now a guesthouse with B&B at $35/70.

Sale (population 14,000)
At the junction of the Princes and South Gippsland highways, Sale is a supply centre for the Bass Strait oil fields. Points of interest include the **Cobb & Co Stables & Market** at 199 Raymond St, a craft market and amusement centre; a **fauna park & bird sanctuary** near Lake Gutheridge; an **art gallery** at 288 Raymond St; and, in Dawson St, the historic **Bon Accord Homestead & Gardens** is now a guesthouse and tearooms.

There's a tourist information centre (☎ (051) 44 1108) on the Princes Highway, open daily; within the centre is an Oil & Gas Display, which shows the development of the Bass Strait industries.

Places to Stay The *Thomson River Caravan Park* (☎ (051) 44 1102) has all the usual facilities, and the *Colonial Club Hotel* (☎ (051) 44 2021) at 105 Foster St has basic pub rooms at $20/25.

SOUTH GIPPSLAND
South Gippsland is an area of great natural beauty, with rolling hills, forested mountains and a rugged and spectacular coastline. The area's major feature is Wilsons Promontory, one of Victoria's most loved national parks. The main road through here is the South Gippsland Highway, but the back roads through the hills, and the coastal route, are more scenic and worth exploring if you have enough time. The Grand Ridge Road, which runs along the ridge of the Strzelecki Ranges and past the wonderful rainforest remnants of the Tarra Bulga National Park, is a spectacular but rough alternative route.

The Strzelecki Ranges
Between the Latrobe Valley and South Gippsland's coastal areas are the beautiful 'blue' rounded hills of the Strzelecki Ranges. The winding Grand Ridge Road traverses the top of these ranges, from behind Trafalgar to the back of Traralgon, providing a fabulous excursion through fertile farmland that was once covered with forests of mountain ash.

A good base for this area is the township of **Mirboo North** which straddles the Grand Ridge Road south of Trafalgar. The town boasts the **Grand Ridge Brewery** in the old Butter Factory building. The complex not only produces a range of quality beers but also features a cosy bar and a good bistro.

There's a caravan park in Mirboo North, opposite the shire hall, which has tent sites for $6.50.

The **Tarra Bulga National Park**, at the eastern end of the Grand Ridge Road, is one of the last remnants of the magnificent forests that once covered this area. There are several good picnic areas and some lovely nature walks, and the 1930s-style guesthouse (☎ (051) 96 6141) has old-fashioned accommodation from $60 a double.

Korumburra (population 2900)

The **Coal Creek Historical Village**, a very popular re-creation of a coal-mining town of the 19th century, is near Korumburra. Coal was first discovered here in 1872 and the Coal Creek Mine operated from the 1890s right up to 1958. The park is open daily and entry costs $9 for adults and $5 for kids.

Port Albert

This quaint little fishing village was one of Victoria's earliest settlements, and has a large number of historic buildings. It's also an excellent and popular fishing spot.

There are two caravan parks, and the *Port Albert Hotel* (☎ (051) 83 2212) has motel units for $45 a double and good bistro meals.

WILSONS PROMONTORY

'The Prom' is one of the most popular national parks in Australia. It covers the peninsula that forms the southernmost part of the Australian mainland. The Prom offers more than 80 km of walking tracks and a wide variety of beaches – whether you want surfing, safe swimming or a secluded beach all to yourself, you can find it on the Prom. Finally there's the wildlife, which abounds despite the park's popularity. There are wonderful birds, emus, kangaroos and, at night, plenty of wombats. The wildlife around Tidal River is very tame and can even become a nuisance. One Lonely Planet staffer was bitten by a wombat but lived to tell the tale.

Information

The National Parks office (☎ (056) 80 9555) at Tidal River is open daily from 8.30 am to 4.30 pm. The displays here are excellent. The park office takes reservations for accommodation and issues camping permits. The office is also where you pay your park entry fee ($6 per car) if the main gate is not staffed.

Activities

It's probably walkers who get the best value from the Prom, though you don't have to go very far from the car parks to really get away from it all. The park office at Tidal River has free leaflets on walks ranging from 15-minute strolls from Tidal River to overnight and longer hikes. You can also get detailed maps of the park.

The walking tracks take you through ever-changing scenery: swamps, forests, marshes, valleys of tree ferns and long beaches lined with sand dunes. For serious exploration, it's really worth buying a copy of *Discovering the Prom on Foot* ($6.95) from the park office.

Don't miss the Mt Oberon walk – it starts from the Mt Oberon car park, takes one hour and is about three km each way. The views from the summit are excellent.

It's a long day walk from the Mt Oberon car park to the tip of the Prom, and by prior arrangement (☎ (056) 80 8529) it's possible to visit the lighthouse. Another popular walk is the Squeaky Beach Nature Walk, a lovely 1½-hour stroll around to the next bay and back.

The northern area of the park is much less visited, simply because all the facilities are at Tidal River. Most of the walks in this area are overnight or longer. All the camp sites away from Tidal River have pit toilets but nothing else in the way of facilities. Fires are totally banned (except in designated fire places in Tidal River between May and October) so you'll need to carry some sort of stove.

Places to Stay

Camping The Tidal River camping ground has 500 sites, and at peak times (school holidays, Easter and long weekends) booking is essential. In fact for the real peak at Christmas a ballot is held in July allocating sites, so you can forget about a casual visit then (although a few short-term sites are usually reserved for overseas visitors).

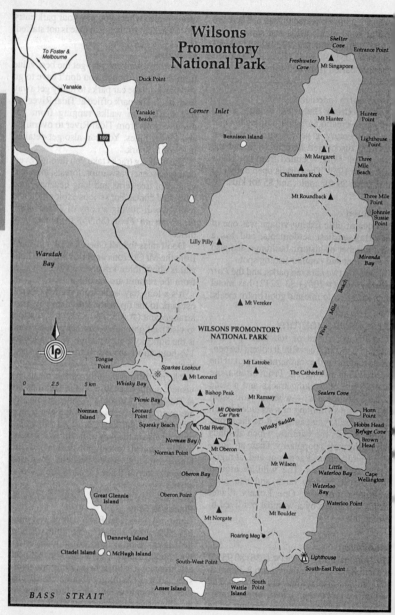

Wilsons Promontory National Park

WILSONS PROMONTORY
NATIONAL PARK

To Foster & Melbourne

Duck Point

Yanakie

Yanakie Beach

189

Corner Inlet

Bennison Island

Shelter Cove

Freshwater Cove

Mt Singapore

Entrance Point

Mt Hunter

Hunter Point

Lighthouse Point

Mt Margaret

Three Mile Beach

Chinamans Knob

Mt Roundback

Three Mile Point

Johnnie Sussie Point

Lilly Pilly

Miranda Bay

Waratah Bay

Mt Vereker

Five Mile Beach

Tongue Point

Sparkes Lookout

Mt Leonard

Mt Latrobe

The Cathedral

Whisky Bay

Picnic Bay

Bishop Peak

Mt Ramsay

Sealers Cove

Norman Island

Leonard Point

Mt Oberon Car Park

Horn Point

Hobbs Head

Squeaky Beach

Tidal River

Windy Saddle

Refuge Cove

Brown Head

Norman Bay

Norman Point

Mt Oberon

Mt Wilson

Little Waterloo Bay

Cape Wellington

Oberon Bay

Waterloo Bay

Great Glennie Island

Oberon Point

Mt Norgate

Mt Boulder

Waterloo Point

Dannevig Island

Roaring Meg

Citadel Island   McHugh Island

Lighthouse

South-West Point

South-East Point

Anser Island

Wattle Island

South Point

BASS STRAIT

0   2.5   5 km

VICTORIA

The charge is $12 per site (up to three people and one car), with a surcharge of $2.40 per extra person. Cheaper off-season rates apply to all periods outside the peak holiday times. For information and booking forms, phone the park office.

Flats & Units There are a number of self-contained flats which can accommodate two to six people. These are usually booked on a weekly basis, and cost from $195 per week for a double bedsitter in the off season up to $540 for a six-bed unit in the peak season.

There are also 'motor huts' and tiny timber cabins with kitchenettes – these share communal bathrooms and you must supply all bed linen. The rate is a very reasonable $32 per night for up to four people, and $48 for up to six. The cabins and motor huts are usually heavily booked, so plan ahead.

Getting There & Away
The closest you can get by bus is to Fish Creek, from where you'll have to hitch the 60 km to Tidal River.

Another alternative is to take a tour with the Amaroo Park Backpackers in Cowes, Phillip Island (☎ (059) 52 2548), which are reasonably priced.

THE GIPPSLAND LAKES
The Lakes District is the largest inland waterway system in Australia. The three main lakes, Lake King, Lake Victoria and Lake Wellington, are all joined and fed by a number of rivers which originate in the High Country. The lakes are actually shallow coastal lagoons which are separated from the ocean by a narrow strip of coastal sand dunes known as the Ninety Mile Beach.

The area is popular for fishing, boating, water-skiing and other water-oriented activities. Obviously, with more than 400 sq km of waterways, the best way to appreciate the area is from a boat. You can join a lakes cruise or hire a boat from various places including Lakes Entrance and Metung.

Most of the Ninety Mile Beach is part of the Gippsland Lakes Coastal Park. Within this area is the Lakes National Park and the bird-watchers' paradise of Rotamah Island.

Bairnsdale (population 10,750)
Bairnsdale, a large commercial centre at the junction of the Princes and Omeo highways, is a popular base both for the mountains to the north and the lakes immediately to the south. For people travelling with energetic children, there is one of the most interesting playgrounds in Victoria – **Howitt Park**, complete with flying foxes – on the Princes Highway on the eastern side of town. **St Mary's Catholic Church**, beside the information centre, has interesting painted murals and is worth a look.

Signposted 42 km north-west of Bairnsdale is the **Mitchell River National Park** with the **Den of Nargun**, a small cave which, according to Aboriginal legend, was haunted by a strange, half-stone creature, known as a 'nargun'. There are some excellent short walks in the park.

There's a good tourist information centre (☎ (051) 52 3234) at 240 Main St, open weekdays from 9 am to 5 pm and weekends from 10 am to 4 pm.

Places to Stay & Eat For an on-site van or tent site, try the *Mitchell Gardens Caravan Park* (☎ (051) 52 4654) on the banks of the Mitchell River. The *Backpackers Hostel* (☎ (051) 52 5097) at 119 McLeod St has bunks at $12 including breakfast, while the *Commercial Hotel* (☎ (051) 52 3031) on the corner of Main and Bailey Sts has basic single rooms for $12, and a good bistro downstairs. The *Orient Hotel* (☎ (051) 52 4030), at 59 Main St, has motel-style rooms at $25/40.

The elegant *Riversleigh Country Hotel* (☎ (051) 52 6996), at 1 Nicholson St, has excellent heritage-style rooms from $65/90 and one of the best restaurants in country Victoria.

Getting There & Away There's a daily train/bus service between Bairnsdale and Melbourne ($31.80), and there are buses to

VICTORIA

Lakes Entrance ($6.40). All the major bus operators stop in Bairnsdale on the coastal route between Melbourne and Sydney.

Metung (population 420)

This interesting little fishing village between Bairnsdale and Lakes Entrance is built on a land spit between Lake King and Bancroft Bay. The town offers hot sulphur springs in two outdoor pools and a wide range of boats can be hired from Riviera Nautica (☎ (051) 56 2243) to tour the lakes. Two boats, the *Spray* and the *Gypsy*, also offer cruises of the lakes.

There is plenty of accommodation to choose from, including the pub (☎ (051) 56 2206) right on the water.

Lakes Entrance (population 4600)

A popular if somewhat old-fashioned tourist town, Lakes Entrance is the main centre of the Lakes District, and also Victoria's largest fishing port.

From the centre of town, a walking bridge crosses Cunningham's Arm to the Ninety Mile Beach. The town's attractions include the **Kinkuna Country Fun Park**; an **antique carriage museum**; the **Wyanga Park Winery**, 10 km north; and **Nyerimilang Park**, a historic homestead and property off the Metung road.

Lots of cruise boats, such as the large *Thunderbird*, operate from here to tour the rivers and lakes – the tourist information centre can advise and make bookings. Boats can also be hired from Riviera Nautica (☎ (051) 56 2243) in Metung, Victor Hire Boats (☎ (051) 55 1888) in Lakes Entrance and Lake Tyers Boat Hire (☎ (051) 56 5666), six km east of the town.

The Lakes Entrance Fishermen's Co-operative, just off the Princes Highway, provides a viewing platform which puts you in the middle of the boats unloading their fish. Sunday morning is the best time to go. The co-op fish shop is guaranteed to sell the freshest fish in town.

From the footbridge in the centre of town, there's a 2.3-km walking track to the actual 'entrance'. Surfers should head for the left-handed reef break at Red Bluff, especially a high tide, or nearby Tracks and Sandy Point

There's a tourist information centre (☎ (051) 55 1966) on the Princes Highway just as you enter the town from the west.

Places to Stay & Eat Lakes Entrance has a huge array of accommodation, especially caravan parks and motels. The *Lakes Main Caravan Park* (☎ (051) 55 2365) in Willis St has an associate-YHA hostel with dorm beds for $8.50 a night, tent sites from $8 and on-site vans from $16. The *Glenara Motel* (☎ (051) 55 1555) at 221 The Esplanade has budget motel rooms from $30/35, and *Homlea Cottages* (☎ (051) 55 1998) at 32 Roadnight St has simple holiday cottages from $25 a double or around $40 for four.

Try *Tres Amigos* at 521 The Esplanade for Mexican meals. The *Kalimna Hotel* has a good bistro overlooking the lakes, or for a splurge try the excellent *Sally's* on the corner of the Esplanade and Bulmer St.

Getting There & Away There are daily V/Line buses between Lakes Entrance and Bairnsdale ($6.40), with bus/train connections to Melbourne ($38.60). Buses also continue east along the Princes Highway daily during school holidays and on Monday, Wednesday, Friday and Saturday at other times.

EAST GIPPSLAND

East Gippsland, also known as the Wilderness Coast, contains some of the most remote and spectacular national parks in the state, ranging from the coastal wilderness areas of Croajingolong to the lush rainforests of the Errinundra Plateau.

While the area was always considered too remote for agriculture, it has provided a rich harvest for the logging industry since late last century. Today, the logging of these forest areas is a sensitive and controversial issue, with an underlying conflict between the region's history of economic dependence on the logging industry and the current promotion of the area as a wilderness zone.

For naturalists interested in seeing East Gippsland, an essential book to buy is the Australian Conservation Foundation's *Car Touring & Bushwalking in East Gippsland*. For shorter visits, the Department of Conservation & Natural Resources publishes a very good map/brochure called *East Gippsland ... A Guide for Visitors*.

Orbost (population 2500)

Orbost is a logging service town, with a very pretty location on the Snowy River.

The excellent Rainforest Information Centre (☎ (051) 54 6375), operated by the Department of Conservation & Natural Resources, is an excellent source of information on forests and national parks in East Gippsland. It has interesting audiovisual displays and landscaped gardens, and is open on weekdays from 9 am to 5 pm, and on weekends from 10 am to 5 pm.

The tourist information office, known as the Slab Hut (☎ (051) 54 2424), is on Nicholson St.

Places to Stay Orbost has a caravan park (☎ (051) 54 1097), with tent sites and on-site vans; the *Commonwealth Hotel* (☎ (051) 54 1077) at 159 Nicholson St, with B&B from $25/35; and a couple of motels.

Getting There & Away V/Line has buses to Bairnsdale ($16.80), Lakes Entrance ($9), Cann River ($11.40), Genoa ($16.80) and east along the coast as far as Narooma.

Marlo & Cape Conran

On the coast 15 km south of Orbost is the sleepy little settlement of Marlo, at the mouth of the Snowy River. It's a popular fishing spot and the route along the coast to Cape Conran, 18 km to the east, is especially pretty as it winds through stands of banksia trees. The beach at Cape Conran is one long beautiful deserted strip of white sand.

Places to Stay Marlo has a couple of caravan parks, while at Cape Conran the Department of Conservation & Natural Resources (☎ (051) 54 8438) runs the *Banksia Bluff Camping Area*, with great sites from $5 to $13, and the superb *Cape Conran Cabins*, a set of seven self-contained timber cabins that sleep up to eight and cost from $45 for four plus $7 per extra adult – you'll need to book.

Baldwin Spencer Trail

This is a drive well worth doing – a 265-km route through more superb forest, including **Errinundra National Park**, north of Orbost on the Bonang Highway.

The route follows the trail of Walter Baldwin Spencer, a noted scientist and explorer who led an expedition through here in 1889. A map/brochure is available from the Rainforest Information Centre in Orbost.

Buchan (population 400)

There are a number of limestone caves around the tiny and beautiful town of Buchan, 55 km north-west of Orbost. The two major ones, maintained by the Department of Conservation & Natural Resources, are the **Royal Cave** and **Fairy Cave**. There are daily tours at 10 am and 1 and 3.30 pm for the Royal Cave, and 11.15 am and 2.15 pm for the Fairy Cave. The tours take around an hour and are well worth the $6.

The department also offers guided tours to more remote and undeveloped caves in the area; phone ☎ (051) 55 9264.

Places to Stay Buchan has a delightful camp site right at the caves, with a swimming pool continuously fed by an icy underground stream flowing from a cave in the hillside. Very refreshing! There's also a pub and a couple of private guesthouses which offer accommodation.

Snowy River National Park

This is one of Victoria's most isolated and spectacular national parks, dominated by deep gorges carved through limestone and sandstone by the mighty Snowy River. The entire park is a smorgasbord of unspoilt and superb bush and mountain scenery.

VICTORIA

The two main access routes are the Gelantipy Rd from Buchan and the Bonang Highway from Orbost. These roads are joined by McKillops Rd which runs across the northern border of the park. Along McKillops Rd you'll come across **McKillops Bridge**, where you can have a dip in the river or camp on its sandy banks. The view from the lookout over **Little River Falls**, about 20 km west of McKillops Bridge, is spectacular.

The classic canoe or raft trip down the Snowy River from Willis or McKillops Bridge to a pull-out point near Buchan takes at least four days and offers superb scenery: rugged gorges, raging rapids, tranquil sections and excellent camping spots on broad sand bars. A number of commercial operators organise raft trips on the Snowy, including World Expeditions (☎ (03) 670 8400) and Peregrine Adventures (☎ (03) 602 3066); the cost is about $480.

Errinundra National Park

This national park contains Victoria's largest areas of temperate rainforest. The park is on a high granite plateau with a high rainfall, deep, fertile soils and a network of creeks and rivers. The main access is via the Bonang Highway from Orbost or the Errinundra road from Club Terrace, both of which are unsealed, steep, slow and winding. There are various walking trails throughout the park, but no other facilities. Contact the rangers at Bendoc (☎ (064) 58 1456) or in Cann River (☎ (051) 58 6351) for more information and to check road conditions.

Croajingolong National Park

Croajingolong, a coastal wilderness park which stretches for about 100 km along the easternmost tip of Victoria, is one of the state's finest national parks. Magnificent unspoiled beaches, inlets, estuaries and forests make this an ideal area for camping, walking, swimming, surfing or just lazing around. The diverse habitat supports a wide range of plants and animals, with over 250 species of birds recorded in the area.

There are several roads leading from the highway to different parts of the park. Some are quite rough and require 4WD; the National Parks office at Cann River will give you more information about vehicular access.

There are camp sites within Croajingolong National Park at Wingan Inlet, Thurra River, Mueller River and Shipwreck Creek. Facilities are minimal and it's a good idea to make reservations with the parks office in Cann River (☎ (051) 58 6351) or Mallacoota (☎ (051) 58 0219).

Mallacoota (population 960)

Mallacoota is at the seaward end of a small lake system and is the main service town for this corner of the state. It is a popular fishing resort and there's good access to the Croajingolong National Park. Abalone and fishing are the town's mainstays, and there are fishing boats for hire.

The town's bank is only open on Mondays and Wednesdays, but there's a nearby general store that acts as a bank on other weekdays.

At Christmas and Easter the town becomes packed out with holiday makers, and accommodation can be hard to come by.

The Mallacoota Information & Booking Service (☎ (051) 58 0788), beside the pub at 57 Maurice Ave, can book tours, cruises and accommodation. Wallagaraugh River Wilderness Cruises (☎ (051) 58 0555) and the MV *Loch Ard* (☎ (051) 58 0455) both offer good cruises through the lakes system.

Places to Stay There's a great deal of holiday accommodation here, including five caravan and camping parks. The *Mallacoota Camping Park* (☎ (051) 58 0300) has hundreds of sites right on the foreshore, costing $8.50. The *Mallacoota Hotel/Motel* (☎ (051) 58 0455) has motel units from $35/45.

Other places include the excellent *Adobe*

Mud-brick Flats (☎ (051) 58 0329) which cost from $38 to $59 for four people plus $10 per extra adult; and *Karbethong Lodge*

(☎ (051) 58 0411), an old-fashioned guesthouse with double rooms from $50 and family units from $60.

VICTORIA

Western Australia

Area	2,525,500 sq km
Population	1,800,000

☎ From September 1997, Perth's existing phone numbers will be prefixed by the additional digit 9 (for example, ☎ 123 4567 becomes ☎ 9123 4567). From April 1998, in regional areas, the last two digits of the current area code will be added to the existing number (for example, ☎ (012) 123 456 becomes ☎ 1212 3456). The area code for the state will be (08). ■

Western Australia's position near the Indian Ocean trading routes occasioned very early European contact. The first known Europeans to land near the Western Australian coast were Dutch – Dirk Hartog in 1616, and those previously shipwrecked on the wild shores (whose wrecked vessels are still being discovered today). Abel Tasman was the first to chart parts of the WA coastline; he charted as far as the Gulf of Carpentaria in Queensland in 1644.

William Dampier was the first Englishman to comprehensively chart the coast. He first visited the area in 1688 on board the *Cygnet*, and his 1697 publication, *New Voyage around the World*, prompted funds for his subsequent trip in 1699 to chart what was then known as New Holland. On this trip, on board the HMS *Roebuck*, he charted from the Houtman Abrolhos Islands as far north as Roebuck Bay, near Broome.

Dampier's reports of a dry, barren land discouraged attempts at settlement and it was not until 1829, three years after Britain had formally claimed the land, that the first British settlers arrived in the Swan Valley, later Perth. Their presence was intended to forestall settlement by other European nations, in particular France.

The arrival of the Europeans had disastrous consequences for the local Aborigines. During the more than 40,000-year Aboriginal occupation of Western Australia, they had managed to live in harmony with nature despite the harshness of the environment, by hunting and gathering in small nomadic groups. Pushed off their traditional lands, many of the Aborigines who were not killed by the colonisers died of European diseases against which they had no immunity.

Western Australia's development as a British colony was painfully slow – hardly surprising, given its distance from the main Australian settlements in the east. It was not until the gold rushes of the 1890s that the colony really began to progress. Today, a larger and far more technologically advanced mineral boom forms the basis of the state's prosperity. As a result, Western Australia, more than any other state, is deeply embroiled in the current Mabo debate because of the conflicting issues of land rights and mining interests (see the Facts about the Country chapter).

There's a lot to see in WA ('double-U Ay' the common appellation for Western Australia). Close to the state's capital, Perth, is the scenic and historical Avon Valley. In the north there's the harsh and beautiful Pilbara, the reefs of Ningaloo and the boom tourist town of Broome, with its fascinating pearling past. At the top end of the state is the wild Kimberley area, one of Australia's last frontiers, while in the east there are the mining and ghost towns of the gold-fields region. The south-west is dotted with beautiful surf

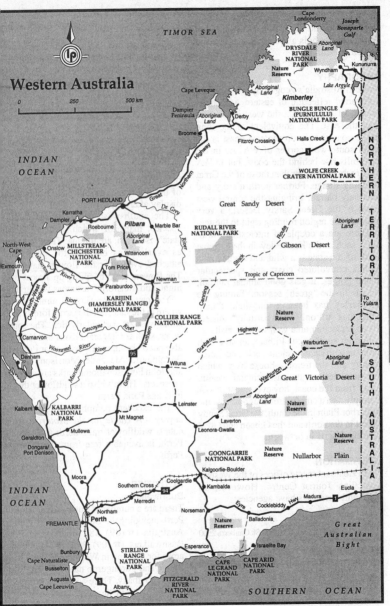

Western Australia

0   250   500 km

and swimming beaches, historic towns, wineries and giant karri forests. The Great Australian Bight is a spectacular, fierce and rugged coastline.

GEOGRAPHY

Western Australia's geography is a little like a distorted reflection of eastern Australia's except, of course, that the west is far drier than the east. The equivalent of the long fertile coastal strip on the east coast is the small south-west corner of WA. As in the east, hills rise behind the coast, but in WA they're much smaller than those of the Great Dividing Range. Further north it's dry and relatively barren. Fringing the central-west coast is the Great Sandy Desert, a very inhospitable region running right to the sea.

There are a couple of interesting variations, such as the Kimberley, in the extreme north of the state – a wild and rugged area with a convoluted coast and spectacular inland gorges. It gets good annual rainfall, but all in the 'green' season. Taming the Kimberley has been a long-held dream which has still only been partially realised. It's a spectacular area well worth a visit.

Further south is the Pilbara, an area with more magnificent ancient rock and gorge country and the treasure-house from which the state derives its vast mineral wealth. Away from the coast, however, most of WA is simply a vast empty stretch of outback: the Nullarbor Plain in the south, the Great Sandy Desert in the north and the Gibson and Great Victoria deserts in between.

INFORMATION

There are no interstate offices of the Western Australian Tourist Centre. However, all states and territories have agencies:

ACT
    Goddard & Partners, 40 Allara St, Canberra 2600 (☎ (06) 248 5214)
New South Wales
    Justravel, MO, 231-247 Pitt St, Sydney 2000 (☎ (02) 261 2800)
Northern Territory
    AANT, 79-81 Smith St, Darwin 0800 (☎ (089) 81 3838)

Queensland
    Justravel, 204 Adelaide St, Brisbane 4000 (☎ (07) 221 5022)
South Australia
    Tourism House, 41 Currie St, Adelaide 5000 (☎ (08) 211 8455)
Tasmania
    RACT, corner Murray and Patrick Sts, Hobart 7000 (☎ (002) 38 2200)
Victoria
    Contal Travel, 253 Flinders Lane, Melbourne 3000 (☎ (03) 654 1400)

WILDFLOWERS

WA is famed for its wildflowers, which bloom from August to October. Even some of the driest regions put on a technicolour display after just a little rainfall.

The south-west alone has over 3000 species, many of which, because of the state's isolation, are unique. They're known as everlastings because the petals stay attached even after the flowers have died. The flowers seem to spring up almost overnight, and transform vast areas within days.

You can find the flowers almost everywhere in the state, but the jarrah forests in the south-west are particularly rich. The coastal parks, such as Fitzgerald River and Kalbarri also put on brilliant displays. Near Perth, the Badgingarra, Alexander Morrison, Yanchep and John Forrest national parks are excellent prospects. There's also a wildflower display in Kings Park, Perth.

The excellent pamphlet *Wildflower Discovery – A Guide for the Motorist*, which details wildflower trails north and south of Perth, is available free from the WATC in Perth.

ACTIVITIES
Bushwalking

There are a number of bushwalking clubs in Perth including the Bushwalkers of Western Australia (☎ (09) 387 6875) and Perth Bushwalkers (☎ (09) 362 1614). Popular areas for walking in WA include the Stirling Range and Porongurup national parks, both north of Albany. There are also a number of coastal parks in the south and south-west such as Cape Le Grand, Fitzgerald River,

Western Australia 803

Valpole-Nornalup and Cape Arid, which have good walking tracks. To the north, the Kalbarri and Karijini (Hamersley Range) national parks provide a stimulating hiking environment.

There are interesting walks in the hills around Perth, and if you're a really enthusiastic walker there's the 640-km Bibbulman Track, which runs along old forest tracks between Perth and Walpole on WA's south-east coast. Information on this and many other tracks is available from CALM (Department of Conservation & Land Management) at 50 Hayman Rd in Como (☎ (09) 367 0333). Two excellent publications are *Discover Wild Places, Quiet Places* (which covers the south-west) and *North-West Bound* (covering Shark Bay to Wyndham).

Bird-watching can be an integral part of bushwalking, and WA is a fascinating destination for the avifauna addict. It is the only state with two Royal Australasian Ornithologists Union (RAOU) observatories – at Eyre and Broome, both splendid locations. The diversity of habitats, from the arid central and northern regions to the forests of the south-west, means that a great number of species can be observed.

Water Sports

Swimming People in Perth often claim that their city has the best surf and swimming beaches of any Australian city. Popular surfing areas around WA include Denmark near Albany; from Cape Naturaliste to Margaret River in the south-west; Bunbury, 180 km south of Perth; and Geraldton to the north. Fine swimming beaches occur right around the WA coast.

Diving Good diving areas include the large stretch of coast from Esperance to Geraldton, and between Carnarvon and Exmouth. You can get to the islands and reefs off the coast in small boats. The more popular diving spots include Esperance, Bremer Bay, Albany, Denmark, Margaret River, Bunbury, Rottnest Island, Shoalwater Islands Marine Park (off Rockingham), Lancelin, Houtman Abrolhos Islands (off Geraldton),

Carnarvon and all around North-West Cape (Exmouth, Ningaloo Reef and Coral Bay).

Fishing The coastal regions of WA offer excellent fishing. Some of the more popular areas include Rottnest Island, Albany, Geraldton and the Houtman Abrolhos Islands, Mackerel Islands, Shark Bay, Carnarvon and the coastline to the north, the North-West Cape and Broome.

Fishing licences are only required if you intend catching marron and rock lobsters or will be using a fishing net. They are available for $10 from the Fisheries Department (☎ (09) 325 5988), 108 Adelaide Terrace, Perth, or country offices.

Heritage Trails Network

The Heritage Trails Network, launched during Australia's Bicentenary in 1988, is an excellent series of road trails covering historical, cultural or natural points of interest throughout the state. A little neglected now, the trails are usually marked with interpretive displays and directional markers. Information on the Heritage Trails Network can be obtained from tourist offices or the WA Heritage Committee (☎ (09) 221 4177), 292 Hay St, East Perth.

GETTING THERE & AWAY

Western Australia is the largest, most lightly populated and most isolated state in the country. Yet in spite of the vast distances that must be travelled, you can drive across the Nullarbor Plain from the eastern states to Perth and then all the way up the Indian Ocean coast and through the Kimberley to Darwin without leaving the bitumen.

Even so, there's absolutely no way of covering all those km cheaply, although the deregulation of the airline industry has certainly helped. Sydney to Perth is 3284 km as the crow flies, and more like 4000 km by road: a one-way economy rail ticket on the route is $230, a discounted air ticket costs $580 return (or even less if you shop around), while a seat on one of the cheaper bus lines costs around $200. (See the Perth Getting

WESTERN AUSTRALIA

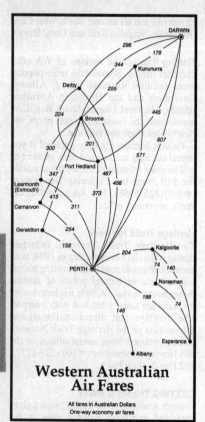

Western Australian Air Fares

All fares in Australian Dollars
One-way economy air fares

the Warburton Road. There are a number of escorted tours, including Austracks 4WD Outback Adventures (☎ 1800 655 200); the cost for their six-day trip is $450. Also operating is Marlu Camping Safaris (☎ (09) 30 1320) which has an 11-day Red Centre tour for $720.

GETTING AROUND

Air

So far deregulation has made little difference to flying within WA. Ansett Australia controls most traffic, with Skywest and local operators in spirited competition on some routes. Ansett has a comprehensive network of flights connecting Perth with most of WA's regional centres. The frequency of some flights seems ridiculous given the state's small population – until you realise how many mining projects are based there.

The chart details the main Western Australian routes and flight costs.

Bus

Greyhound Pioneer (☎ 13 2030) buses run from Perth along the coast to Darwin ($330) and from Perth to Adelaide via Kalgoorlie and the Eyre Highway ($180). Dixon's Westliner (☎ (09) 250 3318) does the Port Hedland to Perth run via Newman and the Great Northern Highway; and Perth to Derby via the coastal route. Dixon's has a 28-day West Pass for $277; some restrictions apply such as a seven-day stopover limit. Kalgoorlie Express (☎ (09) 328 9199) does the Perth to Leinster via the gold fields run ($90).

South-West Coach Lines (☎ (09) 322 5173) in the Transperth bus station, Wellington St, Perth, runs bus services between Perth and the following centres in the state's south-west: Bunbury, Busselton, Augusta, Dunsborough, Nannup, Manjimup and Collie.

Train

Western Australia's internal rail network operated by Westrail, is limited to services between Perth and Kalgoorlie (the Prospector), and Perth and Bunbury in the south (the

There & Away section for details on train travel.)

Hitching across the Nullarbor is not advisable; waits of several days are not uncommon. Driving yourself is probably the cheapest way of getting to WA from the eastern states – if there is a group of you. You'll probably spend around $450 to $500 on fuel, travelling coast to coast; shared among four people that's about $125 each. (See the Nullarbor section later in this chapter.)

Another interesting route into WA is from Yulara near Uluru (Ayers Rock) to Perth via

Australind). Westrail also runs buses to York, Geraldton, Esperance, Augusta, Pemberton, Hyden, Albany and Meekatharra. Reservations are necessary on all Westrail bus/train services (☎ 13 2232).

Perth

Population 1,400,000

Perth is a vibrant and modern city, pleasantly sited on the Swan River, with the port of Fremantle a few km downstream and dormitory cities to the south. It's claimed to be the sunniest state capital in Australia and the most isolated capital city in the world. Of WA's 1.8 million people, around 80% live in and around Perth.

Perth was founded in 1829 as the Swan River Settlement, but it grew very slowly until 1850, when convicts were brought in to alleviate the labour shortage. Many of Perth's fine buildings such as Government House and Perth Town Hall were built with convict labour. Even then, Perth's development lagged behind that of the eastern cities, until the discovery of gold in the 1890s increased the population fourfold in a decade and initiated a building boom.

More recently, WA's mineral wealth has contributed to Perth's growth, and the resultant building boom has spread into the outer suburbs. A somewhat hick, squeaky-clean nouveau-riche image has been tainted by scandals such as 'WA Inc' and the crash of entrepreneurs, but it all seems to add to the town's frontier image.

Orientation
The city centre is fairly compact, situated on a sweep of the Swan River, which borders the city centre to the south and east, and links Perth to its port, Fremantle. The main shopping precinct in the city is along the Hay St and Forrest Place malls and the arcades that run between them. St George's Terrace is the centre of the city's business district.

The railway line bounds the city centre on the northern side. Immediately north of the railway line is Northbridge, a popular restaurant and entertainment enclave with a number of hostels and cheap accommodation. The western end of Perth slopes up to the pleasant Kings Park, which overlooks the city and Swan River. Further to the west, suburbs extend as far as Perth's Indian Ocean beaches such as Scarborough and Cottesloe.

Information
Tourist Offices The Western Australian Tourist Centre (WATC) (☎ 483 1111) is in Albert Facey House in Forrest Place, on the corner of Wellington St and opposite the railway station. The centre is open from 8.30 am to 5.30 pm Monday to Friday and from 9 am to 1 pm Saturday. It has a wide range of maps and brochures on Perth and the rest of WA, and an accommodation and tours reservation service. The Pinnacles Travel Centre, on the corner of Hay and Pier Sts, acts as the information centre on Saturday afternoon and on Sunday until noon.

A number of guides to Perth, including *Hello Perth & Fremantle*, *What's on this week in Perth & Fremantle*, *This Week in Perth & Fremantle – West Coast Visitor's Guide* and the *Map of Perth & Fremantle*, are available free of charge from the tourist centre, and from hostels and hotels. The free *Tourist Guide to Western Australia* is also useful.

Post & Telecommunications Perth's GPO (☎ 326 5211) is in Forrest Place, which runs between Wellington St and the Murray St Mall. There are phones for international calls in the foyer of the GPO. The STD telephone area code for Perth is 09.

Other Offices The Royal Automobile Club of Western Australia (RACWA) (☎ 421 4444) is at 228 Adelaide Terrace. The club's bookshop has an excellent travel section, and detailed regional maps can be obtained at the Road Travel counter.

The YHA (☎ 227 5122) has its office at 65 Francis St in Northbridge.

WESTERN AUSTRALIA

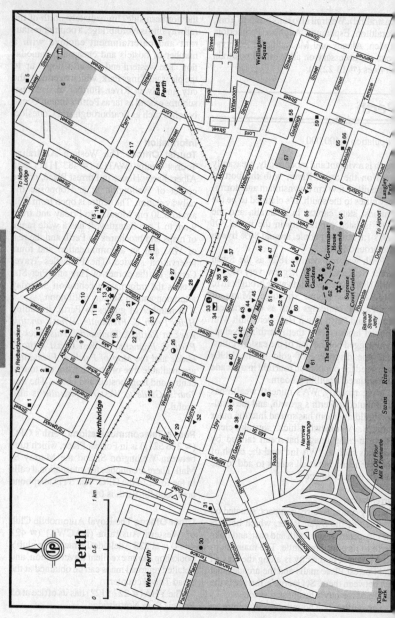

Perth

PLACES TO STAY		21	Brass Monkey Hotel	28	Central Perth Railway
		22	Plaka Shish Kebab		Station
1	12.01 Central	23	Sylvana Pastry	30	Parliament House
2	Perth Travellers Lodge	29	Fast Eddy's	31	Barrack's Arch
3	Budget Backpackers'	32	Shafto Lane Tavern	33	Western Australian
	International	35	Gopal's		Tourist Centre
4	Backpackers'	36	Ann's Malaysian	34	Post Office
	International		Food	38	Cloisters
5	Cheviot Lodge	45	Savoy Tavern	39	His Majesty's
11	Aberdeen Lodge	46	Miss Maud's		Theatre
13	Britannia YHA	52	Granary	40	Thomas Cook
	Backpackers' Hostel	56	Magic Apple	41	American Express
14	Northbridge YHA Hostel			42	Ansett Australia
15	Newcastle Lodge	OTHER		43	Carillon Arcade
16	City Backpackers' HQ			44	City Arcade
	(Lone Star)	6	Perth Oval	49	Old Perth Boy's
17	Newcastle YHA Hostel	7	Army Museum of		School
37	Grand YWCA Central		Western Australia	50	London Court
47	Regatta Hotel	8	Russell Square	51	Qantas Airlines
48	Murray Lodge	10	Aberdeen Hotel	53	Perth Town Hall
58	Jewel House YMCA	18	Claisebrook Railway	54	Deanery
59	Downtowner Lodge		Station	57	Ansett Australia
65	Girls Friendly Society	20	YHA Office	60	Qantas Airlines
	Lodge	24	Western Australian	61	Alan Green Plant
			Museum		Conservatory
PLACES TO EAT		25	Entertainment Centre	62	Supreme Court
		26	Wellington St Bus	63	Government House
9	Mamma Maria's		Station	64	Concert Hall
12	Bar Italia	27	Art Gallery of Western	66	RACWA
19	Northbridge Pavilion		Australia		

WESTERN AUSTRALIA

Bookshops Some good city bookshops include Angus & Robertson, 199 Murray St and 625 Hay St; Dymocks, Hay St Mall; and the Down to Earth Bookshop, 790 Hay St.

Kings Park
There are superb views across Perth and the river from this four-sq-km park. It includes a 17-hectare **Botanic Garden** that displays over 2000 different plant species from WA, and a section of natural bushland. In spring, there's a cultivated display of WA's famed wildflowers.

Free guided tours of Kings Park and the Botanic Gardens are available all year. The park also has a number of bike tracks; bikes can be rented from Koala Bicycle Hire (☎ 321 3061) at the western side of the main car park. An information centre, situated next to the car park, is open daily from 9.30 am to 3.30 pm. The park also has a restaurant with a pleasant coffee shop.

To get there, catch bus No 33 from St George's Terrace, the Green Clipper to Kings Park entrance or walk up Mount St from the city.

City Buildings
Near the corner of King St and St George's Terrace, the **Cloisters** date from 1858 and are noted for their beautiful brickwork. Originally a school, they have now been integrated into a modern office development. On the corner of St George's Terrace and Pier St is the **Deanery** which was built in 1859 and restored after a public appeal in 1980. It is one of the few cottage-style houses that have survived from colonial days. Neither the Cloisters nor the Deanery are open to the public.

Opposite the Deanery, on St George's Terrace, is **Government House**, a Gothic-looking fantasy built between 1859 and 1864. At the corner of St George's Terrace and William St is the grand and once extravagant **Palace Hotel**; it dates back to 1895 and is now a banking chamber.

In the Stirling Gardens off Barrack St is the old **courthouse**, next to the Supreme Court. One of the oldest buildings in Perth, it was built in Georgian style in 1836. Other old buildings include **Perth Town Hall** on the corner of Hay and Barrack Sts (1867-70); the **Central Government Buildings** on the corner of Barrack St and St George's Terrace, which can be recognised by their patterned brick; the restored **His Majesty's Theatre** (originally opened in 1904) on the corner of King and Hay Sts; and the Gothic-style **Old Perth Boys' School**, which was built in 1854 and now houses a National Trust gift shop.

The distinctive **Barracks Arch**, at the western end of St George's Terrace, is all that remains of a barracks built in 1863 to house the Pensioner Guards of the British Army – discharged British army soldiers who guarded convicts.

Parliament House

Tours of the Parliament buildings on Harvest Terrace can be arranged from Monday to Friday through the Parliamentary Information Officer (☎ 222 7222) – you will of course get a more extensive tour when Parliament is not in session. You can get there on the Purple Clipper from St George's Terrace or by the Green Clipper to Harvest Terrace.

Museums

On Francis St, north across the railway lines from the city centre, is the **Western Australian Museum**, which includes a gallery of Aboriginal history, a marine gallery, vintage cars, a 25-metre whale skeleton and a good collection of meteorites, the largest of which weighs 11 tonnes. (The Australian outback is a rich source of meteorites.)

The museum complex also includes Perth's original prison, built in 1856 and used until 1888. Admission to the museum is free and it is open from 10.30 am to 5 pm

Monday to Friday and from 1 to 5 pm Saturday and Sunday.

Three other museums close to town are the **Small World Museum** at 12 Parliament Place, which has the largest collection of miniatures in the country; the **Army Museum of Western Australia** on the corner of Bulwer and Lord Sts, which has a display of army memorabilia; and the **Fire Safety Education Centre & Museum** on the corner of Irwin and Murray Sts, which has displays of fire safety and fire-fighting equipment.

Art Gallery of Western Australia

Housed in a modern building which runs from James St through to Roe St, behind the railway station, the gallery has a fine permanent exhibition of European, Australian and Asian-Pacific art and a wide variety of temporary exhibitions. It is open from 10 am to 5 pm daily, and admission is free.

Perth Zoo

Perth's popular zoo is set in attractive gardens across the river from the city at 20 Labouchere Rd, South Perth. It has a number of interesting collections including a nocturnal house which is open daily from noon to 3 pm, an Australian Wildlife Park, a numbat display and a Conservation Discovery Centre. The zoo is open from 10 am to 5 pm daily and admission is $6 (children $2). You can reach the zoo on bus No 110 (or No 109 on weekends), which leaves from bus stand No 42 on St George's Terrace, or by taking the ferry across the river from Barrack St jetty.

Underwater World

Underwater World, north of the city, at Hillarys Boat Harbour, West Coast Drive, Hillarys, is certainly not your run-of-the-mill aquarium. There is an underwater tunnel aquarium displaying 2500 examples of 200 marine species including sharks and stingrays. Also in the complex are interactive displays such as a Touch Pool, Microworld and an audiovisual theatre. In season they conduct three-hour whale-watching trips out to see humpbacks. Underwater World is open daily from 9 am to 5 pm and entry costs 13.50 for adults, $6.50 for children and 33.50 for families.

Parks & Gardens

On the Esplanade, between the city and the river, is the **Alan Green Plant Conservatory**. It houses a tropical and semitropical controlled-environment display; admission is free. Also close to the city, on the corner of St George's Terrace and Barrack St, are the **Supreme Court Gardens**, a popular place to eat lunch.

The **Queen's Gardens**, at the eastern end of Hay St, is a pleasant little park with lakes and bridges; get there on a Red Clipper bus. The lake in **Hyde Park**, Highgate, is popular for the water birds it attracts, and the park is the site for the annual Hyde Park Festival – catch bus No 60 from bus stand No 2 in Barrack St. **Lake Monger** in Wembley is another hang-out for local feathered friends, particularly the famous black swans. Get there on bus Nos 91, 92 and 95 from opposite the Wellington St bus station (stand No 49). **Bold Park**, west of the city centre, is very popular with the locals.

Beaches

Perth residents claim that their city has the best beaches and surf of any Australian city.

There are calm bay beaches on the Swan River at **Crawley**, **Peppermint Grove** and **Como**. Or you can try a whole string of patrolled surf beaches on the Indian Ocean coast including Perth's very popular nude beach at **Swanbourne** – take bus No 205 or 207 from bus stand No 44 in St George's Terrace.

Some of the other surf beaches include **Cottesloe**, a very safe swimming beach; **Port**; **City**; **Scarborough**, a wide, golden and very popular surf beach which is only for experienced swimmers; **Leighton**; **Floreat**; and **Trigg Island**, another surf beach that is dangerous when rough. Perhaps the best beach of all is on secluded **Carnac Island**, frequented by the odd marooned human and some sea lions. (See also Rottnest Island in the Around Perth section.)

Markets

There are many lively markets around Perth – ideal if you're into browsing and buying. The **Subiaco Pavilion**, on the corner of Roberts and Rokeby Rds near Subiaco railway station, is open Thursday to Sunday. The **Wanneroo Markets**, north of Perth at Prindiville Drive, Wangara, feature a large food hall and a variety of stalls; they're open on Saturday and Sunday.

Other markets include the well-known

Perth skyline

and historic **Fremantle Markets** (see the Fremantle section of this chapter); the weekend **Stock Rd Markets**, in Bibra Lake south of Perth; and **Gosnells Railway Markets**, open Friday to Sunday.

Other Inner-City Attractions

Across Narrows Bridge is one of Perth's landmarks: the finely restored **Old Mill**, built in 1835. It's open every afternoon, except Tuesday and Friday; admission is free.

Between Hay St and St George's Terrace is the narrow, touristy **London Court**, a photographer's delight. Although it looks very Tudor English, it dates from just 1937. At one end of this shopping court St George and the dragon do battle above the clock each quarter of an hour, while at the other end knights joust on horseback.

The **Scitech Discovery Centre** in the City West shopping centre in Railway Parade, West Perth, has a number of hands-on and large-scale exhibits. It is open daily and well worth a visit, although admission is not cheap at $9 for adults and $5 for children.

Perth Suburbs

Armadale The **Pioneer World** at Armadale, 27 km south-east of the city, is a working model of a 19th-century colonial village; it's open daily and admission is $8.50. You can get to Armadale on a bus from Pier St or a local train from Perth railway station.

The **History House Museum**, on Jull St, is a free museum in a 19th-century pioneer's house. About six km south of Armadale, **Tumbulgum Farm** has a number of Australian products for sale, and puts on farm shows and displays of Aboriginal culture.

On Mills Rd in Martin you can ride a miniature railway through the **Cohunu Wildlife Park**, where there are native animals in natural surroundings. There are also plenty of water birds and a large walk-in aviary at the park. Open Wednesday to Sunday (daily during school holidays), the park's about a 35-minute drive from Perth.

Up the Swan River There are many attractions up the Swan River. On Maylands Peninsula, enclosed by a loop of the Swan River, is the beautifully restored **Tranby House**. Built in 1839, it is one of the oldest houses in WA and a fine example of early colonial architecture. It's open from 2 to 5 pm Monday to Saturday and from 11 am to 1 pm and 2 to 5 pm Sunday; admission is $2 for adults and $1 for children.

The **Rail Transport Museum** on Railway Parade, Bassendean, has locomotives and all sorts of railway memorabilia; it is open from 1 to 5 pm on Sunday; entry is $3.

Guildford has a number of historic buildings, including the **Mechanics Hall**, in Meadow St, and the **Folk Museum & Gaol** which is open Sunday from 2 to 5 pm in summer. **Woodbridge**, in Third Ave, was built in 1855 and is a fully restored and beautifully furnished colonial mansion overlooking the river. It's open daily (except Wednesday); there's a $2 entry.

In West Swan is the **Caversham Wildlife Park & Zoo** which has a large collection of Australian animals and birds; it's open from 10 am to 5 pm daily.

The Swan Valley **vineyards** are dotted along the river from Guildford right up to the Upper Swan. Many of them are open for tastings and cellar sales. Olive Farm Winery, 77 Great Eastern Highway, South Guildford, is the oldest in the region. Houghton Winery on Dale Rd, Middle Swan, was established later but produced the first commercial vintage in 1842.

The river cuts a narrow gorge through the Darling Range at **Walyunga National Park** in Upper Swan, off the Great Northern Highway. There are walking tracks along the river and it's a popular picnic spot.

Other Suburbs There's a real potpourri of other options; enquire at the tourist centre for opening times. In Subiaco, the **Museum of Childhood**, at 160 Hamersley Rd, houses an interesting collection. Across the Canning River towards Jandakot Airport, on Bull Creek Drive, Bull Creek, there is the excellent **Aviation Museum** with a collection of aviation memorabilia. In Melville, just off the Canning Highway, is the **Wireless Hill**

Park & Telecommunications Museum. The **Claremont Museum**, in the Freshwater Bay School at 66 Victoria Ave, Claremont, concentrates on local history.

In Cannington, on the road to Armadale, is **Woodloes**, a restored colonial home of 1874. The small **Liddelow Homestead** in Kenwick has also been restored. Yet another early home is the mud-brick and shingle **Stirk's Cottage**, Kalamunda, built in 1881.

Adventure World, 15 km south of Perth at 179 Progress Drive, Bibra Lake, is a large amusement park open daily. At **Cables Water Park**, at Troode St in Spearwood (just off Rockingham Rd, south of the city), cables haul water-skiers along the water at 20 to 50 km/h. It is open daily; an hour's skiing costs $12.

Organised Tours & Cruises
The WATC has the most detailed information about the many tours around Perth; they can also book them for you.

Land-Based Tours Half-day city tours of Perth and Fremantle are about $20, and for around $30 you can get tours to the Swan Valley wineries, Cohunu Wildlife Park or Underwater World and the northern beaches.

A favourite is the free tour of the Swan Brewery (☎ 350 0650), 25 Baile Rd, Canning Vale. The tour takes 1½ hours (followed by a couple of beers) and departs at 10 am on Monday to Thursday and 2.30 pm on Monday to Wednesday. Remember to make reservations.

Safari Treks (☎ 271 1271) does a good half-day tour of the Swan Valley; it's not cheap at $58 but you cover a lot of territory.

A recommended walking tour of Perth and surrounds is the three-hour Perth & Beyond tour through the King's Park (☎ 483 2601).

Cruises A number of cruise companies operate tours from the Barrack St jetty, including Captain Cook Cruises (☎ 325 3341) and Boat Torque (☎ 221 5844). Tours include scenic cruises of the Swan River, winery visits, trips to Fremantle and lunch and dinner cruises.

From September to May, the Transperth MV *Countess II* departs daily except Saturday at 2 pm from the Barrack St jetty on a three-hour cruise towards the Upper Swan River; the cost is $10. Boat Torque also has a three-hour Tranby House river cruise for $15, and Captain Cook Cruises has a three-hour Scenic River Cruise around Perth and Fremantle for $20.

Marine Mammal Observation
There are a number of activities that bring you closer to marine mammals in and around Perth, including sea-lion swimming, and dolphin- and whale-watching.

One informative, laid-back trip is the *Bellbird* Marine Discovery tour (☎ 335 1521). The small fishing boat takes you out to islands in Cockburn Sound on either a half-day or day trip. You can also swim with Australian sea lions (*Neophoca cinerea*) – these are much larger than fur seals and they range through the Southern and Indian oceans. The sea lions found on Carnac Island are nonmating males, barren females and juveniles. The cost is $35 with a healthy lunch included; there are discounts for hostellers.

There is an informative whale-watching trip with Mills Charters (☎ 401 0833), which is run in conjunction with Underwater World aboard the *Blue Water* and *Blue Horizon*. Of course, the actual search is for the humpback whale (*Megaptera novaengliae*) which returns to Antarctic waters after wintering in the waters of north-western Australia. The trip leaves from Hillarys boat harbour and costs $25 and $20 for weekends and weekdays respectively (children $20 and $15). Other operators are Oceanic Cruises (☎ 430 5127) and Boat Torque (☎ 246 1039).

Dolphin watching is done on two-hour cruises with Rockingham Dolphins (☎ 527 1803) from Mangles Bay.

Festivals
Every year around February/March the Festival of Perth offers entertainment in the form of music, drama, dance and films. The Northbridge Festival coincides with this

festival. The Royal Perth Show takes place every September, and the Artrage festival is in October.

Places to Stay

Perth has a wide variety of accommodation catering for all tastes and price brackets. There are numerous caravan parks scattered around the metropolitan area. The main area for budget accommodation is Northbridge, while hotels and motels of all standards and holiday flats are spread throughout Perth.

Camping Perth, like many other large cities, is not well endowed with camp sites convenient to the city centre. However, there are many caravan parks in the suburbs, and many are within a few km of the centre. Some of these include (distances are from the city):

Central Caravan Park (☎ 277 5696), seven km east at 38 Central Ave, Redcliffe; tent camping $12 for two, on-site vans are $25.

Guildford Caravan Park (☎ 274 2828), 19 km northeast at 372 West Swan Rd, Guildford; camping $13 for two, on-site vans from $28.

Karrinyup Caravan Park (☎ 447 6665), 14 km north at 467 North Beach Rd, Gwelup; camping $10 for two, on-site vans from $29.

Kenlorn Caravan Park (☎ 356 2380), nine km southeast at 224 Treasure Rd, Queens Park; tent camping $12 for two, on-site vans are $25.

Hostels There are over 20 budget hostels around Perth – most are reasonably central and many have similar names. Dorm beds range from $9 to $13 – $12 is about average. A twin share room is about $24 to $30.

Northbridge & City Centre The busy, friendly and slightly run-down *Newcastle YHA Hostel* (☎ 328 1135), at 60 Newcastle St, is about a 15-minute walk from the city centre; just go straight up Barrack or William St, crossing the railway line, until you hit Newcastle St, then turn right. The *Northbridge YHA Hostel* (☎ 328 7794), at 42-48 Francis St, is in an old guesthouse near the corner of William St, a little closer to the city. This hostel has friendly hosts, bicycles for

hire and a large outdoor area. It has dorm beds as well as twin and family rooms available.

Around the corner at 253 William St is the large *Britannia YHA Backpackers' Hostel* (☎ 328 6121). The better rooms are at the back on the verandah. Ask for a room away from the main hallways as they are noisy.

Budget Backpackers' International (☎ 328 9468), at 342 Newcastle St, has a comfortable lounge and good kitchen facilities. The staff will pick up travellers from the airport, station and bus depot.

Further along Newcastle St, at No 496, is the small, new *Redbackpackers* (☎ toll-free 1800 679 969). They pick up free of charge from the airport.

Rory's Backpackers (☎ 328 9958), also listed as *Backpackers Perth Inn*, at 194 Brisbane St, is further north of the city centre than other hostels. However, this nice renovated colonial house is very clean and has a pleasant garden and barbecue area. The hostel also has a ski boat to take hostellers out on the water in the summer months.

A good alternative is the *North Lodge* (☎ 227 7588) at 225 Beaufort St. It's clean, friendly and has all the usual facilities and comfortable dorm/twin rooms.

The *Perth Travellers Lodge* (☎ 328 6667) at 156-158 Aberdeen St is actually made up of two recently renovated houses, one for males and one for females. This place takes semipermanent boarders so if you are after international flavour look elsewhere.

The *Aberdeen Lodge* (☎ 227 6137), at 79 Aberdeen St, East Perth, is central and has four-bed dorms. Two other Aberdeen St places are *Backpackers' International* (☎ 227 9977), at the corner of Lake and Aberdeen Sts, and the impressive *12.01 Central* (☎ 227 1201), at the corner of Fitzgerald and Aberdeen Sts. In the relatively modern 12.01 there are dorms and twins. Downstairs is the Whistle Stop Deli, the Junction Cafe and a budget travel bureau.

Also in the Northbridge area is *Cheviot Lodge* (☎ 227 6817) at 30 Bulwer St. Open 24 hours, it is close to the interstate rail terminal, provides a free pick-up service

om Westrail bus station and hires out bicy-
les. There are no bunk beds. A little way out
f the budget strip, at 235 Vincent St in West
erth, is *Beatty Lodge* (☎ 227 1521).

At *City Backpackers' HQ* (also known as
e Lone Star) (☎ 328 7566), on the corner
f Beaufort and Newcastle Sts, most rooms
ave fridges, fans and balconies; twins and
oubles are $12 a night, $70 a week. With
e Lone Star Saloon below, you may need
arplugs. Next door is the ordinary *Newcas-
e Lodge* (☎ 328 5186) at 144-148 Newcastle
t. Dorm beds are $8 so you get what you
ay for!

Close to town is *Murray Lodge* (☎ 325
627), at 119 Murray St, which has all the
sual facilities as well as an open-air barbe-
ue area. The *Jewel House YMCA* (☎ 325
488), at 180 Goderich St (as Murray St
ecomes after Victoria Square), has 206
omfortable, clean and modern rooms. It's
ext to the Perth Dental Hospital and about
15-minute walk from the city centre – the
ed Clipper bus passes. Singles/doubles are
28/36 and weekly rates are six times the
aily rate.

The *Grand YWCA Central* (☎ 221 2682),
379 Wellington St, has recently been
enovated. There is a great variety of
ccommodation; bunk beds are $15 and
ingles/doubles are $25/40. There is also a
estaurant and cafe in the building.

Scarborough This is a good alternative to
Northbridge, being close to the surf. The
Mandarin Gardens (☎ 341 5431), at 20-28
Wheatcroft St in Scarborough, is the pick of
he beach accommodation. It has dorm beds
nd twin rooms. The hostel is within walking
distance (500 metres) of popular Scarbor-
ugh Beach, and it has friendly hosts, a
wimming pool and a sizable recreation
rea.

The *Sunset Beach Cafe & Accommoda-
ion* (☎ 341 6655), on the corner of the
Brighton and West Coast highways, has
orms and twin rooms. A 'big' breakfast
rom the accompanying cafe is $5.90. Also
n Scarborough, at 6 Westborough St, the
Western Beach Lodge* (☎ 245 1624) has male

and female dorms. This small place is clean
and airy.

Hotels There are quite a number of old-fashioned hotels around the centre of Perth. The
Regatta Hotel (☎ 325 5155), centrally
located at 560 Hay St, has friendly staff and
simple but clean singles/doubles for $35/54
with shared bathroom and $47/60 with facil-
ities. Also centrally located is the *Downtowner
Lodge* (☎ 325 6973), at 63 Hill St, opposite
the Perth Mint. The 13 rooms are clean and
pleasant, and it's a very quiet, friendly, nonsmoking place with a TV lounge and car
park. Beds are $17 in twin rooms and there
are weekly rates.

At the back of the Wentworth Hotel is the
Royal Hotel (☎ 481 1000), a renovated Fed-
eration-style building in the city centre. It has
singles for $30 to $45, and doubles for $45
to $60. There are three bars and three restau-
rants in the complex.

In West Perth, the *OBH*, or *Ocean Beach
Hotel* (☎ 384 2555), is a legendary hotel
right on Cottesloe Beach at the corner of Eric
St and Marine Parade. Spacious rooms with
fridge, TV and tea- and coffee-making facilities cost from $35/50; the counter meals,
like the rooms, are renowned.

Motels & Holiday Flats Perth and the surrounding suburbs have an abundance of
motels and holiday flats (see the *Western
Australia Accommodation Listing* available
from the tourist office for more information).

City Waters Lodge (☎ 325 1566), at 118
Terrace Rd down by the river, is conveniently central and good value with cooking
facilities, bathroom, TV, laundry and so on.
Daily costs are $67/72 for singles/doubles.

North of the city centre at 166 Palmerston
St are the self-contained *Brownelea Holiday
Units* (☎ 328 4840) at $40 a double. The
Adelphi Hotel Apartments (☎ 322 4666), at
130A Mounts Bay Rd, has well-equipped
units for $50/60.

Heading south across the bridge to
Applecross, the *Canning Bridge Auto Lodge*
(☎ 364 2511) is at 891 Canning Highway,
with rooms from $55. Along the Swan River

there are the *Swan View Motor Inn* (☎ 367 5755) at 1 Preston St in Como; *Broadwater Resort* (☎ 474 1919) at 6 Bowman St, also in Como; and the *Metro Inn* (☎ 367 6122) at 61 Canning Highway. There is a host of accommodation between the airport and city on the Great Eastern Highway; ask at the WATC.

Places to Eat

Food Centres This terrific Asian idea has really taken off in Perth, and crowded food halls prove that it's a popular alternative to fast food. You can choose quick meals, desserts and drinks from a range of cuisines to eat in the central eating area.

The *Down Under Food Hall* in the Hay St Mall, downstairs and near the corner of William St, has stalls offering Chinese, Mexican, Thai, Indian and many other types of food. This food centre is open Monday to Wednesday from 8 am to 7 pm and Thursday to Saturday from 8 am to 9 pm.

The *Carillon Food Hall*, in the Carillon Arcade on Hay St Mall, is slightly more up-market and has the same international flavour with Italian, Middle Eastern and Chinese food from $5 to $7. It also has sandwich shops, a seafood stall and fast-food outlets.

The large *Northbridge Pavilion* at the corner of Lake and James Sts is another good-value international food hall with Japanese, Italian, Indian, Thai, vegetarian and Chinese food. Open from Wednesday to Sunday, it has some outdoor seating and a couple of bars; the juices at *Naturals* are truly wonderful.

Seafood Perth is famous for its seafood restaurants. A number of well-frequented places in Northbridge are *Simon's* at 73 Francis St; *Harry's Seafood Grill & Garden Restaurant* at 94 Aberdeen St; *Fishy Affair* at 132 James St; and the *Oyster Bar* at 20 Roe St. On the Nedlands foreshore, *Jo-Jo's* claims to have the freshest seafood in town, and *Jessica's*, in the Hyatt at 99 Adelaide Terrace, is also good.

City The city centre is especially good f[or] lunches and light meals. The wholefoo[d] *Magic Apple* at 447 Hay St does deliciou[s] pitta-bread sandwiches, cakes and fres[h] juices.

The busy *Bernadi's*, at 528 Hay St, ha[s] good sandwiches, quiches, home-mad[e] soups and salads. The *Hayashi Japanes[e] BBQ*, at 107 Pier St, has excellent set lunche[s] for around $10. At 117 Murray St, betwee[n] Pier and Barrack Sts, is a pleasant and ver[y] reasonably priced little Japanese restaura[nt] called *Jun & Tommy's*.

Bobby Dazzler's at the Wentworth Hot[el] prides itself on its Australian menu – a goo[d] place for a bite and a drink. The *Granar[y]* downstairs at 37 Barrack St, has an extensiv[e] range of vegetarian dishes from $4 to $6 f[or] lunch.

Further up the road, at 129 Barrack St, [is] the Hare Krishna *Gopal's*, which has a[n] excellent $4 all-you-can-eat vegetarian me[al] from noon to 2.30 pm on weekdays. Not fa[r] away, at No 137, is *Ann's Malaysian Foo[d]*. Also in Barrack St is one of Perth's re[al] surprises, *Mr Samurai* at No 83. Ope[n] Monday to Saturday from 11 am to 6 pm (a[nd] Thursday until 8.30 pm), they serve deliciou[s] beef or tempura with rice, okonomiyaki (Jap[]- anese-style vegetables and prawns wit[h] okonomi sauce) or fried chicken with ric[e]. At an average of $4 this food is highly rec[]- ommended. Down in Murray St, on th[e] corner of Pier St, is *Miss Maud's*, a Swedis[h] restaurant.

The *Venice Cafe* at the St George's Terrac[e] end of the Trinity Arcade (shop No 201) is [a] pleasant European-style cafe with tables ou[t] the front and light meals such as lasagne[,] quiche or home-made pies and salad from $[5] to $6. They also make excellent coffee. Loc[al] tour gurus recommend *King Street Cafe*, i[n] King St, purveyors for the 'cuisine Yuppie'[.]

Perth has the usual selection of counte[r] meals in the city centre area. *Sassella[s] Tavern*, in the City Arcade, off Hay St, doe[s] bistro meals from $8 to $11. The *Savo[y] Tavern*, under the Savoy Plaza Hotel, at 63 [] Hay St, has basic pub fare such as roast bee[f] and vegetables and fish & chips for lunch.

Toward the western (Kings Park) end of the city centre, there's a string of places, including the popular *Fast Eddy's* on the corner of Murray and Milligan Sts. Shafto Lane between Murray and Hay Sts has a number of eateries including *Fasta Pasta*, with a wide selection of pasta dishes from $7.50 to $8.50, and *Iguana's Cafe*, which has a four-course meal after 5.30 pm for only 10.

Kings Park Restaurant and *Frasers Restaurant* are both good for a splurge, and both have great views over the city and the river.

Northbridge North of the city centre, the area bounded by William, Lake and Newcastle Sts is full of ethnic restaurants to suit all tastes and budgets. It is also an area undergoing rapid development due to its popularity. Listed below are some suggested places to eat, but this list is by no means exhaustive. The best bet is just to walk around and take in the sights and smells – you will soon find something to your liking at an appropriate price.

Kim Anh, at 178 William St near the railway station, is a friendly Vietnamese BYO place with an extensive menu including vegetarian food. At 182 William St is the reasonably priced *Tak Chee*, a favourite amongst the locals – always a good sign. They serve delicious Penang-style rice and noodle dishes. Across the street, at No 175, is the *Linh Phong*. Nearby, at 188 William St, is the moderately priced and popular *Romany*, one of the city's really long-running Italian places.

Not far away, at No 197, is *Sylvana Pastry*, a comfortable Lebanese coffee bar with an amazing selection of those sticky Middle Eastern pastries which look, and usually taste, delicious. On the corner of Aberdeen and William Sts is the busy *Bar Italia* which serves excellent coffee and light meals including a good selection of pasta dishes; it is open from breakfast time until 1 am. *Mamma Maria's*, at 105 Aberdeen St on the corner of Lake St, has a pleasant ambience and a reputation as one of Perth's best Italian eateries. Its main courses are priced from

$11.50. There are a couple of pizza places on Lake St, at Nos 71 and 60, which serve tasty food.

Plaka Shish Kebab, at 87 James St, has good souvlaki and kebabs from $4.50 but it is somewhat sterile in atmosphere. Further away, at 193 Brisbane St, is the *Ly Tao* Vietnamese restaurant. At 17 Chinatown or 66 Roe St is the cleverly named *Thai me Down Sport*, open seven days for lunch and dinner for all those spicy Thai favourites. In front of this place is a bewildering array of Asian cuisine squeezed into a rambling food hall, exuding aromatic and pungent smells reminiscent of Singapore, Canton and Bangkok.

Several restaurants and cafes have recently opened up in Leederville, north-west of the city centre. Located on Oxford St, between Vincent and Aberdeen Sts, they include *Villa Bianchi*, *Giardini* and *Palermo*.

Entertainment

Perth has plenty of pubs, discos and nightclubs. The Thursday edition of the *West Australian* has an informative entertainment lift-out called the *Revue*. The *X-press*, a weekly music magazine available free at record shops and other outlets, has a gig guide. Northbridge is definitely the place to go after dark – Friday night there is witness to almost frenetic revelry, while the city centre is dead.

Cinemas & Theatres
Quality films are shown at the *Lumiere Cinema* in the Perth Entertainment Centre, *Cinema Paradiso* at 166 James St and the *Astor*, on the corner of Beaufort and Walcott Sts in Mt Lawley. Popular theatres include *His Majesty's Theatre* on the corner of King and Hay Sts, the *Regal Theatre* at 474 Hay St in Subiaco and the *Hole in the Wall* at the Subiaco Theatre Centre, 180 Hamersley Rd, Subiaco.

Concerts & Recitals
The *Perth Concert Hall* in St George's Terrace and the large *Entertainment Centre* in Wellington St are venues for concerts and recitals by local and international acts.

Pubs & Live Music Three popular places for interesting live music in Northbridge are the *Aqua*, on the corner of William and James Sts; the *Aberdeen Hotel*, at 84 Aberdeen St; and the *Lone Star*, on the corner of Beaufort and Newcastle Sts. The latter has a backpackers' night every Wednesday and live bands on the weekends.

Perth has the usual pub-rock circuit with varying cover charges depending on the gig. Popular venues include *Raffles* on the Canning Highway, Applecross; the *Stadium* inside the Herdsman Hotel; the *Charles Hotel*, Charles St, North Perth; and *Club Original* at the Grosvenor Hotel, corner of Hill and Hay Sts, East Perth.

Discos & Nightclubs In the city centre is *Mangoes*, a piano bar with music and exotic cocktails at 101 Murray St, and the *Loft* nightclub at 237 Hay St. *Havana* is a popular venue at 69 Lake St.

Gay and lesbian places include the *Northbridge Hotel*, corner of Lake and Brisbane Sts; the *Court Hotel*, corner of Beaufort and James Sts; *Connections* (Connies), James St; and *DC's*, Francis St. Check in the *Westside Observer* for venues and activities. Other nightclubs are *Exit* at 187 Stirling St, the *Racket Club* in East Perth on the corner of Aberdeen St, the *James Street Club* (techno music) and the *Hip Club* on the corner of Newcastle and Oxford Sts (backpackers' night every Tuesday).

Spectator Sports The people of Perth, like most other Australians, are parochial in their support of local sporting teams. The West Coast Eagles, Perth's representatives in the Australian Football League, and the Perth Wildcats in the National Basketball League regularly play interstate teams in Perth. Check the *West Australian* for game details.

Casino On an artificial island en route to the airport, off the Great Western Highway at Victoria Park, is Perth's glitzy *Burswood Casino*, open all day, every day. Its set up seems pretty similar to that of other Australian casinos, with gaming tables (roulette and

blackjack), a two-up gallery, Keno, poke machines and extensive off-course betting.

Things to Buy

Perth has a number of excellent outlets fo Aboriginal arts and crafts, including the Cre ative Native Gallery at 32 King St. Othe local crafts can be found at the variou markets around town – see the Market section earlier in this chapter.

For camping and climbing equipment there's Paddy Pallin at 891 Hay St and across the road at No 862, there's also Moun tain Designs.

Getting There & Away

Air Qantas (☎ 13 1313) and Ansett Australi (☎ 13 1300) have flights to and from Sydney Melbourne, Brisbane, Adelaide, Darwin and Alice Springs. Some Sydney and Melbourne flights go direct, and some via Adelaide or in the case of Sydney, via Melbourne.

The standard economy fares are $601 to Sydney, $539 Melbourne, $620 Brisbane $482 Adelaide, $607 Darwin and $468 Alice Springs. As always, check with the airline for special deals; it would be rare that you' have to pay the full economy fare.

Skywest (☎ 334 2288), on the Grea Eastern Highway, fly to WA centres such a Albany, Esperance, Kalgoorlie, Geraldton Monkey Mia and Meekatharra.

Bus Greyhound Pioneer (☎ 13 2030) oper ates daily bus services from Adelaide to Perth from the Westrail Centre on Wes Parade in East Perth (Interstate railway station). The journey from Perth to Darwin along the coast takes around 56 hours by bu and costs $330. Greyhound Pioneer also operates a four-times-weekly service to Darwin via the more direct, inland route through Newman (it saves five hours and i the same price).

Westrail operates bus services to a numbe of WA centres including Albany ($34) Augusta ($28), Bunbury ($17), Collie ($20) Hyden (Wave Rock) ($29; twice weekly) Esperance ($50), Geraldton ($35) and Meekatharra ($64).

A	
B	C	D
E	

Victoria

A Melbourne skyline (PS)

B Luna Park, St Kilda (CK)

C Swanston Walk, Melbourne (TS)

D St Paul's Cathedral, Melbourne (RN)

E Victorian Arts Centre, Melbourne (RI)

A	B
C	D	E
	F	

Victoria

A Mt Buffalo National Park (RB)
B Sovereign Hill, Ballarat (RN)
C Moyne River, Port Fairy (GB)
D Grampians (Geriwerd) National Park (HF)

E River red gums, Hattah-
  Kulkyne National Park (C
F Twelve Apostles, Port
  Campbell National Park (F

Train Along with the Ghan to Alice Springs, the long Indian Pacific run is one of Australia's great railway journeys – a 65-hour trip between the Pacific Ocean on one side of the continent and the Indian Ocean on the other. Travelling this way you see Australia at ground level and by the end of the journey you really appreciate the immensity of the country (or perhaps are only bored stiff).

From Sydney, you cross New South Wales to Broken Hill and then continue on to Adelaide and across the Nullarbor. From Port Augusta to Kalgoorlie, the seemingly endless crossing of the virtually uninhabited centre takes well over 24 hours, including the 'long straight' on the Nullarbor – at 478 km this is the longest straight stretch of railway line in the world. Unlike the trans-Nullarbor road, which runs south of the Nullarbor along the coast of the Great Australian Bight, the railway line actually crosses the Nullarbor Plain.

To Perth, one-way fares from Adelaide are $337 for an economy sleeper, $566 for a 1st-class sleeper or $170 in an economy seat with no meals; from Melbourne $444 economy sleeper, $715 1st-class sleeper or $215 seat only; and from Sydney $495 economy, $850 1st class or $230 seat only.

Advance-purchase fares offer good reductions (around 30%) if you book at least seven days in advance. Melbourne and Adelaide passengers connect with the Indian Pacific at Port Pirie. Cars can be transported between Adelaide and Perth ($290) and most other major cities.

The distance from Sydney to Perth is 3961 km. You can break your journey at any stop along the way and continue on later as long as you complete the one-way trip within two months; return tickets are valid for up to six months. Westbound, the Indian Pacific departs Sydney on Monday and Thursday. Heading east, the train departs Perth on Monday and Friday. Book at least a month in advance.

Between Adelaide and Perth you can also travel on the weekly Trans-Australia railway. Fares are the same as those on the Indian Pacific, and the trip takes 38 hours.

The only rail services within WA are the Prospector from Perth to Kalgoorlie and the Australind from Perth to Bunbury – see the Kalgoorlie and Bunbury sections for details. All rail services run to or from the Westrail terminal in East Perth, as do the Westrail buses.

Train bookings can be made by phone (☎ 13 2232), or through the WATC in Forrest Place.

Car Rental Hertz (☎ 321 7777), Budget (☎ 322 1100), Avis (☎ 325 7677) and Thrifty (☎ 481 1999) are all represented in Perth, along with cheaper local firms including:

ATC, 126 Adelaide Terrace (☎ 325 1833)
Bayswater Car Rental, 160 Adelaide Terrace (☎ 325 1000)
Carousel Rent-a-Car, 318 Charles St, North Perth (☎ 328 8999)
Economic Car Rental, 179 William St (☎ 227 1112)

Hitching Hostel notice boards are worth checking for lifts to points around the country. If you're hitching out of Perth to the north or east, take a train to Midland. For travel south, take a train to Armadale. Trans-Nullarbor hitching is not that easy, and the fierce competition between bus companies and discounted air fares have made those forms of travel much more attractive.

Getting Around

Perth has a central public transport organisation called Transperth which operates buses, trains and ferries. There are Transperth information offices (☎ 13 2213) in the Plaza Arcade (off the Hay St Mall), at the City Bus Port on Mounts Bay Rd at the foot of William St and at the Wellington St bus station. They can all provide advice about getting around Perth and can also supply a system map and timetables. These offices are open from 6.30 am and 8 pm Monday to Friday and from 8 am to 5 pm on Saturday.

To/From the Airport Perth's airport is busy night and day. The city's isolation from the east coast and the airport's function as an international arrival point mean planes arrive and depart at all hours.

The domestic and international terminals are 10 km apart and taxi fares to the city are around $15 and $20 respectively. The privately run Perth Airport Bus (☎ 250 2838) meets all incoming domestic and international flights and provides transport to the city centre, hotels and hostels. Although the operators claim to meet all flights, some travellers have reported that sometimes it doesn't turn up – if this occurs late at night, a taxi into the city is probably your best option.

The airport bus costs $6 from the domestic terminal and $7 from the international terminal. There are scheduled runs to the airport terminals every couple of hours from 4.45 am to 10.30 pm. Call them for hotel and hostel pick-ups and timetable information.

Alternatively, you can get into the city for about $1.90 on Transperth bus Nos 200, 201, 202, 208 and 209 to William St. They depart from the domestic terminal every hour or so (more frequently at peak times) from 5.30 am to 10 pm on weekdays and for nearly as long on Saturday; Sunday services are less frequent. To the domestic terminal, the bus leaves from stand No 39 on St George's Terrace. Some of the backpackers' places pick up at the airport (generally only if you are staying in their accommodation that night) and offer reduced fares into the city.

Bus There are five free City Clipper services which operate every 20 minutes or so from 7 am to 6 pm Monday to Friday. The Yellow Clipper (No 1) passes every eight minutes on weekdays and every 15 minutes on Saturday. All clipper services, except the Blue Clipper, pass through the Wellington St bus station.

(No 1) Yellow Clipper
    These operate around the central area of the city.
(No 2) Purple Clipper
    These operate from the City Bus Port to West Perth.
(No 3) Green Clipper
    These travel between the Wellington St bus station and West Perth.

(No 4) Blue Clipper
    These run from the City Bus Port, Mounts Bay Rd, to the Esplanade along Barrack and William Sts, then down Beaufort St.
(No 5) Red Clipper
    These depart Wellington St bus station to East Perth, near the WACA, and return.

On regular buses, a short ride of one zone costs $1.30, two zones cost $1.90 and three zones $2.30. Zone 1 includes the city centre and the inner suburbs (including Subiaco and Claremont), and Zone 2 extends all the way to Fremantle, 20 km from the city centre. A Multirider ticket gives you 10 journeys for the price of nine.

The Perth Tram (☎ 367 9404) doesn't run on rails – it's a bus that takes you around some of Perth's main attractions (such as the city, Kings Park, Barrack St jetty and the casino) in 1½ hours for $9. The 'tram' leaves from 124 Murray St (near Barrack St) six times a day, seven days a week.

Train Transperth operates suburban train lines to Armadale, Fremantle, Midland and the northern suburb of Joondalup from around 5.20 am to midnight on weekdays with reduced services on weekends. All trains leave from the city station on Wellington St. Your rail ticket can also be used on Transperth buses and ferries within the ticket's area of validity.

Bicycle Cycling is a great way to explore Perth. There are many bicycle routes along the river all the way to Fremantle and along the Indian Ocean coast. Get the free *Along the Coast Ride* and *Around the River Ride* booklets from the WATC in Forrest Place.

At WA Bike Disposals (☎ 325 1176), in Bennett St, you can buy a bike knowing that you get a guaranteed buy-back price after a certain time. Ride Away (☎ 354 2393) by the city side of the Causeway also rents cycles.

Boat Transperth ferries cross the river every day from the Barrack St jetty to the Mend St jetty in South Perth every half an hour (more frequently at peak times) from around am to 7 pm for 70c. Take this ferry to get to the zoo.

The Rottnest Island Getting There & Away section has details on ferries from Perth, Hillarys and Fremantle to Rottnest. See the Organised Tours section earlier for river cruises.

Around Perth

FREMANTLE (population 25,000)
Fremantle ('Freo' to the locals), Perth's port, is at the mouth of the Swan River, 19 km south-west of the city centre. Over the years, Perth has sprawled to engulf Fremantle, which is now more a suburb of the city than a town in its own right. Despite recent development, Freo has a wholly different feeling than gleaming, skyscrapered Perth. It's a place with a real sense of history and a very pleasant atmosphere.

Fremantle was founded in 1829 when the HMS *Challenger* landed, captained by Charles Fremantle. Like Perth, the settlement made little progress until it reluctantly decided to take in convicts. This cheap and hard-worked source of labour constructed most of the town's earliest buildings, some of them amongst the oldest and most treasured in WA. As a port, Fremantle was abysmal until the brilliant engineer C Y O'Connor built an artificial harbour in the 1890s.

In 1987, the city was the site of the unsuccessful defence of what was, for a brief period, one of Australia's most prized possessions – the America's Cup yachting trophy. Preparations for the influx of tourists associated with the competition certainly transformed Fremantle into a more modern, colourful and expensive city. Many of the residents, however, protested at the time that their lifestyle and the character of their community were damaged by the development.

The town has numerous interesting old buildings, some excellent museums and galleries, a lively produce and craft market, and a diverse range of pubs, coffee shops and restaurants. A visit to Fremantle will be one of the highlights of your trip to WA. Make sure you leave yourself enough time to explore, sip coffee in an outdoor cafe and soak in the atmosphere.

Information
There is an information centre in the Fremantle Town Hall shop (☎ 430 2346), near St John's Square, which is open Monday to Friday from 9 am to 5 pm, Saturday from 9 am to 1 pm, and Sunday 10 am to 3 pm. Among the brochures are a number of guides and information on heritage trails and National Trust walking tours – obtain the *Manjaree Track*, *Convict Trail* and *Old Foreshore* brochures if you can.

Fremantle Museum & Arts Centre
The museum is housed in an impressive building on Finnerty St, originally constructed by convict labourers as a lunatic asylum in the 1860s. It houses a fine collection including exhibits on Fremantle's early history, the colonisation of WA and the early whaling industry. It also tells the intriguing story of the Dutch East India Company ships which first discovered the western coast of Australia and in several instances were wrecked on its inhospitable shores. The museum is open from 1 pm to 5 pm Thursday to Sunday; admission is free.

The Arts Centre, which occupies one wing of the building, is open daily from 10 am to 5 pm and Wednesday evening from 7 to 9 pm; admission is free.

Maritime Museum
On Cliff St, near the waterfront, is the Maritime Museum, which occupies a building constructed in 1852 as a commissariat store. The museum has a display on WA's maritime history with particular emphasis on the famous wreck of the *Batavia*. One gallery is used as a working centre where you can see the *Batavia* actually being preserved.

At one end of this gallery is the huge stone facade intended for an entrance to Batavia

Fremantle

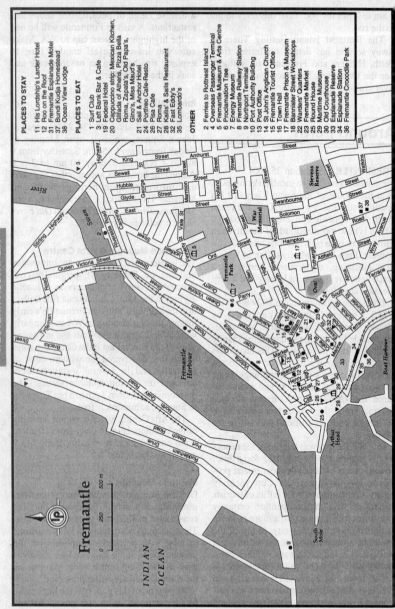

INDIAN OCEAN

0   250   500 m

PLACES TO STAY

11 His Lordship's Larder Hotel
12 Roo on the Roof
31 Federal Hotel
37 Fremantle Esplanade Motel
38 Bundi Kudja Homestead
38 Ocean View Lodge

PLACES TO EAT

1   Surf Club
3   Left Bank Bar & Cafe
19 Federal Hotel
20 Cappuccino strip: Mexican Kitchen,
    Gilfada of Athens, Pizza Bella
    Roma, Zapata's, Old Papa's,
    Gino's, Miss Maud's
21 Sail & Anchor Hotel
24 Portfree Cafe-Resto
26 Pisa Cafe
27 Roma
28 Kailis & Sails Restaurant
32 Fast Eddy's
35 Lombardo's

OTHER

2   Ferries to Rottnest Island
4   Overseas Passenger Terminal
5   Fremantle Museum & Arts Centre
6   Proclamation Tree
7   Energy Museum
8   Fremantle Railway Station
9   Northport Terminal
10 Port Authority Building
13 Post Office
14 St John's Anglican Church
15 Fremantle Tourist Office
16 Town Hall
17 Fremantle Prison & Museum
18 Bannister Street Workshops
22 Warders' Quarters
23 Fremantle Market
25 Round House
29 Maritime Museum
30 Old Courthouse
33 Esplanade Reserve
34 Esplanade Station
36 Fremantle Crocodile Park

Castle in modern-day Jakarta, Indonesia. It was being carried by the *Batavia* as ballast when the vessel sank. This intriguing museum is open Monday to Thursday from 10.30 am to 5 pm and Friday to Sunday from 1 to 5 pm; admission is free, and a visit is a must.

Fremantle Market

A prime attraction is the colourful Fremantle Market on South Terrace at the corner of Henderson St. Originally opened in 1892, the market was reopened in 1975 and draws crowds looking for everything from craft items to vegetables, jewellery and antiques; there is a also a great tavern bar where buskers often perform. The market is open from 9 am to 9 pm on Friday, from 9 am to 5 pm on Saturday, and from 10 am to 5 pm on Sunday.

Round House

On Arthur Head at the western end of High St, near the Maritime Museum, is the Round House. Built in 1831, it's the oldest public building in WA. It actually has 12 sides and was originally a local prison (in the days before convicts were brought into WA). It was also the site of the colony's first hanging.

Later, the building was used to hold Aborigines before they were taken to Rottnest Island. The site provides good views of Fremantle. The Round House shop and information centre is housed in one of the nearby pilots' cottages. The building is open from 10 am to 5 pm daily; admission is free.

Convict-Era Buildings

Many other buildings in Fremantle date from the period after 1850, when convict labour was introduced. The *Convict Trail* brochure, available from the Fremantle Town Hall shop, outlines the places of interest from this era. They include **Fremantle Prison**, one of the unlucky convicts' first building tasks. The entrance on Fairbairn St is picturesque. The prison is open from 10 am to 6 pm daily; admission is $10. Beside the prison gates, at 16 The Terrace, is a small museum on the convict era in WA.

Later Landmarks

Fremantle boomed during the Western Australian gold rush and many buildings were constructed during, or shortly before, this period. They include **Samson House**, a well-preserved 1888 colonial home in Ellen St, which is open from 1 to 5 pm on Thursday and Sunday – tours of the house are run by volunteer guides. The fine **St John's Church** of 1882, on the corner of Adelaide and Queen Sts, features a large stained-glass window.

Other buildings of the era include the **Fremantle Town Hall** (1887) in St John's Square; the former **German consulate building** built in 1902 at 5 Mouat St; the **Fremantle railway station** of 1907; and the old, Georgian-style **customs house** on Cliff St. The **water trough** in the park in front of the station has a memorial to two men who died of thirst on an outback expedition. The **Proclamation Tree**, near the corner of Adelaide and Parry Sts, is a Moreton Bay fig that was planted in 1890.

Other Attractions

Fremantle is well endowed with parks, including the popular **Esplanade Reserve**, beside the picturesque boat harbour off Marine Terrace.

The city is a popular centre for craft workers of all kinds and one of the best places to find them is at the imaginative **Bannister St Workshops**. From the observation tower on top of the **Port Authority Building**, at the end of Cliff St, you can enjoy a panoramic view of the harbour. You must take the escorted tours which are conducted from the foyer every weekday at 2.30 pm only.

The **Energy Museum**, at 12 Parry St, has some entertaining and educational displays tracing the development of gas and electricity. It is open from 10.30 am to 4.30 pm on weekdays and from 1 to 4.30 pm on weekends; admission is free.

For boat freaks only, there is a collection of boats from the last 100 years in B-Shed at Victoria Quay. The collection includes the 12-metre yacht *Australia II*, which won the America's Cup in 1983; admission is free.

WESTERN AUSTRALIA

Finally, there is the **Fremantle Crocodile Park**, where the reptiles have the avarice of entrepreneurs; admission is $8.

Organised Tours
The Fremantle Tram is very much like the Perth Tram and does a 45-minute historical tour of Fremantle with full commentary for $7; a harbour tour is also available for $7 and a top of the Port tour for $10. You can combine the tour with a cruise to Perth, a tour of Perth on the Perth Tram and a return ticket to Fremantle for $34 (☎ 339 8719).

Places to Stay
Bundi Kudja Homestead (☎ 335 3467), 96 Hampton Rd, has dorm beds for $11, and singles and twins for $16/13 per person. It is housed in former nurses' quarters, which were built around 1896 (bundi kudja means 'home of good babies'). There are kitchens, plenty of facilities, a log fire, games room and TV and video lounge.

The *Ocean View Lodge* (☎ 336 2962), 100 Hampton Rd, has singles/doubles for $15/27 and also weekly rates. There are about 200 rooms in this huge complex which also has a gym, sauna, billiard room, swimming pool and barbecue area.

More central is the rather run-down *Roo on the Roof* (☎ 335 1998), 11 Pakenham St, which offers budget (in the worst sense of the word) accommodation from $12.50 and singles from $15.

His Lordship's Larder Hotel (☎ 336 1766), on the corner of Mouat and Phillimore Sts, is a nicely renovated hotel with rooms for $30/50.

For a more homelike place to stay, contact Fremantle Homestays (☎ 319 1256), which can arrange B&B accommodation in houses around Fremantle from $25 to $40 a night for a single and from $50 to $75 for a double. Self-contained single and double units are also available from $200 to $250 per week.

The ritziest hotel in town is the four-star *Fremantle Esplanade Hotel* on the corner of Marine Terrace and Collie St.

Places to Eat
A highlight of Fremantle is its diverse range of cafes, restaurants, food halls and taverns. Many a traveller's afternoon has been whittled away sipping beer or coffee and watching life go by from various kerbside tables.

Along South Terrace, there's a string of outdoor cafes and restaurants including the popular *Old Papa's – Ristorante Luigi's*, at No 17, which has coffee and gelati; the trendy *Gino's* (the place to be seen) at No 1 and the large *Miss Maud's* at No 33. All these places can be crowded on weekends when the weather is fine.

The historic *Sail & Anchor Hotel* (formerly the Freemason's Hotel, built in 1854) at 64 South Terrace, has been impressively restored to much of its former glory. I specialises in locally brewed Matilda Bay beers, and on the 1st floor is a brasserie which serves snacks and full meals.

Also in South Terrace is the *Mexican Kitchen*, next door to Old Papa's, with range of Mexican dishes from $10 to $12. Across the road are *Pizza Bella Roma*, the *Glifada of Athens*, with tasty souvlaki, and the popular licensed Mexican place *Zapata'*, at Shop 30, South Terrace Piazza. A couple of affluent backpackers have recommended *Portfreo Cafe-Resto*, at the corner of Parry St and South Terrace, for its patisseries.

The *Upmarket Food Centre* on Henderson St, opposite the market, has stalls where you can get delicious and cheap Thai, Vietnamese, Japanese, Chinese and Italian food from $5 to $7. Open Thursday to Sunday from about noon to 9 pm, it can be very busy especially on market days.

Roma, at 13 High St, is a reliable Freo institution, which serves home-made Italian fare including its now famous chicken and spaghetti. Even the rich and famous have to queue to eat here. The nearby *Round House Cafe* is good for a cheap breakfast or a quick snack. For Vietnamese food, try the *Vung Tau*, at 19 High St, with meals including vegetarian menu from $6 to $9.

Fast Eddy's, similar to the one in Perth, is at 13 Essex St. Fish & chips from *Cicerello's*

Kailis' or *Lombardo's*, on the Esplanade by the boat harbour, is a Fremantle tradition. The *Fisherman's Kitchen* is at the back of the equally popular *Sails Restaurant*, situated near McDonald's on the waterfront. Both Fisherman's and Cicerello's have restaurant and takeaway sections.

The current places to be seen at are the *Left Bank Bar & Cafe* on Riverside Rd down by the East St jetty and the beachy, trendified *Surf Club* (which has both cheap and expensive sections) out at North Fremantle Beach.

There are typical counter meals available at the *Newcastle Club Tavern* on Market St, the *Federal Hotel* on William St and the *National Hotel* on the corner of Market and High Sts.

Entertainment

There are a number of venues around town with music and/or dancing, the majority concentrated in the High St area.

The *West End Hotel* at 24 High St has music most nights, and poetry on Monday evenings. Across the road at No 39 is the *Orient*, with bands most nights. For Latin and folk music, the *Fly by Night Club*, in Queen St, is frequented by some talented musicians.

Home of the 'big gig' is the *Metropolis* on South Terrace. The *Newport Hotel*, also on South Terrace, has bands most nights. A fair walk further down the road at No 282 is the *Seaview Tavern*. The *Harbourside Hotel* on the corner of Beach Rd and Parry St has thrash bands. The *Railway Hotel* at 201 Queen Victoria St, in North Fremantle, has rock bands or jazz from Thursday to Sunday nights. The *Tarantella* nightclub is on Mouat St between High and Phillimore Sts.

Getting There & Around

The train between Perth and Fremantle runs every 15 minutes or so throughout the day for around $1.90. Bus Nos 106 (bus stand No 35) and 111 (bus stand No 48) go from St George's Terrace to Fremantle via the Canning Highway; or you can take bus No 105 (bus stand No 40 on St George's Terrace), which takes a longer route south of

the river. Bus Nos 103 and 104 also depart from St George's Terrace (southern side) but go to Fremantle via the northern side of the river.

Captain Cook Cruises has daily ferries from Perth to Fremantle for around $12 one way.

Bicycles are available for hire from Fleet Cycles (☎ 430 5414), 66 Adelaide St, and Captain Munchies (☎ 339 6633), 2 Beach St.

ROTTNEST ISLAND

'Rotto', as it's known by the locals, is a sandy island about 19 km off the coast of Fremantle. It's 11 km long, five km wide and is very popular with Perth residents and visitors. The island was discovered by the Dutch explorer de Vlamingh in 1696. He named it 'Rats' Nest' because of the numerous king-size 'rats' he saw there (in fact they were small wallabies called quokkas).

What do you do on Rotto? Well, you cycle around, laze in the sun on the many superb beaches (the Basin is the most popular, while Parakeet Bay is the place for skinny dipping), climb the low hills, go fishing or boating, ride a glass-bottomed boat (the waters off Rotto have some of the southernmost coral in the world and a number of shipwrecks), swim in the crystal-clear water or go quokka spotting.

The Rottnest settlement was established in 1838 as a prison for Aborigines from the mainland – the early colonists had lots of trouble imposing their ideas of private ownership on the nomadic Aborigines. The prison was abandoned in 1903 and the island soon became an escape for Perth society. Only in the last 30 years, however, has it really developed as a popular day trip. The buildings of the original prison settlement are among the oldest in WA.

Information

There is an information centre, open weekdays from 8.30 am to 5 pm, Saturday 9 am to 4 pm and Sunday 10 am to noon and 2.30 to 4 pm. It is just to the left of the jetty at Thomson Bay (the island's largest settlement) as you arrive. There, and at the

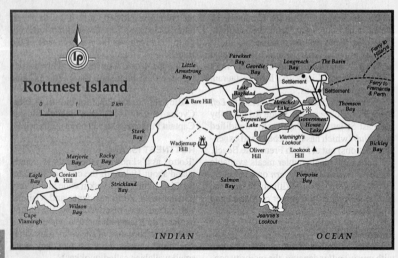

Rottnest Island

WESTERN AUSTRALIA

museum, you can get useful publications, such as a walking tour of the old settlement buildings, heritage trail brochures, information on the various shipwrecks around the island and a cycling guide.

Also, grab a copy of the informative paper *Rottnest Islander* and the brochure *Rottnest: Holiday Island*. Rottnest is very popular in the summer when the ferries and accommodation are both heavily booked – plan ahead.

Things to See & Do
There's an excellent little **museum** with exhibits about the island, its history, wildlife and shipwrecks. You can pick up the walking-tour leaflet here and wander around the interesting old convict-built buildings, including the octagonal 1864 'Quad' where the prison cells are now hotel rooms. **Vlamingh's Lookout** on View Hill, not far from Thomson Bay, offers panoramic views of the island. The island's main lighthouse, built in 1895, is visible 60 km out to sea.

The island has a number of low-lying salt lakes, and it's around them that you are most likely to spot **quokkas**. Bus tours have regular quokka-feeding points where the voracious marsupials seem to appear on demand. Also of interest is the recently restored **Oliver Hill Battery**, west of Thomson Bay.

Some of Rotto's **shipwrecks** are accessible to snorkellers, but to get to most of them requires a boat. There are marker plaques around the island telling the grim tales of how and when the ships sank. Snorkelling equipment, fishing gear and boats can be hired from Dive, Ski & Surf (☎ (09) 292 5167) at Thomson Bay.

There are two-hour and one-hour bus tours around the island for $9 and $6 respectively; they depart daily at 1 and 1.15 pm – again it is wise to book in the peak season. *Underwater Explorer* is a boat with windows below the waterline for viewing shipwrecks and marine life. It departs at regular hourly intervals from the jetty at Thomson Bay; an interesting 45-minute trip costs about $12.

Places to Stay
Most visitors to Rotto come only for the day but it's equally interesting to stay on the island. You can camp for $12 (two people) in hired tents with rubber mattresses or get tent sites at *Rottnest Camping* (☎ (09) 372 9737). Safari cabins are also available from

Quokka

$25 to $35 a night. Book in advance for a cabin or if you want to hire a tent.

The *Rottnest Island Authority* (☎ (09) 372 9729) has over 260 houses and cottages for rent in Thomson Bay and around Geordie, Fays and Longreach bays from $50 (bungalows) to $110 (villas) per night for four-bed accommodation. Reductions of up to 25% are available in off-peak periods.

The *Kingstown Barracks Hostel* (☎ (09) 372 9780), 1.2 km from the ferry terminal, is housed in an old barracks built in 1936; the cost per night is from $13.

Places to Eat

The *Rottnest Island Bistro* has a pleasant balcony overlooking Thomson Bay and serves tasty pasta, roasts, cold meat and salad and light meals from $6 to $9. *Brolley's Restaurant* in the Rottnest Hotel also serves snacks and meals.

The island has a general store and a *bakery* that is famed during the day for its fresh bread and pies. There's also a fast-food centre in the Thomson Bay settlement. The *Geordie Bay Village Store* has Devonshire teas, fish & chips, burgers and sandwiches.

Getting There & Away

Competition has brought prices down for the ferry trip to Rotto. Oceanic Cruises (☎ (09) 430 5127) has done some monopoly busting and its boat, which leaves from the East St jetty, East Fremantle, costs only $12 (plus the $5 landing fee). Set up by rival operator, Boat Torque (☎ (09) 430 7644), is White Dolphin Cruises, which matches Oceanic's prices. You can also take Boat Torque's *Star Flyte* ferry from Perth's Barrack St jetty to Thomson Bay daily; it leaves Perth at 9 am and Northport, North Fremantle, at 10.15 am. The fare is $42 return from Perth and $25 from Fremantle. Boat Torque has another ferry service, *Sea Raider III*, from Hillarys Boat Harbour (north of Perth), which leaves at 8.30 am daily for $30 return. Bookings are essential at peak periods.

You can also fly to Rottnest on the Rottnest Airbus (☎ (09) 478 1322). It leaves Perth Airport four times a day, seven days a week for about $45 return; the trip takes just 15 minutes. There's a connecting bus between Rottnest Airport and Thomson Bay.

Getting Around

Bicycles are the time-honoured way of getting around the island. The number of motor vehicles is strictly limited, which makes cycling a real pleasure. Furthermore, the island is just big enough to make a day's ride fine exercise. You can bring your own bike over on the ferry (free at present from East St jetty) or rent one of the hundreds available on the island from Rottnest Bike Hire (☎ (09) 372 9722) in Thomson Bay, near the hotel – a deposit is required.

Two bus services, the Bayseeker ($2) and the Settlement bus (50c), also run during the summer season – see the information centre for bus timetables and departure points.

NORTH COAST

The coast north of Perth has great scenery with long sand dunes but it quickly becomes the inhospitable terrain that deterred early visitors.

Yanchep

The **Yanchep National Park**, 51 km north of Perth, has natural bushland, some fine

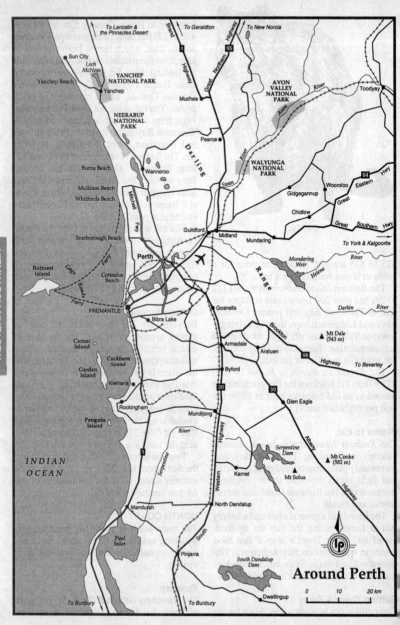

Around Perth

caves (including the limestone Crystal and Yondemp caves), Loch McNess and the Yaberoo Budjara Aboriginal Heritage Trail. Yanchep Sun City is a major marina with a modern shopping complex.

There are a handful of places to stay, including the *Yanchep Inn* (☎ (09) 561 1001), which has singles/doubles from $28/45, and a motel section with rooms from $65. On weekdays, one bus goes to Yanchep from Perth's Wellington St bus station.

Some 43 km north of Yanchep is **Guilderton**, a popular holiday resort beside the mouth of the Moore River. The *Vergulde Draeck* (Gilt Dragon), a Dutch East Indiaman, ran aground near here in 1656. The coast road ends at **Lancelin** (population 530), a small fishing port 130 km north of Perth, but coastal tracks continue north and may be passable with a 4WD. Windswept Lancelin is the finishing point of the annual Ledge Point Windsurfing Race held in January.

Pinnacles Desert

The small seaport of **Cervantes** (population 530), 257 km north of Perth, is the entry point for the unusual and haunting Pinnacles Desert. Here, in coastal **Nambung National Park**, the flat sandy desert is punctured with peculiar limestone pillars, some only a few cm high, others towering up to five metres high. The park is the scene of an impressive display of wildflowers from August to October.

If possible, try to visit the Pinnacles Desert early in the morning. Not only is the light better for photography but you will avoid the crowds that can detract from your experience of the place later in the day, especially in peak holiday times.

Check in Cervantes before attempting to drive the unsealed road into the park – if conditions are bad, a 4WD may be necessary but usually the road is OK, if somewhat bumpy, for normal vehicles. A coastal 4WD track runs north to **Jurien**, a crayfishing centre, and south to Lancelin. The sand dunes found along this coastline are spectacular.

Organised Tours It's possible to save your car's suspension and take a half-day tour from the Cervantes Shell service station (☎ (096) 52 7041) for $12 (plus a $2 park entrance fee). The tour leaves daily at 1 pm (in spring there's a morning tour) and you would be wise to book. If you drive into the Pinnacles Desert yourself, there is a $3 car entrance fee.

Places to Stay Accommodation in the area includes the *Pinnacles Caravan Park* (☎ (096) 52 7060) on the beachfront, with tent sites at $10 for two and on-site vans from $25 for two people. The *Cervantes Pinnacles Motel* (☎ (096) 52 7145), 227 Aragon St, has singles/doubles for $55/68, and *Cervantes Holiday Homes* (☎ (096) 52 7115), on the corner of Valencia Rd and Malaga Court, has self-contained units from $40.

New Norcia

The small community of New Norcia is an incongruity, Australia's very own setting for the *Name of the Rose*. Established as a Spanish Benedictine mission in 1846, it has changed little since and boasts a fine collection of buildings with classic Spanish architecture. The building which houses the museum and art gallery (both worth seeing for their old paintings, manuscripts and religious artefacts) also houses the tourist office (☎ (096) 54 8056). There are daily tours of the monastery for $10 (children $5) which take in the interior of chapels and other cloistered and secret places. You can buy a snack of sourdough bread at the 150-year-old bakehouse.

At the museum, you can get the excellent *New Norcia Heritage Trail* brochure which traces the development of the settlement. Just past the museum is the historic *New Norcia Hotel* (☎ (096) 54 8034) which has interesting decor, including a grand staircase. The Benedictine monks still live and work in New Norcia today. You can experience monastery life by staying in their guesthouse; the cost is $40 per person for bed and all meals.

Moora (population 1700), further north, is

a farming community in an area known for its colourful spring wildflowers. In the nearby **Berkshire Valley**, an old cottage and flour mill built in the mid-19th century have been restored and now operate as a museum.

SOUTH COAST

The coast south of Perth has a softer appearance than the often harsh landscape to the north. This is another very popular beach resort area for Perth residents, many of whom have holiday houses along the coast.

Rockingham (population 36,700)

Rockingham, just 47 km south of Perth, was founded in 1872 as a port, but that function, in time, was taken over by Fremantle. Today, Rockingham is a dormitory city and popular seaside resort with sheltered and ocean beaches. Close by is **Penguin Island**, home to a colony of fairy penguins from late March to early December, and **Seal Island**. You can get to the islands with Rockingham Sea Tours (☎ (09) 528 2004) – check with the tourist centre for details. The naval base of **Garden Island** is close by.

From Rockingham, you can also head inland to the Serpentine Dam and the scenic **Serpentine Falls National Park**, where there are wildflowers and pleasant bushland. You can get to Rockingham on bus No 120 from Fremantle or a No 116 from bus stand No 48 in St George's Terrace, Perth.

The helpful Rockingham tourist centre (☎ (09) 592 3464), at 43 Kent St, is open Monday to Friday from 9 am to 5 pm and weekends from 10 am to 4 pm.

Places to Stay & Eat There are five caravan parks in the Rockingham area; enquire at the tourist centre. One of them, the *Palm Beach Caravan Park* (☎ (09) 527 1515), at 37 Fisher St, has tent sites and on-site vans. Another budget place, the *CWA Rockingham* (☎ (09) 527 9560), 108 Parkin St, is operated by a friendly couple. There are two units available, each sleeping six, from $25 per night. The *Rockingham Motor Lodge* (☎ (09) 527

1230), 20 Lake St, has singles/doubles for $25/38.

For meals, try the local hotels. Otherwise, there is *El Roccos*, at 84 Parkin St, for good Mexican food or the *Silver Dragon* Chinese restaurant on Rockingham Rd.

Mandurah (population 23,300)

Situated on the calm Mandurah Estuary, this is yet another popular beach resort, 74 km south of Perth. Dolphins are often seen in the estuary, and the waterways in the area are noted for good fishing, prawning (March and April) and crabbing.

Things to see in town include the restored limestone **Hall's Cottage** (open Sunday afternoon), built in the 1830s, and the **Western Rosella Bird Park**, open daily from 9 am to 6 pm (admission $4). Full-day and short cruises are available on the *MV Peel Princes* from the jetty in town. Contact the Mandurah tourist bureau (☎ (09) 535 1155), 5 Pinjarra Rd, for ferry schedules, maps and other information.

Prolific bird life can be seen on **Peel Inlet** and the narrow coastal salt lakes, **Clifton** and **Preston**, 20 km to the south. Catch bus No 116 from stand 48 in St George's Terrace Perth, or bus No 117 from Fremantle to Mandurah.

Places to Stay & Eat There is a string of caravan parks around town with tent sites and on-site vans.

The *Brighton Hotel* (☎ (09) 535 1242), on Mandurah Terrace, is the best deal in town with B&B singles/doubles from $25/50; it also serves good counter meals.

There are numerous places to eat around town including *Pronto's Cafe* on the corner of Pinjarra Rd and Mandurah Terrace. You can get good snacks and cakes, and there's an all-you-can-eat pasta night on Friday for $9 – live music is often provided.

A big and tasty serve of fish & chips ($3.50) is available at *Jetty Fish & Chips* by the estuary near the end of Pinjarra Rd. Next door is *Yo-Yo's* with a vast array of ice cream and sundaes.

Pinjarra (population 1800)

Pinjarra, 86 km south of Perth, has a number of old buildings picturesquely sited on the banks of the Murray River. The Murray tourist centre (☎ (09) 531 1438) in Pinjarra is in the historic **Edenvale**, on the corner of George and Henry Sts. About four km from the town is the **Old Blythewood Homestead**, an 1859 colonial farm and a National Trust property. Behind the historic post office is a pleasant picnic area and a **suspension bridge** – wobbly enough to test most people's co-ordination!

Hotham Valley Railway **steam trains** run from Pinjarra to Dwellingup through blooming wildflowers and jarrah forests in winter only (August to October).

Places to Stay & Eat The *Pinjarra Motel* (☎ (09) 531 1811) offers singles/doubles with breakfast for $40/50. The *Exchange Hotel* (☎ (09) 531 1209), George St, has singles for $20.

The *Heritage Tearooms* has light meals such as sandwiches and quiches for around $6.

AVON VALLEY

The green and lush Avon Valley looks very English and was a delight to homesick early settlers. In the spring, this area is particularly rich in wildflowers. The valley was first settled in 1830, only a year after Perth was founded, so there are many historic buildings in the area. The picturesque Avon River is very popular with canoe enthusiasts.

Getting There & Away

The Avon Valley towns all have bus connections to Perth; contact Westrail (☎ (09) 326 2222) for timetable details. Fares from Perth are Toodyay ($9), Northam ($10), York ($9) and Beverley ($12.50). It is also possible to take the Prospector train from Perth to Toodyay ($9.20) and Northam ($11).

Toodyay (population 600)

There are numerous old buildings in this charming and historic town, many of them built by convicts. The local tourist centre (☎ (09) 574 2435) is on Stirling Terrace, in the 1870s **Connor's Mill**, which also houses a working flour mill. It is open from 9 am to 5 pm, except for Sunday 10 am to 5 pm.

Don't miss the **Old Newcastle Gaol Museum** on Clinton St, or the 1862 **St Stephen's Church**. The **Moondyne Gallery** tells the story of bushranger Joseph Bolitho Johns (Moondyne Joe). Close to town is the oldest inland **winery** in WA, which began operating in the 1870s.

Downriver from Toodyay is the **Avon Valley National Park** and along the Perth road is the popular Whitegum Flower farm.

Places to Stay & Eat *Toodyay Caravan Park* *Avonbanks* (☎ (09) 574 2612), Railway Rd, on the banks of the Avon River, has tent sites, air-con on-site vans and chalets. It is noisy and the tent sites are as hard as rock. The *Broadgrounds Park* (☎ (09) 574 2534) has tent sites and a campers' kitchen.

The old convent of *Avondown* is now a budget accommodation place, with singles/doubles for $18/35. Opposite is the *Freemasons Hotel* (☎ (09) 574 2201) with basic rooms and breakfast for $22 per person and reasonably priced counter meals. On the same street is the *Victoria Hotel* (☎ (09) 574 2206) with singles/doubles from $20/40; counter meals are available from $7 to $9.

There are a few eating places on Stirling Terrace: the *Lavender Restaurant*, *Emma's Restaurant* and the *Wendouree Tearooms*. O'Meara's Tavern, also on Stirling Terrace, has the *Cellar Bistro*.

Northam (population 6600)

Northam, the major town of the Avon Valley, is a busy farming centre on the railway line to Kalgoorlie. At one time, the line from Perth ended abruptly here and miners had to make the rest of the weary trek to the gold fields by road.

Northam is packed on the first weekend in August every year for the start of the gruelling 133-km Avon Descent for power boats and canoeists.

WESTERN AUSTRALIA

The tourist bureau (☎ (096) 22 2100), situated at 138 Fitzgerald St, is open daily.

Things to See & Do The 1836 **Morby Cottage** served as Northam's first church and school, and it now houses a museum open on Sunday; entrance fee is $1. The **old railway station**, listed by the National Trust, has been restored and turned into a museum; it is open on Sunday from 10 am to 4 pm and admission is $2. Also of interest in town is the colony of **white swans** on the Avon River, descendants of birds introduced from England early this century.

Near Northam, at Irishtown, is elegant **Buckland House**. Credited with being WA's most impressive stately home, it was built in 1874 and has a fine collection of antiques.

If your funds are up to it then try **ballooning** over the Avon Valley from March to November.

Places to Stay The *Northam Guest House* (☎ (096) 22 2301), 51 Wellington St, has cheap accommodation from $15 per person for the first night and $10 thereafter. On the same street, at No 426, is the *Grand Hotel* (☎ (096) 22 1024) with basic rooms and shared facilities for $20/40.

The *Avon Bridge Hotel* (☎ (096) 22 1023) is the oldest hotel in Northam, and has singles/twins for $20/30 and counter meals from $5. The only motel in town is aptly named the *Northam* (☎ (096) 22 1755), at 13 John St; singles/doubles are $43/50. The *Shamrock Hotel*, at 112 Fitzgerald St, is the best in town with elegant en-suite bedrooms.

Two excellent out-of-town choices are *Buckland House* (☎ (096) 46 1200), in Irishtown, which has singles/doubles for $68/136; and the farmstay *Egoline Reflections* (☎ (096) 22 5811), on the Toodyay road, which has cottage accommodation for $90 and homestead rooms for $80 a double.

Places to Eat Near the tourist bureau are two tearooms, *Lisa's* and *Lucy's*. Next to the Tattersalls Hotel, *Bruno's Pizza Bar* does tasty pizza to eat in or take away. The *Ruen Thai*, 96 Fitzgerald St, is fast becoming

popular as local palates adopt Asian flavours. The *Whistling Kettle*, at 48 Broome Terrace overlooking the river, is a great place to enjoy some home-cooked food.

York (population 1600)
The oldest inland town in WA, York was first settled in 1831 and is one of the highlights of the Avon Valley. A stroll down the main street, with its many restored old buildings, is a real step back in time. The tourist bureau (☎ (096) 41 1301) is at 105 Avon Terrace.

Things to See & Do Places of interest include the excellent 1850s **Residency Museum**, the old **town hall**, **Castle Hotel** which dates from the coaching days, the classy **Motor Museum** (a must for vintage-car enthusiasts – entrance is $6, children $2), the old **police station, jail & courthouse**, and **Settlers' House**. On the edge of town is the **Historic Balladong Farm**, which depicts life during the pioneer era, and the **De Ladera Alpaca Farm**, where you can purchase those oh-so-warm and expensive jumpers. The suspension bridge near town was built in 1906 and it crosses the Avon River. Understandably, the entire town is classified by the National Trust.

Most people drive their own cars to York so they can take in the many heritage drives. You can also get there on the daily Westrail bus; the cost from Perth is $9.20.

Festivals York is the state's festival town with no fewer than a dozen major events. The better-patronised ones are the Jazz Festival and the Flying 50s Vintage & Veteran car race.

Places to Stay The only caravan park around town is *Mt Bakewell Caravan Park* (☎ (096) 41 1421) with tent sites at $10 for two and on-site vans.

The *York YHA Hostel* (☎ (096) 41 1372), at 3 Brook St, is housed in three buildings that originally formed part of the old hospital; dorm beds are $10. The old section of the historic, renovated *Castle Hotel* (☎ (096) 41

1007), on Avon Terrace, is good value with singles/doubles from $25/45.

There are a number of quality B&B and farmstays in the region; enquire at the tourist bureau.

Places to Eat For breakfast go to the *Settler's House* on Avon Terrace. Try *Cafe Bugatti* for cappuccino and Italian food, *York Village Bakehouse & Tearooms* for freshly baked bread and cakes, and *Gilbert's* in the York Palace Hotel for a range of meals; all are on Avon Terrace. The *Castle Hotel* serves good counter meals from $9 to $13 and à la carte meals as well; you can also eat outside at the verandah cafe.

Beverley (population 800)
South of York, also on the Avon River, is Beverley (founded in 1838) which is noted for its fine **aeronautical museum**, open daily from 10 am to 4 pm. Exhibits include a locally constructed biplane, built between 1928 and 1930.

The 706-hectare **Avondale Discovery Farm**, six km west of Beverley, has a large collection of agricultural machinery, a homestead, a workshop and stables. The information centre (☎ (096) 46 1555) is in Vincent St. Further upriver is **Pingelly**, in an area well known for its wildflowers.

Places to Stay The *Beverley Caravan Park* (☎ (096) 46 1200), on Vincent St, has tent sites and on-site vans. The rather ordinary *Beverley Hotel* (☎ (096) 46 1190), at 137 Vincent St, has B&B for $18/35.

THE DARLING RANGE
The hills that surround Perth are popular for picnics, barbecues and bushwalks. There are also some excellent lookouts from which you can see over Perth and down to the coast. **Araleun** with its waterfalls, the fire lookout at **Mt Dale**, and **Churchman's Brook** are all off the Brookton Highway. Other places of interest include the **Zig Zag** at Gooseberry Hill and **Lake Leschenaultia**.

From **Kalamunda** there are more fine

views over Perth. You can get there from Perth on bus No 300 or 302, via Maida Vale from bus stand No 43 in St George's Terrace, or on bus No 292 or 305, via Wattle Grove and Lesmurdie, also from bus stand No 43. Taking one route out and the other back makes an interesting circular tour of the hill suburbs. There's a good walking track at **Sullivan Rock**, 69 km south-east of Perth, on the Albany Highway.

Mundaring Weir
Mundaring (population 1500), in the ranges only 35 km east of Perth, is the site of the Mundaring Weir – the dam built at the turn of the century to supply water to the gold fields over 500 km to the east. The reservoir has an attractive setting and is a popular excursion for Perth residents. There are also a number of walking tracks. The **C Y O'Connor Museum** has models and exhibits about the water pipeline to the gold fields – in its time one of the world's most amazing engineering feats (see the aside in the Gold Country section).

The 1600-hectare **John Forrest National Park** near Mundaring has protected areas of jarrah and marri trees, native fauna, waterfalls and a swimming pool.

Places to Stay The *Mundaring Caravan Park* (☎ (09) 295 1125) is two km west of town on the Great Eastern Highway. The *Mundaring Weir YHA Hostel* (☎ (09) 295 1809), on Mundaring Weir Rd, is eight km south of town and costs $8. The *Mundaring Weir Hotel* (☎ (09) 295 1106) is exceedingly popular with Perth residents for weekend breaks. Its quality units, constructed out of rammed earth, cost $53.

Wheatlands

Stretching north from the Albany coastal region to the areas beyond the Great Eastern Highway (the Perth to Coolgardie road) are the WA wheatlands. The area is noted for its unusual rock formations (the best known of

WESTERN AUSTRALIA

which is the somewhat overrated Wave Rock near Hyden), and for its many Aboriginal rock carvings.

CUNDERDIN & KELLERBERRIN

An earthquake in 1968 badly damaged **Meckering**, a small town 24 km west of Cunderdin; the agricultural museum in Cunderdin has exhibits relating to that event as well as an interesting collection of farm machinery and equipment. The museum is housed in an old pumping station used on the gold-fields water pipeline.

Further to the east is Kellerberrin, which has a historical museum in the old courthouse of 1897 and a lookout on Kellerberrin Hill.

The *Campfire Caravan Park* (☎ (096) 35 1258) in Cunderdin has tent sites and on-site vans. Kellerberrin has a caravan park, motel and hotel.

MERREDIN (population 3100)

Merredin, the largest centre in the wheatbelt, is 260 km east of Perth on the Kalgoorlie railway line and the Great Eastern Highway. It has a tourist centre (☎ (090) 41 1666) on Barrack St. The 1920s railway station has been turned into a charming **museum** with a vintage 1897 locomotive and an old signal box. Also of note in the area is **Mangowine Homestead**, 65 km north of Merredin, restored by the National Trust.

There are also some interesting rock formations around Merredin, including granite outcrops near **Koorda**, 155 km to the north; **Kangaroo Rock**, 17 km to the south-east; **Burracoppin Rock** to the north; and **Sandford Rocks** 11 km east of Westonia.

Places to Stay & Eat

The *Merredin Caravan Park* (☎ (090) 41 1535), on the Great Eastern Highway, has tent sites and on-site vans. The *Merredin Motel* (☎ (090) 41 1886), on Gamenya Ave, has B&B for $25/40. The *Commercial Hotel* on Barrack St has counter meals including a $2 lunch-time special, and *Jason's* Chinese restaurant, on the corner of Bates and Mitch-

ell Sts, has takeaway or eat-in meals for around $6.

SOUTHERN CROSS (population 980)

Although the gold quickly gave out, Southern Cross was the first gold-rush town on the WA gold fields. The big rush soon moved east to Coolgardie and Kalgoorlie. Like the town itself, the streets of Southern Cross are named after the stars and constellations. The **Yilgarn History Museum** in the old courthouse has local displays which are worth a visit. If you follow the continuation of Antares St south for three km, you will see a couple of active open-cut mines.

Situated 378 km east of Perth, this is really the end of the wheatlands area and the start of the desert; when travelling by train the change is very noticeable. In the spring, the sandy plains around Southern Cross are carpeted with wildflowers.

There is a caravan park on Coolgardie Rd, two hotels in Antares St and a motel on Canopus St.

HYDEN & WAVE ROCK

Wave Rock is 350 km south-east of Perth and three km from the tiny town of Hyden, south of Merredin and Southern Cross. It's a real surfer's delight – the perfect wave, 15 metres high and frozen in solid rock marked with different colour bands. Other interesting rock formations in the area bear names like the **Breakers**, **Hippo's Yawn** and the **Humps**. **Mulka's Cave** has Aboriginal rock paintings.

At Wave Rock, the *Wave Rock Caravan Park* (☎ (098) 80 5022) has tent sites, and chalets at $45 for two. *Diep's B&B* (☎ (098) 80 5179), on Clayton St in Hyden, has B&B for around $26 per person, or there's the *Hyden Hotel/Motel* (☎ (098) 80 5052), on Lynch St, with singles/doubles for $48/68.

A Westrail bus to Hyden leaves Perth on Tuesday and returns on Thursday; the trip costs $29 one way and takes five hours.

OTHER TOWNS

There is a fine rock formation, known as

Kokerbin (Aboriginal for 'high place'), 45 km west of the town of Bruce Rock. **Corrigin** (population 720), 68 km south of Bruce Rock, has a folk museum, the aptly named Buried Bone canine cemetery, a craft cottage and a miniature railway. **Jilakin Rock** is 18 km from Kulin, while further south-east there's the town of **Lake Grace**, near the lake of the same name.

Narrogin (population 4600), 192 km south-east of Perth, is an agricultural centre with a courthouse museum, a railway heritage park and the Albert Facey Homestead, 39 km to the east and close to Wickepin – well worth a visit, especially if you have read Facey's popular book *A Fortunate Life*. There are a couple of unusual rock formations nearby.

Dumbleyung (population 300), south-east of Narrogin, also has a museum. Near the town is the lake upon which Donald Campbell broke the world water-speed record (442.08 km/hr) in 1964; today it hosts a variety of bird life.

Wagin (population 1300), 229 km south-east of Perth, has a 15-metre-high fibreglass ram (a tribute to the surrounding merino industry) and a historical village with some fine restored buildings and a vintage tractor display. The Wagin tourist centre (☎ (098) 61 1177) is on Arthur Rd. There is bushwalking around **Mt Latham**, six km to the west.

Katanning (population 4100), south of Wagin, has a large Muslim community, complete with a mosque built in 1980. Other attractions include the old flour mill on Clive St, which houses the tourist centre (☎ (098) 21 2634), and the ruins of an old winery.

Gold Country

Fifty years after its establishment in 1829, the Western Australia colony was still going nowhere, so the government in Perth was delighted when gold was discovered at Southern Cross in 1887. That first strike petered out pretty quickly, but there followed more discoveries and WA profited from the gold boom for the rest of the century. It was gold that put WA on the map and finally gave it the population to make it viable in its own right, rather than just a distant offshoot of the east-coast colonies.

The major strikes were made in 1892 at Coolgardie and nearby Kalgoorlie, but in the whole gold-fields area Kalgoorlie is the only large town left today. Coolgardie's period of prosperity lasted only until 1905 and many other gold towns went from nothing to populations of 10,000 then back to nothing in just 10 years. Nevertheless, the towns capitalised on their prosperity while it lasted, as the many magnificent public buildings grandly attest.

Life on the early gold fields was terribly hard. This area of WA is extremely dry – rainfall is erratic and never great. Even the little rain that does fall quickly disappears into the porous soil. Many early gold

---

Where Water is Like Gold!

It soon became clear to the WA government that the large-scale extraction of gold, the state's most important industry, was unlikely to continue in the Kalgoorlie gold fields without a reliable water supply. Stop-gap measures, like huge condensation plants that produced distilled water from salt lakes, or bores that pumped brackish water from beneath the earth, provided temporary relief. In 1898, however, the engineer C Y O'Connor proposed a stunning solution: he would build a reservoir near Perth and construct a 556-km pipeline to Kalgoorlie.

This was long before the current era of long oil pipelines, and his idea was opposed violently in Parliament and looked upon by some as impossible, especially as the water had to go uphill all the way (Kalgoorlie is 400 metres higher than Perth). Nevertheless, the project was approved and the pipeline laid at breakneck speed.

In 1903, water started to pour into Kalgoorlie's newly constructed reservoir; a modified version of the same system still operates today. For O'Connor, however, there was no happy ending: long delays and continual criticism by those of lesser vision resulted in his suicide in 1902, less than a year before his scheme proved operational. ∎

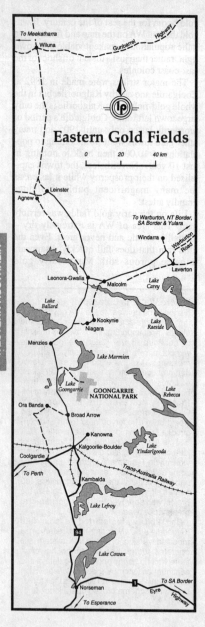

Eastern Gold Fields

0   20   40 km

seekers, driven more by enthusiasm than by common sense, died of thirst while seeking the elusive mineral. Others succumbed to diseases that broke out periodically in the unhygienic shanty towns. The supply of water to the gold fields by pipeline in 1903 was a major breakthrough (see the aside in this section) and ensured the continuation of mining.

Today, Kalgoorlie is the main gold-fields centre and mines still operate there. Elsewhere, a string of fascinating ghost and near-ghost towns and modern nickel mines make a visit to WA's gold country a must.

COOLGARDIE (population 1100)

A popular pause in the long journey across the Nullarbor, and also the turn-off for Kalgoorlie, Coolgardie really is a ghost of its former self. You only have to glance at the huge town hall and post office building to appreciate the size that Coolgardie once was. Gold was discovered here in 1892, and by the turn of the century the population had boomed to 15,000. The gold then petered out and the town withered away just as quickly. However, there's still plenty to interest the visitor.

The helpful Coolgardie tourist bureau (☎ (090) 26 6090), in Bayley St, is open daily from 9 am to 5 pm.

Things to See

The many historical markers scattered in and around Coolgardie describe the past history of its buildings and sites. The **Goldfields Exhibition**, in the same building as the tourist bureau, is open from 9 am to 5 pm daily and has a fascinating display of gold-fields memorabilia. You can even find out about US President Herbert Hoover's days on the WA gold fields. It's an interesting museum and worth the $2.50 admission fee, which includes a film shown at the tourist bureau (in the same building as the museum).

The **railway station** is also operated as a museum, and there you can learn the incredible story of the miner who was trapped 300 metres underground by floodwater in 1907 and rescued by divers 10 days later.

One km west of Coolgardie is the **town cemetery**, which includes many old graves such as that of explorer Ernest Giles (1835-97). Due to the unsanitary conditions and violence in the gold fields, it's said that 'one half of the population buried the other half'.

One of Coolgardie's odd sights is **Prior's Open Air Museum**, diagonally opposite the tourist bureau, but its collection seems a little neglected these days.

Another attraction is **Warden Finnerty's Residence**, restored by the National Trust, which is open daily except Tuesday from 1 to 4 pm and Sunday from 10 am to noon (admission $2). Nearby is the lightning-dissected **Gaol Tree**, complete with leg irons. At the **Camel Farm**, three km west of town on the Great Eastern Highway, you can take camel rides or organise longer camel treks; it is open daily 9 am to 5 pm and admission is $2 (rides are $2.50). About 45 km south of Coolgardie is **Queen Victoria Rock Nature Reserve**, which has interesting transitional vegetation types and limited primitive camping.

Places to Stay & Eat

The *Coolgardie Caravan Park* (☎ (090) 26 6009), 99 Bayley St, has excellent tent sites for $8 and on-site vans. The fine old *Coolgardie YHA Hostel* (☎ (090) 26 6051), at 56-60 Gnarlbine Rd, costs $10.

There are a couple of historic hotels in Bayley St with long, shady verandahs: the *Railway Lodge* (☎ (090) 26 6166), which has singles/doubles for $20/30, and the *Denver City Hotel* (☎ (090) 26 6031), with rooms for $30/45.

The Denver does counter meals from $10, and there are a couple of roadhouses on Bayley St that also do meals. The *Premier Cafe*, on Bayley St, has excellent meals for $7 and the usual snacks and takeaways. There are restaurants in the Motor Inn and Coolgardie Motel.

Getting There & Away

Greyhound Pioneer passes through Cool-

gardie on its Perth to Adelaide run; the one-way fare from Perth to Coolgardie is $70, and to Adelaide it's $180. Goldenlines (☎ (090) 21 2655) runs two buses on weekdays from Kalgoorlie to Coolgardie; the fare is $2.75.

The Prospector from Perth to Kalgoorlie stops at Bonnie Vale railway station, 14 km away, daily except Saturday; the one-way fare from Perth is $53.60, with a meal. For bookings call the tourist bureau or Westrail (☎ (09) 326 2222).

KALGOORLIE-BOULDER

(population 25,000)

Kalgoorlie is a real surprise – today it is a prosperous, humming metropolis. The longest lasting and most successful of WA's gold towns, it rose to prominence later than Coolgardie. In 1893, Paddy Hannan, a prospector from way back, set out from Coolgardie for another gold strike but stopped at the site of Kalgoorlie and found, just lying around on the surface, enough gold to spark another rush.

As in so many places, the surface gold soon petered out, but at Kalgoorlie the miners went deeper and more and more gold was found. There weren't the storybook chunky nuggets of solid gold – Kalgoorlie's gold had to be extracted from the rocks by costly and complex processes of grinding, roasting and chemical action – but there was plenty of it.

Kalgoorlie quickly reached fabled heights of prosperity, and the enormous and magnificent public buildings built around the turn of the century are evidence of its fabulous wealth. After WW I, however, increasing production costs and static gold prices led to Kalgoorlie's slow but steady decline.

With the substantial increase in gold prices since the mid-1970s, mining of lower-grade deposits has become economical and Kalgoorlie is again the largest producer of gold in Australia. Large mining conglomerates have been at the forefront of new open-cut mining operations in the Golden Mile – gone are the old headframes and

PLACES TO STAY

14 York Hotel
17 Windsor Backpackers' Guesthouse
18 Palace Hotel
19 Exchange Hotel
27 Surrey House

PLACES TO EAT

4 Takeaway Food Enclave
8 Victory Cafe

10 Old Australia Hotel
11 Grand Hotel
13 Kalgoorlie Cafe
15 De Bernales
16 Pizza Cantina
20 Matteo's Pizza
21 Criterion
22 Broccoli Forest
23 Top End Thai Restaurant

OTHER

1 Hospital

2 Railway Station
3 Woolworth's
5 Town Hall
6 Ansett Australia
7 Kalgoorlie-Boulder Tourist Centre
9 Post Office
12 RACWA
24 Museum of the Goldfields
25 Goldfields Aboriginal Art Gallery
26 School of Mines Museum
28 Paddy Hannan's Tree

Kalgoorlie

0   125   250 m

corrugated iron homes. Mining, pastoral development and a busy tourist trade ensure Kalgoorlie's continuing importance as an outback centre.

Orientation

Although Kalgoorlie ('Kal' to the locals) sprang up close to Paddy Hannan's original find, the mining emphasis soon shifted a few km away to the Golden Mile, a square mile which was probably the wealthiest gold-mining area for its size in the world. The satellite town of Boulder, five km south of Kalgoorlie, developed to service this area.

The two towns amalgamated in August 1989 into the City of Kalgoorlie-Boulder.

Kalgoorlie itself is a grid of broad, tree-lined streets. The main street (Hannan St), flanked by imposing public buildings, is wide enough to turn a camel train – a necessity in turn-of-the-century gold-field towns. You'll find most of the hotels, restaurants and offices on or close to Hannan St.

Information

There's a helpful tourist centre (☎ (090) 21 1966), on the corner of Hannan and Cassidy Sts, where you can get a good free map of

Kalgoorlie; a number of other area maps are for sale. The office is open from 8.30 am to 5 pm Monday to Friday and from 9 am to 5 pm on weekends. For an account of the fascinating Kalgoorlie story, read *The Golden Mile* by Geoffrey Blainey (Allen & Unwin). Kal's daily paper is the *Kalgoorlie Miner*.

Kal can get very hot in December and January; overall the cool winter months are the best time to visit. From late August to the end of September, however, the town is packed because of wildflower tours and the local horse races, and accommodation of any type can be difficult to find.

The RACWA (☎ (090) 21 1511) is on the corner of Porter and Hannan Sts.

Hannan's North Tourist Mine

One of Kalgoorlie's biggest attractions is the Hannan's North Mine. You can take the lift cage down into the bowels of the earth and make a tour around the drives and crosscuts of the mine, guided by an ex-miner.

The $14 entry fee covers the underground tour, an audiovisual presentation, a tour of the surface workings, and a gold pour. Underground tours are run according to demand daily (more regularly during peak seasons) and the complex is open from 9.30 am to 4.30 pm.

Golden Mile Loopline

You can make an interesting loop around the Golden Mile by catching the 'Rattler', a tourist train complete with commentary which makes an hour-long trip daily at 10 am. On Sunday it also leaves at 11.45 am. It departs from Boulder railway station, passing the old mining works. The cost is $9 for adults and $5 for children.

Museum of the Goldfields

The impressive mine headframe at the northern end of Hannan St marks the entrance to this excellent museum. It is open daily from 10 am to 4.30 pm (admission is free) and has a wide range of exhibits including an underground gold vault and historic photographs. The tiny British Arms Hotel (the narrowest hotel in Australia) is part of the museum.

Other Attractions

The **Mt Charlotte Lookout** and the town's reservoir are only a few hundred metres from the north-eastern end of Hannan St. The view over the town is good but there's little to see of the reservoir, which is covered to limit evaporation. The **Super Pit** lookout, just off the Eastern Bypass near Boulder, gives a good insight into modern mining practices; it is open from 7.30 am to 4.15 pm daily (closed when blasting is in progress).

The **School of Mines Museum**, on the corner of Egan and Cassidy Sts, has a geology display including replicas of big nuggets. It's usually open from 9 am to 4 pm Monday to Friday.

Along Hannan St, you'll find the imposing **town hall** and the equally impressive **post office**. There's an art gallery upstairs in the decorative town hall, while outside is a replica of a statue of Paddy Hannan himself holding a water bag. The original is inside the town hall, safe from nocturnal spray painters.

A few blocks back, west of Hannan St, is Hay St and one of Kalgoorlie's most famous 'attractions'. Although it's quietly ignored in the tourist brochures, Kal has a block-long strip of **brothels** where working ladies beckon passing men to their true-blue (and sometimes pink) galvanised-iron doorways. A blind eye has been turned to this activity for so long that it has become an accepted and historical part of the town.

Kalgoorlie also has a **two-up school** in a corrugated-iron amphitheatre – follow the signs from Hannan St. Two-up is a frenetic, uniquely Australian gambling game where two coins are tossed and bets are placed on the heads or tails result. Amongst the gamblers' yelps, a lot of money seems to change hands. It is open from 2.30 pm until dark, as the owners have lost so much money they can't afford to put the power on. Not!

On Outridge Terrace is **Paddy Hannan's tree**, marking the spot where the first gold strike was made. **Hammond Park** is a small fauna reserve with a miniature Bavarian castle. It's open daily from 9 am to 5 pm. Not far away is a pleasant **arboretum**.

WESTERN AUSTRALIA

Architectural Styles

Kalgoorlie-Boulder boasts an interesting collection of architectural styles, many unconventional. Nowhere is this better represented than along Hannan St. Expect to see curious blends of Victorian gold boom, Edwardian, Moorish and Art-Nouveau styles. The blend of styles from the turn of the century has produced an almost comic mix of ornate facades, colonnaded footpaths, recessed verandahs, stuccoed walls and general overstatement.

Buildings to look out for in Hannan St include the Kalgoorlie Miner and Old Western Argus building (Nos 117-119), Exchange Hotel (No 135), Palace Hotel (Nos 135-139), Exchange Building (Nos 149-151), Lasletts (No 181), York Hotel (No 259 – don't miss its staircase), the town hall, and the City Markets (No 276); around in Maritana St look out for Hannan's Club and the Maritana buildings. ■

The **Goldfields War Museum** in Burt St, Boulder, is open from 10 am to 4 pm weekdays. The Boulder railway station, home to the **Eastern Goldfields Historical Society Museum**, is an 1897 building. It is open from 9 am to 11.30 pm daily.

Organised Tours

Goldrush Tours (☎ (090) 21 2954) are the main tour operators in Kalgoorlie. Book through the tourist centre or from Goldrush Tours directly at Palace Chambers, Maritana St. They have tours of Kal, Coolgardie and nearby ghost towns. There's also a gold-detector tour for avid fossickers, and August and September wildflower tours.

Starting from $25, you can see Kal and the Golden Mile mining operations from the air with Goldfields Air Services.

Places to Stay

There are a number of caravan parks in Kalgoorlie. The closest to the city centre are the *Golden Village Caravan Park* (☎ (090) 21 4162), on Hay St two km south-west of the railway station, which has tent sites and on-site vans; and the *Prospector Caravan Park* (☎ (090) 21 2524), on the Great Eastern Highway, which has tent sites, on-site vans and cabins. The Prospector has a pool, a grassed area for campers and a campers' kitchen – it's one of the best caravan parks in WA.

The popular and central *Windsor Backpackers' Guesthouse* (☎ (090) 21 5483), at the end of the courtyard at 147 Hannan St, is an austere but quiet place with a TV room

and kitchen facilities; rooms are $30 for single or twin. At 9 Boulder Rd is the comfortable *Surrey House* (☎ (090) 21 1340), which has backpackers' beds for $15 per night and singles/doubles for $28/40; a continental breakfast is $4.50 extra per person.

There are several pleasantly old-fashioned hotels right in the centre of Kalgoorlie, including the *Palace Hotel* (☎ (090) 21 2788) on the corner of Maritana and Hannan Sts. Standard rooms cost $30/40 for singles/doubles. The *York Hotel* (☎ (090) 21 2337), 259 Hannan St, has singles/twins for $35/60; it is exceptionally well located in the heart of town.

One particularly interesting place to stay is the *homestay* (☎ (090) 91 1482) at 164 Hay St, a former brothel in the heart of Kal's Rue Pigalle; rooms with a past are $30/50 for B&B singles/doubles and there's a preferred three-night minimum. The tourist bureau has a list of other B&B accommodation.

Places to Eat

There are plenty of counter-meal pubs, restaurants and cafes in Kalgoorlie, particularly along Hannan St. The *York Hotel*, on Hannan St, does solid counter meals in its Steak House from $7 to $10, and meals in the saloon bar for around $6. The *Criterion Bistro* and the *Grand Hotel* also do counter meals and usually have cheap lunch specials.

The more up-market *De Bernales* does tasty food from $12 to $16 and has a pleasant verandah opening onto Hannan St – a good place to sip a beer and watch life go by.

The *Broccoli Forest*, at 75 Hannan St, has

a lunch bar with an interesting menu – most of it vegetarian. Nearby, the *Top End* Thai restaurant, at 71 Hannan St, is good for a splurge – a wide range of prawn, curry and noodle dishes costs from $12 to $15.

At 275 Hannan St is the *Kalgoorlie Cafe*, which has burger-type fast food, or there's the *Victory Cafe*, at 246 Hannan St, for an early breakfast. For pizza, try *Pizza Cantina* at 211 Hannan St, or *Matteo's* at No 123.

On Wilson St, between Brookman and Hannan Sts, is a small enclave of takeaway places including the *Fu Wah* Chinese restaurant and *Thai Food*. In Egan St there is the BYO *Loaded Cactus* Mexican restaurant.

In Boulder, you can get counter meals at *Tattersalls*, on the corner of Bart and Lane Sts, and opposite the *Albion Hotel*. You can also try the *Wah On* Chinese restaurant, next to the Goldfields War Museum, and *Peachy's* takeaway at 16 Burt St.

Things to Buy
The Goldfields Aboriginal Art Gallery, next to the Museum of the Goldfields, has crafts for sale. Kal is a good place to buy actual gold nuggets fashioned into relatively inexpensive jewellery.

Getting There & Away
Air Ansett Australia flies from Perth to Kalgoorlie several times daily; the Apex return fare is $218, and the full return fare is $408. The Ansett office (☎ 13 1300) is at 314 Hannan St.

Skywest has two direct flights a day for $248 (Apex return) or $183 (one-way full fare) – other discounts such as special weekend fares are also available (☎ (090) 91 1446). Goldfields Air Services (☎ (090) 93 2116) fly from Kalgoorlie to Esperance (via Norseman) every Tuesday and return the same day – the one-way fare is $134.

Bus Greyhound Pioneer buses operate through Kalgoorlie on the services from Perth to Sydney, Melbourne and Adelaide; the fare from Perth is around $71. Kalgoorlie Express (☎ (09) 328 9199) also has a twice-weekly Perth to Kalgoorlie service which

heads north to Laverton ($43), Leinster ($49) and Leonora ($31). Check timetables carefully as some of these buses pull into Kalgoorlie at an ungodly hour of the night when everything is closed up, and finding a place to stay can be difficult.

Westrail (☎ (090) 21 2023) runs a bus three times a week from Kal to Esperance – once via Kambalda and Norseman and twice via Coolgardie and Norseman; the trip takes 5½ hours and costs $16.30 to Norseman and $30.40 to Esperance.

Train The daily Prospector service from Perth takes around 7½ hours and costs $55.80, including a meal. From Perth, you can book seats at the WATC in Forrest Place or at the Westrail terminal (☎ (09) 326 2222). It's wise to book as this service is fairly popular, particularly in the tourist season. The Indian Pacific and Trans-Australia trains also go through Kalgoorlie.

Car Rental You can rent cars from Hertz (☎ (090) 91 2625), Budget (☎ (090) 93 2300) and Avis (☎ (090) 21 1722). If you want to explore very far, you'll have to drive or take a tour as public transport is limited.

Getting Around
There's a regular bus service between Kalgoorlie and Boulder (you can get the timetable from the tourist centre).

A taxi from the airport costs around $8. You can hire bicycles from Johnston Cycles (☎ (090) 21 1157), 76 Boulder St – a deposit is required.

NORTH OF KALGOORLIE
The road north is surfaced from Kalgoorlie all the way to Leonora-Gwalia (240 km) and from there to Laverton (130 km north-east) and Leinster (160 km north). Off the main road, however, traffic is virtually nonexistent and rain can quickly close the dirt roads.

Towns of interest include **Kanowna**, just 18 km from Kalgoorlie-Boulder along a dirt road. In 1905, this town had a population of 12,000, 16 hotels, many churches and an hourly train service to Kalgoorlie. Today,

WESTERN AUSTRALIA

apart from the railway station and the odd pile of rubble, absolutely nothing remains!

Broad Arrow now has a population of 20, compared with 2400 at the turn of the century, but one of the town's original eight hotels operates in a virtually unchanged condition. **Ora Banda** has gone from a population of 2000 to less than 50.

Menzies, 132 km north of Kal, has about 110 people today, compared with 5000 in 1900. Many early buildings remain, including the railway station with its 120-metre-long platform and the town hall with its clockless clocktower – unfortunately, the ship bringing the clock from England sank en route.

With a population of 1200, **Leonora** serves as the railhead for the nickel from Windarra and Leinster. In adjoining **Gwalia** (a ghost town), the Sons of Gwalia Goldmine, the largest in WA outside Kalgoorlie, closed in 1963 and much of the town closed with it; due to the increase in gold prices this and other mines in the area have been reopened. At one time, the mine was managed by Herbert Hoover, later to become president of the USA.

The Gwalia Historical Society is housed in the 1898 mine office – this fascinating local museum is open daily. Also of interest is the restored State Hotel, originally built in 1903. South of Leonora-Gwalia, 25 km off the main road, is **Kookynie**, another interesting once-flourishing mining town with just a handful of inhabitants left – in 1905 the population was 1500. Nearby **Niagara** is also a ghost town.

From Leonora-Gwalia, you can turn north-east to **Laverton**, where the surfaced road ends. The population here declined from 1000 in 1910 to 200 in 1970 when the Poseidon nickel discovery (beloved of stockmarket speculators in the late '60s and early '70s) revived mining operations in nearby Windarra. The town now has a population of 1200, and there are many abandoned mines in the area. From here, it is just 1710 km north-east to Alice Springs (see the following section on the Warburton Road/Gunbarrel Highway).

North of Leonora-Gwalia, the road is now surfaced to **Leinster** (population 1000), another modern nickel town. Nearby, **Agnew** is another old gold town that has all but disappeared. From here, it's 170 km north to **Wiluna** (population 230) and another 180 km west to **Meekatharra** on the surfaced Great Northern Highway, which runs 765 km south-west to Perth or 860 km north to Port Hedland. Through the '30s, when arsenic was mined there, Wiluna had a population of 8000 and was a modern, prosperous town. The ore ran out in 1948 and the town quickly declined. Today, the population is mainly Aboriginal.

Warburton Road/Gunbarrel Highway

For those interested in an outback experience, the unsealed road from Laverton to Yulara (the tourist development near Uluru) via Warburton (population 350) provides a rich scenery of red sand, spinifex, mulga and desert oaks. The road, while sandy in places, is suitable for conventional vehicles, although a 4WD would give a much smoother ride. Although this road is often called the Gunbarrel Highway, the genuine article actually runs some distance to the north, but it is very rough and no longer maintained.

You should take precautions relevant to travel in such an isolated area – tell someone reliable of your travel plans and take adequate supplies of water, petrol, food and spare parts. The longest stretch without fuel is between Laverton and Warburton (568 km). Don't even consider doing it from November to March due to the extreme heat. See the Getting Around chapter for more details. Conditions out here should not be taken lightly – in January 1994 a Japanese motorcyclist, equipped with just four leaky one-litre water bottles, nearly met his end here.

Petrol is available at Laverton, Warburton (where basic supplies are also available), Docker River and Yulara. At **Giles**, about 105 km west of the Northern Territory border, is a weather station with a friendly 'Visitors Welcome' sign and a bar – it is well worth a visit.

Note that this road passes through Aboriginal land and a permit from the Central Land Council in Alice Springs is required before you can travel along it. These permits take up to two weeks to issue.

KAMBALDA (population 4200)
Kambalda died as a gold-mining town in 1906, but nickel was discovered there in 1966, and today it is a major mining centre. There are two town centres, East and West Kambalda, about four km apart. The town is on the shores of Lake Lefroy, a large salt pan and a popular spot for land yachting. The view from Red Hill Lookout in Kambalda East is well worth checking out.

The tourist bureau (☎ (090) 27 1446), on Irish Mulga Drive in West Kambalda, can provide information and a map of the area.

NORSEMAN (population 1400)
To most visitors, Norseman is just a crossroads where you turn east for the trans-Nullarbor Eyre Highway journey, south to Esperance along the Leeuwin Way or north to Coolgardie and Perth. The town, however, also has gold mines, some still in operation.

The tourist bureau (☎ (090) 39 0171), at 68 Roberts St, is open daily from 9 am to 5 pm. Next to the tourist bureau is a tourist rest park, open from 8 am to 6 pm.

The **Historical & Geological Collection** in the old School of Mines has items from the gold-rush days; it's open weekdays from 10 am to 4 pm and admission is $2. An interesting gold-mining tour is conducted by Central Norseman Goldmining every weekday at 10 am and 1 pm; the 2½-hour tour costs $5 and bookings can be made at the tourist bureau.

You can get an excellent view of the town and the surrounding salt lakes from the **Beacon Hill Mararoa Lookout**, down past the mountainous tailings dumps, one of which contains 4.2 million tonnes of rock – the result of 40 years of gold mining.

The graffiti-covered **Dundas Rocks** are huge boulders, 22 km south of Norseman.

Also worth a look are the views at sunrise and sunset of the dry, expansive and spectacular **Lake Cowan**, north of Norseman.

South of Norseman, just under halfway along the road to Esperance, is the small township of **Salmon Gums** (population 50), named after the gum trees, prevalent in the area, which acquire a seasonal rich, pink bark in late summer and autumn.

Places to Stay & Eat
The *Gateway Caravan Park* (☎ (090) 39 1500) has tent sites for $11, vans for $26 and on-site cabins at $35. Both the *Norseman Hotel* (☎ (090) 39 1023) and the *Railway Hotel/Motel* (☎ (090) 39 1115) have rooms; and the *Norseman Eyre Motel* (☎ (090) 39 1130) has rooms for $62/69.

Bits & Pizzas has a wide range of eat-in or takeaway meals, and also cooked breakfasts with the works for $7.50. The *BP Roadhouse* at the start of the Eyre Highway has a wide range of food that includes tasty fish & chips.

Getting There & Away
Goldfields Air Services (☎ (090) 93 2116) fly from Kalgoorlie to Esperance via Norseman – the Kalgoorlie to Norseman sector costs $70. For bus information, see the Kalgoorlie Getting There & Away section.

The Nullarbor

It's a little over 2700 km between Perth and Adelaide – not much less than the distance from London to Moscow. The long and sometimes lonely Eyre Highway crosses the southern edge of the vast Nullarbor Plain – Nullarbor is bad Latin for 'no trees' and indeed there is a small stretch where you see none at all. Surprisingly, the road is actually flanked by trees most of the way as this coastal fringe receives regular rain, especially in winter.

The road across the Nullarbor takes its name from John Eyre, the explorer who made the first east-west crossing in 1841. It

WESTERN AUSTRALIA

was a superhuman effort that took five months of hardship and resulted in the death of Eyre's companion, John Baxter. In 1877, a telegraph line was laid across the Nullarbor, roughly delineating the route the first road would take.

Later in the century, miners en route to the WA gold fields followed the same telegraph-line route across the empty plain. In 1896, the first bicycle crossing was made and in 1912 the first car was driven across, but in the next 12 years only three more cars managed to traverse the continent.

In 1941, the war inspired the building of a trans-continental highway, just as it had the Alice Springs to Darwin route. It was a rough-and-ready track when completed, and in the '50s only a few vehicles a day made the crossing. In the '60s, the traffic flow increased to more than 30 vehicles a day and in 1969 the Western Australian government surfaced the road as far as the South Australian border. Finally, in 1976, the last stretch from the South Australian border was surfaced and now the Nullarbor crossing is a much easier drive, but still a long one.

The surfaced road runs close to the coast on the South Australian side. Here, the Nullarbor region ends dramatically on the coast of the Great Australian Bight, at cliffs that drop steeply into the ocean. It's easy to see why this area was a seafarer's nightmare, for a ship driven on to the coast would quickly be pounded to pieces against the cliffs, and climbing them would be a near impossibility.

The Indian Pacific Railway runs north of the coast and actually on the Nullarbor Plain – unlike the main road, which only fringes the great plain.

Crossing the Nullarbor

See the Perth Getting There & Away section for air, rail, hitching and bus information across the Nullarbor.

Although the Nullarbor is no longer a torture trail, with cars getting shaken to bits in potholes and travellers facing the real possibility of dying of thirst while waiting for another vehicle if they break down, it's still wise to prepare adequately and to avoid difficulties whenever possible.

The longest distance between fuel stops is about 200 km, so if you're foolish enough to run low on petrol midway, it can be a long round trip to get more. Getting help for a

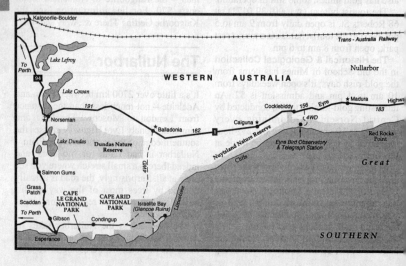

mechanical breakdown can be equally time-consuming and very expensive, so make sure your vehicle is in good shape and that you've got plenty of petrol, good tyres and at least a basic kit of simple spare parts. Carry some drinking water just in case you do have to sit it out by the roadside on a hot summer day.

Take it easy on the Nullarbor – plenty of people try to set speed records and plenty more have made a real mess of their cars when they've run into big kangaroos, particularly at night.

THE EYRE HIGHWAY

From Norseman, where the Eyre Highway begins, it's 725 km to the WA-SA border, near Eucla, and a further 480 km to Ceduna (from an Aboriginal word meaning 'a place to sit down and rest') in South Australia. From Ceduna, it's still another 793 km to Adelaide via Port Augusta. It's a bloody long way!

Balladonia

From Norseman, the first settlement you reach is Balladonia, 193 km to the east. After Balladonia, near the old station, you can see the remains of old stone fences built to

enclose stock. Clay saltpans are also visible in the area. **Newmann's Rocks** (50 km west of Balladonia) are also worth a look. Visits can be arranged by phoning ☎ (090) 39 3456 between 9 am and 4.30 pm. The *Balladonia Hotel/Motel* (☎ (090) 39 3453) has rooms from $58/66 and its dusty caravan park has tent and caravan sites for $8/14.

The road from Balladonia to Cocklebiddy is one of the loneliest stretches of road across the Nullarbor.

Caiguna & Cocklebiddy

The road from Balladonia to Caiguna includes one of the longest stretches of straight road in the world – 145 km. At Caiguna, the *John Eyre Motel* (☎ (090) 39 3459) has rooms for $50/65, and a caravan park with tent and caravan sites from $5/12.

At Cocklebiddy are the stone ruins of an Aboriginal mission. **Cocklebiddy Cave** is the largest of the Nullarbor caves – in 1983 a team of French explorers set a record there for the deepest cave dive in the world. With a 4WD, you can travel south of Cocklebiddy to **Twilight Cove**, where there are 75-metre-high limestone cliffs. The *Wedgetail Inn* (☎ (090) 39 3462) at Cocklebiddy has a

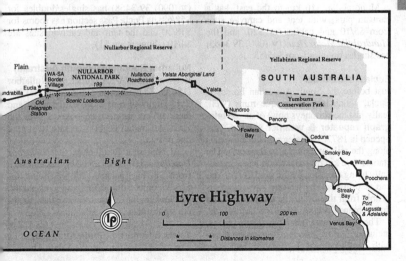

The Eyre Bird Observatory

The *Eyre Bird Observatory* (☎ (090) 39 3450) provides accommodation by prior arrangement only. Established in 1977, it is housed in the Eyre Telegraph Station, an 1897 stone building in the Nuytsland Nature Reserve, surrounded by mallee scrubland and looking onto spectacular sand dunes which separate the buildings from the sea. A wide range of desert flora and fauna is studied, and twitchers can expect to see pink cockatoos, brush bronzewings and the odd furtive mallee fowl. A small museum at the rear of the station has exhibits from the days of the telegraph line and of the legendary stationmaster, William Graham.

Full board costs $45 per person per day (discounts for YHA and RAOU members). Return transport to the bird observatory from Cocklebiddy or the Microwave Tower can be arranged for about $25. If travelling independently, you will need a 4WD to get there, as it is about 50 km south-east of Cocklebiddy. You have to descend the escarpment and then drive through about 12 km of sand to reach the observatory. From the buildings there is a one-km walk, via the dunes, to the beach and the lonely Australian Bight. ■

marauding and contrary goat, expensive fuel, tent and caravan sites for $6/12 and overpriced rooms from $58/66. It also has wedge-tailed eagles overhead!

Madura & Mundrabilla

Madura, 91 km east of Cocklebiddy, is close to the hills of the Hampton Tablelands. At one time, horses were bred here for the Indian Army. There are good views over the plains from the road. The *Madura Hospitality Inn* (☎ (090) 39 3464) has rooms from $60/70 and tent and caravan sites from $5/12.

Mundrabilla, 116 km to the east, has a caravan park, with tent and caravan sites from $5/10 and cabins for $20, and the *Mundrabilla Motor Hotel* (☎ (090) 39 3465) has singles/doubles from $45/55.

Eucla & the Border

Just before the South Australian border is Eucla, which has picturesque ruins (well, really just the chimneys now) of an old **telegraph repeater & weather station**, first opened in 1877. The telegraph line now runs along the railway line, far to the north. The station, five km from the roadhouse, is gradually being engulfed by the sand dunes. You can also inspect the historic jetty, which is visible from the top of the dunes. The sand dunes around Eucla are a truly spectacular sight.

The Eucla area also has many caves, including the well-known **Koonalda Cave** with its 45-metre-high chamber. You enter

by ladder and, like other Nullarbor caves, it's really only for experienced cave explorers.

Many people have their photo taken at Eucla's famous sign which pinpoints distances to international destinations. For connoisseurs of kitsch there's a ferrocement sperm whale (a species seldom seen in these parts), and a five-metre-high fibreglass kangaroo nearby.

The *WA-SA Border Village* (☎ (090) 39 3474) has tent and caravan sites from $6/12, cabins from $35 a double and motel units from $60/68. The *Eucla Motor Hotel* (☎ (090) 39 3468) has singles/doubles for $58/68; its Eucla Pass section has rooms for $18/30 and the tent and caravan sites are $4/10 (showers are $1).

Nullarbor Roadhouse (South Australia)

Between the WA-SA border and Nullarbor (184 km to the east in South Australia), the Eyre Highway runs close to the coast and there are six spectacular lookouts over the Great Australian Bight – be sure to stop at one or two.

At Nullarbor Roadhouse, the *Nullarbor Hotel/Motel* (☎ (086) 25 6271) has tent sites from $8, backpackers' singles/twins for $15/25, units from $55/65 and a restaurant. Just look for the diminutive fibreglass southern right whale.

Yalata & Nundroo (South Australia)

The road passes through the Yalata Aboriginal Reserve (600,000 hectares), and Aborigines often sell boomerangs and other souvenirs by the roadside. You can also buy these in the *Yalata Aboriginal Community Roadhouse* (☎ (086) 25 6990), which also has tent sites from $3.50, singles/doubles from $30/35, a restaurant and a takeaway food service.

Nundroo is really on the edge of the Nullarbor. The *Nundroo Inn* (☎ (086) 25 6120) has a caravan park with tent sites, rooms, a licensed restaurant, takeaway food and a pool.

Penong (South Australia)
Between Nundroo and Penong is the ghost town of **Fowlers Bay**. There is good fishing here, and nearby is **Mexican Hat Beach**.

You can make a short detour south of Penong to see the **Pink Lake**, **Point Sinclair** and **Cactus Beach** – a surf beach with left and right breaks that is a must for any serious surfer making the east-west journey. Although the Point is private property, you can camp there for $4 (bring your own water).

The *Penong Hotel* (☎ (086) 25 1050) has basic singles/doubles from $20/30, and serves counter meals. The service station across the road has a restaurant and takeaways.

Eastbound from Penong to Ceduna, there are several places with petrol and other facilities. Ceduna is effectively the end of the solitary stretch from Norseman, and is equipped with supermarkets, banks and all the comforts (see Ceduna in the South Australia chapter).

The South-West

The southern area of WA, the 'Great Southern', has magnificent coastline pounded by huge seas, rugged ranges, national parks, Albany (the oldest settlement in WA) and, in the south-west, the greenest and most fertile areas of WA – a great contrast to the dry and barren country found in much of the state.

Here, you will find the great karri and jarrah forests, prosperous farming land, wineries and more of the state's beautiful wildflowers.

Many travellers on the road between the east and west coasts of Australia take the direct route through WA via Coolgardie and Norseman. However, if you travel the longer route to or from Perth around the south-west corner of Australia, you will be rewarded by some of the state's most stunning scenery.

There is plenty of accommodation with enough hostels to make a good backpacking loop such as Perth, Augusta, the Big Trees, Albany, Esperance, and return to Perth.

Getting There & Away
Air Skywest (☎ (09) 323 1188 in Perth) has flights to Albany ($146 one way/$200 Apex return) and Esperance ($188/252). Goldfields Air Services has flights between Kalgoorlie and Esperance via Norseman ($137/192).

Bus & Train Westrail has a number of bus services in the region including buses from Kalgoorlie and Perth to Esperance and from Perth to Hyden, Manjimup, Albany and Denmark. There is also a bus and the Australind train service from Perth to Bunbury. From Bunbury, Westrail buses continue to Busselton, Yallingup, Margaret River and Augusta.

South-West Coach Lines (☎ (09) 324 2333) also services the region and has daily services from Perth to Bunbury, Busselton, Dunsborough, Margaret River, Augusta, Nannup and Manjimup.

AUSTRALIND (population 4400)
The holiday resort of Australind is a pleasant 11-km drive north of Bunbury. The town takes its name from an 1840s plan to make it a port for trade with India. The plan never worked but the strange hybrid name (Australia-India) remains.

Australind has the tiny **St Nicholas Church**, which, at just four by seven metres, is said to be the smallest church in Australia.

There's also **Henton Cottage**, built in 1843, and a scenic drive between Australind and Binningup along **Leschenault Inlet**, a good place to catch blue manna crabs. There are three caravan parks at Australind.

INLAND

Inland from the south-west coast, the town of **Harvey** (population 2600) is located in a popular bushwalking area of rolling green hills to the north of Bunbury. This is the home of WA's Big Orange, standing 20 metres high at the Fruit Bowl on the South-Western Highway. There are dam systems and some beautiful waterfalls nearby, and the **Yalgorup National Park**, with its peculiar stromatolites, is north of town. The tourist bureau (☎ (097) 29 1122) is on the South Western Highway.

Further south of Bunbury is **Donnybrook** (population 1600), in the centre of an apple-growing area. It has a deer park to the north and a tourist centre (☎ (097) 31 1720) in an old railway station. Apple-picking work is often available in season (apparently most of the year).

Collie (population 7700), WA's only coal town, has an interesting replica of a coal mine, a historical museum and a steam-loco-motive museum. There is some pleasant bushwalking country around the town and plenty of wildflowers in season. The tourist bureau (☎ (097) 34 2051) is on Throssell St.

Places to Stay

The *Rainbow Caravan Park* (☎ (097) 29 2239), on King St in Harvey, has tent sites and on-site vans, as does the *Mr Marron Holiday Village* (☎ (097) 34 2507) in Porter St, Collie.

In Donnybrook, the *Brook Lodge* (☎ (097) 31 1520), on Bridge St, is a private lodge with kitchen and laundry facilities. Just before the bridge leading to Brook Lodge, at 6 Bridge St, is the comfortable and rambling *Donnybrook Backpackers'* (☎ (097) 31 1844); dorm beds/twins are $11 per night or $66 per week per person.

BUNBURY (population 24,000)

As well as being a port, an industrial town and a holiday resort, Bunbury, WA's second largest town, is also noted for its blue manna crabs and dolphins. The tourist bureau (☎ (097) 21 7922) is in the old 1904 railway station on Carmody Place. It has a detailed walking-tour brochure of Bunbury called *Walk About*.

The town's old buildings include **King Cottage**, which now houses a museum, the **Rose Hotel** and **St Mark's Church**, built in 1842. The interesting **Arts Complex** on Wittenoom St is in a restored 1897 convent building.

Dolphins

You don't have to go to Monkey Mia to interact with dolphins; you can also do so at the Bunbury Dolphin Trust centre on **Koombana Beach**. Visits from a group that regularly feed in the Inner Harbour usually occur several times a day, less frequently in winter; a flag is raised when the dolphins are in.

The area, staffed during the day by helpful volunteers, was set up in 1989, and dolphins started to interact with the public in early 1990. A brochure explains the simple rules of contact with dolphins, or you can ask a ranger.

Places to Stay

There are three caravan parks in town: *Bunbury Village* on the Bussell Highway; *Glade*, also on the Bussell Highway; and the small *Punchbowl* on Ocean Drive. The *Residency Retreat Hostel* (☎ (097) 91 2621) is in a historic residence on the corner of Stirling and Moore Sts. Good dorm beds in this clean hostel are $15 per night and there is one family room for $30.

The efficiently run and friendly *Wander Inn – Bunbury Backpackers* (☎ (097) 21 3242), closer to the city centre at 16 Clifton St (two blocks from the tourist bureau and the Indian Ocean), costs $12 a night for a dorm bed and $28 for a double. The staff provide free transport to the dolphins and a free trip back to Perth once a week.

The *Captain Bunbury Hotel* (☎ (097) 21 2021) at 8 Victoria St has basic rooms for $15/25, and the *Prince of Wales* (☎ (097) 21 2016) on Stephen St has rooms for $25/44 with breakfast. The *Rose Hotel* (☎ (097) 21 4533) is a clean and lavishly restored place; singles/doubles are $29/46 with breakfast.

Places to Eat
The *International Food Hall* on Symmons St is a large place with kebabs, roasts, Italian and Chinese dishes and seafood from $5 to $7; it is open Thursday to Sunday from 11 am to 9 pm. *Drooly's*, at 70 Victoria St, has great pizzas at moderate prices. The *Rose Hotel*, on Wellington St, does good counter meals.

Also in Victoria St are the popular *Memories of the Bond Store*, which has four outlets including a brasserie, and the *China City Garden Restaurant*. If you are after French cuisine then hop into the *Little Frog* on Rose St. *Louisa's* on Clifton St is an award winner – one of Bunbury's best.

Getting There & Around
South-West Coach Lines travels daily between Bunbury and Perth for $16. Westrail also has a daily bus (three hours, $17) and the Australind train (2½ hours, $17.10) runs from Perth.

Bunbury City Transit (☎ (097) 911 955) covers the region around the city as far north as Australind and south to Gelorup.

BUSSELTON (population 9000)
Busselton on the shores of Geographe Bay is another popular holiday resort. The town has a two-km jetty which was once reputed to be the longest timber jetty in Australia. Busselton has a tourist bureau (☎ (097) 52 1091) in the civic centre on Southern Drive.

The old **courthouse** has been restored and now houses an impressive arts centre with a gallery, a coffee shop and artists' workshops. **Wonnerup House**, 10 km east of town, is an 1859 Colonial-style house lovingly restored by the National Trust.

To get to Busselton you can take a Westrail or South-West Coachlines bus. Geographe Bay Coachlines (☎ (097) 54 2026) conducts tours to Cape Naturaliste, Augusta, Cape Leeuwin and Margaret River.

Places to Stay
There is a great deal of accommodation along this stretch of coast. The most central of the many caravan parks is *Kookaburra No 1* (☎ (097) 52 1516) at 66 Marine Terrace. The *Busselton Caravan Park* (☎ (097) 52 1175), on the Bussell Highway, has tent sites for $10 and extremely friendly hosts.

The nearly always full *Motel Busselton* (☎ (097) 52 1908), 90 Bussell Highway, has comfortable units from $28 per B&B double per night. *Villa Carlotta Private Hotel* (☎ (097) 54 2026), at 110 Adelaide St, is good, friendly, organises tours and has singles/doubles for $35/50 with breakfast. Another guesthouse, the *Travellers Rest* (☎ (097) 52 2290), 223 Bussell Highway, has B&B for $20/30.

Places to Eat
There is a stack of places to eat in Busselton including *Michelango's* at the Riviera Motel for Italian food, the *Golden Inn* on Albert St for Chinese food, and hotels such as the *Ship Hotel/Motel*, on Albert St, and the *Esplanade*, on Marine Terrace, for counter meals. Enjoy the succulent seafood at the BYO *Tails of the Bay*, 42 Adelaide St.

DUNSBOROUGH (population 660)
Dunsborough, just to the west of Busselton, is a pleasant little coastal town that is dependent on tourism. The tourist centre (☎ (097) 55 3517) is in the shopping centre.

North-west of Dunsborough, the Cape Naturaliste Rd leads to excellent beaches such as **Meelup**, **Eagle Bay** and **Bunker Bay**, some fine coastal lookouts and the tip of **Cape Naturaliste**, which has a lighthouse and some walking trails. In season you can see humpback whales, southern right whales

WESTERN AUSTRALIA

and dolphins from the lookouts out over Geographe Bay. At scenic **Sugarloaf Rock** there is the southernmost nesting colony of the rare red-tailed tropicbird.

Both South-West Coachlines and Westrail have daily services to Dunsborough; the one-way fare to Perth is $23.

Places to Stay & Eat

Greenacres Caravan Park (☎ (097) 55 3087), on the beachfront at Dunsborough, has tent sites and on-site vans and cabins. Near Dunsborough, in Quindalup, is the well-positioned, refurbished *Dunsborough YHA Resort Hostel* (☎ (097) 55 3107) on the beachfront at 285 Geographe Bay Rd; the rate is $13 per night (dorms, twins and family) and they hire bicycles ($8 per day) and canoes and life jackets ($5 per hour).

The *Forum Food Centre* has a variety of eating places including a fine bakery, home of the 'Naturaliste' filled lamington. *Dunsborough Health Foods* in the shopping centre sells wholemeal salad rolls and delicious smoothies and juices. The *Dunsborough Bakery* has tasty pies and is reputed to be the best pastry filler around.

YALLINGUP

Yallingup, a Mecca for surfers, is surrounded by spectacular coastline and some fine beaches. Surfers can get a copy of the free *Down South Surfing Guide* from the Dunsborough tourist centre. Nearby is the stunning **Yallingup Cave** which was discovered, or rather stumbled upon, in 1899. The cave is open daily from 9.30 am to 3.30 pm and you can look around by yourself or take a guided tour that also explores parts of the cave not usually open to visitors.

The *Yallingup Caravan Park* (☎ (097) 55 2164) on the beachfront at Valley Rd has tent sites and on-site vans. On Caves Rd, *Caves House* (☎ (097) 55 2131), established in 1903, is one of those olde-worlde lodges with ocean views and an English garden. As Yallingup means 'place of lovers', the rooms at Caves House are perfect for honeymooners but are not cheap at $95 for two.

The *Yallingup Store* is known for its burgers, and there's also the *Surfside Restaurant* or the more expensive *Wildwood Winery*, eight km south of Yallingup.

MARGARET RIVER (population 1700)

This area is famous for its wineries. You can buy a copy of the *Margaret River Regional Vineyard Guide* at tourist centres for $2.50. It lists over 35 wineries from Cape Naturaliste to Cape Leeuwin including the renowned Leeuwin Estate, Sandalford and Cape Mentelle. In general the wines are expensive but worth it.

The attractive town of Margaret River is a popular holiday spot due to its proximity to fine surf (Margaret River Mouth, Gnarabup, Suicides and Redgate) and swimming (Prevelly and Grace Town) beaches, some of Australia's best wineries and spectacular scenery.

The Augusta-Margaret River tourist bureau (☎ (097) 57 2911) is on the corner of the Bussell Highway and Tunbridge Rd. It has a wad of information on the area, including an extensive vineyard guide.

There are a number of art and craft places in town including Margaret River Pottery and Kookaburra Crafts. An 1855 National Trust property, **Ellensbrook Homestead**, the first home of the Bussell family, is eight km north-west of town. **Eagle Heritage**, five km south of Margaret River on Boodjidup Rd, has an interesting collection of raptors (birds of prey) in a natural setting; it is open daily 10 am to 5 pm and costs $4.50, children $2.50.

A most interesting tour takes you on a search for forest secrets with the Bushtucker Lady at Prevelly Park (☎ (097) 57 2466). This tour combines walking and canoeing up the Margaret River and teaches Aboriginal culture, bushcraft and flora and fauna. The two-hour exploration costs $12 (children $7.50).

The old coast road between Augusta, Margaret River and Busselton is a good alternative to the direct road which runs slightly inland. The coast here has real variety – cliff faces, long beaches pounded by rolling surf, and calm, sheltered bays.

Places to Stay

The *Margaret River Caravan Park* (☎ (097) 57 2180) on Station Rd has tent sites and on-site vans, and there's also the *Riverview Caravan Park* (☎ (097) 57 2270) on Willmott Ave (its tent sites are on a bit of an angle).

There are plenty of places to stay around Margaret River but unfortunately most are upwards of $50 per night. One exception is *Margaret River Lodge* (☎ (097) 57 2532), a backpackers' hostel about 1.5 km south-west from the town centre at 220 Railway Terrace. It's clean, friendly and modern with all the facilities including a good swimming pool, bicycle and boogie board hire and an open fireplace. There are dorms at $11, four-bed bunk rooms from $12 per person and doubles from $30 for two.

If you want to splash out, the *Croft* (☎ (097) 57 2845), at 54 Wallcliffe Rd, is a comfortable guesthouse run by a very friendly couple; B&B is $65 per double.

Places to Eat

Among the many places to eat in Margaret River is the *Settler's Tavern*, on the Bussell Highway, which has good counter meals from $10 to $12 – it occasionally has live music. The *Margaret River Hotel* has counter meals in its bistro. On the same road, you can also try the *Kebab Company* which has a wide range of kebabs and felafels from $4 to $5. *Eats Diner* and the *Arc of Iris*, both on the Bussell Highway, have been recommended. For continental fare there is the more expensive but licensed *1885* on Farrelly St.

Getting There & Around

There are daily bus services between Perth and Margaret River on South-West Coach Lines and Westrail (both about $26); the trip takes around five hours.

Bikes can be rented on a daily or hourly basis from Margaret River Lodge.

AUGUSTA (population 840)

A popular holiday resort, Augusta is five km north of Cape Leeuwin, which has a rugged coastline, a lighthouse (open daily to the public) with views extending over two oceans (the Indian and the Southern), and a salt-encrusted 1895 waterwheel. The interesting **Augusta Historical Museum** on Blackwood Ave has exhibits relating to local history. The tourist centre (☎ (097) 58 1695) is in a souvenir shop at 70 Blackwood Ave.

Between here and Margaret River to the north, there are some good beaches at **Hamelin Bay** and **Cosy Corner**. Scenic flights over the cape are conducted by Leeuwin Aviation; book with the Margaret River tourist bureau.

'Hidden Wilderness' Caves

There are a number of limestone caves between the Naturaliste and Leeuwin capes. These include **Jewel** (the most picturesque), **Lake**, **Mammoth** and **Moondyne**. Fossilised skeletons of Tasmanian tigers have been found in Moondyne, and a fossil jawbone of *Zygomaturus trilobus*, a giant wombat-like creature, is on display in the cave. Moondyne is unlit and an experienced guide takes the visitor on a caving adventure; all equipment is provided on this two-hour trip which costs $18. Guided cave tours, the only way to see these caves, run daily for $7.50. In all, 120 caves have been discovered between Cape Leeuwin and Cape Naturaliste but only these four, and Yallingup Cave near Busselton, are open to the public.

Places to Stay & Eat

Doonbanks (☎ (097) 58 1517) is the most central caravan park, with tent sites for $10; it is a well-run place in a good setting. There are a number of basic camp sites in the Leeuwin-Naturaliste National Park including ones on Boranup Drive and Conto's Field, near Lake Cave.

The small *Augusta Hostel* (☎ (097) 58 1433) costs $9 per night. It is in a cottage on the corner of the Bussell Highway and Blackwood Ave. Some of the self-contained holiday flats have reasonable rates but they may have minimum booking periods in the high season; enquire at the tourist bureau.

The *Augusta Hotel* does counter meals and has an à la carte restaurant, or head for *Squirrels*, next to the hotel, where you can find delicious burgers piled high with salad, Lebanese sandwiches and various health foods. The *Augusta Moon Chinese restaurant* is in the Matthew Flinders shopping centre on Ellis St.

Between the caves in the Boranup karri forest is the quaint *Arumvale Siding Cafe*, which serves a mean nachos, Devonshire teas and a range of juices.

NANNUP (population 470)

Fifty km west of Bridgetown is Nannup, a quiet, historical and picturesque town in the heart of forest and farmland. The tourist centre (☎ (097) 56 1211) at the old 1922 police station in Brockman St (open daily from 9 am to 3 pm) has an excellent booklet (50c) that points out places of interest around town and details a range of scenic drives in the area, including a Blackwood River Rd drive and numerous forest drives. There is a sawmill (one of the largest in WA), an arboretum, some fine old buildings and several craft shops. The descent of the Blackwood River, from the forest to the sea, is one of Australia's great canoe trips.

Places to Stay & Eat

There is now a backpackers' lodge in Nannup – the rustic *Black Cockatoo Eco-Stay* (☎ (097) 56 1035), 27 Grange Rd, has singles/twins for $10/20. The centrally located and friendly *Dry Brook B&B* (☎ (097) 56 1049) has comfortable singles/doubles for $20/30 with breakfast and is highly recommended.

The *Blackwood Cafe* has good light meals such as quiche, soup and sandwiches. It is on Warren Rd, near the *Nannup Hotel*, which has counter meals.

BRIDGETOWN (population 2000)

This quiet country town on the Blackwood River is in an area of karri forests and farmland. Bridgetown has some old buildings, including **Bridgedale House** which was built of mud and clay by the area's first settler in 1862 and has been restored by the National Trust. There's a panoramic view from **Sutton's Lookout** off Philips St, and there is a local history display in the tourist centre (☎ (097) 61 1740) on Hampton St.

Interesting features of the Blackwood River valley are the burrawangs (grass trees) and large granite boulders. In **Boyup Brook**, 31 km north-east of Bridgetown, there is a flora reserve, a country & western music collection and a large butterfly and beetle display. Nearby is **Norlup Pool** with glacial rock formations, and **Wilga**, which is an old timber mill with vintage engines.

Places to Stay & Eat

Bridgetown Caravan Park (☎ (097) 61 1053), on the South-Western Highway, has tent sites for $12 and on-site vans for $24 for two; backpackers' accommodation is $10. About 20 km out of town, in Greenbushes, there is the *Backpackers YHA – Exchange Hotel* (☎ (097) 64 3509). The *Old Well* (☎ (097) 61 2032) on Gifford St has B&B for $35. Enquire at the tourist centre about the many other B&B possibilities.

Good meals are available at *Riverwood House*, the *Pottery* and *Buckley's Bistro*.

MANJIMUP (population 4400)

Manjimup is the commercial and agricultural centre of the south-west, and is noted for its apple growing and wood chipping. The impressive **Timber Park Complex** on the corner of Rose and Edwards Sts includes various museums, old buildings and the Manjimup tourist bureau (☎ (097) 71 1 831), open daily from 9 am to 5 pm.

One Tree Bridge, or what's left of it after the 1966 floods, is 22 km down the Graphite Rd. It was constructed from a single karri log. The **Four Aces**, 1.5 km from One Tree Bridge, are four superb karri trees believed to be over 300 years old. **Fonty's Pool**, a great spot to cool off during those hot summer days, is 10 km south-west of town along Seven Day Rd.

Nine km south of town, along the South-Western Highway, is the 51-metre-high karri **Diamond Tree Fire Tower**, which you can observe but not climb. There is a nature trail nearby.

Perup, 50 km east of Manjimup, is the centre of a 40,000-hectare forest which has populations of six rare mammals – the numbat, chuditch, woylie, tammar wallaby, ringtail possum and southern brown bandicoot.

Places to Stay & Eat

The *Manjimup Caravan Park* (☎ (097) 71 2093) has a hostel with dorm beds and cooking facilities for $12 per night – it can get busy in apple-picking season (March to June), when beds are $65 weekly. It also has tent sites and on-site vans. Two other caravan parks – *Warren Way* (☎ (097) 71 1060), two km north of town, and *Fonty's Pool* (☎ (097) 71 2105), 10 km south-west of town – also have tent sites and on-site vans.

For meals, try the *Blue Marron Restaurant* for marron and trout, the *Country Kitchen* next to the Timber Park for Devonshire teas, and the *Manjimup Hotel* for counter meals.

Getting There & Away

Westrail has a Perth to Manjimup bus service via Bunbury and Collie, and South-West Coach Lines has a weekday service from Perth to Manjimup; both are about $25 one way.

PEMBERTON (population 930)

Deep in the karri forests is the delightful town of Pemberton. The child-friendly, well-organised Karri visitor centre (☎ (097) 76 1133), on Brockman St, incorporates the tourist centre, pioneer museum and karri forest discovery centre.

Pemberton has some interesting **craft shops**; the pretty **Pemberton Pool**, surrounded by karri trees (ideal on a hot day); and a **trout hatchery** that supplies fish for the state's dams and rivers. The excellent

What to See & Do in Big Tree Country map is available from the tourist centre.

If you are feeling fit, you can make the scary 60-metre climb to the top of the **Gloucester Tree**, the highest fire lookout tree in the world (this is not for the faint hearted and only one visitor in four ascends!). The view makes the climb well worthwhile. To get to the tree just follow the signs from town. Also of interest in the area are the spectacular **Cascades** (when the water level is high), **Beedelup National Park**, the **100-year-old forest** and the **Warren National Park**, where camping is allowed in designated areas.

The scenic **Pemberton Tramway** is one of the area's main attractions. Trams leave Pemberton railway station for Warren River ($11.50) daily at 10.45 am and 2 pm, and for Northcliffe ($18) at 10.15 am on Tuesday, Thursday and Friday. The route travels through lush marri and karri forests with occasional picture stops; a commentary is also provided.

Organised Tours

Southern Forest Adventures (☎ (097) 76 1222) has 4WD tours of the forest and coastal areas around Pemberton from $30. Canoeing trips with the same operator cost from $15. Pemberton Scenic Bus Tours does a forest industry tour from Monday to Friday at 10.30 am, and a daily three-hour scenic bus tour at 2 pm (also at 10.30 am on weekends).

Places to Stay

Camping is permitted in Warren National Park and in some areas of the Pemberton Forest (☎ (097) 76 1200). The picturesque *Pemberton Caravan Park* (☎ (097) 76 1300) has tent sites for $11 and on-site vans for $26.

The *Pemberton YHA Hostel* (☎ (097) 76 1153), in a beautiful forest location at Pimelea, costs $9 a night (nonmembers $10); doubles in cottages are $35 and two other cottages, Pimelea and Zamia, are $55 each (maximum of five people). It's 10 km north-west of town but the hostel provides a courtesy bus to meet the Westrail bus in

Pemberton – call in advance if you need transport.

In town, the centrally located *Warren Lodge* (☎ (097) 76 1105), on Brockman St, has backpackers' beds from $10 and B&B at $40 for two. There are many more up-market options.

Places to Eat

The *Pemberton Patisserie* has tasty pies and cakes, *Chloe's Kitchen* has takeaways including vegetarian food, and the *Mainstreet Cafe* on Brockman St has good, basic and cheap food such as hamburgers and Lebanese rolls. The *Pemberton Chinese Restaurant*, next to the supermarket on Dean St, is only open Thursday to Sunday from 5 pm and has meals from $6. The *Shamrock*, on Brockman St, is a marron and steak restaurant where a three-course meal costs around $25. The *Silver Birch* at the Tammeron Motor Lodge, Widdeson St, also has great three-course meals for $25.

Getting There & Away

Westrail Perth to Pemberton buses operate daily, via Bunbury, Donnybrook and Manjimup and cost $29; the trip takes about five hours. From Albany it is three hours and the cost is $22; the service is twice weekly.

NORTHCLIFFE (population 800)

Northcliffe, 32 km south of Pemberton, has a **pioneer museum** and a **forest park** close to town with good walks through stands of grand karri, marri and jarrah trees – a brochure and map of the trails is available from the tourist centre (☎ (097) 76 7203) by the museum on Wheatley Coast Rd.

The popular and picturesque **Lane Poole Falls** are 19 km south-east of Northcliffe; the 2.5-km track to the falls leaves from the 50-metre Boorara lookout tree. These falls slow to a trickle in the summer months.

Windy Harbour, on the coast 29 km south of Northcliffe, has prefab shacks and a sheltered beach; true to its name, it is very windy. The cliffs of magnificent **D'Entrecasteaux National Park** are accessible from here.

Places to Stay & Eat

Opposite the school is the *Northcliffe Caravan Park* (☎ (097) 76 7193), which has tent sites for $5.50 (power $1 extra). *Northcliffe Hotel* (☎ (097) 76 7089), the only hotel in Northcliffe, has basic accommodation for $16/30.

Out of town, both *Westpool Farm* (☎ (097) 76 7179), on Doublebridges Rd, and *Brook Farm* (☎ (097) 75 1014), on Middleton Rd, have B&B for $22/44. At Windy Harbour, the only place to stay is the *Windy Harbour Camping Area* (☎ (097) 76 7056) where basic tent sites are $4.

The *Hollow Butt* coffee shop, on Zamia St and Wheatley Coast Rd, has microwaved pies, light meals and cakes. Also on Wheatley Coast Rd is *Witchetty's*.

Getting There & Away

The Perth to Albany Westrail bus goes through Northcliffe twice weekly (Wednesday and Saturday), but you need your own transport to get to Windy Harbour.

WALPOLE-NORNALUP NATIONAL PARK

The heavily forested Walpole-Nornalup National Park covers 18,000 hectares around Nornalup Inlet and Walpole; it contains beaches, rugged coastline, inlets and the 'Valley of the Giants', a stand of giant karri and tingle trees, including one that soars 46 metres high. Here four species of rare eucalypts grow naturally within four km of each other and nowhere else in the world – red, yellow and Rates tingle (*Eucalyptus jacksonii, E. guilfoylei, E. cornuta*) and red flowering gum (*E. ficifolia*). Pleasant shady and ferny paths lead through the forest and the area is often frequented by bushwalkers. The Frankland River is popular with canoeists.

There are a number of scenic drives including Knoll Drive and the Valley of the Giants Rd. About 13 km from Walpole via Crystal Springs is Mandalay Beach, where the wreck of the *Mandalay*, a Norwegian barge wrecked here in 1911, can sometimes be seen. It seems to appear every 10 years out of the sands. Details are available from the Walpole tourist bureau (☎ (098) 40 1111) in the Pioneer Cottage or CALM (☎ (098) 40 1027), on the South Coast Highway in Walpole.

An informative CALM publication, *Finding the Magic*, costs $1.50 and includes a tree-spotter's guide. It also outlines the Ocean Drive, which includes the beautiful Conspicuous Cliffs beach, not far from the western end of the Valley of the Giants.

Karri to Coast (☎ (098) 40 1170) and Muir's Tours (☎ (098) 40 1036) run day trips around the area for $60, which includes lunch. The *Naughty Lass* (☎ (098) 40 1215) cruises the inlets and the river systems; morning tea is included, all for a mere $10.

Places to Stay & Eat

There are a number of camping grounds in the Walpole-Nornalup National Park, including tent sites at Peaceful Bay, Crystal Springs and Coalmine Beach. There are CALM huts at Fernhook Falls and Mt Frankland.

In the region are two really interesting places to stay. The *Tingle All Over Backpackers* (☎ (098) 40 1041), on the South Coast Highway in Walpole, has dorms/twins for $12/15 per person. This is a laid-back place that is central to many of the attractions of this area – many walkers and cyclists relax here after the Bibbulman Track.

There is also the *Dingo Flat YHA Hostel* (☎ (098) 40 8073) on Dingo Flat Rd off the Valley of the Giants Rd, 18 km east of Walpole – booking is recommended. You need a car or cycle to get to this hostel, or if you ring ahead they'll pick you up at Bow Bridge (there is a public phone in the local shop). Beds are $8, and the place has great character, with wonderful views over the fields to the forest, especially from the Loft.

You can get counter meals at the *Walpole Motel/Hotel* and there are three street cafes – *Anne's Pantry*, *Golden Wattle Country Kitchen* and the *Carragah*.

DENMARK (population 1600)

Denmark, or Koorabup ('place of the black swan'), has some rare evidence of Aboriginal settlement in Wilson Inlet – 3000-year-old fish traps. Named Denmark by an early explorer to commemorate a friend, the town was first established to supply timber for gold-field developments. About 54 km west of Albany, it has some fine beaches in the area (especially Ocean Beach for surfing) and is a good base for trips into the karri forests.

The Denmark tourist bureau (☎ (098) 48 1265) on Strickland St has heritage trail brochures including the **Mokare Trail** (a three-km trail along the Denmark River) and the **Wilson Inlet Trail** (a six-km trail that starts from the river mouth). There are fine views from **Mt Shadforth Lookout**, while the **William Bay National Park**, 15 km west of Denmark, has fine coastal scenery of rocks and reefs.

Places to Stay

There are several caravan parks in town, the closest being the idyllically located *Rivermouth Caravan Park* (☎ (098) 48 1262), one km south of the town centre on Inlet Drive.

The *Denmark Associate-YHA Hostel* at the Wilson Inlet Holiday Park, over four km south of Denmark, is a bit run down. The dingy dorm accommodation in the park's most dilapidated building is $10 per night – four or five people could band together and get something much better in town.

The *Denmark Guesthouse* (☎ toll-free 1800 671 477), on the South Coast Highway in the centre of town, remains one of the best accommodation bargains in WA. It is a friendly place with a TV lounge and clean rooms for $20/35; en-suite rooms are $32/50. (Show this book for a $5 discount.)

There are many types of chalets and cottages in the Denmark area; the tourist bureau keeps a current list.

Places to Eat

On North St, the *Mary Rose* serves tasty light meals and is a quaint place with a pleasant balcony. For a quick meal or takeaway food, try *Kettle's Deli* on the corner of the highway and Holling Rd.

Beneath the Denmark Guesthouse is the *Tiger & Snake*, open from Wednesday to Sunday from 5 pm, which serves tasty and hearty servings of Indian and Chinese food ($6 and $8 for small and large servings). The *Riverview Coffee Shop*, at 18 Holling Rd, has very good German food – no meal is over $10. Also beside the river, *Scoundrel's Brasserie*, a BYO with blackboard menu, is open later than most places.

Getting There & Around

Westrail's Perth to Albany (via the south coast) service comes through Denmark four times a week and costs $40 one way; the trip takes about seven hours. Contact the tourist bureau about local tours and bike hire.

MT BARKER (population 1500)

Mt Barker is 50 km north of Albany, 64 km south of the Stirling Range and about 20 km west of the Porongurups. There's a tourist bureau at 57 Lowood St (☎ (098) 51 1163), open weekdays from 9 am to 5 pm, Saturday 9 am to 2 pm.

The town has been settled since the 1830s and the old police station and jail building of 1868 is preserved as a museum. You can get a panoramic view of the area from the Mt Barker Lookout, five km south of town.

The region has a good reputation for wine making, and there are many wineries with cellar sales and tastings within a few km of town – see the tourist bureau for locations and opening times. Plantagenet Wines in the centre of town may show you around their winery.

Kendenup, 16 km north of Mt Barker, was the actual site of WA's first gold discovery, though this was considerably overshadowed by the later and much larger finds in the Kalgoorlie area. North of Mt Barker is **Cranbrook**, an access point to the Stirling Range National Park.

Places to Stay & Eat

The *Mt Barker Caravan Park* (☎ (098) 51

1619), Albany Highway, has tent sites at $8.50 and park homes at $30 for two people. The *Plantagenet Hotel* (☎ (098) 51 1008) at 9 Lowood Rd has singles/doubles from $20/36 (in the older hotel section) and good counter meals (beaut steaks) for around $10. The *Mt Barker Hotel* (☎ (098) 51 1477), 39 Lowood Rd, has basic twin rooms at $20.

Getting There & Away

Westrail's Perth to Albany via Williams bus service stops daily in Mt Barker; the fare from Perth is $29 one way.

PORONGURUP & STIRLING RANGE NATIONAL PARKS

The beautiful Porongurup National Park (2401 hectares) has panoramic views, spectacular scenery, large karri trees, 1100 million-year-old granite outcrops and excellent bushwalks. Trails range from the short **Tree in the Rock** stroll and the intermediate **Castle Rock** (two hours) walk to the harder **Hayward** and **Nancy Peaks** (four hours) and the excellent **Devil's Slide** and **Marmabup Rock** (three hours) walks. A scenic six-km drive along the northern edge of the park starts near the ranger's residence.

In the Stirling Range National Park (115,650 hectares), **Toolbrunup** (for views and a good climb), **Bluff Knoll** (at 1073 metres, the highest peak in the range) and **Toll Peak** (for the wildflowers) are popular half-day walks. The 96-km range is noted for its spectacular colour changes through blues, reds and purples. The mountains rise abruptly from the surrounding flat and sandy plains, and the area is known for its fine flora and fauna.

Further information on these parks can be obtained from the following CALM offices: Porongurup National Park, Bolganup Rd, RMB 1112, Mt Barker; Stirling Range National Park, Chester Pass Rd, c/o Amelup via Borden; and South Coast Regional Office, 44 Serpentine Rd, Albany.

Places to Stay

You can camp in the Stirling Range National

Park on Chester Pass Rd, near the Toolbrunup Peak turn-off; call the ranger (☎ (098) 27 9278) for details. Facilities are limited, and tent sites are $4 for two.

Stirling Range Caravan Park (☎ (098) 27 9229), on the north boundary of the park, is also on Chester Pass Rd; there is an associate-YHA hostel here, with beds for $12 in self-contained rammed-earth units ($40 for four).

There is no camping in Porongurup National Park but there's a caravan park (☎ (098) 53 1057) in Porongurup township, and *Karribank Lodge* (☎ (098) 53 1022) on Main St.

ALBANY (population 18,800)

The commercial centre of the southern region, the town of Albany is the oldest European settlement in the state, established in 1826 shortly before Perth. The area was occupied by Aborigines long before and there is much evidence, especially around Oyster Harbour, of their earlier presence.

With its excellent harbour on King George Sound, Albany was a thriving whaling port. Later, when steamships started travelling between the UK and Australia, Albany was a coaling station for ships bound for the east coast. During WW I, it was also the gathering point for troopships of the 1st AIF before they sailed for Egypt, eventually to fight in the Gallipoli campaign.

The coastline around Albany contains some of Australia's most rugged and spectacular scenery. There are a number of pristine beaches in the area where you don't have to compete for space on the sand – try Misery, 'ledge-n-dary' Ledge and Nanarup beaches.

Information

The informative Albany tourist bureau (☎ (098) 41 1088) is in Peels Place. It is open from 8.30 am to 5.30 pm Monday to Friday and from 9 am to 5 pm Saturday and Sunday. If you are in need of some reading material, there is a book exchange diagonally across from the tourist bureau.

Old Buildings

Albany has some fine old colonial buildings – **Stirling Terrace** is noted for its Victorian shopfronts. The 1851 **Old Gaol**, now a folk museum, is open daily; admission is $2 (this includes entry to the 1832 wattle-and-daub Patrick Taylor Cottage, also open daily).

The informative **Albany Residency Museum**, opposite the Old Gaol, was originally built in the 1850s as the home of the resident magistrate; it is open daily from 10 am to 5 pm. Displays include seafaring subjects, flora and flora and Aboriginal artefacts. Housed in another building is 'Sea & Touch', a great hands-on experience for children and adults. Next to this museum is a full-scale replica of the brig *Amity*, the ship that brought Albany's founding party to the area; there is a $2 entry fee.

The restored **old post office**, built in 1870, now houses the Inter-Colonial Museum. It has an interesting collection of communications equipment from WA's past; admission is free.

The farm at **Strawberry Hill**, two km from town, is one of the oldest in the state, having been established in 1827 as the government farm for Albany.

Other historic buildings in town include the railway station, St John's Anglican Church and the courthouse. A guided walking-tour brochure of Albany's colonial buildings is available from the tourist bureau.

Views

There are fine views over the coast and inland from the twin peaks, **Mt Clarence** and **Mt Melville**, which overlook the town. On top of Mt Clarence is the Desert Mounted Corps Memorial, originally erected in Port Said as a memorial to the events of Gallipoli. It was brought here when the Suez crisis in 1956 made colonial reminders less than popular in Egypt.

Mt Clarence can be climbed along a track accessible from the end of Grey St East; turn left, take the first on the right and follow the path by the water tanks. The walk is tough but the views from the top make it worth-

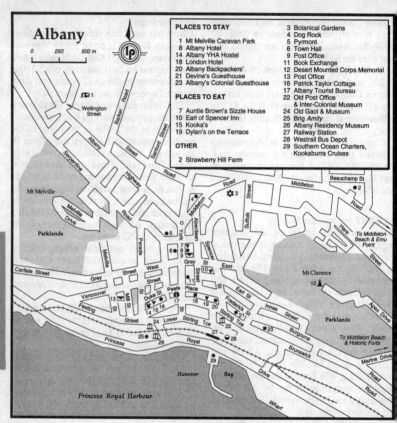

Albany

0   250   500 m

PLACES TO STAY

1 Mt Melville Caravan Park
8 Albany Hotel
14 Albany YHA Hostel
18 London Hotel
20 Albany Backpackers'
21 Devine's Guesthouse
23 Albany's Colonial Guesthouse

PLACES TO EAT

7 Auntie Brown's Sizzle House
10 Earl of Spencer Inn
15 Kooka's
19 Dylan's on the Terrace

OTHER

2 Strawberry Hill Farm
3 Botanical Gardens
4 Dog Rock
5 Pyrmont
6 Town Hall
9 Post Office
11 Book Exchange
12 Desert Mounted Corps Memorial
13 Post Office
16 Patrick Taylor Cottage
17 Albany Tourist Bureau
22 Old Post Office
& Inter-Colonial Museum
24 Old Gaol & Museum
25 Brig *Amity*
26 Albany Residency Museum
27 Railway Station
28 Westrail Bus Depot
29 Southern Ocean Charters,
Kookaburra Cruises

while. The easier way to the top is along Apex Drive.

Spectacular panoramic views are also available from the lookout tower on Mt Melville; the turn-off to the tower is off Serpentine Rd.

Other Attractions

Albany's **Princess Royal Fortress**, on Mt Adelaide, was built in 1893 when the strategic port's perceived vulnerability to an enemy naval squadron was recognised as a potential threat to Australia's security. The restored buildings, gun emplacements and

fine views make it well worth a visit. It is open daily from 7.30 am to 5.30 pm and costs $2. **Dog Rock**, a deformed boulder that looks like a dog's head, is on Middleton Rd.

More bizarre is **Extravaganza**, a museum with a difference, at Middleton Beach. All the exhibits in this cornucopia of trash and treasure are for sale; entry is $5.

Whale-Watching

The whale-watching season is from July to September – southern right whales are observed near the bays and coves of King George Sound. Southern Ocean Charters

(☎ (098) 41 7176) takes trips out to the whales and also operates diving, fishing, underwater photography and snorkelling tours on demand. Remember that whales were still hunted here until 1979 so it will take time for numbers to increase.

Organised Tours & Cruises

The *Silver Star* leaves the Emu Point jetty three times a week for a 2½-hour cruise around King George Sound; the cost is $18.50. The Kookaburra Jet (☎ (098) 42 2174) leaves from the Emu Point Marina three days a week; the two-hour cruise up Oyster Harbour and Kalgan River costs $20.

Escape Tours operates from the tourist bureau and has many local half-day and day tours around Albany from $22.50 to $55. Check with the tourist bureau for information on these and other tours.

Places to Stay

There are caravan parks aplenty in Albany. The closest to the city centre are *Mt Melville Caravan Park* (☎ (098) 41 4616), one km north of town on Wellington St, and the spotless *Middleton Beach Caravan Park* (☎ (098) 41 3593) on Middleton Rd, three km east of town. Both have tent sites and on-site cabins.

The *Albany YHA Hostel* (☎ (098) 41 3949), at 49 Duke St, is only 400 metres from the town centre, and costs $10 a night; the comments in the visitors' book were almost unanimously favourable in spite of the application of those Precambrian 'chores'.

The *Albany Backpackers'* (☎ (098) 41 8848), also centrally located, is on the corner of Stirling Terrace and Spencer St. It's worth going there just to check out the upstairs murals by Australian artist Jack Davies. Shared accommodation costs $12 per night, and twins/doubles are $25 for two. The hostel has all the essentials and it hires out mountain bikes.

The *London Hotel* (☎ (098) 41 1048), on Stirling Terrace, has entered the backpacker market. The opulent staircase and bat-like flurry of freebies belie the characterless singles/doubles in equally bland surrounds

which are $18/30. For your free drink, avoid the Harvey Wallbanger!

Albany also has a number of reasonably priced guesthouses, many of which offer breakfast with accommodation; enquire at the tourist bureau. As an example, Albany's *Colonial Guesthouse* (☎ (098) 41 3704), at 136 Brunswick Rd, charges $25/38 per night including breakfast. At Middleton Beach is the *Middleton Beach Guesthouse* (☎ (098) 41 1295) on Adelaide Crescent; the cost is $32 to $40 per night for two. The *Coraki Holiday Cottages* (☎ (098) 44 7068) are about a 10-minute drive from Albany, on Lower King River Rd on the banks of Oyster Harbour. Self-contained cottages in this extremely pretty setting are from $50 per night.

The tourist bureau has more details, especially on self-catering options.

Places to Eat

You will not starve if you wander along Stirling Terrace. *Dylan's on the Terrace* at No 82 has an excellent range of light meals including hamburgers and pancakes at reasonable prices; it is open late most nights, early for breakfast, and has a takeaway section.

Also on the terrace is *Kooka's*, at No 204 in a restored old house, where you can count on paying $30 for an excellent three-course meal. Other sterling choices are the *Penny Post Restaurant*, the *Harbourfront Steak & Grill*, *Stirling Terrace Dine-In*, *Cafe Bizarre* and three pubs with their ubiquitous counter meals. The *Royal George* wins the Sterling Silver Fork Award for value.

Breakfasts at the *Wildflower Cafe*, on York St, have been recommended. Also in the area is *Eatcha Heart Out* for breakfasts, and next to the tourist bureau is *Cosi's Cafe* for breakfasts and light lunches. There are also a couple of pizza places on York St including *Al Fornetto's* and the *Venice*. At No 280 is *Auntie Brown's Sizzle House* – it has a very good all-you-can-eat smorgasbord for just over $20.

The *Lemon Grass Thai*, at 370 Middleton Rd, has a good range of Thai food (including

WESTERN AUSTRALIA

vegetarian meals). At Middleton Beach there's the *Beachside Cafe*, right on the beach, and, close to the Extravaganza, the *Middleton Beach Fish & Chips*, which has crisp golden chips and a plethora of fish such as groper, snapper, shark and flounder to select from.

Getting There & Away
Skywest flies daily from Perth to Albany; the one-way fare on Skywest is $146 ($200 Apex return). Westrail has daily buses from Perth via various wheatbelt towns for $33, and buses four times a week via Bridgetown, Manjimup and Denmark for $43.

Getting Around
Love's bus service runs around town from Monday to Friday and Saturday mornings. Buses will take you along Albany Highway from Peels Place to the roundabout; others go to Spencer Park, Middleton Beach, Emu Point and Bayonet Head.

You can rent bicycles from Albany Backpackers' in Stirling Terrace for $10 per day.

AROUND ALBANY
South of Albany, off Frenchman Bay Rd, is a stunning stretch of coastline that includes the **Gap** and **Natural Bridge** rock formations; the **Blowholes**, especially interesting in heavy seas when air is blown with great force through the surrounding rock; the **rock climbing** areas of Peak Head and West Cape Howe National Park; steep, rocky coves such as **Jimmy Newhill's Harbour** and **Salmon Holes**, popular with surfers (although they are considered to be quite dangerous); and **Frenchman Bay**, which has a caravan park, a fine swimming beach and a grassed barbecue area with plenty of shade. This is a dangerous coastline and you should be aware of king waves.

Also at Frenchman Bay, 21 km from Albany, is **Whaleworld** at the Cheynes Beach Whaling Station which only ceased operations in 1978. There's the rusting whale chaser *Cheynes 4* and the station impedimenta to inspect after seeing a gore-spattered film on whaling operations. It is open daily from 9 am to 5 pm, but the $4.50 admission is considered a bit rich by some. From the beach, listen carefully and you will hear the haunting, mournful songs of the humpbacks at sea.

National Parks & Reserves
There are a number of excellent natural areas near Albany. From west to east along the coast you can explore many different habitats and see a wide variety of coastal scenery. The 1739-hectare **William Bay National Park** has coastal dunes, granite boulders, heath lands and mature karri forests. **West Cape Howe National Park** is a 3517-hectare

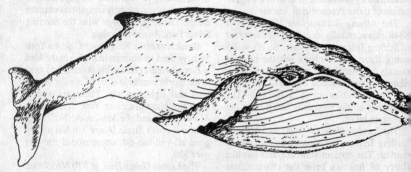

Humpback whale

playground for naturalists, bushwalkers, rock climbers and anglers. **Torndirrup National Park** includes the region's two very popular attractions, the Natural Bridge and the Gap, as well as the Blowholes, Jimmy Newhills Beach and Bald Head.

East of Albany is **Two People's Bay**, a nature reserve with a good swimming beach, scenic coastline and a small colony of noisy scrub birds, a species once thought extinct. Probably the best of the parks, but the least visited of them, is the 3983-hectare **Waychinicup National Park** which includes Mt Manypeaks and other granite formations. Walking in the area is currently restricted because of a dieback problem.

ALBANY TO ESPERANCE (476 km)

From Albany, the South Coast Highway runs north-east along the coast before turning inland to skirt the Fitzgerald River National Park and finally finishes in Esperance.

Ongerup & Jerramungup

Ongerup, a small wheatbelt town, has an annual wildflower show in September/ October with hundreds of local species on show. In Jerramungup you can visit the interesting **Military Museum**.

Bremer Bay

This fishing and holiday town, which sits at the western end of the Great Australian Bight, is 61 km from the South Coast Highway. It is a good spot to observe southern right whales.

The *Bremer Bay Caravan Park* (☎ (098) 37 4018) has camp sites for $12 for two and units for $30. A nice place to stay within Fitzgerald River National Park is *Quaalup Homestead* (☎ (098) 37 4124) on Gairdner Way; camping is $5, single/double units are $25/29 and homestead rooms are $35/39.

Ravensthorpe (population 390)

The small town of Ravensthorpe was once the centre of the Phillips River gold field; later, copper was also mined there. Nowadays, the area is dependent on farming.

The ruins of a disused government smelter and the Cattlin Creek Mine (copper) are near town, and the Ravensthorpe Historical Society has a display in the **Dance Cottage**. If possible, avoid buying petrol here as it seems to be well above normal prices. About 150 km north of Ravensthorpe, the **Frank Hann National Park** has a range of typical sand-plain region flora.

Places to Stay & Eat *Ravensthorpe Caravan Park* (☎ (098) 38 1050) has tent sites at $8 for two and vans from $25 for two. The *Palace Motor Hotel* (☎ (098) 38 1005), classified by the National Trust, has singles/doubles for $20/30; there are more rooms in the motel section. Tempt yourself with the sumptuous selection of cakes at *Ravy's Country Kitchen*.

Hopetoun (population 210)

The fine beaches and bays around Hopetoun are south of Ravensthorpe. It is also the eastern gateway to the Fitzgerald River National Park. The information centre (☎ (098) 38 3088) is in the Blue Groper Hardware & Tackle Store, Veal St.

The *Hopetoun Caravan Park* (☎ (098) 38 3096) has tent sites for $10 and on-site vans for $25, and the *Port Hotel* (☎ (098) 38 3053), Veal St, has beds for $20/40.

Fitzgerald River National Park

This 320,000-hectare park is one of two places in WA with a UNESCO Biosphere rating. The park contains beautiful coastline, sand plains, the rugged Barren mountain range and deep, wide river valleys. The bushwalking is excellent and the wilderness route from Fitzgerald Beach to Whalebone Beach is recommended – there is no trail and no water but camping is permitted. Clean your shoes at each end of the walk to discourage the spread of dieback.

The park contains half the orchids in WA (over 80 species, 70 of which occur nowhere else), 200 species of birds and 1700 species of wildflowers. It is also the home of that floral marvel the royal hakea, and southern right whales are seen offshore from August to September.

You can gain access to the park from Bremer Bay and Hopetoun or from the South Coast Highway along Devils Creek, Quiss and Hamersley Rds. There is accommodation in Bremer Bay, Quaalup and Hopetoun.

ESPERANCE (population 7100)

Esperance, on the coast 200 km south of Norseman, has become a popular resort due to its temperate climate, magnificent coastal scenery, blue waters, good fishing and dazzling white beaches.

Although the first settlers came to the area in 1863, it was during the gold rush in the 1890s that the town really became established as a port. When the gold fever subsided, Esperance went into a state of suspended animation until after WW II. In the 1950s, it was discovered that adding missing trace elements to the soil around Esperance restored it to fertility, and since then the town has rapidly become an agricultural centre.

Information

The Esperance tourist centre (☎ (090) 71 2330), on Dempster St by the museum village, is open daily from 9 am to 5 pm and can book tours along the coast, to the islands and into the surrounding national parks.

Things to See

Esperance, or the Bay of Isles, has some excellent beaches, and the seas offshore are studded with the many islands of the Recherche Archipelago. Distinctive Norfolk Island pines line the foreshore. The **Esperance Municipal Museum** contains the tourist centre and various old buildings, including a gallery, smithy's forge, cafe and craft shop.

The museum itself, between the Esplanade and Dempster St, is open daily from 1.30 to 4.30 pm and contains a Skylab display – a US space station launched in May 1973, which crashed to earth in 1979 and made its fiery re-entry right over Esperance.

The captivating 36-km **Scenic Loop Road** has a number of highlights including

the vistas from Observatory Point and the Rotary Lookout on Wireless Hill; Twilight Bay and Picnic Cove, popular swimming spots; and the Pink Lake, stained by a salt-tolerant algae called *Dunalella salina*.

There are about 100 small islands in the **Recherche Archipelago**, home to colonies of seals, penguins and a wide variety of water birds. There are regular trips to Woody Island, a wildlife sanctuary.

Organised Tours & Cruises

Vacation Country Tours (☎ (090) 71 2227) run a number of tours around Esperance including a town-and-coast tour for $12 and a tour of Cape Le Grand National Park twice a week for $25. More adventurous alternatives are Safari Wheels & Reels (☎ (090) 71 1564), which conducts 4WD safaris and fishing trips to secluded beaches and bays, and the trips run by the YHA to capes Arid and Le Grand.

Tours on the waters of Esperance Bay are a must. Unfortunately, the tug *Cape Le Grand II* (McKenzies Marine, ☎ (090) 71 1772) only heads out if the right numbers front up on the jetty, so even though they advertise daily tours these are at the owner's convenience. McKenzies operates a daily ferry service to Woody Island in January and February.

The *Dive Master II* (☎ (090) 71 5111) goes out on Tuesday and Thursday. Expect to see seals, sea lions, white-bellied sea eagles, Cape Barren geese, dolphins and a host of other wildlife in the two-hour cruise around the Bay of Isles. Trips are weather-dependent and cost $20 (children $10). The *Dive Master II* is also the flagship for the Esperance Diving Academy.

Places to Stay

Half a dozen caravan parks around Esperance provide camping areas and on-site accommodation, the most central being the *Esperance Bay Caravan Park* (☎ (090) 71 2237), on the corner of the Esplanade and Harbour Rd, near the wharf, and the *Esperance Shire Caravan Park* (☎ (090) 71 1251)

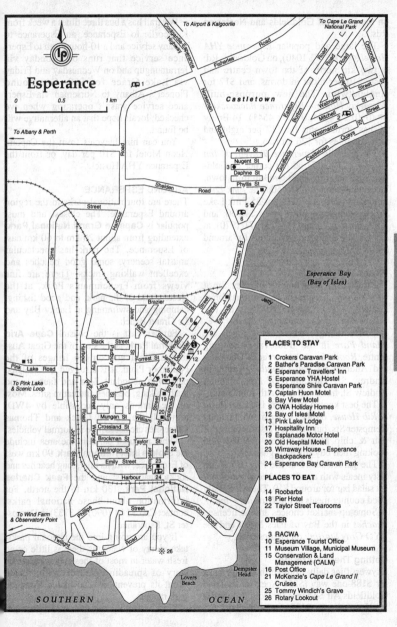

Esperance

0   0.5   1 km

To Airport & Kalgoorlie

To Cape Le Grand National Park

Coolgardie Esperance Highway

Fisheries Road

Norseman Esperance Highway

Ormonde Road

Pink Road

Easton Road

Chapman Street

Walmsley St

Mitchell St

Westmacott Street

Castletown

Castletown Quays

Goldfields Road

Arthur St

Nugent St

Daphne St

Phyllis St

Shelden Road

Harbour Street

Norseman Rd

Esperance Bay
(Bay of Isles)

Sims Street

Jetty

Brazier Street

Hicks Street

Windich Street

The Esplanade

Black Street

Pinbury

Foy Street

Forrest St

Jane St

James Street

Andrew Street

William Street

Mungan St

Crossland St

Brockman St

Taylor Street

Warrington St

Emily Street

Dempster Street

Harbour Road

Williamston Road

Pink Lake Road

To Pink Lake
& Scenic Loop

To Albany & Perth

To Wind Farm
& Observatory Point

Phillips Street

Twilight Beach

Lovers Beach

Dempster Head

SOUTHERN   OCEAN

PLACES TO STAY

1   Crokers Caravan Park
2   Bather's Paradise Caravan Park
4   Esperance Travellers' Inn
5   Esperance YHA Hostel
6   Esperance Shire Caravan Park
7   Captain Huon Motel
8   Bay View Motel
9   CWA Holiday Homes
12 Bay of Isles Motel
13 Pink Lake Lodge
19 Hospitality Inn
19 Esplanade Motor Hotel
20 Old Hospital Motel
23 Wirraway House - Esperance
    Backpackers'
24 Esperance Bay Caravan Park

PLACES TO EAT

14 Roobarbs
18 Pier Hotel
22 Taylor Street Tearooms

OTHER

3   RACWA
10 Esperance Tourist Office
11 Museum Village, Municipal Museum
15 Conservation & Land
    Management (CALM)
16 Post Office
21 McKenzie's Cape Le Grand II
    Cruises
25 Tommy Windich's Grave
26 Rotary Lookout

WESTERN AUSTRALIA

on the corner of Goldfields and Norseman Rds.

The large and popular *Esperance YHA Hostel* (☎ (090) 71 1040), on Goldfields Rd, is two km north of the town centre and costs $10 per night in dorms, and $12 for singles/twins. The new, purpose-built *Wirraway House – Esperance Backpackers* (☎ (090) 71 4724; 018 93 4541), 14 Emily St, has dorm rooms for $12 per night and twins/doubles for $26 for two.

The friendly *Esperance Travellers' Inn* (☎ (090) 71 1677), at the corner of Goldfields Rd and Phyllis St two km from town, has clean rooms for $30/50. The *Pink Lake Lodge* (☎ (090) 71 2075), at 85 Pink Lake Rd, has singles/doubles from $18/30, and *CWA Holiday Homes* (☎ (090) 71 1970), at Lot 85 The Esplanade, has units for around $40.

Places to Eat

The town has a good number of cafes. Sip at *Ollie's on the Esplanade*, *Beachfront Coffee Lounge*, *Taylor Street Tearooms* or the *Village Cafe*, in the museum enclave.

Coffee lounges which serve meals are *Island Fare* in the Boulevard shopping centre, *Roobarbs* at the corner of Dempster and Andrew Sts and *Captain's Cabin*, in Andrew St. The *Spice of Life*, also on Andrew St, has a varied health-food menu.

The best known takeaway is *Pizza, Pasta & Rib House*, on the corner of William and Dempster Sts, but there are also a number of fish & chip places. If you like fish and cooking then buy fillets of gnanagi.

The garden bistro at the *Pier Hotel* has tasty meals with a well-stocked all-you-can-eat salad bar for around $10. There are really good counter meals at the *Travellers' Inn*.

Some up-market choices are the licensed *Peaches* in the Bay of Isles Motel and the BYO *Gray Starling* on Dempster St.

Getting There & Around

Skywest flies daily from Perth to Esperance for $188 one way ($252 Apex return), and Goldfields Air Services fly from Kalgoorlie via Norseman for $137 every Tuesday.

Westrail has a bus three times a week from Kalgoorlie to Esperance, an Esperance to Albany service and a 10-hour Perth to Esperance service that runs on Monday via Jerramungup and on Wednesday and Friday via Lake Grace for $50. Greyhound Pioneer's Albany to Norseman via Esperance service wasn't operating when we checked; locals hope that an alternative will be found.

You can hire bicycles from the Captain Huon Motel for $10 per day, or from the Esperance YHA Hostel.

AROUND ESPERANCE

There are four national parks in the region around Esperance. The closest and most popular is **Cape Le Grand National Park**, extending from about 20 km to 60 km east of Esperance. The park has spectacular coastal scenery, some good beaches and excellent walking tracks. There are fine views from Frenchman's Peak, at the western end of the park, and good fishing, camping and swimming at Lucky Bay and Le Grand Beach.

Further east is the coastal **Cape Arid National Park**, at the start of the Great Australian Bight and on the fringes of the Nullarbor Plain. It is a rugged and isolated park with abundant flora and fauna, good bushwalking, beaches and camp sites. Most of the park is only accessible by 4WD, although the Poison Creek and Thomas River sites are accessible in normal vehicles.

Other national parks in the area include the **Stokes Inlet National Park**, 90 km west of Esperance, with its inlet, long beaches and rocky headlands; and the **Peak Charles National Park**, 130 km to the north. For information about these national parks, contact CALM (☎ (090) 71 3733) in Dempster St, Esperance.

If you are going into the national parks, take plenty of water, as there is little or no fresh water in most of these areas. Also, be wary of spreading dieback; information about its prevention is available from the park rangers.

Limited-facility tent sites are $5 per night

at Cape Le Grand National Park (☎ (090) 75 9022) and they are free at Cape Arid (☎ (090) 75 0055). Apply for permits with the ranger at the park entrances. Between the two national parks is the *Orleans Bay Caravan Park* (☎ (090) 75 0033), a friendly place to stay; camp sites are $9 and park homes are $30.

Just off Merivale Rd, on the way to Cape Le Grand, food is available at *Merivale Farm*.

Up the Coast

Highway 1, which encircles Australia, is sealed almost all the way round. The unsealed section is between Fitzroy Crossing and Halls Creek, in the Kimberley area.

The route from Perth to Darwin may still be a hell of a long way but it's no longer an endurance test. There's also a lot to see if you want to break the journey. But don't underestimate it – from Perth to Port Hedland is 1770 km by the coast, and in summer it can be a very hot and sometimes tedious drive.

Getting There & Away

Air Ansett flies from Perth to Geraldton ($158 one way; $189 Apex return), Carnarvon ($254; $289) and Learmonth for Exmouth ($311; $349), as well as to centres in the Kimberley.

Bus Westrail has bus services from Perth to Geraldton (daily) and Kalbarri (Monday to Friday). Greyhound Pioneer has a daily bus up the coast to Darwin via Geraldton, Carnarvon and Port Hedland – connections to Monkey Mia are also available.

One-way fares from Perth on Greyhound Pioneer are $35 to Geraldton, $100 to Carnarvon, $121 to Shark Bay via the Overlander Roadhouse and $185 to Broome.

PERTH TO GERALDTON (421 km)

From Perth, you follow the Brand Highway past the turn-off to Jurien and the Pinnacles Desert (see North Coast in the Around Perth section for information on this area).

Dongara & Port Denison

The main road comes back to the coast 360 km north of Perth at Dongara (population 1700). This is a pleasant little port with fine beaches, lots of crayfish, a main street lined with Moreton Bay figs, and a tourist centre (☎ (099) 27 1404) housed in the old police station at 5 Waldeck St. **Russ Cottage**, built in 1870, is open on Sunday from 10 am to noon. Just over the Irwin River is Port Denison. The mouth of the Irwin River is a great place to watch birds such as pelicans and cormorants.

Places to Stay & Eat There are a number of places to stay in these coastal towns. There are five caravan parks, two recommended ones being *Dongara-Denison Beach* (☎ (099) 27 1131) and the very friendly *Seaspray* (☎ (099) 27 1165). In Dongara try *Toko's Restaurant* in Moreton Terrace for Mexican fare.

Some 58 km south of Dongara is the *Western Flora Caravan Park* (☎ (099) 55 2030), special because it is in the heart of one of the most diverse and dense floral regions in the world. Several tracks branch out from the park into the wonderland of native plant species; a must for foreign visitors. Powered sites are $10 for two, on-site vans are $25 and two-room chalets with TV are $39.

Greenough

Further north, only about 20 km south of Geraldton, is Greenough, once a busy little mining town but now a quiet farming centre. The excellent Greenough Historical Hamlet contains 11 buildings constructed in the 19th-century and now restored by the National Trust; guided tours are run daily and it is well worth a visit. The Pioneer Museum, open daily from 10 am to 4 pm, has some fine historical displays. In the local paddocks, look out for flood gums, the 'leaning trees' caused by strong salt winds off the ocean.

Inland

There are two road options inland of Dongara and Geraldton. Towns such as **Dalwallinu, Perenjori, Morawa** (population

600) and **Mullewa** (population 740) are part of the Wildflower Way – famous for its brilliant spring display of wildflowers, including wreath leschenaultia, native fox-gloves, everlastings and wattles. This area is also a gateway to the **Murchison gold fields**; there are old gold-mining centres and ghost towns around Perenjori.

The other option is State Highway 116, known locally as the Midlands Scenic Way. It's a good alternative route for travel between Perth and Geraldton – the scenery is more interesting and there is a number of small towns along the way. At **Watheroo**, the old *Watheroo Railway Station* (☎ (096) 51 7007) offers accommodation, meals and activities such as bushwalking, wildflowers, tennis and horse riding. It's well worth the detour. **Coorow** is 262 km north of Perth and nearby is the **Alexander Morrison National Park**. **Carnamah**, near the Yarra Yarra Lakes, is noted for its bird life.

Mingenew (population 360) has a small historical museum in an old primary school. The tourist centre (☎ (099) 28 1081) is on Midlands Rd.

GERALDTON (population 24,400)

Geraldton, the major town in the midwest region, is on a spectacular stretch of coast, with the magnificent Houtman Abrolhos Islands offshore. It's 421 km north of Perth and the area has a fine climate, particularly in the winter. If you are tempted by lobster fresh from the boat then this is the place to come.

Information

The Geraldton-Greenough tourist bureau (☎ (099) 21 3999) is in the Bill Sewell complex on Chapman Rd, diagonally across from the railway station and adjacent to the Northgate shopping centre. It is open from 8.30 am to 5 pm Monday to Friday, from 9 am to 4.30 pm Saturday and 9.30 am to 4.30 pm Sunday.

If you are short of reading material, there are a couple of second-hand book stores in Geraldton: the House of Books at 176 Marine Terrace and the Sun City Book Exchange at 36 Marine Terrace.

Geraldton Museum

The town's excellent museum is in two adjacent buildings on Marine Terrace. The Maritime Museum tells the story of the early wrecks and has assorted relics from the Dutch ships, including items from the

---

Dutch Shipwrecks

During the 17th century, ships of the Dutch East India Company, sailing from Europe to Batavia in Java, would head due east from the Horn of Africa then beat up the western Australian coast to Indonesia. It only took a small miscalculation for a ship to run aground on the coast and a few did just that, usually with disastrous results. The west coast of Australia is often decidedly inhospitable, and the chances of rescue at that time were remote.

Four wrecks of Dutch East Indiamen have been located, including the *Batavia* – the earliest and, in many ways, the most interesting. In 1629, the *Batavia* went aground on the Abrolhos Islands, off the coast of Geraldton. The survivors set up camp, sent off a rescue party to Batavia (now Jakarta) in the ship's boat and waited. It took three months for a rescue party to arrive and in that time a mutiny had taken place and more than 120 of the survivors had been murdered. The ringleaders were hanged, and two mutineers were unceremoniously dumped on the coast.

In 1656, the *Vergulde Draeck* (Gilt Dragon) struck a reef about 100 km north of Perth and although a party of survivors made its way to Batavia, no trace, other than a few scattered coins, was found of the other survivors who had straggled ashore. The *Zuytdorp* ran aground beneath the towering cliffs north of Kalbarri in 1712. Wine bottles, other relics and the remains of fires have been found on the cliff top but again no trace of survivors.

In 1727, the *Zeewijk* followed the ill-fated *Batavia* to destruction on the Abrolhos Islands. Again a small party of survivors made its way to Batavia but many of the remaining sailors died before they could be rescued. Many relics from these shipwrecks, particularly the *Batavia*, can be seen today in the museums in Fremantle and Geraldton. ■

Western Australia

A Perth skyline (PS)

B Dolphins at Monkey Mia (JW)

C Cape Leeuwin lighthouse (JW)

D Near Oxer's Lookout, Karijini (Hamersley Range) National Park (JW)

E The Pinnacles Desert, Nambung National Park (RN)

A
B
C
D

Western Australia

A Bungle Bungle (Purnululu) National Park (JW)

B Pteroglyphs, near Karratha (JW)

C View from Bluff Knoll, Stirling Range National Park (JW)

D Landscape near Kununurra (MK)

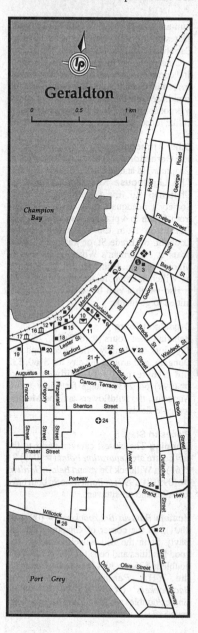

PLACES TO STAY

3 Batavia Backpackers
9 Ocean Centre Hotel
13 Sun City Guesthouse
14 Grantown Guesthouse
15 Victoria Hotel
18 Colonial Hotel
19 Peninsula Guesthouse
    & Backpackers'
20 Geraldton Hotel
25 Hacienda Motel
26 Ocean West Units
27 Goodwood Lodge Units

PLACES TO EAT

8 Cuisine Connection
12 Reflections
23 Los Amigos Restaurant

OTHER

1 Northgate Shopping Centre
2 Geraldton Tourist Bureau
4 Railway Station
5 Westrail Bus Depot
6 RACWA & Greyhound Pioneer
7 Geraldton Art Gallery
10 Post Office
11 Ansett Australia
16 Regional Museum
17 Geraldton Maritime Museum
21 Francis Xavier Cathedral
22 Queen's Park Theatre
24 Hospital

Batavia and the *Zeewijk*, and the carved wooden sternpiece from the *Zuytdorp*, found by a local stockman in 1927 on top of the cliffs above the point where the ship had run ashore. It was not until the 1950s that the wreckage was positively identified as that of the *Zuytdorp*.

The Old Railway Building has displays on flora, fauna and the settlement of the region by Aborigines and, later, Europeans. The museum complex is open Monday to Saturday from 10 am to 5 pm and from 1 to 5 pm on Sunday and holidays; admission is free.

St Francis Xavier Cathedral

Geraldton's St Francis Xavier Cathedral is just one of a number of buildings in Geraldton and WA's midwest designed by Monsignor John Hawes, a strange priest-cum-architect who left WA in 1939 and spent the rest of his life a hermit on an island in the Caribbean (he died in Florida in 1956).

Construction of the Byzantine-style cathedral commenced in 1916, a year after Hawes arrived in Geraldton, but his plans were too grandiose and the partially built cathedral was not completed until 1938. The interior is unlike most cathedrals you will have seen!

Other Attractions

The **Geraldton Art Gallery**, on the corner of Chapman Rd and Durlacher St, is open daily. The **Lighthouse Keeper's Cottage** on Chapman Rd, the Geraldton Historical Society's headquarters, is open Thursday from 10 am to 4 pm. You can look out over Geraldton from the Waverley Heights Lookout, on Brede St, or watch the lobster boats at Fisherman's Wharf, at the end of Marine Terrace. **Point Moore Lighthouse** on Willcock Drive, in operation since 1878, is also worth a visit but visitors aren't permitted to go inside.

Organised Tours

Batavia Coast Tours (☎ (099) 21 7760) has day tours to Monkey Mia, Greenough and Dongara, and around the city for $180, $32 and $16 respectively. Midwest Tours (☎ (099) 64 2939) range far wider to Mt Augustus, the wildflowers and the Murchison gold fields.

Places to Stay

Camping The closest caravan parks to the city centre are *Separation Point* (☎ (099) 21 2763) on Willcock Drive and *Belair Gardens* (☎ (099) 21 1997) at Point Moore; both have tent sites and on-site vans.

Hostels *Batavia Backpackers* (☎ (099) 64 3001), on the corner of Chapman Rd and Bayly St in the Bill Sewell complex, has good facilities and beds for $12 per night; a double is $25. At 305-311 Marine Terrace is the YHA *Peninsula Guesthouse & Backpackers'* (☎ (099) 21 4770) where singles/doubles are $15/25 and backpackers' beds $12.

Chapman Valley Farm Backpackers (☎ (099) 20 5160), 25 km out of town, is in a historic homestead. They pick up from Geraldton at 11 am; beds are $10.

Guesthouses & Hotels Geraldton has plenty of old-fashioned seaside guesthouses, particularly along Marine Terrace. The *Grantown Guesthouse* (☎ (099) 21 3275) at No 172 has singles/doubles for $22/44, which includes breakfast. The friendly *Sun City Guesthouse* (☎ (099) 21 2205) at No 184 offers B&B for $20/30; there is a shabby backpackers' dorm with beds at $10, where you can observe the sea from a back deck which is slowly falling to meet the waters.

Cheap rooms are also available at some of the older-style hotels such as the *Colonial*, the *Victoria* and the *Geraldton*.

Motels & Units The *Hacienda Motel* (☎ (099) 21 2155), on Durlacher St, has rooms at $45/58. The *Mariner Motel* (☎ 21 2544), at 298 Chapman Rd, is cheaper at $30/40. Family units are available at both of these places.

Ocean West Units (☎ (099) 21 1047), on the corner of Hadda Way and Willcock Drive at Mahomets Beach, has self-contained cottages for around $55 per double. *Goodwood Lodge Units* (☎ (099) 21 5666), at the corner of the Brand Highway and Durlacher St, also has self-contained units for $45/55.

Places to Eat

The *Cuisine Connection*, in Durlacher St, is a food hall with Indian, Chinese and Italian food, roasts and fish & chips. The food is excellent and you should be able to get a good feed for $7.

There is a number of small snack bars and cafes along Marine Terrace including *Thuy's Cake Shop* at No 202, which is open from 6 am for breakfast, and *Belvedere* at No 149, with standard cafe food at down-to-earth prices. *Hardy's*, on Chapman Rd in the Bill Sewell complex, is also open for breakfast and lunches, including monster burgers.

The *Sail Inn Snack Bar*, by the museum on Marine Terrace, sells burgers and fish &

chips; it is in a fast-food enclave which includes *Batavia Coast Fish & Chips* (which also sells pizza and chicken).

Chinese restaurants on Marine Terrace include the *Golden Coins* at No 198 and the *Jade House* at No 57. At 105 Durlacher St, *Los Amigos* is a good, straightforward, licensed Mexican place. It's popular, and deservedly so. Fancier restaurants include *Reflections* on Foreshore Drive, and the *Boatshed* for great seafood.

Getting There & Around

Ansett flies from Perth to Geraldton for around $158 one way, or $189 Apex return. Skywest flies the same route for $142/190.

Westrail and Greyhound Pioneer have regular services from Perth to Geraldton for around $35 one way. Westrail services continue north-east to Meekatharra (once a week) or north to Kalbarri (three times a week). Greyhound Pioneer continues on Highway 1 through Port Hedland and Broome to Darwin. Westrail stops at the railway station, while Greyhound Pioneer stops at the Bill Sewell complex.

There is a local bus service (☎ (099) 21 1034) in Geraldton which provides access to all the nearby suburbs.

HOUTMAN ABROLHOS ISLANDS

There are more than 100 islands in this group, located about 60 km off the Geraldton coast, and they are a bird-watcher's paradise. The beautiful but treacherous reefs surrounding the islands have claimed many ships over the years. The islands are also the centre of the area's lobster-fishing industry. Air and diving tours to these protected and spectacular islands are available from Geraldton – check with the tourist bureau for details.

NORTHAMPTON (population 900)

Northampton, 50 km north of Geraldton, has a number of historic buildings and provides access to good beaches at **Horrocks** (22 km west) and **Port Gregory** (47 km north-west). The town was founded to exploit the area's

lead and copper deposits, which were discovered in 1848. The town is now an agricultural centre and is making forays into tourism. An early mine-manager's home, **Chiverton House**, is now a fine municipal museum ($2 entry). The stone building was constructed between 1868 and 1875. Gwalla Church cemetery also tells its grim tales of the early days. The Northampton tourist bureau (☎ (099) 34 1488) is in the Nagle Centre on the main road.

The ruins of the **Lynton Convict Settlement** are about 40 km from Northampton. It was established as a convict-hiring facility in 1853 and abandoned some four years later.

Places to Stay & Eat

There are caravan parks near Northampton (☎ (099) 34 1202), Port Gregory (☎ (099) 35 1052) and Horrocks (☎ (099) 34 3039); all have tent sites, and the Horrocks and Port Gregory caravan parks have on-site vans. The *Killara Holiday Village* at Horrocks has three- to four-bed cottages at $35 per night.

There is budget accommodation in the *Nagle Centre* (☎ (099) 34 1488), formerly the Sacred Heart Convent, for $12 per person in two- and four-bed rooms; it has all the usual facilities. There are three hotels in town, and all offer rooms. The *Lynton Homestead B&B* (☎ (099) 35 1040) is next to the convict settlement, and costs a very reasonable $25 per person.

You can get coffee and a snack at the *Northampton Tourist Cafe* or counter meals at any of the three hotels.

KALBARRI (population 1500)

Kalbarri, a popular spot with backpackers, is on the coast at the mouth of the Murchison River, 66 km west of the main highway. The area is intimately associated with an alluring coastline, scenic gorges and the west coast's Dutch shipwrecks. The *Zuytdorp* was wrecked about 65 km north of Kalbarri in 1712; earlier, in 1629, two *Batavia* mutineers were marooned at Wittecarra Gully, an inlet just south of the town. Although diving on the *Zuytdorp* is very difficult, as a heavy swell and unpredictable currents batter the shoreline, divers from the Geraldton Museum did manage to raise artefacts in 1986.

The Kalbarri tourist bureau (☎ (099) 37 1104) on Grey St provides a wide range of tourist information.

Things to See & Do

The **Rainbow Jungle** is an interesting rainforest and bird park four km south of town towards Red Bluff ($4 adults, $1.50 children), and **Fantasyland** on Grey St ($3.50 adults, $1.50 children) is a collection of dolls, shells and gemstones. Boats can be hired on the river (☎ (099) 37 1245), and tours are made on the river's lower reaches on the *Kalbarri River Queen*.

There are some excellent surfing breaks along the coast – **Jakes Corner**, 3.5 km south of town, is reputed to be amongst the best in the state.

To the south of town there is a string of rugged cliff faces, including **Red Bluff**, **Rainbow Valley**, **Pot Alley**, **Eagle Gorge** and **Natural Bridge**. They can all be reached by car but the road will test your suspension in places.

Kalbarri National Park has over 1000 sq km of bushland including some scenic gorges on the **Murchison River**. From Kalbarri, it's about 40 km to the **Loop** and **Z-Bend**, two impressive gorges. Short walking trails lead down into the gorges from the road access points but there are also longer walks. It takes about two days to walk between Z-Bend and the Loop.

Further east along the Ajana to Kalbarri road are two lookouts: **Hawk's Head** (a must see) and **Ross Graham**. The park puts on a particularly fine display of wildflowers in the spring including everlastings, banksias, grevilleas and kangaroo paws.

Organised Tours

For tours over the Murchison River gorges take a flight with Kalbarri Air Charter. Kalbarri Coach Tours has trips to the Loop, Z-Bend and ocean gorges. The company also runs a canoeing adventure tour into the

gorges ($30) which takes in the Fourways gullies. The more adventurous can absei into the gorge with a bloke called Gorge-ous Gordon; for canoeing, abseiling and flights book at the tourist bureau.

Kyco runs 4WD tours down the coast to Lucky Bay and Wagoe Beach. This recommended tour includes a trip along the sand beach, with views of magnificent sand hills again, book at the tourist bureau.

Places to Stay

Kalbarri is a popular resort, and accommodation can be tight at holiday times. There's a wide selection of caravan parks, holiday units, hotels and motels.

There are four caravan parks around town and all have tent sites, on-site vans and cabins.

The clean and modern *Kalbarri Back packers* (☎ (099) 37 1430), at 2 Mortimer St has shared accommodation from $11 and family and disabled units from $40; it has been recommended by a number of travellers. They organise snorkelling trips to the Blue Holes, one km south of Kalbarri, and have free beer on Friday night. Other budget possibilities are *Av-Er-Rest Backpacker* (☎ (099) 37 1101) on Mortimer St, and the *Murchison River Lodge* (☎ (099) 37 1584 on Grey St.

The *Kalbarri Motor Hotel* (☎ (099) 37 1000), on Grey St, is central and has comfortable singles/doubles for $45/55.

Places to Eat

There are four cafes in town: the *Kalbarri Cafe*, in the main shopping centre; the *Seabreeze* in the Kalbarri Arcade; *River Cafe* near the jetty; and *Lure 'n' Line* in Grey St near the tourist bureau. For fish & chips try *Jonah's* in Grey St, and for pizza go to *Kalbarri Pizza*.

Finlay's Fresh Fish BBQ, on Magee Crescent in an old ice works, is a really special place for a meal (most are less than $10). The decor is no frills but the meals and salads are filling – the atmosphere is, in a word, great There are three licensed restaurants in tow – the *Palm* in the Palm Resort, *Echoes* in the main shopping centre and *Zuytdorp* in the Kalbarri Beach Resort; Echoes is probably the best.

Getting There & Around
Western Airlines has return flights from Perth on Monday, Wednesday and Friday; the one-way fare is $152. Westrail buses from Perth come into Kalbarri on Monday, Wednesday and Friday ($56.50), returning Tuesday, Thursday and Saturday. On Monday, Thursday and Saturday there is a return shuttle into Kalbarri which connects with the Greyhound Pioneer bus at Ajana on the North-West Coastal Highway.

Bicycles can be rented from Murchison Cycles on Porter St – if no-one is there, ask at the Mini-Putt complex next door.

SHARK BAY
Shark Bay World Heritage & Marine Park has some spectacular beaches, important sea-grass beds, the stromatolites at Hamelin Pool and the famous dolphins of Monkey Mia. Shark Bay satisfied all four natural criteria for World Heritage listing.

The first recorded landing on Australian soil by a European took place at Shark Bay in 1616 when the Dutch explorer Dirk Hartog landed on the island that now bears his name. He nailed an inscribed plate to a post on the beach but a later Dutch visitor collected it. It's now in the Rijksmuseum in Amsterdam, although there's a reproduction in the Geraldton Museum.

Denham, the main population centre of Shark Bay, is 132 km off the main highway from the Overlander Roadhouse. Denham is the most westerly town in Australia and was once a pearling port. Today, prawns and tourism are the local moneymakers.

Organised Tours & Cruises
There is a wildlife cruise (weather permitting) to Steep Point on the MV *Explorer*, on demand, for $50 – book at the tourist centre in Denham; minimum of 10 people. Shark Bay Safari Tours (☎ (099) 48 1247) has various tours around Shark Bay and the World Heritage area; again, enquire at the

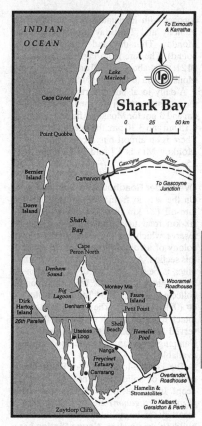

tourist centre. On Tuesday they go out to Big Lagoon ($35) and on Wednesday they do a full-day tour of Cape Peron ($55). Every day, except Monday and Friday, the yacht *Shotover* does a morning and sunset dolphin cruise for $19.

Getting There & Away
North of Kalbarri, it's a fairly dull, boring and often very hot run to Carnarvon. The Overlander Roadhouse, 290 km north of Geraldton, is the turn-off to Shark Bay. Greyhound Pioneer has a connecting return bus service from Denham to Overlander to

connect with interstate buses on Saturday, Monday and Thursday (northbound) and Monday, Thursday and Saturday (south-bound). The fare from Perth to Denham is $121. It's about $25 from Denham and Monkey Mia to the Overlander Roadhouse.

A daily local bus departs Denham (near the tourist centre on Knight Terrace) at 8.45 am and 3 pm for Monkey Mia and returns at 9.15 am and 3.30 pm; the fare is $7 one way. There is an airport bus service; one way to Monkey Mia is $7 and to Denham it is $5.

Overlander Roadhouse to Denham

On the way in from the highway, the first turn-off (27 km from the highway) is the six-km road to **Hamelin Pool**, a marine reserve which has the world's best-known colony of **stromatolites** – see the aside in this section. A boardwalk out to the stromat-olites is being constructed. Information on these unique living-rock formations can be collected from the 1884 **Telegraph Station** (☎ (099) 42 5905). The station is the only intact repeater station left in WA, and it served as a telephone exchange until 1977. Camping, caravan sites and food are also available here.

The 110-km-long stretch of **Shell Beach** consists of solid shells nearly 10 metres deep! In places in Shark Bay, the shells (*Fragum erugatum*) are so tightly packed that they can be cut into blocks and used for building construction. **Nanga Station** has a

pioneer museum and at **Eagle Bluff**, halfway between Nanga and Denham, there are superb cliff-top views.

Denham (population 940)

This town has the Shark Bay tourist centre (☎ (099) 48 1253) at Knight Terrace, which is open Monday to Saturday from 8.30 am to 6 pm, and on Sunday from 9 am. The CALM office (☎ (099) 48 1208), Knight Terrace, has a great deal of information on the World Heritage area. There is also a shell-craft museum and a church and a restaurant made of shell blocks.

A couple of km down the road to Monkey Mia is the shallow and picturesque **Little Lagoon**. About four km from Denham on the Monkey Mia Rd is the turn-off to the fascinating, wild **François Peron National Park**. The park is known for its arid scenery, wilderness feel and landlocked salt lakes; entry is $3 for a day visit. There are two artesian bore tanks – one has water at 35°C and the other at a hot 43°C. These are in the grounds of the **Peron Homestead**, a reminder of the peninsula's grazing days.

Places to Stay You can camp at Denham or 55 km south at Nanga Station. *Denham Seaside Caravan Park* (☎ (099) 48 1242), Knight Terrace, is a friendly place on the foreshore with tent sites for $10 and on-site vans from $32 for two. *Shark Bay Caravan Park* (☎ (099) 48 1387) on Spaven Way and the *Blue Dolphin* (☎ (099) 48 1385) on

---

Stromatolites

The dolphins at Monkey Mia didn't contribute to the listing of Shark Bay as a World Heritage region. Perhaps the biggest single contribution was the existence of stromatolites at Hamelin Pool. The rocky masses of blue-green algae are 'only' some thousands of years old, but are examples of one of the oldest living organisms, having evolved in the Precambrian era over 3 billion years ago – extremely old when you think of *Homo sapiens*'s two-million-year history.

Hamelin Pool is suited to the growth of stromatolites because of the clarity and hypersalinity of the water. In essence, each stromatolite is covered in a form of cyanobacterial microbe, shaped like algae, which waves around during daily photosynthesis. At night the microbe folds over, often trapping calcium and carbonate ions dissolved in the water. The sticky chemicals they exude adds to the coalescence of another layer onto the surface of the stromatolite.

These are the most accessible stromatolites in the world, spectacularly set amidst the turquoise waters of Hamelin Pool. Don't disturb them. ■

Hamelin Rd, in Denham, are similarly priced.

Accommodation in Shark Bay can be very tight and expensive during school holidays. *Bay Lodge & Backpackers* (☎ (099) 48 1278), an associate-YHA hostel in Knight Terrace, on the Denham foreshore, has a great atmosphere and is the best value in town. Bookings are recommended at this popular hostel. Beds in shared units cost $11, two bedroom self-contained units are $46 and a motel room costs from $45.

There are a number of holiday cottages and villas in Shark Bay. *Shark Bay Holiday Cottages* (☎ (099) 48 1206), Knight Terrace, has backpackers' beds for $12 in four-bed self-contained rooms, cottages at $35 for two, and three-bedroom units from $50.

Shark Bay Accommodation Service (☎ (099) 48 1323) has a number of privately owned cottages and units available, usually by the week. At *Nanga Bay Holiday Resort* (☎ (099) 48 3992) there are camp/caravan sites at $10/14 for two. Backpackers' accommodation is $11 ($18 if linen is supplied), cabins for two are $45, chalets for two are $75 (but they fit five), and motel/home units are $80/85.

Places to Eat On Knight Terrace in Denham, the *Shark Bay Hotel* has counter meals, or there's the more expensive shell-block *Old Pearler* restaurant. The *Heritage Resort* serves bar meals and has a good restaurant. At Nanga Station, the *Nanga Barn Restaurant* does sit-down and takeaway meals.

Monkey Mia
This pleasant spot is 26 km north-east of Denham, on the other side of the Peron Peninsula. You pass the Dolphin Information Centre (☎ (099) 48 1366) just as you enter the beach-viewing area; the centre has lots of information on the region and its dolphins and also screens a 45-minute video on Shark Bay.

The Dolphins of Monkey Mia It's believed that bottle-nose dolphins (*Tursiops truncatus*) have been visiting Monkey Mia since the early 1960s, although it's only in the last decade or so that their visits have become world famous.

Monkey Mia's dolphins simply drop by to visit humans; they swim right into knee-deep water and will nudge up against you, and even take a fish if it's offered. The dolphins generally come in every day during the winter months, less frequently during the summer, and more often in the mornings. They may arrive alone or in groups of five or more; as many as 13 were recorded on one occasion.

The entry fee to the reserve is $3 per adult and $2 for children. There are some rules of good behaviour for visitors:

Stand knee deep in water and let them approach you – don't chase or try to swim with them.
Stroke them along their sides with the back of your hand as they swim beside you. Don't touch their fins or their blowhole.
If you get invited to offer them fish by the ranger (feeding times and quantities are regulated) it should be whole, not gutted or filleted. They take defrosted fish only if it has completely thawed.

Places to Stay & Eat *Monkey Mia Dolphin Resort* has a wide range of accommodation including tent and caravan sites for two for $10/15, backpackers' beds in four tented condos for $10, and on-site vans for $30 and $50 for three and four persons respectively; discounts apply in the off season.

At the *Bough Shed Restaurant* in Monkey Mia you can join the elite and watch the dolphins feed as you do. There is a more economical takeaway and a small grocery shop nearby.

CARNARVON (population 6900)
Situated at the mouth of the Gascoyne River, Carnarvon is noted for its tropical fruit (particularly bananas) and fine climate – although it can become very hot in the middle of summer and is periodically subjected to floods and cyclones. Subsurface water, which flows even when the river is dry, is tapped to irrigate riverside plantations. Salt is produced at Lake Macleod near

WESTERN AUSTRALIA

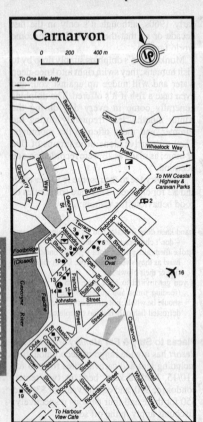

Carnarvon

0   200   400 m

To One Mile Jetty

To NW Coastal
Highway &
Caravan Parks

Wheelock Way

Town
Oval

Gascoyne
River

Footbridge
(Closed)

To Harbour
View Cafe

PLACES TO STAY

2   Carnarvon Tourist Centre
    Caravan Park & Chickenland
8   Port Hotel
12 Backpackers' Paradise
    & Bus Depot
14 Carnarvon Backpackers
17 Carnarvon Hotel
18 Outcamp
19 Hospitality Inn

PLACES TO EAT

4   Carnarvon Fresh Seafoods
5   Lucki's Asian Takeaway
9   Carnarvon Bakery
11 Red Peppers
15 Dragon Pearl Chinese
    Restaurant

OTHER

1   Swimming Pool
3   Boulevard Shopping Centre
6   Jolly's Tyrepower Service
7   Post Office
10 Civic Centre
13 Carnarvon Tourist Bureau,
    Public Toilets &
    Commonwealth Bank
16 Airport

Carnarvon, and prawns and scallops are harvested in the area.

The main street of Carnarvon is 40 metres wide, a reminder of the days when camel trains used to pass through. The Carnarvon tourist bureau (☎ (099) 41 1146), on Robinson St, is open daily from 8.30 am to 5.30 pm; in the off season from 9 am to 5 pm.

Things to See

Carnarvon once had a NASA **tracking station**. It opened in 1964 and ceased operations in 1975; it's open to the public daily. The **Fascine esplanade**, lined with palm trees, is a pleasant place to take a stroll. Carnarvon's **'one mile' jetty** is a popular fishing spot, as is the little jetty at the prawning station. The small, furnished **Lighthouse Keeper's Cottage Museum**, is beside the jetty ($1 entry).

Pelican Point, five km to the south-west, is a popular swimming and picnic spot. Other good **beaches**, also south and off the Geraldton Rd, are Bush Bay (turn-off 20 km) and New Beach (37 km).

Munro's Banana Plantation, on South River Rd, does a very informative plantation tour at 11 am and 2 pm daily (only 11 am at off-peak times). After the tour, you can indulge yourself with fresh-fruit ice cream or smoothies. They also sell a banana cookbook which includes banana cures for such ills as diarrhoea, ulcers and depression.

Organised Tours

Tropical Tripper Tours and Tony's Tour

(Gascoyne Lookabout Safari) depart from the tourist bureau and include half-day tours around town for $13 and an all-day tour that takes in Lake Macleod, Cape Cuvier, the wreck of the *Korean Star* and the blowholes for $30.

The *Dolphin Express* hovercraft runs from Carnarvon to Monkey Mia daily except Monday and Friday; the 2½-hour trip is $60 one way and $90 return. The hovercraft leaves Carnarvon at 7 am and returns at 4 pm – bookings can be made in Carnarvon or Denham.

Places to Stay

Camping You shouldn't have any trouble finding a caravan park in Carnarvon; the closest to the centre of town is the *Carnarvon Tourist Centre Caravan Park* (☎ (099) 41 1438), 90 Robinson St, which has tent sites at $12 for two and on-site vans from $25. The *Marloo Caravan Park* (☎ (099) 41 1439), on Wise St, is well set up for campers as it has a kitchen, laundry and great bathroom facilities; camp sites are $10 for two. The other five caravan parks have similar rates.

Hostels There is plenty of budget accommodation in Carnarvon. The *Carnarvon Backpackers* (☎ (099) 41 1095), an associate-YHA hostel at 46 Olivia Terrace, has dorm beds at $12. *Backpackers' Paradise* (☎ (099) 41 2966) is centrally located next to the tourist bureau on Robinson St, and it has shared accommodation at $12 and a discount for YHA members.

At the *Port Hotel* (☎ (099) 41 1704), on Robinson St, backpackers' accommodation is $10 per night.

Hotels, B&B & Motels Carnarvon has some old-fashioned hotels with old-fashioned prices. The *Port Hotel* has rooms from $25/50 in the older part of the hotel. The *Carnarvon Hotel* (☎ (099) 41 1181), Olivia Terrace, has rooms for $20/35, or for $35/50 in the newer motel part. There are self-contained units in the *Pelican Point Beach Resort*, *Carnarvon Close* and the *Carnarvon Caravan Park*; all are about $55 per night.

The *Gateway Motel* (☎ (099) 41 1532), on Robinson St, has rooms at $75. Or there are self-contained holiday units at the *Carnarvon Beach Holiday Resort* (☎ (099) 41 2226), Pelican Point, at $55 for two. The *Fascine Lodge* and the *Hospitality Inn* cost about the same as the Gateway.

The top accommodation in Carnarvon is the Maslen family's *Outcamp* (☎ (099) 41 2421) at 16 Olivia St, on the Fascine. This is a luxurious B&B in the town's best location. For the great facilities the cost is a mere $40 per person, so treat yourself.

Places to Eat

Try *Carnarvon Fresh Seafoods*, on Robinson St, for fish & chips and hamburgers. On the same street are *Fascine* and *Kaycee's*, both standard coffee lounges. *Chickenland*, also on Robinson St next to the Tourist Centre Caravan Park, is a mini food hall with takeaways and pasta at reasonable prices; you can eat in or take away.

The *Carnarvon Bakery* has home-made pies and sandwiches, while you can get good counter meals at the *Carnarvon* and *Port* hotels. The *Harbour View Cafe*, up at the small boat harbour, is renowned for its excellent seafood – read the visitors' book.

Lucki's Asian Takeaway, on Robinson St, has typical Chinese food. There is also the *Dragon Pearl* Chinese place on Francis St. If you're looking for a more up-market place, you could try the Mexican *Red Peppers* on Robinson St ($16 for a main meal), or the excellent restaurant in the *Tropicana Tavern*.

Getting There & Around

Ansett flies to Carnarvon from Perth for $254 one way ($289 Apex return). Greyhound Pioneer and Dixon's Westliner both pass through Carnarvon on their way north and south. The one-way full fare from Perth to Carnarvon is around $100.

Bicycles are available for hire from Backpackers' Paradise (provide your own helmet). Mopeds can be hired from Jolly's Tyrepower Service in Robinson St.

GASCOYNE AREA

About 14 km north of town, the **Bibbawarra Bore**, an artesian well sunk to a depth of 914 metres, is being developed into a spa bath.

Attractions in the vicinity of Carnarvon include the spectacular **blowholes**, 70 km to the north – they are well worth the trip. There's a fine beach about one km south of the blowholes with a primitive camping ground (no fresh water available) and a sort of local shanty town. You can camp at *Quobba Station* for about $4.50 per person – power is limited but water is available. One km south of the homestead is the **HMAS *Sydney* Memorial** to the ship sunk here by the German raider *Kormoran* in November 1941.

Cape Cuvier, where salt is loaded for Japan, is 30 km north of the blowholes, and nearby is the wreck of the *Korean Star*, grounded in 1988 (do not climb over the wreck as it is dangerous). In 1993 a unique natural phenomenon occurred at Cape Cuvier. Millions of anchovies and pilchards attracted tropical (Bryde's) and pygmy whales feeding alongside a variety of sharks (tiger, hammerhead, mako, bronze whaler, grey nurse and reef sharks) and many species of fish. It seemed that the sharks kept the fish herded up while the whales had their fill.

Remote **Gascoyne Junction** is 164 km inland (east) of Carnarvon in the gemstone-rich Kennedy Range. From here, if you are really adventurous, you can continue on to Buringurrah National Park, 450 km from Carnarvon, to see **Mt Augustus**, the biggest rock (or monadnock) in the world but certainly not the most spectacular. The rock can be climbed (almost a full-day excursion), and there are Aboriginal rock paintings in the area. There's also accommodation close by at *Cobra Station* and *Mt Augustus Station*.

North-West Cape

North-West Cape, a finger of land jutting north into the Indian Ocean, offers a bewildering array of activities for travellers – mainly because of the excellent ecotourism opportunities at Coral Bay, Ningaloo Marine Park and Cape Range National Park. Whale sharks, humpbacks, manta rays and colourful schools of fish can be seen in and around Ningaloo Reef. In addition there are mammals, marine and land reptiles, and abundant bird life.

EXMOUTH (population 3100)

Exmouth was established in 1967, largely as a service town for a US navy communications base, which has recently closed.

The well-organised Exmouth tourist bureau (☎ (099) 49 1176), on Thew St, has a video display. It is open daily from 9 am to 5 pm.

Things to See

There's a shell museum on Pellew St, and the

Interaction with Marine Life

Exmouth is becoming increasingly popular as an ecotourism destination.

Whale sharks can be observed from late March to the end of May. The season begins at the time of coral spawning, when the plankton blooms. The largest numbers of whale sharks are seen off the Tantabiddi and Mangrove Bay areas. The best way to see them is by licensed charter vessel, which heads off after they have been spotted by aircraft.

Manta rays are seen from July until about mid-November, although they are not generally seen every day. The mantas come here for the accumulation of available food and are seen in pods of 20 to 30.

The Murion Islands, 10 km north-east of the cape, are a breeding sanctuary for three species of turtle – green, loggerhead and hawksbill. During dives it is possible to hand feed the 1.5-metre-long potato cod (*Epinephalus tukula*) at the 'cod house'. ■

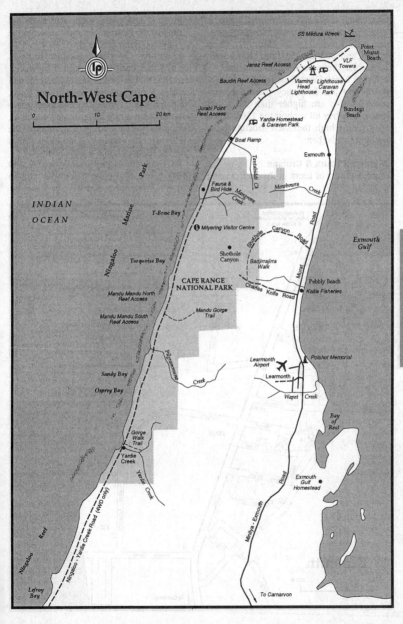

North-West Cape

0   10   20 km

SS Mildura Wreck
Point Murat Beach
VLF Towers
Janz Reef Access
Baudin Reef Access
Vlaming Head Lighthouse
Lighthouse Caravan Park
Bundegi Beach
Jurabi Point Reef Access
Yardie Homestead & Caravan Park
Boat Ramp
Exmouth
Tantabiddi Ck
Mowbowra Creek

INDIAN OCEAN

Park
Marine
Fauna & Bird Hide
Mangrove Creek
T-Bone Bay
Milyering Visitor Centre
Shothole Canyon
Shothole Canyon Road
Badjirrajirra Walk
Exmouth Gulf

Ningaloo
Turquoise Bay

CAPE RANGE NATIONAL PARK

Mandu Mandu North Reef Access
Mandu Mandu South Reef Access
Mandu Gorge Trail
Charles Knife Road
Murat Road
Pebbly Beach
Kalis Fisheries

Sandy Bay
Osprey Bay
Yanginnmup Creek

Learmonth Airport
Learmonth
Wapet Creek
Potshot Memorial

Gorge Walk Trail
Yardie Creek
Yardie Creek

Bay of Rest

Ningaloo – Yardie Creek Road (4WD only)

Minilya – Exmouth Road

Exmouth Gulf Homestead

Ningaloo Reef

Lefroy Bay

To Carnarvon

WESTERN AUSTRALIA

town beach at the end of Warne St is quite popular. North of town, apart from the navy base, is the wreck of the **SS Mildura** beached in 1907, and the **Vlaming Head Lighthouse** from which there are sensational views.

Part of North-West Cape is rendered ugly by 13 very low-frequency transmitter stations. Twelve are higher than the Eiffel Tower, and they all support the 13th, which is 396 metres high, the tallest structure in the southern hemisphere.

Organised Tours & Cruises

There is a host of tours in the area ranging from gulf and gorge safaris to reef and fishing tours. Perhaps the most informative is Ningaloo Safari Tours (☎ (099) 49 1550) – the full-day Over the Top safari (10 hours for $75) has been recommended by travellers. Neil McLeod takes you to Shothole and Charles Knife gorges, Owl's Roost Cave, Ningaloo Reef, Yardie Creek Gorge (where you may spot a rare black-footed wallaby), Turquoise Bay and ends with an ascent of the lighthouse at Vlaming Head. The tour's catering features home-made tucker.

At Exmouth Backpackers (☎ (099) 49 1101) you can arrange a four-day trip to

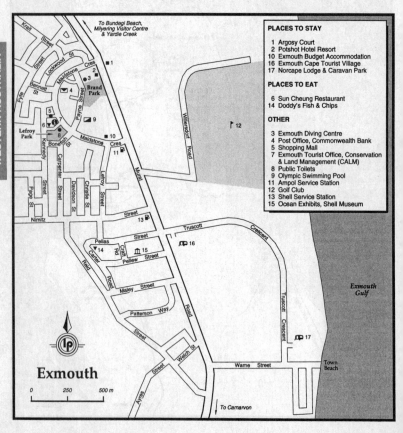

PLACES TO STAY

1 Argosy Court
2 Potshot Hotel Resort
10 Exmouth Budget Accommodation
16 Exmouth Cape Tourist Village
17 Norcape Lodge & Caravan Park

PLACES TO EAT

6 Sun Cheung Restaurant
14 Doddy's Fish & Chips

OTHER

3 Exmouth Diving Centre
4 Post Office, Commonwealth Bank
5 Shopping Mall
7 Exmouth Tourist Office, Conservation & Land Management (CALM)
8 Public Toilets
9 Olympic Swimming Pool
11 Ampol Service Station
12 Golf Club
13 Shell Service Station
15 Ocean Exhibits, Shell Museum

Exmouth

0   250   500 m

WESTERN AUSTRALIA

Karijini (Hamersley Range) National Park for $300; everything is supplied. During the season they do turtle tours, walks in Yardie Creek, and abseiling and rock climbing with the group Adventure Out. Peter Turner tends to make sure that you get out on a trip regardless of numbers.

The Exmouth Diving Centre (☎ (099) 49 1201) provides a wide range of diving possibilities, such as whale-shark observing, with equipment and refreshments included, for $299. Manta rays can be observed at $25 per dive (daily rental of equipment $50), and the centre also organises trips to the Murion Islands to observe turtles.

Near the Walkabout Cafe you will find the Coral Coast Tourist Centre (☎ (099) 49 1625) which incorporates West Coast Safaris and the semisubmersible Ningaloo Coral Explorer which operates over Bundegi Reef. Exmouth Air Charters (☎ (099) 49 2182) conduct scenic flights.

Hour-long boat tours are conducted up the interesting Yardie Gorge on Monday, Wednesday and Saturday and cost $15 (children $8).

Places to Stay

Accommodation in and around Exmouth can be quite expensive, although there are several caravan parks around town. At the *Exmouth Caravan Park* (☎ (099) 49 1331), Lefroy St, tent and caravan sites are $12 a double; it is a bit run down. The *Norcape Lodge Caravan Park* (☎ (099) 49 1908), on Truscott Crescent, has tent and caravan sites for $12/15. At Vlaming Head the *Lighthouse Caravan Park* (☎ (099) 49 1478) has on-site vans for $30. There is some good surfing nearby.

The *Exmouth Cape Tourist Village and Exmouth Backpackers* (☎ (099) 49 1101), on the corner of Truscott Crescent and Murat Rd, has tent sites at $11 for two, on-site vans for $32 a double and excellent backpackers' accommodation for $12 per night; there's also a cold swimming pool. The *Potshot Hotel Resort* (☎ (099) 49 1200), off Payne St, has self-contained units from $30 a

double plus much more expensive options for $40/50.

At Minilya Bridge, seven km south of where the road to Exmouth forks away from the North-West Coastal Highway, is the *Swagman Caravan Facility*. It has typical roadhouse fare, free camping and units for $25/35. This place cops a fair amount of flak from travellers – the large 'Backpackers – No Loitering' sign sets the tone.

Places to Eat

The number of places is growing rapidly in response to increased tourism. There are a number of takeaways in the main shopping area of town including *Cape Rock Cafe*, *Shell's Coffee Bar*, *Judy's Fast Food* and the *Walkabout Cafe*.

Fish & chips are a speciality of this region – in town go to *Doddy's* and out of town try *M G Kailis'* prawn palace, 25 km south, open May to November.

The *Sun Cheung* Chinese restaurant is next door to the tourist bureau. Both the *Potshot Hotel* and *Norcape Lodge* have buffet and à la carte meals.

Getting There & Away

Ansett has a once-daily service between Perth and Exmouth for $349 Apex return ($311 one way), except Saturday. There is a shuttle bus service Monday to Friday which goes from Exmouth to Minilya roadhouse to meet Greyhound Pioneer. The cost one way is $10 – a good option if you don't have your own vehicle. Three times a week there is a Greyhound Pioneer service to Exmouth from Perth (Sunday, Tuesday and Friday). From Exmouth to Perth services are Saturday, Monday and Thursday.

NINGALOO REEF

Running along the western side of the North-West Cape for 260 km is the stunning Ningaloo ('Point of Land') Reef. This miniature, but discontinuous, version of the Great Barrier Reef is actually much more accessible, as in places it is only a few hundred metres offshore. The lagoons enclosed by the reef vary in width from 200 metres to six km. Within the marine park are eight sanctuary zones – no fishing is allowed here. Dugongs are observed, greenback turtles lay their eggs along the cape beach and placid whale sharks, the world's largest fish, can also be seen just beyond the reef's waters.

Every year in June and July, humpback whales pass close by the coast on their way north to their calving grounds, probably near the Monte Bello Islands. In October and November they return to Antarctica.

In November turtles come up the beaches when the tide is right to lay their eggs at night. This usually happens from November to January near the top end of North-West Cape.

You can contact Exmouth's CALM office (☎ (099) 49 1676) in Thew St for more specific information and copies of the excellent *Parks of the Coral Coast* pamphlet, which outlines the area's special fishing regulations.

CAPE RANGE NATIONAL PARK

The park, which runs down the west coast of the cape, includes the modern Milyering visitor's centre, a wide variety of flora and fauna, good swimming beaches, gorges (including scenic Yardie Creek) and rugged scenery.

Milyering (☎ (099) 49 2808) is built in rammed-earth style, is solar powered and has environmentally thoughtful waste disposal.

A comprehensive display of the area's natural and cultural history can be seen here. It is usually open from 10 am to 4 pm during the tourist season.

Basic tent and caravan sites are available in larger camps in the park (☎ (099) 49 1676) at $5 per double per night.

Suitably equipped (4WD) vehicles can continue south to Coral Bay following the coast. The road is signposted and there is a turn-off to the Point Cloates Lighthouse.

CORAL BAY (population 730)

This town, 150 km south of Exmouth, is an important access point for Ningaloo Reef and a popular diving centre. The Glass Bottom Boat and Sub-sea Explorer (☎ (099) 42 5955) trips leave from here; they cost about $15.

Places to Stay & Eat

There are two camping grounds in Coral Bay. The *People's Park Caravan Village* (☎ (099) 42 5933) has tent and caravan sites for $10/14 per double. The friendly *Bay View Holiday Village* (☎ (099) 42 5932) in Robinson St has camping and caravan sites. *Coral Bay Lodge* (☎ (099) 42 5932), on the corner of Robinson and French Sts, has double units from $80, and the *Ningaloo Reef Resort* (☎ (099) 42 5934) has backpackers' accommodation for $10 and cabanas from $80 a double.

There are two places to eat in town. Just as you approach the bay there is the *Bay View Restaurant* and at the end of the road is the *Coral Bay Hotel*.

Station Stays

If you really want to sample a slice of genuine station life out in the red sandy country then head out to one of the station stays. On the Bullara to Giralia road, 43 km from the North-West Coastal Highway, is the 265,000-hectare *Giralia Station* (☎ (099) 42 5937). There is a variety of accommodation here including DB&B for $55 (bookings essential and BYO), shearers' quarters at $10, and camping and caravan sites for $5; all prices are per person. The homestead is central to many features in the Pilbara and Gascoyne regions. If you want to sample activities on the station, which runs 25,000 merino sheep, then just ask.

There are plenty of other places in the region. In the Kennedy Ranges there is *Mt Sandiman Homestead* (☎(099) 43 0546); *Manbery Station* (☎(099) 42 5926) and *Boologooroo Station* (☎(099) 42 5907) are north of Carnarvon; *Nallan Station* (☎(099) 63 1054) is near Cue; and *Wooleen Station* (☎(099) 63 7973) is on the Murchison River. ∎

The Pilbara

The Pilbara (meaning 'fish') contains some of the hottest country on earth, and its iron-ore and natural-gas production accounts for much of WA's prosperity. Gigantic machines are used to tear the dusty red ranges apart. It's isolated, harsh and fabulously wealthy. The Pilbara towns are almost all company towns: either mining centres where the ore is wrenched from the earth or ports from which it's shipped abroad. Exceptions are the beautiful gorges of Karijini (Hamersley Range) and earlier historic mining centres like Marble Bar.

If you are travelling away from the main coastal highway in this area in your own vehicle, always carry a lot of extra water – 20 litres per person is a sensible amount – and adequate fuel. If travelling into remote areas, make sure you tell someone reliable your travel plans, and don't leave your vehicle if you are stranded.

Getting There & Away

Air Ansett flies from Perth to Newman ($312 one way/$357 Apex return), Paraburdoo ($288/318) and Port Hedland ($373/424). Skywest flies from Perth to Mt Magnet ($202/263), Cue ($214/278) and Meekatharra ($258/335). Ansett has regular flights to Learmonth from Perth ($311/349 Apex return).

Bus Greyhound Pioneer has four buses a week from Perth to Port Hedland via Mt Magnet, Cue, Meekatharra and Newman. There's a once-weekly service from the Nanutarra turn-off to Tom Price, leaving Perth on Tuesday, and three services a week to Exmouth from Perth (departing Tuesday, Friday and Sunday).

Westrail has a weekly bus service from Perth to Meekatharra ($64), stopping at Mt Magnet ($53) and Cue ($58).

There is a Monday and Friday bus service to Wittenoom from Karratha operated by Snappy Gum Safaris (☎ (091) 85 1278). You can reach Wittenoom directly from Port Hedland (307 km via the Great Northern Highway), from near Roebourne (311 km off the North-West Coastal Highway) or from the Nanutarra turn-off (377 km off the North-West Coastal Highway). Remember, many of the roads in the Pilbara are unsealed or require a permit.

ONSLOW (population 880)

Onslow has the dubious distinction of being the southernmost Western Australian town to be bombed in WW II and later being used as a base by the British for nuclear testing in the Monte Bello Islands.

There is good swimming and fishing in the area. The **old Onslow ruins**, 48 km from town, were abandoned in 1925. They include a jail and a post office, and are worth a look.

The *Ocean View Caravan Park* (☎ (091) 84 6053) on Second Ave has tent sites at $14 for two and on-site vans from $30. The *Beadon Bay Hotel* (☎ (091) 84 6002), Second Ave, has rooms for $45/55.

There are resorts on the Direction and Mackerel islands (☎ (09) 388 2020), 11 and 22 km offshore respectively.

DAMPIER (population 1800)

Dampier is on King Bay and faces the other 41 islands of the Dampier Archipelago (named after the explorer William Dampier who visited the area in 1699).

Dampier is a Hamersley Iron town and the port for Tom Price and Paraburdoo iron-ore operations. (It will also be the port for the huge Marandoo mineral project.) Gas from the natural-gas fields of the North-West Shelf is piped ashore nearby on the Burrup Peninsula. From there, it is piped to Perth and the Pilbara, or liquefied as part of the Woodside Petroleum project and exported to Japan and South Korea.

An inspection of the port facilities can be arranged (☎ (091) 44 4600). The William Dampier Lookout provides a fine view over the harbour and the Woodside LNG Visitors' Centre (☎ (091) 83 8100) is open weekdays 9 am to 4.30 pm during the tourist season.

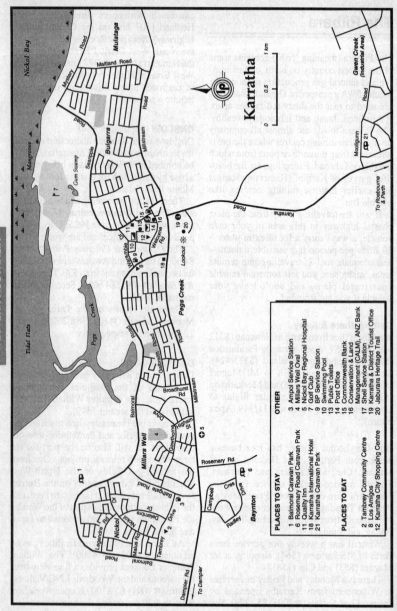

WESTERN AUSTRALIA

Karratha

0   0.5   1 km

Nickol Bay

Mangroves

Tidal Flats

Pegs Creek

Mystery Road

Maitland Road

Bulgarra

Gum Swamp

Seaslope

Millstream Road

Mulataga

Warambie Dr

Welcome Rd

Pegs Creek Lookout

Broadhurst Rd

Higham St

Gawthorne Dr

Balmoral Rd

Galbraith Road

Millstream Road

Millars Well

Rosemary Rd

Balgate Road

Delambre Dr

Nickol Rd

Malus Rd

Legendre Rd

Tambrey Dr

Balmoral Road

Campbell Cres

Radley

Beynton

Dampier Rd

To Dampier

Gwen Creek (Industrial Area)

Mooligunn

Karratha Road

To Roebourne & Perth

PLACES TO STAY

1 Balmoral Caravan Park
6 Rosemary Road Caravan Park
11 Quality Inn
18 Karratha International Hotel
21 Karratha Caravan Park

PLACES TO EAT

2 Tambrey Community Centre
8 Los Amigos
12 Karratha City Shopping Centre

OTHER

3 Ampol Service Station
4 Millars Well Oval
5 Nickol Bay Regional Hospital
7 Golf Club
9 BP Service Station
10 Swimming Pool
13 Public Toilets
14 Post Office
15 Commonwealth Bank
16 Conservation & Land Management (CALM), ANZ Bank
17 Shell Service Station
19 Karratha & District Tourist Office
20 Jaburara Heritage Trail

Nearby **Hearson's Cove** is a popular beach and picnic area, as is **Dampier Beach**. The **Burrup Peninsula** has some 10,000 Aboriginal rock engravings depicting fish, turtles, kangaroos and a Tasmanian tiger. The **Dampier Archipelago** is renowned as a game-fishing Mecca and each year it hosts the Dampier Classic.

Places to Stay & Eat

Apart from the caravan park (☎ (091) 83 1109) on the Esplanade, there is no budget accommodation in Dampier. The *King Bay Holiday Village* (☎ (091) 83 1440) on the Esplanade has expensive units; the *Harbour Lights* restaurant is part of the complex. Also on the Esplanade is the *Mermaid Hotel* (☎ (091) 83 1222).

The *Captain's Galley*, on the Esplanade and overlooking Hampton Harbour, is good for fish & chips. There is a Chinese restaurant in the shopping centre.

KARRATHA (population 11,300)

Karratha (Aboriginal for 'good country') is located 20 km from Dampier, and is the commercial centre for the area. The town was developed due to the rapid expansion of the Hamersley Iron and Woodside LNG projects, and is now the hub of the coastal Pilbara.

There are good views from the lookout at the area known as **TV Hill** (because of the television repeater mast). **Miaree Pool**, 35 km to the south-west, is a scenic place to cool off. The area around town is replete with evidence of Aboriginal occupation – carvings, grindstones, etchings and middens are all located on the **Jaburara Heritage Trail** which starts near the information centre. *Terminalia canescens*, the trees which grow in the creek beds here, are a reminder of the area's formerly very different tropical climate.

Information

The Karratha & District information centre (☎ (091) 44 4600), on Karratha Rd just before you reach the T-intersection of Karratha and Millstream Rds, has heaps of info on what to see and do in the Pilbara.

The Fe-NaCl-NG Festival is held in August each year. The title of the festival combines the chemical abbreviations of the region's main natural resources – iron, salt and natural gas.

Places to Stay & Eat

There are three caravan parks in Karratha: *Balmoral* (☎ (091) 85 3628) and *Rosemary* (☎ (091) 85 1855) are both administered by Fleetwood Caravan Parks, and there's also the *Karratha Caravan Park* (☎ (091) 85 1012) on Mooligunn Rd. The first two parks have tent sites at $12 for two, and they also have cabins.

On Balmoral Rd in Karratha, *Los Amigos*, opposite the BP service station, has Mexican food, and the *Universal* on the same road does good Chinese food. For a snack, there is a number of cafes and takeaway places in the Karratha shopping centre, including *Adrienne's Cafe*. A little out of town, the *Tambrey Community Centre* has a tavern which serves good counter meals; visitors are welcome to use the pool.

ROEBOURNE AREA

The Roebourne area is a busy little enclave of historic towns and modern port facilities. Wickham is the port for the ore produced at Tom Price and Pannawonica, Point Samson is a great fishing spot and Cossack is a very picturesque historic town. European settlement of the North-West began in this area.

Information

Information on the area is available from the Roebourne District tourist bureau (☎ (091) 82 1060), Old Gaol, Queen St, Roebourne. If in Cossack, the Heritage Council officials will help. There is a laundromat in the Victoria Hotel-Mt Welcome Motel complex in Roebourne and a good supermarket in Wickham.

Roebourne (population 1200)

Roebourne is the oldest existing town in the

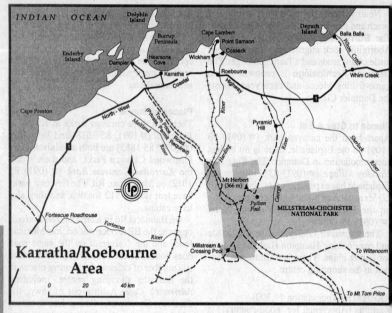

Karratha/Roebourne Area

Pilbara. It has a history of grazing, gold and copper mining, and was once the capital of the North-West. There are still some fine old buildings to be seen, including the **old gaol** (which has an excellent Aboriginal art gallery), an **1894 church** and the **Victoria Hotel**, which is the last of the five original pubs. The town was once connected to Cossack, 13 km away on the coast, by a horse-drawn tram.

Places to Stay & Eat There is the *Harding River Caravan Park* (☎ (091) 82 1063) with tent sites at $8 for two. The *Mt Welcome Motel*, in Roe St, is the main accommodation with singles/doubles for $40/60.

The *Roebourne Diner*, good for eat in and takeaway, and the *Poinciana Room* are in the Victoria Hotel-Mt Welcome Motel. Also on Roe St is a snack bar, open seven days.

Cossack

Originally known as Tien Tsin Harbour, Cossack was a bustling town and the main port for the district in the mid- to late 19th century. Its boom was short lived and Point Samson soon supplanted it as the chief port for the area. The sturdy old buildings date from 1870 to 1898, and much of the ghost town has been restored as a continuing 1988 bicentennial project.

The town now includes an **art gallery**, **museum** and a budget-accommodation house which has a boat-hiring facility. Beyond town, there's a **pioneer cemetery** with a small Japanese section dating from the old pearl-diving days. In fact, this is where pearling actually began; it later moved on to Broome in the 1890s. There are a couple of good lookouts and excellent beaches in the area; the cooler, drier months are best for a visit. Obtain *Cossack Historic Walk* ($1.50) and *Cossack: The First Port in the North-West* (50c) when you get to the town. All proceeds go towards its restoration.

The staircase to the moon reflection can

be viewed from Reader's Point Lookout. It comes across an average of 50 km of marsh and lasts for ages (this effect is also described in the section on Broome). A point for trivia buffs: all seven of the species of mangrove found in the Pilbara occur near the Cossack boat ramp.

Places to Stay The *Cossack Backpackers* (☎ (091) 82 1190) is one of those gems of the road. It's housed in the old police barracks administered by the Heritage Council of WA. The dorm rooms are $9, and there is a kitchen, refrigerator and hot and cold shower. There is also a small shop nearby. Currently for $136 two persons can stay two nights and have the use of a 3.8-metre powerboat. As there are no places to eat bring your own food from Wickham, six km away. If you ring in advance the proprietors will pick up from the bus depot in Wickham. They do two runs each day.

Wickham & Point Samson

Wickham (population 2000) is the Robe River Iron Company town, handling its ore-exporting facilities 10 km away at Cape Lambert, where the jetty is three km long. Ore is railed there from the mining operations inland at Pannawonica.

Point Samson, beyond Wickham, took the place of Cossack when the old port silted up. In turn, it has been replaced by the modern port facilities of Dampier and Cape Lambert. There are good beaches at Point Samson itself and at nearby **Honeymoon Cove**.

Places to Stay & Eat In Wickham, *Wickham Lodge* (☎ (091) 87 1439), on Wickham Drive, has a backpackers' and self-contained units. *Samson Accommodation* (☎ (091) 87 1052), at 56 Samson Rd, Point Samson, has budget beds for $17.50. The *Solveig Caravan Park* (☎ (091) 87 1414), Samson Rd, has powered caravan sites for $15.

It's worth detouring to Point Samson for the seafood. *Trawlers* is a licensed restaurant overlooking the pier. Underneath, in the same building, is *Moby's Kitchen*, where you can get excellent fish & chips and salad.

Whim Creek

The first significant Pilbara mineral find was at Whim Creek, 80 km east of Roebourne. It once had a copper mine and all that is left is the *Whim Creek Hotel* (☎ (091) 76 4953) which has accommodation and a restaurant; tent and caravan sites are free and singles/doubles are $30/35.

MILLSTREAM-CHICHESTER NATIONAL PARK

The impressive 200,000-hectare Millstream-Chichester National Park lies 87 km south of Roebourne, while the Millstream Homestead is 150 km south of Roebourne, 21 km off the road to Wittenoom. The park includes a number of freshwater pools such as **Python Pool**, which was once an oasis for Afghani camel drivers and still makes a good place to pause for a swim.

The **Chinderwarriner Pool**, near the visitor centre in Millstream, is another pleasant oasis with pools, palms (including the unique Millstream palm) and lilies; it is well worth a visit. The lush environment is a haven for birds and other fauna such as flying foxes and kangaroos. Over 20 species of dragonfly and damselfly have been recorded around the pool. The old homestead has been converted into an information centre with a wealth of detail on the Millstream ecosystems and the lifestyle of the Yinjibarndi people.

The park also has a number of walking and driving trails including the 6.8-km Murlunmunyjurna Trail, the eight-km Chichester Range Camel Track and Cliff Lookout Drive.

There are basic camp sites (☎ (091) 84 5144) at Snake Creek (near Python Pool), Crossing Pool and Deep Reach; tent sites are $5 for two and $3 for each extra adult.

WITTENOOM (population 50)

Wittenoom, 288 km south-east of Roebourne, is the Pilbara's tourist centre. It had an earlier history as an asbestos-mining town but mining finally halted in 1966; it is the magnificent gorges of Karijini (Hamersley

Range) National Park which now draw people to the area. The tourist centre is in the Ashburton shire offices on Third Ave (☎ (091) 89 7011). There are no banking facilities so bring plenty of cash to pay for supplies and tours.

Places to Stay & Eat

The *Gorges Caravan Park* (☎ (091) 89 7075), on Second Ave, has tent sites from $9 and on-site vans from $25 for two.

Wittenoom Bungarra Bivouac Hostel (☎ (091) 89 7026), at 71 Fifth Ave, has beds at $7 per night (incidentally, a bungarra is a big goanna). Another budget place is the *Old Convent* (☎ (091) 89 7060), Gregory St, which has an elongated dorm in the front verandah for $8 per person and double rooms at $30 for two. *Nomad Heights* (☎ (091) 89 7068), on First Ave, is a small arid/tropical permaculture farm where you can stay for $6 per night; you can book trips into the gorges from here.

At present you have to bring your own food to Wittenoom as there are no restaurants in town. You can get basic supplies at the camping ground or at the local store.

Some 40 km from Wittenoom, on the Great Northern Highway, is the *Auski Tourist Village Roadhouse* (☎ (091) 76 6988); shady, grassed tent and caravan sites are $8/13. Why Auski? Because it was set up by Aussies and Kiwis.

Warning Even after 25 years, there is a health risk from airborne asbestos fibres. Avoid disturbing asbestos tailings in the area and keep your car windows closed on windy days. If you are concerned, seek expert medical advice before going to Wittenoom.

KARIJINI (HAMERSLEY RANGE) NATIONAL PARK

Wittenoom is at the northern end of the Karijini (Hamersley Range) National Park and the famous **Wittenoom Gorge** is

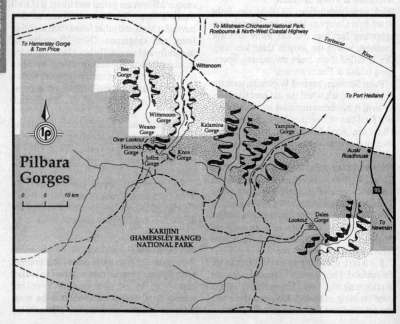

mmediately south of the town. A road runs he 13 km to this gorge, passing old asbestos nines and a number of smaller gorges and pretty pools.

Like other gorges in central Australia, hose of Karijini are spectacular both in their sheer rocky faces and their varied colours. In the early spring, the park is often carpeted with colourful wildflowers. Travel down the Newman road 24 km and there's a turn-off to the **Yampire Gorge** where blue veins of asbestos can be seen in the rock. Fig Tree Soak, in the gorge, was once used by Afghani camel drivers as a watering point. Look carefully at the bird life around the fig tree – if you are lucky you might see a spotted bowerbird feeding on the ripe figs.

The road continues through Yampire Gorge to **Dales Gorge**. On this same route, you can get to **Circular Pool** and a nearby lookout, and by a footpath to the bottom of he **Fortescue Falls**. The walk from Circular Pool along Dales Gorge to the falls is recommended; you will be surprised by the supply of permanent water in the gorge.

The Joffre Falls road leads to **Knox Gorge**; nearby is a 1.5-km return walk to Red Gorge lookout. From the Joffre Falls turn-off it is 16 km to the spectacular **Oxer Lookout** at the junction of the Red, Weano, Joffre and Hancock gorges. If you wish to get down into the gorge proper then take the steps down to Handrail Pool (turn to the right at the bottom) in Weano Gorge. If you want a totally different impression of the impressive scenery in Karijini you can try the Miracle Mile (see Organised Tours below). It starts in Wittenoom early in the morning, going first to Oxer's Lookout and then to Hancock Gorge where the adventure really starts. You descend a steep track into the gorge to Kermit's Pool for a swim before you climb around a waterfall, down the steep Jade's Stairs and around the corner to the end of Hancock Gorge. The next stage is a swim across Junction Pool. Climbing starts again as you head up the 100-foot waterfall into Weano Gorge. All this is not for the faint-hearted.

Following the main road to Tom Price,

you pass through the small **Rio Tinto Gorge**, 43 km from Wittenoom, and just beyond this is the **Hamersley Gorge**, only four km from the road. Mt Meharry (1251 metres), the highest mountain in WA, is near the southeast border of Karijini National Park.

There are several basic camp sites within the Karijini, including Dales Gorge, Weano Gorge and the Joffre intersection ($5 for a tent site for two) – contact the rangers (☎ (091) 89 8157) for more information.

Organised Tours

A number of tours operate out of the area, including Dave's Gorge Tours (☎ (091) 89 7026) from the Wittenoom Bungarra Bivouac Hostel. The one-day circuit tour costs $45 (bring your own lunch) and the Miracle Mile costs $45 ($50 if you are not staying in the hostel). Nomad Heights Backpackers (☎ (091) 89 7068) also runs tours.

Design-a-Tour (☎ (091) 89 7059) has one-day tours of Karijini (Hamersley Range) and the gorges for $55, including lunch (an extra $10 for pick up from Auski). Pilbara Adventure Tours (☎ (091) 73 2544), based in Port Hedland, go to Karijini, as well as Marble Bar and Rudall River National Park.

Snappy Gum Safaris (☎ (091) 85 1278) runs tours to Karijini but mainly concentrate on Millstream-Chichester and the Burrup Peninsula.

TOM PRICE & PARABURDOO

These company-run iron-ore towns lie south-west of Wittenoom. Check with Hamersley Iron (☎ (091) 89 2375) in Tom Price about inspecting the mine works – if nothing else, the scale of it all will impress you.

Mt Nameless, four km west of Tom Price, offers good views of the area especially at sunset. Paraburdoo's airport is the closest commercial airport to Karijini (Hamersley Range) National Park.

The *Tom Price Caravan Park* (☎ (091) 89 1515) has powered caravan sites and on-site vans. *Hillview Lodge* (☎ (091) 89 1625) has overpriced singles/doubles for $85/95.

The *Red Emperor* cafe in the shopping

mall provides reasonable food and the *Tom Price Hotel* has standard counter meals.

PORT HEDLAND (population 11,300)

This port handles a massive tonnage as it is the place from which the Pilbara's iron ore is shipped overseas. The iron-ore trains are up to 2.8 km in length. The town itself is built on an island connected to the mainland by causeways and the main highway into Port Hedland enters along a three-km causeway.

Even before the Marble Bar gold rush of the 1880s, the town had been important. It became a grazing centre in 1864 and during the 1870s a fleet of 150 pearling luggers was based there. By 1946, however, the population had dwindled to a mere 150.

The port is on a mangrove-fringed inlet – there are plenty of fish, crabs, oysters and birds around. The port and iron-ore eyesores are feted at the expense of the prolific natural wonders in the area.

Information

The sleepy tourist bureau (☎ (091) 73 1711), which has a small art gallery and showers ($1.50), is at 13 Wedge St, across from the post office. It's open from 8.30 am to 5 pm during the week and from 8.30 am to 4.30 pm on weekends. It provides an excellent map of the town.

Things to See & Do

Seven km east of the town centre on the waterfront is **Pretty Pool**, a safe tidal pool where shell collectors will have fun – beware of stonefish. Visits can also be made to the **Royal Flying Doctor base**, Richardson St, at 11.15 am on weekdays.

You can visit the wharf area or view it from the 26-metre observation tower behind the tourist bureau (you have to sign a waiver to climb it and you'll need closed-in shoes). From the tower you will see huge ore carriers, stockpiles of ore and a town encrusted in red Pilbara dust. From Monday to Friday, at 9 and 11 am, there is a mind-numbing 1½-hour BHP Iron Ore & Port Tour which leaves

from the tourist bureau (adults $8, children $2).

There are two excellent heritage trails i the area. The *Port Trail* and *Out and Abou Trail* pamphlets are available from the touris bureau ($1 each).

Whale & Turtle Watching

The flatback turtle nests between Octobe and March on some of the nearby beaches including Munda, Cooke Point, Cemeter and Pretty Pool. At Munda up to 20 turtle may nest in a night.

Whale-watching trips are operated by Por Hedland Fishing Charters (☎ (091) 73 2937 in their boat the *Chatham Belle*. These tak six to eight hours, leave on weekends onl and cost $60 per person (lunch is $10 extra trips are dependent on tides. The whal observed is the majestic humpback, often i pods of five to six.

Places to Stay

Camping You can camp by the airport a *Dixon's Caravan Park* (☎ (091) 72 2525 Tent sites are $12 for two and backpackers rooms are $12 per person. The park has pool and a great recreation room wit cooking facilities, tape deck and TV. Mor convenient, but looking like something ou of T S Eliot's *Wasteland*, is the *Cooke Poin Caravan Park* (☎ (091) 73 1271), on Atho St, which is also adjacent to Pretty Pool dusty powered sites are $15 for two.

Hostels *Port Hedland Backpackers'* (☎ (09 73 2198) is at 20 Richardson St, betwee Edgar and McKay Sts. The homely atmc sphere and friendly hosts make up for th lack of luxuries. Dorm beds cost from $10 night and the place has kitchen and laundr facilities. The *Ocean View* (☎ (091) 7 2418), in Kingsmill St, has rooms for $35 pe person. The *Pier Hotel* (☎ (091) 73 1488 on the Esplanade, has $15 beds for back packers. Similar in price is the *Harbou Lodge* (☎ (091) 73 2996), at 11 Edgar S which has a fully equipped kitchen.

Hotels & Motels On the corner of Anderso

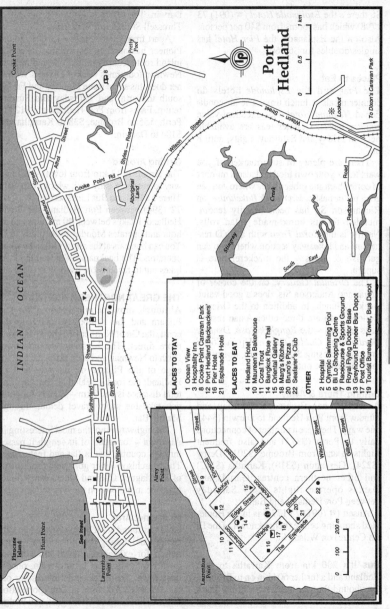

Port Hedland

To Dixon's Caravan Park

Lookout

PLACES TO STAY

1   Ocean View
3   Hospitality Inn
8   Cooke Point Caravan Park
12 Port Hedland Backpackers'
16 Pier Hotel
21 Esplanade Hotel

PLACES TO EAT

4   Hedland Hotel
10 Maureen's Bakehouse
11 Coral Trout
14 Bangkok Rose Thai
15 Oriental Gallery
18 Marg's Kitchen
20 Bruno's Pizza
22 Seafarer's Club

OTHER

2   Hospital
5   Olympic Swimming Pool
6   Bi Lo Shopping Centre
7   Racecourse & Sports Ground
13 Royal Flying Doctor Base
17 Post Office
19 Greyhound Pioneer Bus Depot
    Tourist Bureau, Tower, Bus Depot

St, there's the *Esplanade Hotel* (☎ (091) 73 1798) which has rooms from $40 per person. Also on the Esplanade, the *Pier Hotel* has singles/doubles for $55/60.

Places to Eat

The *Pier* and the *Esplanade* hotels do counter meals at lunch time. The air-conditioned *Hedland Hotel* does excellent-value counter meals. Counter teas are available only on Friday and Saturday nights, until 8 pm.

There are plenty of supermarkets if you want to fix your own food and also a number of coffee bars and other places where you can get a pie or pastie. *Maureen's Bakehouse*, on Richardson St, has been heartily recommended for its home-made salad rolls. Nearby is the *Coral Trout* with a BYO restaurant and takeaway section where you can get fish & chips – the mackerel here is superb.

The *Oriental Gallery*, on the corner of Edgar and Anderson Sts, does a good-value weekday lunch. In addition to the Oriental Gallery there are three other Asian restaurants in town – the *Bangkok Rose*, *Dynasty Gardens* and *Golden Crown*. Up in Cooke Point, on Keesing St, is *Tammi's*, one of the more expensive options in town.

Getting There & Away

Air Ansett has flights on Saturday and Sunday from Port Hedland to Darwin ($445 one way). There are a number of connections daily to Perth ($373) and also frequent flights to and from Broome ($201), Derby ($224), Geraldton ($318), Karratha ($147) and other northern centres. Garuda and Qantas operate flights every Saturday between Port Hedland and Bali.

Ansett (☎ (091) 73 1777) is in the Boulevard shopping centre (better known as the Bi Lo Centre) on Wilson St.

Bus It's 230 km from Karratha to Port Hedland and a further 604 km on to Broome. Greyhound Pioneer has services from Perth to Port Hedland and north on to Broome and Darwin. The office is in the Homestead in Throssell St in South Hedland.

Apart from the coastal route, Greyhound Pioneer has another service that takes the inland route from Perth to Port Hedland via Newman four times weekly. Dixon's Westliner does this same route Monday and Friday south to Perth, and Thursday and Sunday return. Fares from Port Hedland are $124 to Perth, $55 to Broome, $38 to Karratha and $184 to Darwin.

Getting Around

The airport is 13 km from town – the only way to get there is by taxi, which costs $15. There's a Hedland Bus Lines service (☎ (091) 72 1394) between Port Hedland and South Hedland; it takes between 40 minutes and an hour and operates Monday to Saturday ($2). You can hire cars at the airport from the usual operators. The backpackers' hostel lends its bikes out to responsible users.

THE GREAT NORTHERN HIGHWAY

Although most people heading for the Pilbara and the Kimberley travel up the coast, the Great Northern Highway is much more direct. The highway extends from Perth to Newman and then skirts the eastern edge of the Pilbara on its way to Port Hedland; the road is sealed all the way. The total distance is 1636 km – slightly longer if you take the short gravel detour through Marble Bar.

The highway is not the most interesting in Australia – for much of its length it passes through country that is flat and featureless. The Murchison River gold fields and towns of Mt Magnet, Cue and Meekatharra punctuate the monotony on the way to Newman.

Mt Magnet Area

Gold was found at Mt Magnet in the late 19th century and mining is still the town's prime reason for existence. Eleven km north of town are the ruins of **Lennonville**, once a busy town. There are some interesting old buildings of solid stone in **Cue** (population 400), 80 km north of Mt Magnet, and **Walga**

Rock, 48 km to the west, is a large monolith with a gallery of Aboriginal art.

Places to Stay The *Mt Magnet Caravan Park* (☎ (099) 63 4198) has tent sites for $7 and there are three hotels in Mt Magnet's main street.

Cue Caravan Park (☎ (099) 63 1107) has tent sites at $7 for two and the *Murchison Club* (☎ (099) 63 1020), in Austin St, also in Cue, has singles from $30.

Meekatharra (population 1400)

Meekatharra is still a mining centre. At one time it was a railhead for cattle brought down from the Northern Territory and the east Kimberley along the Canning Stock Route. There are ruins of various old gold towns and workings in the area. From Meekatharra, you can travel south via Wiluna and Leonora to the Kalgoorlie gold fields. It's over 700 km to Kal, more than half of it on unsealed road.

Places to Stay The *Meekatharra Caravan Park* (☎ (099) 81 1253) has tent sites and on-site vans, and the *Meekatharra Hotel/Motel* (☎ (099) 81 1021), on Main St, has inexpensive units.

Newman (population 5600)

At Newman, a town which only came into existence in the 1970s, the iron-ore mountain, Whaleback, is being systematically taken apart and railed down to the coast. Guided tours (☎ (091) 75 2888) of these engrossing operations leave across from the tourist centre daily at 8.30 am and 1 pm; safety helmets are provided and the tour is 1½ hours long. Newman is a modern company town built solely to service the mine. The Shire of East Pilbara tourist centre (☎ (091) 75 1924) is in Kalgan Drive.

There are Aboriginal **rock carvings** at Wanna Munna, 70 km from town, and at Punda, off the Marble Bar road. Two nearby pools of note are **Stuart's Pool**, a difficult but adventurous trip by 4WD, and **Kalgan's Pool**, a day outing from town.

Places to Stay & Eat There are several caravan parks in the area, the closest to town being the *Newman Caravan Park* (☎ (091) 75 1428), on Kalgan Drive. In addition to the roadhouses, there are takeaways and two Chinese places.

Marble Bar (population 380)

Reputed to be the hottest place in Australia, Marble Bar had a period in the 1920s when for 160 consecutive days the temperature topped 37°C. On one occasion, in 1905, the mercury soared to 49.1°C. From October to March, days over 40°C are common – though it is dry heat and not totally unbearable.

The town is 203 km south-east of Port Hedland and takes its name from a bar of red jasper across the Coongan River, five km west of town. The tourist centre (☎ (091) 76 1041) is in the BP service station on Francis St.

In town, the 1895 government buildings, made of local stone, are still in use. In late winter, as the spring wildflowers begin to bloom, Marble Bar is actually quite a pretty place and one of the most popular towns in the Pilbara to visit. The **Comet Gold Mine**, 10 km south of Marble Bar, is still in operation and has a mining museum and display centre; it is open daily.

Coppins Gap/Doolena Gorge, about 70 km north-east of Marble Bar, is a deep cutting with impressive views, twisted bands of rock and an ideal swimming hole.

Places to Stay The *Marble Bar Caravan Park* (☎ (091) 76 1067), on Contest St, has tent sites for $14 and on-site vans from $32 for two. There's a range of rooms at the *Ironclad Hotel* (☎ (091) 76 1066), one of the area's most distinctive drinking spots – backpackers' accommodation starts from $20.

PORT HEDLAND TO BROOME

The Great Northern Highway continues on from Port Hedland to Broome. Unfortunately, the 604-km stretch is a contender for the most boring length of roadway in Australia.

About 84 km from Port Hedland is the **De Grey River**, where several bird species can be spotted. Near the Pardoo Roadhouse (154 km) is the turn-off to **Cape Keraudren**, where there is great fishing; caravan sites are $5. *Pardoo Station* (133 km) has station stays, and camping and caravan sites are $7/9. At **Eighty Mile Beach**, 245 km from Port Hedland, backpackers' beds are $10 per person. The *Sandfire Roadhouse* (295 km) is very much an enforced fuel stop for most – pack sandwiches rather than eat the dull, expensive food sold here. On the other hand, **Port Smith** (477 km) comes recommended; camp sites are $5 per person.

Broome

Population 8,900

For many travellers, Broome is Australia's true getaway, with its palm-fringed beaches and cosmopolitan atmosphere. This old port is a small, dusty place noted for its Chinatown and the Japanese influences of early pearlers. Although still isolated, Broome has certainly been discovered. Today it is also something of a travellers' centre with the attendant good and bad characteristics.

Pearling in the sea off Broome started in the 1880s and peaked in the early 1900s when the town's 400 pearling luggers, worked by 3000 men, supplied 80% of the world's mother-of-pearl. Today only a handful of boats operate. Pearl diving was a very unsafe occupation, as Broome's Japanese cemetery attests. The divers were from various Asian countries. The rivalries between the different nationalities were always intense and sometimes took an ugly turn. The *Broome Heritage Trail* pamphlet aligns the history with the present.

Information

The Broome tourist bureau (☎ (091) 92 2222) is just across the sports field from Chinatown. From April to November it's open daily from 9 am to 5 pm, and in the interim it's open from 9 am to 5 pm Monday to Friday and from 9 am to 1 pm on weekends. The bureau publishes a very useful fortnightly guide to what's happening in and around Broome, a *Town Map & Information Guide* and a *Broome Holiday Planner*. You can also get a copy of the useful, free *Broome or Bust!* pamphlet, aimed at budget tourists.

Chinatown

The term 'Chinatown' is used to refer to the old part of town, although there is really only one block or so that is really multicultural and historic. Some of the plain and simple wooden buildings that line Carnarvon St still house Chinese merchants, but most are now restaurants and tourist shops. The bars on the windows aren't there to deter outlaws but to minimise cyclone damage.

The Carnarvon St phone-box sign is in English, Chinese, Arabic, Japanese and Malay. There is a street statue of three men in Carnarvon St – Hiroshi Iwaki, Tokuichi Kuribayashi and Keith Dureau were all involved in the cultured pearl industry.

Pearling

A pearling lugger can occasionally be seen at Streeters jetty off Dampier Terrace, and there are cruises from May to October ($40).

The **Broome Historical Society Museum**, on Saville St, has exhibits both on Broome and its history and on the pearling industry and its dangers. It's in the old customs house and is open Monday to Friday from 10 am to 4 pm, and Saturday and Sunday from 10 am to 1 pm (April to November); reduced hours operate from November to May.

Mother-of-pearl has long been a Broome speciality. Along Dampier Terrace in Chinatown are a number of shops selling pearls.

The **Japanese Cemetery**, near Cable Beach Rd, testifies to the dangers that accompanied pearl diving when equipment was primitive and knowledge of diving techniques limited. In 1914 alone, 33 divers died of the bends, while in 1908 a cyclone killed

PLACES TO STAY

4 Broome's Last Resort
10 Roebuck Bay Hotel Motel
   & Broome Bunkhouse
20 Ocean Lodge
24 Mangrove Motel
26 Auski Tropical Holiday Resort
28 Continental Motel
29 Quality Tropicana Inn
33 Forrest House
34 Roebuck Bay Resort
36 Roebuck Bay Caravan Park

PLACES TO EAT

6 Tong's Chinese Restaurant
8 Bloom's
9 D'Jango's
11 Weng Ho
12 Chin's Chinese Restaurant
   & Bicycle Centre
14 Wing's Restaurant
15 Mango Jack's, Rocky's Pizza,
   Chicken World

OTHER

1 Airport Terminal
2 Hertz
3 Avis
5 Broome Tourist Bureau
7 Sun Pictures
13 Aboriginal Gallery
16 Deluxe Coachlines
17 Courthouse
18 Post Office
19 Ansett Australia
21 Commonwealth Bank
22 Library, Art Gallery
   & Civic Centre
23 Horrie Miller's Wackett Aircraft
25 Broome Travel & Greyhound
   Pioneer
27 Bedford Park
30 Seaview Shopping Centre
31 Ray's Marine
32 Broome Historical Society
   Museum
35 Pioneer Cemetery
37 Flying Boat Wrecks

Broome

0   250   500 m

WESTERN AUSTRALIA

150 seamen caught at sea. The Japanese section of the cemetery is one of the largest and most interesting. Behind the neat Japanese section is the also interesting but now run-down section containing European and Aboriginal graves.

Other Attractions

Across Napier Terrace from Chinatown is Wing's Restaurant with a magnificent **boab tree** beside it. There's another boab tree behind, outside what used to be the old police lock-up, with a rather sad little tale on a plaque at its base. The tree was planted by a police officer when his son (later killed in France in WW I) was born in 1898. The boab tree is still doing fine.

The 1888 **courthouse** was once used to house the transmitting equipment for the old cable station. The cable ran to Banyuwangi in Java, the ferry port across from Bali.

Further along Weld St, by the library and civic centre, is a **Wackett aircraft** that used to belong to Horrie Miller, founder of MacRobertson Miller Airlines, once Ansett WA, now part of Ansett Australia. The plane is hidden away in a modern but absurdly designed building that most people pass without a second glance.

There's a **pioneer cemetery** near Town Beach at the end of Robinson St. Nearby, there's a park and also a small beach which is worth a visit at high tide. In the bay, at the entrance to Dampier Creek, there's a landmark called **Buccaneer Rock**, dedicated to Captain William Dampier and his ship, the *Roebuck*.

If you're lucky enough to be in Broome on a cloudless night when a full moon rises you can witness the **Staircase to the Moon**. The reflections of the moon from the rippling mud flats creates a wonderful golden-stairway effect, best seen from the town beach. The effect is in fact most dramatic about two days after the full moon, as the moon rises after the sky has had a chance to darken. A lively evening market is held on this evening, and the town takes on a carnival air. Check with the tourist bureau for exact dates and times.

Organised Tours & Cruises

There are a number of tours to make in an around Broome. The *Spirit of Broom* (☎ (091) 93 5025) is a small hovercraft which makes daily one-hour flights aroun Roebuck Bay ($45), stopping at variou points of interest.

Out on the water, you can twilight cruis on an original pearl lugger, the *Dampier*, o a replica lugger, the *Willie*, or on a magnifi cent yacht, *Starsand*; all cost $40 an provide beer, wine and nibbles.

There are also some good guided bush walks. Paul Foulkes (☎ (091) 92 1371 concentrates on environmental feature close to Broome, such as the palaeontologic ally important dinosaur footprints ($10), th mangroves ($20), remnant rainforest ($20 a hidden valley ($20) and the coast fror Broome to Cable Beach ($50).

Other unusual options include Harley Davidson motorcycle tours with th incomparable Norm; ask at the touris bureau.

Festivals

Broome is somewhat of a festival centre Some of the many excuses to party include

Shinju Matsuri (Festival of the Pearl) Thi excellent festival commemorates the early pearlin years and the town's multicultural heritage. When th festival is on, around August and September, the tow population swells and accommodation is hard to fin – book ahead. Many traditional Japanese ceremonie are featured, including the Bon Festival. It's we worth trying to juggle your itinerary to be in Broom at this time. It concludes with a beach concert and huge fireworks display. Don't miss the dragon-bo races.

Mango Festival In late November the town cele brates that sticky sweet fruit loved by some b deplored by mothers with small children.

Stompem Ground Late September (in even year, is the time to be in Broome if you wish to listen great music, witness colourful dance and imbib ancient culture – this is the time for Stompem Groun the celebration of Aboriginal culture by the Broom Musicians Aboriginal Corporation. Hail the Bran Nu Dae with the Kimberley's original people. For detai phone (☎ (091) 92 2550.

Places to Stay

Camping Even camping sites can become impossible to find in popular Broome, nor is it particularly cheap. The *Roebuck Bay Caravan Park* (☎ (091) 92 1366) is conveniently central. *Lamb's Vacation Village* (☎ (091) 92 1057), Port Drive, has tent sites for $10 for two and on-site vans for $30. The *Broome Caravan Park* (☎ (091) 92 1776), on the Great Northern Highway four km from town, has tent sites and on-site vans.

Hostels Cheap beds in Broome are scarce but there are two hostel choices. On Bagot St, close to the centre and just a short stagger from the airport, is *Broome's Last Resort* (☎ (091) 93 5000). It's adequate and has a pool, large kitchen and courtesy bus. Theft by outsiders seems to be a problem – in my short stay I had my wallet lifted (the first time in 20 years of travel) and there were several reports of other instances. The accommodation is not cheap – dorm beds are $12 and twins/doubles are $36 for two, all with shared facilities. One plus: the resort offers excellent camping tours into the Kimberley (see Devonian Reef National Parks).

Also close to the centre is the *Broome Bunkhouse* (☎ (091) 92 1221), part of the Roebuck Bay Hotel, on Napier Terrace. Accommodation is rock-bottom, with beds in 20-bed dorms for $12 and four-bed units for $48. The mattresses look as though they saw service on the Western Front in WW I and if there's a band playing at the pub you have the equivalent of pre-dawn artillery fire. There is also a hostel at Cable Beach (see that section for details).

Hotels, Motels & Resorts During school holidays and other peak times finding accommodation can be extremely difficult, so book ahead if possible.

The once legendary *Roebuck Bay Hotel/Motel* (☎ (091) 92 1221), on the corner of Carnarvon St and Napier Terrace in Chinatown, has motel units. The pool is the hotel's saving grace.

The *Continental Hotel* (☎ (091) 92 1002) is a modern place on Weld St, at the corner of Louis St, with rooms from $85 a double. The *Mangrove Motel* (☎ (091) 92 1303) is down near the water, between the Continental and Chinatown. *Forrest House* (☎ (091) 93 5067), at 59 Forrest St, has small double rooms with fan for $45, including breakfast.

The *Roebuck Bay Resort* (☎ (091) 92 1898), on Hopton St, has studio units and the *Auski Tropical Holiday Resort* (☎ (091) 92 1183), in Milner St, has a swimming pool and all mod cons.

One new place is the *Ocean Lodge* (☎ (091) 93 7700), on Cable Beach Rd near the Port Drive turn-off. It has backpackers' rooms for $12 per person and twin rooms for $60. On Saturday evening they have an Aussie tucker night.

Places to Eat

Light Meals & Fast Food Finding a place to stay in Broome may be a hassle but eating out is no sweat at all. *D'Jango's*, on Carnarvon St, has good, healthy food such as vegetarian pasta and excellent smoothies. Lots of people end up there for coffee after the movies at Sun Pictures. *Bloom's*, across the road, serves a very generous cappuccino and has excellent croissants.

Mango Jack's, on Hamersley St, has hamburgers and sandwiches, fish & chips and the like. In the same little shopping centre as Mango Jack's there's *Chicken World* and *Rocky's Pizza*, which turns out pretty average pizzas.

There's an average, pricey bakery in Chinatown, on the corner of Carnarvon and Short Sts. The Seaview shopping centre also has a bakery, as well as Broome's biggest supermarket, Charlie Carters.

Pubs & Restaurants The Roebuck Bay Hotel/Motel has the *Pearlers Restaurant*, an alfresco dining area, and the *Black Pearl*.

Chin's Chinese restaurant, on Hamersley St near Mango Jack's, has a variety of dishes from all over Asia. Prices range from $7 for an Indonesian nasi goreng to $12 for other dishes. There's a popular takeaway section.

Other Chinese specialists are *Wing's*, on Napier Terrace; *Tong's*, just around the corner; *Son Ming* on Carnarvon St; and *Murray's Asian Affair*, on Dampier Terrace.

Annelies is a Swiss restaurant on Napier Terrace near the Roebuck, and according to the locals it's quite a good place. The *Tea House*, situated in a mud-brick building with an outdoor dining area, is at the end of Saville St. It has a great variety of Thai seafood dishes.

Other more expensive places include the restaurants in the resorts and motels. The Continental Hotel has both a good bistro and a decent restaurant, the *Port Light*. The latter serves delectable meals in the $12 to $18 range. The Mangrove reputedly has the best seafood restaurant in town, *Charters*.

Entertainment

In Chinatown, *Sun Pictures*, the open-air cinema dating from 1916, is near Short St and has a program of surprisingly recent releases. It is probably the longest-running picture garden in the world.

Despite an attempt to improve its appearance the *Roebuck Bay Hotel* still rocks along – just stand clear of the occasional fight.

Nightclubs in town include the *Nippon Inn* in Dampier Terrace and *Tokyo Joe's* in Napier Terrace.

Getting There & Away

Air Ansett flies to Broome regularly on its Perth to Darwin route. From Perth the fare is $469, from Darwin $344, from Kununurra $255 and from Port Hedland $201. Ansett's office (☎ (091) 93 5444) is on the corner of Barker and Weld Sts.

Bus Greyhound Pioneer operates through Broome on its Perth to Darwin route. Typical fares from Broome include $185 to Perth, $55 to Port Hedland, $22 to Derby and $160 to Darwin. Its office (☎ (091) 92 1561) is at Broome Travel on Hamersley St.

Car Rental Hertz and Avis have rent-a-car

Broome Bird-Watching

The RAOU Broome Bird Observatory (☎ (091) 93 5600), 18 km from Broome on Roebuck Bay, is a bird-watcher's delight. Officially opened in 1990, it rates as one of Australia's top four nonbreeding grounds for migrant Arctic waders – the others are Rotamah Island in Victoria, the Barren Grounds in NSW and Eyre, also in WA.

Each year Roebuck Bay receives 150,000 migrants from the northern hemisphere. The observatory is a good base from which to seek out birds in a variety of habitats – mangroves, salt marshes, plains, pindan woodland, tidal flats and beaches. Phone to find out the best viewing times. Over 250 species of birds have been spotted in the region, with migratory waders (shore birds) seen there in abundance as well as over 20 species of raptors (birds of prey), including the white-breasted sea eagle, osprey and the rare grey falcon.

The RAOU organises one- to three-hour tours to see birds of the bush, shore and mangroves. In October you can take a walk to see the waders which have just arrived from Siberia; the cost for the one-hour walk is $8 and binoculars are provided. If you are around at the time of banding you can join in and help.

The observatory is along Crab Creek Rd (not signposted), but there is a dry-weather track off the Great Northern Highway about 3.5 km north of town. You can camp near the observatory for $8 for one ($12 for two; power $1 extra), or there are twin units for $36, and a five-bed, self-contained chalet for $50 for two ($10 each extra person).

George Swann of Kimberley Birdwatching (☎ (091) 92 1246) takes trips around town, out to Roebuck Bay, Crab Creek and the local sewage plant. He is almost guaranteed to correctly identify any species of wader you care to point out. To the uninitiated, the waders on the beach look pretty much the same. But if you wish to distinguish between the eastern curlew, sanderling, sandpiper, Asian dowitcher, greenshank, Mongolian plover, red-capped plover and whimbrel you will not be disappointed.

State-of-the-art watching equipment is provided, included tripod-mounted telescopes. Based on a minimum of four persons the cost of a three-hour shore-bird trip is $38, a five-hour Broome environs trip is $64 and an eight-hour creek tour is $100. ■

lesks at the airport but there are better deals available if you just want something for popping around town or out to the beach. Suzuki jeeps are popular. Topless Rentals ☎ (091) 93 5017), on Hunter St, and Woody's (☎ (091) 92 1791), Napier Terrace, are local operations.

Getting Around

To/From the Airport There are taxis to take you from the airport to your hotel. However, the airport is so close to the centre that backpackers staying at the Last Resort, or elsewhere close by, may decide to walk.

Bus There's an hourly Broome Coachlines bus (☎ (091) 92 1068) between the town and Cable Beach. The one-way fare is $2 or you can get 10 fares for $15. The bus goes to all levels of accommodation in town.

Bicycle Cycling is the best way to see the area. There are a number of places that hire bicycles for $6 to $12 a day, including the backpackers' places. The Broome Cycle Centre, on the corner of Hamersley and Frederick Sts, hires bikes, does repairs and gives good advice. Broome is an easy area to ride around; it's flat and you'll usually have no problem riding out to Cable Beach (about seven km) as long as it's not too windy. Stay on the roads, though, or your tyres might be punctured by thorns.

AROUND BROOME

Cable Beach

Six km from town is Cable Beach, the most popular swimming beach in Broome. It's a classic – white sand and turquoise water as far as the eye can see. You can hire surfboards and other beach and water equipment on the beach – parasailing ($35 to $40) is always popular. The northern side beyond the rock is a popular nude-bathing area. You can also take vehicles (other than motorbikes) onto this part of the beach, although at high tide access is limited because of the rocks, so take care not to get stranded.

Two companies, Red Sun and Ships of the Desert, operate camel rides along the beach;

Around Broome

the best time is at sunset. The cost is $20 per hour; book at the tourist bureau.

Also on Cable Beach Rd is the **Broome Crocodile Park**. It's open daily from 10 am to 5 pm, May to November; reduced hours for the rest of the year. There are guided tours at 3 pm weekdays; admission is $9 (children $5, family $22).

The long sweep of Cable Beach eventually ends at **Gantheaume Point**, seven km south of Broome. The cliffs there have been eroded into curious shapes. At extremely low tides dinosaur tracks 120 million years old are exposed. At other times you can inspect casts of the footprints on the cliff top. Anastasia's Pool is an artificial rock pool on the northern side of the point; it fills at high tide.

Willie Creek Pearl Farm This pearl farm is 35 km north of Broome, off the Cape Leveque Rd. It offers a rare chance to see a working pearl farm and is worth the trip (cost of entrance is $12.50). During the Wet the road is open only to 4WD vehicles. There are daily tours from Broome ($40) with Broome Coachlines (☎ (091) 92 1068).

Places to Stay & Eat The *Cable Beach Caravan Park* (☎ (091) 92 2066) is at the beach, and has tent sites from $15. The well-positioned and quiet *Broome Backpackers*, on Lullfitz Drive in Cable Beach, has twins at $32 for two; enquire at the Last Resort in Broome (☎ (091) 93 5000). The very up-market *Cable Beach Club* (☎ (091) 92 2505) is a beautifully designed place covering a large area, although it's not right on the beach.

The resort has an incredibly expensive *restaurant*, and a much cheaper place, *Lord Mac's*, which is a good vantage point for the sunset but not for the food. For a great intimate breakfast try *Carol's Munchies*, which overlooks beautiful Cable Beach.

Dampier Peninsula

It's about 200 km from the turn-off nine km out of Broome to the Cape Leveque Lighthouse at the tip of the Dampier Peninsula. This flora and fauna paradise is a great spot for free humpback whale-watching.

Some 96 km from Broome is the *County Downs Homestead* (☎ (091) 92 4911) which has camp sites, showers and ablution blocks. About halfway (120 km) is a diversion to the **Beagle Bay Aboriginal Community** (☎ (091) 92 4913) which has a beautiful church in the middle of a green. Inside is an altar stunningly decorated with mother-of-pearl. A fee of $5 is charged for entry into the community; petrol and diesel are available seven days.

Just before Cape Leveque is **Lombadina Aboriginal Community** (☎ (091) 92 4942) which has a church built from mangrove wood. One-day and overnight mud-crabbing and traditional fishing tours are available; contact the Broome tourist bureau for details. Petrol and diesel are available every day except Sunday.

Cape Leveque itself, about 200 km from Broome, has a lighthouse and two wonderful beaches. Beyond it is **One Arm Point**, another Aboriginal community (☎ (091) 9. 4930). Take note that the communities won' want you to stay on their land, but if you wan to see their churches or buy something from their shops they will be helpful. Permission to visit other areas must be obtained i advance. Check with the Broome touris bureau about road conditions before settin, out.

Organised Tours Halls Creek & Bungl Bungle Tours (☎ (091) 68 6217), Over th Top Safaris (☎ (091) 93 7700), Flaktra (☎ (091) 92 1487) and Pearl Coast 4W (☎ (091) 93 5786) all operate tours to th peninsula.

Places to Stay There is accommodation a *Kooljaman* (☎ (091) 92 4970), ranging from backpackers' accommodation ($10), a self contained unit, chalets, bark huts an camping. Bush-tucker and mud-crabbin, tours are available, as are all types of vehicl fuel, except LPG.

The Kimberley

The rugged Kimberley, at the northern en of WA, is one of Australia's last frontiers Despite enormous advances in the pas decade this is still a little-travelled and ver remote area of great rivers and magnificen scenery. The Kimberley suffers from cli matic extremes – heavy rains in the We followed by searing heat in the Dry – but th irrigation projects in the north-east hav made great changes to the region.

Nevertheless, rivers and creeks can ris rapidly following heavy rainfall and becom impassable torrents within 15 minutes Unless it's a very brief storm, it's quite likel that the watercourses will remain impassabl for some days. The Fitzroy River ca become so swollen at times that after two o three days of rain it grows from its norma 100-metre width to over 10 km. River an creek crossings on the Great Norther

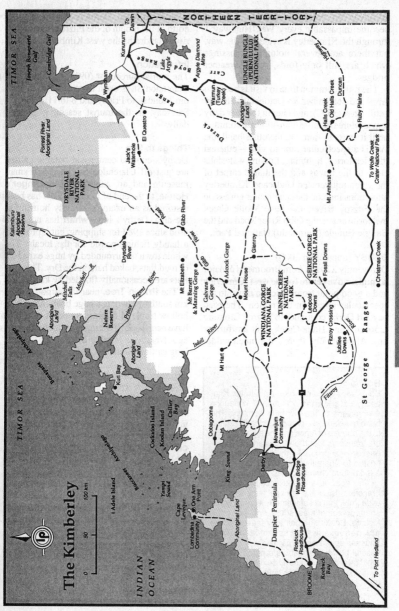

Highway on both sides of Halls Creek become impassable every Wet. Highway 1 through the Kimberley is sealed all the way, but there are several notorious crossings which are still only fords, not all-weather bridges.

The most common time to visit is between April and September. By October it's already getting hot (35°C), and later in the year daily temperatures of more than 40°C are common until it starts to rain. On the other hand, the Wet is a spectacular time to visit – ethereal thunderstorms, lightning, flowing waterfalls close to the towns and the magic carpet of the green rejuvenated landscape. Kimberley attractions include the spectacular gorges on the Fitzroy River, the huge Wolfe Creek meteorite crater, the Gibb River Road and the Bungle Bungle (Purnululu) National Park.

DERBY (population 3000)

Derby, only 220 km from Broome, is a major administrative centre for the west Kimberley and a good point from which to travel to the spectacular gorges in the region. The road beyond Derby continues to Fitzroy Crossing (256 km) and Halls Creek (288 km further on). Alternatively, there's the much wilder

---

Boabs

Boab trees are a common sight in the Kimberley and also in the Victoria and Fitzmaurice river basins of the Northern Territory. The boab or *Adansonia gregorii* is closely related to the baobab of Africa and the eight varieties of *Adansonia* found on the island of Madagascar. It's probable that baobab seeds floated to Australia from Africa, then developed unique characteristics.

The boab is a curious-looking tree with branches rising like witches' fingers from a wide trunk that is sometimes elegantly bottle shaped, sometimes squat and powerful-looking. Boabs shed all their leaves during dry periods, further accentuating their unusual appearance. Evidently it's a successful policy, for boabs are noted for their rapid growth, hardiness and extreme longevity. Derby has some fine boabs, including a number transplanted along Loch St. ■

Gibb River Road. Derby is on King Sound, north of the mouth of the Fitzroy, the mighty river that drains the west Kimberley region.

Information

The tourist bureau (☎ (091) 91 1426), at 1 Clarendon St, is open from 8.30 am to 4.30 pm Monday to Friday and 8 to 11.30 am on Saturday. In the tourist season it is open daily.

Things to See

Derby's cultural centre and botanic garden are just off Clarendon St. There's a small museum and art gallery in **Wharfinger's House**, at the end of Loch St. This has been restored as an example of early housing in the area. Derby's lofty **wharf** has not been used since 1983 for shipping, but it provides a handy fishing possie for the locals. The whole town is surrounded by huge expanses of mud flats, baked hard in the Dry. The mud flats are occasionally flooded by king tides.

The **Prison Tree**, near the airport, seven km south of town, is a huge boab tree with a hollow trunk 14 metres around. It is said to have been used as a temporary lock-up years ago. Nearby is **Myall's Bore**, a 120-metre-long cattle trough.

Organised Tours & Cruises

From Derby there are flights over King Sound to the BHP-owned **Koolan** and **Cockatoo islands**. You can't land there unless invited by a resident, but scenic flights are available to the adjoining islands of the **Buccaneer Archipelago**. Aerial Enterprises (☎ (091) 91 1132) and Derby Air Services (☎ (091) 93 1375) provide two-hour flights for about $110 to the Buccaneer Archipelago; minimum of four. Buccaneer Sea Safaris (☎ (091) 91 1991) does extended tours up the Kimberley coast (including the horizontal falls of Talbot Bay) in a 30-foot aluminium mono-hull. Bush Track Safaris (☎ (091) 91 1547) operates four- to ten-day tours into the remote Walcott Inlet area.

Places to Stay

The *Derby Caravan Park* (☎ (091) 93 1055),

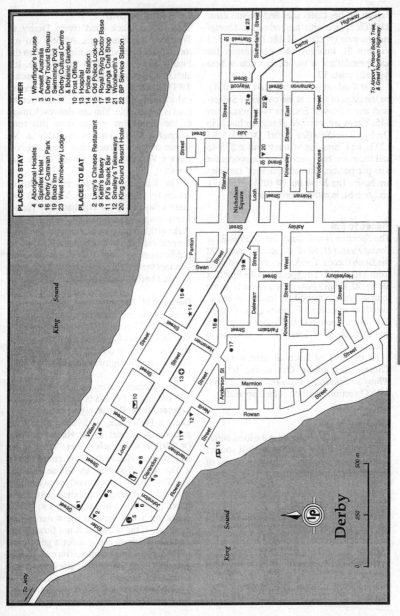

PLACES TO STAY
4 Aboriginal Hostels
6 Spinifex Hotel
16 Derby Caravan Park
19 Boab Inn
23 West Kimberley Lodge

PLACES TO EAT
2 Lwoy's Chinese Restaurant
9 Keith's Bakery
11 PJ's Snack Bar
12 Smalley's Takeaways
20 King Sound Resort Hotel

OTHER
1 Wharfinger's House
3 Ansett Australia
5 Derby Tourist Bureau
7 Swimming Pool
8 Derby Cultural Centre
   & Botanic Garden
10 Post Office
13 Hospital
14 Police Station
15 Old Police Lock-up
17 Royal Flying Doctor Base
18 Ngunga Craft Shop
21 Woolworth's
22 BP Service Station

Derby

WESTERN AUSTRALIA

Rowan St, has camp sites and on-site vans. It is a nice place with free barbecues. *Aboriginal Hostels* (☎ (091) 91 1867), at 233-235 Villiers St, charges $10 per person for accommodation; a two-course dinner here typically costs $7.

West Kimberley Lodge (☎ (091) 91 1031), on the edge of town at the corner of Sutherland and Stanwell Sts, has twin rooms for $45. There are a couple of regular hotels in Derby. The *Spinifex Hotel* (☎ (091) 91 1233), on Clarendon St, has rooms at $35/45 and there are backpackers' triple rooms for $10 per person. The backpackers' facilities are basic. The *Boab Inn* (☎ (091) 91 1044), on Loch St, is rather more motel-like.

Places to Eat

The *Spinifex Hotel*, *Boab Inn* and the *King Sound Resort Hotel* all do counter meals. At the Boab there's a wide choice of good food from $10 to $15. The specials at the Spinifex are $5.50. *Keith's Bakery*, just down from the tourist bureau, is good for lunch and has an excellent selection of sandwiches. *Griffo's Takeaway*, open late, is another place for a quick meal, as is *Smalley's Takeaways* in Clarendon St.

At the end of Loch St there's *Lwoy's Chinese Restaurant*. Out at the jetty is *Wharf's Restaurant & Takeaways* which has a BYO section; seafood is their speciality.

Entertainment

Bands can usually be heard at the local hotels on Thursday, Friday and Saturday. If you are lucky you may be able to make it to one of the legendary marsh parties.

Getting There & Away

Ansett will whisk you to Port Hedland ($224 one way), Perth ($456) or Darwin ($296). Ansett's office (☎ (091) 91 1266) is at 14 Loch St.

Greyhound Pioneer stops in Derby at the tourist bureau. Typical fares are $22 to Broome, $78 to Kununurra, $209 to Perth and $143 to Darwin.

GIBB RIVER ROAD

This is the 'back road' from Derby to Wyndham or Kununurra. At 667 km it's more direct by several hundred km than the Fitzroy Crossing to Halls Creek route. It's almost all dirt, although it doesn't require a 4WD when it has been recently graded (which is not always the case). In the Wet the road is impassable. You can also reach many of the Kimberley gorges from this road without a 4WD. Fuel is available at Mt House and Mt Barnett, and Durack River (Jack's Waterhole) and Home Valley stations.

The Kimberley gorges are the major reason for taking this route. You could also make a day trip to the Windjana and Tunnel Creek gorges (see Devonian Reef National Parks in this section). Get a copy of *The Gibb River Road* from tourist bureaus. There's no public transport along the Gibb River Road – in fact there's very little traffic of any sort, so don't bother trying to hitch.

Derby to Mt Barnett

From Derby the bitumen extends only 62 km. It's 119 km to the Windjana Gorge (21 km) and Tunnel Creek (51 km) turn-off and you can continue down that turn-off to the Great Northern Highway near Fitzroy Crossing.

The Lennard River bridge is crossed at 122 km and at 190 km is the turn-off to the **Lennard River Gorge**, eight km off the road along a 4WD track. At 246 km there's the signposted turn-off to **Mt House Station** (☎ (091) 91 4649), where there's fuel, stores and accommodation (by prior arrangement).

The turn-off to **Adcock Gorge** is at 267 km. This gorge is five km off the road and is good for swimming, with some fine rocks for jumping or diving off, although you should check for rocks beneath the water before doing so. If the waterfall is not flowing too fiercely, climb up above it for a good view of the surrounding country. You can camp at Adcock Gorge although the site is rocky and there's little shade.

Galvans Gorge is less than a km off the road, at 286 km. The small camp site here has some good shade trees, and the gorge itself has a swimming hole.

Mt Barnett & Manning Gorge

The Aboriginal-owned and run Mt Barnett Station is at the 315-km point. There's a roadhouse there (ice is available) and a small general store. It's also the access point for Manning Gorge, which lies seven km off the road along an easy dirt track. There's an entry fee of $4 per person, and this covers you for camping.

The camp site is right by the waterhole, but the best part of the gorge is about a 1¼-hour walk along the far bank – walk around the right of the waterhole to pick up the track, which is marked with empty drink cans strung up in the trees. It's a strenuous walk and, because the track runs inland from the gorge, you should carry some drinking water.

After the hot and sweaty walk, you are rewarded with this most beautiful gorge. It has a waterfall and some high rocks for daredevils.

Mt Barnett to Kununurra

First up after Mt Barnett is the turn-off to the **Barnett River Gorge** at 328 km. This is another good swimming spot, and if you scan the lower level of the cliff face on the far side you should be able to spot a number of Aboriginal paintings.

The **Mt Elizabeth Station** (☎ (091) 91 4644) lies 30 km off the road at the 338-km mark. Homestead accommodation is available but this must be arranged in advance.

At 419 km you come to the turn-off to the spectacular **Mitchell Plateau** (162 km) and the **Kalumburu Aboriginal Mission** (267 km). This is remote, 4WD territory and should not be travelled without adequate preparation; an entry permit is required.

There's some magnificent scenery between the Kalumburu turn-off and Jack's Waterhole on the Durack River Station at 542 km. Apart from fuel, there's also homestead accommodation or camping. The owners, the Sinnamon family, run a number of tours from Durack River Station.

At 599 km you get some excellent views of the **Cockburn Ranges** off to the south, and shortly after is the turn-off to *Home Valley Station* (☎ (091) 61 4322), which has camping ($5) and homestead accommodation.

The large **Pentecost River** is forded at 610 km, but this crossing can be dodgy if there's any amount of water in the river. During the Dry it poses no problems.

El Questro is another station offering a variety of accommodation and riverside camping ($5); it lies 16 km off the road at the 634-km mark. This is also the access point for the **Chamberlain Gorge**, 16 km from the turn-off.

The last attraction on the road to Kununurra is **Emma Gorge** at 645 km. A pleasant camping area lies two km off the road, and from here it's about a 40-minute walk to the spectacular gorge. This gorge is close enough to Kununurra to make it a popular weekend escape for residents of that town.

At 667 km you finally hit bitumen road again, and Wyndham lies 48 km to the north, while it's 52 km east to Kununurra.

Organised Tours

Kununurra's Desert Inn and Kununurra Backpackers run five-day camping trips along the road for $395; these are excellent value and well worth doing. The Desert Inn also operates a two-day camping and walking tour to El Questro on demand ($150).

There are guided trips to the Mitchell Plateau, about 500 km north-west of Kununurra. Highlights include waterfalls, Surveyor's Pool, the *Livistonia eastonii* palm and ancient Wandjina art sites with unique headdress paintings which are typical of Kimberley-style art.

DEVONIAN REEF NATIONAL PARKS

The west Kimberley boasts three national parks, based on gorges which were once part of a western coral 'great barrier reef' in the Devonian era, 350 million years ago. The magnificent **Geikie Gorge** is just 18 km north of Fitzroy Crossing and the Great

WESTERN AUSTRALIA

Northern Highway. Part of the gorge, on the Fitzroy River, is in a small national park only eight km by three km. During the Wet the river rises nearly 17 metres and in the Dry the river stops flowing, leaving only a series of waterholes.

The vegetation around this beautiful gorge is dense and there is also much wildlife, including freshwater crocodiles, wallaroos and the rare black-footed wallaby. Sawfish and stingrays, usually only found in or close to the sea, can also be seen in the river. Visitors are not permitted to go anywhere except along the prescribed part of the west bank, where there is an excellent 1.5-km walking track.

During the April to November Dry there's a 1½-hour boat trip up the river at 9 am and 3 pm. It costs $12 and covers 16 km of the gorge (children $2). There's a weekday bus (☎ (091) 91 5155) to Geikie from Fitzroy Crossing at 8 am which connects with the morning trip. It costs $8 return (children $5).

You can go to the gorge with Darlngunaya Aboriginal guides who show you a lot more than just rocks and water. These Bunuba people reveal secrets of bush tucker, stories of the region and Aboriginal culture. The trip, which includes transport to the gorge, the river trip and lunch beside the Fitzroy River, costs $60.

Alternatively, you can fly over the gorge with Geikie Air Charter (☎ (091) 91 5068) for about $50.

You can visit the spectacular formations of Windjana Gorge and Tunnel Creek from the Gibb River Road, or make a detour on the Leopold Station Rd off the main highway between Fitzroy Crossing and Derby, which only adds about 40 km to the distance.

The walls at the **Windjana Gorge** soar 90 metres above the Lennard River, which rushes through in the Wet but becomes just a series of pools in the Dry. More than likely the deafening screech of corellas and the persistent horseflies will keep you out of the gorge during the middle of the day. Three km from the river are the ruined remains of **Lillimilura**, an early homestead and, from

1893, police station. Nightly camping fees for this gorge are $5 per person (children $1).

Tunnel Creek is a 750-metre-long tunnel which the creek has cut right through a spur of the Napier Range. The tunnel is generally from three to 15 metres wide and you can walk all the way along it. You'll need a good light and sturdy shoes; be prepared to wade through very cold chest-deep water in places. Don't attempt it during the Wet, as the creek may flood suddenly. Halfway through, a collapse has created a shaft up to the top of the range.

Broome's Last Resort hostel (☎ (091) 93 5000) operates popular two-day trips combining Windjana and Tunnel Creek with Geikie Gorge, a good way of seeing three sites in one trip; cost $168. (There have been several recommendations for these tours.) Day trips out to Tunnel Creek and Windjana Gorge can be made from Fitzroy Crossing with Kimberley Safaris.

Jundumurra ('Pigeon')

Windjana Gorge, Tunnel Creek and Lillimilura were the scene of the adventures of an Aboriginal tracker called Jundumurra, nicknamed 'Pigeon'. In November 1894 Pigeon shot two police colleagues and then led a band of dissident Aborigines, skilfully evading search parties for over two years. In the meantime he killed another four men, until in early 1897 he was trapped and killed in Tunnel Creek. He and his small band had hidden in many of the seemingly inaccessible gullies of the adjoining Napier Range. Get hold of a copy of the *Pigeon Heritage Trail* from the Derby or Broome tourist bureaus ($1.50).

FITZROY CROSSING (population 1100)

A tiny settlement where the Great Northern Highway crosses the Fitzroy River, this is another place from which you can get to the gorges and waterholes of the area. The old town site is on Russ St, north-east of the present town. The Crossing Inn, near Brooking Creek, is the oldest pub in the Kimberley.

Places to Stay & Eat

The *Tarunda Caravan Park* (☎ (091) 91 5004), in town, is a reasonable if dusty place, where powered camp sites cost $14 for two. The *Crossing Inn & Caravan Park*

(☎ (091) 91 5080), by the river crossing, has cabins and ordinary motel rooms. It can get pretty noisy as there is a rather colourful, if a little unsavoury, bar next door.

The *Fitzroy River Lodge & Caravan Park* (☎ (091) 91 5141), two km east of town on the banks of the Fitzroy River, is the pick of the bunch and probably the best camp site along the Broome to Kununurra stretch. A camp site is $13 for two and you are allowed to use the pool for free. Air-con safari tents cost $60/73, while motel units cost $80/95.

In the Old Post Office on Geikie Gorge Rd, about four km from town, you'll find *Darlngunaya Backpackers* (☎ (091) 91 5140); dorm beds are $10. All backpackers get picked up and returned to the bus stop at the roadhouse.

It is cheaper to prepare food for yourself in this town. If your margarine is runny and the cheese you bought the day before stinks then the *Homestead* in the Fitzroy River Lodge does reasonable meals.

HALLS CREEK (population 1300)

Halls Creek, in the centre of the Kimberley and on the edge of the Great Sandy Desert, was traditionally the land of the Jaru and Kija people. The graziers took over in the 1870s and virtually turned these people into slave labourers on the stations. When the stations were sold, about a hundred years later, the Aboriginal people drifted to the nearby town and its associated boredom and alcohol. The region was the site of the 1885 gold rush, the first in WA. The gold soon petered out and today the town is a cattle centre, 14 km from the original site where some crumbling remains can still be seen. There's an Aboriginal art shop in the town where you can often see carvers at work making some high-quality artefacts.

Five km east of Halls Creek and then about 1.5 km off the road there's the natural **China Wall** – so called because it resembles the Great Wall of China. This subvertical quartz vein is short but very picturesquely situated.

Halls Creek **Old Town** is a great place for fossicking. All that remains of the once bus-tling mining town are the ant-bed and spinifex walls of the old post office, the cemetery and a huge bottle pile where a pub once stood. 'Old Town' is in fact the general term for the hilly area behind Halls Creek and gold might be found anywhere there. You can swim in **Caroline Pool**, **Sawpit Gorge** and **Palm Springs**.

Although Halls Creek is a comfortable enough little place it's as well to remember that it sits on the edge of a distinctly inhospitable stretch of country.

Places to Stay

The *Halls Creek Caravan Park* (☎ (091) 68 6169), on Roberta Ave towards the airport, has tent sites ($5). Opposite is the *Kimberley Hotel* (☎ (091) 68 6101), which has a variety of rooms from $60/73 and is currently offering backpackers' accommodation at $20. This hotel best exhibits both the rough and smooth sides of this frontier town.

The *Shell Roadhouse* (☎ (091) 68 6060) and the *Halls Creek Motel* (☎ (091) 68 6001), both on the Great Northern Highway, are other options.

Places to Eat

The *Kimberley Hotel* has a pleasantly casual bar with standard counter meals at $10. You can eat out at the tables on the grass. Inside there's a surprisingly swish restaurant with smorgasbord meals at $14. The *Swagman* and *Poinciana* roadhouses both have takeaway and restaurant facilities.

Getting There & Away

It's 371 km north-east to Kununurra, 555 km west to Derby. Greyhound Pioneer passes through Halls Creek early in the morning (northbound) and late at night (southbound).

WOLFE CREEK CRATER NATIONAL PARK

The 835-metre-wide and 50-metre-deep Wolfe Creek meteorite crater is the second largest in the world. To the local Jaru Aboriginal people, the crater, which they call Kandimalal, marks the spot where a snake emerged from the desert.

The turn-off to the crater and Wolfe Creek Crater National Park is 16 km out of Halls Creek towards Fitzroy Crossing and from there it's 130 km by unsealed road to the south. It's accessible without 4WD, and limited supplies and fuel *may* be available at the nearby Carranya Roadhouse (but you can't rely on this being the case). If you can't handle one more outback road you can fly over the crater from Halls Creek for $90 with the local operators – Oasis Air (☎ (091) 68 6088), Kingfisher Aviation (☎ (091) 68 6162) and Crocodile Air (☎ (091) 68 6250).

From Carranya the road, known as the Tanami Track, goes all the way to Alice Springs nearly 900 km away.

BUNGLE BUNGLE (PURNULULU) NATIONAL PARK

The Bungle Bungles are an amazing spectacle which shouldn't be missed – spectacular rounded rock towers, striped like tigers in alternate bands of orange (silica) and black (lichen). The only catch is that the range is hard to get to and because of the fragile nature of the rock formations you are not allowed to climb them.

Echidna Chasm in the north or **Cathedral Gorge** in the south are only about a one-hour walk from the car park at the road's end. However, the soaring **Piccaninny Gorge** is an 18-km round trip that takes eight to 10 hours return to walk. Access to the park costs $11 per adult and $1 for each child; this entitles you to seven nights in the park and fuel for campfires. The restricted gorges in the northern part of the park can only be seen from the air, but they too are a spectacular sight.

Scenic Flights

As the range is so vast, flights and helicopter rides over the Bungles are popular – it's money well spent. The chopper rides cost $115 for a 45-minute flight from Bellburn camp site, or $125 in a faster helicopter from Turkey Creek (Warmun) Roadhouse, on the main highway. This latter flight is a popular option for people without a 4WD. The chopper rides, operated by Heliwork WA

(part of Slingair), are most impressive because they fly right in, among and over the deep, narrow gorges, while the light planes have to remain above 700 metres. Flights from Kununurra are $135 and they fly over Lake Argyle and the Argyle Diamond mine. Out of Halls Creek, the flights to the Bungles only are $100.

Places to Stay

From the main highway it's 55 km to a track junction known as Three Ways, from where it's eight km north to *Kurrajong Camp* and 15 km south to *Bellburn Creek Camp*. At Bellburn Creek Camp there's a ranger station. Fires are forbidden, so you'll need to have your own gas cooking equipment, and the only facilities are long-drop dunnies and a primitive shower set-up at Kurrajong Camp.

Getting There & Away

Although it's only 55 km to Three Ways from the Halls Creek to Kununurra road turn-off, the stretch requires a 4WD and takes two hours. From Three Ways it's another 20 km north to Echidna Chasm and 30 km south to Piccaninny Creek.

The best option if you don't have a 4WD is to take one of the tours from Kununurra. Kununurra Backpackers has popular two-day trips ($168), while East Kimberley Tours charges much the same if you are staying at Desert Inn Backpackers. The three-day option, which includes a lot more walking, is $240; a four-day trip is $350.

WYNDHAM (population 860)

Wyndham, a sprawling town, is suffering from Kununurra's boom in popularity but its **Five Rivers Lookout** on top of Mt Bastion is still a must. From there you can see the King, Pentecost, Durack, Forrest and Ord rivers enter the Cambridge Gulf. The view is particularly good at sunrise and sunset. Wyndham was the starting point for two record-breaking flights to England in 1931. It was also bombed by the Japanese in WW II. When the tide is right you can go down to the water's edge and observe (from a distance) large saltwater crocodiles.

The **Moochalabra Dam** is a popular fishing and picnic spot about 25 km away. Near the town there's a rather desolate and decrepit little **cemetery** where Afghani camel drivers were buried last century. Near the Moochalabra Dam, south of Wyndham, there are some Aboriginal paintings and another prison boab tree. The **Grotto** is a good swimming hole just off the Wyndham to Kununurra road. **Crocodile Hole** is further off the road and has a small population of freshwater crocs. Not far from Wyndham is a well-known bird sanctuary, Marlgu Billabong on Parry's Creek.

Places to Stay

The *Three Mile Caravan Park* (☎ (091) 61 1064) has tent sites. Rooms in the *Wyndham Town Hotel* (☎ (091) 61 1003), on O'Donnell St, cost $65/75, and you can try the *Wyndham Community Club* (☎ (091) 61 1130) for cheaper but more basic rooms.

KUNUNURRA (population 4100)

In the Miriwoong language, this region is known as 'gananoorrang' – Kununurra is the European version of this word. Founded in the 1960s, Kununurra is in the centre of the Ord River irrigation scheme and is quite a modern and bustling little town. In the past it was just a stopover on the main highway and there was little incentive to linger. That has all changed in recent years with the increase in tourism and there are now enough recreational activities, most of them water-based, to keep you busy for a week.

The town is also a popular place to look for work. The main picking season starts in May and ends about September. Ask at the Desert Inn, Kununurra Backpackers or the tourist bureau.

Information

The excellent Kununurra tourist bureau (☎ (091) 68 1177) on Coolibah Drive has information on the town and the Kimberley. It's open from 8 am to 5 pm daily. There's a

1½-hour time change between Kununurra and Katherine in the Northern Territory.

Things to See & Do

The **Waringarri Aboriginal Arts Centre** is on Speargrass Rd, at the turn-off to Kelly's Knob. There are good views of the irrigated fields from **Kelly's Knob Lookout**, close to the centre of town. During the Wet, distant thunderstorms are spectacular when viewed from there, although caution is needed as the Knob itself is frequently struck by lightning.

Lily Creek Lagoon (also called the Diversion Dam), an artificial lake beside the town, has plenty of bird life and several swimming spots. There's good fishing below the Lower Dam (watch for crocodiles) and also on the Ord River at **Ivanhoe Crossing**. If you're swimming there, be careful. **Hidden Valley**, only a couple of km from the centre of town, is a wonderful little national park with a steep gorge, some great views and a few short walking tracks.

The **Packsaddle Plains**, six km out of town, has a zebra rock gallery and a small wildlife park. Further along this road is **Packsaddle Falls**, popular for swimming.

About 250 km south of Kununurra is the huge **Argyle Diamond Mine** which produces around 35% of the world's diamonds, although most are only of industrial quality.

Organised Tours & Flights

Canoe trips on the Ord River, between Lake Argyle and the Diversion Dam, are very popular amongst travellers. A recommended operation, Kimberley Canoeing Experience (☎ 1800 805 010), has three-day self-guided tours for $80, with all gear supplied and transport to the dam included. The company also runs half-day guided trips which feature wildlife and bird-watching.

Kununurra Backpackers has one-hour white-water trips on the Lake Argyle spillway from the end of the Wet onwards. They're $20, or $35 if you need transport to and from Kununurra.

Kununurra Backpackers runs an exciting trip into Andy's Chasm in the Wet and early

WESTERN AUSTRALIA

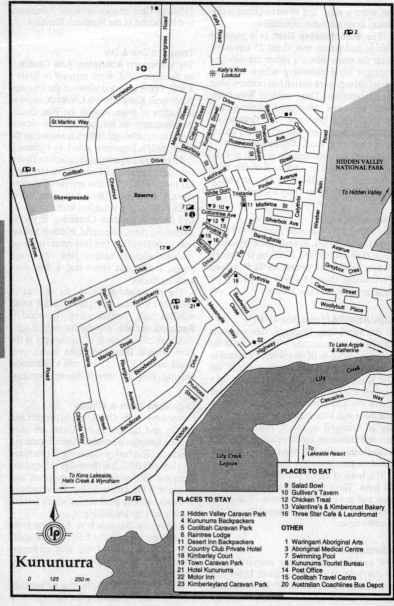

Kununurra

0   125   250 m

PLACES TO STAY

2 Hidden Valley Caravan Park
4 Kununurra Backpackers
5 Coolibah Caravan Park
6 Raintree Lodge
11 Desert Inn Backpackers
17 Country Club Private Hotel
18 Kimberley Court
19 Town Caravan Park
21 Hotel Kununurra
22 Motor Inn
23 Kimberleyland Caravan Park

PLACES TO EAT

9 Salad Bowl
10 Gulliver's Tavern
12 Chicken Treat
13 Valentine's & Kimbercrust Bakery
16 Three Star Cafe & Laundromat

OTHER

1 Waringarri Aboriginal Arts
3 Aboriginal Medical Centre
7 Swimming Pool
8 Kununurra Tourist Bureau
14 Post Office
15 Coolibah Travel Centre
20 Australian Coachlines Bus Depot

Dry – for $30 you can squeeze through rock passages, jump into the abyss and survive.

Barramundi is the major fishing attraction, but other fish are also caught. Half-day boat trips operated by Ultimate Adventures (☎ (091) 68 1610) and Kimberley Sport Fishing (☎ (091) 68 2752) cost $65 and up.

Triple J (☎ (091) 68 2682) operates high-speed boats along the Ord between Lake Argyle and Kununurra. These are a real thrill and pass through beautiful scenery. The cost is from $65 to $85 (including lunch and the bus trip out from Kununurra). Other operators on Lily Creek Lagoon are the *Lakeside Lady* and Triangle Tours ($35).

Flights over the Bungle Bungles are popular and cost $135 a person (discounts apply). They take about two hours and also fly over Lake Argyle, the Argyle and Bow River diamond projects and the irrigation area north of the town. Contact Alligator Airways (☎ (091) 68 1333) or Slingair (☎ (091) 69 1300) in Kununurra, Heliwork WA (☎ (091) 68 1811) in Turkey Creek or Ord Air Charters (☎ (091) 61 1335) in Wyndham.

Places to Stay

Camping Kununurra has a number of caravan parks, a couple of them by Lily Creek Lagoon, with tent sites from $10. The *Town Caravan Park* (☎ (091) 68 1763) is on Bloodwood Drive and has on-site vans for $45; the *Coolibah Caravan Park* (☎ (091) 68 1653) is on the corner of Ivanhoe Rd and Coolibah Drive; and *Kimberleyland* (☎ (091) 68 1280) is on the edge of the lagoon near town. The pick of the parks is *Kona Lakeside* (☎ (091) 68 1031), Lake View Drive, with tent sites for two at $10.

Hostels There are three hostels, each costing about $12 for a dorm bed. *Desert Inn Backpackers* (☎ (091) 68 2702) is on Tristania St, right opposite Gulliver's Tavern in the centre of town. This purpose-built complex has full facilities, including a spa pool. It's a friendly and popular place.

At 112 Nutwood Crescent is *Kununurra Backpackers* (☎ (091) 68 1711). It's in a couple of adjacent houses about five minutes walk from the centre of town. The shaded pool is a big drawcard, but kids aren't welcome.

The associate-YHA *Raintree Lodge* (☎ (091) 68 1372), on Coolibah Drive, doesn't get much business these days.

The *Country Club Private Hotel* (☎ (091) 68 1024), also on Coolibah Drive, has some cheap beds for $10, but no cooking facilities.

Hotels Hotel accommodation is expensive. The *Country Club Private Hotel* (☎ (091) 68 1024) is the cheapest, but at $47/57 a single/double for small air-con rooms with no facilities, even it is pretty overpriced. It does have a pool though. Another place is *Kimberley Court* (☎ (091) 68 1411), on the corner of River Fig Ave and Erythrina St.

The *Hotel Kununurra* (☎ (091) 68 1344), Messmate Way, is the town's main hotel. It has a motel section with rooms from $65/95.

Places to Eat

The *Three Star Cafe*, on Banksia St, offers takeaway tucker and light meals; *Valentine's Pizzeria* and the *Kimbercrust Bakery*, both on Cottontree Ave, are open daily. On Coolibah Drive, the *Salad Bowl* serves good salads, perfect accompaniments to its hamburgers, and there's also *Chicken Treat*, opposite the tourist bureau.

Standard counter meals are available at the *Hotel Kununurra* for $10, and there's also a more expensive dining room. *Gulliver's Tavern*, on the corner of Konkerberry Drive and Cottontree Ave, is a popular drinking place, and, although the counter meals are poor value, its George Room is quite good. The licensed *Chopsticks Restaurant* at the Country Club Private Hotel is about the best in town; main courses cost around $15. *Ivanhoe's Gallery Restaurant* in the Quality Inn is also good.

Getting There & Away

Air Ansett will fly you to Broome for $255 one way, Darwin for $178, and Perth for $571. Its office (☎ (091) 68 1444) is in the Charlie Carter shopping complex.

Ansett will fly you from Kununurra to Darwin or from Darwin to Broome for 50% of the normal fare on presentation of authorised discount cards. Note that there is currently a cheap one-way fare from Darwin to Kununurra on Wednesday ($102 all seasons).

Bus Greyhound Pioneer travels through Kununurra on its Darwin to Perth route. Typical fares are $78 to Derby, $47 to Halls Creek, $47 to Katherine and $85 to Darwin.

LAKE ARGYLE

Created by the Ord River Dam, Lake Argyle is the second biggest storage reservoir in Australia, holding nine times as much water as Sydney Harbour. Prior to its construction, there was too much water in the wet season and not enough in the Dry. By providing a regular water supply the dam has encouraged agriculture on a massive scale.

At the lake there's a **pioneer museum** in the old Argyle Homestead, moved here when its original site was flooded. The *Lake Argyle Tourist Village* has expensive rooms and camp sites. Boats depart from there for the huge lake each morning and afternoon. Downstream of the lake there is now green farmland. Encircling these flat lands are the small reddish mountains typical of the region. There are two cruises: the *Bowerbird* does the two-hour cruise ($22) and the *Silver Cobbler* the half-day cruise ($75).

Index

ABBREVIATIONS

ACT – Australian Capital Territory
NSW – New South Wales
NP – National Park

NT – Northern Territory
Qld – Queensland
SA – South Australia

Tas – Tasmania
WA – Western Australia
Vic – Victoria

MAPS

Adelaide (SA) 543
Adelaide Hills (SA) 557
Airlie Beach (Qld) 459
Albany (WA) 856
Alice Springs (NT) 343
    Around Alice Springs 356-357
    Central Alice Springs 348
    The Ghan (Old & New) 352
Australia
    Air Fares 119
    Principal Bus Routes 121
    Principal Railways 123
Australian Capital Territory 138

Ballarat (Vic) 760-761
    Central Ballarat 763
Barossa Valley (SA) 570
Bendigo (Vic) 771
    Central Bendigo 772
Brisbane (Qld) 382
    Central Brisbane 388-389
Broken Hill (NSW) 290
Broome (WA) 891
    Around Broome 895
Burnie (Tas) 662
Burra (SA) 575
Byron Bay (NSW) 242

Cairns (Qld) 490
    Around Cairns 502
Canberra (ACT) 140
    Central Canberra 146
    Suburbs 153
Cape Tribulation, Around (Qld) 513
Cape York Peninsula (Qld) 521
Capricorn Coast (Qld) 440
Carnarvon (WA) 872
Centre, the (NT) 362
Charters Towers (Qld) 487
Coffs Harbour (NSW) 235
Coober Pedy (SA) 604
Cooktown (Qld) 517
Coolangatta (Qld) 413

Cradle Mountain-Lake St Clair (Tas) 674

Darwin (NT) 304
    Around Darwin 320-321
    Central Darwin 308
Derby (WA) 899
Devonport (Tas) 657
Dubbo (NSW) 283

Eastern Gold Fields (WA) 834
Esperance (WA) 861
Exmouth (WA) 876
Eyre Highway (WA) 842-843

Far North Coast Hinterland (NSW) 250
Fleurieu Peninsula (SA) 560
Flinders Ranges (SA) 594
Fraser Island (Qld) 434
Fremantle (WA) 820

Geelong (Vic) 723
Geraldton (WA) 865
Gippsland (Vic) 790
Gold Coast (Qld) 407
Grampians, the (Vic) 747
Great Keppel Island (Qld) 446
Great Ocean Road & South-West Coast (Vic) 736-737

Hervey Bay (Qld) 431
Hobart (Tas) 619

Kalgoorlie (WA) 836
Kangaroo Island (SA) 565
Karratha (WA) 880
Katoomba, Around (NSW) 212-213
Kata Tjuta (The Olgas) (NT) 366
Kimberley, the (WA) 897
Kings Canyon (NT) 363
Kununurra (WA) 906
Kuranda (Qld) 504

Launceston (Tas) 646
    Around Launceston 651
Lorne (Vic) 738

Mackay (Qld) 454
Magnetic Island (Qld) 477
Manly (NSW) 178
Melbourne (Vic) 699
    Around Melbourne 720-721
    Central Melbourne 688-689
    St Kilda 704
Moreton Bay (Qld) 402
Murray River (Vic) 752
Mt Isa (Qld) 529

Newcastle (NSW) 220
New South Wales 157
    Air Fares 160
Noosa (Qld) 422
Northern Territory 297
    Air Fares 301
North-West Cape (WA) 875
North-West Coast (Tas) 661

Outback Tracks 128

Perth (WA) 806
    Around Perth 826
Phillip Island (Vic) 731
Pilbara Gorges (WA) 884
Port Hedland (WA) 887
Port Macquarie (NSW) 228

Queensland 374-375
    Air Fares 380

Rockhampton (Qld) 442
Roebourne Area (WA) 882
Rottnest Island (WA) 824

Shark Bay (WA) 869
Snowy Mountains (NSW) 267
South Australia 538
    Air Fares 541
Sunshine Coast (Qld) 419

Surfers Paradise (Qld) 409
Sydney
    Around 205
    Central 162-163
    Darling Harbour 170
    Kings Cross 174
    Sydney Harbour & Inner
        Suburbs 176

Tasmania 610

Air Fares 615
Tasman Peninsula (Tas) 634
Townsville (Qld) 470

Uluru (Ayers Rock) (NT) 365
    Around Uluru 365

Victoria (Vic) 682
Victorian Alps (Vic) 784

Western Australia 801
    Air Fares 804
West Coast (Tas) 667
Whitsunday Islands (Qld) 464
Wilpena Pound (SA) 599
Wilsons Promontory (Vic) 794
Wollongong (NSW) 260

Yorke Peninsula (SA) 586
Yulara (NT) 368

Text

Map references are in **bold** type.

Aborigines 12-15, (NT) 296-299, (Qld) 376-376, (SA) 537-537, (Tas) 611
    Aboriginal culture 48-49
    Aboriginal events & festivals (NT) 299
    language 55-56
    tours on Aboriginal land (NT) 299
accommodation 100-106
ACT, *see* Australian Capital Territory
Adaminaby (NSW) 272
Adcock Gorge (WA) 900
Adelaide (SA) 541, **543**
    entertainment 553-554
    getting around 556
    getting there & away 554-555
    organised tours 547-548
    places to eat 550-553
    places to stay 548-550
    shopping 554
    things to see 542-546
    tourist offices 541-542
Adelaide Hills (SA) 556-559, **557**
Adelaide River (NT) 333
Adelaide River Crossing (NT) 322
Agincourt Reef (Qld) 509
Agnew (WA) 840
air travel, *see also* individual states
    arriving & departing 116
    to/from Australia 113-116
    within Australia 118-121, **119**
Aireys Inlet (Vic) 736
Airlie Beach (Qld) 458-463, **459**
Ajana (WA) 869
Akuna Bay (NSW) 208
Albacutya (Vic) 751
Albany (WA) 855-858, **856**

Albury (NSW) 275-276, 279
Alexander Morrison NP (WA) 864
Alexandra Headland (Qld) 420
Alexandria Bay (Qld) 423
Alice Springs (NT) 342-355, **343, 356-357, 348**
Alligator Creek (Qld) 468
Alligator Gorge (SA) 596
Alpine NP (Vic) 783-785
Alpine Walking Track (Vic) 684, 785
Alpine Way (NSW) 272
Alps, the (Vic) 783-789, **784**
American River (SA) 567-568
Anakie (Qld) 451
Andamooka (SA) 602
Angahook-Lorne State Park (Vic) 736
Angaston (SA) 573
Anglesea (Vic) 736
Angourie (NSW) 239
Anna Bay (NSW) 225
Anxious Bay (SA) 592
ANZSES 86-87
Apollo Bay (Vic) 684, 739
Apsley Falls (NSW) 255
Apsley Gorge (Tas) 640
Ararat (Vic) 745
Aratula (Qld) 428
Arcadia (Qld) 476, 477
Archer Bend NP (Qld) 523
Archer River Roadhouse (Qld) 520, 523
Ardrossan (SA) 587
Arkaroo (SA) 593
Arkaroola (SA) 600
Arkhurst Island (Qld) 466
Arltunga Historical Reserve (NT) 357-358
Armadale (WA) 810
Armidale (NSW) 257-258
Arnhem Land (NT) 331-333
Aroona Dam (SA) 600

Aroona Valley (SA) 599
Arrawarra (NSW) 238
art
    Aboriginal 57-76
    European 49-50
Arthur Pieman Protected Area (Tas) 666
Arthur River (Tas) 666
Arthur's Seat (Vic) 729
Asbestos Range NP (Tas) 660
Atherton (Qld) 505
Atherton Tableland (Qld) 493, 501-508
Auburn (SA) 573
Audley (NSW) 204
Austinmer (NSW) 262
Australian Capital Territory 137-155, **138**
    air travel 151
    bus travel 151, 152
    train travel 151-152
Australian Conservation Foundation 84
Australian Rules football 110
Australind (WA) 845-846
automobile associations 82-83
Avon Descent (WA) 829
Avon Valley (WA) 829
Avon Valley NP (WA) 829
Ayers Rock, *see* Uluru
Ayr (Qld) 468

Babinda (Qld) 485
Bairnsdale (Vic) 795-796
Bald Rock NP (NSW) 256
Baldwin Spencer Trail (Vic) 797
Balladonia (WA) 843
Ballarat (Vic) 759-765, **760-761, 763**
Ballina (NSW) 240
Balmain (NSW) 175
Bamaga (Qld) 520, 524
Barcaldine (Qld) 534
Bare Island (NSW) 204

Bargo (NSW) 207
Barkly Homestead (Qld) 532
Barmah State Forest (Vic) 757
Barmera (SA) 583
Barnett River Gorge (WA) 901
Barossa Valley (SA) 569-573,
   570
   wineries 569-571
Barraranna Gorge (SA) 600
Barrier Reef, *see* Great Barrier
   Reef
Barrington Tops NP (NSW) 225
Barron River (Qld) 493, 503
Barrow Creek (NT) 341
Barwon Heads (Vic) 726
basketball 111
Bass Strait Islands (Tas) 678-680
Bat Cave (SA) 580
Batchelor (NT) 333
Batemans Bay (NSW) 264
Bathurst (NSW) 280-281
Bathurst Island (NT) 330-331
Batlow (NSW) 272
Baw Baw NP (Vic) 787
Bay Isles (Qld) 406
Beachport (SA) 578-579
Beaconsfield (Tas) 653
Beagle Bay Aboriginal
   Community (WA) 896
Beaudesert (Qld) 418
Bedarra Island (Qld) 484
Bedourie (Qld) 535
Beech Forest (Vic) 740
Beechworth (Vic) 781-782
Beedelup NP (WA) 851
beer 108, 314
Beerburrum (Qld) 420
Beerwah (Qld) 420
Bega (NSW) 265
Belair NP (SA) 558
Bell's Beach (Vic) 735
Bellara (Qld) 406
Bellarine Peninsula (Vic)
   724-726
Bellbird (NSW) 224
Bellingen (NSW) 232
Bellingen Island (NSW) 233
Bellinger River (NSW) 234
Bells Line of Road (NSW) 209,
   210
Belmont (NSW) 221
Ben Boyd NP (NSW) 266
Ben Lomond NP (Tas) 643-644
Bendigo (Vic) 770-775, **771, 772**
   Bendigo Pottery 775
Berkshire Valley (WA) 828
Bermagui (NSW) 264
Berri (SA) 582
Berrima (NSW) 273

Berry (NSW) 263
Berry Springs (NT) 322
Berry Springs Nature Park (NT)
   322
Berserker Range (Qld) 444
Bethany (SA) 573
Betoota (Qld) 535
Beverley (WA) 831
Bibbulman Track (WA) 803
Bicheno (Tas) 640-641
Big Desert Wilderness (Vic) 751
Binna Burra (Qld) 417
Binningup (WA) 846
Bird Island (Qld) 466
bird-watching
   Broome (WA) 894
   Burketown (Qld) 526
   Cooloola NP (Qld) 425
   Coorong NP (SA) 577
   Croajingolong NP (Vic) 798
   Flinders Ranges (SA) 593
   Hacks Lagoon (SA) 580
   Kellidie Bay Conservation Park
      (SA) 591
   Loch Luna Game Reserve (SA)
      583
   Maria Island NP (Tas) 637
   Moreton Island (Qld) 405
   Orpheus Island (Qld) 480
   Queenscliff (Vic) 725
   Rotamah Island (Vic) 795
   Waikerie (SA) 583
   Wilpena Pound (SA) 598
Birdsville (Qld) 535
Birdsville Track (Qld) 536
Birdsville Track (SA) 601, 607
Birdwood (SA) 558
Black Island (Qld) 466
Black Mountain (ACT) 154
Black Point (NT) 331
Blackall (Qld) 534
Blackall Range (Qld) 426
Blackbutt Reserve (NSW) 221
Blackdown Tableland NP (Qld)
   451
Blackfellows (SA) 592
Blackheath (NSW) 216-217
Blacktown (NSW) 207
Blackwater (Qld) 451
Blinman (SA) 599
Bloomfield (Qld) 515
Bloomfield River Crossing
   (Qld) 515
Bloomfield Track (Qld) 508, 515
Blue Gum Forest (NSW) 210,
   216
Blue Lake (SA) 579
Blue Mountains (NSW)
   210-217

Blue Mountains NP (NSW) 210,
   211
boabs (WA) 898
Bobbin Head (NSW) 208
Bogangar-Cabarita (NSW) 247
Bogong High Plains (Vic) 785
Bomaderry (NSW) 263
Bombah Point (NSW) 225
Bongaree (Qld) 406
Bonnie Doon (Vic) 776
books 91-94
Bool Lagoon Reserve (SA) 580
Boonoo Boonoo NP (NSW) 256
Border Ranges NP (NSW)
   254-255
Bordertown (SA) 580
Boreen Point (Qld) 425
Borroloola (NT) 340
Boston Bay (SA) 590
Boston Island (SA) 591
Botany Bay (NSW) 204
Botany Bay NP (NSW) 204
Bothwell (Tas) 677-678
Bouddi NP (NSW) 218
Boulia (Qld) 535
Bourke (NSW) 286-287
Bow Bridge (WA) 853
Bowen (Qld) 467-468
Bowling Green Bay NP (Qld)
   468
Bowral (NSW) 273
Bowraville (NSW) 232
Boydtown (NSW) 265
Brachina Gorge (SA) 600
Braidwood (NSW) 155, 264
Brammo Bay (Qld) 484
Brampton Island (Qld) 457-458
Bremer Bay (WA) 859
Brewarrina (NSW) 286
Bribie Island (Qld) 406
Bridgetown (WA) 850
Bridport (Tas) 643
Bright (Vic) 782-783
Brisbane (Qld) 380-401, **382,**
   388-389
   entertainment 396-398
   festivals 391
   getting around 400-401
   getting there & away 398-400
   organised tours 390-391
   places to eat 393-396
   places to stay 391-393
   things to see 383-387
   tourist offices 381
Brisbane Forest Park (Qld) 387
Brisbane Ranges NP (Vic) 722
Brisbane River (Qld) 390
Brisbane Water NP (NSW) 218
Broad Arrow (WA) 840

Broadbeach (Qld) 408
Broken Bucket Reserve (Vic) 751
Broken Head Nature Reserve (NSW) 243
Broken Hill (NSW) 289-293, **290**
mines 290-291
Broken Hill Proprietary Company (BHP) 289
Broken River (Qld) 457
Brooklyn (NSW) 209
Broome (WA) 890-895, **891, 895**
Brooms Head (NSW) 238
Brunswick Heads (NSW) 247
Bruny Island (Tas) 630-631
Buccaneer Archipelago (WA) 898
Buchan (Vic) 797
Buckaringa Sanctuary (SA) 597
Buckland (Tas) 637
Bulcock Beach (Qld) 420
Buley Rockhole (NT) 323
Bull Creek (WA) 810
Bulwer (Qld) 405
Bunbury (WA) 846-847
Bundaberg (Qld) 437-438
Bundall (Qld) 415
Bundanoon (NSW) 273
Bundeena (NSW) 206
Bundjalung NP (NSW) 239
Bungendore (NSW) 155
Bungle Bungle (Purnululu) NP (WA) 904
Bunjil's Cave (Vic) 746
Bunya Mountains (Qld) 426
Buringurrah NP (WA) 874
Burketown (Qld) 526
Burleigh Heads NP (Qld) 408
Burnie (Tas) 661-663, **662**
Burning Mountain (NSW) 225
Burra (SA) 574-576, **575**
Burrup Peninsula (WA) 881
bus travel 121-122, **121**, see also individual states
bushwalking 99, (ACT) 145, (NSW) 158, (NT) 300, 310, (Qld) 378, (SA) 539, (Tas) 613, (Vic) 684, (WA) 802
business hours 87
Busselton (WA) 847
Butterfly Gorge NP (NT) 334
Byron Bay (NSW) 241-247, **242**

Cable Beach (WA) 895-896
Caboolture (Qld) 419-420
Cactus Beach (SA) 593
Caiguna (WA) 843-844
Cairns (Qld) 489-501, **490, 502**

Caloundra (Qld) 420
Camden (NSW) 207
Camden Haven (NSW) 227
Camel Cup (NT) 344
camel treks 99
Alice Springs (NT) 349
Cable Beach (WA) 895
Port Macquarie (NSW) 229
Rainbow Valley (NT) 361
Silverton (NSW) 294
Camooweal (Qld) 532
Campbell Town (Tas) 645
Campbell's Creek (Vic) 768
Campbelltown (NSW) 207
Canberra (ACT) 137-152, **140, 146, 153**
entertainment 150-151
getting around 152
getting there & away 151
organised tours 146-147
places to eat 149-150
places to stay 147-148
things to see 141-145
tourist office 139
Canberra Nature Park (ACT) 154
Cannington (WA) 811
canoeing (NSW) 159, 180, (Qld) 379, (SA) 540, (Tas) 613-614
Airlie Beach (Qld) 460
Cairns (Qld) 489
Frankland River (WA) 852
Lower Glenelg NP (Vic) 743
Loxton (SA) 583
Murchison River (WA) 868
Murray River (Vic) 752
North Johnstone River (Qld) 485
North Stradbroke Island (Qld) 403
Ord River (WA) 905
Tully River (Qld) 492
Canowindra (NSW) 284
Canungra (Qld) 417
Cape Arid (WA) 803
Cape Arid NP (WA) 862
Cape Borda (SA) 565
Cape Byron (NSW) 241
Cape Conran (Vic) 797
Cape Crawford (Qld) 527
Cape Cuvier (WA) 874
Cape Hillsborough NP (Qld) 457
Cape Jervis (SA) 560
Cape Keraudren (WA) 890
Cape Kimberley Beach (Qld) 513
Cape Le Grand (WA) 802
Cape Le Grand NP (WA) 862, 863
Cape Naturaliste (WA) 847

Cape Nelson State Park (Vic) 743
Cape Range NP (WA) 878
Cape Schank (Vic) 730
Cape Schank Coastal Park (Vic) 728
Cape Tribulation (Qld) 512, 515, **513**
Cape Woolamai (Vic) 733
Cape York (Qld) 524
Cape York Peninsula (Qld) 520-525, **521**
Capricorn Coast (Qld) 438-452, **440**
car travel 125-132, see also individual states
buying a car 130-132
outback travel 127-129
rental 129-130
Cardwell (Qld) 481
Cardwell Forest Drive (Qld) 481
Carlisle Island (Qld) 457-458
Carnac Island (WA) 811
Carnamah (WA) 864
Carnarvon (WA) 871-873, **872**
Carnarvon NP (Qld) 452
Cascade Waterfalls (SA) 584
Cassilis (NSW) 282
Castlemaine (Vic) 767
Castlereagh (NSW) 209
Cataract Gorge (Tas) 647
Cathedral Range State Park (Vic) 727
Cathedral Rock NP (NSW) 255
caving (Tas) 614
Ceduna (SA) 592-593
Central Tilba (NSW) 264
Cervantes (WA) 827
Cessnock (NSW) 223
Chambers Gorge (SA) 593
Channel Country (Qld) 534-536
Channon, the (NSW) 253
Chapman River (SA) 568
Charleville (Qld) 534
Charlotte Pass (NSW) 272
Charters Towers (Qld) 486-488, **487**
Chatswood (NSW) 208
Cherbourg (Qld) 426
Chewton (Vic) 769
Cheynes Beach (WA) 858
Childers (Qld) 437
Chillagoe (Qld) 505
Chiltern (Vic) 779
Church Point (NSW) 208
Churchill Island (Vic) 733
Cid Harbour (Qld) 467
cinema 50-51
Clare (SA) 574

Clarence River (NSW) 239
Clarence Valley (NSW) 239
Clarendon (SA) 559
Clarks Beach (NSW) 243
Cleland Conservation Park (SA)
557
Clermont (Qld) 451
Cleve (SA) 590
Cleveland (Qld) 401, 404
climate 24
Cloncurry (Qld) 527-528
Clunes (Vic) 765
Cobar (NSW) 288
Cobargo (NSW) 265
Cobourg Peninsula (NT) 331
Cockatoo Island (WA) 898
Cockle Creek (Tas) 633, 673
Cocklebiddy (WA) 843-844
Cocoparra NP (NSW) 278
Coen (Qld) 523
Coffin Bay (SA) 591-592
Coffs Harbour (NSW) 234-238,
235
Cohuna (Vic) 756
Colac (Vic) 744
Coles Bay (Tas) 639-640
Collie (WA) 846
Collingwood River (Tas) 672
Colo River (NSW) 210
Combe Island (Qld) 484
Congo (NSW) 264
Coningham (Tas) 630
convicts 16-18
Conway (Qld) 459
Conway NP (Qld) 458
Coober Pedy (SA) 603-606, **604**
Coochiemudlo Island (Qld) 406
Coochin Creek State Forest
(Qld) 420
Cooee (Tas) 662
Cooee Bay (Qld) 445
Cooinda (NT) 328
Cooktown (Qld) 516-519, **517**
Coolangatta (NSW) 263
Coolangatta (Qld) 410, **413**
Coolgardie (WA) 834-835
Cooloola NP (Qld) 425
Cooloola Wilderness Trail (Qld)
425
Cooma (NSW) 268-269
Coomera (Qld) 410
Coonabarabran (NSW) 285
Coonalpyn (SA) 580
Coonamble (NSW) 285
Coonawarra (SA) 580-581
Cooper Creek (SA) 608
Coorong (SA) 577-578
Coorow (WA) 864
Coral Bay (WA) 878

Corinna (Tas) 666-667
Corowa (NSW) 279
Corrigin (WA) 833
Corroboree Rock Conservation
Reserve (NT) 356
Corryong (Vic) 780
Cossack (WA) 882-883
costs, see money
Cow Bay (Qld) 513
Cowan Water (NSW) 207
Cowell (SA) 590
Cowes (Vic) 730
Cowra (NSW) 284
Cradle Mountain-Lake St Clair
(Tas) 673-677, **674**
Cradle Valley (Tas) 675
Cranbrook (WA) 854
credit cards, see money
Crescent Head (NSW) 231
cricket 110
Croajingolong NP (Vic) 798
Crocodylus Village (Qld) 513
Crowdy Bay NP (NSW) 227
Croydon (Qld) 507, 527
cruises
  Adelaide (SA) 547-548
  Adelaide River Crossing (NT)
  322
  Albany (WA) 857
  Albury (NSW) 275
  Authur River (Tas) 666
  Brisbane River (Qld) 390-391
  Broome (WA) 892
  Cairns (Qld) 493-494
  Coffs Harbour (NSW) 236
  Daintree River (Qld) 512
  Darwin (NT) 310
  Derby (WA) 898
  Echuca (Vic) 756
  Esperance (WA) 862
  Exmouth (WA) 876
  Gippsland Lakes (Vic) 795
  Gordon River (Tas) 671
  Great Barrier Reef (Qld) 494
  Great Keppel Island (Qld) 447
  Hawkesbury River (NSW) 209
  Hobart (Tas) 622
  Lady Musgrave Island (Qld)
  439
  Lake Alexandrina (SA) 564
  Lake Argyle (WA) 908
  Lakes Entrance (Vic) 796
  Loxton (SA) 582
  Mackay (Qld) 453
  Metung (Vic) 796
  Mildura (Vic) 753
  Mission Beach (Qld) 483
  Murray Bridge (SA) 584-585

Murray River (Vic) 752
Nitmuluk (Katherine Gorge)
  NP (NT) 337
Noosa (Qld) 423
Port Macquarie (NSW) 229
Renmark (SA) 582
Shark Bay (WA) 869
Swan Hill (Vic) 755
Swan River (WA) 811
Sydney Harbour (NSW) 177,
  203
Townsville (Qld) 472
Yarra River (Vic) 693
Yellow Water (NT) 328
Cue (WA) 888
Culcairn (NSW) 275
cultural events 87-89
Cumberland Scenic Reserve
  (Vic) 727
Cunderdin (WA) 832
Cunnamulla (Qld) 428
Currie (Tas) 679
Currumbin Sanctuary (Qld) 408
customs 78-79
Cutta Cutta Caves (NT) 338
cycling 99, 133-135, (ACT) 146,
  (NSW) 160, (Tas) 617, (Vic)
  685
  Beechworth (Vic) 781
  Brisbane (Qld) 401
  Canberra (ACT) 152
  Great Victoria Bike Ride (Vic)
  685
  Magnetic Island (Qld) 480
  Melbourne (Vic) 719-721
  Perth (WA) 818
Cyclone Tracy (NT) 306
Cygnet (Tas) 631
Cynthia Bay (Tas) 675

Daintree (Qld) 511-512
Daintree River (Qld) 512
Dalhousie Mound Springs (SA)
  601
Dalwallinu (WA) 863
Daly River (NT) 334
Daly Waters (NT) 340
Dampier (WA) 879
Dampier Archipelago (WA) 881
Dampier Classic (WA) 881
Dampier Peninsula (WA) 896
Danbulla Forest Drive (Qld)
  506
Dandenong Ranges (Vic)
  727-728
Dandenong Ranges NP (Vic) 727
Darling Downs (Qld) 426-429
Darling Point (NSW) 175
Darling Range (WA) 831

Darwin (NT) 302-318, **304, 308, 320-321**
  entertainment 315-316
  festivals 311
  getting around 317-318
  getting there & away 316-317
  organised tours 310-311
  places to eat 313-315
  places to stay 311-313
  shopping 316
  things to see 306-310
  tourist offices 305
Daydream Island (Qld) 465
Daylesford (Vic) 766-767
De Grey River (WA) 890
Deloraine (Tas) 655
Denham (WA) 869, 870
Deniliquin (NSW) 279
Denman (NSW) 224
Denmark (WA) 853-854
D'Entrecasteaux NP (WA) 852
Derby (Tas) 643
Derby (WA) 898-900, **899**
Devil's Marbles Conservation
  Reserve (NT) 341
Deviot (Tas) 653
Devonian Reef NP (WA)
  901-902
Devonport (Tas) 656-660, **657**
Dharug NP (NSW) 209
Diamantina Developmental
  Road (Qld) 535
Diamond Head (NSW) 227
Diamond Island (Tas) 640
Diggers Beach (NSW) 234
Dilli Village (Qld) 435
Dimboola (Vic) 750
Dimbulah (Qld) 505
dinosaur footprints (Qld) 532,
  (WA) 892, 895
disabled travellers 86
  disabled travellers'
  organisations 85-86
Discovery Bay Coastal Park
  (Vic) 743
Diversion Dam (WA) 905
diving 99, (NSW) 159, 180,
  (Qld) 378-379, (SA) 540,
  (Tas) 613, (Vic) 684, (WA)
  803
  Airlie Beach (Qld) 458, 460
  Byron Bay (NSW) 243
  Cairns (Qld) 492
  Cape Tribulation (Qld) 515
  Coral Bay (WA) 878
  Flinders Island (Tas) 679
  Great Barrier Reef (Qld) 492
  Great Keppel Island (Qld) 446
  Great Ocean Road (Vic) 734

Green Island (Qld) 501
Heron Island (Qld) 439
Kangaroo Island (SA) 565
Lade Elliot Island (Qld) 439
Lizard Island (Qld) 519
Lord Howe Island (NSW) 295
Maria Island NP (Tas) 638
Ocean Grove (Vic) 726
Penneshaw (SA) 568
Pondalowie (SA) 587
Port Douglas (Qld) 509
Portsea (Vic) 730
Rottnest Island (WA) 824
Solitary Islands (NSW) 236
Tomahawk (Tas) 643
Townsville (Qld) 472
Whitsunday Island (Qld) 467
Docker River (WA) 840
dolphins, see also whale-
  watching
  Bunbury (WA) 846
  Monkey Mia (WA) 871
  Sorrento (Vic) 730
Donaghys Hill (Tas) 672
Dongara (WA) 863
Donnybrook (WA) 846
Dorrigo (NSW) 233-234
Dorrigo NP (NSW) 233
Dorunda Station (Qld) 527
Double Island (Qld) 508
Double Island Point (Qld) 429
Douglas-Apsley NP (Tas) 640
Dover (Tas) 632
Drayton (Qld) 428
drinks 107-109
Dromana (Vic) 728, 729
Dubbo (NSW) 282-284, **283**
Dugongs (WA) 878
Dumbleyung (WA) 833
Dundubura (Qld) 434
Dungog (NSW) 225
Dunk Island (Qld) 484-485
Dunkeld (Vic) 744
Dunolly (Vic) 765-766
Dunsborough (WA) 847-848

East Beach (Tas) 654
East Coast Trail (Qld) 481
East Gippsland (Vic) 796-799
Eastern MacDonnell Ranges
  (NT) 355-358
Ebor (NSW) 255
Ebor Falls (NSW) 255
Echo Point (NSW) 214
Echuca (Vic) 752, 756-757
economy 47-48
Eden (NSW) 265
Edith Falls (NT) 334
Edithburgh (SA) 587

Edmund Kennedy NP (Qld) 481
Eildon (Vic) 776
Eildon State Park (Vic) 776
Eimeo Beach (Qld) 455
Einasleigh (Qld) 507, 508, 527
El Questro (WA) 901
Elanda Point (Qld) 425
Elbow Hill (SA) 590
electricity 91
Elizabeth Creek (Qld) 508
Ellery Creek Big Hole (NT) 359
Elliston (SA) 592
embassies 77-78
Emerald (Qld) 451
Emerald (Vic) 728
Emily Gap (NT) 356
Emma Gorge (WA) 901
Emu Park (Qld) 445
Engadine (NSW) 206
entertainment 109-111
Epsom (Vic) 775
Errinundra NP (Vic) 797, 798
Erskine Falls (Vic) 737
Esperance (Tas) 632
Esperance (WA) 860-863, **861**
Ettamogah (NSW) 275
Eucla (WA) 844
Eugowra (NSW) 284
Eumundi (Qld) 426
Eungella NP (Qld) 456-457
Eungella Township (Qld) 457
Eureka Rebellion (Vic) 762
Eurong (Qld) 434, 435
Evandale (Tas) 652
Evans Head (NSW) 239
Exmouth (WA) 874-877, **876**
Eyre Bird Observatory (WA) 844
Eyre Highway (WA) 843-845,
  842-843
Eyre Peninsula (SA) 588-593

Fairfield Park (Vic) 685
Falls Creek (Vic) 786
Family Islands (Qld) 484-485
Feathertop Bushwalk (Vic) 785
Fern Tree Gully NP (Vic) 728
Finch Hatton Gorge (Qld) 457
Finke (NT) 361
Finke Gorge NP (NT) 360
Fisherman's Beach (Vic) 735
Fisherman's Wharf (Qld) 408
fishing (NT) 301, (Qld) 379,
  (Tas) 614, (WA) 803
  Ballina (NSW) 240
  Borroloola (NT) 340
  Bothwell (Tas) 677
  Caloundra (Qld) 420
  Dampier Archipelago (WA) 881
  Esperance (WA) 860

Glenelg NP (Vic) 743
Gulf of Carpentaria (Qld) 525
Innes NP (SA) 585
Jurien (WA) 827
Kangaroo Island (SA) 564
Kingston SE (SA) 578
Kununurra (WA) 907
Lake Eildon (Vic) 776
Lake King William (Tas) 677
Lake Macquarie (NSW) 219
Lakes Entrance (Vic) 796
Locks Bay (SA) 592
Mallacoota (Vic) 798
Mary River (NT) 322
Murray Bridge (SA) 584
Narooma (NSW) 264
Norman River (Qld) 527
North Stradbroke Island (Qld)
    402
Pondalwie Bay (SA) 587
Port Albert (Vic) 793
Fitzgerald River (WA) 802
Fitzgerald River NP (WA)
    859-860
Fitzroy Crossing (WA) 902-903
Fitzroy Island (Qld) 501
Five Rivers Lookout (WA) 904
Fleurieu Peninsula (SA) 559-
    564, **560**
Flinders (Vic) 730
Flinders Chase NP (SA) 568-569
Flinders Island (SA) 592
Flinders Island (Tas) 679-680
Flinders Ranges (SA) 593-600,
    594
flora 24-28
Florence Falls (NT) 323
Fogg Dam (NT) 322
food 106-107
football, *see* Australia Rules
    football
Forbes (NSW) 284
Forsayth (Qld) 507, 527
Forster-Tuncurry (NSW) 226
Forty Mile Scrub NP (Qld) 507
fossicking (NT) 301, (Qld) 379
    Capricorn Hinterland (Qld) 451
    Cooper Pedy (SA) 605
    Eumundi (Qld) 426
    Glen Innes (NSW) 258
    South Burnett (Qld) 426
    Tamborine Mountain (Qld) 417
    White Cliffs (NSW) 288
Fossil Bluff (Tas) 664
4WD safaris
    Broken Hill (NSW) 291
    Cape York (Qld) 522
    Cooktown (Qld) 518
    Esperance (WA) 862

Kalbarri (WA) 868
Port Douglas (Qld) 509
Strahan (Tas) 671
François Peron NP (WA) 870
Frank Hann NP (WA) 859
Frankland River (WA) 852
Franklin River (Tas) 672
Franklin-Gordon Wild Rivers
    NP (Tas) 672
Frankston (Vic) 728
Fraser Island (Qld) 423, 429,
    433-437, **434**
Fraser NP (Vic) 776
Fremantle (WA) 819-823, **820**
French Island (Vic) 730
Frenchman Bay (WA) 858
Frenchmans Cap (Tas) 672
Freshwater (Qld) 508
Freycinet NP (Tas) 639-640
Frome Creek (SA) 607
fruit picking
    Griffith (NSW) 277
    Mildura (Vic) 753
Fryerstown (Vic) 769

Gammon Ranges NP (SA) 600
Gantheaume Point (WA) 895
Garden Island (WA) 828
Gascoyne Junction (WA) 874
Gay & Lesbian Mardi Gras
    (NSW) 181
Geelong (Vic) 722-724, **723**
Geeveston (Tas) 632
Geikie Gorge (WA) 901
Gellibrand (Vic) 740
Geoffrey Bay (Qld) 476
geography 23
George Town (Tas) 654
Georgetown (Qld) 507, 527
Geraldton (WA) 864-867, **865**
Germein Gorge (SA) 596
Gerringong (NSW) 262
Ghan, the (NT) 353, **352**
Gibb River Road (WA) 900-901
Gibraltar Falls (ACT) 154
Gibraltar Range NP (NSW)
    255
Giles (WA) 840
Gilgandra (NSW) 285
Gin Gin (Qld) 438
Ginninderra Falls (ACT) 154
Gippsland (Vic) 789-799, **790**
Gippsland Lakes (Vic) 685, 795
Gippsland Lakes Coastal Park
    (Vic) 795-796
Girraween NP (Qld) 428
Gisborne (Vic) 726
Gladstone (Qld) 441
Gladstone (Tas) 642-643

Glass House Mountains (Qld)
    420
Glebe (NSW) 175
Glen Helen Gorge (NT) 359
Glen Innes (NSW) 258
Glenbrook (NSW) 211, 212
Glendambo (SA) 603
Glenelg (SA) 546-547
Glenelg River (Vic) 743
Glenrowan (Vic) 778
Gloucester River (NSW) 225
Goat Island (SA) 582
gold 19-20, (Vic) 758-759, (WA)
    833- 840, **834**
Gold Coast (Qld) 406 -418, **407**
Goldfield Track (Qld) 485
Goldfields Tourist Route (Vic)
    758-759
Goldsborough Valley State
    Forest Park (Qld) 485
Goolwa (SA) 563-564
Goondiwindi (Qld) 428
Gordon Falls Reserve (NSW)
    214
Gordon River (Tas) 671, 672
Gordonvale (Qld) 485-486
Gosford (NSW) 218
Gostwyck (NSW) 257
Goulburn (NSW) 274
Goulburn River NP (NSW) 224
Goulburn Valley (Vic) 777
Gove (NT) 331-333
government 46-47
Govetts Leap (NSW) 216
Grafton (NSW) 239
Grampians (Gariwerd) NP (Vic)
    746-749, **747**
Grand Prix (SA) 546
Great Barrier Reef (Qld) 378,
    448-449, 494
    Agincourt Reef 509
Great Keppel Island (Qld)
    445-450, **446**
Great Mountain Race (Vic) 777
Great Northern Highway (WA)
    888-889
Great Ocean Road (Vic)
    734-741, **736-737**
Great Sandy NP (Qld) 433
Great Western (Vic) 745
Green Island (Qld) 501
Green Mountains (Qld) 417
Greenly Beach (SA) 592
Greenough (WA) 863
Greens Beach (Tas) 653
Gregory Downs (Qld) 532
Gregory NP (NT) 338
Greta (Vic) 778
Griffith (NSW) 277-278

Groote Eylandt (NT) 332
Grose Valley (NSW) 210, 211, 216
Grove (Tas) 631
Guilderton (WA) 827
Guildford (Vic) 769
Gulf Developmental Road (Qld) 507-508
Gulf of Carpentaria (Qld) 525-527
Gulf St Vincent (SA) 560-561
Gulgong (NSW) 281
Gunbower State Forest (Vic) 756
Gundagai (NSW) 274
Gunns Plains Cave Reserve (Tas) 660
Guthega (NSW) 272
Guy Fawkes River NP (NSW) 255
Guyra (NSW) 258
Gwalia (WA) 840
Gympie (Qld) 429

Hacks Lagoon (SA) 580
Hadspen (Tas) 651-652
Hahndorf (SA) 558-559
Halfway Island (Qld) 450
Halls Creek (WA) 903
Halls Gap (Vic) 746
Hamelin Pool (WA) 869, 870
Hamilton (Qld) 535
Hamilton (Vic) 744-745
Hamilton Island (Qld) 466
Hancocks Lookout (SA) 596
hang-gliding 99
   Airlie Beach (Qld) 460
   Apollo Bay (Vic) 739
   Bright (Vic) 782
   Byron Bay (NSW) 243
   Cape Jervis (SA) 560
   Great Ocean Road (Vic) 734
   Waikerie (SA) 583
Hanging Rock (Vic) 726
Hanson Bay (SA) 569
Happy Valley (Qld) 435
Harrietville (Vic) 785
Hartley (NSW) 210, 217
Hartz Mountains NP (Tas) 632
Harvey (WA) 846
Hastings (Tas) 632-633, 730
Hastings Caves State Reserve (Tas) 633
Hat Head (NSW) 231
Hattah (Vic) 751
Hattah-Kulkyne NP (Vic) 751
Hawk's Head (WA) 868
Hawker (SA) 597-598
Hawkesbury River (NSW) 179, 208-209

Hawks Nest (NSW) 226
Hay (NSW) 278-279
Hayman Island (Qld) 466
Headlands (NSW) 262
Healesville (Vic) 727
Healesville Wildlife Sanctuary (Vic) 727
health 95
Heathcote (NSW) 206
Heathcote (Vic) 776
Heathlands (Qld) 524
Helenvale (Qld) 515
Hellyer Gorge (Tas) 666
Henbury Meteorite Craters (NT) 361-363
Hepburn Springs (Vic) 767
Herberton (Qld) 507
Heritage Trails Network (WA) 803
Hermannsburg (NT) 359-360
Heron Island (Qld) 439
Hervey Bay (Qld) 429-433, **431**
Heysen Trail (SA) 539
Hidden Valley NP (WA) 905
Hill End (NSW) 281
Hillwood (Tas) 654
Hinchinbrook Island (Qld) 481-482
Hindmarsh Island (SA) 564
history 12-23
hitching 135-136
Hobart (Tas) 617-627, **619**
   entertainment 626
   festivals 622
   getting around 626-627
   getting there & away 626
   places to eat 624-626
   places to stay 622-624
   things to see 618-622
   tourist office 618
Hogarth Falls (Tas) 671
Holbrook (NSW) 275
holidays 87
Hook Island (Qld) 465
Hopetoun (WA) 859
Horn Island (Qld) 525
Horse Week (NSW) 225
horse-racing 111
   Melbourne Cup (Vic) 694
Horseshoe Bay (Qld) 477-478
Horseshoe Bay (SA) 562
Horsham (Vic) 749
houseboats
   Ballina (NSW) 240
   Echuca (Vic) 757
   Hawkesbury River (NSW) 209
   Lake Eildon (Vic) 776, 777
   Mildura (Vic) 754

Houtman Abrolhos Islands (WA) 867
Howard Springs (NT) 319
Hughenden (Qld) 488
Humpy Island (Qld) 450
Hunter Valley (NSW) 223-225
Hunter Vintage Walkabout (NSW) 223
Huonville (Tas) 631-632
Huskisson (NSW) 263
Hyden (WA) 832

Iluka (NSW) 239
Indera (NSW) 275
Ingham (Qld) 480
Inglewood (Vic) 776
Injune (Qld) 452
Inman Valley (SA) 560
Innamincka (SA) 608
Innes NP (SA) 585, 587-588
Innisfail (Qld) 485
Inskip Point (Qld) 429
Inverell (NSW) 258-259
Inverleigh (Vic) 744
Ipolera (NT) 360
Ipswich (Qld) 427
Irishtown (WA) 830
Iron Range NP (Qld) 523
Irwin River (WA) 863

Jabiru (NT) 327
Jakes Corner (WA) 868
Jamestown (SA) 576
Jamieson (Vic) 776
Jamison Valley (NSW) 211, 214
Jan Juc (Vic) 735
Jardine River NP (Qld) 524
Jenolan Caves (NSW) 217-218
Jerilderie (NSW) 277
Jerramungup (WA) 859
Jervis Bay (NSW) 263
Jervis Bay NP (NSW) 263
Jessie Gap (NT) 356
Jewel Cave (WA) 849
Jim Jim Falls (NT) 328
Jindabyne (NSW) 269
Jip Jip NP (SA) 578
Johanna (Vic) 740
John Forrest NP (WA) 831
John Hayes Rockhole (NT) 356
Jondaryan (Qld) 429
Jourama Falls NP (Qld) 480
Julia Creek (Qld) 488
Junee (NSW) 276
Jurien (WA) 827

Kadina (SA) 586
Kakadu NP (NT) 323-330
Kalang River (NSW) 234

Kalbarri (WA) 867
Kalbarri NP (WA) 803, 868
Kalgoorlie-Boulder (WA) 835-839, **836**
Kambalda (WA) 841
Kanakas (Qld) 376
Kanangra Boyd NP (NSW) 211
Kangaroo Island (SA) 564-569, **565**
Kangaroo Valley (NSW) 263
Kanowna (WA) 839
Kanyaka (SA) 597
Kapunda (SA) 573
Karijini (Hamersley Range) NP (WA) 803, 877, 884
Karratha (WA) 881, **880**
Karumba (Qld) 526-527
Kata Tjuta (The Olgas) (NT) 366-367, **366**
Katanning (WA) 833
Katarapko Game Reserve (SA) 582
Katherine (NT) 334-336
Katoomba (NSW) 214-216, **212-213**
Keep River NP (NT) 338
Keith (SA) 580
Kellerberrin (WA) 832
Kellidie Bay Conservation Park (SA) 591
Kelly, Ned 277
Kelso (Tas) 653
Kempsey (NSW) 231
Kendenup (WA) 854
Kennett River (Vic) 739
Kerang (Vic) 755
Kettering (Tas) 630
Kew (NSW) 227
Khancoban (NSW) 272
Kiama (NSW) 262
Kiandra (NSW) 270
Killarney (Qld) 428
Killiecrankie Bay (Tas) 679
Kimberley, the (WA) 896-908, **897**
Kinaba Island (Qld) 425
Kinchega NP (NSW) 294
King Island (Tas) 678-679
King Sound (WA) 898
Kingaroy (Qld) 426
Kingower (Vic) 776
Kings Canyon (NT) 363, **363**
Kings Cross (NSW) 174-175, **174**
Kings Park (WA) 807
Kingscliff (NSW) 247
Kingscote (SA) 567
Kingston (Tas) 627
Kingston SE (SA) 578

Kondalilla NP (Qld) 426
Kookynie (WA) 840
Koolan Island (WA) 898
Koombana Beach (WA) 846
Koorda (WA) 832
Kooringal (Qld) 405
Korora (NSW) 234
Korumburra (Vic) 793
Kosciusko NP (NSW) 269-270
Ku-ring-gai Chase NP (NSW) 207-208
Kununurra (WA) 905, **906**
Kuranda (Qld) 503, **504**
Kuranda Scenic Railway (Qld) 505
Kutikina Cave (Tas) 672
Kyneton (Vic) 776
Kynuna (Qld) 532
Kyogle (NSW) 254

La Perouse (NSW) 204
Lady Elliot Island (Qld) 439
Lady Musgrave Island (Qld) 439
Lagoon Bay (Tas) 654
Lake Ainsworth (NSW) 241
Lake Alexandrina (SA) 563, 585
Lake Argyle (WA) 905, 908
Lake Barrine (Qld) 506
Lake Barrington (Tas) 656
Lake Bellfield (Vic) 748
Lake Bennett (NT) 333
Lake Bolac (Vic) 744
Lake Bonney (SA) 583
Lake Burley Griffin (ACT) 146
Lake Catani (Vic) 785
Lake Cathie (NSW) 227
Lake Cave (WA) 849
Lake Chisholm (Tas) 665
Lake Condah (Vic) 745
Lake Condah Aboriginal Mission (Vic) 745
Lake Cowan (WA) 841
Lake Dulverton (Tas) 644
Lake Eacham (Qld) 506
Lake Eildon (Vic) 776-777
Lake Eppalock (Vic) 776
Lake Eyre (SA) 601
Lake Garawongera (Qld) 435
Lake Gordon (Tas) 673
Lake Grace (WA) 833
Lake Hattah (Vic) 751
Lake Illawarra (NSW) 262
Lake King William (Tas) 677
Lake Leake (Tas) 645
Lake Macquarie (NSW) 219
Lake McKenzie (Qld) 435
Lake Mountain (Vic) 789
Lake Mountain Reserve (Vic) 727

Lake Mournpall (Vic) 751
Lake Mulwala (Vic) 757
Lake Mungo (NSW) 294
Lake Nagambie (Vic) 777
Lake Pedder (Tas) 673
Lake St Clair, see Cradle Mountain-Lake St Clair
Lake Talbot (NSW) 277
Lake Tinaroo (Qld) 505-506
Lake Wabby (Qld) 435
Lake Wendouree (Vic) 761
Lakefield NP (Qld) 522-523
Lakeland (Qld) 522
Lakes District (Vic) 795
Lakes Entrance (Vic) 796
Lakes NP (Vic) 795
Lakeside (Vic) 728
Lamington NP (Qld) 417-418
Lancelin (WA) 827
Langford Island (Qld) 466
Langi Ghiran State Park (Vic) 745
language 51-56
    Aboriginal 55-56
    Australian English 51-55
Larapinta Drive (NT) 359
Larapinta Trail (NT) 358-359
Lark Quarry Environmental Park (Qld) 532
Larrimah (NT) 339-340
Latrobe Valley (Vic) 789-792
Launceston (Tas) 645-651, **646, 651**
Laura (Qld) 522
Lavers Hill (Vic) 739
Laverton (WA) 840
Lawn Hill NP (Qld) 525, 527, 532
Leeton (NSW) 278
Leeuwin-Naturaliste NP (WA) 849
Leigh Creek (SA) 600
Leinster (WA) 840
Lennonville (WA) 888
Lennox Head (NSW) 240-241
Leonora (WA) 840
Leura (NSW) 213
Leven Canyon (Tas) 660
Liffey Valley (Tas) 652
Lightning Ridge (NSW) 285
Lillian Rock (NSW) 254
Lily Creek Lagoon (WA) 905
Lilydale (Tas) 654
Lilydale Falls Reserve (Tas) 654
Limeburners Creek Nature Reserve (NSW) 231
Lincoln NP (SA) 591
Lindeman Island (Qld) 466-467
Lismore (NSW) 249-251

Litchfield NP (NT) 322-323
literature 50
Lithgow (NSW) 280
Little Desert NP (Vic) 750
Little River Falls (Vic) 798
Liverpool (NSW) 207
Lizard Island (Qld) 519
Loch Ard Gorge (Vic) 740
Loch Luna Game Reserve (SA) 583
Locks Bay (SA) 592
Lombadina Aboriginal Community (WA) 896
London Bridge (Vic) 740
Long Island (Qld) 465
Longford (Tas) 652
Longford Wildlife Park (Tas) 652
Longreach (Qld) 533-534
Lord Howe Island (NSW) 294, 295
Lorne (Vic) 736-739, **738**
Louth (NSW) 288
Low Head (Tas) 653-654
Low Isles (Qld) 509
Lower Glenelg NP (Vic) 743
Loxton (SA) 582-583
Lucinda (Qld) 480
Lune River (Tas) 633
Lyndoch (SA) 571-572

MacDonnell Ranges (NT) 355-360
Mackay (Qld) 453-456, **454**
Maclean (NSW) 239
Macquarie Pass NP (NSW) 262
Macrozamia Grove NP (Qld) 417
Madura (WA) 844
Magnetic Island (Qld) 476-480, **477**
Main Beach (NSW) 241
Main Beach (Qld) 408
Main Range NP (Qld) 427
Maitland (NSW) 224
Major Mitchell Trail (Vic) 744
Malanda (Qld) 506-507
Maldon (Vic) 769-770
Mallacoota (Vic) 798
Mallee, the (Vic) 750-751
Malmsbury (Vic) 726
Mammoth Cave (WA) 849
Mandorah (NT) 319
Mandurah (WA) 828
Manjimup (WA) 850-851
Manly (NSW) 177-179, **178**
Manning Gorge (WA) 901
Manning Valley (NSW) 226-227
Mannum (SA) 584
Mansfield (Vic) 777

Manyallaluk (Eva Valley) (NT) 338
Mapleton Falls NP (Qld) 426
maps 94
Marble Bar (WA) 889
Mareeba (Qld) 505
Margaret River (WA) 848-849
Maria Island NP (Tas) 637-638
Marla (SA) 606
Marlo (Vic) 797
Maroochydore (Qld) 420-421
Marrawah (Tas) 665-666
Marree (SA) 606-607
Mary Kathleen (Qld) 528
Mary River Crossing (NT) 322
Maryborough (Qld) 430
Maryborough (Vic) 765
Marysville (Vic) 727
Mataranka (NT) 339
McKillops Bridge (Vic) 798
McKinlay (Qld) 532
McLaren Vale (SA) 561
McPherson Range (Qld) 416
Meckering (WA) 832
media 94
Medlow Bath (NSW) 210
Meekatharra (WA) 840, 889
Megalong Valley (NSW) 216
Melba Gully State Park (Vic) 739
Melbourne (Vic) 685-721, **688-689, 699, 720-721**
entertainment 713-716
festivals 701-702
getting around 718-721
getting there & away 717-718
organised tours 701
places to eat 707-713
places to stay 702-707
shopping 716-717
things to see 687-698
tourist offices 686
Melbourne Cup (Vic) 694
Melrose (SA) 596
Melville Island (NT) 330-331
Mena Creek (Qld) 485
Menindee (NSW) 294
Menindee Lakes (NSW) 294
Menzies (WA) 840
Mereenie Loop Road (NT) 360
Merimbula (NSW) 265
Merredin (WA) 832
Merriwa (NSW) 282
Metung (Vic) 796
Miall Island (Qld) 450
Michaelmas Cay (Qld) 501
Middle Island (Qld) 450
Middleton (Qld) 535
Midlands Scenic Way (WA) 864

Mildura (Vic) 753-754
Millaa Millaa (Qld) 507
Millers Point (NSW) 167
Millicent (SA) 579
Millstream (WA) 883
Millstream-Chichester NP (WA) 883
Milparinka (NSW) 287-288
Mimosa Rocks NP (NSW) 265
Mingela (Qld) 486
Mingenew (WA) 864
mining (NSW) 290-291, (NT) 326
Minnie Water (NSW) 238
Mintabie (SA) 606
Mintaro (SA) 574
Minyon Falls (NSW) 253
Mirboo North (Vic) 792
Mission Beach (Qld) 482-484
Mitchell Plateau (WA) 901
Mitchell River NP (Vic) 795
Mitta Mitta River (Vic) 785
Mittagong (NSW) 273
Moe (Vic) 791
Mole Creek (Tas) 655-656
Moliagul (Vic) 765-766
Molonglo Gorge (ACT) 154
money 79-81
    costs 80
    credit cards 79-80
    tipping 80-81
Monkey Beach (Qld) 446
Monkey Mia (WA) 871
Montague Island (NSW) 264
Montville (Qld) 426
Moochalabra Dam (WA) 905
Mooloolaba (Qld) 420
Moomba (Vic) 701
Moondyne Cave (WA) 849
Moonta (SA) 587
Moora (WA) 827
Moorook (SA) 583
Mootwingee NP (NSW) 289
Moranbah (Qld) 451
Morawa (WA) 863
Moree (NSW) 285
Moreton Bay (Qld) 401-406, **402**
Moreton Island (Qld) 404-406
Morgan (SA) 583-584
Morialta Conservation Park (SA) 557
Mornington (Vic) 729
Mornington Peninsula (Vic) 728-730
Morphett Vale (SA) 561
Morton NP (NSW) 262-264
Morwell (Vic) 791
Mossman (Qld) 511
motorbike travel 132-133

Mourilyan (Qld) 485
Mrs Macquarie's Point (NSW) 166
Mt Ainslie (ACT) 154
Mt Arapiles (Vic) 684, 749-750
Mt Augustus (WA) 874
Mt Barker (WA) 854
Mt Barnett (WA) 901
Mt Barnett Station (WA) 901
Mt Barney NP (Qld) 418
Mt Bartle Frere (Qld) 485
Mt Baw Baw (Vic) 787
Mt Beckworth (Vic) 765
Mt Beerwah (Qld) 420
Mt Blue Cow (NSW) 272
Mt Bogong (Vic) 789
Mt Boothby Conservation Park (SA) 580
Mt Buffalo (Vic) 785, 787
Mt Buffalo NP (Vic) 785
Mt Buller (Vic) 787-788
Mt Carbine (Qld) 516
Mt Colah (NSW) 208
Mt Coonowrin (Qld) 420
Mt Coot-tha Park (Qld) 386-387
Mt Dandenong (Vic) 728
Mt Donna Buang (Vic) 789
Mt Elizabeth Station (WA) 901
Mt Erica (Vic) 785
Mt Field NP (Tas) 628-629
Mt Gambier (SA) 579
Mt Garnet (Qld) 507
Mt Gower (NSW) 295
Mt Grenfell (NSW) 288
Mt Gunderbooka (NSW) 286
Mt Hotham (Vic) 788-789
Mt House Station (WA) 900
Mt Hypipamee (Qld) 507
Mt Isa (Qld) 528-531, 529
Mt Kaputar NP (NSW) 285
Mt Keira (NSW) 262
Mt Kembla (NSW) 262
Mt Latham (WA) 833
Mt Lidgbird (NSW) 295
Mt Lofty Botanical Gardens (SA) 557
Mt Macedon (Vic) 726
Mt Magnet (WA) 888-889
Mt Magnificent Conservation Park (SA) 561
Mt Majura (ACT) 154
Mt Martha (Vic) 729
Mt Molloy (Qld) 516
Mt Morgan (Qld) 444
Mt Nardi (NSW) 253
Mt Ngungun (Qld) 420
Mt Oldfield (Qld) 467
Mt Olga (NT) 366
Mt Painter (SA) 600

Mt Panorama (NSW) 280
Mt Remarkable (SA) 596
Mt Remarkable NP (SA) 596
Mt Rescue Conservation Park (SA) 580
Mt Richmond NP (Vic) 743
Mt Roland (Tas) 656
Mt Selwyn (NSW) 272
Mt Spec NP (Qld) 480
Mt St Gwinear (Vic) 789
Mt Stirling (Vic) 789
Mt Stromlo Observatory (ACT) 154
Mt Strzelecki (Tas) 680
Mt Surprise (Qld) 507, 527
Mt Tamborine (Qld) 417
Mt Tempest (Qld) 404, 405
Mt Tibrogargan (Qld) 420
Mt Victoria (NSW) 217
Mt Warning NP (NSW) 254
Mt William NP (Tas) 642
Mt Wilson (NSW) 217
Mt York (NSW) 217
Mudgee (NSW) 281
Mudgeeraba (Qld) 417
Mullumbimby (NSW) 253-254
Mundaring Weir (WA) 831
Mundrabilla (WA) 844
Mungo NP (NSW) 294, 754
Mungo Track (NSW) 226
Murchison River (WA) 867
Murgon (Qld) 426
Murramarang NP (NSW) 264
Murray Bridge (SA) 584-585
Murray River (SA) 581-585
  houseboats 581
Murray River (Vic) 751-758, 752
Murray-Sunset NP (Vic) 751
Murrayville (Vic) 751
Murrumbidgee Irrigation Area (NSW) 277
Murrumbidgee River (ACT) 154
Murwillumbah (NSW) 247-248
Musgrave (Qld) 523
music 51
Muswellbrook (NSW) 225
Muttonbird Island (NSW) 234
Myall Lakes NP (NSW) 225-226
Myers Flats (Vic) 775
Mylestom (NSW) 234

Nadgee Nature Reserve (NSW) 266
Nagambie (Vic) 777-778
Nagundie (NSW) 282
Namadgi NP (ACT) 154
Namatjira Drive (NT) 359
Nambour (Qld) 426

Nambucca Heads (NSW) 231-232
Nambung NP (WA) 827
Nanango (Qld) 426
Nannup (WA) 850
Naracoopa (Tas) 679
Naracoorte (SA) 580
Narellan (NSW) 207
Narooma (NSW) 264
Narrabri (NSW) 285
Narrandera (NSW) 276-277
Narrogin (WA) 833
Narromine (NSW) 286
Natimuk (Vic) 749
national parks & reserves 45, see also separate National Parks index
  (NSW) 158, (NT) 300, (Qld) 377, (SA) 539, (Tas) 612, (Vic) 684
  Organisations 83-84
N'Dhala Gorge Nature Park (NT) 357
Neath (NSW) 224
Nelly Bay (Qld) 476
Nelson (Vic) 743
Nelson Bay (NSW) 225
Nelson Falls (Tas) 672
Nepean River (NSW) 207
Nerada (Qld) 485
New England (NSW) 255-259
New England NP (NSW) 255
New Norcia (WA) 827-828
New Norfolk (Tas) 628
New South Wales 156-295, 157, 250
  air travel 160, 160
  bus travel 160
  geography 158
  tourist offices 158
  train travel 160
Newcastle (NSW) 219-223, 220
Newcastle Beach (NSW) 219
Newhaven (Vic) 732
Newman (WA) 889
Newry Island (Qld) 458
Nguiu (NT) 330
Nhill (Vic) 750
Nhulunbuy (NT) 332
Niagara (WA) 840
Nightcap NP (NSW) 253
Nightcap Track (NSW) 253
Nimbin (NSW) 251-252
Nimmitabel (NSW) 269
Ninety Mile Beach (Vic) 795
Ningaloo Reef (WA) 877-878
Nitmiluk (Katherine Gorge) NP (NT) 337-338
Noah Beach (Qld) 513

Noccundra (Qld) 535
Noosa (Qld) 421-425, **422**
Noosa Heads (Qld) 421
Noosa NP (Qld) 423
Noosa River (Qld) 425
Noosaville (Qld) 421
Normanton (Qld) 526
Norseman (WA) 841
North Johnstone River (Qld) 493
North Keppel Island (Qld) 450
North Shields (SA) 590
North Stradbroke Island (Qld) 402-404
North West Island (Qld) 441
North-West Cape (WA) 874-878, **875**
Northam (WA) 829-830
Northampton (WA) 867
Northcliffe (WA) 852
Northern Territory 296-372, **297, 362**
    air travel 301, **301**
    car travel 302
    tourist offices 300
Notley Gorge State Reserve (Tas) 653
Nourlangie Rock (NT) 327-328
Nowra (NSW) 263
Nullarbor Roadhouse (SA) 844
Nullarbor, the (WA) 841-845
Nullum State Forest (NSW) 254
Numinbah Valley (Qld) 410
Nundroo (SA) 844-845
Nuriootpa (SA) 572-573
Nymboida River (NSW) 236, 243
Nyngan (NSW) 286

Oatlands (Tas) 644-645
Ocean Beach (Tas) 671
Ocean Grove (Vic) 726
Old Bar (NSW) 227
Old Noarlunga (SA) 561
Olga River (Tas) 672
Olgas, the see Kata Tjuta
Olympic Games 2000 161
Omeo (Vic) 785-786
One Arm Point (WA) 896
Ongerup (WA) 859
Onslow (WA) 879
Oodnadatta (SA) 607
Oodnadatta Track (SA) 601
opal mining
    Coober Pedy (SA) 603-605
Ophir (NSW) 282
Ora Banda (WA) 840
Orange (NSW) 282
Orbost (Vic) 797
Ord River (WA) 905

Orford (Tas) 637
Organ Pipes NP (Vic) 726
Ormiston (Qld) 401
Ormiston Gorge (NT) 359
Orpheus Island (Qld) 480-481
Otford (NSW) 206
Otway NP (Vic) 739
Otway Ranges (Vic) 739-740
outback **128**
    SA 601-608
    NSW 286-294
    Qld 527-536
Ovens River (Vic) 785
Ovens Valley (Vic) 781
Overland Track (Tas) 675-676
Overlander Roadhouse (WA) 870
Oxenford (Qld) 410, 417
Oxley Wild Rivers NP (NSW) 255

Paddington (NSW) 173-174
Palm Beach (NSW) 208
Palm Beach (Qld) 411
Palm Cove (Qld) 508
Palm Valley (NT) 360
Palmer River (Qld) 516
Palmerston NP (Qld) 485
Paluma (Qld) 480
Pambula (NSW) 265
Paraburdoo (WA) 885-886
Parachilna (SA) 600
Parramatta (NSW) 206-207
Patonga (NSW) 208
Peak Charles NP (WA) 862
Peak Head (WA) 858
Pearling (WA) 890-892
Pekina Creek (SA) 596
Pemberton (WA) 851-852
Penguin (Tas) 661
Penguin Island (WA) 828
Peninsula Coastal Walk (Vic) 730
Penneshaw (SA) 568
Pennington Bay (SA) 568
Penola (SA) 580-581
Penong (SA) 593, 845
Penrith (NSW) 207
Pentecost River (WA) 901
Perenjori (WA) 863
Perisher Valley (NSW) 271-272
Perrys Lookdown (NSW) 216
Perth (Tas) 652
Perth (WA) 805-818, **806, 826**
    entertainment 815-816
    festivals 811-812
    getting around 817-819
    getting there & away 816-817
    places to eat 814-815
    places to stay 812-814

    shopping 816
    things to see 807-811
    tourist offices 805
Perup (WA) 851
Peterborough (SA) 577
Phillip Island (Vic) 730-734, **731**
Phillip Island Wildlife Park (Vic) 732
photography 94-95
Pialba (Qld) 430
Picnic Bay (Qld) 476
Picnic Rocks (Tas) 642
Picton (NSW) 207
Pilbara, the (WA) 879-889, **884**
Pine Creek (NT) 328, 334
Pinjarra (WA) 829
Pinnacles Desert (WA) 827
Pitt Town (NSW) 209
Pittwater (NSW) 179, 207
Point Danger (NSW) 248
Point Labatt (SA) 592
Point Leo (Vic) 730
Point Lonsdale (Vic) 725-726
Point Nepean NP (Vic) 730
Point Samson (WA) 883
Point Sinclair (SA) 593
Point Vernon (Qld) 430
Pondalowie Bay (SA) 587
Pontville (Tas) 627-628
population 48
Porcupine Gorge NP (Qld) 488
Porongurup NP (WA) 802, 854
Port Albert (Vic) 793
Port Arthur (Tas) 633-635
Port Augusta (SA) 588-589
Port Campbell (Vic) 740
Port Campbell NP (Vic) 740-741
Port Clinton (SA) 587
Port Davey (Tas) 673
Port Denison (WA) 863
Port Douglas (Qld) 508-511
Port Elliot (SA) 562
Port Essington (NT) 331
Port Fairy (Vic) 742-743
Port Hacking (NSW) 204
Port Hedland (WA) 886-888, **887**
Port Kembla (NSW) 259
Port Kenny (SA) 592
Port Lincoln (SA) 590-591
Port Macdonnell (SA) 579-580
Port Macquarie (NSW) 227-231, **228**
Port Neill (SA) 590
Port Pirie (SA) 576
Port Sorell (Tas) 660
Port Stephens (NSW) 225
Portarlington (Vic) 725
Portland (Vic) 743
Portsea (Vic) 730

Possession Island (Qld) 524
postal services 89
Princetown (Vic) 740
Proserpine (Qld) 458
Puffing Billy (Vic) 728
Pumpkin Island (Qld) 450
Punsand Bay (Qld) 524
Purnong Rd Bird Sanctuary
    (SA) 584

Queanbeyan (NSW) 155
Queenscliff (Vic) 725
Queensland 373-536, **374-375**
    air travel 379, **380**
    bus travel 379-380
    tourist offices 377
    train travel 380
Queenstown (Tas) 668-670
Quilpie (Qld) 535
Quindalup (WA) 848
quokkas 823
Quorn (SA) 596-597

Rabbit Island (Qld) 458
Radical Bay (Qld) 477
rafting 99, (NSW) 159, (Qld)
    379, (Tas) 613-614
    Cairns (Qld) 489
    Franklin River (Tas) 672
    Mission Beach (Qld) 483
    Mitta Mitta River (Vic) 785
    Murray River (NSW) 266
    North Johnstone River (Qld)
        485
    Nymboida River (NSW) 236,
        243
    Shoalhaven (NSW) 263
    Snowy River (NSW) 266
    Snowy River NP (Vic) 798
    Tully River (Qld) 482, 492
Rainbow Beach (Qld) 429-430
Rainbow Valley Nature Park
    (NT) 361
Rainforests (Qld) 514
Rathdowney (Qld) 418
Ravenshoe (Qld) 507
Ravensthorpe (WA) 859
Ravenswood (Qld) 486
Recherche Archipelago (WA)
    860
Recherche Bay (Tas) 633
Red Cliffs (Vic) 754
Red Hand Cave (NSW) 212
Red Hill (Vic) 729
Red Rock (NSW) 238
Redcliffe (Qld) 401
Redhead Beach (NSW) 221
Redland Bay (Qld) 401
religion 51

Renmark (SA) 582
Richmond (NSW) 209
Richmond (Qld) 488
Richmond (Tas) 629-630
Richmond River (NSW) 240
Ridgley (Tas) 662
River Heads (Qld) 430
Riversleigh (Qld) 530
Robe (SA) 578
Robin Falls (NT) 333
rock climbing (Vic) 684
    Glass House Mountains (Qld)
        420
    Grampians (Gariwerd) NP
        (Vic) 746, 748
    Mt Arapiles (Vic) 749
    Peak Head (WA) 858
    Penneshaw (SA) 568
    Warren Gorge (SA) 597
Rockhampton (Qld) 441-444,
    442
Rockingham (WA) 828
Rockley (NSW) 281
Rocky Cape NP (Tas) 664
Roebourne (WA) 881-882, **882**
Rokeby (Qld) 523
Rokeby-Croll Creek NP (Qld)
    523
Rolleston (Qld) 452
Roma (Qld) 429, 452
Rosebery (Tas) 667
Ross (Tas) 644-645
Ross River (NT) 357
Rosslyn Bay Harbour (Qld) 445
Rossville (Qld) 515
Rotamah Island (Vic) 795
Rottnest Island (WA) 823-825,
    824
Royal Flying Doctor Service
    (NSW) 291
Royal NP (NSW) 204-206
Ruby Gap Nature Park (NT) 358
Rubyvale (Qld) 451
rugby league 110
rugby union 110
Rum Jungle Lake (NT) 333
Rushcutters Bay (NSW) 175
Rushworth (Vic) 776
Russell River (Qld) 493
Rutherglen (Vic) 779-780
Rylstone (NSW) 281

Sacred Canyon (SA) 593
safety 96-98
Sale (Vic) 792
Salmon Gums (WA) 841
Salmon Point (SA) 592
San Remo (Vic) 730
Sandgate (Qld) 401

Sandon Point (NSW) 262
Sapphire (Qld) 451
Sarah Island (Tas) 671
Scamander (Tas) 641
Scarness (Qld) 430
Scone (NSW) 225
Scottsdale (Tas) 643
Seal Bay (SA) 565, 569
Seal Island (WA) 828
Seal Rocks (NSW) 225
Seal Rocks (Vic) 732
Segenhoe (NSW) 225
Serpentine Falls NP (WA) 828
Serpentine Gorge (NT) 359
Seymour (Vic) 777
Shark Bay (WA) 869, **869**
Sharkies (NSW) 262
Sheffield (Tas) 656
Shell Beach (WA) 870
Shellharbour (NSW) 262
Shepparton (Vic) 778
Sherbrooke Forest Park (Vic)
    728
Shoal Bay (NSW) 225
Shoalhaven (NSW) 263-264
shopping 111-112
Shute Harbour (Qld) 458-463
Siding Spring (NSW) 285
Silverton (NSW) 293-294
Simpson Desert (SA) 601
Simpson Desert NP (Qld) 536
Simpson's Gap (NT) 358
Singleton (NSW) 225
Sir Joseph Banks Islands (SA)
    590
Sir Richard Peninsula (SA) 564
Six Foot Track (NSW) 211, 218
Skenes Creek (Vic) 739
skiing 99, (NSW) 266, (Tas)
    614, (Vic) 786-789
    Alpine NP (Vic) 783
    Ben Lomond NP (Tas) 643
    Charlotte Pass (NSW) 272
    Falls Creek (Vic) 786
    Guthega (NSW) 272
    Lake Mountain Reserve (Vic)
        727
    Mt Baw Baw (Vic) 787
    Mt Blue Cow (NSW) 272
    Mt Buffalo (Vic) 785, 787
    Mt Buller (Vic) 787-788
    Mt Hotham (Vic) 788-789
    Mt Selwyn (NSW) 272
    Perisher Valley (NSW) 271
    Smiggin Holes (NSW) 271
    Snowy Mountains (NSW)
        270-272
    Thredbo (NSW) 271
Sleaford Bay (SA) 591

Smeaton (Vic) 765
Smiggin Holes (NSW) 271-272
Smithton (Tas) 665
Smoky Bay (SA) 592
Snowy Mountains (NSW)
    266-273, **267**
    Snowy Mountains Hydroelectric
    Scheme 268
Snowy Mountains (SA) 581
Snowy River (Vic) 797
Snowy River NP (Vic) 797-798
Snug (Tas) 630
soccer 110
Sofala (NSW) 281
Solitary Islands (NSW) 236, 239
Somerset (Qld) 524
Sorell (Tas) 633
Sorrento (Vic) 729-730
South Australia 537-608, **538**
    air travel 540, 554, **541**
    bus travel 540
    tourist offices 539
South Bank (Qld) 385-386
South Burnett (Qld) 426
South Coast Track (Tas) 633, 673
South Gippsland (Vic) 792-793
South Molle Island (Qld)
    465-466
South West Rocks (NSW) 231
South Yarra (Vic) 698-700
South-West NP (Tas) 673
Southbank (Vic) 693
Southern Cross (WA) 832
Southern Reef Islands (Qld)
    439-441
Southport (Qld) 408
Sovereign Hill (Vic) 759-760
Spit, the (Qld) 408
Springbrook NP (Qld) 417
Springbrook Plateau (Qld) 417
Springbrook Village (Qld) 417
Springsure (Qld) 451-452
Springton (SA) 573
Springvale Homestead (NT) 337
Springwood (NSW) 213
St Albans (NSW) 209
St George (Qld) 428
St Helena Island (Qld) 406
St Helens (Tas) 641-642
St Marys (Tas) 641
Standley Chasm (NT) 359
Stanley (Tas) 664-665
Stanthorpe (Qld) 428
Stawell (Vic) 745
Stawell Gift (Vic) 745-746
Stenhouse Bay (SA) 587
Stirling Range NP (WA) 802,
    854
Stockton (NSW) 219, 221

Stokes Inlet NP (WA) 862
Stone Island (Qld) 468
Straddie Classic (Qld) 402
Strahan (Tas) 670
Strathalbyn (SA) 559
Strathgordon (Tas) 673
Streaky Bay (SA) 592
Strelecki Ranges (Vic) 792-793
Strzelecki Track (SA) 601, 607
Sturt NP (NSW) 287
Sturt Stony Desert (SA) 601
Subiaco (WA) 810
sugar growing (Qld) 456
Summerland Beach (Vic) 732
Sunshine Beach (Qld) 421
Sunshine Coast (Qld) 418-426,
    419
Surf Coast Walk (Vic) 735
Surfers Paradise (Qld) 408, **409**
surfing 99, (NSW) 159, (Qld)
    379, (SA) 540, (Tas) 613,
    (Vic) 684
    Apollo Bay (Vic) 684
    Bell's Beach (Vic) 735
    Blackfellows (SA) 592
    Byron Bay (NSW) 243
    Cactus Beach (SA) 593
    Cape Woolamai (Vic) 733
    Diggers Beach (NSW) 236
    Great Ocean Road (Vic) 734
    Greenly Beach (SA) 592
    Jakes Corner (SA) 868
    Lennox Head (NSW) 241
    Margaret River (WA) 848
    Newcastle (NSW) 219
    Noosa NP (Qld) 423
    North Stradbroke Island (Qld)
        402
    Ocean Grove (Vic) 726
    Picnic Rocks (Tas) 642
    Pondalowie Bay (SA) 587
    Port Lincoln (SA) 590
    Yallingup (WA) 848
Surprise Bay (Tas) 678
Swan Hill (Vic) 755
Swan Reach (SA) 584
Swan River (WA) 810, 811, 819
Swansea (Tas) 638-639
Sydney (NSW) 160-203,
    162-163, 176, 205
    entertainment 195-197
    festivals 181
    getting around 201-204
    getting there & away 198-201
    organised tours 180-181
    places to eat 189-195
    places to stay 181-189
    shopping 197-198

Sydney Harbour 175-177
Sydney Harbour Bridge
    167-168
Sydney Opera House 168
    things to see 166-180
    tourist offices 161-164
Sydney to Hobart Yacht Race
    181, 622

Tailem Bend (SA) 585
Talbingo (NSW) 272
Talia (SA) 592
Tallaroo Station (Qld) 527
Tallebudgera (Qld) 415
Tamar Valley (Tas) 653-654
Tamborine Mountain (Qld)
    416-417
Tamworth (NSW) 256
Tanami Track (WA) 904
Tangalooma (Qld) 405
Tantanoola (SA) 579
Tantanoola Caves (SA) 579
Tanunda (SA) 572
Taree (NSW) 226
Tarnagulla (Vic) 765-766
Taroona (Tas) 627
Tarra Bulga NP (Vic) 792
Tasman Peninsula (Tas)
    633-636, **634**
Tasmania 609-680, **610, 661, 667**
    air travel 614-616, **615**
    boat travel 615-616
    bus travel 616
    car travel 617
    tourist offices 612
Tea Gardens (NSW) 226
telephone services 89-90
Tennant Creek (NT) 340-341
Tenterfield (NSW) 259
Terowie (SA) 576
Terrey Hills (NSW) 208
Terrigal (NSW) 218
Tewantin (Qld) 421, 425
Thargomindah (Qld) 535
Tharwa (ACT) 155
Thirlmere (NSW) 207
Thornton Beach (Qld) 513
Thredbo (NSW) 271
Three Sisters (NSW) 214
Three Sisters (Tas) 660
Threeways (NT) 340
Thunder Eggs (Qld) 417
Thursday Island (Qld) 525
Tibooburra (NSW) 287
Tidal River (Vic) 793
Tidbinbilla Nature Reserve
    (ACT) 154
Tidbinbilla Tracking Station
    (ACT) 154

Tilba Tilba (NSW) 264
Timber Creek (NT) 338
time 91
Tingha (NSW) 259
Tintinara (SA) 580
tipping, see money
Tjaynera (Sandy Creek) Falls
    (NT) 323
Tocumwal (NSW) 279
Tolga (Qld) 505
Tolmer Falls (NT) 323
Tom Groggin (Vic) 785
Tom Price (WA) 885-886
Tomahawk (Tas) 643
Toodyay (WA) 829
Toowoomba (Qld) 428-429
Top End, the (NT) 318-332
Torndirrup NP (WA) 859
Torquay (Qld) 430
Torquay (Vic) 735-736
Torres Strait Islands (Qld)
    524-525
tourist offices 81-82, see also
    individual states and capital
    cities
tours 136, see also individual
    capital cities
Tower Hill State Game Reserve
    (Vic) 742
Townsville (Qld) 468-476,
    470
train travel 123-124, 123, see
    also individual states
Traralgon (Vic) 791
Trephina Gorge Nature Park
    (NT) 356-357
Triabunna (Tas) 637
Troubridge Island (SA) 587
Tryon Island (Qld) 441
Tucki Tucki Nature Reserve
    (NSW) 251
Tully (Qld) 482
Tully River (Qld) 482, 492
Tumbarumba (NSW) 272
Tumbling Waters (NT) 322
Tumby Bay (SA) 590
Tumut (NSW) 272
Tunnel Creek (WA) 902
Turramurra (NSW) 208
turtles 438, 439, 458, 480, 878,
    886
Tweed Heads (NSW) 248-249
Tweed Heads (Qld) 410
Tweed Range Scenic Drive
    (NSW) 254
Twelve Apostles (Vic) 740
Twin Falls (NT) 328
Two People's Bay (WA) 859
two-up 315

Ubirr (NT) 327
Ulian Rocks (NSW) 243
Ulladulla (NSW) 263
Uluru (Ayers Rock) (NT)
    364-366, 365
Uluru NP (NT) 364-372
Ulverstone (Tas) 660-661
Umbrawarra Gorge Nature Park
    (NT) 334
Uralla (NSW) 257
Urangan (Qld) 430
Uriarra Crossing (ACT) 154
Urunga (NSW) 234

Valley of the Giants (WA) 852
Valley of the Winds (NT) 366
Vaughan Springs (Vic) 769
Victor Harbor (SA) 562-563
Victoria 681-799, 682
    air travel 717
    bus travel 685, 717
    tourist offices 683-684
    train travel 685, 717-718
Victoria Range (Vic) 748
Victoria River Crossing (NT)
    338
Victoria Valley (Vic) 748
visas 77-78
Vivonne Bay (SA) 569

Wacol (Qld) 427
Wadbilliga NP (NSW) 265
Waddy Point (Qld) 434
Wagga Wagga (NSW) 276
Wagin (WA) 833
Wahgunyah (Vic) 779
Waikerie (SA) 583
Walcha (NSW) 256
Walga Rock (WA) 889
Walgett (NSW) 285
Walhalla (Vic) 791-792
Wallaga Lake NP (NSW) 264
Wallaman Falls NP (Qld) 480
Wallaroo (SA) 586-587
Walls of Jerusalem NP (Tas) 677
Walpole-Nornalup (WA) 803
Walpole-Nornalup NP (WA) 852
Walyunga NP (WA) 810
Wanaaring (NSW) 287
Wangaratta (Vic) 778-779
Wangi Falls (NT) 323
Wanna Munna (WA) 889
Warburton (Vic) 727
Warburton (WA) 840
Warragul (Vic) 791
Warrawong Sanctuary (SA) 558
Warren (NSW) 286
Warren Gorge (SA) 597
Warren NP (WA) 851

Warrnambool (Vic) 741-742
Warrumbungle NP (NSW) 285
Warwick (Qld) 428
Washpool NP (NSW) 255
Watarrka NP (NT) 363-364
Waterfall (NSW) 206
Waterloo Bay (SA) 592
Watheroo (WA) 864
Watsons Bay (NSW) 175
Wauchope (NSW) 231
Wauchope (NT) 341
Wave Rock (WA) 832
Waychinicup NP (WA) 859
Wedderburn (Vic) 776
Wee Jasper (NSW) 274
Weipa (Qld) 520, 523
Weldborough (Tas) 642
Wentworth (NSW) 279
Wentworth (Vic) 754
Wentworth Falls (NSW) 213
Werribee Park (Vic) 721
Werrikimbe NP (NSW) 255
West Cape Howe NP (WA) 858
West Gippsland (Vic) 789-792
West Head (Vic) 730
Westbury (Tas) 654-655
Western Australia 800-908, 801
    air travel 804, 804
    bus travel 804
    geography 802
    tourist offices 802
    train travel 804-805
Western MacDonnell Ranges
    (NT) 358-360
Western Plains Zoo (NSW) 282
whale-watching (SA) 562
    Airlie Beach (Qld) 458
    Albany (WA) 856
    Bremer Bay (WA) 859
    Dampier Peninsula (WA) 896
    Dunsborough (WA) 848
    Eden (NSW) 265
    Fitzgerald River NP (WA) 860
    Hervey Bay (Qld) 430, 432
    Muttonbird Island (NSW) 235,
        236
    Ningaloo Reef (WA) 878
    North Stradbroke Island (Qld)
        402
    Perth (WA) 808, 811
    Port Hedland (WA) 886
    Port Kenny (SA) 592
    Warrnambool (Vic) 741
Wheatlands (WA) 831-833
Wheeler Island (Qld) 484
Whian Whian State Forest
    (NSW) 253
Whim Creek (WA) 883
Whipstick State Forest (Vic) 775

White Cliffs (NSW) 288-289
white-water rafting, *see* rafting
Whitsunday Coast (Qld) 452-468
Whitsunday Fun Race (Qld) 460
Whitsunday Island (Qld) 467
Whitsunday Islands (Qld) 463-467, **464**
Whyalla (SA) 589-590
Wiangaree (NSW) 254
Wickepin (WA) 833
Wickham (WA) 883
Wilberforce (NSW) 209
Wilcannia (NSW) 288
Wilderness Society 84
Wildflower Way (WA) 864
Willabalangaloo Reserve (SA) 582
Willandra NP (NSW) 278
William Bay NP (WA) 853, 858
Williamtown (NSW) 222
Willis (Vic) 798
Willows Gemfield (Qld) 451
Willunga (SA) 561
Wilmington (SA) 596
Wilpena Pound (SA) 598-599, **599**
Wilson Island (Qld) 439-441
Wilsons Promontory (Vic) 793-795, **794**
Wiluna (WA) 840
Wimmera, the (Vic) 745-750
Winchelsea (Vic) 744
Windarra (WA) 840
Windjana Gorge (WA) 902
Windjana Gorge Park (WA) 900
Windorah (Qld) 535
Windsor (NSW) 209
Wineglass Bay (Tas) 639
wineries (Vic) 779
    Barossa Valley (SA) 569-571, **570**

Berri (SA) 582
Corowa (NSW) 279
Fleurieu Peninsula (SA) 561
Geelong (Vic) 722
Great Western (Vic) 745
Griffith (NSW) 277
Hunter Valley (NSW) 223-225
Margaret River (WA) 848
McLaren Vale (SA) 561
Mt Barker (WA) 854
Mudgee (NSW) 281
Rutherglen (Vic) 779-780
Yarra Valley (Vic) 727
Wingham (NSW) 226
Winton (Qld) 532
Wirrabara (SA) 596
Wisemans Ferry (NSW) 209
Witches Falls NP (Qld) 417
Wittenoom (WA) 883-884
Wittenoom Gorge (WA) 884
Wodonga (Vic) 780
Wolfe Creek Crater NP (WA) 903
Wollemi NP (NSW) 211
Wollombi (NSW) 223
Wollomombi Falls (NSW) 255
Wollongong (NSW) 259-262, **260**
women travellers 96
Wonboyn (NSW) 266
Wonderland Range (Vic) 748
Woodenbong (Qld) 418
Woodend (Vic) 726
Woodford (NSW) 210
Woody Island (WA) 860
Woody Point (NSW) 239
Woolgoolga (NSW) 238
Wooli (NSW) 238
Woolloomooloo (NSW) 175
Woomera (SA) 602
Woorim (Qld) 406

Wooyung (NSW) 247
work 98-99
Wujal Wujal (Qld) 515
Wye River (Vic) 739
Wyndham (WA) 904-905
Wynnum (Qld) 401
Wynyard (Tas) 663-664
Wyperfeld NP (Vic) 751
Wyseby (Qld) 452

Yackandandah (Vic) 780-781
Yalata (SA) 844-845
Yalgorup NP (WA) 846
Yallingup (WA) 848
Yamba (NSW) 239
Yampire Gorge (WA) 885
Yanchep (WA) 825-827
Yanchep NP (WA) 825
Yandina (Qld) 426
Yarra River (Vic) 692-693
Yarra Valley (Vic) 727
Yarrawonga (Vic) 757-758
Yass (NSW) 274
Yellow Water (NT) 328
Yengo NP (NSW) 211
Yeppoon (Qld) 444-445
York (WA) 830-831
Yorke Peninsula (SA) 585-588, **586**
Yorketown (SA) 587
You Yangs (Vic) 722
Yourambulla (SA) 593
Yourambulla Rock Shelter (SA) 597
Yowah (Qld) 428
Yulara (NT) 367-372, **368**
Yungaburra (Qld) 506
Yuraygir NP (NSW) 238-239

Zeehan (Tas) 668
Zig Zag Railway (NSW) 280

NATIONAL PARKS

Alexander Morrison NP (WA) 864
Alpine NP (Vic) 783-785
Archer Bend NP (Qld) 523
Asbestos Range NP (Tas) 660
Avon Valley NP (WA) 829

Bald Rock NP (NSW) 256
Barrington Tops NP NSW) 225
Baw Baw NP (Vic) 787
Beedelup NP (WA) 851
Belair NP (SA) 558
Ben Boyd NP (NSW) 266
Ben Lomond NP (Tas) 643-644

Blackdown Tableland NP (Qld) 451
Blue Mountains NP (NSW) 210, 211
Boonoo Boonoo NP (NSW) 256
Border Ranges NP (NSW) 254-255
Botany Bay NP (NSW) 204
Bouddi NP (NSW) 218
Bowling Green Bay NP (Qld) 468
Brisbane Ranges NP (Vic) 722
Brisbane Water NP (NSW) 218
Bundjalung NP (NSW) 239

Bungle Bungle (Purnululu) NP (WA) 904
Buringurrah NP (WA) 874
Burleigh Heads NP (Qld) 408
Butterfly Gorge NP (NT) 334

Cape Arid NP (WA) 862
Cape Hillsborough NP (Qld) 457
Cape Le Grand NP (WA) 862, 863
Cape Range NP (WA) 878
Carnarvon NP (Qld) 452
Cathedral Rock NP (NSW) 255
Cocoparra NP (NSW) 278

Conway NP (Qld) 458
Cooloola NP (Qld) 425
Coorong (SA) 577-578
Cradle Mountain-Lake St Clair (Tas) 673-677
Croajingolong NP (Vic) 798
Crowdy Bay NP (NSW) 227

Dandenong Ranges NP (Vic) 727
D'Entrecasteaux NP (WA) 852
Devonian Reef NPs (WA) 901-902
Dharug NP (NSW) 209
Dorrigo NP (NSW) 233
Douglas-Apsley NP (Tas) 640

Edmund Kennedy NP (Qld) 481
Errinundra NP (Vic) 797, 798
Eungella NP (Qld) 456-457

Fern Tree Gully NP (Vic) 728
Finke Gorge NP (NT) 360
Fitzgerald River NP (WA) 859-860
Flinders Chase NP (SA) 568-569
Forty Mile Scrub NP (Qld) 507
François Peron NP (WA) 870
Frank Hann NP (WA) 859
Franklin-Gordon Wild Rivers NP (Tas) 672
Fraser NP (Vic) 776
Freycinet NP (Tas) 639-640

Gammon Ranges NP (SA) 600
Girraween NP (Qld) 428
Goulburn River NP (NSW) 224
Grampians (Gariwerd) NP (Vic) 746-749
Great Sandy NP (Qld) 433
Gregory NP (NT) 338
Guy Fawkes River NP (NSW) 255

Hartz Mountains NP (Tas) 632
Hattah-Kulkyne NP (Vic) 751
Hidden Valley NP (WA) 905

Innes NP (SA) 585, 587-588
Iron Range NP (Qld) 523

Jardine River NP (Qld) 524
Jervis Bay NP (NSW) 263
Jip Jip NP (SA) 578
John Forrest NP (WA) 831
Jourama Falls NP (Qld) 480

Kakadu NP (NT) 323-330
Kalbarri NP (WA) 803, 868

Kanangra Boyd NP (NSW) 211
Karijini (Hamersley Range) NP (WA) 803, 877, 884
Keep River NP (NT) 338-339
Kinchega NP (NSW) 294
Kondalilla NP (Qld) 426
Kosciusko NP (NSW) 269-270
Ku-ring-gai Chase NP (NSW) 207-208

Lakefield NP (Qld) 522-523
Lakes NP (Vic) 795
Lamington NP (Qld) 417-418
Lawn Hill NP (Qld) 525, 527, 532 check
Leeuwin-Naturaliste NP (WA) 849
Lincoln NP (SA) 591
Litchfield NP (NT) 322-323
Little Desert NP (Vic) 750
Lower Glenelg NP (Vic) 743

Macquarie Pass NP (NSW) 262
Macrozamia Grove NP (Qld) 417
Main Range NP (Qld) 427
Mapleton Falls NP (Qld) 426
Maria Island NP (Tas) 637-638
Millstream-Chichester NP (WA) 883
Mimosa Rocks NP (NSW) 265
Mitchell River NP (Vic) 795
Mootwingee NP (NSW) 289
Morton NP (NSW) 262-264
Mt Barney NP (Qld) 418
Mt Buffalo (Vic) 787
Mt Buffalo NP (Vic) 785
Mt Field NP (Tas) 628-629
Mt Kaputar NP (NSW) 285
Mt Remarkable NP (SA) 596
Mt Richmond NP (Vic) 743
Mt Spec NP (Qld) 480
Mt Warning NP (NSW) 254
Mt William NP (Tas) 642
Mungo NP (NSW) 294, 754
Murramarang NP (NSW) 264
Murray-Sunset NP (Vic) 751
Myall Lakes NP (NSW) 225-226

Namadgi NP (ACT) 154
Nambung NP (WA) 827
New England NP (NSW) 255
Nightcap NP (NSW) 253
Nitmiluk (Katherine Gorge) NP (NT) 337-338
Noosa NP (Qld) 423

Organ Pipes NP (Vic) 726
Otway NP (Vic) 739

Oxley Wild Rivers NP (NSW) 255

Palmerston NP (Qld) 485
Peak Charles NP (WA) 862
Point Nepean NP (Vic) 730
Porcupine Gorge NP (Qld) 488
Porongurup NP (WA) 802, 854-855
Port Campbell NP (Vic) 740

Rocky Cape NP (Tas) 664
Rokeby-Croll Creek NP (Qld) 523
Royal NP (NSW) 204-206

Serpentine Falls NP (WA) 828
Simpson Desert NP (Qld) 536
Snowy River NP (Vic) 797
South-West NP (Tas) 673
Springbrook NP (Qld) 417
Stirling Range NP (WA) 802, 854
Stokes Inlet NP (WA) 862
Sturt NP (NSW) 287

Tarra Bulga NP (Vic) 792
Torndirrup NP (WA) 859

Uluru NP (NT) 364-372

Wallaga Lake NP (NSW) 264
Wallaman Falls NP (Qld) 480
Walls of Jerusalem NP (Tas) 677
Walpole-Nornalup NP (WA) 852
Walyunga NP (WA) 810
Warren NP (WA) 851
Warrumbungle NP (NSW) 285
Washpool NP (NSW) 255
Watarrka NP (NT) 363-364
Waychinicup NP (WA) 859
Werrikimbe NP (NSW) 255
West Cape Howe NP (WA) 858
Willandra NP (NSW) 278
William Bay NP (WA) 853, 858
Wilsons Promontory (Vic) 793-795
Windjana Gorge Park (WA) 900
Witches Falls NP (Qld) 417
Wollemi NP (NSW) 211
Wyperfeld NP (Vic) 751

Yalgorup NP (WA) 846
Yanchep NP (WA) 825
Yengo NP (NSW) 211
Yuraygir NP (NSW) 238-239

THANKS

Thanks also to those travellers who took the time and trouble to write to us about their experiences in Australia. Writers (apologies if we've misspelt your name) to whom thanks must go include:

Wayne Ahrens (Aus), Suzanne Albrecht, Juliette Allain (F), Michael Palsgad Andersen (DK), Rachel Andrew (Aus), David Armstrong (Aus), Melissa-Kate Ashwell (UK), J F Aylard (UK), David Baehr (USA), John Bailey (Aus), Lee Baldwin (Aus), Piero Balestri (I), Andrew Barber (UK), Charlotte Bauer (USA), R D Beale (UK), Alison Beard (UK), Neil Beaumont (Aus), Oliver Berls (D), Danielle R Bernstein (USA), Rhonda Bhattachanga (Aus), Samantha Bianchi (UK), Neville Biffin (Aus), Jonathon Bigley (UK), Lone Biilmann (DK), Anna Blackburn (UK), E Blayden (Aus), Kevin Blott (Aus), Rene Boissevain (Aus), Heather Bond (Aus), Anna Bowden (Aus), Judie Boyd (UK), Kate Brebner (Aus), Seth & Mary Brickner (USA), Lester C Brien (Aus), Jeff Bright (Aus), Greg Brown (Aus), Emma Burnes (UK), Beverly Burns (Aus), Dr N Burrell (Aus), Dirk Bussenschutt (D), W R A Butler (Aus), Alison Buy (UK), Dr Don Campbell (C), Julie Caravella (Aus), Paul Carr (UK), Jonathan Carroll (UK), A W Chambers (Aus), Judy & Peter Chengody (Aus), C Childs (Aus), Sarah Clavel (Aus), Chris Collins (NZ), Mark Cook (UK), Thomas Cooke (UK), Robyn Cooper (Aus) Forrest Cowlishaw (Aus), Michael Cox (UK), Gerard Croix, A C Culberg (Aus), Mike Dancer (Aus), Miss T H Dann (UK), Deni Dante (Aus), Sue Dart (Aus), Evan Davey (Aus), Cheryl Davies (Aus), Anita de Boer (C), Joseph Dean (USA), Nigel Dearing (UK), R Joy Dendry (Aus), Elizabeth Dennison (Aus), Diana & Gavin (Aus), Julie Dickson (UK), P R Diggins (UK), Robert Disney (Aus), Daniel Doody (UK), Doc Dorahy (Aus), Mark Dorrington (Aus), Pauline Downing (Aus), N Duff (Aus), Alison Duncan (Aus), Bruce Dungey (Aus), Anne Dunn (UK), Gill Dunning (UK), Jenny Dwyer (Aus), Nicole Dyer (Aus), Steve Edgeller (Aus), Melany Edworthy (C), Dr J Eggleton (UK), Mayne Ellis (C), Eva (Aus), Anna Evangelou (Aus), Craig Evans (UK), Linda Evans (Aus), Miss R Evans (Aus), Helen Fairall (Aus), Anna Fairfax (Aus), Debra Fallek (USA), Marilyn Farnham-Smith (UK), Peter Farris (Aus), Patrick Fay (UK), Anna Featherstone (Aus), Angela Finnigan (Aus), John Fischbein (Aus), Shelley Flam (C), Emily Follman (Aus), Grant J Fothergill (Aus), Richard Fowkes (UK), David Frank, Audrey Fuller (UK), Jane Galbally (Aus), Evaline Gamage (USA) Elvira Ganter (PNG), N Caleb Gardner (Aus), Paul Gardner (UK), Brian Garth (Aus), Elizabeth Geary (UK), Andrew Gee (Aus), Alison Geldard (Aus), Suzanne Gervay (Aus), Bruce Gilsen (USA), Helen & Brian Gitsham (Aus), Mully Glezer (Isr), Elizabeth Golay (CH), Edna Goldman

(Aus), Vanessa Goldschmidt (D), Diana Gounvenec (UK), Samantha Gowing (Aus), Stefan Graf (D), Yvette Gray (Aus), Manuel Gren (UK), C Guggisberg (CH), Patricia Hackel (USA), Andrew Haines (UK), Nola Cath & Fay Halden (Aus), Meg Hall (Aus), Jane Halond (UK), Lars Hammarberg (S), Bjarne Stig Hansen (DK), John Hanson (Aus), John Harden (Aus), Teresa Harkes (UK), Isabel Hay (Aus), Peter Heath (Aus), Mrs S L Hebdon (UK), Jorg Heikhaus (D), Susan Helmer (Aus), Olivier Henrot (F), Alan & Pam Hislop (Aus), Clare Hodgson (UK), Sharyn Holder (Aus), Stig & Charlotte Holm (DK), Jack Holmes (Aus), Lyle Honess (Aus), Ron Hoore (Aus), Louise Hoskin (UK), Michael Hosking (Aus), Jane Hughes (Aus), Teena Hughes (Aus), J L C Humphrey (Aus), Duncan Husband (Aus), Emma Hutchcroft (UK), Deirdre Hynes (UK), Chris James (UK), Brian Jeppsson (DK), Dionne Johnson (Aus), Garry Johnson (Aus), Ian & Melva Johnson (Aus), Ian & Jacquelin Johnston (UK), B E A Jones (UK), Lars Vincents Jorgensen (DK), Sudarshan Joshi (PNG), Idsert Joukes (NL), Ilene Joyce (USA), Amanda Kanters (NL), Mrs Robyn Karran (Aus), Matthew Keighton (Aus), James Kemp (Aus), Geraldine Keogh (Aus), Paul Keyenberg (B), Tina Kimbacher (A), Kevin Kitto (Aus), Wolfgang Klein, Miranda Kleys, Ingrid Klose (D), R L Knox (Aus), Kristina Kortlander (D), Gudrun Kose (D), Chris Koudounaris (Aus), Rita Kuhl (Aus), Lucy Kunkel (USA), Jasper Kyndi (D), David & Noah Leavitt (USA), Kerry Leech (Aus), Catherine Lewis (UK), Matt Lewis (UK), Peter Lewis (UK), Peter Lindgren (Aus), Mark & Birgit Linnett (Aus), Margaret Lisantey (Aus), R & S Litton (Aus), Karsten Lochert (D), Tor Loege (N), Henry Long (UK), Pat & Pete Lyon, J W Mac Donald (Aus), Scot Macbeth (USA), Kevin MacKeaggan (UK), Barry Maggs (Aus), Simon Mahon (Aus), Katie Malcolm (UK), Nigel Mallett (Aus), Frank Marchetti (C), Stella Marshall (Aus), Barry J Marshmaw (Aus), Sherman McCall (USA), Elizabeth McCallum (C), Don McCasker (Aus), Garry McDougall (Aus), Clare McKenzie (Aus) Richard McNab, James & Doris McNairn (USA), Mrs John R McNeil (USA), Eric Mead (USA), Tanja Meier (Aus), David Menzel (Aus), Chantal Mercier (C), Gudrun Merkle (D), H R Meyer (Aus), Nicole Miran (Isr), Anita Mistonen (C), Jacque Mog (USA), R P & D W Monaghan (Aus), Tony & Gigi Mondello (Aus), Jean-Paul Moonen (NL), Nicole Moran (Isr), Miss L A Morgan (Aus), John Morrow (NZ), Gisela Murdter, Bob & Cynthia Newing (UK), Helena Newton (Aus), H Novak (Aus), Darren O'Byrne (UK), Peter O'Shea (Aus), Caroline & Lorr O'Sullivan (UK), Jeff Oakley (Aus), Miss L Ogden (UK), H T Oosterheerd (NL), Laurence Orsini (F), Andrej Panjkov, Donna Pansino (Aus), Michele Paparelle (I), Sarah Parfitt (Aus), Glengarry Park (Aus), Jose Luis Perez (Sp), Silvana Pessano (I), Anne Phelan (Aus), Chris Pilley (UK), Dianne Pollard (Aus), Lionel Pollard (Aus), Roy

Pollock (Aus), Belinda Pope (NZ), Marg Popovitch (USA), Penny Pretty (Aus), Joanne Price (Aus), Private Hotel Central (Aus), C R T Puckle (UK), Laura Puphet (Aus), Andrew Qualtrough (UK), Kate & Paul Quarry (UK), Wayne Quick (Aus), Janus Ramussen (DK), Bradley A Reback (UK), Mr M H Reeves (Aus), Paul Renshaw (UK), G R Richardson (UK), Colleen Riga (Aus) Joe Roccella (Aus), Sam Rodan (Aus), Allie Rogers (UK), Armando Rossi (I), Julie Rothan (UK), Ruth Salvisberg (D), Dr Rainer Schumacher (D), Steve & Jane Schutt (Aus), Daniela Schwarz (A), Donald Scott-Orr (Aus), Barbara Shepherd (UK), Hedley Shepstone (Aus), Bernard Shirley (Aus), Caroline Shirley (Aus), Trevor Short (Aus), Jonathan Sibtain-Dudler (CH), Maria & Roland Signer (CH), Donna Simpson (Aus), Ravina Sinah (Aus), Jim Sinclair (Aus), Sandra Skelton (Aus), D H Smith (Aus), Greg Smyth (UK), Tania Somsen (NL), Bernard & Lisa Spiquel (F), Karen & Andrew Stansfield (UK), Fernando Stein (Aus), Edward Stekar (C), L F Sternberg (Aus), Paul Stevens (NZ), Donald Stewart (Aus), Jacqueline Stolk, Alexandra Stone (UK), Miss Bid Strachan (UK), Tom Stratton (Aus), Dr David Stredder (Aus), Joanna Sugden (Aus), James Supaibulpipat, Jos & Birgitta Sweers (NL), Benjamin Szeto, John Tansey (Aus), Jane Taylor, Don Townsend (Aus), Ted Trenarther (Aus), Megan Trotter (Aus), Lisa Tuck (UK), Leo Tudisca (Aus), Rosalind Turner (Aus), R Uchara (J), Rand J K Uehara, Armin Uhlig (B), Mark Ungari (Aus), Cheryl Upright (C) Krister Valtonen (S), Martin van Buuren (NL), Edith van der Chijs (NL), Ruud van Leeuwen (NL), Nicole van Wyhe (NL), Peter Vandenesch (D), Mel Veal (UK), Rose-Maree Verhey (NL), Nadia Veuve (CH), Charlotte Wadsworth (UK), Stefan Waldenburg (D), Stephen Walker (UK), Kedi Walton (UK), Lori Warchow, Ian Ward (Aus), Zoe Wareham (UK), Lisa Warlick (USA), Jenny Warner (UK), Philippe Warnery (CH), Watheroo Tavern (Aus), Rob Webster (UK), Lee Sao Wei (Sin), Geoff White (Aus), Lyn Whiteman (Aus), Jane Whitford (Aus), Bob Whitworth (Aus), Roxy Wicherts (Aus), Andrew Willetts (UK), Tim & Nicki Williams (UK), Juliet Wilson (UK), Richie Wilson (Aus), Linda Wissmann (Aus), Sylvia Wolf (Aus), Rosalie & Colin Wood (Aus), Victoria Worsley (Aus), Ann Wright (Aus), Nick Wykeman (UK), Ross S Yosnow (USA).

A – Austria, Aus – Australia, B – Belgium, C – Canada, CH – Switzerland, D – Germany, DK – Denmark, F – France, I – Italy, Isr – Israel, J – Japan, NL – the Netherlands, PNG – Papua New Guinea, S – Sweden, Sin – Singapore, Sp – Spain, UK – United Kingdom, USA – United States of America.

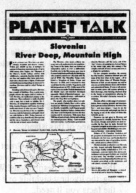

Guides to the Pacific

Bushwalking in Australia
Two experienced and respected walkers give details of the best walks in every state, covering many different terrains and climates.

Bushwalking in Papua New Guinea
The best way to get to know Papua New Guinea is from the ground up – and bushwalking is the best way to travel around the rugged and varied landscape of this island.

Islands of Australia's Great Barrier Reef – Australia guide
The Great Barrier Reef is one of the wonders of the world – and one of the great travel destinations! Whether you're looking for the best snorkelling, the liveliest nightlife or a secluded island hideaway, this guide has all the facts you'll need.

Melbourne – city guide
From historic houses to fascinating churches and from glorious parks to tapas bars, cafés and bistros, Melbourne is a dream for gourmets and a paradise for sightseers.

New South Wales & the ACT
Ancient aboriginal sites, pristine surf beaches, kangaroos bounding across desert dunes, lyre-birds dancing in rainforest, picturesque country pubs, weather-beaten drovers and friendly small-town people, along with Australia's largest and liveliest metropolis (and the host city of the year 2000 Olympic Games) – all this and more can be found in New South Wales and the ACT.

Sydney – city guide
From the Opera House to the surf; all you need to know in a handy pocket-sized format.

Outback Australia
The outback conjures up images of endless stretches of dead straight roads, the rich red of the desert, and the resourcefulness and resilience of the inhabitants. A visit to Australia would not be complete without visiting the outback to see the beauty and vastness of this ancient country.

Victoria – Australia guide
From old gold rush towns to cosmopolitan Melbourne and from remote mountains to the most popular surf beaches, Victoria is packed with attractions and activities for everyone.

Fiji – a travel survival kit
Whether you prefer to stay in camping grounds, international hotels, or something in-between, this comprehensive guide will help you to enjoy the beautiful Fijian archipelago.

Hawaii – a travel survival kit
Share in the delights of this island paradise – and avoid some of its high prices – with this practical guide. It covers all of Hawaii's well-known attractions, plus plenty of uncrowded sights and activities.

Micronesia – a travel survival kit

The glorious beaches, lagoons and reefs of these 2100 islands would dazzle even the most jaded traveller. This guide has all the details on island-hopping across the Micronesian archipelago.

New Caledonia – a travel survival kit

This guide shows how to discover all that the idyllic islands of New Caledonia have to offer – from French colonial culture to traditional Melanesian life.

New Zealand – a travel survival kit

This practical guide will help you discover the very best New Zealand has to offer: Maori dances and feasts, some of the most spectacular scenery in the world, and every outdoor activity imaginable.

Tramping in New Zealand

Call it tramping, hiking, walking, bushwalking or trekking – travelling by foot is the best way to explore New Zealand's natural beauty. Detailed descriptions of over 40 walks of varying length and difficulty.

Papua New Guinea – a travel survival kit

With its coastal cities, villages perched beside mighty rivers, palm-fringed beaches and rushing mountain streams, Papua New Guinea promises memorable travel.

Rarotonga & the Cook Islands – a travel survival kit

Rarotonga and the Cook Islands have history, beauty and magic to rival the better-known islands of Hawaii and Tahiti, but the world has virtually passed them by.

Samoa – a travel survival kit

Two remarkably different countries, Western Samoa and American Samoa offer some wonderful island escapes, and Polynesian culture at its best.

Solomon Islands – a travel survival kit

The Solomon Islands are the best-kept secret of the Pacific. Discover remote tropical islands, jungle-covered volcanoes and traditional Melanesian villages with this detailed guide.

Tahiti & French Polynesia – a travel survival kit

Tahiti's idyllic beauty has seduced sailors, artists and travellers for generations. The latest edition of this book provides full details on the main island of Tahiti, the Tuamotos, Marquesas and other island groups. Invaluable information for independent travellers and package tourists alike.

Tonga – a travel survival kit

The only South Pacific country never to be colonised by Europeans, Tonga has also been ignored by tourists. The people of this far-flung island group offer some of the most sincere and unconditional hospitality in the world.

Vanuatu – a travel survival kit

Discover superb beaches, lush rainforests, dazzling coral reefs and tradional Melanesian customs in this glorious Pacific Ocean archipelago.

Also available:

Pidgin phrasebook.

Lonely Planet Guidebooks

Lonely Planet guidebooks cover every accessible part of Asia as well as Australia, the Paci
South America, Africa, the Middle East, Europe and parts of North America. There are
series: *travel survival kits*, covering a country for a range of budgets; *shoestring gu*
with compact information for low-budget travel in a major region; *walking guides*;
guides and *phrasebooks*.

Australia & the Pacific
Australia
Australian phrasebook
Bushwalking in Australia
Islands of Australia's Great Barrier Reef
Outback Australia
Fiji
Fijian phrasebook
Melbourne city guide
Micronesia
New Caledonia
New South Wales
New Zealand
Tramping in New Zealand
Papua New Guinea
Bushwalking in Papua New Guinea
Papua New Guinea phrasebook
Rarotonga & the Cook Islands
Samoa
Solomon Islands
Sydney city guide
Tahiti & French Polynesia
Tonga
Vanuatu
Victoria

South-East Asia
Bali & Lombok
Bangkok city guide
Cambodia
Indonesia
Indonesia phrasebook
Laos
Malaysia, Singapore & Brunei
Myanmar (Burma)
Burmese phrasebook
Philippines
Pilipino phrasebook
Singapore city guide
South-East Asia on a shoestring
Thailand
Thai phrasebook
Vietnam
Vietnamese phrasebook

Middle East
Arab Gulf States
Egypt & the Sudan
Arabic (Egyptian) phrasebook
Iran
Israel
Jordan & Syria
Middle East
Turkish phrasebook
Trekking in Turkey
Yemen

North-East A
Ch
Beijing city gu
Cantonese phraseb
Mandarin Chinese phraseb
Hong Kong, Macau & Car
Ja
Japanese phraseb
Kc
Korean phraseb
Mong
North-East Asia on a shoest
Seoul city gu
Taiv
Ti
Tibet phraseb
Tokyo city gu

Indian Oce
Madagascar & Como
Maldives & Islands of the East Indian Oc
Mauritius, Réunion & Seyche

Mail Order

onely Planet guidebooks are distributed worldwide. They are also available by mail order from onely Planet, so if you have difficulty finding a title please write to us. US and Canadian residents hould write to Embarcadero West, 155 Filbert St, Suite 251, Oakland CA 94607, USA; European esidents should write to 10 Barley Mow Passage, Chiswick, London W4 4PH; and residents of ther countries to PO Box 617, Hawthorn, Victoria 3122, Australia.

Indian Subcontinent
Bangladesh
India
Hindi/Urdu phrasebook
Trekking in the Indian Himalaya
Karakoram Highway
Kashmir, Ladakh & Zanskar
Nepal
Trekking in the Nepal Himalaya
Nepali phrasebook
Pakistan
Sri Lanka
Sri Lanka phrasebook

Africa
Africa on a shoestring
Central Africa
East Africa
Trekking in East Africa
Kenya
Swahili phrasebook
Morocco, Algeria & Tunisia
Arabic (Moroccan) phrasebook
South Africa, Lesotho & Swaziland
Zimbabwe, Botswana & Namibia
West Africa

Central America & the Caribbean
Baja California
Central America on a shoestring
Costa Rica
Eastern Caribbean
Guatemala, Belize & Yucatán: La Ruta Maya
Mexico

North America
Alaska
Canada
Hawaii

South America
Argentina, Uruguay & Paraguay
Bolivia
Brazil
Brazilian phrasebook
Chile & Easter Island
Colombia
Ecuador & the Galápagos Islands
Latin American Spanish phrasebook
Peru
Quechua phrasebook
South America on a shoestring
Trekking in the Patagonian Andes
Venezuela

urope
altic States & Kaliningrad
ublin city guide
astern Europe on a shoestring
astern Europe phrasebook
nland
rance
reece
ungary
eland, Greenland & the Faroe Islands
eland
aly
lediterranean Europe on a shoestring
lediterranean Europe phrasebook
oland
candinavian & Baltic Europe on a shoestring
candinavian Europe phrasebook
witzerland
rekking in Spain
rekking in Greece
SSR
ussian phrasebook
estern Europe on a shoestring
estern Europe phrasebook

The Lonely Planet Story

Lonely Planet published its first book in 1973 in response to the numerous 'How did you do it?' questions Maureen and Tony Wheeler were asked after driving, bussing, hitching, sailing and railing their way from England to Australia.

Written at a kitchen table and hand collated, trimmed and stapled, *Across Asia on the Cheap* became an instant local bestseller, inspiring thoughts of another book.

Eighteen months in South-East Asia resulted in their second guide, *South-East Asia on a shoestring*, which they put together in a backstreet Chinese hotel in Singapore in 1975. The 'yellow bible' as it quickly became known to backpackers around the world, soon became *the* guide to the region. It has sold well over half a million copies and is now in its 8th edition, still retaining its familiar yellow cover.

Today there are over 140 Lonely Planet titles in print – books that have that same adventurous approach to travel as those early guides; books that 'assume you know how to get your luggage off the carousel' as one reviewer put it.

Although Lonely Planet initially specialised in guides to Asia, they now cover most regions of the world, including the Pacific, South America, Africa, the Middle East and Europe. The list of *walking guides* and *phrasebooks* (for 'unusual' languages such as Quechua, Swahili, Nepali and Egyptian Arabic) is also growing rapidly.

The emphasis continues to be on travel for independent travellers. Tony and Maureen still travel for several months of each year and play an active part in the writing, updating and quality control of Lonely Planet' guides.

They have been joined by over 50 authors 90 staff – mainly editors, cartographers & designers – at our office in Melbourne Australia, at our US office in Oakland California and at our European office in Paris; another five at our office in London handle sales for Britain, Europe and Africa. Travellers themselves also make a valuable contribution to the guides through the feedback we receive in thousands of letters each year.

The people at Lonely Planet strongly believe that travellers can make a positive contribution to the countries they visit, both through their appreciation of the countries culture, wildlife and natural features, and through the money they spend. In addition the company makes a direct contribution to the countries and regions it covers. Since 1986 a percentage of the income from each book has been donated to ventures such as famine relief in Africa; aid projects in India agricultural projects in Central America Greenpeace's efforts to halt French nuclear testing in the Pacific and Amnesty International. In 1993 $100,000 was donated to such causes.

Lonely Planet's basic travel philosophy is summed up in Tony Wheeler's comment 'Don't worry about whether your trip will work out. Just go!'.